T0135251

More information about this subseries at https://link.springer.com/bookseries/1244

Honghai Liu · Zhouping Yin · Lianqing Liu ·
Li Jiang · Guoying Gu · Xinyu Wu ·
Weihong Ren (Eds.)

Intelligent Robotics and Applications

15th International Conference, ICIRA 2022
Harbin, China, August 1–3, 2022
Proceedings, Part I

Editors
Honghai Liu
Harbin Institute of Technology
Shenzhen, China

Lianqing Liu
Shenyang Institute of Automation
Shenyang, Liaoning, China

Guoying Gu
Shanghai Jiao Tong University
Shanghai, China

Weihong Ren
Harbin Institute of Technology
Shenzhen, China

Zhouping Yin
Huazhong University of Science
and Technology
Wuhan, China

Li Jiang
Harbin Institute of Technology
Harbin, China

Xinyu Wu
Shenzhen Institute of Advanced Technology
Shenzhen, China

ISSN 0302-9743 ISSN 1611-3349 (electronic)
Lecture Notes in Artificial Intelligence
ISBN 978-3-031-13843-0 ISBN 978-3-031-13844-7 (eBook)
https://doi.org/10.1007/978-3-031-13844-7

LNCS Sublibrary: SL7 – Artificial Intelligence

This Springer imprint is published by the registered company Springer Nature Switzerland AG
The registered company address is: Gewerbestrasse 11, 6330 Cham, Switzerland

Preface

With the theme "Smart Robotics for Society", the 15th International Conference on Intelligent Robotics and Applications (ICIRA 2022) was held in Harbin, China, August 1–3, 2022, and designed to encourage advancement in the field of robotics, automation, mechatronics, and applications. It aims to promote top-level research and globalize the quality research in general, making discussions, presentations more internationally competitive and focusing on the latest outstanding achievements, future trends, and demands.

ICIRA 2022 was organized by Harbin Institute of Technology, co-organized by Huazhong University of Science and Technology, Shanghai Jiao Tong University, and Shenyang Institute of Automation, Chinese Academy of Sciences, undertaken by State Key Laboratory of Robotics and Systems, State Key Laboratory of Digital Manufacturing Equipment and Technology, State Key Laboratory of Mechanical Systems and Vibration, and State Key Laboratory of Robotics. Also, ICIRA 2022 was technically co-sponsored by Springer. On this occasion, ICIRA 2022 was a successful event this year in spite of the COVID-19 pandemic. It attracted more than 440 submissions, and the Program Committee undertook a rigorous review process for selecting the most deserving research for publication. The advisory Committee gave advice for the conference program. Also, they help to organize special sections for ICIRA 2022. Finally, a total of 284 papers were selected for publication in 4 volumes of Springer's Lecture Note in Artificial Intelligence. For the review process, single-blind peer review was used. Each review took around 2–3 weeks, and each submission received at least 2 reviews and 1 meta-review.

In ICIRA 2022, 3 distinguished plenary speakers and 9 keynote speakers had delivered their outstanding research works in various fields of robotics. Participants gave a total of 171 oral presentations and 113 poster presentations, enjoying this excellent opportunity to share their latest research findings. Here, we would like to express our sincere appreciation to all the authors, participants, and distinguished plenary and keynote speakers. Special thanks are also extended to all members of the Organizing Committee, all reviewers for peer-review, all staffs of the conference affairs group, and all volunteers for their diligent work.

August 2022

Honghai Liu
Zhouping Yin
Lianqing Liu
Li Jiang
Guoying Gu
Xinyu Wu
Weihong Ren

Organization

Honorary Chair

Youlun Xiong   Huazhong University of Science and Technology, China

General Chairs

Honghai Liu   Harbin Institute of Technology, China
Zhouping Yin   Huazhong University of Science and Technology, China
Lianqing Liu   Shenyang Institute of Automation, Chinese Academy of Sciences, China

Program Chairs

Li Jiang   Harbin Institute of Technology, China
Guoying Gu   Shanghai Jiao Tong University, China
Xinyu Wu   Shenzhen Institute of Advanced Technology, Chinese Academy of Sciences, China

Publication Chair

Weihong Ren   Harbin Institute of Technology, China

Award Committee Chair

Limin Zhu   Shanghai Jiao Tong University, China

Regional Chairs

Zhiyong Chen   The University of Newcastle, Australia
Naoyuki Kubota   Tokyo Metropolitan University, Japan
Zhaojie Ju   The University of Portsmouth, UK
Eric Perreault   Northwestern University, USA
Peter Xu   The University of Auckland, New Zealand
Simon Yang   University of Guelph, Canada
Houxiang Zhang   Norwegian University of Science and Technology, Norway

Advisory Committee

Jorge Angeles	McGill University, Canada
Tamio Arai	University of Tokyo, Japan
Hegao Cai	Harbin Institute of Technology, China
Tianyou Chai	Northeastern University, China
Jie Chen	Tongji University, China
Jiansheng Dai	King's College London, UK
Zongquan Deng	Harbin Institute of Technology, China
Han Ding	Huazhong University of Science and Technology, China
Xilun Ding	Beihang University, China
Baoyan Duan	Xidian University, China
Xisheng Feng	Shenyang Institute of Automation, Chinese Academy of Sciences, China
Toshio Fukuda	Nagoya University, Japan
Jianda Han	Shenyang Institute of Automation, Chinese Academy of Sciences, China
Qiang Huang	Beijing Institute of Technology, China
Oussama Khatib	Stanford University, USA
Yinan Lai	National Natural Science Foundation of China, China
Jangmyung Lee	Pusan National University, South Korea
Zhongqin Lin	Shanghai Jiao Tong University, China
Hong Liu	Harbin Institute of Technology, China
Honghai Liu	The University of Portsmouth, UK
Shugen Ma	Ritsumeikan University, Japan
Daokui Qu	SIASUN, China
Min Tan	Institute of Automation, Chinese Academy of Sciences, China
Kevin Warwick	Coventry University, UK
Guobiao Wang	National Natural Science Foundation of China, China
Tianmiao Wang	Beihang University, China
Tianran Wang	Shenyang Institute of Automation, Chinese Academy of Sciences, China
Yuechao Wang	Shenyang Institute of Automation, Chinese Academy of Sciences, China
Bogdan M. Wilamowski	Auburn University, USA
Ming Xie	Nanyang Technological University, Singapore
Yangsheng Xu	The Chinese University of Hong Kong, SAR China
Huayong Yang	Zhejiang University, China

Jie Zhao	Harbin Institute of Technology, China
Nanning Zheng	Xi'an Jiaotong University, China
Xiangyang Zhu	Shanghai Jiao Tong University, China

Contents – Part I

Motion Control and Interactive Technology for Mobile Robots

AI Meets the Challenges of Autism

Autonomous Intelligent Robot Systems for Unconstrained Environments

Rehabilitation and Assistive Robotics

Rehabilitation and Assistive Robotics

Vision-Based Human-Robot Interaction
and Applications

Knowledge-Enhanced Scene Context Embedding for Object-Oriented Navigation of Autonomous Robots

Yongwei Li, Nengfei Xiao, Xiang Huo, and Xinkai Wu[✉]

School of Transportation Science and Engineering, Beihang University, Beijing 100191, China
xinkaiwu@buaa.edu.cn

Abstract. Object-oriented navigation in unknown environments with only vision as input has been a challenging task for autonomous robots. Introducing semantic knowledge into the model has been proved to be an effective means to improve the suboptimal performance and the generalization of existing end-to-end learning methods. In this paper, we improve object-oriented navigation by proposing a knowledge-enhanced scene context embedding method, which consists of a reasonable knowledge graph and a designed novel 6-D context vector. The developed knowledge graph (named MattKG) is derived from large-scale real-world scenes and contains object-level relationships that are expected to assist robots to understand the environment. The designed novel 6-D context vector replaces traditional pixel-level raw features by embedding observations as scene context. The experimental results on the public dataset AI2-THOR indicate that our method improves both the navigation success rate and efficiency compared with other state-of-the-art models. We also deploy the proposed method on a physical robot and apply it to the real-world environment.

Keywords: Autonomous robots · Object-oriented navigation · Knowledge graph · 6-D context vector · Learning

1 Introduction

Nowadays, autonomous robots are widely applied to various scenarios and play an important role in improving services and reducing labor. As an essential capability of autonomous robots, navigation has always attracted the attention of researchers. Classical mobile robot navigation methods usually rely on the Simultaneous Localization and Mapping technology (SLAM), which provides an occupancy grid map that characterizes the geometric information of the environment [1, 2]. However, as more and more autonomous robots are entering human-centered environments with rich semantic information, the traditional methods relying only on geometric maps are difficult to meet people's expectations for interaction and intelligence. In this paper, we will introduce a knowledge-enhanced method to improve the performance of object-oriented navigation for autonomous robots in human-centered environments.

© The Author(s), under exclusive license to Springer Nature Switzerland AG 2022
H. Liu et al. (Eds.): ICIRA 2022, LNAI 13455, pp. 3–12, 2022.
https://doi.org/10.1007/978-3-031-13844-7_1

Object-oriented navigation is defined as navigating to search for a goal object without knowing the precise coordinates of the destination using only visual input [3]. Humans seem to be able to perform this task efficiently, but this is an admittedly huge challenge for robots. Robots are challenging in object-oriented navigation, mainly due to the unstructured environmental information, the wide variety of dynamic objects, and the lack of effective understanding of human-centered scenes. In contrast, human beings have excellent performance in this task, thanks to the massive experience and knowledge they have learned in their daily living environment. As shown in Fig. 1, there are certain common understandings, or "laws", in human-centered scenes. For example, the cellphone is usually with the laptop, the toaster is probably next to the coffee-machine, and the towel is usually placed above the sink. With this prior commonsense knowledge, humans can easily deal with object-oriented navigation. Previous studies have shown that prior knowledge can help robots improve performance on high-level tasks such as object recognition [4], task planning [5], and VQA [6]. Therefore, extracting this knowledge and assisting robots to learn has the potential to improve the robots' object-oriented navigation.

Fig. 1. Examples of common object relationships in human-centered environments.

Existing research on object-oriented navigation by visual input is generally divided into two categories. One category is sensory-based learning [3, 7, 8], which tends to encode the raw data from the sensor into a state vector, and then input it into an end-to-end reinforcement learning (RL) framework for implicit learning. Zhu et al. [3] introduced an actor-critic model and created a simulation framework with high-quality rendering that enables visual interactions for agents. Ran et al. [7] converted the problem of visual navigation to scene classification and improved navigation performance by designing an adaptive weighted control algorithm and a shallow convolutional neural network with higher scene classification accuracy and efficiency. To achieve continuous and unsupervised learning, Wortsman et al. [8] proposed a self-adaptive visual navigation method (SAVN) that learns to adapt to new environments without any explicit supervision. However, the above methods often face many challenges, such as relying on large-scale training data and poor generalization in new environments.

The second category is knowledge-enhanced learning [9–11], which combines raw sensor features and prior semantic knowledge and is expected to enhance the learning ability of the deep learning models. Zeng et al. [9] proposed an active visual object search strategy through a Semantic Link Graph model to enable robots to reason about the location of previously unseen target objects. Aiming at the ineffectiveness of end-to-end learning-based navigation methods in terms of exploration and long-term planning, Chaplot et al. [10] designed an episodic semantic map and used it to explore the environment efficiently. Yang et al. [11] applied Graph Convolutional Networks for incorporating the prior knowledge into a deep reinforcement learning framework. These works have achieved better performance in accuracy and robustness than traditional sensory-based learning methods, simply because the prior semantic knowledge can represent the high-level environment information in a way close to human perception. Recently, Qiu [12] proposed the memory-utilized joint hierarchical object learning for navigation in indoor rooms, in which the introduction of context vectors provided a novel approach for improving object-oriented navigation and had made great progress. Unfortunately, they did not pay attention to the source of reasonable prior object relationships.

We believe that obtaining the complex relationship of objects from large-scale real scenes is essential for improving the task of robot object-oriented navigation. Therefore, we propose a knowledge-enhanced method consisting of knowledge graphs derived from large-scale real indoor environments and a learning framework based on novel scene context embedding. We first build a knowledge graph (named MattKG) containing hierarchical object relationships based on the large-scale real indoor scene dataset Matterport3D [13] and apply the graph convolutional neural networks to encode the key information in MattKG. Furthermore, we develop a novel 6-D scene context vector, which is used to encode the detected objects and the prior knowledge, and send the joint embedding to the baseline model backed by reinforcement learning. Finally, we evaluate the effectiveness of our proposed method on the public dataset AI2-THOR [14] and deploy the proposed approach to a real-world robot. In summary, the main contributions of this paper include:

1) We propose MattKG, a knowledge graph containing hierarchical object relationships in human-centered environments, derived from large-scale real indoor scenes and suitable for high-level tasks on robot-human interactions.
2) We develop a novel 6-D context vector to substitute the raw sensor features as input to the end-to-end learning model. The designed context vector embeds the observation content and the above-mentioned prior knowledge, and it is verified to have better performance on public datasets.
3) Experiments on public datasets show that the proposed method improves the performance of baseline models. We also deploy the proposed method on a real-world robot and apply it to a real human-centered environment.

The remainder of the paper is organized as below. In Sect. 2, we describe the task definition and the proposed method. The experimental results are discussed in Sect. 3. Finally, Sect. 4 summarizes the conclusions and future challenges of this work.

2 Definition and Methodology

2.1 Task Definition

Robot object-oriented navigation is defined as the problem in that the robot starts from a random location L_0 to find a goal object O_o that is not visible in the current field of view. To clarify, the environment is unknown to the robot in advance and the robot relies entirely on real-time visual input for action planning. The action space that the robot can perform during navigation is *Actions* ={*MoveAhead, RotateLeft, RotateRight, LookUp, LookDown* and *Done*}. The navigation process can be represented as a continuous sequence of actions $SeqA = \{a_1, a_2, a_3, ..., a_n\}$, where each action $a \in Actions$ is directly output by the model. The navigation task was considered successful when the goal object was visible and the distance to the robot was less than 1.5 m. For efficient evaluation, the maximum episode for a single navigation task is limited to E_{max}, beyond which the robot will stop navigating regardless of whether the task is successful or not.

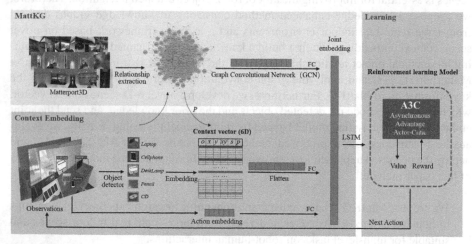

Fig. 2. Overview of the architecture. There are three modules: the MattKG module for embedding prior object relations, the Contextual Embedding module for encoding scenes observed by the robot, and the Learning module for policy learning and agent training.

As displayed in Fig. 2, the proposed framework for object-oriented navigation mainly consists of three modules: MattKG, Context embedding, and End-to-end learning. The MattKG module is used for prior knowledge extraction and reasoning, including our proposed knowledge graph containing object relationships derived from large-scale real scenes. The Context Embedding module is used to encode observations of the robot, where we develop a novel 6-D context vector. The End-to-end Learning module employs Asynchronous Advantage Actor-Critic (A3C) [15] as the backbone network and is implemented based on the baseline model [12]. The detailed implementation of the above modules is described below.

2.2 Knowledge Graph Based on Matterport3D (MattKG)

Reasonable and generalizable semantic knowledge is the key to improving robots' understanding of the environment. However, different scenes such as homes, offices, and shopping malls have their own characteristics and correspond to different domain knowledge. Relying only on commonsense knowledge bases and ontologies is challenging for object-oriented navigation tasks. In this section, we present MattKG, a knowledge graph containing hierarchical object relationships derived from the large-scale real-world indoor environment dataset Matterport3D [13].

The structure of the proposed MattKG is defined as $G = (V, E, w)$, where $V = \{v_1, v_2, v_3, ...\}$ is the set of nodes contained in the graph, and $E = \{e_{(v_1, v_2)} | v_1, v_2 \in V\}$ is the set of edges representing the connectivity between any two nodes in the graph. Unlike existing studies that only exploit connectivity between nodes in knowledge graphs, we also emphasize the quantified relevance of connected nodes. For example, pillow-bed and pillow-sofa are common connected objects, but the frequency of pillows on the sofa and on the bed is usually different. To quantify the relationship among objects, we introduce a weight set w to characterize the correlation of objects connected by edges.

Matterport3D is the largest real indoor RGB-D dataset available, which contains RGB-D images captured from 90 buildings with the Matterport Pro Camera. The scale of Matterport3D covers 46,561 m^2 of floor space, including 2056 rooms and multiple room types. The data provided by the Matterport3D includes 10,800 panoramic views and corresponding depth images, as well as the hundreds of object categories covered in the scene. Rich semantic representation provides a guarantee for us to construct a reasonable knowledge graph containing object-level relationships. We use a detector with Faster R-CNN [16] as the backbone network for object recognition on panoramic images in the dataset. Each type of object is added to the graph as a node, and the nodes of objects that co-occur on the same image are connected in the graph. Furthermore, we count the frequency of co-occurrence of connected objects in the graph as their edge weights across the entire dataset. Neo4j serves as the database and query engine of our proposed MattKG.

To apply our proposed MattKG above to navigation, we employ the Graph Convolutional Network (GCN) [17] to extract the feature representation of the prior graph. For a given graph $G = (V, E)$, assuming it contains n nodes and each node is represented as an m-dimensional feature vector, then the features of the nodes in the graph form a feature matrix $X^{n \times m}$, and the graph structure is represented by the adjacency matrix $A^{n \times n}$. X and A are the inputs of the GCN model, and the output H is the learned feature representation. The classical multilayer GCN propagates according to the following function:

$$H^{(l+1)} = f(\tilde{D}^{-\frac{1}{2}} \tilde{A} \tilde{D}^{-\frac{1}{2}} H^{(l)} W^{(l)}) \tag{1}$$

where $H^{(l)}$ is the feature learned after layer l and $H^{(l)} = X$; $\tilde{A} = A + I$ is the adjacency matrix of an undirected graph with self-connections, and I is the identity matrix; $\tilde{D}$ is the degree matrix of $\tilde{A}$ and $W^{(l)}$ is the trainable weight matrix at layer l; and $f(\cdot)$ denote the activation function.

2.3 6-D Scene Context Embedding

In this section, we develop a 6-D context vector to embed robot observations of the environment as an alternative to traditional pixel-level visual features. Unlike the traditional method, which directly sends the raw RGB image features obtained by the sensor to the end-to-end network for learning, we propose first performing object detection and encoding the detection results into vectors before feeding them into the model. Since the input of the model is replaced by the context vector encoded by the detected object, the prior semantic knowledge in MattKG introduced in Sect. 2.2 is organically integrated.

This novel 6-D context vector embeds the observed object, the relative object position, and its prior relationship to the goal object, and can be denoted as $Embedding = [k, x, y, bbox, S, P]$. It is worth mentioning that this novel 6-D context vector is inspired and extended from [12]. Assuming that the goal object of the current object-oriented navigation task is O_o, and the list of objects detected by the robot in the current frame is Obj, then any object O_i can be encoded according to the above rules as $Embedding_i = [k_{io}, x_i, y_i, bbox_i, S_{io}, P_{io}]$. Respectively, $k_{io} \in \{0, 1\}$ is a binary factor depending on whether object O_i is detected in Obj; x_i and y_i represent the coordinates of detected object O_i in the image; and $bbox_i$ is used to characterize the area covered by the bounding box of object O_i. S_{io} is the cosine similarity between the word embeddings of the observed object O_i and the goal object O_o, where the object label is embedded as vector v by the GloVe [18]. S_{io} is calculated as follows [12]:

$$S_{io} = \frac{v_i \cdot v_o}{||v_i|| \cdot ||v_o||} \tag{2}$$

Additionally, P_{io} is the prior probability of co-occurrence of the observed object O_i and the goal object O_o inferred from the knowledge graph. It represents the correlation between connected objects in the knowledge graph in a probabilistic form, and enhances the interaction between the prior graph and the observed context embeddings. The probability P_{io} follows Bayes' rule and can be calculated as follows:

$$P_{io} = \frac{N_{io} + \lambda}{\sum_{j \in Obj} N_{jo} + \lambda n} \tag{3}$$

where N_{io} is the value on the edge of the observed object O_i and the goal object O_o in the graph, and Obj denotes a set containing n objects detected in the current frame. The parameter λ plays a smoothing role and the value is set to 0.5.

2.4 End-to-End Learning

The above describes our proposed MattKG and novel 6-D context vectors. In this section, we introduce the entire end-to-end learning framework for training agent, and further describe the function and operational details of each module in the framework.

As shown in the overview of the proposed architecture in Fig. 2 above. First, in the MattKG module, we propose an automated pipeline to extract object relationships from large-scale visual datasets and build a prior knowledge graph named MattKG, and then extract node features through a two-layer graph convolutional network. The feature embedding extracted from the prior knowledge graph is denoted as vector Vec_1. Second, in the Context Embedding module, we first utilize the object detector based on ResNet [19] to identify observations as object sets, and then embed the detection results into the vector Vec_2 via the proposed 6-D context vector. The Vec_2 embeds the label of the object detected by the robot in the current frame, the area covered by the object in the image, and the prior relationship to the goal object. Similarly, the current action sequence of the robot is also embedded as a vector Vec_3. Finally, we concatenate the above three vectors to generate a joint embedding which is fed into the End-to-end Learning module based on the reinforcement learning model.

The policy is learned and trained through the Asynchronous Advantage Actor-Critic (A3C) [15] model, and the joint embeddings pass a layer of LSTM [20] to reinforce its temporal features before being fed into the A3C model. For efficient evaluation, the reward function as well as other training settings follow the baseline model.

3 Experiments

In this section, we introduce the evaluation method and discuss the experimental results. We evaluate the performance of the proposed method on the public dataset AI2-THOR [14] and compare it with the baseline model. Furthermore, we deploy the model on a real-world robot to validate its application on autonomous robots.

AI2-THOR is a widely accepted and challenging simulation environment for robotics. It contains rich scene and semantic information to meet the needs of object-oriented navigation. The entire platform provides 120 scenes containing 4 types of rooms: *living rooms, bedrooms, kitchens,* and *bathrooms.* Each room type consists of 30 rooms of different appearances and configurations, with realistic objects distributed throughout the rooms for the robot to interact with. To facilitate training and evaluation, we take the first 20 rooms of each scene type as the training set and the remaining 10 rooms as the test set.

We complete the training on the Ubuntu18.04 system platform with an NVIDIA-3090 GPU, and the experimental results are shown in Fig. 3. Two approaches are trained: the baseline model [12] and our proposed knowledge-enhanced method. For each approach, the agent was trained for 6 million episodes. Success Rate (SR) and SPL were used as metrics to evaluate navigation performance. SR refers to the percentage that the robot successfully finds the target object within the limited episodes. SPL is a comprehensive metric widely used to evaluate the efficiency of robot navigation, it weights the success rate and the expended path length and can be calculated as follows:

$$SPL = \frac{1}{N} \sum_{i=1}^{N} s_i \frac{pl_i}{\max(pl_i, l_i)} \qquad (4)$$

where N is the number of experiments, $s_i \in \{0, 1\}$ is a binary parameter that depends on success, pl_i denotes the ideal shortest path length, and l_i is the path length actually traveled by the agent.

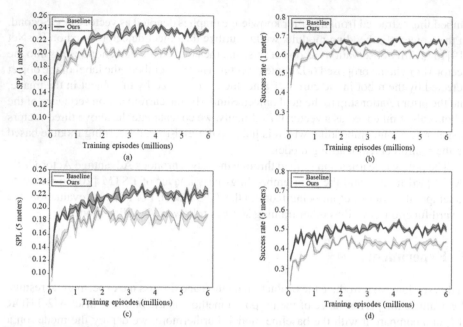

Fig. 3. Experimental results in AI2-THOR. (a). SPL with navigation length of 1 m; (b). Success rate with navigation length of 1 m; (c). SPL with navigation length of 5 m; (d). Success rate with navigation length of 5 m.

We evaluate the performance of the proposed method on the object-oriented navigation task and compare it with the baseline model, and the detailed experimental results are displayed in Fig. 3. The experimental results indicate that our proposed method improves both the navigation success rate and SPL. Compared with the baseline model, the navigation success rate is improved by about 16%, and the SPL is improved by about 12%.

For training 6 million episodes, the baseline model reaches its best performance at about 2 million episodes and the SPL does not increase any more, while our proposed method can achieve the same performance with fewer episodes wand the SPL will continue to improve with subsequent training. Since our proposed method emphasizes the embedding of knowledge graphs, continuous training performance will still improve within a certain range. To distinguish challenges, we record the capability of the model on tasks with navigation lengths greater than 1 m and navigation lengths greater than 5 m, respectively. Analyzing the experimental results of different navigation lengths, it can be seen that our proposed method has a more obvious improvement when the navigation length is greater than 5 m. This is mainly due to our proposed knowledge-enhanced method, which learns to reason about object relationships in the scene by embedding the scene context to achieve longer-distance navigation.

Furthermore, to realize the application of our proposed method in a real environment, we deploy it to a real-world robot (named Rokid). Rokid is a mobile robot with a robotic arm developed in our lab. It is equipped with multiple sensors including RGB-D camera, ultrasonic and IMU, and is capable of vision processing. The entire robot software operating system is based on ROS under Ubuntu18.04. As shown in Fig. 4, equipped with our proposed method, the robot is able to navigate in an unknown environment to objects that are not currently visible in the field of view, such as finding a microwave oven through a refrigerator. This mechanism of learning to reason about object-level relationships helps to reduce path cost and improve navigation efficiency.

Fig. 4. Deploy the proposed model to a real-world robot for application.

4 Conclusion

Object-oriented navigation of autonomous robots in unknown environments has always been a challenging task. In this paper, we propose a knowledge-enhanced approach to address this challenge. We emphasize the key role of prior knowledge in object-oriented navigation and propose a new approach for the acquisition of knowledge graphs containing reasonable object relations and the embedding of scene context in end-to-end learning models. The MattKG we proposed is a knowledge graph containing object-level relationships, which is derived from large-scale real environments and can provide prior domain knowledge for intelligent robots. The developed 6-D scene context vector can fully embed observations and integrate the prior knowledge in the graph, which improves the learning efficiency of the end-to-end navigation model. Experiments on the public dataset AI2-THOR indicate that our proposed method improves both the navigation success rate and SPL compared to the baseline model. In addition, we also deploy the trained model to a real-world autonomous robot and achieve application in a human-centered environment.

Prior knowledge plays an important role in improving object-oriented navigation, but existing knowledge graphs do not include the spatiotemporal properties of objects. Considering the spatiotemporal characteristics of objects is the direction of our future research.

Acknowledgments. This work was partially supported by the National Natural Science Foundation of China (52172376), the Young Scientists Fund of the National Natural Science Foundation of China (52002013), the China Postdoctoral Science Foundation (BX20200036, 2020M680298) and the Project Fund of the GENERAL ADMINISTRATION OF CUSTOMS.P.R.CHINA (2021HK261).

References

1. Taheri, H., Xia, Z.C.: Slam; definition and evolution. Eng. Appl. Artif. Intell. **97**, 104032 (2021)
2. Thrun, S.: Learning metric-topological maps for indoor mobile robot navigation. Artif. Intell. **99**(1), 21–71 (1998)
3. Zhu, Y., et al.: Target-driven visual navigation in indoor scenes using deep reinforcement learning. In: 2017 IEEE International Conference on Robotics and Automation (ICRA), pp. 3357–3364. IEEE (2017)
4. Maillot, N.E., Thonnat, M.: Ontology based complex object recognition. Image Vis. Comput. **26**(1), 102–113 (2008)
5. Serrano, S.A., Santiago, E., Martinez-Carranza, J., Morales, E.F., Sucar, L.E.: Knowledge-based hierarchical pomdps for task planning. J. Intell. Rob. Syst. **101**(4), 1–30 (2021)
6. Marino, K., Chen, X., Parikh, D., Gupta, A., Rohrbach, M.: Krisp: integrating implicit and symbolic knowledge for open-domain knowledge-based vqa. In: Proceedings of the IEEE/CVF Conference on Computer Vision and Pattern Recognition, pp. 14111–14121 (2021)
7. Ran, T., Yuan, L., Zhang, J.: Scene perception based visual navigation of mobile robot in indoor environment. ISA Trans. **109**, 389–400 (2021)
8. Wortsman, M., Ehsani, K., Rastegari, M., Farhadi, A., Mottaghi, R.: Learning to learn how to learn: self-adaptive visual navigation using meta-learning. In: Proceedings of the IEEE/CVF Conference on Computer Vision and Pattern Recognition, pp. 6750–6759 (2019)
9. Zeng, Z., R¨ofer, A., Jenkins, O.C.: Semantic linking maps for active visual object search. In: 2020 IEEE International Conference on Robotics and Automation (ICRA), pp. 1984–1990. IEEE (2020)
10. Chaplot, D.S., Gandhi, D.P., Gupta, A., Salakhutdinov, R.R.: Object goal navigation using goal-oriented semantic exploration. Adv. Neural. Inf. Process. Syst. **33**, 4247–4258 (2020)
11. Yang, W., Wang, X., Farhadi, A., Gupta, A., Mottaghi, R.: Visual semantic navigation using scene priors. arXiv preprint arXiv:1810.06543 (2018)
12. Qiu, Y., Pal, A., Christensen, H.I.: Learning hierarchical relationships for object-goal navigation. arXiv preprint arXiv:2003.06749 (2020)
13. Chang, A., et al.: Matterport3d: learning from rgb-d data in indoor environments. arXiv preprint arXiv:1709.06158 (2017)
14. Kolve, E., et al.: Ai2-thor: An interactive 3D environment for visual ai. arXiv preprint arXiv: 1712.05474 (2017)
15. Mnih, V., et al.: Asynchronous methods for deep reinforcement learning. In: International Conference on Machine Learning, pp. 1928–1937. PMLR (2016)
16. Ren, S., He, K., Girshick, R., Sun, J.: Faster R-CNN: towards real-time object detection with region proposal networks. Adv. Neural Inf. Process. Syst. **28** (2015)
17. Kipf, T.N., Welling, M.: Semi-supervised classification with graph convolutional networks. arXiv preprint arXiv:1609.02907 (2016)
18. Pennington, J., Socher, R., Manning, C.D.: Glove: global vectors for word representation. In: Proceedings of the 2014 Conference on Empirical Methods in Natural Language Processing (EMNLP), pp. 1532–1543 (2014)
19. He, K., Zhang, X., Ren, S., Sun, J.: Deep residual learning for image recognition. In: Proceedings of the IEEE Conference on Computer Vision and Pattern recognition, pp. 770–778 (2016)
20. Hochreiter, S., Schmidhuber, J.: Long short-term memory. Neural Comput. **9**(8), 1735–1780 (1997)

An End-to-End Object Detector with Spatiotemporal Context Learning for Machine-Assisted Rehabilitation

Xuna Wang[1] , Hongwei Gao[1]([✉]) , Tianyu Ma[1] , and Jiahui Yu[2]

[1] School of Automation and Electrical Engineering, Shenyang Ligong University, Shenyang 110159, Liaoning, China
ghw1978@sohu.com

[2] Department of Biomedical Engineering, Zhejiang University, Hangzhou 310027, China

Abstract. Recently, object detection technologies applied in rehabilitation systems are mainly based on the ready-made technology of CNNs. This paper proposes an DETR-based detector which is an end-to-end object detector with spatiotemporal context learning for machine-assisted rehabilitation. To improve the performance of small object detection, first, the multi-level features of the RepVGG are fused with the SE attention mechanism to build a SEFP-RepVGG. To make the encoder-decoder structure more suitable, next, the value of the encoder is generated by using feature maps with more detailed information than key/query. To reduce computation, Patch Merging is finally imported to modify the feature map scale of the input encoder. The proposed detector has higher real-time performance than DETR and obtains the competitive detection accuracy on the ImageNet VID benchmark. Some typical samples from the NTU RGB-D 60 dataset are selected to build a new limb-detection dataset for further evaluation. The results show the effectiveness of the proposed detector in the rehabilitation scenarios.

Keywords: Machine-assisted rehabilitation system · Deep learning · Object detection · Transformer · CNNs

1 Introduction

Clinical medicine shows that the central nervous system has high plasticity. Patients with disabilities can reactivate their limbs through repeated appropriate rehabilitation training. The machine-assisted rehabilitation training system is the product of AI and medicine, which can reduce the burden of care and provide robust assessments. These systems execute human-machine interaction primarily through human biological signals and dynamic signals [1].

The human biological signals require patients to have direct or indirect contact with equipment, and the freedom of rehabilitation exercise is limited [2]. In contrast, many works in the dynamic signal acquisition have solved this problem. Chae SH et al. [3] developed an upper limb home-based rehabilitation system using wearable sensors embedded in a commercial smartwatch. However, like most wearable sensors, this device

H. Liu et al. (Eds.): ICIRA 2022, LNAI 13455, pp. 13–23, 2022.
https://doi.org/10.1007/978-3-031-13844-7_2

cannot detect the overall posture of the human body and the interaction with the outside world. Optical sensor and depth sensor can avoid all of these problems. Chiang AT et al. [4] developed a Kinect-based intervention system, which captured the joint positions using both a Kinect sensor and a motion capture (MOCAP) system.

Object detection technology is needed to capture human motion through environmental sensors. The object detectors used in rehabilitation systems are mostly based on CNN. Its detection framework is mainly divided into two categories: two-stage and one-stage. Typical two-stage detector, such as Faster RCNN [5]. This method still has room for acceleration, and the small object detection effect is not good. Typical one-stage detector, such as YOLOv3 [6], whose small object detection performance is poor. In general, both the two-stage and one-stage detectors generate a set of rectangular boundary boxes through the proposed generator. Then these proposals are used for classification and localization improvement.

Effective use of context information helps to improve detection performance, especially for objects with insufficient detection clues (small objects, occlusion, etc.). The convolution network cannot through the global context information to determine the region of interest. Recently, many works have transplanted Transformer into CV tasks, using the attention mechanism to focus on global information, and achieved good results. DEtection with TRansformer (DETR) [7] is the first end-to-end Transformer detector by eliminating the hand-designed representations and non-maximum suppression (NMS).

For the rehabilitation training of patients with sports disorders, the effect of limb training is significant. Limb detection (arm + hand, thigh + calf) requires high detection performance of small objects and needs to capture the correlation information between various body parts. Besides, the rehabilitation system needs to make real-time feedback for patients' training. Most machine-assisted rehabilitation systems use existing methods without in-depth study on limb detection to obtain dynamic information. We aim to apply DETR to the rehabilitation system and improve it powered by [8–12] to address the above issues. The main contributions of this work are shown as follows:

1. We improve the DETR to achieve an end-to-end object detection with spatiotemporal context learning, which can successfully apply in the rehabilitation system.
2. Feature extraction neural networks combine the SE attention mechanism to fuse multi-level feature maps of RepVGG. This enables the proposed detector to achieve accurate small object detection. The transformer head uses different level feature maps to generate values and keys/queries to enhance the sensitivity of local information. Patch Merging is introduced to reduce the scale of input feature maps and the computational complexity.
3. We conducted many experiments to evaluate the proposed detector. We compare the results with state-of-the-art works on the ImageNet VID benchmark [13]. A subset of limb-related data is selected from the NTU RGB + D 60 dataset [14] to simulate limb detection in the real world.

The rest of the paper is organized as follows: In Sect. 2, we briefly introduce DETR and some works related to its improvement. Then, we describe the main methods of proposed model in Sect. 3. In order to verify that the model can be applied to the rehabilitation system, we make multiple sets of experiments in Sect. 4. Finally, we summarize the model and its development space.

2 Related Work

DETR provides a new pattern that resolve object detection as a set prediction problem by a set of learned parameters equally aggregate global features. The object query gradually learns instance features during the interaction with image features. The bipartite matching allows a direct set prediction to quickly adapt to one-to-one label assignment tasks, thus eliminating traditional post-processing. However, DETR has low accuracy on small objects and slow convergence. The DETR framework is shown in Fig. 1. Our work is to apply the DETR object detection framework to the rehabilitation system and adjust it.

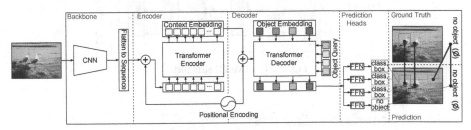

Fig. 1. The DETR framework (Modified from [7])

Object detectors based on Transformer are almost all variants of DETR. Deformable DETR [15] contains a learnable sparse deformable attention for convergence acceleration and a multi-scale architecture for accuracy improvement. Efficient DETR [10] consists of dense proposal generation and sparse set prediction parts, which leverage dense prior to initializing the object containers. Conditional DETR [16] learns a conditional spatial query from the decoder embedding so that each cross-attention head can attend to a band containing a distinct region. Existing modified models fail to take full advantage of the backbone so they have to through overly complex design to improve performance. Moreover, these models are not designed for rehabilitation systems. By contrast, our work is to strive for a concise model used in rehabilitation systems. We improve DETR mainly in feature extraction networks and generating tokens.

The feature extraction network largely determines the accuracy and speed of the model. ResNeXt [17] is constructed by repeating a building block that aggregates a set of transformations with the same topology. MobileNet [18] is based on a streamlined architecture that uses depthwise separable convolutions to build lightweight deep neural networks. RepVGG [8] has a VGG-like inference-time body and a training-time model with multi-branch topology. Due to the good trade-off between speed and accuracy of the RepVGG network, this model selects and improves it as a feature extraction network to meet the requirements of the rehabilitation system.

To apply Transformer in the image processing, there are three types of token-improvement: 1) Change the attention mechanism. Sparse Transformers [19] introduce sparse factorizations of the attention matrix which reduce required time and memory. employ scalable approximations to global self-attention. 2) Change the input sequence of the image. Swin Transformer [12] is a hierarchical Transformer whose representation is computed with Shifted windows and number of tokens is reduced by patch merging layers. 3) CNN combined with Transformer. DETR belongs to this approach which alleviate the problem of poor model performance when training data is insufficient. This model imports the second method while retaining the original one.

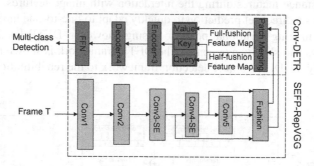

Fig. 2. The overall structure

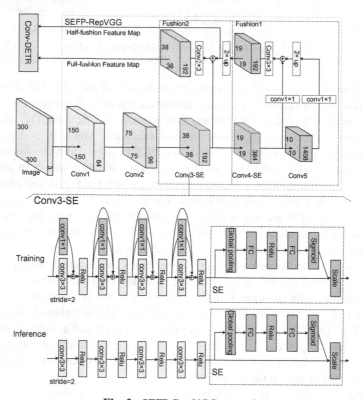

Fig. 3. SEFP-RepVGG network

3   Proposed Method

We introduce DETR into the rehabilitation system to achieve end-to-end object detection and focus on spatiotemporal context information. Besides, we adjust DETR according to the application requirements. The overall structure of the object detector is shown in Fig. 2. It includes two parts. The CNN part is called SEFP-RepVGG and the Transformer part is called Conv-DETR.

3.1   SEFP-RepVGG

For video object detection, many static frames need to be processed in real-time, which requires high memory consumption of the model. By decoupling the architecture of training and reasoning, RepVGG can utilize the advantages of multi-branch model training (high performance) and single-path model reasoning (fast speed and memory saving). In order to achieve real-time detection and a good feature extraction effect, we select the five-level network before the pooling layer of the RepVGG-A2 network as the backbone of the model.

To improve the performance of small object detection, Conv3, Conv4, and Conv5 output feature maps are fused according to the idea of FPN. In order to enhance the fusion of valuable features and suppress the fusion of useless features, the SE attention mechanism is introduced in this part. SE attention mechanism automatically learns the importance of each feature channel and gives it weight. In order to make full use of the SE attention mechanism, the SE attention mechanism is added to the output parts of Conv3 and Conv4 so that the SE attention mechanism can play a role in feature extraction and feature map fusion at the same time. Based on the above work, we get the CNN part of this project, namely the SEFP-RepVGG network, whose structure is shown in the Fig. 3.

In the feature extraction part of the SEFP-RepVGG network, the input image size is $300 \times 300 \times 3$, and the output of each network is $150 \times 150 \times 64$, $75 \times 75 \times 96$, $38 \times 38 \times 192$, $19 \times 19 \times 384$, $10 \times 10 \times 1408$, respectively. The network convolution layers at all levels are 1, 2, 4, 14, 1 respectively. The step of the first convolution layer of each stage is 2, which is used for down-sampling, and the others are 1. To introduce the specific structure of each level, we take Conv3-SE as an example and show it in the lower half of Fig. 3. In the feature fusion part of the SEFP-RepVGG network, deconv is used as the upper sampling method, and add used as the fusion method. The 1×1 convolution layer is used to reduce the number of channels to 192, and the 3×3 convolution layer is used to eliminate the aliasing effect. Both of them do not change the size of the feature map.

3.2   Conv-DETR

When DETR is initialized, the attention module assigns almost consistent attention weight to all pixels in the feature map. Because Transformer is not sensitive to local information, its convergence speed is very slow. The calculation of attention weight in the encoder is a secondary calculation relative to the number of pixels, so DETR has very high computational and storage complexity in processing high-resolution feature maps.

To solve the problem of slow convergence of DETR, this study refers to the idea of ConvTrans to make Transformer focus on more local information. ConvTrans uses a convolution layer with kernel size k and steps size 1 to transform input into key/query. However, ConvTrans is a module constructed for one-dimensional temporal data prediction, which is not suitable for two-dimensional data information of video frames. We use the feature map (the output feature map of up-sampling in Fushion2) that is not fused with the output feature map of Conv3-SE to generate the key/query and apply the Fushion2 output feature map to generate the value. Thereby realize that the detailed information of value is not lost while the encoder assigns the weight of value according to higher semantic information. In order to solve the problem of significant computation of DETR, we use Patch Merging in Swin Transformer to process the feature map before the two feature maps flatten to the sequence. Patch Merging can further reduce the scale of feature maps without losing feature information and constructing hierarchical features. Thus, the Conv-DETR network is obtained, and its architecture is shown in Fig. 4.

When the number of decoders reaches 3, the performance will not decline without the NMS model. And DETR is more sensitive to the number of decoder layers [10]. This part sets up three-layer encoders and four-layer decoders to maximize the retention of detection accuracy while ensuring a real-time network. In addition to the above work, the input vector is embedded in 2D position-coding to further strengthen the attention to the local context information and make the detection more accurate.

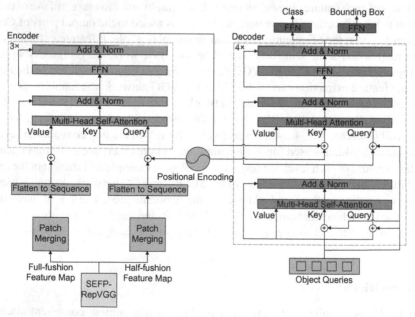

Fig. 4. Structure of the Conv-DETR

Table 1. The verification results of each component on the ImageNet VID

NO	Methods	mAP(%)
1	DETR	55.4
2	RepVGG-DETR	57.3
3	FP-RepVGG- DETR	59.7
4	SEFP-RepVGG- DETR	61.5
5	SEFP-RepVGG-Conv-DETR	64.6

Table 2. The comparison results

NO	Methods	Real-time	mAP(%)
1	TCD [20]	Yes	54.9
2	Patchwork [21]	Yes	58.7
3	EfficientDet-D0 [22]	Yes	59.7
4	TSSD [23]	Yes	65.4
5	Proposed	Yes	64.6

Table 3. Validation results of limb-detection dataset

mAP(%)			FPS
Short-distance	Middle-distance	Long-distance	
97.2%	97.1%	96.7%	29

4   Experimental Results and Discussion

This model is designed for practical rehabilitation application which need multiple object detection and small object detection in real-time. In order to verify whether the model meets the above requirements, three groups of experiments are given successively in this section: 1) Ablation study verifies that each component designed has a positive effect on the model performance; 2) Comparison test, by comparing with State-of-the-Arts, evaluates the object detection level of this model; 3) Applications test inspects whether the model meets application requirements by simulating rehabilitation scenarios. The experimental setting is described in the first part.

4.1 Experimental Settings

During these experiments, we use two datasets. ImageNet VID data set is used as the benchmark data set. Screening limb-related samples from NTU RGB + D dataset as the limb-detection dataset in this experiment. This dataset is used to test the application performance of the model in the rehabilitation system.

Key experimental settings are as follows. This study uses the Python framework and Ubuntu 16.04 64 OS system. Training process in NVIDIA GeForce GTX 2080ti 11 GB GDDR 5X, 32 GB-RAM. For data training, the initial learning rate is 0.0001, the momentum is 0.9, and the weight attenuation is 0.005. As evaluation indexes, average precision (mAP) and the number of frames per second (FPS) are selected.

4.2 Ablation Study

In this section, the ablation experiment is used to test the contribution of the designed components. We use the ImageNet VID benchmark to verify. The following methods are tested: 1) DETR; 2) RepVGG-DETR is obtained by combining RepVGG with three encoders and four decoders of DETR; 3) The output feature maps of Conv3, Conv4 and Conv5 in RepVGG-DETR are fused to obtain FP-RepVGG-DETR; 4) SE attention mechanism is introduced into the feature fusion to obtain SEFP-RepVGG-DETR; 5) The proposed SEFP-RepVGG-Conv-DETR model. The verification results are shown in Table 1.

By comparing the results of method 1 and 2, it can be seen that using RepVGG as the backbone network can improve the detection accuracy. By comparing the results of method 2, 3 and 4, it can be seen that the feature fusion and the SE attention mechanism improve the accuracy of model detection respectively. This improvement mainly is the accuracy of small object detection because the useful detailed information of low-level features makes up for the lack of high-level features. By comparing method 4 and 5, it can be seen that the key/query generated by feature maps with more semantic information enhances the detection accuracy. Besides, Patch Merging is introduced to reduce the scale of the SEFP-RepVGG output feature map, which reduces the computational complexity and does not affect the detection accuracy.

4.3 Comparison with State-of-the-Arts

This part compares the model with the related models in recent years on the ImageNet VID benchmark and obtains the performance level of the model. Since the ImageNet VID dataset includes millions of frames and the amount of data in each category varies greatly, it is difficult to train the dataset directly. In this test, the training program follows [24]. That is to say, using ImageNet VID dataset to perform step-by-step training. The comparison results are shown in Table 2.

The results show that the proposed detector achieves competitive performance compared with others. This work focuses on the feature extraction network, the number of tokens generated, and the generation of key/query for the encoder. The above work alleviates the shortcomings of slow convergence and poor detection performance of the original DETR model. The proposed detector can balance the accuracy and speed of detection.

4.4 Applications in Rehabilitation System

In rehabilitation training, the movement of patients' limbs is the key to detecting the completion of patients' training action. Due to the flexibility of limbs, it is tricky to object detection. In this part, we test the model on the limb-detection dataset to simulate the practical application in rehabilitation training. Every sample is given a set number (1–17) according to the camera height and distance. In order to test the detection performance of this model for different distance objects, we further divide the limb-detection dataset according to the set number as follows: 1) Short-distance detection: samples numbered 2, 3, 9; 2) Long-distance detection: samples numbered 7, 15, 16; 3) Middle-distance detection: residual samples. The experimental results are shown in Table 3.

We can find that the mAP of the long-distance set is slightly lower than the other two verification sets. This is because the tiny body is small and not easy to detect. However, due to the fusion of multi-level features by combining the SE attention mechanism, the remote verification set still has a high mAP. In addition, according to the results of FPS, it can be proved that the model has a good speed in limb detection. Therefore, in multiple combinations of angles and distances, this model can meet the requirements of real-time feedback on the limb movement of patients.

5 Conclusion

To achieve end-to-end object detection with spatiotemporal context learning in the rehabilitation system, we introduce the DETR framework as the object detector and improve it according to the application requirements. This work improves the performance of small object detection by fusing the feature maps with the SE attention mechanism. Besides, we use key/query with more semantic information to assign weights to values with more details. Experiments on multiple datasets show that the speed and accuracy of this model meet the application requirements of the rehabilitation system.

The application of Transformer in object detection makes the joint modeling of vision and language for the rehabilitation system easier. Our work is a preliminary exploration of the Transformer model applied to the rehabilitation system. We hope that future work will maximize the advantages of Transformer in rehabilitation medicine to assist patients with limb disorders and reduce the burden on the medical staff.

Acknowledgments. The authors would like to acknowledge the support from the AiBle project co-financed by the European Regional Development Fund, National Key R&D Program of China (Grant No. 2018YFB1304600), CAS Interdisciplinary Innovation Team (Grant No. JCTD-2018-11), Liaoning Province Higher Education Innovative Talents Program Support Project (Grant No. LR2019058), and National Natural Science Foundation of China (grant No. 52075530, 51575412, and 62006204). LiaoNing Province Joint Open Fund for Key Scientific and Technological Innovation Bases (Grant No. 2021-KF-12-05).

References

1. Kadu, A., Singh, M.: Comparative analysis of e-health care telemedicine system based on internet of medical things and artificial intelligence. In: 2nd International Conference on Smart Electronics and Communication (ICOSEC), pp. 1768–1775 (2021). https://doi.org/10.1109/ICOSEC51865.2021.9591941

2. Debnath, B., O'Brien, M., Yamaguchi, M., Behera, A.: A review of computer vision-based approaches for physical rehabilitation and assessment. Multimedia Syst. **28**(1), 209–239 (2021). https://doi.org/10.1007/s00530-021-00815-4

3. Chae, S.H., Kim, Y., Lee, K.S., Park, H.S.: Development and clinical evaluation of a web-based upper limb home rehabilitation system using a smartwatch and machine learning model for chronic stroke survivors: prospective comparative study. JMIR Mhealth Uhealth **8**(7), e17216 (2020). https://doi.org/10.2196/17216

4. Chiang, A.T., Chen, Q., Wang, Y., Fu, M.R.: Kinect-based in-home exercise system for lymphatic health and lymphedema intervention. IEEE J. Transl. Eng. Health Med. **6**, 1–13 (2018). https://doi.org/10.1109/JTEHM.2018.2859992

5. Ren, S., He, K., Girshick, R., Sun, J.: Faster R-CNN: towards real-time object detection with region proposal networks. IEEE Trans. Pattern Anal. Mach. Intell. **39**(6), 1137–1149 (2017). https://doi.org/10.1109/TPAMI.2016.2577031

6. Redmon, J.,, Farhadi, A.: YOLOv3: an incremental improvement. eprint arXiv:1804.02767 (2018). https://doi.org/10.48550/arXiv.1804.02767

7. Carion, N., Massa, F., Synnaeve, G., Usunier, N., Kirillov, A., Zagoruyko, S.: End-to-end object detection with transformers. In: Vedaldi, A., Bischof, H., Brox, T., Frahm, J.-M. (eds.) ECCV 2020. LNCS, vol. 12346, pp. 213–229. Springer, Cham (2020). https://doi.org/10.1007/978-3-030-58452-8_13

8. Ding, X., Zhang, X., Ma, N., Han, J., Ding, G., Sun, J.: RepVGG: making VGG-style ConvNets great again. In: 2021 IEEE/CVF Conference on Computer Vision and Pattern Recognition (CVPR), pp. 13728–13737. IEEE, New York (2021). https://doi.org/10.1109/CVPR46437.2021.01352

9. Zhang, X., Gao, Y., Ye, F., Liu, Q., Zhang, K.: An approach to improve SSD through skip connection of multiscale feature maps. Comput. Intell. Neurosci. **2020**, 13 (2020). https://doi.org/10.1155/2020/2936920

10. Yao, Z., Ai, J., Li, B., Zhang, C.: Efficient DETR: improving end-to-end object detector with dense prior. eprint arXiv: 2104.01318 (2021). https://doi.org/10.48550/arxiv.2104.01318

11. Li, S., et al.: Enhancing the locality and breaking the memory bottleneck of transformer on time series forecasting. eprint arXiv: 1907.00235 (2019). https://doi.org/10.48550/arxiv.1907.00235

12. Liu, Z., et al.: Swin transformer: hierarchical vision transformer using shifted windows. In: 2021 IEEE/CVF International Conference on Computer Vision (ICCV), pp. 9992–10002. IEEE, New York (2021). https://doi.org/10.48550/arxiv.2103.14030

13. Russakovsky, O., et al.: ImageNet large scale visual recognition challenge. Int. J. Comput. Vis. **115**(3), 211–252 (2015). https://doi.org/10.1007/s11263-015-0816-y

14. Shahroudy, A., Liu, J., Ng, T.-T., Wang, G.: NTU RGB+D: a large scale dataset for 3D human activity analysis. In: 2016 IEEE Conference on Computer Vision and Pattern Recognition (CVPR), pp. 1010–1019. IEEE, New York (2016). https://doi.org/10.1109/CVPR.2016.115

15. Zhu, X., Su, W., Lu, L., Li, B., Wang, X., Dai, J.: Deformable DETR: deformable transformers for end-to-end object detection. eprint arXiv: 2010.04159 (2020). https://doi.org/10.48550/arxiv.2010.04159

16. Meng, D., et al.: Conditional DETR for fast training convergence. In: 2021 IEEE/CVF International Conference on Computer Vision (ICCV), pp. 3631–3640. IEEE, New York (2021). https://doi.org/10.1109/ICCV48922.2021.00363

17. Xie, S., Girshick, R., Dollár, P., Tu, Z., He, K.: Aggregated residual transformations for deep neural networks. In: 2017 IEEE Conference on Computer Vision and Pattern Recognition (CVPR), pp. 5987–5995. IEEE, New York (2017). https://doi.org/10.1109/CVPR.2017.634
18. Howard, A., et al.: MobileNets: efficient convolutional neural networks for mobile vision applications. eprint arXiv: 1704.04861 (2017). https://doi.org/10.48550/arxiv.1704.04861
19. Child, R., Gray, S., Radford, A., Sutskever, I: Generating long sequences with sparse transformers. eprint arXiv: 1904.10509 (2019). https://doi.org/10.48550/arxiv.1904.10509
20. Zhou, N.: Research on video object detection based on temporal characteristics. J. China Acad. Electron. Inf. **16**(02), 157–164 (2021)
21. Chai, Y.: Patchwork: a patch-wise attention network for efficient object detection and segmentation in video streams. In: 2019 IEEE/CVF International Conference on Computer Vision (ICCV), pp. 3414–3423. IEEE, New York (2019). https://doi.org/10.1109/ICCV.2019.00351
22. Tan, M., Pang, R., Le, Q.V.: EfficientDet: scalable and efficient object detection. In: 2020 IEEE/CVF Conference on Computer Vision and Pattern Recognition (CVPR), pp. 10778–10787. IEEE, New York (2019). https://doi.org/10.1109/CVPR42600.2020.0107
23. Chen, X., Yu, J., Wu, Z.: Temporally identity-aware SSD with attentional LSTM. IEEE Trans. Cybern. **50**(6), 2674–2686 (2020). https://doi.org/10.1109/TCYB.2019.2894261
24. Kang, K., et al.: Object detection in videos with tubelet proposal networks. In: 2017 IEEE Conference on Computer Vision and Pattern Recognition (CVPR), pp. 889–897. IEEE, New York (2017). https://doi.org/10.1109/CVPR.2017.101

Skeleton-Based Hand Gesture Recognition by Using Multi-input Fusion Lightweight Network

Qihao Hu[1], Qing Gao[2,3(✉)], Hongwei Gao[1], and Zhaojie Ju[4(✉)]

[1] School of Automation and Electrical Engineering, Shenyang Ligong University,
Shenyang 110159, China
ghw1978@sohu.com

[2] Institute of Robotics and Intelligent Manufacturing and School of Science and Engineering,
The Chinese University of Hong Kong, Shenzhen 518172, China
gaoqing@cuhk.edu.cn

[3] Shenzhen Institute of Artificial Intelligence and Robotics for Society, Shenzhen 518129, China

[4] School of Computing, University of Portsmouth, Portsmouth PO13HE, UK
Zhaojie.Ju@port.ac.uk

Abstract. Skeleton-based hand gesture recognition has achieved great success in recent years. However, most of the existing methods cannot extract spatiotemporal features well due to the skeleton noise. In real applications, some large models also suffer from a huge number of parameters and low execution speed. This paper presents a lightweight skeleton-based hand gesture recognition network by using multi-input fusion to address those issues. We convey two joint-oriented features: Center Joint Distances (CJD) feature and Center Joint Angles (CJA) feature as the static branch. Besides, the motion branch consists of Global Linear Velocities (GLV) feature and Local Angular Velocities (LAV) feature. Fusing static and motion branches, a robust input can be generated and fed into a lightweight CNN-based network to recognize hand gestures. Our method achieves 95.8% and 92.5% hand gesture recognition accuracy with only 2.24M parameters on the 14 gestures and 28 gestures of the SHREC'17 dataset. Experimental results show that the proposed method outperforms state-of-the-art (SOAT) methods.

Keywords: Skeleton-based hand gesture recognition · Multi-input fusion · Joint-oriented feature Second Keyword

1 Introduction

Recently, thanks to the development of machine learning and computer vision, dynamic hand gesture recognition becomes a popular research topic in many fields, e.g., human-computer interaction (HRI), sign language interpretation and medical assistive applications. Over the past decade, with the widespread use of depth cameras and great developing of hand-pose estimation, skeletal data of high accuracy can be generated easily. Skeletal data is a time sequence of 3D coordinates of multiple hand joints. Compared with RGB and RGB-D inputs, skeletal data is more robust to background changes

© The Author(s), under exclusive license to Springer Nature Switzerland AG 2022
H. Liu et al. (Eds.): ICIRA 2022, LNAI 13455, pp. 24–34, 2022.
https://doi.org/10.1007/978-3-031-13844-7_3

and illumination variations. Skeleton-based gesture recognition has shown powerful classification effect in many applications.

One essential problem in dynamic hand gesture recognition is how to extract rich features to fully describe the variations of spatial configurations and temporal dynamics in gestures. Skeleton-based gesture recognition algorithms are developing rapidly, and there are mainly three deep learning methods, namely Convolutional Neural Networks (CNN), Recurrent Neural Networks (RNN) and Graph Convolutional Networks (GCN). The above three methods transform the raw skeletal data into pseudo graph, time series and graph structure for feature extraction, respectively. CNN-based method is of frequently used as a backbone model of real-time gesture detection and recognition because of its compact structure and fast processing speed.

In real applications, a desirable gesture recognition model should be adaptable to the influence caused by the variation of the viewpoints and achieves high recognition accuracy. It also should run efficiently by using a few parameters. To meet those requirements, we propose a multi-input fusion lightweight network, which is a CNN model equipped with a static features branch and a motion feature branch. The proposed model takes into account both the recognition accuracy and the execution speed. Extensive experiments are conducted on public dataset to demonstrate the effectiveness of our proposed method.

Specifically, our research is implemented based on the unique properties of skeletal data. To tackle the issue of viewpoint rotation, we propose a simplified joint distances feature. Meanwhile, to alleviate magnitude changes caused by the distance variations between observer and hand, we introduce the feature of center joint angles. As shown in Fig. 1, joint distances feature and joint angles feature can cope with the variations of input data caused by viewpoints changes. To make full use of the rich spatio-temporal information of skeleton data, motion features generated by joint coordinates and center joint angles are extracted as input features. We adopt a fast slow frame generation method, which is applied to motion branch. Different frame generation method can distinguish the influence of the speed of gestures. At the network structure level, we employ 1D convolutional neural network to embed the above features, and then utilize 2D convolutional neural network to process the fused features. The network structure not only provides small parameter scale and fast running speed, but also can extract spatio-temporal information well. Compared with other similar CNN method, our proposed method has achieved better performance through experimental verification.

The contributions of this paper are as follows:

1. Two geometric features with translation, rotation and scaling invariance are compounded to constitute the static feature module. Besides, motion features are introduced to improve the sensitivity of the model to different temporal and spatial scales, and improve the classification effectiveness.
2. The network architecture combining 1D CNN and 2D CNN is adopted to extract the rich spatio-temporal features, and avoids unnecessary parameters and slow processing speed.
3. Comparative experiment proves that the accuracy of the model is ahead of other advanced CNN-based networks.

The rest of the paper are arranged as follows: We review the related works in Sect. 2. Section 3 introduces the methodology of our model. The fourth section makes ablation studies and comparative experiments to demonstrate the effectiveness of our model. The last section concludes our paper and the future works.

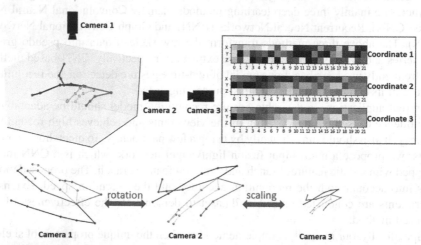

Fig. 1. Variations of Cartesian coordinates caused by viewpoint changes. Camera 1 and Camera 2 have different observation directions, which makes the skeleton rotation. Camera 2 and Camera 3 have different observation distances, which makes the skeleton scaling.

2 Related Works

2.1 Static and Motion Features

In many prior works, static features are frequently applied in recognizing action and gesture tasks, e.g., position, angle, distance, velocity and acceleration. Li et al. [9] propose 2D and 3D joint distance map (JDM) features. Zhang et al. [10] provide a variety of distance and angle features of lines and planes. Liao et al. [4] utilize a set of joint-oriented features for human action recognition. Song et al. [8] propose an early fused Multiple Input Branches (MIB) architecture to capture structure features from skeleton sequences.

Motion features contain rich dynamic information. Chen et al. [11] extract finger articulated features from the hand skeleton by a variational autoencoder (VAE). Choutas et al. [12] introduce a fixed-sized representation that encodes pose motion. Feichtenhofer et al. [5] propose two scales motion features difference of slow and fast motions. Different from these works, our work obtains static and motion features by a center joint-oriented method, which can reduce the noise of skeletal data and consume a small amount of computing resources.

2.2 Skeleton-Based Gesture Recognition

Skeleton-based action recognition has been studied for decades. Yang et al. [1] propose DD-Net solely based on 1D CNNs for easy computation and training, while taking into consideration the integration of location-viewpoint invariant feature Joint Collection Distances (JCD) and two-scale global motion features. Ding et al. [13] encoded five spatial skeleton features into images and then fed those features to a CNN structure. Ke et al. [14] created texture arrays from 3D coordinates of body joints using 4 key body joints as a reference to form the center of a coordinate system by which the 3D positions of body joints are shifted before conversion into cylindrical coordinates. Twelve maps were generated which are fed to 12 CNN streams. Guo et al. [18] propose a normalized edge convolution operation to recognize hand gestures. In [15], a skeleton sequence representation was proposed in the form of a matrix that concatenates the joint coordinates in each instant and arranged those vector representations in a chronological order. Vemulapalli et al. [6] utilize rotations and translations to represent the 3D geometric relationships of body parts in Lie group. Some methods cost huge computing resources [4, 10–12] or contain redundant input [9]. Inspired by [1], we design our method on two aspects: introduce new features for skeleton sequences and propose novel neural network architectures.

3 Methodology

This section will describe the implementation process of the model. The framework of our networks is shown in Fig. 2. Our network takes a hand skeleton sequence as input and predicts the class label of dynamic hand gesture. It consists of two main branches, which process static features and motion features, respectively. In the following, we explain our motivation for designing input features and network structure of the model.

3.1 Modeling Static Feature by Center Joint Oriented Method

Raw skeleton data is a set of 3D Cartesian coordinates of hand joints. For one frame, the nth joint can be donated by $J_n = (J_x, J_y, J_z)$, where $n \in \{0, 1, 2, \ldots, (N-1)\}$ and N is the number of the hand joints. However, the Cartesian coordinate is variant to locations and viewpoints. As Fig. 1 shows, when the position of observer changes, skeletons may rotate or zoom. The Cartesian coordinate will be changed significantly. However, the geometric feature (e.g., distances and angles) is location-viewpoint invariant, and thereby we adopt it as the static feature input of the network. To reduce the computation and decrease the noise interference of bone data, we adopt a joint oriented method to extract static features.

First, a center joint J_0 is selected as original point. For each frame, the Euclidean distance D_n between joints J_0 and J_n can be denoted as.

$$D_n = \|J_n - J_0\|_2, n \in \{1, 2, \ldots, (N-1)\}. \tag{1}$$

The cosine $A_{i,k}$ of the joint angle $J_i - J_0 - J_k$ is denoted as

$$A_{i,k} = cos < \vec{J_i}, \vec{J_k} >, i, k \in \{1, 2, \ldots, (N-1)\}, i \neq k, \tag{2}$$

where $\vec{J_i}$ is the vector from $\vec{J_0}$ to $\vec{J_i}$, and $< \vec{J_i}, \vec{J_k} >$ is the angle of vector $\vec{J_i}$ and $\vec{J_k}$.

Except for the center joint J_0, the other $(N-1)$ joints can generate $(N-1)$ joint oriented distances by formula (1). The collection of those distances is named Center Joint Distances (CJD). The dimension of $CJD : [D_1 D_2 \ldots D_{N-1}]$ is $(N-1)$. Similarly, the collection of all joint angles is named Center Joint Angles (CJA). The CJA feature can be denoted as

$$CJA = \begin{bmatrix} A_{2,1} & & \\ \vdots & \ddots & \\ A_{(N-1),1} & \cdots & A_{(N-1),(N-2)} \end{bmatrix}. \tag{3}$$

In our processing, the CJA is flattened to be a one-dimensional matrix and the dimension of the flattened CJA is

$$d_{CJA} = C_{N-1}^2 = \frac{(N-1)(N-2)}{2}. \tag{4}$$

3.2 Extracting Global and Local Motion Features by Different Frames

Since static features do not contain motion information, we introduce the motion features as another input. Two kinds of motion features can be extracted by calculating the temporal differences of the Cartesian coordinate feature and geometric feature. Inspired by [5], we adopt the slow-fast networks method to extract two scale of velocities:

$$s(t) = x(t+1) - x(t), t = 1, 2, 3, \ldots, T - 1, \tag{5}$$

$$f(t) = x(t+2) - x(t), t = 1, 3, 5, \ldots, T - 2, \tag{6}$$

where $s(t)$ and $f(t)$ are the slow and fast motion at frame t. $x(t)$ is the physical quantity at frame t. $x(t+1)$ and $x(t+2)$ represents the physical quantities 1 frame and 2 frames after frame t, respectively. The frame number of the temporal sequence is denoted as T.

To represent the motion, we introduce Global Linear Velocities (GLV) and Local Angular Velocities (LAV). GLV represent the movements of all hand joints' coordinates $J_n = (J_x, J_y, J_z)$ in the Euclidean space, while LAV represent the rates of change of Center Joint Angles (CJA).

3.3 Dimension Adjustment and Feature Fusion by CNN Embedding

After extracting static and motion features, we adopt embedding method similar to [1]. 1D convolutions are used to transform the features into four embeddings, which are concatenated together to feed in spatiotemporal 2D representation layers. The embedding method can automatically learn the correlation between joint points and reduce the noise interference of skeletal data. In order to fuse different features and eliminate the inconsistency of different time dimensions, we adopt zero padding method and two kinds of different embedding methods.

Specially, dim of static features is $d_{static}*T$ for it is extracted per frame. While dim of slow-motion feature is $d_{motion}*(T-1)$. We employ a zero padding in slow motion feature so that it can match with the frame number of the static features. Same zero padding is employed in fast motion feature as well so that its dimension can be resized to $T/2$. We introduce two embedding operations for features of different dimension.

More formally, let embedding representations of static feature, slow motion features and fast motion features to be e_{static}, e_{slow} and e_{fast}, respectively. The embedding operation is as follows:

$$e_{static} = Embed_s[CJD \oplus CJA], \qquad (7)$$

$$e_{slow} = Embed_s[s(t)], \qquad (8)$$

$$e_{fast} = Embed_f[f(t)], \qquad (9)$$

where $\oplus$ is the concatenation operation. Our network further fuses those embedding features to a representation e by concatenation:

$$e = e_{static} \oplus e_{slow} \oplus e_{fast}. \qquad (10)$$

Rich spatial features are extracted by embedding and feature fusion. Then we use 2D convolutional neural network to extract spatiotemporal features and classification. Our

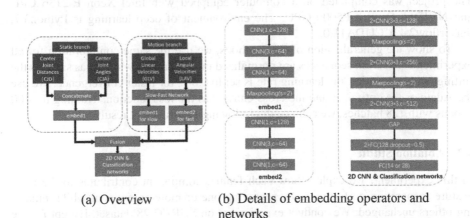

(a) Overview

(b) Details of embedding operators and networks

Fig. 2. The network architecture of our network. "2 * CNN (3 * 3, c = 128)" denotes two 2D Conv-Net layers (kernel size = 3 * 3, channels = 128), and "CNN (1, c = 128) represents a 1D ConvNet layer with a 1-dimension kernel. Other CNN layers are defined in the same way. GAP denotes Global Average Pooling. "Maxpooling(s = 2)" denotes a Maxpooling with 2 strides. FC denotes Fully Connected Layers (Dense Layers in our experiments).

feature fusion network embeds the static features (CJD, CJA) and the two-scale motion features into latent vectors at each frame. Through the embedding, the correlation of joints can be automatically learned. Also, joint-oriented method and embedding process can reduce the effect of skeleton noise. The overall process is shown in Fig. 2.

4 Experiments

4.1 Dataset

The performance of our method is evaluated on SHREC'17 Track dataset[2], which is a challenging gesture dataset with skeletal data. In this subsection, we introduce the experimental dataset in detail.

The SHREC'17 Track dataset [2] use Intel RealSense short range depth camera to collect hand gesture data. The depth images and hand skeletons were captured at 30 frames per second. Each sample gesture has 20 to 50 frames. Each frame of sequences contains a depth image, the coordinates of 22 joints both in the 2D depth image space and in the 3D world space forming a full hand skeleton. We take only 3D hand skeletons sequences as the raw data for all experiments.

The dataset contains sequences of 14 hand gestures performed in two ways: using one finger and the whole hand. Each gesture is performed between 1 and 10 times by 28 participants in 2 ways, resulting in 2800 sequences. Those 2800 sequences are divided into 1960 sequences (70% of the dataset) for training and 840 sequences (30% of the dataset) for testing. We adopt the same evaluation metric.

4.2 Training Details

The project was completed on a computer equipped with Intel Xeon E-2136 CPU and NVIDIA Quadro P5000 GPU. The environment of deep learning is Python3.7, tensorflow2.4.0, CUDA11.0.

To show the generalization of our methods, we use the same configuration for all experiments. Skeleton sequences are normalized into 32 frames which is as same as the settings in [1]. Besides, the learning rate is set to 0.001 for faster convergence. We use the Adam as the optimizer and the cross-entropy as the loss function. Training for 400 epochs with 128 batches, we achieve the following experimental results.

4.3 Ablation Studies

In this experiment, we explore how each feature component contributes to the hand gesture recognition performance by removing one or more component while remaining others unchanged. We conduct experiments on SHREC-28 dataset. Except for the explored parts, other details are set the same for fair comparison.

Table 1 shows the necessity of each input branch. With the increase of branches, the model performance is improved. This phenomenon further confirms the effectiveness of the data preprocessing module. More specifically, similar to video recognition, motion features play an important role in dynamic hand gesture recognition. Without motion feature, a network with solely static feature input only achieves 70.95% accuracy. Besides, we cannot ignore the contributions of the static geometric feature. The CJD feature provides our multi-input network rotation invariability property, while the CJA feature provides scaling invariability property. The ablation studies prove that all of the input branch in our method make the input robust.

Table 1. Contributions of different components

Ablations	CJD	CJA	Motion	Accuracy
	√	√	×	70.95%
	×	×	√	86.43%
	√	×	√	91.31%
	×	√	√	90.83%
Ours	√	√	√	**92.50%**

4.4 Comparison with Previous Methods

The hand gesture classification results of SHREC'17 Track dataset are presented in Table 2 and more details are listed in their confusion matrices. The confusion matrices of 14 gestures and 28 gestures are shown in Fig. 3(a) and (b), respectively.

As shown in Table 2, our network achieves the accuracy of 95.8% for the 14 gestures setting and 92.5% for the 28 gestures setting. The effect of our model outperforms the state-of-the-art models'. This shows that our method has a satisfactory effect on hand gesture recognition. Our model brings 1.2% and 0.6% improvements for 14 gestures and 28 gestures setting compared with the state-of-the-arts. Due to the simple CNN-based structure, our model contains only 2.24M parameters, which is smaller than many

Table 2. Accuracy of SHREC dataset

Method	Parameters	14 Gestures	28 Gestures
Dynamic hand [3]	–	88.2%	81.9%
Key-frame CNN [2]	7.92M	82.9%	71.9%
CNN + LSTM [21]	8–9M	89.8%	86.3%
Parallel CNN [20]	13.83M	91.3%	84.4%
STA-Res-TCN [9]	5–6M	93.6%	90.7%
MFA-Net [11]	–	91.3%	86.6%
NormEdgeConv [18]	–	92.9%	91.1%
DD-Net [1]	**1.82M**	94.6%	91.9%
Our method	2.24M	**95.8%**	**92.5%**

other methods and only 0.42M more than DD-Net [1]. Compared with other methods, the proposed model utilizes multi-features as input and a lightweight network structure, which leads to high classification effect and fast execute speed. Thus, our method is hardware-friendly.

As shown in Fig. 3(a), our network achieves recognition rate higher than 95.0% in 9 of the 14 gestures, and achieves 100.0% recognition rate in 4 of the 14 gestures. All 14 gestures can be classified with more than 90.0% accuracy. Figure 3(b) shows the confusion matrix of 28 gestures setting. The proposed model achieves recognition rate higher than 90.0% in 18 of 28 gestures and recognition rate higher than 95.0% in 13 of 28 gestures. Our model shows high classification accuracy for many different hand gesture categories.

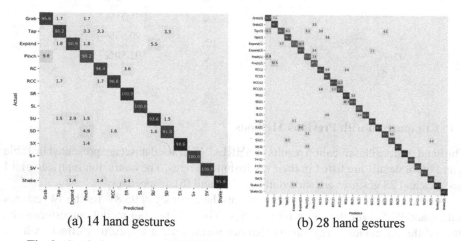

(a) 14 hand gestures   (b) 28 hand gestures

Fig. 3. Confusion matrices of SHREC dataset (14 hand gestures & 28 hand gestures)

5   Conclusion

This paper proposed a pipeline for skeleton-based hand gesture recognition. First, we introduced new static and motion features as robust input for our network. To satisfy calculation speed of some real-time hand detection and recognition applications, a lightweight CNN structure was proposed. Compared with other methods with numerous parameters, our network has simple structure and requires less memory and processing power. Our network showed great accuracy and speed advantages over similar networks on our experimental dataset.

To improve the effectiveness of the algorithm and make it better adapt to different environments, the following aspects can be considered for future work:

- We have verified the effectiveness of the network on the SHREC'17 dataset. Even though the model achieved satisfactory results, it needs to be tested on other benchmark datasets for robustness and generalization;

- More new features can be proposed and fused to the input branch. Besides, new fusion methods can be utilized instead of simple concatenation;
- Other powerful convolutional neural networks, e.g., 3D-CNN, can be used to explore rich spatiotemporal information.

Acknowledgements. The authors would like to acknowledge the support from the AiBle project co-financed by the European Regional Development Fund, National Natural Science Foundation of China (grant No. 52075530, 62006204), Guangdong Basic and Applied Basic Research Foundation (2022A1515011431), and Shenzhen Science and Technology Program (RCBS20210609104516043).

References

1. Yang, F., Wu, Y., Sakti, S., Nakamura, S.: Make skeleton-based action recognition model smaller, faster and better. In: Proceedings of the ACM Multimedia asia, pp. 1–6 (2019)
2. De Smedt, Q., Wannous, H., Vandeborre, J.P., Guerry, J., Le Saux, B., Filliat, D.: Shrec 2017 track: 3D hand gesture recognition using a depth and skeletal dataset. In: 3DOR-10th Eurographics Workshop on 3D Object Retrieval, pp. 1–6 (2017)
3. De Smedt, Q., Wannous, H., Vandeborre, J.P.: Skeleton-based dynamic hand gesture recognition. In: Proceedings of the IEEE Conference on Computer Vision and Pattern Recognition Workshops, pp. 1–9 (2016)
4. Liao, L.C., Yang, Y.H., Fu, L.C.: Joint-oriented features for skeleton-based action recognition. In: 2019 IEEE International Conference on Systems, Man and Cybernetics (SMC), pp. 1154–1159. IEEE (2019)
5. Feichtenhofer, C., Fan, H., Malik, J., He, K.: SlowFast networks for video recognition. In: 2019 IEEE/CVF International Conference on Computer Vision (ICCV), pp. 6202–6211. IEEE (2019)
6. Vemulapalli, R., Arrate, F., Chellappa, R.: Human action recognition by representing 3D skeletons as points in a lie group. In: 2014 IEEE Conference on Computer Vision and Pattern Recognition (CVPR), pp. 588–595. IEEE Computer Society (2014)
7. Gao, Q., Liu, J., Ju, Z., Zhang, X.: Dual-hand detection for human–robot interaction by a parallel network based on hand detection and body pose estimation. IEEE Trans. Industr. Electron. 66(12), 9663–9672 (2019)
8. Song, Y.F., Zhang, Z., Shan, C., Wang, L.: Constructing stronger and faster baselines for skeleton-based action recognition. IEEE Trans. Pattern Anal. Mach. Intell. (2022)
9. Li, C., Hou, Y., Wang, P., Li, W.: Joint distance maps based action recognition with convolutional neural networks. IEEE Signal Process. Lett. 24(5), 624–628 (2017)
10. Zhang, S., et al.: Fusing geometric features for skeleton-based action recognition using multilayer LSTM networks. IEEE Trans. Multimedia 20(9), 2330–2343 (2018)
11. Chen, X., Wang, G., Guo, H., Zhang, C., Wang, H., Zhang, L.: Mfa-net: motion feature augmented network for dynamic hand gesture recognition from skeletal data. Sensors, 19(2), 239 (2019)
12. Choutas, V., Weinzaepfel, P., Revaud, J., Schmid, C.: PoTion: pose motion representation for action recognition. In: 2018 IEEE/CVF Conference on Computer Vision and Pattern Recognition (CVPR), pp. 7024–7033. IEEE (2018)
13. Ding, Z., Wang, P., Ogunbona, P.O., Li, W.: Investigation of Different Skeleton Features for CNN-based 3D Action Recognition. IEEE Computer Society, IEEE Computer Society (2017)

14. Ke, Q., Bennamoun, M., An, S., Sohel, F., Boussaid, F.: A new representation of skeleton sequences for 3D action recognition. In: CVPR 2017, pp. 3288–3297. IEEE Computer Society (2017)
15. Li, C., Zhong, Q., Xie, D., Pu, S.: Skeleton-based action recognition with convolutional neural networks. In: 2017 IEEE International Conference on Multimedia \& Expo Workshops (ICMEW), pp. 597–600. IEEE Computer Society (2017)
16. Huang, Z., Wan, C., Probst, T., Van Gool, L.: Deep learning on lie groups for skeleton-based action recognition. In: Proceedings of the IEEE Conference on Computer Vision and Pattern Recognition, pp. 6099–6108. IEEE Computer Society (2016)
17. Paulo, J.R., Garrote, L., Peixoto, P., Nunes, U.J.: Spatiotemporal 2D skeleton-based image for dynamic gesture recognition using convolutional neural networks. In: 2021 30th IEEE International Conference on Robot & Human Interactive Communication (RO-MAN), pp. 1138–1144. IEEE (2021)
18. Guo, F., He, Z., Zhang, S., Zhao, X., Tan, J.: Normalized edge convolutional networks for skeleton-based hand gesture recognition. Pattern Recog. **118**(6), 108044 (2021)
19. Sabater, A., Alonso, I., Montesano, L., Murillo, A.C.: Domain and view-point agnostic hand action recognition. IEEE Robot. Autom. Lett. **6**(4), 7823–7830 (2021)
20. Devineau, G., Xi, W., Moutarde, F., Yang, J.: Convolutional neural networks for multivariate time series classification using both inter-and intra-channel parallel convolutions. In: Reconnaissance des Formes, Image, Apprentissage et Perception (RFIAP'2018), June 2018
21. Nunez, J.C., Cabido, R., Pantrigo, J., et al.: Convolutional neural networks and long short-term memory for skeleton-based human activity and hand gesture recognition. Pattern Recogn. J. Pattern Recogn. Soc. **76**, 80–94 (2018)
22. Gao, Q., Liu, J., Ju, Z.: Robust real-time hand detection and localization for space human–robot interaction based on deep learning. Neurocomputing **390**, 198–206 (2020)
23. Song, Y.F., Zhang, Z., Shan, C., Wang, L.: Stronger, faster and more explainable: a graph convolutional baseline for skeleton-based action recognition. In: MM 2020: The 28th ACM International Conference on Multimedia pp. 1625–1633. ACM (2020)

Multiple-Point Obstacle Avoidance Based on 3D Depth Camera Skeleton Modeling and Virtual Potential Field for the Redundant Manipulator

Genliang Xiong[1,2(✉)], Lan Ye[2], Hua Zhang[1], and Gao Yanfeng[1]

[1] School of Mechanical and Automotive Engineering, Shanghai University of Engineering Science, Longteng Rd 333, Shanghai 201620, China
xionggenliang7865@163.com
[2] School of Mechanical Engineering, Nanchang University, XuFu Avenue, HongGuTan District, Nanchang 330031, China

Abstract. For use in unstructured domains, highly redundant robotic systems need both deliberative and compliant control schemes, to avoid collision and safely interact with the dynamic environment. Aiming at the shortcoming of the traditional method of path planning using merely on the typical structure of the manipulator, a new algorithm, named the "skeleton extraction based on 3D-depth camera", is proposed for the real-time generation of collision avoidance motions. The algorithm is applied to get the distances of the multiple possible collision points and to establish a new form of a repulsive force, which includes the radial repulsive force and tangential repulsive force. For the redundant manipulator, the equilibrium angles through incremental iteration of the moment instead of inverse kinematics to reduce calculation cost. Finally, the method was tested by a 7-DOF manipulator in MATLAB environment. The results show that the proposed method can avoid local minima traps and eliminate oscillations effectively.

Keywords: Artificial potential field · 7-DOF robot · Skeleton algorithm · 3D depth camera · Obstacle avoidance

1 Introduction

Collaborative robots are finding many applications in fields such as manufacturing, health-care, agricultural production, and social tasks. In particular, the use in unstructured and dynamic environments implies the need for implementing real-time reactive strategies to cope with possible collisions instead of precisely following a predefined path. Such an approach should include features for the detection of possible colliding points [1], multiple-point control [2], modifications of the path as a reaction [3].

For its importance collision avoidance has been one of the most studied fields in robotics, and many different planning and control approaches for obstacle avoidance have been proposed. A large majority of the real-time capable planning concepts are based on the famous artificial potential field (APF) approach introduced in [4] and further elaborated, e.g., in [5, 6]. Compared with the sample-based method such that

© The Author(s), under exclusive license to Springer Nature Switzerland AG 2022
H. Liu et al. (Eds.): ICIRA 2022, LNAI 13455, pp. 35–47, 2022.
https://doi.org/10.1007/978-3-031-13844-7_4

RRT [7], PRM [8], the potential field method plans the same path every time, which has important significance in practical application. In particular, it has obvious advantages in dynamic obstacle avoidance [9] and dynamic target tracking [10], but it is mainly used in mobile robots. Thus, the robot is considered as a particle, and its workspace is described by a global potential function that its gradient guides the robot to the target point. For a manipulator, when it comes to redundant manipulator which is consist of a multiple-link structure, the problem becomes challenging because there exist some inherent limitations such as local minimum traps and oscillations in the presence of obstacles and narrow passages [11]. Furthermore, as the increase of degrees of freedom, the calculation of motion planning increases exponentially.

Many attempts for the limitations of the APF method have been made in a variety of ways [12–14]. The authors [15] proposed a novel method for path planning called Bacteria Potential Field (BPF) based on APF, which uses a BEA to find the shortest path according to the designer criteria and solve the local minima traps limitation. However, this method has a high demand for computing power in online planning applications. Badawy et al. [16] used the potential field method to construct two minimum points in Cartesian space to form a vortex field and select the reference point of the manipulator. Lukas Huber then offers an approach to avoid multiple concave obstacles, that preserves the asymptotic stability and inherits the convergence properties of harmonic potential fields [17]. In [18, 19] proposes an improved adaptive artificial potential field method, which avoids local minimum and oscillation through a priori path combined with RRT random search. Xie et al. [20] constructed the attraction velocity based on the target point at the field force action point, introduced the Pivot algorithm to construct the repulsive velocity and realized the local minimum escape of the manipulator by adding virtual obstacles. Whereas these studies have a common feature, that is, the main research is the end effector of the manipulator for the collision avoidance problem. For the manipulator composed of multiple-link, the collision of any point of the whole arm may occur in the process of planning, but it is seldom discussed.

The paper is organized as follows: In Sect. 2, The skeleton algorithm is presented, where the bounding box, possible collision multiple-points, and distances can be obtained. Section 3 introduces the proposed approach is applied to human-robot collision avoidance based on potential function. Section 4 shows the simulation results, carried out in the Matlab environment, to confirm the effectiveness of the proposed method. Finally, Sect. 5 summarizes and concludes the paper.

2   Skeleton Algorithm Based on 3D Depth Camera

2.1   Building the Skeleton

To avoid collisions between the manipulator and dynamic obstacle, 3D depth cameras are applied to image acquisition to consider all the points of the articulated structure which may collide. In this paper, we adopted the idea of thinning, namely by removing some points from the original image, but still keeping the original shape, until the skeleton of the image is obtained. The problem of analyzing the whole volumes of the parts of the manipulator/obstacle is simplified by considering a skeleton of the structure (Fig. 1), and proper volumes surrounding this skeleton.

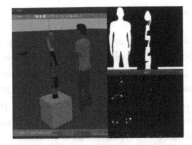

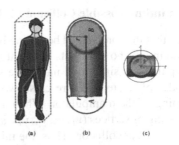

Fig. 1. Skeleton extraction   **Fig. 2.** Bounding box model

For the manipulator, one could derive the skeleton automatically from a proper kinematic description, e.g. via a Denavit-Hartenberg table. However, it would be difficult to check automatically for which segments collision tests are not necessary, especially the redundant robot. Therefore, it is more efficient, and also intuitive and straightforward, to set up the skeleton combined with vision.

2.2 Constructing Bounding Box

In this paper, based on the established skeleton, the bounding box is used for dynamic obstacles (see Fig. 2(a)). When we extract the skeleton of the objective, the 3D coordinates of the evaluation points can be obtained. Based on these points, the two important coordinates can be given:

$$
\begin{aligned}
p_{min} &= \left[x_{min}, y_{min}, z_{min} \right] \\
p_{max} &= \left[x_{max}, y_{max}, z_{max} \right]
\end{aligned}
\tag{1}
$$

Then the center of the bounding box can be calculated by:

$$
c = (p_{min} + p_{max})/2
\tag{2}
$$

We define dimension vector s as the vector from p_{min} to p_{max}, which include information on the length, width, and height of the bounding box:

$$
s = p_{max} - p_{min}
\tag{3}
$$

Combined with the above analysis, the 8 vertex coordinates of the bounding box are easily obtained based on establishing the skeleton using 3D depth cameras.

Aim at safety collision avoidance, a cylindrical bounding box with the skeleton as a central axis, to which add two hemispherical bounding boxes, was constructed for the manipulator. Figure 2(b) shows a segment of the bounding box, which line AB represents the central axis of the skeleton, and r is the bounding box radius. It can be obtained that points A and B are the intersections or endpoints of the skeleton, and the radius r can be directly approximated in the SolidWorks model or calculated by the projection method (see Fig. 2(c)).

In view of the above analysis, the method of the bounding box construction based on the skeleton, not only to the method is simpler, and the complex 3D model distance calculation problem is transformed into a simple space geometry problem, which greatly simplifies the calculation of distance.

2.3   Finding Possible Collision Multiple-Points

Given that the constructed bounding box of the obstacle in part 3.2 is shown in Fig. 3(a), the bounding box consists of eight vertices forming six planes, the skeleton of the manipulator is simplified into three segments and the bounding box is chosen as the cylinder of radius r. There exist two situations for the possible collision point in the planning of the manipulator. When a segment of the manipulator is located in a plane consisting of vertices (v_1, v_3, v_5, v_7), as shown in Fig. 3(b), the endpoints s_2 or s_3 is most likely to occur collision. Thus, the minimum distance is calculated as follows:

$$d = \frac{\overrightarrow{v_7 s_3} \cdot \overrightarrow{n}}{\| \overrightarrow{n} \|} \qquad (4)$$

where $\overrightarrow{n}$ is the unit normal vector of the plane (v_1, v_3, v_5, v_7).

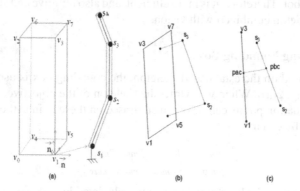

Fig. 3. Schematic diagram of human-robot interaction

Another situation is that a segment of the manipulator moves across two adjacent planes such as (v_1, v_3, v_5, v_7) and (v_0, v_1, v_2, v_3). In this case, the calculation of the minimum distance is not only related to the two endpoints of the skeleton segment but also related to the intersecting line segment of the two planes (see Fig. 3(c)). As anticipated above, the collision points move along the segments of the skeleton. Hence, the direct kinematics computation can be carried out in a parametric way for a generic point on each segment by simply replacing the link length in the homogeneous transformation relating to two subsequent frames with the distance of the collision point from the origin of the previous frame. For each segment in which the structure is decomposed, the distance to all the other segments is calculated with a simple formula. Let P_a and P_b denote the positions of the generic points along with the two segments, whose extremal points are v_1, v_3, and s_2, s_3, respectively.

$$\overrightarrow{P_a} = \overrightarrow{v_1} + t_1 \overrightarrow{u_1} \qquad (5)$$

$$\overrightarrow{P_b} = \overrightarrow{s_2} + t_2 \overrightarrow{u_2} \qquad (6)$$

where the unit vectors $\vec{u_1}$ and $\vec{u_2}$ for the two segments are evaluated as follows:

$$\vec{u_1} = \frac{\vec{v_3} - \vec{v_1}}{\|\vec{v_3} - \vec{v_1}\|} \tag{7}$$

$$\vec{u_2} = \frac{\vec{s_3} - \vec{s_2}}{\|\vec{s_3} - \vec{s_2}\|} \tag{8}$$

and $\{t_1, t_2\}$ are scalar values, with $t_1/\|\vec{v_3} - \vec{v_1}\| \in \{0, 1\}$, $t_2/\|\vec{s_3} - \vec{s_2}\| \in \{0, 1\}$.

The collision points P_{ac} and P_{bc} are found by computing the minimum distance between the two segments. Thus, the common normal line can be calculated as:

$$\overrightarrow{P_{ac}P_{bc}} = \|\vec{s_2} - \vec{v_1} + t_2\vec{u_2} - t_1\vec{u_1}\| \tag{9}$$

$$\overrightarrow{P_{ac}P_{bc}} \times \vec{u_1} = 0 \tag{10}$$

$$\overrightarrow{P_{ac}P_{bc}} \times \vec{u_2} = 0 \tag{11}$$

It is understood that in the case the common normal does not intersect either of the two segments, i.e. $\frac{t_1}{\|\vec{v_3} - \vec{v_1}\|} \in \{0, 1\}$, and $\frac{t_2}{\|\vec{s_3} - \vec{s_2}\|} \in \{0, 1\}$ are both outside the interval $\{0,1\}$, then the distance between the closest extremal points becomes the minimum distance. Thus, this analytical approach is adopted to compute the real-time the collision points pac and P_{bc} for each pair of segments, and the related distance is given by:

$$d_{min} = \|\overrightarrow{P_{ac}} - \overrightarrow{P_{bc}}\| \tag{12}$$

3 Collision Avoidance for the Redundant Manipulator

For the redundant manipulator, it can be described by a point using a generalized coordinate (usually the joint angles). However, the description of the corresponding obstacles is quite cumbersome. Because of the problems of multiple solutions and singularities in the inverse kinematics of the manipulators, the mapping from the workspace to the configuration space is nonlinear. It is difficult to give a distinct description of the obstacle space in Configuration-space, i.e., the "curse of dimensionality" makes that difficult. We consider establishing potential field functions in the workspace instead of the C-space. Based on the skeleton algorithm to obtain the distance in Sect. 2, the repulsive field is designed to realize dynamic obstacle avoidance of manipulators which offers a relatively fast and effective way is introduced in this section.

After constructing the bounding box based on the skeleton algorithm to calculate the distance in real-time, we establish the attractive potential field function of the goal and the repulsive potential filed functions of obstacles in the workspace instead of the configuration space. Then a series of control points on the manipulator are chosen to be influenced by the total potential. A policy is proposed that only the endpoint is attracted to the goal while all selected points are repulsed by obstacles. Afterward, we transfer the potential force of each point in the workspace into the moment in configuration space to make the manipulator move by iteration of joint angles.

3.1 Attractive Potential Field and Force

Here we adopt a policy that only the endpoint is attracted to the goal but all points are repulsed by obstacles. We use $P = \{P_1, P_2,..., P_N\}$ to indicate the evaluation points on the manipulator skeleton, then we define an artificial potential field at each point. We always choose the end effector as the Nth evaluation point. In this paper, an attractive force is defined as a function of the relative position between the manipulator and the target. The simplest method of attractive potential field selection is to make it increase linearly with distance, i.e., the conical potential. However, in this case, the gradients are constant everywhere, and the gradient at the endpoint is 0. Therefore, the gradient is not continuous, which may cause system instability. We also hope that the attractive potential field will be smooth everywhere. So we construct a quadratic potential function which is a parabolic well:

$$U_{att,i}(q) = \frac{1}{2} k_{att} L_i^2(q) \tag{13}$$

where k_{att} is a positive weight scale factor, $L_i(q) = \|p_i(q) - p_i(q_{goal})\|$, which represents the distance between the ith evaluation point in configuration q and the goal configuration q_{goal}. It should be noted that if the start point is very far from the endpoint, the attractive force could be very large. In this case, it may be desirable to have distance functions that grow more slowly to avoid huge velocities far from the goal. Therefore, we usually combine the conical field with the quadratic field structure. We use the conical one when the distance is far, and the quadratic one when it is closer. Due to the limited scope of the workspace, we do not consider this situation in this paper. The negative gradient of the attractive field is the attractive force.

$$f_{att,i}(q) = -\nabla U_{att,i}(q) = -\frac{1}{2} k_{att} \nabla L_i^2(q) = -k_{att}(p_i(q) - p_i(q_{goal})) \tag{14}$$

3.2 Repulsive Potential Field and Force

A repulsive force is defined as a function of the relative position between a robot and an obstacle that is nearest from the robot among obstacles. To compute the repulsive field intensity, we calculate the distance between the multiple-points of the manipulator skeleton and the obstacle from the 3D depth camera. When constructing the repulsive potential field, it is necessary to ensure that the robot and the obstacle repel each other so that the two never touch; meanwhile, when the robot is away from the obstacle, the repulsive force should be gradually reduced. Thus, one of the simplest methods of constructing a repulsive field is to make the repulsive field tend to infinity at the obstacle boundary and to zero at a distance from the obstacle. We define this distance as d_{safe}. It is the safety index derived from the obstacle and the manipulator bounding box within which the repulsive potential is "activated" and can influence the robot. The repulsive force function can be expressed as

$$U_{rep,i}(q) = \begin{cases} 0 & d_i(q) > d_{safe} \\ \frac{1}{2} \eta_i \left(\frac{1}{d_i(q)} - \frac{1}{d_{safe}} \right)^2 & d_i(q) \leq d_{safe} \end{cases} \tag{15}$$

where η_i is a positive weight coefficient, $d_i(q) = \|p_i(q) - p_i(q_{obstacle})\|$, which represents the nearest distance between the ith evaluation point and the obstacle. Suppose the obstacle is convex so that $d_i(q)$ is smooth everywhere, the repulsive force to the robot can be represented by the negative gradient of the repulsive field as follows:

$$
f_{rep,i}(q) = \begin{cases} 0 & d_i(q) > d_{safe} \\ -\eta_i\left(\dfrac{1}{d_i(q)} - \dfrac{1}{d_{safe}}\right)\dfrac{1}{d_i^2(q)}\nabla d_i(q) & d_i(q) \leq d_{safe} \end{cases}
\tag{16}
$$

where $\nabla d_i(q)$ represents the gradient of the shortest distance in the workspace. If b is the point on the obstacle which is closest to the ith evaluation point, then we have:

$$
\nabla d_i(q) = \frac{p_i(q) - b}{\|p_i(q) - b\|}
\tag{17}
$$

Which $\nabla d_i(q)$ is the unit vector from b to $p_i(q)$. It should be noted that if the shape of the obstacle is not convex, the distance function $d(q)$ is not necessarily differentiable everywhere, which means the force vector is discontinuous. So the selection of the evaluation points does not guarantee that the robot and the obstacle do not collide. When the possible collision point is in the middle of the link, A and B are endpoints of the link, E is the middle point. In this case, point E is the closest point to the link rather than A or B, the collision occurs probably. We can select more floating evaluation points to ensure that the nearest distance exists such as Fig. 1 based on the skeleton algorithm.

3.3 Modified Representation of Repulsive Force

There is an inevitable problem when using artificial potential fields to avoid obstacles is the occurrence of the local minimum. As shown in Fig. 4(a)–(b), obstacle, target, robot are on the same line, and the obstacle is in the middle position, or multiple obstacles are symmetrically distributed, the resultant force of repulsion is zero and the robot cannot reach the target point. According to Eq. (16), when the robot moves to the target point under the attractive potential field, but also the repulsive force of the repulsive force field increases with approaching the obstacle. If the target is too close to the obstacle (see Fig. 4(c)), the repulsive force of the robot is much larger than that of the target, the robot cannot move towards the target resulting in the target not accessible, the robot may full into shock. To solve local minimum traps and minimize oscillations, the repulsive field is represented by:

$$
U_{rep,i}(q) = \begin{cases} 0 & d_i(q) > d_{safe} \\ \dfrac{1}{2}\eta_i\left(\dfrac{1}{d_i(q)} - \dfrac{1}{d_{safe}}\right)^2 \dfrac{d_g^n}{1+d_g^n} & d_i(q) \leq d_{safe} \end{cases}
\tag{18}
$$

where distance index $d_g = \frac{L_N(q)}{d_N(q)}$, namely the ratio of the distance from the end evaluation point to the goal to the distance from this evaluation point to the obstacle. It can be seen in Eq. (18), when the robot is far from the objective, i.e., $d_g^n \gg 1$, the expression $\frac{d_g^n}{1+d_g^n}$ is equivalent to approximately 1 and the repulsive field is equivalent to Eq. (15), avoiding

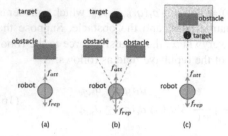
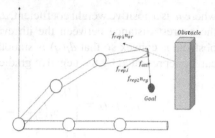

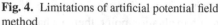

Fig. 4. Limitations of artificial potential field method

Fig. 5. Modified repulsive force

the path increase to propose the distance of the objective. When the manipulator is ready for the objective, i.e. $d_g^n \ll 1$, the expression $\frac{d_g^n}{1+d_g^n} \approx d_g < 1$. That is to say, the repulsive field is weaker than the attractive field to avoid local minimum problems and d_g plays an important role in the weakening of the repulsive field.

Figure 5 shows the Modified repulsive force, given the role of d_g, a tangential repulsive force is added to the repulsive force. The repulsive force is composed of radial force f_{rep1} and tangential force f_{rep2}, which attract the manipulator up to the objective and repel the manipulator of the obstacle.

$$f_{rep,i}(q) = \begin{cases} 0 & d_i(q) > d_{safe} \\ f_{rep1}n_{or} + f_{rep2}n_{rg} & d_i(q) \leq d_{safe} \end{cases} \tag{19}$$

where the unit normal vector n_{or} indicates the direction from the obstacle to the control point of the manipulator and n_{rg} indicates the direction of the manipulator to the objective. The f_{rep1} component, represented by taking the gradient of $d_i(q)$ as follows:

$$f_{rep1} = \eta_i \left(\frac{1}{d_i(q)} - \frac{1}{d_{safe}} \right) \frac{d_g^n}{d_i^2(q)\left(1 + d_g^n\right)} \tag{20}$$

In fact, the tangential repulsive force from obstacle f_{rep2} is equivalent to attraction in the direction of the goal, represented by taking the gradient of d_g as follows:

$$f_{rep2} = \frac{1}{2}\eta_i \left(\frac{1}{d_i(q)} - \frac{1}{d_{safe}} \right)^2 \frac{d_g^{n-1}}{\left(1 + d_g^n\right)^2} \tag{21}$$

3.4 Relation Between Forces and Joint Angles

According to the idea of the traditional artificial potential field method, the forces on each joint must be obtained successively, and then a resultant force can be obtained to determine the direction of movement of the manipulator. Yet it must be to convert the inverse kinematics to the joint coordinate system and then obtain each joint angle. Therefore, the inverse solution will be frequently solved by the manipulator, which is not only difficult and costly to calculate, but also more likely to fail to obtain continuous joint angle values, namely singular solutions, which are not allowed in practical applications. In this paper, we can avoid solving the inverse kinematics. Through the above two sections, we finally get the total potential energy of the ith evaluation point under the configuration q:

$$U_{net,i}(q) = U_{att,i}(q) + U_{rep,i}(q) \tag{22}$$

and the net force is

$$f_{net,i}(q) = -\nabla U_{att,i}(q) - \nabla U_{rep,i}(q) = f_{att,i}(q) + f_{rep,i}(q) \tag{23}$$

For multiple-link manipulators, the net moment vector:

$$\tau_{net} = \sum_{i=1}^{N} J_i^T f_{net,i} \tag{24}$$

where $\tau_{net} = \begin{bmatrix} \tau_1 & \tau_2 & \dots & \tau_m \end{bmatrix}$ and m represents the total number of joints (DoFs), τ_i corresponds to the moment that will change joint angle θ_i, J is the Jacobian matrix, N represents the total number of selected points on the skeleton algorithm of the manipulator. In this paper, we regulate that the only endpoint is attracted to the goal but all points are repelled from obstacles. Thus, the attractive force of Nth point can be expressed as:

$$f_{att}(q) = -\nabla U_{att,N}(q) = k_{att}\left(p_N\left(q_{goal}\right) - p_N(q)\right) \tag{25}$$

By using (23), (24), and (25), the net moment can be calculated as:

$$\tau_{net} = \sum_{i=1}^{N} J_i^T f_{rep,i} + J_N^T f_{att} \tag{26}$$

As well known, the inverse kinematics (IK) of the redundant manipulator is not unique, and the choice of IK affects the obstacle avoidance. Meanwhile the existence of obstacles, the potential field is non-linear and discontinuous. Hence, we compute equilibrium angles through incremental iteration of the moment. Here we use a batch update rule:

$$\theta(t+1) = \theta(t) + \beta\tau_{net}/\|\tau_{net}\| \tag{27}$$

where β is an iterative step in joint space and $\tau_{net}/\|\tau_{net}\|$ is the normalized total moment.

4   Simulation

To evaluate the performance and correctness of this framework, we verify the effectiveness of our method presented in this paper. The method is tested in the MATLAB environment.

we did simulation experiments to verify the advantages of the modified method relative to the traditional APF and some sampling methods such as A^*, D^*. Figure 6 shows some common local minimum traps and oscillations, where green, yellow points each represent initial, goal points, the objects surrounded by blue represent obstacles, and red solid lines represent the paths of the robot. The coordinates of the initial points, goal points, positions of obstacles, and times cost are shown in Table 1.

Figure 6(a)–(b) show obstacle avoidance case in the presence of one obstacle. Figure 6(c)–(d) describes the simulation when there are three obstacles in the scene. As we can see that it only adds two obstacles compared with Fig. 6(a)–(b). Figure 6(a) and (c) show that the robot which needs to reach the same goal point is trapped in local minima and oscillates in the process of moving to the target due to the attractive force and the repulsive force is equal or almost equal but in the opposite direction. Figure 6(b) and (d) show that local minima traps can be avoided and oscillations can be minimized used by the modified repulsive potential field. Figure 6(e) shows the distribution of attractive potential field, repulsive potential field, and combined potential field corresponding to Fig. 6(d). In view of the local minimum in Fig. 6(c), D* and A* are adopted for obstacle avoidance planning in Fig. 6(f) and Fig. 6(g), respectively while at the expense of computing time shown in Table 1.

Figure 7 shows the multiple-point obstacle avoidance realized by the manipulator skeleton. The solid orange line represents the initial position of the robot, the solid gray line is the goal position, and the red cylinder is the obstacle. It can be seen that the obstacle avoidance problem of the manipulator in the narrow space can be realized presented in this paper.

Table 1. The coordinates and times in Fig. 6

	Initial point (cm)	Goal point (cm)	Obstacle center point (cm)	Times (s)
Figure 6(a)	(580, 580)	(50, 300)	(50, 300)	7.4466
Figure 6(b)	(580, 580)	(50, 300)	(50, 300)	56.3251
Figure 6(c)	(580, 580)	(150, 40)	(150, 40)	7.4804
Figure 6(d)	(580, 580)	(150, 40)	(150, 40)	52.4186
Figure 6(e)	(580, 580)	(150, 40)	(150, 40)	245.8535
Figure 6(f)	(580, 580)	(150, 40)	(150, 40)	121.7245

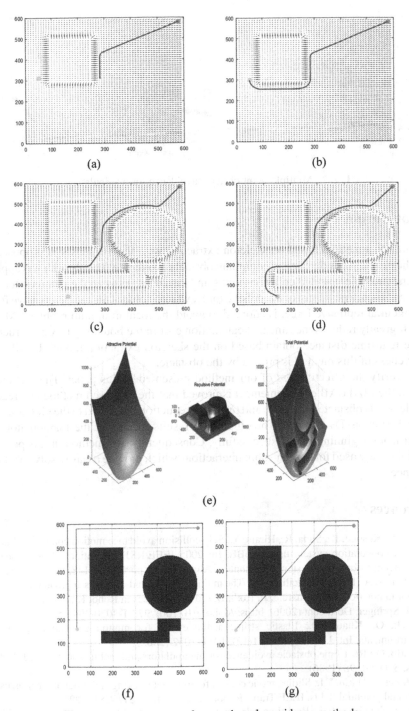

Fig. 6. Comparison test of some obstacle avoidance methods

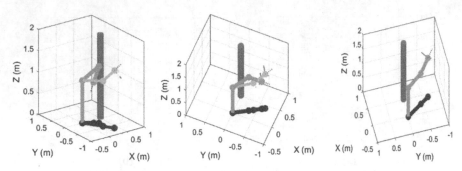

Fig. 7. Multiple-point obstacle avoidance for manipulator

5 Conclusion

In summary, a method based on skeleton extraction with the 3D-sensor is proposed to solve the problem of non-contact compliant obstacle avoidance. The algorithm is applied to get the multiple possible collision points and distances between the manipulator and obstacles. Then, a new form of a repulsive force, which includes the radial repulsive force and tangential repulsive force, is adopted to avoid the local minimum problem. Meanwhile, it greatly reduces the time and calculation cost in the bounding box construction and the real-time distance obtain based on the skeleton extraction model. Finally, the effectiveness of this method is proved by the obstacle.

We verify the effectiveness of our method presented in this paper. The method is tested in the MATLAB environment. It is proved that the proposed method can realize multiple points obstacle avoidance and time cost reduction compared to the global search approach such as D∗ and A∗. The simulation results mean that the manipulator can avoid it from beginning to end successfully. Consequently, the method in this paper is potential widely used for human-robot interactions which provide a way to solve obstacle avoidance.

References

1. Seto, F., Kosuge, K., Suda, R., Hirata, Y.: Self-collision avoidance motion control for human Robot cooperation system using RoBE. In: 2005 IEEE/RSJ International Conference on Intelligent Robots and Systems, Edmonton, Alta, Canada, pp. 3143–3148. IEEE (2005)
2. De Santis, A., Pierro, P., Siciliano, B.: The multiple virtual end-effectors approach for human-robot interaction. In: Lennarčič, J., Roth, B. (eds.) Advances in Robot Kinematics, pp. 133–144. Springer, Dordrecht (2006). https://doi.org/10.1007/978-1-4020-4941-5_15
3. Brock, O., Khatib, O.: Elastic strips: a framework for motion generation in human environments. Int. J. Robot. Res. 21(12), 1031–1052 (2002)
4. Khatib, O.: Real-time obstacle avoidance for manipulators and mobile robots. Int. J. Robot. Res. 5(1), 90–98 (1986)
5. Guldner, J., Utkin, V.I.: Sliding mode control for gradient tracking and robot navigation using artificial potential fields. IEEE Trans. Robot. Autom. 11(2), 247–254 (1995)
6. Yan, P., Yan, Z., et al.: Real time robot path planning method based on improved artificial potential field method. In: Proceedings of the 37th Chinese Control Conference, Wuhan, China, pp. 25–27. IEEE (2018)

7. Xu, J.J., Duindam, V., Alterovitz, R., Goldberg, K.: Motion planning for steerable needles in 3D environments with obstacles using rapidly-exploring random trees and backchaining. In: 4th IEEE Conference on Automation Science and Engineering Key Bridge Marriott, Washington DC, USA, pp. 41–46. IEEE (2008)
8. Kavralu, L.E., Svestka, P., Latombe, J.C., Overmars, M.H.: Probabilistic roadmaps for path planning in high-dimensional configuration spaces. IEEE Trans. Robot. Autom. 12(4), 566–580 (1996)
9. Tzafestas, S.G., Tzamtzi, M.P., Rigatos, G.G.: Robust motion planning and control of mobile robots for collision avoidance in terrains with moving objects. Math. Comput. Simul. 59(4), 279–292 (2002)
10. Ge, S.S., Cui, Y.J.: Dynamic motion planning for mobile robots using potential field method. Auton. Robot. 13, 207–222 (2002)
11. Weerakoon, T., Ishii, K., Forough Nassiraei, A.A.: An artificial potential field based mobile robot navigation method to prevent from deadlock. J. Artif. Intell. Soft Comput. Res. 5(3), 189–203 (2015)
12. Wang, Q.Z., Cheng, J.Y., Li, X.L.: Path planning of robot based on improved artificial potential field method. In: Proceedings of the 2017 International Conference on Artificial Intelligence, Automation and Control Technologies, Wuhan, China, pp. 1–6 (2017)
13. Li, H., Wang, Z.Y., Ou, Y.S.: Obstacle avoidance of manipulators based on improved artificial potential field method. In: Proceeding of the IEEE International Conference on Robotics and Biomimetics, Dali, China, pp. 564–569 (2019)
14. Zhu, Z.X., Jing, S., Zhong, J.F., Wang, M.: Obstacle avoidance path planning of space redundant manipulator based on a collision detection algorithm. J. Northwestern Polytech. Univ. 38(1), 183–189 (2020)
15. Oscar, M., Ulises, O.R., Roberto, S.: Path planning for mobile robots using bacterial potential field for avoiding static and dynamic obstacles. Expert Syst. Appl. 42(12), 5177–5191 (2015)
16. Badawy, A.: Dual-well potential field function for articulated manipulator trajectory planning. Alex. Eng. J. 55(2), 1235–1241 (2016)
17. Huber, L., Billard, A., Slotine, J.: Avoidance of convex and concave obstacles with convergence ensured through contraction. IEEE Robot. Autom. Lett. 4(2), 1462–1469 (2019)
18. He, Z.C., He, Y.L., Zeng, B.: Obstacle avoidance path planning for robot arm based on mixed algorithm of artificial potential field method and RRT. Ind. Eng. J. 20(2), 56–63 (2017)
19. Zhu, J., Yang, M.Y.: Path planning of manipulator to avoid obstacle based on improved artificial potential field method. Comput. Meas. Control 26(10), 205–210 (2018)
20. Xie, L., Liu, S.: Dynamic obstacle-avoiding motion planning for manipulator based on improved artificial potential filed. Control Theory Appl. 35(9), 1239–1249 (2018)

A Novel Grasping Approach with Dynamic Annotation Mechanism

Shuai Yang [ID], Bin Wang[⊠], Junyuan Tao, Qifan Duan, and Hong Liu

State Key Laboratory of Robotics and System, Harbin Institute of Technology, Harbin 150001, China
wbhit@hit.edu.cn

Abstract. The Grasping of unknown objects is a challenging but critical problem in the field of robotic research. However, existing studies only focus on the shape of objects and ignore the impact of the differences in robot systems which has a vital influence on the completion of grasping tasks. In this work, we present a novel grasping approach with a dynamic annotation mechanism to address the problem, which includes a grasping dataset and a grasping detection network. The dataset provides two annotations named basic and decent annotation respectively, and the former can be transformed to the latter according to mechanical parameters of antipodal grippers and absolute positioning accuracies of robots. So that we take the characters of the robot system into account. Meanwhile, a new evaluation metric is presented to provide reliable assessments for the predicted grasps. The proposed grasping detection network is a fully convolutional network that can generate robust grasps for robots. In addition, evaluations based on datasets and experiments on a real robot show the effectiveness of our approach.

Keywords: Grasping dataset · Annotation · Grasping detection

1 Introduction

The ability of robots to grasp objects autonomously with the help of the visual perception system is very important, and it is of great significance for industrial production, logistics distribution, and family service. Grasping detection is the key to this ability and also the fundamental problem in robotics. Although a lot of work in the field of grasping detection has achieved good results, there are still many shortcomings. An important problem is that the present approach only considers the influence of object shape on grasping, and ignores the effects of the mechanical parameters of grippers and the absolute positioning accuracy of robots, which play a vital role in practical grasping tasks.

In this paper, we propose a novel grasping approach that consists of a grasping dataset and a grasping detection network to tackle the above problem. Our approach has a dynamic annotation mechanism, which means that annotations of our dataset can be dynamically adjusted according to actual task needs. To implement this mechanism, our dataset provides basic annotation and an annotation transformation algorithm. Unlike previous works [1–3] our basic annotation does not represent the grasping pose but the grasping region on the object, and it is independent of the gripper and robot platform. In order to make the dataset can adapt to a specific robot to achieve better performance in real robot grasping tasks, we adjust basic annotation to decent annotation which is closely related to gripper and robot through the annotation transformation algorithm. With the help of annotation transform, we fuse the mechanical parameters of the antipodal gripper and the absolute positioning accuracy into the grasping region, and transform the grasping region to the dense grasping pose label which is suitable for model training. In addition, we present an original evaluation metric which gives accurate assessments for predicted grasps.

In order to realize the full potential of our dataset, a grasping detection network is developed in this work. We construct our model as a generation model similar to [4, 5] instead of an object detection model like [6, 7] to realize higher speed and grasping precision. Inspired by [8–10], our grasping detection network contains three parts: feature extraction module, multi-scale fusion module, and decoding module. Experiments demonstrating the adaptability of our dataset and the effectiveness of our grasping detection network are conducted on both datasets and a practical robot platform.

2   Related Work

Grasping Datasets. Cornell Grasping Dataset [1] is a famous grasping dataset in the field of deep-learning-based robot grasping. It proposes to use oriented rectangle annotation which is widely used in follow-up works [4, 5, 7] instead of point annotation [11] as the grasping representation. Jacquard Dataset [12] is constructed as a large-scale grasping dataset based on ShapeNet [13] through synthetic methods, which contains more than 50k images of 11k objects and 1 million unique successful grasp positions annotated with oriented rectangles. One disadvantage of these datasets is that they mainly consider parallel-jaw and ignore other end effectors. Dex-Net-2.0 [2] and 3.0 [14] construct datasets according to a parallel-jaw and a suction-based end effector respectively. Similarly, GraspNet-1Billion [3] contains 88 objects and over 1.1 billion grasp poses for parallel-jaw, and SuctionNet-1Billion [15] is built for suction-based grasping based on data provided by GraspNet-1Billion. But they can't adapt to the size change of end effectors. Although the previous work builds corresponding datasets for different end-effectors, they cannot automatically adapt to the size variation of the gripper and the absolute positioning accuracy of the robot, which will seriously affect the performance of the actual grasping task. In this work, we propose a novel dataset to address these issues.

Deep Learning Based Grasping Detection. Much of the early works in this field, such as [6, 7, 16], are based on object detection algorithms. ROI-GD [17] presents a two-stage method, which provides Regions of Interest (ROIs) through a region proposal network in the first stage and then detects grasps based on ROIs in the second stage. In order to improve the accuracy, a multi-object grasping detection network [18] is developed based on the single-shot detection approach, hierarchical feature fusion, and attention mechanism. The grasping detection problem is decoupled into two sub-tasks in [19], and two modules are proposed to estimate the orientation and action of the gripper respectively. Based on generation and segmentation methods, GG-CNN [4] is proposed to predict the quality, opening size, and angle for every pixel. Similar to GG-CNN, GR-ConvNet [5] is also a generative method but it has a deeper decoder that is built based on residual networks. GR-ConvNet provides better representation and grasping accuracy than GG-CNN. Inspired by these methods, we present a generative-based grasping detection network to obtain robust grasping estimates.

3 Dataset

In this section, we first describe the primary features of our dataset, and then the dynamic annotation mechanism is explained, which includes the basic-decent annotation of our dataset as well as the algorithm used to transform the annotations according to gripper and robot. Finally, the metric for grasp assessment is introduced in the last subsection.

3.1 Overview

Previous grasping datasets only focus on two aspects, the data from different sensors such as RGB images from color cameras, depth images or point clouds from depth cameras, and the annotation to represent the grasping pose on the corresponding data. It is worth noting that most of them only give appropriate annotations based on collected data, such as [1, 12]. And there are also some grasping datasets [2, 14] that take into account not only the data but also the robot gripper, but unfortunately, only a robot gripper with particular parameters was taken into account. Therefore, such grasping datasets are not easily generalized to grippers with different mechanical sizes. In addition, the existing grasping datasets do not take the control error of the robot into account, which makes the robot grasping system not robust enough in practical applications.

To overcome these issues, we propose a novel grasping dataset named Adaptive Grasping Dataset with a dynamic annotation mechanism. It can automatically adapt to grippers with different mechanical parameters and robot systems with different absolute positioning accuracies. Adaptive Grasping Dataset contains 40 different objects with 1553 high-quality RGB-D images captured by Intel Realsense D435 depth camera. For each RGB-D Image, our Adaptive Grasping Dataset provides corresponding basic annotations. Meanwhile, an annotation transform program is provided in the dataset, it can help users optimize the basic annotations according to the different mechanical parameters of grippers and the absolute positioning accuracies of their robot systems. We show some of the objects of our dataset in Fig. 1.

Fig. 1. Some objects of Adaptive Grasping Dataset.

3.2 Basic and Decent Annotation

The core design idea of our Adaptive Grasping Dataset is to enable the dataset to automatically adjust the annotation according to the mechanical parameters of the gripper and the control precision of the robot system, so as to improve the performance of the whole robot system in the implementation of the practical grasping task. For that purpose, we designed two annotation forms: basic annotation and decent annotation. The former is already provided in the dataset, while the latter requires the user to use the annotation transformation algorithm provided in the dataset to generate according to their robot platform parameters. Basic annotation is generated through manual annotation, which is only related to the objects in RGB-D images and has nothing to do with the real robot platform that completes the capture task. It contains all possible grasping information in the dataset, but it is difficult to be directly used for the training of the grasping detection network because it does not directly represent the grasping pose. And because basic annotation does not contain the hardware information of the robot platform, it's not suitable for the actual robot grasping task. However, decent annotation is calculated according to basic annotation and hardware information of the robot, so the grasping information contained in the decent annotation is applicable to the corresponding robot platform. In addition, we design decent annotation as a dense pixel-level annotation to achieve better training performance.

In order to explain the basic and decent annotation, we first describe the gripper model used in our work. Similar to [3, 20, 21], we adopt a simplified gripper model, as shown in Fig. 2, it contains two primary mechanical parameters: w_g and h_g that denote the maximum opening length and thickness of the robot gripper respectively.

To easily predict the pose of the gripper, with the help of camera intrinsic parameters we adopt a representation with five parameters $\{v_g, d_g, x_g, y_g, \theta_g\}$ to uniquely determine the orientation and translation of the gripper under the camera frame, where v_g denotes the Z-axis of the gripper frame, d_g denotes the distance from camera optic center to the center of gripper frame, x_g and y_g denote the pixel position projected by the center of gripper frame on the image, θ_g denotes the in-plane rotation angle around v_g. Because v_g is generally approximated as the Z-axis of the camera frame in practical application and d_g can be obtained directly from depth images captured by the depth camera, we only need to estimate the remaining three parameters.

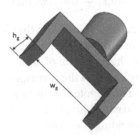

Fig. 2. Model of our gripper. The w_g is the maximum opening length of the robot gripper and h_g is the thickness of the robot gripper.

Basic annotation is designed to represent the graspable region in RGB-D image rather than the grasping pose as in the previous work. As shown in Fig. 3, inspired by the widely used 5-dimensional oriented grasp rectangle employed [1], We describe our basic annotation as

$$label_{bsc} = \{x, y, w, h, \theta\}. \tag{1}$$

where x and y denote the center of the graspable region. w and h denote the side length of the graspable region. θ denotes the angle of the graspable region.

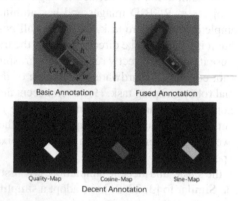

Fig. 3. Visualization of our basic annotation, fused annotation, and the corresponding decent annotation. The basic annotation describes a grasping region rather than a grasping configuration and the decent annotation represents all possible grasps in this region for a specific gripper.

Decent annotation needs to have three characteristics: first, it can be automatically generated according to basic annotation. Secondly, the generation process of it needs to take the robot parameters into account. Finally, it should provide dense annotation information for training. Inspired by the data processing method used in previous works [4, 5], we define our decent annotation as Fig. 3. And the Mathematical representation for our decent annotation to be:

$$label_{dct} = \{m_q, m_c, m_s\} \tag{2}$$

where m_q, m_c, and m_s are 2-dimensional matrices that have the same number of rows and columns as RGB-D Image in our dataset. m_q denotes the map of grasping quality named quality-map, its elements have values of 0 or 1 and represent the probability of whether the corresponding positions on the corresponding RGB-D image can be the center of the robot gripper. m_c and m_s denote the $\cos 2\theta$ and $\sin 2\theta$ named cosine-map and sine-map respectively. m_θ can be easily figured out from m_c and m_s, and its elements are the gripper angles of the corresponding positions on the corresponding RGB-D image if those positions can afford good grasping configurations. We use $\{m_c, m_s\}$ instead of m_θ to ensure that the grasping angle is unique and symmetric in its domain.

3.3 Annotation Transform

We propose a two-stage algorithm to realize the transformation from basic annotation to decent annotation named annotation transfer. The first stage is called parameter fusion, which integrates the mechanical parameters $\{w_g, h_g\}$ of the robot gripper and the absolute positioning accuracy of the robot system into the annotation. The result of parameter fusion named $label_{fus}$ is expressed in the same data structure as the basic annotation. And the algorithm of the parameter fusion stage proposed to transform $label_{bsc}$ to $label_{fus}$ is,

$$label_{fus} = \{x, y, w_g - w - 2a_r, h - h_g - 2a_r\}. \tag{3}$$

where a_r denotes the absolute positioning accuracy of the robot system. Figure 3 illustrates the transformation results of the parameter fusion stage. With the help of parameters w_g, h_g, and a_r, we fuse the characteristics of a specific robot platform into the annotation of our Adaptive Grasping Dataset without introducing new variables.

The second stage is called style transfer, which is to transform the grasping region processed in the parameter fusion stage into decent annotation. Decent annotation can be viewed as three single-channel images of the same size as RGB-D images in our dataset. We first initialize the elements of $label_{dct}$ to zero and then fill the region represented by $label_{fus}$ in $label_{dec}$ with the corresponding value. Specifically, we assign one to the elements in the region of m_q represented by $label_{fus}$. And the elements in the region of m_c and m_s represented by $label_{fus}$ is replaced by $\cos 2\theta$ and $\sin 2\theta$ respectively.

3.4 Evaluation

There are several ways to evaluate the prediction performance of grasp pose. Previous work [2, 4] used the actual robot grasping results as the judgment basis for the success of grasping. Although this method can intuitively express the overall grasping performance of the robot system, its evaluation results are affected by the robot hardware, which is not conducive to the comparison of grasping estimation networks. And [1, 4, 5] adopt the rectangle metric that has too high error tolerance to accurately evaluate grasping performance. In this work, we propose a novel metric named boundary metric to evaluate the grasp accuracy.

We first illustrate how we get gripper pose $\{x_g, y_g, \theta_g\}$ from predicted results $\{m_q, m_c, m_s\}$. We believe that the positions of all elements with values greater than 0.95 in m_q are the predicted center $\{x_g, y_g\}$ of gripper frame. And then we get the corresponding in-plane rotation angle θ_g of gripper from m_c and m_s according to trigonometric functions.

Then we transform our gripper model $\{w_g, h_g\}$ into the image according to the predicted gripper pose $\{x_g, y_g, \theta_g\}$. We consider a gripper pose as correct if:

1. Gripper center (x_g, y_g) is in the graspable region $label_{fus}$;
2. The gripper does not interfere with $label_{bsc}$;
3. The edge of the gripper intersects the grasping region at the boundary h.

We show the evaluation process of predicted gripper pose and the results evaluated by boundary metric in Fig. 4.

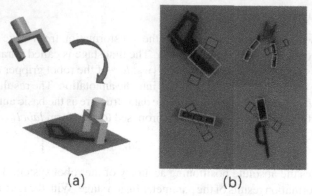

Fig. 4. (a) The evaluation process of the predicted gripper pose. (b) The results of predicted grasps evaluated by boundary metric. The Grasp in the upper left corner is considered to be successful and others are cases of failure.

4 Grasping Detection Network

In this section, we first introduce the structure of our three-part grasping detection network, and then the loss function applied for error backpropagation is described.

4.1 Network Structure

Inspired by [4], we build our end-to-end grasping detection network as a full convolutional neural network with semantic segmentation network structure. Most semantic segmentation networks [9, 22–25] have very complex structures, resulting in poor real-time performance. In order to improve the inference speed, we take the FCN structure proposed by [8] as the basic structure of our model, which is a network with good real-time performance and segmentation result.

Our grasping detection pipeline can be divided into three parts: feature extraction module, multi-scale fusion module, and decoding module. We take the deep residual network proposed by [26] as our feature extraction module, which has the excellent ability for feature extraction and stable convergence due to the skip connections and after-addition activation structure [27], compared with VGG [28], inception [29] and other widely used feature extraction networks. As shown in Fig. 5, our multi-scale fusion module consists of three deconvolution layers, which are connected with the features of the feature extraction module through cross-layer connections. And the decoding module is a light multi-task network that consists of a set of independent 1x1 convolutions, which are used to decode the features from the multi-scale fusion network into quality-map, cosine-map, and sine-map.

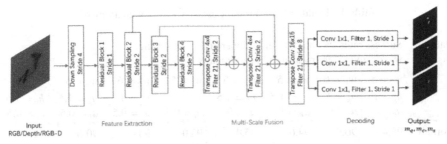

Fig. 5. Structure of our grasping detection network.

4.2 Loss Function

We treat the prediction of quality-map as a binary classification problem, so we use the binary cross-entropy loss function for the training of quality-map. For cosine-map and sine-map, we select mean squared error as the loss function because they need to be regressed to the label $\{\widehat{m_c}, \widehat{m_s}\}$. Then the loss function used to train our grasping detection network to be:

$$loss = \alpha * BCE\left(\widehat{m_q}, m_q\right) + \beta * (MSE\left(\widehat{m_c}, m_c\right) + MSE\left(\widehat{m_s}, m_s\right)) \qquad (4)$$

where α and β are the coefficients used to balance the errors.

5 Experiments

In this section, we first train a remarkable grasping network on our dataset and another famous dataset to show the ability of our Adaptive Grasping Dataset to adapt to the mechanical parameters of the gripper and the absolute positioning accuracy of the robot platform. Then we benchmark our grasping detection network as well as several representative grasping methods on our dataset and give the comparison results. Finally, we conduct grasping experiments on a practical robot platform to demonstrate the effectiveness of our dataset, grasping detection network, and boundary metric.

5.1 Comparison Experiment of Datasets

Cornell Grasping Dataset [1] is a widely used grasping dataset, which is composed of 885 RGB-D images with more than 8k 5-dimensional grasp rectangle labels. According to [4, 18] and other methods, it has good performance in robot grasping task. Since Cornell Grasping Dataset is very close to our data set in terms of volume and the category of objects, we use it as a contrast to evaluate our Adaptive Grasping Dataset. To verify the adaptability of the gripper and robot, we set up four grippers with different mechanical parameters and two robots with different absolute positioning accuracies, and then we transform the dataset according to the above settings. We select GR-ConvNet from [5] as the evaluating network, which has excellent performance on Cornell Grasping Dataset, and the results evaluated by the boundary metric are reported in Table 1. It is obvious that the model trained on our dataset is more robust to the changes of mechanical parameters of the gripper and the absolute positioning accuracy of the robot.

Table 1. Evaluation of different datasets with boundary metric

Dataset	Success rates (%) on different gripper and robot settings w_g, h_g and a_r are measured in centimeters							
	$w_g = 5$ $h_g = 1$ $a_r = 0$	$w_g = 6$ $h_g = 1$ $a_r = 0$	$w_g = 5$ $h_g = 1.5$ $a_r = 0$	$w_g = 6$ $h_g = 1.5$ $a_r = 0$	$w_g = 5$ $h_g = 1$ $a_r = 0.5$	$w_g = 6$ $h_g = 1$ $a_r = 0.5$	$w_g = 5$ $h_g = 1.5$ $a_r = 0.5$	$w_g = 6$ $h_g = 1.5$ $a_r = 0.5$
Cornell	95.4	96.0	94.6	95.4	93.0	94.4	90.6	92.6
Ours	96.6	97.2	96.8	96.0	96.0	95.8	96.4	96.4

5.2 Comparison Experiment of Methods

We adopt two generative methods GG-CNN from [4] and GR-ConvNet from [5] with their original implementations as contrasts. And our model is trained with Adam optimizer on a computer running Ubuntu 18.04 with an Intel Core i9–9900 CPU and an NVIDIA GeForce RTX 2080Ti graphics card. Grasping detection networks are trained on our dataset and assessed by our boundary metric. Table 2 shows the performance of our method in comparison to other models on our dataset. As we can see, our grasping detection network achieves a higher success rate than others so the effectiveness of our three-part network structure is proven. Unlike other networks, through the cross-layer connection structures, the high-level features are enhanced by low-level features in our network. And because the grasping detection is closely related to the object shape embedded in low-level features, our network achieves better performance.

Table 2. Evaluation of different methods with boundary metric

Methods	Success rates (%)
GG-CNN [4]	92.4
GR-ConvNet [5]	96.0
Ours	97.2

5.3 Robot Grasping Experiment

To conduct our grasping experiments, we take 7-DoF KUKA LBR iiwa as our robot platform and equip it with a self-developed antipodal gripper, see Fig. 6. An Intel Realsense D435 depth camera mounted above the grasping area captures images for the grasping detection network. We provide 20 grasping scenes that contain several novel objects with random orientations and positions for the robot to grasp and use the percentage of objects that are successfully lifted as the metric to evaluate our model and dataset. The following Table 3 demonstrates that grasping detection networks trained on our dataset have higher success rates than networks trained on Cornell Grasping Dataset, and our network achieves the best performance in the two datasets. At the same time, we can also see that the results of our boundary metric are very consistent with the results of practical robot experiments.

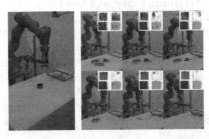

Fig. 6. Grasping experiments on real robot. The left picture shows our experiment environment and right picture illustrates the process that robot picking up multiple objects and placing them in a box.

Table 3. Success rates of practical robot experiments

Datasets	Success rates (%)		
	GG-CNN [4]	GR-ConvNet [5]	Our method
Cornell [1]	90	93	93
Ours dataset	91	95	97

6   Conclusion

In this paper, a novel grasping approach for antipodal grippers with a dynamic annotation mechanism is developed. With the help of our dynamic annotation mechanism, the Adaptive Grasping Dataset in our approach can be adjusted automatically according to a specific robot platform. In order to accurately evaluate the quality of predicted grasps, we present an original criterion named boundary metric. In addition, we propose a grasping detection network to predict grasps. Experiments demonstrate that our dataset has the ability to adapt to the mechanical parameters of grippers and the absolute positioning accuracy of robots, so it has better performance in the practical grasping task. And the effectiveness of our grasping detection network and the accuracy of our boundary metric are also proved by adequate experiments. In order to further improve the actual generalization ability of robot grasping methods, how to make grasping methods automatically adapt to different types of grippers such as dexterous hands and three-finger grippers should be considered in the future research.

References

1. Yun, J., Moseson, S., Saxena, A.: Efficient grasping from RGBD images: learning using a new rectangle representation. In: 2011 IEEE International Conference on Robotics and Automation, pp. 3304–3311. IEEE, Shanghai, China (2011)
2. Mahler, J., et al.: Dex-net 2.0: deep learning to plan robust grasps with synthetic point clouds and analytic grasp metrics. In: Robotics: Science and Systems, MIT Press, Massachusetts, USA (2017)
3. Fang, H.S., Wang, C., Gou M., Lu, C.: GraspNet-1Billion: a large-scale benchmark for general object grasping. In: 2020 IEEE/CVF Conference on Computer Vision and Pattern Recognition, pp. 11441–11450. IEEE, Seattle, WA, USA (2020)
4. Morrison, D., Corke, P., Leitner, J.: Closing the loop for robotic grasping: a real-time, generative grasp synthesis approach. In: Robotics: Science and Systems. MIT Press, Pittsburgh, Pennsylvania, USA (2018)
5. Kumra, S., Joshi, S., Sahin, F.: Antipodal robotic grasping using generative residual convolutional neural network. In: 2020 IEEE/RSJ International Conference on Intelligent Robots and Systems, pp. 9626–9633. IEEE, Las Vegas, USA (2020)
6. Redmon, J., Angelova, A.: Real-time grasp detection using convolutional neural networks. In: 2015 IEEE International Conference on Robotics and Automation, pp. 1316–1322. IEEE, Seattle, WA, USA (2015)
7. Chu, F.J., Xu, R., Patricio, V.: Real-world multiobject, multigrasp detection. IEEE Robot. Autom. Lett. 3(4), 3355–3362 (2018)
8. Shelhamer, E., Long, J., Darrell, T.: Fully convolutional networks for semantic segmentation. IEEE Trans. Pattern Anal. Mach. Intell. 39(4), 640–651 (2016)
9. Zhou, Z., Siddiquee, M.M.R., Tajbakhsh, N., Liang, J.: UNet++: redesigning skip connections to exploit multiscale features in image segmentation. IEEE Trans. Med. Imaging 39(6), 1856–1867 (2020)
10. Huang, G., Liu, Z., Laurens, V., Weinberger, K.Q.: Densely connected convolutional networks. In: 2017 IEEE Conference on Computer Vision and Pattern Recognition, pp. 2261–2269. IEEE, Honolulu, HI, USA (2017)
11. Le, Q.V., Kamm, D., Kara, A.F., Ng, A.Y.: Learning to grasp objects with multiple contact points. In: 2010 IEEE International Conference on Robotics and Automation, pp. 5062–5069. IEEE, Anchorage, AK, USA (2010)
12. Depierre, A., Dellandrea, E., Chen, L.: Jacquard: a large scale dataset for robotic grasp detection. In: 2018 IEEE/RSJ International Conference on Intelligent Robots and Systems, pp. 3511–3516. IEEE, Madrid, Spain (2018)
13. Chang, A.X., et al.: ShapeNet: an information-rich 3D model repository Computer Science. CoRR abs/1512.03012 (2015)
14. Mahler, J., Matl, M., Liu, X., Li, A., Gealy, D., Goldberg, K.: Dex-Net 3.0: computing robust vacuum suction grasp targets in point clouds using a new analytic model and deep learning. In: 2018 International Conference on Robotics and Automation, pp.5620–5627. IEEE, Brisbane, QLD, Australia (2018)
15. Cao, H., Fang, H.S., Liu, W., Lu, C.: SuctionNet-1Billion: a large-scale benchmark for suction grasping. IEEE Robot. Autom. Lett. 6(4), 8718–8725 (2021)
16. Kumra, S., Kanan, C.: Robotic grasp detection using deep convolutional neural networks. In: 2017 IEEE/RSJ International Conference on Intelligent Robots and Systems, pp. 769–776. IEEE, Vancouver, BC, Canada (2017)
17. Zhang, H., Lan, X., Bai, S., Zhou, X., Tian, Z., Zheng, N.: ROI-based robotic grasp detection for object overlapping scenes. In: 2019 IEEE/RSJ International Conference on Intelligent Robots and Systems, pp. 4768–4775. IEEE, Macau, China (2019)

18. Wu, G., Chen, W., Cheng, H., Zuo, W., Zhang, D., You, J.: Multi-object grasping detection with hierarchical feature fusion. IEEE Access **7**, 43884–43894 (2019)
19. Gou, M., Fang, H.S., Zhu, Z., Xu, S., Wang, C., Lu, C.: RGB matters: learning 7-DoF grasp poses on monocular RGBD images. In: 2021 IEEE International Conference on Robotics and Automation, pp. 13459–13466. IEEE, Xi'an, China (2021)
20. Pas, A.T., Gualtieri, M., Saenko, K., Platt, R.: Grasp pose detection in point clouds. Int. J. Robot. Res. **36**(13–14), 1455–1473 (2017)
21. Liang, H., et al.: PointNetGPD: detecting grasp configurations from point sets. In: 2019 International Conference on Robotics and Automation, pp. 3629–3635. IEEE, Montreal, QC, Canada (2019)
22. Chen, L.C., Papandreou, G., Kokkinos, I., Murphy, K., Yuille, A.L.: DeepLab: semantic image segmentation with deep convolutional nets, atrous convolution, and fully connected CRFs. IEEE Trans. Pattern Anal. Mach. Intell. **40**(4), 834–848 (2017)
23. Cao, J., Anwer, R.M., Cholakkal, H., Khan, F.S., Pang, Y., Shao, L.: SipMask: spatial information preservation for fast image and video instance segmentation. In: Vedaldi, A., Bischof, H., Brox, T., Frahm, J.-M. (eds.) ECCV 2020. LNCS, vol. 12359, pp. 1–18. Springer, Cham (2020). https://doi.org/10.1007/978-3-030-58568-6_1
24. Xie, E., Wang, W., Yu, Z., Anandkumar, A., A, J.M., Luo, P.: SegFormer: simple and efficient design for semantic segmentation with transformers. In: 35th Conference on Neural Information Processing Systems, pp. 12077–12090. MIT Press, Virtual Conference (2021)
25. Wu, S., Zhong, S., Liu, Y.: Deep residual learning for image steganalysis. Multi. Tools Appl. **77**(9), 10437–10453 (2017). https://doi.org/10.1007/s11042-017-4440-4
26. He, K., Zhang, X., Ren, S., Sun, J.: Deep residual learning for image recognition. In: 2016 IEEE Conference on Computer Vision and Pattern Recognition, pp. 770–778. IEEE, Las Vegas, NV, USA (2016)
27. He, K., Zhang, X., Ren, S., Sun, J.: Identity mappings in deep residual networks. In: Leibe, B., Matas, J., Sebe, N., Welling, M. (eds.) ECCV 2016. LNCS, vol. 9908, pp. 630–645. Springer, Cham (2016). https://doi.org/10.1007/978-3-319-46493-0_38
28. Simonyan, K., Zisserman, A.: Very deep convolutional networks for large-scale image recognition. CoRR, abs/1490.1556 (2014)
29. Szegedy, C., Ioffe, S., Vanhoucke, V., Alemi, A.: Inception-v4, inception-resnet and the impact of residual connections on learning. In: 31th AAAI Conference on Artificial Intelligence, pp. 4278–4284. AAAI Press, San Francisco California USA (2017)

Tracking and Counting Method for Tomato Fruits Scouting Robot in Greenhouse

Guanglin Dai, Ling Hu, Pengbo Wang(✉), and Jiacheng Rong

School of Mechanical and Electric Engineering, Jiangsu Provincial Key Laboratory of Advanced Robotics, Soochow University, Suzhou 215123, China
pbwang@suda.edu.cn

Abstract. The quantity of tomatoes is closely related to their yield information, and a powerful inspection robot that can automatically count tomatoes is urgently necessary for the hot and harsh environment of greenhouses. With the continuous progress of computer vision technology, the use of deep learning algorithms for counting tomatoes can greatly improve the inspection speed of the inspection robot. This paper propose a tomato fruit counting method for greenhouse inspection robots, which tracks the position of tomatoes in the image by the spatial displacement information of the robot, while 3D depth filtering can effectively avoid the interference of background tomatoes on the counting. The main advantages of this method are: (1) it can realize the tracking of bunched fruits and the counting of single fruits at the same time; (2) it can avoid the interference of background tomatoes. The experimental results of the greenhouse showed that the accuracy rates of bunch and single fruit counting were higher than 84% and 86% respectively, which greatly improved the inspection speed compared with manual counting and basically meet the counting requirements of the current greenhouse.

Keywords: Greenhouse scouting robot · Tomato tracking and counting · YOLOV5

1 Introduction

Tomato is one of the three major world trade vegetables and occupies an important position in the global vegetable trade. China is the largest tomato producing country in the world, but the production per unit area in China is very low, which is in contrast to developed countries. In recent years, in order to increase the yield per unit area of tomato, it is very important to manage tomatoes scientifically, in addition to using greenhouse cultivation. The use of inspection robots to obtain tomato growth data instead of manual labor can greatly reduce labor costs and improve tomato growing efficiency. The number of tomatoes as an important characteristic of tomato growth process, counting greenhouse tomatoes can not only reasonably arrange the picking cycle, but also make marketing plans in advance to improve economic efficiency.

With the continuous development of computer vision technology and deep learning algorithms, robots are gradually used in agricultural scenes to improve crop growing

© The Author(s), under exclusive license to Springer Nature Switzerland AG 2022
H. Liu et al. (Eds.): ICIRA 2022, LNAI 13455, pp. 60–68, 2022.
https://doi.org/10.1007/978-3-031-13844-7_6

efficiency and reduce manual growing costs [1, 2]. The use of computer vision technology instead of the human eye for fruit counting is very widely used in scenes such as orchards and greenhouses.

Suchet Bargoti [3] et al. at the Field Robotics Centre, University of Sydney, Australia presented an image processing framework for fruit detection and counting using orchard image data,including two feature learning algorithms: multiscale multilayered perceptrons (MLP) and convolutional neural networks (CNN), finally achieved the best detection F1-score of 0.861 with WS detection. Xu Liu [4] et al. from the GRASP lab at the University of Pennsylvania presented a novel fruit counting pipeline that combines deep segmentation, frame to frame tracking, and 3D localization to accurately count visible fruits across a sequence of images, the model had an L1 loss of 203, finally achieved an error mean of -0.2% and a standard deviation of 7.8% after the 3D reconstruction correction step. P.J. Ramos [5] et al. from the National Coffee Research Center of Colombia proposed a hand-held non-destructive coffee bean counting method, which can achieve coffee bean counting in some areas through image segmentation algorithms and edge processing methods, which linked the fruits that were counted automatically to the ones actually observed with an R^2 higher than 0.93 one-to-one. Nicolai Häni [6] et al. from University of Minnesota proposed a new fruit detection and counting method based on semantic segmentation and a modular end-to-end system for apple orchard yield estimation, achieved yield estimation accuracies ranging from 95.56% to 97.83%. Manya Afonso [7] et al. from Wageningen University used the MASK-RCNN algorithm to accurately identify tomato fruits and classify their maturity, and found that MASK-RCNN can learn the depth data of objects, finally achieved 91% detection accuracy in a single image. Raymond Kirk [8] et al. from University of Lincoln presented a novel multi-object, multi-class fruit tracking system to count fruit from image sequences.

In this study, we propose a tomato fruit counting method for a greenhouse inspection robot, which tracks the position of tomato in the image through the spatial displacement information of the inspection robot. The method is mainly divided into three steps: (1) use the trained fruit detection model to identify the bunch of fruits and single fruits in the picture, and each bunch of fruits will generate an information list; (2) process the tomato information list and delete duplicate labels; (3) convert the list of information to the number of tomatoes.

2   Material and Method

2.1   Tomato Sample and Scouting Robot

In this study, the tomato we selected is a cherry tomato named "jiaxina" from nijiawan greenhouse, Xiangcheng District, Suzhou City, Jiangsu Province. As shown in Fig. 1(a), the tomatoes are planted in a ridge and its fruit grow in a bunch. After artificial agronomic treatment, the mature tomato fruits were in a fixed height range from the ground. There is a track between the two ridges of tomatoes, which is used for vehicles such as greenhouse scouting robot and tomato picking robot. As shown in Fig. 1(b), the scouting robot which we currently use is mainly composed of a depth camera (Realsense D435i), a lifting pole and a greenhouse track chassis. The lifting rod can meet the inspection requirements of tomato fruits with different heights. The chassis contains a set of RFID system. When the tags at both ends of the track were read, it can control the opening and closing of the inspection function. At the same time, the chassis can move on the track at a constant speed.

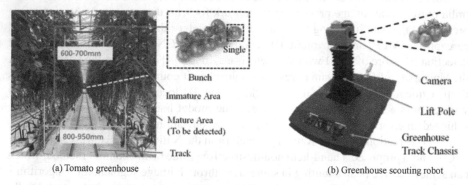

(a) Tomato greenhouse   (b) Greenhouse scouting robot

Fig. 1. Tomato greenhouse environment and scouting robot.

2.2 Image Acquisition

The images of tomatoes were acquired by a depth camera mounted on the scouting robot, and the images consist of RGB images of tomatoes and depth images aligned with them, and both the color and depth images were 1280 * 720 pixels. Special attention should be paid to the fact that the position of the camera relative to the scouting robot was fixed during the scouting robot movement. As shown in Fig. 2, the camera axis was perpendicular to the monopoly plane, the camera was 500–650 mm away from the ridge plane, and the height of the camera was 1650 mm above the ground, so that the tomatoes in the mature were appear exactly within the field of view of the camera.

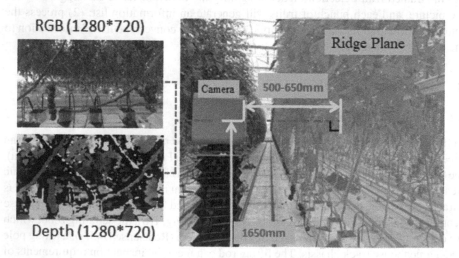

Fig. 2. Position of depth camera.

2.3   Tomato Fruit Detection

Yolov5 is a single-stage target detection algorithm, which has been updated in many iterations and has great superiority in speed and accuracy. In this study we choose YOLOV5 [9] as the tomato fruit detection algorithm. A sufficient amount of dataset should be trained before tomato detection, and we used the scouting robot to drive on the track at a uniform speed (0.1 m/s) and saved color pictures at 5 frames per second. To meet the diversity of samples, we selected data samples from October 2021 to December 2021 for three time periods: 6:00–8:00 AM, 12:00–14:00 PM, and 16:00–17:00 PM, which include different weather lighting environments of sunny, cloudy, and rainy days. After nearly three months of data collection, a total of about 15, 000 images were obtained, and finally 3000 images containing different backgrounds and different fruit ripeness were selected.

In this study we need to train two models, one for the detection of bunches of fruits and one for the detection of single fruits. The filtered images were labeled twice using Labelme software, once with the bunch fruit in the image and once with the single fruit in the image. The labeled images were trained using yolov5. In this study, the ratio of training set, verification set and test set is 1:1:19.

Once the model was trained, we can detect the tomatoes in the greenhouse. As shown in Fig. 3, the detection of tomatoes was divided into 3 main steps: the first step detects tomato bunches, the second step detects the number of individual fruit in each bunch, and the third step assigns an information list to each tomato bunch. Finally, we used the list [*frame, ID, x, y, w, h, a, D, s*] to mark each tomato bunch detected, frame represents the number of frames of the current image, the *ID* represents the total number of tomato bunches detected from the beginning to the present, *x, y, w, h* represent the pixel coordinates of the center point and the length and width of the target rectangle box obtained from the tomato bunch detected, *a* represents the number of single fruit of the current tomato bunch after single detection, *D* represents the average value of the depth of each single fruit in the current bunch, and *s* represents the accumulated distance traveled by the scouting robot on the track from the beginning of detection to the present.

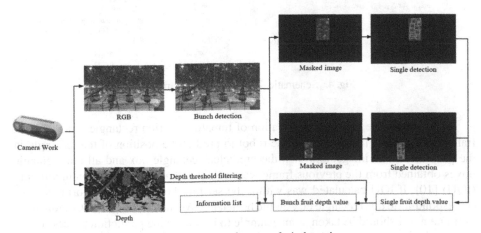

Fig. 3.   Flow chart of tomato fruit detection.

The main use of the depth map in the fruit detection process was to filter the background mis-detected tomatoes after getting the depth values of bunch and single fruit. In order to prevent the following tracking error caused by the incomplete fruit of the tomato bunches at the edge of the image, we set invalid areas on both sides of the image, if x is less than 100 or greater than 1180, then the list of information obtained will be deleted.

2.4 Tracking and Counting of Tomato Fruit

After the fruit detection step, the tomatoes detected in each frame of the picture will correspond to an information list. During the inspection process, the same bunch of tomatoes may be identified in multiple frames of the image, which means that a bunch of tomatoes may correspond to multiple lists. Tracking counting is the process of removing these duplicate labels. As is shown in Fig. 4, take frame n and frame n + 1 as examples, at this time, the scouting robot walks s_n and s_k respectively. It is assumed that three strings of tomatoes are found in each frame.

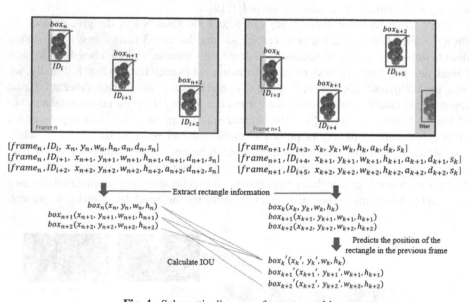

Fig. 4. Schematic diagram of tomato tracking.

In this study, we used the information of tomato detection rectangle in the current frame and the shift information of the robot to predict the position of the rectangle in the previous frame image, and then the predicted rectangle box and all the rectangle boxes obtained from the previous frame were calculated as the intersection union ratio (IOU) [10]. If IOU calculated was within the set threshold, then the information list corresponding to this rectangle box should be deleted. As shown in Fig. 4, ID_{i+3} tomatoes in frame n + 1 should be taken as an example to introduce the prediction process of the rectangular box.

The rectangular box corresponding to the information list of ID_{i+3} tomato is box_k. First, converted the pixel coordinates (x_k, y_k) of the center point of the box to the coordinates (X_k, Y_k) under the camera coordinate system. In Eq. (1) and Eq. (2), c_x, c_y, f_x, f_y are camera internal parameters.

$$X_K = \frac{d_k * x_k - c_x * d_k}{f_x} \tag{1}$$

$$Y_k = \frac{d_k * y_k - c_y * d_k}{f_y} \tag{2}$$

The moving distance of the scouting robot from frame n to frame n + 1 is calculated by the cumulative displacement difference (Eq. (3)). In Eq. (4) and Eq. (5), x_k' and y_k' respectively represent the pixel coordinates of the center point predicted in frame n of box_k, finally, x_k' and y_k' are calculated (Eq. (6) and Eq. (7)).

$$s = s_k - s_n \tag{3}$$

$$X_K - s = \frac{d_k * x_k' - c_x * d_k}{f_x} \tag{4}$$

$$Y_k = \frac{d_k * y_k' - c_y * d_k}{f_y} \tag{5}$$

$$x_k' = \frac{d_k * s_k - s * f_x}{d_k} \tag{6}$$

$$y_k' = y_k \tag{7}$$

After predicting the position of box_k in frame n, we calculated the IOU of the predicted new box_k' and all rectangular boxes of frame n in turn. If the IOU calculated was greater than 0.8, the information list corresponding to box_k was considered to be a duplicate list. On the contrary, if the IOU calculated was less than 0.8, the list should be retained. In order to prevent the tomato in a frame image from being successfully detected, each list must be calculated with all the information lists in the previous 30 frames until it is considered as a duplicate list.

2.5 Result Output

After patrol inspection, the number of information lists retained is the total number of tomato bunches, and the sum of value a in each information list is the total number of single tomato fruit. At the same time, the images of each tomato bunch and the corresponding information list were saved as patrol inspection record.

3 Result and Discussion

As shown in Table 1, in order to verify the reliability of the algorithm, we selected three tracks in different areas of the greenhouse to count the tomato fruits, and compared the number of fruits obtained with the actual number of fruits obtained by manual counting. It was found that the algorithm has high accuracy in tomato fruit counting. From the experimental results, the accuracy of single fruit counting is lower than that of bunch fruit counting, which is due to the problem of mutual shading of single fruits. Although the inspection process can identify single fruits from different angles, the shading between fruits will still affect the counting.

Table 1. Experimental results of counting tomatoes by described method.

	test1	test2	test3
Speed	0.1 m/s	0.1 m/s	0.1 m/s
Actual number of bunch fruits	30	68	86
Number of detected bunch fruits	34	75	98
Accuracy of bunch fruit counting	86.7%	91.2%	87.2%
Actual number of single fruit	356	664	704
Number of single fruit detected	302	586	593
Accuracy of single fruit counting	84.8%	88.3%	84.2%

In addition, we set up a group of comparative experiments, using the current mainstream crowd counting algorithm (Deepsort) to count the tomatoes in the greenhouse. Deepsort [11] is a classical multi-target tracking algorithm based on Tracking by Detection strategy. Its main principles are Hungarian algorithm and Kalman filter. We used the color video stream recorded by the inspection robot on the same track at the same time to do experiments. First, the trained yolov5 model was used to identify the bunch fruit in each frame of images, then deepsort tracked the position of the bunch fruits in the image, and the final output detection results are shown in Table 2. In the tracking process, each tracked bunch fruit was given a label. We cut out the bunch fruit rectangle of the same label for single fruit detection, so that we can get the number of single fruit of each bunch fruit.

From Table 2, we can find that the accuracy of bunch fruits counting of deepsort is lower than that of Table 1, but the number of detected tomatoes is higher than that of Table 1. The reason is that deepsort does not have the function of deep filtering, and many background tomatoes are included in the final number. Comparing the two counting methods, it is easy to find that the number of bunches of fruit counted is higher than the actual number. Because the bunch tomatoes were not successfully identified in several consecutive frames during the process of being tracked, and when they were identified again they were no longer successfully tracked, and then the algorithm defined them as newly identified bunches of fruit, so that the number of bunches of fruit is higher than the actual number. Therefore, improving the accuracy of target recognition in a single frame image is very important for target tracking and counting.

Table 2. Experimental results of counting tomatoes by Deepsort algorithm.

	test1	test2	test3
Speed	0.1 m/s	0.1 m/s	0.1 m/s
Number of detected bunch fruits	49	116	144
Accuracy of bunch fruit counting	61.2%	58.6%	59.7%
Number of single fruit detected	265	586	593
Accuracy of single fruit counting	74.3%	77.4%	79.2%

4 Conclusion and Future Work

We proposed a tomato fruit counting method for a greenhouse inspection robot that uses the spatial displacement information of the inspection robot to track the position of tomatoes in an image to achieve the function of tomato fruit tracking and counting. This method uses a trained fruit detection model to identify each bunch of fruits in the image and calculate the number of single fruits in each bunch. At the same time, 3D deep filtering can effectively avoid the interference of background tomatoes. Then, the displacement information and coordinate transformation of the inspection robot are used to eliminate the repeated list representing the same string of tomatoes. Finally, the retained list can be converted into the quantity information of tomato fruits. Then, the duplicate list representing the same bunch of tomatoes is removed by coordinate transformation and the displacement information of the inspection robot, and the retained list is converted into the quantity information of tomato fruits.

The tomato fruit counting method proposed in this paper has the following two advantages: (1) it can realize the tracking of bunched fruits and the counting of single fruits at the same time; (2) Depth information filtering can effectively reduce the interference of background tomato fruit.

Our future work will mainly focus on how to improve the accuracy of string fruit and single fruit recognition, especially how to solve the occlusion problem of single fruit. We may train and use different models for different periods, or modify the network to improve the recognition accuracy.

Funding. This research was fundeded by National Key Research and Development Program of China (2017YFD0701502).

References

1. Yangyang, Z., Jianlei, K., Xuebo, J., et al.: Crop deep: the crop vision dataset for deep-learning-based classification and detection in precision agriculture. Sensors **19**(5), 1058 (2019)
2. Tian, H., Tianhai, W., Yadong, L., et al.: Computer vision technology in agricultural automation—a review. Inf. Process. Agri. **7**(1), 1–19 (2020)
3. Bargoti, S., Underwood, J.P.: Image segmentation for fruit detection and yield estimation in apple orchards. J. Field Robot. **34**(6), 1039–1060 (2017)
4. Liu, X., Chen, S.W., Aditya, S., et al.: Robust fruit counting: combining deep learning, tracking, and structure from motion. In: 2018 IEEE/RSJ International Conference on Intelligent Robots and Systems (IROS), pp. 1045–1052(2018)
5. Ramos, P.J., Prieto, F.A., Montoya, E.C., et al.: Automatic fruit count on coffee branches using computer vision. Comput. Electron. Agric. **137**, 9–22 (2017)
6. Häni, N., Roy, P., Isler, V.: A comparative study of fruit detection and counting methods for yield mapping in apple orchards. J. Field Robot. **37**(2), 263–282 (2020)
7. Afonso, M., Fonteijn, H., Fiorentin, F. S., et al.: Tomato fruit detection and counting in greenhouses using deep learning. Front. Plant Sci. 1759 (2020)
8. Kirk, R., Mangan, M., Cielniak, G.: Robust counting of soft fruit through occlusions with re-identification. In: Vincze, M., Patten, T., Christensen, H.I., Nalpantidis, L., Liu, M. (eds.) Computer Vision Systems. ICVS 2021. LNCS, vol. 12899, pp. 211–222 (2021). https://doi.org/10.1007/978-3-030-87156-7_17
9. Redmon, J., Divvala, S., Girshick, R., et al.: You only look once: unified, real-time object detection. In: Proceedings of the IEEE Conference on Computer Vision and Pattern Recognition, pp. 779–788 (2016)
10. Jiang, B., Luo, R., Mao, J., et al.: Acquisition of localization confidence for accurate object detection. In: Proceedings of the European Conference on Computer Vision (ECCV), pp. 784–799 (2018)
11. Wojke, N., Bewley, A., Paulus, D.: Simple online and realtime tracking with a deep association metric. In: 2017 IEEE International Conference on Image Processing (ICIP), pp. 3645–3649 (2017)

Interaction, Control and Application Technologies of Welfare Robots

Safety Assistance Strategy of Nursing Robot in Stand-To-Sit Movement

Zexin Li[✉], Baiqing Sun, Yong Li, and Qiuhao Zhang

School of Electrical Engineering, Shenyang University of Technology, Shenyang, China
Edanscholar@163.com

Abstract. Stand-to-sit movement(SST) refers to the process from stand to sit, and the interaction of SST usually refers to the process of contact between people and the seat. SST is a relaxed and natural movement for normal people with healthy lower limbs, and they will not perceive any difficulties. However, for those people with lower limb disabilities, they have certain handicaps in SST. When they perform SST, owing to their lower extremity muscles could not work properly, they would receive a violent shock from the seat after touching the seat surface, which is a huge threat to the safety of the interactor. This paper mainly studies the safety assistance method of the nursing robot in the process of contact between the human body and the seat in SSI. We propose a lumped parameter model of human-robot interaction based on the vertical dimension to describe the post-contact process. On the basis of completing the modeling, we constructed the safety auxiliary control system of the nursing robot, and verified the effectiveness of the control system through the simulation experiment of the control system.

Keywords: Stand-to-sit movement · Lumped parameter model · Muscle strength · Biomechanics

1 Introduction

Stand-to-sit movement(SST) refers to the process from stand to sit, and the interaction of SST usually refers to the process of contact between people and the seat. SST is a relaxed and natural movement for normal people with healthy lower limbs, and they will not perceive any difficulties. However, for those people with lower limb disabilities or insufficient lower limb muscle strength, they have certain handicaps in SST. When they perform SST, owing to their lower extremity muscles could not work properly, they would receive a violent shock from the seat after touching the seat surface, which is a huge threat to the safety of the interactor. If these people with lower extremity disabilities have diseases such as osteoporosis themselves, they may fall to the ground as a result, and even cause fractures, damage other organs of the body or muscle and ligament tissue. The nursing robot can control the vertical movement of the chair surface to generate an appropriate impulse when the user interacts with the chair surface to offset the huge impact force generated by the contact between the hip and the chair surface and protect the safety of the user. Providing auxiliary nursing robots during interaction is of great

H. Liu et al. (Eds.): ICIRA 2022, LNAI 13455, pp. 71–79, 2022.
https://doi.org/10.1007/978-3-031-13844-7_7

significance for people with lower limb disabilities, whether it is to improve the quality of life or prevent accidents such as accidental falls. The development of the nursing robot mainly includes the dynamic analysis of the human-robot motion process in theory and the construction of the safety auxiliary control system of the nursing robot in practice.

However, in terms of STS, the technical research and development of nursing robots is still in a blank period. After consulting the literature, it is found that the current related research mainly analyzes the movement process from sit to stand, which is exactly the opposite of the movement process that needs to be studied. For instance, Geravand et al. developed a six-link biomechanical model for STD research and utilized it in the STD auxiliary strategy formulation [1]. Josip et al. designed a three-link model and reconstructed the trajectory of the thighs, calves and torso in STD with several low-cost inertial sensors [2]. STD and STS are distinct, but they are so similar especially in the situation when the human body is no longer in contact with the seat, and the two movements can be described by the same model in such circumstance. By way of illustration, the three-link model established by Hemami et al. can describe STS and STD simultaneously [3]. In addition, the mathematical model proposed by Jayeshkumar, which is also a three-link mathematical model is applicable to STS and STD [4]. However, similar to the models used by the CUHK-EXO exoskeleton robot, the designers of these models generally did not consider the impact of the seat. This can largely be explained that when the human body is not in contact with the seat, in order for STS and STD to share the same model, they must omit the contact process between the body and the seat. But for our research in STS, from the perspective of reducing the impact of the seat, the contact process is of great significance. After consulting a large amount of literature, we found that few studies focused on the contact process between the body and the seat. Kazunori et al. proposed an optimal control model to describe STS: when the body is not in contact with the seat, it is equivalent to a three-link dynamic structure, and when the body is in contact with the seat, the structure of links and joints is used [5]. Although these researchers considered the contact between the body and the seat when modeling, they essentially simplified the original three-link mechanical model based on the changes in the scene, and did not reflect the relative displacement and interaction force between body and seat.

This paper mainly studies the safety assistance method of the nursing robot in the process of contact between the human body and the seat in STS. After referring to related literatures [6–10], we propose a lumped parameter model of human-robot interaction based on the vertical dimension to describe the post-contact process. On the basis of completing the modeling, we constructed the safety auxiliary control system of the nursing robot, and verified the effectiveness of the control system through the simulation experiment of the control system.

2   Method

2.1   The Intelligent Assistant Model of Nursing Robot

In SST, the human body can be regarded as a mass, and the nursing robot can also be regarded as a mass. The human body and the nursing robot are connected by two groups of spring and damping. The first group includes the spring and damping of the soft part of the both human thigh and chair surface, while the second group of spring and damping includes the hard part of the both human thigh skeleton and chair surface. The value of the above spring and damping depends on the relative displacement of the human body and the nursing robot. As the relative displacement changes, the spring damping value also changes linearly.

In the first stage of the post-contact process, the influence of the second group of spring and damping is not considered, only the influence of the first group of spring and damping is in the consideration. The human body is subjected to the spring and damping force from the soft part of the chair surface and its own gravity. The nursing robot is subjected to the spring and damping force from the soft part of the human thigh, its own gravity and the force that controls the lifting motor to the robot.

In the second stage of the post-contact process, it is considered that the spring and damping force of the first stage is a fixed value which is the maximum spring and damping force value in the whole stage, and the influence of the second group of spring damping is also considered. The human body is subjected to the spring and damping force of the hard part of the nursing robot, the maximum value of the spring and damping force from the robot in the previous stage, and its own gravity. The nursing robot is subjected to the spring and damping force from the hard part of the human thigh bone, the maximum value of the spring and damping force from the human in the first stage, its own gravity and the force that controls the lifting motor to the robot.

Based on the above force analysis, the value assistance model of the nursing robot is established. The human-robot dynamics equation in the first stage of the post-contact process is:

$$m_{man}\ddot{y}_{man} = K_{soft}(y_{man} - y_{bot}) + C_{soft}(\dot{y}_{man} - \dot{y}_{bot}) - m_{man}g \tag{1}$$

$$m_{bot}\ddot{y}_{bot} = K_{soft}(y_{bot} - y_{man}) + C_{soft}(\dot{y}_{bot} - \dot{y}_{man}) - m_{bot}g + f_{bot} \tag{2}$$

where m_{man} is the mass of the human body except for the calf, y_{man} is the displacement of the human thigh, y_{bot} is the speed of the human thigh, $\ddot{y}_{man}$ is the acceleration of the human thigh, m_{bot} is the mass of the robot, y_{bot} is the displacement of the robot, and $\dot{y}_{bot}$ is the speed of the robot, $\ddot{y}_{bot}$ is the acceleration of the robot motion, K_{soft} is the spring coefficient connecting the human body and the soft part of the robot, C_{soft} is the damping coefficient connecting the human body and the soft part of the robot, and f_{bot} is the force that controls the lifting motor of the robot on the robot.

The human-robot dynamics equation of the second stage of the post-contact process is:

$$m_{man}\ddot{y}_{man} = K_{hard}(y_{man} - y_{bot}) + C_{hard}(\dot{y}_{man} - \dot{y}_{bot}) - m_{man}g + f_{soft1} \tag{3}$$

$$m_{bot}\ddot{y}_{bot} = K_{hard}(y_{bot} - y_{man}) + C_{hard}(\dot{y}_{bot} - \dot{y}_{man}) - m_{bot}g + f_{bot} + f_{soft2} \tag{4}$$

where K_{hard} is the spring coefficient connecting the hard part of the human body and the robot, C_{hard} is the damping coefficient connecting the human body and the hard part of the robot, f_{soft1} is the maximum value of the spring and damping force that human receives from the robot in the first stage, and f_{soft2} is the maximum value of the spring and damping force that the robot receives from human in the first stage.

The safety auxiliary model of the nursing robot can obtain the calculation expression of the impact force, and the expression of the force of the seat on the human body in the first stage of the post-contact process is:

$$F_{chair} = K_{soft}(y_{man} - y_{bot}) + C_{soft}(\dot{y}_{man} - \dot{y}_{bot}) \tag{5}$$

The expression of the force of the seat on the human body in the second stage of the post-contact process is:

$$F_{chair} = K_{hard}(y_{man} - y_{bot}) + C_{hard}(\dot{y}_{man} - \dot{y}_{bot}) + f_{soft1} \tag{6}$$

where F_{chair} is the impact force received by the person from the seat.

2.2 Model Predicted Intelligent Auxiliary Control System

As shown in Fig. 1, the basic structure of the control system consists of six parts: the state observer A, the object model, filtering process, the optimal controller, the state observer B, and the object output.

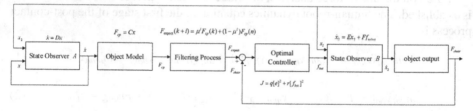

Fig. 1. Block diagram of intelligent auxiliary control system based on model prediction.

The state observer A observes the state variables when the nursing robot does not consider the auxiliary motion in the system. The observed state variable expression is:

$$x = \begin{bmatrix} y_{man} \\ \dot{y}_{man} \\ \ddot{y}_{man} \\ y_{bot} \\ \dot{y}_{bot} \\ \ddot{y}_{bot} \end{bmatrix} \tag{7}$$

where x is the integrated representation of the state variables in the state observer A.

In the state equation, these state variables can be regarded as a whole, and the known state variables in the current sampling period and the unknown state variables in the next sampling period in the future are regarded as a linear correspondence, and the state observation can be obtained. The calculation expression that can get the state variable in the state observer A is:

$$\dot{x} = Dx \tag{8}$$

where $\dot{x}$ is the state of the state variable x in the current sampling period of the state observer A in the next sampling period. D is the constant.

The object model refers to the theoretical calculation model of the control object. Its expression in the state space equation is:

$$F_{cp} = Cx \tag{9}$$

where F_{cp} is the predicted output of the force of the seat on the human body, and C is the constant.

The filtering process refers to the operation of filtering the predicted value of the force of the seat on the human body. The desired output change curve is obtained by filtering. The calculation expression of the expected force of the seat on the human body is:

$$F_{expect}(k + i) = \mu^i F_{cp}(k) + (1 - \mu^i) F_{cp}(n) \tag{10}$$

where F_{expect} is the expected output of the force of the seat on the human body, k is the number of current sampling periods, i is the number of remaining sampling periods, n is the total number of sampling periods, and μ is the filter coefficient.

The optimal controller controls the given control quantity of the safety auxiliary control system. The performance index of the optimal controller is divided into two parts. The task of the first half is to ensure that the output of the system is as close to the expected value as possible, and the task of the second half is to ensure that the given amount of the control system is as low as possible to reduce energy loss. The first half includes the weight coefficient q, r and the control error e, and the performance index expression of the optimal controller is:

$$J = q[e]^2 + r[f_{bot}]^2 \tag{11}$$

where J is the performance index of the optimal controller.

After determining the performance index of the optimal controller, the optimal solution can be solved for the optimal controller. The solution expression of the optimal controller is:

$$\frac{\partial J(f_{bot})}{\partial f_{bot}} = 0 \tag{12}$$

State observer B observes the state variables of the human and nursing robot including f_{bot}, which has the same composition as the state observer A. The calculation expression of the state variable in the state observer B is:

$$\dot{x}_2 = Ex_2 + Ff_{robot} \tag{13}$$

where $\dot{x}_2$ is the state of the state variable x_2 in the current sampling period of the state observer B in the next sampling period. E, F is the constant.

Object output refers to the direct output of system objects. The control object in the safety assistance system is the force of the seat on the human body, and the calculation method can refer to the control object model.

The realization of the safety assistance of the control system starts from the acquisition of the initial state variables, and the state variables at the moment when the human body touches the seat is obtained through the sensor, including the displacement, speed and acceleration of the human and the robot. Input the obtained state variables into the state observer A, so that the state observer A starts to calculate the prediction sequence of the future state variable x in a loop. The obtained prediction sequence is the state of the human and the nursing robot in the future sampling period without considering the robot-assisted force.

The predicted state variable sequence is input to the object model, and after calculation, the sequence of F_{cp} without considering the robot-assisted force is output. The obtained F_{cp} sequence is filtered to obtain the F_{expect} sequence, and the F_{expect} of the next cycle is taken from this sequence. The control error e of the system is obtained by making the difference with the output F_{chair} of the current cycle system (the force of the seat on the human body in the first cycle is 0).

Input the control error e into the optimal controller to calculate f_{bot} that controls the robot in the next cycle. Then input the state variable output by the state observer B in the previous cycle (the initial state variable is used in the first cycle) and the f_{bot} output by the controller into the state observer B to obtain the state variable x_2 of the next cycle of the final simulated real system. The state variable x_2 obtained here will not only become the input of the state observer A in the next sampling period, but also become a part of the input of the state observer B in the next sampling period.

Finally, the state variable x_2 is substituted into the object model to simulate the real environment to obtain the output F_{chair} of the system, and at the same time, F_{chair} is fed back to the input part of the optimal controller for calculating the error.

3 Experiment

The control system constructed in this paper is based on the process after the human body is in contact with the seat. Therefore, before simulating the control system, it is necessary to obtain the state variables of the human body generated during the pre-contact process, which include the displacement, velocity, and acceleration of the human body at the moment of contact with the seat. We use the DataLog angle data acquisition system to obtain the posture information in STS. The acquisition system is divided into two parts, including an angle data acquisition terminal and a wired angle data acquisition module installed on the human body. The wired angle data acquisition module can sense the change of angle through the internal strain element, while the angle data acquisition terminal can support up to 8 channels of analog signal input and 4 channels of digital signal input according to requirements. The experimental equipment is set up as shown in the Fig. 2.

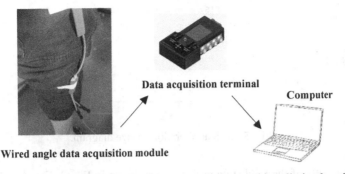

Data acquisition terminal

Computer

Wired angle data acquisition module

Fig. 2. Schematic diagram of experimental equipment and installation location

We performed a STS experiment to obtain the initial variables for the simulation. Experiment content: After installing the sensor according to Fig. 2, arrange the subject to stand 10 cm in front of the chair (chair height: 0.45 m; chair length: 0.40 m; chair width: 0.40 m) to stand still for 4–5 s, then sit and remain still until the sensor turns off. The sensor measures the changes in angle, angular velocity, and angular acceleration. These data will first be directly transmitted to the acquisition terminal through the transmission line for storage.

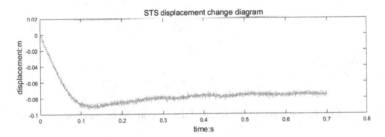

Fig. 3. STS displacement change diagram.

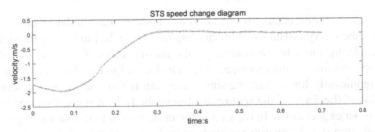

Fig. 4. STS speed change diagram.

After the experiment is over, it will be uploaded to the host computer through the built-in memory card of the terminal. Finally, in the host computer, the displacement, velocity and acceleration are calculated through geometric relationship conversion. The

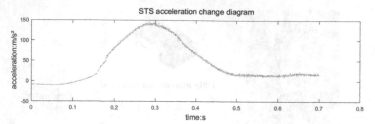

Fig. 5. STS acceleration change diagram.

acquisition results of the final state variables are shown in Fig. 3, Fig. 4 and Fig. 5. We take the time node when the acceleration first suddenly changes as the initial point of the post-contact process.

Based on the above theoretical and experimental data preparation, we simulated the safety auxiliary control system. We built a simulation platform in Matlab, simulated the six basic structures of the intelligent auxiliary control system through the simulation program, and completed the simulation of the intelligent auxiliary process. The sampling period of the simulation was set to 0.01 s, and the simulation results are shown in Fig. 6.

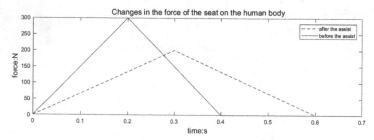

Fig. 6. Changes in the force of the seat on the human body.

4 Discussion

Refer to the simulation results in Fig. 6. The red line is the simulation curve without considering the safety assistance of the nursing robot, and the blue line is the simulation curve considering the safety assistance of the nursing robot. We found that after the nursing robot performs safety assistance, the maximum force of the seat on the human body is significantly lower than the simulation data before the safety assistance, and the duration of the force of the seat on the human body is also greatly extended. This fully meets our expectations. In the simulation environment built, the nursing robot can theoretically improve the energy conversion rate from the human body to the seat, and can obtain more ideal data than before assistance in terms of energy transfer time and energy transfer peak value. Although the simulation of the entire safety auxiliary control system is based on the test in the virtual environment, it can also verify the feasibility of the nursing robot to complete the auxiliary tasks under the safety auxiliary control system to a certain extent.

5 Conclusion

We build a lumped parameter model of human-robot interaction to study the process of the human body before and after contact with the seat in STS. Based on this model, we constructed the control system of the nursing robot and obtained the ideal control effect in the simulation experiment, which shows high reliability. We believe that the established model can simulate STS in the real environment with low error, and the established nursing robot control system can effectively assist the interactor in STS, providing a theoretical basis for subsequent research.

References

1. Geravand, M., Korondi, P.Z., Werner, C., et al.: Human sit-to-stand transfer modeling towards intuitive and biologically-inspired robot assistance. Auton. Robot. **41**(3), 575–592 (2017)
2. Musić, J., Kamnik, R., Munih, M.: Model based inertial sensing of human body motion kinematics in sit-to-stand movement. Simul. Model. Pract. Theory **16**(8), 933–944 (2008)
3. Hemami, H., Jaswa, V.C.: On a three-link model of the dynamics of standing up and sitting down. IEEE Trans. Syst. Man Cybern. **8**(2), 115–120 (1978)
4. Gandhi, J.: Mathematical model of human sit-to-stand and stand-to-sit motion analysis. New Jersey Institute of Technology (1998)
5. Wada, K., Matsui, T.: Optimal control model for reproducing human sitting movements on a chair and its effectiveness. J. Biomech. Sci. Eng. **8**(2), 164–179 (2013)
6. Coermann, R.R.: The mechanical impedance of the human body in sitting and standing position at low frequencies. Hum. Fact. **4**(5), 227–253 (1962)
7. Cho, Y., Yoon, Y.S.: Biomechanical model of human on seat with backrest for evaluating ride quality. Int. J. Ind. Ergon. **27**(5), 331–345 (2001)
8. Jan, M., Qassem, W., Othman, M., Gdeisat, M.: Human body model response to mechanical impulse. Med. Eng. Phys. **19**(4), 308–316 (1997)
9. Liang, C.C., Chiang, C.F.: A study on biodynamic models of seated human subjects exposed to vervibration. Int. J. Ind. Ergon. **36**(10), 869–890 (2006)
10. Rosen, J., Arcan, M.: Modeling the human body/seat system in a vibration environment. J. Biomech. Eng. **125**(2), 223–231 (2003)

Motion Planning Method for Home Service Robot Based on Bezier Curve

Yu Shu[1], Donghui Zhao[1]([✉]), Zihao Yang[1], Junyou Yang[1], and Yokoi Hiroshi[2]

[1] Shenyang University of Technology, Shenyang 110870, China
zhaodonghui@sut.edu.cn
[2] The University of Electro-Communications, Tokyo 1820021, Japan

Abstract. Aiming at the problems of collision, non-smoothness, and discontinuity of the trajectory generated by the motion planning of the service robot in the home environment, this paper proposes a robot motion planning system consisting of three parts: path planning, trajectory generation, and trajectory optimization. First, use the A* algorithm based on graph search to quickly plan a passable global path in a complex home environment as the initial value of trajectory generation; secondly, construct an objective function based on Minimum Snap to generate the initial trajectory to be optimized; finally, Using the convex hull property of the Bezier curve, the safety corridor is constructed and the time distribution is adjusted by the trapezoidal velocity curve method, which solves the overshoot phenomenon that occurs in the solution process of the trajectory generation. The Minimum Snap method based on the Bezier Curve is constructed to optimize the trajectory and finally generate A continuous and smooth motion trajectory with minimal energy loss suitable for service robots. The feasibility and effectiveness of this method are proved by simulation experiments.

Keywords: Service robot · Trajectory optimization · Bezier curve

1 Introduction

In recent years, with the increase in the number of the aging population, service robots play a great advantage in taking care of the daily life of the elderly and are widely used in the home environment [1]. The home environment is relatively complex and unstructured, which puts higher requirements on the motion planning of service robots. The motion planning of mobile robots consists of two parts: path planning and trajectory optimization.

At present, the path planning algorithms of mobile robots mainly include two categories: search-based and sampling-based. Search-based methods mainly include A* algorithm [2,3], D* algorithm [4], the main feature of this kind of algorithm is to expand from the starting point to the endpoint until it reaches the endpoint. The sampling-based method is another kind of commonly used path planning method, among which the most classic is the rapidly exploring random tree algorithm [5], but since it uses random sampling, the planned path is not the optimal path. Due to the high center of gravity of the service robot, it is necessary to ensure the stability of the robot's movement, which puts forward higher requirements for the trajectory optimization of the robot. Through the differential flat method [6], polynomials can be used to optimize the trajectory of various robots [7]. However, the generated trajectory only considered the smoothness and continuity constraints of the intermediate points, and did not consider the shape of the trajectory, that is, whether a collision will occur.

In this paper, a motion planning method for service robots in the home environment is proposed. By imposing security corridor constraints on position and redistributing time by trapezoidal velocity method, a trajectory optimization method based on the Minimum Snap of Bezier curve is constructed, which effectively solves the motion planning problem of robots in the home environment.

2   Motion Planning

2.1   Overall Structure

The motion planning method of the home service robot proposed in this paper consists of three parts: path planning, trajectory generation, and trajectory optimization, and the overall structure block diagram is shown in Fig. 1. Firstly, the A* algorithm is used to realize the initial path planning and get a set of discrete waypoints that do not collide with the obstacles. On this basis, an objective function based on Minimum Snap is constructed to generate a continuous, smooth, and to-be-optimized trajectory. However, the generated trajectory suffers from a certain amount of overshoot. Therefore, the Bezier curve is introduced, the safety corridor is constructed according to the obstacle distribution, the time is redistributed using the trapezoidal velocity curve method, and the trajectory optimization of Minimum Snap based on the Bezier curve is constructed using the transformation relationship between the Bezier and polynomial functions to finally generate a continuous, smooth motion with minimum energy loss applicable to the home service robot trajectory. The trajectory is input to the robot trajectory tracker, and the service robot can then track the trajectory.

2.2   Trajectory Generation Based on Minimum Snap

When the home environment information is known, given the initial state and the target state, the A* algorithm is used to obtain a path consisting of a series of discrete waypoints that are sparse and do not contain temporal information. To better control the service robot's motion, the sparse waypoints need to be transformed into continuous and smooth curves. In this paper, we use a higher-order polynomial function for trajectory generation. The polynomial coefficients are calculated so that the overall polynomial trajectory satisfies the continuity and smoothness constraints while minimizing the energy function. To be able to restrict the snap and satisfy the equation semi-positive definite, construct a 7th order polynomial objective function.

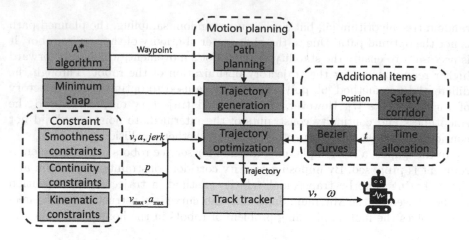

Fig. 1. Block diagram of the overall structure of motion planning.

Let the path be divided into a total of h segments, then any of these segments can be expressed as:

$$q(t) = q_0 + q_1 t + q_2 t^2 + \cdots + q_7 t^7 = \sum_{i=0}^{7} q_i t^i \tag{1}$$

where $q(i)$ is the coefficient of the polynomial($i = 0, 1, \cdots, 7$), and t is the time of current trajectory.

The Minimum Snap minimization objective function of the whole trajectory is constructed, that is $Z(t)$, the integral of the square of the change of snap in the corresponding time segment of each trajectory, and its expression is:

$$Z(T) = \int_{T_{j-1}}^{T_j} \left(f^{(4)}(t) \right)^2 \mathrm{d}t = Q_j^T L_j Q_j \tag{2}$$

where Q_j is the coefficient matrix of jth trajectory polynomial; L_j is the information matrix of jth trajectory polynomial.

The problem of minimization of the objective function is modeled as a mathematical Quadratic Programming (QP) problem. After constructing the objective function to be optimized, to make the final generated trajectory continuous, the continuity equation constraint is constructed at the end of the jth segment trajectory and the beginning of the $(j+1)^{th}$ segment trajectory as:

$$f_j^{(k)}(T_j) = f_{j+1}^{(k)}(T_j) \tag{3}$$

The position of the trajectory at the path junction of each segment of the trajectory is relatively fixed, and the smoothness equation constraint is constructed:

$$f_j^{(k)}(T_j) = c_j^{(k)} \tag{4}$$

where c represents the x and y axes.

Formula (3) and Formula (4) are substituted for Formula (2), and the coefficients q of each trajectory satisfying the constraint conditions are calculated. The coefficients are substituted into the state equations of each segment to solve the state quantities of the whole trajectory in all directions, and finally, the trajectory to be optimized is obtained.

2.3   Trajectory Optimization Based on Bezier Curve

The trajectory generated based on the Minimum snap method does not impose restrictions on the whole trajectory position. The generated trajectory may collide with the obstacle because of the dense obstacles in the home environment. And the trajectory generated based on the Minimum snap method does not consider the speed and acceleration running limit of the robot itself. Based on the above problems, the trajectory optimization is carried out using the Minimum snap method based on the Bezier Curve, and the mathematical properties of the Bezier Curve are used to construct a safe corridor, and kinematic constraints are imposed according to the parameters of the robot, and the time is redistributed using the trapezoidal velocity curve. The Bezier curve polynomial is established as follows:

$$E_j(t) = p_j^0 e_n^0(t) + p_j^1 e_n^1(t) + \cdots + p_j^n e_n^n(t), t \in [0,1] \qquad (5)$$

where p_j^i is the $(i+1)^{th}$ control points of a convex hull polygon, $e_n^i(t)$ is the Berstein basis function.

There is a transformation relationship between the Bezier curve and the polynomial curve, such as the formula (6). Therefore, we can use the Bezier property to impose additional velocity and acceleration constraints, and then transform them into polynomial curves to solve them. This will greatly shorten the calculation time and improve the solution quality.

$$\sum_{i=0}^{n} p_i \frac{n!}{(n-i)!i!}(1-t)^{n-i}t^i = q_0 + q_1 t + \cdots + q_n t^n \qquad (6)$$

The objective function of the original trajectory will start at the first control point and end at the last control point after the Bezier Curve transformation. By restricting the control points of the Bezier curve to the rectangular safety zone, the generated trajectory will be surrounded by the convex envelope formed by the control points due to the convex envelope nature of the Bezier curve [8], and then the whole trajectory must be located within the safety zone and must be collision-free. To avoid collision between trajectory and obstacles, the trajectory expected to be planned must be in Corridor. If the passable safety region is added to the QP problem as a constraint, the trajectory of the solution will naturally be in Corridor. As shown in Fig. 2, a collision-free safe corridor is constructed with the waypoints searched by the A* algorithm as the center, and a trajectory is generated in the corridor, so the trajectory must be safe and collision-free. The inequality constraint expression is as follows:

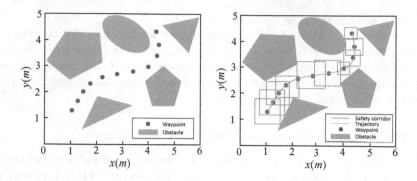

Fig. 2. Establishment of global security corridor.

$$\delta_{\mu j}^- \leq d_{\mu j}^{0,i} m_j \leq \delta_{\mu j}^+ \tag{7}$$

where $d_{\mu j}^{0,i}$ is the control point of the Bezier curve of order r^{th} and i on the jth trajectory on the μ axis, $\delta_{\mu j}^-, \delta_{\mu j}^+$ is the minimum and maximum limit position of safety corridor.

Based on the linear relationship between the high-order control points and the low-order control points of the Bezier curve, the dynamic inequality constraints are constructed as follows:

$$\begin{cases} v_m^- \leq d_{\mu j}^{1,i} \leq v_m^+ \\ a_m^- \leq d_{\mu j}^{2,i} m^{-1} \leq a_m^+ \end{cases} \tag{8}$$

where v_m^-, v_m^+ is the minimum and maximum speed; a_m^-, a_m^+ is the minimum and maximum acceleration.

Equality constraints are imposed on the position, velocity, acceleration and jerk of the starting point and end point, which are expressed as:

$$\begin{cases} d_{\mu j}^{r,i} m_j^{1-r} = g_{\mu j}^{(r)} \\ d_{\mu j}^{r,i} = \frac{n!}{(n-r)!} \left(d_{\mu j}^{r-1,i+1} - d_{\mu j}^{r-1,i} \right) & r \geq 1 \end{cases} \tag{9}$$

where m_j^{1-r} is the scalar coefficient of order $1-r$ of the jth segment, $g_{\mu j}^{(l)}$ is the jth segment r^{th} order on the axis is a certain value.

To ensure the position, velocity, acceleration, and jerk of every two Bezier Curve joints, a continuity equality constraint is imposed, which is expressed as:

$$d_{\mu j}^{r,n} m_j^{1-r} = d_{\mu j+1}^{r,0} m_{j+1}^{1-r} \tag{10}$$

Most current time allocation methods use uniform motion to calculate time, as shown in Fig. 3(a), time is allocated in proportion to the path length [9], but the solver is not easy to solve. In Fig. 3(c), the blue and orange colors are different time allocations to produce different trajectories. In this paper, the trapezoidal velocity profile method is used to allocate time, where the mobile robot starts from the starting point, accelerates smoothly to the maximum speed, moves at a uniform speed, and decelerates smoothly near the endpoint. The velocity profile is shown in Fig. 3(b), and the robot acceleration function is designed as follows:

$$a = g_s \left(1 - \cos\left(t\right)\right) \tag{11}$$

where g_s is the expected maximum jerk value.

By constructing the objective function of minimizing energy and imposing linear equality constraints and linear inequality constraints, the whole trajectory optimization problem is expressed as:

$$\begin{aligned}
\min \quad & P^T Q_o P \\
\text{s.t.} \quad & A_{eq} P = B_{eq} \\
& A_{ie} P \leq B_{ie} \\
& P_l \in \Omega_l, \quad l = 1, 2, \ldots, h
\end{aligned} \tag{12}$$

where $P = [P_1, P_2, \cdots, P_h]$ consists of the feasible region Ω_l in section l that satisfies the waypoint constraint and the safety corridor constraint.

The QP solver is used to solve the above problems, and finally, a continuous, smooth, collision-free, and executable trajectory suitable for home service robot is generated.

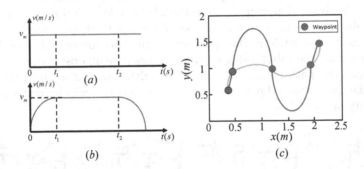

Fig. 3. Time allocation. (a) Uniform time allocation velocity curve. (b) Trapezoidal time allocation velocity curve. (c) Trajectories produced by different time allocation. (Color figure online)

3 Experiment

To validate the proposed method, Ubuntu 16.04 is used as the bottom operating system, and C++ programming is used in the ROS stage simulation environment on I5-7200HQ 8G memory portable computer. In the ROS Stage simulator, To build the robot navigation environment model in the home environment, the Gmapping algorithm is used to build the map, and the map can be started by configuring the parameter file and providing the related topic topics subscribed.

Using Rviz visualization tool in ROS to display simulation results. Service robot $v_{max} = 0.25\,\mathrm{m/s}$, $a_{max} = 0.25\,\mathrm{m/s}^2$. Firstly, the starting point and the target point are selected, and then the robot trajectory is planned by using the A* algorithm and the trajectory optimization algorithm proposed in this paper under simple obstacles and complex obstacles. The simulation results in a simple environment and a complex environment are shown in Figs. 4 and 5.

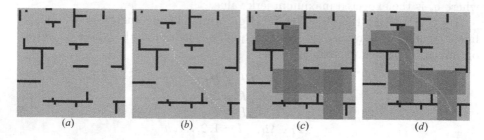

Fig. 4. Simulation results in a simple environment. (a) Environment map. (b) A* algorithm planning path. (c) Safe corridor generation. (d) Optimized trajectory.

In the simulation results, the white discrete points are the paths planned by A*, the light blue area is the safety corridor extended according to waypoints, and the green trajectory is the optimized trajectory within the safety corridor. Analyzing the simulation results, There are 24 obstacles in a simple environment, the path planned by the A* algorithm has 7 steep path turns, which is not good for robot execution, while in the optimized path there are only 2 smooth turns, which is good for the robot's stable driving. There are 49 obstacles in a complex environment, the path planned by the A* algorithm has 12 steep turns and 90° turns, while the optimized path has only 3 smooth turns, which greatly improves the stability of the robot.

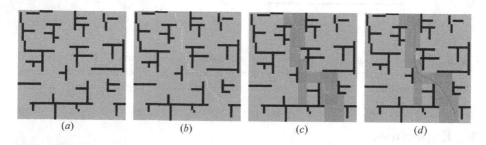

Fig. 5. Simulation results in a complex environment. (a) Environment map. (b) A* algorithm planning path. (c) Safe corridor generation. (d) Optimized trajectory.

The simulation results show that the optimized trajectory of the motion planning method proposed in this paper is better than the traditional A* planning in terms of smoothness and safety, and the obtained trajectory is far away from obstacles and improves safety. Especially in an environment with complex obstacles, the optimization effect is more obvious and more beneficial to the application of service robots in the home environment.

4 Conclusion

In this paper, a motion planning method for service robots in the home environment is proposed. Trajectory optimization based on Bezier curve Minimum Snap is constructed, security corridor constraint is imposed, and trapezoidal velocity curve is introduced to redistribute time. The feasibility of this method is tested in ROS. By comparing the effect of this method with the traditional method, we can see that the proposed motion planning method can plan a smoother and safer path in both simple and complex environments, and is suitable for the motion planning of service robots in the home environment.

References

1. Tagliavini, L., et al.: On the suspension design of paquitop, a novel service robot for home assistance applications. Machines **9**(3), 52 (2021)
2. Guruji, A.K., Agarwal, H., Parsediya, D.K.: Time-efficient A* algorithm for robot path planning. Procedia Technol. **23**, 144–149 (2016)
3. Yang, R.J., Cheng, L.: Path planning of restaurant service robot based on a-star algorithms with updated weights. In: 2019 12th International Symposium on Computational Intelligence and Design (ISCID), pp. 292–295. IEEE, Hangzhou (2019)
4. Ferguson, D., Stentz, A.: Using interpolation to improve path planning: the field D* algorithm. J. Field Robot. **23**(2), 79–101 (2006)
5. Wang, W., et al.: An improved RRT path planning algorithm for service robot. In: 2020 IEEE 4th Information Technology, Networking, Electronic and Automation Control Conference (ITNEC), pp. 1824–1828. IEEE, Chongqing (2020)
6. Zhou, J., et al.: Pushing revisited: differential flatness, trajectory planning, and stabilization. Int. J. Robot. Res. **38**(12–13), 1477–1489 (2019)
7. Shomin, M., et al.: Fast, dynamic trajectory planning for a dynamically stable mobile robot. In: 2014 IEEE/RSJ International Conference on Intelligent Robots and Systems, pp. 3636–3641. IEEE, Illinois (2014)
8. Preiss, J.A., et al.: Downwash-aware trajectory planning for large quadrotor teams. In: 2017 IEEE/RSJ International Conference on Intelligent Robots and Systems (IROS), pp. 250–257. IEEE, Vancouver (2017)
9. Mellinger, D., et al.: Minimum snap trajectory generation and control for quadrotors. In: 2011 IEEE International Conference on Robotics and Automation, pp. 2520–2525. IEEE, Shanghai (2011)

A Current Location Confidence Algorithm for Service Robot in Elder-Care Environment

Zihan Zhang, Donghui Zhao$^{(\boxtimes)}$, Zihao Yang, and Junyou Yang

Shenyang University of Technology, Shenyang 110870, China
zhaodonghui@sut.edu.cn

Abstract. Identifying the wrong location is one of the prerequisites for mobile service robots to work safely and stably. This paper proposes a current location confidence algorithm (CLCA) suitable for mobile service robots in the elder-care environment. In this method, the laser data is matched with the grid map information to obtain the current location confidence, which is used in the safety module to identify the wrong location. Compared with other laser-based methods, the CLCA is not limited by the geometric features of the map, so it is particularly applicable for the elder-care environment with complex space scenes. To verify the feasibility of the CLCA, we have experimented with calculating the current location confidence of the robot. The experimental results show that this method can identify the wrong location and take safety measures.

Keywords: Location confidence · Service robot · Elder-care environment

1 Introduction

Due to the ageing population and increasing number of only children, there is a huge demand for service robots under the relative shortage of professional nursing staff [1]. For the elderly, safety when interacting or getting along with robots is critical. If the robot continues to navigate or grab under the wrong location, it may lead to a failure of the task or even cause an accident. Therefore, the accurate location of the robot is crucial to ensuring the safety of the daily life of the elderly.

The elder-care environment is more complicated than the ordinary indoor environment because of the dynamic obstacles such as the elderly and other service robots [2]. At the same time, there are usually carpets, water stains and other terrains, which will affect the location based on the dead reckoning algorithm [3]. In addition, when the robot interacts with people, it may be kidnapped artificially, resulting in discontinuous location data. These factors put forward higher requirements for identifying the wrong location in the elder-care environment.

H. Liu et al. (Eds.): ICIRA 2022, LNAI 13455, pp. 88–97, 2022.
https://doi.org/10.1007/978-3-031-13844-7_9

Vision and laser sensors are always used to judge whether the indoor location is accurate. In the elder-care environment, because the elderly always have nocturnal actions, such as going to the toilet and taking medicine, the vision sensor that can only work with insufficient light is unsuitable [4]. Thus, the laser sensor is more suitable for this scenario [5]. Researchers have proposed several solutions to identify the wrong location based on the laser. Weerakoon et al. extracted geometric features of an indoor environment such as straight lines and inflection points by a laser sensor. The wrong location can be identified by matching current features with theoretical features [6]. In addition, Zhao et al. also proposed a prediction-based method to extract geometric features quickly [7]. However, these methods need regular geometric features, unsuitable for the elderly-care environment with complex space scenes.

Therefore, this paper proposes a current location confidence algorithm (CLCA) to identify the wrong location, which is not limited by the geometric features. The method is based on the Scan-to-Map process of Cartographer, and can quantify the accuracy of real-time location information [8]. It uses laser data to match the grid map information suitable for the elder-care environment with complex space scenes. We divide this method into the offline and online parts to speed up the calculation of location confidence. The offline part expands the grid map and extracts the proportion of obstacle grids on the map. The online part establishes a geometric model to calculate the robot's current location confidence. In addition, we set up a safety module, which will gave an error reason and take safety measures when the location confidence is lower than the threshold.

2 Current Location Confidence Algorithm

In this paper, we propose the CLCA for mobile service robots, and the system block diagram of this algorithm is shown in Fig. 1. The location confidence is described by calculating the distance between the hit grid by each sampling laser data and its nearest obstacle grid. The CLCA is divided into offline and online parts through whether the robot works during calculation. The offline part includes the expansion of the map and the setting of the laser's sample numbers N_l. In the online part, the geometric model is first established to match the laser measurement value with the expansion map. Secondly, the robot's current location data score S_k is calculated, and it is mapped into the location confidence based on the geometric model LCG in the interval $[0, 100]$. Finally, the LCG is output into the safety module which will identify the wrong location and take safety measures.

2.1 Offline Part of the CLCA

In the offline part, the system expands the grid map, calculates the value v of each grid, and sets the laser's sample numbers N_l according to the complexity of the map.

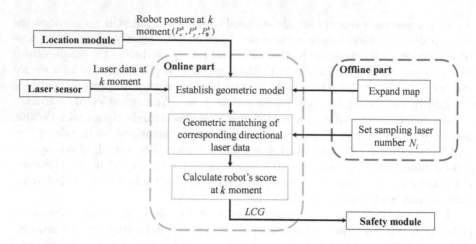

Fig. 1. System block diagram of the CLCA

Expand Map. When the system receives the message *map*, it will expand the grid map. Each expanded grid in the map holds the distance between itself and its nearest obstacle grid d. The less the d is, the earlier the grid is expanded. (The first expanded grids are the obstacle grid with $d = 0$.)

As shown in Fig. 2, it shows the expansion processes of the grid map. The black grid is the obstacle grid OG, the gray grid is the expanded grid EG, the white grid is the free grid FG, the grids in the red box are the grids to be expanded GTE, and the green arrow is the grid to be expanded next time in GTE. Figure 2 (a) and (b) show the first two expansion processes of the map, where all grids in GTE are expanded because they have the same d. As shown in Fig. 2 (c) and (d), only the grids with the minor d will be expanded next time. We set the expansion radius as r which determined by the robot's size. When the d of the expanded grid is more than r or the expanded grid exceeds the map boundary, the expansion is finished, and the system will calculate the v in every EG, as shown in formula (1).

$$v = 100(1 - \frac{d}{r}) \tag{1}$$

When the expansion is finished, we set the unexpanded grid's $v = 0$ To extract the proportion of OG on the grid map, we save all the grids with $v = 100$, and set their total number to N_{OG}.

Set Sample Numbers of the Laser. The N_l is the number of lasers required for each location confidence calculation, and the CLCA can adaptively set it according to the received map. For maps of the same size, the number of OG can represent the complexity of the map's space scene. The more the number of OG, the more N_l is required to ensure sufficient calculation accuracy. At the same time, the number of N_l should not be too large. Although a large number

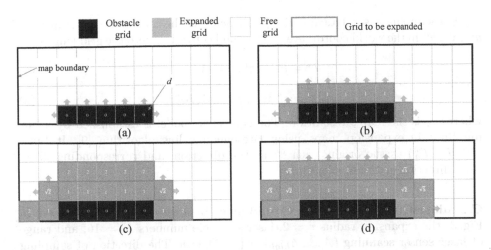

Fig. 2. Expansion processes of the grid map. (a) First expansion. (b) Second expansion. (c) Third expansion. (d) Fourth expansion. (Color figure online)

of N_l can improve the accuracy and safety of the system, it will also increase the calculation cost of the system. Therefore, we can adjust the k_n to ensure the balance between cost and safety. We set the grid map's width as M_w and height as M_h, then the N_l can be set according to the proportion of OG as:

$$N_l = \left\lceil k_n \frac{N_{OG}}{M_w \times M_h} \right\rceil \tag{2}$$

where k_n is the proportionality factor set by the computer's running speed, and the symbol $\lceil \ \rceil$ can assure the N_l is an integer.

2.2   Online Part of the CLCA

This section introduces the online part of the CLCA. We establish a geometric model according to the laser data, robot's current location point, and expansion maps. Based on this model, the system uses the geometric matching method to calculate the robot's LCG.

Establish Geometric Model. In this paper, a geometric model is established to describe the accuracy of the location data. When the robot's posture at k moment is $(P_x^k, P_y^k, P_\theta^k)$ and range of laser sensor scanning is $(A_{low}, A_{high}]$, we take N_l lasers with the same interval angle a_{inc}. The angle of the nth sampling laser data in the robot coordinate system a^n is shown in formula (3):

$$a_{inc} = \frac{A_{high} - A_{low}}{N_l}$$
$$a^1 = A_{low} \tag{3}$$
$$a^n = a^1 + (n-1)a_{inc}, \text{n} = [1, N_l]$$

The sampling laser data at a^n is z_k^n. To facilitate the calculation, we transform a^n into θ^n in the world coordinate system, and convert z_k^n into the grid length x_k^n:

$$\theta^n = P_\theta^k + a^n, \mathrm{n} = [1, N_l] \tag{4}$$

$$x_k^n = z_k^n \times r_m, n = [1, N_l] \tag{5}$$

where r_m is the map's resolution. The geometric model is established by drawing lines in expansion maps using Bresenham's line algorithm [9]. It takes $(P_x^k, P_y^k, P_\theta^k)$ as the origin, each θ^n as the direction, and corresponding x_k^n in each direction as the line length.

Calculate Current Location Confidence. In the geometric model shown in Fig. 3, the expansion radius $r = 2$, laser's sample numbers $N_l = 16$, and range of laser sensor scanning $(A_{low}, A_{high}] = (-180, 180]$. The direction of sampling laser data is θ^n, as shown by the dotted green lines. In addition, the blue lines are drawn by Bresenham's line algorithm, and each blue line has a length of x_k^n and an angle of θ^n. When the line hits FG or outside the map boundary, the score of the current sampling laser data is set to 0, and when the line hits EG or OG, the score is set to v saved in the hit grid. Taking the three lines l_1, l_2, l_3 shown in Fig. 3 as an example, the scores of the hit grids are as follows: s_1 of l_1 is 50, s_2 of l_2 is 0, and s_3 of l_3 is 100. The S_k can be obtained by adding the score of each line:

$$S_k = s_1 + s_2 + \ldots + s_{N_l} = v_1 + v_2 + \ldots + v_{N_l} \tag{6}$$

To intuitively express the accuracy of the location data, we map S_k into the current location confidence LCG:

$$LCG = \frac{S_k}{N_l} \tag{7}$$

The flow chart of the CLCA is shown as Algorithm 1. Before the system works, we define the message type $map, pose, laser$. In the flow chart, Step1 to Step9 are the offline part, Step10 to Step20 are the online part. The function $map.expend()$ is used to expend map, $grid.calculate()$ is used to calculate v, and $setLaserNum()$ is used to set N_l. Step13 and Step14 establish the geometric model, and Step15 is the Bresenham's line algorithm which return the hit $grid$. The LCG is calculated in Step19, and it is output to the safety module in Step20.

2.3   Safety Module

In this paper, a safety module is set up to identify the wrong location and take safety measures. We divide the reasons why the robot's LCG is lower than the threshold in the elder-care environment into two types: (1) The robot passed the terrain such as carpet and water stains which increased the accumulated error

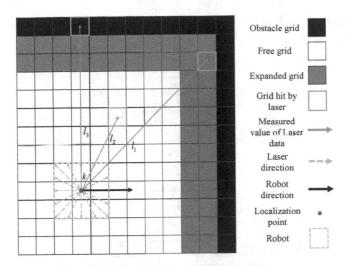

Fig. 3. Calculate current location confidence base on the geometric model. (Color figure online)

Algorithm 1. The current location confidence algorithm

Require: $map, pose, laser, r$
 1: $map.expend(r)$
 2: $N_{OG} = 0$
 3: **for** $grid \in map$ **do**
 4: $\quad grid.v \leftarrow grid.calculate(d, r)$
 5: $\quad$ **if** $v = 100$ **then**
 6: $\quad\quad N_{OG} + +$
 7: $\quad$ **end if**
 8: **end for**
 9: $N_l \leftarrow setLaserNum(map, N_{OG})$
10: $S_k = \emptyset$
11: $n = 1$
12: **for** $n \leq N_l$ **do**
13: $\quad \theta_n \leftarrow setLaserDir(N_l, n, laser, pose)$
14: $\quad x_n \leftarrow setLaserLen(N_l, n, laser)$
15: $\quad grid \leftarrow bresenham(x_n, \theta_n, pose)$
16: $\quad S_k.push(grid.v)$
17: $\quad n + +$
18: **end for**
19: $LCG \leftarrow calculateLC(S_k, N_l)$
20: **return** LCG

---

of the dead reckoning algorithm, resulting in a gradual decrease of the LCG. (2) The robot was kidnapped to another position in the process of human-robot interaction, resulting in a sudden reduction of the LCG. Therefore, the reason can be judged according to the decreased magnitude of the LCG when the system raises an alarm.

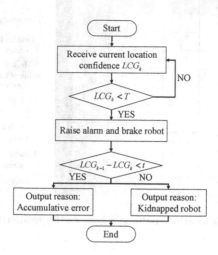

Fig. 4. System flow chart of the safety module.

The system flow chart of the safety module is shown in the Fig. 4. We set the alarm threshold T as the average value of LCG when the deviation between the current pose and real pose equals the robot's size. Whenever this module receives LCG_k, it judges the size relation between LCG_k and T. If $LCG_k \geq T$, the system will wait for the location confidence of the next moment. Otherwise, this module will raise the alarm and brake the robot. In this time, the system will continue to analyze the reason according to the decreased magnitude and the output threshold t. When the robot is kidnapped, its LCG tends to drop sharply, and the decline often exceeds 30. Instead, the accumulative error will slowly reduce the LCG, so t is generally set between 10 and 20.

3   Experiment

To fully evaluate the performance of the CLCA, we have done comprehensive experiments in the Stage simulation environment. The algorithm runs on the PC of the Ubuntu18.04 system and is implemented on the ROS platform. In the simulation experiments, the robot picks up a 2d laser rangefinder with a viewing angle of 360° and a detection distance of 5 m, as shown in Fig. 2. When the system receives map, it will expand the map and set the laser's sample numbers. Then, the robot can start working, and the system will calculate LCG according to the $pose$ and $laser$ received at each moment.

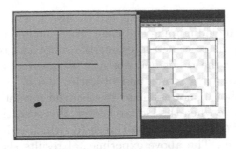

Fig. 5. Stage simulation environment.

The *LCG* calculation experiment is shown in Fig. 6. The time interval for each calculation is 1s, $T = 60$, and $t = 20$. Figure 6 (a) shows the *LCG* calculation when the robot ran with accurate location data. At the $40th$ moment, we stopped the robot to simulate the process of the human-robot interaction, and kidnapped it to another position on the map at the $60th$ moment. As shown in Fig. 6 (b), the *LCG* had a sudden reduction, and the system raised the alarm and braked the robot. At the same time, the system gave the reason as kidnapped robot. In addition, as shown in Fig. 6 (c) and (d), we add a fixed error to the odometer location data at every moment to simulate the robot passing the carpets or water stains in the elder-care environment. The robot started running at the $11th$ moment, and the *LCG* gradually decreased due to accumulated errors. At the $20th$ moment, the system raised the alarm and gave the reason as accumulated error. Because the error of the robot odometer is still increasing, the *LCG* continues to change.

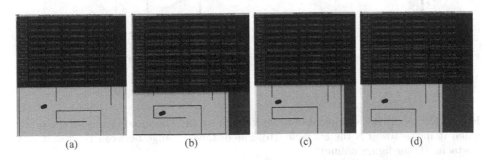

| (a) | (b) | (c) | (d) |

Fig. 6. Experiment of current location confidence calculation. (a) *LCG* calculation with accurate location data. (b) *LCG* calculation under kidnapped robot alarm. (c) *LCG* calculation with odometer error. (d) *LCG* calculation under accumulated error alarm.

In addition, we did a comparative experiment to verify the effectiveness and significance of the CLCA. In this experiment, the robot moved to the obstacle at a constant speed v_r, and was kidnapped to a position close to the obstacle in this process. Figure 7 (a) shows the speed change, where t_1 is the kidnapping start time and t_2 is the kidnapping end time. The blue line represents the robot normal motion, and the red line represents the robot motion with the CLCA. The distance between the robot and obstacle is shown in Fig. 7 (b). d_r is the initial distance between the robot and obstacle, and d_r' is the distance after kidnapping. If the robot do not estimate whether the current location is reliable, it will continue to move when the kidnap is over. However, the CLCA can brake the robot when its LCG is below the threshold, which reduces the risk of the robot hitting obstacles. The above experimental results show that the CLCA can independently identify the low LCG and take safety measures, proving this method's correctness and feasibility.

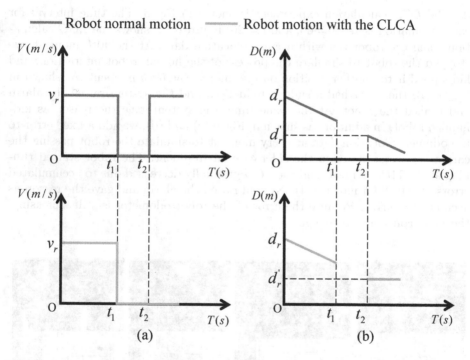

Fig. 7. Comparative experiment of robot kidnapped. (a) The speed change of the robot when it moves towards the obstacle. (b) The distance change between the robot and obstacle. (Color figure online)

4   Conclusion and Future Work

This paper proposes a current location confidence calculation algorithm for mobile service robots in the elder-age environment. By matching laser data with map information, the accuracy of the current location data can be described to identify the wrong positioning quickly. In this method, the calculation of location confidence is divided into online and offline parts to reduce the memory required for system operation. At the same time, the laser's sample numbers are adjusted according to the complexity of the spatial scene, which can further speed up the calculation and improve the system's security and robustness. The algorithm proposed in this paper is verified by simulation experiments, and the results show that the robot can raise the alarm for the wrong location and identify its causes.

In future work, we will improve the application range of the system. There may be some areas with similar spatial structures in the environment, so the system needs other sensors to judge whether the robot has been kidnapped to these areas.

References

1. Robinson, H., et al.: The psychosocial effects of a companion robot: a randomized controlled trial. J. Am. Med. Dir. Assoc. **14**(9), 661–667 (2013)
2. Bemelmans, R., et al.: How to use robot interventions in intramural psychogeriatric care. A feasibility study. Appl. Nurs. Res. **30**(1), 154–157 (2016)
3. Tian, Q., et al.: A multi-mode dead reckoning system for pedestrian tracking using smartphones. IEEE Sens. J. **16**(7), 2079–2093 (2016)
4. Llorca, D.F., et al.: Vision-based traffic data collection sensor for automotive applications. Sensors **10**(1), 860–875 (2010)
5. Tang, J., et al.: NAVIS - an UGV indoor positioning system using laser scan matching for large-area real-time applications. Sensors **14**(7), 11805–11824 (2014)
6. Weerakoon, T., Ishii, K., Nassiraei, A.A. F.: Geometric feature extraction from 2d laser range data for mobile robot navigation. In: 2015 IEEE 10th International Conference on Industrial and Information Systems (ICIIS), pp. 326–331. IEEE, Sri Lanka (2015)
7. Zhao, Y., Xiong, C.: Prediction-based geometric feature extraction for 2D laser scanner. Robot. Auton. Syst. **59**(6), 402–409 (2011)
8. Dwijotomo, A., et al.: Cartographer SLAM method for optimization with an adaptive multi-distance scan scheduler. Appl. Sci. **10**(1), 347 (2020)
9. Jia, Y., Zhang, H., Jing, Y.: A modified Bresenham algorithm of line drawing. J. Image Graph. **13**(1), 158–161 (2008)

A Smart Home Based on Multi-heterogeneous Robots and Sensor Networks for Elderly Care

Tianqi Zhang[1] , Donghui Zhao[1](✉) , Junyou Yang[1], Shuoyu Wang[2],
and Houde Liu[3]

[1] Shenyang University of Technology, Shenyang 110870, China
putongdeyu@126.com
[2] Kochi University of Technology, Kochi 7828502, Japan
[3] Tsinghua University, Beijing 100084, China

Abstract. To tackle behavioral assistance for elderly care in daily life, our laboratory rollout seven homecare robots: walking support robot, gait rehabilitation robot, intelligent wheelchair robot, excretory support robot, personal care robot, intelligent bed, and transport robot. By integrating the multi-heterogeneous robot systems (MHRS) and distributed sensor networks, we propose a novel smart home for elderly care that can cover most life behaviors. Furthermore, to realize that the MHRS can efficiently serve multi-user within the architecture of the smart home. A self-organizing MHRS architecture is proposed. This architecture combines specific tasks to establish a robot group communication mechanism, and multi-robot in the group can complete adaptive control according to the user's real-time position, ensuring assist safety and adaptability. Finally, we conducted experiments in the proposed smart home to rising transfer, standing transfer, and behavior assistance. The experiments show the proposed smart home has the auxiliary capabilities for basic activities of daily living (ADLs), instrumental activities of daily living (IADLs), enhanced activities of daily living (EADLs) even continuous assistance in safety and comfortable way, which can be used in homes, hospitals, rehabilitation center and other scenes for elderly care.

Keywords: Elderly care · Multi-robot system · Homecare robots · Smart home

1 Introduction

As the burgeoning older adult population, several emerging technologies have been used to facilitate the development of aging-in-place, among which the smart home technology for elderly care is an important one [1].

Recently, mobile robots have been integrated into a few smart elderly-care homes through wireless communications to relieve the demanding workload of care from family caregivers, healthcare providers, and support independent living, such as the Sony AIBO robot [2], RoboEarth [3], Kukanchi [4], the RiSH [5] and the Intelligent Space [6].

Meanwhile, the multi-heterogeneous robot systems (MHRS) architecture is mainly divided into centralized, distributed, and hybrid [7]. However, under the conditions

© The Author(s), under exclusive license to Springer Nature Switzerland AG 2022
H. Liu et al. (Eds.): ICIRA 2022, LNAI 13455, pp. 98–104, 2022.
https://doi.org/10.1007/978-3-031-13844-7_10

of multi-robot cooperation, real-time allocation of multi-priority tasks and multi-task demands occurring in parallel for the elderly care scene, the above three architectures all have limitations. The MHRS architecture in the scene of elderly care needs to establish an efficient and adaptive communication mechanism and effectively solve the problems of multi-robot safety adaptive cooperation in the nursing process.

To summarize, smart home environments offer a better quality of life to the elderly by employing robotic control and assistive services. These previous research projects can provide general frameworks for smart home systems. However, due to the functional limitations of intelligent devices such as robots and the heterogeneity of interfaces, the auxiliary functions of these smart elderly-care homes are limited, and it is impossible to perform continuous behavior assistance and multiple users' simultaneous assistance. Meanwhile, the special physical condition and safe nursing requirements of elderly with weak motion capability put forward strict requirements on the performance of homecare robots, and the compliance and safety of nursing behaviors must be ensured. Therefore, it is urgent to break through the single robot nursing technology and create a novel robot system for elderly care. In this paper, we established a smart home for elderly care based on multi-heterogeneous nursing robots and sensor networks. In addition, we proposed a self-organizing MHRS architecture that provides an efficient communication mechanism for multi-robot adaptive cooperative control under specific tasks in the scene of elderly care.

2 Overall Concept of MHSH Architecture

Although several smart homes integrated with robots previously studied can provide services for the elderly to a certain extent, they all have shortcomings in functionality, security, and service continuity. A smart living environment is expected to provide not only in-home services and rehabilitation training but also living comfort and a good user experience. The multiple homecare-robot smart home (MHSH) architecture, as shown in Fig. 1, by integrating a smart home, seven heterogeneous homecare robots, and data management system, contributes to raising the living standards of the elderly. The whole system provides the following services: (1) Basic activities of daily living (ADLs) Service: safe and comfortable auxiliary services for getting up, standing up, walking, carrying things, and excretion (2) Enhanced activities of daily living (EDLs) Services: the fall detection system and remote monitoring service; (3) Enhanced activities of daily living (IDLs) Service: gait rehabilitation training and self-diagnosis services. The components of the smart home are as follows:

2.1 Homecare Robot

Seven homecare robots are shown in Fig. 1. According to the daily requirements, the user operates telecontroller to call the different robots. Based on indoor positioning and path planning technology, the robot comes to the human side and help the users to implement task and transfer based on the optimal transfer method.

2.2 Sensor Network and Home Gateway

The sensor network consists of four parts: Positioning and Communication Sensors, Intelligent Perception Sensors, Medical Evaluation Sensors, and Body Sensors. The home gateway is a personal computer that serves as a data management system in the smart elderly-care home. It receives sensor data from the robot and the sensor network. It also enables communication with the cloud server and the remote caregivers.

2.3 Smart Home Environment

The smart home environment includes 3 areas: recreation area, living area, and rehabilitation area. The smart home testbed will be used by multiple users, including simple indoor behavior, and complex behavior consisting of multiple simple behaviors.

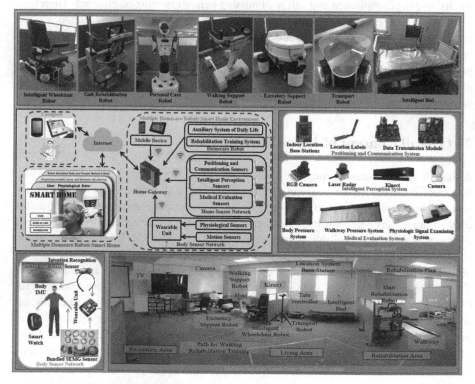

Fig. 1. The overall architecture of the smart elderly-care home.

3 Multi-heterogeneous Robot System Architecture

In this section, we introduce the self-organizing MHRS architecture, as shown in Fig. 2. Because the nursing demands sent by some users are complicated and need the cooperation of multiple robots, therefore, we regard the demands of users in the scene of elderly are as a series of compound tasks $\{T_m, m = 1, \ldots, N_T\}$, each compound task will be decomposed into a list of sub-tasks $\{t_m, m = 1, \ldots, N_t\}$, treating the task allocation problem in this scenario as a decompose-then-allocate problem as described in [8]. The overall process is as follows:

Centralized Task Allocation: As the coordinator of the architecture, the central controller will receive the user's demands, the robot's position, occupancy, and other related information, then centrally assign the tasks sent by the users according to the task value, which is calculated by Eq. (1). A low task value means that the task is easier to assign. Z_m is all the skills needed to complete task T_m. s_p is the skill required for the task $t_{n,m}$, which represents the corresponding task t_m executed by Robot r_n. The effort corresponding to a skill is directly proportional to the work estimate $\omega_{m,p}$, which is defined as a function of the different actions required for the skill and depending on the skill, the parameters considered for the work estimate may differ, and is inversely proportional to the expertise $\lambda_{n,p}$ of the robot, which represents the robot's expertise parameter for s_p. The time cost factor of the task is directly proportional to the estimated completion time $S_{n,m}$ of the task. α ($\alpha > 0$) is the time scaling factor. The constraint on $v_{n,m}$ is given by Eq. (2). Considering the energy of the system, when the remaining energy E_{remain} of the system is less than the energy required to complete the task, $v_{n,m}$ is null. It indicates that the robot will give up on the current task, which can effectively avoid dangerous behavior.

$$v_{n,m} = \sum_{s_p \in Z_m} \left[\frac{\omega_{m,p}}{\lambda_{n,p}} \right] \cdot \alpha S_{n,m} \tag{1}$$

$$\textbf{\textit{Subject to}} \; E_{remain} \leq w v_{n,m} = \text{NULL} \tag{2}$$

Robot Alliance: When the task T_m is assigned, the central controller stops giving guidance to each robot. Robot r_1, Robot r_2 ...... Robot r_n forms a robot group according to the task vector to complete one task. Each robot group should include at least two heterogeneous nursing robots.

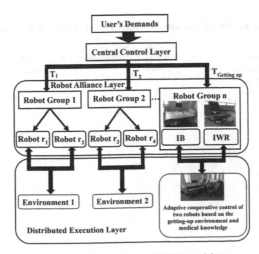

Fig. 2. The self-organizing MHRS architecture.

Distributed Execution: Each robot will perform its own subtasks. Meanwhile, when interacting with the environment, each robot will adjust itself timely according to the situation in the nursing process, for adapting to specific users and ensuring safety.

When multiple users in the smart home make demands for auxiliary care at the same time, the self-organizing multi-robot system architecture proposed in this paper can handle these tasks in parallel, and establish a robot group communication mechanism in combination with specific tasks. Multi-robots in the group can complete adaptive control according to the real-time position of users.

4 Experiment

The goal of the comprehensive experiments is to determine how well the proposed smart elderly-care home when multi-heterogeneous homecare robots care for users.

4.1 Performance Comparison of the Smart Home

MHSH aims to help patients to complete basic indoor activities based on the multi-heterogeneous robot architecture. Compared to the traditional smart home, MHSH pays more emphasis on safe auxiliary behavior for daily activities and a higher comfort experience. Therefore, we propose that the user perform complex behavior by operating multi-heterogeneous robots. The comparison between MHSH and previous studies in functional practicability and universality of applicable objects is shown in Table 1, this paper uses symbols "√" to express the corresponding smart home has a certain function, symbols "○" indicate that the smart home lacks a certain function. The results show that the functions of MHSH is more closely to people's real requirements in daily life; the applicable object includes a variety of user groups: the elderly, people with inconveniences in lower extremities, including stroke, foot drooping, hemiplegic, plantar repair and so on.

Table 1. Functional comparison of smart elderly-care home.

Project	Assisted getting-up	Assisted standing up and sitting down	Auxiliary walking	Auxiliary excretion	Transportation	Grasp	Medical care	Emergency behavior monitoring	Emotional interaction
MHSH	√	√	√	√	√	√	√	√	√
Sony AIBO [2]	○	○	○	○	○	○	√	○	○
RoboEarth [3]	○	○	○	○	○	○	○	○	√
KuKanchi [4]	○	○	○	○	○	○	○	√	○
RiSH [5]	○	○	○	○	○	○	√	○	√
Intelligent Space [6]	○	○	√	○	√	○	○	○	○

4.2 Experiments on Real Robotics

Ancillary Services of ADLs, EDLs, and IDLs. We performed some service experiments based on MHSH in a real family environment: ADLs, IDLS, and EDLs, as shown in Fig. 3 (yellow line). Based on seven homecare robots, we can easily help users to complete many kinds of daily activities, which are closer to life and basic requirements. We can conclude that the smart elderly-care home proposed in this paper can not only helps patients to complete rise, stand, walk, and other simple behaviors, but also can implement food delivery, auxiliary excretion, and other complex behaviors.

Continuous Safety Ancillary. Experiments of continuous behavior assistance on our proposed MHSH are shown in Fig. 3 (blue line). Different tasks of the types of assistive excretion and return, assistive fetching, assistive walking, and transportation indoors, and assistive rehabilitation training were initialized at different locations in the environment. Simplified implementation for assistive excretion and return and assistive transportation tasks were implemented in which the robot assigned to execute the task looked for robot loaded monitoring system using the camera, the proximity sensor, the pressure sensors, and if the abnormal data was found to generate an alarm sound.

Adaptive Cooperative Control in the Nursing Process. The adaptive adjustment of the robot in the nursing process is shown in Fig. 3 (green line). When performing a transfer task that requires cooperation between two robots, the user may switch from one state to another. At this time, it is necessary to set the transfer point, transfer posture, and transfer trajectory in advance according to the user's physical condition. In the process of real-time dynamic assistance, two robots are needed to track according to the user's real-time dynamic transfer point, transfer position, and transfer trajectory, to assist the user to provide the optimal transfer.

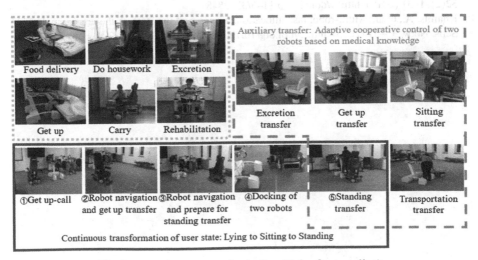

Fig. 3. Experiments on real robotics. (Color figure online)

5 Conclusion

Aiming at the limitations of the smart home in terms of functionality and service continuity, we independently developed seven heterogeneous homecare robots, and combined with sensor networks, established a smart home for elderly care that can cover most life behaviors. Because of the particularity of multi-robot serving multi-user in the scene of elderly care, we propose a self-organizing MHRS architecture to effectively solve key problems of multi-robot security adaptive cooperation in the scene of elderly care. The architecture of the smart home based on multi-heterogeneous robots and sensor networks can be applied to nursing centers, hospitals, and other places for the elderly.

References

1. Yong, K.C., et al.: Emerging smart home technologies to facilitate engaging with aging. J. Gerontol. Nurs. **45**(12), 41–48 (2020). https://doi.org/10.3928/00989134-20191105-06
2. Kertész, C., et al.: Exploratory analysis of sony Aibo users. AI Soc. **34**(3), 625–638 (2018)
3. Marco, D.D., Tenorth, M., et al.: RoboEarth action recipe execution. Intell. Syst. Comput. **193**, (2013). https://doi.org/10.1007/978-3-642-35485-4_9
4. Mohd, N.N.S., et al.: Robotic services at home: an initialization system based on robots' information and user preferences in unknown environments. Int. J. Adv. Rob. Syst. **11**(7), 112 (2014). https://doi.org/10.5772/58682
5. Do, H.M., et al.: RiSH: a robot-integrated smart home for elderly care. Robot. Auton. Syst. **101**, 74–92 (2018). https://doi.org/10.1016/j.robot.2017.12.008
6. Zhang, Y., Tian, G.: Exploring the cognitive process for service task in smart home: a robot service mechanism. Futur. Gener. Comput. Syst. **102**, 588–602 (2020). https://doi.org/10.1016/j.future.2019.09.020
7. Rizk, Y., et al.: Cooperative heterogeneous multi-robot systems: a survey. ACM Comput. Surv. **52**(2), 1–31 (2019). https://doi.org/10.1145/3303848
8. Khamis, A., et al.: Multi-robot task allocation: a review of the state-of-the-art. Coop. Robots Sens. Netw. 31–51 (2015). https://doi.org/10.1007/978-3-319-18299-5_2

A Study of Virtual Reality Systems for Attention Stabilization

Chao Fei, Baiqing Sun[⊠], Yong Li, and Qiuhao Zhang

Shenyang University of Technology, Shenyang 110870, China
sunbaiqing@sut.edu.cn

Abstract. The main idea of this paper is to design an attention quality testing system based on the combination of virtual reality technology and eye-tracking technology, through which a visual attention stability testing method is established and the feasibility of the system and method is verified. The relationship between attention and eye movements and prefrontal cerebral blood flow was investigated by simultaneous acquisition of prefrontal blood oxygen concentration in the attentional stability test experiment. After the experimental data analysis, the eye-movement signal can accurately capture the information of attention shifting occurred, and find the evidence that attention shifting excited the prefrontal brain area, and find the relationship between attention, eye-movement and prefrontal. It verified the rationality of the combined method of virtual reality technology and eye-tracking technology in the content of attentional stability test, and provided scientific data support and experimental suggestions for future attention deficit disorder to conduct attentional stability test.

Keywords: Virtual reality · Attention stabilization · Eye tracking

1 Introduction

Appropriate attention levels are critical for the correct completion of other higher cognitive processes [1, 2]. Attentional stability is the duration for which attention can be sustained on the same object or the same activity. The concept of attentional stability is the same as sustained attention [3]. Sustained attention is the ability to maintain attention on a repetitive task over time. In the process of performing a task, people have a drift of attention, which is called "mind wandering" (MW) episodes. Patients with attention deficit hyperactivity disorder (ADHD) also have a higher incidence of MW episodes [4]. Although ADHD symptoms diminish with age, more than half of ADHD patients continue to exhibit clinical features of ADHD in adulthood, and the severity increases with age, resulting in interference with the ability to perform daily tasks in adults [5]. Therefore, studies of attentional stability are important for the early diagnosis of ADHD.

Current research on attentional stability usually involves sustained attention paradigms, such as The Integrated Visual and Auditory Continuous Performance Test (IVA-CPT) [6], Test of Variables of Attention (TOVA) [7], Sustained Attention to Response Task (SART) [8], etc. These tests involve presenting a variety of short-term

H. Liu et al. (Eds.): ICIRA 2022, LNAI 13455, pp. 105–113, 2022.
https://doi.org/10.1007/978-3-031-13844-7_11

stimuli to the subject on a computer screen and instructing the subject to respond to a predefined "target" stimulus. Many indicators are often recorded in these tasks, including omission errors (failure to detect the target stimulus) and commission errors (response to non-target stimuli). In the SART, for example, only one digit at a time appears on the computer screen, and subjects are asked to press a button when the target digit "3" appears. Because the SART is simple, the subject's attention is often diverted from the judgment of the digit. The timing and frequency of MW events can be assessed by counting the number of consecutive missed targets and reaction times. Although the current method of sustained attention has good specificity and sensitivity, it is a widely accepted and used method. However, computer operation is required during the test, which will cause the subjects to be disturbed by the external environment during the test, which will have a negative impact on the data results. Although current computer-based tests of sustained attention perform well on the temporal dimension, the computer is unable to perform accurate capture when short shifts in attention occur. And the visual sustained attention task requires subjects to provide feedback to visual stimuli through physical control of mouse/keyboard buttons. No consideration was given to the importance of eye movements as a manifestation of feedback on visual tasks.

Virtual reality technology is a promising tool for neuropsychological assessment [9, 10] and testing of cognitive processes [11]. Assessments based on virtual reality technology may be a good alternative to computerized neuropsychological assessments. In 2016, Iriarte et al. developed a virtual reality classroom to administer visual and auditory attention tests to 1272 children and adolescents aged 6–16 years, obtaining to attention-related normative data [12]. The use of virtual reality technology to build the testing environment allows for the blocking of external environmental distractions, independent assessment of distractors, and the accurate collection of information about the subject's attention.

The frontal lobe of the brain is mainly responsible for movement, attention, executive function and so on. Imaging and neurophysiological experiments have also proved that the dorsolateral prefrontal cortex (DLPFC) and the posterior parietal cortex (PPC) are two brain regions activated in the process of visual spatial information processing and attention orientation [13]. Functional near infrared spectroscopy (fNIRS) is an effective optical neuroimaging method to monitor the hemodynamic response of brain activation. In 2013, Harrivel used fNIRS to monitor attention status and proved that fNIRS can be used to distinguish between task participation period and rest period [14]. In 2015, Durantin used fNIRS to collect the prefrontal cortex in SART task. The results showed that fNIRS was correlated with MW and could assist in judging the state of attention [15].

In this paper, we used a virtual reality device to build a visual attentional stabilization experiment, captured attentional information through an eye-movement sensor and used fNIRS to measure prefrontal hemodynamics synchronously during the task. The rationale for combining virtual reality and eye-tracking techniques in attentional stabilization tests was validated, and the relationship between attention, eye movements and prefrontal lobes was found.

2 Attention Stability Test Platform

2.1 Hardware Platform

The experimental platform is composed of virtual reality (VR) equipment (built-in eye tracking sensor), functional near infrared spectrometer, router and two computers, as shown in Fig. 1. The two computers establish wireless connection with VR equipment and functional near infrared spectrometer through router, and record VR equipment data and functional near infrared spectrometer data respectively.

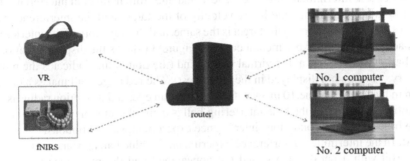

Fig. 1. Structural diagram of experimental platform

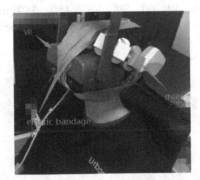

Fig. 2. Wearing mode of the equipment

The VR equipment uses Pico Neo 2 eye version, and the functional near infrared spectrometer uses WOT-100 produced by Hitachi. Among them, VR equipment is used to receive the test instructions sent by No. 1 computer, play the corresponding test scheme, and package and upload the subject's eye movement data to No. 1 computer through wireless router. The sampling rate of eye movement sensor is 50 Hz. No. 1 computer is used to input the subject information and send test instructions to VR equipment. According to the real-time feedback information of VR equipment, display the eye movement of the current subject, and save the relevant data in the database. WOT-100 has 16 channels to collect prefrontal hemodynamic data at a sampling rate of 5 Hz. No. 2 Computer receives and stores the hemodynamic data collected by WOT-100 wirelessly.

The wearing mode of the equipment is shown in Fig. 2. In order to ensure the quality of the test signal, medical elastic bandage is used for binding during the test.

2.2 Test Program

The test protocol was based on a conceptual design visual tracking test, in which a moving target was set up in virtual reality, and the subject's eyes were allowed to gaze at the moving target, while interferers were designed to interfere with the target. Four experiments were designed in this study, including: no interference test, continuous interference test, intermittent interference test, and intermittent random interference test.

In the four experiments, the linear velocity of the target and the interference were both 1.48 m/s, the trajectory of the target is the same, and the trajectory of the interference differs according to the experimental content. Figure 3a shows the display effect of the target ball during the test at the virtual reality end (the dotted line indicates the motion trajectory, which is not displayed in the actual test). The red target ball makes a circular motion in the vertical plane, 10 m away from the human eye, and its motion radius is 3 m. The motion trajectory of the blue interfering ball is a circular motion with a radius of 5 m. The blue ball in the continuous interference experiment was continuously present in its orbit. In the intermittent interference experiment, the blue ball appears intermittently on its orbit with a period of 6 s, and the appearance and disappearance time of 3 s each. Intermittent random interference is shown in Fig. 3b. The starting point of the blue jamming ball is located in the orbit of the red ball target, and the blue jamming ball and the red target ball make 30°, 60°, 90°, 120°, 150°, 180° angles with the center of the circle as the vertex, and appear randomly and do centripetal motion, and the time interval of appearance is 3 s.

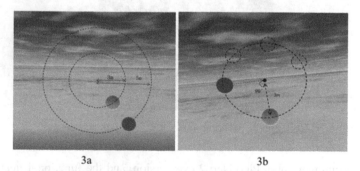

3a   3b

Fig. 3. Operational trajectory diagram

2.3 Experimental Subjects and Screening

The vision of all participants changed from normal to corrected to normal, and all participants had no eye diseases such as red green blindness. Since the virtual reality tools used in this experiment may cause some subjects to have discomfort symptoms, the virtual reality sickness questionnaire (VRSQ) [16] should be conducted on the subjects before the experiment, and the questionnaire results should be used as a measure of whether this experiment can be conducted. The process of questionnaire is to first let the subjects wear virtual reality equipment and perform a series of tasks, and then score the questionnaire after the task is completed. The questionnaire gives subjective scores on the overall discomfort, fatigue, eye fatigue, difficulty in concentrating vision, headache, head distension, blurred vision and blurred vision in the direction of eye movement and disorientation, and calculates the results.

3 Experiment and Data Analysis

3.1 Experiment

Fifteen participants, aged between 23 and 27 years (M = 24.4, SD = 2.1). All participants had normal or corrected vision and no eye disease and red-green color blindness. A video explaining the experimental procedure and precautions was given prior to the start of the test, and the fNIRS equipment was informed that it was a non-invasive and non-invasive collection device. Each participant was given an information sheet and consent form to sign prior to the experiment.

The experiments were conducted in the order of no interference experiment, continuous interference experiment, intermittent interference experiment and intermittent random interference experiment. Each experiment was tested for 180 s. A 10-min break was taken between each experiment.

3.2 Data Analysis

Data Pre-processing. There are three species of hemodynamic data collected in this experiment, namely deoxygenated-hemoglobin (Hb), oxygenated-hemoglobin (HbO2) and total-hemoglobin (HbT). The highest absroption of near infrared light at 600–900 nm in blood is HbO2, which has good scattering properties, and therefore the HbO2 signal has a higher signal-to-noise ratio than the other signals. The current study is also the most extensive in the analysis of HbO2, so this study uses the HbO2 signal for analysis. Normal human physiological activities including respiration, heartbeat cycles etc. at low frequency oscillations around 0.5 Hz and ultra-low frequency oscillations around 0.016 Hz can interfere with the data [16], so the data were filtered by band stop filters at 0.016 Hz to 0.5 Hz.

Blood Oxygen Data Analysis. Analysis of differences between the presence and absence of interferers. Multiple comparison analysis of the HBO_2 data for 16 channels showed that only 5 individuals had 1 to 4 channels that did not show significant differences ($P > 0.05$). 10 individuals showed significant differences for all channels ($P < 0.05$). 10 individuals had significant differences of 100% and 5 individuals had significant differences of 93.75% to 75% for the 16 channels.

Differences in data between different disturbances were analyzed using the same method. 8 individuals showed significant differences for all channels ($p < 0.05$). 8 individuals had 2 to 4 channels that did not show significant differences ($P > 0.05$). The statistical variability of 16 channels had 8 individuals with a significant difference of 100% and 8 individuals with a significant difference of 93.75% to 81.25%.

The results of the HbO_2 data analysis showed that different experiments differed in prefrontal activation in humans. The variability between different experiments is analyzed below using eye movement data.

Eye Movement Data Analysis. A histogram of the total time subjects disengaged from the target in different experiments is shown in Fig. 4. As the complexity of the interference increased, the total time to disengage from the target increased for 75% of the individuals. The disengagement time was further explored using ANOVA. Because there was only a single effect of interference, a one-way ANOVA was used, and assuming no significant differences between the raw data groups, the results of the analysis are shown in Table 1. From this table, it can be seen that the disengagement time increases as the complexity of the interference increases.

In order to explore the significance of the differences between the groups in depth, multiple comparisons were performed and the significance level was set to 0.05. The results of the analysis are shown in Table 2, with no significant differences between the no interference and continuous interference experiments (P > 0.05) and no significant differences between intermittent and random interference (P > 0.05).

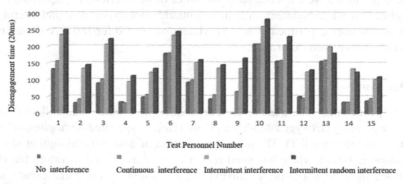

Fig. 4. Statistics of disengagement time from the target with different disturbances

Table 1. One-way ANOVA results

	Average	Standard deviation
No interference	86.13	64.319
Continuous interference	95.67	60.515
Intermittent interference	164.73	52.947
Intermittent random interference	175.73	55.947

Table 2. Results of the multiple comparison analysis

	1	2
No interference	86.133333	
Continuous interference	95.666667	
Intermittent interference		164.733333
Intermittent random interference		175.733333
Sig	0.657615	0.609179

Correlation Analysis of Oculomotor Signals and HbO₂. The relationship between attention and the prefrontal lobe of the brain was determined by analyzing changes in prefrontal HbO_2 concentration when attention shifts (gaze point off the target).

According to the current method used to analyze HbO_2 data, the change in HbO_2 data is relatively slow. In this experiment, the moment of disengagement when the eye's gaze point is not on the target sphere was used as the synchronization marker point, and the period of data from 3 s before this moment to 3 s after the eye's gaze point returns to the target object was used for analysis. As shown in Fig. 5, 6. The black line in the figure is the eye movement data, when this data is 0, it means that the attention has shifted, where the dashed lines on the left and right side represent the range of 3 s before and after the extraction of the attention shift time. the HbO_2 data will take this range for the analysis.

Only two periods of attentional shifts are marked in the figure: the first is a short period of attentional shifts: throughout the test period, attentional shifts started at 22 s and the duration of attentional shifts was 40 ms. The second is a longer period of

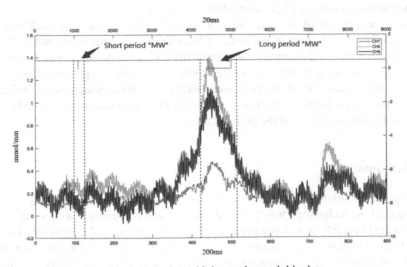

Fig. 5. Right prefrontal lobe oxyhemoglobin data

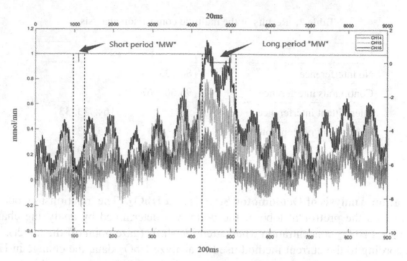

Fig. 6. Left prefrontal lobe oxyhemoglobin data

attentional shifts: the test time was at 88.66 s and the duration of attentional shifts was 11.34 s.

Short shifts in attention occurred: the results showed that the peak of HbO_2 during attention shift duration below 100 ms was not higher than the average peak of HbO_2 during attention stabilization. There was no significant difference between the data during attention stabilization and attention shift by ANOVA analysis ($p > 0.05$).

The peak value of HbO_2 during the prolonged shift of attention was higher than the average peak value of HbO_2 during the stable period of attention. And by ANOVA analysis, there was a significant difference between the data during attention stabilization and during the occurrence of attention shift ($P < 0.05$).

From the analysis of the data, we can conclude that no significant difference in HbO_2 was found in the case of the onset of brief shifts in attention, and due to the low sampling frequency of the currently used oximetry collection device, it was not possible to determine whether the brief shifts in attention were related to the prefrontal lobe. In the case of prolonged attention shifts, prefrontal HbO_2 concentrations increased significantly and activation of prefrontal brain regions occurred. This suggests an association between prolonged attention shifts and the prefrontal lobes.

4   Conclusion

In this paper, an attentional stability test method combining virtual reality technology and eye tracking technology was designed, and a visual attentional stability experiment was designed to verify the validity and feasibility of the method and experimental design. The relationship between eye-movement data and prefrontal HbO_2 concentration during attention shifting was also investigated in depth, providing a technical means and testing method for in-depth study of attention problems, and providing a valid reference for future visual attention stability testing of ADHD patients.

References

1. Posner, M.I., Petersen, S.E.: The attention system of the human brain. Annu. Rev. Neurosci. **13**(1), 25–42 (1990)
2. Fuster, J.M.: The prefrontal cortex—an update: time is of the essence. Neuron **30**(2), 319–333 (2001)
3. Cohen, R.A.: Sustained Attention. Springer, New York (2011)
4. Peterson, B.S., Potenza, M.N., Wang, Z., et al.: An FMRI study of the effects of psychostimulants on default-mode processing during Stroop task performance in youths with ADHD. Am. J. Psychiatry **166**(11), 1286–1294 (2009)
5. Ornoy, A., Spivak, A.: Cost effectiveness of optimal treatment of ADHD in Israel: a suggestion for national policy. Heal. Econ. Rev. **9**(1), 24 (2019)
6. Tinius, T.P.: The integrated visual and auditory continuous performance test as a neuropsychological measure. Arch. Clin. Neuropsychol. **18**(5), 439–454 (2003)
7. Greenberg, L.M., Waldmant, I.D.: Developmental normative data on the test of variables of attention (TOVA™). J. Child Psychol. Psychiatry **34**(6), 1019–1030 (1993)
8. Robertson, I.H., Manly, T., Andrade, J., et al.: Oops!': performance correlates of everyday attentional failures in traumatic brain injured and normal subjects. Neuropsychologia **35**(6), 747–758 (1997)
9. Parsons, T.D., Courtney, C.G., Dawson, M.E.: Virtual reality stroop task for assessment of supervisory attentional processing. J. Clin. Exp. Neuropsychol. **35**(8), 812–826 (2013)
10. Henry, M., Joyal, C.C., Nolin, P.: Development and initial assessment of a new paradigm for assessing cognitive and motor inhibition: the bimodal virtual-reality stroop. J. Neurosci. Meth. **210**(2), 125–131 (2012)
11. Chan, C.L.F., Ngai, E.K.Y., Leung, P.K.H., et al.: Effect of the adapted virtual reality cognitive training program among Chinese older adults with chronic schizophrenia: a pilot study. Int. J. Geriatr. Psychiatry J. Psychiatry Late Life Allied Sci. **25**(6), 643–649 (2010)
12. Iriarte, Y., Diaz-Orueta, U., Cueto, E., et al.: AULA—advanced virtual reality tool for the assessment of attention: normative study in Spain. J. Atten. Disord. **20**(6), 542–568 (2016)
13. Schall, J.D.: The neural selection and control of saccades by the frontal eye field. Phil. Trans. R. Soc. London. Ser. Biolog. Sci. **357**(1424), 1073–1082 (2002)
14. Harrivel, A.R., Weissman, D.H., Noll, D.C., et al.: Monitoring attentional state with fNIRS. Front. Hum. Neurosci. **7**, 861 (2013)
15. Durantin, G., Dehais, F., Delorme, A.: Characterization of mind wandering using fNIRS. Front. Syst. Neurosci. **9**, 45 (2015)
16. Kim, H.K., Park, J., Choi, Y., et al.: Virtual reality sickness questionnaire (VRSQ): motion sickness measurement index in a virtual reality environment. Appl. Ergon. **69**, 66–73 (2018)
17. Zhang, Y., Brooks, D.H., Franceschini, M.A., et al.: Eigenvector-based spatial filtering for reduction of physiological interference in diffuse optical imaging. J. Biomed. Opt. **10**(1), 011014 (2005)

Design and Verification of an Active Lower Limb Exoskeleton for Micro-low Gravity Simulation Training

Yingxue Wang[1], Jingshuo Gao[1], Zhuo Ma[1], Yuehua Li[2], Siyang Zuo[1], and Jianbin Liu[1(✉)]

[1] Key Laboratory of Mechanism Theory and Equipment Design, Ministry of Education, Tianjin University, Tianjin, China
jianbin_liu@tju.edu.cn
[2] Tianjin Key Laboratory of Microgravity and Hypogravity Environment Simulation Technology, Tianjin, China

Abstract. Exploring the most economic method to achieve micro-low gravity simulation training has been troubling researchers for a long time. Hence, this paper presents an active lower limb exoskeleton to counteract gravity of astronauts with a very low cost compared to conventional ways. It includes two link rods, fixing modules, servo motors used in hip and ankle, which is designed as common structures of lower limb exoskeletons. Note that selected servo motors can feed back driving torque and rotating angle at the same time, which makes exoskeleton more integrated and light. Different from common control methods applied in assistive exoskeleton to help wearers walk or run, zero-force control is used in the exoskeleton to counteract gravity for micro-low gravity simulation training of astronauts. Healthy volunteers are recruited to wear this exoskeleton and their surface electromyography (sEMG) signals are recorded during the process. Experimental results show that the proposed lower limb exoskeleton can averagely counteract gravity of more than 60% for each subject in static and dynamic states.

Keywords: Micro-low gravity simulation · Counteracting gravity · Exoskeleton · Zero-force control

1 Introduction

Exploding space has become the common objective of more and more countries all over the world, with rapid development of science and technology. Many astronauts have been sent into space on missions, which requires both physical and mental excellence of them [1]. Consequently, there are hundreds of training projects that need to be done in preparation, one of which is adaptation to the space environment.

Existing on Earth, the human body has adapted to the gravitational field, while outer space environment without gravitational field has many effects. For its lack of gravitational field, the outer space environment has many negative effects, which can be

H. Liu et al. (Eds.): ICIRA 2022, LNAI 13455, pp. 114–123, 2022.
https://doi.org/10.1007/978-3-031-13844-7_12

divided into short-term ones and long-term ones. Long-term effects include osteoporosis [2], muscle atrophy [3], cardiovascular disorder [4] and head displacement of body fluids [5]. In the short term, the absence of gravitational field can disrupt the nervous system and change external sense of touch. External touch is the perception of force by muscles, skin and bones. To avoid irreversibly harmful effects, adequate training is essential for astronauts, therefore, a slightly low gravity environment must be artificially created to achieve the training effect.

It is known that being able to achieve effective movement in the absence of gravity is the basis for completing various space missions. Therefore, it is very necessary to conduct sufficient training before space missions [6, 7]. For safety and economical reasons, astronauts are usually trained on the ground. Traditional training methods of micro-gravity simulation on the ground mainly include counteracting gravity by using water and cable [6], as well as achieving weightlessness by free fall in falling tower and parabolic motion in flight [7]. However, there are certain disadvantages in the cost of building, maintenance and preparing time. Therefore, the method of using exoskeletons to achieve micro-gravity simulation has been developed as the more economical way [8, 9]. Bing et al. proposed an exoskeleton robotic system based on the completely passive gravity compensation technique that a person wearing such a passive exoskeleton experiences a realistic reduced gravity feeling when people moves [8]. In addition, to provide assistance across activities of daily living, Kai et al. presented a bi-articular anti-gravity exosuit. And results show that this exosuit can assist hip and knee extension with up to 26% of the natural knee torque and up to 35% of the knee power [9].

In this paper, an active lower limb exoskeleton for micro-gravity simulation is proposed, which consists of two servo motors, link rods, and fixing modules. Zero-force control strategy [10], which is commonly used in industrial manipulator, was transplanted to the exoskeleton system to counteract gravity of human body. And then the whole motion perception of the body presents a state of weightlessness. Actively counteracting gravity performance of this exoskeleton was verified in the experiments, where several healthy volunteers were recruited to measure surface electromyography (sEMG).

2   System Design of the Exoskeleton

In reference to analysis of weightlessness training on the surface of astronauts and the structure of human lower limbs, this paper proposes a micro-gravity simulation active lower limb exoskeleton for weightlessness simulation training. In addition to meet the safety and comfort requirements for conventional human-computer interaction, the exoskeleton design should meet functional design requirements. In the process of working, the goal of active lower limb exoskeleton is to counteract gravity. Thus, it needs to detect the posture and position of human lower limb and generate torque for real time. Then the torque can be quickly passed to the human lower limb by link rods in the exoskeleton, and decreasing the perception of gravity in muscle and bone. In addition, exoskeleton's structural design is also important. Effective modeling and designing of exoskeleton is very critical to ensure the perfect function of joint movement due to the complexity of the structure. Meanwhile, the exoskeleton should be to fit closely with the human lower limbs and assure no interference between the human body and the exoskeleton, as shown in Fig. 1.

2.1 Mechanical Structure Design

The essential of designing lower limb exoskeleton lies in three joints (hip, knee, and ankle) based on the analysis of human body structure and human gait. This exoskeleton contains such well-designed joints to be suitable for human physical body. Link rods between each joint of this exoskeleton, which is corresponding to thigh, calf and foot of human body, are all mad of aluminum alloy material. In fact, ignoring the slight effect of human foot to gait, ankle in this exoskeleton was designed as a passive joint, while knee and hip joints can be driven by servo motor. Hence, the motion forms of exoskeleton depend on the flexion and extension of hip and knee joints.

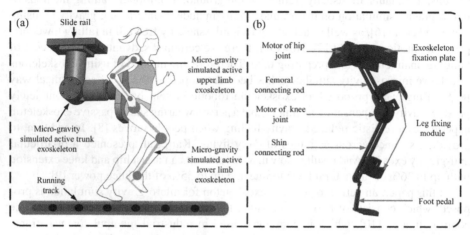

Fig. 1. (a) System design of micro-gravity simulation applied in the whole body. (b) Mechanical structure design of active lower limb exoskeleton to counteract micro-gravity.

Mechanical structure design of active exoskeleton was designed in Fig. 1(b). It consists of direct current servo motors placed in hip and knee joints, leg fixing modules, foot pedal, and link rods that can be designed differently according to the body shape of the subjects. The hip and knee joints are articulated by the motors increasing to increase the original driving power of the exoskeleton, and a ball bearing connection is adopted between foot pedal and link rod that is parallel to shank. Considering the comfort of the subjects wearing the exoskeleton, sponge pads are placed between the exoskeleton and the lower limbs of the human body. Because of high specific strength, aluminum alloy is selected as the processing material for the link rods in active lower limb exoskeleton.

2.2 Control System Design

The structure of this exoskeleton required to achieve counteracting gravity was designed as conventional ones. The exoskeleton can be attached to human lower limb in a parallel way. Most of the common exoskeletons can assist the physical body to move after the recognition of human intention while the exoskeleton proposed in this paper need to follow and counteract the movement of human lower limbs in real time. Therefore, zero-force control was adopted as the control strategy of the exoskeleton,which is a hybrid control strategy based on force and position.

The zero-force control strategy is first applied in the industrial field and is often used in flexible manipulator. In working process, the mechanical arm needs to be manipulated frequently, namely the so-called "manual teaching", which is to move it to reach appropriate position through manual operation input. Through this control strategy, mechanical arm can quickly detect the external force and make corresponding changes with the help of the interaction between human and mechanical arm, almost not affected by gravity, friction and inertia force. When the external force is withdrawn, it can reach a stable state again in the current position. For better fulfillment of zero-force control, movement and force analysis for this exoskeleton is essential. Hence, simplified two rod model is applied, as shown in Fig. 2.

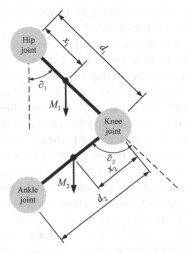

Fig. 2. Movement and force analysis in simplified two rod model.

In this model, the human thigh and the link rod connecting hip and knee in the exoskeleton are simplified as the rod one, while the human calf and the link rod connecting knee and ankle in the exoskeleton are simplified as the rod two. In this case, M_1 is the gravity of the rod one, and M_2 is the gravity of the rod two. The center of gravity of two rods both are in the medium position. ∂_1 is the rotation angle of the rod one at its initial vertical position, and ∂_2 is the rotation angle of the rod two at its initial position. x_1 is the distance from the center of mass of the rod one to the hip, and x_2 is the distance from the center of mass of the rod two to the knee. Therefore, heavy torque can be derived in following formula:

$$G = \begin{bmatrix} G_1 \\ G_2 \end{bmatrix} = \begin{bmatrix} (M_1 x_1 + M_2 x_2) \sin \partial_1 + M_2 x_2 \sin(\partial_1 + \partial_2) \\ M_2 x_2 \sin(\partial_1 + \partial_2) \end{bmatrix} \qquad (1)$$

The entire exoskeleton is actively driven by a hip motor and a knee motor. To maintain the current state, the driving torques generated by the two motors completely counteract the gravity, therefore, the driving torque can be obtained in $T = G$ formula.

3 Experimental Verification

3.1 Lifting Leg in Testing Platform

A testing platform, which can effectively simulate the really physical movement of human hip and knee, has been established in previous works [11], which can help us check out the function of the exoskeleton in preparation. Note that human lower limb model in this platform can move as expected velocity after pre-set program was input in the controller. The testing platform can collect the force and displacement of the cable in real time, so as to obtain the energy consumption. Based on this, the effect of counteracting gravity can be quantified and shown.

Before the experiment, it is necessary to complete pretreatments. The pretreatment consists of two part, one is the identification of the gravity parameters of the models in the platform, and the other is tensing the driving wire. During the determination of gravity parameters, the driving cable in models needs to be removed. Before the experiment, exoskeleton needs to be attached to models. At this time, the upper computer controls the joint motor to output a certain torque, and the joints in models rotate a certain angle. The angle and torque data could be transmitted to the upper computer through the serial port, which is recorded as pose one. The next step is to change the output torque and repeat the above steps, recording it as pose two. In the cases that the two pose angles and joint torques are known, the gravity parameters can be derived.

In this experiment, the speed of lower limb models' movement is set as high speed, medium speed and low speed, and the corresponding PWM wave frequency of stepping motor is set as 6400 Hz, 3200 Hz and 1600 Hz, considering that the rang of rotation angle of human lower limb joints (hip forward flexion is about 30°, knee backward flexion is about 50°). Movement process as medium speed and experimental results of three different speeds are shown in Fig. 3.

As can be seen in the Fig. 3, in the case of monitoring thigh or calf without wearing the exoskeleton, the angle changes with the increasing of the displacement of the driving cable, and the tensile force gradually increases. However, in comparison of wearing the exoskeleton, the amplitude of the tension force decreased significantly in all of three conditions with different speed. Counteracting efficiency of the exoskeleton can be shown in the Table 1.

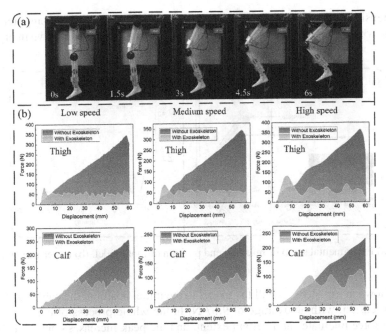

Fig. 3. (a) The process of lifting leg at the medium speed. (b) Force-displacement curves of three different speeds with and without exoskeleton.

Table 1. Efficiency of counteracting gravity of models in testing platform.

Testing platform	Low speed	Medium speed	High speed
Thigh model	71.37%	70.08%	67.34%
Calf model	41.15%	39.22%	34.13%

3.2 Resetting End Position of the Model

The experiments of lifting leg verified that exoskeleton could output the torque to counteract gravity. However, whether it can respond quickly to the falling leg needs further experimental verification. The experiment of resetting end position is designed for the such purpose. In fact, in the process of falling leg, gravity does positive work and the exoskeleton doesn't need to provide torque.

To explore how much tensional force is needed to reset end position of lower limb model equipped with the exoskeleton in testing platform, experimental setup is built in Fig. 4(a). First, driving cable was removed in testing platform. Second, one end of a cable was fixed in the foot model and the other end was fixed into the digital display tension meter mounted on the moving bench. The retightening force of the cable was adjusted to about 5 N, and then the bench moves at a uniform speed (3 mm/s). When the leg model was downward vertically, it returned to initial position. During the experiment, the digital display tension meter transmitted the tensional force of the cable to the computer in real time. The whole experiment is repeated for three times, and results are shown in Fig. 4(b).

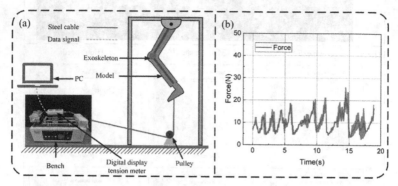

Fig. 4. (a) Experimental setup of resetting end position of foot model. (b) Experimental results.

As shown in Fig. 4(b), to pull the model to the initial position, the cable has to exert a certain tension, with an average of 9.67 N. In the whole process of experiment, the tensional force fluctuates at a certain extent, and the peak increases continuously, and the highest peak is about 20 N. Therefore, it can be concluded that the exoskeleton can make leg model resetting.

3.3   Counteracting Gravity

After the exoskeleton functions were verified, wearing test is conducted. First, three healthy male adults are recruited and their information is shown in Table 2. Second, they are informed about the whole process of experiments. Two counteracting gravity tests in static and dynamic states are done. The two groups of tests utilized the same movement, which is raising thigh to the level and calf close to thigh. In the dynamic test, the whole process is completely at uniform speed. In the static test, the action is maintained for ten seconds. Then, counteracting gravity of the left legs each subjects are recorded. Finally, once subjects reported feeling uncomfortable, the test must be terminated.

Table 2. Information of subjects.

Number	Age	Height (cm)	Weight (kg)
A	23	180	75
B	27	173	68
C	26	169	63

The sEMG signals are measured to estimate counteracting gravity performance. As shown in Fig. 5(a, b), there were five measured muscles, which named rectus femoral muscle, vastus medial muscle, vastus lateral muscle, internal gastrocnemius muscle, external gastrocnemius muscle. Before fitting the electrodes, the fitting part are wiped with alcohol wipes. Then the sEMG sensor is connected with the signal acquisition card. RMS (Root Mean Square) of sEMG signals with and without gravity counteracted are illustrated in Fig. 5(c, d). The sEMG signals were subjected to low-pass filtering (0–300 Hz) and RMS processing (with an average range of 0.1s). The sampling frequency is 1000 Hz.

Experimental results are shown in Table 3. The proposed lower limb exoskeleton can averagely counteract gravity of more than 60% for each subject in the static and dynamic states. And for the subject B, more than 85% gravity can be counteracted by this exoskeleton. This exoskeleton shows a very excellent performance in counteracting gravity and becomes an economical way of micro-low gravity simulation training.

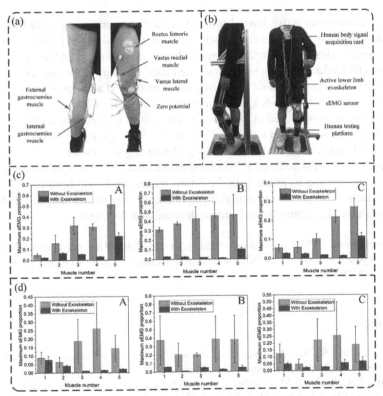

Fig. 5. (a) Electrode installation position. (b) Experimental setup. (c) Results of counteracting gravity in the static state. (d) Results of counteracting gravity in the dynamic state.

Table 3. Real counteracting gravity performance.

State	Sub.	Lateral femoral muscle	Medial femoral muscle	External gastrocnemius muscle	Internal gastrocnemius muscle	Rectus femoral muscle	Avg.
Static	A	50.60%	58.06%	82.92%	89.90%	57.48%	68%
	B	91.24%	93.41%	95.82%	97.08%	77.71%	91%
	C	50.59%	58.06%	82.93%	93.89%	57.48%	69%
Dynamic	A	14.30%	35.00%	94.43%	94.64%	85.60%	65%
	B	85.14%	95.33%	76.54%	93.41%	87.70%	88%
	C	59.31%	53.59%	87.81%	78.03%	64.09%	69%

4 Conclusion

This paper presents an active lower limb exoskeleton to counteract gravity for using in outer space. Based on common design way, structure of exoskeleton is established. This exoskeleton includes two link rods, fixing modules, servo motors used in hip and ankle. It is known that selected servo motors can feed back driving torque and rotating angle at the same time, which makes exoskeleton more integrated and lightweight. Different from common control methods applied in assistive exoskeleton to help wearers walk or run, zero-force control is used in lower limb exoskeleton with counteracting gravity for micro-low gravity simulation training of astronauts. Through experiments wearing the exoskeleton, in which limbs of subjects keep certain angle or move as certain speed, it can be proved that the developed exoskeleton reduces the cost of weightlessness training without compromising its efficacy. In the future, a deep study will be done to eliminate the side-effects of long-time utilization. In addition, the way of attaching exoskeleton to human limbs will be promoted to decrease donning and doffing time.

Acknowledgements. This work was supported by National Natural Science Foundation of China under Grant No. 51905374 & 62133010 and Natural Science Foundation of Tianjin under Grant No. 17JCQNJCO4800.

References

1. Chao, J., Chen, S., Xue, L.: Study on technology of space flight training simulator and its engineering implementation. Space Med. Med. Eng. **21**, 233–239 (2008)
2. Spector, E.R., Smith, S.M., Sibonga, J.D.: Skeletal effects of long-duration head-down bed rest. Aviat. Space Environ. Med. **80**(5), A23–A28 (2009). https://doi.org/10.3357/ASEM.BR02.2009
3. Fitts, R.H., Riley, D.R., Widrick, J.J.: Physiology of a microgravity environment invited review: microgravity and skeletal muscle. J. Appl. Physiol. **89**(2), 823–839 (2000). https://doi.org/10.1152/jappl.2000.89.2.823
4. Tuday, E.C., Berkowitz, D.E.: Microgravity and cardiac atrophy: no sex discrimination. J. Appl. Physiol. **103**(1), 1–2 (2007). https://doi.org/10.1152/japplphysiol.00010.2007

5. Diedrich, A., Paranjape, S.Y., Robertson, D.: Plasma and blood volume in space. Am. J. Med. Sci. **334**(1), 80–86 (2007). https://doi.org/10.1097/MAJ.0b013e318065b89b
6. Omer, A.M.M., Lim, H.O., Takanishi, A.: Simulation study of a bipedal robot jumping motion approach on moon gravity. In 2010 IEEE International Conference on Robotics and Biomimetics, pp. 218–222. IEEE, December 2010
7. Chen, C.I., Chen, Y.T., Wu, S.C., Liu, D.S., Ni, C.Y.: Experiment and simulation in design of the board-level drop testing tower apparatus. Exp. Tech. **36**(2), 60–69 (2012). https://doi.org/10.1111/j.1747-1567.2011.00755.x
8. Qiao, B., Chen, Z.: A passive exoskeleton robotic simulator for reduced-gravity locomotion training of astronaut. J. Astronautics **35**(4), 474–480 (2014)
9. Schmidt, K., et al.: The myosuit: Bi-articular anti-gravity exosuit that reduces hip extensor activity in sitting transfers. Front. Neurorobot. **11**, 57 (2017). https://doi.org/10.3389/fnbot.2017.00057
10. Dong, K., Liu, H., Zhu, X., Wang, X., Xu, F., Liang, B.: Force-free control for the flexible-joint robot in human-robot interaction. Comput. Electr. Eng. **73**, 9–22 (2019). https://doi.org/10.1016/j.compeleceng.2018.10.014
11. Gao, J., Zhang, Y., Liu, J.: A novel human lower limb simulation test system for gravity-counteracting exoskeletons. In: 2021 4th International Conference on Intelligent Robotics and Control Engineering (IRCE), pp. 16–19. IEEE, September 2021

Trajectory Tracking Control of Omnidirectional Robot Based on Center of Gravity Offset Parameter Estimation

Yina Wang[1]([✉]), Sainan Liu[1], Junyou Yang[1], and Shuoyu Wang[2]

[1] Shenyang University of Technology, Shenyang, Liaoning, China
wang.yina@sut.edu.cn
[2] Kochi University of Technology, Kochi, Japan

Abstract. Omnidirectional mobile robot is applied in people's daily life. In order to properly assist users, the robot must accurately track the predetermined trajectory. However, the robot's tracking accuracy is severely compromised center of gravity shifts induced by the user. An acceleration proportional differential control strategy based on parameter estimation has been proposed in this paper when the center of gravity of the robot is different from its geometric center. The present paper first investigates the dynamic of mechanical structure and constructs a new dynamic model by considering the interference of the center of gravity shift. Secondly, a parameter estimation strategy is designed to estimate the dynamic center of gravity in real time. Then, an acceleration proportional differential controller with center of gravity offset compensation is designed to control the robot. Next, based on Lyapunov stability theory, stability analysis is carried out to prove the asymptotic stability of the proposed control algorithm. Finally, simulation validation shows that the control accuracy of the proposed method is more accurate than proportional differential and adaptive control because they can estimate the center of gravity offset parameters in real time.

Keywords: Center of gravity shifts · Parameter estimation · Trajectory tracking

1 Introduction

In recent years, omnidirectional mobile robots (OMRs) are increasingly presented in the fields of industry, agriculture, national defense and service due to their advantages of moving in all directions in the same posture [1–3]. In robotics, an effective motion control strategy is required in order to implement various operational tasks efficiently. Therefore, it has become the research hotspot in the field of robotics.

Since OMR is a typical coupled system, most of the current research on its tracking control scheme. Wang C et al. design of target tracking motion controller with input and output state constraints based on model predictive control (MPC) guarantees the point stability of OMR and the effectiveness of trajectory tracking [4]. A dual closed-loop tracking strategy based on dynamics was designed in [5] for an OMR using a time-varying gain extended state observer and an integral sliding mode control method.

© The Author(s), under exclusive license to Springer Nature Switzerland AG 2022
H. Liu et al. (Eds.): ICIRA 2022, LNAI 13455, pp. 124–133, 2022.
https://doi.org/10.1007/978-3-031-13844-7_13

Chao R et al. introduce a trajectory tracking control design with friction compensation [6]. Jeong et al. propose robust tracking control of OMR with motion and dynamic uncertainty based on sliding mode disturbance observer [7]. In [8], an adaptive sliding mode controller was applied to an OMR. A MPC scheme with friction compensation is proposed [9]. [10] presented an adaptive robust controller.

Although the controllers proposed in reference [4–10] have achieved good trajectory tracking effect, the problem of center of gravity offset is not considered. When the mobile robot is in use, its center of gravity will be changed because the user's posture changes. This causes a certain deviation between the actual running trajectory and the reference trajectory and seriously affect the actual work performance of robot. To address this problem, in [11], the shift of the center of gravity was regarded as uncertainty, and a strong-feedback accelerated controller was designed to restrain the impact of the shift of the center of gravity. Based on the recalculation and the experimental evaluation of multirotor hybrids, Emil et al. [12] present a general method for estimating the center distance of multiple rotors and adjusting for position drift. In [13, 14], the center of gravity shift was transformed into a random disturbance, and a new self-adapting law was proposed to adjust the unknown parameters of the tracking controller. However, they only considered the impact of the center of gravity shift on the inertia array, and did not consider the impact of the center of gravity shift on the transformation array. In [15], an adaptive zero offset angle recognition algorithm has been developed to compensate for deviations caused by changes in the center of gravity of the robot. In [16], the center of gravity offset is treated as an uncertain parameter, and a robust controller is designed to solve it. In [17], the least square method is used to estimate the center of gravity offset parameters. In [18–21], a nonlinear geometric adaptive controller is proposed for quadrotors when its location of center of gravity is different from geometric center, but none of their subjects is OMR.

Based on the above analysis, in this paper, the trajectory tracking control design with the center of gravity shift compensation is proposed for a four wheeled OMR. A dynamic model is derived from the center of gravity offset considered. The control efforts consist of two parts. One part is used to compensate the center of gravity offset effects, in which parameters of center of gravity offset are estimated based on the Contrast model. The other part of the control efforts is for the trajectory tracking control, which is derived based on acceleration PD control. Stability analysis is also studied. Finally, simulations are conducted to verify the effectiveness of the proposed control design in the center of gravity offset.

The remainder of this paper is organized as follows. In Sect. 2, a dynamic model with center of gravity offset for the four-wheeled OMR is derived. The control design as well as stability analysis is presented in Sect. 3. In Sect. 4, simulation details, simulation results and discussions of the proposed control design are presented, and conclusion is presented in Sect. 5.

2 System and Modeling of OWTR

Figure 1 shows the configuration for the geometric model of the OMR. The four omni-directional wheels are equally spaced at the corners of the robot. They are driven by direct-current (DC) motors. and θ is the angle between the axes x and the first omni-directional wheel, V is the moving direction and G is the mass center, C represents a geometrical Centre of the OWTR, r represents a distance between C and G, l_i represent a distance between the center of gravity and the i omnidirectional wheel, l is the distance from the center of the robot to the four omnidirectional wheels.

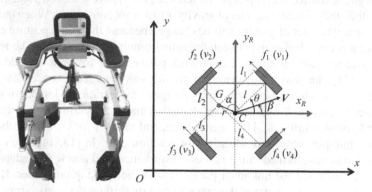

Fig. 1. Structural model of the robot

According to the coordinate system relationship in Fig. 1, we can get the dynamic equation of the center of gravity of the robot is as follows:

$$K_G F = \begin{bmatrix} -\sin\theta & \cos\theta & l - r\cos\alpha \\ \cos\theta & \sin\theta & -l + r\sin\alpha \\ -\sin\theta & \cos\theta & -l - r\cos\alpha \\ \cos\theta & \sin\theta & l + r\sin\alpha \end{bmatrix}^T \begin{bmatrix} f_1 \\ f_2 \\ f_3 \\ f_4 \end{bmatrix} = \begin{bmatrix} M+m & 0 & 0 \\ 0 & M+m & 0 \\ 0 & 0 & I+mr^2 \end{bmatrix} \begin{bmatrix} \ddot{x}_G \\ \ddot{y}_G \\ \ddot{\theta} \end{bmatrix} = M_G \ddot{X}_G \tag{1}$$

M is the mass of the robot, m is the mass of the human, I is the inertia of the robot, $\ddot{x}_G$ and $\ddot{y}_G$ are the accelerations of the position of the robot's center of gravity in x and y directions, and $\ddot{\theta}$ is the angular acceleration of the robot's rotation.

The relationship between acceleration at the center of gravity and acceleration at the center of the robot can be obtained:

$$\ddot{X}_G = \begin{bmatrix} \ddot{x}_G \\ \ddot{y}_G \\ \ddot{\theta} \end{bmatrix} = \begin{bmatrix} 1 & 0 & -r\sin(\alpha+\theta) \\ 0 & 1 & r\cos(\alpha+\theta) \\ 0 & 0 & 1 \end{bmatrix} \begin{bmatrix} \ddot{x}_C \\ \ddot{y}_C \\ \ddot{\theta} \end{bmatrix} + \begin{bmatrix} 1 & 0 & -r\cos(\alpha+\theta) \\ 0 & 1 & -r\sin(\alpha+\theta) \\ 0 & 0 & 1 \end{bmatrix} \begin{bmatrix} \dot{x}_C \\ \dot{y}_C \\ \dot{\theta} \end{bmatrix} = T\ddot{X}_C + \dot{T}\dot{X}_C \tag{2}$$

$\dot{x}_G, \dot{y}_G$ are the speed at which the center of gravity of the robot in x direction and y direction. $\dot{\theta}$ is the angular velocity of the robot's rotation. Based on Eqs. (1) and (2), the dynamic model of the central position of the robot can be obtained as follows:

$$K_G F = M_G T \ddot{X}_C + M_G \dot{T} \dot{X}_C \tag{3}$$

3   Controller Design

The purpose of the present study was designing an acceleration PD with center of gravity offset estimation and compensation controller that could track the predefined paths to ensure that the robot can transport people from an arbitrary initial position to the destination position when the robot is in an environment with uncertainty of center of gravity shift caused by user's sitting position. The control block diagram is shown in Fig. 2.

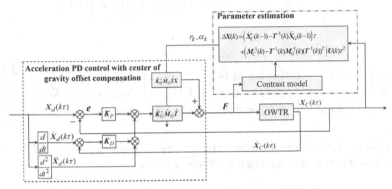

Fig. 2. Block diagram of the proposed control design

3.1   Acceleration PD Controller with Center of Gravity Offset Compensation

Let the desired motion trajectory be X_d, and the actual motion trajectory be X_C. Therefore, we define the tracking error as follows:

$$e = X_d - X_C \tag{4}$$

The purpose of the present section is to design an acceleration PD controller such that the tracking error e and its time derivative $\dot{e}$ tend toward zero as much as possible.

For the dynamic in Eq. (4), an acceleration PD controller with the compensation term is proposed.

$$F = K_G^+(\theta)M_GT(\theta)\left(K_Pe + K_D\dot{e} + \ddot{X}_d\right) + K_G^+(\theta)M_G\dot{T}(\theta)\dot{X}_C \tag{5}$$

$K_P = diag\left(k_{Px}, k_{Py}, k_{P\theta}\right)$ is the position deviation factor, $K_D = diag\left(k_{Dx}, k_{Dy}, k_{D\theta}\right)$ is the velocity deviation factor.

According to Eq. (5), $K_G^+, M_G, T, \dot{T}$ are related to the r, α. r and α are unknown. A parameter estimation method is used to estimate the r, α.

3.2   Estimation of Parameters

A new parameter estimation method is introduced to estimate the real-time center of gravity offset at the current time. The estimated value of the real-time center of gravity offset of the robot can be obtained from the driving force and real-time position input of the four wheels of the robot.

The following equation is established by comparing the relationship between the position difference between the model and the actual robot and the center of gravity offset at the current time:

$$\Delta X(k) = \left(\dot{X}'_C(k-1) - T^{-1}(k)\dot{X}_G(k-1)\right)\tau$$
$$+ \left(M_C^{-1}(k) - T^{-1}(k)M_G^{-1}(k)(T^{-1}(k))^T\right)U(k)\tau^2 \qquad (6)$$

where,

$$\Delta X(k) = \begin{bmatrix} \Delta x(k) \\ \Delta y(k) \\ \Delta \theta(k) \end{bmatrix} = \begin{bmatrix} x'_C(k) - x_C(k) \\ y'_C(k) - y_C(k) \\ \theta'(k) - \theta(k) \end{bmatrix}, U(k) = \begin{bmatrix} \Delta u_{Cx}(k) \\ \Delta u_{Cy}(k) \\ \Delta u_{C\theta}(k) \end{bmatrix} = K_C(k) \begin{bmatrix} f_1(k) \\ f_2(k) \\ f_3(k) \\ f_4(k) \end{bmatrix}.$$

The relationship between the robot reference model position $X'_C(k)$ and the driving force $F(k)$ on the four omnidirectional wheels at time k:

$$X'_C(k) = X'_C(k-1) + \dot{X}'_C(k-1)\tau + \left(M_C^{-1}K'_C(k)F(k)\right)\tau^2 \qquad (7)$$

where,

$$M_C = \begin{bmatrix} M & 0 & 0 \\ 0 & M & 0 \\ 0 & 0 & I \end{bmatrix}, K'_C(k) = \begin{bmatrix} -\sin\theta'_{k-1} & \cos\theta'_{k-1} & -\sin\theta'_{k-1} & \cos\theta'_{k-1} \\ \cos\theta'_{k-1} & \sin\theta'_{k-1} & \cos\theta'_{k-1} & \sin\theta'_{k-1} \\ l & -l & -l & l \end{bmatrix}.$$

θ'_{k-1} is the attitude angle of the $t = (k-1)\tau$ time comparison robot model, the sampling time is τ.

The relationship between the OWTR's position $X'_C(k)$ and the driving force $F(k)$ on the four omnidirectional wheels at time k:

$$X_C(k) = X_C(k-1) + \left(T^{-1}(k)\dot{X}_G(k-1)\right)\tau + \left(T^{-1}(k)M_G^{-1}(k)K_G(k)F(k)\right)\tau^2 \quad (8)$$

where,

$$K_G(k) = \begin{bmatrix} -\sin\theta_{k-1} & \cos\theta_{k-1} & -\sin\theta_{k-1} & \cos\theta_{k-1} \\ \cos\theta_{k-1} & \sin\theta_{k-1} & \cos\theta_{k-1} & \sin\theta_{k-1} \\ l - r_k\cos\alpha_k & -l + r_k\sin\alpha_k & -l - r_k\cos\alpha_k & l + r_k\sin\alpha_k \end{bmatrix},$$

$$M_G(k) = \begin{bmatrix} M+m & 0 & 0 \\ 0 & M+m & 0 \\ 0 & 0 & I+mr_k^2 \end{bmatrix}, T(k) = \begin{bmatrix} 1 & 0 & -r_k\sin(\alpha_k+\theta_{k-1}) \\ 0 & 1 & r_k\cos(\alpha_k+\theta_{k-1}) \\ 0 & 0 & 1 \end{bmatrix}.$$

Parameters r and α are estimated by Newton iterative method using Eqs. (6). The estimation process are as follows:

Step 1: Select the initial values of r and α, calculate the Jacobian matrix and obtain the initial value of the Jacobian matrix $F_0'(r_k, \alpha_k)$, $F_0'(r_k, \alpha_k)^{-1}$.

Step 2: Use the following formula for Jacobian iteration:

$$r_{k+1} = r_k - F'(r_k)^{-1}F'(r_k), \; \alpha_{k+1} = \alpha_k - F'(\alpha_k)^{-1}F'(\alpha_k)$$

Step 3: when the absolute value of the difference between the two iterations is less than 10^{-7}, end the iteration.

3.3 Convergence Analysis of Tracking Errors

First, we let the state vector of the robot tracking system be as follows.

$$\chi = \begin{bmatrix} \chi_1^T & \chi_2^T \end{bmatrix}^T = \begin{bmatrix} e^T & \dot{e}^T \end{bmatrix}^T \tag{9}$$

Then, we can get the following state equation.

$$\begin{aligned} \dot{\chi}_1 &= \chi_2 \\ \dot{\chi}_2 &= -K_P\chi_1 - K_D\chi_2 + \delta(t), \; \delta(t) = \hat{K}_1^+\tilde{K}_1\ddot{X}_C + \hat{K}_1^+\tilde{K}_2\dot{X}_C \end{aligned} \tag{10}$$

That is,

$$\begin{bmatrix} \dot{\chi}_1 \\ \dot{\chi}_2 \end{bmatrix} = \begin{bmatrix} 0 & I \\ -K_P & -K_D \end{bmatrix} \begin{bmatrix} \dot{\chi}_1 \\ \dot{\chi}_2 \end{bmatrix} + \begin{bmatrix} 0 \\ \delta(t) \end{bmatrix} \tag{11}$$

Let, $A = \begin{bmatrix} 0 & I \\ -K_P & -K_D \end{bmatrix}$, $\Delta_x = \begin{bmatrix} 0 \\ \delta(t) \end{bmatrix}$.

Equation (11) can be rewritten as

$$\chi = A\chi + \Delta_x \tag{12}$$

Theorem 1. *If we consider an acceleration PD controller (5) with estimating and compensating parameters of the center of gravity offset, for an omnidirectional mobile robot (3) affected by the center of gravity offset, the attitude and speed tracking errors converge to zero when t tends to infinity.*

Proof. For any given positive definite symmetric matrix Q, there exists a positive definite symmetric matrix P that satisfies the Lyapunov equation $PA + A^TP = -Q$. For simplicity, in our analysis, set.

$$P = \begin{bmatrix} K_PP_{22} + K_D & I \\ I & P_{22} \end{bmatrix}, Q = -2 \begin{bmatrix} K_P & 0 \\ 0 & K_DP_{22} - I \end{bmatrix}, P_{22} = \begin{bmatrix} p_{44} & p_{45} & p_{46} \\ p_{54} & p_{55} & p_{56} \\ p_{64} & p_{65} & p_{66} \end{bmatrix}$$

$$p_{22}^2 = (p_{44} + p_{45} + p_{46})^2 + (p_{54} + p_{55} + p_{56})^2 + (p_{64} + p_{65} + p_{66})^2$$

In order to analyze the stability of the controller, a reasonable Lyapunov function is given as

$$V = \frac{1}{2}\chi^T P \chi \tag{13}$$

Taking the first order derivative of (13) with respect to t, we have

$$
\begin{aligned}
\dot{V} &= \chi^T \left(PA + A^T P \right) Q\chi + 2\chi^T P \Delta_x \\
&= -\chi^T Q\chi + 2\chi^T P \Delta_x \\
&\le -\chi^T Q\chi + 2\sqrt{3 + p_{22}^2}\, \delta_{max} \|\chi\| \\
&\le -(1 - \gamma)\lambda_{min}(Q)\|\chi\|^2 - \left(\gamma\lambda_{min}(Q)\|\chi\| - 2\sqrt{1 + p_{22}^2}\, \delta_{max} \right)\|\chi\| \\
&\le -(1 - \gamma)\lambda_{min}(Q)\|\chi\|^2, \forall \|\chi\| \ge \frac{2\sqrt{1 + p_{22}^2}\, \delta_{max}}{\gamma\lambda_{min}(Q)}
\end{aligned}
\tag{14}
$$

where $\gamma \in (0, 1)$ and $\lambda_{min}(Q) = 2\min(k_{pi}, k_{di}p_{22} - 1)$, $i = x, y, \theta$.

4 Simulations and Discussion

Computer simulations were presented to show the tracking performance and effectiveness of the designed controller under the influence of center of gravity offset.

Parameters of the robot are given as follows: $M = 80$ kg, $m = 50$ kg, $I = 0.7$.
Asteroid trajectory is selected for the mobile robot:

$$x_d = 4\sin^3(\frac{\pi t}{5}),\ y_d = 4\cos^3(\frac{\pi t}{5}),\ \theta_d = 0.7t.$$

Under the same initial conditions and the influence of center of gravity offset, acceleration PD control [11], adaptive control (AC) [14] and controller with parameter estimation and center of gravity offset compensation (PD with C) are used for simulation. The starting pose of the indoor carrier robot was assumed as $X_C = \begin{bmatrix} -1 & 3 & 0 \end{bmatrix}^T$. Parameters of center of gravity offset are set as follows: $r = 0.3 - 0.3\cos(t)$, $\alpha = 0.2t$.

The controller gains are chosen as follows:
$k_{px} = 10.5$, $k_{py} = 10$, $k_{p\theta} = 20$, $k_{dx} = 2$, $k_{dy} = 2$, $k_{d\theta} = 5$, $w = diag(38\ 28.05\ 16)$, $R = diag(140\ 140\ 140)$, $K = diag(170\ 170\ 8)$.

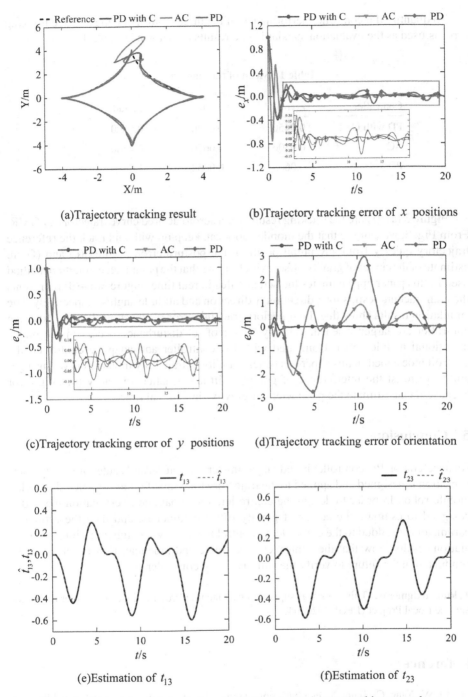

(a)Trajectory tracking result

(b)Trajectory tracking error of x positions

(c)Trajectory tracking error of y positions

(d)Trajectory tracking error of orientation

(e)Estimation of t_{13}

(f)Estimation of t_{23}

Fig. 3. Comparison of simulation results for robot trajectory tracking control

To quantify the controller performance of the three controllers, the average tracking error is used as the evaluation standard. The results are shown in Table 1.

Table 1. Mean of tracking errors

Controller	e_x(m)	e_y(m)	e_θ(rad)
PD with C	0.0450	0.0440	0.0200
AC	0.0506	0.0620	0.4100
PD	0.0665	0.0652	1.0580

Figure 3 (a)–(f) are the tracking results for asteroid desired curve trajectory of OMR. From Fig. 3, we can see that the mobile robot can keep up with and track the reference trajectory quickly from any initial position, the posture error. Figure 3(e) and (f) are estimate of the center of gravity offset, which shows that the parameter estimation method used in this paper approximates the actual value in real time. Figure 3(a)–(d) represents the path tracking results for x direction, y direction and attitude angles, respectively. The simulation results show that the trajectory tracking error of PD controller and adaptive controller are larger when the gravity center offset disturbance occurs in the omni-directional mobile robot. Compared with PD controller and adaptive controller, the controller designed in this paper has better stability of trajectory tracking curve, stronger ability to resist the interference of gravity shift and smaller trajectory tracking error because it can estimate the parameters of gravity shift in real time.

5 Conclusion

An acceleration PD controller based on parameter estimation and center of gravity compensation is designed and applied to the trajectory tracking of omni-directional wheeled mobile robot. In order to design the controller, a new parameter estimation method is designed to estimate the center of gravity offset parameters, and then the estimated parameters are added to the controller to control the robot with high precision. The simulation results show that the controller is effective and practical. Experiments will be conducted in the future to verify the validity of the controller.

Acknowledgments. This work was supported by Liaoning Provincial Department of Education Service Local Project (LFGD2020004).

References

1. Li, W., Yang, C., Jiang, Y., et al.: Motion planning for omnidirectional wheeled mobile robot by potential field method. J. Adv. Transp. (2017)
2. Jiang, S.Y., Lin, C.Y., Huang, K.T., et al.: Shared control design of a walking-assistant robot. IEEE Trans. Control Syst. Technol. **25**(6), 2143–2150 (2017)

3. Thi, K.D.H., Nguyen, M.C., Vo, H.T., et al.: Trajectory tracking control for four-wheeled omnidirectional mobile robot using Backstepping technique aggregated with sliding mode control. In: 2019 First International Symposium on Instrumentation. Control, Artificial Intelligence, and Robotics (ICA-SYMP), pp. 131–134. IEEE, Thailand (2019)
4. Wang, C., Liu, X., Yang, X., et al.: Trajectory tracking of an omni-directional wheeled mobile robot using a model predictive control strategy. Appl. Sci. **8**(2), 231 (2018)
5. Yang, H., Wang, S., Zuo, Z., et al.: Trajectory tracking for a wheeled mobile robot with an omnidirectional wheel on uneven ground. IET Control Theory Appl. **14**(7), 921–929 (2020)
6. Ren, C. and Ma, S.: Trajectory tracking control of an omnidirectional mobile robot with friction compensation. In: 2016 IEEE/RSJ International Conference on Intelligent Robots and Systems (IROS), pp. 5361–5366. IEEE, Korea (2016)
7. Jeong, S., Chwa, D.: Sliding-mode-disturbance-observer-based robust tracking control for omnidirectional mobile robots with kinematic and dynamic uncertainties. IEEE/ASME Trans. Mechatron. **26**(2), 741–752 (2020)
8. Morales, S., Magallanes, J., Delgado, C., et al.: LQR trajectory tracking control of an omnidirectional wheeled mobile robot. In: 2018 IEEE 2nd Colombian Conference on Robotics and Automation (CCRA), pp.1–5. IEEE, Colombia (2018)
9. Conceição, A.G.S., Dórea, C.E., Martinez, L., et al.: Design and implementation of model-predictive control with friction compensation on an omnidirectional mobile robot. IEEE/ASME Trans. Mechatron. **19**(2), 467–476 (2013)
10. Dong, F., Jin, D., Zhao, X., et al.: Adaptive robust constraint following control for omnidirectional mobile robot: an indirect approach. IEEE Access **9**, 8877–8887 (2021)
11. Wang, Y., Xiong, W., Yang, J., et al.: A robust feedback path tracking control algorithm for an indoor carrier robot considering energy optimization. Energies **12**(10), 2010 (2019)
12. Fresk, E., Wuthier, D., Nikolakopoulos, G.: Generalized center of gravity compensation for multirotors with application to aerial manipulation. In: 2017 IEEE/RSJ International Conference on Intelligent Robots and Systems (IROS), pp. 4424–4429. IEEE, Canada (2017)
13. Chang, H., Wang, S., Sun, P.: Stochastic adaptive tracking for a rehabilitative training walker with control constraints considering the omniwheel touchdown characteristic. Int. J. Control **93**(5), 1159–1171 (2020)
14. Tan, R., Wang, S., Jiang, Y., et al.: Adaptive control method for path-tracking control of an omni-directional walker compensating for center-of-gravity shifts and load changes. Int. J. Innov. Comput. **7**(7B), 4423–4434 (2011)
15. Su, Y., Wang, T., Zhang, K., et al.: Adaptive nonlinear control algorithm for a self-balancing robot. IEEE Access **8**, 3751–3760 (2019)
16. Inoue, R.S., Terra, M.H., Leão, W.M., et al.: Robust recursive linear quadratic regulator for wheeled mobile robots based on optical motion capture cameras. Asian J. Control **21**(4), 1605–1618 (2019)
17. Wang, Y., Wang, S., Ishida, K., et al.: High path tracking control of an intelligent walking-support robot under time-varying friction and unknown parameters. Adv. Robot. **31**(14), 739–752 (2017)
18. Sharma, M., Kar, I.: Adaptive geometric control of quadrotors with dynamic offset between center of gravity and geometric center. Asian J. Control **23**(4), 1923–1935 (2021)
19. Shen, Z., Ma, Y., Song, Y.: Robust adaptive fault-tolerant control of mobile robots with varying center of mass. IEEE Trans. Industr. Electron. **65**(3), 2419–2428 (2017)
20. Kumar, R., Deshpande, A.M., Wells, J.Z., et al.: Flight control of sliding arm quadcopter with dynamic structural parameters. In: 2020 IEEE/RSJ International Conference on Intelligent Robots and Systems (IROS), pp. 1358–1363. IEEE, USA (2020)
21. Falanga, D., Kleber, K., Mintchev, S., et al.: The foldable drone: a morphing quadrotor that can squeeze and fly. IEEE Robot. Autom. Lett. **4**(2), 209–216 (2018)

Force Coordination Control of Dual-Arm Robot Based on Modified Sliding Mode Impedance Control

Yina Wang[1]([✉]), Xiangling Huang[1], Zhongliang Liu[1], Junyou Yang[1], Kairu Li[1], and Shuoyu Wang[2]

[1] Shenyang University of Technology, Shenyang, Liaoning, China
wang.yina@sut.edu.cn
[2] Kochi University of Technology, Kochi, Japan

Abstract. In order to realize the precise control of the contact force and position between the two manipulators and the object when the dual-arm robot cooperatively carry the target object, a modified sliding mode control method with force coordination performance based on impedance control is proposed in this paper. Firstly, the motion constraint relationship and dynamic model of the dual-arm robot are obtained according to the relative position relationship of the dual-arm robot when carrying objects. Next, the force of the controlled object is analyzed and decomposed by Newton's second law, and the terminal contact force of dual arms is obtained. Then, we integrate the hyperbolic tangent sliding mode control algorithm into the position-based impedance control method to realize the dual control of force and position, and the stability and convergence analysis of the proposed cooperative control system is given. Finally, we verified through simulation that this control scheme can realize the precise control of the position and contact force the manipulator.

Keywords: Dual-arm robot · Modified sliding mode · Coordination impedance control

1 Introduction

The manipulator has been widely used in industry with the development of social science and technology [1, 2]. However, due to the complexity of production tasks and the limitations of single manipulator, many tasks cannot be completed, dual-arm robot have gradually entered people's production and life [3]. Compared with single-arm robot, dual-arm robot has the advantages of greater load capacity and higher dexterity [4], and can complete more complicated work [5]. Since the kinematics and dynamics model of dual-arm robot becomes more complicated than that of single-arm robot, its control problem is more difficult. Therefore, the effective control of dual-arm robot is the main research focus of researchers at home and abroad.

The multi-DOF dual-arm robot is a highly coupled nonlinear system, and its dynamic modeling is more complicated than that of the traditional single-arm robot [6]. There are many uncertain factors such as parameter uncertainty, joint friction and so on in our model. Therefore, many control methods are designed or robot systems with uncertain factors [7]. Among them, the sliding mode control method is widely used in robot systems with parameter uncertainties and external disturbances because of its high adaptability and robustness [8, 9]. However, due to the existence of discontinuity, the system will produce chattering phenomenon, so how to diminish its chattering while maintaining its original advantages is a problem worth studying. Lin et al. [10] proposed to replace the discontinuous symbolic function in the control signal with a saturation function to reduce the influence of chattering. Recently, the chattering phenomenon can be diminished by the controller which combines advanced control methods such as neural network and fuzzy control [11, 12]. In the references [13], a dynamic surface control method of uncertain dual-arm robot based on adaptive neural network is proposed, which realizes the precise control of the position of the object at the end of the dual-arm robot in the uncertain system.

In the process of cooperation between dual-arm robot, the force contact is inevitable, and the fine position deviation of the robot end effector may lead to a huge contact force on the surface of the operated object, which may damage the object [14]. Therefore, the control goal is not only to realize the precise control of the end trajectory, but also to consider the tracking effect of the end contact force of the manipulator. To realize the dual control of position and force, Raibert and Craig proposed a hybrid control method of position and force [15]. This method task space is divided into position control subspace and force control subspace. However, the mixed position and force control method ignores the dynamic coupling between the manipulator and the environment, it is impossible to accurately control the commanded position or force. To solve this problem, Hogan [16] proposed an impedance control method. Impedance control establishes a dynamic relationship between position and force and is widely used in flexible control of manipulator, because of its stable and excellent control performance [17]. Jiao et al. [18] put forward a new adaptive hybrid impedance control method based on master-slave structure, which can adapt the stiffness of the object to adjust the internal force. However, because the master-slave structure is a completely closed chain structure, it is unrealistic in practical application. Lin et al. [19] proposed a double-loop method which combines the robust model arrival control with the dynamic trajectory adaptive method to realize the unified control of manipulator's motion/force/impedance in unknown environment. Li et al. [20] proposed a dual-arm cooperative impedance control method based on time delay estimation and adaptive fuzzy sliding mode, this scheme can track the expected trajectory of the target object and meet the requirements of the expected contact force between the end of both arms and the target object.

According to the understanding of the research status of cooperative control of dual-arm robots at home and abroad, we propose a modified sliding mode control based on impedance control for the position/force coordination control of the two-arm robot to transport objects. The proposed approach can realize the dual control of force and position when dual-arm robots carry objects cooperatively. The rest of the paper is arranged as follows. In Sect. 2, we introduce a model of the dual-arm robot system. In Sect. 3, we present the design of a modified sliding mode impedance controller based on the dual-arm coordinated operation system. In Sect. 4, we present the results of simulation experiments, and conclusion is presented in Sect. 5.

2   The Model of Dual-Arm Robot

2.1   Motion Constraint Relationship of the Dual-Arm Robot

As shown in Fig. 1, the dual-arm robot system consists of two manipulators R_1 and R_2. It is assumed that both manipulators are rigidly attached to the load, so that there is no slippage between the grasping point and the object to be grasped.

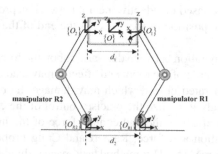

Fig. 1. The dual-arm robot

When two-arm robots cooperate to operate the object, the robot and the object form a closed chain system. $\{O_{R1}\}$ and $\{O_{R2}\}$ are the base coordinate systems of manipulators R_1 and R_2, respectively. The pose transformation matrix from $\{O_{R2}\}$ to $\{O_{R1}\}$ is:

$$^{R1}T_{R2} = Trans(-d_2, 0, 0) \tag{1}$$

$\{O_1\}$ and $\{O_2\}$ are respectively the coordinate systems of robot end-effector, The pose transformation matrix from $\{O_2\}$ to $\{O_1\}$ is:

$$^1T_2 = Rot(z, \pi) \times Trans(d_1, 0, 0) \tag{2}$$

The constraints between the robot end-effectors can be obtained from Eqs. (1) and (2) shown as:

$$^{R1}T_2 = {}^{R1}T_1 {}^1T_2 \tag{3}$$

where, $^{R1}T_2$ is the pose of the end effector of the robot R_2 in the coordinate system $\{O_{R1}\}$. $^{R1}T_1$ is the pose of the end effector of the robot R_1 in the coordinate system $\{O_{R1}\}$.

Equations (3) is the motion constraints between robots, at the same time, they are related to the kinematics. If the configuration of the robot or the position of the end effector is known, the forward kinematics and the reverse kinematics of the robot can be solved through the motion constraints, and it is unnecessary to model and solve the kinematics of the robot.

2.2 Force Analysis of the Object

The force analysis of the target object manipulated by the dual-arm is shown in Fig. 2. where, m denotes the quality of the manipulated target object. F_1 and F_2 are the robot manipulators apply forces to the object. F_{s1} and F_{s2} are friction forces to rigidly hold the load up. F_{s1y}, F_{s2y}, F_{s1z} and F_{s2z} denote the components of the friction forces in y and z directions, respectively. μ is the coefficient of friction.

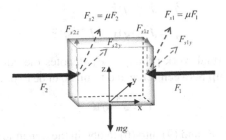

Fig. 2. Diagram of the force analysis of the object

The dynamic model of the object is obtained by Newton's second law as follows:

$$\begin{cases} m\ddot{x}_m = F_2 - F_1, \\ m\ddot{y}_m = F_{s1y} + F_{s2y} \\ m\ddot{z}_m = F_{s1z} + F_{s2z} - mg \end{cases} \tag{4}$$

where, x_m, y_m and z_m denote the trajectory of the center of mass of the object in xyz direction, respectively, $g = 9.8$ m/s. To keep the balance of objects, the following conditions should be met:

$$\begin{aligned} F_{s1y}^2 + F_{s1z}^2 < (\mu F_1)^2 \\ F_{s2y}^2 + F_{s2z}^2 < (\mu F_2)^2 \end{aligned} \tag{5}$$

2.3 Dynamic Model of Dual-Arm Robot

By the use of Lagrange multipliers, the joint space combinative dynamics model of the dual-arm robot can be written in compact form as:

$$M(q)\ddot{q} + C(q, \dot{q})\dot{q} + G(q) = \tau + w - J^T(q)F \tag{6}$$

where, $M(q) = diag[M_1(q_1), M_2(q_2)] \in R^{6\times6}$, $C(q) = diag[C_1(q_1), C_2(q_2)] \in R^{6\times6}$ and $G(q) = [G_1^T(q_1), G_2^T(q_2)]^T \in R^{6\times1}$ represent the mass matrix, the Coriolis force and centrifugal force matrix and the gravity matrix of the dual-arm robot, respectively. $\tau(q) = [\tau_1^T, \tau_2^T]^T \in R^{6\times1}$ is the control torque input matrix in joint space of the dual-arm robot. $F = [F_1, F_{s1y}, F_{s1z}, F_2, F_{s2y}, F_{s2z}]^T$ is an external environmental force. $J(q) = diag[J_1(q_1), J_2(q_2)] \in R^{6\times6}$ is Jacobian matrix of dual-arm robot. w is the disturbance torque. $q = [q_1^T, q_2^T]^T \in R^{6\times1}$ denotes the joint angle of the dual-arm robot.

The forward kinematics of the manipulator can be expressed as:

$$\dot{x} = J(q)\dot{q} \tag{7}$$

where, $x = [x_1^T, x_2^T]^T$ denotes the position of the end of the manipulator in Cartesian coordinate system.

The inverse kinematics of the manipulator can be expressed as:

$$\dot{q} = J^{-1}(q)\dot{x}$$
$$\ddot{q} = \dot{J}^{-1}(q)\dot{x} + J^{-1}(q)\ddot{x} \tag{8}$$

According to the virtual work principle, F_x denotes the control force at the end-effectors. The relationship between force and torque can be expressed as:

$$\tau = J^T(q)F_x \tag{9}$$

Substituting Eq. (7), (8) and (9) into (6) to obtain the dynamic equation in Cartesian coordinate system:

$$M_x(q)\ddot{x} + C_x(q,\dot{q})\dot{x} + G_x(q) = F_x + W - F \tag{10}$$

where,

$$M_x(q) = J^{-T}(q)M(q)J^{-1}(q); \; C_x(q,\dot{q}) = J^{-T}(q)(C(q,\dot{q}) - M(q)J^{-1}(q)\dot{J}(q))J^{-1}(q);$$
$$G_x(q) = J^{-T}(q)G(q); \; F_x = J^{-T}(q)\tau; \; W = J^{-T}(q)w.$$

Next, the controller design will be completed in Cartesian coordinate system.

3 Modified Sliding Mode Coordination Impedance Control for Dual-Arm Robot

3.1 Cooperative Impedance Control

We assumed that the rigid connection established the constraint relationship between the two manipulator and the object. However, in practical application, the rigid connection would cause a great contact force between the manipulator and the object, which will damage the object. In other word, the contact between the manipulator ends and the object should be flexible. Therefore, in this section, we propose an impedance control to realize the flexible control of manipulator operating objects.

The purpose of impedance control is to modify the original dynamics of an object to the desired dynamics. The expected dynamics of impedance is generally linear, the second-order system is:

$$M_m(\ddot{X}_d - \ddot{X}_c) + B_m(\dot{X}_d - \dot{X}_c) + K_m(X_d - X_c) = F_c - F_d \tag{11}$$

where, F_c indicates the actual contact force between the robot end and the object; F_d indicate the expected contact force between the robot end and the object; M_m, B_m and

K_m indicate mass, damping and stiffness matrix respectively; X_d, $\dot{X}_d$ and $\ddot{X}_d$ indicate the actual position, speed and acceleration of the end of the manipulator respectively; X_c, $\dot{X}_c$ and $\ddot{X}_c$ indicate the initial expected position, speed and acceleration of the end of the manipulator respectively.

The impedance control can modify the original reference trajectory according to the force error to meet the contact force requirement at the end of the manipulator. The expression form of the actual acceleration vector of the target object can be obtained:

$$\ddot{X}_d = \ddot{X}_c + M_m^{-1}[F_c - F_d + B_m(\dot{X}_c - \dot{X}_d) + K_m(X_c - X_d)] \tag{12}$$

The corrected X_d, $\dot{X}_d$ and $\ddot{X}_d$ are obtained and used as the expected input of the inner loop position controller, as shown in Fig. 3.

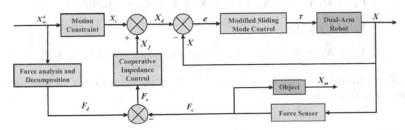

Fig. 3. Control flow chart of dual-arm robot

3.2 Modified Sliding Mode Control Based on Impedance Control

In order to improve the adaptability and robustness of the control system, and effectively eliminate the chattering caused by the traditional sliding mode control, we use the continuous hyperbolic tangent function instead of the switching function to greatly reduce the chattering degree of the control signal switching.

The hyperbolic tangent function is defined as:

$$\tanh(\frac{x}{\varepsilon}) = \frac{e^{\frac{x}{\varepsilon}} - e^{-\frac{x}{\varepsilon}}}{e^{\frac{x}{\varepsilon}} + e^{-\frac{x}{\varepsilon}}} \tag{13}$$

where, $\varepsilon > 0$, the value of ε determines the steepness of hyperbolic tangent function. In addition, the hyperbolic tangent function satisfies:

$$x \tanh(\frac{x}{\varepsilon}) \geq 0$$

$$|x| - x \tanh(\frac{x}{\varepsilon}) \leq \rho\varepsilon \tag{14}$$

where, ρ is a constant, $\rho = 0.2785$.

The design steps of the modified sliding mode control based on hyperbolic tangent function are follows:

Firstly, the expected trajectory X_d, $\dot{X}_d$ and $\ddot{X}_d$ corrected by the impedance controller is taken as the expectation of the modified sliding mode controller, and the tracking error function of the position of the end of the manipulator is defined as:

$$e = X_d - X \tag{15}$$

Then, the sliding surface S is designed as:

$$S = \dot{e} + \Lambda e, \Lambda = diag(\lambda_1, \lambda_2 \cdots \lambda_6), \lambda_i > 0 \tag{16}$$

According to the dynamics model established by Eq. (10), the sliding mode impedance controller based on the hyperbolic tangent function can be obtained:

$$\begin{cases} F_x = M_x \ddot{X}_r + C_x \dot{X}_r + G_x - W + F + KS + \eta \tanh(\frac{S}{\varepsilon}) \\ \dot{X}_r = \dot{X}_d + \Lambda e \\ \ddot{X}_d = \ddot{X}_c + M_m^{-1}[F_d - F_c - B_m(\dot{X}_d - \dot{X}_c) - K_m(X_d - X_c)] \end{cases} \tag{17}$$

where, $K = diag\{k_1, \cdots k_6\}, k_i > 0, i = 1, \cdots 6$ is the gain matrix of sliding mode controller, $\varepsilon > 0, \eta > 0$.

3.3 Stability and Convergence Analysis

Substituting the control rate (17) into the dynamic model (10) can be obtained:

$$M_x(q)\dot{S} + C_x(q, \dot{q})S + KS + \eta \tanh(\frac{S}{\varepsilon}) = 0 \tag{18}$$

Since $M_x(q)$ is positive definite matrix, we define Lyapunov function:

$$V = \frac{1}{2}S^T M_x S \tag{19}$$

Take derivative on both sides:

$$\begin{aligned} \dot{V} &= \frac{1}{2}S^T \dot{M}_x S + S^T M_x \dot{S} = \frac{1}{2}S^T (\dot{M}_x - 2C_x)S + S^T C_x S + S^T M_x \dot{S} \\ &= S^T C_x S + S^T M_x \dot{S} = S^T (C_x S + M_x \dot{S}) = -S^T (KS + \eta \tanh(\frac{S}{\varepsilon})) \end{aligned} \tag{20}$$

According to the control rate (17) and the hyperbolic tangent function characteristic (14), thus the inequality term satisfies $\dot{V} = -S^T (KS + \eta \tanh(\frac{S}{\varepsilon})) < 0$ and we get:

$$\begin{aligned} \dot{V} &= -S^T (KS + \eta \tanh(\frac{S}{\varepsilon})) \leq -S^T KS - \eta\|S\| + \eta\rho\varepsilon \leq -S^T KS + \eta\rho\varepsilon \\ &\leq -\lambda_{\min}(K)S^T S + \eta\rho\varepsilon \leq -\frac{2\lambda_{\min}(K)}{\lambda_{\max}(M_x)}\frac{1}{2}\lambda_{\max}(M_x)S^T S + \eta\rho\varepsilon \leq -2\lambda V + \beta \end{aligned} \tag{21}$$

where, $\lambda_{\max}(M_x)$ and $\lambda_{\min}(K)$ are the maximum eigenvalue of M_x and the minimum eigenvalue of K, respectively. $\lambda = \frac{2\lambda_{\min}(K)}{\lambda_{\max}(M_x)}, \beta = \eta\rho\varepsilon$.

Theorem 1. *Let f, $V : [0, \infty) \in R$, if $\dot{V} \leq -\alpha V + f$, $\forall t \geq t_0 \geq 0$, $\alpha \in R$, then its solution can be obtained:*

$$V(t) \leq e^{-\alpha(t-t_0)}V(t_0) + \int_{t_0}^{t} e^{-\alpha(t-\zeta)}f(\zeta)d\zeta \tag{22}$$

Therefore, in accordance with Eq. (21) and Theorem 1 (22), we can obtain:

$$V(t) \leq e^{-2\lambda(t-t_0)}V(t_0) + \beta e^{-2\lambda t}\int_{t_0}^{t} e^{2\lambda\zeta}d\zeta = e^{-2\lambda(t-t_0)}V(t_0) + \frac{\beta}{2\lambda}(1 - e^{-2\lambda(t-t_0)}) \tag{23}$$

Finally, we can get:

$$\lim_{t \to \infty} V(t) \leq \frac{\beta}{2\lambda} = \frac{\eta\rho\varepsilon}{2\lambda} \tag{24}$$

According to the Eq. (24), we can know that the tracking error and the error derivative converge gradually. The convergence accuracy depends on η, ε and λ.

4 Simulation

4.1 Simulation Environment

In order to verify the cooperative improvement synovial control algorithm of two manipulators based on impedance control proposed in this paper, this paper takes Matlab/Simulink as the simulation experiment platform, and uses Robotics Toolbox build two three-freedom manipulator models of the same model, and carries out the simulation experiment verification.

Suppose there is a target object in space, its length $l = 1$ m, its mass is 1 kg, and it is in the world coordinate system (0.2, 1, 0). Install two flat three-degree-of-freedom manipulator bases at (0.5, 0, 0) and (–0.5, 0, 0), as shown in Fig. 4. Assuming that two robotic arms are in the initial state, the distance between their ends is 1m, just touching the two ends of the target object.

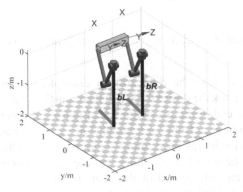

Fig. 4. Matlab modeling dual-arm robot

4.2 Simulation Results

Take the manipulator R_1 as an example for analysis. The simulation results of controller torque of each joint of the dual-arm robot based on the sliding mode control method are shown in Fig. 5. It can be seen from the figure that compared with the symbolic function sliding mode control method, the hyperbolic tangent function sliding mode control used in this paper can obviously smooth the joint torque and eliminate the chattering phenomenon.

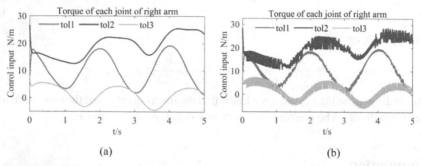

Fig. 5. The Controller torque of dual-arm robot. (a) the controller torque results for the control method of tanh(x); (b) the controller torque results for the control method of sign(x)

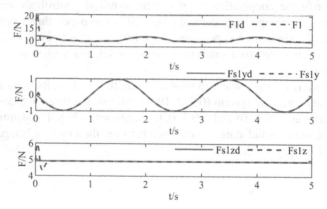

Fig. 6. The result of the tracking of contact force at the end of dual-arm robot

As shown in Fig. 6, Take the right arm for example, the force tracking control algorithm can quickly track the desire force and then remains in a relatively stable force tracking state until the end of the operation task. Figure 7 shows the position error of operated object, it can be seen from the figure that the controller used in this paper can obviously make the error in this paper more stabilize and smooth. Figure 8 shows the comparison between the expected trajectory and the actual trajectory of the operated object, and the trajectory of the end of the dual-arm robot to complete coordinated transport task of the target object. Therefore, it can be concluded that the end-effectors

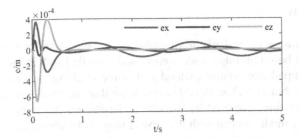

(a) The position error for the control method of tanh(x)

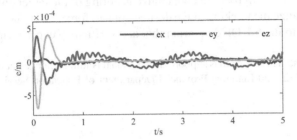

(b) The position error for the control method of sign(x)

Fig. 7. The position error of operated object

of the dual-arm robot can complete coordinated transport task of the target object using the control scheme in this paper, and at the same time can realize the tracking of the desired contact force.

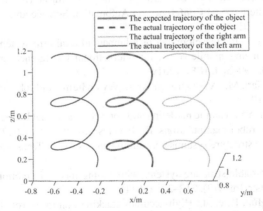

Fig. 8. The result of the expected trajectory and the actual trajectory of the object

5 Conclusion

In this paper, aiming at the task of carrying objects with dual-arm robots in cooperation, a control method based on impedance control and modified sliding mode controller is proposed. The impedance control method with force tracking performance is applied to the dual-arm robot to realize flexible control, so that the dual-arm robot can stably output the control force required by the object. Replacing the switching function of traditional sliding mode control with hyperbolic tangent function can reduce the chattering phenomenon of the system output and keep the tracking accuracy of the object. The simulation results show that the control scheme can realize the desired trajectory movement of the dual-arm robot in cooperative handling of the target object, and at the same time can realize the tracking of the desired contact force. Next, the control method will be extended to the 6-DOF dual-arm robot and verified by experiments.

Acknowledgments. This research is supported by National Natural Science Foundation of China (Grant No. 62003222) and Liaoning Provincial Department of Education Service Local Project (LFGD2020004).

References

1. Harun-Or-Rashid, M.: Design and development of a robotic arm for sorting colored object. In: 2021 International Conference on Automation, Control and Mechatronics for Industry 4.0 (ACMI), pp. 1–5. IEEE (2021)
2. Oke, A.O., Afolabi, A.: Development of a robotic arm for dangerous object disposal. In: International Conference on Computer Science and Information Technology, pp. 153–160. IEEE (2014)
3. Do, H.M., Park, C., Kyung, J.H.: Dual arm robot for packaging and assembling of IT products. In: 2012 IEEE International Conference on Automation Science and Engineering (CASE), pp. 1067–1070. IEEE (2012)
4. Shut, R., and Hollis, R.: Development of a humanoid dual arm system for a single spherical wheeled balancing mobile robot. In: International Conference on Humanoid Robots (Humanoids), pp. 499–504. IEEE (2019)
5. Saeedvand, S., Jafari, M.: A comprehensive survey on humanoid robot development. Knowl. Eng. Rev. **34** (2019)
6. Lv, N., Liu, J., Jia, Y.: Dynamic modeling and control of deformable linear objects for single-arm and dual-arm robot manipulations. IEEE Trans. Robot. 1–13 (2022)
7. Utkin, V.: Variable structure systems with sliding modes. IEEE Trans. Autom. Control **22**(2), 212–222 (2003)
8. Sabanovic, A.: Variable structure systems with sliding modes in motion control—a survey. IEEE Trans. Industr. Inf. **7**(2), 212–223 (2011)
9. Jin, M., Jin, Y., Hun, P., et al.: High-accuracy tracking control of robot manipulators using time delay estimation and terminal sliding mode. Int. J. Adv. Robot. Syst. **8**(4), 65–78 (2011)
10. Lin, C., Guo, H., Meng, S., Ding, X.: Sensorless control of PMSM based on modified sliding mode observer. In: 2016 IEEE Vehicle Power and Propulsion Conference (VPPC), pp. 1–5. IEEE (2016)
11. Xu, J., Wang, Q, Lin. Q.: Parallel robot with fuzzy neural network sliding mode control. Adv. Mech. Eng. **10**(10) (2018)

12. Su, X., Wen, Y., Shi, P.: Event-triggered fuzzy control for nonlinear systems via sliding mode approach. IEEE Trans. Fuzzy Syst. **29**(2), 336–344 (2019)

13. Pham, D.T., et al.: Adaptive neural network based dynamic surface control for uncertain dual arm robots. Int. J. Dyn. Control **8**(3), 824–834 (2020). https://doi.org/10.1007/s40435-019-00600-2

14. Uchiyama, M., Dauchez, P.: Symmetric kinematic formulation and non-master/slave coordinated control of two-arm robots. Adv. Robot. **7**(4), 361–383 (1992)

15. Raibert, M.H., Craig, J.J.: Hybrid position/force control of manipulators. (1981)

16. Hogan N.: impedance control - an approach to manipulation. I- theory. II - implementa-tion. III - applications. J. Dyn. Syst. Measure. Control **107**, 1–24 (1985)

17. Ott, C., Mukherjee, R., Nakamura, Y.: Unified impedance and admittance control. In: 2010 IEEE international conference on robotics and automation, pp. 554–561. IEEE (2021)

18. Jiao, C., Wei, X., Zhao, H., Xiaojie, S.U.: Adaptive hybrid impedance control for a dual-arm robot manipulating an unknown object. In: IECON 2020 The 46th Annual Conference of the IEEE Industrial Electronics Society, pp. 2754–2759. IEEE (2020)

19. Lin, Y., Chen, Z., Yao, B.: Unified motion/force/impedance control for manipulators in unknown contact environments based on robust model-reaching approach. IEEE/ASME Trans. Mechatron. **26**(4), 1905–1913 (2021)

20. Li, D.J., Xu, D.G., Gui, W.H.: Cooperative impedance control of two manipulators based on time delay estimation and adaptive fuzzy sliding mode controller. Control Decis. **36**(6), 13 (2021)

Finger Disability Recognition Based on Holistically-Nested Edge Detection

Dianchun Bai, Xuesong Zheng[✉], Tie Liu, Kairu Li, and Junyou Yang

Shenyang University of Technology, Shenyang, China
1124184833@qq.com

Abstract. In order to relieve the medical pressure, when patients with finger disability see a doctor, the degree of finger disability can be identified and judged by the equipment first, and then the doctor carries out the next step of diagnosis and treatment. Aiming at the problem that the traditional recognition algorithm is not ideal, this paper proposes a finger disability recognition algorithm based on Holistically-nested edge detection algorithm. On the basis of extracting the edge of hand image with Holistically-nested edge detection algorithm, the similarity judgment is made between the experimental object's hand edge detection image and the standard hand edge detection image. The degree of finger joint integrity was analyzed by different similarity judgment, and then the degree of finger disability was judged. In order to verify the effectiveness of the method, 50 people's hand images were collected to establish a sample database of hand images, and a total of 600 simulated severed finger images were tested. The accuracy of finger disability recognition was 96.6%. This algorithm can effectively identify the degree of finger disability and improve the medical efficiency.

Keywords: Finger recognition · Edge detection · Similarity algorithm · Image recognition

1 Introduction

As the population increases year by year, the number of people with physical disabilities is also increasing, among which the proportion of disabled fingers is the largest. At present, the total amount of health resources in China is insufficient, high-quality medical resources are concentrated, and there is a shortage of manpower [1, 2]. Therefore, efficient intelligent medical care has become a hotspot, and ARTIFICIAL intelligence is widely used in disease screening, diagnosis and treatment. Mainly through image classification, target detection, image segmentation and so on to help doctors get image information faster. In order to make rational use of medical power and relieve medical pressure, the hand recognition test can be carried out first to judge the degree of finger disability when the patient sees a doctor, and then the doctor makes the next diagnosis.

With the development of computer technology, research on hand recognition has attracted more and more attention from researchers. Some representative studies are as follows:

H. Liu et al. (Eds.): ICIRA 2022, LNAI 13455, pp. 146–154, 2022.
https://doi.org/10.1007/978-3-031-13844-7_15

Robert P.Miler published the first patent on hand recognition in 1960 and developed the first set of palm feature acquisition system with the function of recognizing palm features in 1971. Most existing hand recognition systems were improved and perfected on his basis [3]. In 1999, Jain and Ross proposed a hand shape recognition algorithm based on skin color processing and light compensation, adding Euclidean feature distance into the recognition algorithm, and improving the hand shape recognition rate through light processing [4]. In 2005, Xiong Wei et al. designed a hand recognition method in free state (without fixed stake). In the process of hand image collection, hands do not need to be fixed or bound, but only need to open five fingers and put the palm close to the background plate to obtain a better hand image [5]. In 2008, Miguel Adan first used contour matching algorithm for hand shape recognition. The modified algorithm adopts the hand contour full matching calculation method, and its recognition rate reaches 99.5% in the case of complicated hand feature data processing [6].

Nowadays, the domestic hand shape recognition technology has also been greatly improved. In 2005, Gu Li proposed a hand shape recognition algorithm combining template matching and multi-feature fusion [7]. In 2006, Qiang Li designed a hand feature recognition algorithm, which integrates palmprint and hand shape features for recognition [8]. In 2009, Weiqi Yuan designed using finger width as the recognition characteristic value. With accurate positioning and no less than three finger width values, the effective recognition rate can reach more than 90%, and when six finger width values are selected, the recognition rate can reach 94.03% [9]. In 2014, Lantao Jing designed the hand-shape recognition technology of facial phase to process the hand-shape image under difficult acquisition conditions, and completed the non-ideal hand-shape recognition technology [10].

In this paper, a kind of edge detection based on HED fingers disability degree of recognition algorithm, can effectively extract the edge of the palm of your hand, to avoid the influence of noise interference, aHash algorithm is used to calculate the subjects the processed image is edge detection and standard hand edge detection, the processed image similarity by similarity judgment fingers the existence of each joint, Then the degree of finger disability of experimental subjects was identified.

2 Data Collection

In the hardware part of this paper, Hikvision MV-SC7016M-06S-WBN series industrial camera is used, and the frame rate is 60 FPS and the resolution is 1440×1080. First, the palm was placed flat on the experimental table, and the five fingers were naturally tensited. A complete palm model was selected through the camera, as shown in Fig. 1. The finger joints marked in the figure include the metacarpophalangeal joint (MCP), proximal interphalangeal joint (PIP) and distal interphalangeal joint (DIP).

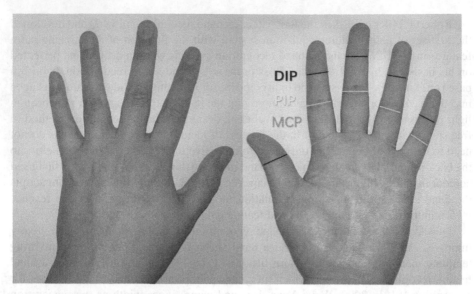

Fig. 1. Complete palm model and finger joint schematic diagram

In this paper, finger amputation simulation was carried out for partial occlusion of fingers, and a camera was used to take photos of the hands to create a hand database. The collected hand figure is shown in Fig. 2.

This hand image has the characteristics of uniform illumination and single background. The distance between the lens and the palm is fixed when the hand image is collected. In the process of collection, the five fingers of the palm of the collected person are required to open naturally first, and part of the fingers are covered to simulate the broken finger. There were 4 images of proximal interphalanx joint (PIP) and distal interphalanx joint (DIP),4 images of proximal interphalanx joint (PIP) but not distal interphalanx joint (DIP), 4 images of proximal interphalanx joint (PIP) and distal interphalanx joint (DIP), and a total of 600 simulated finger amputation images. Different hand image, finger opening degree is slightly different. Because the thumb joint is slightly different from the other four fingers, the thumb will not be analyzed in this experiment.

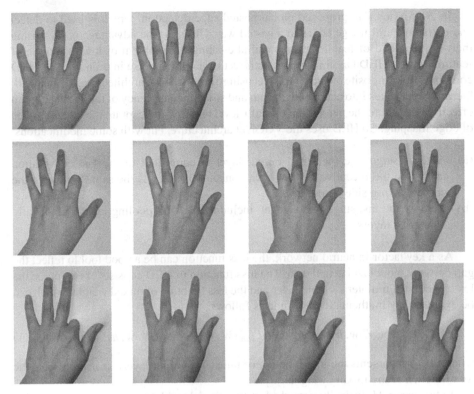

Fig. 2. Part of hand acquisition images

3 Finger Disability Evaluation Algorithm

In this paper, in order to finger disability identification, this paper proposes a finger disability degree evaluation algorithm, first of all subjects on edge detection, and then use aHash algorithm to calculate similarity finger, hand edge detection after the image through the experiment with the model hand edge detection after the similarity to determine the degree of disability, finger similarity is higher, the lower the degree of disability.

3.1 Edge Detection

The edges of the image is of great importance to the human visual system, it is important basis of human discriminant object, is the most basic of the image, the most important characteristic, is the computer vision, pattern recognition and so on important basis in the field of study, through the image edge detection can filter out the useless information, greatly reduces the data image analysis and processing.

Early edge detection algorithms mostly determine boundaries according to changes in image edge gradient, such as Sobel operator and Canny operator [11, 12]. Although these methods can also extract the edge of the image, it is difficult to ensure the high robustness of finger recognition when there are other interference factors such as background and illumination in the actual scene.

In 2015, Xie et al. proposed global nested edge detection, which is used to detect and extract natural image edges in a nested way. HED has the advantage of increasing the receptive field of feature images and alleviating the problem of low resolution of feature images. HED has amazing robustness to annotation noise in training [13]. HED combines the composite blocks of ResNet using a new network architecture, a framework hierarchy that takes into account the depth and stride inconsistency of the architecture to effectively generate the perception of multi-level features and capture the inherent scale of edge mapping. So HED uses the VGGNet architecture, but with some modifications:

(a) At each stage, the measured output layer is connected to the last convolution layer, and the receptive field of each convolution layer is the same as that of the corresponding side output layer;

(b) Remove the last stage of VGGNet, including the fifth pooling layer and all fully connected layers.

As a key factor in neural network, the loss function can be a good tool to reflect the gap between model and actual data. The loss function in HED consists of two parts: the loss function of unilateral output layer and the loss function of mixed weight, which can be expressed by mathematical formula as follows:

$$(W, w, h)^* = \arg\min\left(L_{side}(W, w) + L_{fuse}(W, w, h)\right) \tag{1}$$

where, L_{side} represents the loss function of unilateral output layer; L_{fuse} represents the loss function of the mixing weights.

In this paper, Holistically-nested edge detection algorithm is used to detect the edge of the palm. By comparing with the results of Canny edge detection algorithm, it can be seen that Holistically-nested edge detection algorithm has a much better detection effect on the palm than Canny. Useless edge information is filtered out. Figure 3 shows the comparison of Canny edge detection and Holistically-nested edge detection on the model hand in this experiment.

 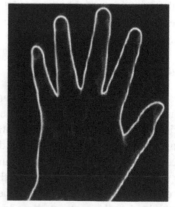

Fig. 3. Canny edge detection (left) and Holistically-nested edge detection (right)

HED is performed on part of hand images, and the images obtained are shown in Fig. 4

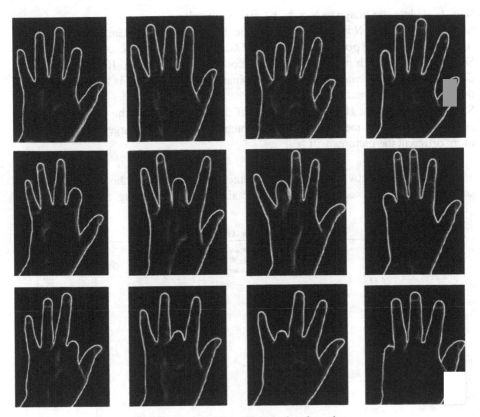

Fig. 4. Partial effect of hand edge detection

3.2   Finger Similarity

Based on edge detection was carried out on the experimental object, use finger aHash algorithm to calculate similarity, the algorithm design is simple, mainly USES the low frequency component of images, by narrowing the image to remove high frequency components, keep low frequency information, and image gray scale method is used to remove the color of the image to further remove high frequency components. On this basis, the pixel mean value of gray-scale image is calculated. Iterate over each pixel of the grayscale image and compare it with the mean value of pixels. If it is larger than the mean value, 1 is recorded. Otherwise, write down 0 and the resulting binary string is the

Hash value of the image, also known as the image fingerprint. The specific algorithm is described as follows:

Step 1: Reduce the image to N × N, n2 pixels in total;
Step 2: Convert n × N images into grayscale images, denoted as Ga;
Step 3: Calculate the pixel average value of Ga of grayscale image, denoted as Pavg;
Step 4: Traverse each pixel PI in Ga, and compare PI with Pavg. If PI ≥ Pavg, write down 1; otherwise, write down 0, and the binary string of N2 bits is the aHash value of the image, which is marked as Ha.
Step 5: Calculate the Hamming distance of the hash values of the two pictures. The smaller the distance, the more similar the pictures will be. The larger the distance, the more different the pictures will be.

The similarity between the image and the model hand after the edge detection of some hands is calculated, and the results obtained are shown in Fig. 5.

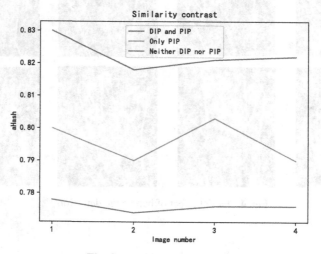

Fig. 5. Partial hand similarity

3.3 Finger Disability Recognition

For finger disability recognition, we judge the degree of finger disability by the similarity between the image of the experimental hand edge detection and the model hand edge detection. The higher the similarity, the lower the degree of disability. Among them, the distal interphalangeal joint (DIP) and the proximal interphalangeal joint (PIP) are the key nodes, and the specific recognition process of finger disability degree is shown in Formula (2). R is the mean hash similarity of the fingers of the subject and the model hand, S is the similarity threshold of the fingers when DIP and PIP exist, T is the similarity threshold of the fingers when DIP does not exist PIP, when J = 1, at this time, the proximal interphalanx and distal interphalanx exist, and the degree of finger disability is the first finger disability, when J = 2, At this time, the proximal interphalangeal joint exists, while the distal interphalangeal joint does not exist, and the degree of finger disability is the disability of the first two knuckles. When J = 3, neither the proximal interphalangeal joint nor the distal interphalangeal joint exists, and the degree of disability is the disability of the whole finger.

$$J = \begin{cases} 1, R \geq S \\ 2, T \leq R \leq S \\ 3, R < S \end{cases} \tag{2}$$

4 Experimental Results

This time, 50 people were selected, with 12 finger images for each of them, and a total of 600 finger images were selected. The mean similarity calculation was conducted between the hand image with HED edge detection in the hand shape database and the hand image with HED edge detection in the standard model, and the results were obtained as shown in Fig. 6.

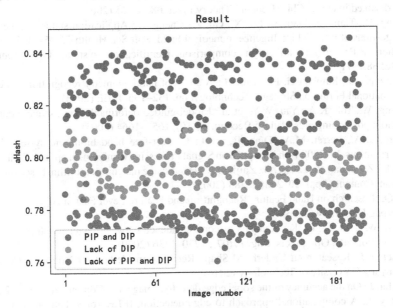

Fig. 6. Schematic diagram of similarity results

When the threshold S is 0.835 and T is 0.782, the recognition accuracy of finger disability degree reaches the highest at this time, the accuracy rate is 96.6%.

5 Conclusion

This paper proposes a recognition algorithm based on the HED finger disability degree, in the use of hand Holistically-nested edge detection algorithm to extract image edge, on the basis of through experiment object edge detection after the image with the model hand edge detection after the image average hash similarity evaluation to analyze the existence of the interphalangeal joint near side and then recognize the subjects fingers degree of disability. The accuracy rate of the algorithm is 96.6%, which has good recognition ability. It provides a new treatment method for the patients with hand disability, and a new idea for the rational use of medical power and relief of medical pressure. In this paper, finger disability recognition is carried out in a fixed environment. It is necessary to identify finger disability in a more complex environment, which is the research goal in the future.

Funding. This research was funded by National Natural Science Foundation of China, grant number 62003222.

References

1. Chen, G., Xu, X.: General situation and development of production and supply of articles for the disabled in china. Chin. Rehabil. Theory Pract. **08**, 63–65 (2002)
2. Wang, H., Tian, X., Mao, Y., Lu, X., Gu, Z., Cheng, L.: Application status, problems and suggestions of artificial intelligence in medical Field. Soft Sci. Health **32**(05), 3–5+9 (2018)
3. Miller, R.P.: Finger dimension comparison identification system. US Patent, No. 3576538.1971
4. Ayurzana, O., Pumbuurei, B., Kim, H.: A study of hand-geometry recognition system. In: International Forum on Strategic Technology, pp. 132–135. IEEE (2013)
5. Xiong, W., Toh, K.A., Yau, W.Y., et al.: Model-guided deformable hand shape recognition without positioning aids. Pattern Recogn. **38**(10), 1651–1664 (2005)
6. Morales, A., Ferrer, M.A., Díaz, F., et al.: Contact-free hand biometric system for real environments. In: 2008 16th European on Signal Processing Conference, pp. 1-5. IEEE (2008)
7. Gu, L., Zhenquan, Z., Zheng, G., Zaijian, W.: Hand shape matching algorithm based on feature fusion. Comput. Appl. **10**, 2286–2288 (2005)
8. Li, Q.: Research on Hand Feature Recognition and Feature Level Fusion Algorithm. Beijing Jiaotong University (2006)
9. Yuan, W., Zhu, C., Li, K.: Analysis of correspondence between finger width selection and recognition rate. Opt. Precis. Eng. **17**(07), 1730–1736 (2009)
10. Lanctao, J.: Research on Underhand Shape Recognition Method for Non-ideal Condition. Shenyang University of Technology (2014)
11. Kittler, J.: On the accuracy of the sobel edge detector. Image Vis. Comput. **1**(1), 37–42 (1983)
12. Canny, J.: A computational approach to edge detection. IEEE Trans. Pattern Anal. Mach. Intell. **8**(06), 679–698 (1986)
13. Xie, S., Tu, Z.: Holistically-nested edge detection. In: Proceedings of the 2015 IEEE International Conference on Computer Vision, pp. 1395–1403. IEEE, Piscataway (2015)

Electrocardiograph Based Emotion Recognition via WGAN-GP Data Enhancement and Improved CNN

Jiayuan Hu and Yong Li[✉]

Shenyang University of Technology, Shenyang 110870, China
liyong@sut.edu.cn

Abstract. Emotion recognition is one of the key technologies for the further development of human-computer interaction, and is gradually becoming a hot spot in current AI research. At the same time, physiological signals are objective external manifestations of emotions, and emotion recognition based on physiological signals often lacks high-quality training samples and suffers from inter-sample category imbalance. In this paper, 140 samples of electrocardiogram (ECG) signals triggered by Self-Assessment Manikin (SAM) emotion self-assessment experiments were collected using International Affective Picture System (IAPS). To cope with the problem of small data size and data imbalance between classes, Wasserstein Generative Adversarial Network-Gradient Penalty (WGAN-GP) was used to add different number samples for different classes to achieve class balance in the training set, and by continuously adding -samples, the training set to different sizes, using three classifiers to train different sizes of training set samples separately. The results show that the accuracy and weighted F1 values of all three classifiers improve after increasing the data, where higher accuracy and F1 values can be obtained using the proposed Multi Attention-CNN(MA-CNN) as a classifier before and after increasing the samples.

Keywords: Electrocardiograph · Emotion elicitation · Data augmentation · Emotional recognition

1 Introduction

Emotion is a generic term for a set of subjective cognitive experiences, a mental state, and a physiological state resulting from the combination of multiple feelings, thoughts, and behaviours [1]. Research has demonstrated that if B perceives A's emotions, B's behaviour toward A may change, at which point it may influence or determine A's emotional experience [2]. Therefore, it makes sense to give robots and computers the ability to understand human emotions during human-computer interaction. Emotion recognition has a wide range of applications in the medical field, distance education, security and health detection, healthcare, and human-computer interaction [3–6]. For example, in the field of education, if a computer can even grasp the emotional state of a student, it can provide appropriate learning programs as a way to improve student acceptance

H. Liu et al. (Eds.): ICIRA 2022, LNAI 13455, pp. 155–164, 2022.
https://doi.org/10.1007/978-3-031-13844-7_16

and learning efficiency. Similarly, doctors can improve the efficiency and accuracy of diagnosis by understanding the emotional state of their patients, especially when dealing with those who cannot express their emotions clearly, such as the elderly and autistic patients [7, 8]. In a driving environment, the driver's emotional state can be understood in time to alert the driver to make adjustments [9]. Emotion recognition is mostly based on non-physiological signals, such as expression, posture, and physiological signals, such as EEG and ECG [10–13]. However, non-physiological signals are easily artifacts and their validity and reliability are usually difficult to guarantee [14], while physiological signals are not easily controlled subjectively and can objectively reflect the true emotional state. Among them, ECG signals are rich in physiological information, and heart rate variability reflects the corresponding modulation of autonomic and humoral regulation by the cardiovascular system. Since changes in emotional state directly affect the autonomic nervous system and humoral regulation, changes in individual emotions can be reflected in heart rate variability, i.e., heart rate variability can be used for emotion recognition Picard et al. [15] demonstrated through a series of experiments that it is feasible to extract certain effective combinations of features from specific human physiological signals and use them for emotion recognition studies. In addition, ECG acquisition devices are more portable than EEG acquisition devices, which has greatly facilitated the marketability and commercialization of human-computer emotion communication. While multimodal emotion recognition methods typically perform better, unimodal methods have the advantage of shorter processing times and simpler data collection [16]. The use of deep learning as a classifier has increased in recent years with the development of deep learning. However, inefficiencies in physiological signal acquisition have led to a scarcity of high-quality samples, and it has been found in practice that different categories of people have different difficulties in evoking emotions, such that the amount of data obtained for each emotion category is often unbalanced. In the case of small samples, the classification performance of the classifier is severely degraded, and the imbalance in sample categories makes the classifier extremely inaccurate in identifying fewer categories.

For the problem of small samples, data augmentation is a technique to generate new data from limited data by synthesis or transformation. Data augmentation techniques are an effective means to overcome data deficiencies and improve model generalization [17]. 2014 Goodfellow et al. proposed GAN [18] to expand the samples, but it still has shortcomings. In 2017, WGAN-GP was proposed based on GAN [19], which has remarkable capabilities in image generation and other aspects.

To solve the problems of small sample size and category imbalance in emotion recognition, this paper obtains the ECG signals of experimenters under different emotions through experiments and proposes the following innovations.

(1) WGAN-GP is used as an enhancement to the ECG signal and a different number of samples are added to different categories to achieve category balancing, thus solving the problem of category imbalance.
(2) Attention-based multi-channel convolutional neural networks were used to classify the data before and after enhancement to achieve higher classification accuracy.

The rest of this paper is organized as follows. Section 2 describes the training process of WGAN-GP and the structure of the improved classification network MA-CNN. Section 3 describes the experiments related to the acquisition of emotional arousal and physiological signals. Section 4 introduces the basic structure of the MA-CNN classification network using the training results of WGAN-GP and shows the results based on the three classification networks before and after adding different amounts of data, marking the effectiveness of the data enhancement, and comparing the results of the MA-CNN classification network with the other two classification networks to verify the effectiveness of the MA-CNN. Finally, conclusions are drawn in Sect. 5.

2 WGAN-GP

2.1 GAN

The GAN network mainly consists of generator G and discriminator D. The training process is as follows: the generator takes the random noise z obeying a certain distribution as input and generates G(z) of new samples by learning the distribution D(x) of real samples x. Meanwhile, the discriminator takes the samples from the generator and real samples as input and discriminates the probability that G(z) comes from x. The output is the linear function value y. The structural diagram of the GAN model is shown in Fig. 1. The optimal loss function of this model can be expressed as:

$$\min_{G} \max_{D} L(D, G) = E_{x_r \sim P_r}[D(x_r)] + E_{x_G \sim P_G}[D(x_G)] \tag{1}$$

where P_r denotes the data distribution of the real sample x_r and P_G denotes the data distribution of the generator-generated sample G(z). The sum of the two in the formula represents the Jensen-Shannon scatter between the real data and the generated data.

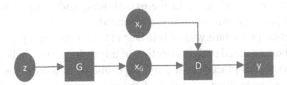

Fig. 1. Schematic diagram of GAN

2.2 WGAN-GP

GAN often suffers from training instability and poor robustness in practical training, and the training of the model depends on hyperparameter tuning of the generator and discriminator, and there is no metric to quantify the progress of training, which may lead to model collapse. To solve these problems, Arjovsky et al. proposed the WGAN [20] model by introducing the Wasserstein distance. However, WGAN uses weight cropping to restrict the absolute value of discriminator parameter updates to not exceed a predetermined fixed constant. It cannot fit complex data samples, resulting in a great waste of resources, and also easily leads to problems such as gradient disappearance or gradient explosion. The literature [19] used Gradient Penally to improve the original weight cropping to satisfy the continuity condition, which successfully solved the problem of gradient disappearance or explosion, and the improved WGAN-GP has faster convergence, a more stable training process, and higher quality of generated samples compared with other GAN models. WGAN The loss function of -GP consists of two parts: the loss term and the gradient penalty term of the native WGAN, which can be expressed as:

$$\min_{G} \max_{D} L(D, G) = E_{x_r \sim P_r}[D(x_r)] + E_{x_G \sim P_G}[D(x_G)] + \lambda E_{x_p \sim P_{penalty}}[||\nabla_{x_P} D(x_P)|| - 1]^2$$

$$(2)$$

where λ is the gradient penalty factor $P_{penalty}$ belongs to the gradient coefficients in P_r and P_G the sampling space between $\nabla_{x_p} D(x_p)$ is the discriminator gradient. In this loss function, weight clipping is not strictly required to be less than or equal to 1, but it is sufficient to approximate 1, and the convergence can be accelerated by using the parametric calculation.

3 Experiment

In this paper, we conducted an experiment on visual emotional arousal based on IAPS, a picture database that can provide a standardized set of pictures for the study of emotion and attention that has been widely used in psychological research. We selected 20 images (10 from each class, high and low value) from the IAPS library as experimental material for the emotion evocation material, with the 20 being chosen on the principle of covering as many value coordinates as possible. Subjects' physiological signals during emotional arousal were collected along with the results of the completed SAM self-assessment questionnaire. Informed consent and confidentiality agreements were signed by the subjects participating in the experiment, under the premise of ensuring that no privacy or personal information was revealed.

The experimental procedure was as follows: (1) Experimental preparation: the subjects wore instruments related to the collection of physiological signals, Fig. 2 shows the location of the electrodes placed during the experiment. In a quiet and non-disturbing environment, the subjects were informed of the requirements and basic procedures of the experiment and pressed the experimental button to start the experiment; (2) Picture display: after 10 s of calming down, the picture was displayed on the computer screen for 5 s, after 20 s of (3) The participant was asked to fill out the SAM questionnaire within 15 s to assess his or her mood when seeing the previous picture. After another 10 s of emotional calm, a second picture appeared for 5 s. The following 20 s of emotional calm were followed by 1–15 s of self-assessment; (4) 10 s were given for the subject's calm mood; (5) The (2) (3) process was repeated until the 20 pictures were shown and one experiment was completed. In the experiment, the baseline ECG signal was collected for 10 s during the emotional calmness and the ECG signal for 5 s during the image display. the BIOPAC-MP160 was used as the ECG signal acquisition device. The CH3236TDY physiological electrodes were used to connect the skin to the BIOPAC-MP160 device. Diagram of the experimental scenario where a total of 140 (7 subjects * 20 images) samples were taken. Of these, 86 were high value samples and 54 were low value samples.

To perform emotion evocation experiments, a portable biosensor needs to be properly worn. The BIOPAC-MP160 was connected to the subject's body via the CATHAY CH3236TDY physiological electrode piece for a more efficient acquisition of bioelectric signals. The ECG module- ECG was connected to the left lower chest position as shown in Fig. 2. Before the start of the experiment, the seat was adjusted to a comfortable position and ECG signals were collected during the experiment.

Fig. 2. Electrode position and experimental scenario

For each ECG sample, heart rate variability features were collected using Neurokit2 [21] then features were selected using a chi-square test [22]. The final mean heart rate, maximum heart rate, median heart rate, and heart rate variability (HRV) data from the original samples were selected: pNN50, HRV_S, HRV_SD2, HRV_CSI, HRV_CVI, HRV_C2a, HRV_SDNN, for a total of 10 features, giving an experimental sample dimension of 140×10. In which the data set is randomly divided, 60% as the training set, 20% as the validation set, and 20% as the test set.

4 Emotion Recognition

4.1 WGAN-GP Settings

WGAN-GP is used for data augmentation, and the structure of the generator and discriminator of WGAN-GP is shown in Fig. 3. The generator is a 3-layer fully connected network with 64, 32, and 10 neurons. The discriminator is also a 3-layer fully connected layer with 32, 64, and 1 neuron, using LeakyReLU as the activation function, and the last layer is a fully-connected layer with 1 node and no activation function. The learning rate of the Adam optimizer used for the discriminator is 0.0001 and the learning rate of the Adam optimizer used for the generator is 0.0002.

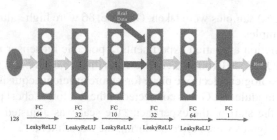

Fig. 3. Structure of generator and discriminator

The Generator loss in Fig. 4 indicates the loss variation of the generator and the Critic loss indicates the loss variation of the discriminator. After epochs = 750, the training was stopped and gradually smoothed out after epoch = 600 with no obvious fluctuations, meeting the training completion criteria.

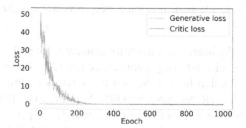

Fig. 4. Generators and discriminator losses

4.2 Attention-Based and Multi-convolutional Neural Network

To obtain feature information for different combinations of feature signals, three convolutional kernels at different scales are used in the first layer. An attention mechanism, the coordinate attention (CA) module [23], is also introduced to obtain both spatial aspects as well as inter-channel feature information. The CA structure is shown in Fig. 5. CA implements two functions in turn, the coordinate information embedding and the coordinate attention generation module. In this paper, a classification network MA-CNN is proposed by combining multi-scale convolution with the CA module, and the structure of its MA-CNN is illustrated in Fig. 6. The steps of the CA module are as follows: (1) Firstly, for the input feature map, feature extraction is performed for each feature channel using adaptive averaging pooling layers for horizontal and vertical directions respectively; (2) The generated feature maps are stitched together and then 1 × 1 convolution is used to generate both vertical and horizontal, (3) Dividing the intermediate feature map into two feature maps along the spatial direction and converting the number of channels using 1 × 1 convolution respectively; (4) Obtaining the attention weights for the vertical and horizontal spatial directions and multiplying them with the input feature map to obtain the feature map with the attention weights.

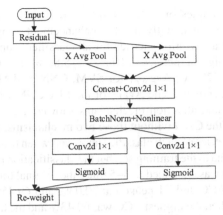

Fig. 5. The structure of CA

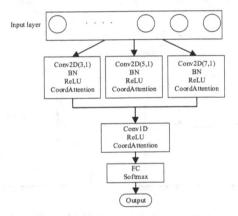

Fig. 6. MA-CNN structure diagram

4.3   ECG Signal Preprocessing

For the experimentally obtained ECG signal data, to address the imbalance between data categories and to compare the effect on classifier performance after adding samples of different sizes generated by WGAN-GP to the training set. Generated data were added to the original training set and the original training set of high and low value samples was expanded to 100, 200, 300, ..., 900, and the training set was expanded to N (200, 400, 600, ..., 1800) samples. Where when the number of samples is 84 is the training set before data augmentation. The expanded samples were trained with SVM and CNN and MA-CNN classifiers, respectively, and then classified on the test set to obtain accuracy and weight F1(WF1) values, respectively. To avoid the chance of generating samples, 10 times the same size of sample data were generated for the training set, and in these 10 same-size training sets, each classifier was trained and tested separately to obtain ACC and WF1 [24], as well as their mean and standard deviation Std_{ACC}, Std_{WF1}, As shown in Table 1, Table 2, and Fig. 7. The bold numbers in Tables 1 and 2 indicate the highest accuracies for adding samples of different sizes. From the first column of the table compared to the other columns, firstly, the data enhancement using WGAN-GP resulted in an increase in both classification metrics for all classifiers compared to the pre-data enhancement, with the highest increases of 17.24%, 5.86%, and 10.71% for Avg_{Acc} and 13.53%, 6.25% and 24.52% for Avg_{WF1} for SVM, CNN, and MA-CNN respectively. 6.25% and 24.52% respectively. The Avg_{F1} of the MA-CNN with the addition of the multiscale convolution and attention mechanisms showed a greater increase than the Avg_{Acc} and Avg_{WF1} of the CNN without these two mechanisms. Finally, it can be seen that the classification metrics of each classifier improved when tested by adding different amounts of generated data to the training set, but the classification performance no longer improved when the data was enhanced to 3–5 times the original training set. When using SVM as the classifier, ACC and F1 peaked at 70.03% and 69.45% at N = 200. When using CNN as the classifier, the highest ACC was 60.43% and the highest F1 was 59.68% when N = 600. When using MA-CNN as the classifier, the highest values of ACC and F1 were 85.69% and 87.43% respectively at N = 800.

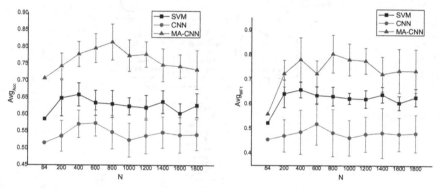

Fig. 7. Avg_{Acc}, Std_{Acc} and Avg_{WF1} and Std_{WF1} of SVM, CNN, and MA-CNN when adding samples of different sizes

Table 1. Avg_{Acc} and Std_{Acc} for different classifiers when adding different numbers of samples

N		84	200	400	600	800	1000	1200	1400	1600	1800
SVM	Avg_{Acc}	0.5862	0.6483	**0.6586**	0.6345	0.6310	0.6241	0.6207	0.6379	0.6034	0.6276
	Std_{Acc}	0.0000	0.0534	0.0343	0.0371	0.0400	0.0254	0.0363	0.0335	0.0293	0.0356
CNN	Avg_{Acc}	0.5157	0.5357	0.5714	**0.5743**	0.5473	0.5241	0.5369	0.5472	0.5393	0.5407
	Std_{Acc}	0.0000	0.0457	0.0406	0.0385	0.0491	0.0500	0.0525	0.0464	0.0525	0.0457
MA-CNN	Avg_{Acc}	0.7071	0.7428	0.7785	0.7962	**0.8142**	0.7742	0.7785	0.7472	0.7428	0.7336
	Std_{Acc}	0.0000	0.0375	0.0368	0.0427	0.0532	0.0463	0.0376	0.0485	0.0352	0.0574

Table 2. Avg$_{WF1}$ and Std$_{WF1}$ for different classifiers when adding different numbers of samples

N		84	200	400	600	800	1000	1200	1400	1600	1800
SVM	Avg$_{WF1}$	0.5222	0.6413	**0.6575**	0.6341	0.6308	0.6226	0.6203	0.6381	0.6041	0.6273
	Std$_{WF1}$	0.0000	0.0563	0.0318	0.0357	0.0386	0.0226	0.0355	0.0316	0.0284	0.0354
CNN	Avg$_{WF1}$	0.4553	0.4700	0.4853	**0.5178**	0.4824	0.4626	0.4766	0.4825	0.4769	0.4803
	Std$_{WF1}$	0.0000	0.0656	0.0895	0.0845	0.0952	0.0718	0.0716	0.1011	0.0676	0.0756
MA-CNN	Avg$_{WF1}$	0.5587	0.7235	0.7806	0.7232	**0.8039**	0.7806	0.7755	0.7219	0.7349	0.7353
	Std$_{WF1}$	0.0000	0.0546	0.0895	0.0523	0.0770	0.0648	0.0526	0.0701	0.0896	0.0874

5 Conclusion

For emotion recognition based on physiological signals, this paper first organizes experiments to obtain ECG signals evoked by IAPS, and obtains 140 samples, 86 high valence samples and 54 validity samples. Sample expansion data were generated by adding WGAN-GP, and three classification models were used respectively. The experimental results show that the data augmentation algorithm based on WGAN-GP for ECG data augmentation can improve the performance of the classifier. The MA-CNN model with multiscale convolution and attention channels outperformed the SVM and the CNN without multiscale convolution and attention channels before and after sample augmentation, while the SVM, CNN and MA-CNN models were no longer optimised when the training samples were increased to 400, 600 and 800 respectively. Based on the research in this paper, the next step is to prepare for more experiments to acquire EEG and other signals for emotion recognition using the proposed model.

References

1. Picard, R.W.: Affective computing: challenges. Int. J. Hum. Comput. Stud. **59**, 55–64 (2003)
2. Wang, S.H., Phillips, P., Dong, Z.C., Zhang, Y.D.: Intelligent facial emotion recognition based on stationary wavelet entropy and Jaya algorithm. Neurocomputing **272**, 668–676 (2018)
3. Seo, J., Laine, T.H., Oh, G., Sohn, K.A.: EEG-based emotion classification for Alzheimer's disease patients using conventional machine learning and recurrent neural network models. Sensors (Switzerland) **20**, 1–27 (2020)
4. Belkacem, A.N., Jamil, N., Palmer, J.A., Ouhbi, S., Chen, C.: Brain computer interfaces for improving the quality of life of older adults and elderly patients. Front. Neurosci. **14**, 1–11 (2020)
5. Joshi, A., Bhattacharyya, P., Ahire, S.: Sentiment resources: lexicons and datasets, 85–106 (2017)
6. Chaturvedi, I., Satapathy, R., Cavallari, S., Cambria, E.: Fuzzy commonsense reasoning for multimodal sentiment analysis. Pattern Recognit. Lett. **125**, 264–270 (2019)
7. Bal, E., et al.: Emotion recognition in children with autism spectrum disorders: relations to eye gaze and autonomic state. J. Autism Dev. Disord. **40**, 358–370 (2010)
8. Harms, M.B., Martin, A., Wallace, G.L.: Facial emotion recognition in autism spectrum disorders: a review of behavioral and neuroimaging studies. Neuropsychol. Rev. **20**, 290–322 (2010)

9. Zheng, W.L., Lu, B.L.: A multimodal approach to estimating vigilance using EEG and forehead EOG. J. Neural Eng. **14** (2017)
10. Kessous, L., Castellano, G., Caridakis, G.: Multimodal emotion recognition in speech-based interaction using facial expression, body gesture and acoustic analysis. J. Multimodal User Interfaces **3**, 33–48 (2010)
11. Busso, C., et al.: Analysis of emotion recognition using facial expressions, speech and multi-modal information. In: ICMI 2004 - Sixth International Conference on Multimodal Interfaces, pp. 205–211 (2004)
12. Salankar, N., Mishra, P., Garg, L.: Emotion recognition from EEG signals using empirical mode decomposition and second-order difference plot. Biomed. Sig. Process. Control **65**, 102389 (2021)
13. Hasnul, M.A., Aziz, N.A.A., Alelyani, S., Mohana, M., Aziz, A.A.: Electrocardiogram-based emotion recognition systems and their applications in healthcare—a review. Sensors **21** (2021)
14. Kim, K.H., Bang, S.W., Kim, S.R.: Emotion recognition system using short-term monitoring of physiological signals. Med. Biol. Eng. Comput. **42**, 419–427 (2004)
15. Picard, R.W., Healey, J.: Affective wearables. Pers. Technol. **1**(4), 231–240 (1997)
16. Pantic, M., Caridakis, G., André, E., Kim, J., Karpouzis, K., Kollias, S.: Multimodal emotion recognition from low-level cues. Cogn. Technol. J. 115–132 (2011)
17. Lata, K., Dave, M., KN, N.: Data augmentation using generative adversarial network. SSRN Electron. J. 1–14 (2019)
18. Goodfellow, I., et al.: Generative adversarial nets. In: Advances in Neural Information Processing Systems, vol. 27 (2014)
19. Gulrajani, I., Ahmed, F., Arjovsky, M., Dumoulin, V., Courville, A.: Improved training of Wasserstein GANs. Advances in Neural Information Processing Systems, December 2017, pp. 5768–5778 (2017)
20. Arjovsky, M., Chintala, S., Bottou, L.: (WGAN) Wasserstein generative adversarial network Junhong Huang. In: ICML, pp. 1–44 (2017)
21. Makowski, D., et al.: NeuroKit2: a Python toolbox for neurophysiological signal processing. Behav. Res. Methods **53**(4), 1689–1696 (2021). https://doi.org/10.3758/s13428-020-01516-y
22. Mchugh, M.L.: The chi-square test of independence lessons in biostatistics. Biochem. Medica **23**, 143–149 (2013)
23. Hou, Q., Zhou, D., Feng, J.: Coordinate attention for efficient mobile network design. In: Proceedings of the IEEE/CVF Conference on Computer Vision and Pattern Recognition, pp. 13713–13722 (2021)
24. Chinchor, N., Sundheim, B.M.: MUC-5 EVALUATION METRIC S Science Applications International Corporation 10260 Campus Point Drive, MIS A2-F San Diego, CA 92121 Naval Command, Control, and Ocean Surveillance Center RDT & E Division (NRaD) Information Access Technology Project TE. System, pp. 69–78 (1992)

Multi-objective Optimization of Intelligent Wheelchair Paths Taking into Account User Preferences

ShanFeng Cheng and Yong Li[(⊠)]

Shenyang University of Technology, Shenyang 110870, China
liYong@sut.edu.cn

Abstract. For the optimization of an intelligent wheelchair driving path, most studies focus on the length of the path. Although a few studies have taken user preferences and comfort into account, the length of the path has not been involved in the meantime. Namely, we can say user preferences are not considered when considering path length, while no consideration of user preferences when considering path length, which leads to conflicts between the path length of intelligent wheelchairs and user preferences. Therefore, this study proposes a multi-objective optimization method for intelligent wheelchair path considering user preferences. Firstly, an intelligent wheelchair path preference recognition framework based on evidence network is proposed. Secondly, A* and artificial potential field fusion path planning method is used to generate a certain scale of paths, and the user's path preference and path length are calculated, so as to build a mathematical model for multi-objective optimization. Finally, the model is solved by multi-objective PSO. The results show that the proposed method can realize the optimization of the intelligent wheelchair path with consideration of user preference and path length.

Keywords: Evidence network · User preferences · Path planning · Multi-objective optimization

1 Introduction

In the field of robotics, intelligent wheelchairs are becoming a solution for a growing number of elderly and disabled people. Common path planning methods include artificial potential field path planning method [1], A*algorithm [2] and Dijkstra algorithm [3]. The above methods comprehensively consider path length optimization, generally have good performance in distance, time cost and other aspects, and also achieve collusion-free safe navigation. A research and development team from Shanghai Jiao Tong University proposed a navigation method that combines global path planning with online replanning and behavior control to solve the autonomy and safety problems of intelligent wheelchair navigation in a dynamic environment, and verified their method with good path optimization and safety [4]. However, this method only considers path optimization and safety, without considering user preference and comfort. Y. Morales et al. [5] considered the comfort level of people when they took wheelchairs as vehicles. With linear velocity

H. Liu et al. (Eds.): ICIRA 2022, LNAI 13455, pp. 165–173, 2022.
https://doi.org/10.1007/978-3-031-13844-7_17

and linear acceleration, angular velocity and angular acceleration, and distance between people and obstacles selected as the factors affecting human comfort, according to the definition of comfort level, the comfort model is obtained. Y.Morales et al. obtained an environmental comfort zone model and planned the comfort level of the path based on the length and visibility of the path. A balanced navigation model for passengers and pedestrians is proposed in [6]. The model takes into account the comfort requirements of passengers and pedestrians. Kuu-young Young et al. [7] proposed a motion guidance system for robot walkers based on comfort. The system includes a path planner that takes into account human factors: the distance between people and obstacles, and formulates corresponding control strategies for their execution to produce a path that generates comfort. But these methods only consider user comfort, with no path length optimization. Li Yong et al. [8] proposed a path preference recognition method based on evidence network, which mainly deduces the user's path preference through fusion. Most of the research on intelligent wheelchair driving path is about the optimization of the path length. Although a small number of studies have considered user comfort and user personality preferences, there are also many shortcomings and deficiencies. Based on the contradiction between path length and user preference, this study proposed a multi-objective optimization method for intelligent wheelchair path length considering user preference.

2 Path Length Calculation

2.1 Simulation Scenarios

The size of the actual indoor environment is 6 m × 6 m. There is a triangle object, a rectangular table and four octagonal benches placed in the indoor environment. There are also two interior walls. The realistic indoor environment maps the simulation scene in this paper. The realistic environment size of 6 m × 6 m is mapped into a simulation grid of 400 × 400, as shown in Fig. 1, so that the size of each grid is 1.5 cm × 1.5 cm. The starting point coordinate is [40,60], and the end point coordinate is [360, 360].

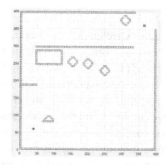

Fig. 1. Simulation scene diagram

2.2 Calculation of Path Length

In this paper, the path planning method combining A* algorithm and artificial potential field method is used to generate paths. A* algorithm is used in global path planning to obtain global path information and find the current global sub-target point [9]. The current global sub-target point guides artificial potential field method to perform local path planning again [10]. The process is repeated until the target point is found. Therefore, the problem that artificial potential field method falls into local small value and the target is unreachable can be solved and safe collision-free path can be generated [11].

The length of the entire path can be calculated by summing up the Euclidean distance of all the path segments by calculating the length of the entire path segments based on Euclidean distance. Path P is $[p_1, p_2, p_3 \ldots p_n]$, where the continuous coordinate points are (x_i, y_i) and (x_{i+1}, y_{i+1}), and a path is connected by multiple ordered line segments. Then the length of the entire path can be calculated using Eq. (1).

$$L = \sum_{i=1}^{n} \sqrt{(x_{i+1} - x_i)^2 + (y_{i+1} - y_i)^2} \tag{1}$$

3 Path Preference Calculation Based on Evidence Network

The user's path preference in this paper is finally obtained through fusion inference based on the evidence network-based intelligent wheelchair path preference recognition framework. The evidence-network-based intelligent wheelchair path preference recognition framework mentioned above is shown in Fig. 2. The circle represents node, the diamond represents evaluation function, among which obstacle distance (OD), obstacle number (OQ), obstacle shape (OS) and channel width (CW) are input nodes. ODS is a composite node of obstacle distance and obstacle shape. O is the composite node of the obstacle property. P is the output node [12].

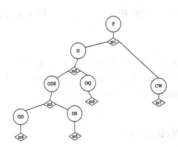

Fig. 2. Wheelchair path preference recognition framework based on evidence network

3.1 Path Segmentation

There are problems when calculating path preference. Due to the number of path factors (the channel width (CW), number of obstacles (OQ), shape of obstacles (OS) and distance between obstacles and users (OD)) is changing when the robot goes through the path, we need to divide the whole path into segments, ensuring that each segment has the same amount of factors. Therefore, the path of a certain size should be segmented according to the following three principles:

(1) The maximum threshold is set as 0.4 m from the wheelchair robot to the obstacle. When the distance of the obstacle is greater than 0.4 m, the repulsive force field of the obstacle is set as 0, so the 0.4-m threshold is used as the segmentation point.
(2) At the same time, in such segmentation, the distance from the obstacle is less than 0.4 m, and soon more than 0.4 m will affect the segmentation. As shown in Fig. 3, the blue part and the pink part are the parts with thresholds greater than 0.4 m. The Euclidean distance between the geometric centers of two obstacles in the simulation scene was selected as the segmentation basis (the Euclidean distance between the geometric center of the rectangle and the geometric center of the octagon).
(3) The path needs to be segmented when it has channel. When the coordinates of the wheelchair robot are greater than (30, 220) and (300, 270), it is the path factor of the passage width of the wheelchair robot. As shown in Fig. 3, the red part of the path is the path factors of channel width through which the robot passes.

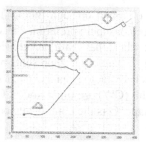

Fig. 3. Path segment description diagram (Color figure online)

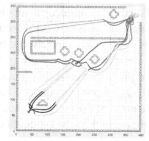

Fig. 4. Path segment diagram

Paths of a certain size are randomly generated in the simulation scene, and the 6 paths in the scene are segmented according to the above 3-segmented principle. The segmented results of the 6 paths are shown in Fig. 4.

3.2 Calculation of Path Preferences

The four path factors of channel width (CW), number of obstacles (OQ), obstacle shape (OS) and distance between obstacles and users (OD) are identified by obstacle coordinate points [13]. The geometric center of the wheelchair robot was taken as the center of the obstacle search circle, and the search radius of the circle was 0.5 m. The search circle moved synchronously with the wheelchair robot, and the shortest Euclidean distance from the robot to the obstacle was afterwards determined. When identifying the shape of an obstacle, the angle of the obstacle can be calculated by calculating the cosine value of the angle between the three coordinate points of the obstacle. When the included angle of the edge line of the obstacle is acute angle, it is a triangle obstacle, when the included angle of the edge line of the obstacle is 90°, it is a rectangular obstacle, when the included angle of the edge line of the obstacle is 135°, it is an octagonal obstacle. The number of obstacles can be obtained by adding the number of obstacles passed by the robot in the current path segment. See Sect. 3.1 for identification of path factors of channel width.

After the wheelchair robot identifies the four path factors, based on the experimental data of path factor preference in literature [8], the evidence network is adopted to conduct fusion inference operation for the four path factor variables in order. The fusion inference process is shown in Fig. 5, the four factors of preference data fusion reasoning, and gradually eliminate the indirect variable, finally obtain reliability values of the decision variables, the reliability value will be converted to mathematical expectation, so as to get the path to the user preferences. Taking path 1 as an example, the path preference result is shown in formula (2) below.

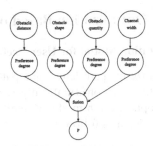

Fig. 5. Path preference fusion inference based on evidence network

$$P_{total} = \frac{0.2375+0.4675+0.4471+0.6768+0.1+0.1}{6} = 0.3382 \qquad (2)$$

Based on the path preference calculation method of path 1 above, the preferences of the other five paths in Fig. 4 can also be calculated. Table 1 below shows the path preferences and path lengths of the six paths. There is a contradiction between user preference and path length in 6 paths. Therefore, multi-objective optimization of user preference and path length is needed.

Path preference reflects the user's preference level for the path. The goal of optimizing path preference is to maximize the preference value as much as possible. For the convenience of description, the maximization problem is transformed into a minimization problem.

$$\frac{1}{P_{total}} = \frac{N}{\sum\limits_{j=1}^{n} \frac{P_j}{M}} \qquad (3)$$

Table 1. User preference and path length

Path	Path length	Path preference
Path1	470.22	0.3382
Path2	832.31	0.3675
Path3	512.82	0.4097
Path4	873.27	0.3659
Path5	532.48	0.3705
Path6	468.58	0.3028

In formula (3), preference p_{total} is converted to the reciprocal of preference, where N is the number of segments in the path. M is the preference level of the network identified framework. The smaller the reciprocal, the higher the user's preference for the path.

4   Multi-objective Path Optimization Based on MOPSO

4.1   Multi-objective Optimization Model for User Preferences and Path Length

In this paper, we hope to optimize the path length and path preference. For the convenience of description, the objective function is uniformly transformed into a minimization problem. The multi-objective optimization model of intelligent wheelchair path length and user preference can be expressed as follows.

$$\begin{cases} \min f_1 = \sum_{i=1}^{n} \sqrt{(x_{i+1} - x_i)^2 + (y_{i+1} - y_i)^2} \\ \min f_2 = \dfrac{1}{P_{total}} = \dfrac{N}{\sum_{j=1}^{n} \frac{P_j}{M}} \end{cases} \tag{4}$$

Since Coello et al. [14] proposed the application of elementary particle swarm to solving multi-objective particle swarm in 2004, a large number of preliminary results on MOPSO have been proposed after learning from the successful experience of other algorithms in the field of multi-objective optimization. In this paper, by changing the guided search range of A* algorithm, the gain coefficients of repulsion field and gravitational field of artificial potential field method, paths of different sizes can be generated randomly. At this time, the three variables: A* algorithm's guided search domain S_f, repulsive field gain coefficient K_r and gravitational field gain coefficient K_a are taken as the position of the generated particle $[S_f, K_r, K_a]$.

Multi-objective path optimization steps based on MOPSO:

(1) For each particle in the generated particle swarm, initialize the particle position and velocity;

(2) The path preference value and path length value of the objective function of each particle are calculated, and the initial non-dominated solution is added into the archive;

(3) Determine the particle global optimal position G_{best} and individual optimal position P_{best};
(4) Update the velocity and position of particles;
(5) Update the non-dominated solution set and delete redundant inferior solutions;
(6) Judge the current iteration state. If the termination condition has been reached, it will end; otherwise, go to (3).

4.2 Results and Discussion

Multi-objective optimization of user preference and path length for intelligent wheelchair robot was carried out using multi-objective particle swarm optimization. MOPSO's initialization parameters are set as follows: the maximum iteration number is 100, and the starting point and ending point of the intelligent wheelchair robot are [40, 60] and [360, 360]. The generation path of intelligent wheelchair after multi-objective optimization is shown in Fig. 6 below.

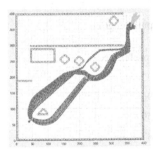

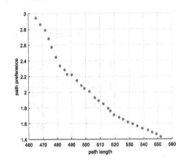

Fig. 6. Simulation results after optimization   **Fig. 7.** Objective function

The results of multi-objective optimization are shown in Fig. 7, which is a set of optimal solutions corresponding to the objective function of path length and path preference, also known as Pareto frontier [15]. It can be seen from Fig. 7 that the changing trend of the optimal solution set is that the reciprocal of path preference decreases with the increase of path length, that is to say, the longer the path length, the greater the path preference (user preference).

Six optimal solutions are randomly selected from the optimal solution set in Fig. 7. The six paths generated by the six optimal solutions are shown in Fig. 8. The path length and objective function of path preference corresponding to the six optimal solutions are shown in Table 2. Figure 4 shows the simulation results without multi-objective optimization, and Fig. 8 shows the simulation results after multi-objective optimization. By comparing Fig. 4 and Fig. 8, it can be seen that the two objective functions of path length and path preference in Fig. 8 have been optimized. Next, by comparing the objective function in Table 1 and Table 2, it can be concluded in more detail that in Table 1, the objective optimization of path length and path preference often exists in the optimization of path length, and the path preference cannot be taken into account. When optimizing the path preference, the path length cannot be taken into account. There is a contradiction between the two objective functions. The objective function in Table 2 is a set of optimal solutions, which is a set of compromise solutions that can well balance the conflicts between path preference and path length. This set of solutions can realize the optimization of intelligent wheelchair path with both user preference and path length taken into account.

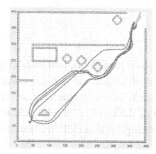

Fig. 8. Simulation results after optimization

Table 2. User preference and path length

Path	Path length	Path preference
Path1	464.03	0.3397
Path2	468.31	0.3496
Path3	494.77	0.4659
Path4	499.08	0.4887
Path5	506.27	0.5191
Path6	516.10	0.5581

5   Conclusion

This study proposes a multi-objective optimization method for intelligent wheelchair path length considering user preference. MOPSO was used for path length and preference multi-objective optimization. Table 1 shows the objective function data without multi-objective optimization. By comparing the objective functions in Table 1 and Table 2, it can be concluded that there are contradictions between the two objective functions in Table 1, and there are conflicts between path length and path preference. It only realizes the optimization of one of the two objective functions of path length and path preference. In Table 2, the objective function is a set of optimal solutions and a set of compromise solutions, which can well balance the conflict between path preference and path length. This set of solutions can realize the optimization of the intelligent wheelchair path with consideration of user preference and path length. The effectiveness of the method is proved. Finally, different simulation scenarios should be set up in the future research to prove that the algorithm has strong adaptability.

References

1. Li, G., Yamashita, A., Asama, H., et al.: An efficient improved artificial potential field based regression search method for robot path planning. In: IEEE International Conference on Mechatronics and Automation, pp. 1227–1232. IEEE (2012)
2. Fu, B., Chen, L., Zhou, Y., et al.: An improved A* algorithm for the industrial robot path planning with high success rate and short length. In: Robotics and Autonomous Systems. **106**, 26–37 (2018)
3. Fusic, S.J., Ramkumar, P., Hariharan, K.: Path planning of robot using modified dijkstra Algorithm. In: National Power Engineering Conference (NPEC), pp. 1–5 IEEE (2018)
4. Shiomi, M., Iio, T., Kamei, K., et al.: Effectiveness of social behaviors for autonomous wheelchair robot to support elderly people in Japan. Plos One **10**(5), e0128031 (2015)
5. Morales, Y., Kallakuri, N., Shinozawa, K., et al.: Human-comfortable navigation for an autonomousrobotic wheelchair. In: International Conference on Intelligent Robots and Systems, pp. 2737–2743 (2013)
6. Morales, Y., Miyashita, T., Hagita, N.: Social robotic wheelchair centered on passenger and pedestrian comfort. Robot. Autonomous Syst. **87**, 355–362 (2017)
7. Young, K.-Y., Cheng, S.-L., Ko, C.-H., Tsou, H.-W.: Development of a comfort-based motion guidance system for a robot walking helper. J. Intell. Rob. Syst. **100**(2), 379–388 (2020). https://doi.org/10.1007/s10846-020-01168-2
8. Li, Y., Sun, Z., Sun, B., et al.: Path preference recognition for intelligent robotic wheelchair based on evidence network. In: IEEE International Conference on Intelligence and Safety for Robotics (ISR). pp. 204–209. IEEE (2018)
9. Liu, X., Zhang, D., Zhang, T., Cui, Y., Chen, L., Liu, S.: Novel best path selection approach based on hybrid improved A* algorithm and reinforcement learning. Appl. Intell. **51**(12), 9015–9029 (2021). https://doi.org/10.1007/s10489-021-02303-8
10. Orozco-Rosas, U., Montiel, O., Sepúlveda, R.: Mobile robot path planning using membrane evolutionary artificial potential field. Appl. Soft Comput. **77**, 236–251 (2019)
11. Sang, H., You, Y., Sun, X., et al.: The hybrid path planning algorithm based on improved A* and artificial potential field for unmanned surface vehicle formations. In: Ocean Engineering, vol. 233 (2021)
12. Xu, H., Smets, P.: Reasoning in evidential networks with conditional belief functions. Int. J. Approximate Reasoning **14**(2–3), 155–185 (1996)
13. Gao, J., Du, H., et al.: Obstacle's shape recognition based on ultrasonic ranging. J. Beijing Sci. Technol. Univ. **24**(04),16–20 (2009)
14. Coello, C.A.C., Pulido, G.T., Lechuga, M.S.: Handling multiple objectives with particle swarm optimization. IEEE Trans. Evol. Comput. **8**(3), 256–279 (2004)
15. Vigliassi, M.P., Massignan, J.A.D., Delbem, A.C.B., et al.: Multi-objective evolutionary algorithm in tables for placement of SCADA and PMU considering the concept of Pareto Frontier. Int. J. Electr. Power Energy Syst. **106**, 373–382 (2019)

Motion Control and Interactive Technology for Mobile Robots

What and Where to See: Deep Attention Aggregation Network for Action Detection

Yuxuan He⬤, Ming-Gang Gan(✉), and Xiaozhou Liu⬤

State Key Laboratory of Intelligent Control and Decision of Complex Systems,
School of Automation, Beijing Institute of Technology,
Beijing 100081, People's Republic of China
aganbit@126.com

Abstract. With the development of deep convolutional neural networks, 2D CNN is widely used in action detection task. Although 2D CNN extracts rich features from video frames, these features also contain redundant information. In response to this problem, we propose Residual Channel-Spatial Attention module (RCSA) to guide the network what (object patterns) and where (spatially) need to be focused. Meanwhile, in order to effectively utilize the rich spatial and semantic features extracted by different layers of deep networks, we combine RCSA and deep aggregation network to propose Deep Attention Aggregation Network. Experiment resultes on two datasets J-HMDB and UCF-101 show that the proposed network achieves state-of-the-art performances on action detection.

Keywords: Action detection · Residual channel-spatial attention · Feature aggregation · Deep neural network

1 Introduction

Human action detection is one of the most active research topics due to its wide applications to video surveillance, robot vision [1, 2, 7–11], human computer interaction, etc. The main goal of detecting human actions is automatically predicting the start, end and spatial extent of various actions by predicting sets of linked detection windows in time (called tubes) where each action is enclosed.

Most of the action detection methods are based on image object detection methods - using a 2D CNN as the backbone to extract features and then feed these features into an anchor-based or anchor-free detector to locate and classify actions [13, 14]. In order to correctly classify and locate actions accurately at the same time, researchers have proposed some network architectures that combine low/mid-level features and high-level features [20]. F. Yu [20] combined the ideas of deeper and wider of neural network architecture by iterative deep aggregation and hierarchical deep aggregation. However, these features also contain a large amount of redundant information, which makes action detection more difficult. How to select the indicative information for action detection from the rich information has become a challenging problem.

Y. He and X. Liu—Contributing author(s).

© The Author(s), under exclusive license to Springer Nature Switzerland AG 2022
H. Liu et al. (Eds.): ICIRA 2022, LNAI 13455, pp. 177–187, 2022.
https://doi.org/10.1007/978-3-031-13844-7_18

In this paper, we propose a lightweight residual channel-spatial attention module ($RCSA$) that captures channel-spatial attention. In order to comprehensively use spatial information and semantic information to improve the network's action localizing and classification performance, we also propose Deep Aggregation Attention Network ($DAAN$) by combing RCSA and deep aggregation network.

Our main contributions are: (1) The proposal of RCSA. Attention is constructed in the channel dimension and the spatial dimension with the spatial attention branch does not add any additional parameters, which reduce the amount of training parameters; (2) The proposal of DAAN, in which low/mid-level features and high-level features are aggregated layer by layer and combined with RCSA to automatically select the required information from the rich feature maps; (3) Comparison experiments and ablation study have been conducted on J-HMDB [4] and UCF-101 [15] datasets. To the best of our knowledge, the results show that the proposed network achieves state-of-the-art performances.

2   Related Work

2.1   Attention in Computer Vision

The attention mechanism was first proposed in the field of Natural Language Processing and achieved outstanding results. With the rise of computer vision research, visual attention has also been extensively studied in recent years [3, 16, 18]. J. Hu [3] proposed the Squeeze-and-Excitation structure, which provided an effective feature dimension decomposition method for processing multi-dimensional feature tensors in visual attention. CBAM [18] is a continuation of SENet. However, the channel-wise attention plays the main role in CBAM and the contribution of spatial-wise attention to the network is very small. NonLocal [16] is based on the self-attention mechanism and uses the similarity between position pairwise information as the spatial position weight. However, the NonLocal module needs to map the input features through multiple convolutional layers or fully connected layers, which causes an increase in the amount of training parameters and the cost of computing resources. We propose to use the trilinear operation without additional learnable parameters to calculate the spatial attention weights, which achieves better performance while the training time is less than the NonLocal block. Then we combine it with the channel-wise attention to filter the feature maps channelly and spatially.

2.2   Action Detection

The purpose of video action detection technology is to locate and classify the actions that appear in the video. More recently researchers have combined the features extracted by the 3D network and the 2D network [17, 19], then feed these fusion features to detectors. However, these methods need to train both 3D and 2D CNN in the end-to-end training, which requires a large number of training samples and computing resources. Therefore, we choose 2D CNN as the backbone and improve the relevance of the extracted features to the action detection task by soft attention. The high-level features of deep convolutional networks contain rich semantic information, which is indicative of action recognition. However, a point in the low-resolution high-level feature maps a large area in the high-resolution low/mid-level feature. Only using the low-resolution high-level feature to locate the action area will cause a greater shift. Therefore, we propose DAAN that combines low/mid-level features with high-level features and integrate it with the proposed residual attention module RCSA which strengthens the indicative information for action detection from the rich fusion features. The experimental results on the two datasets show that our proposed DAAN has outstanding performance in action detection.

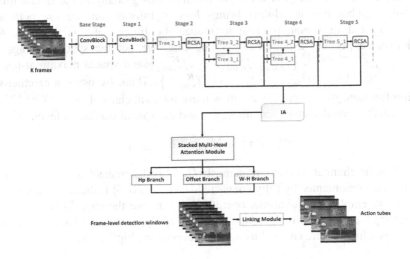

Fig. 1. The overview of the proposed Deep Attention Aggregation Network.

3 Method

We propose a novel Deep Attention Aggregation Network(DAAN) for action detection, using attention mechanism to modulate the features extracted from the input video and output spatial-temporal action tubes. We present the Residual Channel-Spatial Attention module to apply channel-wise attention and spaial-wise attention to the feature extractor. We follow the idea of iterative deep aggregation and hierarchical deep aggregation [20] to fuse the shallow layer features and deep layer features of deep convolutional networks. After features extracted, we conduct a three branches anchor-free detector and adopt the linking algorithm introduced by V. Kalogeiton [5]. The overview of our network is illustrated in Fig. 1.

3.1 Channel-wise Attention Module

Channel-wise attention module is aim to guide our model 'what' is notable. This module is based on an important assumption: each channel of a feature map can be considered as a feature detector and corresponds to a visual pattern. Given feature maps

$F \in \mathbb{R}^{C \times H \times W}$ of length K as input, denoted as $\{f_1, f_2, \cdots, f_k\}$, where C represents the number of channels, H and W are the height and width of the features maps. In the most deep convolutional networks used as feature extractor, all the channels are equivalent and can get equal attention. But we argue that not all features are useful. Some channels do not pay attention to features that are conducive to action detection so these channels should be suppressed and those channels that are conducive to action detection should be enhanced.

Therefore, we propose a channel-wise attention module to enhance channels that are beneficial to action detection and suppress feature channels that are useless for action detection. First, we pool the input feature maps globally in the spatial dimension. Since global pooling always brings loss of information, we use both average pooling and maximum pooling to reduce the impact of this problem. After global average pooling and global max pooling, we get the spatial average features $F_{s,avg} \in \mathbb{R}^{C \times 1 \times 1}$, $\{f_{s,avg}^1, f_{s,avg}^2, \cdots, f_{s,avg}^K\}$ and spatial maximum features $F_{s,max} \in \mathbb{R}^{C \times 1 \times 1}$, $\{f_{s,max}^1, f_{s,max}^2, \cdots, f_{s,max}^K\}$. Then, by using a channel-wise attention function, we can get the attention mask for each channel $w_{c,i} \in \mathbb{R}^{C \times 1 \times 1}, i \in [1, C]$ from the spatial average feature $F_{s,avg}$ and the spatial maximum feature $F_{s,max}$,

$$W_c = \sigma \left(G_c \left(F_{s,avg}, F_{s,max} \right) \right) \tag{1}$$

where W_c is the channel-wise attention mask, $G_c(\cdot)$ is the channel-wise attention function which is implemented by fully connected layers and $\sigma(\cdot)$ is the sigmoid activation function. We employ convolutional operation to generate the channel-wise attention. After getting the channel-wise attention mask, we apply each channel attention mask to the corresponding feature channel using channel-wise multiplication,

$$F_c' = W_c \odot F = \sigma \left(G_c \left(SGAP \left(F \right), SGMP \left(F \right) \right) \right) \odot F \tag{2}$$

where $F_c' \in \mathbb{R}^{C \times H \times W}$ represents the channel-wise attention enhancement feature maps, W_c is the channel-wise attention masks, F is input feature maps and $\odot$ means channel-wise multiplication.

3.2   Spatial-wise Attention Module

Different from the channel-wise attention module, the purpose of the spatial-wise module is to guide the network "where" is worth paying attention to. We follow the idea of self-attention mechanism and use the method of self-attention to capture the long-distance dependence between spatial positions. Inspired by H. Zheng [22], we propose a lightweight three-branch spatial-wise attention module, including query branch, key branch and value branch. Therefore, in the self-attention method, for the input x_i of any position, the response of that position depends on the global area information. Compared with the convolution operation, the self-attention operation can better capture the long-distance dependence of the spatial dimension in the input visual information.

As shown in Fig. 2, given stacked feature maps $F \in \mathbb{R}^{C \times H \times W}$ of length K as input, denoted as $\{f_1, f_2, \cdots, f_k\}$. To model the spatial dependencies $c(x_i, x_j)$, we use global spatial information at each position j, $j = \{1, 2, \cdots, HW\}$.

$$\sum_{i=1}^{HW} \sum_{j=1}^{HW} c(x_i, x_j) = softmax(F_r \times scale) \times F_r^T \qquad (3)$$

We first reshape the input feature map in the spatial dimension to obtain the feature map $F_r \in \mathbb{R}^{HW \times C}$. After F_r is multiplied by a scale value, we use the softmax function to regularize F_r in the space dimension, which is used as a query. Then use F_r as the key and value. After the query and the key are multiplied, the softmax function is used to regularize the spatial dimension to obtain the spatial-wise attention mask. Then, the spatial-wise attention mask is multiplied by the F_r and reshaped as $C \times H \times W$, and the feature map of spatial attention modulation is obtained.

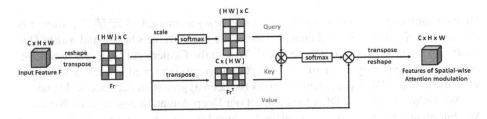

Fig. 2. The details of spatial-wise attention module. The spatial-wise attention module constructed by three branches: query branch, key branch and value branch. ⊛ means matrix multiplication. ⊗ is element-wise multiplication.

3.3 Residual Channel-Spatial Attention Module

Considering the relationship between channel-wise attention and spatial-wise attention, we construct three different types of residual channel-spatial attention modules, respectively placing channel-wise attention module and spatial-wise attention module in sequential or parallel. The input feature maps first pass through channel-wise attention module and spatial-wise attention module to get channel-wise attention mask and spatial-wise attention mask respectively, and then the two attention masks are merged to obtain channel-spatial attention-modulated feature maps F'_{cs},

$$F'_{cs} = \alpha * M_s(F) + \beta * M_c(F) \qquad (4)$$

where F'_{cs} represents channel-spatial attention-modulated feature maps, M_s is spatial-wise attention module, M_c is channel-wise attention module, F is input feature maps, α and β are two weight parameters that can be learned. The channel-wise attention module M_c and the spatial-wise attention module M_s are as described in Sect. 3.1, 3.2.

There are two different arrangements for sequential channel-spatial attention module: channel-spatial module and spatial-channel module. The input feature maps first pass through channel attention module to obtain feature maps with enhanced channel attention, and then pass through spatial attention module to obtain feature maps with enhanced channel-spatial attention F'_{cs}, or reverse the order. Note that many of the values in the features after attention mask processing often approach zero. These stacked processed features can make back propagation difficult. In order to solve this problem, we propose the Residual Channel-Spatial Attention module, as shown in equation below.

$$F_{cs}^{''} = F + \gamma * M_s\left(M_c\left(F\right)\right) \tag{5}$$

where $F_{cs}^{''}$ is output feature maps of the Residual Channel-Spatial Attention module, F is input feature maps of the Residual Channel-Spatial Attention module, M_{cs} is the Residual Channel-Spatial Attention module and γ is a learnable parameters. In this way, through this residual connection, the original information of the input feature F is preserved.

3.4   Deep Attention Aggregation Network

Given a short clip of K video frames $\{v_1, v_2, \cdots v_K\}$ as input, $v \in \mathbb{R}^{c \times h \times w}$, where c is the number of video frame's channels, h and w are video frame's height and width. This short clip of video frames is denoted as V. We use the CenterNet [23] as the backbone. After comprehensively evaluating the effect and processing speed of each architecture, we choose to use DLA [20] architecture as the deep aggregation network backbone.

We follow the idea of DLA to construct our Deep Attention Aggregation Network. We integrate IDA with HDA to construct a deep layer aggregation structure to better fuse shallow stage expression with deep stage representations. Then, we combine the channel-spatial attention with the deep layer aggregation structure, from the bottom to the top level to enhance the features layer by layer using attention masks. We apply Residual Channel-Spatial Attention module to each stage of aggregation node, so that the attention modulated features can be fused stage by stage through HDA and iteratively improved through IDA while focusing on favorable feature channels and spatial positions in a learning manner. The overview of Deep Attention Aggregation Network is shown in Fig. 1.

Inspired by MOC [12], we propose a three-branch action detector, which contains Heat point Branch($Hp\ Branch$), Offset Branch and Width-Height Branch ($W - H\ Branch$). Hp Branch locates the center of the action region from the feature map of the key frame and predicts the action specific score of this tubelet. The resolution of the feature map input to the detector has been greatly compressed, so the location of the heat point on the feature map will cause errors compared with the groundtruth on the original image. To address this issue, Offset Branch will predict the offsets of the heat point on original frames. W-H Branch regresses the width and height of the bounding box based on the heat point on each frame.

4   Experiments

4.1   Datasets and Evaluation Metrics

J-HMDB. JHMDB is a subset of the HMDB51 dataset which is a action recognition benchmark with 51 action classes. JHMDB contains 928 trimmed videos from 21 action classes from our daily life, including kick ball and swing baseball. For the video are trimmed, the challenge on this dataset focus on the action recognition and spatial detection. We report results averaged on the three splits following [5].

UCF101-24. The UCF101-24 dataset is a subset of larger UCF101 action classification dataset and contains spatio-temporal action instance annotations for 3207 videos from 24 sports classes. Because of these spatial-untrimmed and temporal-untrimmed videos, the dataset is more challenging for action detection. Following [5], we report the performance for the first split only.

Implementation Details. We implement our model in Pytorch. During training, we train our network using a batch size of 12 videos for 25 epochs on JHMDB and 40 videos for 12 epochs on UCF101-24 using Adam optimizer. We set the initial learning rate to 0.0003 on JHMDB, whereas 0.0005 on UCF101-24. The learning rate is reduced by a factor of 10 when the performance of the model no longer improves on the validation set. The input clip length is set to $K = 7$ and the frame is resized to 288×288.

Evaluation Metrics. We report the frame-level Average-Precision, frame-mAP, and the video-level Average-Precision, video-mAP, on the two datasets. Frame-mAP measures the area under the precision-recall curve of each frame and video-mAP measures the area under the precision-recall curve of the action tubes predictions. We set the threshold of the intersection-over-union(IoU) to 0.5 for frame-mAP. For video-mAP, we set various threshold of the IoU to 0.2, 0.5 and 0.75. We also report average results over multiple IoU thresholds with the protocol 0.5:0.95.

4.2 Comparison with State-of-the-Arts

We compare our network Residual Deep Attention Aggregation Network with existing state-of-the-art action detection methods on the datasets JHMDB and UCF101.

Through the experimental results shown in the Table 1, our DAAN has achieved outstanding results in frame-level and video-level detection on both JHMDB and UCF101 compared with those frame-level methods which apply action detector on each frame without considering temporal context. Moreover, our method has comparable performance to those 3D methods [6,17]. Compared with ACT [5] and Two-in-one [21], which proposed for action detection task, our DAAN also achieves better results in the video-level action detection. In particular, our DAAN compares the outperform results obtained by MOC [12] in frame-level and video-level action detection, which shows that DAAN not only improves the ability of the network to locate the action area, but also improves the accuracy of the network's recognition of actions through the attention mechanism. Compared with the 21M learnable parameters of MOC, our network only improves the number of parameters by 0.3%. The video-level performance of our method on the UCF101 dataset does not exceed the MOC when the IoU is 0.75. We argue that this is because videos in UCF101 dataset is longer and temporal-untrimmed. The ACT detection window linking algorithm we use smoothes the temporal dimension after linking the detection windows, which averages the coordinates of the detection windows of the adjacent frames as new detection windows for linking. Our method generates attention maps based on the information of each video frame and lack of

Table 1. Comparison with the state-of-the-art methods on JHMDB dataset by frame-mAP and video-mAP with various IoU threhold.

Method	JHMDB					UCF101-24				
	Frame-mAP	Video-mAP				Frame-mAP	Video-mAP			
	0.5	0.2	0.5	0.75	0.5:0.95	0.5	0.2	0.5	0.75	0.5:0.95
2D Methods										
ROAD	–	73.8	72.0	44.5	41.6	–	73.5	46.3	15.0	20.4
ACT	65.7	74.2	73.7	52.1	44.8	69.5	76.5	49.2	19.7	23.4
Two-in-one	–	–	74.7	53.3	45.0	–	78.5	50.3	22.2	24.5
MOC	70.8	77.3	77.2	71.7	59.1	78.0	82.8	53.8	**29.6**	28.3
DAAN	**71.3**	**78.8**	**78.5**	**73.7**	**59.7**	**80.0**	**84.1**	**54.4**	29.1	**28.9**
3D Methods										
C3D	–	–	–	–	–	41.4	47.1	–	–	–
I3D	73.3	–	**78.6**	–	–	76.3	–	**59.9**	–	–

temporal information from adjacent frames. After smoothing, the action tubes are off-set, which leads to a decrease in the performance of the model. How to modulate the attention maps from the temporal dimension is our future work.

4.3 Ablation Study

In this subsection, we carried out experimental analysis on the effectiveness of channel attention module and spatial attention module, the arrangement of attention modules, and the effectiveness of deep attention aggregation network architecture. For efficient exploration, we only conduct experiments on the first split of JHMDB dataset.

Experiment results are shown in Fig. 3, in which we compare eight different attention module by its video-mAP results. In Fig. 3, 'DAAN+RCSA' is the methods Deep Attention Aggregation Netowrk with residual sequential channel-spatial attention module, 'Spatial-wise attention only' and 'Channel-wise attention only' are only employ spatial-wise attention module and channel-wise attention module, 'Channel + SpatialConv' is the method of combining channel-wise attention module and two sequential convolution layers with kernel size of 3×3 as the spatial attention module, 'DAAN+CBAM' and 'DAAN+NonLocal' are methods which replace RCSA with CBAM module and NonLocal module, 'Parallel C-S' is the method which place channel-wise attention and spatial-wise attention module in a parallel way, 'Sequential S-C' is the method with sequential spatial-channel attention module. From the Fig. 3 we can see that the DAAN with RCSA has achieved the best results. The experiment results indicate that the combination of channel-wise attention and spatial-wise attention can achieve better results than using channel-wise attention or spatial-wise attention alone. Channel-wise attention focus on the semantic information in features and ignore appearance information, while spatial-wise attention focus on appearance information and ignore semantic information. The comparison with the results of 'Channel+SpatialConv' shows that the method based on self-attention is better than the traditional convolutional layer to generate spatial-wise attention mask. We argue that the

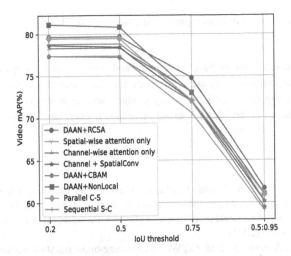

Fig. 3. Ablation study of different attention module

receptive field of the response of each spatial position in the traditional convolutional layer is only the surrounding regions and the size of receptive field is limited. The self-attention-based method measures the relationship between each spatial position and all other spatial positions. Therefore, the receptive field is expanded from the local area to the global area, which better measure spatial importance of each position to get the spatial attention mask.

As shown in Fig. 3, it can be seen that the effect of sequential channel-spatial module is better than sequential spatial-channel module and parallel channel-spatial module. We argue that sequential spatial-channel module modulates feature maps in the spatial dimension first so the features in each channel has changed. Then channel-wise attention module generates channel-wise attention mask through spatial maximum pooling and average pooling based on the spatial-wise modulated feature maps. If the features in each channel has changed, the channel weight vector will also be affected.

5 Conclusion

In this paper, we propose the Deep Attention Aggregation Network for action detection, which utilizes attention mechanism to adaptively modulate the features of each layer of the deep convolutional network. The framework fuses the shallow and deep presentations of the network to provide rich and effective feature representation. In particular, we introduce a residual channel-spatial attention module which generates attention mask on the dimensions of channel and space to make the network focus on the action area and recognize the action effectively. Experiments are conducted on two action detection benchmarks: J-HMDB and UCF-101. Our method shows outstanding performance on both datasets compared with other existing methods. In addition, time dimension information is significant for action detection and recognition. Our future work is exploring the attention on time dimension, improving network performance through temporal attention reference.

Acknowledgments. This work is supposed by the National Key R&D Program of China under Grant 2020YFB1708500

Declarations. We declare that we have no financial and personal relationships with other people or organizations that can inappropriately influence our work, there is no professional or other personal interest of any nature or kind in any product, service and/or company that could be construed as influencing the position presented in, or the review of, the manuscript entitled.

References

1. Chen, Z., Li, J., Wang, S., Wang, J., Ma, L.: Flexible gait transition for six wheel-legged robot with unstructured terrains. Robot. Auton. Syst. **150**, 103989 (2022)
2. Chen, Z., et al.: Control strategy of stable walking for a hexapod wheel-legged robot. ISA Trans. **108**, 367–380 (2021)
3. Hu, J., Shen, L., Albanie, S., Sun, G., Wu, E.: Squeeze-and-excitation networks. IEEE Trans. Pattern Anal. Mach. Intell. PP(99) (2017)
4. Jhuang, H., Gall, J., Zuffi, S., Schmid, C., Black, M.J.: Towards understanding action recognition. In: IEEE International Conference on Computer Vision (2014)
5. Kalogeiton, V., Weinzaepfel, P., Ferrari, V., Schmid, C.: Action tubelet detector for spatiotemporal action localization. In: IEEE International Conference on Computer Vision, ICCV 2017, Venice, Italy, October 22–29, 2017, pp. 4415–4423 (2017). https://doi.org/10.1109/ICCV.2017.472
6. Köpüklü, O., Wei, X., Rigoll, G.: You only watch once: a unified CNN architecture for real-time spatiotemporal action localization. CoRR abs/1911.06644 (2019)
7. Li, J., Wang, J., Peng, H., Hu, Y., Su, H.: Fuzzy-torque approximation-enhanced sliding mode control for lateral stability of mobile robot. IEEE Trans. Syst. Man Cybern. Syst. **52**(4), 2491–2500 (2022). https://doi.org/10.1109/TSMC.2021.3050616
8. Li, J., Wang, J., Peng, H., Zhang, L., Hu, Y., Su, H.: Neural fuzzy approximation enhanced autonomous tracking control of the wheel-legged robot under uncertain physical interaction. Neurocomputing **410**, 342–353 (2020)
9. Li, J., Wang, J., Wang, S., Yang, C.: Human-robot skill transmission for mobile robot via learning by demonstration. Neural Computing and Applications pp. 1–11 (2021). https://doi.org/10.1007/s00521-021-06449-x
10. Li, J., Qin, H., Wang, J., Li, J.: Openstreetmap-based autonomous navigation for the four wheel-legged robot via 3D-lidar and CCD camera. IEEE Trans. Industr. Electron. **69**(3), 2708–2717 (2022). https://doi.org/10.1109/TIE.2021.3070508
11. Li, J., Zhang, X., Li, J., Liu, Y., Wang, J.: Building and optimization of 3d semantic map based on lidar and camera fusion. Neurocomputing **409**, 394–407 (2020)
12. Li, Y., Wang, Z., Wang, L., Wu, G.: Actions as moving points. In: Vedaldi, A., Bischof, H., Brox, T., Frahm, J.-M. (eds.) ECCV 2020. LNCS, vol. 12361, pp. 68–84. Springer, Cham (2020). https://doi.org/10.1007/978-3-030-58517-4_5
13. Peng, X., Schmid, C.: Multi-region two-stream R-CNN for action detection. In: Leibe, B., Matas, J., Sebe, N., Welling, M. (eds.) ECCV 2016. LNCS, vol. 9908, pp. 744–759. Springer, Cham (2016). https://doi.org/10.1007/978-3-319-46493-0_45
14. Saha, S., Singh, G., Sapienza, M., Torr, P.H.S., Cuzzolin, F.: Deep learning for detecting multiple space-time action tubes in videos. In: Wilson, R.C., Hancock, E.R., Smith, W.A.P. (eds.) Proceedings of the British Machine Vision Conference 2016, BMVC 2016, York, UK, 19–22 September 2016 (2016)

15. Soomro, K., Zamir, A.R., Shah, M.: Ucf101: a dataset of 101 human actions classes from videos in the wild. Comput. Ence (2012)
16. Wang, X., Girshick, R.B., Gupta, A., He, K.: Non-local neural networks. In: 2018 IEEE Conference on Computer Vision and Pattern Recognition, CVPR 2018, Salt Lake City, UT, USA, 18–22 June 2018, pp. 7794–7803 (2018). https://doi.org/10.1109/CVPR.2018.00813
17. Wei, J., Wang, H., Yi, Y., Li, Q., Huang, D.: P3d-CTN: pseudo-3D convolutional tube network for spatio-temporal action detection in videos. In: 2019 IEEE International Conference on Image Processing (ICIP) (2019)
18. Woo, S., Park, J., Lee, J.-Y., Kweon, I.S.: CBAM: convolutional block attention module. In: Ferrari, V., Hebert, M., Sminchisescu, C., Weiss, Y. (eds.) ECCV 2018. LNCS, vol. 11211, pp. 3–19. Springer, Cham (2018). https://doi.org/10.1007/978-3-030-01234-2_1
19. Yang, X., Yang, X., Liu, M., Xiao, F., Davis, L.S., Kautz, J.: STEP: spatio-temporal progressive learning for video action detection. In: IEEE Conference on Computer Vision and Pattern Recognition, CVPR 2019, Long Beach, CA, USA, June 16–20, 2019. pp. 264–272 (2019). https://doi.org/10.1109/CVPR.2019.00035
20. Yu, F., Wang, D., Shelhamer, E., Darrell, T.: Deep layer aggregation. In: 2018 IEEE/CVF Conference on Computer Vision and Pattern Recognition (CVPR) (2018)
21. Zhao, J., Snoek, C.G.M.: Dance with flow: two-in-one stream action detection. In: 2019 IEEE/CVF Conference on Computer Vision and Pattern Recognition (CVPR) (2020)
22. Zheng, H., Fu, J., Zha, Z., Luo, J.: Looking for the devil in the details: learning trilinear attention sampling network for fine-grained image recognition. In: IEEE Conference on Computer Vision and Pattern Recognition, CVPR 2019, Long Beach, CA, USA, 16–20 June 2019, pp. 5012–5021 (2019). https://doi.org/10.1109/CVPR.2019.00515
23. Zhou, X., Wang, D., Krähenbühl, P.: Objects as points. CoRR abs/1904.07850 (2019)

Road Environment Perception for Unmanned Motion Platform Based on Binocular Vision

Xu Liu, Junzheng Wang[(⊠)], and Jiehao Li

State Key Laboratory of Intelligent Control and Decision of Complex Systems,
School of Automation, Beijing Institute of Technology, Beijing 100081, China
wangjz@bit.edu.cn

Abstract. In order to enable the unmanned motion platform to obtain
real-time environmental semantic information and obstacle depth information, a real-time semantic segmentation and feature point matching
based on binocular cameras are considered. This method firstly takes
advantages of a real-time semantic segmentation network to obtain the
road scene information and the region of obstacles on the road such
as vehicles or pedestrians. Then, feature matching is performed on the
region of interest (ROI) of left and right views. In the experiment part,
firstly we conduct simulation verification on the KITTI dataset, and then
we conduct binocular camera calibration, rectification, segmentation and
stereo matching based on Oriented FAST and Rotated BRIEF (ORB)
method on the actual system. The experiment results proves that the
method is real-time and robust.

Keywords: Semantic segmentation · Binocular vision · Stereo
matching · Unmanned motion platform · Road environment perception

1 Introduction

The three key technologies common to autonomous driving and robots are environment perception, decision planning and executive control [8,10,11,13,24].
Among them, environment perception is a prerequisite for robots to be able to
make decisions, plan and execute control, and largely determines the effect of
robots in practical applications [2,3,9,12,14,21,23]. Improving the robot's ability to perceive the target and the environment has always been a hot topic in
robotics and artificial intelligence.

To make robots more intelligent, it is crucial to obtain both semantic information and depth information at the same time. With the development of neural
network technology and the improvement of computer performance, semantic
segmentation technology can be deployed on mobile robots. In 2014, FCN [17]
appeared for the first time to talk about the application of convolutional network
to semantic segmentation. Inspired by this, many classic networks like PSPNet
[27] sprung up like mushrooms. Later, in order to apply it to mobile robots,

H. Liu et al. (Eds.): ICIRA 2022, LNAI 13455, pp. 188–199, 2022.
https://doi.org/10.1007/978-3-031-13844-7_19

researchers did not blindly pursue the accuracy rate, but reduced the network model to improve the inference speed, and achieved a balance between accuracy and speed. In the field of real-time semantic segmentation, a series of excellent networks have emerged [4,5,15,16], such as ENet [20], SegNet [1], BiSeNet V2 [25] etc.

In order to enable the unmanned motion platform to obtain real-time environmental semantic information and obstacle depth information, we propose a method combining real-time semantic segmentation technology and feature point matching based on binocular cameras in this paper. The main contributions of our work can be listed as follows:

1) Sparse stereo matching is performed in the region of interest generated by the semantic segmentation network. This matching method is efficient, real-time, and robust.
2) The semantic information of the environment and the depth information of obstacles are fused and provided to the planning module of the unmanned motion platform at the same time.

The rest of the paper is organized as follows: Sect. 2 expounds the basic principles, as well as a brief introduction of key steps of binocular vision. Section 3 describes an architecture of real-time semantic segmentation network BiSeNet V2. Section 4 gives a description of experiments and the work is concluded in Sect. 5.

2   Binocular Stereo Vision

2.1   Principles of Stereo Vision

Binocular imaging is similar to human eyes. There is a difference between the images captured by the left and right cameras. This difference is inversely proportional to the distance of the object, so depth information can be perceived for the environment perception system. The binocular structure is usually divided into two types: parallel type and non-parallel type. The division is based on whether the main optical axes of the two cameras are parallel or not.

The parallel type is a binocular structure model established in an ideal situation. The model requires that the two cameras are exactly the same. In other words, the imaging planes of the two cameras are parallel and coplanar.

As shown in the Fig. 1(a), point $P(X, Y, Z)$ is a point in 3-dimensional space, and $P_l(x_l, y)$ and $P_r(x_l, y)$ are the projection points of point P on the left camera image plane and the right camera plane, respectively. According to the principle of triangular similarity, we can get:

$$\begin{cases} x_1 = f * \frac{X}{Z} \\ x_r = f * \frac{X-b}{Z} \\ y = b * \frac{Y}{7} \end{cases} \tag{1}$$

Let the disparity $d = x_r - x_l$, and after deformation, we can get:

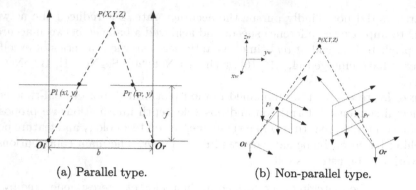

Fig. 1. The model of the binocular camera.

$$\begin{cases} X = b * \frac{x_l}{d} \\ Y = b * \frac{y}{d} \\ Z = b * \frac{f}{d} \end{cases} \tag{2}$$

The above formula shows that, given any point on the camera image plane, combined with the baseline length b, the camera focal length f and the disparity d, the three-dimensional coordinates corresponding to the point can be obtained. Furthermore, it can be seen that the depth is inversely proportional to the disparity. The baseline length b is the distance between cameras.

Since the parallel structure is an idealized model while it is more of a non-parallel binocular structure in practice. As shown in Fig. 1(b), there is a certain angle between the imaging planes of the two cameras in the non-parallel binocular structure, so the main optical axis is not parallel.

Let the coordinates of a point $P(x_w, y_w, z_w)$ in the world coordinate system be $P_{cl}(x_{cl}, y_{cl}, z_{cl})$ and $P_{cr}(x_{cr}, y_{cr}, z_{cr})$ in the left and right camera coordinate systems respectively, then there are:

$$\begin{bmatrix} x_{cr} \\ y_{cr} \\ z_{cr} \\ 1 \end{bmatrix} = \begin{bmatrix} R_r & T_r \\ 0 & 1 \end{bmatrix} \begin{bmatrix} x_w \\ y_w \\ z_w \\ 1 \end{bmatrix} \tag{3}$$

where R_r and T_r represent the rotation and translation matrices of the right camera respectively.

$$\begin{bmatrix} x_{cl} \\ y_{cl} \\ z_{cl} \\ 1 \end{bmatrix} = \begin{bmatrix} R_l & T_l \\ 0 & 1 \end{bmatrix} \begin{bmatrix} x_w \\ y_w \\ z_w \\ 1 \end{bmatrix} \tag{4}$$

where R_l and T_l represent the rotation and translation matrices of the left camera respectively.

By eliminating x_w, y_w and z_w from the two equations simultaneously, we can obtain:

$$\begin{bmatrix} x_{\mathrm{cl}} \\ y_{\mathrm{cl}} \\ z_{\mathrm{cl}} \\ 1 \end{bmatrix} = \begin{bmatrix} R_1 R_{\mathrm{r}}^{-1} T_1 - R_1 R_{\mathrm{r}}^{-1} T_{\mathrm{r}} \\ 0 \qquad\qquad 1 \end{bmatrix} \begin{bmatrix} x_{\mathrm{cr}} \\ y_{\mathrm{cr}} \\ z_{\mathrm{cr}} \\ 1 \end{bmatrix} \tag{5}$$

where

$$\begin{cases} R_{\mathrm{t}} = R_1 R_{\mathrm{r}}^{-1} \\ T_{\mathrm{t}} = T_1 - R_1 R_{\mathrm{r}}^{-1} T_{\mathrm{r}} \end{cases} \tag{6}$$

Then the positional relationship between the two cameras can be expressed as:

$$P_{\mathrm{cl}} = \begin{bmatrix} R_{\mathrm{t}} & T_{\mathrm{t}} \\ 0 & 1 \end{bmatrix} P_{\mathrm{cr}} \tag{7}$$

The transformation relationship between the coordinates of P in the right camera coordinate system and in the right camera coordinate system can be obtained. Now we set the left camera coordinate system as the world coordinate system for the sake of simplicity. Based on the above derivation, we can get that the point P in the right pixel image coordinate system can be expressed as:

$$Z_1 \begin{bmatrix} x_{\mathrm{r}} \\ y_{\mathrm{r}} \\ 1 \end{bmatrix} = \begin{bmatrix} f_{\mathrm{r}} & 0 & 0 & 0 \\ 0 & f_{\mathrm{r}} & 0 & 0 \\ 0 & 0 & 1 & 0 \end{bmatrix} \begin{bmatrix} R_{\mathrm{t}} & T_{\mathrm{t}} \\ 0 & 1 \end{bmatrix} \begin{bmatrix} X_1 \\ Y_1 \\ Z_1 \\ 1 \end{bmatrix} \tag{8}$$

where f_r represents the focal length of the right camera, (X_l, Y_l, Z_l) represents the coordinates of point P in the new world coordinate system, (x_r, y_r) represents the coordinates of P in the right pixel image coordinate system.

Let

$$\begin{bmatrix} R_{\mathrm{t}} & T_{\mathrm{t}} \\ 0 & 1 \end{bmatrix} = \begin{bmatrix} r_1 & r_2 & r_3 & t_{\mathrm{x}} \\ r_4 & r_5 & r_6 & t_{\mathrm{y}} \\ r_7 & r_8 & r_9 & t_{\mathrm{z}} \end{bmatrix} \tag{9}$$

We can get:

$$Z_1 \begin{bmatrix} x_{\mathrm{r}} \\ y_{\mathrm{r}} \\ 1 \end{bmatrix} = \begin{bmatrix} f_{\mathrm{r}} & 0 & 0 & 0 \\ 0 & f_{\mathrm{r}} & 0 & 0 \\ 0 & 0 & 1 & 0 \end{bmatrix} \begin{bmatrix} r_1 & r_2 & r_3 & t_{\mathrm{x}} \\ r_4 & r_5 & r_6 & t_{\mathrm{y}} \\ r_7 & r_8 & r_9 & t_{\mathrm{z}} \end{bmatrix} \begin{bmatrix} X_1 \\ Y_1 \\ Z_1 \\ 1 \end{bmatrix} \tag{10}$$

$$Z_1 \begin{bmatrix} x_{\mathrm{r}} \\ y_{\mathrm{r}} \\ 1 \end{bmatrix} = \begin{bmatrix} r_1 f_{\mathrm{r}} & r_2 f_{\mathrm{r}} & r_3 f_{\mathrm{r}} & t_{\mathrm{x}} f_{\mathrm{r}} \\ r_4 f_{\mathrm{r}} & r_5 f_{\mathrm{r}} & r_6 f_{\mathrm{r}} & t_{\mathrm{y}} f_{\mathrm{r}} \\ r_7 & r_8 & r_9 & t_{\mathrm{z}} \end{bmatrix} \begin{bmatrix} Z_1 * \frac{x_1}{f_1} \\ Z_1 * \frac{y}{f_1} \\ Z_1 \\ 1 \end{bmatrix} \tag{11}$$

In the formula above, f_l represents the focal length of the left camera, and (x_l, y_l) represents the coordinates of P in the left pixel image coordinate system.

According to formula (11), it can be solved to get the coordinates of P in the world coordinate system.

$$\begin{cases} X_1 = Z_1 * \frac{x_1}{f_1} \\ Y_1 = Z_1 * \frac{y_1}{f_1} \\ Z_1 = \frac{f_1(f_r t_x - x_r t_z)}{x_r(r_7 x_1 + r_7 x_1 + r_9 f_1) - f_r(r_1 x_1 + r_2 y_1 + r_3 f_1)} \end{cases} \tag{12}$$

2.2 Key Steps of Realizing a Binocular System

The measurement of depth information through the binocular system requires three steps: stereo calibration, stereo rectification, and stereo matching. The purpose of stereo calibration is to obtain the internal and external parameters of the two cameras, the stereo rectification is to obtain the left and right views aligned in parallel, and stereo matching is a key step to obtain the disparity map.

Camera Calibration. We can establish a transformation relationship between the coordinates (X, Y, Z) of point in the 3-dimensional space and the coordinates (u, v) of the corresponding point on the 2-dimensional image:

$$S \begin{bmatrix} u \\ v \\ 1 \end{bmatrix} = H \begin{bmatrix} X \\ Y \\ 1 \end{bmatrix} \tag{13}$$

Matrix H contains 8 unknowns. Combining with formula (13), it is known that when the coordinates of 4 points on the image are available and the corresponding 3-dimensional coordinates are solvable, we can solve the matrix H [26].

$$H = \begin{bmatrix} h_1 & h_2 & h_3 \end{bmatrix} = \lambda K \begin{bmatrix} r_a & r_b & t \end{bmatrix} \tag{14}$$

$$K = \begin{bmatrix} \alpha & \gamma & u_0 \\ 0 & \beta & v_0 \\ 0 & 0 & 1 \end{bmatrix} \tag{15}$$

where K is the camera internal parameter matrix, $\alpha = f/d_x$, $\beta = f/d_y$, γ is the deviation of the pixel on the x, y axis, h_1, h_2, h_3 are the column vectors of the matrix H, λ is the constant coefficient. From formula (14), we can get:

$$\begin{cases} r_a = \lambda K^{-1} h_1 \\ r_b = \lambda K^{-1} h_2 \\ t = \lambda K^{-1} h_3 \end{cases} \tag{16}$$

Since r_a and r_b are the rotation column vectors around the x and y axes respectively, it can be seen that r_a and r_b are orthogonal with the modulus of 1. Then there are the following constraints:

$$\begin{cases} r_a^T r_b = 0 \\ \|r_a\| = \|r_b\| = 1 \end{cases} \tag{17}$$

After collecting 10 photos of the calibration plate at different angles, the internal parameter matrix can be obtained by using the constraint condition (17). Combined with the matrix H, the rotation matrix R and the translation matrix T can be obtained.

Lens distortion factor is not taken into account. After solving the ideal parameters according to the above steps, it is necessary to optimize the distortion taking into account the final calibration result. For the influence of the camera distortion, the maximum likelihood estimation is used to optimize the parameters.

After calibrating the left and right cameras respectively, we will get the respective rigid body transformation matrices of the left and right cameras: R_l, T_l, R_r, T_r. Then R_t, T_t of the right camera relative to the left camera can be obtained through formula (18).

$$\begin{cases} R_\mathrm{t} = R_1 R_\mathrm{r}^{-1} \\ T_\mathrm{t} = T_1 - R_1 R_\mathrm{r}^{-1} T_\mathrm{r} \end{cases} \tag{18}$$

Stereo Rectification. In non-ideal cases, the binocular stereo vision model is a non-parallel structure. So the left and right planes are not parallel and line-aligned. In order to calculate the disparity of each point, it is necessary to convert the left and right planes into parallel and line-aligned. Of course, before performing stereo correction, two images need to be corrected. The correction is to eliminate the influence of tangential distortion and radial distortion on the images.

Stereo Match. Stereo matching is the core link of stereo binocular vision. Stereo matching contains feature matching and dense matching. Feature matching has high speed, high efficiency, high precision, and is not sensitive to lighting changes. The disadvantage is that reconstruction requires fitting. The advantage of dense matching is that reconstruction does not require fitting, but it is slow, inefficient, and greatly affected by illumination [7].

3   Real-time Semantic Segmentation Network

Semantic segmentation technology can help the unmanned platform distinguish the surrounding environment such as road areas, pedestrians, and vehicles at the pixel level. There are certain requirements for accuracy and speed, so we select the real-time semantic segmentation network BiSeNet V2 with excellent performance recently to detect the surrounding environment. Specifically, for a 2048×1024 input, BiSeNet V2 achieves an average IoU of 72.6% on the Cityscapes test set, at 156 FPS on an NVIDIA GeForce GTX 1080 Ti card.

Different from the two structures of dilation backbone and Encoder-Decoder backbone, BiSeNet V2 proposes a two-pathway architecture as shown in Fig. 2. This structure not only avoids the time-consuming heavy computation complexity and memory footprint but also consumes less memory access cost with few

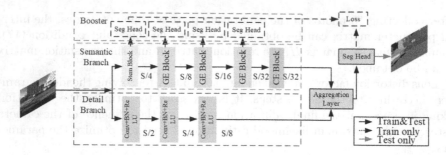

Fig. 2. BiSeNet V2 network structure.

connections shortcoming. To achieve high accuracy and high efficiency. Both of the low-level details and high-level semantics are taken into consideration. One pathway called Detail Branch is designed to capture the spatial details with wide channels and shallow layers. The other pathway called Semantic Branch with narrow channels and deep layers to capture high-level semantics context.

4   Experiment Results

4.1   Experiments on the KITTI Dataset

The stereo 2015 benchmark in the KITTI vision benchmark suite consists of 200 training scenes and 200 test scenes [19]. For the 200 training scenes, we can utilize a pair of stereo-rectified left and right views and a disparity map obtained by 3D-Lidar. The scenes have the same type of semantic labels as Cityscapes. In our experiments, the semantic segmentation network is first pretrained on the Cityscapes dataset and then trained on the KITTI dataset.

Figure 3 shows the key steps of our algorithm. Firstly, Fig. 3(a) is input to the trained network to obtain the segmentation results shown in Fig. 3(b). It can be seen that areas such as roads, cars, and trees are well divided. Then, according to the segmentation results, we extract the obstacle on the road as the region of interest. With the regions of interest of the left and right views gained, we perform ORB [22] feature matching. The matching results are shown in Fig. 3(c). The semantic information and depth information obtained from this are fed back to the decision-making planning system to realize the road environment perception system of the unmanned platform. According to the description in the literature [22,25], our proposed algorithm is able to process road environment information in real time.

Accuracy Evaluation Experiment. According to the obtained matching point coordinates, we search for the true value on the disparity map obtained by the 3D-Lidar to evaluate the accuracy of our method. A total of 16 pairs of well-matched feature points (yellow) were detected corresponding to Fig. 4.

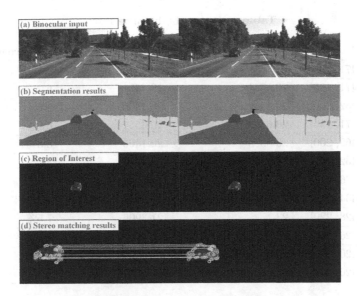

Fig. 3. Steps of our proposed method.

Fig. 4. Disparity maps calculated by 3D-Lidar (Color figure online).

Fig. 5. Stereo matching results without segmentation.

Since the depth information will not produce a large mutation, smoothing filtering is used to filter out the noise points with large differences. After filtering, 12 groups of points are left. The measurement results are shown in Table 1. It can be seen from the results that the error is almost within 5%, which meets the needs of practical applications. It should be noted that, the error is less than 1% when replacing ORB with SIFT [18]. But SIFT costs a long time while ORB is real-time.

Unsegmented Contrast Experiment. The results shown in the Fig. 5 are the matching results obtained without the segmentation steps. It can be seen

Table 1. Results of disparity test

NO	Coordinates	Measurements (pixel)	Truth value (pixel)	Relative error
1	[471, 190]	20.6638	19.4531	6.2%
2	[471, 190]	20.6641	19.4531	6.2%
3	[462, 200]	20.8662	20.1406	3.6%
4	[471, 190]	20.6632	19.4531	6.2%
5	[462, 200]	20.8693	20.1406	3.6%
6	[462, 200]	20.869	20.1406	3.6%
7	[476, 194]	20	19.1602	4.4%
8	[434, 219]	22.1987	21.3125	4.2%
9	[428, 229]	23	21.3906	7.5%
10	[426, 229]	21	21.3867	1.8%
11	[420, 231]	22.4798	21.3203	5.4%
12	[420, 231]	22.4789	21.3203	5.4%

Fig. 6. Unmanned motion platform.   **Fig. 7.** Binocular calibration.

that the points with better matching are mostly concentrated in the surrounding environment such as trees, but there are fewer matching points in the obstacle area where we need to obtain depth information. This not only wastes computing resources, but also makes it difficult to acquire useful depth information.

4.2   Experiments on the Unmanned Platform

After validation experiments on the KITTI dataset, we test it on the actual system as shown in the Fig. 6. Capture checkerboard images and take advantage of MATLAB toolbox [6] for stereo calibration. Figure 7 generated by Matlab toolbox illustrates the positional relationship between the calibration board and the camera coordinate system. The reprojection error is 0.15 pixels, which meets the actual use accuracy requirements. The calibration results are shown in the Table 2.

Table 2. Results of binocular calibration

Parameter	Left	Right
Focal Length	[1.0456e+03, 1.0472e+03]	[1.0470e+03,1.0488e+03]
Principle Point	[6.4474e+02,5.0116e+02]	[6.4749e+02,4.9520e+02]
Radial Distortion	[−0.1321, 0.2229, −0.1372]	[−0.1244, 0.1838, −0.1000]
Tangential Distortion	[4.2571e−04, 0.0011]	[9.6750e−04, 9.1139e−04]
R	[0.9999, −0035, 0.0048; 0.00350, 0.9999, −0.0086; −0.0048, 0.0086, 0.9999]	
T	[−2.3970e+02, 1.0741, 1.6559]	

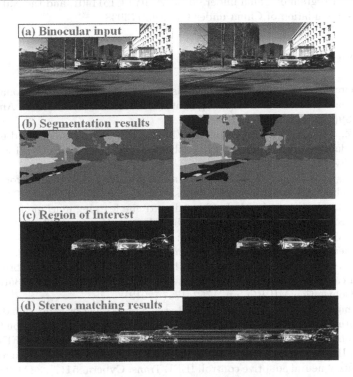

Fig. 8. Experiments on the unmanned motion platform.

Figure 8 illustrates our experiments on the unmanned motion platform. According to the results of stereo matching, we get the average disparity of 2 cars in front of our platform. The left is $32.7 pixels$ while the right is $32.0 pixels$. Based on the camera parameters, the depth is calculated to be 7.66 m and 7.83 m.

5   Conclusion

In this paper, semantic segmentation and stereo matching are combined to provide both the semantic information of the environment and the depth information of obstacles for unmanned motion platform. The obstacle region obtained by semantic segmentation is used for sparse matching, which solves the problem of poor environmental robustness and slow processing speed of dense matching. The proposed method can better adapt to light changes and noise problems. Finally, some demonstrations are conducted on a public dataset and unmanned motion platform to verify the feasibility and accuracy of the developed method. In future work, we will consider the sensor fusions of instance segmentation or edge detection technology to improve the accuracy and robustness.

Acknowledgements. This work was supported by the National Key Research and Development Program of China under Grant 2019YFC1511401, and the National Natural Science Foundation of China under Grant 62173038.

References

1. Badrinarayanan, V., Kendall, A., Cipolla, R.: Segnet: a deep convolutional encoder-decoder architecture for image segmentation. IEEE Trans. Pattern Anal. Mach. Intell. **39**(12), 2481–2495 (2017)
2. Chen, Z., Li, J., Wang, J., Wang, S., Zhao, J., Li, J.: Towards hybrid gait obstacle avoidance for a six wheel-legged robot with payload transportation. J. Intell. Robot. Syst. **102**(3), 1–21 (2021)
3. Chen, Z., Li, J., Wang, S., Wang, J., Ma, L.: Flexible gait transition for six wheel-legged robot with unstructured terrains. Robot. Auton. Syst. **150**, 103989 (2022)
4. Dai, Y., Li, J., Wang, J., Li, J.: Towards extreme learning machine framework for lane detection on unmanned mobile robot. Assem. Autom. **42**(3), 361–371 (2022)
5. Dai, Y., Wang, J., Li, J., Li, J.: Mdrnet: a lightweight network for real-time semantic segmentation in street scenes. Assem. Autom. **41**(6), 725–733 (2021)
6. Fetić, A., Jurić, D., Osmanković, D.: The procedure of a camera calibration using camera calibration toolbox for matlab. In: 2012 Proceedings of the 35th International Convention MIPRO, pp. 1752–1757 (2012)
7. Hirschmuller, H.: Accurate and efficient stereo processing by semi-global matching and mutual information. In: 2005 IEEE Computer Society Conference on Computer Vision and Pattern Recognition (CVPR 2005), vol. 2, pp. 807–814. IEEE (2005)
8. Huang, H., Yang, C., Chen, C.L.P.: Optimal robot environment interaction under broad fuzzy neural adaptive control. IEEE Trans. Cybern. **51**(7), 3824–3835 (2021)
9. Li, J., Li, R., Li, J., Wang, J., Wu, Q., Liu, X.: Dual-view 3D object recognition and detection via lidar point cloud and camera image. Robot. Auton. Syst. **150**, 103999 (2022)
10. Li, J., Qin, H., Wang, J., Li, J.: Openstreetmap-based autonomous navigation for the four wheel-legged robot via 3D-lidar and CCD camera. IEEE Trans. Industr. Electron. **69**(3), 2708–2717 (2022)
11. Li, J., Wang, J., Peng, H., Hu, Y., Su, H.: Fuzzy-torque approximation-enhanced sliding mode control for lateral stability of mobile robot. IEEE Trans. Syst. Man Cybern. Syst. **52**(4), 2491–2500 (2022)
12. Li, J., Wang, J., Peng, H., Zhang, L., Hu, Y., Su, H.: Neural fuzzy approximation enhanced autonomous tracking control of the wheel-legged robot under uncertain physical interaction. Neurocomputing **410**, 342–353 (2020)
13. Li, J., et al.: Parallel structure of six wheel-legged robot trajectory tracking control with heavy payload under uncertain physical interaction. Assem. Autom. **40**(5), 675–687 (2020)

14. Li, J., Wang, J., Wang, S., Yang, C.: Human-robot skill transmission for mobile robot via learning by demonstration. Neural Comput. Appl. 1–11 (2021). https://doi.org/10.1007/s00521-021-06449-x

15. Li, J., Wang, S., Wang, J., Li, J., Zhao, J., Ma, L.: Iterative learning control for a distributed cloud robot with payload delivery. Assem. Autom. **41**(3), 263–273 (2021)

16. Li, J., Zhang, X., Li, J., Liu, Y., Wang, J.: Building and optimization of 3d semantic map based on lidar and camera fusion. Neurocomputing **409**, 394–407 (2020)

17. Long, J., Shelhamer, E., Darrell, T.: Fully convolutional networks for semantic segmentation. IEEE Trans. Pattern Anal. Mach. Intell. **39**(4), 640–651 (2015)

18. Lowe, D.G.: Distinctive image features from scale-invariant keypoints. Int. J. Comput. Vision **60**(2), 91–110 (2004)

19. Menze, M., Heipke, C., Geiger, A.: Joint 3D estimation of vehicles and scene flow. ISPRS Ann. Photogram. Rem. Sens. Spat. Inf. Sci. **2**, 427 (2015)

20. Paszke, A., Chaurasia, A., Kim, S., Culurciello, E.: Enet: a deep neural network architecture for real-time semantic segmentation. arXiv preprint arXiv:1606.02147 (2016)

21. Peng, G., Yang, C., He, W., Chen, C.P.: Force sensorless admittance control with neural learning for robots with actuator saturation. IEEE Trans. Ind. Electron. **67**(4), 3138–3148 (2019)

22. Rublee, E., Rabaud, V., Konolige, K., Bradski, G.: Orb: an efficient alternative to sift or surf. In :2011 International Conference on Computer Vision, pp. 2564–2571. IEEE (2011)

23. S. Wang, Z. Chen, J. Li, J. Wang, J. Li, and J. Zhao. Flexible motion framework of the six wheel-legged robot: experimental results. IEEE/ASME Transactions on Mechatronics, pages 1–9, 2021

24. Yang, C., Peng, G., Cheng, L., Na, J., Li, Z.: Force sensorless admittance control for teleoperation of uncertain robot manipulator using neural networks. IEEE Trans. Syst. Man Cybernet. Syst. **51**(5), 3282–3292 (2021)

25. Yu, C., Gao, C., Wang, J., Yu, G., Shen, C., Sang, N.: Bisenet v2: bilateral network with guided aggregation for real-time semantic segmentation. Int. J. Comput. Vision **129**(11), 3051–3068 (2021)

26. Z. Zhang. Flexible camera calibration by viewing a plane from unknown orientations. In: Proceedings of the Seventh IEEE International Conference on Computer Vision, vol. 1, pp. 666–673 (1999)

27. Zhao, H., Shi, J., Qi, X., Wang, X., Jia, J.: Pyramid scene parsing network. In: 2017 IEEE Conference on Computer Vision and Pattern Recognition (CVPR), pp. 6230–6239 (2017)

Design and Control of a Porous Helical Microdrill with a Magnetic Field for Motions

Yaozhen Hou, Huaping Wang[✉], Qing Shi, Shihao Zhong, Yukang Qiu, Tao Sun,
Qiang Huang, and Toshio Fukuda

The Intelligent Robotics Institute, School of Mechatronical Engineering, Beijing Institute of
Technology, 5 South Zhongguancun Street, Haidian District, Beijing 100081, China
wanghuaping@bit.edu.cn

Abstract. Magnetically controlled microrobots have attracted wide attention in
noninvasive therapy. However, it is challenging to design a microrobot with both
low motion resistance and multi-mode motions control. Here, we design a 100 μm
helical drill-like microrobot with biodegradable materials GelMA and HAMA.
The microrobot is optimized with surface pores to reduce the resistance and alternately rotates and oscillates in composite magnetic fields. Inspired by the dimpled
surface of the golf ball to reduce the pressure drag via fluid transition, the microdrill
is modified with 98 dimples over its surface to effectively reduce the movement
resistance. Considering hyperviscosity tasks, a control strategy to dynamically
switch rotating and oscillating composite magnetic fields is performed with visual
recognition of the local environment, which actuates the microdrill to move flexibly. The experiment demonstrates that the swimming step-out frequency of the
dimpled microdrill is improved 44.5% to 13 Hz, and swimming velocity of the
dimpled microdrill is improved by 13.7% to 25.3 μm/s. Furthermore, the microdrills can be degraded by collagenase in a concentration of 0.35 mg/mL, which
shows good biocompatibility and is anticipated to be applied in microsurgery and
untethered therapies in the future. (This work was supported by National Key
R&D Program of China under grant number 2019YFB1309701, and0 National
Natural Science Foundation of China under grant number 62073042).

Keywords: Magnetic microrobot · Helical microstructure · Composite magnetic
field control · Motions in high-viscosity fluids · Vascular therapy

1 Introduction

In the past ten years, due to the progress of micromanufacturing and operating systems,
various microrobots have emerged that can be used in several fields and have been noted
to be of great interest in the biomedical field. A microrobot needs to be designed with
low motion resistance to ensure that it moves in a stable manner posture in fluids and
avoids deviation from its path caused by body wobbling due to fluid interference [1–4].

Prototype helical microstructures have been designed for tasks in low-Reynolds
fluids. They are propelled because their nonreciprocal motions can break spatial and
temporal symmetries [5, 6]. A single–helical microrobot has the advantages of a simple

H. Liu et al. (Eds.): ICIRA 2022, LNAI 13455, pp. 200–208, 2022.
https://doi.org/10.1007/978-3-031-13844-7_20

shape and small surface area. It can produce corkscrew motion to reduce the viscous resistance in low-Reynolds environments, so it is suitable for use in targeted drug delivery [7]. However, its hollow structure may lead to wobbling under fluid fluctuation, which can disrupt its motion.

To improve the motion stability, a double-helical microrobot has been designed that has a high volume–surface ratio and ideal mechanical properties [8]. The solid core structure ensures a stable corkscrew motion in a fluctuating fluid. Considering the need for biocompatibility and biodegradability for in vivo work, the biological hybrid microrobot seems to be an ideal choice. Nevertheless, most biological hybrid microrobots have poor mechanical properties compared with double–helical microrobots, and are prone to being twisted or broken during movement by the shear stress of fluids [9]. Therefore, under limited mechanical characteristics, it remains challenging to design a surface-optimized microrobot with reduced movement resistance that can be fabricated with biomaterials that facilitate recovery and degradation.

A rotating magnetic field can provide torque for a helical microrobot to rotate. Therefore, the rotation of the microrobot can be transformed into translation with only a low field strength in a low-Reynolds environment, which is convenient for use in cargo transportation and other applications [10, 11]. Compared with a rotating magnetic field, an oscillating magnetic field can actuate a microrobot to oscillate in a plane [12]. The oscillation of the microrobot makes it exert forces in both the forward and lateral directions. If the microrobot encounters obstacles or is towed by them, its oscillation actuates it to move reciprocally in perpendicular directions to penetrate. Hence, there are few microrobots that can rotate strongly enough to overcome high viscous resistance to move flexibly and linearly, and that can oscillate to penetrate viscous obstacles.

In this paper, we design a drill-like magnetic helical microrobot whose surface is modified by dimpling to effectively reduce resistance. To make the microrobot move effectively and flexibly in fluids, we propose a closed-loop control algorithm for rotating and oscillating a composite magnetic field to actuate the microrobot to rotate and oscillate alternately. The microdrill is fabricated by combining the soft materials gelatin–methacryloyl (GelMA) and hyaluronic acid (HAMA) to show its biocompatibility and biodegradability.

2 Materials and Methods

The magnetic microdrill control system includes a surface-optimized microstructure and a set of self-designed eight-axis electromagnets to realize a five-degree-of-freedom (5-DOF) motion control of the microdrill. To reduce the resistance in high–viscosity fluids, we dimpled the surface of the microdrill to optimize it. We used a magnetic control strategy based on a composite field that rotates and oscillates. The microdrill achieves both rotation and oscillation in high–viscosity fluids, to achieve complex tasks.

2.1 Magnetic Control System Setup

Hardware. The eight-axis magnetic control system is integrated under an optical microscope (OM) (IX73, Olympus, Inc.,). Four of the axes were placed in a horizontal plane each at an angle of 90°. The other four were positioned diagonally at an angle of 40° from the horizontal plane. Each electromagnet can be controlled individually with a set of current controllers (STM32), by changing the current of the electromagnetic coil to acquire the desired magnetic field strength. In a spherical central workspace with a diameter of 30 mm, the system can generate a maximum rotational magnetic field intensity of 30 mT and a maximum magnetic field gradient of 1.6 T/m. The motions are monitored with an inverted lens and a digital camera (DP21, Olympus, Inc.,) mounted on the OM. By recognizing the structural features of the microdrill, the control system is able to control the movement of the microdrill.

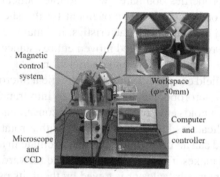

Fig. 1. Picture of the magnetic microrobots control system.

Generation of the Composite Magnetic Field. According to the various structural features and complex tasks required for microrobots, the three typical forms of magnetic fields are a rotating magnetic field, oscillating magnetic field and magnetic field gradient. The helical microdrills in this paper mainly rely on rotating magnetic fields to achieve locomotion. If a rotation field is applied, the microdrill will rotate around its long axis, which is also the rotational axis of the magnetic field. The helix on the microdrill produces a nonreciprocal motion, thus propelling itself forward.

To rotate the microdrill, generating rotating magnetic fields is crucial. The magnetic field B after rotation can be expressed as:

$$\mathbf{B}(\theta) = \mathbf{B}_0\mathbf{A} \tag{1}$$

The microdrill was also actuated by an oscillating magnetic field that can be expressed as:

$$\boldsymbol{B}_0(t) = \boldsymbol{B}_0\big[|\cos(2\pi ft)|\boldsymbol{n} + \sin(2\pi t)\boldsymbol{u}\big] \tag{2}$$

where $\boldsymbol{u}$ is the unit vector perpendicular to the space vector $\boldsymbol{n}$ in the oscillation plane.

For soft-magnetic electromagnets, the induced magnetic field is related to the current through every electromagnet in the system. The magnetic field in the workspace can be calculated from equation:

$$\boldsymbol{B} = \sum_{k=1}^{8} \boldsymbol{B}_k = \sum_{k=1}^{8} f(x, y, z, \alpha, \beta, \gamma)\boldsymbol{I}_k \tag{3}$$

where B_k is the magnetic field intensity generated by the unipolar coil, I_k is the current and $f(x, y, z, \alpha, \beta, \gamma)$ represents the pose function of an electromagnet pole.

According to Maxwell's equations, the microdrills in this paper are mainly affected by the torque T due to the external magnetic field, which can be expressed as:

$$T_m = m \times B \tag{4}$$

where m is the magnetic moment vector of the microdrill, and B is the magnetic induction intensity. Owing to the drift caused by friction in the locomotion of the microdrill, closed-loop motion control is implemented using visual feedback and certain navigation angle compensation is added to achieve precise locomotion control. The workflow of the closed-loop control is shown in Fig. 2.

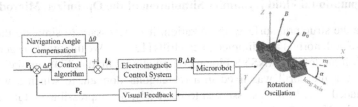

Fig. 2. Diagram of the actuation strategy and closed-loop method of the magnetic field system.

2.2 Structure Design and Surface Optimization

The design of the 3D microdrill is shown in Fig. 3(a). It has a length L = 100 μm, outer diameter Do = 40 μm, inner diameter Di = 14 μm and pitch λ = 72 μm. The geometry is chiral, which affects the rotation-translation coupling. We determined the ratios L/λ and Do/Di to be 1.39 and 2.67, respectively. At the top of the microdrill, we designed a tip with a taper of 53° to increase the drilling effectiveness. Inspired by the dimpled surface of a golf ball, which reduces the pressure drag through fluid transition, we made 98 dimples exerted by the surrounding fluid. This in turn reduces the movement resistance of the microdrill. The diameter of each dimple is 2 μm and the depth is 0.8 μm. An SEM image of the microdrill in Fig. 3(b) shows the complete structure and local features of the dimples.

To fabricate the microdrill, we chose a compounded photoresist containing 70% (v/v) GelMA and 30% (v/v) HAMA as the precursor and 5% (w/v) lithium phenyl-2,4,6-trimethylbenzoylphosphinate (LAP) as the photoinitiator. The photoresist was crosslinked using a high precision 3D photolithography system (Nanoscribe, Photonic Professional GT) to form a 3D microstructure. The fabrication process is shown in Fig. 3(c).

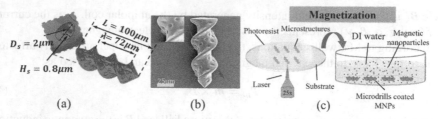

Fig. 3. (a) Structural design and parameters of microdrill. (b) SEM of a microdrill with dimples optimization. (c) Fabrication and magnetization of the microdrills.

3   Experimental Results and Discussion

3.1   Computational Fluid Dynamics Simulation of the Optimized Microdrill

To validate the structural surface optimization, it is necessary to simulate the motion resistance of both normal and dimpled microdrills [13–17]. We imported the geometrical 3D microdrill model into ANSYS Fluent computational fluid (CFD) simulation. In the CFD model, a microdrill was fixed in a rectangular domain, to which a water flow field was added. The flow was assumed to be steady, incompressible and laminar. The incompressible Navier-Stokes equations govern the induced flow field in a fluidic domain $\Omega(t)$ and are subject to continuity as follows:

$$\rho(\frac{\partial U}{\partial t} + (U - \dot{x}_{mesh}) \cdot \nabla U) = -\nabla p + \mu \nabla^2 U \tag{5}$$

$$\nabla \cdot U = 0 \tag{6}$$

where U and $\dot{x}_{mesh}$ are the fluid and mesh velocities, ρ is the fluid density, and p is the hydrostatic pressure.

We simulated the dimpled microdrill and the undimpled microdrill swimming in water, as shown in Fig. 4(a)–(b). In Fig. 4(c), each curve represents the flow velocity through the microdrill surface. The results show that the red curve has a higher flow velocity than the green curve, which means that fluid flow through the dimpled surface is faster than the fluid flow through the smooth surface. Because the drag force of fluid

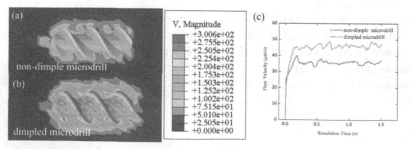

Fig. 4. (a)–(b) Flow velocity nephogram of two microdrills. (c) Flow velocity comparison of non-dimple microdrill and dimpled microdrill in water.

flow is directly related to the flow velocity, a faster flow velocity represents lower drag force [18]. Therefore, the simulation results have verify that the dimpled microdrill has a lower drag force than the non-dimple microdrill.

3.2 Mobility of Microdrills

According to Lighthill [15], the geometry and surface properties of the microdrill and the fluid properties affect the step-out frequency. We first tested the step-out frequency of the dimpled microdrill and the non-dimple microdrill by increasing the magnetic field input frequency from 1 to 20 Hz with a 1 Hz step at 10 mT, as shown in Fig. 5(a). Below a frequency of 9 Hz, the velocities of both of the dimpled microdrill and the non-dimple microdrill increase linearly with the increasing driving frequency. When the driving frequency exceeded 9 Hz, the velocity of non-dimpled microdrill showed an inflexion point and began to decrease with increasing driving frequency. At this time, the non-dimple microdrill reaches its step-out frequency and begins to oscillate. For the dimpled microdrill, which can catch up with higher driving frequency and its velocity increase synchronously with the increase of the driving frequency. When the driving frequency is 13 Hz, the dimpled microdrill reaches its step-out frequency and began to oscillate. When the driving frequency continues to increase to 20 Hz, the velocities of both the dimpled microdrills and the non-dimple microdrill almost decrease to 0, and both of them just oscillate in situ. In Fig. 5(b)–(d), we compared the movement distance of the dimpled microdrill and the non-dimple microdrill at 10 mT and 6 Hz. Figure 5(b) shows the initial distance between the two types microdrills at 210 μm. As the two microdrills moved forward, their gaps were increased to 425 μm, which took 7 s, as shown in Fig. 5(c). In Fig. 5 (d), the front microdrill was 660 μm ahead of the back microdrill. We can see that by moving for 10 s, the dimpled microdrill was more than 500 μm ahead of the non-dimpled microdrill.

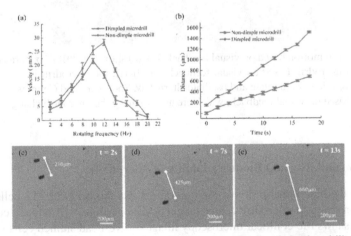

Fig. 5. (a) Comparison of the step-out frequency between the dimpled microdrill and the non-dimple microdrill. (b) Differences in the moving distance between the dimpled microdrill and the non-dimple microdrill. (c)–(e) are screenshots from the motion comparison experiments.

3.3 Magnetic Actuation and Control Based on Visual Feedback

In this experiment, we tested the mobility of the microdrill using target points through visual feedback control. We planned for the microdrill to move in a graphical path tracing the word "B I T", as shown in Fig. 6(a)–(c). The path "B I T" included small offset angle steering in Route "B" via 3-4-5 ($\alpha = 10°$). The microdrill swam from point 3 toward point 4 along the direction 185° from the positive x-axis. Subsequently, the microdrill steered counterclockwise 170° to swim toward point 5. The angle between the two trajectories is 10°. This means that the navigation angle of the microdrill could be finely controlled, which also kept the targeted motion stable. In Route "I", the microdrill passed through point 3 as it swam from point 1 to point 2 and returned to the point 3. In Route "T", the trajectory of the microdrill is 1–2–3–4.

We also verified the ability of the microdrill to switch motion modes at a fixed position. This process was based on visual feedback to ensure that the microdrill could accurately switch the motion mode at the fixed point. In Fig. 6(d)–(f), the microdrill started to rotate from spot A at 10 mT and 10 Hz. When it reached spot B, under visual feedback, the microdrill changed its motion from rotation to oscillation at 10 mT and 10 Hz. Then the microdrill rotated toward spot C. At spot C, the microdrill oscillated repeatedly at 10 Hz. This process demonstrates that control strategy is feasible and effective. This also laid the foundation for the later experiments.

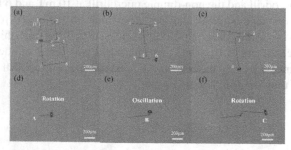

Fig. 6. Microdrill motion based on visual feedback. (a)–(c) shows the "BIT" pattern is drawn by the motion of microdrill based on visual feedback. In (d)–(f), the microdrill is actuated by the composite magnetic field to rotate and oscillate alternately. Spot A, B, and C represent the settled target points based on visual feedback, which are used to make the microdrill change motion.

3.4 Biocompatibility and Biodegradability of Microdrills

To evaluate the biocompatibility of the microdrills, we spread NIH-3T3 cells in petri dishes within arrays of microdrill coated magnetic nanoparticles to produce a co-culture. Figure 7(a) shows the confocal microscopy image of live-dead stained cells seeded on the microstructures coated with magnetic nanoparticles. The results indicate that cells could adhere to the surface of microdrills and grow around them. Negligible red-stained cells demonstrate excellent biocompatibility with the polymerized microstructures that is consist of GelMA, HAMA, and magnetic materials, as shown in Fig. 7(b). Because gelatin and hyaluronic acid are natural biological molecules in the skin, collagenase was selected as a degradation catalyst to study the biodegradation properties. Figure 7(c) shows the time-resolved degradation process of microdrills at a collagenase concentration of 0.35 mg/ml. In the case of proteolytic cleavage of amide bonds of peptide domains in gelatin and hyaluronic acid, the microdrills almost disappear after 5 h, leaving only parts of the structure embedded in the glass substrate.

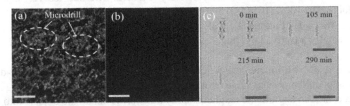

Fig. 7. (a) Live (green) and dead (red) NIH-3T3 cells treated with microdrills coated magnetic nanoparticles are shown in (a) and (b), (c) shows the biodegradation of the microdrills by the collagenase. The scale bars represent 100 μm. (Color figure online)

4 Conclusions

We designed a drill-like magnetic helical microrobot and optimized its surface with dimples. Through actuation by the composite magnetic field to rotate and oscillate alternately, the movement resistance is notably reduced. To validate the effectiveness of the surface optimization, the movement distances and average velocity of the dimpled and normal microdrills were compared. The dimpled microdrill moved 561 μm farther than the normal microdrill in 10 s of motion, the swimming step-out frequency of the dimpled microdrill is improved 44.5%, and the swimming velocity of the dimpled micro-drill is improved by 13.7%. Furthermore, we validated the biocompatibility of the microdrill by coculturing NIH-3T3 cells and the biodegradability of the microdrill by treating it with collagenase. The results show that the microdrill is friendly to the human body and suitable for further biomedical applications.

References

1. Nelson, B.J., Kaliakatsos, I.K., Abbott, J.J.: Microrobots for minimally invasive medicine. Ann. Rev. Biomed. Eng. **12**, 55–85 (2010)
2. Næss, I.A., Christiansen, S., Romundstad, P., Cannegieter, S., Rosendaal, F.R., Hammerstrøm, J.: Incidence and mortality of venous thrombosis: a population-based study. J. Thrombosis Haemostasis. **5**(4), 692–699 (2007)
3. Sun, Y., et al.: A three-dimensional magnetic tweezer system for intraembryonic navigation and measurement. IEEE T. Robot. **34**(1), 240–247 (2018)
4. Fischer, P., et al.: Biocompatible magnetic micro- and nanodevices: fabrication of FePt nanopropellers and cell transfection. Adv. Mater. **32**(25), 1–9 (2020)
5. Feng, L., Arai, F., et al.: Untethered octopus-inspired millirobot actuated by regular tetrahedron arranged magnetic field. Adv. Intell. Syst. **2**, 1900148 (2020)

6. Koepele, C., Cappelleri, D., et al.: 3D-printed microrobots with integrated structural color for identification and tracking. Adv. Intell. Syst. **2**(5), 1–9 (2020)
7. Simi, M., Dario, P., et al.: Magnetically activated stereoscopic vision system for laparoendoscopic single-site surgery. IEEE-ASME T. Mech. **18**(3), 1140–1151 (2013)
8. Menciassi, A., et al.: A power-efficient propulsion method for magnetic microrobots. Int. J. Adv. Robot Syst. **11**(116), 1–9 (2014)
9. Iacovacci, V., Lucarini, G., Ricotti, L., Dario, P., Dupont, P.E., Menciassi, A.: Untethered magnetic millirobot for targeted drug delivery. Biomed. Microdevice **17**(3), 1–12 (2015). https://doi.org/10.1007/s10544-015-9962-9
10. Zheng, Z., Wang, H., Fukuda, T., et al.: Ionic shape-morphing microrobotic end-effectors for environmentally adaptive targeting, releasing, and sampling. Nat. Commun. **12**, 1598–1609 (2021)
11. Diller, E., et al.: Millimeter-scale flexible robots with programmable three-dimensional magnetization and motions. Sci. Robot. **4**(29), 4494–4505 (2019)
12. Shen, Y., et al.: An agglutinate magnetic spray transforms inanimate objects into millirobots for biomedical applications. Sci. Robot. **5**(48), 8191–8203 (2020)
13. Xu, T., Hao, Z., Huang, C., Yu, J., Zhang, L., Wu, X.: Multi-modal locomotion control of needle-like microrobots assembled by ferromagnetic nanoparticles. IEEE-ASME T MECH (2022)
14. Lighthill, J.: Flagellar hydrodynamics. SIAM Rev. **18**, 161–230 (1976)
15. Honda, T., Arai, K., Ishiyama, K.: Micro swimming mechanisms propelled by external magnetic fields. IEEE Trans. Magn. **32**(5), 5085–5087 (1996)
16. Abbott, J., Nelson, B.J., et al.: How should microrobots swim? Int. J. Robot Res. **66**, 157–167 (2009)
17. Hart, J.: Comparison of turbulence modeling approaches to the simulation of a dimpled sphere. Procedia Eng. **147**, 68–73 (2016)
18. Asproulis, N., Drikakis, D.: Surface roughness effects in micro and nanofluidic devices. J. Comput. Theor. Nanosci. **7**(9), 1825–1830 (2010)

Optimal Control Method of Motor Torque Loading Based on Genetic Algorithm

Shaohua Niu⬛, Wencai Zhang⬛, Tianzhen Li⬛, and Gan Zhan⁽✉⁾⬛

Beijing Institute of Technology, Beijing 100081, China
{shh,3220200178,1120180096}@bit.edu.cn
zhonghangzhuoyuan@163.com

Abstract. This paper designs an automatic calibration method and system of motor torque for the problem of low loading accuracy of motor torque. The system uses genetic algorithm to optimize PID parameters and load control and measurement of the motor. The genetic algorithm is realized in the simulation platform, and the iterative operation is carried out by setting different cross probability and mutation probability parameters. The results are substituted into the motor model to analyze the response speed and anti-interference ability of the motor to the given random signal, and the optimal PID parameters are obtained as the configuration parameters of the motor torque automatic calibration system. The experimental results show that compared with the traditional motor torque calibration loading control, the accuracy of the system torque calibration error is improved and the error range is controlled within $\pm0.003\,\text{N}\cdot\text{m}$, which verifies the effectiveness and feasibility of this method.

Keywords: Motor torque calibration accuracy · Genetic algorithms · PID parameters · Loading control · Response speed · Anti interference ability

1 Introduction

In recent years, the motor has been widely used in many fields as the power source of the system, such as robot control [2,6,7,9,10,14,21,29–31,34], Stewart simulator [1,3,4,11–13,19,25,26], aerospace and servo visual system [5,15–18,20, 23,24]. Especially in the aerospace field, the motor is usually required to have the characteristics of low power consumption, large output torque, high precision and high reliability [8]. In the process of motor calibration, when the loading motor applies different loading torques to the motor under test, due to the existence of inertia of the motor under test, a large coupling torque, that is, excess torque, will be generated between the loading motor and the motor under test [33]. The

This work was supported by the National Key R&D Program of China under Grant No. 2018AAA0101000.

excess torque on the motor drive shaft will affect the loading accuracy of the motor servo loading system, which is one of the main sources of calibration errors in the process of motor calibration. Therefore, how to effectively eliminate the influence of excess torque is one of the main problems to be solved in the motor calibration loading system.

At present, the main methods to eliminate excess torque are structure method and control method [22]. In the structural method, excessive torque is suppressed by changing the connection stiffness between the loading motor and the motor under test, such as adding a spring rod [27]. The control law is to use the control algorithm to compensate the excess torque between the motors to eliminate the purpose. PID control method is widely used in motor calibration loading system. However, in the actual loading calibration process, there are many interference factors, the system work presents nonlinear characteristics, the traditional PID control method is difficult to meet the requirements of high precision loading control. Wang X [28] proposed a control strategy combining adaptive controller and feedforward compensation controller to improve the motor loading accuracy. Zhang K [32] designed a dynamic sliding mode controller to eliminate excess torque. In order to realize high-precision loading control of the motor, the PID controller is optimized based on genetic algorithm. Simulation and experiment verify that the method can effectively improve the detection accuracy of the motor torque automatic calibration system.

The main contribution of this paper is to design an automatic motor torque calibration system, optimize the motor parameters through genetic algorithm, and improve the loading accuracy of the motor. Its structure is as follows; The working principle of the system is introduced in Sect. 2. In Sect. 3, the basic principle of genetic algorithm is described in detail. In Sect. 4, the motor parameters are optimized based on genetic algorithm, and the effectiveness of the parameters is verified by simulation. In Sect. 5, the feasibility of the algorithm is verified by experiments. Finally, conclusions is drawn in Sect. 6.

2   Working Principle of Motor Automatic Calibration System

Motor automatic calibration system is composed of the loading test bed body, the torque sensor, load, motor, and other components of the motor to be tested, as shown in Fig. 1. Torque sensor, loading motor and motor under test are fixedly connected to the corresponding fixture seat through bellows coupling. Firstly, the motor loading parameters are set in the industrial computer. The industrial computer acts on the loading motor through the programmable multi axis controller (PMAC), and the PMAC collects the torque sensor information and the torque signal of the tested motor to the industrial computer. The industrial computer processes, stores and displays the data, and optimizes the instructions through the control algorithm according to the collected information. So that the loading motor can still be high precision torque tracking when the motor is moving. The difference between the measured value feedback from the torque

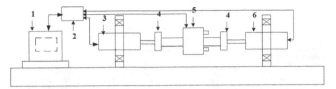

1: Industrial Personal Computer(IPC) 2: Programmable Multi Axis Controller(PMAC)
3: Loading Motor 4: Coupling 5: Torque Sensor 6: Tested Motor

Fig. 1. Structure diagram of automatic motor torque calibration equipment.

sensor and the expected loading torque value is used as the optimization input instruction, and the torque difference is eliminated by the control algorithm to make the loading precision of the motor meet the requirements.

3   Optimization of PID Parameters by Genetic Algorithm

Genetic algorithm is a kind of simulation mechanism of heredity and variation of organisms in nature random search optimization method, in solving complex combinatorial optimization problem to get better optimization results [35]. In the application of genetic algorithm, it can be roughly divided into five basic elements:

(1) Coding. Each individual of the initial population is coded. Binary code is adopted in this paper to make genetic operation easy to implement.
(2) Initial population setting. Usually to shorten the time to find the optimal solution, we set the individual to a certain range.
(3) Setting of fitness function. In this paper, the error e, adjustment time t_s and overshoot σ Displayed equations are centered and set on a separate line, produced by PID parameters on the system are taken as fitness indexes and they are allocated in a certain proportion to form a fitness function to evaluate individuals. The fitness function is shown in Eq. 1:

$$\begin{cases} fitness = \int_0^\infty (W_1 \cdot e(t) + W_2 \cdot t_s + W_3 \cdot \sigma)dt \\ (W_1 + W_2 + W_3 = 1, (W_1 > W_2, W_3)) \end{cases} \tag{1}$$

In genetic algorithm, the most commonly used roulette algorithm is used for individual selection. The corresponding probability of individual is shown in Eq. 2:

$$p_i = \frac{f_i}{\sum\limits_{i=1}^{n} f_i} \tag{2}$$

where f_i represents individual $i(i = 1, 2, 3 \ldots, n)$ corresponding fitness, and finally, these individuals were allocated to the roulette wheel according to the probability proportion, and randomly selected for subsequent genetic operations.

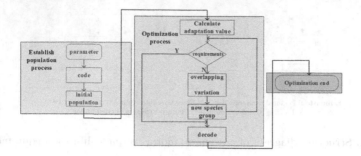

Fig. 2. Flow chart of genetic algorithm.

(4) Genetic manipulation. In this paper, only crossover operator and mutation operator can be used to complete the optimal design of parameters.
(5) Control parameter design. The initial population, the number of evolution, crossover probability, mutation probability and so on are assigned.

In this paper, genetic algorithm is used to optimize the PID parameters required by the experiment. First, the PID parameter range is determined and its individual binary encoding is carried out. The number of individuals and fitness function of the initial population were selected, and then a new population was selected by fitness function after the genetic operation of crossover and mutation. The optimal PID parameters are obtained after the set number of iterations. The optimization process is shown in Fig. 2.

4   Optimization Simulation of Loading Control System

The system adopts the double closed-loop servo control method. The outer ring takes the value collected by the torque sensor as the feedback quantity, and the inner ring is the current ring. The error of torque loading control is limited within a certain range, and the control flow chart is shown in Fig. 3. The Experiments using loading electric machine related parameters as shown in Table 1.

Thus, the transfer function of the motor mathematical model can be obtained as shown in Eq. 3.

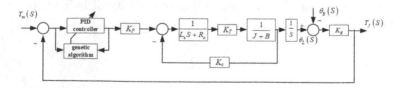

Fig. 3. Control block diagram of loading system.

Table 1. Parameters of loading motor.

Parameter	Values	Units
Armature inductance	0.195	L_a/mH
Motor resistance	1.51	Ra/Ω
Back EMF constant	0.004	$K_e/(V/rpm)$
Inductance torque constant	0.042	$K_T/(N \cdot m/A)$

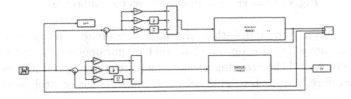

Fig. 4. The simulation diagram.

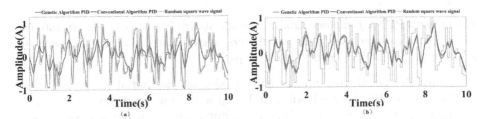

Fig. 5. (a) represents simulation diagram of optimized PID parameter (1) and (b) represents simulation diagram of optimized PID parameter (2).

$$G(s) = \frac{9.97 \times 10^3}{S^2 + 9.67S + 54.80} \qquad (3)$$

where G(s) represents the ratio of output (the output torque T_f) to input (the rated torque T_m).

Assuming the population size used in the genetic algorithm is 30 and the evolutionary algebra $M = 100$, two groups of different crossover probability (P_c) and variation probability (P_m) are selected according to experience, namely (1) $P_c = 0.9$, $P_m = 0.033$ and (2) $P_c = 0.6$, $P_m = 0.01$, respectively. In order to avoid too large the PID parameters selection, can be set parameters in the range of [0, 20], so that you can shorten the time of the initial optimization. The PID parameters obtained from the above two groups of parameters through genetic algorithm are (1) P1 = 6.9688, I1 = 8.8720, D1 = 0.2188, (2) P2 = 8.6761, I2 = 10.3743, D2 = 1.4402 respectively. The random signal is used to simulate the irregular change of motor speed as input, and the built motor model is used for simulation. The simulation diagram are shown in the Fig. 4. The simulation results are shown in the Fig. 5.

Fig. 6. Flow chart of automatic motor calibration.

It can be seen from Fig. 5 that the anti-interference ability and response speed of parameter (1) are better than that of parameter (2) and traditional PID parameters, and the tracking accuracy and response speed also reach ideal results. Therefore, parameter (1) is selected as the motor control parameter.

5 Automatic Calibration Experiment of Motor Torque

The optimal PID parameters obtained by the above simulation are input into the test upper computer as system parameters to calibrate the motor. The specific working process is divided into three steps;

(1) Enter the positioning and ranging mode, set the initial torque value by the host at the torque loading end, adjust the torque evenly to the motor under test until it just makes the motor rotate at a uniform speed, and automatically store the positioning torque value.

(2) Enter the driving torque mode, set the initial torque value by the host at the torque loading end, gradually increase the current of the motor under test until it can rotate uniformly for the whole cycle, and record the current value. The clockwise and counterclockwise currents should be tested at the same moment. Start test of current entering next torque after recording.

(3) Enter the torque holding mode, set the saved current value as the rated current to the loading motor, the motor under test applies the reverse torque, so that the motor under test can not rotate, and the measured value is fed back to the driving end through the torque sensor for automatic storage record.

Finally, the torque value in the positioning and ranging mode is compared with the torque value in the holding torque. When the error is less than the given error, it indicates that the loading precision of the loading motor meets the conditions and the motor calibration is successful. The specific process is shown in Fig. 6.

According to the above steps, we give the motor a certain load torque, and we can measure the torque value W, current value I and torque values W1, W2 and W3 fed back by the torque sensor. The errors E1, E2 and E3 between the feed-back torque values W1, W2 and W3 and the measured torque value W are shown in Fig. 7.

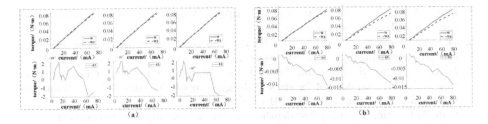

Fig. 7. Motor torque value and error diagram.

It can be seen from Fig. 7(a) that when the current increases to 7.248 mA, the motor starts to rotate uniformly for the whole cycle. When the reverse loading torque of the loading motor is 0.0035 N · m, the motor is just stationary, which is equal to the measured torque value in the first step. As the current gradually increasing, the difference between the expected torque and the measured torque value always varies between ±0.003 N · m. The traditional PID parameter is used as the motor control parameter, the torque values W4, W5 and W6 feedback from the torque sensor are measured according to the same steps. Feedback torque value W4, W5 and W6 and the error between the measured torque value E4 and E5, E6 in Fig. 7(b). It shows that the difference between the expected torque and the measured torque is ±0.015 N · m as the current increases. Compared with Fig. 7(a), the calibration error of traditional PID is much greater than that of PID parameter optimization based on genetic algorithm, indicating that the motor optimized based on genetic algorithm has higher loading accuracy and smaller calibration error.

6   Conclusion

Aiming at the problem of insufficient motor torque loading accuracy, the genetic algorithm is adopted to optimize the traditional PID parameters, and then the optimized PID parameters are used as the configuration parameters of the loading motor. The experiment shows that the PID parameter optimization method based on genetic algorithm can effectively reduce the traditional PID calibration error, and the calibration error of the experimental system after optimization is within ±0.003 N · m.

References

1. Chen, Z., Li, J., Wang, J., Wang, S., Zhao, J., Li, J.: Towards hybrid gait obstacle avoidance for a six wheel-legged robot with payload transportation. J. Intell. Robot. Syst. **102**(3), 1–21 (2021)
2. Chen, Z., Li, J., Wang, S., Wang, J., Ma, L.: Flexible gait transition for six wheel-legged robot with unstructured terrains. Robot. Auton. Syst. **150**, 103989 (2022)
3. Chen, Z., Wang, S., Wang, J., Xu, K.: Attitude stability control for multi-agent six wheel-legged robot. IFAC-PapersOnLine **53**(2), 9636–9641 (2020)

4. Chen, Z., et al.: Control strategy of stable walking for a hexapod wheel-legged robot. ISA Trans. **108**, 367–380 (2021)
5. Dai, Y., Wang, J., Li, J., Li, J.: MDRNet: a lightweight network for real-time semantic segmentation in street scenes. Assem. Autom. **41**(6), 725–733 (2021)
6. Deng, C., Wang, S., Chen, Z., Wang, J., Ma, L., Li, J.: CPG-inspired gait generation and transition control for six wheel-legged robot. In: 2021 China Automation Congress (CAC), pp. 2310–2315. IEEE (2021)
7. Gan, M.G., He, Y.: Adaptive depth-aware visual relationship detection. Knowl.-Based Syst. **247**, 108786 (2022)
8. Kou, B., Zhao, X., Wang, M., Chen, W.: Overview of negative-saliency permanent magnet synchronous motors and its control technology. Proc. CSEE **39**(8), 2414–2425 (2019)
9. Li, J., Dai, Y., Wang, J., Su, X., Ma, R.: Towards broad learning networks on unmanned mobile robot for semantic segmentation. In: 2022 IEEE International Conference on Robotics and Automation (ICRA), pp. 1–7. IEEE (2022)
10. Li, J., Wang, J., Peng, H., Hu, Y., Su, H.: Fuzzy-torque approximation-enhanced sliding mode control for lateral stability of mobile robot. IEEE Trans. Syst. Man Cybern. Syst. **52**(4), 2491–2500 (2022)
11. Li, J., Wang, J., Peng, H., Zhang, L., Hu, Y., Su, H.: Neural fuzzy approximation enhanced autonomous tracking control of the wheel-legged robot under uncertain physical interaction. Neurocomputing **410**, 342–353 (2020)
12. Li, J., et al.: Parallel structure of six wheel-legged robot trajectory tracking control with heavy payload under uncertain physical interaction. Assem. Autom. **40**(5), 675–687 (2020)
13. Li, J., et al.: Neural approximation-based model predictive tracking control of non-holonomic wheel-legged robots. Int. J. Control Autom. Syst. **19**(1), 372–381 (2021)
14. Li, J., Wang, J., Wang, S., Yang, C.: Human–robot skill transmission for mobile robot via learning by demonstration. Neural Comput. Appl. 1–11 (2021). https://doi.org/10.1007/s00521-021-06449-x
15. Li, J., Wang, S., Wang, J., Li, J., Zhao, J., Ma, L.: Iterative learning control for a distributed cloud robot with payload delivery. Assem. Autom. **41**(3), 263–273 (2021). https://doi.org/10.1108/AA-11-2020-0179
16. Li, J., Li, R., Li, J., Wang, J., Wu, Q., Liu, X.: Dual-view 3D object recognition and detection via lidar point cloud and camera image. Robot. Auton. Syst. **150**, 103999 (2022)
17. Li, J., Qin, H., Wang, J., Li, J.: OpenStreetMap-based autonomous navigation for the four wheel-legged robot via 3D-LiDAR and CCD camera. IEEE Trans. Industr. Electron. **69**(3), 2708–2717 (2022)
18. Li, J., Shi, X., Li, J., Zhang, X., Wang, J.: Random curiosity-driven exploration in deep reinforcement learning. Neurocomputing **418**, 139–147 (2020)
19. Li, J., Wu, Q., Wang, J., Li, J.: Neural networks-based sliding mode tracking control for the four wheel-legged robot under uncertain interaction. Int. J. Robust Nonlinear Control **31**, 4306–4323 (2021)
20. Li, J., Zhang, X., Li, J., Liu, Y., Wang, J.: Building and optimization of 3d semantic map based on lidar and camera fusion. Neurocomputing **409**, 394–407 (2020)
21. Peng, G., Yang, C., He, W., Chen, C.P.: Force sensorless admittance control with neural learning for robots with actuator saturation. IEEE Trans. Ind. Electron. **67**(4), 3138–3148 (2019)
22. Rui, L., Jian-fang, J., Rui-feng, Y.: Overview on control strategies of load simulator. Chin. Hydraul. Pneumatics **10**, 12–16 (2012)

23. Su, H., et al.: Improving motion planning for surgical robot with active constraints. In: 2020 IEEE/RSJ International Conference on Intelligent Robots and Systems (IROS), pp. 3151–3156 (2020)
24. Su, H., et al.: Internet of Things (IoT)-based collaborative control of a redundant manipulator for teleoperated minimally invasive surgeries. In: 2020 IEEE International Conference on Robotics and Automation (ICRA), pp. 9737–9742 (2020)
25. Wang, R., Chen, Z., Xu, K., Wang, S., Wang, J., Li, B.: Hybrid obstacle-surmounting gait for hexapod wheel-legged robot in special terrain. In: 2021 6th IEEE International Conference on Advanced Robotics and Mechatronics (ICARM), pp. 1–6. IEEE (2021)
26. Wang, S., Chen, Z., Li, J., Wang, J., Li, J., Zhao, J.: Flexible motion framework of the six wheel-legged robot: experimental results. IEEE/ASME Trans. Mechatron. (2021)
27. Wang, X., Feng, D.: Experimental research on DC load simulator test bed with elastic rod. Electr. Mach. Control 16(09), 91–94 (2012)
28. Wang, X.y., Zhang, G.w., Li, Z.s.: Composite control for electric load simulator based on parameter estimation. Small Special Electr. Mach. 44(11), 57–61 (2016)
29. Xue, J., Li, J., Chen, Z., Wang, S., Wang, J., Ma, R.: Gait planning and control of hexapod robot based on velocity vector. In: 2021 6th IEEE International Conference on Advanced Robotics and Mechatronics (ICARM), pp. 616–620. IEEE (2021)
30. Yang, C., Chen, C., Wang, N., Ju, Z., Fu, J., Wang, M.: Biologically inspired motion modeling and neural control for robot learning from demonstrations. IEEE Trans. Cogn. Dev. Syst. 11(2), 281–291 (2018)
31. Yang, C., Luo, J., Liu, C., Li, M., Dai, S.L.: Haptics electromyography perception and learning enhanced intelligence for teleoperated robot. IEEE Trans. Autom. Sci. Eng. 16(4), 1512–1521 (2018)
32. Zhang, K., Wang, L., Fang, X.: Feedback linearization adaptive dynamic sliding mode control of linear synchronous motor for CNC machine tools. J. Electr. Eng. Technol. 1–9 (2021). https://doi.org/10.1007/s42835-021-00930-2
33. Zhao, W., Tang, Q., Zhang, M.: Disturbance torque suppression and improved dynamic loading performance for electric torque loading simulator. J. Harbin Eng. Univ. 37(11), 1586–1593 (2016)
34. Zhihua, C., Shoukun, W., Kang, X., Junzheng, W., Jiangbo, Z., Shanshuai, N.: Research on high precision control of joint position servo system for hydraulic quadruped robot. In: 2019 Chinese Control Conference (CCC), pp. 755–760. IEEE (2019)
35. Zhou, M., Sun, S.: Principle and Application of Genetic Algorithm. National Defense Industry Press, Beijing (1999)

A Multi-AGV Scheduling Model with Obstacle Impact Factor in Uncertain Workshop Environment

Wen-Bin Wu and Guang-Zhong Cao[✉]

Guangdong Key Laboratory of Electromagnetic Control and Intelligent Robots, College of Mechatronics and Control Engineering, Shenzhen University, Shenzhen 518000, China
gzcao@szu.edu.cn

Abstract. In order to improve the accuracy of the optimal solution obtained by the scheduling model in uncertain workshop environment, a multi-AGV scheduling model with obstacle impact factor is proposed. The multi-AGV scheduling model takes minimum total length of driving path of AGVs and maximum utilization rate of AGVs as the optimization goal and the obstacle impact factor is obtained according to the area and shape of obstacles. The genetic algorithm (GA) with a custom coding method is adopted to obtain the optimal solution of the multi-AGV scheduling model. The improved A* algorithm improves the quality of the driving path of AGVs transporting materials by setting virtual obstacle area and turning penalty factor. The simulation result shows the model that introduces obstacle impact factor is 41% more accurate than the model without obstacle impact factor.

Keywords: Automated guided vehicles · Scheduling model · Obstacle impact factor

1 Introduction

Combining the characteristics of flexible manufacturing workshops, studying the task scheduling and path planning of multi-AGV is a key issue to improve the efficiency of workshop logistics and is of great significance to achieve high-quality development.

There has been some research on the scheduling of flexible manufacturing workshops. Abderrahim et al. [1] established a scheduling model in an AGV-based job-shop manufacturing facility, and achieved completion time minimization and battery management. Zhao et al. [2] designed the AGV scheduling model of the unmanned factory, planned the collision-free path through the A* algorithm, and determined the AGV priority to deal with the collision problem. Ji Shouwen et al. [3] established a two-level programming model for the integrated scheduling problem, and designed two two-level optimization algorithms to solve the model. Yuan et al. [4] comprehensively considered the constraints of machines, workpieces and AGVs, established a dual-resource integrated scheduling model and verified the effectiveness of the model through workshop examples. Tang et al. [5] designed a two-layer genetic algorithm to solve the scheduling model with the shortest order completion time as the goal, which improved the picking efficiency of the unmanned warehouse. In addition, Simulated Annealing Algorithm [6], multi-objective particle swarm optimization algorithm [7] were also used to solve the scheduling model.

The above scheduling model can realize the task allocation of AGV, but does not take into account the impact of the actual workshop environment on the AGV driving route, resulting in deviations in the calculation results. In order to reduce the influence of the uncertainty of the actual workshop environment, this paper introduces the obstacle influence factor into the scheduling model, and uses the GA with self-defined coding method to solve it. The improved A* algorithm is used to complete the path planning, and the actual effect of the model is verified on MATLAB.

2 Mathematical Modelling

2.1 Derivation of the Model

The scheduling model of flexible manufacturing shop containing AGVs can be described as: there are W AGVs and N workstations in the manufacturing workshop, and AGVs are responsible for transporting materials to the workstations. The following assumptions must be satisfied:

1. The initial location of the AGV and material is in the warehouse, and the AGV returns to the warehouse after finishing transportation task.
2. Each AGV can transport the corresponding materials from the warehouse to multiple workstations, but each workstation allows one AGV to be distributed, and cannot be repeatedly distributed.
3. The number of AGVs is lower than the number of workstations.
4. Collisions and failures during AGV transportation are not taken into account.
5. All AGVs and machines are available at zero time.

$$d_m = \sum_{m=1}^{W} (d_{me} + d_{ml}) \delta \tag{1}$$

$$\eta = \frac{\sum_{m=1}^{W} d_{ml}}{d_m} \tag{2}$$

$$J = \alpha * min\left(\sum_{m=1}^{W} d_m\right) + \beta * max(\eta) \tag{3}$$

Symbols relevant to mathematical modelling is shown in Table 1. Equation (1) shows that the total travel distance of all AGVs in the system is equal to the sum of the no-loaded travel distances and loaded travel distances of all AGVs. Equation (2) means that the AGV utilization rate is equal to the ratio of the total loaded distance traveled by the AGV to the total distance traveled by the AGV. Equation (3) shows that an optimization model is established with the optimization goal of minimizing the AGV travel distance and maximizing the utilization rate of AGV.

Table 1. The description of relevant symbols

Parameter	Description
N	number of workstations
W	number of AGVs
m	AGV serial number
d_m	Total distance traveled by all AGVs
d_{me}	m_{th} AGV distance without load
d_{ml}	m_{th} AGV distance with load
α	weight coefficient of minimum travel distance
β	weight coefficient of AGV utilization rate
η	AGV utilization rate
δ	obstacle impact factor

2.2 Derivation of the Obstacle Impact Factor

To represent the impact of obstacles on the distance of the driving path, the obstacle impact factor δ is introduced. The first factor affecting the path traveled by the AGV is the area of the obstacle. The larger the ratio of the area of the obstacle to the total area of the workshop, the greater the likelihood of affecting the driving route of the AGV.

Similarly, irregularly shaped obstacles can also have a great impact on the AGV's route. To better represent the impact of obstacle shape on travel distance, θ_k is defined as the virtual area of the obstacle S_v, which is the product of the maximum length and maximum width of the obstacle as shown in Fig. 1.

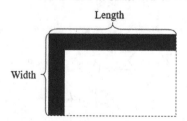

Fig. 1. A virtual area of an irregularity obstacle

$$\theta_k = \frac{S_v}{S_k} \tag{4}$$

$$\theta = \frac{\sum \theta_k}{ON}(\theta_k < 1) \tag{5}$$

Equation (4) shows the calculation of ratio of the virtual area to the actual area (black part) of the k_{th} obstacle. Equation (5) shows the average of θ_k ($\theta_k < 1$), and ON is the number of θ_k that satisfies the condition.

$$\delta = 1 + (\frac{S_o}{S} \times ln(\theta + e)) \qquad (6)$$

Formula (6) indicates that how to calculate obstacle impact factor δ. S_o is the total area of the obstacle, and S is the total area of the manufacturing workshop, which considers the contribution of the obstacle area to the δ. θ is the average of the virtual-to-real ratio of all obstacles, which takes into account the contribution of irregular obstacles to δ.

3   Scheduling Algorithm

The solution of Scheduling model is a typical NP-hard problem. GA is adopted for NP-hard problems by imitating the inheritance and evolution of natural organisms [9].

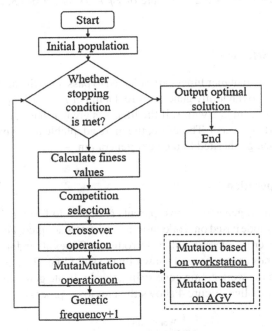

Fig. 2. Flowchart of GA

Figure 2 shows the flowchart of GA. Firstly, the initial population is randomly generated based on workstation sequencing and AGV task assignment. Secondly, the fitness of each chromosome is calculated and compare the fitness with a random number to select the chromosome for genetic manipulation. New populations will generate by using workstation-based crossover operation and hybrid mutation operation. An elite strategy is used to select outstanding parents. Finally, the optimal solution is output.

3.1 Encoding and Decoding

In this paper, a double-layer coding method based on numbers of workstations and AGVs is adopted. The code of feasible solution consists of two parts. The first part is the workstation code, which represents the order in which the AGV travels to the workstation, and its gene string length is N. The second part represents the number of AGV, which has a gene string length of W.

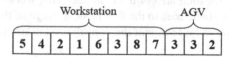

Fig. 3. Chromosome encoding diagram including workstation and AGV

Figure 3 represents a chromosome encoding with 8 workstations and 3 AGV. Left-to-right order is introduced into decoding calculation. The AGV gene string represents the route of 1_{th} AGV is 5->4->2, the route of 2_{th} AGV is 1->6->3, and the route of 3 AGV is 8->7.

3.2 Competition Selection

A subset of the elite with higher fitness are selected to pass on to the next generation. The function rand is used to randomly generate a real number r ($r \in [0, 1]$). The individual's fitness will be used to compare with r. If the fitness is greater than r, it is retained for the next generation, and vice versa. Therefore, the more adaptable an individual, the greater the probability of being inherited to the next generation.

3.3 Crossover Operation

In a crossover operator, genes from two parents are taken to form a child chromosome [10]. The crossover mode based on workstation crossover is adopted. For the workstation-based crossover, *OX* cross operator will be introduced. Genes at random locations on two paternal chromosomes are exchanged shown by the solid line. Because the workstation number is unique in the workstation gene string, the duplicate genes must be exchanged as shown by the dotted line. Figure 4 shows the crossover process.

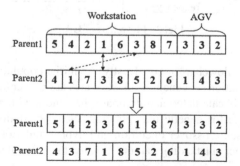

Fig. 4. Crossover process based on workstation

3.4 Mutation Operation

In order to expand the local search area, the hybrid mutation mode based on workstation mutation and AGV mutation is adopted. If $rand(0, 1) \leq 0.5$, workstation-based mutation is adopted; otherwise agv-based mutation is used.

For the workstation-based mutation, two integers are randomly generated in the range of 1 to N. The genes corresponding to these two numbers will be exchanged. Assuming that the mutation genes is the fifth gene and the sixth gene. Figure 5 shows the workstation-based mutation under hypothetical conditions.

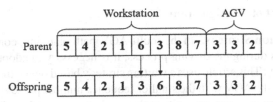

Fig. 5. Workstation-based mutation

For the agv-based mutation, two integers are randomly generated in the range of $N + 1$ to $N + W$ as shown in Fig. 6.

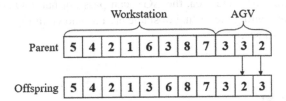

Fig. 6. Agv-based mutation

4 Path Search Algorithm

4.1 A* Algorithm Overview

Path planning aims to find a collision-free optimal path from the origin to the destination. In this study, AGV operate in 2D workspace. In static path planning, compared with D* lite algorithm [11], particle swarm optimization algorithm [12] and neural network algorithm [13], A* algorithm has the advantages of fast efficiency, high flexibility and high precision. Therefore, the actual map is constructed by the grid method, and the path planning algorithm selects the A* algorithm.

The grid method divides the manufacturing workshop map into an equally large square grid, storing the map information in the form of an array, where 0 indicates the obstacle and 1 indicates the presence of obstacles. The A* algorithm approaches the target quickly under the guidance of the heuristic function, and is an efficient path planning algorithm.

$$f(n) = g(n) + h(n) \tag{7}$$

A* algorithm evaluates the surrounding grids of the current gird through the evaluation Eq. (7), and select the grid to be expanded according to the priority. The larger the value of $f(n)$, the lower the priority of the grid; the smaller the value of $f(n)$, the higher the priority of the grid [14].

4.2 Improvement of A* Algorithm

Conflict Elimination Strategy. In the multi-AGV path planning, considering the possible path conflicts during the driving process, it is necessary to adopt the path conflict elimination strategy. This article uses a waiting strategy based on the time window. When the AGV conflicts, the AGV with the smaller sequence number passes first, and the AGV with the bigger sequence number waits at the conflict point until conflict resolution.

Virtual Obstacle Area. A* algorithm picks the smallest f(n) to join the open list for each iteration, and if an irregular obstacle is encountered, a path as shown in Fig. 7 appears. Therefore, the area contained in the maximum length and maximum width of the irregular obstacle is set to the virtual obstacle area as shown in Fig. 8. If the target point is in the virtual obstacle area, the AGV can pass normally. Otherwise, it cannot pass. The path after setting the virtual obstacle area as shown in Fig. 9 greatly reduces the running path distance.

Fig. 7. Irregular obstacles   **Fig. 8.** Virtual zones   **Fig. 9.** Improved path

Turn Penalty Factor. When encountering an unsatisfied grid, A* algorithm will change the direction of AGV, leading to an inflection point. A path with more inflection points will affect the driving efficiency of AGV, so the turn penalty factor σ added to the evaluation function. When there is a turn, $\sigma = 1.5$, otherwise $\sigma = 1$. When the AGV turns to the next grid, $f(n)$ will be larger, reducing the likelihood of being chosen.

$$f(n) = \sigma g(n) + h(n) \tag{8}$$

5 Simulation of Scheduling Model

This paper uses the grid method to map the AGV manufacturing space. The result of the route planning is a list of grids from the origin to the destination. Seeing Fig. 10, the 2D map (*100 × 100*) shows the distribution of obstacles, warehouse, and workstations. The warehouse is located in the upper left corner of the map, indicated by the letter D. Simulation takes place in MATLAB and runs on an Intel Core i5-6200U CPU 2.30GHz PC. Experimental settings are: population size $NP = 200$, genetic algebra $G = 500$, number of AGV $W = 4$, number of workstations $N = 10$.

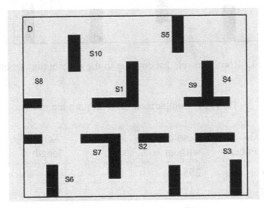

Fig. 10. Map of the manufacturing floor which has black obstacles

The obstacle impact factor δ is calculated to be 1.16. The weight coefficient of minimum driving distance is $\alpha = 0.9$, and the weight cofficient of AGV utilization rate is $\beta = 0.1$. The optimal solution obtained by the GA is recorded in Table 2.

Table 2. Optimal solution

AGV number	Solution routes
1	D → S2 → S3 → S4 → S9 → D
2	D → S5 → S1 → D
3	D → S7 → S6 → D
4	D → S10 → S8 → D

Routes of the AGVs are generated based on the scheme, as shown in Fig. 11. The total path length calculated in the model and the total path length after the actual path planning are shown in Table 3.

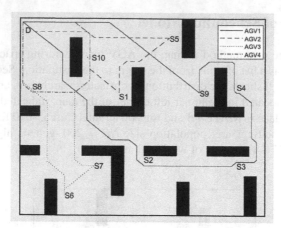

Fig. 11. Routes traveled according to the distribution scheme

Table 3. Comparison of Total path length

AGV number	Results without δ	Results with δ	Actual length
1	255	300	311
2	147	171	166
3	187	217	203
4	96	111	149
all	455	799	829

The actual path length after path planning is 829. The total path length calculated without the obstacle impact factor is 455 and accuracy is 55%, and the total path length calculated using the δ is 799 and accuracy is 96%. Compared with the model without δ, the calculation results of the model with δ are 41% more accurate. Obviously, the calculation results of the multi-AGV scheduling model with the obstacle impact factor are closer to the actual situation.

6   Conclusions

In this paper, the multi-AGV scheduling model with the goal of minimizing the total length of the path and the maximum AGV utilization rate has been studied. The obstacle impact factor has been added to the model, so that the multi-AGV scheduling model results were more in line with the actual manufacturing workshop. The custom GA algorithm has been used to solve the model. The improved A* algorithm has been used for path planning. A 2D map of the flexible manufacturing workshop has been established on MATLAB using the gird method. Experiment has shown that the scheduling model was effective and improved the accuracy of calculation results.

Acknowledgement. This work was supported in part by the National Natural Science Foundation of China under Grant NSFC U1813212, in part by the Science and Technology Planning Project of Guangdong Province, China under Grant 2020B121201012.

References

1. Abderrahim, M., Bekrar, A., Trentesaux, D., Aissani, N., Bouamrane, K.: Manufacturing 4.0 operations scheduling with AGV battery management constraints. Energies **13**(18), 4948 (2020)
2. Zhao, X.F., Liu, H.Z., Lin, S.X., Chen, Y.K.: Design and Implementation of a multiple AGV scheduling algorithm for a job-shop. Int. J. Simul. Model. **19**(1), 134–135 (2020)
3. Shouwen, J., Di, L., Zhengrong, C., Dong, G.: Integrated scheduling in automated container terminals considering AGV conflict-free routing. Transp. Lett. Int. J. Transp. Res. **13**(7), 501–513 (2020)
4. Yuan, M.H., Li, Y.D., Pei, F.Q., Gu, W.B.: Dual-resource integrated scheduling method of AGV and machine in intelligent manufacturing job shop. J. Central South Univ. **28**(8), 2423–2435 (2021)
5. Tang, H.T., Cheng, X.Y., Jiang, W.G., Chen, S.W.: Research on equipment configuration optimization of AGV Unmanned Warehouse. IEEE Access **9**, 479646–547959 (2021)
6. Xu, Y., Qi, L., Luan, W., Guo, X., Ma, H.: Load-In-Load-Out AGV route planning in automatic container terminal. IEEE Access **8**, 157081–157088 (2020)
7. Barak, S., Moghdani, R., Maghsoudlou, H.: Energy-efficient multi-objective flexible manufacturing scheduling. J. Clean. Prod. **283**, 124610 (2021)
8. Wang, F., Zhang, Y., Zuqiang, S.: A novel scheduling method for automated guided vehicles in workshop. Int. J. Adv. Rob. Syst. **3**(16), 1–13 (2019)
9. Xu, W.X., Guo, S.S.: A Multi-Objective and Multi-Dimensional optimization scheduling method using a hybrid evolutionary algorithm with a sectional encoding mode. Sustainability **11**(5), 1329 (2019)
10. Chaudhry, I.A., et al.: Integrated scheduling of machines and automated guided vehicles (AGVs) in flexible job shop environment using genetic algorithms. Int. J. Ind. Eng. Comput. **13**, 343–362 (2022)
11. Deng, X., Li, R.F., Zhao, L.J., Wang, K., Gui, X.C.: Multi-obstacle path planning and optimization for mobile robot. Expert Syst. Appl. **183**, 115445 (2021)
12. Farooq, B., Bao, J.S., Raza, H., Sun, Y.C., Ma, Q.W.: Flow-shop path planning for multi-automated guided vehicles in intelligent textile spinning cyber-physical production systems dynamic environment. J. Manuf. Syst. **59**, 98–116 (2021)
13. Cabezas-Olivenza, M., Zulueta, E., Sanchez-Chica, A., Teso-Fz-Betono, A., Fernandez-Gamiz, U.: Dynamical analysis of a navigation algorithm. Mathematics **9**(23), 3139 (2021)
14. Cai, J.M., Li, X.K., Liang, Y., Ouyang, S.: Collaborative optimization of storage location assignment and path planning in robotic mobile fulfillment systems. Sustainability **13**(10), 5644 (2021)

Type Synthesis of Six Degrees of Freedom Parallel Mechanism with Decoupled Translation and Rotation

Ya Liu[1] (iD), Wenjuan Lu[2], Jiahao Zeng[1], Jianhua Cong[1], Bo Hu[1], and Daxing Zeng[2]([envelope]) (iD)

[1] School of Mechanical Engineering, Yanshan University, Qinhuangdao 066004, China
[2] The DGUT Innovation Center of Robotics and Intelligent Equipment, Dongguan 523808, China
zengdx@dgut.edu.cn

Abstract. A type synthesis method of six degrees of freedom (DOFs) parallel mechanism (PM) with decoupled translation and rotation (DTR) is proposed by analyzing the input and output characteristics of partially decoupled parallel mechanism (PDPM). Firstly, based on the requirements of Jacobian matrix of PDPM, the direct Jacobian matrix and inverse Jacobian matrix are constructed by the screw theory, so as to determine the actuation wrench screw (AWS) that represents the force or couple acting on the moving platform by the actuated twist screw (ATS) of the limb. According to the AWS and the connectivity, the ATS representing the driving pair and the non-actuated twist screw (NATS) representing the non-driving pair on the corresponding limb are obtained, and then the configuration of the limb structure screw system is completed. Finally, according to the limb combination principle of PDPM, six limbs are selected in turn to connect the moving platform and the fixed platform, and then a variety of six DOFs PMs with DTR are obtained. The six DOFs PM with DTR can be used as the main structure of the joint rehabilitation robot, which provides an idea to solve the problem that the rotation center of the robot joint is inconsistent with the actual physiological center of human joint. This kind of mechanism has the characteristics of compact structure and simple control that shows wide application prospects.

Keywords: Type synthesis · Parallel mechanism · Partially decoupled · Actuation wrench screw

1 Introduction

Parallel mechanisms (PMs) have received widespread attention and application in the world because of their excellent characteristics in bearing capacity, accuracy, and stiffness [1]. However, the majority of PMs have strong kinematic coupled, which makes the mechanism complex in control design, path planning and assembly, so the popularization and application of PMs face certain obstacles [2]. Therefore, the PMs with good kinematic decoupled characteristics has become one of the research hotspots in the field of mechanism in recent years.

© The Author(s), under exclusive license to Springer Nature Switzerland AG 2022
H. Liu et al. (Eds.): ICIRA 2022, LNAI 13455, pp. 228–239, 2022.
https://doi.org/10.1007/978-3-031-13844-7_23

Type synthesis is the focus and difficulty in the field of PMs research, and it is also the cornerstone and source of the original innovation of the mechanism. At present, the popular type synthesis methods of PMs in the world include: the enumeration method based on the formula for degrees of freedom (DOFs) [3], the Lie group of displacements [4], the G_F set theory [5], the position and orientation characteristics set [6], the integration of configuration evolution [7], and the screw theory [8].

Zeng et al. proposed a new method of type synthesis for decoupled parallel mechanism, including the programming and distribution of branches' motions, configuration design and combination of branches [9]. Cao et al. proposed a methodology for the structural synthesis of fully-decoupled three-rotational and one-translational PMs by analyzing the characteristics of the input-output relationships for fully-decoupled PMs [10]. Xu et al. analyzed systematically the principle of full decoupling of two rotational DOFs for a two-rotation and one-translation PM and two-rotation PM with three supporting branches [11]. Qu et al. proposed a novel method for type synthesis of lower-mobility decoupled parallel mechanism with redundant constraints [12]. Wang et al. proposed a new synthesis method of three translational and two rotational decoupled hybrid mechanism with large bearing capacity, based on the screw theory and the atlas method [13]. Kuo et al. developed a systematic approach for synthesizing the structures of f-DOF ($f \leq$ 6) PMs with fully decoupled projective motion on the basis of the geometrical reasoning of the projective motion interpreted by screw algebra [14].

It is convenient to study some problems of space mechanism with screw theory. Compared with other methods, screw theory has the advantages of clear geometric concept, clear physical meaning, simple expression form and convenient algebraic operation, etc. Moreover, screw theory is easy to transform with other methods (such as vector method, matrix method and motion influence coefficient method). It is a better one among many mathematical tools.

Based on the screw theory, this paper carries out the type synthesis research of six DOFs PM with decoupled translation and rotation (DTR). The kinematic model of PMs is analyzed in Sect. 2, the type synthesis principle of the six DOFs PM with DTR is proposed in Sect. 3, the type synthesis process of six DOFs PM with DTR is given in Sect. 4, and the conclusions are drawn in Sect. 5.

2 The Kinematic Model of PMs

At a certain moment, the output motion of PMs moving platform can be expressed by a linear combination of each twist screw of the limb, that is

$$\mathbf{v} = \sum_{j=1}^{F_i} \dot{q}_{ij} \$_{ij} \quad i = 1, 2, \cdots, n \tag{1}$$

where, $\mathbf{v}$ represents the output twist screw of the moving platform, F_i represents the connectivity of i-th limb kinematic chain, $\$_{ij}$ represents the j-th single DOF kinematic pair instantaneous twist screw of i-th limb kinematic chain, $\dot{q}_{ij}$ represents the j-th single DOF kinematic pair vector of i-th limb kinematic chain, n represents the number of single open chain limb.

The force or couple acting on the moving platform by the driving pair is defined as the actuation wrench screw (AWS). When the form of the AWS is $\$_{ai} = (L_{ai}\ M_{ai}\ N_{ai}\ ;\ P_{ai}\ Q_{ai}\ R_{ai})$, it represents an acting force; when the form of the AWS is $\$_{ai} = (0\ 0\ 0\ ;\ L_{ai}\ M_{ai}\ N_{ai})$, it represents an acting force couple. And, for the same limb, the reciprocal product of AWS and non-actuated twist screw (NATS) representing the non-driving pair is zero.

The AWS of the i-th limb kinematic chain does the reciprocal product with the left and right sides of Eq. (1) at the same time, which is expressed as:

$$\left[\boldsymbol{\Pi}\$_{ai}\right]^{\mathrm{T}} v = \dot{q}_{i1}\left[\boldsymbol{\Pi}\$_{ai}\right]^{\mathrm{T}}\$_{i1} \tag{2}$$

where, $\$_{i1}$ represents the actuated twist screw (ATS) of the i-th limb, that is, driving pair twist screw of the i-th limb (assuming that the driving pair of each limb is assembled on the fixed platform and is the first kinematic pair); $\dot{q}_{i1}$ represents the instantaneous speed of the i-th limb driving pair.

Simplify Eq. (2) is as follows:

$$J_{\mathrm{dir}} V = J_{\mathrm{inv}} \dot{q} \tag{3}$$

$$
\begin{aligned}
V &= \left[v_X\ v_Y\ v_Z\ \omega_X\ \omega_Y\ \omega_Z\right]^{\mathrm{T}} \\
\dot{q} &= \left[\dot{q}_{11}\ \dot{q}_{21}\ \dot{q}_{31}\ \dot{q}_{41}\ \dot{q}_{51}\ \dot{q}_{61}\right]^{\mathrm{T}} \\
J_{\mathrm{dir}} &= \left[\$_{a1}\ \$_{a2}\ \$_{a3}\ \$_{a4}\ \$_{a5}\ \$_{a6}\right]^{\mathrm{T}} \\
J_{\mathrm{inv}} &= \begin{bmatrix} \$_{a1} \circ \$_{11} & 0 & \cdots & 0 \\ 0 & \$_{a2} \circ \$_{21} & \cdots & 0 \\ \vdots & \vdots & & \vdots \\ 0 & 0 & \cdots & \$_{a6} \circ \$_{61} \end{bmatrix}
\end{aligned} \tag{4}
$$

where, V represents the output velocity vector of the moving platform, $\dot{q}$ represents the input velocity vector of the limb active joint, J_{dir} represents the direct Jacobian matrix of PM, J_{inv} represents the inverse Jacobian matrix of PM.

From Eqs. (3) and (4), the inverse Jacobian matrix J_{inv} is a diagonal matrix, and if it is a full rank matrix, then there is

$$\dot{q} = J_{\mathrm{inv}}^{-1} J_{\mathrm{dir}} V = J^{-1} V \tag{5}$$

$$J^{-1} = J_{\mathrm{inv}}^{-1} J_{\mathrm{dir}} = \begin{bmatrix} \$_{a1}/(\$_{a1} \circ \$_{11}) \\ \$_{a2}/(\$_{a2} \circ \$_{21}) \\ \vdots \\ \$_{a6}/(\$_{a6} \circ \$_{61}) \end{bmatrix} \tag{6}$$

where, J represents the Jacobian matrix of PM.

From Eqs. (5) and (6), the direct Jacobian matrix for six DOFs PM with DTR can be expressed as

$$
J_{dir} = \begin{bmatrix} \$_{a1} \\ \$_{a2} \\ \$_{a3} \\ \$_{a4} \\ \$_{a5} \\ \$_{a6} \end{bmatrix} = \begin{bmatrix} L_{a1} & M_{a1} & N_{a1} & 0 & 0 & 0 \\ L_{a2} & M_{a2} & N_{a2} & 0 & 0 & 0 \\ L_{a3} & M_{a3} & N_{a3} & 0 & 0 & 0 \\ 0 & 0 & 0 & L_{a4} & M_{a4} & N_{a4} \\ 0 & 0 & 0 & L_{a5} & M_{a5} & N_{a5} \\ 0 & 0 & 0 & L_{a6} & M_{a6} & N_{a6} \end{bmatrix} \tag{7}
$$

3 The Type Synthesis Principle of Six DOFs PM with DTR

When the AWS is a couple, the driving pair is prismatic pair or revolute pair. When the driving pair is revolute pair, the limb needs to have another revolute pair at the same time to form a 2R parallel sub chain (hereinafter referred to as 2R parallel sub chain revolute pair), which is equivalent to the linear combination of a revolute pair and a prismatic pair, and the effect is the same as using prismatic pair as the driving pair [15]. However, in order not to destroy the decoupled characteristics of the mechanism, it should be noted that 2R parallel sub chain as the driving pair will bring the driving action in the other direction. Therefore, the structure screw system of the limb must be a prismatic pair that is colinear with the direction of the limb negative driving, so as to eliminate the influence of the negative driving on mechanism decoupled characteristics. When the AWS is force, the driving pair is revolute pair.

Combined with above analysis, the six DOFs PM with DTR type synthesis is completed based on the screw theory. The specific principles are as follows:

(1) According to the characteristics of six DOFs PM with DTR, the inverse Jacobian matrix and the direct Jacobian matrix form is determined, and then the moving platform output DOFs driving by each limb is determined. Finally, the AWS form of corresponding limb is obtained.
(2) The ATS of limb is determined according to the AWS of corresponding limb. When the AWS is a force line vector screw, the driving pair can be a prismatic pair or a 2R parallel sub chain revolute pair, and the corresponding ATS is a couple screw or a force line vector screw. When the AWS is a couple screw, the driving pair can only be a revolute pair, and the corresponding ATS is a force line vector screw.
(3) Based on the characteristic that the reciprocal product of the NATS and the AWS is zero in each limb, the NATS system can be deduced according to the reciprocal screw theory, and then all the structure types of the limb can be deduced according to the different connectivity.
(4) According to the constrained screw theory of PM and the limb rotation conditions of decoupled PM [16], the desired six DOFs PM with DTR can be obtained by selecting six limbs in turn to connect the fixed platform and the moving platform.

The type synthesis principle of the six DOFs PM with DTR is shown in Fig. 1.

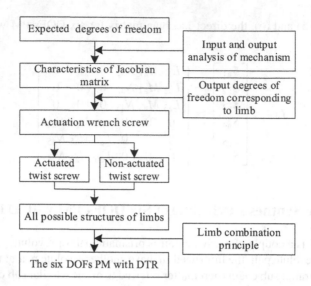

Fig. 1. The type synthesis principle diagram of the six DOFs PM with DTR.

4   The Type Synthesis Process of Six DOFs PM with DTR

4.1   Limb Type Synthesis Conditions

In the following type synthesis process, it is assumed that the first, second and third limb provide the translational driving for the moving platform, and the fourth, fifth and sixth limb provide the rotational driving for the moving platform. In order to simplify the structure and limit the space, the mechanism type synthesis meets the following conditions:

(1) The case of redundant kinematic pairs in the limbs isn't considered, that is, it is considered only that limb connectivity is six.
(2) Only one arrangement case is given for a kind of limbs, that is, it isn't considered that the arrangement order of limb kinematic pairs changes.
(3) Only the basic kinematic pairs are considered, and the case of composite kinematic pair replacing basic motion pair can be seen in Ref. [17].
(4) The axes of adjacent kinematic pairs are perpendicular or parallel, which is not the case in practical engineering application. It can be designed and considered according to specific conditions.
(5) The driving pair is directly connected with the fixed platform to ensure that the form of the ATS will not change with the motion of the limb.

As shown in Fig. 2, the limb coordinate system o_i-$x_iy_iz_i$ ($i = 1, 2, ..., 6$) is established on the limb, where the point o_i is the center point of the fixed platform. In order to ensure structure symmetry and simplify calculation, the projection (o_iB_i) of the x_i axis (o_iA_i) in the fixed platform plane (XOY plane) be homogeneous (60° to each other), the z_i axis is in the $A_io_iB_i$ plane and perpendicular to o_iA_i, and the y_i axis is determined by the right-hand rule, $\angle A_i o_i B_i = \alpha$. The fixed coordinate system $O\text{-}XYZ$ is established on the fixed platform, the point O is the center point of the fixed platform, the Z axis is the normal direction of the fixed platform, the X axis coincides with $o_1 B_1$, and the Y axis is determined by the right-hand rule.

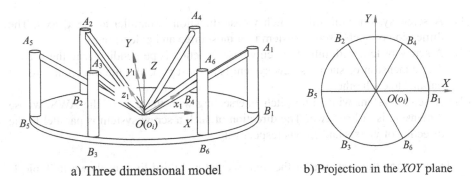

a) Three dimensional model   b) Projection in the XOY plane

Fig. 2. The limb coordinate system and the fixed coordinate system.

4.2 The Type Synthesis of the First, Second and Third Limb

It can be seen from Eq. (7) that the AWS of the first, second and third limb in the $O\text{-}XYZ$ can be expressed as:

$$\$_{ai} = \left(L_{ai} \; M_{ai} \; N_{ai} \; ; 0\,0\,0 \right) \quad (i = 1,\, 2,\, 3) \tag{8}$$

In the $O\text{-}XYZ$, the AWS $\$_{ai}$ ($i = 1, 2, 3$) represents a force screw passing through the origin O. Let the direction of the AWS $\$_{ai}$ coincides with the direction of x_i ($i = 1, 2, 3$), in the respective limb coordinate system $o_i\text{-}x_i y_i z_i$ ($i = 1, 2, 3$), then the AWS $\$_{ai}$ of the first, second and third limb can be expressed by the unified form as

$$\$_{ai}^{o_i} = \left(1\,0\,0 ; 0\,0\,0 \right) \quad (i = 1,\, 2,\, 3) \tag{9}$$

According to the analysis in Sect. 3, it is clear that there are three types of i-th ($i = 1, 2, 3$) limb ATS (type A, type B and type C):

$$\begin{cases} \$_{qi1}^{o_i} = \left(0\,0\,0 ; 1\,0\,0 \right) \\ \$_{qi2}^{o_i} = \left(0\,1\,0 ; d_{qi2}\,0\,e_{qi2} \right) \quad (i = 1,\, 2,\, 3) \\ \$_{qi3}^{o_i} = \left(0\,0\,1 ; d_{qi3}\,e_{qi3}\,0 \right) \end{cases} \tag{10}$$

Substituting Eqs. (9) and (10) into Eq. (4), the element of the inverse Jacobian matrix is as follows

$$\boldsymbol{J}_{invii} = \begin{cases} \$_{ai}^{o_i} \circ \$_{qi1}^{o_i} = 1 \\ \$_{ai}^{o_i} \circ \$_{qi2}^{o_i} = d_{qi2} \quad (i = 1,\, 2,\, 3) \\ \$_{ai}^{o_i} \circ \$_{qi3}^{o_i} = d_{qi3} \end{cases} \tag{11}$$

Since d_{qi2} and d_{qi3} are variables related to the choice of the coordinate system origin, J_{inv11} isn't zero in all three cases in Eq. (11) as long as the position of the driving pair is adjusted so that d_{qi2} and d_{qi3} aren't zero.

According to the type synthesis principle of the six DOFs PM with DTR in Sect. 3, the possible NATS system of limbs are as follows:

(1) A screw system with finite pitch whose direction is parallel to the x_i axis. The dimension of such a screw system is at most three and at least one.
(2) A screw system with infinite pitch whose direction is perpendicular to the x_i axis. The dimension of such a screw system is at most two, and the directions are not parallel to each other.
(3) A screw system with finite pitch intersecting with the axis of the AWS, whose dimension is at least two. The direction of such a screw system is parallel to the direction of y_i axis and z_i axis respectively.

In summary, the structure of the first, second and third limb is shown in Table 1. The kinematic pair with underlined represents the driving pair, the subscripts x_i, y_i and z_i represents the direction of the axis of kinematic pair, T represents the prismatic pair, and R represents the revolute pair, the same below.

4.3 The Type Synthesis of the Fourth, Fifth and Sixth Limb

It can be seen from Eq. (7) that the AWS of the fourth, fifth and sixth limb in the $O\text{-}XYZ$ can be expressed as:

$$\$_{ai} = \begin{pmatrix} 0\,0\,0\,;\, L_{ai}\,M_{ai}\,N_{ai} \end{pmatrix} \quad (i = 4,\ 5,\ 6) \tag{12}$$

In the $O\text{-}XYZ$, the AWS $\$_{ai}$ ($i = 4, 5, 6$) represents a couple screw. Let the direction of the AWS $\$_{ai}$ coincides with the direction of x_i ($i = 4, 5, 6$), in the respective limb coordinate system $o_i\text{-}x_i y_i z_i$ ($i = 4, 5, 6$), then the AWS $\$_a$ of the fourth, fifth and sixth limb can be expressed by the unified form as

$$\$_{ai}^{o_i} = \begin{pmatrix} 0\,0\,0\,;\, 1\,0\,0 \end{pmatrix} \quad (i = 4,\ 5,\ 6) \tag{13}$$

According to the analysis in Sect. 3, the ATS of i-th ($i = 4, 5, 6$) limb can only be

$$\$_{qi1}^{o_i} = \begin{pmatrix} 1\,0\,0\,;\, 0\,e_{qi1}\,f_{qi1} \end{pmatrix} \quad (i = 4,\ 5,\ 6) \tag{14}$$

Substituting Eqs. (13) and (14) into Eq. (4), the element of the inverse Jacobian matrix is as follows

$$J_{invii} = \$_{ai}^{o_i} \circ \$_{qi1}^{o_i} = 1 \quad (i = 4,\ 5,\ 6) \tag{15}$$

The NATS system is obtained according to the type synthesis principle of the six DOFs PM with DTR in Sect. 3. The structure of the fourth, fifth and sixth limb is shown in Table 2.

Table 1. The structure of the first, second and third limb.

Category	Type of kinematic pairs	Type of limbs		Number
Type A	Including three prismatic pairs	$\underline{T}_{x_i}T_{y_i}T_{z_i}R_{x_i}R_{y_i}R_{z_i}$		1
	Including two prismatic pairs	$\underline{T}_{x_i}T_{y_i}R_{x_i}R_{y_i}1R_{y_i}2R_{z_i}$	$\underline{T}_{x_i}T_{y_i}R_{x_i}1R_{x_i}2R_{y_i}R_{z_i}$	4
		$\underline{T}_{x_i}T_{z_i}R_{x_i}R_{y_i}R_{z_i}1R_{z_i}2$	$\underline{T}_{x_i}T_{z_i}R_{x_i}1R_{x_i}2R_{y_i}R_{z_i}$	
	Including one prismatic pair	$\underline{T}_{x_i}R_{x_i}R_{y_i}1R_{y_i}2R_{z_i}1R_{z_i}2$	$\underline{T}_{x_i}R_{x_i}1R_{x_i}2R_{y_i}R_{z_i}1R_{z_i}2$	4
		$\underline{T}_{x_i}R_{x_i}1R_{x_i}2R_{y_i}1R_{y_i}2R_{z_i}$	$\underline{T}_{x_i}R_{x_i}1R_{x_i}2R_{x_i}3R_{y_i}R_{z_i}$	
Type B	Including two prismatic pairs	$\underline{R}_{y_i}R_{y_i}2T_{y_i}T_{z_i}R_{x_i}R_{z_i}$		1
	Including one prismatic pair	$\underline{R}_{y_i}1R_{y_i}2T_{y_i}R_{x_i}1R_{x_i}2R_{z_i}$	$\underline{R}_{y_i}1R_{y_i}2R_{y_i}3T_{y_i}R_{x_i}R_{z_i}$	4
		$\underline{R}_{y_i}1R_{y_i}2T_{z_i}R_{x_i}R_{z_i}1R_{z_i}2$	$\underline{R}_{y_i}1R_{y_i}2T_{z_i}R_{x_i}1R_{x_i}2R_{z_i}$	
	Excluding prismatic pair	$\underline{R}_{y_i}1R_{y_i}2R_{x_i}1R_{x_i}2R_{z_i}1R_{z_i}2$	$\underline{R}_{y_i}1R_{y_i}2R_{x_i}1R_{x_i}2R_{x_i}3R_{z_i}$	4
		$\underline{R}_{y_i}1R_{y_i}2R_{y_i}3R_{x_i}R_{z_i}1R_{z_i}2$	$\underline{R}_{y_i}1R_{y_i}2R_{y_i}3R_{x_i}1R_{x_i}2R_{z_i}$	
Type C	Including two prismatic pairs	$\underline{R}_{z_i}1R_{z_i}2T_{y_i}T_{z_i}R_{x_i}R_{y_i}$		1
	Including one prismatic pair	$\underline{R}_{z_i}1R_{z_i}2T_{y_i}R_{x_i}R_{y_i}1R_{y_i}2$	$\underline{R}_{z_i}1R_{z_i}2T_{y_i}R_{x_i}1R_{x_i}2R_{y_i}$	4
		$\underline{R}_{z_i}1R_{z_i}2T_{z_i}R_{x_i}1R_{x_i}2R_{y_i}$	$\underline{R}_{z_i}1R_{z_i}2R_{z_i}3T_{z_i}R_{x_i}R_{y_i}$	
	Excluding prismatic pair	$\underline{R}_{z_i}1R_{z_i}2R_{x_i}1R_{x_i}2R_{y_i}1R_{y_i}2$	$\underline{R}_{z_i}1R_{z_i}2R_{x_i}1R_{x_i}2R_{x_i}3R_{y_i}$	4
		$\underline{R}_{z_i}1R_{z_i}2R_{z_i}3R_{x_i}R_{y_i}1R_{y_i}2$	$\underline{R}_{z_i}1R_{z_i}2R_{z_i}3R_{x_i}1R_{x_i}2R_{y_i}$	

4.4 Example of Six DOFs PM with DTR

Since six DOFs limb has no constraints on the moving platform, a six DOFs PM with DTR can be obtained by selecting any one type in each limb from Table 1 and Table 2 and connecting it to the moving platform and fixed platform. A six DOFs PM with DTR is obtained by type synthesis, as shown in Fig. 3. The structure of the first, second and third limb is $\underline{T}_{x_i}T_{y_i}T_{z_i}R_{x_i}R_{y_i}R_{z_i}$ ($i = 1, 2, 3$), and the structure of the fourth, fifth and sixth limb is $\underline{R}_{x_i}T_{x_i}T_{y_i}T_{z_i}R_{y_i}R_{z_i}$ ($i = 4, 5, 6$).

Table 2. The structure of the fourth, fifth and sixth limb.

Type of kinematic pairs	Type of limbs		Number
Including three prismatic pairs	$\underline{R}_{x_i}T_{x_i}T_{y_i}T_{z_i}R_{y_i}R_{z_i}$		1
Including two prismatic pairs	$\underline{R}_{x_i}T_{x_i}T_{y_i}R_{y_i1}R_{y_i2}R_{z_i}$	$\underline{R}_{x_i1}R_{x_i2}T_{x_i}T_{y_i}R_{y_i}R_{z_i}$	6
	$\underline{R}_{x_i}T_{x_i}T_{z_i}R_{y_i}R_{z_i1}R_{z_i2}$	$\underline{R}_{x_i1}R_{x_i2}T_{x_i}T_{z_i}R_{y_i}R_{z_i}$	
	$\underline{R}_{x_i}T_{y_i}T_{z_i}R_{y_i}R_{z_i1}R_{z_i2}$	$\underline{R}_{x_i}T_{y_i}T_{z_i}R_{y_i1}R_{y_i2}R_{z_i}$	
Including one prismatic pair	$\underline{R}_{x_i}T_{x_i}R_{y_i1}R_{y_i2}R_{z_i1}R_{z_i2}$	$\underline{R}_{x_i1}R_{x_i2}T_{x_i}R_{y_i}R_{z_i1}R_{z_i2}$	12
	$\underline{R}_{x_i1}R_{x_i2}T_{x_i}R_{y_i1}R_{y_i2}R_{z_i}$	$\underline{R}_{x_i1}R_{x_i2}R_{x_i3}T_{x_i}R_{y_i}R_{z_i}$	
	$\underline{R}_{x_i}T_{y_i}R_{y_i1}R_{y_i2}R_{z_i1}R_{z_i2}$	$\underline{R}_{x_i}T_{y_i}R_{y_i1}R_{y_i2}R_{y_i3}R_{z_i}$	
	$\underline{R}_{x_i1}R_{x_i2}T_{y_i}R_{y_i}R_{z_i1}R_{z_i2}$	$\underline{R}_{x_i1}R_{x_i2}T_{y_i}R_{y_i1}R_{y_i2}R_{z_i}$	
	$\underline{R}_{x_i}T_{z_i}R_{y_i1}R_{z_i1}R_{z_i2}R_{z_i3}$	$\underline{R}_{x_i}T_{z_i}R_{y_i1}R_{y_i2}R_{z_i1}R_{z_i2}$	
	$\underline{R}_{x_i1}R_{x_i2}T_{z_i}R_{y_i}R_{z_i1}R_{z_i2}$	$\underline{R}_{x_i1}R_{x_i2}T_{z_i}R_{y_i1}R_{y_i2}R_{z_i}$	
Excluding prismatic pair	$\underline{R}_{x_i}R_{y_i1}R_{y_i2}R_{z_i1}R_{z_i2}R_{z_i3}$	$\underline{R}_{x_i}R_{y_i1}R_{y_i2}R_{y_i3}R_{z_i1}R_{z_i2}$	7
	$\underline{R}_{x_i1}R_{x_i2}R_{y_i}R_{z_i1}R_{z_i2}R_{z_i3}$	$\underline{R}_{x_i1}R_{x_i2}R_{y_i1}R_{y_i2}R_{z_i1}R_{z_i2}$	
	$\underline{R}_{x_i1}R_{x_i2}R_{y_i1}R_{y_i2}R_{y_i3}R_{z_i}$	$\underline{R}_{x_i1}R_{x_i2}R_{x_i3}R_{y_i}R_{z_i1}R_{z_i2}$	
	$\underline{R}_{x_i1}R_{x_i2}R_{x_i3}R_{y_i1}R_{y_i2}R_{z_i}$		

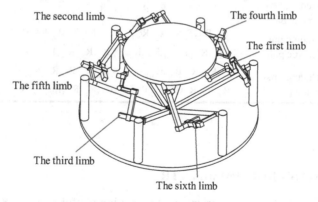

Fig. 3. Example of six DOFs PM with DTR.

5 Conclusions

(1) Based on the screw theory, the type synthesis theory of six DOFs PM with DTR is proposed. The mechanism type synthesis principle is given by analyzing the Jacobian matrix conditions of the six DOFs PM with DTR.

(2) Based on the proposed type synthesis method and principle, the type synthesis of the six DOFs PM with DTR is completed. Each limb of the six DOFs PM with DTR is obtained by type synthesis, and then each limb is connected with the moving platform and the fixed platform to obtain the six DOFs PM with DTR.

(3) The six DOFs PM with DTR can be used as the main structure of the joint rehabilitation robot, which provides an idea to solve the problem that the rotation center of the robot joint doesn't coincide with the actual physiological center of human joint and has wide application prospect.

Acknowledgement. This work was supported in part by the National Natural Science Foundation, China, under Grant 51905464, 51775473, in part by the Scientific Research Capacity Improvement Project of Key Developing Disciplines in Guangdong Province of China, under Grant 2021ZDJS084, in part by the National Key Research and Development Program, China, under Grant 2018YFB1307903, in part by the Dongguan Sci-tech Commissoner, under Grant 20211800500242, in part by the KEY Laboratory of Robotics and Intelligent Equipment of Guangdong Regular Institutions of Higher Education, under Grant 2017KSYS009, and in part by the Innovation Center of Robotics and Intelligent Equipment, China, under Grant KCYCXPT2017006, and in part by the Dongguan Social science and Technology Development (Key) Project, under Grant 20185071021602.

References

1. Lambert, P., Da Cruz, L., Bergeles, C.: Mobility of overconstrained parallel mechanisms with reconfigurable end-effectors. Mech. Mach. Theory **171**, 104722 (2022)
2. Sharifzadeh, M., Arian, A., Salimi, A., et al.: An experimental study on the direct & indirect dynamic identification of an over-constrained 3-DOF decoupled parallel mechanism. Mech. Mach. Theory **116**, 178–202 (2017)
3. Hess-Coelho, T.A.: Topological synthesis of a parallel wrist mechanism. J. Mech. Des. **128**(1), 230–235 (2006)
4. Li, Q., Huang, Z., Hervé, J.M.: Type synthesis of 3R2T 5-DOF parallel mechanisms using the Lie group of displacements. IEEE Trans. Robot. Autom. **20**(2), 173–180 (2004)
5. He, J., Gao, F., Meng, X., et al.: Type synthesis for 4-DOF parallel press mechanism using G_F set theory. Chin. J. Mech. Eng. **28**(4), 851–859 (2015)
6. Yang, T., Liu, A., Shen, H., et al.: On the correctness and strictness of the position and orientation characteristic equation for topological structure design of robot mechanisms. J. Mech. Robot. **5**(2), 021009 (2013)
7. Fan, C., Liu, H., Zhang, Y.: Type synthesis of 2T2R, 1T2R and 2R parallel mechanisms. Mech. Mach. Theory **61**, 184–190 (2013)
8. Zhen, H., Liu, J., Zeng, D.: A general methodology for mobility analysis of mechanisms based on constraint screw theory. Sci. China Ser. E: Technol. Sci. **52**(5), 1337–1347 (2009)
9. Zeng, D., Wang, H., Fan, M., et al.: Type synthesis of three degrees of freedom rotational generalized decoupling parallel mechanism. J. Mech. Eng. **53**(03), 17–24 (2017)
10. Cao, Y., Chen, H., Qin, Y., et al.: Type synthesis of fully-decoupled three-rotational and one-translational parallel mechanisms. Int. J. Adv. Rob. Syst. **13**, 79 (2016)
11. Xu, Y., Wang, B., Wang, Z., et al.: Investigations on the principle of full decoupling and type synthesis of 2R1T and 2R parallel mechanisms. Trans. Can. Soc. Mech. Eng. **43**(2), 263–271 (2018)

12. Qu, S., Li, R., Ma, C., Li, H.: Type synthesis for lower-mobility decoupled parallel mechanism with redundant constraints. J. Mech. Sci. Technol. **35**(6), 2657–2666 (2021). https://doi.org/10.1007/s12206-021-0536-x
13. Wang, S., Li, S., Li, H., et al.: Type synthesis of 3T2R decoupled hybrid mechanisms with large bearing capacity. J. Mech. Sci. Technol. **36**(4), 2053–2067 (2022)
14. Kuo, C., Dai, J.: Structure synthesis of a class of parallel manipulators with fully decoupled projective motion. J. Mech. Robot. **13**, 031011 (2021)

15. Zeng, D., Hou, Y., Lu, W., et al.: Type synthesis method for the translational decoupled parallel mechanism based on screw theory. J. Harbin Inst. Technol. **21**(01), 84–91 (2014)
16. Zeng, D., Huang, Z.: Type synthesis of the rotational decoupled parallel mechanism based on screw theory. Sci. Chin. Technol. Sci. **54**(4), 998–1004 (2011)
17. Huang, Z., Li, Q.: Type synthesis of symmetrical lower-mobility parallel mechanisms using the constraint-synthesis method. Int. J. Robot. Res. **22**(1), 59–79 (2003)

Limited Time Fault Tolerant Control for Attitude Stabilization of Quadrotor UAV

Yibo Li[✉] and Tao Li

Shenyang Aerospace University, Shenyang, Liaoning, China
Liyibo_sau@163.com

Abstract. Aiming at the situation of external disturbance and actuator failure in the attitude control of quadrotor UAV, an adaptive fault-tolerant control (FTC) method based on finite-time disturbance observer is proposed. First, the UAV dynamic model is decoupled into attitude subsystem and position subsystem; a finite-time disturbance observer is designed to observe the external unknown disturbances and actuator fault signals in the system in real time, and the observations are combined with the design of a non-singular fast terminal sliding mode controller, which not only realizes the detection of the unknown external disturbances in the system. It suppresses and compensates for the influence of actuator failure, and improves the tracking speed and control accuracy of the system. The stability of the control system is proved based on Lyapunov theory. Finally, the effectiveness of the proposed method is verified by simulation.

Keywords: FTC · Disturbance observer · Non-singular synovial control · UAV

1 Introduction

UAVs have attracted great attention due to their applications in civil and military applications. UAVs are more used in dangerous situations such as forest firefighting and military strikes [1], which greatly increases the probability of actuator failure of UAVs. In order to ensure that the quad-rotor UAV can achieve the ideal performance under normal and fault conditions, one of the main goals of the research is to adapt to the actuator failure, that is, fault-tolerant control [2]. Therefore, FTC is becoming a major issue for further research.

FTC methods can be divided into passive FTC (PFTC) and active FTC (AFTC). Passive methods emphasize the concept of robustness to deal with assumed failures, such as Quantitative Feedback Theory (QFT) [3], Model Predictive Control (MPC) [4] and Sliding Mode Control (SMC) [5]. Literature [6] proposed a new satellite attitude estimation method based on the second-order sliding mode variable structure prediction filter, which has high accuracy. In literature [7], an adaptive fuzzy sliding mode controller was developed to improve the robustness of the four-rotor UAV control system under actuator failure. In literature [8], a control strategy based on integral sliding mode control (ISMC) is proposed for the affine nonlinear system with interference.

H. Liu et al. (Eds.): ICIRA 2022, LNAI 13455, pp. 240–249, 2022.
https://doi.org/10.1007/978-3-031-13844-7_24

Compared with the passive method, AFTC actively responds to failures by reconfiguring the controller online. At present, there are multi-model observers [9], Thau observers [10] and predictive filtering [11] for the detection and diagnosis methods of aircraft faults. AFTC requires fault detection and diagnosis equipment to provide fault data online [12]. Literature [13] proposed an extended state observer based on non-singular terminal sliding mode to provide spacecraft reconstruction information. Literature [14] proposed an observer for hypersonic vehicle to estimate fault information in a fixed time, with high convergence speed and finite time stability. In [15], based on the information provided by fault detection and identification, the addition and scaling of control inputs are used to compensate for faults. In the literature [16], a new sliding mode surface was designed, and a fixed-time FTC strategy was proposed for the rendezvous and docking of spacecraft under interference and driver failure.

Inspired by the above work, this paper studies the attitude stability and fault-tolerant control of quad-rotor UAVs, and designs a timing controller based on time series prediction. Firstly, a mathematical model of a quadrotor UAV is established, and a time sequence module is used to collect the actuator signals after different failures through preset failure types. Based on previous experiments, the designed controller can accurately estimate disturbances and faults in a short period of time, and then use the timing controller to redistribute output signals to the healthy actuators, and ultimately maintain the stability of the drone.

The rest of this article is structured as follows. In the next part, the mathematical model of UAV is established. The third part is the design of attitude and position controllers based on non-singular terminal sliding mode control. The fourth part is the design of Limited Time Fault Tolerant Controller. The fifth part is the UAV fault simulation experiment. Then the sixth part draws conclusions.

2 Mathematical Model of Quadrotor UAV

The quad-rotor UAV model is shown in Fig. 1. It is a typical under-actuated system that maintains the robustness and stability of the UAV by controlling altitude, yaw, pitch and roll. If any failure involving the driver or propeller occurs and affects the thrust, the control becomes difficult and the UAV may fall to the ground. The earth coordinate system $R_N(n_x, n_y, n_z)$ and the body coordinate system $R_B(b_x, b_y, b_z)$ not only coincide with their origins, but also satisfy the right-hand rule.

Fig. 1. Quadrotor UAV

Based on the rotation matrix R_B^N the conversion matrix from the earth coordinate system to the body coordinate system can be obtained as:

$$\begin{bmatrix} \cos\theta\cos\psi & \cos\theta\sin\psi & -\sin\theta \\ \sin\theta\cos\psi\sin\theta - \sin\psi\cos\phi & \sin\theta\sin\psi\sin\phi + \cos\psi\cos\phi & \cos\theta\sin\psi \\ \sin\theta\cos\psi\cos\phi + \sin\psi\sin\phi & \sin\theta\sin\psi\cos\phi - \cos\psi\sin\phi\cos\theta & \cos\theta\cos\phi \end{bmatrix}$$

where: ϕ, θ, ψ is the roll, pitch and yaw angle. The lift generated by each rotor of the airframe $F_i = bw_i^2$, $i = 1, 2, 3, 4$ determined by the rotor lift coefficient b and the square of the rotor motor speed, d is the rotor anti-torque coefficient.

$$\Omega = -\Omega_1 - \Omega_2 + \Omega_3 + \Omega_4$$
$$U_1 = b(\Omega_4^2 - \Omega_3^2) = F_4 - F_3$$
$$U_1 = b(\Omega_2^2 - \Omega_1^2) = F_2 - F_1$$
$$U_3 = d(\Omega_1^2 + \Omega_2^2 - \Omega_3^2 - \Omega_4^2)$$
$$U_4 = b(\Omega_1^2 + \Omega_2^2 + \Omega_3^2 + \Omega_4^2) = \sum_{i=1}^{4} F_i \tag{2-1}$$

The nonlinear model of the quadrotor UAV as:

$$\ddot{\phi} = \frac{I_y - I_z}{I_x}\dot{\theta}\dot{\psi} - \frac{I_r}{I_x}\dot{\theta}\Omega + \frac{lU_1}{I_x} - \frac{K_4}{I_x}\dot{\phi} \quad \ddot{X} = (\cos\theta\cos\psi\cos\phi + \sin\phi\sin\psi)\frac{U_4}{m} - \frac{K_1}{m}\dot{X}$$
$$\ddot{\theta} = \frac{I_z - I_x}{I_y}\dot{\theta}\dot{\psi} + \frac{I_r}{I_y}\dot{\phi}\Omega + \frac{lU_2}{I_y} - \frac{K_5}{I_y}\dot{\theta} \quad \ddot{Y} = (\cos\phi\sin\theta\sin\psi - \sin\phi\sin\psi)\frac{U_4}{m} - \frac{K_2}{m}\dot{Y}$$
$$\ddot{\psi} = \frac{I_x - I_y}{I_z}\dot{\theta}\dot{\phi} + \frac{U_3}{I_z} - \frac{K_6}{I_z}\dot{\psi} \quad \ddot{Z} = (\cos\phi\cos\theta)\frac{U_4}{m} - g - \frac{K_3}{m}\dot{Z} \tag{2-2}$$

3 Controller Design

FTC provides an optimal strategy to reconfigure the controller based on a series of failures (including motor saturation). Fault-tolerant control can be attached to other controllers, and the stability of the controller when the control output reaches saturation is proved in the literature. However, the heading yaw control may not be critical because it is independent of the altitude control. It can be seen from Fig. 2 of the system structure that the attitude and position parameters are finally controlled by the fault-tolerant controller to control the motor current.

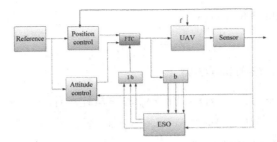

Fig. 2. System structure diagram

3.1 Attitude Controller Design

The controller is designed according to formula (2-2), taking the roll channel as an example, the system state equation as:

$$x_2 = \dot{x}_1; \; \dot{x}_2 = a_1 x_4 x_6 + b_1 U_2 \tag{3-1}$$

when the expected value of the roll angle is $\phi_d = x_{1d}$, the error variable is defined as $e_1 = x_{1d} - x_1$, and the derivative of the error variable is obtained:

$$\dot{e}_1 = \dot{x}_{1d} - \dot{x}_1 = \dot{x}_{1d} - x_2 \tag{3-2}$$

Take the virtual control quantity α_1, and define the error variable of the virtual control quantity α_1 as:

$$e_2 = x_2 - \alpha_1 \tag{3-3}$$

Take the Lyapunov function $V_1(x_1, e_1) = \frac{1}{2}(\lambda_1 x_1^2 + e_1^2), \; (\lambda_1 > 0)$. Deriving it:

$$\dot{V}_1(x_1, e_1) = \lambda_1 x_1 e_1 + e_1 \dot{e}_1 = e_1(\lambda_1 x_1 + \dot{e}_1) \tag{3-4}$$

Substituting formulas (3-2) and (3-3) into (3-4):

$$\dot{V}_1(x_1, e_1) = e_1(\lambda_1 x_1 + \dot{x}_{1d} - e_2 - \alpha_1) \tag{3-5}$$

when $\alpha_1 = \lambda_1 x_1 + \dot{x}_{1d} + k_{3\phi} e_1 (k_{3\phi} > 0)$:

$$\dot{V}_1(x_1, e_1) = -k_{3\phi} e_1^2 - e_1 e_2 \tag{3-6}$$

In order to eliminate $-e_1 e_2$, take the Lyapunov function $V_2 = V_1 + \frac{1}{2} e_2^2$ and derive it to obtain:

$$\dot{V}_2 = \dot{V}_1 + e_2 \dot{e}_2 \tag{3-7}$$

Select the Sliding surface as:

$$S_\phi = e_2 \tag{3-8}$$

Substituting formula (3-8) into (3-3):

$$\dot{V}_2 = \dot{V}_1 + s_\phi \dot{s}_\phi \tag{3-9}$$

Substituting formula (3-3) into (3-9):

$$\dot{V}_2 = \dot{V}_1 + s_\phi(\dot{x}_2 - \dot{\alpha}_1) = \dot{V}_1 + s_\phi(\dot{x}_2 - \lambda_1 \dot{x}_1 - \ddot{x}_{1d} - k_{1\phi}\dot{e}_1)$$
$$\dot{s}_\phi = \dot{x}_2 - k_{1\phi}\dot{e}_1 - \ddot{x}_{1d} - \lambda_1 e_1 \tag{3-10}$$

Substituting formula (3-10) into (3-1):

$$U_2 = \frac{-k_{1\phi} \cdot \text{sgn}(s_\phi) - k_{2\phi} \cdot s_\phi + \ddot{x}_{1d} + k_{3\phi} \cdot \dot{e}_1 + \lambda_1 \chi_1 - a_1 x_4 x_6}{b_1} \tag{3-11}$$

Proof of stability:

Substituting formula (3-6), (3-8), (3-11) into (3-10):

$$\dot{V}_2 = -k_{3\phi}e_1^2 - k_{2\phi}e_2^2 - e_1 e_2 - k_{1\phi} \cdot e_2 \cdot \text{sgn}(e_2) \tag{3-12}$$

When $s_\phi \to 0$, $s_\phi \dot{s}_\phi < 0$, The system state point can reach the sliding surface. $e_2 \to 0$,

$$\dot{V}_2 = -k_{3\phi}e_1^2 - k_{2\phi}e_2^2 - e_1 e_2 - \varepsilon \cdot e_2 \cdot \text{sgn}(e_2) < -k_{3\phi}e_1^2 < 0 \tag{3-13}$$

3.2 Position Controller Design

The position loop includes height z channel, horizontal x channel, and horizontal y channel. Taking the height channel as an example, the system state equation as:

$$x_4 = \dot{x}_3; \ \dot{x}_4 = \cos x_1 \cos x_3 U_1 / m - g \tag{3-14}$$

Take the expected value $z_d = x_{3d}$ of the height channel, define the error variable $e_3 = x_{3d} - x_3$, and derive the error variable e_3 to obtain:

$$\dot{e}_3 = \dot{x}_{3d} - \dot{x}_3 = \dot{x}_{3d} - x_4 \tag{3-15}$$

Define the error variable of the virtual control quantity α_3 as:

$$e_4 = x_4 - \alpha_3 \tag{3-16}$$

Take Lyapunov function $V_3 = \frac{1}{2}e_3^2$ and derivate it to get:

$$\dot{V}_3 = e_3 \dot{e}_3 \tag{3-17}$$

Selected $\alpha_3 = \dot{x}_{3d} + k_{3z}e_3 \ (k_{3z} > 0)$:

$$\dot{V}_3 = -k_{3z}e_3^2 - e_3 e_4 \tag{3-18}$$

Choose Lyapunov function $V_4 = V_3 + \frac{1}{2}e_4^2$ and obtain the derivative:

$$\dot{V}_4 = \dot{V}_3 + e_4 \dot{e}_4 \tag{3-19}$$

Select sliding surface $s_z = e_4$, So the index approach rate as:

$$U_1 = \frac{-k_{1z} \cdot \text{sgn}(s_z) - k_{2z} \cdot s_z + \ddot{x}_{3d} + k_{3z} \cdot \dot{e}_3 + g}{\cos x_1 \cos x_3} \tag{3-20}$$

Proof of stability:

Substituting formula (3-15), (3-17), (3-18) into (3-19):

$$\dot{V}_4 = -k_{3z}e_3^2 - k_{2z}e_4^2 - e_3e_4 - k_{1z} \cdot e_4 \cdot \text{sgn}(e_4) \tag{3-21}$$

When $s_\phi \to 0$, $s_\phi \dot{s}_\phi < 0$, the system state point can reach the sliding surface, as: $e_2 \to 0$:

$$\dot{V}_4 = -k_{3z}e_3^2 - k_{2z}e_4^2 - e_3e_4 - k_{1z} \cdot e_4 \cdot \text{sgn}(e_4) < -k_{3z}e_3^2 < 0 \tag{3-22}$$

According to the Lyapunov stability criterion, the system is gradually stable.

4 Adaptive Timing Fault-Tolerant Controller Design

The main design idea of the adaptive timing fault-tolerant controller is: first set an interval sampling frequency, and sample the attitude and position from the UAV take-off. When the actuator fails, the controller can predict no one based on the sampled data. The attitude and position information of the UAV is first transmitted to the adaptive timing fault-tolerant controller, and the system is redefined as:

$$\dot{x}_1 = x_2 H(x_1) \dot{x}_2 = P^T Eu - C(x_1, x_2)x_2 + \overline{d} \tag{4-1}$$

$H(x)$ is $[\phi\ \theta\ \psi]^T$, P is a positive definite symmetric matrix, $C = w^{-T} J w^{-1}$, w is the coordinate conversion matrix of the pitch angle, J is the inertia matrix.

Define the integral synovial model as:

$$s = x_2(t) - x_2(t_0) - \int_{t0}^{t} H^{-1}(x_1)(P^T u - c(x_1, x_2))d\tau \tag{4-2}$$

Take the integral of the above formula (4-2):

$$\dot{s} = H^{-1}(P^T Eu + \overline{d} - P^T u) \tag{4-3}$$

Substituting formula (4-1) and (4-2) into (4-3):

$$H(x_1)\dot{s} = P^T Eu + \overline{d} - c(x_1, x_2)s + F \tag{4-4}$$

When the quadrotor UAV attitude control system has external interference and actuator failure:

$$u_1 = u + u_{er} \tag{4-5}$$

$$\mathbf{u}_{er} = \begin{cases} -\mathbf{W}^T \left(\dfrac{(\hat{\mu}_0 + \hat{\mu}_1 \|\mathbf{F}\|)\mathbf{s}}{\|\mathbf{s}\|} + k_1 \mathbf{s}^{\frac{\delta_1}{\delta_2}} + k_2 \mathbf{s}^\delta \right) & \text{if } \|\mathbf{s}\| \geq \xi \\ -\mathbf{W}^T \left(\dfrac{\hat{\mu}_0^2 \mathbf{s} + \hat{\mu}_2 \|\mathbf{F}\|}{\xi} + k_1 \mathbf{s}^{\frac{\delta_1}{\delta_2}} + k_2 \mathbf{s}^\delta \right) & \text{otherwise} \end{cases} \tag{4-6}$$

where: $k_1, k_2 > 0, \delta > 1, 0 < \delta_1 < \delta_2, \hat{\mu}_1$ and $\hat{\mu}_2$ is estimated value. Select the adaptive law as:

$$\hat{\mu}_0 = c_0(\|s\| - \eta\hat{\mu}_0) \quad \hat{\mu}_1 = c_1(\|F\|\|s\| - \eta_1\hat{\mu}_1) \quad \hat{\mu}_2 = c_2(\frac{\|F\|\|s\|}{\xi} - \eta_2\hat{\mu}_2) \qquad (4\text{-}7)$$

Select the Lyapunov function as:

$$V_1 = \frac{1}{2}s^T Hs + \frac{e_0}{2c_0}(\hat{\mu}_0 - \mu_0)^2 + \frac{e_0}{2c_1}(\hat{\mu}_1 - \mu_1)^2 \qquad (4\text{-}8)$$

Derivation of Eq. (4-8):

$$\dot{V}_1 = \frac{1}{2}s^T \dot{H}s + s^T H\dot{s} + e_0(\hat{\mu}_0 - \overline{\mu}_0)(\|s\| - \eta\hat{\mu}_0) + e_0(\hat{\mu}_1 - \overline{\mu}_1) \times (\|F\|\|s\| - \eta_1\hat{\mu}_1)$$

$$= s^T(P^T Eu + \overline{d} + F) + s^T P^T Eu_1 + e_0(\hat{\mu}_0 - \overline{\mu}_0)(\|s\| - \eta\hat{\mu}_0) + e_0(\hat{\mu}_1 - \overline{\mu}_1)$$

$$\times (\|F\| - \eta_1\hat{\mu}_1) \qquad (4\text{-}9)$$

If $(\hat{\mu}_i - \mu_i)^2 \geq 1, (i = 0, 1)$:

$$\left[(\hat{\mu}_i - \mu_i)^2\right]^{\frac{\delta_1 + \delta_2}{\delta_2}} - (\hat{\mu}_i - \mu_i)^2 \leq 0 \qquad (4\text{-}10)$$

According to the Lyapunov criterion, the system is gradually stable.

5 Simulation Experiment

In this section, through comparison with other traditional controllers, numerical simulation will verify the effectiveness of the proposed controller. The moments of inertia of the quadrotor drone in the x, y, and z directions are 0.0211, 0.0219, and 0.0366, respectively. The total weight of the fuselage is 1.4 kg, the initial angular velocity is 0, and the initial height coordinates are the origin of the coordinates. When the system can fly normally and return to its actual position without failure. The actual flight trajectory is shown in Fig. 3.

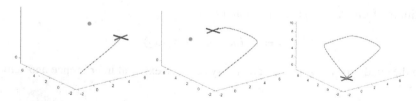

Fig. 3. UAV flight track

The actual simulation time is 70 s. The UAV can be installed on a predetermined trajectory to fly if there is no failure. It can be seen from Fig. 4 that the overshoot on the x-axis and y-axis is small, indicating that the UAV is level. The direction has high stability. Figure 5 show the motor current when the drone is actually hovering. The UAV reaches the predetermined height in 300 ms, and the current is the largest at this time. When the M1 motor propeller fails and the rotation speed decreases, the height of the entire UAV drops. At this time, the timing observer compares the current of each actuator with the current that theoretically it should give the required command. As the fault occurs, the current of M1 gradually decreases, and the current of the remaining three motors increases. The increase in motor current causes the propeller to increase in speed, which will generate greater torque at the frame and cause unstable flight attitude.

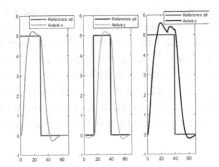

Fig. 4. x, y, z axis motion track

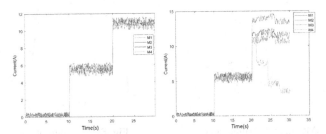

Fig. 5. Motor normal current and motor fault current

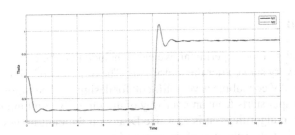

Fig. 6. Pitch angle change curve

Figure 6 is the pitch angle change curve of the aircraft. The main propeller and the longitudinal axis of the aircraft generate an angle during the flight. The torque received is decomposed into vertical and horizontal directions. The vertical direction is used to offset its own weight to maintain high stability. horizontal direction is used to generate forward thrust. In the 10th second or so, when the motor M1 fails, the fault-tolerant controller can respond quickly, and the overshoot of the system is about 5%. It can be seen that the designed controller has strong robustness.

Figure 7 shows the height changes of the sliding film control algorithm when the motors M1 and M2 fail respectively. It can be seen from the figure that after 10 s of introducing a fault, the sliding film control algorithm cannot maintain a stable flight attitude, and the UAV will quickly fall after a fault. Figure 8 is the introduction of the control algorithm in this article, and a fault-tolerant observer is established in the simulation link, Perform the second experiment again. In the 10th and 50th s the faults are introduced respectively, and it can be seen that the height of the drone has dropped from 15 to 5 at the beginning. The fault system can be introduced twice to quickly deal with the measures, the first time the height is kept at about 10, and the second time at about 5. Because the motor failure directly affects the speed of the propeller, it is impossible for the UAV to completely restore the stable position before the failure. The difficulty of synovial control is that the system does not strictly move from the synovial surface to the equilibrium point, so the height of the aircraft drops rapidly in about 30 s.

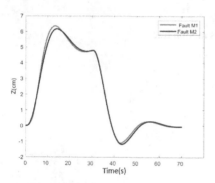 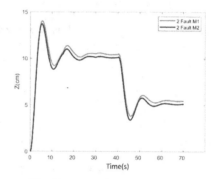

Fig. 7. SMC height change curve   **Fig. 8.** FTC height change curve

6 Conclusion

Based on the results of the experiment, we can conclude that the controller designed in this paper can be very stable after the motor fails. The difficulty of sliding mode control in the process of UAV concubine is very difficult for designers. The timing state observer designed in this paper starts from another way of thinking. By combining previous data and time prediction algorithms, it is effective Deal with the fault in less time, avoiding the trouble caused by the selection of the synovial surface.

In the future work, we plan to analyze the coexistence of partial failures and multiple failures, and apply this method to more complex models. Further breakthroughs are needed in time-based prediction methods, and the advantages of neural networks are used to improve the robustness of current observers. When the types of faults increase or when the motor is saturated, can the reliability of the time prediction algorithm be improved to prevent more serious situations from causing unnecessary losses.

References

1. Song, Z.K., Ling, S., Sun, K.B.: Adaptive fault tolerant attitude tracking control for miniature rotorcrafts under actuator saturation. Aerosp. Sci. Technol. **69**, 27–38 (2017)
2. Sharifi, F., Mirzaei, M., Gordon, B.W., Zhang, Y.: Fault tolerant control of a quadrotor UAV using sliding mode control. In: Control and Fault-Tolerant Systems, October 2010
3. Gharib, M.R., Moavenian, M.: Full dynamics and control of a quadrotor using quantitative feedback theory. Int. J. Numer. Model Electron. **29**(3), 501–519 (2016)
4. Yao, P., Wang, H.L., Ji, H.X.: Multi-UAVs tracking target in urban environment by model predictive control and improved grey wolf optimizer. Aerosp. Sci. Technol. **55**, 131–143 (2016)
5. Ding, S.H., Liu, L., Zheng, W.X.: Sliding mode direct yaw-moment control design for in-wheel electric vehicles. IEEE Trans. Ind. Electron. **64**(8), 6752–6762 (2017)
6. Cao, L., Ran, D.C., Chen, X.Q., Li, X.B., Xiao, B.: Huber second-order variable structure predictive filter for satellites attitude estimation. Int. J. Control Autom. Syst. **17**(7), 1781–1792 (2019)
7. Barghandan, S., Badamchizadeh, M.A., Jahed-Motlagh, M.R.: Improved adaptive fuzzy sliding mode controller for robust fault tolerant of a quadrotor. Int. J. Control Autom. Syst. **15**(1), 427–441 (2017)
8. Rubagotti, M., Estrada, A., Castanos, F., Ferrara, A., Fridman, L.: Integral sliding mode control for nonlinear systems with matched and unmatched perturbations. IEEE Trans. Autom. Control **56**(11), 2699–2704 (2011)
9. Ducard, G.J.: Fault-Tolerant Flight Control and Guidance Systems: Practical Methods for Small Unmanned Aerial Vehicles. Springer, London (2009). https://doi.org/10.1007/978-1-84882-561-1
10. Benosman, M.: A survey of some recent results on nonlinear fault tolerant control. Math. Probl. Eng. (2010)
11. Nobahari, H., Nasrollahi, S.: Nonlinear predictive controllers for continuous systems. J. Guid. Control Dyn. **17**(3), 553–560
12. Yin, S., Zhu, X.: Intelligent particle filter and its application to fault detection of nonlinear system. IEEE Trans. Ind. Electron. **62**, 3852–3861 (2015). https://doi.org/10.1109/TIE.2015.2399396
13. Li, B., Hu, Q.L., Yang, Y.S.: Continuous finite-time extended state observer based fault tolerant control for attitude stabilization. Aerosp. Sci. Technol. **84**, 204–213 (2019)
14. Yu, X., Li, P., Zhang, Y.M.: The design of fixed-time observer and finite-time fault tolerant control for hypersonic gliding vehicles. IEEE Trans. Ind. Electron. **65**(5), 4135–4144 (2018)
15. Merheb, A.-R., Noura, H., Bateman, F.: Active fault tolerant control of quadrotor UA V using sliding mode control. In: Proceedings of the International Conference on Unmanned Aircraft Systems, Orlando, FL, USA, pp. 156–166 (2014)
16. Jiang, B.Y., Hu, Q.L., Friswell, M.: Fixed-time rendezvous control of spacecraft with a tumbling target under loss of actuator effectiveness. IEEE Trans. Aerosp. Electron. Syst. **52**(4), 1576–1586 (2016)

Leg Mechanism Design of a Jumping Robot with Variable Reduction Ratio Joint

Yicheng Weng[1], Xuechao Chen[1,2,3,4](✉), Zhangguo Yu[1,2,3,4], Haoxiang Qi[1], Xiaoshuai Ma[1], Min Zhu[5], and Qiang Huang[1,2,3,4]

[1] School of Mechatronic Engineering, Beijing Institute of Technology, Beijing 100081, China
chenxuechao@bit.edu.cn
[2] Key Laboratory of Biomimetic Robots and Systems, Ministry of Education, Beijing 100081, China
[3] International Joint Research Laboratory of Biomimetic Robots and Systems, Ministry of Education, Beijing 100081, China
[4] State Key Laboratory of Intelligent Control and Decision of Complex System, Beijing 100081, China
[5] Beijing University of Civil Engineering and Architecture, Beijing 102627, China

Abstract. In order to improve the dynamic motion ability of the biped robot, a joint with high torque output and high backdrivability is required. In this paper, a new leg mechanism using a joint with continuously variable reduction ratio inspired by human joint structure is proposed. This mechanism possesses high actuation capability and high impact resistance ability. Based on the characteristics of jumping motion, the parameters of the joint are optimized to increase the jumping height of the robot. A contrast simulation was implemented on a one-legged model to show the advantages of the variable reduction ratio joint over fixed reduction ratio joint. The newly designed joint can increase the jumping height of the robot by 21% comparing with a model without the mechanism. A prototype of one-legged robot using the designed joint with continuously variable reduction ratio has been developed. Vertical jump experiment on the prototype is realized with a height of 42 cm.

Keywords: Mechanical design · Variable reduction ratio joint · Jumping robot

1 Introduction

Legged robots are the frontiers and hotspots in the field of robotics, and they have important scientific significance and application value. However, most biped robots currently only have partial movement abilities such as walking, jogging and small jumps. They have a single movement form, low environmental adaptability, and limited movement speed. In this context, the research on the highly dynamic motions of biped robots, such as running and jumping, has increasingly become the focus of attention.

This work was supported in part by the National Key Research and Development Project under Grant No. 2018YFE0126200.

For jumping motion, the actuation system needs to provide the joint with sufficient torque and speed to reach the preset take-off speed [1–5]. However, motor-driven jumping robots face the problem of motor power limitation, that is, the maximum torque and maximum speed of the motor cannot be achieved at the same time. When the motor speed reaches a certain value, the maximum torque it can output will begin to decrease. We can adjust the reduction ratio, which is the link between the motor and the joint, to optimize the distribution of the torque and speed of the motor to the joint in different motion phases. Therefore, the joints with variable reduction ratio, compared with the joints with fixed reduction ratio, can make the best use of the motor's ability and improve the jumping performance of the robot. Another advantage of the variable reduction ratio joint is that it has better backdrivability after the robot touches the ground after jumping, which can effectively reduce the ground impact received by the robot and help the robot reach balance faster [6].

Researchers have designed a variety of variable mechanisms on the robot to achieve their goals, including reproducing the complex motion of the human body, improving structural strength, optimizing mass distribution, reducing energy consumption, etc. [7–16]. Among them, some researches have designed different joint mechanisms with variable reduction ratio and conducted dynamic motion experiments based on these mechanisms. Their mechanical design includes multi-stage gear, spring structure, linear motors and multi-link design, etc. [12–16]. These designs have achieved specific goals, but they have a certain degree of redundancy in structure, resulting in heavier weight and lower controllability, which is not conducive to dynamic motions like running and jumping. Therefore, it is very necessary to design a lightweight joint mechanism with good stability and high controllability.

The contribution of the paper is to propose a design of variable reduction ratio joint and an optimization method that conforms to the characteristics of jumping motion with demonstration of simulation and experiment.

The construction of this paper is as follows. Sect. 2 proposes the mechanical design of the joint with variable reduction ratio. Sect. 3 presents the parameter optimization process based on dynamic simulation, followed by a contrast simulation and experiments in Sect. 4. Finally, the paper is concluded in Sect. 5.

2   Leg Mechanism with a Variable Reduction Ratio Joint Realized by Ball Screw - Push Rod Mechanism

In order to make the best use of motor capabilities during the take-off phase, and to make the joint act with good backdrivibility when touching the ground, we designed a joint mechanism with variable reduction ratio.

Different from the joints of traditional robots, which are directly driven by the motors at the joints, the joint movement of the human body is not driven by simple joint force, but involves complex coordinated movements of bones, muscles and ligaments. Among them, the stretching and relaxation of muscles provides the most power. For example, flexion of the knee joint is accomplished by pulling and pushing the hamstrings.

Inspired by the structure of the human body, we design a variable reduction ratio joint realized by ball screw - push rod mechanism. As shown Fig. 1, Two fixed points are determined on the upper leg and lower leg respectively. A motor-ball screw - push rod structure is installed between the fixed points. The motor housing and the end of the push rod are respectively connected to the two fixed points. We define r as the distance from the fixed point of lower leg to the joint axis, $S_0 + r$ as the distance from the fixed point of upper leg to the joint axis, S as the distance between two fixed points. There is a small deflection angle θ_0 between the installation position of the push rod and the central axis of the lower leg to prevent the dead point of mechanical motion when the joint angle $\theta = 180°$. The motor drives the push rod, imitating muscle stretch and relax, to achieve the flexion and extension of the joint. Due to the change of the joint angle, the reduction ratio of the motor to the joint is variable.

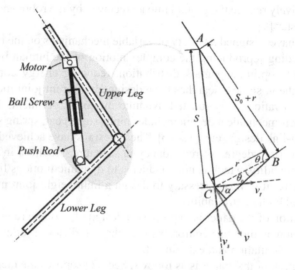

Fig. 1. The proposed joint mechanism with variable reduction ratio

As shown in Fig. 1, through the designed ball screw - push rod mechanism, the motor speed and torque are converted to the linear speed and thrust of the push rod, driving the joints to move. We define the absolute speed of the fixed point of the lower limb as v, according to its effect on the lower leg, it is divided into a vertical component v_s and a horizontal component v_t. The vertical component is also the linear velocity of the push rod, which can be given by

$$v_s = \frac{Qn}{60000} \tag{1}$$

where Q is the lead of the screw, n is the speed of the motor, 60000 is the coefficient to transform the speed from RPM to m/s.

We define α as the angle between v_t and v, then transfer it to a triangle composed of three points A, B, and C. It can be obtained by the law of sine

$$\frac{\sin \alpha}{S_0 + r} = \frac{\sin(\theta - \theta_0)}{S} \tag{2}$$

In the triangle, S can be obtained by the law of cosines

$$S = \sqrt{S_0^2 + 2r^2 + 2S_0 r - (2S_0 r + 2r^2)\cos(\theta - \theta_0)} \tag{3}$$

We define ω as angular velocity of joints, ω can be given by

$$\omega = \frac{v}{r} = \frac{v_s}{r\sin\alpha} = \frac{Qn}{60000 \cdot r\sin\alpha} \tag{4}$$

The reduction ratio k can be expressed as the ratio of the motor speed and the joint speed, which can be given by

$$k = \frac{n}{\omega} \cdot 0.105 = \frac{60000 \cdot r\sin\alpha}{Q} \cdot 0.105 \tag{5}$$

where 0.105 is the coefficient to transform the speed from RPM to rad/s. Finally, by substituting Eq. (2) and Eq. (3) into Eq. (5), we obtain

$$k = \frac{6300r(S_0 + r)\sin(\theta - \theta_0)}{Q\sqrt{S_0^2 + 2r^2 + 2S_0 r - (2S_0 r + 2r^2)\cos(\theta - \theta_0)}} \tag{6}$$

It can be seen from Eq. (6) that once the mechanism parameters of the joint Q, r, S_0, θ_0 are determined, the reduction ratio k will change with the change of the joint angle θ. This realizes the joint characteristic of variable reduction ratio.

3   Mechanism Parameter Optimization

3.1   One-Legged Robot Modeling

We use a one-legged robot model with one actuating joint to verify the effectiveness of the designed variable reduction ratio joint. As shown in Fig. 2, the robot model consists of two links of equal length: the upper leg and the lower leg. To simulate the real robot state, the center of mass (CoM) of the lower leg is set at the geometric center. The installation position of the motor push rod and the electrical components is on the upper part of the upper leg. We regard the upper leg and these components as a whole, so the CoM of the equivalent upper leg is set close to the hip joint. We only consider the movement of the robot in two dimensions, it has three DoF (degree of freedom) in the pitch direction. The hip and ankle joints are both passive revolute joints. These two joints are restricted to move in the vertical direction. The knee joint is an active variable reduction ratio joint with one DoF in the pitch direction. The posture of the robot is determined by the angles of the ankle and knee joints. Due to the limitation of the mechanism, we obtain the relationship between the ankle joint angle q_1 and the knee joint angle q_2

$$q_2 = 2q_1 \tag{7}$$

The dynamic equation of the robot can be expressed as

$$M(\dot{q}, q)\ddot{q} + H(\dot{q}, q) = S^T\tau + J^T F_{ext} \tag{8}$$

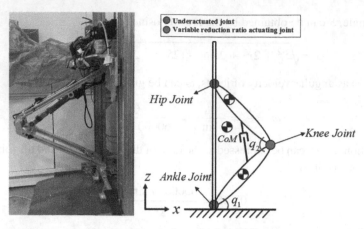

Fig. 2. The one-legged robot platform

where M denotes the inertia matrix, H denotes the centripetal, coriolis forces and gravity vector, τ represents the joint torque matrix, S^T denotes the selection matrix, J denotes the geometric jacobian matrices, F_{ext} denotes the extra force matrix.

After deforming Eq. (8), we obtain the inverse dynamic equation

$$\tau = (S^T)^{-1}(M(\dot{q}, q)\ddot{q} + H(\dot{q}, q) - J^T F_{ext}) \tag{9}$$

During the ground phase, since the ankle joint is always in contact with the ground, we establish a fixed base at the ankle joint. We define $q = \{q_1, q_2\}$ as the state space of the robot, then the external force is applied to the hip joint, we ignore the friction between the hip joint and the vertical slide, and only consider the horizontal supporting force, then the external force vector can be given by

$$F_{ext} = [F_N, 0] \tag{10}$$

since the ankle joint is a passive joint and the knee joint is an active actuating joint, the selection matrix S^T can be given by

$$S^T = \begin{bmatrix} 0 & 0 \\ 0 & 1 \end{bmatrix} \tag{11}$$

During the flight phase, the ankle joint is off the ground, we build a floating base at the ankle joint. In this case, $q = \{p_z, q_1, q_2\}$, where p_z denotes the distance between the hip joint and the ground. S^T can be given by

$$S^T = \begin{bmatrix} 0 & 0 & 0 \\ 0 & 0 & 0 \\ 0 & 0 & 1 \end{bmatrix} \tag{12}$$

3.2 Mechanism Parameter Optimization

Among the four parameters of the variable reduction ratio joint, Q is the lead of the ball screw. The optional values include 2 mm, 5 mm, and 10 mm. For the consideration of mechanical structure, we choose 10 mm. r, S_0, θ_0 are all mechanism design parameters, we will optimize them based on simulation below.

Aiming to increase the jumping height of the robot, we adopted a nonlinear optimization method to optimize the take-off trajectory and joint parameters. We use a process optimization method based on optimal control to optimize this problem. Specifically, as shown in Fig. 3, we take the jerk of the knee joint as the control value u, the position, velocity and acceleration of the knee joint as the state quantities x_1, x_2, x_3, and the joint parameters r, S_0, θ_0 as the static parameters, to perform a single-phase optimization. The state equation can be derived as

$$
\begin{cases}
\dot{x}_1 = x_2 \\
\dot{x}_2 = x_3 \\
\dot{x}_3 = u
\end{cases}
\tag{13}
$$

The equality and inequality constraints can be given by

$$
\begin{cases}
x_1(t_0) = \pi/3, x_2(t_0) = 0, x_3(t_0) = 0 \\
\pi/3 < x_1(t) < \pi, -50 < x_2(t) < 50, -500 < x_3(t) < 500 \\
t_0 = 0, t_0 < t < t_f, -10000 < u(t) < 10000 \\
10 < r < 410, 10 < S_0 < 410, 5 < \theta_0 < 30
\end{cases}
\tag{14}
$$

where t_0 and t_f are the initial and terminal moment of the take-off movement. The position, velocity and acceleration of the CoM C, $\dot{C}$, $\ddot{C}$ can be calculated from the state of the joint. In order to maximize the jump height, we set the cost function J to

$$
J = -\dot{C}_z(t_f)
\tag{15}
$$

where $-\dot{C}_z(t_f)$ refers to the vertical speed of the CoM at the moment of take-off. In the joint mechanism shown in Fig. 1, S can be calculated from r, S_0, θ_0. Using inverse dynamics in Eq. (9), we can calculate the joint torque τ from the joint motion state q, $\dot{q}$, $\ddot{q}$. The reduction ratio k is determined by Eq. (6), then we can obtain the motor torque T and speed n

$$
T = \tau/k
\tag{16}
$$

$$
n = \frac{\dot{q} \cdot k}{0.105}
\tag{17}
$$

According to the characteristic of the motor, the maximum output torque of the motor $T_{\max}$ is determined by n. We define T_r as the ratio of the actual torque of the motor to the maximum torque of the motor

$$
T_r = \frac{T}{T_{\max}}
\tag{18}
$$

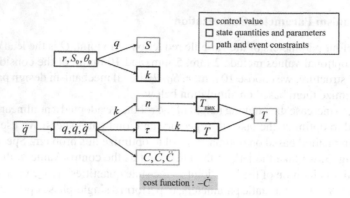

Fig. 3. Nonlinear optimization process

In the parameter optimization process, the length of the push rod cannot exceed the telescopic limit of the push rod. In the process of joint trajectory optimization, the actual speed and torque of the motor cannot exceed the limit of the motor. At the same time, in order to meet the take-off conditions, the vertical velocity of the *CoM* at the take-off moment must be positive, and the vertical acceleration of the *CoM* must be $-g$. According to the constraints above, we specify the path and event constraints in the nonlinear optimization process as

$$\begin{cases} 208.5 < S < 308.5, -5000 < n < 5000, 0 < T_r < 1 \\ \dot{C}_z(t_f) > 0, \ddot{C}_z(t_f) = -g \end{cases} \tag{19}$$

The results of nonlinear optimization are given in Fig. 4 and Table 1. Under the optimized trajectory and mechanism parameters, the one-legged robot reached the maximum jumping height of 52 cm (maximum vertical velocity of the *CoM* at the moment of take-off).

Table 1. Parameter of leg mechanism

r[mm]	43
S_0[mm]	187
θ_0[deg]	5

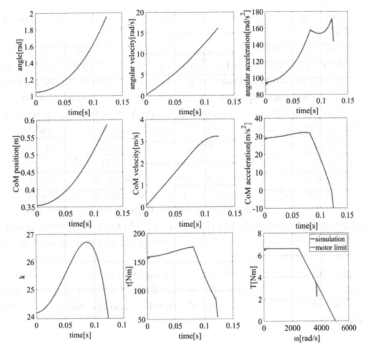

Fig. 4. The result of nonlinear optimization. The first row shows the angle, angular velocity, and angular acceleration of the knee joint. The second row shows the position, velocity, and acceleration of the *CoM* of the robot. The third row shows the change of the joint reduction ratio, the joint torque, the comparison of the joint and the motor limit from left to right.

4   Simulation and Experiment

4.1   Simulation and Evaluation

We establish two comparison one-legged robot models to simulate high jump at the maximum jump height respectively in order to evaluate the superiority of the variable reduction ratio joint over fixed reduction ratio joint. The first model uses a variable reduction ratio knee joint applying the optimized parameters in Sect. 3, and the second model uses a fixed reduction ratio joint. In view of the fact that the reduction ratio of the force-controlled joint should not be too large in real applications, we take the average value of the range of the reduction ratio of the designed variable reduction ratio joint, and the result is 18, which is used as the reduction ratio of the fixed reduction ratio joint.

During the take-off phase, we optimize joint trajectory to achieve the maximum *CoM* vertical speed at the take-off moment to improve jumping height. After the take-off condition is reached, the robot enters the flight phase. The joint angles are taken as the condition to switch from ground phase to flight phase. Then, we use the PD controller to adjust the robot's posture and then maintain it. Joint torque of the robot can be given by

$$\tau = K_p(q_{ref} - q) + K_d(0 - \dot{q}) \qquad (20)$$

where q_{ref} is the given posture. Joint speed is set to zero to maintain the robot posture. The results of simulation are given in Fig. 5.

In the take-off phase, thanks to the optimized mechanism parameter r, the reduction ratio range of the variable reduction ratio joint is in the optimal range, which is manifested in the joint torque maintaining a certain peak height and duration, that is, a larger moment of impulse. This avoids the torque peak being too small due to the reduction ratio being too small, and the motor torque inflection point being reached too quickly due to the reduction ratio being too large. At the same time, by optimizing S_0 and θ_0, the change trend of the reduction ratio of the variable deceleration ratio joint is consistent with the demand of jumping motion, that is: a larger torque is required at the initial stage of the jump, corresponding to the reduction ratio reaches the peak value from the initial value; a larger angular velocity is required at the later stage of the jump, corresponding to the reduction ratio decreasing. The common effect of the above is that the velocity of CoM at the take-off moment is improved from 2.92 m/s to 3.20 m/s, compared with fixed reduction ratio joint. Correspondingly, the jump height is increased from 52 cm to 43 cm, which is an increase of 21%.

In the flight phase, the reduction ratio of the variable reduction ratio joint is further reduced, using a smaller reduction ratio than the fixed reduction ratio joint to deal with the impact of the landing, which improves the robot's backdrivability and helps the robot to reach balance faster.

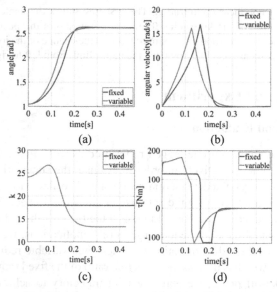

Fig. 5. Simulation results of the two contrast models doing high jump. (a) curve of knee joint angle. (b) curve of knee joint angular velocity. (c) curve of knee joint reduction ratio. (d) curve of knee joint torque

4.2 Experiment

In experiment, we use the jumping method in Sect. 4.1 to realize the vertical jump of the robot by sending current commands to the motors. At the same time, we recorded the angle and torque of the knee joint at a frequency of 1000 Hz. As shown in Fig. 7, the joint maintains a large torque output for a period of time during the take-off phase, and returns to the initial posture quickly under impact, which verifies the effectiveness of the leg mechanism (Fig. 6).

Fig. 6. Snapshots of vertical jump experiment with variable reduction ratio joint

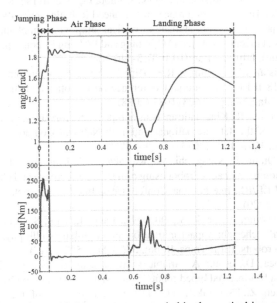

Fig. 7. Joint angles and joint moments recorded in the vertical jump experiment

Finally, we achieved a jump with a robot height of 42 cm, and the reason for the 10 cm gap in the jump height between the experiment and the simulation is considered to be the friction on the guide rails, the friction on the joints and the model error of the robot.

5 Conclusion

In this paper, we designed a leg mechanism with variable reduction ratio joint inspired by the human joint structure. We also propose a nonlinear optimization method for the key parameters of this mechanism. Dynamic simulation of the one-legged model shows that the installation of the optimized mechanism resulted in a 21% increase in jump height. This mechanism also exhibits good backdrivability. In experiment, we realized the vertical jump of 42 cm on the one-legged prototype.

However, this paper only investigates the effect of this mechanism in two-dimensional space and limited experimental conditions. Future work is to explore the effect of this structure under bipedal multi-actuated joint model in three dimensions. The application of the mechanism in walking, running and other motions will also be done and implemented to robots.

References

1. Nunez, V., Drakunov, S., Nadjar-Gauthier, N., Cadiou, J.C.: Control strategy for planar vertical jump. In: 12th International Conference on Advanced Robotics, pp. 849–855 (2015)
2. Nunez, V., Nadjar-Gauthier, N.: Humanoid vertical jump with compliant contact. In: Tokhi, M.O., Virk, G.S., Hossain, M.A. (eds.) Climbing and Walking Robots, pp. 457–464. Springer, Heidelberg (2006). https://doi.org/10.1007/3-540-26415-9_55
3. Sripada, A., Vistapalli, J., Kumar, R.P.: Biped robot vertical jumping with control constraints. In: 2018 IEEE International Conference on Robotics and Biomimetics (ROBIO), Kuala Lumpur, Malaysia, pp. 1683–1687 (2018)
4. Janardhan, V., Kumar, R.: Kinematic analysis of biped robot forward jump for safe locomotion. In: Proceedings of the 1st International and 16th National Conference on Machines and Mechanisms, pp. 1078–1082 (2013)
5. Mineshita, H., Otani, T., Sakaguchi, M., Kawakami, Y., Lim, H., Takanishi, A.: Jumping motion generation for humanoid robot using arm swing effectively and changing in foot contact status. In: IEEE/RSJ International Conference on Intelligent Robots and Systems(IROS), pp. 3823–3828 (2020)
6. Wensing, P.M., Wang, A., Seok, S., Otten, D., Lang, J., Kim, S.: Proprioceptive actuator design in the MIT cheetah: impact mitigation and high-bandwidth physical interaction for dynamic legged robots. IEEE Trans. Robot. 33(3), 509–522 (2017)
7. Rodriguez-Cianca, D., et al.: A variable stiffness actuator module with favorable mass distribution for a bio-inspired biped robot. Front. Neurorobot. 13, 20 (2019)
8. Roozing, W., Ren, Z., Tsagarakis, N.G.: Design of a novel 3-DoF leg with series and parallel compliant actuation for energy efficient articulated robots. In: 2018 IEEE International Conference on Robotics and Automation (ICRA), Brisbane, QLD, pp. 1–8 (2018)
9. Olinski, M., Gronowicz, A., Ceccarelli, M.: Development and characterisation of a controllable adjustable knee joint mechanism. Mech. Mach. Theory 155, 104101 (2021)

10. Seok, S., et al.: Design principles for energy-efficient legged locomotion and implementation on the MIT cheetah robot. IEEE/ASME Trans. Mechatron. **20**(3), 1117–1129 (2015)
11. Ha, S., Coros, S., Alspach, A., Kim, J., Yamane, K.: Computational co-optimization of design parameters and motion trajectories for robotic systems. Int. J. Robot. Res. **37**(13–14), 1521–1536 (2018)
12. Okada, M., Takeda, Y.: Synthesis and evaluation of non-circular gear that realizes optimal gear ratio for jumping robot. In: 2013 IEEE/RSJ International Conference on Intelligent Robots and Systems, Tokyo, pp. 5524–5529 (2013)
13. Tomishiro, K., et al.: Design of robot leg with variable reduction ratio crossed four-bar linkage mechanism. In: 2019 IEEE/RSJ International Conference on Intelligent Robots and Systems (IROS), Macau, China, pp. 4333–4338 (2019)
14. Ming, A., Nozawa, S., Sato, R., Yu, Z., Shimojo, M.: Development of leg mechanism using a knee joint with variable reduction ratio adaptive to load. In: 2013 IEEE International Conference on Robotics and Biomimetics (ROBIO), Shenzhen, China, pp. 1574–1579 (2013)
15. Qi, H., et al.: A vertical jump optimization strategy for one-legged robot with variable reduction ratio joint. In: 2020 IEEE-RAS 20th International Conference on Humanoid Robots (Humanoids), Munich, Germany, pp. 262–267 (2021)
16. Chevallereau, C., Wenger, P., Aoustin, Y., Mercier, F., Delanoue, N., Lucidarme, P.: Leg design for biped locomotion with mono-articular and bi-articular linear actuation. Mech. Mach. Theory **156**, 104–138 (2021)

Adaptive Method of Position-Pose for the Robot to Locate the End face's Hole of the Blade

Zhang Kaiwei[1], Tu Dawei[1], Shi Ben[1], and Zhang Xu[1,2(✉)]

[1] School of Mechatronic Engineering and Automation, Shanghai University, Shanghai, China
zhangxu@hust-wuxi.com
[2] Huazhong University of Science and Technology Wuxi Research Institute, Jiangsu, China

Abstract. In order to realize the automatic measurement and positioning drilling of the end face's hole of the turbine blade, a system of automatic measurement, positioning and drilling is built by using a binocular vision laser scanner, drilling tool, and industrial robot et al., and an adaptive method of position-pose for the robot to locate the end face's hole of the blade is proposed. In this method, the laser scanning is used to measure the point cloud of the end face of the blade, and the position coordinates and the normal vector of the hole are determined. The drill calibration algorithm and hand-eye calibration algorithm are used to realize the parameterization of the system. Based on the coordinate system transformation principle, through the projection transformation of the normal vector determines the optimal pose of positioning the end face's hole for the coordinate system of the drill tool central point, and the optimal position-pose solution of the robot carries the relevant equipment to locate the end face's hole of any complex blade is automatically solved. The experimental results showed that the method of controlling the tool central point of the drill to locate the given position, the error was less than 1 mm, which was better than the 1.5 mm of the traditional method. The linear direction of the drill was highly perpendicular to the plane of the target drilling position, which met the operational requirement of the workpiece.

Keywords: Laser scanning · Coordinate system transformation · Robot positioning · Blade hole

1 Introduction

At present, the national turbine blade drilling has been carried out by manually driven three-dimensional and horizontal drilling machines. Determining the drilling position of the end face's hole of the blade depends on the traditional method to manually move the blade to the positioning fixture, then using the flashlight illuminates the gap between the card and the blade body to judge the position of the end face's hole of the blade with the naked eye. The whole positioning drilling process not only has high labor intensity, low timeliness and insufficient degree of automation, but also the determination process of the end face's hole of the blade is easy to cause a positioning deviation of about 1.5 mm, which will have a certain impact on the subsequent turbine blade installation. Using the multi-degree of freedom and programmable control characteristic of the robot [1], with the binocular vision laser scanner and drilling tool et al. to build the automatic measurement and positioning drilling system [2–5], through the laser scanning measurement to determine the position coordinates and the normal vector of the end face's hole of the blade, and the drill is guided to carry out an accurate positioning operation. It is expected to solve the shortcomings of current blade positioning drilling and realize the automation of workpiece operation.

However, to control the robot to move to a certain position, its position coordinates and pose parameters need to be known, so the normal vector measured by laser scanning needs to be converted. Since there are countless pose solutions for transforming the normal vector to the parameter of the robot, and affected by the flatness of the blade itself, the end face of the blade often tilts in different directions and angles. At the same time, when the blade is clamped to the fixture, there are often changes of multiple positions and angles of the blade. Moreover, the constructed automatic measurement and positioning drilling system of the end face's hole of the blade also needs to ensure that the robot carries relevant equipment to have enough rigidity and stability without any interference to carry out the drilling operation with the best positioning pose. Therefore, how to automatically determine the best position-pose solution to ensure the stable positioning and drilling operation of the robot from the countless position-pose solutions of the robot when there is any blade existing complex condition will be an urgent problem to be solved.

In recent years, experts and scholars at home and abroad have carried out in-depth research on the problem of robot positioning and made contributions to determine the solution of the robot. Jiang Hongchao [6] proposed to use the D-H method to study the kinematics of the manipulator, by the analytical method to carry out the inverse solution, which is based on the analysis of the motion characteristics of the manipulator, but the solution process is complex, and the solution is not unique. Li Xianhua [7] proposed the geometric method to solve the first three joints of the manipulator and the inverse transformation method to solve the last three joints to give the combination principle of the solution, the accuracy of the obtained solution is easily affected by the establishment process of the coordinate system. Yao Haifeng [8] proposed the iterative search method, which used reverse order for the forward solution and gradually homing for the reverse solution, which has certain application limitation. Liu Guangrui [9] proposed the joint solution method of analytical method and BP neural network, which improved the accuracy and efficiency of the inverse kinematics solution of the robot, but the accuracy of the result is affected by the network training sample data.

Aiming at the above issues, this paper proposed an adaptive method of position-pose to guide the robot to locate the end face's hole of the arbitrary complex blade. Through the positioning experiment of seven-point calibration board and the positioning experiment of the end face's hole of the blade, the effectiveness and feasibility of the proposed adaptive method were verified, and to control the robot to locate the target position had higher positioning accuracy than the traditional method, and met the requirement of workpiece positioning and drilling.

2 System Structure Design and Parameterization

2.1 System Structure

The system structure mainly includes two modules: The laser scanning measurement module and the blade conveying module, as shown in Fig. 1. The laser scanning measurement module includes the industrial robot, drilling tool (includes spindle and drill) and the binocular vision laser scanner. The industrial robot is used to realize programmable control and multi-degree of freedom movement. The drilling tool and the binocular vision laser scanner are built on the flange to achieve the measurement and positioning of the end face's hole of the blade; The blade conveying module includes the mobile guide rail, turntable, fixture and turbine blade. The mobile guide rail is used to convey the 360° rotating turntable, fixture and turbine blade to the working scope of the robot.

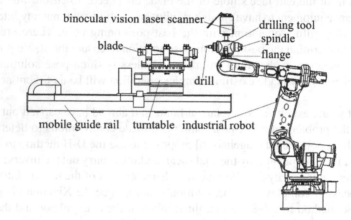

Fig. 1. System structure

During operation, the turbine blade is clamped on the turntable through the fixture, and the blade is transported to the specified position by the mobile guide rail at speed v_1. The robot with the relevant equipment at speed v_2 moves to three different positions, which keep the binocular vision laser scanner 700 mm away from the end face of the blade. Scanning and measuring the end face of the blade to obtain the three-dimensional point cloud, the position coordinates (X, Y, Z) and normal vector $\vec{n}$ of the end face's hole of the blade are determined by PolyWorks fitting point cloud to the standard blade model. According to the position coordinates and normal vector, the robot automatically solves the position-pose of positioning the end face's hole of the blade, then controlling the robot locates the corresponding hole.

2.2 System Calibration

The purpose of the system calibration is to realize the parameterization of the system. Since the calibration data of the binocular vision laser scanner is known, and the position-pose relationship of the flange and the binocular vision laser scanner, the flange and the drill TCP (Tool Central Point) is unknown, TCP calibration and hand-eye calibration are required [10].

TCP calibration. The default tool center point of the robot is located in the center of the flange, and the default tool coordinate system is consistent with the direction of the base coordinate system. As shown in Fig. 2, the "four points method" is used to select a fixed point in the robot workspace, controlling the TCP coincides with the fixed point in four different position-poses to establish equation to calculate the TCP coordinates with the condition that the four coordinates of the TCP are equal in the base coordinate system. According to the position-pose transformation relationship:

$$T_{be_i} * T_{e_i t} = T_{bt} (i = 1, 2, 3, 4) \tag{1}$$

where $T_{bt}, T_{be_i}, T_{e_i t}$ respectively represent the position-pose relationship of the robot base and the TCP, the flange and the robot base, and the flange and the TCP coordinate system. According to Eq. (1), the TCP coordinates $P_{et}(x_1, y_1, z_1)$ can be obtained。

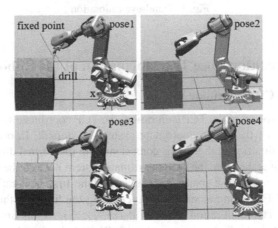

Fig. 2. TCP calibration

Hand-eye Calibration. Since the binocular vision laser scanner is built at the end of the flange, As shown in Fig. 3, a seven-point calibration board is used to control the TCP to contact point 0, 2 and 4 to record the corresponding position-pose, and establish the position-pose relationship ${}_o^b T$ between the target and the base. Moving the robot to take images and record the position-pose relationship ${}_e^b T$ between the flange and the base. According to the calibration parameters of the binocular vision laser scanner, the position-pose relationship ${}_o^c T$ between the target and the binocular vision laser scanner can be obtained:

$${}_o^b T = {}_e^b T * {}_c^e T * {}_o^c T \tag{2}$$

where ${}^e_c T$ represents the position-pose relationship between the binocular vision laser scanner and the flange. Then:

$$ {}^e_c T = {}^b_e T^{-1} * {}^b_o T * {}^c_o T^{-1} \tag{3} $$

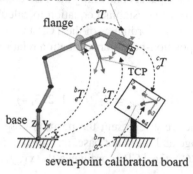

Fig. 3. Hand-eye calibration

3 Adaptive Position-Pose Transformation of the Robot

3.1 Construct TCP Coordinate System

According to the process of the TCP calibration, the TCP coordinate system is consistent with the direction of the flange coordinate system by default. In order to effectively control the linear direction of the drill is consistent with the normal direction of the hole when the drill locates the hole, the TCP coordinate system needs to be reestablished. As shown in Fig. 4, marking the spatial coordinates of the first TCP calibration is P_1, $P_1 = P_{et}(x_1, y_1, z_1)$. Extending a certain distance along the hilt with the drill. Repeating the process of the TCP calibration to obtain $P_2(x_2, y_2, z_2)$. At this time, lineP_1P_2 is the central axis line of the drill. As shown in Fig. 5, P1 is defined as the origin of the TCP coordinate system, the direction of vector $\overrightarrow{P_1P_2}$ is consistent with the Z direction of TCP coordinate system, and the unit vector of $\overrightarrow{P_1P_2}$ is recorded as $\overrightarrow{z}(z^1, z^2, z^3)$. $P_3(x_2, y_2 + a, z_2)$ can be obtained by moving point P_1 by a unit along the Y direction of the flange coordinate system, then the length $|\overrightarrow{P_1P_2}|$, $|\overrightarrow{P_1P_3}|$:

$$ \left|\overrightarrow{P_1P_2}\right| = \sqrt{(x_2 - x_1)^2 + (y_2 - y_1)^2 + (z_2 - z_1)^2} \tag{4} $$

$$ \left|\overrightarrow{P_1P_3}\right| = \sqrt{(x_2 - x_1)^2 + (y_2 + a - y_1)^2 + (z_2 - z_1)^2} \tag{5} $$

According to the spatial position relationship of P_1, P_2 and P_3, through P3 to draw a line is perpendicular with the side of P_1P_2, then:

$$ S = \frac{1}{2} * \left|\overrightarrow{P_1P_2}\right| * |P_3N| \tag{6} $$

$$S = \frac{1}{2} * \left| \overrightarrow{P_1 P_2} \right| * \left| \overrightarrow{P_1 P_3} \right| * \sin\theta \tag{7}$$

$$\overrightarrow{P_1 P_2} * \overrightarrow{P_1 P_3} = \left| \overrightarrow{P_1 P_2} \right| * \left| \overrightarrow{P_1 P_3} \right| * \cos\theta \tag{8}$$

$$P_3 N = \tan\theta * d \tag{9}$$

where S represents the triangular area composed of P_1, P_2 and P_3, θ Indicates $\angle P_2 P_1 P_3$. The distance d and vector $\overrightarrow{P_1 N}$ can be obtained from Eq. (6), (7), (8), (9).Assume $\overrightarrow{P_1 N} = (\overrightarrow{P_1 N_x}, \overrightarrow{P_1 N_y}, \overrightarrow{P_1 N_z})$, then:

$$\overrightarrow{NP_3} = \left\{ (x_2 - x_1 - \overrightarrow{P_1 N_x}), \ (y_2 + a - y_1 - \overrightarrow{P_1 N_y}), \ (z_2 - z_1 - \overrightarrow{P_1 N_z}) \right\}$$

The unit vector of $\overrightarrow{NP_3}$ is $\overrightarrow{y}$ (y^1, y^2, y^3), defining the Y direction of TCP coordinate system is consistent with $\overrightarrow{y}$. Since $\overrightarrow{y}$ and $\overrightarrow{z}$ are coplanar, the unit vector $\overrightarrow{x}$ in the X direction of TCP coordinate system can be obtained:

$$\overrightarrow{x} = \overrightarrow{y} \otimes \overrightarrow{z} \tag{10}$$

Recording $\overrightarrow{x}$ as (x^1, x^2, x^3), according to the calculated relevant parameters, the position-pose relationship $^e_t T$ between the TCP and the flange coordinate system can be obtained:

$$^e_t T = \begin{bmatrix} x^1 & y^1 & z^1 & x_1 \\ x^2 & y^2 & z^2 & x_2 \\ x^3 & y^3 & z^3 & x_3 \\ 0 & 0 & 0 & 1 \end{bmatrix}$$

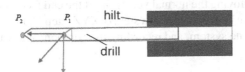
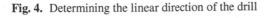

Fig. 4. Determining the linear direction of the drill   **Fig. 5.** TCP coordinate system

3.2 The Calculation of the Robot Positioning Parameters

The projection transformation of the normal vector $\overrightarrow{n}$. It can be seen from 1.2 and 2.1 when the end face of the blade is not inclined at any angle and is fixed in the positive direction, the Z direction of the TCP coordinate system, the normal direction of the hole and the X direction of the base coordinate system are parallel each other, which is a necessary condition to ensure that the robot carries relevant equipment to locate the end face's hole of the blade with the best positioning operation pose (at this time, the binocular vision laser scanner is synchronously fixed above the robot in the positive direction). Due to the relatively fixed position-pose relationship among the flange, TCP and the binocular vision laser scanner coordinate system, in order to ensure the robot carries relevant equipment to locate the end face's hole of any complex blade has the best position-pose. Taking the end face of the blade without any angle inclination and positive fixation as the benchmark, to control the Z direction of the TCP coordinate system to follow the normal vector $\vec{n}$ deflection, and project $\vec{n}$ in the base coordinate system, a coordinate system of the end face's hole that can control the TCP coordinate system to coincide with it is established at the hole.

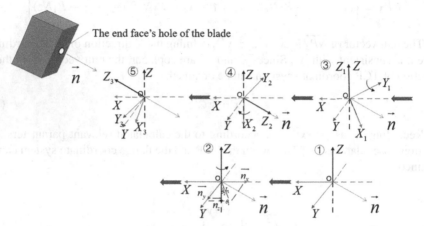

Fig. 6. The projection transformation model of the normal vector $\vec{n}$

In order to better reflect the accuracy of the positioning method in this paper, the normal vector $\vec{n}$ is transformed by projection with any large angle inclination of the blade end face, as shown in Fig. 6. Moving the normal vector $\vec{n}$ of the end face's hole of the blade measured by scanning to the base coordinate system o-XYZ (step 1). Projecting $\vec{n}$ on each axis of the base coordinate system, and recording the component as (n_x, n_y, n_z)(step 2), then:

$$L_1 = \sqrt{n_x^2 + n_y^2} \tag{11}$$

$$\theta_1 = \arctan(\frac{n_y}{n_x}) \tag{12}$$

$$\theta_2 = \arctan(\frac{L_1}{n_z}) \tag{13}$$

Where L_1 represents the oblique side length of the right triangle formed by n_x and n_y, θ_1 represents the tangent angle formed by n_x and n_y, θ_2 represents the tangent angle formed by L_1 and n_z. According to the rotation formula of the coordinate system around the axis, rotating the base coordinate system around the Z axis (step 2) and Y_1 axis (step 3) counterclockwise by $180° - \theta_1$ and $180° - \theta_2$. The corresponding coordinate systems after rotation are o-$X_1Y_1Z_1$ and o-$X_2Y_2Z_2$, and the corresponding rotation matrix R'_Z, R'_{Y_1}:

$$R'_Z = \begin{bmatrix} \cos(\theta_1 - 180^0) & -\sin(\theta_1 - 180^0) & 0 \\ \sin(\theta_1 - 180^0) & \cos(\theta_1 - 180^0) & 0 \\ 0 & 0 & 1 \end{bmatrix} \tag{14}$$

$$R'_{Y_1} = \begin{bmatrix} \cos(\theta_2 - 180^0) & 0 & \sin(\theta_2 - 180^0) \\ 0 & 1 & 0 \\ -\sin(\theta_2 - 180^0) & 0 & \cos(\theta_2 - 180^0) \end{bmatrix} \tag{15}$$

$$R' = R'_Z * R'_{Y_1} = \begin{bmatrix} \cos\theta_1\cos\theta_2 & \sin\theta_1\cos\theta_2 & \sin\theta_2 \\ \sin\theta_1 & -\cos\theta_1 & 0 \\ \cos\theta_1\sin\theta_2 & \sin\theta_1\sin\theta_2 & -\cos\theta_2 \end{bmatrix} \tag{16}$$

where R' represents the fusion transformation matrix of the coordinate system rotating around the Z axis first and then around the Y_1 axis. At this time, the Z_2 direction of the obtained coordinate system is the same as the $\overrightarrow{n}$ direction. Rotating the coordinate system 180° around the X_2 axis (step 4). At this time, the obtained coordinate system o-$X_3Y_3Z_3$ is the feed pose when the TCP coordinate system is positioned to the end face's hole of the blade, which is marked as hole's pose coordinate system. Corresponding rotation matrix R'_{X_2}:

$$R'_{X_2} = \begin{bmatrix} 1 & 0 & 0 \\ 0 & \cos180^0 & -\sin180^0 \\ 0 & \sin180^0 & \cos180^0 \end{bmatrix} = \begin{bmatrix} 1 & 0 & 0 \\ 0 & -1 & 0 \\ 0 & 0 & 1 \end{bmatrix} \tag{17}$$

Marking the fusion transformation matrix of the whole process of projection transformation normal vector $\overrightarrow{n}$ to determine the hole's pose coordinate system is R:

$$R = R'_Z * R'_{Y_1} * R'_{X_2} = R' * R'_{X_2} = \begin{bmatrix} \cos\theta_1\cos\theta_2 & -\sin\theta_1\cos\theta_2 & \sin\theta_2 \\ \sin\theta_1 & \cos\theta_1 & 0 \\ \cos\theta_1\sin\theta_2 & -\sin\theta_1\sin\theta_2 & -\cos\theta_2 \end{bmatrix} \tag{18}$$

The Conversion of the Robot Positioning Parameters. According to 1.2 and 2.1, the coordinate system of base, flange, TCP, and the binocular vision laser scanner and the position-pose relationship between them are known. According to the determined system parameters, the position-pose relationship T between the hole's pose coordinate system and the robot base coordinate system is:

$$T = \begin{bmatrix} R & P \\ 0 & 001 \end{bmatrix} = \begin{bmatrix} \cos\theta_1\cos\theta_2 & -\sin\theta_1\cos\theta_2 & \sin\theta_2 & X \\ \sin\theta_1 & \cos\theta_1 & 0 & Y \\ \cos\theta_1\sin\theta_2 & -\sin\theta_1\sin\theta_2 & -\cos\theta_2 & Z \\ 0 & 0 & 0 & 1 \end{bmatrix} \tag{19}$$

The position-pose relationship between the flange and the base coordinate system can be obtained in real time according to the robot, which is recorded as NewRT:

$$NewRT *_t^e T = T \tag{20}$$

NewRT represents a 4 * 4 matrix, which can be converted to obtain the position coordinates $(X\cdot, Y\cdot, Z\cdot)$ and four elements $(w\cdot, x\cdot, y\cdot, z\cdot)$ required by the robot to locate the end face's hole of any blade.

4   Experiment and Result Analysis

In this paper, the rapid programming control language of the robot is redeveloped by using the VS2015 development platform and configured OpenCv3.3.0, PCL1.8.1, and TC31-ADS to integrate the unified C++ language compiling environment to develop the automatic measurement and positioning drilling software system of blade end face hole. IRB6700-300/2.7 industrial robot is adopted, its positioning accuracy is 0.1 mm; The binocular vision laser scanner constructed by DSV450-500-FL-30 line laser module and MER-500-14GC camera is selected, with a scanning accuracy of 0.037 mm and the working distance of 700 mm. The experimental platform is shown in Fig. 7.

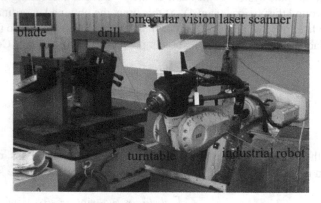

Fig. 7. Experimental platform

4.1   The Positioning Experiment of Seven-Point Calibration Board

Selecting the center of circle 1 with the obvious white cross line in the seven-point calibration board to use laser scanning measurement and control robot to position, to test whether in 3.2 algorithm can effectively control TCP under the condition of the robot with relevant equipment to accurately locate any given target position. In order to better reflect the effectiveness of the algorithm in this paper, the seven-point calibration board fixed on the turntable with an inclination of 15°, scanning the point cloud of the seven-point calibration board at three different positions of the turntable at 0°, 10° and −10° respectively by the binocular vision laser scanner. Using PCL to respectively solve the position coordinates and normal vector of the center of circle 1 in the corresponding turntable position, as shown in Fig. 8 (a); The robot's position coordinates and pose parameter of the center of circle 1 in the corresponding turntable position is determined through t 3.2 algorithm; To control the robot to locate the center of circle 1, as shown in Fig. 8 (b); Measuring the deviation $|\Delta X|$, $|\Delta Y|$, $|\Delta Z|$ between the TCP coordinates$(X', Y', Z')$and the coordinates (X,Y, Z) of the center of circle 1; Measuring the perpendicularity h between the linear direction of the drill and the plane adjacent to the center of circle 1, the parameters are shown in Table 1.

Table 1. Multi-position scanning measurement and positioning results of circle 1 (unit/mm)

Turntable position		0°	10°	-10°
Circle 1 coordinates	X	2074.83	2086.35	2067.29
	Y	−94.56	−72.83	−116.64
	Z	2606.91	2606.91	2606.91
TCP coordinates	X'	2075.02	2086.70	2067.51
	Y'	−94.55	−72.46	−116.48
	Z'	2606.81	2606.84	2606.75
Error	$|\Delta X|$	0.19	0.35	0.22
	$|\Delta Y|$	0.01	0.37	0.16
	$|\Delta Z|$	0.1	0.07	0.16
Verticality	h	89.98°	89.12°	89.34°

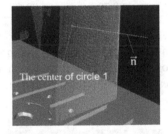

(a) . Point cloud of seven-point calibration board   (b) . The positioning scene of circle 1

Fig. 8. The positioning experiment of the center of circle 1

It can be seen from the parameters in Table 1 that when the position of the seven points calibration board changes at a large angle, the error of the TCP positioning the target position does not exceed 1 mm, and the perpendicularity between the linear direction of the drill and the plane adjacent to the center of circle 1 can reach 89.98°.

4.2   The Positioning Experiment of the End face's Hole of the Blade

In order to further verify the feasibility of 2.2 algorithm to position the actual blade end face hole, a blade with a drilled hole is fixed on the turntable, controlling the turntable at three different positions of 0°, 10° and −10°, respectively to scan and measure the point cloud at the end face of the blade, to determine the central position coordinates and the normal vector of the blade end face hole through PolyWorks fitting the standard blade module, as shown in Fig. 9 (a); The robot's position coordinates and pose parameter to locate the centre of the hole in corresponding turntable position is determined through the 3.2 algorithm; To control the robot to locate the hole, as shown in Fig. 9 (b). As the 4.1, measuring the deviation between the TCP coordinates and the center of hole, and the perpendicularity, the parameters are shown in Table 2.

Table 2. Multi-position scanning measurement and positioning results of the blade (unit/mm)

Turntable position		0°	10°	−10°
Hole's coordinates	X	1991.87	1998.45	1990.23
	Y	−169.82	−221.02	−170.19
	Z	2561.10	2561.10	2561.10
TCP coordinates	X'	1992.12	1988.65	1989.26
	Y'	−169.43	−221.35	−170.53
	Z'	2560.98	2560.99	2561.82
Error	$|\Delta X|$	0.25	0.2	0.03
	$|\Delta Y|$	0.39	0.33	0.34
	$|\Delta Z|$	0.12	0.11	0.7
Verticality	h	89.6°	88.7°	88.6°

According to the analysis for Table 2, even if the blade end face tilts in different directions and angles, the error that the TCP positions the target hole does not exceed 1 mm, and the perpendicularity between the linear direction of the drill and the plane of the hole position area can reach 89.6°.

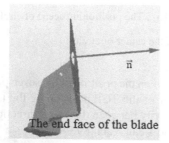

(a) . Registration with the point cloud

(b). Scence of the position

Fig. 9. The positioning experiment of the end face's hole of the blade

5 Conclusion

Aiming at the shortcomings of the current turbine blade positioning and drilling, this paper built an automatic measurement, positioning and drilling system of the end face's hole of the blade, and put forward an adaptive method of position-pose for the robot to locate the end face's hole of the blade. TCP calibration algorithm and hand-eye calibration algorithm were used to realize the parameterization of the system; The point cloud of the end face of the blade was measured by the laser scanning, and the position coordinates and normal vector of the hole were determined; Based on the principle of coordinate system transformation, through constructing the coordinate system to project and transform the normal vector $\vec{n}$, the optimal position-pose of the robot with the relevant equipment to locate the end face's hole of any blade was automatically obtained. Through the positioning experiment of the seven-point calibration board and the end face's hole of the blade, the results showed that the TCP located the target position's error was less than 1 mm, which was better than the 1.5 mm of the traditional method; The linear direction of the drill was highly perpendicular to the plane of the target drilling position, which met the working requirement of the workpiece.

Acknowledgement. This research is partially supported by the National Natural Science Foundation of China (Grant Nos. 62176149 and 51975344).

References

1. Jianxin, C.: Current situation and future of industrial robot application. Sci. Technol. Commun. **5**(02), 212–213 (2013)
2. Zai, L., Hongnan, Z., et al.: Reference hole detection and positioning method based on line laser scanning. Chin. J. Instrum. **42**(12), 184–190 (2021)
3. Yao, G.: Simulation of industrial robot pickup technology based on visual guidance. Mech. Eng. Autom. (06), 37–39+42 (2020)
4. Shi, X., Le, T., et al.: Intelligent positioning and drilling technology of aviation radiator based on machine vision. Measur. Control Technol. **39**(08), 129–133 (2020)
5. Shi, J.: Research on automatic positioning of open-air down the hole drill. Changsha: Central South University (2015)
6. Jiang, H., Liu, S., et al.: Inverse kinematics analysis of six degrees of freedom modular manipulator. J. Zhejiang Univ. (Eng. Ed.) **44**(07), 1348–1354 (2010)
7. Xianhua, L., Yongcun, G., et al.: Inverse kinematics solution and verification of modular 6-DOF manipulator. J. Agric. Mach. **44**(04), 246–251 (2013)
8. Yao, H., Liu W., et al.: Research on drilling positioning method of rock drilling robot with improved configuration. China Mech. Eng. **31**(18): 2254–2261+2267 (2020)
9. Liu, G., Meng, S., et al. Inverse solution algorithm and error analysis of 6R modular robot. Mech. Des. Manuf. (2021)
10. Caidong, W., Zhihang, L., et al.: Robot TCP self-calibration method is based on the hand-eye relationship. Mach. Tools Hydraulics **47**(17), 6–11 (2019)

An AGV Positioning Algorithm for Reducing the Number of Reflectors

Yi Luo, Guang-Zhong Cao[✉], Chao Wu, and Zhi-Yong Hu

Guangdong Key Laboratory of Electromagnetic Control and Intelligent Robots,
College of Mechatronics and Control Engineering, Shenzhen University, Shenzhen
518060, China
gzcao@szu.edu.com

Abstract. Aiming at the problem of low global positioning precision and a large
number of reflectors in the global feature map, an AGV positioning algorithm
for reducing the number of reflectors is proposed. First, the global feature map
is constructed by the reflectors. Next, the reflection points are obtained by lidar
scanning, in which abnormal reflection points are removed through preprocessing.
The local coordinates of the reflector are clustered and fitted by combining the
reflection intensity of the reflector point. Then, the global coordinates of the reflectors are obtained by matching the local coordinates of the reflector with the global
feature map. Finally, the initial position of the AGV is obtained through the static
pose calculation algorithm, and the dynamic position of the AGV is solved by the
two-point positioning algorithm. The experimental results show that, compared
with the traditional algorithm, the positioning algorithm based on reflectors in this
paper decreases the global position precision by 42.0% and 16.1% in the X-axis
and Y-axis, respectively, and the number of reflectors used for the positioning
algorithm is reduced from three or more to two.

Keywords: AGV · Position calculation · Two-point positioning · Reflector

1 Introduction

As an important part of industrial production, Automated Guided Vehicle (AGV) greatly
improves the efficiency of cargo handling and the productivity of workers, and is widely
used in industrial fields such as cargo handling, automated manufacturing, and aerospace
[1, 2].

The primary problem of AGV is the low positioning precision. High-precision positioning is the foundation for completing other tasks [3]. According to the taxonomy of
sensors, the positioning methods of AGV can be divided into visual positioning [4], QR
code positioning [5], magnetic positioning [6], lidar positioning, etc. Among them, lidar
positioning is gradually becoming the mainstream positioning method, due to its advantages of low maintenance cost, high precision positioning, strong ability to adapt to the
environment and so on. Lidar positioning can be sorted into two types, one is natural
positioning, that is, by scanning and matching the surrounding environment information

© The Author(s), under exclusive license to Springer Nature Switzerland AG 2022
H. Liu et al. (Eds.): ICIRA 2022, LNAI 13455, pp. 274–284, 2022.
https://doi.org/10.1007/978-3-031-13844-7_27

to obtain the position of the AGV at the current moment [7]. The other is positioning based on reflectors. The positioning algorithm is utilized to calculate the global position of the AGV in the environment by scanning the previously placed reflectors [8]. Compared with natural positioning, positioning based on reflectors has high precision positioning, flexible path, no cumulative error, low cost and so on. Therefore, studying the positioning based on reflectors is important for improving the performance of AGV in the industrial field.

At present, the common positioning algorithms using reflectors include triangular positioning method [9], trilateral positioning method [10] and their related improvements [11] and so on. In order to improve the AGV positioning precision, Wang Sen et al. [12] proposed a new positioning algorithm, SORLA, which solves the AGV position through singular value decomposition. Guo Shuai et al. [13] proposed to integrate the scanning data of the two lidars for solving the problem of triangular positioning blind spots. Xu Zhen et al. [14] proposed an adaptive weight positioning algorithm that combines natural road signs with the natural environment, which is mainly used in construction sites. The above positioning algorithms all require the use of three or more reflectors, which will result in too many reflectors in the global feature map. But, the number of reflectors excess overabundance can decline the operating efficiency of the positioning algorithm, and even lead to positioning failure. Chen Hua et al. [15] presented a positioning algorithm based on Taylor series iteration, which needs no less than the position of two reference objects and the initial position of itself to be estimated, but it is susceptible to accumulative errors. All existing positioning algorithms can obtain the global position of the AGV. However, to ensure high-precision positioning of AGV and reduce the number of reflectors, the above algorithms cannot be satisfied.

In this paper, we propose a positioning algorithm for reducing the number of reflectors. The global position of the AGV is obtained according to the triangular geometric relationship formed by the global position of the two reflectors and the AGV. In order to avoid the combination with other sensors, only lidar is used to locate the AGV. To avoid the influence of sensor noise and improve the positioning precision of the AGV, the global feature map is matched with the local reflector for one-to-one distance matching or coordinate matching.

The second section describes the framework of the AGV positioning algorithm in this paper. The third section describes the principle of the AGV positioning algorithm used to reduce the number of reflectors in detail, and analyzes its feasibility. The fourth section analyzes its reliability by comparing with the existing positioning algorithm through simulation. The fifth section concludes the paper.

2   The AGV Positioning Process Based on the Reflector

The AGV positioning process based on the reflector is divided into four parts, which are preprocessing, cluster fitting, data matching, and the position calculation, as shown in Fig. 1.

Specifically, to determine the global coordinates of reflectors, a global map featuring reflectors is first constructed. Then, the data of reflection point are acquired by lidar, and the abnormal reflection points are removed by preprocessing. After coordinate transformation, they are evenly distributed around the local coordinate system with the lidar center as the origin. Then, clustering and fitting is performed, and the reflection points belonging to the same reflector are gathered in the same class. Then, the local coordinates of reflectors are determined according to the geometric relationship between the reflection points and the center of the reflector, to obtain the local position of the reflector. On this basis, data matching is carried out, and the global position of the local reflectors is obtained by completing the one-to-one distance and coordinates matching with the global feature map. Finally, the global position of the AGV is obtained through the position calculation algorithm.

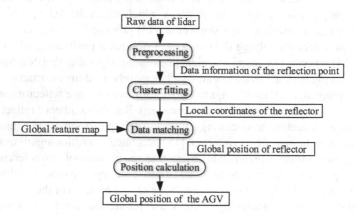

Fig. 1. The AGV positioning process based on the reflector

3   Algorithm Model

3.1   Preprocessing

The continuous and evenly distributed reflection points are obtained by scanning the surrounding environment. Each reflection point p in the local coordinates includes information such as angle θ, distance D, and reflection intensity R. The corresponding point set is $p_i = \{\theta_i, D_i, R_i\}_{i=1}^{N}$, where i is the sequence number of the reflection points, and N is the total number of the reflection points of a frame. After the reflection point information is received and the coordinate transformation is completed, it is evenly distributed around the local coordinate system with lidar as the origin. Then the data information of adjacent reflection points is compared. If a single reflection point changes abruptly, it is classified as abnormal points and eliminated to ensure the accuracy of the information.

3.2   Clustering and Fitting

Clustering. When the lidar scans the reflector, the reflection intensity of the reflection points will be much greater than that of other reflection points. The specific effect is shown in Fig. 2. The protruding part in Fig. 2 is the reflector, and its reflection intensity is all greater than 1000. The clustering and fitting part is divided into two parts, which are clustering and fitting. The clustering part is to find the reflection points belonging to the same reflector according to the reflection intensity of the reflector, and put them into the arrays G_{total} and G_j, where $G_{total} = \{G_j\}_{j=1}^{M}$, j is the serial number of the local reflector, and M is the total number of the reflector obtained by the lidar scanning one frame. The specific algorithm is shown in Algorithm 1.

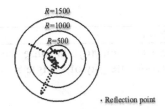

Fig. 2. Intensity distribution map of reflection point

Algorithm 1: Clustering algorithm

Input: Establish an objective function $f(p_i)$. Initialize the parameters k, h, j to 0, where k is the reflection point number of G_j, h is the starting reflection point number of G_j. Initialize the intensity threshold R_{th} to 500, the angular threshold θ_{th} to 3 times the angular resolution of the lidar, the distance threshold D_{th} to the radius of the reflector.

Output: G_{total}.

1: for i=1, 2, …, N do
2:   if $R_i > R_{th}$ then
3:     $G_j = \{p_i\}$, $h=i$, $k=1$.
4:   else if $k \,!\!=0$ && $R_i > R_{th}$ && $D(p_i\text{-}p_h) < D_{th}$ && $\theta(p_i\text{-}p_h) < \theta_{th}$ then
5:     $G_j = \{p_i\}$.
6:     if $k == S_{max}$ then
7:       $G_{total} = \{G_j\}$, $k=0$, $j=j+1$.
8:     else
9:       $k=k+1$.
10:    end if
11:   else if $k == S_{min}$ then
12:     $G_{total} = \{G_j\}$, $k=0$, $j=j+1$.
13:   end if
14: end for
return G_{total}.

Where $D(p_i - p_h)$ and $\theta(p_i - p_h)$ are used to calculate the distance difference and the angle difference between p_i and p_h separately, S_{max} and S_{min} are the maximum and minimum number of detectable reflection points in the reflector, respectively.

Fitting The fitting part is to gain the center data C_j according to G_j, and C_j includes the local coordinates $[x, y]$ of the reflector, the distance d, and the angle α, where the corresponding point set is $C_j = \{x_j, y_j, d_j, \alpha_j\}_{j=1}^{M}$. The internal relationship is shown in Eq. 1. The specific algorithm is shown in Algorithm 2.

$$\begin{cases} x_j = d_j * \cos(\alpha_j) \\ y_j = d_j * \sin(\alpha_j) \end{cases} \tag{1}$$

Alogrithm2 : Fitting alogrithm

Input: Establish an objective function $f(G_j)$. Initialize the parameters R_{total}, H to 0, where R_{total} is the total reflection intensity of a single reflector, H is total number of reflection points in G_j.

Output: C_j.

1: for $h = 1$ to H do
2:    Obtain R_{total} in G_j.
3: end for
4: for $h = 1$ to H do
5:    Obtain the intensity weight W_h of each reflection point in G_j, and then obtain α_j
        of the center of the reflector according to Eq. 2.
6: end for
7: for $h = 1$ to H do
8:    Obtain d_j according to Eq. 3.
9: end for
10: Obtain x_j and y_j according to Eq. 1.
11: $C_j = \{x_j, y_j, d_j, \alpha_j\}$.
return C_j.

$$\alpha_j = \alpha_j + \frac{W_h \theta_h}{H} \tag{2}$$

$$d_j = d_j + \frac{d_h \cos(\theta_h - \alpha_j)}{H} \tag{3}$$

3.3 Data Matching

In the process of AGV positioning and navigation, the coordinate system is divided into the global coordinate system XOY and the local coordinate system xoy. The global coordinate system is a two-dimensional coordinate system set according to the entire motion area of the AGV. The global feature map and the global position of the AGV are based on this coordinate system, which is usually fixed. The local coordinate system is established with the lidar installed on the AGV body as the origin, and its y-axis is the forward direction of the AGV, which changes continuously with the movement of the AGV, as shown in Fig. 3. The global coordinates $[X, Y]$ of three reflectors in the local coordinate system are gained by one-to-one distance and coordinates matching with the global feature map. The specific effects are as shown in Fig. 4.

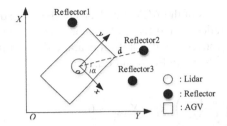

Fig. 3. Local coordinate systems and global coordinate systems

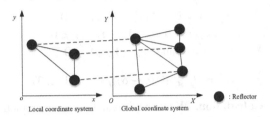

Fig. 4. Data matching

3.4 Position Calculation

The position calculation algorithm is divided into the static position calculation and the dynamic position calculation. When the AGV is in the initial static, to ensure the precision of the initial position of the AGV, the global position of three reflectors obtained by matching is passed into the static position calculation algorithm to obtain the position of the AGV. After the AGV starts to move, the global position information of two reflectors is transmitted to the dynamic position calculation algorithm composed of two-point positioning algorithm to obtain the global position of the AGV.

Static Position Calculation. After completing the data matching section, the global coordinates $[X_1, Y_1]$, $[X_2, Y_2]$, $[X_3, Y_3]$ of the three reflectors, the absolute distances between the center of the reflectors and the lidar d_1, d_2, d_3, the angles $\alpha_1, \alpha_2, \alpha_3$ of the center of the reflector in the global coordinate system are gained. First, the X-axis and Y-axis distances formed between the reflector and the reflector are calculated, which are represented by variables L_{X13}, L_{Y13}, L_{X23}, and L_{Y23}, respectively. Then find the relationship between the coordinates of the reflector and its distance, and using the variables r_{13} and r_{23} to express. The calculation formula is shown in Eq. 4.

$$\begin{cases} r_{13} = X_1^2 - X_3^2 + Y_1^2 - Y_3^2 - d_1^2 + d_1^2 \\ r_{23} = X_2^2 - X_3^2 + Y_2^2 - Y_3^2 - d_3^2 + d_2^2 \end{cases} \tag{4}$$

According to the relationship formed in the trilateration positioning, the global coordinates $[X_{\text{pose}}, Y_{\text{pose}}]$ of the AGV are obtained, as shown in Eq. 5.

$$\begin{cases} X_{\text{pose}} = (L_{Y13}r_{23} - L_{Y23}r_{13})/(2L_{X23}L_{Y13} - 2L_{X13}L_{Y23}) \\ Y_{\text{pose}} = (L_{X13}r_{23} - L_{X23}r_{13})/(2L_{X13}L_{Y23} - 2L_{X23}L_{Y13}) \end{cases} \tag{5}$$

After the global coordinates of the AGV are obtained, the angle difference between the angle formed by each reflector and the global coordinates of the AGV and the angle α of the corresponding reflector is the deflection angle θ_{pose} of the AGV. The specific calculation methods are shown in Eq. 6 and Eq. 7.

$$\begin{cases} \theta_i = \arctan\left(\frac{Y_i - Y_{\text{pose}}}{X_i - X_{\text{pose}}}\right), X_i - X_{\text{pose}} > 0 \\ \theta_i = \arctan\left(\frac{Y_i - Y_{\text{pose}}}{X_i - X_{\text{pose}}}\right) + \pi, (X_i - X_{\text{pose}}) < 0 \text{ and } (Y_i - Y_{\text{pose}}) \geq 0 \\ \theta_i = \arctan\left(\frac{Y_i - Y_{\text{pose}}}{X_i - X_{\text{pose}}}\right) - \pi, (X_i - X_{\text{pose}}) < 0 \text{ and } (Y_i - Y_{\text{pose}}) < 0 \\ \theta_i = \frac{\pi}{2}, (X_i - X_{\text{pose}}) = 0 \text{ and } (Y_i - Y_{\text{pose}}) > 0 \\ \theta_i = -\frac{\pi}{2}, (X_i - X_{\text{pose}}) = 0 \text{ and } (Y_i - Y_{\text{pose}}) < 0 \\ \theta_i = 0, (X_i - X_{\text{pose}}) = 0 \text{ and } (Y_i - Y_{\text{pose}}) = 0 \end{cases} \tag{6}$$

$$\theta_{\text{pose}} = \theta_{\text{pose}} + (\theta_i - \alpha_i)/3 \ (i = 1, 2, 3) \tag{7}$$

Dynamic Position Calculation. When the data matching is completed, the global coordinates of the two reflectors $[X_1, Y_1], [X_2, Y_2]$, the distances d_1 and d_2 between the center of the reflector and the center of the lidar, and the angles α_1 and α_2 of the reflector in the local coordinate system are transmitted, where $Y_2 \geqslant Y_1$. The two reflectors used to two-point positioning algorithm are respectively defined as reflector 1 and reflector 2, and the absolute distance between reflector 1 and reflector 2 is L_{12}. First, a coordinate system $x_1 o_1 y_1$ with reflector 1 as the origin is constructed, and its positive direction of the y_1-axis is the direction from reflector 1 to reflection 2. The position relationship between the coordinate system $x_1 o_1 y_1$ and the AGV is shown in Fig. 5, where the forward direction of the AGV is any pose.

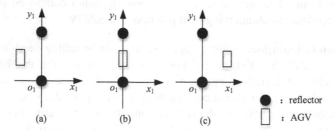

Fig. 5. The position relationship between the coordinate system $x_1 o_1 y_1$ and the AGV: (a) the AGV is on the left side of the y_1-axis. (b) the AGV is in the middle of the y_1-axis. (c) the AGV is on the right side of the y_1-axis.

Obtain the interior angle β at reflector 1 in the triangle formed between reflector 1, reflector 2 and the AGV, as shown in Eq. 8. Then, according to the angle difference γ_1 obtained by subtracting α_1 from α_2, the position $[X_S, Y_S]$ of the AGV in the coordinate system $x_1 o_1 y_1$ is judged. The specific relationship is shown in Eq. 9.

$$\beta = a\cos((d_1^2 + L_{12}^2 - d_2^2)/(2 \cdot d_1 \cdot L_{12})) \tag{8}$$

$$\begin{cases} X_S = -d_1 \sin\beta, \ 0 \le \gamma_1 < \pi \\ X_S = d_1 \sin\beta, \quad -\pi \le \gamma_1 \le 0 \ \text{or} \ \pi \le \gamma_1 < 2*\pi \\ Y_S = d_1 \cos\beta \end{cases} \tag{9}$$

Obtain the angle γ_2 formed by the reflector 1 and the reflector 2, according to Eq. 6. Then, the global coordinates $[X_{pose}, Y_{pose}]$ of the AGV are obtained, according to γ_2 and the global coordinates $[X_1, Y_1]$ of the reflector 1, as shown in Eq. 10.

$$\begin{cases} X_{pose} = \sin\gamma_2 * X_S + \cos\gamma_2 * Y_S + X_1 \\ Y_{pose} = -\cos\gamma_2 * X_S + \sin\gamma_2 * Y_S + Y_1 \end{cases} \tag{10}$$

After the global coordinates of the AGV are obtained, the deflection angle θ_{pose} of the AGV is obtained according to Eq. 6 and Eq. 7.

4 Experiment and Analysis

The material of the reflector used in this experiment is 3M diamond grade reflective film, which is a full prism structure and has the advantages of high reflectivity, long distance detection, and low loss. To improve the efficiency of the program operation and improve the fitting precision, a cylindrical reflector was used for experiments.

The sensor used in this experiment is a single-line lidar, which can scan 360° in all directions. The specific parameters of lidar are shown in Table 1.

Table 1. Specific parameters of single-line lidar

Measuring distance (m)	Reflection intensity	Operating frequency (Hz)	Minimum angular resolution (°)	Distance precision (mm)
0.1–30	32–4095	10–50	0.014	±1

The operating frequency is set to 10 Hz, and the angular resolution is 0.18°. In order to verify this algorithm, a laser range finder is used to measure the distance and angle of the reflector in the coordinate system xoy, and the measured value is used as a reference value. The ranging range is 0.05–150 m, and the precision is 1mm.

The following experiments are designed in combination with the positioning algorithm in this paper.

1) AGV static position experiment

When the global feature map remains unchanged, the proposed algorithm is used to obtain the global position of the AGV and compare it with the trilateration algorithm. The experimental results in Table 2 show the deviation of the static position calculation. The X-axis deviation, Y-axis deviation and angle deviation are selected as the evaluation criteria.

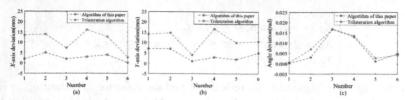

Fig. 6. AGV static global position deviation: a) the X-axis deviation. b) the Y-axis deviation. c) the Angle deviation.

Table 2. Maximum deviation of the static position calculation

Algorithm	X-axis maximum deviation(mm)	Y-axis maximum deviation(mm)	Angle maximum deviation(rad)
The proposed algorithm	5.0	7.0	0.0167
Trilateration algorithm	13.9	16.7	0.0168

By analyzing Table 2 and Fig. 6, it can be seen that the maximum deviation of the X-axis, the Y-axis and the angle are 5.0 mm, 7.0 mm and 0.0167 rad in the proposed algorithm, respectively. Using the trilateration algorithm, it can be known that the maximum deviation of the X-axis, the Y-axis and the angle are 13.9 mm, 16.7 mm and 0.0168 rad, respectively. Compared with the trilateration algorithm, the mean deviation of the X-axis of the proposed algorithm is reduced by 70.1%, the mean deviation of the Y-axis is reduced by 63.7%, and the mean deviation of the angle is reduced by 11.2%.

2) AGV dynamic position experiment

Through repeated experiments, the global coordinates of reflectors in Table 3 are substituted into the two-point positioning algorithm, and the global coordinates of the AGV were obtained. The specific effects are shown in Table 4, and the position deviation is selected as the precision index.

Table 3. Global coordinates of reflectors

Number	X-axis coordinate(m)	Y-axis coordinate(m)
1	−1.000	0
2	−1.000	1.000
3	1.000	0
4	1.000	1.000

Table 4. AGV dynamic position calculation algorithm results

Algorithm	X-axis maximum deviation (mm)	Y-axis maximum deviation (mm)	Angle maximum deviation (rad)
Two-point positioning algorithm	8.0	14.0	0.0080
Trilateration algorithm	13.9	16.7	0.0168

Analysis of Table 4 shows that the maximum deviation of the X-axis, the Y-axis and angle are 8 mm, 14 mm and 0.008 rad respectively. Compared with the trilateration algorithm, the deviation of the X-axis decreases by 42%, and the deviation of the Y-axis decreases by 16.1%, and the angle deviation is reduced by 52.1%. The number of reflectors is reduced from three or more to two.

5 Conclusion

In order to verify the accuracy of the initial pose, the experimental results of the static pose solution algorithm and the trilateration positioning algorithm are compared to prove that the influence of the static position algorithm on the global position precision of the AGV. The dynamic position calculation algorithm only uses the geometric relationship of the AGV and two reflectors, the global coordinates of the AGV are obtained. Then, the experimental results of the dynamic position calculation algorithm are compared with the trilateration positioning algorithm to prove the influence of the dynamic position calculation algorithm on the algorithm operating efficiency and the AGV global positioning accuracy. The experimental results demonstrate that the algorithm effectively reduces the number of reflectors, and the positioning accuracy of the AGV is improved at the same time.

Acknowledgement. This work was supported in part by the National Natural Science Foundation of China under Grant NSFC U1813212, in part by the Science and Tech-nology Planning Project of Guangdong Province, China under Grant 2020B121201012.

References

1. Liu, X., Zhang, J., Jiang, S., et al.: Accurate localization of tagged objects using mobile RFID-augmented robots. IEEE Trans. Mob. Comput. **20**(4), 1273–1284 (2019)
2. Ullrich, G.: The history of automated guided vehicle systems. In: Ullrich, G. (ed.) Automated Guided Vehicle Systems, pp. 1–14. Springer, Heidelberg (2015). https://doi.org/10.1007/978-3-662-44814-4_1
3. Song, Q., Zhao, Q., Wang, S., et al.: Dynamic path planning for unmanned vehicles based on fuzzy logic and improved ant colony optimization. IEEE Access **8**, 62107–62115 (2020)
4. Mu, X., He, B., Zhang, X., et al.: Visual navigation features selection algorithm based on instance segmentation in dynamic environment. IEEE Access **8**, 465–473 (2020)

5. Yu, X., Fan, Z., Wan, H., et al.: Positioning, navigation, and book accessing/returning in an autonomous library robot using integrated binocular vision and QR code identification systems. Sensors 19(4), 783 (2019)
6. Su, S., Dai, H., Cheng, S., et al.: Improved magnetic guidance approach for automated guided vehicles by error analysis and prior knowledge. IEEE Trans. Intell. Transp. Syst. 22(11), 6843–6852 (2021)
7. Chen, X., Läbe, T., Milioto, A., et al.: OverlapNet: loop closing for LiDAR-based SLAM. arXiv preprint arXiv, 2105.11344 (2021)
8. Ronzoni, D., Olmi, R., Secchi, C., et al.: AGV global localization using indistinguishable artificial landmarks. In: 2011 IEEE International Conference on Robotics and Automation, pp. 287–292. IEEE (2011)
9. Pierlot, V., Van, D.M.: BeAMS: a beacon-based angle measurement sensor for mobile robot positioning. IEEE Trans. Robot. 30(3), 533–549 (2014)
10. Zeng, X., Yu, B., Liu, L., et al.: Advanced combination localization algorithm based on trilateration for dynamic cluster network. IEEE Access 7, 180965–180975 (2019)
11. Cotera, P., Velazquez, M., Cruz, D., et al.: Indoor robot positioning using an enhanced trilateration algorithm. Int. J. Adv. Robot. Syst. 13(3), 110 (2016)
12. Wang, S., Chen, X., Ding, G., et al.: A lightweight localization strategy for LiDAR-guided autonomous robots with artificial landmarks. Sensors 21(13), 4479 (2021)
13. Guo, S., Fang, T., Song, T., et al.: Tracking and localization for omni-directional mobile industrial robot using reflectors. Adv. Manuf. 6(1), 118–125 (2018)
14. Xu, Z., Guo, S., Song, T., et al.: Robust localization of the mobile robot driven by lidar measurement and matching for ongoing scene. Appl. Sci. 10(18), 6152 (2020)
15. Hua, C., Zhao, K., Dong, D., et al.: Multipath map method for TDOA based indoor reverse positioning system with improved Chan-Taylor algorithm. Sensors 20(11), 3223 (2020)

Research on Local Optimization Algorithm of 5-Axis CNC Machining Tool Axis Vector Based on Kinematic Constraints

Jianxin Xiao[1,2(✉)], Zhen Gong[1,2], Bingran Li[1,2], and Hui Zhang[1,2]

[1] Department of Mechanical Engineering, Tsinghua University, Beijing 100084, China
xiaojianxincumt@126.com

[2] Beijing Key Lab of Precision/Ultra-Precision Manufacturing Equipment and Control, Tsinghua University, Beijing 100084, China

Abstract. In this study, a local optimization method of the five-axis CNC machining tool axis vector based on kinematic constraints is proposed, which realizes the smoothing of the trajectory of the driving rotation axis in the machine tool coordinate system, so as to realize the smooth machining of the machine tool and reduce the occurrence of vibration. Firstly, this study proposes an optimization interval selection method based on kinematic parameters, that is, the tool path that does not meet the characteristics of the speed, acceleration or jerk of the rotating axis is defined as the tool path that needs to be optimized, and an algorithm based on bidirectional scanning is proposed to determine the start and end positions of each optimization interval. Secondly, the tool axis vector optimization method based on ruled surface is used to optimize the tool axis vector, and a ruled surface space is established at each tool position point, and the tool axis optimization is limited within a certain range, to minimize the dynamic characteristics of the rotary axis as the optimization goal to realize the optimization of the tool axis. Finally, the proposed method is verified by experiments, and the smoothing of the rotating drive shaft of the machine tool is realized.

Keywords: Tool axis vector · Local optimization · Rotary drive shaft

1 Introduction

Five-axis CNC machine tools are widely used in the manufacture of key components in major engineering fields such as aerospace, automotive energy, and shipbuilding, and have put forward higher and higher requirements for processing efficiency and processing quality [1, 2]. Compared with three-axis, the advantage of five-axis CNC machining is that the tool can be processed in any posture, the vector of the tool axis reflects the position of the rotary axis. The actual machine tool can be divided into translation axis and rotary axis. The characteristics of the rotary axis are worse than the driving ability of the translation axis [3]. In the process of machining, it is necessary to ensure the machining characteristics of the rotating shaft. If the driving characteristics of the machine tool are not satisfied, it will cause vibration or noise of the machine tool,

© The Author(s), under exclusive license to Springer Nature Switzerland AG 2022
H. Liu et al. (Eds.): ICIRA 2022, LNAI 13455, pp. 285–296, 2022.
https://doi.org/10.1007/978-3-031-13844-7_28

which will seriously affect the machining quality of the parts [4]. This research will optimize the direction of the tool axis vector in the tool path file to meet the driving characteristics of the machine tool's rotary axis and achieve high-quality and efficient machining of parts.

In the optimization process, the tool axis vector minimizes the overcut or undercut between the tool and the machining surface, and avoids the collision between the tool and the part. Many scholars have conducted research on the optimization of the tool axis. Morishige [5] proposed a three-dimensional parameter space (C-space) method, which is determined according to the principle of avoiding interference collisions. Wang [6] used the visual grid diagram in the process of constructing the feasible region of the tool axis vector, and carried out the smoothness processing of the tool axis vector according to this, and obtained the tool axis vector in the sense of the workpiece coordinate system under the condition of no interference. Farouki [7] proposed that while maintaining a constant cutting speed, the change characteristics of the rotation axis were optimized by using the extremely small rotating frame, and the vector smoothness of the tool axis was optimized in the workpiece coordinate system. The above methods are all optimized in the workpiece coordinate system, However, there is a nonlinear relationship between the workpiece coordinate system and the machine tool coordinate system. As a result, the tool axis that is smooth in the workpiece coordinate system may not be smooth when rotating in the machine tool coordinate system, causing the overload of the machine tool. Jianwei Ma [8] et al. first determined the area that needs to be optimized for the tool direction according to the relationship between the angle change of the rotation axis and the change of the tool path arc length. the tool axis vector equalization method based on the quaternion method is adopted, and the tool axis vector is optimized by using the kinematic characteristics of the rotary feed axis. Castagnetti [9] proposed to establish a feasible domain of the tool axis vector without interference in the workpiece coordinate system, and then convert the feasible domain of the tool axis vector to the machine tool coordinate system through the inverse kinematics of the machine tool, and obtain the feasible domain DAO of the rotary axis, and the minimum angular displacement of the rotary axis is used as the objective function to optimize the motion of the A and C axes in the DAO. The smooth processing improves the processing efficiency of the workpiece. Hu [10] established the feasible region of the tool axis vector in the machine tool coordinate system according to the geometric constraints, and then established three objective functions with the minimum acceleration of the A axis, the minimum acceleration of the B axis, and the minimum acceleration of the A and B axes, and combined the workpiece clamping method to reduce the maximum acceleration of the A-axis and B-axis of the machine tool. Jiyun Qin [11] proposed an effective five-axis toolpath optimization algorithm for the machining of parts with sudden curvature, which smoothed the machine tool rotation axis motion caused by the sharp change of the tool orientation on the helical toolpath, and improved the machining efficiency and surface quality. Gongzhen (Gong, Li et al. 2022) [12] established the characteristic index of the sum of squares of jerk to identify the area that can be optimized, and achieved the smoothing of the rotating shaft by establishing the ruled surface and the kinematic characteristics of the drive shaft as constraints.

In the current tool axis vector optimization algorithm, it includes global optimization and local optimization. In order to better reflect the characteristics of the tool path of the machine tool, this study proposes an optimization interval selection method based on kinematic parameters. By dividing all the tool position points that do not meet the speed, acceleration and jerk of each rotary axis into the tool axis vector optimization area, the tool path that needs to be optimized is identified in principle. Secondly, a method based on bidirectional scanning is proposed to determine the starting position and end position of the optimization interval. Finally, the smoothing of the rotating shaft is realized based on the kinematic characteristics of the ruled surface and the drive shaft as constraints.

The organization structure of the paper is as follows: Sect. 2 introduces the architecture of the proposed method, Sect. 3 introduces the proposed kinematic constraint-based tool axis vector optimization interval identification method, the fourth section introduces the tool axis vector optimization method, the fifth section describes the experimental results, and the sixth section summarizes the conclusions.

2   The Proposed Method

This paper proposes a local optimization method of tool axis vector for five-axis CNC machining based on kinematic constraints, which is divided into two parts: tool axis vector optimization interval selection and tool axis vector optimization method. In the aspect of tool axis vector optimization interval selection, an interval selection method based on kinematic parameters is proposed, that is, the area that does not meet one of the following characteristics is defined as the tool path that needs to be optimized: the area that exceeds the speed constraint of the rotating drive shaft, the area that exceeds the acceleration of the rotating drive shaft, and the area that exceeds the jerk of the rotating drive shaft. In the selection of the interval, a bidirectional scanning algorithm is proposed to determine the start and end positions of each optimized interval. Through the optimized interval identification method proposed in this study, the areas that do not satisfy the rotating drive shaft can be identified. In terms of tool axis vector optimization method, this study adopts the optimization method based on ruled surface, and connects a point on each tool axis within the optimization interval, which is recorded as the tool axis vector reference line. At each optimized tool location point, the tool location point and the tool axis vector reference line are connected to form a ruled surface, which can prevent the optimized tool axis from interfering, and optimize the tool axis through the characteristics of the machine tool rotation axis (Fig. 1).

3   Tool Axis Vector Optimization Interval Selection

In five-axis machining, because the transformation from the workpiece coordinate system to the machine tool coordinate system is non-linear, the smooth change of the tool axis vector in the workpiece coordinate system cannot guarantee the smoothness of each rotating axis of the machine tool coordinate system. Take the AC five-axis cradle machine tool as an example, as shown in Fig. 2.

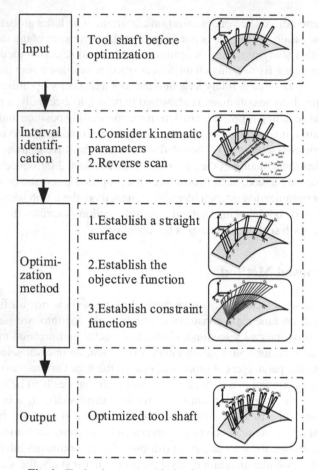

Fig. 1. Tool axis vector optimization method structure.

In the actual five-axis machining, the above-mentioned tool position data is expressed in the workpiece coordinate system, and the same ensures the synchronization of the tool nose point and the tool axis direction, and can be expressed as formula (1) in the actual workpiece coordinate system.

$$P(u) = [R(R_x(u), R_y(u), R_z(u)), O(O_x(u), O_y(u), O_z(u))]$$ (1)

Among them, A is the trajectory of the tool position in the workpiece coordinate system, and B is the trajectory of the tool axis in the workpiece coordinate system. The actual processing needs to convert the workpiece coordinate system to the machine tool coordinate system. Taking the five-axis A-C cradle CNC machine tool as shown in Fig. 2 as an example, the expression under the machine tool coordinate system is as shown in formula (2).

$$q(u) = [q_x(u), q_y(u), q_z(u), q_a(u), q_c(u)]$$ (2)

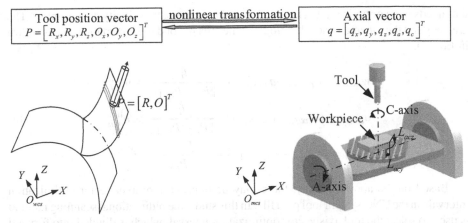

Fig. 2. Five-axis AC turntable structure machine tool.

Among them, $[q_x(u), q_y(u), q_z(u)]$ is the position of the translation axis under the parameter in the machine tool coordinate system, and $[q_a(u), q_c(u)]$ is the position of the rotary axis under the parameter u under the machine tool coordinate system. Through the inverse transformation of machine tool kinematics, the tool position in the workpiece coordinate system is converted into the position of each drive axis in the machine tool coordinate system.

In actual processing, the speed, acceleration and jerk of the AC rotary drive shaft need to be smoothed. For this reason, in order to simplify the operation, set the acceleration of the machine tool to be large enough and the acceleration and deceleration time to be short enough, that is, the movement between the two tool position points can be regarded as a uniform movement. The speed of uniform motion is the feed rate, and the kinematic equation of the machine tool can be established as shown in formula (3).

$$\begin{bmatrix} w_{axis,i} \\ a_{axis,i} \\ j_{axis,i} \end{bmatrix} = \left(\begin{bmatrix} q_{axis,i} \\ w_{axis,i} \\ a_{axis,i} \end{bmatrix} - \begin{bmatrix} q_{axis,i-1} \\ w_{axis,i-1} \\ a_{axis,i-1} \end{bmatrix} \right) \cdot \frac{f_i}{\|P_i - P_{i-1}\|} \tag{3}$$

Among them, $q_{axis,i}, w_{axis,i}, a_{axis,i}, j_{axis,i}$ are the angle, angular velocity, angular acceleration and angular jerk of the rotating axis at the i th tool position point respectively, $axis$ represents the A axis or C axis, and f_i is the feed at the i th tool position point Speed, P_i is the position of the i th tool location point in the machine tool coordinate system.

In the process of five-axis CNC machining, the number of tool positions can reach a massive level, and the constant change of the tool axis vector at each tool position makes the drive axis of the machine tool change. If the tool axis vector is globally optimized, it needs to occupy a large number of operation units, and the optimization efficiency will be greatly reduced. In this study, the method of local optimization is used, that is, the area that needs to be optimized is firstly searched, and the tool axis vector is optimized for the optimized area. For the selection of the optimization area, this study proposes an optimization interval selection method based on kinematic parameters, that is, the area that does not meet one of the following characteristics is set as the tool position point that needs to be optimized: ① The area beyond the kinematic velocity constraint; ② The area beyond the kinematic acceleration; ③ The area beyond the kinematic jerk, as shown in Eq. (4).

$$w_{axis,i} = (q_{axis,i} - q_{axis,i-1}) \cdot \frac{f_i}{\|P_i - P_{i-1}\|} > w_{axis}^{limit}$$

$$a_{axis,i} = (w_{axis,i} - w_{axis,i-1}) \cdot \frac{f_i}{\|P_i - P_{i-1}\|} > a_{axis}^{limit} \qquad (4)$$

$$j_{axis,i} = (a_{axis,i} - a_{axis,i-1}) \cdot \frac{f_i}{\|P_i - P_{i-1}\|} > j_{axis}^{limit}$$

Based on the above strategy, there may be multiple tool axis vector optimization intervals in the CNC system tool path file. In this study, the bidirectional scanning method is used to select the tool axis vector optimization interval, which is divided into forward scan and reverse scan. Forward scanning method: starting from the first tool position, forward scanning cycle, the purpose of forward scanning cycle is to determine the starting point of each optimization interval.When it encounters the conditions that do not meet the formula (4), it is defined as the starting point of the tool axis vector optimization interval; Reverse scan method: starting from the last tool position, reverse scan cycle, the purpose of reverse scan cycle is to determine the end point of each optimization interval, when the condition that does not meet the formula (4) is encountered, it is defined as the end point of the tool axis vector optimization interval. After forward and reverse scanning, the section on the tool path that needs to be optimized by the tool axis can be brought out.

4 Tool Axis Vector Optimization Method

Section 3 completes the identification of the interval that needs to be optimized for the tool axis vector in the tool path file, and then needs to optimize the tool axis vector for the identified interval. In this study, the tool axis vector optimization algorithm based on ruled surface is used for optimization [12]. In the tool axis vector interval to be optimized, each tool position point corresponds to a tool axis vector. First, calculate a point equidistant from the tool position point at each tool axis vector position, and set it as the tool axis vector reference point. The calculation expression is shown in formula (5).

$$Q_i = (Q_{x,i}, Q_{y,i}, Q_{z,i})^T = P_i + |TL| \cdot T_i \qquad (5)$$

Q_i represents the position of the tool axis vector reference point, P_i represents the position of the tool location point, i represents the number of the tool path, TL represents the length between the tool axis vector reference point and the tool location point, and T represents the unit tool axis vector. Next, connect the adjacent tool axis vector reference points to obtain a continuous polyline, which is the tool axis vector reference line. The ruled surface is defined as the surface swept by the moving straight line. The purpose of establishing the ruled surface is that the subsequent tool axis changes within the ruled surface range, which can prevent the changed tool axis from interfering. Take tool point

P_2 as an example, take P_2Q_1 as the initial line segment, and let Q_1 slide on the tool axis vector reference line to form a ruled surface, As shown in Fig. 3, all line segments on the ruled surface represent the direction of the tool axis vector.

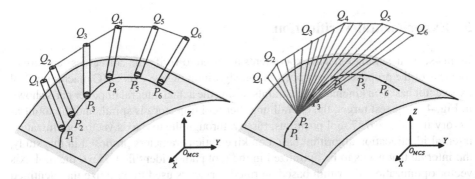

Fig. 3. Establishment of ruled surface.

The ruled surface is established, the range of the tool axis change is determined, and the minimum sum of the squares of the angular jerk of the rotary axis is the objective function as shown in formula (6), The constraint of tool axis optimization is that the drive axis needs to be adjusted in the ruled surface, and the kinematics of the axis drive axis are limited within the drive capability of the machine tool, including the angular velocity, angular acceleration and angular jerk are smaller than the machine tool limit, as shown in formula (7).

$$\min(\sum_{i \in S} \Omega_i) = \min(\sum_{i \in S} \sqrt{j_{A,i}^2 + j_{C,i}^2}) \tag{6}$$

$$\begin{bmatrix} \max\limits_{i \in S} w_{axis,i} \\ \max\limits_{i \in S} a_{axis,i} \\ \max\limits_{i \in S} j_{axis,i} \end{bmatrix} = \begin{bmatrix} \max\limits_{i \in S}(q_{axis,i} - q_{axis,i-1}) \\ \max\limits_{i \in S}(w_{axis,i} - w_{axis,i-1}) \\ \max\limits_{i \in S}(a_{axis,i} - a_{axis,i-1}) \end{bmatrix} \cdot \frac{f_i}{\|P_i - P_{i-1}\|} \leq \begin{bmatrix} w_{axis}^{limit} \\ a_{axis}^{limit} \\ j_{axis}^{limit} \end{bmatrix} \tag{7}$$

Based on the ruled surface method, in the optimization process, there is a ruled surface at each tool position. The starting and ending positions of the tool axis vector reference line corresponding to the ruled surface are respectively a certain point before and after the point, which is represented by S in the above formula to ensure enough optimization space. Based on the above formula, the tool axis vector in the optimization interval can be optimized, and after optimization, a new tool axis vector position that is equidistant from the tool position point is obtained, The new tool axis vector calculation expression is shown in formula (8–9).

$$T_i' = \begin{bmatrix} T_{X,i}' \\ T_{Y,i}' \\ T_{Z,i}' \end{bmatrix} = \frac{Q_i' - P_i}{\|Q_i' - P_i\|} \tag{8}$$

$$A'_i = \arccos(T'_{Z,i})$$
$$C'_i = \arctan(-T'_{X,i}/T'_{Y,i}) + n\pi \tag{9}$$

5 Experimental Verification

In this section, simulation and experiments are used to verify the correctness and effectiveness of the proposed local optimization algorithm of five-axis CNC machining tool axis vector based on kinematic constraints. Using the actual integral impeller parts shown in Fig. 4 as the test target, the overall impeller tool trajectory is spiral, and the tool trajectory includes 20757 tool positions. Firstly, through the tool axis vector optimization interval identification algorithm based on kinematic parameters proposed in this study, the interval that needs to be optimized in the tool path is identified. Next, the tool axis vector optimization algorithm based on ruled surface is used to optimize the identified optimization interval.

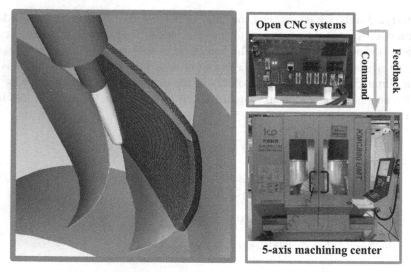

Fig. 4. Rotor type integral impeller experimental test platform.

There are many tool point trajectories, taking the section 18520 to 18560 of the tool path as an example, this interval is the optimized area of the tool axis vector identified by the interval, and the optimization result is shown in Fig. 5. It can be concluded that the angular position of the AC axis of the machine tool is smoother, and the angular velocity, angular acceleration and angular jerk are smoother than the original trajectory, and the maximum value is effectively suppressed. It reflects the smoother movement of the machine tool axis, and the vibration generated during the processing is significantly reduced.

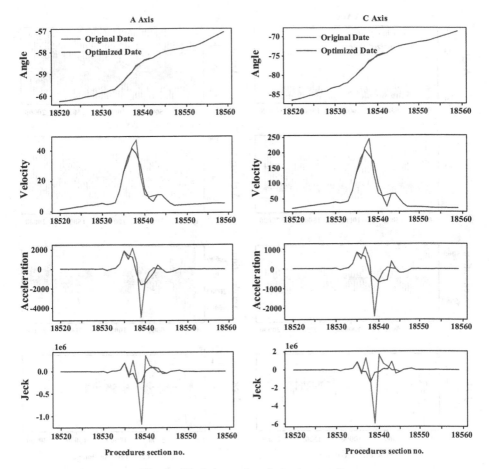

Fig. 5. Single interval optimization results.

Similar optimization is carried out on all 20757 tool positions to realize the overall optimization of the helical tool path. The overall optimization results are shown in Fig. 6. From the figure, it can also be concluded that the angular velocity, angular acceleration and angular jerk of the machine tool drive shaft after optimization are reduced, which reflects the optimization effect of the algorithm in this study.

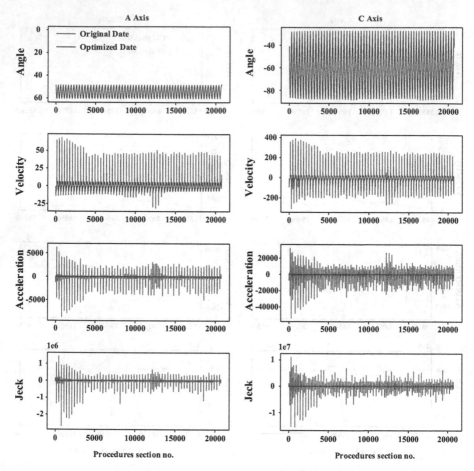

Fig. 6. Overall optimization result of NC program.

6 Summary

The characteristics of the five-axis CNC rotary axis are worse than that of the translation axis. The impact of the rotary axis during the machining process seriously affects the performance of the machine tool and the surface quality of the workpiece. Therefore, it is necessary to optimize the tool axis vector representing the rotary axis of the machine tool. In this study, a local optimization method of the tool axis vector of five-axis CNC machining based on dynamic constraints is proposed, which realizes the smoothing of the trajectory of the driving rotation axis in the machine tool coordinate system. Firstly, an optimization interval selection method based on kinematic parameters is proposed, that is, by judging the speed, acceleration and jerk of the rotary axis at the tool position point, if there is any item that does not meet the performance of the machine tool's rotary axis, that is, the tool position point is defined as the point that needs to be optimized. In order to further determine the optimized area of the tool axis, a method based on bidirectional scanning is proposed. The starting position of the optimized section is determined by forward scanning, and the end position of the optimized section is determined by reverse scanning. Secondly, the tool axis is optimized by the tool axis vector optimization method based on the ruled surface. A ruled surface space is established at each tool position, and the tool axis optimization is limited to a certain range to prevent the optimized tool axis from interfering. The optimization goal is to minimize the kinematics of the rotary axis to realize the optimization of the tool axis. Experiments show that the proposed algorithm based on local optimization can realize the smoothness of the rotary drive shaft in the machine tool coordinate system, and effectively reduce the speed, acceleration and jerk indicators at each tool position. It shows the correctness and effectiveness of the algorithm in this study.

Acknowledgements. This work is supported by the National Natural Science Foundation of China (Grant No. 51875312).

References

1. Huang, T., Zhang, X.-M., Leopold, J., Ding, H.: Tool orientation planning in milling with process dynamic constraints: a minimax optimization approach. J. Manuf. Sci. Eng. Trans. Asme, 140(11) (2018). https://doi.org/10.1115/1.4040872

2. Yu, D.-Y., Ding, Z.: Post-processing algorithm of a five-axis machine tool with dual rotary tables based on the TCS method. Int. J. Adv. Manuf. Technol. **102**(9–12), 3937–3944 (2019). https://doi.org/10.1007/s00170-019-03490-y

3. Xu, J., Zhang, D., Sun, Y.: Kinematics performance oriented smoothing method to plan tool orientations for 5-axis ball-end CNC machining. Int. J. Mech. Sci. **157**, 293–303 (2019). https://doi.org/10.1016/j.ijmecsci.2019.04.038

4. Chao, S., Altintas, Y.: Chatter free tool orientations in 5-axis ball-end milling. Int. J. Mach. Tools Manuf **106**, 89–97 (2016). https://doi.org/10.1016/j.ijmachtools.2016.04.007

5. Morishige, K., Takeuchi, Y., Kase, K.: Tool path generation using C-space for 5-axis control machining. J. Manuf. Sci. Eng.-Trans. Asme **121**(1), 144–149 (1999). https://doi.org/10.1115/1.2830567

6. Wang, N., Tang, K.: Automatic generation of gouge-free and angular-velocity-compliant five-axis toolpath. Comput. Aided Des. **39**(10), 841–852 (2007). https://doi.org/10.1016/j.cad.2007.04.003

7. Farouki, R.T., Li, S.: Optimal tool orientation control for 5-axis CNC milling with ball-end cutters. Comput. Aided Geometric Design **30**(2), 226–239 (2013). https://doi.org/10.1016/j.cagd.2012.11.003

8. Ma, J.-W., Hu, G.-Q., Qin, F., Su, W.-W., Jia, Z.-Y.: Optimization method of tool axis vector based on kinematical characteristics of rotary feed axis for curved surface machining. Int. J. Adv. Manuf. Technol. **100**(5–8), 2007–2020 (2018). https://doi.org/10.1007/s00170-018-2738-7

9. Castagnetti, C., Duc, E., Ray, P.: The Domain of Admissible Orientation concept: a new method for five-axis tool path optimisation. Comput. Aided Des. **40**(9), 938–950 (2008). https://doi.org/10.1016/j.cad.2008.07.002

10. Hu, P., Tang, K.: Improving the dynamics of five-axis machining through optimization of workpiece setup and tool orientations. Comput. Aided Des. **43**(12), 1693–1706 (2011). https://doi.org/10.1016/j.cad.2011.09.005

11. Qin, J.-Y., Jia, Z.-Y., Ma, J.-W., Ren, Z.-J., Song, D.-N.: An efficient 5-axis toolpath optimization algorithm for machining parts with abrupt curvature. Proc. Inst. Mech. Eng. Part C-J. Mech. Eng. Sci. **231**(9), 1609–1621 (2017). https://doi.org/10.1177/0954406215620824

12. Gong, Z., Li, B., Zhang, H., Ye, P.: Tool orientation optimization method based on ruled surface using genetic algorithm. Int. J. Adv. Manuf. Technol. **118**(1–2), 571–584 (2021). https://doi.org/10.1007/s00170-021-07934-2

Research on Modeling and Application of Milling Process Information of Blisk Blade

Shujie Liu[1,2(✉)], Tong Zhao[1,2], and Hui Zhang[1,2]

[1] Department of Mechanical Engineering, Tsinghua University, Beijing 100084, China
liushuji18@mails.tsinghua.edu.cn
[2] Beijing Key Lab of Precision/Ultra-Precision Manufacturing Equipment and Control, Tsinghua University, Beijing 100084, China

Abstract. Blisks with integral structure are key component of the power system. Blade profile usually possesses high complexity and is hard to be milled. There are problems of vague data system and low interconnection in the process information management, which seriously impedes the improvement of the intelligence of milling process. This paper presents a modular information schema in the view of machining features, and the data integration model of blade milling process information is established. Furthermore, the composition of blade milling process database is proposed. Take the advantage of the CAM software specially for 5-axis milling blade and relational database technology, a prototype software system for data management of blade milling process, which is able to realize the function of automatic extraction, storage, and correlation interaction for relevant process data, is developed. It has been tested and verified that the data management model and prototype system are feasible and available by collecting and storing the process data of some simulated blade profiles. The work in this paper can be accepted as a technical support to the integrating information management, and the machining efficiency improvement of intelligent milling unit for the complex blade parts.

Keywords: Blisk · Blade milling · Information integration · Data management

1 Introduction

Blisk parts are the key components of power plants such as aircraft engines. Because of good thrust weight ratio, reliability, and efficiency, they have been widely used in aerospace, power equipment and other fields.

NC (numerical control) milling is a dominant processing method for blisks that are small and medium-sized, with high-precision, integral blank, suitable cutting properties [1]. Compared to other processing methods, such as ECM, EDM, NC milling has the comprehensive advantages of short prep time, flexibility, agility, high reliability of process implementation, processing efficiency, stable machining accuracy and low environmental pollution. It is widely used in the field of blisk manufacturing.

There are many process technologies involved in blisk blade milling. In the earlier research, the concentration is generally focused on particular and given terms,

© The Author(s), under exclusive license to Springer Nature Switzerland AG 2022
H. Liu et al. (Eds.): ICIRA 2022, LNAI 13455, pp. 297–306, 2022.
https://doi.org/10.1007/978-3-031-13844-7_29

such as hard-cut material, simplified or local geometry, special machining conditions. These works can provide support for process optimization, but there are deficiencies in generalization ability.

In the face of diversified structural types of blade profile processing, the advantages of integrated utilization of process data and process experience should be brought into play [2, 3]. Process information modeling can provide data basis for the inheritance of complex process experience, and the integration of the whole process flow is an important guarantee to promote process design and increase productivity. Thus, process information modeling and data integration of blade milling have become an urgent task to improve the NC machining capacity and efficiency of blade parts.

2   Blade Milling Process Information Integration Model

2.1   Blade Milling Process Information Integration

For the sake of the process description of each link and module for systematic connection and integration [4], it is necessary to clarify the main functional requirements of process information integration. Based on the process information structure of blade milling, this paper presents a design scheme with the main frame of "CAD-CAPP-ERP-CAM-CNC-IPS", as shown in Fig. 1.

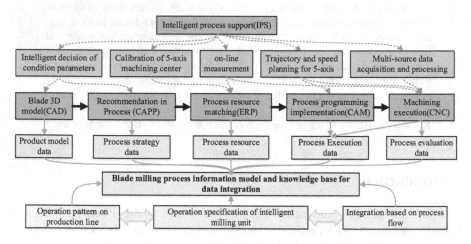

Fig. 1. Main frame of blade milling process integration

(1) CAD blade model. The main works in this part is to establish the expression mode of blade features based on machining region decomposition [5], and realize the discrete substitution of continuous machining features of blade profile, in order to bring out the effect of classification and outline for process data, and provide conditions for process design. (2) CAPP process recommendation. The general target of work in this aspect is to obtain the available and acceptable process parameters for emerging product in the basis of historical process data, giving full play to the supporting role of similarity

between process data. In a word, it is always conceived that the data such as structure, material, accuracy and others of machined volume and machining features could conduct feasible and rational recommendation, and also verification for the application of machine tools, CNC systems, measuring equipment, strategies, cutting tools, conditions parameters and other key process elements, so as to reduce the uncertainty and fuzziness of process programming, and improve the accuracy and work efficiency [6, 7]. (3) ERP process resource matching. Following the CAPP aspect, the key process elements recommended by CAPP should be selected and confirmed from the resource database correspondingly and promptly by the integration of resource data and milling process flow. (4) CAM process programming. Next to ERP, it is the turn of making reasonable planning for the process parameters and routes in the blade milling strategy, and then generating the NC program that is suitable for the machining center in CAM software based on the process recommendation of CAPP and the matching results of ERP process resources. (5) CNC Machining execution. When NC program have been generated by CAM software, it is necessary yet to make some modifications adaptively in combination with the functional factors of machine tool and NC system, such as adding appropriate function code instructions to improve the interpolation accuracy of operation and the smoothness of tool shaft and tool path [8], verifying the rationality of NC program, checking the interference in operating, examining the match relationship between tooling fixture, tool shank, work-piece and other components. By doing all above, it will form the finalized NC program for the whole blade profile machining based on the combination of machining characteristics and process strategy. (6) IPS intelligent process support aspect. During the stages of the process flow listed above, many process technologies in the form of function modules embedded into the process system are very important for producing an up to standard blisk by the way of interacting with information stream. For the process function modules such as condition parameter decision [9], machine tool calibration, on-line measurement, trajectory and speed planning and multi-source data acquisition and utilization, the integrated management of intelligent milling unit could be realized by setting a reasonable and effective data embedding mode, and also reflecting the data input and output functions into the blade milling process system, in the way of promoting the operation of the process system in a data-driven way.

2.2 Feature-Oriented and Modular Information Model for Blade Milling

The data representation of milling process system can be constructed on the basis of quantifying process system parameters, which can be obtained and improved by means of determination empirically and optimization intelligently. In a deeper level, a knowledge and data system for global characteristics of blade milling process can be established.

However, although the data generated and contained in the whole process domain has the superiority of comprehensive information, it is too large and monolithic, and the data flow between each other is not clear enough. It is a practicable way to extract the characteristics of information elements based on the process link, and select the data with typical characteristics in the procedure of conducting integrated analysis, so as to provide the basis for the establishment of process data flow.

According to the principle of stratifying and grading, the theoretical set in the data structure of the process system is classified to determine the data circulation, analyze and summarize the connotation and extension of the process content.

In view of the information representation of blade milling process system, and taking the content of blade milling process as the object, a blade milling process information model that is constructed on the basis of machining feature information element is formed. It includes 9 parts: design model, feature set, theory set, strategy set, parameter set, resource set, process set, evaluation set and product evaluation see Fig. 2.

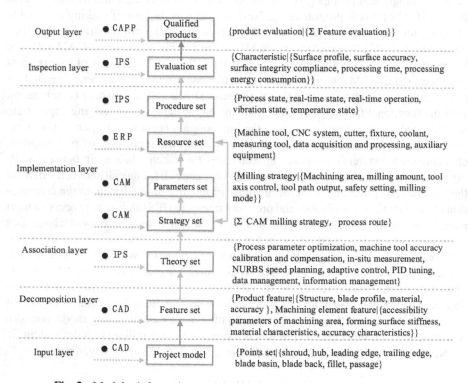

Fig. 2. Modular information model of blade milling for machining features

Among them, The project model represents the input of Blisk products to the milling process system; The feature set represents the expression of process characteristics and demand information of Blisk products; The theory set refers to the process links and fields being improved in intelligent milling unit, as well as the data management and information control unit designed for interacting information; The strategy set represents the milling strategy adopted for the specific machining feature element of the blisk based on the specific CAM software, as well as the process route formed with all the adopted milling strategies and their sequencing; Parameters set refers to the set of parameters designated in series used for forming the milling NC code of specific machining feature element under a certain milling strategy; Resource set refers to the set of a series of process equipment and auxiliary equipment used to complete the milling of specific machining feature elements; The procedure set represents the current particular state of the tooling equipment used in the milling process of a machining feature element and the state parameters of the process system generated in this mode; The evaluation set indicates the process effect produced by the specific machining feature element after the action of the process system; The product output represents the evaluation of the overall processing effect of the blisk based on the comprehensive effects of various processing characteristics.

3 Blade Milling Process Information Data Management

In order to test the applicability of the blade milling process information model, aiming at the blade milling process data management, the compositions of the blade milling process database is designed, the workshop deployment scheme of the blade milling process information model is proposed, and a prototype system is carried out by using the relational database. The data acquisition and storage demonstrate the feasibility of the system.

3.1 Composition of Blade Milling Process Database

The blade milling process database consists of five parts: product model database, process strategy database, process resource database, process procedure database and product evaluation database, as shown in Fig. 3.

The product model database consists of four parts, that is, basic information database, point information database, product feature database and machining area database. In the Basic information database, the basic product information adopts the two-level mode of "product model and product sample". The "model" represents the commonness of similar products, and the "sample" represents multiple processed objects of multiple processing batches of products for the same model. The product model is the parent entity, and the product sample is the child entity. The product sample is recorded according to the single sample of the task batch. The product model is stored in the form of data point set. The three-dimensional model is decomposed to form a point cloud information database. By calling the product 3D point cloud information dataset, it supports the subsequent research on relevant algorithms. The data input of this part is based on the specific CAM software in the way of dealing with the IGS file of the product 3D model, automatically extracting and entering the product 3D point cloud information data into the database. Product features mainly reflect the overall profile of the blade. The setting of product feature attributes is designated according to the Group Code in process classification. The machining area is used to describe the processing scope and requirements in a single work step. The machining area comes from product features, and the union and combination of machining areas should be the overall product features. In the feature set, based on the division of machining area, it is mapped and associated with the process route in the strategy set.

The process strategy database records the overall product processing element milling strategy, process route, process parameters, etc. The process strategy database consists of three parts, that is, milling strategy database, process route database and condition parameter database. Milling strategy database. The milling strategy set is used to describe the milling function of the process programming software. Process route database. The process route database is used to record the process route of product samples. Condition parameter database. The condition parameter database is used to record the configuration parameters of each milling strategy under the product sample process route. The milling strategy should first be set in the milling strategy database, and the concrete data of condition parameter will be associated with the milling strategy in the milling strategy database. The data attribute of milling parameter is set according to the full record principle based on the specific strategy of the process software, with the milling strategy as the entity and the configuration parameter item as the attribute. The input data of this part is directly imported based on CAM software, which can generate process parameter files in the form of XML.

The process resource database consists of machine tool database, NC system database, tool system database, fixture system database, coolant database, measuring tool database, etc. Machine tool database. Machine tool is the main mechanical execution carrier of five axis milling for the blade, and machine tool database is used to record the characteristic information of machine tool. NC system database. Numerical control system is the main control and execution carrier of five axis milling of blisk, and it is also the direct carrier of five axis milling theory. Tool system database. The tool system is the main cutting execution carrier of blade milling. It cooperates with the machine tool and directly interacts with the work-piece to realize the milling action. The tool system is composed of two parts, cutting tool and shank. Therefore, the entity of the tool system is divided into three items, that is, tool, shank and tool assembly. Fixture system database. The fixture system is the work-piece positioning function carrier in the five axis milling of blisk, which ensures the necessary positioning accuracy of the work-piece and realizes the motion transmission of the axial work-piece controlled by the machine tool. Coolant database. Coolant is the carrier of protection function for work-piece and tool in five axis milling of blisk, which ensures the surface quality of work-piece and prolongs the service life of tool. Measuring tool database. The measuring tool is a special function carrier to ensure the five axis milling of the blisk, such as laser interferometer, R-test, ball-bar instrument, tool setting instrument, etc. through measurement, the accuracy of machine tool, work-piece, cutting tool and other information can be determined to assist in the determination of the current process state. Data acquisition equipment is the carrier of state recording function in five axis milling of blisk, which realizes the effective monitoring and state extraction of process procedure, and provides technical means for enriching process samples. Data acquisition equipment is entered as measuring equipment.

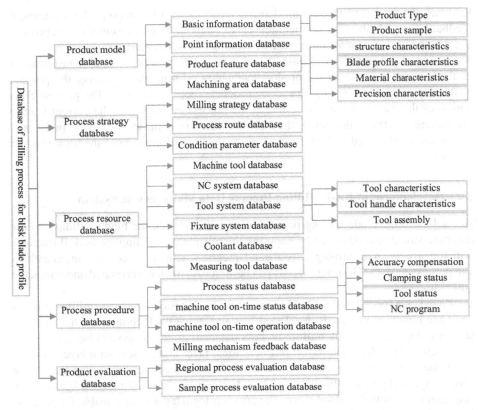

Fig. 3. Database composition of blade milling process system

The process database records the process state, real-time state, real-time operation, vibration state, temperature state and other information, covering the current characteristic milling process state of the current machining feature. The process procedure database mainly includes process status database, machine tool on-time status database, machine tool on-time operation database, milling mechanism feedback database, etc. Process status database. Process status records the state of process system during blade feature milling, including machining NC program, machine tool accuracy compensation, clamping status, cutting tool status, NC program for measurement and other entity contents. Machine tool accuracy compensation is used to record the correction of machine tool accuracy by using calibration module during blade feature machining. The clamping status is used to record the installation error of the blank during the processing of blade. The cutting tool status is used for the actual state of the tool during the current feature machining. The measurement NC program is used to record the in-situ measurement program and results of blade machining. Machine tool on-time status database. The on-time state of the machine tool records the control system parameters of each axis of the machine tool during machining blade features. Machine tool on-time operation database. The on-time operation database of the machine tool records the operation state and process of each axis and feed during blade feature processing. Milling mechanism feedback database. The milling mechanism feedback database records the mechanical feedback states of vibration, temperature, force, sound and light presented by the process system and its components during the machining of blade features.

The product evaluation database is used to record the process evaluation information of the machining area and the product evaluation information, including the process evaluation of the machining area and the product process evaluation. The process evaluation of the machining area is aimed at the process evaluation of the current feature processing, and the evaluation of the machining feature sequence evaluation in the process route is integrated to form the process evaluation information of the blisk product sample.

3.2 Development of Blade Milling Process Data Management System

According to the blade milling process information model, the blade milling process database structure is designed by adopting the relational modeling method. It interacts with the process programming software and integrates with the process resources and on-site processing data. The relevant data can be stored, extracted, correlated and interacted automatically.

Based on a special 5-axis CAM software for blade profile, the blade milling process database prototype system is developed by using MySQL, Python and other tools, as shown in Fig. 4. The blade milling process database prototype system has a three-tier architecture, including data layer, business logic layer and presentation layer. Among them, the data layer is the basic module that undertakes the functions of data acquisition and storage, and provides functions such as database access, file parsing and generation, and interaction with CAM software. The business logic layer is responsible for processing the data according to the business logic. The presentation layer is mainly an interface module, which is responsible for data display and receiving user input.

The operating platform of the prototype system is Windows 10 system, the hardware environment is 4G memory/512G hard disk, the data platform is MySQL relational database management system, the development software is Python 3.8, which is realized

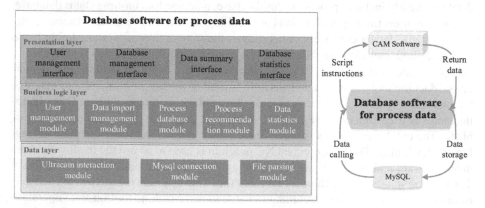

Fig. 4. Software structure of blade milling process database

by object-oriented programming, and the process support platform is a specific CAM software.

The blade milling process database prototype system is an independent software, which is not a subsystem of CAM software. The prototype system can control CAM through script instructions. For example, the process database can use script commands to let CAM export model feature data files from a project, and the prototype system interacts directly with MySQL database. Generally speaking, there are three ways of data interaction. First is the part that needs to be automatically extracted and imported into the database by CAM, such as blade feature data, model point cloud data, regional feature data, strategy data and tool data. After the user inputs a regional range, CAM exports the corresponding regional feature data, which involves two-way interaction with CAM; Second is the data that needs to be imported through files, such as milling mechanism feedback data, machine tool real-time operation data, etc.; Third is that referenced from other databases, but can be modified by users.

3.3 Application of Data Management System

The 5-axis process programming is carried out for the multi blade products designed by simulation, and the process data are collected and stored. The data type covers the model characteristics, process strategies and parameters, process resources and other contents of CAD, CAM and CNC. The management system can realize the automatic decomposition and upload of process data of special CAM software, with clear data classification and easy operation and maintenance.

4 Conclusion

The data integration management of blade milling process is directly applied to the information integration of intelligent milling unit, which provides technical support for the standardized management, systematic integration, in-depth integration and intelligent interaction of 5-axis milling process data of blisk, and effectively connects the long cycle of "Blade 3D model (CAD)-Recommendation in Process (CAPP)-Process resource matching (ERP)- Process programming implementation (CAM)-Machining execution (CNC)-Intelligent process support (IPS)". For the process flow and links that are difficult to control, the integration of intelligent milling units based on process data is realized by establishing a global oriented integral disc blade profile milling process data management module, so as to support the intelligent improvement of milling process, the standardized management of milling process and the improvement of process design efficiency. At the same time, it can also support the improvement and optimization of functions for process programming software. This paper proposes a process information model for blade milling, realizes and applies data management, which can provide technical support for realizing the intellectualization of complex component processing technology.

Intelligent manufacturing is the inevitable trend and main direction of manufacturing industry. The process development mode based on information modeling will become an important motive force leading manufacturing to intelligence. In terms of equipment intelligence, process intelligence, management intelligence and service intelligence, with the development of digital twin, online technology and other technologies, the processing technology system is inevitably required to have diversified abilities of perception, learning, analysis, prediction, decision-making, communication and coordinated control, stronger dynamics, and change from equipment flexibility to data flexibility. Data modeling for industrial process and process integration in complex industrial environment will also play an increasingly important role.

Acknowledgements. This work is supported by the National Natural Science Foundation of China (Grant No. 51875312).

References

1. González-Barrio, H., Calleja-Ochoa, A., Lamikiz, A.: Manufacturing processes of integral blade rotors for turbomachinery, processes and new approaches. Appl. Sci. **10**(9), 3063 (2020)
2. Nandakumar, S., Shah, J.J.: Recognition of multi axis milling features: Part I-topological and geometric characteristics. J. Comput. Inf. Sci. Eng. **4**(3), 242–250 (2004)
3. Nandakumar, S., Shah, J.J.: Recognition of multi-axis milling features: Part II—algorithms & implementation. J. Comput. Inf. Sci. Eng. **5**(1), 25–34 (2005)
4. Ma, H., Zhou, X., Liu, W., Li, J., Niu, Q., Kong, C.: A feature-based approach towards integration and automation of CAD/CAPP/CAM for EDM electrodes. Int. J. Adv. Manuf. Technol. **98**(9–12), 2943–2965 (2018). https://doi.org/10.1007/s00170-018-2447-2
5. Huang, R., Zhang, S., Bai, X.: Multi-level structuralized model-based definition model based on machining features for manufacturing reuse of mechanical parts. Int. J. Adv. Manuf. Technol. **75**, 1035–1048 (2014)
6. Deja, M., Siemiatkowski, M.S.: Machining process sequencing and machine assignment in generative feature-based CAPP for mill-turn parts. J. Manuf. Syst. **48**, 49–62 (2018)
7. Liang, Y., Zhang, D., Ren, J., Chen, Z.C., Xu, Y.: Accessible regions of tool orientations in multi-axis milling of blisks with a ball-end mill. Int. J. Adv. Manuf. Technol. **85**(5–8), 1887–1900 (2016). https://doi.org/10.1007/s00170-016-8356-3
8. Brecher, C., Lohse, W.: Evaluation of toolpath quality: user-assisted CAM for complex milling processes. CIRP J. Manuf. Sci. Technol. **6**(4), 233–245 (2013)
9. Zhang, N., Shi, Y., Yang, C.: Multi-objective optimization of processing parameters for disc-mill cutter machining blisk-tunnel based on GRA-RBF-FA method. J. Northwest. Polytech. Univ. **37**(1), 160–166 (2019)

Structural Design and Gait Planning of Mobile Robot Based on the Rubik's Cube Mechanism

Jiahao Zeng[1] , Wenjuan Lu[2], Xingyan Li[1], Shihao Dong[1], Ya Liu[1] ,
and Daxing Zeng[2](✉)

[1] School of Mechanical Engineering, Yanshan University, Qinhuangdao 066004, China
[2] The DGUT Innovation Center of Robotics and Intelligent Equipment, Dongguan 523808, China
zengdx@dgut.edu.cn

Abstract. In order to improve the obstacle-crossing ability, motion stability and load-bearing capacity of mobile robots for different terrains, the Rubik's Cube mechanism (RCM) with strong coupling and variable topology is introduced into the field of mobile robots, and a wheel-legged mobile robot (WLMR) based on RCM is proposed. A new type of chute third-order RCM is proposed and applied to the wheel-leg conversion module, then a WLMR with polymorphism is constructed by combining wheel-leg conversion module, mechanical leg and Mecanum wheel. Moreover, in order to ensure the stability of the robot during movement, gait planning analysis of the WLMR in different modes is carried out. Eventually, the prototype experiments are performed to verify the efficiency of the WLMR's straight travel, in-situ rotation, obstacle-crossing and morphology transformation in complex environments. This research not only provides a reference for the design of polymorphous mobile robots, but also opens up ideas for the application of the RCM in daily production and life.

Keywords: Rubik's cube mechanism · Mobile robot · Morphology transformation · Gait planning

1 Introduction

As an important field of robotics research, mobile robots integrate multiple functions such as visual recognition, trajectory planning, and mobile obstacle-crossing [1]. According to the movement mode, the existing mobile robots are mainly divided into the following four types: wheeled robots, legged robot, crawler robots and wheel-legged robots. Among them, the wheel-legged mobile robot (WLMR) [2, 3] combines the advantages of wheeled robots and legged robots, which can not only move quickly on flat or soft ground, but also cross obstacles on complex unstructured ground.

There are three basic types of the existing WLMRs: wheel-leg coordination type, wheel-leg shape independent type, and wheel-leg structure variable type. (1) Wheel-leg coordination type: This type of mobile robot mainly moves by virtue of the coordinated action of wheels and legs. For example, BJELONIC et al. [4] developed a quadruped

© The Author(s), under exclusive license to Springer Nature Switzerland AG 2022
H. Liu et al. (Eds.): ICIRA 2022, LNAI 13455, pp. 307–316, 2022.
https://doi.org/10.1007/978-3-031-13844-7_30

robot, which is equipped with four non-steerable and torque-controlled wheels on four legs; MORIHIRO et al. [5] proposed a WLMR composed of six open-chain mechanisms. (2) Wheel-leg shape independent type: This type of mobile robot can transform its shape to adapt to different terrains according to needs. For example, NAKAJIMA et al. [6] developed a robot with two large wheels and four legs; Zhang et al. [7] put the wheels on the mechanical legs of the robot, and proposed a hexapod wheel-leg compound robot that can switch multiple operation modes. (3) Wheel-leg structure variable type: This type of mobile robot can change the structure of the wheel part to turn the wheels into mechanical legs. For example, Taiwan University has proposed two transformable wheel-legged robots: Quattroped [8] and TurboQuad [9].

However, mobile robots still have certain limitations in obstacle-crossing ability, motion stability, and load-bearing capacity, especially their weak adaptive ability when dealing with complex environments. In order to improve the adaptability of robots to different terrains, many scholars have introduced the concept of metamorphosis into the research of mobile robots based on the metamorphic mechanisms. For example, Dai et al. [10] launched the metamorphic dexterous hand for the first time in the world, and used it in the waist structure of the crawling robot to develop a metamorphic robot that can adapt to different environments; Zhen et al. [11] proposed a new type of quadrupedal metamorphic crawling robot, which can meet the requirements of movement in different terranes through the combination of waist activity and gait. Although some progress has been made in the research on mobile metamorphic robots, the study on multi-configuration and highly adaptable mobile robots is still in the ascendant.

As a metamorphic mechanism with strong coupling and variable topology, the Rubik's Cube mechanism (RCM) has hundreds of millions of states [12]. In view of the characteristics of free combination of sub-pieces of RCM [13], it is applied to the field of mobile robots. Thus, a new third-order RCM is proposed, which is introduced into the design of mobile robots to carry out the research of WLMRs based on RCM. It mainly includes: designing a new chute third-order RCM, and a WLMR with polymorphism is constructed; gait planning and gait stability analysis of the WLMR in different modes are carried out; the motion feasibility of the mobile robot in complex environments is verified through prototype experiments.

2   Structural Design of the WLMR

2.1   The Design of the Chute Third-Order RCM

The classic third-order RCM is shown in Fig. 1. It is mainly composed of 12 edge pieces, eight corner pieces, six center pieces, six bolts, six springs and one center cross. The center piece is pressed inward by screws and springs. There are flanges inside the edge piece and corner piece. The center piece is inward against the corner pieces and edge pieces of the corresponding layer, and all the sub-pieces of the Rubik's Cube are interlocked. When the RCM is in the non-orthogonal state [14], all sub-pieces on the rotating layer are regarded as a component, which form a rotating pair with the central cross, and there is only one rotational degree of freedom at the same time; in the orthogonal state, each sub-piece belongs to multiple rotating layers, and all sub-pieces can rotate around the common ball pair with three rotational degrees of freedom.

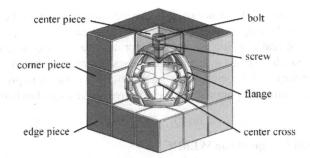

Fig. 1. The structure of the classic third-order RCM.

Due to the existence of the flange of the arc surface, the classic third-order RCM has problems such as small internal space, difficult processing, and strict precision requirements. Based on this, a new type of chute three-order RCM is proposed, as shown in Fig. 2. The positioning structure between the sub-pieces of the chute third-order RCM is changed from the internal flange structure to the chute structure, and cylindrical columns are set on the three sides of the corner piece. The contact surface between each edge piece and the corner piece is provided with a chute, and the contact surface between the edge piece and the center piece is provided with columns. The four contact surfaces between the center piece and the adjacent corner pieces are provided with chutes to meet the rotation requirements of the corresponding layer.

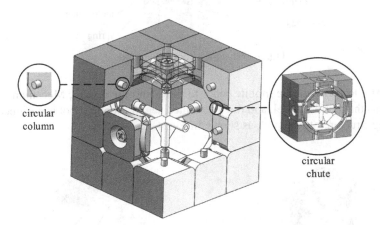

Fig. 2. The structure of the chute third-order RCM.

Compared with the way that all the sub-pieces in the classic RCM move in the same spherical orbit formed by the flange, the sub-pieces of each layer of the new RCM move in an independent circular orbit matched with the columns of the corresponding layer. In the non-orthogonal state of the chute RCM, the column can rotate along the circular chute formed by the edge piece and the center piece of the middle layer; in the orthogonal state, the corner pieces and edge pieces of the cube can rotate along the circular chutes in three directions respectively, so as to realize the metamorphic function of rotating each layer of the cube and changing the position of the sub-pieces.

On the basis of realizing the functions of normal rotation and metamorphic transformation, the new chute RCM effectively increases the space inside the Rubik's Cube, reduces the requirement for accuracy, and each sub-piece is easier to process due to the elimination of the complex spherical surface. The overall structure has better mechanical characteristics.

2.2 The Overall Design of the WLMR

The wheel-leg conversion module is designed based on the optimized chute RCM, and its structure is shown in Fig. 3. The wheel-leg conversion module consists of corner piece, edge piece, center piece, center bracket, motor, motor connector and spring. The axis of the internal motor output shaft is coincident with the rotation axis of the center piece. The motor is fixed on the central bracket, and its output shaft is connected with the motor connector. The robot can drive the corresponding rotating layer to rotate through motor to realize the transformation of robot's wheeled form and hexapod form.

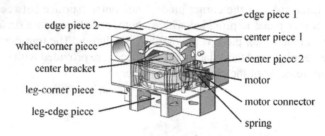

Fig. 3. Wheel-leg conversion module.

In order to facilitate the mobile robot to move and turn better, Mecanum wheel is selected as the mobile wheel, and the mechanical leg of mobile robot is designed based on the leg structure of hexapod, as shown in Fig. 4.

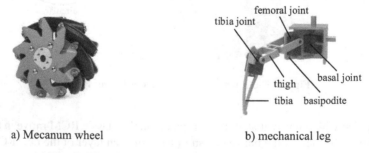

a) Mecanum wheel   b) mechanical leg

Fig. 4. The wheeled and legged structure of the WLMR

Eventually the wheels and mechanical legs are installed on the corresponding cubes of the wheel-leg conversion module. The mechanical legs and wheels of the robot will not only change their positions with the rotation of the wheel-leg conversion module, but also can move independently. At the same time, the mobile robot has more flexibility and adaptive ability. Therefore, the robot can convert among different forms through the wheel-leg conversion module. And its three forms are hexapod form, wheel-legged form and wheeled form, as shown in Fig. 5 respectively.

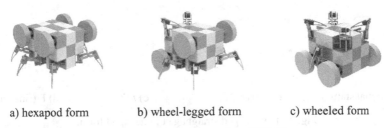

a) hexapod form   b) wheel-legged form   c) wheeled form

Fig. 5. The three forms of the WLMR.

The three forms of mobile robots have different ways of moving. In the wheeled form, the robot can move in any direction in the plane through the control of Mecanum wheels. In the hexapod form, the robot can move on the irregular road surface by the movement of six mechanical legs. In the wheel-legged form, the robot can achieve obstacle crossing in complex environment through the coordination of the wheel and the mechanical leg, and the robot can make use of the high power of the wheel and the flexibility of the mechanical leg to ensure high stability when crossing obstacles.

3 Gait Planning of the WLMR

In the hexapod form, mobile robots can move through different gaits. The four-legged gait is made as an example to study the gait planning because of its good stability. The robot's six mechanical legs are divided into three groups: R1 and L3 are leg group I, then L1 and R2 are leg group II, lastly L2 and R3 are leg group III, as shown in Fig. 6.

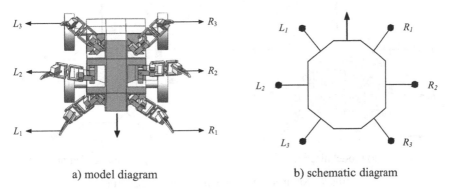

a) model diagram   b) schematic diagram

Fig. 6. Number of the robot in hexapod form.

The robot's straight gait and in-situ rotation gait are shown in Fig. 7 and Fig. 8 respectively. The foot of the robot is solid when it is in contact with the ground, and the foot is hollow when it is lifted off the ground. In the analysis, the time when the robot switches the support leg is ignored, and the robots before and after the switch are at the same time.

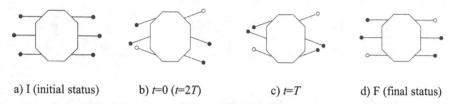

a) I (initial status)   b) $t=0$ ($t=2T$)   c) $t=T$ d) F (final status)

Fig. 7. Four-legged straight gait in hexapod form.

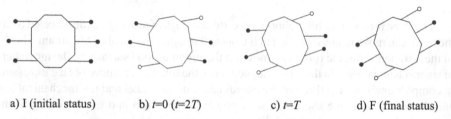

a) I (initial status)   b) $t=0$ ($t=2T$)   c) $t=T$ d) F (final status)

Fig. 8. Four-legged rotating gait in hexapod form.

In hexapod form, two wheels of the robot are in contact with the ground, and the two wheels and four mechanical legs can realize the robot's obstacle crossing through the alternate conversion of supporting state and swinging state. The robot's mechanical legs are divided into two groups: L_2, R_2 leg group I, L_3, R_3 leg group II, as is shown in Fig. 9. And its obstacle-crossing gait diagram is shown in Fig. 10.

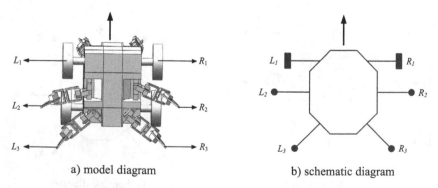

a) model diagram   b) schematic diagram

Fig. 9. Number of the robot in wheel-legged form.

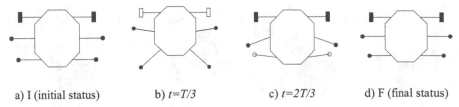

a) I (initial status)   b) $t=T/3$ c) $t=2T/3$ d) F (final status)

Fig. 10. Obstacle-crossing gait of robot in wheel-legged form.

The robot can change its form under the action of the wheel-leg conversion module to adapt to different terrains. The robot will lift to a certain height under the action of the mechanical leg in the middle, and the position of the wheels and legs will be exchanged under the action of the motor inside the wheel-legged conversion module.

4 Experimental Verification

By optimizing the structure and appearance of the robot, an experimental prototype was developed. In order to facilitate the experimental analysis, the lateral rotation of the robot is cancelled. At the same time, the front and rear rotation layers of the wheel-leg conversion module can normally rotate to convert the wheeled and legged form. As for the specific driving implementation, the steering gear is used as the driver of the mechanical leg joint and the wheel-leg conversion module, and the DC motor is used as the driver of the Mecanum wheel. The prototype of the mobile robot is shown in Fig. 11.

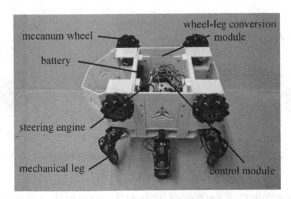

Fig. 11. Structure diagram of mobile robot prototype.

The mobile robot has three forms, and different forms can adapt to different terrain. The feasibility of its form conversion function can be proved by the prototype experiment. Three forms of the prototype and the transformation process are shown in Fig. 12, and the process is consistent with the simulation results. Figure 12a), Fig. 12b) and Fig. 12d) are hexapod form, wheel-legged form and wheeled form respectively in this figure.

a) t=0 s   b) t=4 s   c) t=8 s   d) t=12 s

Fig. 12. Morphological transformation experiment of the robot.

Experiments were carried out on the three-legged walking and rotating gait of the robot prototype in the hexapod form, and the processes are shown in Fig. 13 and Fig. 14 respectively. The experiment shows that the robot can go straight and turn normally on the unstructured ground covered with stones.

a) t=0 s   b) t=2 s   c) t=4 s

Fig. 13. Straight gait experiment of robot in hexapod form.

a) t=0 s   b) t=2 s   c) t=4 s

Fig. 14. Rotating gait experiment of robot in hexapod form.

Finally, the experiment of the robot climbing the steps in the form of wheels and legs is carried out, as shown in Fig. 15. The experiment shows that the robot can successfully achieve obstacle-crossing with a height of 120 mm.

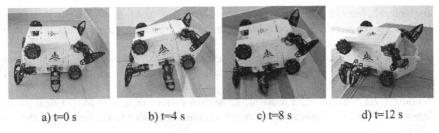

a) t=0 s   b) t=4 s   c) t=8 s   d) t=12 s

Fig. 15. Obstacle-crossing experiment of robot in wheel-legged form.

5 Conclusion

Traditional mobile robots have limitations in obstacle-crossing ability, motion stability and load-bearing capacity, which make it difficult to be applied on a large scale. Based on the RCM with strong coupling and variable topology, a polymorphous WLMR is proposed. By optimizing the rotation mode of the classic third-order RCM, a new type of chute third-order RCM is designed, which is introduced into the wheel-leg conversion module. Then a WLMR with polymorphism is constructed by combining wheel-leg conversion module, mechanical leg and Mecanum wheel. Gait planning analysis of the WLMR in different modes is carried out to ensure the stability of the robot during movement. The prototype experiments are performed to verify the efficiency of the WLMR's straight travel, in-situ rotation, obstacle-crossing and morphology transformation in complex environments. This research not only provides a reference for the design of polymorphous mobile robots, but also opens up ideas for the application of the RCM in daily production and life.

Acknowledgement. This work was supported in part by the National Natural Science Foundation, China, under Grant 51905464, 51775473, in part by the Scientific Research Capacity Improvement Project of Key Developing Disciplines in Guangdong Province of China, under Grant 2021ZDJS084, in part by the National Key Research and Development Program, China, under Grant 2018YFB1307903, in part by the Dongguan Sci-tech Commissoner, under Grant 20211800500242, in part by the KEY Laboratory of Robotics and Intelligent Equipment of Guangdong Regular Institutions of Higher Education, under Grant 2017KSYS009, and in part by the Innovation Center of Robotics and Intelligent Equipment, China, under Grant KCYCXPT2017006, and in part by the Dongguan Social science and Technology Development (Key) Project, under Grant 20185071021602.

References

1. Vijaychandra, A., Alex, C., Mathews, M., Sathar, A.: Amphibious wheels with a passive slip mechanism for transformation. In: ICARM, Osaka, Japan, pp. 960–965 (2019)
2. Ding, X.L., Li, K.J., Xu, K.: Dynamics and wheel's slip ratio of a wheel-legged robot in wheeled motion considering the change of height. Chin. J. Mach. Eng. **25**(5), 1060–1067 (2012)
3. Ding, X.L., Xu, K.: Design and analysis of a novel metamorphic wheel-legged rover mechanism. J. Central South Univ. Sci. Technol. **40**, 91–101 (2009)

4. Bjelonic, M., Sankar, P.K., Bellicoso, D., Vallery, H., Hutter, M.: Rolling in the deep – hybrid locomotion for wheeled-legged robots using online trajectory optimization. IEEE Robot. Autom. Lett. **5**(2), 3626–3633 (2020)
5. Morihiro, Y., Takahashi, N., Nonaka, K., Sekiguchi, K.: Model predictive load distribution control for leg/wheel mobile robots on rough terrain. Int. Fed. Autom. Control **51**(22), 441–446 (2018)
6. Nakajima, S., Nakano, E., Takahashi, T.: Motion control technique for practical use of a leg-wheel robot on unknown outdoor rough terrains. In: IROS, Osaka, Japan, pp. 1353–1358 (2004)
7. Zhang, C.Y., Guo, S., Zhao, F.Q.: Motion analysis and gait research of a new wheel-legged compound robot. J. Mech. Eng. **55**(15), 145–153 (2019)
8. Chen, S.C., Huang, K.J., Chen, W.H., Shen, S.Y., Li, C.H.: Quattroped: a leg-wheel transformable robot. IEEE/ASME Trans. Mechatron. **19**(2), 730–742 (2013)
9. Chen, W.H., Lin, H.S., Lin, Y.M., Lin, P.C.: TurboQuad: a novel leg-wheel transformable robot with smooth and fast behavioral transitions. IEEE Trans. Rob. **33**(5), 1025–1040 (2017)
10. Zhou, F.L., Xu, H.J., Zou, T.A., Zhang, X.: A wheel-track-Leg hybrid Locomotion Mechanism based on transformable rims. In: AIM, Munich, Germany, pp. 315–320 (2017)
11. Dai, J.S., Wang, D.L.: Geometric analysis and synthesis of the metamorphic robotic hand. J. Mech. Des. **129**(11), 1191–1197 (2007)
12. Liu, C., Tan, X.C., Yao, Y.A., Fu, Z.Y.: Design and analysis of a novel deformable wheel-legged robot. J. Mech. Eng. **58**(3), 65–74 (2022)
13. Zeng, D.X., Li, M., Wang, J.J., Hou, Y.L., Lu, W.J., Huang, Z.: Overview of Rubik's cube and reflections on its application in mechanism. Chin. J. Mech. Eng. **31**(4), 9–20 (2018)
14. Zeng, D.X., et al.: Analysis of structural composition and representation of topological structures of RCM. Mech. Mach. Theory **136**, 86–104 (2019)

Design and Evaluation of the Terrestrial Gait of the Bionic Robotic Duck

Zhengyu Li[ID], Liwei Shi[(✉)][ID], and Shuxiang Guo

Key Laboratory of Convergence Medical Engineering System and Healthcare Technology,
The Ministry of Industry and Information Technology, School of Life Science, Beijing Institute
of Technology, No. 5, Zhongguancun South Street, Haidian District, Beijing 100081, China
{lizhengyu,shiliwei}@bit.edu.cn

Abstract. With the exploration of the ocean, amphibious robots can integrate
the advantages of underwater and land robots, and can achieve detection on land,
underwater, and seabed. This topic proposed the idea of bionic waterfowl, designed
a set of amphibious bionic waterfowl robot prototype, and built the machinery platform and control system platform. The robot's dynamic leg and head and neck are
moved by modeling; two kinds of land gait designs and simulation analysis of the
robot are carried out by ADAMS software. In the simulation process, by adjusting
the leg bending angle and joint rotation frequency of the two basic gaits designed,
the robot can have a certain ability to overcome obstacles, and can run smoothly
on horizontal ground and slopes with different angles. progress. Finally, according
to the experimental results, the relationship curves between the leg bending angle
and the anterior distance and the joint rotation frequency and the anterior distance
were fitted. The bionic duck robot can choose the most suitable gait through the
expression of fitting curve under different land environment conditions.

Keywords: Bionic duck robot · Gait design · Adams simulation

1 Introduction

Since the 21st century, land resources have become increasingly scarce, and the ocean
accounts for 70% of the earth surface area, so human beings have set their sights on
the vast sea. At present, more and more scientific researchers have devoted themselves
to the exploration and exploitation of marine resources. But it's not enough just to
have people involved, we need to rely on the right tools to explore the vast ocean.
Now humans have developed a variety of underwater robots. At present, most of the
platforms on the sea use unmanned boats, submersibles, underwater robots and other
equipment to assist humans in exploring the resources of the ocean, and achieve the
goal of underwater research. However, these underwater operating equipment have poor
adaptability to complex terrains such as sand spits, sand dams, barrier islands, tidal flats,
etc. Therefore, amphibious robots are required to cooperate in related work.

Different underwater vehicles have different propulsion methods. The traditional
propulsion method usually takes propeller propulsion as the main propulsion mode [1].

Propeller propulsion has many advantages, such as large thrust, fast real-time response, relatively simple structure, and so on. But it also has some disadvantages, such as low propulsion efficiency, high power consumption, high noise, large volume and weight [2]. But fish which can live in the water, the process that fishes swing their bodies and tail fins is a way of propulsion based on lift force [3].

And amphibians often use resistance-based propulsion methods. For example, turtles and crabs move forward by flapping [4]. Squid and jellyfish move forward by jetting water [5]. Research on bionic underwater vehicles was being carried out gradually in recent years [6].

Xing et al. designed a miniature bio-inspired Amphibious Spherical Robot (ASRobot) with a Legged, Multi-vectored Water-jet Composite Driving Mechanism (LMWCDM). They studied locomotory performance of the robot in amphibious field environments. And the results demonstrate that the robot prototype possesses the high locomotory performance [7].

Guo et al. proposed a decentralized method of spherical amphibious multi-robot control system based on blockchain technology. They set up the point-to-point information network based on long range radio technology of low power wide area network, and designed the blockchain system for embedded application environment and the decentralized hardware and software architecture of multi-robot control system. On this basis, the consensus plugin, smart contract and decentralized multi-robot control algorithm were designed to achieve decentralization. The experimental results of consensus of spherical amphibious multi-robot showed the effectiveness of the decentralization [8].

Zheng et al. design an artificial multi-robot cooperative mode and explore an electronic communication and collaborate devices, the control method is based in particular on underwater environment and also conduct a detailed analysis of control motion module [9].

Shi et al. used a fuzzy Proportional-Integral-Derivative (PID) control algorithm to design an underwater motion control system for a novel robot. Moreover, they compared PID with fuzzy PID control methods by carrying out experiments on heading and turning bow motions to verify that the fuzzy PID is more robust and exhibits good dynamic performance. They also carried out experiments on the three-dimensional (3D) motion control to validate the design of the underwater motion control system [10].

Yin et al. used the adaptive ability of reinforcement learning to propose a two-layer network framework based on reinforcement learning to realize the control of amphibious spherical robots. Through the cooperation of the planning layer and the control layer, the adaptive motion control of the amphibious spherical robot can finally be realized. Finally, the proposed scheme was verified on a simulated amphibious spherical robot [11].

Zhou et al. proposed a two-dimensional trajectory tracking control framework for biomimetic spherical robots (BSR) in a constrained workspace. Meanwhile, the research presents the general dynamics models of the robot and the thrusters allocator scheme to ensure the force generated by the propellers within the feasible range. Finally, they assess the performance and feasibility of the proposed control framework through the simulations [12].

Shi *et al.* developed a small-sized quadruped robotic rat (SQuRo), which includes four limbs and one flexible spine, They proposed a control framework for multimodal motion planning, and the appropriate control parameters were tuned through optimization with consideration to the stability and actuation limits. The results obtained through a series of experimental tests reveal that SQuRo achieves a superior motion performance compared with existing state-of-the-art small-sized quadruped robots [13].

Shi *et al.* proposed key movement joints (KMJs) to capture a decent representation of the rat with a reduced-order model. By extracting the primary KMJs, they determined the number and distribution of robotic joints for the design of a bioinspired spine mechanism. To meet the demand of high biomimicry degree, they generated an optimal compensation term to minimize the trajectory error introduced by simplifying the model. And they calculated the optimal minimum motion cycle based on the constraints of equilibrium under extreme conditions to ensure high flexibility without compromising the stability. The proposed method was successfully verified through simulation and experimental tests with a robotic rat endowed with the bioinspired spine mechanism [14].

In this paper, a bionic amphibious robot is proposed, and its mechanical system is designed, which is divided into head, body, and legs. The land motion gait is designed and optimized based on the bionic duck robot model, and a virtual simulation platform is established by Adams software to simulate and evaluate the designed gait.

The rest of this paper is organized as follows. Section 2 introduces the mechanical structure of the robot. In Sect. 3, the terrestrial gait analysis, included walking gait and running and jumping gait are designed. And in Sect. 4, the designed land gaits are kinematically simulated. Finally, the conclusion is summarized in Sect. 5.

2 Mechanical Structure of the Bionic Robotic Duck

2.1 Head Structure

The head is a structure with 3 degrees of freedom, which is shown in Fig. 1, including two vertical DOF structures and one horizontal DOF structure. The design of the head, as an auxiliary structure of the whole bionic duck robot structure, plays the role of controlling the direction, maintaining the balance and assisting the movement.

Fig. 1. Head structure

2.2 Legs Structure

The legs of the bionic Robotic Duck are mainly divided into dynamic legs and soles and auxiliary legs three parts, as shown in Fig. 2.

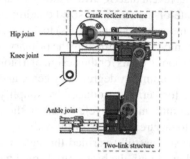

Fig. 2. Legs structure

2.3 Webbed Structure

As shown in Fig. 3, the structure of the webbed is composed of a telescopic rod, which is controlled by a servo motor. There are three branches of the telescopic rod, and they are all fixed in the barrel.

Fig. 3. Webbed structure

3 Overland Gait Design

The gait design of the bionic robotic duck is mainly based on the movement of bipeds, and is improved according to the mechanical structure of the robot. When walking on the road, the robot will choose different gait and pace according to different task requirements and land environment, so that it can complete it most efficiently. In this paper, there are two kinds of forward gaits of robots on land, namely slow walking gait and running and jumping gait. The most suitable gait can be selected according to different terrain environments.

3.1 Walking Gait Design

The walking gait is the most stable gait when the bionic duck robot moves forward on land, as shown in Fig. 4. When the robot moves forward, it always maintains three or more contact points with the land to ensure its stability. When the hip joint is in a horizontal position, and the thigh is kept in a vertical state, it is set to a standing posture.

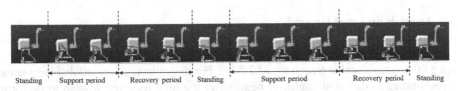

Standing   Support period   Recovery period   Standing   Support period   Recovery period   Standing

Fig. 4. Walking gait cycle

3.2 Running and Jumping Gait Design

As shown in Fig. 5, the running and jumping gait is adjusted accordingly on the basis of the slow walking gait. By changing the frequency of hip rotation, it turns faster than in a walking gait.

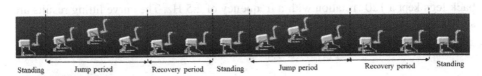

Standing   Jump period   Recovery period   Standing   Jump period   Recovery period   Standing

Fig. 5. Running and jumping gait cycle

4 Simulation and Evaluation of the Gait

4.1 Simulation Experiment of the Gait

There are two main gaits in the land gait, including the walking gait and the running and jumping gait. The step function is used in the simulation, which is shown in formula (1).

$$Step(x, x_0, h_0, x_1, h_1) \tag{1}$$

Among them, x is represented as an independent variable, which can be time or any time function; x_0 and x_1 are the start and end values of the independent variable x, which can be constants, function expressions or design variables; h_0 and h_1 are the start value and end value of the step function respectively, which can be constants, function expressions or design variables.

4.2 Analysis of the Gait

This simulation design is designed with 4s as a cycle. In Adams, the kinematics and dynamics of the robot are collected through its detection module; in the post-processing module, the collected simulation data is graphically processed, including the front and near Distance, speed, torque of the robot, angular velocity of rotation, etc. After that, Matlab was used to fit the relevant data and find the relevant laws.

Gait Analysis on Level Ground

Under the condition of level ground, the influence on the forward distance was explored by changing the bending angle of the robot's back legs, in which the robot's front legs kept a 60° rotation with a frequency of 2.5 Hz. For the collected forward displacements corresponding to different angles of bending of the hind legs, use Matlab to perform curve fitting on the data points in different functional ways, as shown in Fig. 6(a). The fitted linear function expression is as follows:

$$f(x) = 0.8305x - 2.943 \tag{2}$$

According to different needs, the desired bending angle of the back leg can be found. Among them, when the robot adopts a walking gait on the level ground, the maximum distance that the robot can move in one step is about 105 mm.

Also, under the condition of level ground, the influence on the forward distance was explored by changing the bending angle of the robot's front legs, in which the robot's back legs kept a 120° rotation with a frequency of 2.5 Hz. The curve fitting results are shown in Fig. 6(b). The fitted Gaussian function expression is as follows:

$$f(x) = 101.4 * e^{(-((x-69.57)/53.86)^2)} \tag{3}$$

According to different needs, you can find the desired front leg bending angle.

Under the condition of level ground, the influence on the forward distance is explored by changing the rotation angle of the robot's hip joint, and other parameters remain unchanged. The curve fitting results are shown in Fig. 6(c). The fitted Gaussian function expression is as follows:

$$f(x) = 65.33 * e^{(-((x+20.36)/170.1)^2)} \tag{4}$$

Still under the condition of level ground, the influence of the rotation frequency of the robot's hip joint on the forward distance is explored by changing the frequency of the robot's hip joint, in which the robot's front legs maintain a 40° rotation and the back legs maintain an 80° rotation. The curve fitting results are shown in Fig. 6(d). The fitted Gaussian function expression is as follows:

$$f(x) = 1774 * e^{(-((x-70.81)/34.28)^2)} \tag{5}$$

In addition, the jump height of the hip joint rotating robot at different frequencies is also measured, the curve fitting results are shown in Fig. 6(e). The fitted Gaussian function expression is as follows:

$$f(x) = 0.1529 * x^{1.998} + 2.768 \tag{6}$$

The corresponding rotation frequency can be selected according to the height of different obstacles so that the robot can complete the goal of traveling.

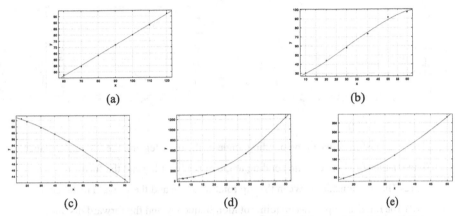

(a)

(b)

(c)   (d)   (e)

(a)The relationship between the bending angle of the back leg and the forward distance

(b)The relationship between the bending angle of the front leg and the forward distance

(c) The relationship between the hip rotation angle and the forward distance

(d) The relationship between joint rotation frequency and the forward distance

(e) The relationship between joint rotation frequency and the jump height

Fig. 6. The relationship under level ground condition

Gait Analysis on Slopes

The gait simulation experiments of the bionic robotic duck were carried out on the inclined planes of 5°, 15° and 25°, respectively. Similar to the situation in the plane, the bending angle of the robot's back legs, the bending angle of the front legs, and the rotation frequencies of the hip and knee joints are adjusted respectively. And according to the data points obtained from the experiment, the corresponding fitting curve can be obtained (Fig. 7).

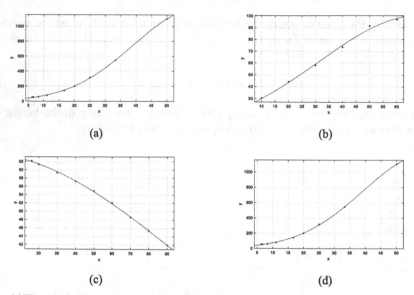

(a)   (b)

(c)   (d)

(a)The relationship between the bending angle of the back leg and the forward distance

(b)The relationship between the bending angle of the front leg and the forward distance

(c) The relationship between the hip rotation angle and the forward distance

(d) The relationship between joint rotation frequency and the forward distance

Fig. 7. The relationship under 5° slope condition

Under the condition of a 5° slope, the bionic duck robot can still walk as smoothly as on a level ground (Fig. 8).

The 15° slope has little effect on the robot's walking gait, but the running-jumping gait is not as stable as it is on a level ground (Fig. 9).

Under the condition of a 25° slope and the robot can walk smoothly, the bending angle of the robot's back legs is more severely limited, and the maximum bending angle is only 87°, but the bending angle of the front legs is still not affected. The angle does not cause the robot's center of gravity to change. In the running and jumping gait, the front distance is further reduced, and more energy is used to work against gravity.

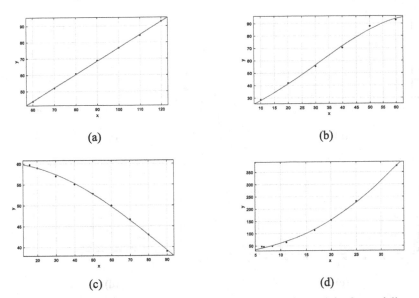

(a)

(b)

(c)

(d)

(a)The relationship between the bending angle of the back leg and the forward distance

(b)The relationship between the bending angle of the front leg and the forward distance

(c) The relationship between the hip rotation angle and the forward distance

(d) The relationship between joint rotation frequency and the forward distance

Fig. 8. The relationship under 15° slope condition

It can be seen from the simulation results that the robot can complete the gait of walking, running and jumping on flat ground and slopes of different angles. When the robot encounters an obstacle, it can jump from the top of the obstacle by running and jumping to achieve the purpose of crossing the obstacle, and the appropriate rotation frequency can be selected according to the fitted functional relationship and the height of the obstacle. However, since the running and jumping gait is completely suspended in the air for a period of time after jumping, it will generate a large force on the joints when landing, so the mechanical structure of the bionic duck robot requires high strength. In addition, the running and jumping gait is to increase the frequency of joint rotation, so this requires the motor to provide a larger frequency. To sum up, the walking gait will be used as the common gait of the bionic duck robot. When the robot needs to overcome obstacles or walk quickly, it can choose the running and jumping gait.

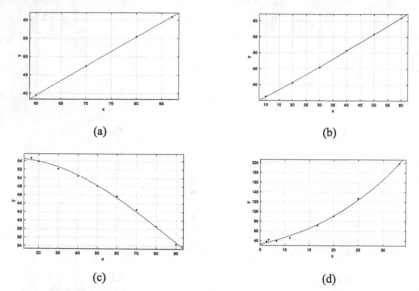

(a)The relationship between the bending angle of the back leg and the forward distance

(b)The relationship between the bending angle of the front leg and the forward distance

(c) The relationship between the hip rotation angle and the forward distance

(d) The relationship between joint rotation frequency and the forward distance

Fig. 9. The relationship under 25° slope condition

5   Result

Based on the previously completed bionic duck robot model, this study designs two novel gaits, which enable the robot to walk in various complex terrain conditions. The designed gait was then simulated and evaluated using Adams software. According to the needs of different environments, robots can carry out a combination of various gaits to complete tasks such as land survey, exploration, search and rescue, and have broad research prospects. However, limited by the time limit of the research, the gait of the bionic duck robot designed in this research still needs to be improved and improved. In the follow-up research, other software needs to be used for simulation verification. Besides, only the land gait simulation has been achieved. In the future, the actual control experiments will be carried out.

References

1. Wang, X., Song, W., You, M., et al.: Bionic single-electrode electronic skin unit based on piezoelectric nanogenerator. ACS Nano **2**(8), 8588–8596 (2018)
2. Zhong, J., Luo, M., Liu, X., et al.: Frog-inspire jumping robot actuated by pneumatic muscle actuators. Adv. Mech. Eng. **10**(6), 2–5 (2018)
3. Li, R., et al.: Computational investigation on a self-propelled pufferfish driven by multiple fins. Ocean Eng. **197**, 106908 (2020)

4. Roper, D.T., et al.: A review of developments towards biologically inspired propulsion systems for autonomous underwater vehicles. Proc. Inst. Mech. Eng. Part M J. Eng. Marit. Environ. **225**(2), 77–96 (2011)
5. Richards, C.T., Clemente, C.J.: Built for rowing: frog muscle is tuned to limb morphology to power swimming. J. R. Soc. Interface **10**, 20130236 (2013)
6. Wang, Y., Zhu, J., Wang, X., et al.: Hydrodynamics study and simulation of a bionic fish tail driving system based on linear hypocycloid. Int. J. Adv. Robot. Syst. **15**(2) (2018)
7. Xing, H., et al.: Design, modeling and control of a miniature bio-inspired amphibious spherical robot. Mechatronics **77**(1), 102574 (2021)
8. Guo, S., Cao, S., Guo, J.: Study on decentralization of spherical amphibious multi-robot control system based on smart contract and blockchain. J. Bionic Eng. **18**(6), 1317–1330 (2021). https://doi.org/10.1007/s42235-021-00073-0
9. Zheng, L., Guo, S., Piao, Y., Gu, S., An, R.: Collaboration and task planning of turtle-inspired multiple amphibious spherical robots. Micromachines **11**, 71 (2020)
10. Shi, L., et al.: A fuzzy PID algorithm for a novel miniature spherical robots with three-dimensional underwater motion control. J. Bionic Eng. **17**(5), 959–969 (2020). https://doi.org/10.1007/s42235-020-0087-3
11. Yin, H., et al.: The vector control scheme for amphibious spherical robots based on reinforcement learning. In: 2021 IEEE International Conference on Mechatronics and Automation (ICMA), pp. 594–599 (2021)
12. Zhou, M., et al.: Trajectory tracking control for a biomimetic spherical robot based on ADRC. In: 2021 IEEE International Conference on Mechatronics and Automation (ICMA), pp. 319–324 (2021)
13. Shi, Q., et al.: Development of a small-sized quadruped robotic rat capable of multimodal motions. IEEE Trans. Robot. (2022). https://doi.org/10.1109/TRO.2022.3159188
14. Shi, Q., et al.: Implementing rat-like motion for a small-sized biomimetic robot based on extraction of key movement joints. IEEE Trans. Robot. **37**(3), 747–762 (2021)

AI Meets the Challenges of Autism

Realtime Interpersonal Human Synchrony Detection Based on Action Segmentation

Bowen Chen[1], Jiamin Zhang[2], Zuode Liu[1], Ruihan Lin[1], Weihong Ren[1], Luodi Yu[2,3], and Honghai Liu[1(✉)]

[1] Harbin Institution of Technology (Shenzhen), Shenzhen, China
honghai.liu@hit.edu.cn
[2] South China Normal University Autism Research Center, Guangzhou, China
[3] Center for Autism Research, School of Education, Guangzhou University, Guangzhou, China

Abstract. IS (Interpersonal Synchrony), where the follower (participant) tries to behave the same action along with the raiser (human or metronome), is an essential social interaction skill. The evaluation of interpersonal synchronization is valuable for early autism screening. However, the research on IS evaluation is limited, and the current approaches usually evaluate the IS task with "motion energy" that is calculated by imprecise corner detection of the participant, which is not robust in an uncontrollable clinical environment. Moreover, these approaches need to manually mark the start and the end anchor of the specified action segment, which is labor-intensive. In this paper, we construct a realtime action segmentation model to automatically recognize the human-wise action class frame by frame. A simple yet efficient backbone is utilized to classify action class straightly instead of extracting the motion features (e.g. optical flow) with high computational complexity. Specifically, given an action video, a sliding window stacks frames in a fixed window size to feed a Resnet-like action classification branch (ACB) to classify the current action label. To further improve the accuracy of action boundary and eliminate the over-segmentation noises, we incorporate a boundary prediction branch (BPB), cooperating with majority-voting strategy, to refine the action classification generated by ACB. Then we can calculate the IS overlap easily by comparing two action timelines belonging to raiser and follower. To evaluate the proposed model, we collect 200K annotated images belonging to 40 subjects who perform 2 tasks (nod and clap) in 2 conditions (interpersonal and human-metronome). The experiment results demonstrate that our model achieves 87.1% accuracy at 200 FPS and can locate the start and end of action precisely in realtime.

Keywords: Interpersonal synchrony · Action segmentation · Autism disorders

1 Introduction

Interpersonal Synchrony(IS) is defined as time-aligned and form-aligned behavior that occurs in the process of social interaction [1]. Take daily conversation as an example, both parties of the conversation tend to unconsciously adjust posture and speech rate to coordinate with each other [20]. IS exists in various social situations, and the implementation of IS can promote the development of individual prosocial behavior [21]. Prosocial behavior generally refers to behaviors that have postive effects on others or society, which is an essential factor affecting one's social participation [5,22].

There has been increasing evidence showing that communicative deficits linked to interpersonal synchrony deficits affect a large number of people on the autism spectrum disorders (ASD) [3,7,11]. On this basis, IS has the potential to be used as a biomarker for early clinical evaluation of individuals with ASD and as an educational intervention method to improve their social skills [2,12]. Therefore, the measurement of interpersonal synchrony synchronization is of great significance for clinical practice with individuals with ASD [16].

Although interpersonal synchrony has a certain psychology research basis, there are few methods to analyze the synchronization data. A labor-intensive way is using subjective observational tools to label individual movements manually on clinical observations for detection [10]. With the development of computer-vision, more and more machine-assisted methods were proposed to analyze ASD biomarkers with a higher performance while saving lots of labours [15,18,23]. In IS task, for example, "motion energy" is defined by summing the gray pixel difference between continuous video frames to detect individual motion synchronization levels [17]. However, these vision-based methods are still complicated in data processing with limited accuracy and robustness.

Action segmentation classifies actions at frame level for untrimmed videos and is suitable for precisely analyzing continual actions. Based on action segmentation, our method first generates two action timelines belonging to the clinician and child (or child only for the human-metronome environment), respectively. Then, we can evaluate the synchronization quickly by computing the overlap between the raiser's and follower's timelines. Over-segmentation noises exist widely in action segmentation tasks. Inspired by [9], we incorporate a boundary prediction branch (BPB), cooperating with majority-voting strategy, to refine the Action Classification generated by ACB. As a result, not only the BPB smoothes the Action Classifications, but also the boundaries are classified more precisely.

Overall, we build a framework to evaluate the motor synchronization for untrimmed automatically IS task recordings at a finer level. The framework is the first attempt to introduce action segmentation into IS task. Our contributions can be summarized as follows:

- We first adopt action segmentation to analyze IS protocol automatically, saving intensive labor on marking action start and end. Unlike the existing methods, we classify action straightly instead of extracting low-level vision features, improving the model's robustness in uncontrollable protocol environments.
- Considering the characteristics of the IS task, we take classical but efficient strategy, temporal sliding window, as our temporal feature extractor, avoiding calculating costly optical flow. This architecture also enables the model to

realize realtime action segmentation. We prove that sliding window remains advantageous when solving periodic short segment tasks.

- To evaluate our pipeline, we collect 40 IS videos and annotate 3 actions (two foreground actions and background action) with above 200,000 frames for children and clinicians in human-metronome and human-human environments. Our method finally achieves 87.1% action accuracy on the dataset, which is comparable to the non-realtime method.

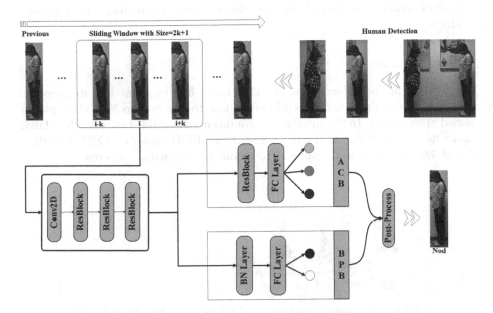

Fig. 1. The pipeline of the proposed action segmentation method. The method first detect humans via YOLO-v5 [19] and then crop video human-wise. For individual single-human videos, the framework slides a temporal window with size = $2k + 1$ on frames to generate frame stacks as the temporal condition of the center frame. The Resnet [8] backbone extracts features of stacked frames and then inputs features into two branches, ACB and BPB, to predict action labels and boundary probabilities, respectively. With Action Classifications and boundary probabilities, the Post-Process procedure refines the Action Classification and outputs the action labels of the video frame by frame.

2 Protocol Details

2.1 Action Definition

Previous studies on interpersonal synchrony have found that different actions, rhythmic presentation, and synchronization targets all have an impact on the accuracy of synchronization [24] patterns, nodding generally produces higher synchronization accuracy than clapping does, and the motion patterns that require coordination of hands and legs tend to be the most complicated. In terms of rhythm presentation, the subjects were more likely to follow the rhythm presented in auditory form than in visual form. Children's interpersonal motor synchronization level following adult actions is higher than that following peers whose motor skills are immature with predictable patterns. Taking the above mentioned factors into consideration, we decided to measure nodding and clapping in the condition of metronome and interpersonal condition. A multi-condition, multi-action, and multi-speed design was implemented to measure behavioral synchronization of autistic children and age-matched neurotypical children.

2.2 Apparatus

The settings of the IS scenarios are illustrated in Fig. 2. In the interpersonal condition, the clinician and the child stand face to face on two 30 × 30 cm planar spaced 80 cm apart. In the metronome condition, the child stands on the planar where he does actions, as shown in Fig. 2. An RGB camera (SONY cx680) is placed 3.0 m away from the subject to record the evaluation process.

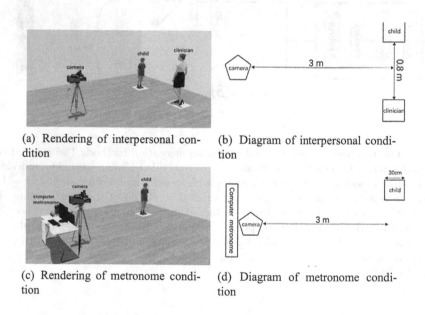

(a) Rendering of interpersonal condition

(b) Diagram of interpersonal condition

(c) Rendering of metronome condition

(d) Diagram of metronome condition

Fig. 2. The scenario of interpersonal and metronome condition.

2.3 Protocol Procedure

1. The child was invited to stand on the designated spot on the floor, and the clinician instructed the child to perform the two actions and described the testing procedures to the child.

2. In the metronome condition, the child was instructed to sync the beginning of each target action to a computer metronome beat. In the interpersonal condition, the child was asked to synchronize their actions with the clinician who followed the metronome beats through a Bluetooth headset.
3. We used various strategies throughout the sessions to make sure each child comprehended the task, including visual demonstrations of the activities by the clinician, use of videos to illustrate the activities, as well as practice trials with manual feedback whenever needed.
4. The order sequence of actions and conditions was randomized while each participant always started from the slow rate. There are three rate for each movement: fast rate (774 ms per beat), medium rate (1035 ms per beat), and slow rate (1384 ms per beat). In every trial, four beats were presented at the beginning to allow participants to familiarize with the beat rate. sented to allow participants to familiarize themselves with the rate.

3   Method

In this section, we introduce our approach to action segmentation. At first, we detect humans in original videos by YOLO-v5 and crop videos human-wise. On the single-person video, inspired by [9], our framework adopts a boundary-based refinement neural network to classify action class frame by frame. Specifically, our proposed approach consists of a spatial-temporal feature extractor based on sliding-window and two branches, an Action Classification Branch (ACB) and a Boundary Prediction Branch (BPB), as illustrated in Fig. 1. The ACB branch supplies the raw prediction of action, and the BPB branch suggests whether one frame is an action boundary or not. Then, the Post-Process module fuses the outputs from both branches and predicts the final decision of the action class. Let $V = [f_1, \ldots, f_T]$, where V is the cropped single-person video and the T is the temporal length of the V. Given V, our goal is to classify frame-level action classes $C = [C_1, \ldots, C_T]$. For each frame, we predict action boundaries $B = [b_1, \ldots, b_T]$ as a refiner to improve the prediction of ACB.

3.1   Network Architecture

Action Classification Branch. Given one temporal window with N ($N < T$) RGB frames from V, we stack frames as feature maps with $N * 3$ channels and input them into our backbone to classify the action class of the center frame. We choose Resnet pretrained on ImageNet as our backbone. We can adjust the number of residual blocks, a network unit that contains multiple convolution layers and shortcut connections, in individual layer to control the complexity of the backbone. In this paper, we choose Resnet-34 as our backbone.

Boundary Prediction Branch. Boundary Prediction Branch (BPB) has been proved efficient in addressing the over-segmentation errors in action segmentation. Prediction Refinement (PR) can smooth the noise among barriers, i.e., the turning point from one action to the next. Inspired by [9], we adopt a similar BPB-PR stragegy but with different network architecture. We take BPB as a binary classification problem instead of a probability regression problem to introduce Focal Loss into boundary prediction. To take advantage of the shallow feature extractors, we utilize the features generated by the third layer of the Resnet as the input of BPB. In BPB, a Batch Normalization Layer, a Full Connect Layer, and a softmax activation function map the input into boundary classification.

Prediction Refinement. We refine the predictions by a majority voting strategy. Because of the lack of boundary examples, the boundary prediction accuracy can not be guaranteed. However, the majority voting strategy is insensitive to over-retrieval. If we take an inner-action frame as a boundary wrongly, the segment label is also determined by majority-voting and the wrong boundary will be eliminated as long as the ACB's predictions are stable. Similar to these approaches, we get the boundary predictions B and action label predictions frame-by-frame at first. At last, we count the action frame instances within a segment under the assumption that there is only one action between two boundaries. The segment label will be determined as the class which owns the most frames.

3.2   Loss Function

Our loss function can be formulated as

$$L = L_a + \lambda L_b \tag{1}$$

where the L_a represents classification loss for ACB while the L_b is the boundary loss for BPB. The λ is a balanced weight of the L_b. We discuss classification loss at first.

Classification Loss. The previous temporal convolution-based works usually adopt cross-entropy loss and smoothing loss for the ACB branch. However, we remove the smoothing loss in our method. Our method predicts actions in a sliding window with a small and fixed temporal receptive field. Therefore, we cannot apply the smooth loss to the whole video. Besides, the smoothing loss within the sliding window is harmful. In our experiments, the probabilities in a frame stack are stable only if the action class changes. In this case, the smooth loss will weaken the boundary regressor and may cause the miss of the boundary retrieval. The classification loss is defined as:

$$L_c = \frac{1}{T} \sum_t -log(y_{t,c}), \tag{2}$$

where $y_{t,c}$ is the predicted probability for the ground-truth label at time t.

Boundary Loss. Boundary Prediction is a binary classification task, the previous researches adopt binary cross-entrophy loss as boundary loss. However, the cross-entropy loss ignores the distribution of the samples and easily be dominated by large sample. Barriers in the action timelines is rare compared to the normal action frames. It cause the extreme imbalance bias in training BPB. Focal loss [14] has been proved efficient for lots of unbalance scenarios. We replaced the binary cross-entropy loss with focal loss. The boundary loss is defined as:

$$L_b = -(1 - \hat{y}_t)^\gamma log\hat{y}_t, \tag{3}$$

where γ is a tunable parameter to adjust the priority of positive samples.

4   Experiments and Discussion

4.1   Dataset and Evaluation Metrics

We collected and annotated 40 IS videos containing 28 TD (typical development) and 12 ASD to build an action segmentation dataset. The protocol was carried out in the South China Normal University Autism Research Center (SCNUARC). The experiments have passed the ethical review, and we pledged not to disclose any personal information about the subjects. The videos were captured at 25 fps, around 15–25 s. There are two foreground actions, "nod" and "clap", in our dataset. They are all annotated with a consistent annotation standard. The total frames of our dataset are above 200000. The foreground actions own 24733 and 17807 frames, respectively. For the evaluation metrics, we adopt the frame-wise accuracy, segment-wise edit distance and F1 score as described in [6]. Frame-wise accuracy is a primary evaluation metric that only calculates the percentage of correct predictions. The segmental edit distance is a metric for measuring the difference between ground truth segments and predicted segments by Levenshtein Distance [13]. When calculating the segment F1 scores averaged per class, the segment which owns a temporal Intersection over Union (IoU) larger than a certain threshold will be classified as correct. In this paper, we choose 0.1,0.25 and 0.5 as F1 thresholds.

4.2   Implementation Details

We train the entire framework using the SGD optimizer with a learning rate of 0.001 and batch size of 128. The results are reported after training 50 epochs. The learning rate will be downgraded 10 times per 20 epochs. The action segmentation results from the ACB are refined using predicted action boundaries from the BPB only in the inference stage.

4.3   Results and Discussions

In this section, we evaluate the effectiveness of the proposed method. Our model achieves more than 87% accuracy in action segmentation for both child and clinician in 200 fps running on RTX3090. Our network can accurately localize the start and end of action segments. The critical action, "nod" and "clap" can also be detected in an untrimmed video. To evaluate our network's ability, we use the widely-used MS-TCN as baseline. The original MS-TCN utilizes RGB and optical flow as input, which is unfair for realtime methods. Therefore, we only input RGB features into MS-TCN as method MS-TCN (RGB-only). Besides, we also report the results of (1) Our Method without BPB, (2) Our Method with BPB, which replaces focal loss to cross-entropy(CE) loss (3) Our Method (4) MS-TCN (Dual-stream).

Table 1. The action segmentation results.

Methods	Acc	Edit distance	F1@{0.1,0.25,0.5}		
MS-TCN (RGB-only)	81.7	72.8	75.0	**73.8**	**65.3**
Our Method w/o BPB	83.5	71.3	75.1	67.7	53.5
Our Method w/ BPB (CE)	85.6	73.2	76.0	69.8	55.4
Our Method w/ BPB (Focal)	**87.1**	**75.3**	**77.2**	71.2	55.6
MS-TCN (Dual-stream)	85.4	81.3	84.3	81.9	72.8

As shown in Table 1, we find that our method can obtain an accuracy improvement compared with other variants. Furthermore, as an ablation study, we can find that the BPB and Focal loss can improve the action segmentation.

Compared to the MS-TCN (RGB-only), our method is better when only extracting RGB features. Instead of stack frames straightly, the RGB features input into MS-TCN is computed from I3D [4] model, which is pre-trained by a substantial professional action dataset Kinetics-400. It should have performed better than Resnet-50 pretrained from ImageNet. We argue that MS-TCN's architecture with a big temporal receptive field is not fit for our task. Our task is a set of short periodical segments, which means the individual segment is analyzed independently. MS-TCN can capture long-term temporal relations thanks to the stacked dilated temporal convolution structures. However, too-long temporal relations may confuse the model instead. MS-TCN (RGB-only) also performs an improvement, especially F1@0.5 compared to our method. We argue that the solid pretrained RGB features give MS-TCN a more robust recognition accuracy. In our task, there is only one action in a single video. A more accurate action boundary is more critical than action recognition accuracy. When we utilize optical flow, the MS-TCN (Dual-stream) performs a big margin improvement than all compared methods. It proves that optical flow is a powerful tool to model the motion, i.e., the movements performed by the human in our scenario. However, the extraction of optical flow is offline and computing-intensive.

5 Conclusion

We present a new method to analyze interpersonal synchronization in the untrimmed video. The method first introduce action segmentation into IS tasks, and detect the start and end of specific actions saving lots of labor. Based on our method, the synchronization rate can be easily calculated. In order to execute our method in real-time, we give up the optical flow extraction and classify the action straightly with a sliding window and simple Resnet backbone. The method can handle 200 frames per second on RTX 3090. To further improve the accuracy of our method, we incorporate a boundary prediction branch as a complementary. Focal loss is utilized to address the unbalance problem in boundary prediction. After the post-process module, our pipeline outputs predictions better than widely-used action segmentation methods.

6 Future Works

We need to give up the optical flow extraction to make our system real-time. However, from the experiment results, we can observe that dynamic motion features significantly benefit the segmentation model. Moreover, the human pose is a strong prior knowledge in IS tasks and a characteristic clue for dynamic motion. Therefore, exploring the dynamic temporal skeleton displacement pattern should be beneficial for IS task.

References

1. Bernieri, F.J.: Coordinated movement and rapport in teacher-student interactions. J. Nonverbal Behav. **12**(2), 120–138 (1988)
2. Bertamini, G., Bentenuto, A., Perzolli, S., Paolizzi, E., Furlanello, C., Venuti, P.: Quantifying the child-therapist interaction in ASD intervention: an observational coding system. Brain Sci. **11**(3), 366 (2021)
3. Brezis, R.S., Noy, L., Alony, T., Gotlieb, R., Cohen, R., Golland, Y., Levit-Binnun, N.: Patterns of joint improvisation in adults with autism spectrum disorder. Front. Psychol. **8**, 1790 (2017)
4. Carreira, J., Zisserman, A.: Quo vadis, action recognition? a new model and the kinetics dataset. In: proceedings of the IEEE Conference on Computer Vision and Pattern Recognition, pp. 6299–6308 (2017)
5. Cirelli, L.K., Trehub, S.E., Trainor, L.J.: Rhythm and melody as social signals for infants. Ann. N. Y. Acad. Sci. **1423**(1), 66–72 (2018)
6. Farha, Y.A., Gall, J.: MS-TCN: multi-stage temporal convolutional network for action segmentation. In: IEEE Conference on Computer Vision and Pattern Recognition, pp. 3575–3584 (2019)
7. Fitzpatrick, P., Frazier, J.A., Cochran, D.M., Mitchell, T., Coleman, C., Schmidt, R.: Impairments of social motor synchrony evident in autism spectrum disorder. Front. Psychol. **7**, 1323 (2016)
8. He, K., Zhang, X., Ren, S., Sun, J.: Deep residual learning for image recognition. In: Proceedings of the IEEE conference on computer vision and pattern recognition, pp. 770–778 (2016)

9. Ishikawa, Y., Kasai, S., Aoki, Y., Kataoka, H.: Alleviating over-segmentation errors by detecting action boundaries. In: Proceedings of the IEEE/CVF Winter Conference on Applications of Computer Vision, pp. 2322–2331 (2021)
10. Kaur, M., Srinivasan, S.M., Bhat, A.N.: Comparing motor performance, praxis, coordination, and interpersonal synchrony between children with and without autism spectrum disorder (ASD). Res. Dev. Disabil. **72**, 79–95 (2018)
11. Kellerman, A.M., Schwichtenberg, A., Abu-Zhaya, R., Miller, M., Young, G.S., Ozonoff, S.: Dyadic synchrony and responsiveness in the first year: Associations with autism risk. Autism Res. **13**(12), 2190–2201 (2020)
12. Koehne, S., Hatri, A., Cacioppo, J.T., Dziobek, I.: Perceived interpersonal synchrony increases empathy: insights from autism spectrum disorder. Cognition **146**, 8–15 (2016)
13. Levenshtein, V.I., et al.: Binary codes capable of correcting deletions, insertions, and reversals. In: Soviet physics doklady, vol. 10, pp. 707–710. Soviet Union (1966)
14. Lin, T.Y., Goyal, P., Girshick, R., He, K., Dollár, P.: Focal loss for dense object detection. In: IEEE International Conference on Computer Vision, pp. 2999–3007 (2017). https://doi.org/10.1109/ICCV.2017.324
15. Liu, J., et al.: Early screening of autism in toddlers via response-to-instructions protocol. IEEE Trans. Cybern. **52**, 3914–3924 (2020)
16. McNaughton, K.A., Redcay, E.: Interpersonal synchrony in autism. Curr. Psychiatry Rep. **22**(3), 1–11 (2020)
17. Noel, J.P., De Niear, M.A., Lazzara, N.S., Wallace, M.T.: Uncoupling between multisensory temporal function and nonverbal turn-taking in autism spectrum disorder. IEEE Trans. Cogn. Dev. Syst. **10**(4), 973–982 (2017)
18. Qin, H., et al.: Vision-based pointing estimation and evaluation in toddlers for autism screening. In: International Conference on Intelligent Robotics and Applications, pp. 177–185 (2021)
19. Redmon, J., Divvala, S.K., Girshick, R.B., Farhadi, A.: You only look once: Unified, real-time object detection. In: 2016 IEEE Conference on Computer Vision and Pattern Recognition, CVPR 2016, Las Vegas, NV, USA, June 27–30, 2016. pp. 779–788. IEEE Computer Society (2016). https://doi.org/10.1109/CVPR.2016.91
20. Richardson, M.J., Marsh, K.L., Isenhower, R.W., Goodman, J.R., Schmidt, R.C.: Rocking together: Dynamics of intentional and unintentional interpersonal coordination. Hum. Mov. Sci. **26**(6), 867–891 (2007)
21. Tarr, B., Launay, J., Cohen, E., Dunbar, R.: Synchrony and exertion during dance independently raise pain threshold and encourage social bonding. Biol. Let. **11**(10), 20150767 (2015)
22. Twenge, J.M., Baumeister, R.F., DeWall, C.N., Ciarocco, N.J., Bartels, J.M.: Social exclusion decreases prosocial behavior. J. Pers. Soc. Psychol. **92**(1), 56 (2007)
23. Wang, Z., Liu, J., He, K., Xu, Q., Xu, X., Liu, H.: Screening early children with autism spectrum disorder via response-to-name protocol. IEEE Trans. Ind. Informatics **17**(1), 587–595 (2021). https://doi.org/10.1109/TII.2019.2958106
24. Zhang, L., Wei, K., Li, J.: Interpersonal motor synchronization in children. Adv. Psychol. Sci. **30**, 623–634 (2022). (in Chinese)

Graph Convolutional Networks Based on Relational Attention Mechanism for Autism Spectrum Disorders Diagnosis

Junbin Mao[1], Yu Sheng[1], Wei Lan[3], Xu Tian[1], Jin Liu[1(✉)], and Yi Pan[2(✉)]

[1] Hunan Province Key Lab on Bioinformatics, School of Computer Science and Engineering, Central South University, Changsha 410083, China
liujin06@csu.edu.cn
[2] Faculty of Computer Science and Control Engineering, Shenzhen Institute of Advanced Technology, Chinese Academy of Sciences, Shenzhen 518055, China
yi.pan@siat.ac.cn
[3] School of Computer, Electronics and Information, Guangxi University, Nanning 530004, China

Abstract. Nowadays, Autism spectrum disorder (ASD) is a neurodevelopmental disorder that severely affects social communication. The diagnostic criteria depend on clinicians' subjective judgment of the patient's behavioral criteria. Obviously, it is an urgent problem to establish an objective diagnosis method for patients with ASD. To address this problem, we propose a novel graph convolutional network(GCN) method based on relational attention mechanism. Firstly, we extract functional connectivity (FC) between brain regions from functional magnetic resonance (fMRI) effects that respond to blood oxygenation signals in the brain. Considering the different relationships between subjects, population relations are then modeled by graph structural models as a way to jointly learn population information. Finally, for individual-specific information, a relational attention mechanism is used to generate relationships between subjects and GCN is utilized to learn their unique representational information. Our proposed method is evaluated 871 subjects (including 403 ASD subjects and 468 typical control (TC) subjects) from the Autism Brain Imaging Data Exchange (ABIDE). The experimental results show that the mean accuracy and AUC values of our proposed method can obtained 90.57% and 90.51%, respectively. Our proposed method has achieved state-of-the-art performance in the diagnosis of ASD compared to some methods published in recent years. Overall, our method is effective and informative in guiding clinical practices.

Keywords: Autism spectrum disorder · Graph convolutional network · Relational attention mechanism · Functional magnetic resonance images

H. Liu et al. (Eds.): ICIRA 2022, LNAI 13455, pp. 341–348, 2022.
https://doi.org/10.1007/978-3-031-13844-7_33

1   Introduction

Autism spectrum disorder is a neurodevelopmental brain disorder. Currently, the diagnosis of ASD relies primarily on the behavioral symptoms of the patient. This approach requires a subjective diagnosis by a specialized physician. Therefore, it is necessary to develop an objective and accurate diagnostic method for the classification of ASD [2].

Functional magnetic resonance imaging (fMRI) is a non-invasive technique for functional brain imaging [11]. The fMRI-based extracted FC reflects the interrelationship and temporal connectivity between different brain regions and is therefore commonly extracted as a feature in ASD classification tasks [8,13]. Functional connectivity can be calculated by time series of regions of interest (ROI) of existing brain atlas.

Graph neural networks have received increasing attention due to their powerful graph learning capabilities for modeling non-Euclidean structured data. Parisot *et al.* [10] used the similarity of demographic information to define the structure of the population graph and used FC as a node feature to achieve the classification of ASD by graph node classification. Wang *et al.* [12] used graph convolutional networks for ASD prediction of FC with different brain altas. However, none of the above graph convolutional neural networks generate information relations adaptively for different individuals in the population, such that they cannot learn the unique information of individuals well.

Based on the above analysis, to improve the ASD recognition performance of GCN, we propose a novel graph convolutional neural network based on relational attention mechanism to classify ASD subjects based on FC data extracted from fMRI.

2   Methods

The overall flow chart of our proposed ASD diagnosis method is shown in Fig. 1. As can be seen from Fig. 1, our proposed method mainly consists of five steps: a) data acquisition and preprocessing, b) population graph construction by demographic information and FC, c) relationship attention mechanism to generate individual relationships and information learning by graph convolutional neural network, and d) multilayer perceptron(MLP) for classification. Next, we describe our proposed method in detail.

2.1   Data Acquisition and Preprocessing

The fMRI data of each subject used in this study are provided by the Autism Brain Imaging Data Exchange (ABIDE). We select 871 subjects who met the imaging quality and phenotypic information criteria used by Abraham et al. [1], including 403 ASD subjects and 468 typical control (TC) subjects.

We then use the Pearson correlation coefficient (PCC) to calculate the brain area correlations of the subjects based on their time series in different brain regions. Afterwards, we obtain a functional connectivity matrix for each subject with row and column dimensions consistent with brain area dimensions. The upper triangle of the matrix for each subject is then used as the feature representation.

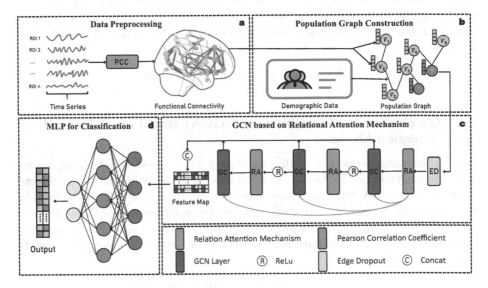

Fig. 1. An overall flow chart of GCN based on relational attention mechanism for ASD diagnosis

2.2 Population Graph Construction

We perform graph reconstruction using demographic information and FC, expecting to obtain an adjacency matrix of the basic population graph. Specifically, we use similarity distance measure based on Gaussian kernel for FC between subjects to generate a similarity connectivity matrix. The matrix $S \in \mathbb{R}^{N \times N}$, where N is the number of subjects. The formula for calculating the adjacency matrix is defined as follows:

$$S_{i,j} = \exp\left(-\frac{\|n_i - n_j\|_2^2}{2\sigma^2}\right) \tag{1}$$

where n_i and n_j represent the feature vector representations of subjects i and j, respectively; σ is the width of Gaussian kernel; Specifically, for a class of demographic information D, we consider subjects i and j to be intrinsically linked if D_i and D_j are similar to identical to each other. After that, we use the subject' multiple types of demographic information links to construct a phenotypic relationship matrix $P \in \mathbb{R}^{N \times N}$, where N is the number of subjects. The formula is defined as follows:

$$P\left(D_m(i), D_m(j)\right) = \begin{cases} 1, \text{ if } D_m(i) = D_m(j) \\ 0, \text{ if } D_m(i) \neq D_m(j) \end{cases} \tag{2}$$

where $P(D_m(i), D_m(j))$ represents the phenotypic connectivity of m-th demographic information between subject i and j, $D_m(i)$ represents the m-th demographic information of subject i, θ is a constant parameter. Finally, the population graph A of subjects can be obtained from the similarity concatenation matrix S and the phenotypic relationship matrix P by matrix dot product, as follows:

$$A(i,j) = S_{i,j} \sum_{m=1}^{M} P(D_m(i), D_m(j)) \tag{3}$$

2.3   Graph Convolutional Network (GCN) Based on Relational Attention Mechanism

Due to the static properties of the population graph constructed above, we use a relational attention mechanism to learn specific information between subjects. Specifically, we first filter more valuable subject relationships from the population graph by threshold, and then generate more informative relationships by learning their unique information from between pairs of subjects through the relationship attention mechanism. The relational attention mechanism can be expressed as follows:

$$\alpha_{ij} = \frac{1}{M} \sum_{m=1}^{M} \frac{\exp\left(\sigma\left(a_m^T [W_m h_i \| W_m h_j]\right)\right)}{\sum_{k \in N_i} \exp\left(\sigma\left(a_m^T [W_m h_i \| W_m h_k]\right)\right)} \tag{4}$$

where α_{ij} is the normalize relational attention weight and N_i is the neighboring population with which subject i is associated. h_i and h_j are the subject's feature vector, T denotes the transpose, $\|$ denotes the concatenate operation, M is the number of heads in the multi-head relational attention mechanism, a_m is the relational attention operator of the m-th head, and W_m is the learnable weight parameter of the m-th head, σ is activation function.

GCN Model: The population graph consists of edges (relationships) and nodes (subjects) to characterize the connections between nodes and nodes in the population graph. For the node features X in the population graph, the adjacency matrix G, we can obtain the representation of the graph convolution on the population graph: $X * G = UG_\theta U^T X$, where U is the eigenvector obtained by decomposing the graph Laplace matrix and $G_\theta = \text{diag}\left(U^T G\right)$.

To reduce calculation costs $O\left(N^2\right)$, Chebyshev graph convolution uses Chebyshev polynomials to approximate the spectral graph convolution. Introducing the polynomial, let $G_\theta = \sum_{i=0}^{k-1} \theta_i \Lambda^i, \theta \in R^k$, where k is the order of the Chebyshev polynomial. So that the following equation is obtained:

$$X * G = \sum_{i=0}^{k-1} \theta_i T_i(\tilde{L}) X \tag{5}$$

where $\tilde{L} = \frac{2L}{\lambda_{max}} - I$, $\tilde{L}$ is the rescaled graph Laplace operator. Similar to CNN, the polynomial $T_k(\tilde{L})$ is a K-order domain aggregator that aggregates the information of neighboring nodes at K steps from the central node.

2.4 MLP for Classification

After learning the population information of the disease by Chebyshev graph convolution, we obtain the deep feature representations generated by the three-layer graph convolution layer. Then, we fuse the three-layer features into one feature map by concat operation. Finally, we classify the feature map using a 2-layer MLP. The first layer of MLP weights $W_1 \in \mathbb{R}^{I \times H}$, The Second layer of MLP weights $W_2 \in \mathbb{R}^{H \times C}$, where I is the dimension of the input feature map, H is the number of hidden neurons, C is the number of classes of subjects.

3 Experiments Settings

To validate and evaluate the superiority and stability of our proposed method. We perform a 5-fold cross-validation experiment on the ABIDE (871 subjects) public dataset and repeat the experiment 10 times. We first compare with traditional machine learning methods and deep learning methods that have recently achieved relatively good results in disease prediction. Then, to validate the robustness of our method, we evaluate the dataset on ABIDE with multiple atlas. Finally, to verify the validity of our proposed relational attention mechanism, we conducted ablation experiments on it.

4 Results and Discussion

4.1 Ablation Experiments

In this section, to verify the effectiveness of our proposed relational attention mechanism, we perform ablation experiments to validate it. Specifically, we use one-three layer graph convolution network to experiment, and select the best performance as the backbone, on which the relational attention mechanism is added separately for experimental validation. The results are listed as follows:

Table 1. The performance of ablation experiments with different GCN layers.

Method	ACC (%)	AUC (%)	SEN (%)	SPE (%)
1 GCN Layer	78.9 ± 0.42	79.03 ± 0.42	78.48 ± 1.26	79.58 ± 1.32
2 GCN Layer	80.07 ± 1.21	80.00 ± 1.27	80.94 ± 1.93	79.06 ± 2.93
3 GCN Layer	81.69 ± 0.71	81.72 ± 0.74	81.32 ± 0.85	82.68 ± 0.63
Ours	$\mathbf{90.57 \pm 0.68}$	$\mathbf{90.51 \pm 0.64}$	$\mathbf{91.399 \pm 1.47}$	$\mathbf{89.87 \pm 1.69}$

As can be seen in Table 1, our method improves 9% in classification performance based on the three-layer graph convolution layer, which fully demonstrates the effectiveness of the relational attention mechanism.

4.2 Effect of Different Brain Atlas

In this section, we use the FC of several atlas from the ABIDE dataset, including the seven atlases of ez, tt, aal, ho, cc200, cc400, and dosenbach. Validation by FC of seven atlas enables to effectively evaluate the robustness of our method under different heterogeneous data. The results are listed as follows:

Table 2. The performance of multi-atlas experiments for ASD/TC classification.

Atlas	ACC (%)	AUC (%)	SEN (%)	SPE (%)	ROIS
tt	89.36 ± 0.53	89.27 ± 0.56	90.41 ± 1.15	88.14 ± 1.43	97
ho	90.47 ± 0.67	90.41 ± 0.66	91.18 ± 1.51	89.65 ± 1.51	111
ez	90.55 ± 0.78	90.51 ± 0.81	91.11 ± 1.28	89.90 ± 1.83	116
aal	**90.57 ± 0.68**	**90.51 ± 0.64**	**91.39 ± 1.47**	**89.87 ± 1.69**	**116**
dosenbach	90.62 ± 0.72	90.56 ± 0.76	91.30 ± 0.73	89.83 ± 1.54	161
cc200	90.80 ± 0.63	90.73 ± 0.64	91.67 ± 1.07	89.80 ± 1.25	200
cc400	90.84 ± 0.87	90.72 ± 0.89	92.26 ± 0.71	88.18 ± 1.28	392

From Table 2, it can be seen that the performance results of the seven atlases are relatively close, and it can be concluded that our proposed method has some robustness under heterogeneous data. Also, the results in Table 2 show that there is a small improvement in the performance of the model as the number of brain regions increases. It can be concluded that the detailed division of brain functional connectivity better reflects the information of the disease.

4.3 Comparison with Other Methods

In this section, we report the classification performance of our method on ASD/TC compared to traditional machine learning methods, The results are listed as follows:

Table 3. The performance of different methods for ASD/TC classification.

Method	ACC (%)	AUC (%)	SEN (%)	SPE (%)
RBF-SVC [3]	66.70	–	62.38	72.35
LDA [9]	77.70	–	76.00	82.80
PGCN [10]	69.80 ± 3.35	70.32 ± 3.90	73.35 ± 7.74	80.27 ± 6.48
Multi-GCN [7]	69.24 ± 5.90	70.04 ± 4.22	70.93 ± 4.68	74.33 ± 6.07
InceptionGCN [5]	72.69 ± 2.37	72.81 ± 1.94	80.29 ± 5.10	74.41 ± 6.22
LSTMGCN [6]	74.92 ± 7.74	74.71 ± 7.92	78.57 ± 11.6	78.87 ± 7.79
EV-GCN [4]	85.90 ± 4.47	84.72 ± 4.27	88.23 ± 7.18	79.90 ± 7.37
Ours	**90.57 ± 0.68**	**90.51 ± 0.64**	**91.39 ± 1.47**	**89.87 ± 1.69**

According to Table 3, we can see that even compared to the state-of-the-art method EV-GCN, our proposed method has a performance improvement of almost 5%. Also, from the standard deviation of 10 experiments, we can conclude that our method shows a high stability.

5 Conclusion

In this study, we propose a novel graph convolutional network based on relational attention mechanism to classify ASD. We evaluate and validated our method on ABIDE and achieve state-of-the-art performance. Subsequently, we demonstrated the effectiveness and rationality of our method through ablation experiments, comparison experiments with other methods, and different brain atlas experiments. Overall, our study provide important guidance and lay a foundation for further exploration of the direction of ASD diagnosis.

Acknowledgment. This work is supported in part by the Natural Science Foundation of Hunan Province under Grant (No.2022JJ30753), the Science and Technology Base and Talent Special Project of Guangxi (No. AD20159044), the Shenzhen Science and Technology Program (No. KQTD20200820113106007) and the National Natural Science Foundation of China under Grant (No.61877059).

References

1. Abraham, A., et al.: Deriving reproducible biomarkers from multi-site resting-state data: an autism-based example. Neuroimage **147**, 736–745 (2017)
2. Amendah, D., Grosse, S.D., Peacock, G., Mandell, D.S.: The economic costs of autism: a review. Autism Spectrum Disorders 1347–1360 (2011)
3. Brahim, A., Farrugia, N.: Graph fourier transform of fMRI temporal signals based on an averaged structural connectome for the classification of neuroimaging. Artif. Intell. Med. **106**, 101870 (2020)
4. Huang, Y., Chung, A.C.S.: Edge-variational graph convolutional networks for uncertainty-aware disease prediction. In: Martel, A.L., et al. (eds.) MICCAI 2020. LNCS, vol. 12267, pp. 562–572. Springer, Cham (2020). https://doi.org/10.1007/978-3-030-59728-3_55
5. Kazi, A., et al.: InceptionGCN: receptive field aware graph convolutional network for disease prediction. In: Chung, A.C.S., Gee, J.C., Yushkevich, P.A., Bao, S. (eds.) IPMI 2019. LNCS, vol. 11492, pp. 73–85. Springer, Cham (2019). https://doi.org/10.1007/978-3-030-20351-1_6
6. Kazi, A., et al.: Graph convolution based attention model for personalized disease prediction. In: Shen, D., et al. (eds.) MICCAI 2019. LNCS, vol. 11767, pp. 122–130. Springer, Cham (2019). https://doi.org/10.1007/978-3-030-32251-9_14
7. Kazi, A., Shekarforoush, S., Kortuem, K., Albarqouni, S., Navab, N., et al.: Self-attention equipped graph convolutions for disease prediction. In: 2019 IEEE 16th International Symposium on Biomedical Imaging (ISBI 2019), pp. 1896–1899. IEEE (2019)
8. Liu, J., Sheng, Y., Lan, W., Guo, R., Wang, Y., Wang, J.: Improved ASD classification using dynamic functional connectivity and multi-task feature selection. Pattern Recogn. Lett. **138**, 82–87 (2020)

9. Mostafa, S., Tang, L., Wu, F.X.: Diagnosis of autism spectrum disorder based on eigenvalues of brain networks. IEEE Access **7**, 128474–128486 (2019)
10. Parisot, S., et al.: Disease prediction using graph convolutional networks: application to autism spectrum disorder and Alzheimer's disease. Med. Image Anal. **48**, 117–130 (2018)
11. Takerkart, S., Auzias, G., Thirion, B., Ralaivola, L.: Graph-based inter-subject pattern analysis of FfMRI data. PLoS ONE **9**(8), e104586 (2014)
12. Wang, Y., Liu, J., Xiang, Y., Wang, J., Chen, Q., Chong, J.: Mage: automatic diagnosis of autism spectrum disorders using multi-atlas graph convolutional networks and ensemble learning. Neurocomputing **469**, 346–353 (2022)
13. Wang, Y., Wang, J., Wu, F.X., Hayrat, R., Liu, J.: Aimafe: autism spectrum disorder identification with multi-atlas deep feature representation and ensemble learning. J. Neurosci. Methods **343**, 108840 (2020)

Outlier Constrained Unsupervised Domain Adaptation Algorithm for Gaze Estimation

Hanlin Zhang, Xinming Wang, Weihong Ren, Ruihan Lin, and Honghai Liu[✉]

School of Mechanical Engineering and Automation,
Harbin Institute of Technology, Shenzhen, China
honghai.liu@hit.edu.cn

Abstract. In recent years, gaze estimation has been applied to numerous application areas, such as driver monitor system, autism assessment, and so on. However, current practical gaze estimation algorithms require a large amount of data to obtain better results. The collection of gaze data requires specific equipment, and the collection process is cumbersome, tedious and lengthy. Moreover, in some scenarios, like the autism assessment scenario, it is impossible to obtain the gaze training data of autistic children due to their social communication disorders. Therefore, we need to generalize a model trained on public datasets to a new scenario without gaze ground truth labels. In this study, we tackle this problem by leveraging adversarial learning to implement domain adaptation. Besides, we propose an outlier loss to supervise the outputs of the target domain. We test our domain adaptation algorithm on the XGaze-to-MPII domain adaptation task, and achieve a performance improvement of 14.7%.

Keywords: Gaze estimation · Domain adaptation · Generative adversarial network · Outlier

1 Introduction

Eye gaze is a crucial cue indicating people's attention or their interests, helping us to understand the visual world and to interact with computer systems [20]. Due to the characteristics of the eye gaze, gaze estimation algorithms have been exploited in various applications, such as driver monitor system [17], autism screening system [22], and marketing research [19].

With the expansion of the gaze estimation application scenarios and the increase in demand, various gaze estimation algorithms have been proposed to estimate the eye gaze. Recently, appearance-based methods have been widely used to obtain eye gaze. However, present appearance-based methods have to train on large datasets. The collection procedure of the datasets is quite complex, tedious and lengthy. The researchers have to build up customized equipment to show the gaze target for subjects to stare at. Datasets preferably cover different periods, angles and illumination conditions to make the models perform well, like [24,26]. In some scenarios, these conditions are hard to achieve, and even the ground truth labels of the eye gaze are difficult to obtain, like the autism screening scenario. Due to social communication disorders, autistic patients will not follow our instructions to stare at the target object. Thus, the ground truth labels cannot be obtained. Those models applied in the field of autism cannot be trained on scenario-specific datasets and have to be trained on public datasets.

Due to the differences in subjects, background environments, and illuminations between public datasets and practical scenarios, the performance of gaze estimation models that are trained on public datasets usually dramatically degrades in unseen scenarios. Therefore, we have to implement domain adaptation to improve the performance of the model. Different domain adaption techniques have been proposed to reduce the domain shift between different domains, including fine-tune, maximum mean discrepancy [11], or correlation distance [13]. Unlike those scenarios that can obtain gaze ground truth labels, those models applied in the field of autism can only be generalized in an unsupervised manner. To reduce the domain shift between public datasets and practical scenarios, several works have been proposed by utilizing adversarial learning [21], collaborative learning [10], and synthetic images [7], which boost the research of the unsupervised domain adaptation (UDA) for gaze estimation.

In this study, to reduce the domain shift between public datasets and unlabeled application scenarios, we leverage the adversarial learning framework [4] to implement domain adaption, which is responsible for extracting domain invariant features between the source domain and target domain to perform robust gaze estimation. The conventional CNNs composed of feature extractors and fully connected layers can be easily adapted into this framework. Inspired by [10], we propose an outlier loss to supervise the outputs of the target domain in order to obtain a better result in the target domain. To summarize, we make the following contributions:

- We leverage the adversarial learning framework to perform unsupervised domain adaptation for gaze estimation, improving gaze estimation accuracy in unlabeled scenarios.
- We propose an outlier loss to supervise the target domain's outputs that lack gaze ground truth labels to obtain good gaze estimation performance in the target domain.

The remaining parts of this paper are organized as follows. In Sect. 2, we present the current research on gaze estimation and unsupervised domain adaptation. In Sect. 3, we present the methodology of our study. In Sect. 4, we present the experiments. And in Sect. 5, we conclude the paper.

2 Related Work

2.1 Gaze Estimation

Technically, gaze estimation is the procedure of determining the fixation points where someone is looking at the monitor or the eye's visual axis in 3D space. In recent years, many gaze estimation algorithms have been proposed. These algorithms can generally be classified into two main categories: 3D model-based gaze estimation algorithms and appearance-based algorithms.

3D model-based gaze estimation algorithms require users to implement eyeball parameters calibration. Researchers proposed to use RGBD camera [14,27] or RGB camera combined with infrared light source [18] to obtain the eyeball parameters. Even though the model-based methods can achieve relatively high gaze estimation accuracy compared with appearance-based methods, the customized equipment limits its application prospects. Therefore, more and more researchers favor appearance-based methods that only require off-the-shelf cameras.

Zhang et al. [25] proposed to use CNN to predict eye gaze from eye images. Although this method does not achieve a quite good result, it can handle the head movement problem and does not require user calibration. Zhang et al. [26] also proposed an algorithm that took high dimensional features from the whole face images. Lian et al. [9] proposed a multi-stream multi-task CNN model to perform gaze estimation.

Appearance-based methods are based on deep learning. One main problem of these methods is that training a mapping function requires a large amount of data. Thus, several datasets have been proposed. Zhang et al. proposed the first full-face dataset called MPIIFaceGaze [26] and a large dataset that contains 1.1M images called ETH-XGaze [24]. Funes Mora et al. proposed a video dataset called EYEDIAP [2].

2.2 Unsupervised Domain Adaptation

Since labeled data are difficult to obtain in some scenarios, unsupervised domain adaptation has been explored in recent years. Unsupervised domain adaptation approaches can be categorized into two techniques: adversarial learning and self-training.

Adversarial learning-based approaches are based on generative adversarial networks (GAN) [4]. Inspired by GAN, a lot of such methods have been proposed, such as ADDA [16], GVBGD [1], CDAN [12]. Briefly, the main idea of such methods is to narrow the gap between the source domain and the target domain by playing a min-max game. Self-training-based methods are inspired by semi-supervised learning [8] that train the models by using their reliable predictions of themselves. Such methods include Pseudo-label [8], Mean Teacher method [15].

With the increase in the number of gaze estimation applications, many researchers sought to improve the performance of gaze estimation algorithms in unlabeled scenarios. Many methods have been proposed, such as adversarial learning combined with Bayesian neural network [21], collaborative learning [10], learning specific gaze representations [23], gaze redirection [6], and so on. Here, we also employ the adversarial learning framework to implement the unsupervised domain adaptation for gaze estimation.

3 Methodology

3.1 Task Definition

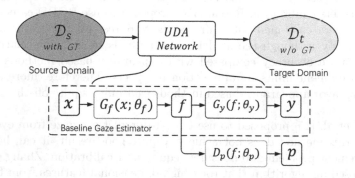

Fig. 1. Illustration of unsupervised domain adaptation for gaze estimation

Before discussing the domain adaptation method we used, we first state the problem scenario. As shown in Fig. 1, We denote the source domain data as $\mathcal{D}_s = \{(x_i^s, y_i^s)|_{i=1}^{N_s}\}$, where x_i^s and y_i^s denote the ith training image and corresponding gaze label that consists of pitch and yaw angle, N_s is the number of images. The target domain data that contains no ground-truth gaze label is denoted as $\mathcal{D}_t = \{(x_i^t)|_{i=1}^{N_t}\}$, where N_t is the number of images, x_i^t is the ith image.

The baseline gaze estimator consists of a feature extractor denoted as $G_f = (x; \theta_f)$ and a gaze estimator denoted as $G_y = (f; \theta_y)$. x is the input of the UDA network, f is the learned feature representation, y is the prediction of gaze and p is the domain classification result. $D_p = (f; \theta_p)$ is the discriminator.

3.2 Adversarial Learning

To implement unsupervised domain adaptation, we employ the DANN framework [3], as shown in Fig. 2. The feature extractor $G_f = (x; \theta_f)$ learns feature representations f^s and f^t from source domain inputs x^s and target domain inputs x^t. Then the feature representations are fed into the gaze estimator $G_y = (f; \theta_y)$ and the domain discriminator $D_p = (f; \theta_p)$ respectively to predict the gaze vector that consists of pitch and yaw angle and the probability that judges whether the inputs come from the source domain.

Since the images of the target domain lack of gaze labels, in order to ensure the predictive capability of the model, we use L_1 loss (1) to supervise the outputs corresponding to the source domain images.

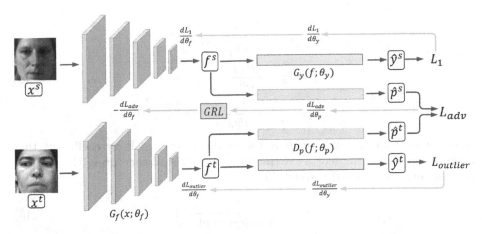

Fig. 2. Illustration of the adversarial learning method. The models in the upper half and the model in the lower half are the same. The red arrows represent the information flow of the forward propagation. The orange arrows represent the information flow of the backpropagation. $G_f(x; \theta_f)$ represents the feature extractor consisting of convolutional and fully connected layers. $G_y(f; \theta_y)$ that contains only fully connected layers is the gaze estimator. $D_p(f; \theta_p)$ is the discriminator that contains fully connected layers. GRL is the gradient reversal layer. x^s and x^t are the inputs from the source domain and target domain. f^s and f^t are the learned feature representations corresponding to the source and target inputs. $\hat{y}^s$ and $\hat{y}^t$ are the gaze predictions corresponding to the source domain and target domain. $\hat{p}^s$ and $\hat{p}^t$ are the domain classification results corresponding to the source inputs and target inputs. (Color figure online)

$$L_1 = \frac{1}{N_s} \sum_{i=1}^{N_s} |\hat{y}_i^s - y_i^s| \tag{1}$$

For the discriminator, its goal is to differentiate images from the source domain or target domain. When the feature extractor confuses the discriminator, the domain shift between the source domain and target domain has been narrowed, and the performance of the gaze estimator will be improved. In order to fool the discriminator, the gradient reversal layer is inserted between the feature extractor and discriminator, making the gradient passed by multiplying a negative coefficient. In this way, the feature extractor is optimized towards maximizing the adversarial loss function. In the view of stochastic gradient descent algorithm, the way of parameter update of feature extractor, discriminator and gaze estimator is shown in Eq. (2).

$$\theta_f = \theta_f - u\left(\frac{\partial L_1}{\partial \theta_f} - \alpha\frac{\partial L_{adv}}{\partial \theta_f}\right)$$

$$\theta_y = \theta_y - u\frac{\partial L_1}{\partial \theta_y} \tag{2}$$

$$\theta_p = \theta_p - u\frac{\partial L_{adv}}{\partial \theta_p}$$

where u is the learning rate, α is the gradient reversal layer coefficient that is used to balance the feature extractor and discriminator during the training process and is computed through Eq. (3).

$$\alpha = \frac{2}{1 + \exp(-\gamma \cdot p)} - 1 \tag{3}$$

where γ is used to adjust the balance of feature extractor and discriminator, p is the training progress.

For the adversarial loss function, we use the binary cross-entropy (4).

$$L_{adv} = -\frac{1}{N_t}\sum_{i=1}^{N_t}\log(1 - D_p(G_f(x_i;\theta_f);\theta_p)) - \frac{1}{N_s}\sum_{i=1}^{N_s}\log(D_p(G_f(x_i;\theta_f);\theta_p)) \tag{4}$$

However, as [21] points out, the term $\log(1 - D_p(G_f(x_i;\theta_f);\theta_p))$ may cause vanishing gradient when we minimize (4). Therefore, we modify (4) to (5).

$$L_{adv} = -\frac{1}{N_t}\sum_{i=1}^{N_t}\log(D_p(G_f(x_i;\theta_f);\theta_p)) \tag{5}$$

3.3   Outlier Loss

Inspired by [10], after each epoch of training, we use the trained model to build the normal distribution on the source domain and the target domain through the following equations:

$$\mu_k = \frac{1}{N}\sum_{i=1}^{N}\hat{y}_{i,k-1}, \sigma_k^2 = \frac{1}{N-1}\sum_{i=1}^{N}(\hat{y}_{i,k-1} - \mu_k)^2 \tag{6}$$

where μ_k is the mean value of the normal distribution of kth epoch, σ_k^2 is the variance, N represents the number of source domain images or target domain images, $\hat{y}_{i,k-1}$ represents the prediction of the source domain data or target domain data in $(k-1)$th epoch.

Empirically, in training epoch k, we define the target domain output $\hat{y}_i^t$ as the reliable output when $|\frac{\hat{y}_i^t - \mu^t}{\sigma^t}| \leq \mu_{1-\epsilon}^t$ and the source domain output $\hat{y}_i^s$ as the reliable output when $|\frac{\hat{y}_i^s - \mu^s}{\sigma^s}| \leq \mu_{1-\epsilon}^s$. ϵ indicates the significance level of judging an output as an outlier. After filtering out the outliers, we punish them

---

Algorithm 1: Adversarial Training Process

Input: Source domain data $\mathcal{D}_s = \{(x_i^s, y_i^s)|_{i=1}^{N_s}\}$, Target domain data
$\mathcal{D}_t = \{(x_i^t)|_{i=1}^{N_t}\}$, Source domain pretrained model $G_s = (x; \theta_f^s, \theta_y^s)$
Output: Target domain model $G_t = (x; \theta_f^t, \theta_y^t)$
Initialization: $\theta_f^t = \theta_f^s$, $\theta_y^t = \theta_y^s$, $\theta_p^s = \mathcal{N}(0, \sigma I)$, $\theta_p^t = \mathcal{N}(0, \sigma I)$, total training
epochs T
for $i \leftarrow 1$ **to** T **do**

    Sample a batch of data from source and target: $(x^s, y^s) \sim \mathcal{D}_s, (x^t) \sim \mathcal{D}_t$
    if $i > 1$ **then**

        Update θ_y^t with (x^s, y^s) and (x^t): $\theta_y^t \leftarrow \theta_y^t - u(\frac{\partial L_1}{\partial \theta_y} + \frac{\partial L_{outlier}}{\partial \theta_y})$

        Update θ_p^t with (x^s) and (x^t): $\theta_p^t \leftarrow \theta_p^t - u\frac{\partial L_{adv}}{\partial \theta_p}$

        Update θ_f^t with (x^s, y^s) and (x^t): $\theta_f^t \leftarrow \theta_f^t - u(\frac{\partial L_1}{\theta_f} + \frac{\partial L_{outlier}}{\partial \theta_f} - \alpha\frac{\partial L_a dv}{\partial \theta_f})$

    else

        Update θ_y^t with (x^s, y^s) and (x^t): $\theta_y^t \leftarrow \theta_y^t - u\frac{\partial L_1}{\partial \theta_y}$

        Update θ_p^t with (x^s) and (x^t): $\theta_p^t \leftarrow \theta_p^t - u\frac{\partial L_{adv}}{\partial \theta_p}$

        Update θ_f^t with (x^s, y^s) and (x^t): $\theta_f^t \leftarrow \theta_f^t - u(\frac{\partial L_1}{\theta_f} - \alpha\frac{\partial L_{adv}}{\partial \theta_f})$

    end

    Use i-th epoch model to build normal distributions $\mathcal{N}_t(\mu_t, \sigma_t^2)$ and
    $\mathcal{N}_s(\mu_s, \sigma_s^2)$ with source domain data $\mathcal{D}_s = \{(x_i^s, y_i^s)|_{i=1}^{N_s}\}$ and target domain
    data $\mathcal{D}_t = \{(x_i^t)|_{i=1}^{N_t}\}$
end

---

with a larger gradient. But practically we found that only when we define the reliable interval as $\frac{\hat{y}_i^t - \mu^t}{\sigma^t} < \mu_{1-\epsilon}^t$ and $\frac{\hat{y}_i^s - \mu_s}{\sigma^s} > \mu_{1-\epsilon}^s$, can the outlier loss improve the performance of domain adaptation. Thus, the overall outlier loss is shown as follows:

$$L_{outlier} = \mathbb{1}_{[\frac{\hat{y}_i^t - \mu^t}{\sigma^t} < \mu_{1-\epsilon}^t]} |\frac{\hat{y}_i^t - \mu^t}{\sigma^t}| + \mathbb{1}_{[\frac{\hat{y}_i^s - \mu^s}{\sigma^s} > \mu_{1-\epsilon}^s]} |\frac{\hat{y}_i^s - \mu^s}{\sigma^s}| \qquad (7)$$

In conclusion, the overall loss function of the unsupervised domain adaptation is:

$$L_{total} = \lambda_1 \cdot L_1 + \lambda_2 \cdot L_{adv} + \lambda_3 \cdot L_{outlier} \qquad (8)$$

where λ_1, λ_2, λ_3 are the loss trade-off parameters.

Finally, we summarize the training process in Algorithm 1. After training, we will discard the discriminator pathway and only use the baseline gaze estimator to predict gaze.

4 Experiments

4.1 Datasets

In order to evaluate our UDA method, we use two of the most popular gaze estimation datasets to perform domain adaptation: ETH-XGaze [24] and MPI-IFaceGaze [26]. The characteristics of these two datasets are described as follows:

ETH-XGaze. ETH-XGaze dataset contains 1.1M images collected from 110 participants (63 males and 47 females). The data is collected in a laboratory where it is easy to control the illumination conditions. Besides, the researchers set up multiple cameras to capture the participants' gaze images from different angles, which can cover a wide range of headpose. The gaze angle range of pitch covers $-70°-70°$, and the gaze angle range of yaw covers $-120°-120°$.

MPIIFaceGaze. MPIIFaceGaze dataset contains 45,000 images collected from 15 participants. The data is collected with laptops and covers different genders (9 males and 6 females), varying illuminations and facial appearances. During the collection procedure, participants were asked to fixate on moving dots randomly shown on the screen. The gaze angle range of pitch covers $-40°-20°$, and gaze angle range of yaw covers $-40°-40°$.

4.2 Implementation Details

During the training process, we use 80% images of each person in MPIIFaceGaze to implement domain adaptation and 20% images to evaluate the performance of the adapted model. The number of images of the ETH-XGaze dataset we used in training is the same as those in MPIIFaceGaze. And each image is resized to 224×224.

As for the details of the model, we use Resnet-50 [5] as the backbone of feature extractor. Followed the output of Resnet-50, we concat a fully connected layer to reduce the feature dimension to 256 dimensions. The details of gaze estimator and discriminator are as follows: (1) $G_y(f; \theta_y)$(FC(2)); (2) $D_p(f; \theta_p)$(FC(128), BatchNorm(128), LeakyReLU(0.2), Dropout(0.5), FC(1), Sigmoid).

As for the hyperparameters, we set learning rate $u = 1^{-5}$, training epochs $T = 15$, batch size $b = 32$, loss trade-off parameters $\lambda_1 = 1, \lambda_2 = 1, \lambda_3 = 0.01$ respectively. We use SGD optimizer with momentum $m = 0.9$.

4.3   Results

Table 1. UDA results

Methods	Error/degree
Source only	7.10
DANN [3]	6.52
Ours	**6.05**

The unsupervised domain adaptation results are shown in Table 1. The result of source only is acquired by directly applying the source domain pretrained model to the target domain. The error of this source domain pretrained model tested on the source domain is 4.4°. We can see that by directly applying the source domain pretrained model to the target domain, the accuracy of the model will degrade due to the existence of domain shift. After adapting the model using DANN in an unsupervised manner, the error of the model tested on the target domain drops to 6.52°, and the model achieves a performance improvement of 8.2%.

Since the adversarial learning based domain adaptation method is not stable in the task of regression domain adaptation, it will produce many outlier results during the process of feature alignment. Thus, our proposed outlier loss can help punish the outlier prediction result with a larger gradient, helping the model converges to get a better result. After introducing the outlier loss, the error of the model drops to 6.05°. It achieves a performance improvement of 7.2% compared with DANN and a performance improvement of 14.7%.

5   Conclusion and Future Work

In this study, we use the generative adversarial learning framework to implement unsupervised domain adaptation for gaze estimation. By introducing the outlier loss, we further improve the performance of the gaze estimation model. We test our method on XGaze-to-MPII domain adaptation task, and achieve a performance improvement of 14.7%.

We found that even though we employ the DANN framework and outlier loss to improve the performance of the gaze model, the gaze estimation performance on some images is still unsatisfactory, such as images with large eyepose, images with dim illumination conditions, and so on. Therefore, we will further find ways to distill the essential features of gaze estimation and integrate them into the process of UDA to improve the precision of the model performance.

References

1. Cui, S., Wang, S., Zhuo, J., Su, C., Huang, Q., Tian, Q.: Gradually vanishing bridge for adversarial domain adaptation. In: Proceedings of the IEEE/CVF Conference on Computer Vision and Pattern Recognition, pp. 12455–12464 (2020)

2. Funes Mora, K.A., Monay, F., Odobez, J.M.: Eyediap: a database for the development and evaluation of gaze estimation algorithms from RGB and RGB-D cameras. In: Proceedings of the Symposium on Eye Tracking Research and Applications, pp. 255–258 (2014)
3. Ganin, Y., Lempitsky, V.: Unsupervised domain adaptation by backpropagation. In: International Conference on Machine Learning, pp. 1180–1189. PMLR (2015)
4. Goodfellow, I., et al.: Generative adversarial nets. In: Advances in Neural Information Processing Systems, vol. 27 (2014)
5. He, K., Zhang, X., Ren, S., Sun, J.: Deep residual learning for image recognition. In: Proceedings of the IEEE Conference on Computer Vision and Pattern Recognition, pp. 770–778 (2016)
6. He, Z., Spurr, A., Zhang, X., Hilliges, O.: Photo-realistic monocular gaze redirection using generative adversarial networks. In: Proceedings of the IEEE/CVF International Conference on Computer Vision, pp. 6932–6941 (2019)
7. Lahiri, A., Agarwalla, A., Biswas, P.K.: Unsupervised domain adaptation for learning eye gaze from a million synthetic images: an adversarial approach. In: Proceedings of the 11th Indian Conference on Computer Vision, Graphics and Image Processing, pp. 1–9 (2018)
8. Lee, D.H., et al.: Pseudo-label: the simple and efficient semi-supervised learning method for deep neural networks. In: Workshop on Challenges in Representation Learning, ICML, vol. 3, pp. 896 (2013)
9. Lian, D., et al.: RGBD based gaze estimation via multi-task CNN. In: Proceedings of the AAAI Conference on Artificial Intelligence, vol. 33, pp. 2488–2495 (2019)
10. Liu, Y., Liu, R., Wang, H., Lu, F.: Generalizing gaze estimation with outlier-guided collaborative adaptation. In: Proceedings of the IEEE/CVF International Conference on Computer Vision, pp. 3835–3844 (2021)
11. Long, M., Cao, Y., Wang, J., Jordan, M.: Learning transferable features with deep adaptation networks. In: International Conference on Machine Learning, pp. 97–105. PMLR (2015)
12. Long, M., Cao, Z., Wang, J., Jordan, M.I.: Conditional adversarial domain adaptation. In: Advances in Neural Information Processing systems, vol. 31 (2018)
13. Sun, B., Feng, J., Saenko, K.: Return of frustratingly easy domain adaptation. In: Proceedings of the AAAI Conference on Artificial Intelligence, vol. 30 (2016)
14. Sun, L., Liu, Z., Sun, M.T.: Real time gaze estimation with a consumer depth camera. Inf. Sci. **320**, 346–360 (2015)
15. Tarvainen, A., Valpola, H.: Mean teachers are better role models: weight-averaged consistency targets improve semi-supervised deep learning results. In: Advances in Neural Information Processing Systems, vol. 30 (2017)
16. Tzeng, E., Hoffman, J., Saenko, K., Darrell, T.: Adversarial discriminative domain adaptation. In: Proceedings of the IEEE Conference on Computer Vision and Pattern Recognition, pp. 7167–7176 (2017)
17. Vicente, F., Huang, Z., Xiong, X., De la Torre, F., Zhang, W., Levi, D.: Driver gaze tracking and eyes off the road detection system. IEEE Trans. Intell. Transp. Syst. **16**(4), 2014–2027 (2015)
18. Villanueva, A., Cabeza, R.: A novel gaze estimation system with one calibration point. IEEE Trans. Syst. Man Cybern. Part B Cybern. **38**(4), 1123–1138 (2008)
19. Wang, B., Hu, T., Li, B., Chen, X., Zhang, Z.: Gatector: a unified framework for gaze object prediction. arXiv preprint arXiv:2112.03549 (2021)
20. Wang, K., Zhao, R., Ji, Q.: Human computer interaction with head pose, eye gaze and body gestures. In: 2018 13th IEEE International Conference on Automatic Face & Gesture Recognition (FG 2018), pp. 789–789. IEEE (2018)

21. Wang, K., Zhao, R., Su, H., Ji, Q.: Generalizing eye tracking with Bayesian adversarial learning. In: Proceedings of the IEEE/CVF Conference on Computer Vision and Pattern Recognition, pp. 11907–11916 (2019)
22. Wang, Z., Liu, J., He, K., Xu, Q., Xu, X., Liu, H.: Screening early children with autism spectrum disorder via response-to-name protocol. IEEE Trans. Industr. Inf. **17**(1), 587–595 (2019)
23. Yu, Y., Odobez, J.M.: Unsupervised representation learning for gaze estimation. In: Proceedings of the IEEE/CVF Conference on Computer Vision and Pattern Recognition, pp. 7314–7324 (2020)
24. Zhang, X., Park, S., Beeler, T., Bradley, D., Tang, S., Hilliges, O.: ETH-XGaze: a large scale dataset for gaze estimation under extreme head pose and gaze variation. In: Vedaldi, A., Bischof, H., Brox, T., Frahm, J.-M. (eds.) ECCV 2020. LNCS, vol. 12350, pp. 365–381. Springer, Cham (2020). https://doi.org/10.1007/978-3-030-58558-7_22
25. Zhang, X., Sugano, Y., Fritz, M., Bulling, A.: Appearance-based gaze estimation in the wild. In: Proceedings of the IEEE Conference on Computer Vision and Pattern Recognition, pp. 4511–4520 (2015)
26. Zhang, X., Sugano, Y., Fritz, M., Bulling, A.: It's written all over your face: full-face appearance-based gaze estimation. In: Proceedings of the IEEE Conference on Computer Vision and Pattern Recognition Workshops, pp. 51–60 (2017)
27. Zhou, X., Cai, H., Li, Y., Liu, H.: Two-eye model-based gaze estimation from a Kinect sensor. In: 2017 IEEE International Conference on Robotics and Automation (ICRA), pp. 1646–1653. IEEE (2017)

Assessment System for Imitative Ability for Children with Autism Spectrum Disorder Based on Human Pose Estimation

Hanwei Ma[1,2], Bowen Chen[1], Weihong Ren[1], Ziheng Wang[1], Zhiyong Wang[3], Weibo Jiang[1], Ruihan Lin[1], and Honghai Liu[1(✉)]

[1] State Key Laboratory of Robotics and System,
Harbin Institute of Technology, Shenzhen, China
honghai.liu@hit.edu.cn
[2] Peng Cheng Laboratory, Shenzhen, China
[3] State Key Laboratory of Mechanical System and Vibration,
Shanghai Jiao Tong University, Shanghai, China

Abstract. Autism spectrum disorders is a range of neurodevelopmental conditions primarily characterized by difficulties in social interactions, differences in communication, and presentations of rigid and repetitive behavior. The evidence shows that the functional social behavior of children with autism can be enhanced by early intervention. However, traditional intervention methods meet problems, e.g., assessment results are varied from one clinician to another while sometimes children are lack of interest in intervention. To address these problems, we design a computer-aided motion imitation assessment system based on human pose estimation in this paper. The system is implemented by Unity3D. We recruit 10 people (5 people with imitation ability defect and 5 people without imitation ability defect) participated in the experiment, and the result shows that the system can effectively evaluate the motion imitation ability. Finally, three future development directions of the system are further discussed for better application in autistic early intervention.

Keywords: Autism spectrum disorder · Imitative ability · Early intervention · Human pose estimation

1 Introduction

Autism spectrum disorder (ASD) is a range of neurodevelopmental conditions primarily characterized by difficulties in social interactions, differences in communication, and presentations of rigid and repetitive behavior [1]. Children with ASD would bring about enormous costs for families and governments, including special education services and parental productivity loss [9]. ASD individuals

Supported by Peng Cheng Laboratory.

can be severely stressed due to the difficulty of proper mutual communication and being misunderstood. Because of the lack of necessary social skills, their personal lives will be impacted, and their career opportunities will be hampered, also resulting in a burden on society. It is noted that the incidence of autism is far beyond the public imagination. In the United States, the incidence rate was 1/5000 in 1975 and then increased to 1/45 in 2018 [12]. The number is still growing rapidly at an alarming rate. In 2014, the incidence rate was found to be 1/68 [2]. As for China, the prevalence was 1/142 in 2017, with ten million in total, of which a substantial proportion were children aged 0–14 years old. This ASD crisis has attracted increasing attention worldwide. Onetheless, there doesn't exist any clinical proven medicines for ASD.

Recent literature proved that some symptoms of ASD can be alleviated through human intervention training, and the effect is significant, especially in early childhood [9]. Therefore, it is of great significance for early screening, diagnosis, and early intervention of autism for children. In the field of early screening and diagnosis of autism, it is a generally considered reliable way that qualified professional clinicians to observe and record behaviors of children following specified protocols, such as autism diagnostic interview-revised and autism diagnostic observation schedule, which are considered to be the most standard tools in autism screening and diagnosis. However, the above methods are restricted by the following problems. Firstly, the qualified clinicians is rare and can not meet the demand of early diagnosis of autism. Secondly, the diagnosis is subjective and heavily relied on the clinician's experience. Therefore, the diagnose maybe unstable if the clinician changed. With the development of computer vision, more and more computer-aided screening efforts have been made in order to cope with the above challenges, such as response-to-instructions protocol proposed by [8], response-to-name protocol proposed by [15], vision-based pointing estimation and evaluation [11], and so on. These methods achieve a higher performance with a lower cost compared to traditional human-based protocols.

In the field of early intervention for autism, the challenges mentioned above in the field of early screening and diagnosis of autism also exist. Inspired by their use of computer-assisted methods to screen and diagnose autism to meet those challenges, we naturally introduced computer-assisted methods into the early intervention of children with autism. Besides, the research over the past decade has provided enough demonstrations that individuals with ASD have a strong interest in technology-based interventions [7]. Motion imitation is a commonly used subject of intervention. On the one hand, due to weaker imitation skills for the autistic group revealed by research studies, and on the other hand, imitation of body movements was concurrently and predictively associated with expressive language skills [13]. Therefore, it is essential to design a computer-aided motion imitation assessment system for autism intervention. The main contributions of the paper are summarized as follows:

1. We design a motion imitation ability assessment system implemented by Unity3D based on human pose estimation.

2. Ten participants are invited to evaluate the proposed system. The experimental results demonstrate that our system can evaluate the imitative ability effectively.
3. Three development directions of the proposed system for better autism early intervention are further discussed.

2   Method

2.1   System Design

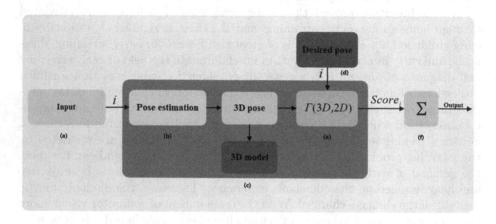

Fig. 1. Overall pipeline.

Figure 1 illustrates the overall pipeline of our computer-aided assessment system based on motion imitation for autism intervention. On the whole, the system works in a typical game design, and the more obstacles they pass, the higher their scores will be for participants. The pose of the 3D model in Fig. 1c is one-to-one corresponding to the pose of the participants, which is linked through the 3D human pose estimation network, which takes the real-time color image (Fig. 1a) of the participants captured by the camera as the input. The "obstacles" mentioned above is an intuitive and figurative expression that is embodied in the system as it is considered that the obstacle can be passed if the similarity calculated by a specific algorithm (Fig. 1e) between the 3D model pose and the desired pose (Fig. 1d) is greater than the threshold which is a hyperparameter. Finally, the scores reflecting the participants' ability to imitate will be derived from the number of obstacles that participants have passed.

In more detail, the desired pose is the 2D pose which is vertically projected from the 3D model pose, and it is pre-defined before the system runs. Suppose we define N desired poses, and they can be described by a set $P_{desired} = (p_{desired}^1, p_{desired}^2, \ldots, p_{desired}^N)$. Because the system performs the same process for each desired pose $P_{desired}^i$, we can focus on the desired pose to examine the pipeline, where $i \in [1, N]$. The system takes, as input, a color image of size $w \times h$ and produces, as output, the score corresponding to $P^i_{desired}$. First, a 3D pose estimation network (Fig. 1b) predicts a set of 3D locations of anatomical keypoints denoted as $P^i_{predicted}$ for input image, including participant, and more details about it are in Sect. 2.2. Driven by the predicted 3D keypoints, the 3D model will move synchronously with the participants, and implementation details can be found in Sect. 2.3. Then, the score $Score_i$ for current pose $P^i_{desired}$ will be uniquely determined by the abstract function $\Gamma(P^i_{predicted}, P^i_{desired})$ (Fig. 1e) which takes the pose of 3D model and the desired pose as inputs, and specific algorithm is shown in Sect. 2.4. Finally, the total score for N desired can be calculated as

$$Score_{total} = \frac{1}{N} \Sigma^N_{i=1} Score_i. \tag{1}$$

2.2   Human Pose Estimation Model

Human pose estimation (HPE) aims to locate the human body parts and build human body representation from input data such as images, videos, signals from other devices, etc. It provides an intuitively effective way to enable machines to have an insightful understanding of the behaviors of humans. For example, HPE provides geometric and motion information about the human body, which has been applied to a wide range of applications (e.g., human-computer interaction, motion analysis, augmented reality (AR), virtual reality (VR), healthcare, etc.) [4]. With the blooming of deep learning techniques and the continuous exploration of researchers from around the world in applying deep learning technology to solve the task of HPE, the performance boundary of HPE has been pushed forward significantly in recent years [3]. At present, both 2D HPE and 3D HPE have achieved high-performance estimation, especially for single-person human pose estimation [10, 14, 16]. Therefore, HPE has a great application prospect in the field of intervention for children with autism, especially tasks related to keypoints of the human body. For example, in this system, we will use the existing HPE network to drive the 3D model (Fig. 1c) in the game scene and evaluate the motion imitation ability of children with autism.

A heatmap-based 3D single-person pose estimation model will be involved in this system to solve the human pose estimation task (Fig. 1b). The model can real-time compute 3D pose from RGB images captured by the camera. Its architecture is illustrated in Fig. 2, which has three inputs named $input1$ $input4$ and $input7$, and four outputs in the form of heatmap representing different meanings. For this system, the three inputs of the above network are color images of size $448 \times 448 \times 3$, and only the third and fourth outputs will be used for the inference of human body keypoints. For clarity, we denote the third output as $offset3D$ with dimension $B \times (K \times 3 \times H) \times H \times H$ and the fourth output as $heatmap3D$ with dimension $B \times (K \times H) \times H \times H$, where B represents the batch size, H represents the heatmap size, and K represents the number of human body keypoints to be detected.

Parsing human keypoints or parts from the output of this network requires the following two steps. The first step is to roughly locate the keypoints through

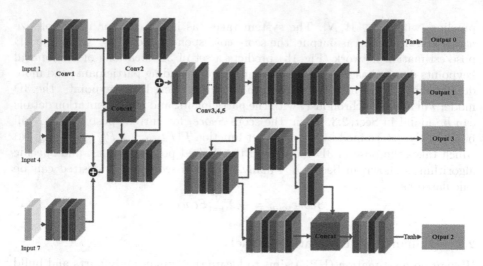

Fig. 2. Illustrating the architecture of the HPE network. Its backbone network is resnet34 proposed by [6]. The "convx" is the layer consisting of residual blocks in resnet34. The green, gray, yellow, blue, and black blocks represent convolutional layer, batch normalization, relu, max pooling and transposed convolution, respectively. The "+"will add the input feature maps. The "concat" will concatenates the input feature maps. (Color figure online)

the *heatmap3D*, and the second step is to accurately locate the keypoints through *offset3D*. More specifically, *heatmap3D* represents 3D heatmaps corresponding to K keypoints and each keypoint corresponds to a 3D heatmap with dimension $H \times H \times H$. We denote the pre-refinement and post-refinement coordinates of the k *th* keypoint as $(x^k_{rough}, y^k_{rough}, z^k_{rough})$ and $(x^k_{refine}, y^k_{refine}, z^k_{refine})$ respectively. $(x^k_{rough}, y^k_{rough}, z^k_{rough})$ can be obtained by performing the *argmax* operation on k *th* *heatmap3D* which returns the maximum value whose value represents the confidence of the keypoint and the subscript corresponding to the maximum value. *offset3D* represents 3D arrays corresponding to 3 coordinates of k *th* keypoints and each coordinate corresponds to a 3D array $Array_c$ with dimension $H \times H \times H$, where $c \in \{x, y, z\}$. Then, the refinement of the coordinates of the keypoints of the human body is done by indexing, and the process is given as follows:

$$c^k_{refine} = Array_c[x^k_{rough}, y^k_{rough}, z^k_{rough}]. \tag{2}$$

Traverse c and $(x^k_{refine}, y^k_{refine}, z^k_{refine})$ can be determined.

2.3 Implementation

Unity is a cross-platform game engine developed by Unity Technologies, which can be used to create three-dimensional (3D) and two-dimensional (2D) games as well as interactive simulations and other experiences. In addition, the Barracuda package is a lightweight cross-platform neural network inference library for Unity, which can integrate the HPE model mentioned in Sect. 2.2 into a Unity-based project. Therefore, the whole system can be implemented by Unity3D from input to output, either by calling built-in resources or by customizing $c\#$ scripts and attaching them to corresponding resources in the scene.

Fig. 3. Scene in Unity3D. The 3D model is on the track full of obstacles.

Figure 3 shows how the motion ability assessment system is designed in the Unity3D scene, which is mainly composed of a 3D model perpendicular to xz plane and a track along the z axis. The 3D model is driven by the coordinates of keypoints predicted by HPE model in Sect. 2.2 and reflects the current pose of the participant in real- time. In order to prevent abnormal jittering of keypoints and unreasonable rotation of joints, coordinate smoothing algorithms and joint rotation algorithms have been considered when driving 3D models. As for the track, N obstacles with our desired pose on it are distributed equidistantly on it. This means that participants need to make the same pose as the obstacle when passing through the obstacle. When the system starts, the 3D model will slide forward along the track over time. If the participants want to get higher scores, they should cross as many obstacles as possible.

2.4   Imitation Ability Assessment

In this section, we will introduce how the function Γ in the Fig. 1e calculates scores. This part is the key to the system because it is directly related to how to evaluate the motion imitation ability of children with autism. Since the whole game scene is designed along the z-axis, the 2D pose can be obtained by the vertical projection of the 3D pose, which can be represented by the mapping is as follows:

$$(P_{2D}^x, P_{2D}^y) = (P_{3D}^x, P_{3D}^y, P_{3D}^z) \times \begin{pmatrix} 1 & 0 & 0 \\ 0 & 1 & 0 \\ 0 & 0 & 0 \end{pmatrix} \quad (3)$$

In order to calculate the similarity in the same dimension, we update the 3D pose inferred from the HPE model to a 2D pose through this transformation. Then, the score $Score_i$ for current pose $P_{desired}^i$ will be uniquely determined by the following formula

$$Score_i = \Gamma(P_{predicted}^i, P_{desired}^i). \quad (4)$$

We need to define pose similarity in order to determine whether the participant can pass the obstacle, and only the similarity between $P_{predicted}^i$ and $P_{desired}^i$ is large enough to pass the obstacle. Therefore, we need to define a pose metric $Sim(P_{predicted}^i, P_{desired}^i | \Lambda, \eta)$ to measure the pose similarity, and a threshold η as scoring criterion, where Λ is a parameter set of function $Sim(\cdot)$. Our scoring criterion can be written as follows:

$$\Gamma(P_{predicted}^i, P_{desired}^i | \Lambda, \eta) = 1[Sim(P_{predicted}^i, P_{desired}^i | \Lambda) > \eta]. \quad (5)$$

If $Sim(\cdot)$ is greater than η, the output of $\Gamma(\cdot)$ should be 1, which indicates that the participant can pass the obstacle and get the point because he performs the same human pose as we desire.

Next, we introduce how the function $Sim(\cdot)$ is calculated, and its definition refers to the pose similarity calculation method proposed by [5]. First, We assume that the box for $P_{desired}$ is $B_{desired}$. Then, we introduce a soft matching function as follows:

$$C_{sim}(P_{predicted}, P_{desired} | \sigma_1) =$$
$$\begin{cases} \Sigma_{j=1}^K \tanh \frac{c_{predicted}^j}{\sigma_1} & \text{if } k_{predicted}^j \text{ is within B}(k_{desired}^j) \\ 0 & \text{otherwise,} \end{cases} \quad (6)$$

where $k_{desired}^j$ represents jth keypoint in $P_{desired}$, K is the number of keypoints in the human body, $c_{predicted}^j$ represents the confidence of jth keypoint in $P_{predicted}$, $B(k_{desired}^j)$ is a square box centered on $k_{desired}^j$, and the side length of $B(k_{desired}^j)$ is $\frac{1}{10}$ of the original box $B_{desired}$. Equation 6 shows that the similarity is not only related to the position relationship of keypoints, but also related to the confidence of keypoints. This pose metric $C_{sim}(\cdot)$ softly counts the number of joints matching between $P_{predicted}$ and $P_{desired}$, which will form one part of the function for calculating similarity $Sim(\cdot)$.

In addition, the spatial distance between $P_{predicted}$ and $P_{desired}$ is considered, which can be written as

$$D_{sim}(P_{predicted}, P_{desired} | \sigma_2) = \Sigma_{j=1}^K \exp[-\frac{(k_{predicted}^j - k_{desired}^j)^2}{\sigma 2}]. \quad (7)$$

This pose metric $D_{sim}(\cdot)$ represents the Euclidean distance between $P_{predicted}$ and $P_{desired}$, which will form another one part of the function for calculating similarity $Sim(\cdot)$.

Combining Eqs. 6 and 7, the final similarity function $Sim(\cdot)$ can be written as

$$
\begin{aligned}
Sim(P_{predicted}, P_{desired}|\Lambda) = \\
C_{sim}(P_{predicted}, P_{desired}|\sigma_1) + \lambda D_{sim}(P_{predicted}, P_{desired}|\sigma_2),
\end{aligned}
\tag{8}
$$

where λ is an adjustable parameter used to adjust the contribution of the two similarity indicators (Eqs. 6–7) to the total similarity and $\Lambda = \{\sigma_1, \sigma_2, \lambda\}$. By combining Eqs. 1, 4, 5, 8, the task of how to evaluate the motion imitation ability of children with autism proposed by Fig. 1e in the system can be solved.

3 Experiment

3.1 Preparation

Hardware. Our system is deployed on a computer with CPU AMD Ryzen 7 3700X 8-Core Processor 3.59 GHz, GPU NVIDIA GeForce GTX 1660 SUPER, and 16 GB of RAM. INTEL REALSENSE DEPTH CAMERA D455 is used in our system as input device.

Software. Our system is implemented by Unity3D with version 2019.3.13f1 on the windows10 platform, and the editor for $c\#$ scripts editing is Visual Studio 2022.

Data Sources. The subjects participating in our experiment are mainly composed of my fellow disciples. To see if the system can assess motion imitation, these participants will show different motion imitation abilities in the experiment because we don't really have a sub-normal level of motion imitation, like some children with autism. During the experiment, they need to face the camera as directly as possible so that they can be in the center of the image captured by the camera. The image will be resized to 448×448 before inputting to the HPE model, which is achieved by reducing height to 448 while maintaining aspect ratio and cropping width to 448 from the center.

3.2 Process

Firstly, we need to define N desired pose in advance and $N = 10$ in this experiment. In order to achieve the above purpose, we need a person to do the predefined pose and drive the 3D model. Then, save the position information of the keypoints and project the 3D model onto the plane of the obstacle so that the desired pose of the obstacle appears in the participants' field of vision. After completing the desired pose definition, participants can show themselves on the track, and all they need to do is do what they see. Then, the system will automatically calculate the participants' imitation ability score for this round and after passing the last obstacle on the track.

3.3   Result

For convenience, we denote N obstacles as $O_1, O_2, \cdots, O_N$. Totally 10 people participated in this experiment and denote them as $P_1, P_2, \cdots, P_{10}$ respectively. Among them, $P_1, P_2, \cdots, P_5$ will show different degrees of deficits in motion imitation ability in the experiment, while the rest as a control group will behave normally. Finally, their performance in the experiment is shown in Table 1.

Table 1. Score details of 10 participants on the track with 10 obstacles. The member in column "participant" with "*" are people with motion imitation deficits.

Participant	O_1	O_2	O_3	O_4	O_5	O_6	O_7	O_8	O_9	O_{10}	Score
P_1^*	1	0	1	0	1	0	0	0	0	0	0.3
P_2^*	0	1	0	0	1	0	1	0	1	0	0.4
P_3^*	0	1	0	0	0	1	0	0	1	0	0.3
P_4^*	1	0	1	1	0	0	0	0	1	0	0.4
P_5^*	1	1	1	0	1	0	1	0	0	1	0.6
P_6	1	1	1	1	1	1	1	1	1	1	1.0
P_7	1	1	1	1	1	1	1	1	1	0	0.9
P_8	1	1	1	1	1	0	1	1	1	1	0.9
P_9	1	1	1	1	1	1	1	1	1	1	1.0
P_{10}	1	1	1	1	1	1	1	0	1	1	0.9

From Table 1 we can see that the participants with the defect scored significantly lower than the participants without the defect. Therefore, the assessment system for imitative ability proposed by us can effectively evaluate the motion imitation ability of participants.

4   Conclusion

In this paper, a computer-aided motion imitation assessment system for autism intervention is proposed, which is mainly based on human pose estimation and implemented by the game development engine Unity3D. Compared with traditional intervention methods, its assessment is more objective for excluding subjective factors brought by doctors, and it can stimulate the children's fun more because the children will surprisingly find that the 3D model on the screen shows the same pose as themselves. Finally, ten people participated in the experiment, and the results showed that the system proposed by us could effectively evaluate the motion imitation ability. This has enormous application value in the field of autism early intervention for children with autism.

In our future work, it would be of great significance for computer-aided autism intervention to optimize the system in the following three directions.

First of all, social elements should be added to the system, such as encouraging and praising children if they perform well, which is an important part of autism intervention. Second, improve the accuracy and speed of human pose estimation models, which will improve the performance of the entire system. Third, enrich the game content and scenes following autism intervention guidelines, which will enlarge the intervention categories and environments.

References

1. Bailey, A., et al.: A clinicopathological study of autism. Brain J. Neurol. **121**(5), 889–905 (1998)
2. Chauhan, A., et al.: Prevalence of autism spectrum disorder in Indian children: a systematic review and meta-analysis. Neurol. India **67**(1), 100 (2019)
3. Chen, H., Feng, R., Wu, S., Xu, H., Zhou, F., Liu, Z.: 2D human pose estimation: a survey, April 2022
4. Choe, M., Yoo, J., Lee, G., Baek, W., Kang, U., Shin, K.: Deep learning-based human pose estimation: a survey (2 2022)
5. Fang, H.S., Xie, S., Tai, Y.W., Lu, C.: RMPE: regional multi-person pose estimation, November 2016
6. He, K., Zhang, X., Ren, S., Sun, J.: Deep residual learning for image recognition. In: IEEE Conference on Computer Vision and Pattern Recognition, pp. 770–778 (2016)
7. Jaliaawala, M.S., Khan, R.A.: Can autism be catered with artificial intelligence-assisted intervention technology? A comprehensive survey. Artif. Intell. Rev. **53**(2), 1039–1069 (2020)
8. Liu, J., et al.: Early screening of autism in toddlers via response-to-instructions protocol. IEEE Trans. Cybern. 1–11 (9 2020)
9. Liu, X., Wu, Q., Zhao, W., Luo, X.: Technology-facilitated diagnosis and treatment of individuals with autism spectrum disorder: an engineering perspective. Appl. Sci. **7**(10), 1051 (2017)
10. Pavllo, D., Feichtenhofer, C., Grangier, D., Auli, M.: 3D human pose estimation in video with temporal convolutions and semi-supervised training. In: CVPR, November 2019
11. Qin, H., et al.: Vision-based pointing estimation and evaluation in toddlers for autism screening. In: Liu, X.-J., Nie, Z., Yu, J., Xie, F., Song, R. (eds.) ICIRA 2021. LNCS (LNAI), vol. 13015, pp. 177–185. Springer, Cham (2021). https://doi.org/10.1007/978-3-030-89134-3_17
12. Scassellati, B., Admoni, H., Matarić, M.: Robots for use in autism research. Annu. Rev. Biomed. Eng. **14**, 275–294 (2012)
13. Stone, W.L., Ousley, O.Y., Littleford, C.D.: Motor imitation in young children with autism: what's the object? J. Abnorm. Child Psychol. **25**(6), 475–485 (1997)
14. Sun, K., Xiao, B., Liu, D., Wang, J.: Deep high-resolution representation learning for human pose estimation (2019)
15. Wang, Z., Liu, J., He, K., Xu, Q., Xu, X., Liu, H.: Screening early children with autism spectrum disorder via response-to-name protocol. IEEE Trans. Industr. Inform. **17**, 587–595 (2021)
16. Zheng, C., Zhu, S., Mendieta, M., Yang, T., Chen, C., Ding, Z.: 3D human pose estimation with spatial and temporal transformers. In: IEEE/CVF International Conference on Computer Vision, pp. 11656–11665 (2021)

Vision-Based Action Detection for RTI Protocol of ASD Early Screening

Yuhang Shi[1], Weihong Ren[1], Weibo Jiang[1], Qiong Xu[2], Xiu Xu[2], and Honghai Liu[1(✉)]

[1] Harbin Institute of Technology (Shenzhen), Shenzhen, China
{yuhangshi,weibojiang}@stu.hit.edu.cn,
{renweihong,honghai.liu}@hit.edu.cn
[2] Department of Child Health Care, Children's Hospital of Fudan University,
Shanghai, China
{xuqiong,xuxiu}@fudan.edu.cn

Abstract. Autism Spectrum Disorder (ASD) is a congenital neurodevelopmental disorder, and the number of ASD has been increasing in recent decades worldwide. Early screening is essential for proper treatment and intervention in toddlers with ASD. However, manual early screening methods for ASD are costly and inefficient. Stereotyped behavior is one of the clinical manifestations of ASD toddlers. In this paper, we propose a vision-based action detection network, named OstAD, for response-to-instruction (RTI) protocol to assist professional clinicians with an early screening. Our network adopts a temporal attention branch to aggregate contextual features, and proposes a spatial attention branch to generate local frame-level features of the toddlers. Experimental results demonstrate that the proposed OstAD model can detect typical actions of ASD toddler with mAP 72.6% and 75.9% accuracy, and achieves the excellent results in the RTI screening.

Keywords: Action detection · Early screening · RTI protocol

1 Introduction

Autism Spectrum Disorder (ASD) is a congenital neurodevelopmental disorder, which is common in childhood. Over the past decade, the number and prevalence of ASD have been increasing dramatically. Several studies indicate that 1/45 children in the United States has autism in 2018, while as for China the number is 1/142 in 2017 [1]. At present, the cause of ASD is still unknown and the children with autism can not be effectively and completely cured, which brings about enormous costs of time and money for the family and society. Fortunately, early screening and intervention for ASD has been proven to be significant in ameliorating the current state of autism [2]. This current mainstream early screening method for ASD is to observe the behavior of children by professional clinicians [3]. In the process of clinical diagnosis, they use some medical

H. Liu et al. (Eds.): ICIRA 2022, LNAI 13455, pp. 370–380, 2022.
https://doi.org/10.1007/978-3-031-13844-7_36

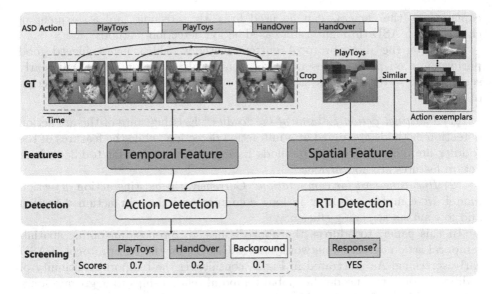

Fig. 1. Overview of our framework for ASD early screening.

assessment scales, such as autism diagnostic observation schedule (ADOS), to score the performance of children. However, traditional manual methods require medical rehabilitation professionals and have long screening cycles. It faces the challenge of the imbalance number of autism and doctors [4]. Therefore, intelligent automatic systems for early screening of ASD have attracted huge research interest.

Relevant studies have shown that children with autism usually have three core manifestations: interaction disorder, narrow interests, and stereotypical and repetitive behaviors. Stereotyped behavior as the most intuitive and obvious feature of autistic children has high clinical application value in the early screening of ASD. Beside, with the rapid development of artificial intelligence and computer vision, action recognition [5] and action detection [6] have achieved good performance on some public datasets [7,8]. In early screening of ASD, action detection for the stereotyped behavior of children to assist professionals provides an efficient and low-cost screening method. Thus, vision-based action detection for ASD has strong practical significance.

In this paper, we are interested in the action detection for autism children. Our research is based on the Response to Instruction (RTI) protocol which is designed for assisting the early screening of ASD [9]. In RTI protocol, the professional clinician sits across from the toddler and interact with the child on the tabletop via some toys and games. The professional clinician gives some instructions to children in the interaction. The doctor evaluates the language comprehension and social communication abilities of the children by observing whether the toddler responds to the his instructions. Their actions during the interaction are recorded by three cameras on a platform. These video streams captured by the cameras can be used for early screening and assessment of children with ASD through vision-based action detection methods.

Based on the above protocol, current methods, which have achieved good performance on public datasets, have a potential to be applied to ASD early screening. However, there are still two major open challenges for action detection of toddler:

(1) *Indistinct action features of the toddler:* Existing state-of-the-art action detection methods are aimed at adult action detection, while the features of the toddler are indistinct. These methods have poor robustness for toddler whose action features are not obvious.

(2) *High time cost for computation:* Currently, the existing action detection model are complex, resulting in long computational time for action detection and low autism screening efficiency.

In this paper, to address the above issues, we propose an online spatial-temporal action detection network, named OstAD, for the RTI protocol of ASD early screening. As illustrated in Fig. 1, considering the temporal continuity of toddlers action, we encode the global temporal relationships to aggregate long-range historical information. Meanwhile, to suppress the noise and enhance the action features of the toddler, we propose a spatial-attention module to obtain high-accuracy action detection results. Based on the above action detection results and the RTI protocol, our model can achieve effective autism screening for children.

The main contributions in this work are as follows.

- To the best of our knowledge, our work is the first action detection method in RTI protocol for autism, which can automatically analyze the RTI protocol, and achieve screening ASD toddlers from the behavioral videos of suspected autistic children. Unlike the existing methods, our method can process the video stream online, and we don't require manually trimming video.
- We propose an online spatial-temporal action detection network, named OstAD, for the RTI protocol of ASD early screening. The proposal network adopts a sliding window to generate contextual and temporal features. We utilize a spatial-attention module to generate local frame-level features of the toddlers to improve the detection accuracy.

The reminder of this paper is organized as follows. In Sect. 2, we briefly review some existing researches on ASD early screening and vision-based action detection. In Sect. 3, we present our online spatial-temporal action detection network and technical details. In Sect. 4, we present the experimental setup and results for action detection and early screening. Discussions and conclusion of the paper are presented in Sect. 5.

2   Related Work

In this section, we briefly review the relate works including ASD early screening methods and vision-based action detection methods.

2.1   ASD Early Screening

In the field of early screening of children with autism, many researchers have conducted extensive research on ASD, including electroencephalogram, functional magnetic resonance imaging (fMRI), galvanic skin response, Inertial Measurement Unit (IMU), and Computer Vision (CV).

Based on time-frequency spectrogram images of electroencephalography signals, [10] uses Convolutional Neural Networks (CNN) for feature extraction and classification to automatically identify and diagnose ASD. [11] designs a deep learning method for detecting the ASD biomarker from neuroimaging fMRI images, so that it aids doctors in screening autism with a quantifiable method that does not rely on behavioral observations. [12] proposes a wearable wristband for acquiring physiological signals of galvanic skin response and heart rate variability. It uses a support vector machine to analyze the recorded physiological signals, so that it predicts emotional state of children with autism. [13] uses wearable sensors to capture stereotyped motor movements in children with autism, so that it utilizes CNN to learn discriminative features from multi-sensor IMU signals.

Based on the clinical symptomatic of autism, there are some methods using CV analysis to quantify the behavior of child, so that they aid in ASD screening. O-GAD [14] adopts a temporal pyramid network to predict the temporal action of ASD and whether the video clip contains high-risk stereotyped repetitive behavior or not. [15] proposes a gaze estimation method based on a multi-sensor visual system for the children with autism, so that it transforms the joint attention detection of autism and doctors into a geometric problem. [16] introduces a coarse-to-fine framework which uses a ResNet-50 to predict coarse-level pose classification, then it proposes a hierarchical infant pose classifier using 3D keypoints to refine its results.

2.2   Vision-Based Action Detection

TCANet [17] utilizes a progressive boundary refinement module to capture local and global temporal features. KFS [18] adopts mid-level action unit from each video to generate the frame-wise features, and the features are used to select the key frame and predict incomplete actions. G-FRNet [19] proposes an end-to-end multi-stage architecture with a sequence-level refinement loss, so that each stage can make a prediction and refine the previous prediction. ETSN [20] introduces a temporal series pyramid network to generate local and global frame-level features, and then uses an unsupervised approach to refine the prediction. [21] first divides a video into consecutive units of equal length, then in the unit-level manner, it proposes a short-term looking back scheme for the online detection of action start.

3   Approach

In this section, we introduce our OstAD model for the action detection of early children with autism spectrum disorder in the response-to-instruction protocol.

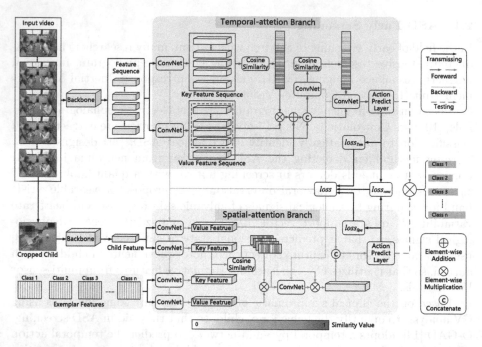

Fig. 2. Framework of the proposed OstAD method for action detection in ASD early screening. Given an untrimmed video, the temporal branch using a sliding window to aggregate contextual features, while the spatial branch aggregates category features based on the obtained category exemplars.

The pipeline of our framework illustrated in Fig. 2 can be summarized as: Firstly, given an untrimmed video, we detect the toddler in original videos by YOLO-v5 [22] and crop videos child-wise. Then, we use I3D [23] to extract long-range temporal features and local frame-level features of cropped child. And based on the exemplar consultation, we use historical frames of cropped child as exemplars. In the temporal-attention branch, the temporal features are transformed to the key space and value space, and we aggregate temporal information in value space according to the similarity in key spaces. At the same time, in the spatial-attention branch, the key feature from child is used to aggregate category features based on the obtained category exemplars. During test, the trained temporal module and spatial module both predict the action scores of toddler in frames, which are fused for action prediction.

Our network for RTI protocol consists of two main components: a temporal attention module and a spatial attention module.

3.1   RTI Protocol

The Response to Instruction (RTI) protocol for early screening of autism is first proposed by [9]. The detailed RTI protocol can be summarized as follows. A toddler with suspected autism is playing with toys. Meanwhile, the clinician sits opposite the toddler, and the clinician will give the toddler a voice command that is repeated twice. There are four rounds of tests corresponding to different voice commands. The responds of toddlers can be rated as two levels. The toddler responds to the voice command from clinician, so that it is a normal reaction. If the toddler does not respond, it is considered autistic tendencies.

3.2   Network Architecture

Temporal Attention Branch. In the RTI protocol for early screening, the suspected autistic toddler often appears repetitive action, and these actions show temporal continuity. Inspired by the advance of sliding window in encoding the long-range historical information [24], we propose a temporal attention module which transforms the feature sequence to key feature sequence and value feature sequence with two convolution layers. Then, we compute the cosine similarity in key space, and aggregate temporal information in value space according to the similarity. In the end, the temporal attention branch uses a convolution layer with similarity to conduct action prediction.

Spatial Attention Branch. Since in the RTI protocol of early screening, the suspected autistic toddler is held by his mother, the action range of toddler is relatively fixed, while the video captured by the camera are wide. Caused by the background noise in the screening environment, the features of the toddler are indistinct. To suppress the noise and enhance the action features of the toddler, we first use YOLO-v5 [22] to detect and crop the toddlers out from the image. Then, we use I3D to extract frame-wise feature of toddler, and we employ the K-Means clustering algorithm to generate exemplar features of the action of toddlers. Both frame feature and exemplar features are converted to key space and corresponding value space. We measure the similarity between child frame feature and exemplar, so that all exemplary features are aggregated. In the end, we use a convolution layer to predict the classification score.

3.3   Loss Function

After obtaining the action predictions of temporal attention branch and spatial attention branch, we use a multi-task loss function to train our proposed model. The overall loss $\mathcal{L}_{total}$ defined as

$$\mathcal{L}_{total} = \mathcal{L}_{tem} + \lambda_1 \mathcal{L}_{spa} + \lambda_2 \mathcal{L}_{cons}, \tag{1}$$

where $\mathcal{L}_{tem}$, $\mathcal{L}_{spa}$ are the temporal and spatial classification losses, and λ_1, λ_2 are hyper-parameters.

We use the cross-entropy loss for classification between both prediction $\{y^T, y^S\}$ and ground truth labels y:

$$\mathcal{L}_{tem} = -\sum_{i=0}^{C} y \log y^T, \mathcal{L}_{spa} = -\sum_{i=0}^{C} y \log y^S, \qquad (2)$$

where C is the number of toddler actions in the RTI screening protocol.

$\mathcal{L}_{cons}$ is a consistency loss between predictions of temporal attention branch and spatial attention branch:

$$\mathcal{L}_{cons} = \frac{1}{2} \sum_{i=0}^{C} (y^T \log \frac{y^S}{y^T} + y^S \log \frac{y^T}{y^S}), \qquad (3)$$

4   Experiment

4.1   Dataset and Metrics

We carry out experiments on the RTI action detection dataset, including action annotations for 16 children of 22 early screening videos. The ASD early screening videos include a toddler, his mother, a doctor, and a observer. The action category of the toddler in the RTI dataset mainly contains "PlayToys", "HandOver", and "Backgrond". The duration of the complete protocol for a suspected toddler is around 2–5 min per video. Notably, the dataset contains a total of 103, 180 valid and meaningful action frames. The frame rate of each video is 30 fps, and the pixels of each frame are 1280×720.

We adopt the frame-wise accuracy and mean average precision (mAP) to measure the performance of online action detection algorithms. For each frame, we collect and rank action prediction scores to compute precision and recall. We compute the average precision (AP) at different recall rates for each class of actions, and then we take the mean of the APs of all action classes to obtain mAP.

4.2   Implementation Details

We optimize the entire network using the Adam optimizer with a learning rate of 0.001 and batch size of 128. The learning rate will be downgraded 10 times per 20 epochs. We adopt weight decay of 0.0001 to train. Video frames are extracted with a frame rate of 30 fps. The original image size is 1280×720, in order to speed up, we adjust the space size to 640×360. In inference, the temporal attention branch is multiplied by 0.7, while the balance coefficient of spatial attention branch is 0.3.

Table 1. Action detection results on the RTI dataset, measured by Acc(%) and mAP(%).

Method	Temporal-attention Module	Spatial-attention Module	Acc	mAP
Colar [25]	-	-	68.3	66.8
OstAD	✓		67.2	64.9
		✓	62.3	58.3
	✓	✓	**75.9**	**72.6**

4.3   Results and Discussions

In this section, we compare our OstAD with the state-of-the-art methods on RTI action detection dataset. The baseline Colar [25] uses the ResNet50-I3D architecture to encode RGB and optical flow. As shown in Table 1, our method achieve mAP 72.6% which outperforms the baseline result by 6% for action detection of suspected toddlers. Besides, our method achieve online inference speed of 40.6 fps on a Quadro RTX 6000.

We conduct various ablation experiments on RTI video dataset to evaluate the effectiveness of different modules in our method.

Effectiveness of Temporal Attention Module: To prove the effectiveness of our temporal attention module for action detection, we conduct ablation experiments without using the module. As observed, the results demonstrate that the temporal attention branch produces 13.6% improvement on frame-wise accuracy and 14.3% improvement on mAP over the results without this branch. This supports our claim that, in the RTI protocol for early screening, temporal context information for actions is an informative clue for action detection of suspected autistic toddlers.

Effectiveness of Spatial Attention Module: The above experimental results demonstrate the superior of spatial attention module. Compared with single temporal branch using, the spatial attention module can further improve the temporal attention module by 8.6% on frame-wise accuracy and 7.7% on mAP, which is a considerable performance promotion. The experimental results indicate that the spatial attention module is indispensable, and suppressing the background noise and enhancing the action features of the toddler are important for action detection in RTI early ASD screening.

Table 2. Assessment scores results of action detection in the RTI screening.

ASD	#3	#6	#7	#13	#15	#18	#20	#22
GT	0	2	0	0	4	3	2	4
Predict	0	1	0	0	4	3	1	4
TD	#1	#2	#9	#12	#16	#17	#19	#21
GT	0	0	0	3	1	0	0	1
Predict	0	0	1	3	1	0	0	1

In the aspect of RTI screening, our method achieves accuracy of 12/16. Following the standard settings of RTI protocol, we report the action predictions of toddlers and summarize the results in Table 2, containing 8 TD (typical development) and 8 ASD. For the 8 ASD toddlers, we successfully detect responses to instructions in 5 of them, while for the #6 and #20 toddlers, our methods detect one more response action. As for the TD toddlers, our method correctly detects the responsive action from 7 out of 8 toddlers. Notably, in the RTI protocol, the more responsive actions of the child, the lower the assessment score. It is difficult to accurately detect the action due to the indistinct action features of the toddler. The results indicate that our method can clearly detect the action of toddlers in the RTI protocol and is robust to background noises.

5   Conclusion

In this paper, we propose an online spatial-temporal action detection network, named OstAD, for the RTI protocol of ASD early screening. Considering the temporal continuity of toddlers action, we encode the global temporal relationships to aggregate long-range historical information. Meanwhile, to suppress the noise and enhance the action features of the toddler, we propose a spatial-attention module to obtain high-accuracy action detection results. Based on the above action detection results and the RTI protocol, our model can achieve effective autism screening for children. As the uncertainty of toddlers is unpredictable and the actions are indistinct, it is difficult to filter out the action of toddlers from the complex RTI protocol. It is worth noting that our OstAD achieves the excellent results in the RTI screening, and it demonstrates robustness to toddler whose action features are not obvious and background noise.

References

1. Wang, Z., Liu, J., He, K., Xu, Q., Xu, X., Liu, H.: Screening early children with autism spectrum disorder via response-to-name protocol. IEEE Trans. Industr. Inf. **17**(1), 587–595 (2019)
2. Zwaigenbaum, L., et al.: Early identification of autism spectrum disorder: recommendations for practice and research. Pediatrics **136**(Supplement_1), S10–S40 (2015)

3. Fernell, E., Eriksson, M.A., Gillberg, C.: Early diagnosis of autism and impact on prognosis: a narrative review. Clin. Epidemiol. **5**, 33 (2013)
4. Lord, C., Cook, E.H., Leventhal, B.L., Amaral, D.G.: Autism spectrum disorders. Neuron **28**(2), 355–363 (2000)
5. Jiang, S., Qi, Y., Zhang, H., Bai, Z., Lu, X., Wang, P.: D3D: dual 3-D convolutional network for real-time action recognition. IEEE Trans. Industr. Inf. **17**(7), 4584–4593 (2020)
6. Q. Liu and Z. Wang, "Progressive boundary refinement network for temporal action detection," in AAAI Conference on Artificial Intelligence, vol. 34, no. 07, 2020, pp. 11 612–11 619
7. Heilbron, F.C., Escorcia, V., Ghanem, B., Niebles, J.C.: ActivityNet: a large-scale video benchmark for human activity understanding. In: IEEE Conference on Computer Vision and Pattern Recognition, pp. 961–970 (2015)
8. Jiang, Y.-G., et al.: Thumos challenge: action recognition with a large number of classes (2014)
9. Liu, J., et al.: Early screening of autism in toddlers via response-to-instructions protocol. IEEE Trans. Cybern. (2020)
10. Tawhid, M.N.A., Siuly, S., Wang, H., Whittaker, F., Wang, K., Zhang, Y.: A spectrogram image based intelligent technique for automatic detection of autism spectrum disorder from EEG. PLoS ONE **16**(6), e0253094 (2021)
11. Husna, R.N.S., Syafeeza, A., Hamid, N.A., Wong, Y., Raihan, R.A.: Functional magnetic resonance imaging for autism spectrum disorder detection using deep learning. Jurnal Teknologi **83**(3), 45–52 (2021)
12. Krupa, N., Anantharam, K., Sanker, M., Datta, S., Sagar, J.V.: Recognition of emotions in autistic children using physiological signals. Heal. Technol. **6**(2), 137–147 (2016). https://doi.org/10.1007/s12553-016-0129-3
13. Rad, N.M., et al.: Deep learning for automatic stereotypical motor movement detection using wearable sensors in autism spectrum disorders. Signal Process. **144**, 180–191 (2018)
14. Y. Tian, X. Min, G. Zhai, and Z. Gao, "Video-based early asd detection via temporal pyramid networks," in 2019 IEEE International Conference on Multimedia and Expo (ICME). IEEE, 2019, pp. 272–277
15. Zhang, W., Wang, Z., Cai, H., Liu, H.: Detection for joint attention based on a multi-sensor visual system. In: 2018 25th International Conference on Mechatronics and Machine Vision in Practice (M2VIP), pp. 1–6. IEEE (2018)
16. Zhou, J., Jiang, Z., Yoo, J.-H., Hwang, J.-N.: Hierarchical pose classification for infant action analysis and mental development assessment. In: ICASSP 2021–2021 IEEE International Conference on Acoustics, Speech and Signal Processing (ICASSP), pp. 1340–1344. IEEE (2021)
17. Qing, Z., et al.: Temporal context aggregation network for temporal action proposal refinement. In: IEEE Conference on Computer Vision and Pattern Recognition, pp. 485–494 (2021)
18. Wang, H., Yuan, C., Shen, J., Yang, W., Ling, H.: Action unit detection and key frame selection for human activity prediction. Neurocomputing **318**, 109–119 (2018)
19. Wang, D., Yuan, Y., Wang, Q.: Gated forward refinement network for action segmentation. Neurocomputing **407**, 63–71 (2020)
20. Li, Y., et al.: Efficient two-step networks for temporal action segmentation. Neurocomputing **454**, 373–381 (2021)

21. Wang, T., Chen, Y., Lv, H., Teng, J., Snoussi, H., Tao, F.: Online detection of action start via soft computing for smart city. IEEE Trans. Industr. Inf. **17**(1), 524–533 (2020)
22. Redmon, J., Divvala, S.K., Girshick, R.B., Farhadi, A.: You only look once: unified, real-time object detection. In: 2016 IEEE Conference on Computer Vision and Pattern Recognition, CVPR 2016, Las Vegas, NV, USA, 27–30 June 2016. IEEE Computer Society, pp. 779–788 (2016). https://doi.org/10.1109/CVPR.2016.91
23. Carreira, J., Zisserman, A.: Quo vadis, action recognition? A new model and the kinetics dataset. In: IEEE Conference on Computer Vision and Pattern Recognition, pp. 6299–6308 (2017)
24. Shou, Z., Wang, D., Chang, S.-F.: Temporal action localization in untrimmed videos via multi-stage CNNs. In: IEEE Conference on Computer Vision and Pattern Recognition, pp. 1049–1058 (2016)
25. Yang, L., Han, J., Zhang, D.: Colar: effective and efficient online action detection by consulting exemplars. arXiv preprint arXiv:2203.01057 (2022)

Multi-task Facial Landmark Detection Network for Early ASD Screening

Ruihan Lin[1], Hanlin Zhang[1], Xinming Wang[1], Weihong Ren[1], Wenhao Wu[1], Zuode Liu[1], Xiu Xu[2], Qiong Xu[2], and Honghai Liu[1(✉)]

[1] School of Mechanical Engineering and Automation Harbin Institute of Technology, Shenzhen, China
honghai.liu@hit.edu.cn
[2] Department of Child Health Care, Children's Hospital of Fudan University, Shanghai, China

Abstract. Joint attention is an important skill that involves coordinating the attention of at least two individuals towards an object or event in early child development, which is usually absent in children with autism. Children's joint attention is an essential part of the diagnosis of autistic children. To improve the effectiveness of autism screening, in this paper, we propose a multi-task facial landmark detection network to enhance the stability of gaze estimation and the accuracy of the joint attention screening result. In order to verify the proposed method, we recruit 39 toddlers aged from 16 to 32 months in this study and build a children-based facial landmarks dataset from 19 subjects. Experiments show that the accuracy of the joint attention screening result is 92.5%, which demonstrates the effectiveness of our method.

Keywords: Autism · Joint attention · Multi-task facial landmark detection

1 Introduction

Autism spectrum disorders (ASD) is one of the most common neurodevelopmental disorders in the world, characterized by severe impairments in social communication and unusual, restricted, or repetitive behaviors [8]. So far, the effective treatment is early detection and intervention, which can help to alleviate the symptoms and effects of ASD [11,13]. Furthermore, with the development of computer vision and deep learning, research on vision-based automatic auxiliary screening methods applied in traditional treatment has been focused on. Joint attention (JA) is one of the essential protocols in the early screening process to find out whether the children look into others' eyes and orient their attention to follow others' gazing cues. The test of JA protocol [22] can be described as follows: The child sits on a chair accompanied by a parent and play with toys on the table, and the clinician sits opposite the child and gives instructions in clear and brief tones. Firstly, let the child play with toys for 2 min. Secondly, when

H. Liu et al. (Eds.): ICIRA 2022, LNAI 13455, pp. 381–391, 2022.
https://doi.org/10.1007/978-3-031-13844-7_37

the child shifts attention to toys completely, the clinician takes the toy from the child's hands and turns his or her attention to the clinician by calling name or clapping. Then, the clinician gives the instruction 'look at here!' and points at the designated area. Finally, whether the child's gaze follows the clinician's instruction is the judgment. The test is conducted for 4 rounds, and there is 1-minute rest between each round. The clinician records the score in each round according to the child's performance.

Over the past few years, appearance-based gaze estimation methods, which are proven to achieve excellent effects in unconstrained environments [1, 18], have been applied in the paradigm of joint attention detection. However, the existing gaze estimation model lands in a predicament in children-oriented tasks, despite being state-of-the-art on the public datasets. Through the comparative experiments, the comparison of results indicates that the main reason the existing models can not achieve satisfactory results in the early autism screening is that the pre-process of the network can not obtain accurate and stable facial landmarks to normalize the faces or eyes for the follow-up tasks. Specifically, the facial landmarks can affect the accuracy and robustness of a gaze estimation model. We conclude three challenges for obtaining children's facial landmarks as follows: (1) It is hard to estimate facial landmarks under heavy occlusion. (2) The data distribution of children's faces has individual differences; (3) The facial features of children are quite different from those of adults, such as the ratio among the five sense organs.

To cope with the above challenges, we propose a multi-task facial landmark detection network termed MFLDN. The MFLDN contains two branches. We estimate the head state and then regress landmarks with the help of head-state results. Considering the effect of faces with heavy occlusion, we divide the head state into two classes and apply head pose instead of gaze for faces with heavy occlusion. As noticed in Fig. 3, we define the faces with yaw angle of head pose between $-50°$ to $50°$ and pitch angle between $-50°$ to $50°$ as 'Front', and the remains are defined as 'Side'. Finally, we recruited 39 toddlers between the ages of 16 and 32 months for this study. We built a children-based facial landmarks dataset from videos of 19 subjects selected to verify the influence of dataset distribution. The experiments show the evaluation details. The experiment results compared with the previous methods show the effectiveness and efficiency of our method, with an accuracy of 92.5%.

The main contributions of this paper can be summarized as follows

(1) We proposed a multi-task network including facial landmark detection and head-state classification for the JA screening task of autistic children.
(2) Our proposed facial landmark detection method was applied into JA screening paradigm, improving the stability of gaze estimation and the accuracy of JA screening result.
(3) Based on the work of Wang et al. [19] in the ASD screening system, we built a facial landmarks dataset for children.

2   Related Work

In this section, we briefly review the related works on diagnosis of autism with machine vision and facial landmark detection in this area.

2.1   Application of Visual Methods in the Field of Autism

The informational expression of pathological manifestations of ASD is significant for the clinical diagnosis and treatment of clinical professionals [20]. Traditional autism screening methods are performed by professional clinicians to observe the behavioral characteristics of the tested children in a series of designed screening paradigms. The screening results are highly subjective, and the screening process takes a long time. In recent years, computer vision-based artificial intelligence technology has been successfully applied in the early screening of children with autism, which shows the great promise of visual methods in this field [5]. Liu et al. [10] proposed a protocol to examine children's responses to instructions and an evaluation method that combined skeleton point and target detection. The experiments showed that the ASD classification accuracy rate reached 95%. Wang et al. [19] proposed a paradigm named 'Response To Name' and used cameras arranged at multiple angles to obtain children's gaze for behavior analysis. Li et al. [9] applied a gaze estimation method based on the joint prediction of head pose and gaze estimation in the screening of children with autism, and the accuracy of ASD screening was 94.8%.

In addition, vision-based auxiliary therapy methods have also achieved good results in the intervention and treatment of children with autism. Researchers [12] from the Cyprus University of Technology constructed a VR-based Cave environment to train and enhance the social skills of autistic children. Zhang et al. [21] developed a gaze-driven interactive system to evaluate the cognitive ability of the tested patients from multiple perspectives and provide guidance for the personalized, customized intervention plan.

2.2   Facial Landmark Detection

With the development of CNN, facial landmark detection algorithms based on CNN are mainly divided into coordinate regression model and heat map regression model.

The coordinate regression model [16,17,24] usually extracts image features through CNN and directly maps the coordinates of each landmark through the fully-connected layer. Coordinate regression model can learn the intrinsic relationship between landmarks to a certain extent, but too strong hidden prior knowledge makes the inference results inaccurate. The heatmap regression model generates a high-resolution heatmap for each landmark separately, then regresses the landmarks with the highest probability in the heatmaps [2,4,14]. The heatmap regression model has higher accuracy, but it is computationally expensive for a high-resolution feature map. In contrast, the coordinate regression model is fast and robust but not accurate enough. PIPNet [7] combines the advantages of heatmap regression and coordinate regression. PIPNet is based on low-resolution heatmaps, eliminating the need for the upsampling module, reducing computational cost, and learning the positional relationship with neighbor landmarks.

3   Methodology

As mentioned in the introduction, we propose a multi-task facial landmark detection network to improve the effectiveness of screening. The overall architecture of the network is shown in Fig. 1. We use ResNet-18 as the backbone to extract the information from the input images. The feature map created by the third layer is fed to the fully-connected layer for the head-state classification. We use the feature map obtained from the fourth layer to regress facial landmarks.

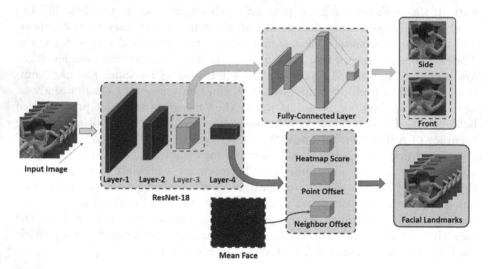

Fig. 1. The overall architecture of MFLDN. MFLDN has two branches. The upper branch classifies the head state, and the lower branch detects the facial landmarks. The mean face is the average coordinates of landmarks on the dataset.

3.1   Facial Landmark Detection

As is shown in Fig. 1, we use the PIPNet [7] to detect facial landmarks, which can be computationally efficient and achieves comparable accuracy to heatmap regression. ResNet-18 [6] is used as the backbone network. The regression stage consists of three modules, namely heatmap regression, offset regression, and neighbor offset regression. The heatmap regression module directly regresses the maximum probability grid in the low-resolution feature map obtained from down-sampling. The offset regression module is applied to estimate the offset to the top-left corner of the grid to get a specific localization. The neighbor regression module is presented to consider the positional relationship of neighbor landmarks, which means each landmark predicts the offsets of its C neighbors. The number C of neighbor landmarks is defined by computing the Euler distances among landmarks.

The loss of heatmap regression can be enforced as L2 loss. The L1-loss is used for both offset predictions and neighbor offset predictions. The final outputs are consist of a score map of size $N \times H \times W$, an offset map of size $2N \times H \times W$ and a neighbor offset map of size $2CN \times H \times W$, where the N is the number of facial landmarks and the C is the number of neighbor landmarks predicted. The heatmap score, the offset predictions, and the neighbor offset predictions are independent and can be computed in parallel.

The training loss of the facial landmark detection can be formulated as

$$L_{landmark} = L_S + \alpha L_O + \beta L_N, \tag{1}$$

where L_S is the loss of score map, L_O is for offset predictions, L_N is for neighbor offset predictions, and α, β are balancing coefficients.

Concretely, L_S for the score map is formulated as

$$L_S = \frac{1}{NHW} \sum_{i=1}^{N} \sum_{j=1}^{H} \sum_{k=1}^{W} (s_{ijk} - \hat{s_{ijk}})^2, \quad s_{ijk} \in \{0, 1\} \tag{2}$$

where s_{ijk} and $\hat{s_{ijk}}$ denote the ground truth and predicted score values, respectively, and NHW is the normalization term.

L_O for the offset map is formulated as

$$L_O = \frac{1}{2N} \sum_{s_{ijk}=1} \sum_{l=1}^{2} |o_{ijkl} - \hat{o_{ijkl}}|, \quad o_{ijkl} \in [0, 1] \tag{3}$$

where o_{ijkl} and $\hat{o_{ijkl}}$ denote the ground truth and predicted offset values, respectively, and $2N$ is the normalization term.

L_N for the offset map is formulated as

$$L_N = \frac{1}{2CN} \sum_{n_{ijk}=1} \sum_{l=1}^{2} \sum_{m=1}^{C} |n_{ijklm} - \hat{n_{ijklm}}|, \quad n_{ijklm} \in [0, 1] \tag{4}$$

where n_{ijklm} and $\hat{n_{ijklm}}$ denote the ground truth and predicted neighbor offset values, respectively, $2CN$ is the normalization term.

3.2 Head-State Classification

Children's behaviors have individual differences, which means the faces will be detected with difficulty in an unconstrained environment. When the gaze estimation network can not obtain the eye features because of the occlusion, the gaze vector fluctuates dramatically. To avoid the negative effect of faces under heavy occlusion, we divide the head state into two classes. One is the frontal views; the other is the no-frontal views. As is shown in Fig. 3, we define the head state of images in the Euler angle range (Yaw$[-50°, 50°]$, Pitch$[-50°, 50°]$) as 'Front' and the remains are defined as 'Side'.

Figure 1 gives the architecture of MFLDN. The feature extracted from the former three layers is used to predict the head state for the downstream tasks. The branch of head-state classification ends with a global average pooling layer and a fully-connected layer with softmax. The Binary Cross Entropy (BCE) loss is suitable for this binary classification task. The loss function is formulated as

$$L_{classification} = -\sum_{n=1}^{N} [y_n \cdot \log \sigma(x_n) + (1 - y_n) \cdot \log(1 - \sigma(x_n))], \quad N = 2 \quad (5)$$

where y_n and x_n denote the ground truth and the prediction. The function σ is the Sigmoid function.

3.3 Loss Function

As the losses of two branches are computed above, the total loss is jointed together. To balance the two branches, the total loss of MFLDN can be defined as

$$L_{total} = \gamma L_{landmark} + \phi L_{classification}, \quad (6)$$

where γ and ϕ are balancing coefficients. The γ and ϕ need to be adjusted accordingly so that the loss values of $L_{landmark}$ and $L_{classification}$ are comparable. In the training process, the score map, the offset predictions, the neighbor offset predictions, and the class prediction are computed at the same time, and then the total loss is calculated between the ground truth and the predictions.

4   Experiments and Results

In this section, we introduce the Children-based Facial Landmarks Dataset and the details of the evaluation method. The overall architecture of the auxiliary screening algorithm is shown in Fig. 2. In the experiment, we focus on the gaze response of the child when the clinician gives instructions. In order to evaluate the effectiveness of the algorithm, we apply two downstream tasks, which consist of head pose estimation and gaze estimation. WHENet [23], an end-to-end head pose estimation network, is used to predict 3D head pose through the no-frontal faces. For the gaze estimation network, the MPIIFaceGaze is taken to train in ResNet-14. After 24 epochs of training, the average angle error in the test set achieves 4.85°.

4.1   Children-Based Facial Landmark Dataset

Aiming to cope with the problem that existing pretrained models can not achieve a satisfactory results when applied in children's face tasks, we built a children-based facial landmarks dataset within both the normal children and the autistic children.

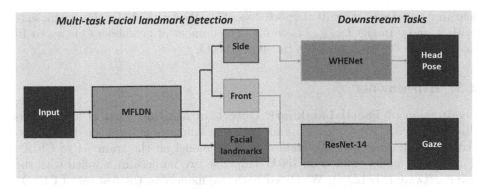

Fig. 2. The overall architecture of the auxiliary screening algorithm. We use MFLDN to detect facial landmarks and classify the head state. There are two branches. By feeding the whole face images to the ResNet-14, we can obtain an accurate gaze vector. The WHENet can predict the head pose from images labeled as 'Side'. Finally, we concatenate the result of two branches as the output.

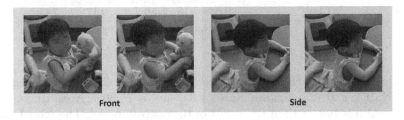

Fig. 3. The classes of the head state.

In this experiment, 39 toddlers aged from 16 to 32 months, of which 26 are diagnosed with ASD, were recruited from the children's hospital of Fudan University to participate in this experiment. We choose 19 toddlers involving 7 who are autistic and the comparison group of TD toddlers as the data collection objects to build the CFLD (Children-based Facial Landmarks Dataset). The Microsoft Kinect captures the experimental videos from 5 min to 10 min. The CFLD contains 9228 images, consisting of 4926 images labeled as 'Front' with 83 facial landmarks and 4302 images labeled as 'Side'. We divide the CFLD into a train set and a test set according to the different subjects.

4.2   Implementation Details

The input images are face images, which are cropped according to the bounding box predicted by face detector [3]. Then, the size of input images is resized to 256×256. To obtain more information and ensure the area of face images can include all landmarks, we enlarge the face images by 10%. We use ResNet-18 pretrained on ImageNet as our default backbone. We train our model with the Adam optimizer for total 60 epochs with an initial learning rate of 0.0001. The learning rate decayed by 10 at epoch 30 and 50. We set the balancing coefficients both α and β in the $L_{landmarks}$ to 0.1. The number of neighbors C is set to 10 according to the best model in the experiments.

4.3 Experiments

Evaluation of Facial Landmark Detection Module First of all, we conducted comparative experiments to verify the influence of different dataset distributions and features. We trained the test model on the train set of CFLD. The control model trained on 300 W [15]. The two models are applied with the same network (MFLDN). We tested both two models on the test set of CFLD.

Table 1. The comparison of MFLDN on CFLD, which trained on different datasets. The results are in NME (%), using inter-ocular distance for normalization.

Method	Pre-trained Dataset	Backbone	NME (%)	FR (%)	AUC (%)
MFLDN	CFLD	ResNet-18	**2.56**	0.17	74.97
	300 W	ResNet-18	3.28	/	/

Table 1 shows that the proposed model achieves a 2.58% Normalized Mean Error (NME), a 0.12% Failure Rate (FR), and a 75.30% Area Under Curve (AUC), which is better than the result of the control model. The model trained on CFLD dataset is accurate and robust enough for the application in the JA screening method.

Evaluation of Head-State Classification Module. Before the evaluation is conducted, we applied for and passed an ethical review, and pledged not to disclose any personal information about the subjects before and after the experiment. Furthermore, before each experiment, we obtained informed consent from every child's parents.

According to the JA protocol mentioned in the introduction, to illustrate the effectiveness of the head-state classification, we compared the result of the auxiliary screening algorithm (Fig. 2) with the one of the algorithm without the head-state classification module. The details of the evaluation method are as follows. When the clinician attracts the toddler's attention and gives the instructions, the JA screening algorithm starts and detects the toddler's face to estimate gaze direction. The rotation angle of the gaze and the duration computed by the number of frames are employed in experiments. If the gaze is not available, the head pose is used to show the toddler's attention. The gaze of each frame is considered as the response gaze once it meets the conditions as shown in (7). If the response lasts N_{frame} consecutive frames, we record the score as '0' otherwise as '1'. The assessment will take 4 rounds, and both the clinician and the algorithm will record the scores for comparison.

$$\begin{cases} MIN_{yaw} \le \theta_{yaw} \le MAX_{yaw} \\ MIN_{pitch} \le \theta_{pitch} \le MAX_{pitch} \end{cases} \tag{7}$$

where the MIN_{yaw}, MIN_{pitch}, MAX_{yaw} and MAX_{pitch} are set to 60°, 20°, 90° and 45°, respectively. The N_{frame} is 10.

4.4 Results and Discussion

There are 20 toddlers, different from the subjects in CFLD, who participate in this experiment. The ratio between TD children and ASD children is 1:1. The comparative results of different algorithms used in JA screening are shown in Table 2.

Table 2. The JA screening results of different algorithms (score)

TD subject	A	B	C	D	E	F	G	H	I	J	Acc
Ground truth	0	0	0	3	0	0	0	0	2	1	/
Ours$_{w/o}$ Sect. 3.2	0	1	0	3	0	0	0	0	0	1	90%
Ours	0	1	0	3	0	0	0	0	1	1	**95%**
ASD subject	K	L	M	N	O	P	Q	R	S	T	Acc
Ground truth	4	4	3	3	2	3	4	2	4	4	/
Ours$_{w/o}$ Sect. 3.2	2	3	3	3	0	3	3	2	3	3	80%
Ours	3	4	3	3	0	3	4	2	4	3	90%

As can be seen, with the help of the head-state classification module, our auxiliary screening algorithm achieves the highest accuracy (TD:95%, ASD:90%) in this experiment. The experimental results show the improvement of 10% for the accuracy of the evaluation of JA tasks compared with the algorithm without the head-state classification module. Comparing our result with the ground truth, the average accuracy of ours to score the JA task for all subjects is 92.5%. The head-state classification module focus on refining the head pose to provide the front faces for facial landmark detection and avoid the influence of occlusion. Meantime, we test the effect of the head-state classification. The accuracy of classification achieves 95.7%. There are several critical problems. Firstly, the end-to-end head pose predictor pretrained on public datasets is unstable and can not match the children-oriented task. Secondly, for child B in the TD children, when he wore a mask and paid attention to the camera, the facial landmark detector couldn't predict accurate landmarks for gaze estimation when the face was occluded. Thus, the accuracy and robustness of the auxiliary screening algorithm for JA need to be improved.

5   Conclusion

In this work, we propose a multi-task facial landmark detection network for the JA screening paradigm to solve the occlusion problem, improving the stability of gaze estimation and the accuracy of JA screening. In order to verify the influence of different dataset distributions and features, we recruited 39 toddlers between the ages of 16 and 32 months and built a children-based facial landmarks dataset from 19 toddlers, termed CFLD. Experiments show that a normal gaze estimation model can achieve competitive results on the remaining 20 subjects when the facial landmark detector trained on CFLD is deployed. In the future, we will consider analyzing the gaze performance of children with autism through multi-views. We believe the auxiliary screening algorithm can be more accurate when combining multi-view data with well-constructed deep learning models.

References

1. Cheng, Y., Wang, H., Bao, Y., Lu, F.: Appearance-based gaze estimation with deep learning: a review and benchmark. arXiv preprint arXiv:2104.12668 (2021)
2. Dapogny, A., Bailly, K., Cord, M.: DeCaFA: deep convolutional cascade for face alignment in the wild. In: IEEE International Conference on Computer Vision, pp. 6893–6901 (2019)
3. Deng, J., Guo, J., Ververas, E., Kotsia, I., Zafeiriou, S.: RetinaFace: single-shot multi-level face localisation in the wild. In: IEEE Conference on Computer Vision and Pattern Recognition, pp. 5203–5212 (2020)
4. Dong, X., Yang, Y.: Teacher supervises students how to learn from partially labeled images for facial landmark detection. In: IEEE International Conference on Computer Vision, pp. 783–792 (2019)
5. Hazlett, H.C., et al.: Early brain development in infants at high risk for autism spectrum disorder. Nature **7641**, 348–351 (2017)
6. He, K., Zhang, X., Ren, S., Sun, J.: Deep residual learning for image recognition. In: IEEE Conference on Computer Vision and Pattern Recognition, pp. 770–778 (2016)
7. Jin, H., Liao, S., Shao, L.: Pixel-in-pixel net: towards efficient facial landmark detection in the wild. Int. J. Comput. Vision **12**, 3174–3194 (2021)
8. Kaliouby, R.E., Picard, R., Baron-Cohen, S.: Affective computing and autism. Ann. N. Y. Acad. Sci. (1), 228–248 (2006)
9. Li, J., et al.: Appearance-based gaze estimation for ASD diagnosis. IEEE Trans. Cybern. (2022)
10. Liu, J., et al.: Early screening of autism in toddlers via response-to-instructions protocol. IEEE Trans. Cybern. (2020)
11. Magiati, I., Charman, T., Howlin, P.: A two-year prospective follow-up study of community-based early intensive behavioural intervention and specialist nursery provision for children with autism spectrum disorders. J. Child Psychol. Psychiatry **8**, 803–812 (2007)
12. Matsentidou, S., Poullis, C.: Immersive visualizations in a VR cave environment for the training and enhancement of social skills for children with autism. In: International Conference on Computer Vision Theory and Applications (VISAPP), pp. 230–236. IEEE (2014)

13. Ming, S., Mulhern, T., Stewart, I., Moran, L., Bynum, K.: Training class inclusion responding in typically developing children and individuals with autism. J. Appl. Behav. Anal. **1**, 53–60 (2018)
14. Newell, A., Yang, K., Deng, J.: Stacked hourglass networks for human pose estimation. In: Leibe, B., Matas, J., Sebe, N., Welling, M. (eds.) ECCV 2016. LNCS, vol. 9912, pp. 483–499. Springer, Cham (2016). https://doi.org/10.1007/978-3-319-46484-8_29
15. Sagonas, C., Tzimiropoulos, G., Zafeiriou, S., Pantic, M.: 300 faces in-the-wild challenge: The first facial landmark localization challenge. In: IEEE international conference on computer vision workshops. pp. 397–403 (2013)
16. Sun, Y., Wang, X., Tang, X.: Deep convolutional network cascade for facial point detection. In: IEEE Conference on Computer Vision and Pattern Recognition, pp. 3476–3483 (2013)
17. Trigeorgis, G., Snape, P., Nicolaou, M.A., Antonakos, E., Zafeiriou, S.: Mnemonic descent method: a recurrent process applied for end-to-end face alignment. In: IEEE Conference on Computer Vision and Pattern Recognition, pp. 4177–4187 (2016)
18. Wang, X., Zhang, J., Zhang, H., Zhao, S., Liu, H.: Vision-based gaze estimation: a review. IEEE Trans. Cogn. Dev. Syst. (2021)
19. Wang, Z., Liu, J., He, K., Xu, Q., Xu, X., Liu, H.: Screening early children with autism spectrum disorder via response-to-name protocol. IEEE Trans. Industr. Inf. **1**, 587–595 (2019)
20. Wang, Z., Liu, J., Zhang, W., Nie, W., Liu, H.: Diagnosis and intervention for children with autism spectrum disorder: a survey. IEEE Trans. Cogn. Dev. Syst. (2021)
21. Zhang, H., et al.: Gaze-driven interaction system for cognitive ability assessment. In: International Conference on Intelligent Control and Information Processing (ICICIP), pp. 346–351. IEEE (2021)
22. Zhang, W., Wang, Z., Liu, H.: Vision-based joint attention detection for autism spectrum disorders. In: Sun, F., Liu, H., Hu, D. (eds.) ICCSIP 2018. CCIS, vol. 1005, pp. 26–36. Springer, Singapore (2019). https://doi.org/10.1007/978-981-13-7983-3_3
23. Zhou, Y., Gregson, J.: WHENet: real-time fine-grained estimation for wide range head pose. arXiv preprint arXiv:2005.10353 (2020)
24. Zhu, S., Li, C., Change Loy, C., Tang, X.: Face alignment by coarse-to-fine shape searching. In: IEEE Conference on Computer Vision and Pattern Recognition, pp. 4998–5006 (2015)

An Eye Movement Study of Joint Attention Deficits in Children with Autism Spectrum Disorders

Wang Jing, Lin Zehui, Wang Yifan, Wei Ling[✉], and Su Linfei

Department of Psychology, School of Health, Fujian Medical University, Fuzhou 350108, China
ysyang-78@163.com

Abstract. Using eye tracking technology to explore the underlying processing mechanisms of joint attention in children with autism spectrum disorders (ASD). The experiment selected 32 ASD children and 34 IQ-matched typically developing (TD) children. By freely viewing different hand-up (palm-up, does not respond to intention information; palm-down, grasping action, response intention information) action videos to explore whether hand movements affect joint attention in children with ASD. The results showed that (1) ASD children and TD children had significantly greater dwell time and fixation counts to the post-cued target than non-targets; (2) Hand movements would affect the joint attention of ASD children and TD children. The dwell time and fixation counts were significantly greater in palms down condition than those with palms up. This suggests that children with ASD have joint attention, and this joint attention is based on intentional information.

Keywords: Autism spectrum disorder · Joint attention · Eye tracking · Potential processing mechanisms

1 Introduction

Autism spectrum disorder (ASD) is a complex, pervasive and multifactorial neurodevelopmental disorder. The diagnosis of ASD is based on the observation of abnormal behaviors. The diagnostic criteria focus on social and communication impairment, restricted interests and repetitive and stereotyped behaviors (American Psychiatric Association 2013). Previous studies have shown that joint attention impairment is one of the prominent features of individuals with ASD (Dawson et al. 2012). Joint attention (JA) refers to the use of gestures, eye orientation, language and other cues in social interaction to achieve joint attention to an object or event with others. Joint attention can tell others what they are talking about and the position of the object they are interested in in the environment. Being able to help people understand other people's inner states (such as intentions, emotions, beliefs, desires) is an important prerequisite for the development of language and social learning (Mundy et al. 1990; Tomasello 1995a; Caruana et al. 2017). The impairment of joint attention in ASD patients seriously damages their social

© The Author(s), under exclusive license to Springer Nature Switzerland AG 2022
H. Liu et al. (Eds.): ICIRA 2022, LNAI 13455, pp. 392–402, 2022.
https://doi.org/10.1007/978-3-031-13844-7_38

function. Therefore, it is of great theoretical and practical significance to understand the potential processing mechanism of joint attention in ASD individuals.

Although some studies suggest the existence of complete joint attention in individuals with ASD (Billeci et al. 2016; Kuhn et al. 2010; Rutherford and Krysko 2008; Nation and Penny 2008), it is not clear that the note whether the underlying processing pattern of cues is automatic or reflexive or is predicted based on understanding the intentions of others. Reflexive attention refers to the presence of an attentional cue effect even if the attentional cue is not predictive of the target position or the direction of the attentional cue is opposite to the target position (Friesen and Kingstone 1998). Previous studies have found that ASD individuals rarely have abnormal attentional following when using the Posner cue paradigm (Nation and Penny 2008), which seems to suggest that individuals with ASD seem to have a cue effect on eye fixation comparable to TD. So does this equivalence mean that individuals with ASD can understand the intention behind the turning of the eyes as well as those with TD?

Chawarska et al. (2003) found that ASD individuals and TD individuals had the same pattern of responses to cues through the cuing paradigm. Even if cue accuracy was 50%, their search latency for consistent cues was significantly lower than that for inconsistent cues, and the response latencies of ASD individuals were smaller than those of TD individuals regardless of consistent or discordant conditions, however, there was no significant difference in fixation latencies between ASD and TD individuals when the cues were not eyes but non-biological physical cues. This may be because when the cue is the eyes in the face, the TD individual may consider the intention of the person behind the cues, and the ASD individual may process it only as a physical cue, ignoring the intention factor. When gaze direction was found not to predict target position, ASD patients were more dependent on eye cue movements than TD individuals to trigger attention shifts (Ristic et al. 2005), and a study found that children with ASD were more sensitive to arrows and gaze cues Responding reflexively, children with TD are able to suppress responses to non-predictive cues (Senju et al. 2004). These studies all seem to suggest that children with ASD respond to social (eyes) and nonsocial (arrows) cues using the same, learned, nonsocial mechanisms, but this is also only speculated from behavioral reaction times, the underlying ASD individuals The psychological mechanism remains unclear. This study was conducted to further explore the underlying processing mechanisms of joint attention in children with ASD.

Many studies use action intention to explore whether ASD individuals can understand the behaviors of others in tasks involving mental states as TD individuals can, and respond to the objects and motor behaviors that others look at by prospectively observing the areas or objects that people may take action on (Biro 2013). According to many scholars, this behavior reflects an understanding of the goal-orientation or "about sex" of the actor's behavior, and is therefore an important organizer of social cognition and the basis for a more complex process of developing social understanding and social reciprocity (Cannon and Woodward 2012). (Vivanti et al. 2014) used an eye-tracking paradigm to explore the understanding of action information in individuals with ASD by manipulating the actor's movements. Therefore, this study explored the potential processing mechanism of common attention in children with ASD by manipulating actors' movements and head direction cues in videos.

2   Method

2.1   Participants

Thirty-three children with ASD were recruited in a special education school in Fujian Province, and all the children could provide a clinical diagnosis certificate from a tertiary hospital. Excluding 1 child who could not cooperate with the experiment, there were 32 valid subjects, including 27 boys and 5 girls, with an average age ($M \pm SD$) of 11.79 ± 2.49 years old. All subjects had no other mental diseases and normal vision or corrected vision. The CARS score ($M \pm SD$) for all children was 30.69 ± 6.26. The mean IQ of children with ASD tested by PPVT was 33.72 (±23.04).

There were 35 preschoolers from a kindergarten in Fujian, one of which was deleted due to the low sampling rate. Finally, there were 34 effective subjects, including 26 boys and 8 girls, with an average age ($M \pm SD$) of 4.29 ± 0.94 years old. The average score of IQ measured by PPVT was 28.88 (±18.26), which was not significantly different from that of ASD children ($t = -0.94, p > .05$).

There were 35 preschoolers from a kindergarten in Fujian, one of which was deleted due to the low sampling rate. Finally, there were 34 effective subjects, including 26 boys and 8 girls, with an average age ($M \pm SD$) of 4.29 ± 0.94 years old. The average score of IQ measured by PPVT was 28.88 (±18.26), which was not significantly different from that of ASD children ($t = -0.94, p > .05$) (Table 1).

Table 1. Demographic information of subjects in Experiment 1

	ASD ($n = 32$)	TD ($n = 34$)	Comparison coefficient	p-value
Age	11.79 ± 2.49	4.29 ± 0.94	$t(60) = -16.02$	<.000
Gender: (male female)	27,5	26,8	—	—
PPVT	33.72 ± 23.04	28.88 ± 18.27	$t(60) = -0.94$	>.05
CARS	30.69 ± 6.26		—	—

2.2   Instruments

The EyeLink Portable Duo portable eye tracker is used to collect data, and the telemetry mode with a sampling rate of 1000 Hz is used, and the tracking accuracy is about 0.5° of viewing angle.

2.3   Materials

The experimental material is a video shot in a real-world scene. In order to exclude the influence of other irrelevant factors, the distance and angle between the camera and the actor remained unchanged during the shooting, and the shooting environment was carried out in a closed room; during the shooting, the actors' expressions and movements were all expressed in relaxed and natural conditions.

The experimental material is a video stimulation sequence (the video is an actor showing an incomplete action for 5 s). At the beginning of the video, the actor sits in the center of the sofa and bows his head, with his hands naturally placed on his knees. After 1s, the actor raises his head, and one hand naturally faces one side. The direction of the object is carried out, and the actor's hand is very close to the object at the end of the video. The experimental conditions were controlled by controlling the orientation of the actor's one-handed hand. There were two types of hand conditions for the actor, one with the palm facing down, doing the action of grasping the object; the other with the palm facing up, doing the upward grasping action. In the end, there are 16 videos in total, 8 videos with palms up and 8 videos with palms down, balancing gender and left and right hands, as shown in Fig. 1.

A palm up condition   B palm down condition

Fig. 1. Example pictures of two stimuli in the experiment

2.4 Procedure

There were two main subjects, one explained the experimental process to the subjects and controlled the software of the eye tracker in the computer, and the other subjects comforted the subjects by the side. The experimental environment is quiet and comfortable, and the light is suitable. Each subject conducts the experiment separately, and the specific process is as follows: (1) Calibration: The subject sits on a chair with his eyes looking straight ahead, adjusts the seat according to the sampling range of the eye tracker and the subject's comfort level, and explains the experimental procedure to the children, using the 5-point calibration standard, if the calibration fails to meet the standard, re-calibrate; (2) After the calibration is completed, the instruction is displayed: "Children, please look at the front computer screen carefully", after which the Eyelink Bulider program will automatically play all stimuli sequence: The central fixation cross appears for 1 s first, then disappears for 5 s of video stimuli, and then continues to appear for 1 s of the central fixation point, followed by video stimuli, and randomly play all video sequences until the end, the experimental flow chart is shown in Fig. 2.

While the participants were watching the video, the two subjects did not ask them to respond, and when the participants were observed to be distracted or their movements were too large to deviate from the tracking range of the tracker, they were reminded to look at the screen, and the experiment was done after all the videos were played. Finish. After the experiment, the subjects were given a small gift.

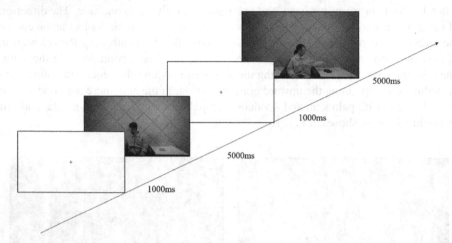

Fig. 2. Example picture of experiment 1 process

2.5 Design

The freely viewing paradigm was adopted, and the experiment was a 2 (subject type: ASD children, TD children) × 2 (one-handed cues: palm up, palm down) two-factor mixed experimental design.

2.6 Areas of Interest, Data Analysis Indicators and Statistical Methods

The time for selecting the dynamic interest area is after the actor starts to turn his head, and then divides into four interest areas: the actor's head, the target object, the non-target object and the actor's hand interest area. Analysis metrics include:

- (1) IA dwell time: refers to the sum of the duration of all fixation points of the participant in the area of interest. This indicator can usually reflect the time dimension of the participant's orientation to a certain type of situation;
- (2) IA fixation count: refers to the sum of all fixations in the area of interest. This indicator can reflect the breadth of the participants' orientation towards a certain type of situation;
- (3) Number of attentional transitions between areas of interest: refers to the number of transitions of the participant's gaze between two areas of interest (Fig. 3).

Fig. 3. Experiment 1 example picture of interest area (1 is the full video interest area; 2 is the head interest area, 3 is the object interest area)

2.7 Experimental Results and Data Analysis

Eye movement indicators such as fixation latency, first fixation duration, fixation time and fixation times were processed using the Data Viewer software that comes with the eye tracker. At the same time, combined with SPSS 24, repeated measures analysis of variance was performed on eye movement data such as attention cues under different conditions.

3 Results

3.1 Gaze in the Dynamic Object Area of Interest

For the dynamic object area of interest, a repeated measures variance of 2 (subject type: ASD children; TD children) × 2 (one-handed cues: palm up; palm down) × 2 (object type: target object; non-target object) analyze (Table 2).

Table 2. ASD and TD children's gaze on the dynamic interest area of objects ($M \pm SD$)

Index	Subject type	Palm up non-target	Palm up target	Palm down non-target	Palm down target
Dwell time (ms)	TD	61 ± 55	355 ± 268	66 ± 93	465 ± 326
	ASD	14 ± 26	217 ± 270	11 ± 29	262 ± 297
Fixation count	TD	0.24 ± 0.21	0.90 ± 0.59	0.27 ± 0.33	1.17 ± 0.70
	ASD	0.06 ± 0.10	0.60 ± 0.58	0.05 ± 0.11	0.75 ± 0.64

- (1) Gaze time

The main effect of subject type was significant $F(1,64) = 9.45, p < .05, \eta_p^2 = 0.13$, and the TD children's fixation time on the object area was significantly longer than that of the ASD children. The main effect of one-handed cues was significant $F(1,64) = 6.97$, $p < .05, \eta_p^2 = 0.10$, and the dwell time to the object area was significantly longer when the palm was facing down than when the palm was facing up. The main effect of object type was significant $F(1,64) = 83.46, p < .001, \eta_p^2 = 0.57$, and the fixation time of the ROI of the target object was significantly longer than that of the non-target object. The interaction between one-handed cues and object type was significant $F(1,64) = 8.95, p < .01, \eta_p^2 = 0.12$, further simple effect test found that for the target region, the fixation time of the target region with the hand facing down was significantly greater than that with the hand facing up, but there was no significant difference between the two conditions without the target region. Whether palm up or palm down, the fixation time of the target object is longer than that of the non-target object. Other effects are not significant.

- (2) Fixation count

The main effect of subject type was significant $F(1,64) = 11.19, p < .01, \eta_p^2 = 0.15$, and the number of TD children's fixation on the object area was significantly greater than that of ASD children. The main effect of single-handed cues was significant $F(1,64) = 9.82$, $p < .01, \eta_p^2 = 0.13$, and fixation count on the object area was significantly greater when the palm was facing down than when the palm was facing up. The main effect of object type is significant $F(1,64) = 121.46, p < .001, \eta_p^2 = 0.66$, the fixation times of the target object area of interest is significantly greater than the fixation time of non-target objects. The interaction between one-handed cues and object type was significant $F(1,64) = 10.55, p < .01, \eta_p^2 = 0.1$, and further simple effect test found that for the target object area, the number of times the subjects looked at it when the palm was facing down was significantly greater than when the palm is facing up, the non-target object area has no significant difference between the two conditions; no matter whether the palm is facing up or the palm is facing down, the subjects fixate on the target object more frequently than the non-target object. The remaining effects were not significant.

3.2   Pay Attention to the Number of Conversions

2 (subject type: ASD children; TD children) × 2 (one-handed cues: palm up; palm downward) repeated measures ANOVA (Table 3).

- (1) Attention transition between head-hand ROIs

The main effect of subject type was significant $F(1,64) = 24.91, p < .001, \eta_p^2 = 0.28$. The number of attention transitions between head-hand interest areas in TD children was significantly greater than that in ASD children. The remaining effects were not significant.

Table 3. Attention transitions ($M \pm SD$) in children with ASD and TD

Subject type	Palm up			Palm down		
	Head-hand	Hand-target object	Head-target object	Head-hand	Hand-target object	Head-target object
TD	3.09 ± 2.09	2.53 ± 1.93	1.79 ± 1.68	3.53 ± 2.35	2.88 ± 2.52	2.15 ± 1.96
ASD	1.25 ± 1.34	0.91 ± 1.03	1.00 ± 1.70	1.25 ± 1.59	0.81 ± 1.15	1.47 ± 1.87

- (2) Attention transition between hand-target object area of interest

The main effect of subject type was significant $F(1,64) = 26.61, p < .001, \eta_p^2 = 0.29$, and the number of attention transitions between hand and target object interest area of TD children was significantly greater than that of ASD children. The remaining effects were not significant.

- (3) Attention transition between head-target object area of interest

Subject type edge was significant $F(1,64) = 3.29, p = .08, \eta_p^2 = 0.28$, TD children had more attention transitions between head-target object interest areas than ASD children. The main effect of one-handed cues was significant $F(1,64) = 5.10, p < .05, \eta_p^2 = 0.07$, and the number of attention transitions between the head-target area of interest with the palms down was significantly greater than that with the palms up. The remaining effects were not significant.

3.3 Model Building Between IQ and CARS Scales and Attention

Calculate the regression model between the fixation time of the target object area after the head starts to turn and the PPVT IQ of ASD children. The results show that the fixation time of ASD on the target area is related to IQ ($r^2 = 0.05, p > .05$), CARS score ($r^2 = 0.05, p > .05$) and age ($r^2 = 0.01, p > .05$). The gaze time of the ASD children on the actor's head was not significantly related to IQ ($r^2 = 0.03, p > .05$), CARS score ($r^2 = 0.00, p > .05$) and age ($r^2 = 0.01, p > .05$).

4 Discussion

From a social cognition perspective, the development of shared attention is thought to be closely related to the development of the ability to understand the mental states of others, such as emotions, thoughts, and intentions (Tomasello 1995b). Intent understanding in particular has been the focus of many studies. According to the social cognitive model, children do not develop joint attention skills until they understand the intentions of others and that their actions are goal- orientation. Children with autism have problems with shared attention, possibly because they have difficulty understanding intent (Tomasello et al. 2006). Previous studies have suggested that the processing of social stimuli, such as the eyes, is atypical in children with ASD, who respond to social (eyes) and nonsocial (arrows) cues with the same, learned, and asocial mechanisms, such as children with ASD are able to respond more quickly to eye cues, possibly because TD individuals spend more time responding to social eye movements (Chawarska et al. 2003).

This study found that children with ASD can shift their attention to the target object according to cues, and the actor's hand movements will affect their gaze pattern on the target. When the palm is facing down, the ASD children's gaze on the target object is significantly greater than when the palm is facing up, which suggests that children with ASD have reactive joint attention abilities based on understanding the intentions of others, which is consistent with the findings of Krogh-Jespersen et al. (2018). The latter experiment found that children can predict the most likely outcome of goal- orientation action based on the trajectory information of the actor's hand movements in the video material, that is, lock their attention to the target in advance before the actor's hand touches the toy, which is consistent with this experiment. What's more, their video material also shows the actor's internal state by turning his head while holding out a hand.

Studies have shown that individuals with ASD have a complete ability to understand the consequences of actions, and when they see that others are not performing the action in the most efficient way, they will stare at other people for a longer time (Vivanti et al. 2011), which Explain that children with ASD can not only understand the action itself, but also consider the rationale for the action based on contextual information. Similar to Falck-Ytter's (2010) study, he found that young children with autism can predict other people's action goals, and can predict goals based on hand cues. These studies seem to suggest that children with ASD retain the ability to understand other people's intentions through movement.

When the cues are clear and single, although ASD children can shift their attention according to the cues and understand the intentions of others, there are still deficiencies in the overall processing of reactive joint attention, which is mainly manifested in the time and frequency of fixation of the target object by ASD children Compared with the TD children, the number of attention transitions between various interest areas was significantly smaller than that of the TD children. There may be two reasons for the reduction in the number of attentional transitions: on the one hand, because of impaired social orientation, children with ASD are more inclined to look at non-social stimuli than social stimuli (Parish-Morris et al. 2013); On the one hand, because of the attentional dissociation disorder, it is difficult for their attention to leave the current focus area and then focus on new areas/stimuli (Qianjiaqun, Wang Enguo 2022), so the number of attentional transitions decreases.

5   Conclusion

Children with ASD have the ability of reactive joint attention and can shift their attention according to cues, and this ability is based on understanding the intention of others' actions. However, compared with TD children, their reactive joint attention is impaired as a whole, which is manifested in the fixation time on the target is shorter, and the number of transitions between the cue and the target is lower.

Funding. This study was supported by the Fujian Provincial Natural Science Foundation Project (2020J01656).

References

Fifth Edition: Diagnostic and statistical manual of mental disorders. Am. Psychiatric Assoc. **21**, 591–643 (2013)

Dawson, G., Bernier, R., Ring, R.H.: Social attention: a possible early indicator of efficacy in autism clinical trials. J. Neurodev. Disord. **4**(1), 1–12 (2012)

Mundy, P., Sigman, M., Kasari, C.: A longitudinal study of joint attention and language development in autistic children. J. Autism Dev. Disord. **20**(1), 115–128 (1990)

Tomasello, M.: Joint attention as social cognition. In: Moore, C., Dunham, P. (eds.) Joint Attention: Its Origins and Role in Development, pp. 103–130. Lawrence Erlbaum, Hillsdale (1995)

Caruana, N., Ham, H.S., Brock, J., Woolgar, A., Mcarthur, G.: Joint attention difficulties in autistic adults: an interactive eye-tracking study. Autism **22**(4), 1–11 (2017)

Billeci, L., et al.: Disentangling the initiation from the response in joint attention: an eye-tracking study in toddlers with autism spectrum disorders. Transl. Psychiatry **6**(5), e808 (2016)

American Psychiatric Association: Diagnostic and Statistical Manual of Mental Disorders: DSM-5. American Psychiatric Association, Washington, DC (2013)

Kuhn, G., Benson, V., Fletcher-Watson, S., Kovshoff, H., Mccormick, C.A., Kirkby, J., et al.: Eye movements affirm: automatic overt gaze and arrow cueing for typical adults and adults with autism spectrum disorder. Exp. Brain Res. **201**(2), 155–165 (2010)

Rutherford, M.D., Krysko, K.M.: Eye direction, not movement direction, predicts attention shifts in those with autism spectrum disorders. J. Autism Dev. Disord. **38**(10), 1958–1965 (2008)

Nation, K., Penny, S.: Sensitivity to eye gaze in autism: is it normal? Is it automatic? Is it social? Dev. Psychopathol. **20**(1), 79–97 (2008)

Friesen, C.K., Kingstone, A.: The eyes have it! Reflexive orienting is triggered by nonpredictive gaze. Psychon. Bull. Rev. **5**(3), 490–495 (1998)

Chawarska, K., Klin, A., Volkmar, F.: Automatic attention cueing through eye movement in 2-year-old children with autism. Child Dev. **74**(4), 1108–1122 (2003)

Ristic, J., Mottron, L., Friesen, C.K., Iarocci, G., Burack, J.A., Kingstone, A.: Eyes are special but not for everyone: the case of autism. Cogn. Brain Res. **24**(3), 715–718 (2005)

Senju, A., Tojo, Y., Dairoku, H., Hasegawa, T.: ReXexive orienting in response to eye gaze and an arrow in children with and without autism. J. Child Psychol. Psychiatry **45**(3), 445–458 (2004)

Biro, S.: The role of the efficiency of novel actions in infants' goal anticipation. J. Exp. Child Psychol. **116**(2), 415–427 (2013)

Cannon, E.N., Woodward, A.L.: Infants generate goal-based action predictions. Dev. Sci. **15**, 292–298 (2012)

Vivanti, G., Trembath, D., Dissanayake, C.: Atypical monitoring and responsiveness to goal-directed gaze in autism spectrum disorder. Exp. Brain Res. **232**(2), 695–701 (2014). https://doi.org/10.1007/s00221-013-3777-9

Tomasello, M.: Joint attention as social cognition. In: Moore, C., Dunham, P.J. (eds.) Joint Attention: Its Origins and Role in Development, pp. 1–14. Lawrence Erlbaum Associates, Hillsdale (1995)

Tomasello, M., Hare, B., Lehmann, H., Call, J.: Reliance on head versus eyes in the gaze following of great apes and human infants: the cooperative eye hypothesis. J. Hum. Evol. **52**(3), 314–320 (2006)

Krogh-Jespersen, S., Kaldy, Z., Valadez, A.G., Carter, A.S., Woodward, A.L.: Goal prediction in 2-year-old children with and without autism spectrum disorder: an eye-tracking study. Autism Res. **11**(6), 870–882 (2018)

Vivanti, G., Mccormick, C., Young, G.S., Nadig, A., Ozonoff, S., Rogers, S.J.: Intact and impaired mechanisms of action understanding in autism. Dev. Psychol. **47**(3), 841–856 (2011)

Falck-Ytter, T.: Young children with autism spectrum disorder use predictive eye movements in action observation. Biol. Let. **6**(3), 375–378 (2010)

Parish-Morris, J., Chevallier, C., Tonge, N., Letzen, J., Pandey, J., Schultz, R.T.: Visual attention to dynamic faces and objects is linked to face processing skills: a combined study of children with autism and controls. Front. Psychol. **4**, 185 (2013)

Recent Development on Robot Assisted Social Skills Intervention of Children with ASD

Lei Cai[1], Xiaolong Zhou[1,2(✉)], Zhuoyue Shen[1], and Yujie Wang[1]

[1] College of Electrical and Information Engineering, Quzhou University, Quzhou 324000, China
xiaolong@ieee.org
[2] Key Lab of Spatial Data Mining and Information Sharing of Ministry of Education, Fuzhou 350108, China

Abstract. Children with autism spectrum disorder (ASD) have significant challenges in social interaction. With the rapid development of intelligent robot technology, robot assisted ASD children therapy has penetrated into the intervention of social skills. In this paper, we mainly focus on reviewing the recent development on robot assisted social skills intervention of children with ASD. First, five kinds of robots for ASD children assisted diagnosis and treatment are introduced and the respective advantages and disadvantages are analyzed. Then, five robot assisted social skill intervention scenarios are reviewed and analyzed. Finally, the future research directions on robot assisted ASD children diagnosis and treatment are proposed.

Keywords: ASD children · Robot-assisted diagnosis and treatment · Social skills intervention

1 Introduction

Autism, also known as autism or autism spectrum disorder (ASD), is a representative disease of generalized developmental disorder and a serious neurodevelopmental disorder. It usually occurs in early childhood and the time of occurrence is not clearly defined. Stereotyped behavior and narrow interests, language and communication barriers and social barriers are the three main clinical manifestations. According to the data from the "Report on the Development of China's Autism Education Rehabilitation Industry" [1], the incidence rate of autism in China has reached 0.7%. At present, there are more than 10 million people with ASDs, including more than 2 million children under the age of 12.

Social skills deficiency is a core challenge for children with ASDs. Due to the great differences in skill level, cognitive ability, coping ability and the type and number of specific challenges shown by patients with each spectrum disorder, a single scheme is not effective for all patients. Many children affected by autism can benefit from other interventions, such as speech and other professional treatments. The ABA training method [2] has strong purpose for the specific behavior of patients, but the training form and content are single. There is still a large gap between the real social environment and

H. Liu et al. (Eds.): ICIRA 2022, LNAI 13455, pp. 403–412, 2022.
https://doi.org/10.1007/978-3-031-13844-7_39

the experimental environment, so it is difficult for patients to overcome psychological obstacles.

With the development of science and technology, more and more new technologies have been applied to assist the intervention experiments of children with ASD, in which robot has become one of the important research tools. A large number of studies [3] have proved that robot technology has a good effect in the fields of early diagnosis, monitoring and recording, emotion recognition, social skills, behavior correction and game interaction of children with ASD. Huijnen et al. [4] and others [5, 6] pointed out that robots can more accurately collect data and analyze the symptoms of children with ASD. Therefore, robot technology plays an irreplaceable role in promoting the diagnosis and treatment of children with ASD. This paper summarizes the research results on the application of robots in the social skills of children with ASD, hoping to provide reference for the social skills intervention of children with ASD in China.

2   ASD Children Assisted Diagnosis and Treatment Robots

2.1   KASPER Robot

As shown in Table 1, the KASPAR Robot [7–9] developed by the Adaptive System Research Group at the University of Hertfordshire has a simplified human-like appearance that communicates with autistic children through gestures, expressions and language. The first KASPAR Robot was introduced in 2005, now has been developed for five generations. As versions continue to upgrade, researchers have successively used Wii Remote control, touch skin patch, speaker and other technologies on the Robot. The new generation of robots is manufactured using modern manufacturing methods such as laser cutting and 3D printing, incorporating an RFID reader, a FSR sensor, and a strong neodymium magnet in the hand. At the same time, the new generation of robots [10] is able to make WiFi connections without having to be fixed on a computer, greatly improving their ability to interact with autistic children.

2.2   NAO Robot

The NAO robot produced by Aldebaran Company of France is often used in all kinds of robot-assisted autism diagnosis and treatment experiments. It is the earliest autism diagnosis and treatment robot introduced into China. The NAO robot has mature performance, voice, motion and other functions, can express anger, fear, sadness, happiness, excitement and pride, and can deduce its emotional changes by learning the body language and expression of the interactors. The head of the NAO robot [11] is not very human-like. Therefore, autistic children will not feel threatened and have a strong attractiveness to autistic children, but NAO robots also have deficiencies [12]. It is a limitation that the robot cannot turn its eyes, which makes autistic children unable to notice the eyes of the robot and prevents it from acting as a human agent.

Table 1. Overview of assisted diagnosis and treatment robots for ASD children

Robot model	R & D institutions	Major function
KASPAR	Adaptive systems research group at the University of Hertfordshire	KASPER can make a positive contribution to learning and improving body awareness and prolonging children's attention span
NAO	France Aldebaran company	It can realize dialogue with people, playing music, action communication and even emotional communication
KIBO	The research team at the Tufts University	Children with autism can be helped by creating an environment for practicing and using social and coding skills
Rero	Unknown	Help children imitate actions, follow instructions, name objects, focus and match colors
Rehabilitation robot for ASD children based on Beidou	Tianjin Key Laboratory of intelligent signal and image processing	Through intelligent interaction, children can concentrate, improve their interest in learning and stimulate their enthusiasm

2.3 KIBO Robot

The research team of the University of Tofz, led by Dr. Marina UmaSchi Beers [13], dedicated to the design and development of KIBO robots for the target group of 4–7 years old. KIBO is a screenless robot platform, which reduces the complexity and coding understanding of the operation. It has a simple visual interface, which can effectively promote face-to-face interaction with children with autism, thereby promoting children's communication with the outside world.

2.4 Rero Robot

As a commercial robot, the Rero [14] robot is used as an interactive medium. The robot is selected based on its reconfigurable ability and the ability to be developed into multiple forms. It is mobile, voice-enabled, controllable, programmable and attractive. Furthermore, five interactive modules have been developed to help children imitate actions, follow instructions, name objects, and focus and match colors.

2.5 Beidou-Based Autism Children Rehabilitation Robot

The Beidou-based rehabilitation robot [15] for autistic children developed in China has similar appearance and intelligent interaction with human. Its program design includes

Beidou signal processing, voice signal processing, rudder control and motor control, which makes it easier for autistic children to receive external information and improve their social ability.

2.6 Trends and Difficulties of Robot Development

Compared with the previous research on assistant diagnostic and therapeutic robots, the robots developed now are not only simple interactive, but more intelligent. They can deduce children's emotional changes and concentration based on their facial expressions and behavior. However, there are still many difficulties and they are in a dynamic stage of development. Currently, new trends in the development of autistic robots include the ability to detect user moods and preferences, and to adjust their behavior to these factors in real time, as well as the ability to perceive and respond appropriately to user behavior. At the same time, the design, portability, safety and reliability of the robot need to be further improved, which is an important direction for the future development of autism diagnosis and treatment robots.

3   Robot Assisted Social Skills Intervention for ASD Children

The research of using robots to help children with ASD began in 1976. Weir and Emanue [7] used remote control robot to improve the social behavior of a 7-year-old child with ASD, and achieved good results. Since then, researchers have devoted themselves to developing more flexible and intelligent robots, enhancing the social skills of children with ASD, and through the interaction between robots and children with ASD, achieving social means such as improving their emotional understanding and communication skills. Therefore, the design and development of robot has certain pertinence, and the social related ability of children with ASD can be improved by exploring several fields of social skills [17], such as imitation, joint attention, emotion recognition and expression, rotation and cooperation, active communication, etc.

3.1   Imitation

Impaired imitation and motor skills are regarded as the core symptoms of autistic children. Therefore, it is important to use robots to help children improve their imitation ability [18]. Taheril et al. [19] conducted a test in a $10 \times 5 \times 3$ m^3 playroom. Twenty children with ASD learned actions in two modes of robot-child interaction (mode A) and teacher-child interaction (mode B), and finally scored by their parents. Obviously, autistic children in mode A got higher scores. The research of Duquette [20] shows that the four children with ASDs participating in the test have reduced repetitive fixed behavior, have more eye contact with the robot Tito, have more emotional fluctuations, and are willing to follow. Zheng et al. [21] proposed an imitation skill process for robot intervention of children with ASDs (including Nao robot, camera for posture recognition, posture recognition algorithm and feedback mechanism for evaluating imitation posture). Four children with ASD and six normal children were tested, and each group selected robots and human therapists to show a set of arm movements (including raising one hand, waving, raising both hands and extending the arm to the side). The results showed that ASD children focused on robots 11% more than human therapists, and ASD children scored higher in imitating robots than human therapists.

3.2 Joint Attention

The main defect of ASD children is their social skills, and joint attention (JA) plays an important role in social interaction. JA refers to a set of behaviors that enable two partners to pay attention to the third entity, object or event through voice or non-voice [22]. The behavioral dimension of JA [23] has been replaced by various labels. Many studies have shown that it is urgent to improve JA of ASD children. HOANG-LONGCAO et al. [24] By comparing the JA status of ASD children's interaction with adults and social robots, it can be found that when interacting with social robots, both eye attention and behavioral motivation are improved. Yun et al. [25] selected 15 children with ASD in South Korea, and randomly divided 8 of them into the experimental group (robots iRo, biQ and CARO participated in the intervention training process), and 7 into the control group (two nurses participated in the intervention training process). They were trained in social skills, and found that the eye contact frequency of ASD children in the experimental group increased significantly, which was better than that of the control group. Twenty-four autistic male children aged 4–6 years were diagnosed in Guangzhou Women's and Children's Medical Center [26]. All of them met the diagnostic criteria of DSM-5. The score of the Child Autism Rating Scale (CARS) was higher than 36. Schizophrenia and obsessive-compulsive disorders were excluded. Twenty-four children were randomly divided into two groups, 12 in the experimental group, 12 in the control group, and 12 in the floor time social training [27]. David et al. [28] studied the use of social robots in Cluj-Napoca, Romania. Five children with ASD participated in their study. The researchers hypothesized that the more social cues (e.g., head direction, pointing, and verbal cues) the robot used in child robot interaction, the better the child's performance in maintaining joint attention. The results are consistent with the hypothesis. After testing, it was found that the group of JA with humanoid robot was in better condition and had more remission.

3.3 Emotion Recognition and Expression

Children with autism tend to hide their emotions, while others' emotions are escaping and hiding. Emotional cognitive impairment of ASD group is also a manifestation of empathy deficit [29]. For example, a robot called Milo can depict various emotions, such as happiness, sadness, anger and fear. Through facial expressions, children choose the appropriate emotions and use a tablet based multi-choice interface. The recognition ability of ASD children's emotional expression shows that in the social skills treatment environment, the humanoid robot (Zeno) [30] uses gestures to convey emotional expression, which will significantly affect the accuracy of emotional expression prediction. Kozima et al. [31] also shows that ASD children like to show their joy to robots and are willing to convey this emotion to adults. Vanstraten et al. [32] evaluate the emotional state results of 4–8-year-old autistic children playing puzzle games with robots. The researchers studied the effects of robot intonation and body appearance, and pointed out that both of these aspects will affect children's emotional state. ASD children are more interested in humanoid robot emotional expression.

3.4 Rotation and Cooperation

Due to the presence of social disorders, autistic children have common difficulties in acquiring and expressing social rules. Many ASD children do not understand and master the basic social rules of rotation and cooperation. Rotation behavior [33] refers to operating one by one according to specific rules and sequences. Cooperation refers to the operation with partners. Because many ASD children cannot understand these two operations, they often destroy the game and process and are often isolated. Therefore, it is very vital to use robots to help ASD children master this social skill. Through its status as a clear social existence, it is more animated than typical toys, but its social complexity is less than that of people. Robots [14] can arouse children's initiative more easily. Autistic children show more social participation when interacting with robots than when interacting with people [34]. An autonomous humanoid robot KASPAR [8] plays a binary cooperative video game with ASD children. Under specific rules, autistic children are allowed to participate in both cooperative game forms and social interactions with other players. Experiments show that [7] ASD children can persist many times. This research shows that humanoid robots can help children with the ASD to improve their ability to take turns and cooperate.

3.5 Active Communication

The most inadequate skill for ASD children is active communication, because they are afraid of contact with others and are unwilling to communicate their ideas to others actively. Because of its unique construction, robots can easily make autistic children drop their psychological alert and communicate with them in order to improve their social skills. Some robots [35] have the function of sensory processing, which can judge the initiative and appropriateness of behavior in the process of communication through the touch of children. In another study, Taheri et al. [36] observed that after the robot assisted the group game program, the language communication of autistic children's group increased significantly. Saadatzi et al. [37] conducted a study using social robots and virtual technology to guide ASD children to learn. After the test, the researchers observed that participants responded positively to the performance of robot peers (such as "thank you" and "well done"). One of the participants kept greeting and hugging the robot at the end of the meeting.

3.6 Advantages and Disadvantages of Robot-Assisted Intervention in Social Interaction of ASD Children

Robots have brought many positive reactions since they were used to treat autistic children. Many studies [20, 21, 23, 30, 33] have shown that ASD children tend to put down their vigilance and have greater interest and enthusiasm when facing robots, which is conducive to improving the social skills of autistic children and helping them to better integrate into society. However, the defects of robots cannot be ignored. The range of robot action is often large, which is easy to hurt ASD children by mistake. Moreover, at present, the robot vision detection and line of sight tracking technology for ASD children is not mature, so it cannot better help ASD children. In addition, in practical application, the lack of robot intelligence, language, emotion and flexibility may also hinder the treatment of autism. If ASD children feel irritable and tired of the stiff words, rigid actions and repeated expressions shown by the robot, their cognition will collapse seriously.

4 Future Development Direction of Robots for Assisted Diagnosis and Treatment of ASD Children

4.1 Combination of Big Data and Treatment of Children with ASD

The rise of big data [38] has made it easier to share information. Many problems arise when using robots to assist autistic children in their personal treatment. However, with the development of large data, a network platform has already been set up so that cases of children with Robot-Assisted Autism can be uploaded all over the world. Many problems can be solved through data analysis and mining, thus constantly correcting the instructions of the robot, optimizing the computational model of human-computer interaction [39], and making it more effective in the treatment of ASD children.

4.2 Portable Robot Development

Existing robots, such as Nao, KIBO, are often larger and can be used in treatment rooms or laboratories. Autistic children, however, have limited time to stay there, which limits the effectiveness of treatment. So, in the future, we should develop easy-to-carry robots. Because robots as tools to increase interaction with therapists or others may prove very effective. A portable robot at your child's hand might help your child open up to peers and family members. Using robots in clinics opens up communication between children and therapists, and the same phenomenon may prove beneficial in families and schools.

4.3 Development of Semi-autonomous Robots

Today's robots are used to treat children with ASD either by an experienced therapist or by pre-typing instructions. Treatment emergencies can be tricky or even impossible to resolve to interrupt treatment. This mode of treatment not only severely depletes the therapist's energy, but also makes it difficult to achieve the desired results. Therefore, the rise of semi-autonomous robots can solve this problem very well, give the robot semi-autonomous ability, can solve problems independently and well in the face of emergencies, let the robot continue to optimize its own models and algorithms while assisting children with ASD, so as to promote the progress of treatment.

4.4 Affordable Robots that Tend to Be Customized

The prevalence of autistic children varies, leading to differences in robotic assistance, and current mainstream robots are often targeted at mass treatment. So future robots should be more personalized and make treatment plans for every ASD child. Correspondingly, the cost of robots should be reduced by developing powerful platforms that ordinary families can afford. Not only will it tend to be personalized, but also to be civilian, which will drive progress in the treatment of autism as a whole.

5 Conclusion

With the development of robots and human-computer interaction, the use of robots to assist children with autism will become more and more common. Although there are still many problems in the current treatment of robots, with the development of the times and the progress of science and technology, the prospects for these problems to be solved are very bright. The advantages of robotic assisted therapy will be further enlarged to better help children with autism recover to health and move to society!

Acknowledgement. This work was supported by National Natural Science Foundation of China (61876168), Key Lab of Spatial Data Mining and Information Sharing of Ministry of Education (Grant No. 2022LSDMIS02), and National College Students' Innovation and Entrepreneurship Training Program (202111488019).

References

1. WUCAILU CHILDREN'S BEHAVIOR CORRECTION CENTER: Report on the Development of Autism Education and Rehabilitation Industry in China. Beijing Normal University Press, Beijing (2015)
2. Ding, D.W., Zhong, Y., Cheng, X.N., et al.: Effect of applied behavioral analysis training on the quality of life of autistic children. Chin. J. Clin. Psychol. **3**, 564–566 (2015)
3. Chen, J., Xiao, C.P.: Application of robot technology in intervention of autistic children. Chin. J. Clin. Psychol. **25**(4), 789–792 (2017)
4. Huijnen, C.A.G.J., Lexis, M.A.S., de Witte, L.P.: Matching robot KASPAR to autism spectrum disorder (ASD) therapy and educational goals. Int. J. Soc. Robot. **8**(4), 445–455 (2016). https://doi.org/10.1007/s12369-016-0369-4
5. Boucenna, S., et al.: Interactive technologies for autistic children: a review. Cogn. Comput. **6**(4), 722–740 (2014). https://doi.org/10.1007/s12559-014-9276-x
6. Leaf, J.B., Sato, S.K., Javed, A., et al.: The evidence-based practices for children, youth, and young adults with autism report: concerns and critiques. Behav. Interv. **36**(2), 457–472 (2021)
7. Wainer, J., Dautenhahn, K., Robins, B., Amirabdollahian, F.: A pilot study with a novel setup for collaborative play of the humanoid robot KASPAR with children with autism. Int. J. Soc. Robot. **6**(1), 45–65 (2013). https://doi.org/10.1007/s12369-013-0195-x
8. Robins, B., Dickerson, P., Stribling, P., et al.: Robot-mediated joint attention in children with autism: a case study in robot-human interaction. Interact. Stud. **5**(2), 161–198 (2004)
9. Wainer, J., Robins, B., Amirabdollahian, F., et al.: Using the humanoid robot KASPAR to autonomously play triadic games and facilitate collaborative play among children with autism. IEEE Trans. Auton. Ment. Dev. **6**(3), 183–199 (2014)

10. Wood, L.J., Zaraki, A., Robins, B., Dautenhahn, K.: Developing Kaspar: a humanoid robot for children with autism. Int. J. Soc. Robot. **13**(3), 491–508 (2019). https://doi.org/10.1007/s12369-019-00563-6
11. Otterdijk, M., Korte, M., Smeekens, I., et al.: The Effects of long-term child-robot interaction on the attention and the engagement of children with autism. Robotics **9**, 1–15 (2020)
12. Hirokazu, K., Yuichiro, Y., Yuko, Y., et al.: The impact of robotic intervention on joint attention in children with autism spectrum disorders. Mol. Autism **9**, 46 (2018)
13. Albo-Canals, J., Martelo, A.B., Relkin, E., et al.: A pilot study of the KIBO robot in children with severe ASD. Int. J. Soc. Robot. **10**, 71–383 (2018)
14. Kerstin, D., Nehaniv, C.L., Walters, M.L., et al.: KASPAR-a minimally expressive humanoid robot for human-robot interaction research. Appl. Bionics Biomech. **6**(3), 369–397 (2009)
15. Xiong, G.H., Wang, Y., Li, X.W., et al.: Beidou based rehabilitation robot for autistic children. China Equipment Eng. **404**(19), 149–150 (2018)
16. Scassellati, B., Admoni, H., Matarić, M.: Robots for use in autism research. Annu. Rev. Biomed. Eng. **14**, 275–294 (2012)
17. Cabibihan, J.-J., Javed, H., Ang, M., Aljunied, S.M.: Why robots? A survey on the roles and benefits of social robots in the therapy of children with autism. Int. J. Soc. Robot. **5**(4), 593–618 (2013). https://doi.org/10.1007/s12369-013-0202-2
18. Zhang, Y.D., Zhao, C.J., Zhao, M., et al.: Application progress of social robot in the care of children with autism spectrum disorders. J. Nurs. **35**(15), 107–110 (2020)
19. Taheri, A., Meghdari, A., Mahoor, M.H.: A close look at the imitation performance of children with autism and typically developing children using a robotic system. Int. J. Soc. Robot. **13**, 1125–1147 (2021)
20. Duquette, A., Michaud, F., Mercier, H.: Exploring the use of a mobile robot as an imitation agent with children with low-functioning autism. Autonom. Robots **24**(2), 147–157 (2008)
21. Zhi, Z., Young, E.M., Swanson, A.R., et al.: Robot-mediated imitation skill training for children with autism. IEEE Trans. Neural Syst. Rehabil. Eng. **24**(6), 682–691 (2016)
22. Mundy, P.: Joint attention and social-emotional approach behavior in children with autism. Dev. Psychopathol. **7**(1), 63–82 (1995)
23. Wetherby, A.M., Prizant, B.M., Carpenter, M., et al.: Joint attention, cultural learning, and language acquisition: implications for autism. Autistic Spectrum Disorders: A Transactional Developmental Perspective 31–54 (2000)
24. Cao, H.L., Simut, R.E., Desmet, N., et al.: Robot-assisted joint attention: a comparative study between children with autism spectrum disorder and typically developing children in interaction with NAO. IEEE Access **8**, 223325–223334 (2020)
25. Yun, S., Choi, J., Park, S., et al.: Social skills training for children with autism spectrum is order using a robotic behavioral intervention system. Autism Res. **10**(7), 1306–1323 (2017)
26. Yang, S.Y., Gan, Y.Y., Chen, W.X., et al.: Effect of humanoid robot on assisted rehabilitation of autistic children. Mod. Diagn. Treat. **31**(9), 1345–1347 (2020)
27. Sun, B.X., Lu, L.D.: Application of "floor time" in the intervention of emotional and behavioral problems of autistic children. Mod. Spec. Educ. **9**, 57–59 (2017)
28. David, D.O., Costescu, C.A., Matu, S., Szentagotai, A., Dobrean, A.: Developing joint attention for children with autism in robot-enhanced therapy. Int. J. Soc. Robot. **10**(5), 595–605 (2018). https://doi.org/10.1007/s12369-017-0457-0
29. Wang, Z., Tian, J., Zhu, Z.Q.: Emotion cognition intervention effects in children with autism spectrum disorder: a meta-analysis. Psychol. Techniques Appl. **9**(6), 330–342 (2021)
30. Marinoiu, E., Zanfir, M., Olaru, V., et al.: 3D human sensing, action and emotion recognition in robot assisted therapy of children with autism. In: 2018 IEEE/CVF Conference on Computer Vision and Pattern Recognition (CVPR). IEEE (2018)
31. Kozima, H., Michalowski, M.P., Nakagawa, C.: A playful robot for research, therapy, and entertainment. Int. J. Soc. Robot. **1**, 3–18 (2009)

32. Van Straten, C., Smeekens, I., Barakova, E., et al.: Effects of robots' intonation and bodily appearance on robot-mediated communicative treatment outcomes for children with autism spectrum disorder. Pers. Ubiquit. Comput. **22**, 379–390 (2018)
33. Hu, M.J., Guan, W.J., Li, Y.Y.: Pre research on the rotation behavior of autistic children by single attempt teaching method research. Mod. Spec. Educ. **22**, 63–72 (2019)
34. Robins, B., Dautenhahn, K., Boekhorst, R.T., et al.: Robotic assistants in therapy and education of children with autism: can a small humanoid robot help encourage social interaction skills? Univ. Access Inf. Soc. **4**(2), 105–120 (2005)
35. Fan, X.Z.: Review on the research of robot intervention in social skills of children with autism spectrum disorders. Mod. Spec. Educ. **14**, 34–37 (2015)
36. Taheri, A., Meghdari, A., Alemi, M., et al.: Human-robot interaction in autism treatment: a case study on three pairs of autistic children as twins, siblings, and classmates. Int. J. Soc. Robot. **10**, 93–113 (2017)
37. Saadatzi, M.N., Pennington, R.C., Welch, K.C., Graham, J.H.: Small-group technology-assisted instruction: virtual teacher and robot peer for individuals with autism spectrum disorder. J. Autism Dev. Disord. **48**(11), 3816–3830 (2018). https://doi.org/10.1007/s10803-018-3654-2
38. Wang, Y.Z., Jin, X.L., Cheng, X.Q.: Network big data: current situation and prospect. Chin. J. Comput. **36**(6), 1125–1138 (2013)
39. Feng, R.F., Wang, R.J., Xu, W.X.: Research and implementation of an intelligent human-computer interaction model. Comput. Eng. Appl. **42**(24), 91–93 (2006)

Assistive Robot Design for Handwriting Skill Therapy of Children with Autism

Xiansheng Huang(iD) and Yinfeng Fang(✉)(iD)

Hangzhou Dianzi University, Hangzhou 310018, China
{xiansheng.huang,yinfeng.fang}@hdu.edu.cn

Abstract. The complex handwriting skill needs reasonable planning along with fine motor skill. However, most children with Autism Spectrum Disorder (ASD) possess motor deficits adversely affecting handwriting. Specifically, it can be divided into extreme finger force, unsmooth handwriting, uncoordinated fingers and other problems, addressable through intervention and robots can provide efficient and engaging ASD intervention environments for children with Autism. The work presented in this paper aims at targeted training of the skills required for writing by developing a multifunctional hand-held robot. The robot is composed of pressure sensor, optical flow sensor, led and other components and its interactive system includes finger strength training game and trajectory training game. Children with autism complete the training by engaging in emotional touch behaviors through an interactive game system. This study conducted a usability study with 8 right-handed healthy volunteers. The results showed significant improvements in finger strength control, fine motor and trajectory control. In particular, the results of trajectory training show that more visual feedback early in training can help them understand and adapt to the game more quickly. It can be expected that the system can be also applied for children with autism for motor training.

Keywords: Robot-assisted autism therapy · Fine motor skill · Visual feedback

1 Introduction

Autism Spectrum Disorder (ASD) is characterised by impairments in social interactions and communication, usually accompanied by restricted interests and repetitive behaviors [1]. A substantial increase in the prevalence of (ASD) has been observed over the past few decades, sparking claims that autism has become an "epidemic" [2,3]. 80–90% of children with ASD show motor abnormality to some degrees and motor skill impairments, which was directly correlated with severity of social and communication impairments. Studies also pointed that the cause of impairments in motor functioning are related to abnormal cerebellum or functional connectivity abnormalities in the cerebral cortex [4]. Probably due

H. Liu et al. (Eds.): ICIRA 2022, LNAI 13455, pp. 413–423, 2022.
https://doi.org/10.1007/978-3-031-13844-7_40

to the plasticity on the nervous system, early intervention in rehabilitation are proved to be effective in ameliorating the severity of the condition [5]. However, motor dysfunction has only recently been the focus of research on autism spectrum disorders.

The complex handwriting skill relies in facts on fine motor skill, precise in spatial and temporal, therefore ASD children (ASDC) have difficulties in producing good quality handwriting. ASDC generally have the following problems such as wrong pen holding posture, hold the pen too hard/weak, weak/illegible handwriting strokes, slow speed of handwriting and so on [6]. In this context, interactive robots seem to be a promising tool to support the therapeutic activity. In fact, research suggests that ASDC who interact with robots will behave in a positive way, but they do not have such response when interacting with peers, caregivers or teachers [7].

Motor learning theory is an important tool used to study motor function rehabilitation training [8,9]. The currently generally accepted theory is that enhanced feedback can effectively improve motor learning ability, where enhanced feedback refers to external feedback such as visual, auditory, and tactile sensations [10]. As such, many people have designed assistive robots to improve motor skills in ASDC. Palsbo and Hood-Szivek [11] used a haptic robot that was passively trained according to preset handwriting to improve fine motor skills of eighteen children with motor impairments (AHDH, attention deficit disorder, cerebral palsy and ASD) including five ASDC. For the ASDC, progress was observed in writing speed and letter reversal, but it does not involve the coordination of finger strength. Masakazu Nomura et al. [12] developed a system named iWakka to training ASDC's adjustability for grasping force (AGF). Eight participants with autism were involved in this study. The AGF of the four participants who could use iWakka by themselves was improved after training. Lee et al. [13] designed a study to improve the control of hand force using a sphere which could change colour. Eight children had to apply the required force and maintain it until the end of the test. They performed the experiment with and without feedback from the ifbot (an interactive robot). It pointed out that children performed better with robot feedback. At present, few studies involve the coordination between the five fingers while training writing. Given the inherent appeal of robots to ASDC, who able to drive attention and keep motivation on training tasks.

In this framework, this study developed an experimental device that can acquire the pressure of five fingers and the trajectory data of hand movement in real time, which will be used to simulate the force of holding the pen and the direction of the handwriting. To verify the feasibility of this device, this study invited 8 right-handed healthy volunteers to conduct the experiment. The results showed significant improvements in finger strength control, fine motor and trajectory control, can be further applied to children with autism.

2   Material and Methods

2.1   System Architecture

The system includes an assistive robot and an corresponding games for inter-action. The assistive robot is specially designed for ASDC which embeds the dedicated hardware capable of sampling, digitizing and wirelessly transmitting the data of pressure measurements and hand movement trajectory to the PC in real-time (see Fig. 1). This robot can simulate the problems encountered by ASDC in writing to the greatest extent, and can help to train the strength coor-dination of the five fingers, the control of the grasping force and the cognitive training of the writing trajectory. To be able to ensure that ASDC attracts attention and maintains motivation on sensorimotor tasks, interesting interac-tions and engaging scenarios are added to the UI interface.

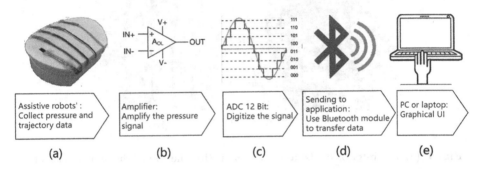

Fig. 1. The modular sensor architecture, embedded inside an assistive robot, is repre-sented here. (a) Force is measured at the prescribed contact point of the object through force sensing resistors (FSRs) and trajectory is collected by moving this robot through a ADNS-3080 sensor. (b) The force signal is amplified. (c) Then the force signal is sampled and filtered by a micro-controller. (d) After that, all the data are transmitted to a remote host. (e) Finally, the data are used to animate an avatar inside a graphical game environment.

2.2   Hardware Design

The hardware architecture for assistive robot is composed of power management circuit, pressure sensor, operational amplifier, optical flow sensor, microcontroller chip, and Bluetooth module (see Fig. 2). When the child uses the robot, the pressure signal is amplified by the operational amplifier and sent to the A/D converter of the STM32 (12 bits resolution) for digitization, and the trajectory signal is sent to the SPI (Serial Peripheral Interface) of the STM32. The STM32 processes the signal and passes it through the Bluetooth module HC-04 sends the signal to the PC. Additionally, this study designed an ergonomic 3D printed shell that allows the ASDC to be used comfortably. The FSRs are reasonably arranged on the top of the 3D printed shell with hot melt adhesive. Other components are embedded inside the shell (see Fig. 3).

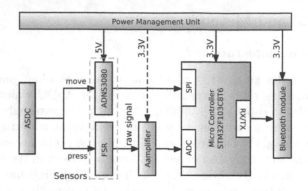

Fig. 2. The hardware architecture for assistive robot

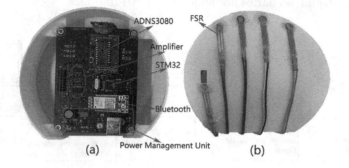

Fig. 3. (a) The interior of the assistive robot. (b) The top of the assistive robot.

This study takes a kind of FSR (Interlink Electronics, Camarillo, CA, US)) to measure the force. The FSR is made of robust polymer film are utilized in this study, which converts the change of pressure into specific resistance change. This series of sensors provide a relatively large sensitivity range (0.2–20 N), the sensing signal grows logarithmically with increasing pressure. However, it loses repeatability at high force range due to unavoidable hysteresis. However, for smaller forces (0–10 N), their transfer function is almost linear. Besides, it has properties of low drift, softness and low cost.

An optical flow sensor ADNS-3080 (Avago Technologies, San Jose, CA, US) is employed in this study to collect the trajectory of the robot as it moves. The ADNS-3080 is a high performance optical mouse sensors, which has a resolution of up to 1600 cpi; the speed of 40 ips is 6400 frames per second; the acceleration of gravity is 15 g. Therefore, it can provide smooth handwriting for ASDC.

2.3 Software Design

Following a methodology specifically designed for therapeutic exergames [14], this study designed two types of fine motor virtual games (see Fig. 4) for interaction, focusing on finger strength and coordination and hand trajectory movement operation. All games have time constraints and must be performed in Complete within a certain period of time (e.g. 15 s). Game performance is assessed by scores.

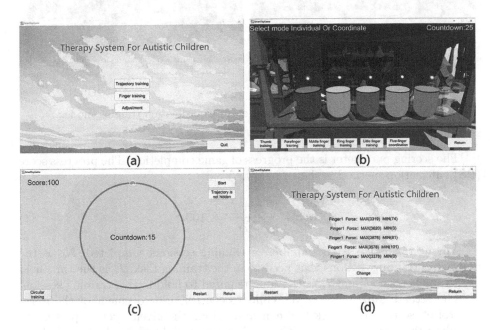

Fig. 4. (a) Home of the game. (b) Finger training game. (c) Trajectory training game. (d) The interface for adjusting the corresponding relationship between the pressure value and the liquid level

In the first game, children can choose five fingers for individual training or finger coordination training (see Fig. 4 (b)). Use fingers to press the pressure sensor, and the liquid level in the five corresponding water bottles will change with the pressure signals (see Fig. 5). When the liquid level reaches the required position (where the black line is) and maintains it for a period of time, a training session can be completed (the black line will change position after completion). The target water level in this training mode is given with a fixed strategy. Complete 5 training sessions within the specified 20 s will get full marks and record the remaining time and the pressure data (from game start to completed). If the training task is not completed, it will be scored according to progress, and the pressure data within these 20 s is recorded. This game is designed to exercise finger coordination and how to apply force reasonably.

Take into account that the strength range of each person's fingers is different. Therefore, by collecting the range of the strength of each finger, it is used to adjust the corresponding function relationship between the force exerted by the finger and the level of the liquid level, so that the training is more targeted and universal (see Fig. 4 (d)).

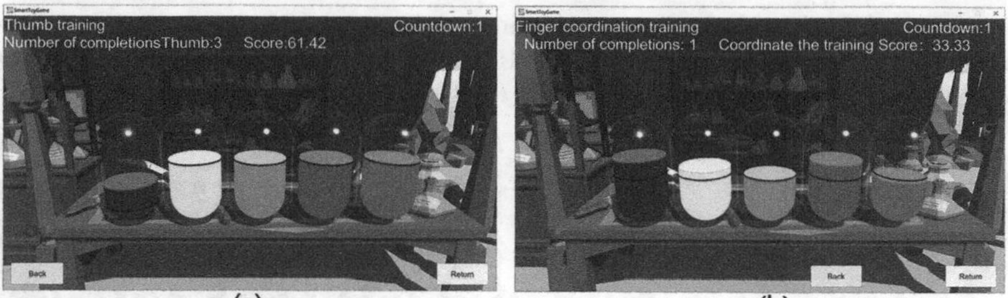

Fig. 5. (a) One-finger training mode. (b) Coordination training mode.

The scoring parameter is the progress of game completion. The progress score (PS) calculation method is shown below.

$$PS = \frac{N_C + \frac{T_c}{T_o}}{N_O} \times 100 \tag{1}$$

Among them, N_C is the number of training sessions completed, N_O is the number of training sessions that need to in the training task, T_c is the time held in a training session, and T_o is the time required to hold in this training session.

The second game requires the child to control the movement of the assistive robot, so that the black ball can move along the given circular pattern to complete the task (see Fig. 6). This task requires children to draw a circle as accurately as possible within 15 s. If the time to draw a circle exceeds 15 s, it will be scored as 0, and if the time is within 15 s, it will be scored according to accuracy. The data recording method is the same as the first game. This game is designed to exercise children's accurate control of time and space when writing.

The scoring parameter is the roundness score (RS). The RS calculation method is shown below.

$$D_i = \sqrt{(x_i - x_o)^2 + (y_i - y_o)^2} \tag{2}$$

$$RS = \frac{R - \sqrt{\frac{\sum\limits_{i=1}^{N}(D_i - R)^2}{N}}}{R} \times 100 \tag{3}$$

Among them, D_i is the distance between the point (x_i, y_i) controlled by the assistive robot and the center of the circle (x_o, y_o), and R is the radius of the circle.

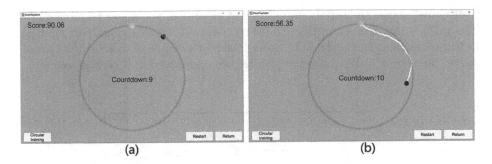

Fig. 6. (a) The task without visual feedback. (b) The task with visual feedback

It can also choose whether to hide the trajectory option, in order to explore the impact of additional visual feedback on children's training (see Fig. 6 (a)). Early stages of motor learning may rely on incoming information to calibrate motor errors, while later stages of motor learning may rely more on proprioception [15]. Among them, the improvement of proprioception is beneficial to motor learning and rehabilitation.

2.4 Experimental Setup

In this experiment, eight subjects volunteered for the experience, all of them right-handed. Before data recording, the research assistant explained the purpose of the experiment, the rules of the game, and the scoring mechanism to the participants. Each participant needs to use the assistive robot to collect the range of finger strength to initialize and calibrate the device. Afterwards, each participant was required to complete a pre-test and a separate training session to get used to the game flow. Start the training task after a 5–10 min rest. Each participant needs to carry out 5 sessions of training, rest for 1–2 min after completing each session. Each training session needs to complete the training task of individual five-finger one time, the coordination task one time and the training task of drawing trajectory three times (For this trajectory training, four participants did not use visual feedback, and the other four participants used visual feedback). After the training, participants were required to complete a questionnaire.

3 Result

Each participant completed the entire training session in an average of 20 min, and none of the participants felt fatigued.

Figure 7 shows the mPS values of 8 participants in the finger training game. The mPS is the average of five PS values obtained by volunteers participating in finger training. In this training game, the performance of most of the participants' fine motor skills of the hands have been improved to a certain extent.

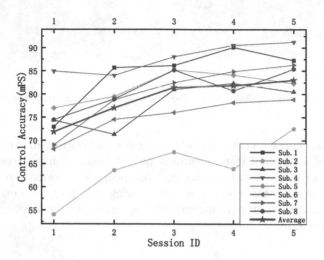

Fig. 7. The changes of control accuracy along the training session across eight subjects. The average curve shows control accuracy averaged from subject 1–8 mPS indicates mean PS.

In the trajectory training game, eight participants were equally divided into a visual feedback group (VG) and a non-visual feedback group (NVG). Figure 8 shows the RS values for the two groups and Fig. 9 shows the time of complete a session. The mRS represents the average score of volunteers in 15 circle-drawing tasks (5 trainings, 3 circles per training). The mRemaining time is the average time spent.

In terms of motion accuracy, VG can quickly achieve high accuracy, and the performance can gradually increase. The NVG motion accuracy improves slowly, but in the end it can reach a similar level. It shows that visual feedback can better assist training in the early stage of learning. In terms of exercise time, although 15 s were specified in the training, the scores obtained by the participants gradually increased, but the time spent did not change much, and even decreased. In general, the participants have improved the planning of space and time to a certain extent, which also verifies that the system is helpful to writing to a certain extent.

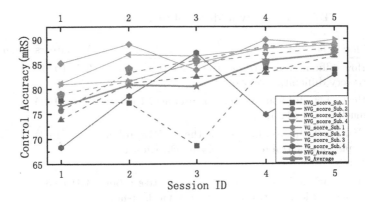

Fig. 8. Changes in mRS values during trajectory training game for eight participants.

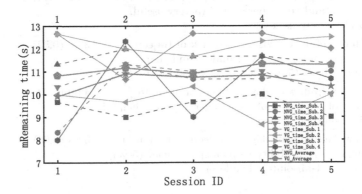

Fig. 9. Changes in mRemaining time during trajectory training game for eight participants.

This study collected participants' feedback about the assistive robot and virtual games with a 5 point-Likert scale questionnaire including eight questions. Table 1 shows the survey questions and responses from the participants. The answers to questions 1–4 indicated that the assistive robot and the corresponding interactive game were well received by the participants. They felt that the operation of the assistive robot was not difficult and that the visual feedback of the game could bring them more interest. But when it comes to finger training game, some people find it a little difficult. Answers to questions 5–6 indicate that they are interested in using the device with sensory feedback to play video games, and that sensory feedback can help them understand the operation of the game. The answers to questions 7–8 show that this training games can improve hand fine motor and handwriting skills to a certain extent.

Table 1. Survey feedback of volunteers group (N = 8)

NO.	Questions	Volunteers mean (SD)
1	How difficult was it to use the assistive robot? (5-very difficult, 1-very easy)	2.75 (0.89)
2	How much did you like the UI interface? (5-very much, 1-not at all)	3.75 (0.71)
3	How much did you like to use the assistive robot to play finger training? (5-very much, 1-not at all)	2.75 (1.04)
4	How much did you like to use the assistive robot to play trajectory training? (5-very much, 1-not at all)	3.31 (0.64)
5	How useful were feedback of pressure to help you understand your operations? (5-very useful, 1-absolutely useless)	4.31 (0.64)
6	How useful were visual feedback of trajectory (white line) to help you understand your operations? (5-very useful, 1-absolutely useless)	3.38 (0.52)
7	How helpful was playing finger training to control the power of your fingers? (5-very helpful, 1-absolutely helpless)	4.00 (0.53)
8	How helpful was playing trajectory training to improve your ability to plan space-time? (5-very helpful, 1-absolutely helpless)	3.88 (0.64)

4   Conclusion and Future Work

In this study, by analyzing the training process and results of eight volunteers, the following points can be drawn: (1) After the training, the control and coordination of the participants' fingers and the ability of handwriting were improved; (2) Most expressed great interest in using the device with haptic feedback to play video games; (3) Participants said that early visual feedback helped them understand and adapt to the game more quickly. The overall ability of volunteers can be improved through special training on the three abilities required for writing skills. As a conclusion, this study develops an effective tool for developing ASDC's fine motor skills and the ability to plan space-time.

In this study discussed with the rehabilitation center for ASDC and related experts and concluded that robots are attractive to ASDC and the colorful interactive interface can attract ASDC to a certain extent. In addition, this assistive robot goes a long way in helping children with autism learn effectively and reducing the workload of therapists. It can also collect all the data during training in real time, so as to further understand how the game plays an auxiliary and therapeutic role in nature.

At present, the interactive game content of the system is not enough, and some games that require the combination of finger force and dynamic programming will be added, such as connecting dots into lines, letters recognition and other games. At the same time, it is also necessary to improve the appearance design of the device to adapt to different hand size.

References

1. American Psychiatric Association: Diagnostic and Statistical Manual of Mental Disorders. American Psychiatric Publishing, Arlington (2013)
2. Fombonne, E.: Is there an epidemic of autism? Pediatrics **107**(2), 411–412 (2001)
3. Fombonne, E.: Epidemiological controversies in autism. Swiss Arch. Neurol. Psychiatry Psychother. **171**(1) (2020)
4. Jouaiti, M., Hénaff, P.: Robot-based motor rehabilitation in autism: a systematic review. Int. J. Soc. Robot. **11**(5), 753–764 (2019). https://doi.org/10.1007/s12369-019-00598-9
5. Izadi-Najafabadi, S., Rinat, S., Zwicker, J.G.: Rehabilitation-induced brain changes detected through magnetic resonance imaging in children with neurodevelopmental disorders: a systematic review. Int. J. Dev. Neurosci. **73**(1), 66–82 (2019)
6. Verma P., Lahiri U.: Deficits in handwriting of individuals with autism: a review on identification and intervention approaches. Rev. J. Autism Dev. Disorders **9**(1), 70–90 (2021)
7. Esteban, P.G., et al.: How to build a supervised autonomous system for robot-enhanced therapy for children with autism spectrum disorder. Paladyn (Warsaw). **8**(1), 18–38 (2017)
8. Krakauer, J.W.: The applicability of motor learning to neurorehabilitation. Oxford Textbook of Neurorehabilitation, Oxford, UK (2015)
9. Lotze, M., Braun, C., Birbaumer, N., Anders, S., Cohen, L.G.: Motor learning elicited by voluntary drive. Brain **126**(4), 866–872 (2003)
10. Crum, E.O., Baltz, M.J., Krause, D.A.: The use of motor learning and neural plasticity in rehabilitation for ataxic hemiparesis: a case report. Physiother. Theory Pract. **126**(11), 1256–1265 (2020)
11. Palsbo, S.E., Hood-Szivek, P.: Effect of robotic-assisted three-dimensional repetitive motion to improve hand motor function and control in children with handwriting deficits: a nonrandomized phase 2 device trial. Am. J. Occup. Ther. **66**(6), 682–690 (2012)
12. Nomura, M., Kucharek, N., Zubrycki, I., Granosik, G., Morita, Y.: Adjustability for grasping force of patients with autism by iWakka: a pilot study. In: 2019 12th International Workshop on Robot Motion and Control (RoMoCo), pp. 50–55. IEEE (2019). https://doi.org/10.1109/RoMoCo.2019.8787382
13. Lee, J., Obinata, G., Aoki, H.: A pilot study of using touch sensing and robotic feedback for children with autism. In: 2014 9th ACM/IEEE International Conference on Human-Robot Interaction (HRI), PP. 222–223. ACM/IEEE (2014). https://doi.org/10.1145/2559636.2563698
14. Pirovano, M., Surer, E., Mainetti, R., Lanzi, P.L., Borghese, N.A.: Exergaming and rehabilitation: a methodology for the design of effective and safe therapeutic exergames. Entertain. Comput. **14**, 55–65 (2016)
15. Ea, F., Rich, S.: Role of kinesthetic and spatial-visual abilities in perceptual-motor learning. J. Exp. Psychol. **66**(1), 6–11 (1963)

Children with ASD Prefer Observing Social Scenarios from Third-Person Perspective

Su Linfei[1], Lin Zehui[1], Li Youyuan[1], Liu Tao[2], and Wei Ling[1(✉)]

[1] Fujian Medical University, Fuzhou 350108, China
linfeisu1105@163.com, 1508088859@qq.com, mocuihle273725@163.com,
ysyang-78@163.com
[2] Zhejiang University, Hangzhou 310058, China
liu_tao@zju.edu.cn

Abstract. This study employed visual tracking technology to explore the effects of a third-person perspective on the fixation condition of social scenarioss in children with autism spectrum disorder (ASD). This study selected 24 ASD children and 24 psychologically age-matched typically developmenting (TD) children as control group, and used eprime 3.0 to present experiment image cosist of social stimuli (a person's smiling expression) and non-social stimuli (Circumscribed Interests, control objects) by pairing. The results reported that: first, children with autism spend significantly longer looking at the images of social scenarios in the third-person perspective than objects; second, children with autism spend significantly longer looking at image in the third-person perspective than in the first-person perspective; third, when the distractor is Circumscribed Interests, children with ASD spend shorter time to the first fixation of both social scenarios and objects than TD children in the first-person perspective.

Keywords: Autism spectrum disorder · Third-person perspective · Social information processing

1 Introduction

Autism Spectrum Disorders (ASD) is a neurodevelopmental disorder that has two core symptoms: social communication disorder and Restricted, Repetitive Behaviors and Interests (RRBIs) [1]. Some researchers reported that the fixation way of social information is attended to may be an important factor in their successful socialization and communication and that reduced social attention in individuals with ASD is strongly associated with their social disorder [2–4]. However, social motivation theory reported that individuals with ASD don't have a natural tendency to attend to social stimuli, and there is no consensus among researchers regarding this finding [5].

It has been found that typically developing (TD) individuals have an attentional bias for social scenarios, but children with ASD have reduced attentional allocation to social stimuli in many contexts [6–8]. For example, children with ASD have a lower tendency to observe and describe scenarioss of complex social interactions with faces

H. Liu et al. (Eds.): ICIRA 2022, LNAI 13455, pp. 424–435, 2022.
https://doi.org/10.1007/978-3-031-13844-7_41

and heads than TD or language-delayed peers [9]. It is well known that the eyes play a distinct important role in social interactions and communication of our real world, and individuals with TD are very sensitive to and show higher motivation for social messages conveyed by the eyes (e.g., emotions, attention, intentions) because of their perception of eye contact as beneficial [10]. In contrast, individuals with ASD are lessly insensitive to eyes [11], resulting in diminished motivation to look at eyes [10].

However, some other researchers have refuted the theory, which does not believe that social motivation theory can be used to generalize to explain the reduced fixtion at social information in individuals with ASD, and some studies have found no difference in the amount of face-gazing effort between children with ASD and control children [12]. Other studies have interpreted this from a cultural perspective, such as for Chinese, looking straightly in others' eyes is rude or impolite [13]. Others consider that children with ASD perceive the eyes are threated [14], so they draw on the contents of their peripheral vision to obtain eye information instead of loking eyes straightly, similar to a compensatory strategy.Wang compared the effects of different perspective orientations on the gaze of children with ASD, which model faces looking directly at children with ASD and controlling for the direction of the model's gaze, results found that the ASD group spent significantly less time looking at the eyes for the 0° perspective than for the 30° and 60° perspectives. The study found that children with ASD would avoid the gaze if a faces looking directly at them, but if not, children with ASD showed a decrease in eye avoidance [15]. In addition, it is important to emphasize that previous studies have used individual faces singally, and it has been reported that children with autism have a impairments in sociality that may result from attentional processes specific to social stimuli, specifically, differential allocation of attention to different components (e.g., reduced attention to the face but increased attention to the body) [8]. Social material just presenting faces singally can't objectively reflect the real-life cognitive processing of social information in children with ASD, and the gaze aversion hypothesis states that individuals with ASD actively avoid eyes to alleviate the discomfort caused by direct eye gaze [16]; therefore, future research should appropriately introduce information about characters rather than lonely faces to avoid excessive rejection of lonely face presentation by children with ASD.

However, previous studies have some shortcomings: first, previous studies have mostly studied only social deficits but not focusing on the relationship between social and nonsocial deficits. Althought some researchers have compared the influence of nonso-cial information on social information without exploring the inner connection between the two in-depth. Second, most previous studies have examined the timing of eye gaze by children with ASD when seeing the faces of others from the first-person perspec-tive, while less attention has been paid to the behavioral patterns of children with ASD when perspectiveing social scenarioss from the third-person perspective. Most of the faces used in previous studies were clear full faces [17], and these face images were all straightforward to the perspective of the child with ASD, but them have a major draw-back is that it only measures focal vision, therefore, it can't detect the attention allocated to the edges of the visual field [18]. In the future, the gaze of children with ASD on social information should be explored from multiple angles and perspectives.Like making a possible real-life scenario, the third perspective, which is a image consist of two people talking to each other, when children with ASD are perspectiveing the social scenarios from a third-person perspective situation, enriches the research base of children with ASD gaze on social scenarioss. Therefore, this study hopes to initially explore the relationship between social and non-social deficits and the behavioral patterns of children with ASD perspectiveing social scenarioss from a third-person perspective.

Other studies have used non-social information to explore the effects of social attention in children with ASD, such as Circumscribed Interests (CI), to which individuals with ASD can show unusual attention and intense obsession [19], but in this area some researchers have suggested that the presence of CIs interferes with children with ASD's attention to social information, thereby reducing attention to social information [20]. Others believe that children with ASD don't pay attention to social information because they have no motivation to it [21]. And other researchers have compared biological movements to nonsocial movements [22], as well as the presentation of objects in static social images or geometric shapes, a decrease in social information gaze was also observed in children with ASD [23–25]. Despite the large number of studies reporting social attention deficits in children with ASD, little is known about the relationship between social and nonsocial processing gaze processing in children with ASD.

Based on this, this study aimed to investigate the effects of different perspectives (first-person perspective vs. third-person perspective) on social scenarios gaze patterns of children with ASD. This study adopted a visual preference paradigm to examine the gaze of children with ASD on social information characters (busts of pepole smiling faces taken in real scenarios) and non-social information objects (CI, control objects). We proposed two hypotheses in this study: **hypothesis 1**: children with ASD avoid social information and children with ASD will pay more attention to non-social information objects, especially CI; **hypothesis 2a**: based on social motivation theory, if children with ASD lack social motivation, then there is no difference between first-person and third-person perspective gaze; **hypothesis 2b**: based on the eye threat hypothesis, if children with ASD just avoid the first-person perspective, then in the third-person perspective, children with ASD would gaze more at social scenarios.

2 Methods

2.1 Subjects

Thirty-three children with ASD diagnosed by a tertiary care hospital were recruited from a special education school, and 33 children with TD were recruited from a kindergarten. Based on the subjects' cooperation and the completion of the experiment, a total of 48 valid subjects were finally screened, including 24 children with ASD (22 boys and 2 girls) and 24 children with TD (22 boys and 2 girls). All subjects had normal visual acuity or corrected visual acuity, and other diseases were excluded. The Peabody Picture Vocabulary Test (PPVT) was used to assess the intelligence level of the subjects, and the Childhood Autistic Rating Scale (CARS) was used to assess the autism level of the subjects. Details of the subjects' information are shown in Table 1.

Table 1. Basic information of subjects ($M \pm SD$)

Basic Information	ASD($n = 24$)	TD($n = 24$)	t
Physiological Age (years)	12.63 ± 2.3	3.46 ± 0.51	19.6^{***}
Score of PPVT	32.8 ± 23.1	31.3 ± 21	0.27
Score of CARS	31.7 ± 4.47	15.3 ± 0.48	17.64^{***}

2.2 Experimental Materials

Experimental materials were images of real scenarios containing objects and people, and pictures of people and objects were presented on both the left and right sides of the computer screen. The position (left and right) in which the objects and person pictures appeared on the screen, and the gender of the person were balanced. The objects stimulus pictures were CI and control object (CO), both from the photographic website (https://699 pic.com/), and the CI selected for this study used the Cambridge University Obsessions Questionnaire (CUQQ).The CIs were assessed by parents or teachers of children with ASD, and the CIs were selected from computer, fan, and vehicle according to the high to low selection rate, and the COs were selected from dishes, sofa, and green plants according to the low to high selection rate. The pictures of people were taken by ourselves, and the expressions of people in the scenarios were happy, and the two environments of office and outdoor were chosen for the shooting scenarios. The object Scenarios and character Scenarios were matched out of 12 groups of pictures, 6 groups of pictures containing CI Scenarios and character Scenarios, and 6 groups of pictures containing CO Scenarios and character Scenarios, see Fig. 1. all pictures were processed by Photoshop and the size was 1024×768 pixels.

A   B

Fig. 1. Example of Experimental Image (A: a two-person scenario with CI; B: a two-person scenario with CO)

2.3 Experimental Design

2 (subject type: children with ASD, children with TD) × 2 (distractor type: CI, CO) × 2 (perspective type: third-person perspective, first-person perspective) × 2 (information type: social information, non-social information) mixed-factor design.

2.4   Experimental Procedures

Subjects were 60–70 cm away from the computer display. Using SMI RED500 eye-tracker to record the data of eye-tracking, and 5-point calibration was used, and the experiment began with the main subject explaining to the subject the instruction phrase: "XXX (subject's name) please look at the picture on the screen." When the subject was ready to start the experiment, there are two images of practiced trials from each of the various experimental conditions, and then the formal experiment was started, with each image presented 5 s, and then presented a "+" white screen 1s. A total of 12 groups of pictures (excluding practice trials) were presented, each experimental conditions has 6 groups, and each subject watched all images. The images were presented randomly for different experimental conditions. Subjects just expected to look the computer screen whithout any task. The procedure is shown in Fig. 2.

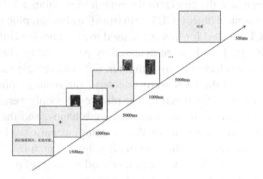

Fig. 2.   Experimental flow chart

2.5   Experimental Apparatus

Subjects' gaze behavior was eye-tracked using an SMI RED500 eye-tracker with a sampling rate of 500 Hz. Stimulus material was presented using a 20-in. desktop computer display with a screen resolution of 1680 × 1050 pixels.

2.6   Areas of Interest and Analysis Metrics

Area of interest: left and right full image, object, head, body, and person. See Fig. 3 for details.

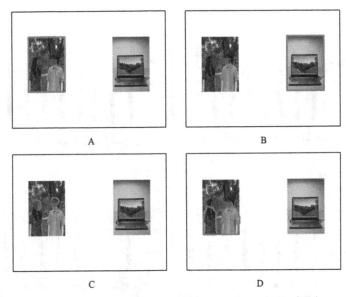

Fig. 3. Example of areas of interest (AOI) (A: full-image of people, B: full-image of object, C: head, D: body, the area except people is the background)

Analysis indexes: (1) gaze time: the sum of all gaze time and eye-hopping time between entering an area of interest and leaving this area of interest; (2) fixation count: the total number of gaze points falling on the area of interest; (3) dwell time ratio: the dwell time ratio of the full map area of interest is the ratio of the dwell time of the full map area of interest to the total dwell time presented in the full map; the dwell time ratio of the local area of interest is the ratio of the dwell time of the local area of interest to the dwell time of the full map area of interest, and because of the size difference between different areas of interest, the dwell time ratio is further area normalized, i.e., the dwell time ratio is then divided by the area ratio of the area of interest to the full map area of interest. (4) time to first fixation time (TFF): the time spent on the first fixation to the area.

3   Results

3.1   Analysis of Social Information, Non-social Information Full Map

A 2 (subject type: ASD, TD) × 2 (interferer type: CI, CO) × 2 (perspective type: third-person perspective, first-person perspective) × 2 (information type: social, non-social) repeated measures ANOVA was performed on the oculomotor metrics of the full figure, and the results are shown in Fig. 4.

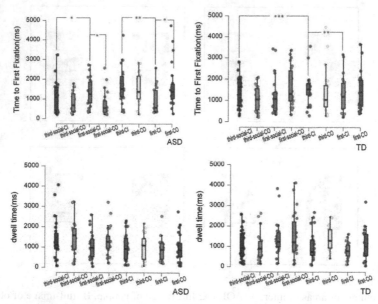

Fig. 4. Subjects' fixation condition on different types of pictures

(1) TFF

ANOVA revealed a significant subject type main effect, $F(1,41) = 4.49, p < 0.05, \eta_p^2 = 0.176$; and interactions for subject type, information type, perspective type, and distractor type, $F(1,41) = 7.21, p < 0.05, \eta_p^2 = 0.256$. All other main effects and interactions were not significant.

Further simple effects analysis revealed that under the first-person perspective, children with ASD had significantly shorter TFF for characters appearing simultaneously with CI than for characters appearing simultaneously with CO ($p = 0.044$), and children with ASD had significantly shorter TFF for characters appearing simultaneously with CI than children with TD ($p = 0.005$); children with ASD had significantly shorter TFF for CI than for CO ($p = 0.000$) and also perceived the CI significantly shorter than in the case of the third-person perspective ($p = 0.007$). In the third-person perspective, children with ASD had significantly shorter TFF for characters presented in pairs with CI than children with TD ($p = 0.027$) and also significantly shorter TFF for the first-person perspective ($p = 0.038$); children with TD had significantly shorter TFF for CI than for the first-person perspective ($p = 0.001$). children with ASD had significantly shorter TFF than children with TD.

(2) gaze time

ANOVA revealed a significant main effect of information type, $F(1,41) = 9.7, p < 0.01$, $\eta_p^2 = 0.316$; the interaction between subject type, information type, and perspective type was significant, $F(1,41) = 8.5, p < 0.01, \eta_p^2 = 0.288$. All other main effects and interactions were not significant.

Further simple effects analysis revealed that under the first-person perspective, TD children gaze time significantly longer at people ($p = 0.046$) and also significantly longer at objects ($p = 0.002$) than under the third-person perspective. Under the third-person perspective, children with ASD had significantly longer gaze time for people than children with TD ($p = 0.028$), children with ASD had significantly longer gaze time for people than objects ($p = 0.027$), and children with TD had significantly longer gaze time for objects than for the first-person perspective ($p = 0.026$). Subjects' gaze time was significantly longer for people than for objects.

3.2 Detailed Analysis of Social Information

A repeated-measures ANOVA was performed on the social information 2 (subject type: children with ASD, children with TD) × 2 (distractor type: CI, CO) × 2 (perspective: third-person perspective, first-person perspective) × 3 (AOI: background, body, head), and the results are shown in Fig. 5.

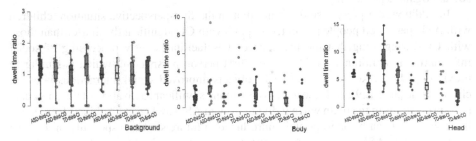

Fig. 5. Ratio of subjects' gaze time for different types of interest areas

On the gaze time ratio, the ANOVA results found a significant main effect of area of interest type, $F(1,36) = 313, p < 0.001, \eta_p^2 = 0.97$; main effect of perspective type, $F(1,36) = 44, p < 0.01, \eta_p^2 = 0.71$, interaction of subject type, perspective type, and area of interest, $F(1,36) = 11.6, p < 0.01, \eta_p^2 = 0.58$. All other main effects and interactions were not significant.

Further simple effect analysis revealed that the gaze time ratio for the body was significantly biger for ASD children than TD children in the first-person perspective ($p = 0.011$). Under the third-person perspective, TD children had a significantly biger gaze time ratio to the head than ASD children ($p = 0.000$); ASD children had a significantly biger gaze time ratio to the figure's head than in the first-person perspective ($p = 0.037$); TD children had a significantly biger gaze time ratio to the body, head than in the first-person perspective ($p = 0.000$). The subjects' gaze time ratios for the area of interest were ranked from largest to smallest: head, body, and background. Subjects' gaze time ratio for pictures in the third-person perspective was significantly biger than that of the first-person perspective.

4 Discussion

4.1 Early Processing of Social Scenarios by Children with ASD

The results of this study showed that children with ASD had significantly shorter TFF for characters in both the first-person and third-person perspectives than children with

TD. However, children with ASD also had significantly shorter TFF for CIs in the first-person perspective than children with TD, and this result did not occur in the third-person perspective. This suggests that children with ASD are able to perceive social information early, but shift their attention to CI when the model looks directly at the child with ASD (first-perspective condition). Some previous studies have supported the results of the present study, Hernandez found that individuals with ASD increased their face gaze time only in conditions where the actor's gaze was not direct [26]. Since the visual preference paradigm chosen for the present study, reported by Qi, such a presentation would allow subjects to engage in "forced selection," and the less gaze time on social stimuli in this condition could be due to avoidance of social stimuli by children with ASD, or it could be due to an over-preference for CIs over-preference [27]. Since TFF is an indicator of early processing stages [28], the results of this study found that children with ASD actively engage in the early processing of social information but avoid first-perspective social cognitive processing.

In addition, the present study found that in the first-perspective situation, children with ASD perceived people presented in pairs with CIs significantly shorter than those with COs, suggesting that the presence of CIs facilitates early processing of social information in children with ASD in the first-person perspective, which is similar to previous findings, Koegel found that CI objects improved social interactions between children and peers [29], and researchers also found significant activation of the amygdala and syrinx gyrus in the brain when individuals with ASD looked at CI objects [30]. It can be seen that CI can be appropriately introduced in future studies, especially in the case of children with ASD who have direct eye gaze, as a way to facilitate early processing of social information in children with ASD, but the present study did not find that children with ASD gaze more at CI-related social information on gaze duration indicators, which may be due to the fact that the CI objects selected for the present study were not specific to each child with ASD specifically assessed, but rather for this study group. The effect of CIs on children with ASD's attention to social scenarios could be further tested in the future by assessing CIs for each ASD subject.

4.2 Perspective Influences Children with ASD's Gaze on Social Scenarios

The results of this study found that children with ASD gazed at third-perspective characters for significantly more time than children with TD; and children with ASD gazed at people more often in the third-perspective rather than in the first-perspective condition. This indicates that children with ASD do not avoid social information in the third-perspective situation and actively engage in social cognitive processing. When the first-perspective situation, children with ASD and the model's eyes were in a reciprocal gaze, the gaze time ratio on the peoples' body was significantly biger for children with ASD than TD, whereas the gaze time ratio on the figure's head was significantly biger for children with ASD than TD in the third-perspective situation. The results of the present study showed that children with ASD did not gaze at reduced social information in all situations, especially the head, and since researchers usually consider the head to be the significant social information [31], Wang also found that children with ASD showed an increase in attention allocation to the eyes when performing an active task (facial identity judgment task) compared to a passive task (perspectiveing the same stimuli)

/

[15]. The results of the present study do not support the social motivation theory [5], the present study found that children with ASD do not avoid social information, direct eye avoidance of direct eye gaze, and that children with ASD gaze at social information is atypical, but does not mean that they lack social motivation, as the results of the present study show that in the third perspective, children with ASD not only attended to social information more than nonsocial information but also attended to the head of the salience area more than TD children, as shown in the present study. Therefore, it is hypothesized that children with ASD may perceive themselves as participating in this process in the third perspective, for example, in their daily lives, they watch their parents and teachers talking in the third perspective, and in addition, in this case, they do not need to make direct eye contact, so they do not avoid looking at the social Scenarios in the third perspective.

To sum up, future researchers should focus on the social processing function of children with ASD, especially the social processing function of the third perspective. In addition, special education teachers can also use the third perspective presentation of social information to teach or intervene with children with ASD, such as avoiding looking directly at the students during lectures or showing some instructional videos so that the social stimuli in the videos do not look directly at the students, which may promote children with ASD to pay more attention to social information and instructional content. Furthermore, the results of this study can be applied in the future in conjunction with artificial intelligence (AI), such as creating a humanoid robot that gradually evolves from a third-perspective to a first-perspective state of presenting instructional information, thereby promoting the development of socially relevant skills in children with ASD.

5 Conclusion

The following conclusions are drawn from this study: first, children with ASD will promote their fixation on people in the third-person perspective, which shows that the gaze time of ASD children on people is significantly longer than on objects in the third perspective; second, in the first perspective, CI It will promote ASD children to perceive social information earlier, and it is shown that in the first perspective, ASD children's perception time of people paired with CI is significantly shorter than that of people paired with CO.

Funding. This study was supported by the Key Project of the 13th Five-Year Plan of Fujian Province (FJJKCGZ18-828).

References

1. American Psychiatric Association. Diagnostic and Statistical Manual of Mental Health Disorders, 5th ed., pp. 26–284. American Psychiatric Association Publishing, Washington, D.C. (2013)
2. Riby, D.M., Hancock, P.J.: Viewing it differently: social scenarios perception in Williams syndrome and autism. Neuropsychologia **46**(11), 2855–2860 (2008)
3. Falck-Ytter, T., von Hofsten, C.: How special is social looking in ASD: a review. Progress in Brain Res. **189**, 209–222 (2011)

4. Frazier, T.W., et al.: A meta-analysis of gaze differences to social and nonsocial information between individuals with and without autism. J. Am. Acad. Child Adolescent Psychiatry **56**(7), 546–555 (2017)

5. Chevallier, C., Kohls, G., Troiani, V., Brodkin, E.S., Schultz, R.T.: The social motivation theory of autism. Trends Cogn. Sci. **16**(4), 231–239 (2012)

6. Fletcher-Watson, S., Leekam, S.R., Benson, V., Frank, M.C., Findlay, J.M.: Eye-movements reveal attention to social information in autism spectrum disorder. Neuropsychologia **47**(1), 248–257 (2009)

7. Chita-Tegmark, M.: Social attention in ASD: A review and meta-analysis of eye-tracking studies. Res. Dev. Disabil. **48**, 79–93 (2016)

8. Guillon, Q., Hadjikhani, N., Baduel, S., Rogé, B.: Visual social attention in autism spectrum disorder: insights from eye tracking studies. Neurosci. Biobehav. Rev. **42**, 279–297 (2014)

9. Chawarska, K., Macari, S., Shic, F.: Decreased spontaneous attention to social scenes in 6-month-old infants later diagnosed with autism spectrum disorders. Biol. Psychiat. **74**(3), 195–203 (2013)

10. Dubey, I., Ropar, D., Hamilton, A.F.: Measuring the value of social engagement in adults with and without autism. Mol. Autism **6**(1), 1–9 (2015)

11. Moriuchi, J.M., Klin, A., Jones, W.: Mechanisms of diminished attention to eyes in autism. Am. J. Psychiatry **174**(1), 26–35 (2017)

12. Ewing, A.V., Clarke, G.S., Kazarian, S.G.: Stability of indomethacin with relevance to the release from amorphous solid dispersions studied with ATR-FTIR spectroscopic imaging. Eur. J. Pharm. Sci. **60**, 64–71 (2014)

13. Zhang, J., Wheeler, J.J., Richey, D.: Cultural validity in assessment instruments for children with autism from a Chinese cultural perspective. Int. J. Spec. Educ. **21**, 109–114 (2006)

14. Tanaka, J.W., Sung, A.: The, "eye avoidance" hypothesis of autism face processing. J. Autism Dev. Disord. **46**(5), 1–15 (2013)

15. Wang, Q.L.: Effects of gaze direction on gaze processing in children with autism. Doctoral dissertation, Minnan Normal University (2013)

16. Hutt, C., Ounsted, C.: The biological significance of gaze aversion with particular reference to the syndrome of infantile autism. Syst. Res. Behav. Sci. **11**(5), 346–356 (1966)

17. Yi, L., et al.: Abnormality in face scanning by children with autism spectrum disorder is limited to the eye region: evidence from multi-method analyses of eye tracking. J. Vis. **13**(10), 227–232 (2013)

18. Grynszpan, O., Nadel, J.: An eye-tracking method to reveal the link between gazing patterns and pragmatic abilities in high functioning autism spectrum disorders. Front. Hum. Neurosci. **8**, 1067 (2015)

19. Leekam, S.R., Prior, M.R., Uljarevic, M.: Restricted and repetitive behaviors in autism spectrum disorders: a review of research in the last decade. Psychol. Bull. **137**(4), 562 (2011)

20. Sasson, N.J., Turner-Brown, L.M., Holtzclaw, T.N., Lam, K.S., Bodfish, J.W.: Children with autism demonstrate circumscribed attention during passive viewing of complex social and nonsocial picture arrays. Autism Res. **1**(1), 31–42 (2008)

21. Traynor, J.M., Gough, A., Duku, E., Shore, D.I., Hall, G.: Eye tracking effort expenditure and autonomic arousal to social and circumscribed interest stimuli in autism spectrum disorder. J. Autism Dev. Disord. **49**(5), 1988–2002 (2019)

22. Klin, A., Lin, D.J., Gorrindo, P., Ramsay, G., Jones, W.: Two-year-olds with autism orient to non-social contingencies rather than biological motion. Nature **459**(7244), 257–261 (2009)

23. Chevallier, C., et al.: Measuring social attention and motivation in autism spectrum disorder using eye-tracking: stimulus type matters. Autism Res. **8**(5), 620–628 (2015)

24. Pierce, K., Conant, D., Hazin, R., Stoner, R., Desmond, J.: Preference for geometric patterns early in life as a risk factor for autism. Arch. Gen. Psychiatry **68**(1), 101–109 (2011)

25. Pierce, K., Marinero, S., Hazin, R., McKenna, B., Barnes, C.C., Malige, A.: Eye tracking reveals abnormal visual preference for geometric images as an early biomarker of an autism spectrum disorder subtype associated with increased symptom severity. Biol. Psychiatry **79**(8), 657–666 (2016)
26. Hernandez, R.N., Feinberg, R.L., Vaurio, R., Passanante, N.M., Thompson, R.E., Kaufmann, W.E.: Autism spectrum disorder in fragile X syndrome: a longitudinal evaluation. Am. J. Med. Genet. A **149**(6), 1125–1137 (2009)
27. Qi, Y.F., Liang, L., Mo, S.L., Wang, F.X.: Visual attention to stimuli of restrictive interest in children with autism: an eye movement study. Spec. Educ. Chin. **5**(5), 29–34 (2016)
28. Banire, B., Al-Thani, D., Qaraqe, M., Khowaja, K., Mansoor, B.: The effects of visual stimuli on attention in children with autism spectrum disorder: an eye-tracking study. IEEE Access **8**, 225663–225674 (2020)
29. Koegel, L.K., Vernon, T.W., Koegel, R.L., Koegel, B.L., Paullin, A.W.: Improving social engagement and initiations between children with autism spectrum disorder and their peers in inclusive settings. J. Positive Beh. Interv. **14**(4), 220–227 (2012)
30. Grelotti, D.J., et al.: fMRI activation of the fusiform gyrus and amygdala to cartoon characters but not to faces in a boy with autism. Neuropsychologia **43**(3), 373–385 (2005)
31. Shic, F., Bradshaw, J., Klin, A., Scassellati, B., Chawarska, K.: Limited activity monitoring in toddlers with autism spectrum disorder. Brain Res. **1380**, 246–254 (2011)

Early Screening of ASD Based on Hand Gesture Analysis

Qiang Zhou[1], Jing Li[1(✉)], Qiong Xu[2], Huiping Li[2], Xiu Xu[2], and Honghai Liu[3]

[1] School of Computer Science and Engineering, Tianjin University of Technology, Tianjin, China
jing.li.2003@gmail.com
[2] Department of Child Health Care, Children's Hospital of Fudan University, Shanghai, China
[3] State Key Laboratory of Robotics and System, Harbin Institute of Technology, Shenzhen, China

Abstract. Neurodevelopmental disorder refers to behavioral and cognitive impairment during development, which is manifested as significant difficulties in intelligence, motor or social skills. Among these disorders, autism spectrum disorder (ASD), language disorder (LD) and mental retardation (MR) are easily misclassified due to their similar symptoms, which can be very detrimental to later treatment. Therefore, it is important to screen and classify these types of patients correctly. Traditionally, diagnosis of these disorders has relied on the American Psychiatric Research Association's DSM-5, but these methods require professionals and special assessments to diagnose patients, which can take a lot of time and cost. Nowadays, thanks to the development of deep learning, many researches have used some biological signals (such as electroencephalogram, facial expression and gesture, etc.) for the early diagnosis of neurodevelopmental diseases and have achieved good results. In this work, we proposed a method based on deep learning, which can well distinguish different types of patients only by children's hand gestures. In order to verify the effectiveness of the method, we conducted a series of experiments on the TASD dataset, and finally the classification accuracy of these three types of patients reached 99.42%. It proves that using only hand gestures is also effective in the screening of ASD, LD, and MR.

Keywords: Autism spectrum disorder · Language disorder · Mental retardation · Hand gesture recognition · Deep learning

1 Introduction

Neurodevelopmental disorders are a common health problem in children. Autism spectrum disorder (ASD), language disorder (LD) and mental retardation (MR) are all neurodevelopmental disorders, which occur in early childhood and result in communication disorders. Early diagnosis and intensive intervention are essential to optimize treatment outcomes for these diseases, especially in children. Often, detection of such diseases relies on specialized medical expertise with diagnostic equipment by child observation, parental interviews, and professional analysis. Because of similar symptoms, ASD is

© The Author(s), under exclusive license to Springer Nature Switzerland AG 2022
H. Liu et al. (Eds.): ICIRA 2022, LNAI 13455, pp. 436–444, 2022.
https://doi.org/10.1007/978-3-031-13844-7_42

easily confused with LD and MR, which hinders the treatment of the disease. Shattuck et al. [1] showed that the increased prevalence of ASD from 1994 to 2003 was associated with a decrease in the prevalence of MR and LD, and part of the patients previously classified as MR and LD were misclassified as ASD.

The clinical diagnosis of ASD is characterized by social communication disorders and stereotyped behavior deficits. In recent years, the number of ASD patients keeps increasing, and the global prevalence of autism is slightly less than 1% [2]. At this time, it is very important to strengthen early diagnosis and intervention for patients. In the past, testing for such diseases required special diagnostic equipment and evaluation by professionals, a manual method that costs a lot of time and money. Recently, many machine learning (especially deep learning) methods have been proposed for early diagnosis of ASD. Li et al. [3] proposed a deep learning-based method to diagnose ASD children from raw video sequences by integrating the appearance-based features of facial expressions, head pose, and head trajectory. Baygin et al. [4] proposed hybrid lightweight deep feature extractor to detect ASD using Electroencephalogram (EEG) signals. Zunino et al. [5] classified ASD through the videos of children's hand gesture. Liu et al. [6] proposed a the response-to-instructions (RTIs) protocol to diagnose ASD by analyzing children's hand movement and gaze direction.

Patients with mental retardation (MR) have neurodevelopmental deficits characterized by limited intellectual functioning and adaptive behavior. Intellectual functioning, generally called intelligence, includes the ability to learn, the ability to express language and so on. Adaptive behavior is manifested by the lack of social, conceptual and social practice skills [7]. Traditionally, diagnosing mentally retarded patients relies on a comprehensive assessment by a professional, which is subjective and time consuming. Shukla et al. [8] proposed a new framework for detecting developmental disorders from facial images, which can help identify MR patients. Aggarwal et al. [9] proposed a classification model that can directly distinguish children with mental retardation (MR) from Typically Developed (TD).

Language disorder (LD), a common developmental disorder in children with a prevalence of 5–8%, is classified as a communication disorder, which affects the ability to transmit the verbal and non-verbal information between individuals. Traditionally, recognizing LD requires professional diagnosis. Zhang et al. [10] proposed a solution to fast screen children's LD based on an evaluation of comprehensive speech ability and a deep learning framwork.

Hand gestures are earlier than language in children's early development, and studies have shown that hand gestures can predict language changes [11]. Hand gestures and language contain non-verbal and verbal information of an integrated communication system [12], which provides a theoretical basis for using children's hand gestures to identify ASD, LD and MR patients with communication disorders.

In this paper, we classify the patients with ASD, LD, and MR by detecting and recognizing their hand gestures based on deep learning methods. The contributions of the paper are summarized as follows:

1) We proposed a visual-based method to screen the patients with ASD, LD, and MD.
2) By integrating hand detection and hand gesture recognition, we can distinguish different types of patients with an accuracy of 99.42% only based on input images.

The rest of the paper is organized as follows. Section 2 introduces the work related to the diagnosis of neurodevelopmental disorders and hand gesture recognition. Section 3 introduces the proposed framework. Section 4 gives the experimental setting and results. We conclude in Sect. 5.

2 Related Works

2.1 Diagnosis of Neurodevelopmental Disorders

DSM-5 [13], provided by the American Psychiatric Research Association, is the main diagnostic basis for the diagnosis of neurodevelopmental diseases. However, this method mainly relies on professionals and special evaluation methods to diagnose patients, which takes a lot of time and is easily affected by subjective factors. In order to solve this kind of problem, there are many studies using some biological characteristics (such as facial expression, EEG, gesture) as diagnostic basis and proving their effectiveness [14–16]. However, the acquisition of EEG signals depends on specialized equipment, which is expensive and inconvenient. Therefore, machine learning methods based on visual cues (e.g., facial expression) have been proposed for the diagnosis since only a face image is required as the input. Nevertheless, it still raises the privacy issues. In contrast, hand gesture-based methods can obtain satisfactory results based on extracting hand gesture information from RGB images with hands.

2.2 Hand Gesture Recognition

Hand gestures are part of body language, and each type of hand gestures has its own specific meaning. There are mainly two methods to collect hand gesture data, one is based on wearable glove sensors and the other is based on vision sensors [17]. Wearable sensor-based methods put sensors on the hand, detect hand movement and finger bending, and then process the data collected by the sensors. The methods can achieve high accuracy and fast speed, but the sensors are expensive [18] and may cause discomfort to the user. Vision sensors shoot RGB images or depth images by a camera, and then deep neural networks are used to recognize hand gestures. Here, data acquisition is relatively simple, but the performance is easily affected by light conditions and shooting angles.

With the development of deep learning, there are many works using pre-trained deep learning models such as VGGNet [19], ResNet [20], and ConvNeXt [21] for hand gesture recognition, which can achieved good results. Zunino et al. [5] used GoogleNet[22] as the backbone network to extract image features, and then put the features into LSTM to obtain timing information and classification results. Yang et al. [23] reformed ResNet18 and proposed a dynamic thinning network for gesture recognition and prediction, which improved the model efficiency without affecting the accuracy.

Based on the works mentioned above, in this paper, we propose a framework that can distinguish children with ASD, MR, and LD based on hand gestures. The framework adopts YOLOv5 (The 5th Edition of YOLO [24]) to detect a child's hands from the input image and uses pre-trained ResNet50 [20] for gesture recognition. We obtain the classification accuracy of 99.42%, which demonstrates the proposed framework can distinguish the children with ASD, MR, and LD successfully.

3   Method

The proposed method is illustrated in Fig. 1. It is mainly composed of three stages, i.e., hand detection, hand gesture recognition and classification.

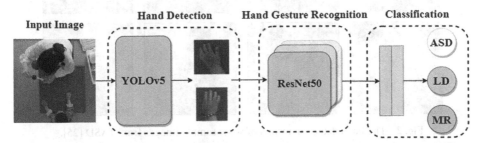

Fig. 1. The overview of the proposed framework. It consists of hand detection, hand gesture recognition and classification.

3.1   Hand Detection

Hand detection can be regarded as an object detection task. Generally, object detection algorithms can be mainly classified into two categories: i) two-stage object detection; and 2) one-stage object detection. Two-stage detection methods firstly generate some candidate regions as the samples and then classify them through the convolutional neural network.They can achieve high detection accuracy, but the detection speed is slow and training takes a lot of time. In contrast, one-stage detection algorithms, represented by the YOLO algorithm [24], can achieve fast detection speed. As the latest version of YOLO, YOLOv5 has greatly improved the training speed and detection accuracy, so we choose it to detect the hands from the original input images. The YOLOv5 has four versions, and we use the pre-trained YOLOv5s for hand detection in this work.

As shown in Fig. 2, the original images contain doctors and children. In order to exclude the factors that may interfere with the classidication results, we detect and crop the children's hand from the input images by YOLOv5 since it is fast and stable. To make YOLOv5 suitable for our task, we manually tagged the regions of children's hands and used them to fine-tune the model. Afterwards, all the images in the dataset were sent to the model for hand detection.

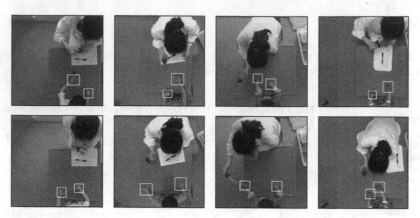

Fig. 2. The hand detection results of some sample images from TASD [25].

3.2 Hand Gesture Recognition and Classification

With the rapid development of deep learning, many deep learning architectures have been proposed, where ResNet [20] has been widely applied because it improves the network performance while reducing network parameters. Therefore, we choose ResNet50 as our backbone network to recognize different hand gestures.

As shown in Fig. 1, the size of the obtained hand images may be different, so we resize each image to 224 × 224 since the mainstream network adopts the size as the image input. Then, the resized hand image is input into ResNet50 to extract hand gesture features. Finally, the extracted features are passed through a fully connected layer and a softmax layer for classification. Figure 3 shows the heatmap of children's hand gestures. We can find that the model assigns more weights to the position of children's fingers and palms.

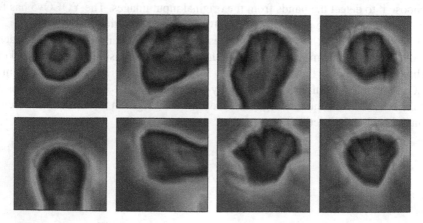

Fig. 3. Heatmap generated after model training.

4   Experiments and Results

4.1   Dataset

Qin et al. [25] designed a platform to collect 19 children's hand gesture data. In a room, a doctor and a child sat opposite to each other on two chairs, with a 0.6 m × 0.6 m × 0.6 m table between them. An RGB camera (Logitech BRIO C1000e) was placed 1.0 m above the table to record video information of the interaction. First, the doctor plays with the child in order to familiarize the child with the environment, then blows bubbles with bubble water to attract the child's attention, and finally takes the bubble water out of the child's reach to observe whether the child has relevant gestures to express his hope that the doctor will continue blowing bubbles. Here, we only use the data from 5 children. Figure 2 provides some sample images.

4.2   Experiments

For the hand detection task, the YOLOv5 model is pre-trained on the COCO dataset [26]. In order to adapt the model to our task, we adopted the Roboflow tool to annotate part of the data and generate YOLO labels, then used the annotated data to fine-tune the weights of YOLOv5s, and finally the fine-tuned model was applied to the whole dataset. After detecting and cropping hand images from the original data, we obtained a dataset of more than 4000 hand images.

Table 1. Classification accuracy of different models.

Model	Accuracy	Parameters (M)	Epoch time (s)
VGG16	98.97%	**14.72**	23
ConvNeXt-T	99.41%	27.82	23
ResNet50	**99.42%**	25.56	**17**

For hand gesture recognition and classification, we use 80% of the images for training and 20% for testing. In addition, due to the relatively small amount of data, the training strategy of 10-fold cross-validation is used for training. In the training stage, we use the Cross-Entropy loss as the loss function, and select AdamW [27] as the optimizer, with a learning rate of 0.0005 and weight decay rate of 0.05. In the test phase, we obtain the classification accuracy by averaging the results of ten folds. In our experiments, we compare the performance of three mainstream deep neural networks, i.e., VGG16 [19], ResNet50 [20] and ConvNeXt-T [21]. We use the pre-trained weights of VGG16 and ResNet50, which are officially provided by Pytorch, but we revise the fully connected layer and add a softmax layer, and we can get the confidence of each category after fine-tuning our own gesture dataset. We use the same parameters of ConvNeXt-T as in [21], and we add a softmax layer to fine-tune it to get the final results. We compare the classification accuracy using these three backbone networks, the number of parameters and the operation time of each epoch, and give the results in Table 1, ResNet50 achieves the best results of 99.42%, and the classification rate of ConvNeXt-T is slightly lower. Although the number of parameters trained by VGG16 is small, the running time of each epoch is relatively long due to the large amount of calculation of the model. Considering these three factors, we finally choose ResNet50 for our task.

4.3 Results

We trained 50 epochs for each fold.Fig. 4 shows the accuracy and loss in the training process. Thanks to the optimization strategy of AdamW [27], the accuracy curve is relatively stable in the training process. The loss and accuracy corresponding to each epoch are the average of ten folds. As we can see, the accuracy of the validation set is slightly better and the loss of the validation set is much lower than that of the training set. The main reason is that the process of the training is earlier than that of the verification.

Table 2. Accuracy at different thresholds.

Threshold	0.5	0.6	0.7	0.8	0.9
Accuracy	**99.42%**	99.34%	99.25%	99.17%	99.04%

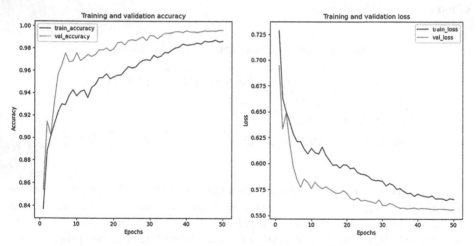

Fig. 4. Average accuracy and loss during training

Finally, in order to verify the robustness of our method, we set a threshold to the final classification confidence. If the classification confidence is lower than the threshold, the result can be considered wrong; vice versa. We set the threshold ranging from 0.5 to 0.9 since the result is untrustworthy when the confidence is lower than 0.5. As seen in Table 2, the classification accuracy reaches the highest 99.42% when the threshold is set as 0.5. Even if the threshold is set as 0.9, we still achieve the classification accuracy of 99.04%, indicating that our model is very robust.

5 Conclusion

In this paper, we classify the patients with ASD, LD, and MR by detecting and recognizing their hand gestures based on deep learning methods. To verify the effectiveness of the proposed method, we conducted a series of experiments and the results show that the classification accuracy of the proposed method is 99.42%, which proves that our method is effective. In the future, we will expand the dataset since a larger dataset can help the model achieve higher training accuracy and better generalization ability. Moreover, we will add the attention mechanism into our model since it pays more attention to useful information. Finally, we will adopt multimodal data such as children's facial expressions and poses to further improve the model.

Acknowledgments. This work was supported by the National Natural Science Foundation of China under Grant 61963027.

References

1. Shattuck, P.T.: The contribution of diagnostic substitution to the growing administrative prevalence of autism in US special education. Pediatrics **117**(4), 1028–1037 (2006)
2. Lord, C., et al.: Autism spectrum disorder. Nat. Rev. Dis. Primers. **6**(1), 1–23 (2020)
3. Li, J., et al.: Automatic classification of ASD children using appearance-based features from videos. Neurocomputing **470**, 40–50 (2022)
4. Baygin, M., et al.: Automated ASD detection using hybrid deep lightweight features extracted from EEG signals. Comput. Biol. Med. **134**, 104548 (2021)
5. Zunino, A., et al.: Video gesture analysis for autism spectrum disorder detection. In: 24th International Conference on Pattern Recognition, pp. 3421–3426 (2018)
6. Liu, J., et al.: Early screening of autism in toddlers via response-to-instructions protocol. IEEE Trans. Cybern. (2020)
7. Lee, K., Cascella, M., Marwaha, R.: Intellectual disability. https://europepmc.org/article/NBK/nbk547654 (2019)
8. Shukla, P., et al.: A deep learning frame-work for recognizing developmental disorders. In: IEEE Winter Conference on Applications of Computer Vision, pp. 705–714 (2017)
9. Aggarwal, G., Singh, L.: Classification of intellectual disability using LPC, LPCC, and WLPCC parameterization techniques. Int. J. Comput. Appl. **41**(6), 470–479 (2019)
10. Zhang, X., Qin, F., Chen, Z., Gao, L., Qiu, G., Shuo, L.: Fast screening for children's developmental language disorders via comprehensive speech ability evaluation—using a novel deep learning framework. Ann. Transl. Med. **8**(11), 707–707 (2020). https://doi.org/10.21037/atm-19-3097
11. Iverson, J.M., Goldin-Meadow, S.: Gesture paves the way for language development. Psychol. Sci. **16**(5), 367–371 (2005)
12. Ramos-Cabo, S., Vulchanov, V., Vulchanova, M.: Gesture and language trajectories in early development: an overview from the autism spectrum disorder perspective. Front. Psychol. **10**, 1211 (2019)
13. Edition, F.: Diagnostic and statistical manual of mental disorders. Am. Psychiatric. Assoc. **21**, 591–643 (2013)
14. Sheikhani, A., et al.: Detection of abnormalities for diagnosing of children with autism disorders using of quantitative electroencephalography analysis. J. Med. Syst. **36**(2), 957–963 (2012)

15. Guha, T., et al.: On quantifying facial expression-related atypicality of children with autism spectrum disorder. In: IEEE International Conference on Acoustics, Speech and Signal Processing, pp. 803–807 (2015)
16. Stieglitz Ham, H., et al.: Exploring the relationship between gestural recognition and imitation: evidence of dyspraxia in autism spectrum disorders. J. Autism Dev. Disord. **41**(1), 1–12 (2011)
17. Mitra, S., Acharya, T.: Gesture recognition: a survey. IEEE Trans. Syst. Man Cybern. Part C (Applications and Reviews) **37**(3), 311–324 (2007)
18. Kaur, H., Rani, J.: A review: study of various techniques of Hand gesture recognition. In: IEEE 1st International Conference on Power Electronics, Intelligent Control and Energy Systems, pp. 1–5 (2016)
19. Simonyan, K., Zisserman, A.: Very deep convolutional networks for large-scale image recognition. arXiv preprint arXiv:1409.1556 (2014)
20. He, K., Zhang, X., Ren, S., Sun, J.: Deep residual learning for image recognition. In: Proceedings of the IEEE Conference on Computer Vision and Pattern Recognition, pp. 770–778 (2016)
21. Liu, Z., Mao, H., Wu, C.Y.: A ConvNet for the 2020s. In: Proceedings of the IEEE/CVF Conference on Computer Vision and Pattern Recognition, pp. 11976–11986 (2022)
22. Szegedy, C., et al.: Going deeper with convolutions. In: Proceedings of the IEEE Conference on Computer Vision and Pattern Recognition, pp. 1–9 (2015)
23. Yang, J., et al.: Dynamic iterative refinement for efficient 3D hand pose estimati-on. In: Proceedings of the IEEE/CVF Winter Conference on Applications of Computer Vision, pp. 1869–1879 (2022)
24. Redmon, J., et al.: You only look once: Unified, real-time object detection. In: Proceedings of the IEEE Conference on Computer Vision and Pattern Recognition, pp. 779–788 (2016)
25. Qin, H., et al.: Vision-based pointing estimation and evaluation in toddlers for autism screening. In: Liu, X.-J., Nie, Z., Yu, J., Xie, F., Song, R. (eds.) ICIRA 2021. LNCS (LNAI), vol. 13015, pp. 177–185. Springer, Cham (2021). https://doi.org/10.1007/978-3-030-89134-3_17
26. Chen, X., et al.: Microsoft coco captions: data collection and evaluation server. arXiv preprint arXiv:1504.00325 (2015)
27. Loshchilov, I., Hutter, F.: Fixing weight decay regularization in adam (2018)

A Coarse-to-Fine Human Visual Focus Estimation for ASD Toddlers in Early Screening

Xinming Wang[1], Zhihao Yang[1], Hanlin Zhang[1], Zuode Liu[1], Weihong Ren[1], Xiu Xu[2], Qiong Xu[2], and Honghai Liu[1(✉)]

[1] School of Mechanical Engineering and Automation, Harbin Institute of Technology, Shenzhen, China
honghai.liu@hit.edu.cn
[2] Children's Hospital of Fudan University Department of Child Health Care, Shanghai, China

Abstract. Human visual focus is a vital feature to uncover subjects' underlying cognitive processes. To predict the subject's visual focus, existing deep learning methods learn to combine the head orientation, location, and scene content for estimating the visual focal point. However, these methods mainly face three problems: the visual focal point prediction solely depends on learned spatial distribution heatmaps, the reasoning process in post-processing is non-learnable, and the learning of gaze salience representation could utilize more prior knowledge. Therefore, we propose a coarse-to-fine human visual focus estimation method to address these problems, for improving estimation performance. To begin with, we introduce a coarse-to-fine regression module, in which the coarse branch aims to estimate the subject's possible attention area while the fine branch directly outputs the estimated visual focal point position, thus avoiding sequential reasoning and making visual focal point estimation is totally learnable. Furthermore, the human visual field prior is used to guide the learning of gaze salience for better encoding target-related representation. Extensive experimental results demonstrate that our method outperforms existing state-of-the-art methods on self-collected ASD-attention datasets.

Keywords: Coarse-to-fine learning · Gaze analysis · Human visual focus estimation · Multi-task learning · Early screening

1 Introduction

Gaze, as a perception function, can be used to evaluate other people's attention and reveal underlying cognitive mechanisms. Consequently, gaze analysis is widely applied to cognition evaluation [13], driver monitor system (DMS) [16], and autism spectrum disorder (ASD) diagnosis [8,15]. In general, gaze can be parameterized as a vector, including the eye and (1) the gaze direction, or (2) the visual focal point. Estimating gaze in the wild is a challenge due to large variations in input images. A way to learn the former gaze parameter is vision-based gaze direction estimation [14] but tends to degrade when the input facial appearance is illuminated in the wild. In contrast, a convolution neural network (CNN) based method which simulates the gaze following behavior to predict the visual focal point, proposed by [11], is more robust in non-restricted scenes. Thus in this paper, we investigate this kind of method to estimate human visual focus in the wild. How to estimate the visual focal point of the observed subject? When humans infer other people's attention, a common sense is that following the observed subject's gaze direction and searching for a rough attention area would be easy for the observer to find the exact visual focal point depending on scene context. It is analog to this perception mechanism that existing human visual focus estimation methods [2,3,6,7,11] mainly consist of four parts: the gaze salience module, the scene salience module, the fusion module, and the post-processing module. Gaze salience representation and scene salience representation are respectively extracted from the first two modules. Then, the estimated heatmap, which means the spatial distribution probability of the visual focal point, is computed from the fusion module, using dot product operation or CNNs on the fusion representation of scene salience and gaze salience. Finally, in post-processing, the visual focal point is predicted as the highest point on the estimated heatmap using the argmax operation.

Though existing methods have made significant advances, there are still three problems to be considered. (1) The post-processing module is non-learnable. Existing methods search for the prediction as to the point with the largest value on the predicted heatmap through the argmax operation, based on the assumption that the true visual focal point is consistent with the point having the highest probability in the spatial distribution heatmap. However, the groundtruth is not always the same as the point with the largest value in the heatmap. For instance, the heatmap indicates the prediction is on the person sitting opposite the subject, while the true visual focal point is on the bookshelf. Therefore, simply finding the point with the highest value on the heatmap is arbitrary. (2) Sequential reasoning can lead to incorrect estimates. In the post-processing module, the visual focal point is directly inferred from the learned heatmaps. Once the heatmap is estimated with significant error, the subsequent visual focus estimation is with errors too. The sequential reasoning is also a reason that leads to the wrong prediction. (3) When encoding gaze salience representation, extra prior knowledge could be introduced to guide the learning process. A prior knowledge is that the human visual span is more likely a cone, which can be simply represented as a sector in 2D image plane and can guide the learning of gaze salience feature map for better representing target-related information.

Based on these observations, we propose a coarse-to-fine human visual focus estimation method for addressing the problems mentioned above to improve estimation performance in the wild. The proposed method contains five modules in comparison to existing methods. In addition to a scene salience module, a gaze salience module, and a fusion module, we introduce a coarse-to-fine module that contains heatmap regression for encoding coarse spatial information of the visual focal point and a point regression for encoding fine accurate point positions. Using this multi-task scheme, the proposed model can directly output the predicted visual focal point through a mapping function with trained parameters, and the final visual focal point prediction does not entirely rely on the learned heatmap. Besides, the optimization of both the coarse branch and the fine branch can improve basic representation, further boosting estimation accuracy. In addition, for better encoding gaze salience representation, we introduce a FOV-guided regression module to guide the learning of gaze salience for better extracting target-related information. Thus, the gaze salience representation is more reasonable in spatial distribution.

Our contributions can be summarized as follows:

- we propose a coarse-to-fine human visual focus estimation method to avoid sequential reasoning and non-differentiable post-processing to improve estimation accuracy.
- we also introduce a FOV-guided regression module, which utilizes the human visual field prior as supervision to guide the generation of gaze salience for better encoding target-related information.
- we demonstrate the superiority of our model by results on ASD-attention dataset, outperforming existing state-of-the-art methods.

2   Related Work

This section reviews related works about human visual focus estimation from methodology improvement, priors to enhance accuracy, and its applications.

Methodology improvement could enchance estimation performance. Before neural network widely used, early work [17] used gaussian process regressor to estimate gaze vectors and object depth information from head pose. Then, a potential area that contains candidate objects is the intersection of gaze direction and object depth. Instead of predicting visual focal point positions, the model output the bounding box of the target object, which is refined by salience. But the restricted experimental scenes, subjects are sitting and facing to the camera, limit the generalization of this method. [11] firstly proposes a CNN-based method for detecting gaze targets in the wild, which encode gaze and scene representation respectively and fuse them using dot product operation. Furthermore, the benchmark Gazefollow is released in this paper. [12] further proposes a method for estimating the target that does not appear in the same image with the observer. A transformation module is proposed to learn the gaze location density through encoding geometric relationships between views. Gaze direction could be learned from full face images since the coupling exists between head pose and eye orientation in social interaction scene, but accurate gaze estimation can improves detection accuracy when eye region is detecable. [2] proposes a multi-task method which includes gaze angle estimation, human visual focus estimation and inside or outside frame target classification. This model achieves good performance using the selective training strategy that updates each task on different datasets. [1] points that the post-processing module is non-differentiable and replaces the argmax operation with integral regression, but the results still can be further boosted. Temporal modeling can benefit human visual focus estimation since gaze behavior is naturally a time-series signals. [3] proposes to encode temporal gaze representation using convolutional long-short term memory (convLSTM) for improving estimation accuracy in the VideoAttentionTarget dataset. This spatial part of this method further improves detection accuracy in the Gazefollow dataset towards the human level. Besides, based on this model, the authors propose to retrieve gaze shift events in toddlers using predicted visual focal points. Also, shared attention is detected based on this model in VideoCoAttdataset [5]. These two additional experiments further approve the potential of this method. For estimating visual focus of a group people, [19] proposes a multi-stream CNN based group gaze estimation. This model firstly detects all faces in a image and then predicts gaze saliency map of each person. Then, the superimposed heatmap is fed into holistic branch while each heatmap is fed into aggregation branch, the final output is the fusion of outputs from the two branches. [7] generates multi-scale gaze direction field maps based on the predicted gaze direction in 2D image. The prediction heatmap is regressed using an encoder-decorder module with the input as the concatenatation of multiple direction field maps and the original image. [9] proposes a top-view gaze saliency representation for detecting objects beyond the camera field of view in 3D space. As for time consuming, [4] makes real-time inference using MobileNetV2 with less loss of accuracy. Instead of learning the heatmap of visual focal point, [18] directly learns sightline from raw images, the line connecting from eye to gaze target. By transforming the learned sightline into polar domain, the learned heatmap is reweighted to eliminate dataset bias.

3   Method

We introduce our coarse-to-fine human visual focus estimation method, which consists of five modules in this section, as shown in Fig. (1-a). Firstly, the scene salience module extracts scene saliency information from full images and head position encodings. Meanwhile, the gaze salience module encodes gaze saliency area from head images and head position encodings. The scene salience contains possible objects drawing subjects' attention, such as an object with significantly different colors from the environment. The gaze salience indicates the potential area of interest to subjects. The scene salience and gaze salience are fused in the fusion module. Lastly, spatial distribution heatmaps and accurate point positions are predicted parallelly through coarse and fine regression in the coarse-to-fine regression module. The final output of this model is the predicted point position of fine regression in the coarse-to-fine regression module.

3.1   Coarse-to-Fine Regression Module

We propose a coarse-to-fine regression module shown in Fig. (1-b) to address the sequential reasoning problem and the non-differentiable problem. If estimated

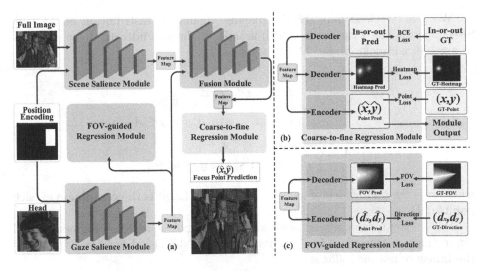

Fig. 1. a) shows the overview of the proposed method, which consists of five modules: the scene salience module, the gaze salience module, the FOV-guided regression module, the fusion module, and the coarse-to-fine regression module. The scene salience module encodes scene context from original images, while the gaze salience module extracts gaze area information from head images and encodings. Then, the FOV-guided regression module is to guide the learning of gaze salience representation under the supervision of prior knowledge FOV. Next, the scene salience and gaze salience are fused in the fusion module. Lastly, the fused feature representation is regressed to spatial distribution heatmaps and point positions parallelly by coarse regression and fine regression. Overall, we propose the coarse-to-fine regression module (b) to address the sequential reasoning problem and non-differentiable problem and prior knowledge FOV is utilized in the FOV-guided regression module (c) to guide the learning of gaze salience representation.

heatmaps from the fusion module are erroneous, the subsequent predicted points would also have errors. Besides, point estimation would be more accurate if it had learnable parameters.

As shown in Fig. (1-b), we use a multi-task scheme for simulating a coarse-to-fine strategy. In order to solve the problem of sequential reasoning and non-differentiation, the visual focal point position is directly learned from the feature maps $\mathcal{F}_b$, rather than inferred from the spatial distribution heat map. Specifically, feature maps $\mathcal{F}_b$ generated from the encoder in the fusion module are decoded into spatial distribution heatmaps $\hat{H}_i$ using deconvolutions for coarse regression. Meanwhile, these feature maps are also regressed into a vector $\hat{P}_i = (\hat{x}, \hat{y})$ representing predicted point positions in the image plane for fine regression. Furthermore, $\mathcal{F}_b$ is encoded into $\hat{O}_i$ to classify whether the visual focus is inside the image or not. Finally, the module predicts heatmaps and points through forwarding inference, calculates the loss between prediction and groundtruth, and updates the module parameters through gradient backpropagation.

We generate heatmaps H_i by placing a gaussian distribution on P_i [10]. Specifically, given $P_i = (x, y)$ which stands for the groundtruth point positions in normalized image plane, H_i is computed by:

$$H_i^{(x,y)} = \begin{cases} e^{-\frac{(x-x)^2+(y-y)^2}{2\sigma^2}}, & x, y \in A \\ 0, & x, y \notin A \end{cases}$$

$$A = \begin{cases} x - 3\sigma < x < x + 3\sigma \\ y - 3\sigma + 1 < y < y + 3\sigma + 1 \end{cases} \tag{1}$$

where σ is the bandwidth of gaussian kernel and (x, y) is the coordinate of each point in H_i.

We employ mean squared error loss for both coarse and fine regression, and binary cross entropy loss for classifying whether the visual focal point is inside the image or not, as follows:

$$\mathcal{L}_f = \frac{1}{n} \sum_{i=1}^{n} (\hat{P}_i - P_i)$$

$$\mathcal{L}_c = \frac{1}{n} \sum_{i=1}^{n} (\hat{H}_i - H_i) \tag{2}$$

$$\mathcal{L}_o = \frac{1}{n} \sum_{i=1}^{n} (O_i \cdot log(O_i) + (1 - O_i) \cdot log(1 - O_i))$$

where $\hat{H}_i, H_i, \hat{P}_i, P_i, O_i, O_i$ are the predicted spatial distribution heatmap, the groundtruth, the predicted point positions and the groundtruth, encodings of the point is inside the image or not and its groundtruth of i_{th} samples in a batch with batchsize $= n$.

3.2 Fov-Guided Regression Module

We aim to guide the gaze salience module to learn gaze field related information, leading to a gaze salience representation which is more likely a sector area that contains the sight line. In 3D space, the human visual field can be simply considered as a cone, while a sector in 2D image plane. Inspried by the defination filed of view in [6,7], we generate fov $F_i^{(x,y)}$ as groundtruth to supervise the learning of gaze salience as follows:

$$F_i^{(x,y)} = max(1 - \frac{\alpha \theta_i^{(x,y)}}{\pi}, 0)$$

$$D_i^{(x,y)} = (d_x, d_y) = (x - x_h, y - y_h) \tag{3}$$

$$\theta_i^{(x,y)} = arccos(\frac{(x - x_h) \cdot (d_x, d_y)}{\|(x - x_h, y - y_h)\|_2 \cdot \|(d_x, d_y)\|_2})$$

Given groundtruth visual focal point (x, y) and head position (x_h, y_h), we firstly compute the groundtruth gaze direction (d_x, d_y), then the angle between the vector from (x, y) pointing to (x, y) and to (d_x, d_y) is calculated, which is $\theta^{(x,y)}$. Lastly, the groundtruth F_i could be generated by adjusting α to change the shape to a sector.

Due to the effective usage of the coarse-to-fine regression module, we also use the multi-task scheme here. Feature maps $\mathcal{F}_g$ encoded from Gaze Saliency Module are decoded into estimated FOV $\hat{F}_i$. Meanwhile, $\mathcal{F}_g$ are further encoded into estimated planar gaze direction $\hat{D}_i$. We use cosine similarity loss mean squared error loss to optimize the regression for gaze direction and fov:

$$\mathcal{L}_{fov} = \frac{1}{n} \sum_{i=1}^{n} (\hat{F}_i - F_i)$$

$$\mathcal{L}_d = \frac{1}{n} \sum_{i=1}^{n} \left(\frac{\hat{D}_i \cdot D_i}{\|\hat{D}_i\|_2 \cdot \|D_i\|_2} \right) \tag{4}$$

The overall loss function is:

$$\mathcal{L} = \lambda_1 \mathcal{L}_c + \lambda_2 \mathcal{L}_f + \lambda_3 \mathcal{L}_{fov} + \lambda_4 \mathcal{L}_d + \lambda_5 \mathcal{L}_o \tag{5}$$

where λ_1, λ_2, λ_3, λ_4 and λ_5 are their weights respectively. The ratio of them is empirically set to 100:10:1:1:1. The $\mathcal{L}_o$ is binary cross entropy classification loss (BCE loss) for gaze inside or outside classification. For other hyperparameters, the parameters σ and α in computing groundtruth heatmaps and FOVs are empirically set to 6 and 3.

4   Experiments

4.1   Datasets and Metrics

For evaluation, we evaluate our model on self-collected ASD-attention dataset here in detail. We propose a dataset for detecting children's attention with Autism Spectrum Disorder (ASD), named ASD-attention. The proposed dataset contains 1663 images recorded from clinical diagnosis scenes under the response to name [15] and response to instruction [8] clinical protocol. During the diagnosis, children with interact with their parents under the guidance of a therapist. The multi-party interaction naturally includes gaze-based social interaction like joint attention and shared attention. Thus, this dataset can be used to validate the proposed model for the ASD community. In addition, we provide groundtruth of the head bounding box, five possible gaze target positions, and whether the subject is looking inside or outside the image for each child. The distribution of head location and target location is shown in Fig. 2.

We use **MinDist**, **AvgDist**, **AvgAng** and **Out of frame AP** to evaluate our proposed model. We calculate the minimum (MinDist) and mean (AvgDist)

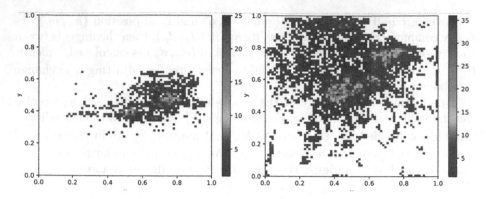

Fig. 2. The normalized distribution of head positions and visual focal points of the ASD-attention.

of L_2 dist of all prediction points and groundtruths. We also compute the mean angle (AvgAng) of all gaze direction predictions pointing from head centers to point predictions and the groundtruth directions pointing from head centers to groundtruth points. For datasets with groundtruth whether subjects are looking inside or outside the image, we additionally use the average precision (AP) to evaluate the performance of out-of-frame classification. The area under curve (AUC) is not used in this paper because the prediction is directly computed by the model instead of using argmax operation on heatmaps.

4.2 Evaluation on ASD-attention Dataset

Table 1. Evaluation on the ASD-attention dataset.

Method	MinDist ↓	AvgDist ↓	AvgAng ↓	AP ↑
Random	0.00206	0.4713	22.98°	0.979
Center	0.00208	0.2954	10.73°	–
Lian *et al.* [7]	0.00156	0.2323	10.22°	–
Chong *et al.* [3]	0.00021	0.1098	4.06°	0.982
Ours	0.00092	**0.0947**	**3.96°**	**0.993**

Table 1 shows the results of model against others on the proposed ASD-attention dataset. Spatial part of the model [3] and the model [7] are also validated. We achieve 0.0947, 3.96° and 0.9993 for AvgDist, AvgAng and AP respectively, with a minimal degrade for MinDist in comparsion to [3]. In comparsion to [7], we attain a 59.2% and a 61.3% improvement for AvgDist and AvgAng (Fig. 3).

Fig. 3. Visualization of an original image and our result against methods [3,7] on the ASD-attention dataset, from left to right. For each prediction visualization, we show the head bounding box, the prediction and the **groundtruth**.

The picture shows the response-to-name protocol. Parents call the child's name and observe whether the child turns his head and pays attention to the parent to assess the possibility of the child who has ASD. Our model predicts that the child's focus is on his parent's face, while other methods incorrectly estimate the gaze point on the doctor or on the parent's leg, which is not what we expected. These results prove the potential of our method for visual focal point estimation in multi-person social scenarios.

5 Summary and Future Work

In this paper, we propose a coarse-to-fine human visual focus estimation method. First, we propose a coarse-to-fine module to address the sequential problem and the non-differentiable problem limiting the estimation accuracy, which employs a multi-task scheme to predict spatial distribution heatmap and visual focal point position parallelly. Secondly, the prior knowledge, the human visual field, is utilized to guide the learning of gaze salience for covering areas related to the gaze target. We validate our model on the ASD-attention dataset. The state-of-the-art results achieved by our model against other methods further approve the effectiveness and the generalization ability of the proposed model. Visual salience is mostly data-driven. In future work, a top-down graph neural network could be considered to analyze the relation of visual focus and the scene context for improving interpretability.

References

1. Cao, Z., Wang, G., Guo, X.: Stage-by-stage based design paradigm of two-pathway model for gaze following. In: Lin, Z., et al. (eds.) PRCV 2019. LNCS, vol. 11858, pp. 644–656. Springer, Cham (2019). https://doi.org/10.1007/978-3-030-31723-2_55
2. Chong, E., Ruiz, N., Wang, Y., Zhang, Y., Rozga, A., Rehg, J.M.: Connecting gaze, scene, and attention: generalized attention estimation via joint modeling of gaze and scene saliency. In: Ferrari, V., Hebert, M., Sminchisescu, C., Weiss, Y. (eds.) ECCV 2018. LNCS, vol. 11209, pp. 397–412. Springer, Cham (2018). https://doi.org/10.1007/978-3-030-01228-1_24
3. Chong, E., Wang, Y., Ruiz, N., Rehg, J.M.: Detecting attended visual targets in video. In: 2020 IEEE/CVF Conference on Computer Vision and Pattern Recognition, CVPR 2020, Seattle, WA, USA, 13–19 June, 2020, pp. 5395–5405. Computer Vision Foundation / IEEE (2020)

4. Dai, L., Liu, J., Ju, Z., Gao, Y.: Attention mechanism based real time gaze tracking in natural scenes with residual blocks. IEEE Trans. Cogn. Dev. Syst. **14**, 1 (2021)
5. Fan, L., Chen, Y., Wei, P., Wang, W., Zhu, S.: Inferring shared attention in social scene videos. In: 2018 IEEE Conference on Computer Vision and Pattern Recognition, CVPR 2018, Salt Lake City, UT, USA, 18–22 June, 2018, pp. 6460–6468. Computer Vision Foundation/IEEE Computer Society (2018)
6. Fang, Y., Tang, J., Shen, W., Shen, W., Gu, X., Song, L., Zhai, G.: Dual attention guided gaze target detection in the wild. In: IEEE Conference on Computer Vision and Pattern Recognition, CVPR 2021, virtual, June 19–25, 2021. pp. 11390–11399. Computer Vision Foundation / IEEE (2021)
7. Lian, D., Yu, Z., Gao, S.: Believe it or not, we know what you are looking at! In: Jawahar, C.V., Li, H., Mori, G., Schindler, K. (eds.) ACCV 2018. LNCS, vol. 11363, pp. 35–50. Springer, Cham (2019). https://doi.org/10.1007/978-3-030-20893-6_3
8. Liu, J., et al.: Early screening of autism in toddlers via response-to-instructions protocol. IEEE Trans. Cybern., 1–11 (2020)
9. Massé, B., Lathuilière, S., Mesejo, P., Horaud, R.: Extended gaze following: Detecting objects in videos beyond the camera field of view. In: 2019 14th IEEE International Conference on Automatic Face Gesture Recognition (FG 2019), pp. 1–8 (2019)
10. Newell, A., Yang, K., Deng, J.: Stacked hourglass networks for human pose estimation. In: Leibe, B., Matas, J., Sebe, N., Welling, M. (eds.) ECCV 2016. LNCS, vol. 9912, pp. 483–499. Springer, Cham (2016). https://doi.org/10.1007/978-3-319-46484-8_29
11. Recasens, A., Khosla, A., Vondrick, C., Torralba, A.: Where are they looking? In: Cortes, C., Lawrence, N., Lee, D., Sugiyama, M., Garnett, R. (eds.) Advances in Neural Information Processing Systems. vol. 28. Curran Associates, Inc. (2015)
12. Recasens, A., Vondrick, C., Khosla, A., Torralba, A.: Following gaze in video. In: IEEE International Conference on Computer Vision, ICCV 2017, Venice, Italy, 22–29 October, 2017, pp. 1444–1452. IEEE Computer Society (2017)
13. Tan, G., Xu, K., Liu, J., Liu, H.: A trend on autism spectrum disorder research: eye tracking-eeg correlative analytics. IEEE Trans. Cogn. Dev. Syst., 1 (2021)
14. Wang, X., Zhang, J., Zhang, H., Zhao, S., Liu, H.: Vision-based gaze estimation: a review. IEEE Trans. Cogn. Dev. Syst., 1 (2021)
15. Wang, Z., Liu, J., He, K., Xu, Q., Xu, X., Liu, H.: Screening early children with autism spectrum disorder via response-to-name protocol. IEEE Trans. Industr. Inf. **17**(1), 587–595 (2021)
16. Yang, L., Dong, K., Dmitruk, A.J., Brighton, J., Zhao, Y.: A dual-cameras-based driver gaze mapping system with an application on non-driving activities monitoring. IEEE Trans. Intell. Transp. Syst. **21**(10), 4318–4327 (2020)
17. Yücel, Z., Salah, A.A., Meriçli,, Meriçli, T., Valenti, R., Gevers, T.: Joint attention by gaze interpolation and saliency. IEEE Trans. Cybern. **43**(3), 829–842 (2013)
18. Zhao, H., Lu, M., Yao, A., Chen, Y., Zhang, L.: Learning to draw sight lines. Int. J. Comput. Vis. **128**(5), 1076–1100 (2020)
19. Zhuang, N., Ni, B., Xu, Y., Yang, X., Zhang, W., Li, Z., Gao, W.: Muggle: multi-stream group gaze learning and estimation. IEEE Trans. Circuits Syst. Video Technol. **30**(10), 3637–3650 (2020)

Space Robot and Space Mechanism

Motion Parameters and State Estimation of Non-cooperative Target

Ziyang Zhang, Guocai Yang[(✉)], Minghe Jin, and Shaowei Fan

State Key Laboratory of Robotics and System, Harbin Institute of Technology, Harbin 150001, China

gc_yang@outlook.com

Abstract. This paper proposes a state estimation method of non-cooperative target, which can be used to identify the target satellite motion. Firstly, tumbling motion of the target is analyzed, while dynamic of non-cooperative target is built. Secondly, an estimate method based on least squares method is proposed to identify the kinematic and dynamic parameters. Both of them are based on least squares methods. Thirdly, with parameters estimated, error state Kalman filter is used to estimate the angular velocity and filter attitude of the target at the same time. Finally, a simulation experiment is carried out to verify the effectiveness of the method. Simulation results reveal the method proposed by this paper can identify parameter and estimate motion state accurately, which is meaningful for non-cooperative target capture.

Keywords: Non-cooperative target · Parameters identification · Motion estimation · ESKF

1 Introduction

These days, with the continuous deepening of human exploration of space, space is getting more crowded. Due to more and more space objects, on-orbit capture is getting more attention [1]. Currently, most of study focuses on cooperative target, which means the motion of the target is slow and smooth, with known motion parameters, such as the moment, the pose of capture point relative to the center of the target and so on. However, lots of space objects are non-cooperative, their attitude control system may not work. The momentum used to be stored in the wheels and gyros are in danger of being released to the satellite. As a result, non-cooperative targets are always in complex motion state [3], which also has been confirmed by the ground experiment and observations [4]. Expect for complex motion state, there is another difficulty in motion state estimation of non-cooperative target, that is no prior knowledge about motion parameters, including the pose of grasping point at the target coordinate frame, the moment of inertia and so on [4]. However, for a safe and effective approach to capture targets, these parameters are necessary. Due to these difficulty, capturing and servicing tasks for a non-cooperative target have not been finished successfully in space, and non-cooperative target motion parameters and state estimation has been a hot area for research for several years [5].

H. Liu et al. (Eds.): ICIRA 2022, LNAI 13455, pp. 457–469, 2022.
https://doi.org/10.1007/978-3-031-13844-7_44

Researchers have put forward many methods in motion parameters estimation. Palimaka et al. [6] proposed a method for estimating the mass characteristic parameters of unknown space objects, which is necessary to predict angular velocity of tumbling space objects. Tanygin et al. [7] used the weighted recursive least squares method to estimate the motion parameters of unknown space objects, including position of the mass center of the spacecraft, the initial velocity, and the inertia ratio. In angle filter design area, many researchers have proposed effective methods. To solve quaternion normalization problem, Lefferts et al. [8] proposed Multiplicative Extended Kalman Filter(MEKF), which uses quaternion multiply to update state variable during filter. Kim et al. [9] combined the least squares method with the extended Kalman filter. it performs target parameter estimation and attitude filtering at the same time, so that the parameter estimation gradually converges, with the target attitude filtering and angular velocity estimation are also gradually accurate. Farhad et al. [10, 11] proposed an adaptive estimation method, which uses Kalman filter to estimate the ratio of the inertial parameters of the target spacecraft together with the motion state. This method can be used to estimate the motion of the spacecraft whose inertial parameters are unknown.

This paper focuses on motion parameters and motion state estimation of noncooperative space target, which is the premise of on-orbit service to non-cooperative target. Section 2 analyzes the motion characteristics of non-cooperative tumbling targets and establishes motion equations. Section 3 studies the estimation of target motion parameters and proposes an estimation method based on the least squares method. Section 4 studies attitude filtering and angular velocity estimation method, which applies an error state Kalman filter to perform task. Section 5 performs simulation experiments to verify the performance of the proposed method.

2   Non-cooperative Tumbling Target Motion Characteristics Analysis

The non-cooperative tumbling target is in a microgravity environment in space, so its influence by the external torque can be ignored. The non-cooperative target performs nutation motion in space, while the momentum moment axis is fixed in space, spins around the maximum inertia axis at a constant angular velocity. At the same time, the spin axis rotates around the angular moment axis, as shown in Fig. 1. According to Euler's dynamic equations, we have:

$$\frac{d\boldsymbol{H}}{dt} + \boldsymbol{\omega} \times \boldsymbol{H} = 0 \tag{1}$$

where $\boldsymbol{H}$ is the of the momentum of the target, and $\boldsymbol{\omega}$ is the angular velocity of the target. Inertia matrix of the target is $\boldsymbol{I} = \mathrm{diag}\left([I_x, I_y, I_z]^{\mathrm{T}}\right)$, angular velocity is $\boldsymbol{\omega} = [\omega_x, \omega_y, \omega_z]^{\mathrm{T}}$. Turns Eq. (1) from matric to scalar former, we have:

$$\begin{aligned}
\frac{d\omega_x}{dt} + k_x\omega_y\omega_z &= 0 \\
\frac{d\omega_y}{dt} + k_y\omega_x\omega_z &= 0 \\
\frac{d\omega_z}{dt} + k_z\omega_x\omega_z &= 0
\end{aligned} \tag{2}$$

Angular moment axis

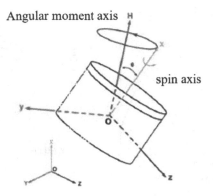

spin axis

Fig. 1. Nutation motion of target

where $k_x = \frac{(I_z - I_y)}{I_x}$, $k_y = \frac{(I_x - I_z)}{I_y}$, $k_z = \frac{(I_y - I_x)}{I_z}$. Since the inertia of the satellite is often distributed symmetrically along the z-axis, I_y and I_x are often set to the same value [2].

In order to further analyze the rotational motion of the target in space, a coordinate frame $\{Bt\}$ is established with the target's spin axis as the Z-axis, and the target's angular momentum is expressed as:

$$H = I_x \omega_x O_{Bt} X_{Bt} + I_y \omega_y O_{Bt} Y_{Bt} + I_z \omega_z O_{Bt} Z_{Bt} \tag{3}$$

Assume $I_x = I_y = I_t$, we have:

$$H = I_t \omega_h + I_z \omega_z O_{Bt} Z_{Bt} \tag{4}$$

In which

$$\omega_h = \omega_x O_{Bt} X_{Bt} + \omega_y O_{Bt} Y_{Bt} \tag{5}$$

It can be seen that the angular momentum consists of two parts, which are the spin angular rate ω_z and the angular rate of spin axis ω_h. The spin axis also moves in a circular motion, and its instantaneous rotational speed is the synthesis of the two angular rates. It can be known from Eq. (5) that the calculation equation of the nutation angle of the target is:

$$\theta = \arccos\left(\frac{I_z \omega_z}{H}\right) \tag{6}$$

It can be seen from above that without external force, the nutation angle of the target remains constant. The motion of the target is simulated in the simulation software, and results are as follows (Fig. 2):

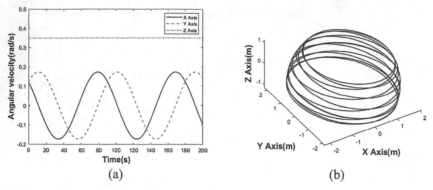

Fig. 2. Simulation results of tumbling target (a) angle velocity of the target. (b) the trajectory of grasping point on the target.

From above results, it can be seen that the trajectory of the grasping point is complicated, so it's necessary to estimate its motion state and parameters before capturing.

3 Target Motion Parameters Estimation

The motion of the target can be decomposed into the rotational motion around the angular momentum axis and the translational motion of the mass center. Correspondingly, its motion parameters are also divided into rotational motion related parameters (PPAM) and mass center motion related parameters (PPACM) [2]. In this section, it is assumed that the position of the target grasping point and the rotation matrix of the grasping point frame relative to the inertial frame have been obtained by the vision system, and the motion parameters are estimated based on the above data with observation noise.

3.1 Mass Center Motion Related Parameters Estimation

As shown in Fig. 3, coordinate frame $\{A\}$ is assumed to be inertial, while coordinate frame $\{B\}$ is attached to the body of the target with the origin of the target center of mass. Coordinate frame $\{C\}$ is with the grasping point as the origin and the same direction as frame $\{B\}$. Because the satellite frame $\{B\}$ is parallel to the grasping point frame $\{C\}$, we have $R_B^A = R_C^A$. Further, the expression of the grasping point r_s in the inertial frame can be derived:

$$r_s^A = r_c^A + R_B^A \rho^B \tag{7}$$

where r_c^A is the expression of the target centroid in the frame $\{A\}$, and ρ is the position vector between the grasping point and the target centroid. The position vector ρ^B in frame $\{B\}$ is constant. It can be obtained from Eq. (7), if the value of ρ^B can be estimated, the position of the target center of mass can be estimated with information about the position and attitude of the grasping point.

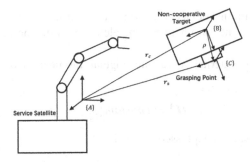

Fig. 3. The body-diagram of service satellite and non-cooperative target

When the target is not subjected to force, it moves in a straight line at a uniform speed in space, and its position vector $r_c(t) = r_{c0} + v_c t$, where r_{c0} is the initial position vector of the target center of mass, and v_c is the linear velocity of the target. These two parameters are related to the motion of the center of mass. Set the parameter to be estimated to p_c, then we have:

$$p_c = \left[r_{c0}^{w'}, v_c^{w'}, \rho_i^{b'} \right]'$$ (8)

Therefore, Eq. (8) can be rewritten as the homogeneous form of the grasping point position and the parameter to be estimated:

$$r_s^A(t) = \Phi_c(t) p_{ci}$$ (9)

where $\Phi_c(t) = \left[I_3, t I_3, R_B^A \right]$. At each observation moment, the observed value of the grasping point position vector $r_s^A(t)$ and coefficient matrix $\Phi_c(t)$ can be obtained, denoted as $\hat{r}_s^A(t)$ and $\hat{\Phi}_c(t)$. Substituting the measured value for the true value in Eq. (9), we have

$$\hat{r}_s^A(t) = \hat{\Phi}_c(t) p_{ci}$$ (10)

Collect multiple sets of data, we have

$$\hat{\Phi}_{c_{vec}} \hat{p}_{ci} = \hat{r}_{s_{vec}}^A$$ (11)

Using the least squares method to solve the above equation, the optimal estimation of p_{ci} can be obtained as follow:

$$\hat{p}_{ci} = \left(\hat{\Phi}_{c_{vec}}^T \hat{\Phi}_{c_{vec}} \right)^{-1} \hat{\Phi}_{c_{vec}}^T \hat{r}_s^A(t)$$ (12)

3.2 Rotational Motion Related Parameters Estimation

According to the analysis in Sect. 2, in order to predict the rotational motion of the target, it is necessary to know the initial angular velocity of the target and the ratio coefficients of the moment of inertia k_x, k_y, and k_z. Since it's impossible to exert external force on the target without additional device, the moment of inertia matrix cannot be completely estimated. Fortunately, the ratio between the elements of the inertia matrix can still be estimated.

In the absence of external force, the angular momentum of the target remains constant, we have:

$$H^A = constant[3, 1] \tag{13}$$

The angular momentum expressed in $\{B\}$ is:

$$H^B = R_A^B H^A \tag{14}$$

According to the conservation law of angular momentum. we have:

$$H^B = J^B \omega_t^B \tag{15}$$

Combine Eqs. (14) and (15), we have

$$R_A^B H^A = J^B \omega_t^B \tag{16}$$

In Eq. (16), R_A^B can be obtained by observing the pose of the grasping point, and J^B is the moment of inertia of the target in the target with frame $\{B\}$, which needs to be estimated. ω_t^B is target angular velocity represented of in frame $\{B\}$. Estimated value of ω_t^B can be obtained by differentiating the target attitude. Its calculation method is as follows:

According to quaternion differential kinematics [12], the relationship between the quaternion derivative and the angular velocity is as follows:

$$\dot{q}_t = \tfrac{1}{2} Q \omega_t \tag{17}$$

In which

$$Q = \begin{bmatrix} q_4 & -q_3 & q_2 \\ q_3 & q_4 & -q_1 \\ -q_2 & q_1 & q_4 \\ -q_1 & -q_2 & -q_3 \end{bmatrix} \tag{18}$$

Therefore, the estimation of the target angular velocity is:

$$\hat{\omega}_t = 2Q^\# \dot{q}_t \tag{19}$$

where $Q^\#$ is Moore-Penrose Inverse of Q. Since the estimation of the target attitude contains noise, after the differential derivation process, the high-frequency noise is enlarged, resulting in a large error in the estimation of the angular velocity. Therefore, the RC low-pass filter processor needs to be used to denoise the estimation of the angular velocity.

Once an initial estimation of the angular velocity is obtained, the moment of inertia ratio can be obtained. Let J_{ij} denote the element of the i-th row and the j-th column of the moment of inertia matrix J. J can be completely determined by six elements due to the symmetry of the moment of inertia matrix. Let x to be the unknown parameter vector, i.e.,

$$x = \left(J_{11} \ \ J_{12} \ \ J_{13} \ \ J_{22} \ \ J_{23} \ \ J_{33} \ \ H_1 \ \ H_2 \ \ H_3 \right)^T \in \mathbb{R}^9 \tag{20}$$

It is worth noting that if x can satisfy Eq. (16), then any vector proportional to x can satisfy the equation, too. Therefore, it is necessary to reduce the order of the estimated parameters. Instead of estimate x directly, a lower-order parameter vector x_b is estimated, i.e.,

$$x_b = \left(1 \ \ \tfrac{J_{12}}{J_{11}} \ \ \tfrac{J_{13}}{J_{11}} \tfrac{J_{22}}{J_{11}} \ \ \tfrac{J_{23}}{J_{11}} \ \ \tfrac{J_{33}}{J_{11}} \ \ \tfrac{H_1}{J_{11}} \ \ \tfrac{H_2}{J_{11}} \ \ \tfrac{H_3}{J_{11}} \right)^T \in \mathbb{R}^9 \tag{21}$$

Rewrite the Eq. (16) as follows:

$$A x_b = 0 \tag{22}$$

In which $A \in \mathbb{R}^{3n \times 9}$, and

$$A = \begin{bmatrix} \Theta_1 & -R_{A1}^B \\ \vdots & \vdots \\ \Theta_n & -R_{An}^B \end{bmatrix} \tag{23}$$

$$\Theta_i = \begin{bmatrix} \omega_{tix} & \omega_{tiy} & \omega_{tiz} & 0 & 0 & 0 \\ 0 & \omega_{tix} & 0 & \omega_{tiy} & \omega_{tiz} & 0 \\ 0 & 0 & \omega_{tix} & 0 & \omega_{tiy} & \omega_{tiz} \end{bmatrix} \tag{24}$$

where n is total number of observed data sets.

In most cases Eq. (22) is a homogeneous incompatible equation, which can be solved using the least squares method. The square of the modulus of the left-hand side of Eq. (22) is:

$$\|A x_b\|^2 = (A x_b)^T A x_b$$
$$= x_b^T A^T A x_b \tag{25}$$

The optimal x_b can be obtained by solving follow equation:

$$B x_b = 0 \tag{26}$$

After getting parameters vector x_b, the target inertia matrix expressed in frame $\{B\}$ can be obtained. Then, the inertia matrix J need to be diagonalized to get principal moments of inertia. Do eigenvalue decomposition of the inertia matrix, we get:

$$J = R_{B_{diag}}^B J_{diag} R_{B_{diag}}^{BT} \tag{27}$$

Through the above formula, the principal moments of inertia ratio of the target can be obtained, which can be used to calculate the coefficients k_x, k_y, k_z required by Eq. (2).

4 Attitude Filtering and Angular Velocity Estimation

Since the observation of the position and attitude of the grasping point is usually noisy, the observation of the target position, attitude and speed contains lots of noise. Therefore, it is necessary to select an appropriate filter for noise reduction processing.

State variable is made of quaternions and angular velocity, i.e., $X = \begin{bmatrix} q & \omega \end{bmatrix}^T$. The measurement variable contains only attitudes of target, i.e., $Z = q^T = \begin{bmatrix} q_1, q_2, q_3, q_4 \end{bmatrix}^T$.

The error state Kalman filter (ESKF) is used to filter attitude and estimate angular velocity. ESKF represents the true quaternion as the product of the error quaternion and the nominal quaternion, i.e.,

$$q(t) = \delta q(a(t)) \otimes q_{\text{ref}}(t) \tag{28}$$

where q(t) is the true quaternion of the target, $q_{\text{ref}}(t)$ is the nominal quaternion of the target, $a(t)$ is the error vector expressed in terms of modified Rodrigues parameters (MRPs). The idea of ESKF is to use normalized quaternion $q_{\text{ref}}(t)$ to represent the singular-free reference pose of the target. Only the error vector $a(t)$ is updated in each prediction step, while $q_{\text{ref}}(t)$ is updated and $a(t)$ is set to zero in each observation step. The difference between the true quaternion and the reference quaternion is represented by a three-element error vector with no singularity and no redundant constraints.

$a(t)$ in Eq. (28) is MRPs, its derivative in the form of quaternion and derivative of quaternion is:

$$\frac{da_p}{dt} = \dot{a}_p = \frac{4}{1+q_1}\dot{\bar{q}} - \frac{4}{(1+q_1)^2}\dot{q}_1\bar{q} \tag{29}$$

Represent quaternions and their derivatives in terms of a_p and ω, we have:

$$\dot{a}_p = \left(-\tfrac{1}{2}[\omega\times] + \tfrac{1}{8}\omega \cdot a_p\right)a_p + \left(1 - \tfrac{1}{16}a_p^T a_p\right)\omega \tag{30}$$

Due to short discrete steps, second-order minors $\omega \cdot a_p$ and $a_p^T a_p$ can be ignored, so we have:

$$\dot{a}_p \approx -\tfrac{1}{2}[\omega\times]a_p + \omega \tag{31}$$

Derivative of angular velocity is:

$$\dot{\omega} = J^{-1}(-\omega \times J\omega + W_\omega) \tag{32}$$

where W_ω represents the influence of process noise, such as extern force acting on target and so on. So state equation of ESKF is:

$$\begin{bmatrix} \dot{a}_p \\ \dot{\omega} \end{bmatrix} = \begin{bmatrix} -\tfrac{1}{2}[\omega\times] & I_{3\times3} \\ 0_{3\times3} & \Phi_\omega \end{bmatrix}\begin{bmatrix} a_p \\ \omega \end{bmatrix} + \begin{bmatrix} 0_{3\times3} \\ J^{-1} \end{bmatrix}W_\omega = A_a\begin{bmatrix} a_p \\ \omega \end{bmatrix} + B_a W_\omega \tag{33}$$

In which

$$\Phi_\omega = \begin{bmatrix} 0 & k_x\omega_z & k_x\omega_y \\ k_y\omega_z & 0 & k_y\omega_x \\ k_z\omega_y & k_z\omega_x & 0 \end{bmatrix} \tag{34}$$

Discretizing Eq. (33), we have:

$$x(k) = \Phi(k)x(k-1) + \Gamma(k)W(k)$$

where $\Phi(k) = \exp(A_a T)$, $\Gamma(k) = \exp(B_a T)$, T is discrete period.

In measurement equation, the target attitude quaternion observation value $\breve{q}(k)$ is selected to be the observation value, then the error Rodrigues vector of the measurement equation is:

$$\delta q(\breve{a}_p(k)) = \breve{q}(k) \otimes q_{\text{ref}}(k)^*$$

Therefore, measurement equation of ESKF is:

$$y(k) = H(k)x(k) + V = [I_{3\times3}\ 0]\begin{bmatrix} a_p \\ \omega \end{bmatrix} + V_{ap}$$

where V_{ap} represents influence of measurement noise of attitude of the target, which may be caused by inaccuracy of grasping attitude recognition method and so on.

After mzseasurement update, we will update the reference quaternion with the error vector and reset error vector, i.e.:

$$\hat{q}(k) = \delta q\left(\hat{a}_p^+(k)\right) \otimes q_{\text{ref}}(k)$$

$$\hat{a}_p^+(k) = 0_{3\times1}$$

$$q_{\text{ref}}(k+1) = \hat{q}(k)$$

5 Simulation Experiment

In this section, a simulation experiment is carried out to verify the correctness of the method in this section. Firstly, dynamic model of the target is built in Adams as shown in Fig. 4:

Fig. 4. Adams model of non-cooperative target

Table 1. Mass properties and initial state of target

Parameters of target	Value
Mass M	1500 kg
Inertia matrix J	diag(1606.7, 1009.5, 783.7) kg·m
Position vector ρ^b	(−1.8000, 0.0100, −0.0200) m
Initial centroid pose r_c^w	(0.0477, 0.8783, 2.3878] m
Centroid velocity v_c^w	(0.01, 0.02, 0.03) m/s
Centroid initial angular velocity w	(1.2, −1.2, 1.4)°/s

It's mass properties and initial state are as shown in Table 1:

Set the observation time to 10 s, record the position and attitude of the grasping point. The observation position error is ±5 mm, while the attitude quaternion error is ±0.001. The estimation and estimation error obtained by the method in Sect. 3 are shown in Table 2:

It can be seen from the simulation results that the proposed parameters-estimation method can get effective estimation of the non-cooperative roll target parameters, initial position and velocity. Next, the first-order differential processing is performed on the target attitude to obtain a preliminary estimation of the angular velocity, and the moment of inertia ratio is obtained according to the preliminary estimation of the attitude and angular velocity. The true value of the moment of inertia ratio in this project is [1.000, 0.628, 0.488], while the estimated value using this method is [1.000, 0.621, 0.485]. It can be seen that the estimation method of the inertia ratio adopted in this paper is effective within the allowable range of error.

Finally, ESKF is used to filter attitude of target and filter angular velocity. Parameters of filter is shown as Table 3.

Table 2. The estimation results of the proposed parameters-estimation method

		x	y	z
Position vector of grasping point ρ^b	Ture value	−1.8000	0.0100	−0.0200
	Estimated value	−1.80247	0.01213	−0.0223
	Error	−0.14%	−21.30%	−11.50%
Initial centroid pose r_c^w	Ture value	0.0447	0.8783	2.3878
	Estimated value	0.0429	0.8766	2.3910
	Error	4.03%	0.19%	−0.13%
Centroid velocity v_c^w	Ture value	0.01	0.02	0.03
	Estimated value	0.01008	0.02001	0.02998
	Error	−0.84%	−0.03%	0.08%

Table 3. Parameters of filter

Parameters of filter	Value
Initial value of covariance matrix P_0	diag(0.1,0.1,0.1,1,1,1)
Process noise of covariance matrix Q	diag(0.001,0.001, 0.001,0.001, 0.001,0.001)
Measurement noise of covariance matrix R	diag(0.1,0.1,0.1)

Figure 5 shows simulation result. Figure 6 shows quaternion errors before and after filtering. Figure 7 shows estimation errors of angular velocity.

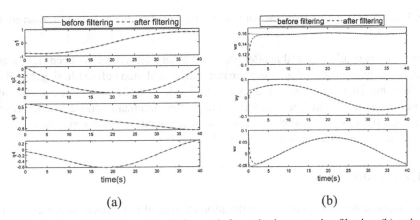

(a)   (b)

Fig. 5. Simulation results (a) the values before and after attitude quaternion filtering. (b) estimated and true angular velocity.

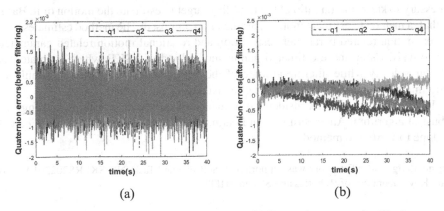

(a)   (b)

Fig. 6. (a) Quaternion errors before filtering. (b) Quaternion errors after filtering

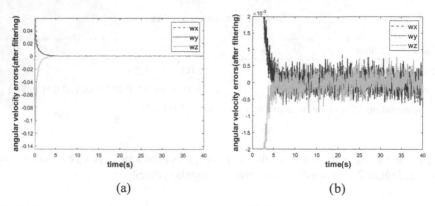

Fig. 7. (a) Estimation errors of angular velocity. (b) Partial enlargement of estimation errors.

Simulation results reveal that after filtering, quaternion errors have been significantly reduced. It is worth noting that noises are normally distributed before filtering, but biased after filtering. This is caused by the lag due to filtering. At the same time estimations of the angular velocity converge to the true value. After stabilization the estimated error of the angular velocity is ±0.0005 rad/s. Within the allowable range of error, the estimation about quaternion and angular velocity is effective.

6   Conclusion

In this paper, a motion parameters estimation method of non-cooperative target is proposed, while a kind of filter to filtering attitude and estimate angular velocity of non-cooperative target is designed. Firstly, the nutation motion of the target is analyzed, and the trajectory of the grasping point on the target is shown. a conclusion is drawn that it's necessary to know inertia ratio of the tumbling target to estimate the motion of it. Based on that, a method to estimate motion parameters is proposed. The method estimates mass center motion related parameters estimation and rotational motion related parameters respectively. Using these estimated parameters, a kind of ESKF, which estimates the angular velocity while filtering attitude of the target, is designed. Finally, simulation experiment is carried out to verify the effectiveness of the method.

In the future, we will consider the influence of outlier observations and improve robust of algorithm. An experiment on floating satellite ground verification device will be done to verify the method.

Acknowledgment. This work was supported by Self-Planned Task (No. SKLRS202201A02) of State Key Laboratory of Robotics and System (HIT).

References

1. Flores-Abad, A., Ma, O., Pham, K., et al.: A review of space robotics technologies for on-orbit servicing. Prog. Aerosp. Sci. **68**, 1–26 (2014)

2. Zhou, B.Z., Cai, G.P., Liu, Y.M., et al.: Motion prediction of a non-cooperative space target. Adv. Space Res. **61**(1), 207–222 (2018)
3. Kawamoto, S.: Research on a space debris removal system. NAL Res. Prog. 2002–2003 (2003)
4. Benninghoff, H., Boge, T.: Rendezvous involving a non-cooperative, tumbling target-estimation of moments of inertia and center of mass of an unknown target. In: 25th International Symposium on Space Flight Dynamics (2015)
5. Flores-Abad, A., Wei, Z., Ma, O., et al.: Optimal control of space robots for capturing a tumbling object with uncertainties. J. Guid. Control. Dyn. **37**(6), 2014–2017 (2014)
6. Palimaka, J., Burlton, B.V.: Estimation of spacecraft mass properties using angular rate gyro data. In: AIAA/AAS Astrodynamics Conference, Hilton Head Island, USA (1992)
7. Tanygin, S., Williams, T.: Mass property estimation using coasting maneuvers. J. Guid. Control. Dyn. **20**, 625–632 (1997)
8. Lefferts, E.J., Markley, F.L., Shuster, M.D.: Kalman filtering for spacecraft attitude estimation. J. Guid. Control. Dyn. **5**(5), 417–429 (1982)
9. Kim, D.H., Yang, S., Cheon, D., et al.: Combined estimation method for inertia properties of STSAT-3. J. Mech. Sci. Technol. **24**(8), 1737–1741 (2010)
10. Aghili, F.: Optimal control for robotic capturing and passivation of a tumbling satellite with unknown dynamics. In: AIAA Guidance, Navigation and Control Conference and Exhibit (2008)
11. Aghili, F.: Optimal trajectories and robot control for detumbling a non-cooperative satellite. J. Guid. Control. Dyn. **43**(5), 981–988 (2020)
12. Bar-Itzhack, I., Deutschmann, J., Markley, F.: Quaternion normalization in additive EKF for spacecraft attitude determination. In: Navigation and Control Conference (1991)

Event-Triggered Adaptive Control for Practically Finite-Time Position-Constrained Tracking of Space Robot Manipulators

Zhiwei Hao[1,2]([✉]), Xiaokui Yue[1], Li Liu[1], and Shuzhi Sam Ge[2]

[1] School of Astronautics, Northwestern Polytechnical University,
Xi'an, Shaanxi 710072, China
haozwbetter@mail.nwpu.edu.cn
[2] Department of Electrical and Computer Engineering, National University
of Singapore, Singapore 117576, Singapore

Abstract. This paper investigates the problem of event-triggered adaptive tracking control for space manipulator systems under pre-determined position constraints. This control scheme aims to overcome external perturbations, reduce the burden of data-transmission, and achieve constrained tracking. Focusing on the constraints of system performance, quadratic Lyapunov functions (QLF) are stitched with a set of asymmetric time-receding horizons (TRH) with fixed settling time, serving as a sufficient condition for the practically prescribed finite-time stability (PPFS) of target plants. By introducing event-triggered conditions, the control signals are transformed into non-periodically updated variables, promoting signaling efficiency while preserving the desired system performance. Complex nonlinearities are integrated and compensated adaptively, providing an ingenious design process and simplifying the construction of the controller. Finally, simulations demonstrate the effectiveness of the proposed scheme.

Keywords: Robot manipulators · Time-receding horizon ·
Event-triggered mechanism · Adaptive control

1 Introduction

In past decades, the great curiosity about the universe has continuously impelled humans to pursue diverse space activities [1,2]. The complex environment and the high-cost of astronaut training make it necessary for space operations to be performed unmanned. As space robots become ever delicate and multifunctional, much more requirements and specifications are called for novel applications from control science [3,4]. Meanwhile, complicated spatial environments

This work was supported in part by the Innovation Capability Support Program of Shaanxi (No. 2019TD-008); and in part by the China Scholarship Council (No. 202106290148).

present many unknowns for robot dynamics, for which advanced control techniques have opened up a host of solutions, such as fuzzy-adaptive control [5], sliding mode control [6], and impedance control [7], etc.

With the increasing demands on space robots, scholars are no longer limited to the pursuit of stability, but brings up sustained interests in the dynamic performance [8,9]. Barrier Lyapunov functions (BLFs), as a well-established methodology derived from rigorous stability analysis, open up a new field of state-constrained control [10]. Based on that, a finite-time fuzzy controller in the presence of input saturation was proposed for n-linked robots [11]. As improvements of the BLF, many studies are devoted to the constraining performance, such as deformation of function expressions, adjustment of constraint symmetry, and specification of time-depending properties, significantly expanding its practicality [12–15]. Studies in [16] combined asymmetric barrier functions (ABF) and neural networks to validate the resulting robust controller on a spatial robot. The work of [17] solved the uniformly ultimately bounded tracking of robots with uncertain parameters, input saturation, and output constraints through ABFs. The improvement of state-constraints presents numerous challenges and opportunities for space engineering. Besides, implementing constraints requires strict initial conditions, while conventional BLFs with constant barriers cannot fully exert the dynamic-constraining advantages.

In addition to performance constraints, researchers then turn attention to signal transmission efficiency. Event-triggered mechanisms (ETM) were motivated by the use of embedded microprocessors with limited resources that will accumulate information and actuate the controller updates [18]. ETM provides rules to reduce the number of actuator updates, preferable for many digital system applications. Unlike periodical sampling, a properly designed ETM facilitates the retention of the desired properties of the nominal system [19]. In [20], the event-triggered strategy was embedded in an adaptive estimator and controller based on fuzzy logic. In [21], ETM was embedded in a fuzzy controller for time-delay teleoperation systems, alleviating the interacting burden. The rise of ETM has injected new blood into the control community, while the exclusion of the Zeno behavior (infinite sampling in a finite period) has always been its key.

In this paper, we develop an event-triggered adaptive control scheme for tracking of space robots. First, an ETM with modified thresholds is proposed for efficient data transmission, where the Zeno behavior is strictly excluded. Second, pre-determined asymmetric time-receding horizons stitched into quadratic Lyapunov functions (QLF) are designed to constrain system outputs from arbitrary initial conditions. Last but not least, system nonlinearities are encapsulated and adaptively compensated, avoiding the deduction of cumbersome derivatives.

2   Problrm Formulation

The dynamics of a disturbed n-degree-of-freedom (DOF) space robot manipulator can be expressed as

$$M(q)\ddot{q} + C(q,\dot{q})\dot{q} + d = u \tag{1}$$

where $q \in \mathbf{R}^n$ denotes the generalized position vector with its time derivatives representing the velocity and acceleration, respectively. $M(q)$ is the inertia matrix and $C(q, \dot{q})$ is the Coriolis and centrifugal terms. $u \in \mathbf{R}^n$ is the control input vector, and $d \in \mathbf{R}^n$ represents the bounded disturbance. System in Eq. (1) has the following properties:

Property 1. *The $\dot{M}(q) - 2C(q, \dot{q})$ is a skew-symmetric matrix, i.e.,*

$$y^T(\dot{M} - 2C)y = 0, \quad \forall y \in \mathbf{R}^n \tag{2}$$

Property 2. *The $M(q)$ is a positive-definite real symmetric matrix, satisfying*

$$\lambda_{\min} \|x\|^2 \leq x^T M x \leq \|M\| \|x\|^2, \quad \forall x \in \mathbf{R}^n \tag{3}$$

where $\lambda_{\min}$ is a positive constant, representing the minimum eigenvalue of M, and $\|\bullet\|$ expresses the Euclidean-norm here and hereafter.

To move on, follows are specific definitions, lemmas, and an assumption.

Definition 1. *[14] For the robotic dynamics in Eq. (1), if there exist $\iota > 0$ and $0 < T_s < \infty$ for all $x_0 = x(0)$ such that $\|x(t)\| \leq \iota, t \geq T_s$, where T_s is a time constant, then the solution of Eq. (1) is called practically prescribed finite-time stable (PPFS).*

Definition 2. *The time-receding horizon (TRH) $f(t)$ is a real value function that follows three properties: 1) $f(t) > 0, \forall t \geq 0$; 2) $\dot{f}(t) \leq 0$ and 3) $\lim_{t \to T_f} f(t) = f_{T_f}$ and $f(t) = f_{T_f}$ for any $t \geq T_f, f_{T_f} > 0$.*

Lemma 1. *[22] For any time-varying scalar value $s(t)$ constrainted in the compact set $\Omega_s := \{-f_1(t) < s(t) < f_2(t)\}$, where $f_1(t)$ and $f_2(t)$ are positive real functions, two inequalities hold that*

$$(s + f_1)(f_2 - s) \leq 2f_1 f_2 - f_1 s + f_2 s \tag{4}$$

$$(s + f_1)(f_2 - s) \leq \frac{(f_1 + f_2)^2}{4} \tag{5}$$

Lemma 2. *[15] For any vector $s \in \mathbf{R}^m, m = 1, 2, \cdots,$ there exists a positive scalar function $f(t)$ such that*

$$0 \leq \|s\| - \frac{s^T s}{\sqrt{s^T s + h(t)^2}} < h(t) \tag{6}$$

Lemma 3. *[20] For any constant $\varepsilon > 0$ and $\beta \in \mathbf{R}$, it holds*

$$0 \leq |\beta| - \beta \tanh\left(\frac{\beta}{\varepsilon}\right) \leq 0.2785\varepsilon \tag{7}$$

Assumption 1. *The reference trajectory $y_d(t)$ of the robotic system is continuous and bounded by $y_{dl} \leq y_d \leq y_{du}$ (with y_{dl} and y_{du} are constant), and $\dot{y}_d$ is also bounded but availability may be not required.*

The object of this paper is to provide good tracking of the general position q in Eq. (1) relative to the reference trajectory $y_d(t)$ without violating position constraints by means of a non-periodically updated controller.

3 Event-Triggered Adaptive Tracking Control for Space Robot

In this section, a TRH-based event-triggered adaptive controller for disturbed n-DOF robot manipulators is developed through backstepping (see Fig 1 for a sketch). The following subsections describe the main results in detail.

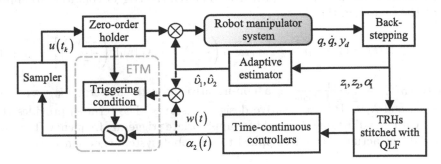

Fig. 1. Closed-loop system overview diagram

3.1 Controller Design

Let $x_1 = q$ and $x_2 = \dot{q}$, the robot dynamics in Eq. (1) can be rewritten into

$$\begin{aligned}
\dot{x}_1 &= x_2 \\
\dot{x}_2 &= M^{-1}(x_1)(u - C(x_1, x_2)x_2 - d)
\end{aligned} \tag{8}$$

To begin, the system tracking error signals are determined as

$$z_1 = x_1 - y_d, \quad z_2 = x_2 - \alpha_1 \tag{9}$$

where $\alpha_1 \in \mathbf{R}^n$ denotes the virtual control signal of the first-order subsystem of Eq. (8). From the overall framework of the paper, we give priority to all the control variables appearing in the design process. The time-continuous virtual control signals α_1 and α_2 corresponding to Eq. (8) are expressed as

$$\alpha_1 = -k_1 W_1^T z_1 - \frac{W_1^T z_1 \varepsilon_1 \hat{v}_1}{\sqrt{\|W_1 z_1\|^2 + h_1^2(t)}}, \quad \alpha_2 = -k_2 M z_2 - \frac{z_2 \varepsilon_2 \hat{v}_2}{\sqrt{\|z_2\|^2 + h_2^2(t)}} \tag{10}$$

where, for $i = 1, 2$, k_i and ε_i are positive control gains, W_1 is a time-varying matrix to be given, $h_i(t)$ is a user-designed positive function satisfying $\int_0^t h_i(\tau)\,d\tau \leq \bar{h}_i < \infty$, $\left|h_i(t)\right| \leq \underline{h}_i$, where $\bar{h}_i$ and $\underline{h}_i$ are positive constant, and $\hat{v}_i$ is the estimate of an unknown parameter v_i^* to be defined.

Remark 1. In backstepping, $\dot{z}_2$ contains the terms of $\dot{\alpha}_1$ and $\dot{y}_d$. For different tasks, deducing these derivatives may be cumbersome. In response, the proposed controller lies in avoiding this difficulty as well as in achieving the system stability through a simple construction.

Considering the process of data transmission, a modified ETM is introduced into the robot system. Signals in the ETM update discontinuously, thus an auxiliary control signal needs to be provided to match the trigger condition to implement the sampling, that is

$$w(t) = (1 + \eta_0) \left[\alpha_2 - e_0 \tanh\left(\frac{z_2^T e_0}{\varpi}\right) - \lambda_1 \tanh\left(\frac{z_2^T \lambda_1}{\varpi}\right) \right] \quad (11)$$

where $e_0(t) = \frac{1_n}{\sum_{i=1}^{2}|z_i|+\mu_0}$ is a non-negative adjustment term, μ_0, ϖ, $0 < \eta_0 < 1$, and $\lambda_1 \in \mathbf{R}^n$ are positive design constants. The term e_0 provides the ETM with an adjustable threshold for appropriate triggering frequency. To move forward, the actual controller applied to the robot system is designed as

$$u(t) = w(t_k), \quad \forall t \in [t_k, t_{k+1}) \quad (12)$$

where $\{t_k, k \in \mathbf{R}^+\}$ are triggering instants. The update of $u(t)$ occurs only at the trigger instant, otherwise the value taken at the previous instant is kept by a zero-order holder. The adaptive laws are given as

$$\dot{\hat{v}}_1 = \gamma_1 \frac{\left\|z_1^T W_1\right\|^2}{\sqrt{\left\|z_1^T W_1\right\|^2 + h_1^2(t)}} - \sigma_1 \hat{v}_1, \quad \dot{\hat{v}}_2 = \gamma_2 \frac{\left\|z_2\right\|^2}{\sqrt{\left\|z_2\right\|^2 + h_2^2(t)}} - \sigma_2 \hat{v}_2 \quad (13)$$

with σ_i being a positive parameter and $\hat{v}_i^0 = \hat{v}_i(0) \geq 0$. The event-triggered sampling is built on the following measurement error

$$e_u(t) = w(t) - u(t) \quad (14)$$

while the triggering condition is given as

$$t_k = \inf\left\{t \in \mathbf{R}^+ \mid |e_{u,i}(t)| \geq \eta_0 |u_i(t)| + \lambda_0 e_{0,i}(t) + \tau_{0,i}, i = 1, \cdots, n\right\} \quad (15)$$

where the subscript $*_i$ denotes the i-th element of a vector $*$, $\lambda_0 > 0$ meeting $\lambda_0 \leq 1 - \eta_0$, and $\tau_0 \leq (1 - \eta_0)\lambda_1$. Without loss of generality, it is assumed that the first event occurs at $t_0 = 0$.

3.2   Stability Analysis

To start with, we define the following TRH for asymmetric constraints, that is

$$f(t) = \begin{cases} \left(f_0 - \frac{t}{T_f}\right) e^{1 - \frac{T_f}{T_f - t}} + f_{T_f}, & t \in [0, T_f) \\ f_{T_f}, & t \in [T_f, +\infty) \end{cases} \quad (16)$$

where $f_0 > \frac{5}{4}$ and $f_{T_f} > 0$ are designable parameters, and $T_f > 0$ denotes the preassigned settling time constant. It can be clearly seen that $f(t) \in \mathcal{C}^1$.

In view of Eqs. (9) and (16), the following Lyapunov functions are constructed:

$$V_1 = z_1^T K_1 z_1, \quad V_2 = \frac{1}{2} z_2^T M z_2, \quad V_{\tilde{\upsilon}} = \frac{1}{2} \tilde{\upsilon}^T \Gamma \tilde{\upsilon} \tag{17}$$

where $\tilde{\upsilon} = [\tilde{\upsilon}_1 \ \tilde{\upsilon}_2]^T$ with $\tilde{\upsilon}_i = \upsilon_i^* - \hat{\upsilon}_i \ (i = 1, 2)$, $\Gamma = \mathrm{diag}\left(\frac{\varepsilon_1}{\gamma_1}, \frac{\varepsilon_2}{\gamma_2}\right)$, and

$$K_1 = \mathrm{diag}\left(\frac{1}{(f_{1L} + z_{1,1})(f_{1U} - z_{1,1})}, \frac{1}{(f_{2L} + z_{1,2})(f_{2U} - z_{1,2})}, \right.$$
$$\left. \cdots, \frac{1}{(f_{nL} + z_{1,n})(f_{nU} - z_{1,n})}\right)$$

where TRHs $f_{iL}, f_{iU}, i = 1, 2, \cdots, n$ indicate lower/upper bounds corresponding to the i-th element of z_1.

By applying the Eqs. (8), (9) and (10), the time derivative of V_1 can be deduced that

$$\dot{V}_1 = \sum_{i=1}^{n} \left[\frac{z_{1,i} \dot{z}_{1,i} [2 f_{iL} f_{iU} + z_{1,i}(f_{iU} - f_{iL})]}{[(f_{iL} + z_{1,i})(f_{iU} - z_{1,i})]^2} \right.$$
$$\left. - z_{1,i}^2 \frac{\dot{f}_{iL} f_{iU} + f_{iL} \dot{f}_{iU} + z_{1,i}\left(\dot{f}_{iU} - \dot{f}_{iL}\right)}{[(f_{iL} + z_{1,i})(f_{iU} - z_{1,i})]^2} \right] \tag{18}$$
$$= z_1^T W_1 (z_2 + \alpha_1 - \dot{y}_d + \eta_1 z_1)$$

where $W_1 = \mathrm{diag}(W_{1,1}, \cdots, W_{1,n})$ and $\eta_1 = \mathrm{diag}(\eta_{1,1}, \cdots, \eta_{1,n})$ with

$$W_{1,i} = \frac{2 f_{iL} f_{iU} + z_{1,i}(f_{iU} - f_{iL})}{[(f_{iL} + z_{1,i})(f_{iU} - z_{1,i})]^2}, \eta_{1,i} = \frac{\dot{f}_{iL} f_{iU} + f_{iL} \dot{f}_{iU} + z_{1,i}\left(\dot{f}_{iU} - \dot{f}_{iL}\right)}{2 f_{iL} f_{iU} + z_{1,i}(f_{iU} - f_{iL})}.$$

Define an operation $|a|_v := a \circ \mathrm{sgn}(a)$ for any $a \in \mathbf{R}^n$, where $\mathrm{sgn}(a) = [\mathrm{sgn}(a_1), \cdots, \mathrm{sgn}(a_n)]^T$ and $\circ$ is the Hadamard product. Letting $\varphi_1 = |z_2|_v + |\dot{y}_d|_v + |\eta_1 z_1|_v$, it is not hard to derive from the Extreme Value Theorem that

$$0 < \varphi_{1L} \leq \|\varphi_1\| \leq \varphi_{1U} \tag{19}$$

Defining $v_1^* = \frac{\varphi_{1U}}{\varepsilon_1}$, recalling the Lemma 2, and substituting Eqs. (10) and (19) into (18) yields

$$
\begin{aligned}
\dot{V}_1 \leq & - k_1 z_1^T W_1 W_1^T z_1 + \left(\left\| z_1^T W_1 \right\| \varphi_{1U} - \frac{\left\| W_1^T z_1 \right\|^2 \varepsilon_1 v_1^*}{\sqrt{\left\| W_1^T z_1 \right\|^2 + h_1^2(t)}} \right. \\
& \left. + \frac{\left\| W_1^T z_1 \right\|^2 \varepsilon_1 \tilde{v}_1}{\sqrt{\left\| W_1^T z_1 \right\|^2 + h_1^2(t)}} \right) \\
\leq & - k_1 z_1^T W_1 W_1^T z_i + \varphi_{1U} h_i + \frac{\left\| W_1^T z_1 \right\|^2 \varepsilon_1 \tilde{v}_1}{\sqrt{\left\| W_1^T z_1 \right\|^2 + h_1^2(t)}}
\end{aligned}
\tag{20}
$$

Retrospecting Eqs. (14) and (15), it holds

$$
u(t) = \frac{w(t) - \xi_0(t)\lambda_0 e_0(t) - \xi_0(t)\tau_0}{1 + \eta_0 \xi_1(t)}
\tag{21}
$$

where $\xi_0(t)$ is a continuous scalar function satisfying $\xi_0(t_k) = 0, \xi_0(t_{k+1}) = \pm 1$, and $\xi_1(t) = \pm \xi_0(t)$ taking the same sign as e_u. Note that $z_2^T w \leq -k_2 z_2^T z_2 - \frac{z_2^T z_2 \varepsilon_2 \tilde{v}_2}{\sqrt{\|z_2\|^2 + h_2^2(t)}} \leq 0$, which leads to

$$
\frac{z_2^T w}{1 + \eta_0 \xi_1} \leq \frac{z_2^T w}{1 + \eta_0}
\tag{22}
$$

Similarly, let $\varphi_2 = |C\alpha_1|_v + |d|_v + |M\dot{\alpha}_1|_v$, which also holds $0 < \varphi_{2L} \leq \|\varphi_2\| \leq \varphi_{2U}$. Then, applying Eqs. (11), (21), (22) and α_2 in Eq. (10), the time derivative of V_2 can be obtained as

$$
\begin{aligned}
\dot{V}_2 = & z_2^T (u - C(\alpha_1 + z_2) - d - M\dot{\alpha}_1) + z_2^T \frac{\dot{M}}{2} z_2 \\
\leq & \frac{z_2^T w}{1 + \eta_0} + z_2^T \left(-\frac{\xi_0 \lambda_0 e_0}{1 + \eta_0 \xi_1} - \frac{\xi_0 \tau_0}{1 + \eta_0 \xi_1} + \varphi_2 \right) \\
\leq & - k_2 z_2^T M z_2 + \varphi_{2U} h_2 + \frac{z_2^T z_2 \varepsilon_2 \tilde{v}_2}{\sqrt{\|z_2\|^2 + h_2^2(t)}} - z_2^T e_0 \tanh\left(\frac{z_2^T e_0}{\varpi}\right) \\
& - z_2^T \lambda_1 \tanh\left(\frac{z_2^T \lambda_1}{\varpi}\right) - z_2^T \frac{\xi_0 \lambda_0 e_0 + \xi_0 \tau_0}{1 + \eta_0 \xi_1}
\end{aligned}
\tag{23}
$$

By adding and subtracting $|z_2^T e_0|$ and $|z_2^T \lambda_1|$ simultaneously, and recalling Lemma 3, further expand Eq. (23) yields

$$
\dot{V}_2 \leq -k_2 z_2^T M z_2 + \varphi_{2U} h_2 + \frac{z_2 \varepsilon_2 \tilde{v}_2}{\sqrt{\|z_2\|^2 + h_2^2(t)}} + 0.557\varpi
\tag{24}
$$

Taking the time derivatives of $V = V_1 + V_2 + V_{\tilde{v}}$ and substituting Eq. (13), one has

$$\dot{V} \leq - k_1 z_1^T W_1 W_1^T z_i - k_2 z_2^T M z_2 + \sum_{j=1}^{2} \varphi_{jU} h_j + \frac{\|W_1 z_1\|^2 \varepsilon_1 \tilde{v}_1}{\sqrt{\|W_1 z_1\|^2 + h_1^2(t)}}$$

$$+ \frac{z_2 \varepsilon_2 \tilde{v}_2}{\sqrt{\|z_2\|^2 + h_2^2(t)}} + 0.557\varpi - \Gamma \tilde{v}^T \dot{v}$$

$$\leq - k_1 z_1^T W_1 W_1^T z_i - k_2 z_2^T M z_2 + \sum_{j=1}^{2} \varphi_{jU} h_j + \tilde{v}^T \Gamma_\sigma \hat{v} + 0.557\varpi$$

$$\leq - \mu V + \Delta + \sum_{j=1}^{2} \varphi_{jU} h_j$$

(25)

where $\mu = \min\left\{ \frac{4k_1}{\bar{f}^2}, k_2 \lambda_{min}(M), \frac{\lambda_{max}(\Gamma_\sigma)}{2} \right\}$, $\Delta = \frac{\lambda_{max}(\Gamma_\sigma)\|v^*\|^2}{2} + 0.557\varpi$, $\Gamma_\sigma = \text{diag}\left(\frac{\sigma_1 \varepsilon_1}{\gamma_1}, \frac{\sigma_2 \varepsilon_2}{\gamma_2} \right)$, $\bar{f} = f_{iL} + f_{iU}$ and $\lambda_{max/min}$ represents the maximum/minimum eigenvalue. Integrating Eq. (25) over $[0, t]$ yields

$$0 \leq V(t) \leq \frac{\Delta + \sum_{j=1}^{2} \varphi_{jU} h_j}{\mu} + \left(V_0 - \frac{\Delta + \sum_{j=1}^{2} \varphi_{jU} h_j}{\mu} \right) e^{-\mu t}$$

(26)

Since $V_1 \leq V$, it is not hard to deduce that

$$|z_{1,1}| \leq \frac{f_{1U} + f_{1L}}{2} \sqrt{\frac{\Delta + \sum_{j=1}^{2} \varphi_{jU} h_j}{\mu} + \left(V_0 - \frac{\Delta + \sum_{j=1}^{2} \varphi_{jU} h_j}{\mu} \right) e^{-\mu t}}$$

(27)

From the Barbalat's lemma, one knows that $\lim_{t \to \infty} h_i(t) = 0$. Thus, $z_{1,1}$ will utimately bounded within $|z_{1,1}| \leq \frac{f_{1U} + f_{1L}}{2} \sqrt{\frac{\Delta}{\mu}}$. Accordingly, z_1 and z_2 are ultimately uniformly bounded (UUB). The boundedness of $\alpha_i, w, u, \hat{v}$ can be derived sequentially without further development here. Moreover, the TRHs can be adjusted so that $-f_{1L}(t) < z_{1,i}(t) < f_{1U}(t), t \geq 0, i = 1, \cdots, n$ are always true. Let $b_{il} = y_{dl} + f_{1L}$ and $b_{iu} = y_{du} + f_{1U}$, it is undoubted that $x_{1,i}$ is restricted to $(-b_{il}, b_{iu})$, which derives the PPFS of the system.

3.3 Fesibility Analysis

For $t \in (t_k, t_{k+1})$, it can be deduced from Eq. (15) that $\frac{d}{dt}|e_{u,i}| = \frac{d}{dt}(e_{u,i}^2)^{\frac{1}{2}} = \text{sgn}(e_{u,i})\dot{e}_{u,i} \leq |\dot{w}_i|$. From the fact that $e_{u,i}(t_k) = 0$, $\lim_{t \to t_{k+1}} e_{u,i}(t) = \eta_0 |u_i(t_{k+1})| + \lambda_0 e_{0,i}(t_{k+1}) + \tau_{0,i}$, and $w \in \mathcal{C}^1$ implying $|\dot{w}_i| \leq \Sigma$ $(\Sigma > 0)$, taking the derivative of Eq. (11) yields

$$|\dot{w}_i| = \lim_{t_{k+1}-t_k \to 0} \left| \frac{e_{u,i}(t_{k+1}) - e_{u,i}(t_k)}{t_{k+1} - t_k} \right|$$

$$= \lim_{t_{t+1}-t_k \to 0} \left| \frac{\eta_0 |u_i(t_{k+1})| + \lambda_0 e_{0,i}(t_{k+1}) + \tau_{0,i}}{t_{k+1} - t_k} \right| \leq \Sigma \qquad (28)$$

In turn, it can be deduced that $T_{\min} = inf[t_{k+1} - t_k] \geq \frac{\tau_0}{\Sigma}$, which implies the avoidance of the Zeno behavior. Finally, integrating all the above, we propose the following theorem:

Theorem 1. *Consider the robot system in Eq. (1) with Assumptions 1, the simple structural TRH-based event-triggered adaptive controller in Eq. (12), and the estimator in Eq. (13). Then, for any initial conditions $q(0), \dot{q}(0)$, a UUB tracking is achieved while the closed-loop system is PPFS. Elements in general position q is constrained by compact sets $\Omega_{q_i} = \{q_i | q_i \in (-b_{il}(t), b_{iu}(t))\}$, $i = 1, \cdots, n$. All signals are bounded and no Zeno behavior occurs.*

4   Numerical Simulations

As shown in Fig. 2, we verify the effectiveness of the proposed controller through a planar free-flying space robot manipulator, where $q = [\phi_0, \phi_1, \phi_2]^T = [q_1, q_2, q_3]^T$. Corresponding paramters are listed in Table 1. External disturbances are $d = [0.1 \sin(1.5t + \frac{\pi}{3}), 0.5 \sin(2t), 0.6 \sin(t + \frac{\pi}{2})]$.

The initial conditions are given as $q(0) = [1.2, -1, 0.7]$ and $\dot{q}(0) = [0, 0, 0]$. The reference trjactory is $y_d = [0, 0.2 \sin(t), 0.2 \cos(t)]^T$. Controller gains are selected as $k_1 = 2.5, k_2 = 3, \varepsilon_1 = \varepsilon_2 = 1, \gamma_1 = 1, \gamma_2 = 1.2$ and parameters for ETM are $\mu_0 = 1 = \eta_0 = 0.1, \lambda_0 = 0.8, \lambda_1 = 0.7 \times 1_3, \tau_0 = 0.5 \times 1_3, \varpi = 8$. We choose $f_{1U,0} = 3.5, f_{1L,0} = 2, f_{1U,T_f} = f_{1L,T_f} = 0.5$ in TRHs $f_{1U}(t)$ and $f_{1L}(t)$ for ease of observation. The simulation results of the example space robot are shown below.

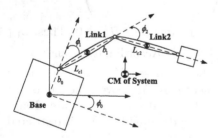

Fig. 2. 3-DOF space manipulator

Table 1. System parameters

Object	Mass (kg)	Moment of Inertia (kgm^2)	Dimension (m)
Base	540	45	1×1
Link1	10	0.83	1
Link2	70	8.37	1
b_0	N/A	N/A	0.5
b_1	N/A	N/A	0.5
L_{c1}	N/A	N/A	0.5
L_{c2}	N/A	N/A	1

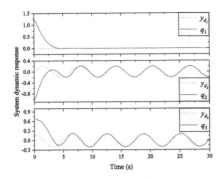

Fig. 3. General position tracking

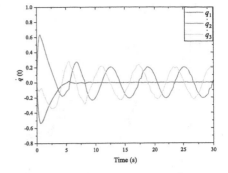

Fig. 4. General velocities

As seen in Fig. 3, all the generalized position elements exhibit good tracking performance, and dynamics response of $\dot{q}$ is displayed in Fig. 4. Specifically, the dynamics of all $z_1 = [z_{1,1}, z_{1,2}, z_{1,3}]^T$ in Fig. 5 are always contained in the envelope shaped by TRHs. To save space, we set the $f_{1U,1L}$ corresponding to $z_{1,i}$ to be the same and merge them in one graph, while separately designing of TRHs could yield better performance. Figure 6 illustrates the control inputs of the manipulator system. Unlike the general time-continuous curves, the control input subjected to ETM presents non-periodically jumping dynamics, which effectively relieves the signaling burden. Figure 7 shows the amplitude of each triggering interval, where a total of 341 triggers occurred in the first 30 s. Finally, The profiles of the σ-modification-based adaptive estimators exhibit gradual convergence trends (see Fig. 8). So far, the simulation results demonstrate the effectiveness of the proposed control method.

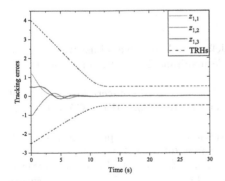

Fig. 5. Tracking errors under constraints

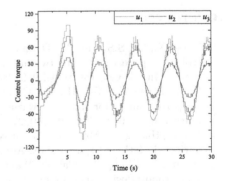

Fig. 6. Control inputs

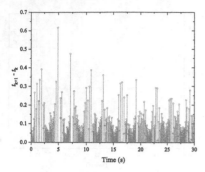

Fig. 7. Triggering intervals

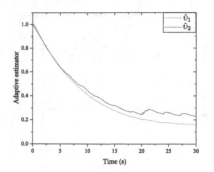

Fig. 8. Adaptive estimator

5   Conclusions

To address the position-constrained tracking of disturbed space robot manipulators and to reduce the data transmission of the closed-loop system, this work is devoted to proposing a simple structural event-triggered adaptive control method. TRHs have been designed to restrict the tracking dynamics within an asymmetric contracting envelope, relaxing initial conditions and providing PPFS to robot systems. By introducing a ETM with modified thresholds, discontinuous control inputs could guarantee good tracking performance while significantly reducing the burden of data transmission. Both the undesired Zeno behavior and cumbersome derivative operations have been averted during backstepping, ensuring the effectiveness and easy solvability of this method. Future work will embark on developing dual-channel event-triggered control techniques for high-order multi-input and multi-output systems.

References

1. Yang, X., Ge, S.S., He, W.: Dynamic modelling and adaptive robust tracking control of a space robot with two-link flexible manipulators under unknown disturbances. Int. J. Control **91**(4), 969–988 (2018)
2. Hao, Z., Yue, X., Wen, H., Liu, C.: Full-state-constrained non-certainty-equivalent adaptive control for satellite swarm subject to input fault. IEEE/CAA J. Automatica Sinica **9**(3), 482–495 (2022)
3. Lu, Y., Huang, P., Meng, Z.: Adaptive anti-windup control of post-capture combination via tethered space robot. Adv. Space Res. **64**(4), 847–860 (2019)
4. Huang, P., Zhang, F., Cai, J., Wang, D., Meng, Z., Guo, J.: Dexterous tethered space robot: design, measurement, control, and experiment. IEEE Trans. Aerospce Electron. Syst. **53**(3), 1452–1468 (2017)
5. Ma, Z., Huang, P., Kuang, Z.: Fuzzy approximate learning-based sliding mode control for deploying tethered space robot. IEEE Trans. Fuzzy Syst. **29**(9), 2739–2749 (2021)
6. Yan, W., Liu, Y., Lan, Q., Zhang, T., Tu, H.: Trajectory planning and low-chattering fixed-time nonsingular terminal sliding mode control for a dual-arm free-floating space robot. Robotica **40**(3), 625–645 (2022)

7. Uyama, N., Hirano, D., Nakanishi, H., Nagaoka, K., Yoshida, K.: Impedance-based contact control of a free-flying space robot with respect to coefficient of restitution. In: 2011 IEEE/SICE International Symposium on System Integration (SII), pp. 1196–1201. Kyoto (2011)
8. Jia, Y.-H., Hu, Q., Xu, S.-J.: Dynamics and adaptive control of a dual-arm space robot with closed-loop constraints and uncertain inertial parameters. Acta. Mech. Sin. **30**(1), 112–124 (2014). https://doi.org/10.1007/s10409-014-0005-1
9. Mali, P., Harikumar, K., Singh, A.K., Krishna, K.M., Sujit, P.B.: Incorporating prediction in control barrier function based distributive multi-robot collision avoidance. In: 2021 European Control Conference (ECC), pp. 2394–2399. IEEE, ELECTR NETWORK (2021)
10. Tee, K.P., Ge, S.S., Tay, E.H.: Barrier Lyapunov Functions for the control of output-constrained nonlinear systems. Automatica **45**(4), 918–927 (2009)
11. Kong, L., He, W., Yang, W., Li, Q., Kaynak, O.: Fuzzy approximation-based finite-time control for a robot with actuator saturation under time-varying constraints of work space. IEEE Trans. Cybern. **51**(10), 4873–4884 (2021)
12. Tee, K.P., Ge, S.S.: Control of state-constrained nonlinear systems using Integral Barrier Lyapunov Functionals. In: 2012 IEEE 51st IEEE Conference on Decision and Control (CDC), pp. 3239–3244. IEEE, Hawaii (2012)
13. Lu, S., Li, D., Liu, Y.: Adaptive neural network control for uncertain time-varying state constrained robotics systems. IEEE Tran. Syst. Man Cybern. Syst. **49**(12), 2511–2518 (2019)
14. Liu, Y., Liu, X.P., Jing, Y.W., Chen, X.Y., Qiu, J.L.: Direct adaptive preassigned finite-time control with time-delay and quantized input using neural network. IEEE Trans. Neural Networks Learn. Syst. **31**(4), 1222–1231 (2020)
15. Liu, Y., Li, H.: Adaptive asymptotic tracking using barrier functions. Automatica **98**, 239–246 (2018)
16. Mishra, P.K., Dhar, N.K., Verma, N.K.: Adaptive neural-network control of mimo nonaffine nonlinear systems with asymmetric time-varying state constraints. IEEE Trans. Cybern. **51**(4), 2042–2054 (2021)
17. Wu, Y., Huang, R., Wang, Y., Wang, J.: Adaptive tracking control of robot manipulators with input saturation and time-varying output constraints. Asian J. Control **23**(3), 1476–1489 (2020)
18. Dimarogonas, D.V., Frazzoli, E., Johansson, K.H.: Distributed event-triggered control for multi-agent systems. IEEE Trans. Autom. Control **57**(5), 1291–1297 (2012)
19. Astrom, K.J., Bernhardsson, B.: Comparison of Riemann and Lebesgue sampling for first order stochastic systems. In: 41st IEEE Conference on Decision and Control, pp. 2011–2016. IEEE, Las Vegas (2002)
20. Wang, A., Liu, L., Qiu, J., Feng, G.: Event-triggered robust adaptive fuzzy control for a class of nonlinear systems. IEEE Trans. Fuzzy Syst. **27**(8), 1648–1658 (2019)
21. Wang, Z., Lam, H.K., Chen, Z., Liang, B., Zhang, T.: Event-triggered interval type-2 fuzzy control for uncertain space teleoperation systems with state constraints. In: 2020 IEEE International Conference on Fuzzy Systems (FUZZ-IEEE), pp. 1–8. IEEE, (2020)
22. Lindgren, G., Rootzen, H.: Extreme values - theory and technical applications. Scand. J. Stat. **14**(4), 241–279 (1987)

A Compliant Strategy of a Underactuated Gripper to Grasp a Space Cooperative Target Based on Hybrid Impedance Control

Shaowei Fan, Peng Lv, Qiang Liu$^{(\boxtimes)}$ (ID), Jiaping Sun, and Cong Ming

Harbin Institute of Technology, Harbin 15001, China
14S008022@hit.edu.cn

Abstract. This paper proposes a compliant strategy for a underactuated gripper to grasp constrained space cooperative target based on the hybrid impedance control. The underactuated gripper is equipped with a differential mechanism and has characteristics of large misalignment tolerance, passive compliant grasp. The strategy consists of two parts: task planning and end effector control algorithm. In the task planning, through the analysis of the contact force and moment caused by the pose misalignment in a single direction, a grasping method of stepwise correcting pose is proposed to avoid the wrong pose correction caused by the complex contact state during the grasping process. In the control algorithm, a six-DOFs hybrid impedance control with variable desired force and variable impedance parameters is designed. The hybrid impedance control algorithm is designed separately in translational direction and rotation direction, to improve the control coupling between the orientation and the position. The underactuated gripper with the compliant strategy can mitigate the impact effect by increasing the interacting time. A set of numerical simulations and capture experiments verify validity of proposed strategy, the correctness of the algorithm and the compliance of the gripper.

Keywords: Hybrid impedance control · Space target capturing · Compliant grasping · Underactuated gripper · Impact mitigation

1 Introduction

The space manipulator is equipped with special tools to execute space tasks, such as repairing malfunctioning satellites [1], on-orbit refueling [2] and replacing ORU [3]. Before carrying out these tasks, the target satellite needs to be captured. Using the space end effector to assist or replace astronauts to complete the capture operation is the current research focus of space robot technology [4]. Due to the effects of visual deviation, control deviation etc., the actual position of the target may not coincide with the desired position during capturing. The position control will result in a large contact force and damage the end effector system and the target. The compliant control algorithm can effectively improve this phenomenon and is popular for the end effector to accomplish the task compliantly. In the past few decades, there have been many research achievements

© The Author(s), under exclusive license to Springer Nature Switzerland AG 2022
H. Liu et al. (Eds.): ICIRA 2022, LNAI 13455, pp. 482–492, 2022.
https://doi.org/10.1007/978-3-031-13844-7_46

on the control algorithm of force compliance. most of them are based on the impedance control [5], the hybrid force/position control [6] and the hybrid impedance control [7].

Liu et al. designed an impedance control based on the friction identification and the compensation in Cartesian space by analyzing the tolerance need of the end effector screwing operation, the position accuracy of the end effector and the contact force requirements. This method improves the contradiction between position accuracy need and contact force need [8]. He et al. designed a large workpiece assembly strategy based on the hybrid impedance control. By updating the compliant frame, it solves the problem that the contact force will generate a contact torque when there is no rotation deviation, resulting in a rotation deviation of the workpiece [9]. Li et al. designed a hybrid force/ position control algorithm based on genetic neural network to solve the problem that due to the multi-input multi-output, nonlinearity and rigid-flex coupling of Heavy-Duty end effector, the appropriate impedance parameters cannot be obtained [10].

For the rigid hands, the current efforts in this respect are mainly directed towards the multi-fingered human-like hand [11–14], typical example, dexterous robot hands [13–15]. However, too many fingers will make the gripper too complex, costly, non-compacted and heavy-weight. The less-finger rigid gripper (less than 5 fingers) performs better to execute manipulations for some special tasks than dexterous robot hands [16]. The innovation of the gripper is to reduce the impact and collision.

To solve the above problems, this paper designs a underactuated gripper and researches a compliant strategy to grasp a space cooperative target based on hybrid impedance control. The paper is organized as follows: Sect. 2 introduces the mechanical structure of the underactuated gripper and the analysis and planning of the constrained target grasping task. Section 3 introduces the 6-DOFs hybrid impedance control algorithm. Section 4 introduces the algorithm of variable desired force and variable impedance parameters. Section 5 verifies the effectiveness of the strategy through simulation and capture experiments. Section 6 summarizes the conclusion.

2 Gripper Mechanism and Planning of Grasping Task

2.1 Gripper Mechanism

The structure of gripper is composed of the finger mechanism, the differential mechanism, the drive system and the mechanical power output mechanism, as Fig. 1. The finger mechanism plays a main role in grasping. It has three fingers. As a passive compliant mechanism, the differential mechanism can achieve a compliant grasp of the target, reduce the impact of contact force and overcome the shortcomings of the current rigid end-effector. It adopts the steel wire rope-pulley and divides the input into two outputs to connect the fingers on both sides. It can be seen that compared with the three outputs, this scheme ensures the centering of the fingers during the closing process and accelerates the correction of deviation of target pose, in term of the characteristics of the handle on the cooperative target.

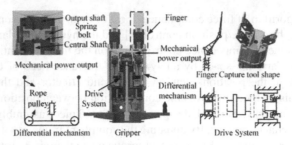

Fig. 1. Mechanical structure of gripper

2.2 Analysis and Planning of Grasping Constrained Target

According to the characteristics of the mechanical structure, the grasp task is divided into the finger closing stage and the shaft-hole assembly stage. The static frame $\{x\,y\,z\}$ is established on the gripper, as shown in Fig. 2.

In the stage of closing the fingers, the contact force and moment caused by the target's single direction deviation is shown in Table 1. "1" and "0" in the table represent the contact force/moment generated or not generated under the corresponding direction deviation and the contact force/moment when there is no pose deviation is [0,0,1,0,0,0]. The generated contact force/moment is expressed in the static frame. According to the characteristics of the data in the table, there are two problems:

(1) When there is only a position deviation in the x direction, the generated contact force/moment is the same as the contact force/moment generated without the pose deviation, so the position deviation in the x direction cannot be corrected according to the contact force/moment. (2) The yaw and pitch angle deviations can generate moments in the x, y and z directions. Therefore, it is difficult to correct the rotation deviation according to T.

In order not to reduce the misalignment tolerance of the gripper, the position deviation should be corrected initially before moving to the grasping position of the base knuckles. The deviation in the y direction can be corrected according to F_y. The position deviation in the x direction cannot be corrected by the finger mechanism. Here, the wedge-shaped surface is used to correct the position deviation in the x direction.

First, the gripper approaches the target along the z axis direction until it contacts the surface for the first time, Then the gripper moves along the x axis direction until it contacts with the surface for the second time. According to the position of the gripper in the x axis direction at the time of contact, the correct position of the target in this direction is estimated as $(x_1 + x_2)/2$. The grasping strategy of the finger closing stage is as follows:

(1) The gripper moves to the grasping position; (2) Close fingers. When contacting with the handle, the y direction force is compliant and the position deviation is initially corrected. When the fingers on both sides contact the handle, the adjustment process ends; (3) Estimate the correct position in the x direction and correct the initial position deviation in this direction; (4) The gripper moves to the base grasping position. The fingers are closed until the base knuckles is vertical. Then, the gripper moves along the y axis until it contacts the handle The force control is used to track the desired force in

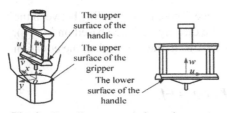

Fig. 2. Coordinate system for task analysis.

Table 1. The contact force and moment

	F_x	F_y	F_z	T_x	T_y	T_z
dx	0	0	1	0	0	0
dy	0	1	1	1	0	0
$d\alpha$	1	1	1	1	1	1
$d\beta$	1	1	1	1	1	1
$d\gamma$	0	1	1	1	0	0

the y direction, so that the base knuckles is always vertical and the yaw angle deviation is corrected according to T_z. When T_z is close to zero, the deviation correction process ends; (5) The fingers continue to close and track the desired force in the y direction. When the base knuckles deviates from the vertical state by a certain angle, it stops closing. Then, the pitch angle deviation is corrected according to T_y. When T_y is close to zero, the deviation correction process ends;(6) The fingers continue to close and zero-force tracking is performed in the y direction until the fingers on both sides contact the handle at the same time.

The strategy of the shaft-hole assembly stage is as follows:

(1) The gripper approaches the target at a slow speed in the z direction. When it contacts tapered guide, the position deviation in the x direction is corrected according to F_x; (2) When the F_x is zero, it is assumed that the input shaft of the handle inserted into the center hole of the output shaft of the gripper. Since the diameter of the hole is larger than the shaft diameter, the position of the gripper in the x direction should be offset by 0.5 mm. The gripper continues to move, ignoring the impact of the contact force/moment generated by the bolt; (3) When the lower end of the handle contacts with the wedge-shaped surface, the desired position and speed in the z direction are adjusted according to F_z.

3   Six DOFs Hybrid Impedance Control

This paper designs the inertia M, damping B, stiffness K and proposes a position-based impedance control. The control uses environmental force as the control input to design the desired end-effector trajectory x_d and achieve the compliant grasping x. The impedance formula is:

$$M(\ddot{x} - \ddot{x}_d) + B(\dot{x} - \dot{x}_d) + K(x - x_d) = -F_e \tag{1}$$

Traditional impedance control [17] cannot control the force. One solution is to add the desired force term and remove the stiffness term. The hybrid impedance control algorithm divides the task space into a position control subspace and a force control subspace. Force control F_e is applied to the force control subspace to achieve tracking of the desired force. The formula is:

$$M(\ddot{x} - \ddot{x}_d) + B(\dot{x} - \dot{x}_d) = F_d - F_e \tag{2}$$

The end effector has six DOFs in Cartesian space. There is no coupling between the positions, so the position impedance control can be directly designed based on Eq. (1). The frame of the compliant track is $\{c\}$ and the desires frame is $\{d\}$, then the equation in the position direction is as follows:

$$M_P \Delta \ddot{p} + B_P \Delta \dot{p} + K_P \Delta p = -f \tag{3}$$

where M_P, B_P, K_P are the position impedance matrixes. K_P is the zero matrix during force control. f is the environmental force during position control and the error between the environmental force and the desired force during force control.

The trajectory of the compliant frame expressed by $p_c = p_d + \Delta p$, $\dot{p}_c = \dot{p}_d + \Delta \dot{p}$, $\ddot{p}_c = \ddot{p}_d + \Delta \ddot{p}$. p_d is the desired position. Δp is the compliance value of the position. The relationship between the Euler angle velocity $\dot{\varphi}$ and the angular velocity ω is,

$$\omega = T(\varphi)\dot{\varphi}, T(\varphi) = \begin{bmatrix} 0 & -\sin\alpha & \cos\alpha\cos\beta \\ 0 & \cos\alpha & \sin\alpha\cos\beta \\ 1 & 0 & -\sin\beta \end{bmatrix} \tag{4}$$

Compared with the equation designed based on the impedance equation, the relationship between the compliance value of the rotation direction and the contact torque is independent of $T(\varphi)$. The control equation is as follows:

$$M_o \Delta \ddot{\varphi} + B_o \Delta \dot{\varphi} + K_o \Delta \varphi = -T^T (\Delta \varphi)^d n \tag{5}$$

where M_o, B_o, K_o are the rotation impedance matrixes. K_o is the zero matrix during force control. $^d n$ is the contact end-effector moment in the desired frame. $^d n$ is the environmental moment during impedance control. $^d n$ is the error between the environmental moment and the desired moment during force control. $\Delta \varphi$ is the Euler angle of the compliant frame relative to the desired frame. The compliant trajectory is designed by $\Delta \varphi$, $\Delta \dot{\varphi}$, $\Delta \ddot{\varphi}$.

4 Variable Desired Force Algorithm and Variable Impedance Parameter Algorithm

When the position control is converted into the force control, there will be a large impact between the end-effector and the target. For this, the desired force is

$$F_{dt}(t) = \begin{cases} F_d(-2(\frac{t-t_{init}}{t_{end}-t_{init}})^3 + 3(\frac{t-t_{init}}{t_{end}-t_{init}})^2), & t_{init} \leq t \leq t_{end} \\ F_d, t > t_{end} \end{cases} \tag{6}$$

where t_{init}, t_{end} are the start time of the planning desired force and the end time of the planning desired force. Before the pose correction in the finger closing phase, the impact force will be generated at the initial moment of pose correction. The initial damping is B_{init} and the initial inertia is M_{init}. To avoid vibration during the system closing to the steady state, a cubic polynomial is used to attenuate the initial inertia value

$$M(t) = \begin{cases} -2(M_{end} - M_{init})(\frac{t-t_{init}}{t_{c1}-t_{init}})^3 + 3(M_{init} - M_{end})(\frac{t-t_{init}}{t_{c1}-t_{init}})^2 + M_{init}, \, t_{init} \leq t \leq t_{c1} \\ M_{end}, \, t > t_{c1} \end{cases}$$

(7)

In order to shorten the pose adjustment time and reduce the anti-interference ability, so sufficient damping B_{end} should be ensured during steady state. A linear function is used to quickly attenuate the damping. When the contact force is less than the threshold F_{max}, the damping should be increased to B_{end}. This process uses a cubic polynomial to make a smooth transition, as follows:

$$B(t) = \begin{cases} B_{init}, \, t_{init} \leq t < t_{c1} \\ k(t - t_{c1})^2/(2(t_{c2} - t_{c1})) + B_{init}, \, t_{c1} \leq t < t_{c2} \\ k(t_{c2} - t_{c1})/2 + B_{init} + k(t - t_{c2}), \, t_{c2} \leq t \leq t_{end}, F_e > F_{max} \\ C_{B3}\bar{t}^3 + C_{B2}\bar{t}^2 + C_{B1}\bar{t} + C_{B0}, \, 0 \leq \bar{t} \leq 1, F_e \leq F_{max} \end{cases}$$

(8)

where k is the slope of the linear function; t_{c2} is the end time of quadratic polynomial planning; C_{B0} is the damping attenuation through linear function; $C_{B_0} = k(2t_{c3} - t_{c2} - t_{c1})/2 + B_{init}$; $\bar{t} = (t - t_{c3})/(t_{end} - t_{c3})$; $C_{B1} = k(t_{end} - t_{c3})$; t_{end} is the moment when cubic polynomial planning damping ends; $C_{B2} = 3(B_{end} - C_{B0}) - 2k(t_{end} - t_{c3})$, $C_{B3} = -2(B_{end} - C_{B0}) + k(t_{end} - t_{c3})$.

5   Simulation and Capture Experiment

5.1   Simulation Results

Build a simulation model through simulation software, as shown in Fig. 3. During yaw and pitch angle deviation correction, the desired force of 2 N is maintained in the y direction of the base. When the position deviation in the z direction and roll angle deviation are corrected. The desired force of 2 N is maintained in the y direction. The target's attitude deviation is $[\Delta x, \Delta y, \Delta \alpha, \Delta \beta, \Delta \lambda] = [-20 \text{mm}, -19 \text{mm}, -3°, 3°, 3°]$ and parameters are $M = Diag(25, 25, 1, 0.2, 0.2, 1)$, $B = Diag(100, 50, 10, 5, 3, 5)$, $K = Diag(5, 5, 0, 0, 0, 0)$. The pose compliance during grasping is shown in the Fig. 4 and the contact force/moment is shown in the Fig. 5. The effect of variable desired force and variable impedance parameters on contact moment are shown in the Fig. 6. The entire grasping process time is 190 s. The finger closing stage is 169 s. At 15 s, the end effector moves to the grasping position.

During 15 s to 28 s, the preliminary adjustment of the z direction position is completed. At 45 s and 60 s, the input shaft of the handle is in contact with the wedge-shaped groove. The adjustment amount in the x direction is estimated to be 17.8 mm according to the contact position. During 80 s to 97 s, the yaw angle deviation is adjusted. During 104 s–124 s, the pitch angle deviation is adjusted. During 149–169 s the z direction position deviation and roll angle deviation are adjusted. The shaft-hole assembly stage takes 21 s. At this stage, the gripper moves along the y direction at a speed of 2 mm/s. At about 173.3 s, the input shaft collided with the tapered guide.

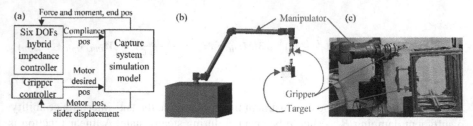

Fig. 3. The simulation model and the experiment system design

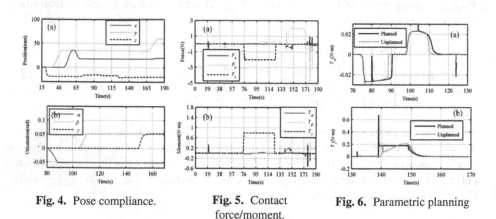

Fig. 4. Pose compliance.   **Fig. 5.** Contact force/moment.   **Fig. 6.** Parametric planning

At about 177 s, the input shaft collided with the bolt. At about 180.5 s, the lower end of the handle is in contact with the wedge-shaped surface. The simulation results show that the effectiveness of the compliance capture strategy based on hybrid impedance control. The contact force does not exceed 5 N and the contact torque does not exceed 0.9 Nm. At the initial planning time 124 s and 139 s of the desired force, the contact impact can be well reduced. In Fig. 6, the initial moment of inertia value planned in the yaw direction is 80 s; the initial moment of inertia value planned in the pitch direction is 104 s; the initial moment of inertia value planned in the z direction position and roll direction is 149 s. It can be seen that the algorithm of variable the desired force and variable impedance parameters reduces the contact impact. And through planning damping, the correction time of yaw and pitch angle deviation is reduced.

5.2 Capture Experiments

The capture experiment is divided into three phases, namely the pre-capture phase, the capture phase and the locking phase. The frames of the gripper and the force sensor are shown in Fig. 7(e), the orientation is descripted by the Euler angles Z-Y-X. The force and moment measured by the force sensor are expressed in the sensor frame. The pose of the gripper is represented by the gripper frame. In the pre-capture phase, the gripper controlled by the Hybrid Impedance Control of Eq. (3) go forward to the target satellite in $-z$ direction and simultaneously has an adjustment motion in $+y$ direction, as shown in Fig. 7 (c). The adjustment motion mainly is caused by the contact between the finger and the target handle. The contact force is measured by the sensors shown in Fig. 7 (a). The moment measured by the sensor as shown in Fig. 7 (b) and the force are acted on the gripper together and generate a rough pure force, that is, zero moment. The little orientation adjustment shown in Fig. 7 (d) illustrates the above idea. The process of pre-capture phase is shown from Fig. 7 (e)-1 to Fig. 7 (e)-3 and six the effectiveness of the proposed control is verified by the compliant adjustment in $+y$ direction.

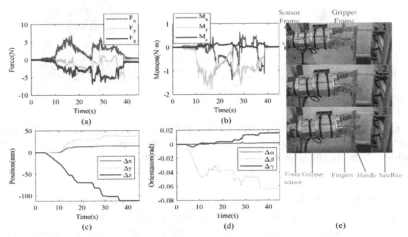

Fig. 7. Pre-capture phase: (a) end-effector force; (b) end-effector moment; (c) the gripper position;(d) the gripper orientations;(e) the executing process of the gripper in this phase

In the capture phase, the gripper stops moving, but remains in Hybrid Impedance Control of Eq. (3). The fingers of the gripper were controlled to close at the 6th second and the displacement of the two-finger side slider is shown in Fig. 8 (c). Stop the movement when the fingers move enough to completely envelop the handle. At the 12th second, give the target an angular velocity, as shown in Fig. 8 (f)-1. When the handle collides with the single finger, due to the existence of the differential mechanism, the single-fingered finger produces a compliant motion in the y direction and the two-finger side finger is accelerated to close, as shown in Fig. 8 (f)-2 and Fig. 8 (c). In the event of a crash, the impact forces and moments measured in Fig. 8 (a) and Fig. 8 (b) showed a slowly increasing process in the direction of compliance, demonstrating that the compliant motion of the single finger slowed down the crash impact. Due to the existence of the differential mechanism, the action time of the impact is longer and the response of the impact force is weakened. The impact interacting time of the proposed gripper is 11 s, as shown in Fig. 8 (a), (b). It is far longer than the rigid collision time 0.1 s [28]. The longer impact interacting time mainly is contributed to the mechanical structure characteristics of the designed differential mechanism.

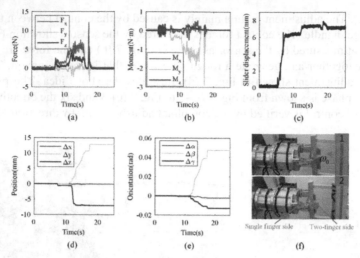

Fig. 8. Capture phase: (a) end-effector force; (b) end-effector moment; (c) the variable impedance parameters displayed by the spring displacement; (d) the gripper position; (e) the gripper orientations; (f) the executing process of the gripper in this phase

As shown in Fig. 8 (d), the adjustment amount in the y direction increases slowly relative to the z direction and the differential mechanism buffers the impact of the collision, so that the adjustment amount of the gripper under impedance control will not change abruptly, making the control system unstable. The target is given an initial angle velocity $\omega_0 = 5°/s$ to simulate the collision impact.

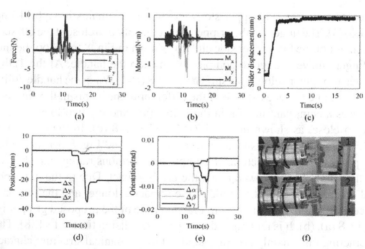

Fig. 9. Locking phase: (a) end-effector force; (b) end-effector moment; (c) the variable impedance parameters displayed by the spring displacement;(d) the gripper position;(e) the gripper orientations;(f) the executing process of the gripper in this phase

After stepwise correcting pose, the initial adjustment of the position deviation in the x direction and the y direction is over and the gripper stops at the target position in the hybrid impedance mode and steps into the locking phase. The fingers contact and collide with the handle during the closing process, resulting in the close force in the $-z$ direction, as shown in Fig. 9. Since the final adjustment of the gripper prototype has not yet been completed, only the locking process as shown in Fig. 9(f)-1 to Fig. 9(f)-2 is executed.

The gripper suffers the force in $+y$ direction, the impact in $+y$ direction and the close force in $-z$ direction and then make the compliant pose adjustments by the six DOFs hybrid impedance control law and the y direction impact shock is rapidly reduced by the differential mechanism compliant motion. The above phases verify the effectiveness of the grasping method of stepwise correcting pose.

6 Conclusion

This paper designs a underactuated gripper and proposes a compliant grasping strategy of stepwise correcting pose based on hybrid impedance control. The strategy consists of task planning and control algorithms. The strategy is proposed for the gripper to grasp the space satellite target to improve the error correction of the pose deviation caused by the complex contact force and moment. According to the mechanical structure characteristics, the grasp task is divided into the finger closing of the pre-capture phase and the shaft-hole assembly of the locking phase. The mechanical structure characteristics designed for the gripper can increase interacting time of collision impact and mitigate the impact effect. The six-DOFs hybrid impedance control with variable desired force and variable impedance parameters is designed to improve the algorithm switch impact of the hybrid impedance strategy. The longer interacting time of impact can effectively improve the gripper pose jump problem. Finally, based on the simulations and the capture experiments, the effectiveness of the designed gripper and the proposed strategy are verified.

References

1. Ohkami, Y., Oda, M.: NASDA's activities in space robotics. European Space Agency-Publications-ESA SP **440**, 11–18 (1999)
2. Rembala, R., Ower, C.: Robotic assembly and maintenance of future space stations based on the ISS mission operations experience. Acta Astronaut. **65**(7–8), 912–920 (2009)
3. Potter, S.D.: Orbital express: leading the way to a new space architecture. In: Proc. Space Core Tech Conference, Colorado Spring, CO (2002)
4. Flores-Abad, A., Ma, O., Pham, K., Ulrich, S.: A review of space robotics technolo-gies for on-orbit servicing. Prog. Aerosp. Sci. **68**, 1–26 (2014)
5. Hogan, N.: Impedance control (An approach to manipulation) Part I, II, III. Trans the ASME J. Dymamic Syst. Meas. Control **107**(4), 481–489 (1985)
6. Raibert, M., Craig, J.J.: Hybrid position/force control of manipulators. ASME J. Dynamic Syst. Meas. Control **102**, 126–133 (1981)
7. Anderson, R., Spong, M.W.: Hybrid impedance control of robotic manipulators. IEEE J. Robot. Autom. 1073–1080 (1987)

8. Liu, D., Liu, H., Liu, Y.: Research on impedance control of flexible joint space ma-nipulator on-orbit servicing. IEEE Int. Conf. Robot. Biomim. **2019**, 77–82 (2019)
9. He, G., Shi, S., Wang, D.: A strategy for large workpiece assembly based on hybrid impedance control. In: 2019 IEEE International Conference on Mechatronics and Auto-mation (ICMA) (2019)
10. Li, L., Xie, L., Luo, X.: Compliance control using hydraulic heavy-duty manipulator. IEEE Trans. Industr. Inf. **2**(15), 1193–1201 (2019)
11. Mattar, E.: A survey of bio-inspired robotics hands implementation: new directions in dexterous manipulation. Robot. Auton. Syst. **61**(5), 517–544 (2013)
12. Bridgwater, L.B., et al.: The robonaut 2 hand-designed to do work with tools. In: 2012 IEEE International Conference on Robotics and Automation, pp. 3425–3430. IEEE (2012)
13. Della Santina, C., et al.: Toward dexterous manipulation with augmented adaptive synergies: the pisa/IIT softhand 2. IEEE Trans. Rob. **34**(5), 1141–1156 (2018)
14. Zaidi, L., et al.: Model-based strategy for grasping 3D deformable objects using a multi-fingered robotic hand. Robot. Auton. Syst. **95**, 196–206 (2017)
15. Pfeifer, R., Iida, F., Gomez, G.: Designing intelligent robots—on the implications of embodiment. J. Robot. Soc. Japan **24**(7), 783–790 (2006)
16. Kim, B.H., et al.: A biomimetic compliance control of robot hand by considering structures of human finger. In: Proceedings 2000 ICRA. Millennium Conference. IEEE International Conference on Robotics and Automation. Symposia Proceedings (Cat. No. 00CH37065), vol. 4, pp. 3879–3886. IEEE (2000)
17. Lasky, T.A., Hsia, T.C.: On force-tracking impedance control of robot manipulators. In: Proceedings. 1991 IEEE International Conference on Robotics and Automation, pp. 274–280. IEEE Computer Society (1991)
18. Liu, X.F., et al.: Dynamics and control of capture of a floating rigid body by a spacecraft robotic arm. Multibody Sys. Dyn. **33**(3), 315–332 (2015)

Multi-agent Pathfinding with Communication Reinforcement Learning and Deadlock Detection

Zhaohui Ye, Yanjie Li$^{(\boxtimes)}$, Ronghao Guo, Jianqi Gao, and Wen Fu

Harbin Institute of Technology Shenzhen, Shenzhen, China
autolyj@hit.edu.cn

Abstract. The learning-based approach has been proved to be an effective way to solve multi-agent path finding (MAPF) problems. For large warehouse systems, the distributed strategy based on learning method can effectively improve efficiency and scalability. But compared with the traditional centralized planner, the learning-based approach is more prone to deadlocks. Communication learning has also made great progress in the field of multi-agent in recent years and has been be introduced into MAPF. However, the current communication methods provide redundant information for reinforcement learning and interfere with the decision-making of agents. In this paper, we combine the reinforcement learning with communication learning. The agents select its communication objectives based on priority and mask off redundant communication links. Then we use a feature interactive network based on graph neural network to achieve the information aggregation. We also introduce an additional deadlock detection mechanism to increase the likelihood of an agent escaping a deadlock. Experiments demonstrate our method is able to plan collision-free paths in different warehouse environments.

Keywords: Multi-agent path finding · Reinforcement learning · Communication learning · Deadlock detection

1 Introduction

In modern warehouse system, the performance of multi-agent path planning determines the efficiency of the system. Multi-robot path planning in warehouse environment can be abstracted as a multi-agent path finding (MAPF) problem. At present, there are two main types of MAPF algorithms. One is the centralized planning method, which uses a global planner to plan paths for all agents with global information [12]. The other is the distributed method in which each agent makes decisions according to its own observation [8], so as to realize the decoupling of the planning process and reduce the computational complexity.

In recent years, methods based on reinforcement learning and imitation learning have been applied to solve MAPF problems [7,8,10]. In the reinforcement-learning methods, the MAPF problem is modeled as a partially observable

Markov process. In most of these methods, each agent regards other neighbor agents as a part of the environment, which inevitably leads to the instability of the environment. The imitation learning method trains the network using supervised data generated by the centralized optimal planner to imitate the centralized planner [5,10]. But imitation learning methods have fitting error of observed values and the generalization error of unseen observed values. Recently, with the development of communication learning [1,15], researchers have begun to introduced communication methods to MAPF problem [5]. But there are two problems in these methods. One is that there will be redundant messages in the information sharing process, which will affect the decision-making of agents. The other is that current communication methods need to communicate with all agents within a certain range. This will increase the training consumption.

In this work, we use reinforcement learning with multi-agent communication to solve the MAPF problem. We introduce a priority-based mechanism to select the communication objectives and mask unnecessary communication links to ensure the effectiveness of the communication message. And we propose a new hyper network to aggregate the communication messages. In order to solve the deadlocks, a new deadlock detection mechanism is introduced, and auxiliary information is used to highlight the abnormal state in the learning process, so that the agent can learn to escape from the deadlock state. Finally, it is tested in warehouse simulation environment with different structures and different number of agents to prove the validity and scalability of the method.

2   Related Work

2.1   Learning Based Methods

In the MAPF domain, Sartoretti et al. proposed PRIMAL framework [11] which combines reinforcement learning with imitation learning based on the centralized planner ODrM*. Although PRIMAL scales well to arbitrarily large team sizes, it does not perform well in structured and densely occupied worlds. Many recent works utilize centralized planners or single-agent path finding algorithms like A* to guide the training process [7,10]. However, these methods do not take into account the solution of deadlock situations. In addition, most of these methods treats other agents as dynamic obstacles when planning. From the perspective of a single agent, its local system is incomplete because of the unobserved state of other agents and will lead to the instability of the training environment. The information sharing is critical to the performance of the system, but the solutions based on reinforcement learning alone cannot solve this problem.

2.2   Multi Agents Communication Learning

The communication learning algorithm realizes the information sharing by communication. The topological structures of the early works are all based on the fully connected or star-shaped structure [1,4,15], which will lead to excessive computational consumption. Therefore, ATOC [3] adopts a grouping communication method and conducts autonomous grouping through a circular attention binary network. The subsequent LSC [13] algorithm proposes a layered communication structure, which divides each agent into several groups with two levels.

Recently, Graph Neural Networks (GNN) has been used to achieve communication. GNN models the multi-agent system as a graph to capture the relationship between agents [5]. The original GNN directly uses the adjacency matrix for message aggregation, while DGN uses the attention mechanism to aggregate communication messages [2]. In the field of MAPF, Qingbiao Li et al. [5] proposed an algorithm that combines convolutional neural network and GNN and uses imitation learning to train the network. Their latest work combines GNN with attention mechanism to improve the communication effectiveness [6]. On the basis of PRIMAL, Ziyuan Ma et al. [9] used potential selection of the shortest path as heuristic guidance, and used graph convolutional network for communication. The above MAPF methods combined with communication learning do not consider that redundant communication connections will impair agent's decision-making.

3   Problem Formulation

3.1   MAPF Definition

A standard MAPF problem is defined as follows: the environment is set as a two-dimensional discrete four-connected grid environment. Given a set of N agents $V = \{v_1, ..., v_n\}$, for each agent, it has its own starting point s^i and goal point g^i. The starting point and goal point of each agent do not coincide and are randomly assigned in each episode.

The path finding problem is modeled as a sequential decision problem, in which the agent chooses an action at each time step. The allowed action set contains up, down, left, right and stagnation. Each action may lead to conflicts and collisions. All actions that lead to conflicts and collisions will make the participating agents stay at the position of the previous moment. In addition, the agent that reaches the goal point will only take stationary actions.

3.2   Observation Space

The environment is modeled as a partially observable environment in this work. Each agent can only perceive its surrounding environment. The observation of each agent will be limited by a field of view (FOV) in the range of $f \times f$, which is initially set to 9×9 in our work. The obtained local observations will be divided into several channels as Fig. 1 shows. Each observation channel is composed of a matrix of $f \times f$. The first channel only contains the information of other agents in the FOV and the second channel represents the static obstacles. The third channel represents the goal point in the FOV. If the goal point is not in the FOV, the goal point will be projected to the boundary of the FOV. The next

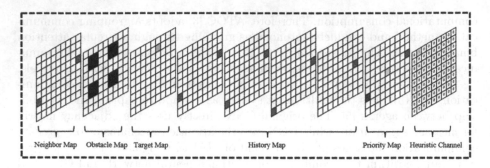

Fig. 1. Observation space of each agent

k channels represent the positions of other agents within the FOV of the last k time steps. In addition, there will be a channel to record the priority status of surrounding agents for the selection of communication objectives. The last channel is used as an auxiliary heuristic channel to indicate whether the agent has fallen into abnormal states.

3.3 Communication Setting

Each agent can communicate with the agents within the communication radius. The communication topology model is similar to the neighborhood structure in DGN [2]. Each agent communicates with neighbor agents through the communication message through a multi-hop communication network. Unlike DGN and the communication methods currently used in MAPF [5,6,9], our method will only communicate with specific agents within the communication range. Compared with the traditional GNN communication method, this method does not need to model the multi-agent system as a fully connected graph, thus the computational consumption can be reduced.

3.4 Reward Design

Table 1. Reward function design

Actions	Reward
Move (Closer/Further)	-0.05, -0.1
No Movement (on/away goal)	0, -0.075
Oscillation/Deadlock	-0.3, -0.5
Collision	-0.5
Finish episode	$+10$

The reward setting is shown in Table 1. Before the agent reaches the goal point, the agent will get a penalty of -0.05 if one step will bring it closer to the goal point, -0.1 if it is further away from the goal point, and -0.075 if it stays at a non-goal point for one step. Colliding with obstacles or other agents will be punished by -0.5, oscillation between two positions will be punished by -0.3, and entering a deadlock state will be punished by -0.5. An agent will get a reward $+10$ for reaching the goal point.

4   Communication Reinforcement Learning Based on Priority with Deadlock Detection

In this section, we will elaborate on the priority-based communication reinforcement learning MAPF solution method. The communication objective agents are selected by priority. Then we use a hyper network to aggregate the messages transmitted by each agent. At the same time, an additional deadlock detection mechanism is used to improve the possibility of jumping out of a deadlock state.

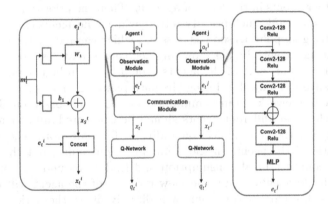

Fig. 2. The neural network consists of 3 modules which are observation module (blue), communication module (red) and Q-Network (Color figure online)

4.1   DQN Framework

The basic reinforcement learning framework of this paper is based on the D3QN algorithm. The network is mainly divided into three modules, namely the observation module, the communication module, and the final decision network part. The observation module consists of four convolutional layers, where the two middle layers are combined into a residual block. Except for the priority channel and the heuristic channel in the input channels, all previous channels will enter the convolution layer first, and we will preprocess the heuristic auxiliary channel input into two vectors. One vector indicates whether the next action will be closer to the goal point, the other vector indicates whether the current agent has problems of staying, wandering and deadlock. These two vectors will be concatnated together with the output of the convolution module as one observation vector, and then the output of the observation processing module will be obtained after passing the vector through several fully connected layers.

The output of the observation module will then enter the communication module. The messages received by each agent are aggregated in this module, and concatnated with the original state value to form the final state tensor. The state tensor is input into the decision-making network to obtain the Q-value function, and the action corresponding to the maximum Q-value is selected.

4.2 Priority Based Communication Selection

In order for the agent to select communication objectives, it is first necessary to assign a priority to each agent. A greedy-based priority assignment strategy is used here. The priority assignment here is not like the traditional priority-based path planning algorithm [14] in which the priority of the agent is fixed. For agent v_i, we calculate the Manhattan distance from its current position to the goal point at time step t as mh_t^i. And we define the crowding degree d_t^i as the number of other agents in the FOV of agent v_i. Then the priority p_t^i of agent v_i is defined as $p_t^i = d_t^i/mh_t^i$. Such priority setting will let the agents closer to the goal point reach the goal point as soon as possible, which can reduce the possibility of collision. The agent with higher crowding degree will have less room for choice, so the message of this part of the agents should be given higher priority. These priorities change dynamically during the path planning process.

The basic framework of our communication module is based on GNN. First, the distance between different agents should be calculated, and then we set all distances beyond the communication radius to 0. Some works choose to communicate with all the agents in the communication radius, but this will bring unnecessary computational consumption and lead to redundancy of messages. Therefore, all the agents within the view radius 1 of the agent will be selected first, because this part of the agent will directly affect the action decision of the current agent. Among the remaining agents, the m agents with the highest priority are selected for communication.

In addition, we noticed that in the communication methods applied to MAPF [5,9], the negative impact of the agent reaching the goal is not considered. When an agent approaches the agent that stays at the goal, avoidance tactics may be employed. Therefore, the communication link of the agent that has reached the goal point is masked, so that only effective information will be transmitted. After this process, we get the adjacency matrix A_t

$$\mathbf{A}_t = \begin{bmatrix} (S_t^1) \\ \vdots \\ (S_t^n) \end{bmatrix} \tag{1}$$

where

$$\mathbf{S}_t^i = \begin{bmatrix} \mathbf{a}_t^{i1} \cdots \mathbf{a}_t^{in} \end{bmatrix} \tag{2}$$

a_t^{ij} represents whether agent v_i will receive the comminication message of agent v_j. The adjacency matrix A_t is also called graph shift operator (GSO) which is used to represent the connectivity of each node in GNN.

4.3   Hyper Cross Network Communication

GNN can effectively process communication messages between agents. The previous part modeled the entire multi-agent system as a neighborhood-based graph model, this part will use GNN to aggregate the messages obtained by each agent. Different from the traditional linear aggregation method and the aggregation method based on the attention mechanism [16], we introduce a super cross network to aggregate the communication messages between agents. Compared with linear aggregation, this kind of super network introduces nonlinear information. The red block in Fig. 2 represents the structure of the super network.

Assuming that the state vector of each agent of the previous observation module is e_t^i, then the state set of the entire multi-agent system is expressed as,

$$\mathbf{E}_t = \begin{bmatrix} (e_t^1) \\ \vdots \\ (e_t^i) \end{bmatrix} \tag{3}$$

Then for agent v_i, its message representation is obtained as

$$m_t^i = S_t^i E_t = \sum_{j:v_j \in V} a_t^{ij} e_t^j \tag{4}$$

Then input the obtained m_t^i into the weight generator network and the bias generator network, and get the weight w_i and bias b_i of the hyper network. Then the output of the feature interaction process is $xS = w_i e_t^i + b_i$. Finally, the xS and e_t^i vectors are concatnated. This step is equivalent to the common self-loop process in GNN, which is used to retain the information of the agent itself in the information of feature aggregation. The concatnated state will pass through a fully connected layer to obtain the final feature input into the Q-network.

4.4   Abnormal Status Detection

Communication-based methods can effectively reduce the deadlock situations in MAPF problems, but it is still not completely avoided. Therefore, on the basis of our previous work [17], here we introduce a new deadlock detection mechanism to embed the abnormal situation in the auxiliary observation channel. First, if the agent stays at the non-goal position for more than three time steps, it is determined that the agent is in a stagnant state. In addition, the agent trained by the reinforcement learning may wander on the map. Here we detect whether the agent has wandered between two positions in the past four time steps.

The above two detections have been proved in our past work to effectively assist the agent's decision-making process [17], but still fail to deal with the deadlock state. Deadlock can be divided into two situations. One is deadlock in a stagnant state, where multiple agents lock up and stagnate on the passage. The other is that two agents make avoidance decisions to each other at the same time, and is similar to a wandering situation. In order to effectively detect deadlock, following the idea of crowding degree above, the crowding degree here is calculated as the number of agents within a radius of 2 of each agent's FOV. If it is detected that the agent is in a stagnant or wandering state, and the crowding degree greater than or equal to 1 continues to remain unchanged or increased for multiple steps, this agent is pre-marked as deadlock.

Pre-marked deadlock state does not guarantee that the agent must be in a true deadlock state, because the deadlock state must be caused by multiple agents preempting passage resources. Therefore, after pre-marking process, we will perform another round of checking. If two or more pre-marked deadlock agents appear in the vicinity, it is confirmed that these agents are in a deadlock state. If a pre-marked agent is not surrounded by other pre-marked agents, this determines that the agent is in a non-deadlock state. Then we will add the deadlock state information in the heuristic auxiliary channel, and impose relevant penalties on the deadlock state to encourage the agent to learn to jump out of the deadlock state.

5   Experiments

In this section we will present our training and testing environments, along with the corresponding test results.

5.1   Training and Testing Setting

Our training environment is defined as a 14×14 warehouse environment, with a total of 5 agents. The training environment is shown in the Fig. 3. The white grid represents the passable grid, and the black grid represents static obstacles. The starting point will be assigned to the white grid, and the goal point will be assigned to the black grid. The goal point of each agent is regarded as an obstacle to other agents and only accessible to the agent itself. We use the curriculum learning to simplify the learning process. That is, the maximum distance between the assigned starting point and the goal point will gradually increase as the training progresses. The longest step size of each episode is 200. In each episode, we only store the states and actions of the agents labeled 0 into the buffer. And as soon as the agent labeled 0 reaches the goal point, we reset the entire environment to start a new episode. We will update the network every 20 steps, and evaluate the entire model every 8000 steps.

The trained model will be tested under different map sizes, obstacle density and number of agents. The map size is set to 46×46 or 58×58, and the number of agents is set from 10 to a maximum of 80 to test the effect of the algorithm with large number of agents. In addition to testing under the structure of the training map, we also test the model on two other maps to evaluate the generalization

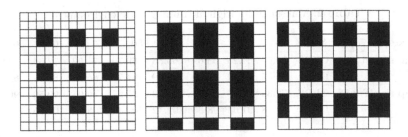

Fig. 3. Three kinds of map structures. The left map structure is used for training. The middle and right ones are more complex and only for evaluating.

performance. The other two kinds of structures can also be seen on Fig. 3. Both two maps increase the density of obstacles, and set a single passage in the map to test the cooperation between the agents. For each environment setting, we will test at least 200 cases. We use two metrics to evaluate the model. One is success rate which is calculated as $SuccessRate = n_{success}/n$, where n is the round of testing, and $n_{success}$ is the number of successful cases. A case is successful if and only if all agents successfully plan paths to the goal points. We set an upper limit of 200 steps per episode, beyond which it is considered to be a failure. We use makespan to measure the efficiency of learning algorithms. Makespan represents the time step when all the agents reach their goals.

5.2   Experiment Results

We compare the performance of our model with one of the state-of-the-art reinforcement learning methods, DHC [9]. Based on PRIMAL [11], DHC uses multi-head attention mechanism to realize communication between agents. First we will test our model and DHC under the environment structure as Fig. 3 shows. The result can be seen in Fig. 4 and Table 2.

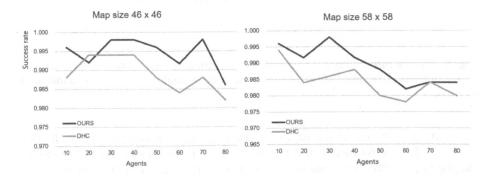

Fig. 4. Success rate in original training style environment with different scales and agent numbers

Table 2. Makespan in original training style environment

Makespan	Agents	10	20	30	40	50	60	70	80
Map size 46 × 46	OURS	56.69	62.25	65.62	66.88	69.30	71.52	72.66	74.98
	DHC	66.87	74.60	79.50	83.99	84.72	85.22	85.79	87.96
Map size 58 × 58	OURS	72.36	76.68	81.60	83.89	85.97	89.95	90.56	90.56
	DHC	81.18	91.63	98.85	102.42	104.41	108.26	109.15	110.14

In the environment with low density of obstacles, the success rates of the two models are maintained at a high level, and the gap is not large. It is worth noting that when the number of agents in the environment increases, the success rate of the two algorithms can still be maintained at a high level. Because in these cases, the agent can obtain more information to assist decision-making by communicating. However, there is a certain gap in the makespan of the two models, which shows that our communication method can filter out redundant information to a certain extent, and help the agent to better extract communication information for decision-making. In order to further illustrate the effect of the communication and deadlock detection module in our algorithm, we trained several variants of the algorithm for testing. The test results are shown in the Fig. 5. It can be seen that after adding the communication module and deadlock detection module, the success rate of the algorithm is greatly improved, which proves the effectiveness of these two modules in our algorithm.

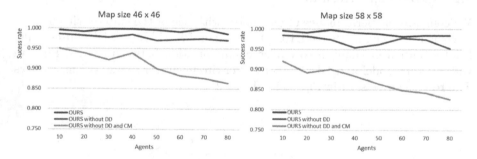

Fig. 5. Success rate in original training style environment with different map size and agent numbers. DD means deadlock detection module and CM means communication module.

Next, we test our model in a more complex environment to verify the performance for environments that are more prone to deadlocks. At this stage, we randomly generate one of the two environment structures in Fig. 4 per test, both of which greatly increase the obstacle density and are more prone to deadlock state. The results are shown in the Fig. 6. Compared with the DHC algorithm, the success rate of our algorithm in this environment has greatly improved. The improvement not only comes from the efficiency of communication, but more importantly, the deadlock detection mechanism provides the agent with additional abnormal state information, so that the agent has a greater possibility to jump out of the deadlock. In addition, after removing the communication and the deadlock detection module, it can be seen that in a complex environment, the success rate of the algorithm will be seriously reduced. This can prove the generalization performance of our algorithm in different environments, as well as the ability to solve such a single-passage environment that can easily cause deadlock.

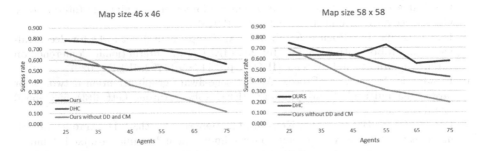

Fig. 6. Success rate in complex environments with different map size and agent numbers.

6 Conclusions

In this paper, we propose a method for solving MAPF problems with reinforcement learning combined with communication. We used a priority-based method to select the communication objectives for the agent, and introduced a new network structure to perform the information aggregation to better extract features in communication messages. At the same time, we introduce a deadlock detection mechanism to help the agent notice the current abnormal state. The solution success rate and efficiency of our algorithm are verified in the relatively simple environment. The generalization performance of our model and the ability to solve an environment prone to deadlocks are verified in more complex environments with single passages.

Our future work will focus on the generation mechanism of communication messages to ensure the effectiveness and simplicity of communication messages. And we will also try to improve the unlocking mechanism of agents when deadlock occurs.

Acknowledgment. This research was supported by National Key R&D Program of China 2018YFB1305500, National Natural Science Foundation (61977019, U1813206) and Shenzhen basic research program (JCYJ20180507183837726, JSGG20201103093802006).

References

1. Foerster, J., Assael, I.A., De Freitas, N., Whiteson, S.: Learning to communicate with deep multi-agent reinforcement learning. In: Advances in Neural Information Processing Systems 29 (2016)
2. Jiang, J., Dun, C., Huang, T., Lu, Z.: Graph convolutional reinforcement learning. In: International Conference on Learning Representations (2019)
3. Jiang, J., Lu, Z.: Learning attentional communication for multi-agent cooperation. In: Advances in Neural Information Processing Systems 31 (2018)
4. Kim, D., Moon, S., Hostallero, D., Kang, W.J., Lee, T., Son, K., Yi, Y.: Learning to schedule communication in multi-agent reinforcement learning. In: International Conference on Learning Representations (2018)
5. Li, Q., Gama, F., Ribeiro, A., Prorok, A.: Graph neural networks for decentralized multi-robot path planning. In: 2020 IEEE/RSJ International Conference on Intelligent Robots and Systems (IROS), pp. 11785–11792. IEEE (2020)
6. Li, Q., Lin, W., Liu, Z., Prorok, A.: Message-aware graph attention networks for large-scale multi-robot path planning. IEEE Robot. Autom. Lett. **6**(3), 5533–5540 (2021)
7. Liu, Z., Chen, B., Zhou, H., Koushik, G., Hebert, M., Zhao, D.: Mapper: multi-agent path planning with evolutionary reinforcement learning in mixed dynamic environments. In: 2020 IEEE/RSJ International Conference on Intelligent Robots and Systems (IROS), pp. 11748–11754. IEEE (2020)
8. Long, P., Fan, T., Liao, X., Liu, W., Zhang, H., Pan, J.: Towards optimally decentralized multi-robot collision avoidance via deep reinforcement learning. In: 2018 IEEE International Conference on Robotics and Automation (ICRA), pp. 6252–6259. IEEE (2018)
9. Ma, Z., Luo, Y., Ma, H.: Distributed heuristic multi-agent path finding with communication. In: 2021 IEEE International Conference on Robotics and Automation (ICRA), pp. 8699–8705. IEEE (2021)
10. Riviere, B., Hönig, W., Yue, Y., Chung, S.J.: Glas: global-to-local safe autonomy synthesis for multi-robot motion planning with end-to-end learning. IEEE Robot. Automation Lett. **5**(3), 4249–4256 (2020)
11. Sartoretti, G., Kerr, J., Shi, Y., Wagner, G., Kumar, T.S., Koenig, S., Choset, H.: Primal: Pathfinding via reinforcement and imitation multi-agent learning. IEEE Robot. Automation Lett. **4**(3), 2378–2385 (2019)
12. Sharon, G., Stern, R., Felner, A., Sturtevant, N.R.: Conflict-based search for optimal multi-agent pathfinding. Artif. Intell. **219**, 40–66 (2015)
13. Sheng, J., et al.: Learning structured communication for multi-agent reinforcement learning. arXiv preprint arXiv:2002.04235 (2020)
14. Silver, D.: Cooperative pathfinding. In: Proceedings of the AAAI Conference on Artificial Intelligence and Interactive Digital Entertainment, vol. 1, pp. 117–122 (2005)
15. Sukhbaatar, S., Fergus, R., et al.: Learning multiagent communication with backpropagation. In: Advances in Neural Information Processing Systems 29 (2016)
16. Wu, Z., Pan, S., Chen, F., Long, G., Zhang, C., Philip, S.Y.: A comprehensive survey on graph neural networks. IEEE Trans. Neural Networks Learning Syst. **32**(1), 4–24 (2020)
17. Xu, Y., Li, Y., Liu, Q., Gao, J., Liu, Y., Chen, M.: Multi-agent pathfinding with local and global guidance. In: 2021 IEEE International Conference on Networking, Sensing and Control (ICNSC), vol. 1, pp. 1–7 (2021)

Agile Running Control for Bipedal Robot Based on 3D-SLIP Model Regulation in Task-Space

Shengjun Wang(ID), Zehuan Li, Haibo Gao, Kaizheng Shan(ID), Jun Li(ID), and Haitao Yu(✉)(ID)

State Key Laboratory of Robotics and Systems,
Harbin Institute of Technology, Harbin, China
`yht@hit.edu.cn`

Abstract. To achieve agile running of a biped robot, dynamic stability, joint coordination, and real-time ability are required. In this paper, a task-space-based controller framework is constructed with a reduced-order 3D-SLIP model. On the top layer, a 3D-SLIP model based planner is employed for center-of-mass trajectory planning. The planner built with optimization for table divided apex state, and a neural network is used to fit the optimized table for real-time planning. On the bottom layer, a task-space-based controller with full-body dynamics is utilized, which solves the quadratic programming for the optimized joint torque in real-time. A 12-DOF biped robot model with a point-foot is used for simulation verification. The simulation result show that stable running and single-cycle apex state change running can achieved with the framework.

Keywords: Biped robot · Dynamic running · Motion control · 3D-SLIP model

1 Introduction

Legged robot is regarded as a compensation for wheeled and tracked robots in automation applications for better terrain adaptation in unstructured environments such as disaster rescue and wild exploration that are usually dangerous for humans. Biped-robot control is difficult due to the high dimension underactuated non-linear dynamic models and complex multi-contact conditions. With years of research, some efficient control methods have been proposed to solve these problem, such as the reduced-dimension model with the task space control method, zero-dynamic model optimization-based method, whole-body trajectory optimization method, and deep-learning method recently. This article proposes a dual-layer control framework for agility running control, which is applied in a biped robot running simulation. The simulation robot contains 12-DOF, which

This work was supported in part by the National Natural Science Foundation of China under Grant 52175011.

are minimal required for 3D motion and makes the system lack of redundant joints for stabilization.

In the domain of legged robots, The reduced dimension method is the earliest investigated to handle the full-body dynamic model's complexity and high computing ability requirement. For walking, the Inverted Pendulum model [1] and the Linear Inverted Pendulum [2,3] based on simplified COM(the Center Of Mass) are used for walking control. The Capture Point model [4–6] is another concept with simple dynamics feature that is used in walking. For running, the SLIP(Spring-Loaded Inverted Pendulum) model was developed and applied in single-legged robot bouncing control by Raibert [7].

For the simplicity and the efficiency of the SLIP model, it has been widely studied in legged robot running control. Gayer provides an approximate solution for the SLIP model [8], which facilitates the cyclic solution calculation. Aside from analytical methods, numerical [9] and neural-network-based methods [10] are applied in 3D-SLIP planning.

The reduced dimension method only provides a low dimension feature trajectory. The control system can be easily controlled with simple feedback control when the system model approximates the reduced dimension model. Whole-body coordination is usually used when the legged system differs from the ideal model. The task-space-based controller is widely used [11,12], first applied in redundant robot arms [13]. The method is not trajectory optimized; however, fast calculation and real-time optimization characters make this method popular.

The remainder of this paper is structured as follows. In Sect. 2, the 3D-SLIP mode is studied to construct an apex planner and verified with a simulation on the reduced-dimension model. In Sect. 3, a task-space-based control framework is proposed for the biped robot control. In Sect. 4, a simulation is achieved for the framework verification. In the last section, a conclusion is composed for this paper's work and the possibly improvement in the future work.

2   3D-SLIP Model and Apex Controller Optimization

2.1   3D-SLIP Model and Gait Cycle

The apex is the crucial state for the running gait cycle, representing the running cycle's main feature. The 3D-SLIP model is built for running cycle description, in which three stages are used for the process. The first stage is, dropping down at the apex with only the gravity until the foot touches down; the second stage is foot-supporting from shoot-in to shoot-out; the third stage is lifting from lift-off to the next apex. The 3D-SLIP model is a hybrid dynamic model with two events for model separation. Two differential equations describe the air condition and the ground supporting condition. Suppose the body mass is m, and the free length of the spring leg is l_0. The differential process from one apex to the next is described:

$$\begin{cases} \ddot{\mathbf{p}}_{\text{com}} = \mathbf{g} & , air \\ \ddot{\mathbf{p}}_{\text{com}} = \frac{k}{m}\left(l_0 \frac{1}{\|\mathbf{l}\|} - 1\right) + \mathbf{g} & , ground \end{cases} \tag{1}$$

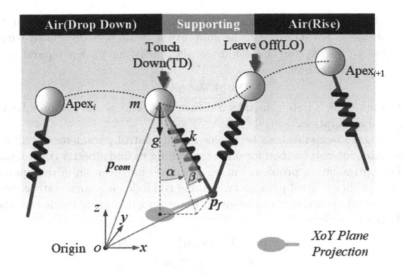

Fig. 1. 3D-SLIP model and gait cycle.

where $\mathbf{p_{com}} \in \mathbb{R}^3$ represents the vector from the original point to the COM(center of mass) point, $\mathbf{\ddot{p}_{com}} \in \mathbb{R}^3$ is the acceleration vector, $\mathbf{g} = [0, 0, -9.8]^{\mathbf{T}}$ is the gravity vector. $\mathbf{l} = \mathbf{p_{com}} - \mathbf{p_f}$ is the vector from the contact point to the COM point, $\mathbf{p_f} \in \mathbb{R}^3$ is the coordinate of the contact point, and k is the stiffness of the leg.

Switching between the ground phase and the air phase corresponding to events TD(Touch Down) and LO(Lift Off), the condition is described:

$$\begin{cases} C_{TD} : \mathbf{p_{com}}\mathbf{e_z^T} - l_0 \cos{(\beta)} \cos{(\alpha)} = 0 \ , \ \mathbf{\ddot{p}_{com}}\mathbf{e_z^T} \leqslant 0 \\ C_{LO} : ||\mathbf{l}|| = l_0 \ , \ \mathbf{l}^T \mathbf{\dot{p}_{com}} \geqslant 0 \end{cases} \tag{2}$$

$\mathbf{e_z^T}$ is the unit vector in the z-direction, α and β is the touch-down angle as shown in Fig. 1.

2.2 Apex Mapping and Controller Optimization

In the 3D-SLIP model, the apex state includes the position and velocity of the COM point. v_x, v_y and h are chosen to represent the apex state, which is the velocity of x,y-direction and height of the COM point. For the $i - th$ apex of a running process, the apex state is defined as respectively:

$$\mathbf{s}_i = \left[h_i, v_{xi}, v_{yi} \right]^T \tag{3}$$

The apex mapping is defined as the mapping from $apex_i$ to the $apex_{i+1}$ with control parameter described as follow:

$$\mathbf{s}_{i+1} = f\left(\mathbf{s}_i, \mathbf{u}_i\right) \tag{4}$$

$\mathbf{u}_i$ is the 3D-SLIP control parameter, including the touch-down angles and supporting stiffness. For simplicity, the supporting stiffness is decoupled with two parameters k_1 and k_2 for the compress and thrusting phases separately. The control vector is written:

$$\mathbf{u}_i = \left[\alpha, \beta, k_1, k_2\right]^T \tag{5}$$

The apex mapping is determined by a differential process and can be solved with numericical integration.

The target apex state can be reached with control parameter coordination. The optimization can be used for offline searching to find a better control parameter. The optimization problem can be described as: given an initial apex state and find a proper control parameter, making the following apex state stable and close to desired apex state, and ensuring the supporting angle inside the fraction cone. It can be written:

$$\begin{cases} \underset{u}{min} .\|\mathbf{Q}\left(f\left(\mathbf{s}_i, \mathbf{u}\right) - \mathbf{s}_{des}\right)\|_2 \\ s.t. \dfrac{\sin(\beta)^2 + \cos(\beta)^2 \sin(\alpha)^2}{\cos(\alpha)\cos(\beta)} \leqslant \mu \end{cases} \tag{6}$$

$\mathbf{Q} = \mathrm{diag}\left(q_h, q_{vx}, q_{vy}\right)$ is the weight matrix corresponding to apex state: apex height, the velocity of xy-direction, and the apex height is an essential feature for stable running. μ is the ground friction coefficient. An optimized control parameter can be solved with the gradient-descent optimization method.

An optimized control table is built for an online controller. The target apex state range is equal to the initial apex state. The height is bounded to $h \in [1.1, 1.5]$, the forward direction velocity is bounded to $v_x \in [-3.0, 3.0]$, and another direction is bounded to $v_y \in [-1.0, 1.0]$. The chosen space is divided into grid $6 \times 10 \times 10$, result in 360000 groups. Two Intel Xeon Platinum 8136@2.5 GHz servers and 12 h are used for the optimization. A 6-layer Feedforward Neural Network is used to fit the optimized strategy table for fast calculation.

$$u_i = FNN_6\left(s_i, s_{i+1}\right) \tag{7}$$

A simulation based on the 3D-SLIP model is made for controller verification. In the simulation, the target apex height and velocity changed every cycle, and the simulated trajectory followed the target apex state well as sown in Fig. 2.

3   Task-Space Based Robot Running Control

3.1   Robot Dynamic Model

The dynamic equation of robot is calculated using the rigid body tree iteration with real-time robot state [17]. In this article, the robot is composed of a underactuated floating-base state $\mathbf{q}_{torso} \in SE\left(3\right)$ and actuated joint vector $\mathbf{q}_{joint} \in \mathbb{R}^6$. The system state is described: $\mathbf{q} = \left[\mathbf{q}_{torso}^T, \mathbf{q}_{joint}^T\right]^T$. The corresponding velocity and acceleration state are written $\dot{\mathbf{q}} \in \mathbb{R}^{12}$, $\ddot{\mathbf{q}} \in \mathbb{R}^{12}$. The dynamic equation of the whole robot is:

$$\mathbf{H}\left(\mathbf{q}\right)\ddot{\mathbf{q}} + \mathbf{C}\left(\mathbf{q}, \dot{\mathbf{q}}\right)\dot{\mathbf{q}} + \mathbf{G}\left(\mathbf{q}\right) = \mathbf{S}_a^T \tau + \mathbf{J}_s\left(\mathbf{q}\right)^T \mathbf{F}_s \tag{8}$$

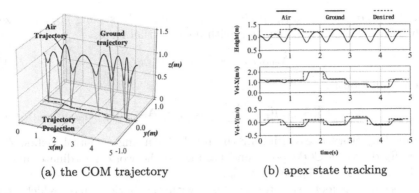

(a) the COM trajectory   (b) apex state tracking

Fig. 2. SLIP simulation with NN-based policy

$\mathbf{H}(q) \in \mathbb{R}^{12 \times 12}$ is the mass matrix calculated with the real-time configuration; $\mathbf{C}(q, \dot{q})$ is the Coriolis concerned coefficient; $\mathbf{G}(q)$ is the gravity part. $\mathbf{F_s} = \begin{bmatrix} \mathbf{F_{s1}^T}, & \mathbf{F_{s2}^T}, & ... \end{bmatrix}^T$ is the ground reaction force vector; $\mathbf{J}_s(q) \in \mathbb{R}^{3 \times 12}$ is the Jacobian Matrix corresponding to the ground reaction force. $\tau \in \mathbb{R}^6$ is the active joint control force vector; $\mathbf{S}_a = [\mathbf{0}_{6 \times 6}, \ \mathbf{1}_{6 \times 6}]$ is the selection matrix that maps the active force into the equation.

3.2   Task-space Based Cost Function Design

The COM trajectory is the most crucial reference trajectory and can only be controlled in the ground phase. The desired COM position $\mathbf{p}_{com}^{des}$, velocity $\dot{\mathbf{p}}_{com}^{des}$, and acceleration $\ddot{\mathbf{p}}_{com}^{des}$ are fetched from planar in real-time. The COM task can be written:

$$\mathbf{a}_{com}^{task} = \ddot{\mathbf{p}}_{com}^{des} + \mathbf{P}_{com} \left(\mathbf{p}_{com}^{des} - \mathbf{p}_{com}^{real} \right) + \mathbf{D}_{com} \left(\dot{\mathbf{p}}_{com}^{des} - \dot{\mathbf{p}}_{com}^{real} \right) \tag{9}$$

where $\mathbf{p}_{com}^{real}$ and $\dot{\mathbf{p}}_{com}^{real}$ is the COM position and velocity estimated by the robot state, $\mathbf{a}_{com}^{task}$ is the desired COM acceleration in the task space.

The cost function of COM trajectory is defined as the error between desired task-space COM acceleration and the acceleration calculated applying a specified force that is to be optimized. The quadratic form of the COM cost function is:

$$c_{com}^{lin} = || \sum m_i \mathbf{a}_{com}^{task} - \dot{f}_{Ml}(\dot{\mathbf{q}}) ||_{\mathbf{Q}_{com}^{lin}} \tag{10}$$

where m_i is the mass of the $i - th$ rigid body in rigid body tree, $\mathbf{Q}_{com}^{lin}$ is the weight matrix, $f_{Ml}(\dot{\mathbf{q}})$ is a function for centroidal linear momentum calculation, which can be calculated [14] by:

$$f_{Ml}(\dot{\mathbf{q}}) = \mathbf{A}_{cmml} \dot{\mathbf{q}} \tag{11}$$

where $\mathbf{A}_{cmml}$ is the linear centroidal momentum matrix. The derivation of linear momentum is:

$$\dot{f}_{Ml}(\dot{\mathbf{q}}) = \mathbf{A}_{cmml} \ddot{\mathbf{q}} + \dot{\mathbf{A}}_{cmml} \dot{\mathbf{q}} \tag{12}$$

where $\dot{\mathbf{A}}_{cmmL}\dot{\mathbf{q}}$ is a constant, and it can be calculated by setting $\dot{f}_{Ml}\,(\dot{\mathbf{q}})$ to zero, which means the COM acceleration with non-external force.

$$\dot{\mathbf{A}}_{cmml}\dot{\mathbf{q}} = -\mathbf{A}_{cmml}\ddot{\mathbf{q}}|_{\mathbf{F}_s=0} \tag{13}$$

The cost function is:

$$c_{com} = \|\mathbf{A}_{cmml}\ddot{\mathbf{q}} - \left(\sum m_i a_{com}^{task} - \dot{\mathbf{A}}_{cmml}\dot{\mathbf{q}}\right)\|_{\mathbf{Q}_{com}} \tag{14}$$

The foot trajectory is essential for the touch-down angle control, define $\mathscr{W}_{com}$ an axis fixed on the COM point and parallel to the world coordinate, and the planning of the foot is based on $\mathscr{W}_{com}$.

The swing leg foot trajectory is built with the bezier curve, which starts from leave-off and ends at touch-down. The trajectory is separated into three segments (see Fig. 3): the first segment (AB) ends at another leg's touch-down; the second segment (BC) ends at another leg's leave-off; the third segment (CD) ends at touch-down. The desired foot position $\mathbf{p}_{foot}^{des}$, velocity $\dot{\mathbf{p}}_{foot}^{des}$, and acceleration $\ddot{\mathbf{p}}_{foot}^{des}$ are updated dynamically. The foot's desired task-space acceleration is calculated with a simple PD controller:

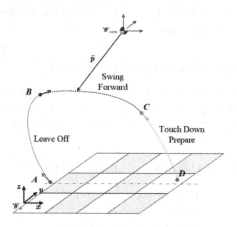

Fig. 3. Swing leg trajectory.

$$\mathbf{a}_{foot}^{task} = \mathbf{P}_{foot}\left(\mathbf{p}_{foot}^{des} - \mathbf{p}_{foot}^{real}\right) + \mathbf{D}_{foot}\left(\dot{\mathbf{p}}_{foot}^{des} - \dot{\mathbf{p}}_{foot}^{real}\right) + \ddot{\mathbf{p}}_{foot}^{des} \tag{15}$$

where $\mathbf{p}_{foot}^{real}$ and $\dot{\mathbf{p}}_{foot}^{real}$ are the position and velocity of swing foot at the coordinate $\mathscr{W}_{com}$ in real-time. The cost function is the error between the task-space foot acceleration and the foot acceleration optimized.

$$c_{foot} = \|\mathbf{a}_{foot}^{task} - \dot{f}_{fv}\,(\dot{\mathbf{q}})\|_{\mathbf{Q}_{foot}} \tag{16}$$

where $f_{fv}\,(\dot{q})$ is the foot velocity estimation function with joint actuation, computed with joint-space state by jacobian mapping $f_{fv}\,(\dot{q}) = J_f\dot{q}$. The derivation is:

$$\dot{f}_{fv}\,(\dot{\mathbf{q}}) = \mathbf{J}_f\ddot{\mathbf{q}} + \dot{\mathbf{J}}_f\dot{\mathbf{q}} \tag{17}$$

where $\mathbf{J}_f$ is the Jacobian Matrix for the corresponding foot, $\dot{\mathbf{J}}_f\dot{\mathbf{q}}$ is also a constant that can be calculated with non-external force.

$$\dot{\mathbf{J}}_f\dot{\mathbf{q}} = \mathbf{J}_f\ddot{\mathbf{q}} - \dot{f}_{fv}(\dot{\mathbf{q}})|_{\mathbf{F}_c=0,\tau=0} \tag{18}$$

Angular centroidal momentum is also necessary for achieving stable running, which is only controllable in the ground phase and remains conservative in the air. The controller has to control the angular centroidal momentum to zero until the leave-off. The desired angular centroidal momentum derivation is calculated with a PD controller:

$$\dot{\mathbf{L}}_{com}^{task} = \mathbf{D}_{com}^{L}\left(0 - \mathbf{L}_{com}^{real}\right) \tag{19}$$

where $\mathbf{L}_{com}^{real}$ is the angular centroidal momentum estimated from real-time robot state. The cost function is formated:

$$c_{com}^{ang} = ||\dot{\mathbf{L}}_{com}^{task} - \dot{f}_{Ma}(\dot{\mathbf{q}})||_{\mathbf{Q}_{com}^{ang}} \tag{20}$$

where $f_{Ma}(\dot{\mathbf{q}})$ is the estimation function for angular centroidal momentum, and it is linear to the real-time robot state:

$$f_{Ma}(\dot{\mathbf{q}}) = \mathbf{A}_{cmma}\dot{\mathbf{q}} \tag{21}$$

where $\dot{\mathbf{A}}_{cmma}\dot{\mathbf{q}}$ is a constant calculated at non-external force condition:

$$\dot{\mathbf{A}}_{cmma}\dot{\mathbf{q}} = -\mathbf{A}_{cmma}\ddot{\mathbf{q}}|_{\mathbf{F}_s=0} \tag{22}$$

The stability of the angular momentum makes sure the system does not revolute severely. And the whole body may revolute slowly without torso angle control, therefore the torso angle should be controlled, and the desired value in the task space is:

$$\alpha_{tor}^{task} = P_{tor}\left(\theta_{tor}^{des} - \theta_{tor}^{real}\right) + D_{tor}\left(\dot{\theta}_{tor}^{des} - \dot{\theta}_{tor}^{real}\right) \tag{23}$$

where θ_{tor}^{des} and θ_{tor}^{real} is the desired torso angle and velocity usually set to be zero, $\dot{\theta}_{tor}^{des}$ and $\dot{\theta}_{tor}^{real}$ is the actual torso angle and velocity estimated in real-time. The cost function n task space is formatted:

$$c_{tor} = ||\alpha_{tor}^{task} - \mathbf{S}_\theta\ddot{\mathbf{q}}||_{\mathbf{Q}_{tor}} \tag{24}$$

where $\mathbf{S}_\theta$ is the torso angle selection matrix

3.3   QP Optimization Formulation and the Control Framework

Combining the aforementioned cost functions together, the optimization problem is formatted:

$$\begin{cases} \min. \ c_{com}^{lin} + c_{foot} + c_{com}^{ang} + c_{tor} \\ s.t. \ \mathbf{H}(\mathbf{q})\ddot{\mathbf{q}} + \mathbf{C}(\mathbf{q},\dot{\mathbf{q}})\dot{\mathbf{q}} + \mathbf{G}(\mathbf{q}) = \mathbf{S}_a^T\tau + \mathbf{J}_s(\mathbf{q})^T\mathbf{F}_s \\ \mathbf{J}_c(\mathbf{q})\ddot{\mathbf{q}} = \mathbf{k} \\ \tau_{\min} \leqslant \tau \leqslant \tau_{\max} \\ F_{fx} \leqslant \mu F_N/\sqrt{2} \\ F_{fy} \leqslant \mu F_N/\sqrt{20} \end{cases} \tag{25}$$

The objective function is the quadratic formulation, and the constraints condition are all linear that can be solved using the active-set method [15]. The constraints include the floating-base dynamic equation, the ground contact constraint, the friction cone constraint, and the joint torque limit constraint. $\mathbf{J}_c(\mathbf{q})$ is the ground constraint matrix, $\mathbf{k}$ is the constant derivated from contact constraint, F_N is the contact force orthogonal to the contact plane, F_x and F_y is the friction force in XY-plane.

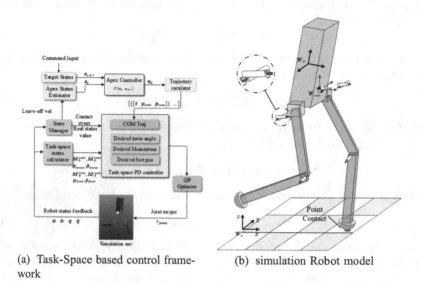

(a) Task-Space based control framework

(b) simulation Robot model

Fig. 4. Robot model and control framework

As shown in Fig. 4(a), a dual-layer controller is applied in simulation. The upper layer is a discrete apex controller that works when the robot leaves off into the air. It estimates the apex state of this cycle and plans a trajectory that approaches the desired apex state in the next cycle. The lower layer controller is a real-time multi-joint coordinator, which solves an optimization problem for real-time control. The framework can be easily extended to the other gaits and deployed to physical robots with critical computing requirements.

4   Simulation

In the simulation, the controller is applied to a biped robot with a floating-base torso and two 3-DOF legs, which are the least required for biped 3D running (see Fig. 4(b)). The dynamic parameters of the simulation biped are shown in Table 1.

The Dynamic simulation and control are implemented with the framework RigidbodyDynamics [16] in Julia language. The running process is rendered in Pybullet (see Fig. 6) (Fig. 5).

Table 1. Robot dynamic properties.

Torso	Mass: 20 kg
	Inertia Matrix: $diag(0.37, 0.29, 0.128)$
Thigh & shank	Mass: 2 kg
	Length: 0.5 m

Fig. 5. Simulation result.

4.1   Running with Constant Target

Running with constant velocity and height is the most common task mode. In this experiment, a constant target running is implemented for controller verification. The robot is released from a specified initial height while the target height is 1 m, and the target velocity in the forward direction is set to be 1.9 m/s. The target side-velocity changes direction according to the touch-down leg. As shown in the result, the whole system works under the gravity-only condition and behaves as following a parabolic trajectory when the robot leaves off in the air. The apex state can be calculated after the leave-off moment, which can be used instantly for the next cycle planning and the foot touch-down angle calculation.

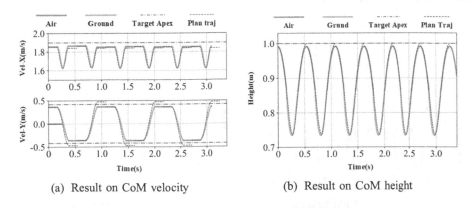

(a) Result on CoM velocity   (b) Result on CoM height

Fig. 6. Constant vlocity and height running simulation

Stable running of the robot also requires centroidal momentum stability. In the air phase, the robot only governed by gravity, which will continue rotating according to the leave-off momentum. Therefore, low centroidal momentum at leave-off is necessary to maintain a reasonable touch-down torso angle. The momentum curve at running is shown in Fig. 7(a), which was disturbed at contact and returned to zero nearby before leave-off.

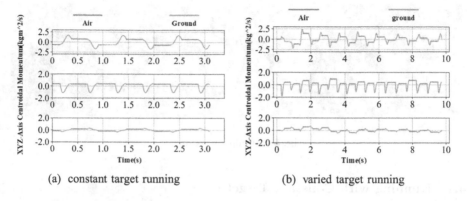

(a) constant target running   (b) varied target running

Fig. 7. Result of momentum change in simulation

4.2   Running with Varied Target

The single-cycle apex reaching is an experiment for biped running agility verification, which requests the robot reach target state in a single cycle. In this experiment, the targe apex state is commanded in the t $= 0.0$ s to ($v_x = 2.0, h_{apex} = 1.0$) and in the t $= 5.0$ s to ($v_x = 1.6, h_{apex} = 1.1$), which reached the target in a single cycle and kept stable. Apex height is first guaranteed in trajectory planning, as shown in Fig. 8.

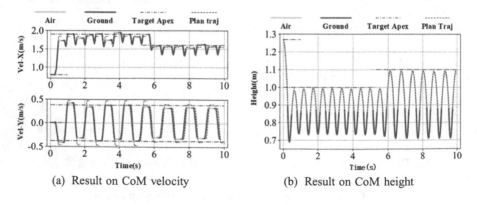

(a) Result on CoM velocity   (b) Result on CoM height

Fig. 8. Constant vlocity and height running simulation

5 Conclusion

In this paper, an apex mapping table of the 3D-SLIP model is created with control parameter optimization, and a neural-network-based apex controller is constructed with the apex mapping table for real-time control. The planner is applied in the biped robot COM trajectory and touch-down angle planning while leaving the ground, and the planned trajectory is regarded as the objective in the task space. A quadratic programming problem is constructed for the joint torque optimization. The biped running simulation based on the control framework is implemented for verification.

For future work, this framework will be transplanted to a physics robot for verification. The dynamic programing method will be considered to resist the disturbance of contact uncertainty. The foot trajectory will also be studied to reduce the foot-ground impact.

References

1. Kuo, A.D., Donelan, J.M., Ruina, A.: Energetic consequences of walking like an inverted pendulum: step-to-step transitions. Exercise Sport Sci. Rev. **33**(2), 88–97 (2005)
2. Kajita, S., Tani, K.: Study of dynamic biped locomotion on rugged terrain-derivation and application of the linear inverted pendulum mode. In: Proceedings. 1991 IEEE International Conference on Robotics and Automation, pp. 1405–1406. IEEE Computer Society (1991)
3. Kajita, S., et al.: Biped walking stabilization based on linear inverted pendulum tracking. In: 2010 IEEE/RSJ International Conference on Intelligent Robots and Systems, pp. 4489–4496. IEEE (2010)
4. Pratt, J., Carff, J., Drakunov, S., Goswami, A.: Capture point: a step toward humanoid push recovery. In: 2006 6th IEEE-RAS International Conference on Humanoid Robots, pp. 200–207. IEEE (2006)
5. Krause, M., Englsberger, J., Wieber, P.-B., Ott, C.: Stabilization of the capture point dynamics for bipedal walking based on model predictive control. IFAC Proc. Vol. **45**(22), 165–171 (2012)
6. Morisawa, M., Kajita, S., Kanehiro, F., Kaneko, K., Miura, K., Yokoi, K.: Balance control based on capture point error compensation for biped walking on uneven terrain. In: 2012 12th IEEE-RAS International Conference on Humanoid Robots (Humanoids 2012), pp. 734–740. IEEE (2012)
7. Raibert, M.H., Benjamin Brown Jr, H., Chepponis, M., Koechling, J., Hodgins, J.K.: Dynamically stable legged locomotion. Technical report, Massachusetts Inst of Tech Cambridge Artificial Intelligence Lab (1989)
8. Geyer, H., Seyfarth, A., Blickhan, R.: Spring-mass running: simple approximate solution and application to gait stability. J. Theor. Biol. **232**(3), 315–328 (2005)
9. Albert, W., Geyer, H.: The 3-d spring-mass model reveals a time-based deadbeat control for highly robust running and steering in uncertain environments. IEEE Trans. Rob. **29**(5), 1114–1124 (2013)
10. Xin, S., Delhaisse, B., You, Y., Zhou, C., Shahbazi, M., Tsagarakis, N.: Neural-network-controlled spring mass template for humanoid running. In: 2018 IEEE/RSJ International Conference on Intelligent Robots and Systems (IROS), pp. 1725–1731. IEEE (2018)

11. Wensing, P.M., Orin, D.E.: Generation of dynamic humanoid behaviors through task-space control with conic optimization. In: 2013 IEEE International Conference on Robotics and Automation, pp. 3103–3109. IEEE (2013)
12. Wiedebach, G., et al.: Walking on partial footholds including line contacts with the humanoid robot atlas. In: 2016 IEEE-RAS 16th International Conference on Humanoid Robots (Humanoids), pages 1312–1319. IEEE (2016)
13. Baerlocher, P., Boulic, R.: Task-priority formulations for the kinematic control of highly redundant articulated structures. In: Proceedings of the 1998 IEEE/RSJ International Conference on Intelligent Robots and Systems. Innovations in Theory, Practice and Applications (Cat. No. 98CH36190), vol. 1, pp. 323–329. IEEE, 1998
14. Kajita, S., e al.: Resolved momentum control: Humanoid motion planning based on the linear and angular momentum. In Proceedings 2003 ieee/rsj International Conference on Intelligent Robots and Systems (IROS 2003) (cat. no. 03ch37453), vol. 2, pp. 1644–1650. IEEE (2003)
15. Kuindersma, S., Permenter, F., Tedrake, R.: An efficiently solvable quadratic program for stabilizing dynamic locomotion. In: 2014 IEEE International Conference on Robotics and Automation (ICRA), pp. 2589–2594. IEEE (2014)
16. Koolen, T., Deits, R.: Julia for robotics: simulation and real-time control in a high-level programming language. In: 2019 International Conference on Robotics and Automation (ICRA), pp. 604–611. IEEE (2019)
17. Featherstone, R.: Rigid body dynamics algorithms. Springer (2014)

The Multi-objective Optimization of a Multi-loop Mechanism for Space Applications

Chuanyang Li[1], Changhua Hu[1], Rongqiang Liu[2], Zhonghao Qin[1], Huiyin Yan[2], Hongwei Guo[2], and Hong Xiao[2(✉)]

[1] PLA Rocket Force University of Engineering, Xi'an 710025, China
li_chuanyang@yeah.net
[2] State Key Laboratory of Robotics and System, Harbin Institute of Technology, Harbin 150080, China
{liurq,guohw,xiaohong}@hit.edu.cn

Abstract. The double-tripod multi-loop mechanism (DTMLM) is expected to construct modular system for space applications, such as space capturing, thus requiring good performance, including good dynamics characteristics, kinematics features, and high actuation-transmission efficiency. This paper proposes local and global performance indicators in terms of kinematics and dynamics, by means of concept of the output-array ellipsoid. Then, the kinematics-and dynamics- performance drawings are plotted and then employed to indicate the relationship between the indicators and rod parameters. A multi-objective-optimization procedure is represented to calculate the weight coefficient of the indicators. The diagram of comprehensive evaluation indicators is henceforth plotted. Due to the optimization, $r = 3d_0$ is better for the DTMLM structures in space applications, which provides strong support in further structure-design process.

Keywords: Kinematics-performance index · Dynamics-performance index · Multi-objective optimization

1 Introduction

To implement non-cooperative, multi-loop mechanisms offer high mobility, high stiffness, high load-carrying capacity, large workspace, and high adaptability. Li et al. [1] proposed a novel multi-loop mechanism for space applications, dubbed the double-tripod multi-loop mechanism (DTMLM) [2].

Multi-objective parameter optimization plays important roles in the design process. Scholars have done a lot of researches in this regard. Hamida et al.

Supported by The Youth Fund of PLA Rocket Force University of Engineering (2021QN-B023) and The Youth Fund of the Natural Science Foundation of Shaanxi (2022JQ-316).

[3] proposed a combined methodology for type and size optimization of a cable driven parallel robot. Venkateswaran et al. [4] represents an optimization approach to deal with design problems of tensegrity mechanism, robot modules, and the size of the leg mechanism. Wang et al. [5] analyzes the design parameters of the proposed a planar cable parallel robot by multi-objective optimization in terms of the largest total orientation wrench closure workspace and the highest global stiffness magnitude index. This paper focuses on the multi-objective optimization of the DTMLM, which provides strong support in parameters optimization in the design process.

2   The Architecture of the DTMLM

The DTMLM, as shown in Fig. 1, has six revolute, three prismatic, and three SRS joints [1]. Each SRS joint, in turn, consists of two concentric spherical joints, coupled by a revolute joint. The mechanism carries one base platform (BP) and one moving platform (MP), represented by identical equilateral triangles in Fig. 1. The two platforms and the middle plane $B_1 B_2 B_3$ are connected by links $A_i B_i$ and $B_i D_i$, for $i = 1, 2, 3$. All six links carry the same length l. Especially, the two platforms are symmetrically located with respect to the plane $B_1 B_2 B_3$ at any possible posture [6].

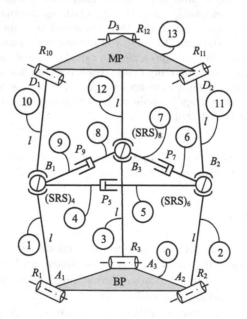

Fig. 1. The Configuration of the DTMLM

3   Kinematics Performance Index

3.1   The Generalized-Velocity Ellipsoid

According to mobility analysis in our early work [6], we have

$$\mathbf{t} = \begin{bmatrix} \boldsymbol{\omega} \\ \dot{\mathbf{c}} \end{bmatrix} \mathbf{J}\dot{\mathbf{q}} = \begin{bmatrix} \mathbf{J}_{\omega} \\ \mathbf{J}_v \end{bmatrix} \dot{\mathbf{q}}, \quad \dot{\mathbf{q}} = [\dot{\theta}_1, \dot{\theta}_2, \dot{\theta}_3]^T \tag{1}$$

where $\mathbf{t}$, a six-dimensional array, denotes the generalized-velocity array of the center of the MP, $\mathbf{J}$ the Jacobain matrix; while $\dot{\mathbf{q}}$ is the actuated-joint-rate array, in which $\dot{\theta}_i$ indicates the angular-velocity of the ith actuator.

Here, the input actuated-joint-rate array is set as a unit vector, an n-dimensional unit sphere then being obtained as,

$$\dot{\mathbf{q}}^T \dot{\mathbf{q}} = 1 \tag{2}$$

Thus, we have

$$\mathbf{j}^T (\mathbf{J}_j^{-1})^T \mathbf{J}_j^{-1} \mathbf{j} = 1 \tag{3}$$

where $\mathbf{j}$ denotes $\boldsymbol{\omega}$ or $\dot{\mathbf{c}}$, while j is ω or v.

Let $\mathbf{J}_j = \mathbf{A}_j \Lambda_j \mathbf{B}_j$, in which $\mathbf{A}_j$ and $\mathbf{B}_j$ are 6×6 Unitary Matrices, Λ_j a 6×6 real diagonal matrix, we have

$$\mathbf{j}^T (\mathbf{A}_j^{-1})^T (\Lambda_j \Lambda_j^T)^{-1} \mathbf{A}_j^{-1} \mathbf{j} = 1 \tag{4}$$

Rewrite Eq.(4) as,

$$\begin{cases} \boldsymbol{\omega}^T (\mathbf{A}_{\omega}^{-1})^T (\Lambda_{\omega} \Lambda_{\omega}^T)^{-1} \mathbf{A}_{\omega}^{-1} \boldsymbol{\omega} = 1 \\ \dot{\mathbf{c}}^T (\mathbf{A}_v^{-1})^T (\Lambda_v \Lambda_v^T)^{-1} \mathbf{A}_v^{-1} \dot{\mathbf{c}} = 1 \end{cases} \tag{5}$$

where $\boldsymbol{\omega}_i = [\omega_1, \omega_2, \omega_3]^T$, and $\dot{\mathbf{c}}_i = [v_1, v_2, v_3]^T$.

Let

$$\mathbf{A}_j^{-1} = \begin{bmatrix} a_{j11} & a_{j12} & a_{j13} \\ a_{j21} & a_{j22} & a_{j23} \\ a_{j31} & a_{j32} & a_{j33} \end{bmatrix} \tag{6a}$$

$$\Lambda_j = \begin{bmatrix} \delta_{j1} & 0 & 0 \\ 0 & \delta_{j2} & 0 \\ 0 & 0 & \delta_{j3} \end{bmatrix} \tag{6b}$$

in which, $\delta_{j1} > \delta_{j2} > \delta_{j3}$.

Then we have,

$$\frac{t_{j1}^2}{\delta_{j1}^2} + \frac{t_{j2}^2}{\delta_{j2}^2} + \frac{t_{j3}^2}{\delta_{j3}^2} = 1 \tag{7}$$

where t_{ji} is the components of the generalized-velocity array $\mathbf{j}$.

$$\begin{cases} t_{j1} = a_{j11} j_1 + a_{j12} j_2 + a_{j13} j_3 \\ t_{j2} = a_{j21} j_1 + a_{j22} j_2 + a_{j23} j_3 \\ t_{j3} = a_{j31} j_1 + a_{j32} j_2 + a_{j33} j_3 \end{cases} \tag{8}$$

The above equations shows that the three main axes of the velocity ellipsoid determine the velocity-transmission capability in the same directions. Different velocities at the center of the PM in light of the inputing unit velocity vector in different directions. Some produce faster motions, while others slower.

When the closer the velocity ellipsoid is to a sphere, the better the overall performance of the DTMLM is. Therefore, in order to evaluate the motion speed transmission performance of DTMLM, $\mathbf{k}$ is introducted to define the kinematics performance index as below. The smaller the $\mathbf{k}$ value, the better the kinematic performance.

$$\mathbf{k} = \begin{bmatrix} k_\omega \\ k_v \end{bmatrix} = \begin{bmatrix} \frac{\delta_{\omega 3}}{\delta_{\omega 1}} \\ \frac{\delta_{v 3}}{\delta_{v 1}} \end{bmatrix} \tag{9}$$

Equation (9) shows the speed-transfer ability at a specific posture thus being a local index. Here $\mathbf{k}_q$ is introduced to define the global kinematics performance index, for analyzing the overall velocity transfer capability of the DTMLM, as

$$\mathbf{k}_q = \begin{bmatrix} k_{q\omega} \\ k_{qv} \end{bmatrix} = \begin{bmatrix} \frac{\int_S k_\omega dS}{\int_S dS} \\ \frac{\int_S k_v dS}{\int_S dS} \end{bmatrix} \tag{10}$$

where S denotes the workspace of the DTMLM.

3.2   The Kinematics-Performance Atlas

The DTMLM possesses two independent parameters d_0 and r due to its kinematics model. The local and global kinematics-performance indexes are calculated and then plotted in Figs. 2 and 3, respectively.

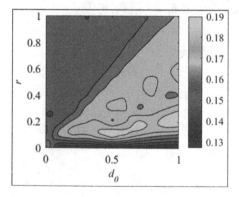

Fig. 2. The local kinematics-performance index

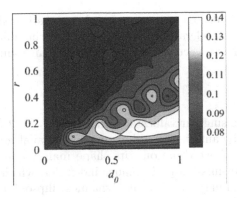

Fig. 3. The global kinematics-performance index

4 Dynamics Performance Index

4.1 The Generalized-Velocity Ellipsoid

From the dynamics model in our early work [2], we have

$$\mathbf{I}(\mathbf{q})\ddot{\mathbf{q}} = -\mathbf{C}(\mathbf{q},\dot{\mathbf{q}})\dot{\mathbf{q}} + \boldsymbol{\tau} + \boldsymbol{\delta} + \boldsymbol{\gamma} \tag{11}$$

in which,

$$\mathbf{I}(\mathbf{q}) = \mathbf{T}^{T}\mathbf{M}\mathbf{T} \in \mathbb{R}^{3\times3}$$
$$\mathbf{C}(\mathbf{q},\dot{\mathbf{q}}) = \mathbf{T}^{T}\mathbf{M}\dot{\mathbf{T}} + \mathbf{T}^{T}\mathbf{W}\mathbf{M}\mathbf{T} \in \mathbb{R}^{3\times3} \tag{12}$$
$$\boldsymbol{\tau} = \mathbf{T}^{T}\mathbf{w}^{A}, \boldsymbol{\delta} = \mathbf{T}^{T}\mathbf{w}^{D}, \boldsymbol{\gamma} = \mathbf{T}^{T}\mathbf{w}^{G}$$

where $\mathbf{M}$ denotes the 6×6 inertia dyad, $\mathbf{T}$ the 6×3 twist-shaping matrix [7];$\boldsymbol{\tau}$, $\boldsymbol{\delta}$, and $\boldsymbol{\gamma}$ denote the generalized actuated-, dissipative-, and gravity-force arrays, respectively.

Rewrite Eq. (11), the $\ddot{\mathbf{q}}$ is represented as

$$\ddot{\mathbf{q}} = -\mathbf{I}^{-1}\mathbf{C}\dot{\mathbf{q}} + \mathbf{I}^{-1}\boldsymbol{\tau} + \mathbf{I}^{-1}\boldsymbol{\delta} + \mathbf{I}^{-1}\boldsymbol{\gamma} \tag{13}$$

The DTMLM is expected to be used in space manipulations, thus the gravity and dissipative terms in the dynamics model playing negligible roles; in addition, the velocity term in the same model has less impact on the dynamics-transmission performance. To simplify the process, Eq. (13) is simplified as

$$\ddot{\mathbf{q}} = \mathbf{I}^{-1}\boldsymbol{\tau} \tag{14}$$

See the actuated-torque array as a unit vector, an n-dimensional unit sphere is obtained, i.e.,

$$\boldsymbol{\tau}^{T}\boldsymbol{\tau} = 1 \tag{15}$$

Then,

$$\ddot{\mathbf{q}}\boldsymbol{\tau}^{T}\boldsymbol{\tau}\ddot{\mathbf{q}} = 1 \tag{16}$$

The singular value decomposition of **I** is then substituted into the equation, and the set of output accelerations corresponding to the unit-joint-input torque are then obtained. These vectors, in turn, structure an n-dimensional ellipsoid. That is,

$$\frac{\mathbf{I}_1^2}{\sigma_1^2} + \frac{\mathbf{I}_2^2}{\sigma_2^2} + \frac{\mathbf{I}_3^2}{\sigma_3^2} = 1 \tag{17}$$

where σ_i denotes the singular values of **I**, in which, $i = 1, 2, 3$, $\sigma_1 > \sigma_2 > \sigma_3$.

Obviously, the dynamics ellipsoid is applied to analyze the dynamic performance. From the above equations, its shape mainly depends on the matrix **I**. The dynamics-transmission-performance index K_I, which obtained from the ratio of the minor and major axes of the dynamics ellipsoid, represents dynamics isotropy. That is,

$$K_I = \frac{\sigma_3}{\sigma_1} \tag{18}$$

The smaller the K_I, the better the dynamics-transmission performance of the mechanism. However, K_I represents the dynamics-transmission ability of the mechanism in a specific posture thus being a local index. In order to analyze the overall dynamics performance of the DTMLM, the global dynamics-performance index K_{Iq} is introduced, as

$$K_{Iq} = \frac{\int_S k_I dS}{\int_S dS} \tag{19}$$

4.2   The Dynamics-Performance Atlas

The DTMLM possesses two independent parameters d_0 and r due to its dynamics and kinematics models. The local and global dynamics-performance indexes are calculated and then plotted in Figs. 4 and 5, respectively.

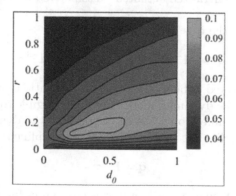

Fig. 4. The local dynamics-performance index

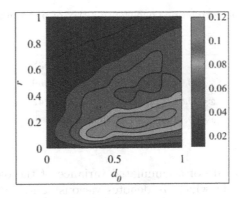

Fig. 5. The global dynamics-performance index

5 Multi-objective Optimization

The original data is standardized by the Z-Score method, as shown in Table 1. The specific value of the correlation coefficient matrix is calculated and put in Table 2. The greater the relationship between the phase, the stronger the correlation. It can be seen that x_3 and x_4 have more correlation, and while x_1 and x_2 less.

Table 1. The standardized data of performance indicators.

Serial number	x_1	x_2	x_3	x_4
1	0.5426	−0.6443	−0.2382	−0.8271
2	−0.8145	−0.7752	0.0818	−0.5039
3	−0.8181	−0.8013	−0.1344	−0.6264
⋮	⋮	⋮	⋮	⋮
120	0.7932	−0.1718	−0.2861	−0.1888
121	0.5428	−0.6443	−0.5745	−0.5719

Derivative and calculate the characteristic value and vector of correlation coefficient matrix **R**. The characteristic value shows the contribution rate of the matrix on the characteristic vector. Thus, a comprehensive performance index is introduced. The number of main components is determined according to the accumulated variance contribution rate of the characteristic value. Generally, it is greater than or equal to 85%. The contribution rate of the accumulated variance of the main component of K is

$$M_i = \frac{\sum_{i=1}^{p} \lambda_i}{\sum_{j=1}^{p} \lambda_j} \qquad (20)$$

Table 2. The correlation coefficient matrix of performance index.

	x_1	x_2	x_3	x_4
x_1	1	0.6415	0.8178	0.7438
x_2	0.6415	1	0.7632	0.7969
x_3	0.8178	0.7632	1	0.9242
x_4	0.7438	0.7969	0.9242	1

The contribution rate of accumulated variance of the owner component is as shown in Table 3, in which a_1 denotes various contribution rate, while a_2 cumulative component contribution rate. Among them, the variance rate of the first main component is 83.75%, which is less than 85%, which is not met to determine the main component conditions; The main component is two. Obviously, the first two main ingredients represent all indicators. The unit feature vector is seen as the indicator for representation of the first and the second main components. The contribution rate then is used as the coefficient of each main component. Thus, the evaluation equation of the indicator is:

Table 3. The calculation results.

Eigenvalues	Unit characteristic vector	a_1	a_2
3.3501	[0.4771, 0.4767, 0.525, 0.5191]	0.8375	0.8375
0.3684	[0.7022, −0.6883, 0.1211, −0.1358]	0.0921	0.9296
0.217	[−0.4971, −0.5417, 0.4094, 0.5403]	0.0543	0.9839
0.0645	[−0.1793, 0.0745, 0.7363, −0.6482]	0.0161	1

$$F = 0.4643K + 0.3359K_q + 0.4508K_I + 0.4223K_{Iq} \tag{21}$$

Based on the analysis above, the relationship between the comprehensive-evaluation-performance indicator and the structure parameter d_0 and r is finally plotted in Fig. 6.

As shown in Fig. 6, the points with excellent-comprehensive-evaluation indicators are concentrated on the top left, although individual unsuitable inferiority appears at the bottom. Particularly, each point in the phase-wide domain is equivalent, thereby working conditions should be considered in the design process. For the DTMLM for space manipulations, $r = 3d_0$ is applied according to the multi-objective optimization in this paper.

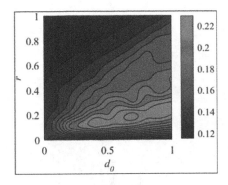

Fig. 6. The comprehensive evaluation performance index

6 Conclusions

Based on the kinematics and dynamics analysis in our early works, this paper established the kinematics- and dynamics-transmission-performance, and the corresponding global indicators of the DTMLM. The performance maps are plotted, to indicate the relationship between the link parameters and the performance indicators, which lays the foundation for the optimization of multi-objective parameters.

The correlation of various indicators are analyzed through the main component analysis method and the performance pictures, thereby obtaining the weight coefficient. The diagram of comprehensive evaluation indicators is henceforth obtained. Therefore, the multi-objective optimization of the DTMLM is finished, as well as, a set of structural parameters of the same mechanism are preferred.

References

1. Li, C., Guo, H., Tang, D., Yan, H., Liu, R., Deng, Z.: A 3-R(SRS)RP multi-loop mechanism for space manipulation: Design, kinematics, singularity, and workspace," ASME Tans. J. Mech. Robot. **12**(1) (2020)
2. Li, C., et al.: On the actuation modes of a multiloop mechanism for space applications. IEEE/ASME Trans. Mechatron. (2022). https://doi.org/10.1109/TMECH.2021.3121723
3. Hamida, I.B., Laribi, M.A., Mlika, A., Romdhane, L., Zeghloul, S., Carbone, G.: Multi-objective optimal design of a cable driven parallel robot for rehabilitation tasks. Mech. Mach. Theory **156**, 104141 (2021)
4. Venkateswaran, S., Chablat, D., Hamon, P.: An optimal design of a flexible piping inspection robot. J. Mech Robot. **13**(3) (2021)
5. Wang, R., Li, Y.: Analysis and multi-objective optimal design of a planar differentially driven cable parallel robot. Robotica **39**(12), 2193–2209 (2021)
6. Li, C., et al.: Mobility and singularity analyses of a symmetric multi-loop mechanism for space applications. Proc. Inst. Mech. Eng. C J. Mech. Eng. Sci. **235**(22), 6205–6218 (2021)
7. Angeles, J.: Fundamentals of robotic mechanical systems. Springer (2002). https://doi.org/10.1007/978-0-387-22458-9_4

Mechanism Design, Control and Application of Reconfigurable Robots

A Flexible Rod-Driven Multimode Spatial Variable Geometry Truss Manipulator for Morphing Wings

Yingzhong Tian[1,2], Xiangping Yu[1,2], Long Li[1,2], Wenbin Wang[3], and Jieyu Wang[1,2(✉)]

[1] School of Mechatronic Engineering and Automation, Shanghai University, Shanghai, China
jywang2021@shu.edu.cn

[2] Shanghai Key Laboratory of Intelligent Manufacturing and Robotics, Shanghai University, Shanghai, China

[3] School of Mechanical and Electrical Engineering, Shenzhen Polytechnic, Shenzhen, China

Abstract. In this paper, a flexible rod-driven VGTM for morphing wings is designed. The mechanism contains two parts: flexible parallel mechanism and VGTM. The flexible drive reduces the drives' number and weight of the mechanism. The VGTM not only reduces the weight of the mechanism but also simplifies the control model. The mechanism can realize multiple deformations including span length, sweep, dihedral and wingtip. It has the advantages of simple structure, light weight, simple control method and many deformation methods. We analyze the degrees of freedom of the mechanism using the screw theory, which demonstrates the deformation ability of the mechanism. The kinematic modeling and control strategy analysis were completed, which demonstrates the feasibility and advantages of this mechanism for morphing wings. And the deformation mode and prototype of the mechanism are also presented in this paper.

Keywords: Parallel mechanism · VGTM · Morphing wings · DOF · Kinematic

1 Introduction

The adoption of morphing wings can greatly improve the flight performance of the aircraft and achieve various mission requirements. Morphing concepts can be categorized into: a) wing plane deformation, including span, sweep [1, 2], b) wing off-plane deformation, including twist, dihedral and wingtip [3–5] and c) airfoil deformation, including chord, thickness and bend [6–8].

Since the morphing wings have many advantages, scholars have studied them extensively. R.M. Ajaj et al. adopted the gear rack structure (traditional mechanical structure) to achieve wing span length changes, effectively improving the cruise time of the aircraft [9]. Traditional mechanical structures have the advantages of large bearing capability and convenient driving approach, but they have large weight and limited deformation mode. Thomas Georges et al. used a memory alloy to drive the crank mechanism, thereby changing the wing thickness [10]. Smart materials (such as shape memory alloy) and

H. Liu et al. (Eds.): ICIRA 2022, LNAI 13455, pp. 529–540, 2022.
https://doi.org/10.1007/978-3-031-13844-7_50

flexible mechanisms have the advantage of lightweight, but their carrying capacity are very weak. The Variable geometry truss manipulator (VGTM) was also used in the morphing wing field [11]. It has the advantages of lightweight and strong carrying capacity, but requires a multitude of drives and complex control models. Especially when the VGTM is used to realize the continuous deformation of multiple mechanisms, its disadvantages are more obvious. Therefore, this paper takes the adaptive VGTM as the wing skeleton to achieve a large wing carrying capacity with a lighter weight. Meanwhile, the flexible rod driven mode is adopted to reduce the number of drives and the control difficulty.

The flexible rod-driven VGTM has the advantages of lightweight, small number of drives and simple drive mode. On the premise of ensuring the wing bearing, it can realize multiple deformations including span length, sweep, dihedral and wingtip. As shown in Fig. 1, several deformation units can be installed inside the wing. The more deformation units, the greater deformation of the wing can achieve.

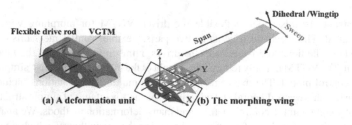

Fig. 1. Morphing wing and deformation unit

2   Structure Description

Each deformation unit contains two parts: flexible drive parallel mechanism and VGTM, as shown in Fig. 2(a). Figure 2(b) is a model of the deformation unit. The structural composition of these two parts is detailed in Fig. 2(c) and Fig. 2(d).

The flexible rods are firmly attached to the moving platform and connected to the base by the roller, as shown in Fig. 2(c). The flexible rod passes through the base and is driven by a linear motor. The position and posture of the moving platform can be controlled by changing the extension length of the flexible rods and the length difference between the rods, so as to achieve the purpose of morphing.

As shown in Fig. 2(d), VGTM consists of 8 branches (i. e., 8-UPU parallel mechanism), each branch chain is connected to the corresponding two platforms through the U pair (Hooke joint), and the P pair (prismatic pair) on the branch chain can be locked. Unlocking specific P pair can make the mechanism have the deformation ability. After the deformation is completed, lock the P pair to bear the large load. The eight clades of the VGTM form four planes, with three branches within each plane. For example, the branches 1, 2, and 3 are in one plane. Because the triangle structure is stable and has good carrying capacity, the center of adjacent U pairs in this paper coincides at one point, so that each plane is composed of two triangles. For the convenience of description, in

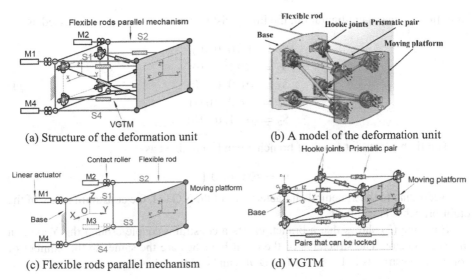

(a) Structure of the deformation unit

(b) A model of the deformation unit

(c) Flexible rods parallel mechanism

(d) VGTM

Fig. 2. Structure of the VGTM driven by flexible rods

the later section, the four planes are referred to as unit 1 (including branches 1,2, and 3), unit 2 (including branches 3,4, and 5), unit 3 (including branches 5,6, and 7), and unit 4 (including branches 7,8, and 1).

3   Degree of Freedom and Control Analysis

In this section, the screw theory is used to analyze the degree of freedom (DOF) of the rigid parallel mechanism, as shown in Fig. 3.

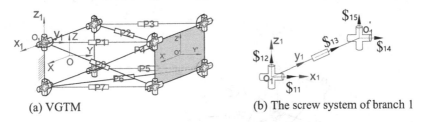

(a) VGTM

(b) The screw system of branch 1

Fig. 3. Degree of freedom analysis

A branch has two U-pairs and a P-pair. The U pair has two rotation screws, and the P pair has a translation screw. The coordinate system is established shown in Fig. 3(b), the origin is at the central point of the U pair, x_1 axis and z_1 axis are parallel to the first and second rotation axes of U pair respectively, and the y_1 axis follows the right-hand rule. In the general configuration, the limb twist system of branch 1 is expressed as

$$\begin{aligned}
\$_1 &= (1\,0\,0;\,0\,0\,0)\\
\$_2 &= (0\,0\,1;\,0\,0\,0)\\
\$_3 &= (0\,0\,0;\,0\,e_3\,0)\\
\$_4 &= (1\,0\,0;\,0\,0\,f_4)\\
\$_5 &= (0\,0\,1;\,d_5\,0\,0)
\end{aligned} \tag{1}$$

The limb constraint screw of branch 1 can be obtained as

$$\$_1^r = (0\,0\,0;\,0\,1\,0) \tag{2}$$

According to the structural characteristics of the VGTM, the constraint screw of the eight branches is identical.

Equation (2) shows that a branch exerts a constraint couple around the Y-axis on the end-effector. The structures of the eight branches are the same, so the number of common constraints is $1(\lambda = 1)$. The DOF can be obtained as

$$M = d(n - g - 1) + \sum_{i=1}^{8} f_i + v - \xi = 5 \tag{3}$$

The d, n, g, f_i, v and ξ respectively represent the order of mechanism ($d = 6-\lambda$), the number of members including the base ($n = 18$), the number of moving pairs ($g = 24$), the sum of DOF of moving pairs of branch i ($f_i = 5$), the number of parallel redundancy constraints ($v = \sum_{1}^{p} q_i - \lambda \cdot p - k = 8 - 8 - 0 = 0$, q_i represent the number of constraints of branch i, p are the number of branches, k is the order of the constraint screw in addition to the common constraint), and ξ is the passive DOF ($\xi = 0$).

The DOF needs to be checked because that the screw theory and the modified G-K formula based on the theory have the instantaneous characteristic [12].

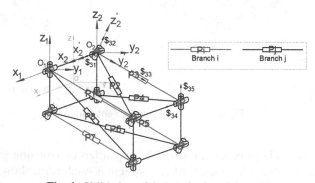

Fig. 4. Validation of the continuity of the DOF

Next, we perform the DOF analysis of the VGTM in special cases. As shown in Fig. 4, we assume that the mechanism has a limited displacement along the Z-axis.

The coordinate system of some branches will deflect, because the x and y axes of each branch coordinate system are always parallel to the two rotation axes of the U pair. For example, in Fig. 4, the coordinate system o_2-$x_2y_2z_2$ transforms into the coordinate system o_2-$x'_2y'_2z'_2$. Therefore, the DOF of the VGTM may change. In the respective frame, the constraint screw of branches can be obtained as

$$\$^r_i = (-b_{i5}\,0\,0;\,0\,d_{i5}\,0)$$
$$\$^r_j = (0\ \ 0\,0;\,0\,1\,0) \tag{4}$$

Equation (4) shows that branches i ($i = 1,3,5,7$) exert a constraint force which is parallel to the Xi-axis on the moving platform [12]. And branches j ($j = 2,4,6,8$) exert a constraint couple which is parallel to the Yi-axis on the moving platform.

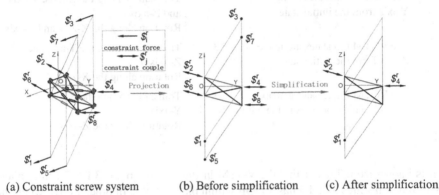

(a) Constraint screw system   (b) Before simplification   (c) After simplification

Fig. 5. Simplification of the constraint screw system

The constraint screw system of the mechanism is shown in Fig. 5(a) and (b), the constraint force $\$_i{}^r$ is perpendicular to plane O-YZ and the constraint couple $\$_j{}^r$ is parallel to plane O-YZ. Because two parallel constraint forces can be equivalent to a combination of a force and couple [12], the constraint screw system can be regarded to one constraint force and two constraint couples as shown in Fig. 5 (c), which are linearly independent ($k = 1 + 2 = 3$). Therefore, the number of common constraints is 0 ($\lambda = 0$) and the number of parallel redundancy constraints is 5 ($v = \sum_1^p q_i - \lambda \cdot p - k = 8 - 0 - 3 = 5$).

The DOF can be obtained as

$$M = d(n - g - 1) + \sum_{i=1}^{g} f_i + v - \xi = 6 \times (18 - 24 - 1) + 40 + 5 - 0 = 3 \tag{5}$$

At this time, the mechanism can translate along the Y axis, the Z axis and rotate around the X axis. The DOF of the mechanism is discontinuous, and the movements in different configurations are shown in Table 1.

Table 1. DOF of the VGTM in different states

Order	The state of the VGTM	DOF	Types of DOF
1	In the initial state	5	Translation along the X-axis, Y-axis and Z-axis Rotation along the X-zxis and Z-axis
2	The VGTM translates along the X-axis from the initial state	3	Translation along the X-axis and Y-axis Rotation along the Z-axis
3	The VGTM rotates along an axis parallel to the X-axis from the initial state	3	Translation along the Y-axis and Z-axis Rotation along the X-zxis
4	The VGTM translates along the Y-axis from the initial state	5	Translation along the X-axis, Y-axis and Z-axis Rotation along the X-zxis and Z-axis
5	The VGTM translates along the Z-axis from the initial state	3	Translation along the Y-axis and Z-axis Rotation along the X-zxis
6	The VGTM rotates along an axis parallel to the Z-axis from the initial state	3	Translation along the X-axis and Y-axis Rotation along the Z-axis

It is known from Table 1 that the VGTM in states 2 and 6 has 3 DOF within plane O-XY, and it in states 3 and 5 has 3 DOF within plane O-YZ. In other words, when the VGTM moves in one plane (the two U-pairs on each branch are no longer parallel), the movement to the other plane is constrained. This characteristic enables the mechanism to resist the load from another plane direction after deformation in one plane.

As mentioned above, the VGTM has 3 or 5 % of freedom in different states. The DOF of the deformation unit depends on the VGTM. The actuation of the four flexible rods is actually changing the length of the four limbs of the VGTM. The maximum DOF of the deformation unit is 5 (when VGTM is in states 1 and 4 in Table 1). Therefore, specific P pairs of 8 branches should be locked during the deformation. The DOF analysis of

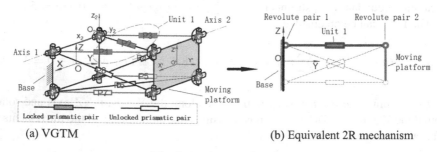

(a) VGTM   (b) Equivalent 2R mechanism

Fig. 6. Equivalent of VGTM

the VGTM in different locking states can explain how to control the mechanism with 4 drive rods.

As shown in Fig. 6(a), if the P pair of the unit 1 is locked, the constraint screw system of unit 1 in the o_2-$x_2y_2z_2$ frame can be obtained as

$$\$_1^r = (0\ 0\ 0;\ 0\ 1\ 0)$$
$$\$_2^r = (0\ 1\ 0;\ 0\ 0\ 0)$$
$$\$_3^r = (0\ 1\ 0;\ 0\ 0\ f_1) \tag{6}$$
$$\$_4^r = (\frac{-e_{24}}{\sqrt{d_{24}^2 + e_{24}^2}}\ \frac{d_{24}}{\sqrt{d_{24}^2 + e_{24}^2}}\ 0\ ;\ 000)$$

The reverse screw system of the constraint screw system is as follows.

$$\$_1^{rr} = (1\ 0\ 0;\ 0\ 0\ 0)$$
$$\$_2^{rr} = (0\ 0\ 0;\ 0\ 0\ 1) \tag{7}$$

According to Eq. (7), if the locking unit 1, the DOF of VGTM is 2. In this state, the platform is able to rotate around the x_2-axis and translate along the z_2-axis. By analyzing the structural characteristics, it is not difficult to find that the two U pairs connected to the base can only rotate around the axis 1, and the two U pairs connected to the moving platform can only rotate around the axis 2. At this time, the two groups of U pairs become two R pairs with rotation axes parallel to each other, so that the VGTM can be equivalent to a 2R mechanism by projecting to the coordinate planes, as shown in Fig. 6 (b).

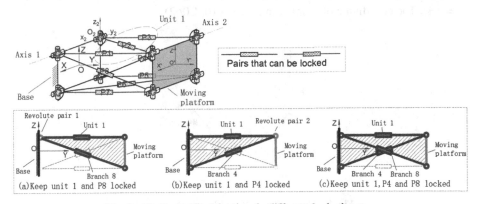

Fig. 7. Equivalent mechanism in different locked states

The DOF of VGTM is 1 in the state shown in Fig. 7(a) and (b), and it can rotate around the rotational axis 1 and 2, respectively. When the unit 1, P7 and P8 are locked, the VGTM is a statically determinate truss in the O-YZ plane (DOF = 0). Similarly, the equivalent mechanisms can be obtained by locking other units and corresponding rods. In summary, the VGTM can be effectively controlled by 4 actuators.

4 Kinematic Modeling and Control Strategy Analysis

Through the analysis of the DOF and control mode of the mechanism, we can see that the mechanism can only deform in a plane, so we just need to establish the kinematic modeling in the plane. This section takes the deformation in the plane O-YZ as an example.

4.1 Kinematic Modeling

When the flexible rods are active, the relationship between the moving distance of rods and the pose of the end-effector should be established to control the enclosed mechanism. Since the movement of rods is related to its own large nonlinear deformation, it is difficult to build a kinematic model used for real-time control by using the deformation governing equations of the flexible members, especially for the mechanisms with multiple flexible members in a parallel structure.

Therefore, a simplified approximate kinematic model can be established based on the constant curvature assumption (i.e., the virtual middle backbone between soft panels follows an arc shape) to compute the moving distance of rods [13]. The constant curvature method is a common method for modeling the motion of the continuum/soft robot whose mobility is fully or partly realized by the nonlinear deformation of soft members. The method is adopted here to establish the relationship between the extended length of soft rods (s_i, s_j) and the pose of the moving platform (y_m, z_m, α).

In the previous study [14], we have completed the constant curvature kinematics modeling of the plane mechanism, and the results are shown below ($s_i = s1 = s2$, $s_j = s3 = s4$). The coordinate of point O in Fig. 8 is (0, $L0/2$).

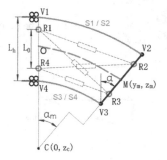

Fig. 8. Constant curvature kinematics modeling

$$(0, z_c) = (0, \frac{y_m^2 + z_m^2 - L_0/4}{2z_m - L_0}) \tag{8}$$

$$\begin{cases} s_i = \frac{1}{2}L_h\alpha + (\frac{L_0}{2} - z_c)\arctan(\frac{y_m}{z_m - z_c}) \\ s_j = -\frac{1}{2}L_h\alpha + (\frac{L_0}{2} - z_c)\arctan(\frac{y_m}{z_m - z_c}) \end{cases} \tag{9}$$

Accurate closed-loop control can be achieved by installing sensors in the mechanism joint to detect and adjust the position of the manipulator in real time. The pose of the moving platform can be controlled by detecting the position of the branches in the plane.

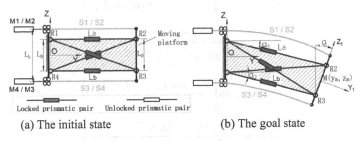

(a) The initial state   (b) The goal state

Fig. 9. Branch control model

As shown in Fig. 9, the length of branches La, Lb and the angles (α_1, α_2) with the Y-axis can be detected in real time by displacement sensors and angle sensors (La, Lb correspond to unit 1 and 3 in Sect. 2 respectively). The positions of La and Lb (L_a, L_b, α_1, α_2) correspond one-to-one to the positions of the moving platform (y_m, z_m, α). M is the central point of the moving platform and α is the angle with the Z-axis.

Therefore, we only need to establish the equation relationship between (L_a, L_b, α_1, α_2) and (y_m, z_m, α) to achieve accurate closed-loop control of the manipulator.

In Fig. 9 (b), the homogeneous transformation matrix from the coordinate system O-YZ to the coordinate system M-Y_1Z_1 is as follows.

$$
{}^O_M T = \begin{bmatrix} 1 & 0 & 0 & 0 \\ 0 & \cos\alpha & -\sin\alpha & y_m \\ 0 & \sin\alpha & \cos\alpha & z_m \\ 0 & 0 & 0 & 1 \end{bmatrix} \tag{10}
$$

The equation of the homogeneous transformation of point R2 and R3 can be obtained as

$$
\begin{aligned}
{}^O R_2 &= {}^O_M T {}^M R_2 \\
{}^O R_3 &= {}^O_M T {}^M R_3
\end{aligned} \tag{11}
$$

i.e.,

$$
\begin{bmatrix} 0 \\ L_a \cdot \cos\alpha_1 \\ \frac{L_0}{2} - L_a \cdot \sin\alpha_1 \\ 1 \end{bmatrix} = \begin{bmatrix} 1 & 0 & 0 & 0 \\ 0 & \cos\alpha & -\sin\alpha & y_m \\ 0 & \sin\alpha & \cos\alpha & z_m \\ 0 & 0 & 0 & 1 \end{bmatrix} \begin{bmatrix} 0 \\ 0 \\ \frac{L_0}{2} \\ 1 \end{bmatrix}
$$

$$
\begin{bmatrix} 0 \\ L_b \cdot \cos\alpha_2 \\ -\frac{L_0}{2} - L_b \cdot \sin\alpha_2 \\ 1 \end{bmatrix} = \begin{bmatrix} 1 & 0 & 0 & 0 \\ 0 & \cos\alpha & -\sin\alpha & y_m \\ 0 & \sin\alpha & \cos\alpha & z_m \\ 0 & 0 & 0 & 1 \end{bmatrix} \begin{bmatrix} 0 \\ 0 \\ -\frac{L_0}{2} \\ 1 \end{bmatrix} \tag{12}
$$

According to Eq. (12), the equation relationship between $(L_a, L_b, \alpha_1, \alpha_2)$ and (y_m, z_m, α) can be obtained as

$$\alpha_1 = \arctan\left[\frac{L_0 \cdot (1 - \cos\alpha) - 2z_m}{L_0 \cdot (1 - \sin\alpha) + 2y_m}\right]$$

$$L_a = \frac{y_1 - \sin\alpha \cdot \frac{L_0}{2}}{\cos\left\{\arctan\left[\frac{L_0 \cdot (1-\cos\alpha) - 2z_m}{L_0 \cdot (1-\sin\alpha) + 2y_m}\right]\right\}}$$

$$\alpha_2 = \arctan\left[\frac{L_0 \cdot (\cos\alpha - 1) - 2z_m}{L_0 \cdot \sin\alpha + 2y_m}\right]$$

$$L_b = \frac{\sin\alpha \cdot L_0 + 2y_m}{2\cos\left\{\arctan\left[\frac{L_0 \cdot (\cos\alpha - 1) - 2z_m}{L_0 \cdot \sin\alpha + 2y_m}\right]\right\}} \tag{13}$$

Using the same method, the mechanism control model in the O-XY plane can also be solved, which will not be described in this paper to avoid repetition.

4.2 Control Strategy

Kinematic modeling of the mechanism has been completed in Sect. 4.1, and the control strategies are analyzed in this section.

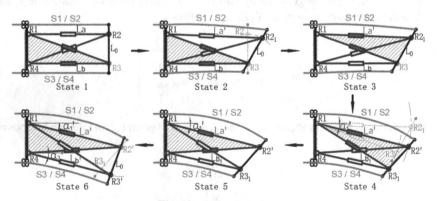

Fig. 10. Control strategy

As shown in Fig. 10, the mechanism needs to be deformed from state 1 to state 6, and the position parameter of the target state is $(L_a', L_b', \alpha_1', \alpha_2')$. In state 1, the triangle R1-R3-R4 is locked and the driver drives the moving platform to rotate around R3 with a radius of L_0 so that L_a becomes the target length L_a' in state 2 (If S1 and S2 elongate, and S3 and S4 shorten, L_a will elongate, and in turn L_a will shorten). As shown in state 3, after L_a reaches the target length L_a', the triangle R1-R2$_1$-R3 is locked, and the length of L_a' no longer changes. As shown in state 4, the triangle R1-R2$_1$-R3 rotates around R1 driven by the flexible rod so that the rod L_a' reaches the target angle α_1' (if S1, S2 elongate and S3 and S4 shorten, the triangle R1-R2$_1$-R3 rotates clockwise, and in turn the triangle will rotate counterclockwise). As shown in state 5, when the rod L_a' reaches the target angle α_1', the triangle R1-R2'-R4 is locked and α_1' will not change anymore. In state 6, the flexible rod drives the moving platform to rotate around R2' to control the position of L_b' to the target state. When both L_a and L_b reach the target position, all the branches are locked, so that the mechanism has a large bearing capacity. Similarly, we can first control L_b to reach the target length L_b' and the target angle α_2' by locking the triangles R1-R2-R4 and R2-R3-R4, respectively, and then actuate L_a to reach the target pose.

Through the above steps, we can control the rods La and Lb, and thus control the pose of the moving platform. If the deformation is large and the first round of deformation cannot reach the target state, the above steps need to be repeated. Due to the limited space of the paper, this situation will be analyzed in our future work.

5   The Prototype and Deformation Mode

As shown in Table 2, different forms of deformation can be realized by changing the mounting position and deformation plane of the deformation unit on the wing. The green section in the deformation model represents the mounting position. The prototype shows deformations in different planes.

Table 2. The prototype and deformation mode.

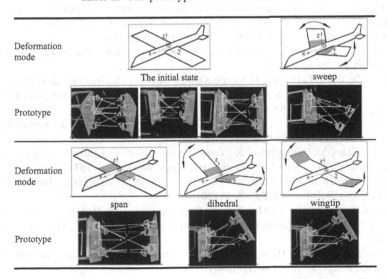

6   Conclusion

In this paper, a flexible rod-driven VGTM for morphing wing has been designed. First, the deformation ability of the mechanism has been demonstrated by the degree-of-freedom analysis. Second, the kinematic and control strategy analysis has been completed. Finally, the deformation form and the prototype have been presented.

The flexible rod driving approach reduces the drives' number and weight of the mechanism. The VGTM is adopted on the premise of ensuring carrying. It not only reduces the weight of the mechanism but also simplifies the control model. The mechanism enables the wing to achieve multiple deformations including sweep, span, dihedral, and wingtip.

In the future, we will analyze the multi-segment deformation unit and the multi-step deformation strategy, and we will also complete the driving force analysis and parameter optimization.

Acknowledgement. The authors acknowledge for the funding from National Natural Science Foundation of China (No. 52105002).

References

1. Vale, J., et al.: Aero-structural optimization and performance evaluation of a morphing wing with variable span and camber. J. Intell. Mater. Syst. Struct. **22**(10), 1057–1073 (2011)
2. Chen, S., et al.: Numerical simulation on the radar cross section of variable-sweep wing aircraft. J. Aerosp. Technol. Manag. **7**(2), 170–178 (2015)
3. Jenett, B., et al.: Digital morphing wing: active wing shaping concept using composite lattice-based cellular structures. Soft Rob. **4**(1), 33–48 (2017)
4. Lazos, B.S., Visser, K.D.: Aerodynamic comparison of Hyper-Elliptic cambered span (HECS) Wings with conventional configurations. In: Proceedings of the 24th Applied Aerodynamics Conference 2006, pp. 3469. AIAA, San Francisco, CA (2006)
5. Xiaoyu, C., et al.: Design and analysis of wingtip of variant vehicle. Journal of Modern Machinery **04**, 59–63 (2021)
6. Perkins, D., Reed, J., Havens, J.: Morphing wing structures for loitering air vehicles. In: 45th AIAA/ASME/ASCE/AHS/ASC Structures, Structural Dynamics & Materials Conference 2004, p. 1888. AIAA, USA (2004)
7. Brailovski, V., Terriault, P., Georges, T., Coutu, D.: SMA Actuators for Morphing Wings. Phys. Procedia **10**, 197–203 (2010)
8. Sen, M., Chao, Y., Changchuan, X., Yang, M.: Design of rigid variable wing and design of rigid variable wing. Journal of Vibration and Shock **40**(21), 157–167 (2021)
9. Ajaj, R.M., Friswell, M.I., Bourchak, M., Harasani, W.: Span morphing using the GNATSpar wing. Aerosp. Sci. Technol. **53**, 38–46 (2016)
10. Georges, T., Brailovski, V., Morellon, E., Coutu, D., Terriault, P.: Design of shape memory alloy actuators for morphing laminar wing with flexible extrados. J. Mech. Des. **131**, 1–9 (2009)
11. Moosavian, A., Xi, F., Hashemi, S.M.X.: Design and Motion Control of Fully Variable Morphing Wings. J. Aircr. **50**(4), 1189–1201 (2021)
12. Huang, Z., Liu, J., Li, Y.: Discuss the degrees of freedom of mechanism. Science Press, BeiJing (2011)
13. Webster, R.J., Jones, B.A.: Design and kinematic modeling of constant curvature continuum robots: a review. Int. J. Robot. Res **29**(13), 1661–1683 (2010)
14. Xi, F., Zhao, Y., Wang, J., Wang, W., Tian, Y.: Two actuation methods for a complete morphing system composed of a VGTM and a compliant parallel mechanism. J. Mech. Robot. **13**(2), 1–39 (2021)

Obstacle Avoidance Planning and Experimental Study of Reconfigurable Cable-Driven Parallel Robot Based on Deep Reinforcement Learning

Xu Wang, Yuan Li$^{(\boxtimes)}$, Bin Zi, Qingjun Wu, and Jiahao Zhao

Hefei University of Technology, Hefei 230000, China
yuanli@hfut.edu.cn

Abstract. Cable-driven parallel robot (CDPR) is widely used in the fields of hoisting and cargo handling. However, it is very easy to be interfered with and restricted by obstacles in the space, which affects the working performance of the robot. This paper takes the reconfigurable cable-driven parallel robot (RCDPR) as the research object and adopts deep reinforcement learning (DRL) to solve the obstacle avoidance planning problem. The model of RCDPR is structured, and kinematic analysis is performed to obtain the state transform function. An improved Soft AC algorithm is employed by expected SARSA and adaptive target values, which enhances the utilization of samples. An environment for RCDPR obstacle avoidance tasks is built, and then the improved Soft AC algorithm is used to train the robot to avoid obstacles in the environment. Finally, the simulation and experimental study of the paths and trajectories generated by the policy neural network are performed to verify the feasibility and effectiveness of the proposed algorithm. The results show that RCDPR can realize autonomous planning and intelligent obstacle avoidance by DRL.

Keywords: Cable-driven parallel robot · Reconfigurable · Deep reinforcement learning · Obstacle avoidance planning

1 Introduction

The cable-driven parallel robot (CDPR) uses multiple flexible cables to coordinately control the motion state of the end effector instead of rigid links. In recent years, CDPRs have achieved many successful applications in the engineering field due to the advantages of large workspace, reconfiguration, small inertia, and high payload to weight ratio [1]. The cables of a CDPR are easily interfered with by obstacles in the workspace because they can only bear the tensile force and are widely distributed in the workspace. The problem of obstacle avoidance planning for CDPRs has become particularly important and has been widely concerned and researched, especially in the field of palletizing and hoisting [2].

Lahouar et al. [3] proposed a path-planning method for a 4-cable-driven parallel manipulator which has two planning modes. When the robot is far from an obstacle, it moves toward the goal straightly, otherwise the robot moves around the obstacle. Bak

© The Author(s), under exclusive license to Springer Nature Switzerland AG 2022
H. Liu et al. (Eds.): ICIRA 2022, LNAI 13455, pp. 541–551, 2022.
https://doi.org/10.1007/978-3-031-13844-7_51

et al. [4] employed three steps to perform path planning of CDPRs with obstacles. They visualized the actual workspace of CDPRs firstly. Then they found a feasible path by a modified RRT algorithm. Finally, they made the path shorter and less winding with a post-processing algorithm. The above are all researches on obstacle avoidance planning in the workspace of CDPRs with a fixed configuration. In some cases, no feasible path exists when the process points or the goal point are not in the workspace. Therefore, some scholars study obstacle avoidance planning by flexibly changing the configuration and workspace of CDPRs.

Gagliardini et al. [5] designed a kind of RCDPRs whose cable connection points on the base frame can be positioned at a large but discrete set of possible locations. For different situations, different robotic configurations can be selected to plan an obstacle avoidance path. However, the different configurations are discrete and cannot be changed during the movement of RCDPRs. To obtain better obstacles avoidance capability, Qian et al. [6] proposed a kind of modular CDPRs, which can be reconfigured to several configurations continuously. This approach increases the flexibility of the robot but requires repetitive manual planning for different obstacle avoidance tasks. As above, RCDPRs have advantages in obstacle avoidance and need an intelligent algorithm to realize automatic planning.

Deep reinforcement learning (DRL) is considered to be the most likely learning paradigm to achieve autonomous learning of complex behaviors, which is very suitable for dealing with time series decision-making problems [7]. For the past few years, DRL algorithms and applications have developed rapidly [8, 9]. Haarnoja et al. [10] came up with soft actor critic (Soft AC) algorithm based on maximum entropy theory, improved the convergence, and verified in a quadruped robot. Target at sparse reward in robot tasks, Andrychowicz et al. [11] proposed hindsight experience replay (HER) trick to generate successful experiences by amending the target points in the failed experiences. This method avoids manually designing complex reward functions.

In this paper, an improved soft AC algorithm is proposed and applied to the obstacle avoidance planning of the RCDPR with HER for the robot to learn to generate motion paths under different states and obstacles automatically. The structure of RCDPR is described and kinematic analysis is completed in Sect. 2. In Sect. 3, a modified algorithm is proposed based on the improvements of Soft AC and enhances the utilization of samples. The obstacle avoidance planning task is constructed, and the training of neural networks is completed in Sect. 4. Then the obstacle avoidance experiment is conducted. Finally, the conclusions are summarized in Sect. 5.

2   Structure Description and Kinematic Analysis

The model of the RCDPR is shown in Fig. 1, which mainly consists of a circular orbit, three mobile modules, three flexible cables, and an end-effector. Every mobile module is made up of a pillar, a cable drum, pulleys, and two servomotors. The mobile modules can rotate along a circular trajectory on the circular orbit and change the configuration of the robot by mobile servomotors. For each cable, one end is rolled in a drum, and the other end connects the end-effector directly through pulleys. Under the end-effector's gravity, its position will be changed when cable drums adjust the length of cables by cable servomotors.

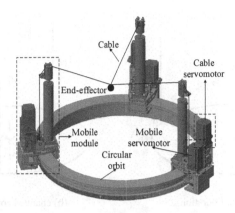

Fig. 1. 3D model of the RCDPR

The schematic diagram of RCDPR is shown in Fig. 2. A global coordinate frame O-XYZ is attached to the center of the circular orbit. The ratio of the orbit is set to 0.65 m and the height of pillars is set to 0.8 m. In the initial configuration three mobile modules are evenly distributed on the circular orbit and module 1 is in the positive direction of the X-axis. θ_1, θ_2, and θ_3 separately denote three angular displacements of mobile modules.

The inverse kinematics equation of the RCDPR can be expressed as Eq. (1).

$$l_i = \left\| \overrightarrow{EA_i} \right\|_2 = \left\| \overrightarrow{OA_i} - \overrightarrow{OE} \right\|_2, \, i = 1, 2, 3 \tag{1}$$

where l_i represents the length of cables. $A_i = \left[\text{Rcon}(\theta_i + \theta_i^0) \; \text{Rsin}(\theta_i + \theta_i^0) \; H \right]^T$ respectively indicate the coordinates of cable exit points of the pulleys anchored on the frame, in which $\theta_i^0 = 2\pi(i-1)/3$. And $E = \left[x_e \, y_e \, z_e \right]^T$ denotes the coordinates of the end effector.

The forward kinematics equation of RCDPR can be derived by Eq. (1) and expressed as Eq. (2) which refers to the solution of the spatial pose for the end-effector with known cable length and configuration changes.

$$\begin{cases} x_e = \dfrac{(l_1^2 - l_3^2) \cdot (s_3 - s_2) - (l_2^2 - l_3^2) \cdot (s_3 - s_1)}{2R(s_3 - s_2) \cdot (c_3 - c_1) - 2R(s_3 - s_1) \cdot (c_3 - c_2)} \\[3mm] y_e = \dfrac{(l_1^2 - l_3^2) \cdot (c_3 - c_2) - (l_2^2 - l_3^2) \cdot (c_3 - c_1)}{2R(c_3 - c_2) \cdot (s_3 - s_1) - 2R(c_3 - c_1) \cdot (s_3 - s_2)} \\[3mm] z_e = H - \sqrt{l_3^2 - (Rc_3 - x_e)^2 - (Rs_3 - y_e)^2} \end{cases} \tag{2}$$

where $s_i = \sin(\theta_i + \theta_i^0)$ and $c_i = \cos(\theta_i + \theta_i^0)$.

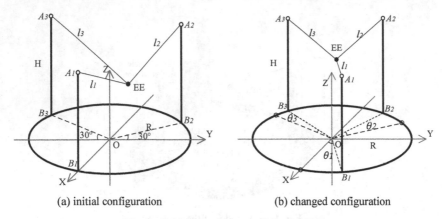

(a) initial configuration   (b) changed configuration

Fig. 2. Schematic diagram of the RCDPR

3   Improved Soft AC Algorithm

Reinforcement learning obtains a Markov chain while an agent interacts with an environment in discrete timesteps. At each timestep t the agent receives a state s_t of environment, gives an action a_t by a policy function $\pi(a|s)$, then gets a scale reward $r_t = r(s_t, a_t)$ and next state s_{t+1}. In generally, the interaction is a finite-horizon Markov decision process whose maximum timesteps is set as T, and the whole process is defined as an episode $\tau = (s_0, a_0, r_0, s_1, \cdots, s_{T-1}, a_{T-1}, r_{T-1}, s_T)$. The return from initial state is defined as accumulated rewards with a discounting factor $\gamma \in [0, 1]$, $R(\tau) = r_0 + \gamma \cdot r_1 + \gamma^2 \cdot r_2 + \gamma^3 \cdot r_3 + \cdots + \gamma^{T-1} \cdot r_{T-1}$. An action-value function [12] for a policy π is defined as the value of taking action a in state s under the policy π, which is referred to as $Q^\pi(s, a)$:

$$Q^\pi(s, a) = \mathbb{E}_\tau \left[\sum_{t=0}^{T-1} \gamma^t \cdot r(s_t, a_t) | \pi, s_0 = s, a_0 = a \right] \tag{3}$$

Obviously, the return that the agent can expect to receive in future depend on what actions it will take. The goal of RL is to find out the optimal policy $\pi^*(a|s)$ by iterating that can maximum action-value function:

$$\pi^* = \arg \max_\pi Q^\pi(s, a) \tag{4}$$

3.1   Soft AC and Expected SARSA

The Soft AC algorithm stochastically selects action a in state s according to a stochastic policy $\pi(a|s)$. The Q function parameters can be updated as Eq. (5) by state-action pairs $\{(s_t, a_t, r_t, s_{t+1})\}$ and next action $a_{t+1} \sim \pi(a|s_{t+1})$:

$$\hat{Q}(s_t, a_t) \leftarrow Q(s_t, a_t) + \alpha \cdot \left[r_t + \gamma \cdot Q(s_{t+1}, a_{t+1}) - Q(s_t, a_t) \right] \tag{5}$$

Many approaches in RL make use of the recursive relationship known as the Bellman equation:

$$Q(s_t, a_t) = r(s_t, a_t) + \gamma \mathbb{E}_{a_{t+1} \sim \pi} \left[Q(s_{t+1}, a_{t+1}) \right] \tag{6}$$

In Soft AC, the Q value under a random action replaces the expected Q value with respect to the policy, which will introduce a large variance to the Q function estimation. Expected SARSA [12] uses the expected value, taking into consideration how likely each action is under the current policy. And the update rule is set as:

$$\widehat{Q}(s_t, a_t) \leftarrow Q(s_t, a_t) + \alpha \cdot \left[r_t + \gamma \cdot \mathbb{E}_{a_{t+1} \sim \pi} \left[Q(s_{t+1}, a_{t+1}) \right] - Q(s_t, a_t) \right] \tag{7}$$

The Q Function approximators are parameterized by ϕ, which can be optimized by minimizing the loss function:

$$Loss = \frac{1}{2} \left(Q_\phi(s, a) - \widehat{Q}(s, a) \right)^2 \tag{8}$$

The action space of the agent in the robot task is usually low-dimension and continuous, such as torque or angular displacement of each joint. Assuming that each dimension is independent of the others, the action can be uniformly discretized to obtain the expected value of the Q function concerning the policy function,

$$\mathbb{E}_{a_{t+1} \sim \pi} \left[Q_\phi(s_{t+1}, a_{t+1}) \right] \approx \sum_{k=1}^{m} \pi \left(a_{t+1,k} | s_{t+1} \right) \cdot Q_\phi \left(s_{t+1}, a_{t+1,k} \right) (k = 0, 1, 2, \cdots, m) \tag{9}$$

3.2 Adaptive Policy Target

The policy network is parameterized of by φ, and we can find a better policy parameter through maximum expected Q function according to Eq. (4):

$$\varphi' = \arg \max_\varphi \mathbb{E}_{a \sim \pi_\varphi} \left[Q_\phi(s, a) \right] \tag{10}$$

Since the neural network is implicitly expressed, we make a qualitative analysis of the above formula. To maximize the integral value, the policy function should conform to the changing trend of the Q function, where the Q value is large, and the probability corresponding to the action is large and vice versa. So, the policy function is undated from the perspective of the mean and variance to make it as close as possible to the changing trend of the Q function.

For mean, the action with the largest Q value is taken as the target mean by interval random discretization,

$$\widehat{\mu} \approx \arg \max_{a_k} \left\{ Q_\phi(s, a_k) \right\} (k = 0, 1, 2, \cdots, m) \tag{11}$$

Normalize the probability distribution of discrete points, and estimate the target variance for different dimensions,

$$\omega_k = Q_k / \sum_{k=1}^{m} Q_k \tag{12}$$

$$\hat{\sigma}^2 \approx \sum_{i=1}^{m} \omega_k \cdot (a_k - \hat{\mu})^2 \tag{13}$$

Finally, parameter φ can be optimized by stochastic gradients.

3.3 Deep Expected SRASA

Table 1. Pseudocode of deep expected SARSA algorithm

Algorithm: Deep Expected SARSA

input: $\phi_1 \smallsetminus \phi_2 \smallsetminus \varphi$ ▷ Initial parameters
$\bar{\phi}_1 \leftarrow \phi_1 \smallsetminus \bar{\phi}_2 \leftarrow \phi_2$ ▷ Initialize target network weights
$\mathcal{D} \leftarrow \varnothing$ ▷ Initialize an empty replay pool
for each iteration **do**
  for each environment step **do**
    $a_t \sim \pi_\varphi (a_t | s_t)$ ▷ Sample action from the policy
    $\mathcal{D} \leftarrow \mathcal{D} \cup \{(s_t, a_t, r_t = r(s_t, a_t), s_{t+1} = f(s_t, a_t))\}$ ▷ Store the transition in the replay pool
  end for
  for each gradient step **do**
    $\hat{Q}_{\phi_i} = \mathbb{E}_{(s_t, a_t) \sim \mathcal{D}} \left[r_t + \gamma \cdot \mathbb{E}_{a_{t+1} \sim \pi_\varphi} \left[Q_{\bar{\phi}_i} (s_{t+1}, a_{t+1}) \right] \right]$ for $i \in \{1, 2\}$ ▷ the target Q function
    $J_Q(\phi_i) = \frac{1}{2} \left(Q_{\phi_i}(s_t, a_t) - \min \left(\hat{Q}_{\phi_1}(s_t, a_t), \hat{Q}_{\phi_2}(s_t, a_t) \right) \right)^2$ for $i \in \{1, 2\}$ ▷ Loss function of Q
    $\phi_i \leftarrow \phi_i - l_Q \cdot \nabla_{\phi_i} J_Q(\phi_i)$ for $i \in \{1, 2\}$ ▷ Update the Q function parameters
    $\hat{\mu} \approx \arg\max_{a_k} \{ Q_{\phi_i}(s_t, a_k) \}, \ \hat{\sigma}^2 \approx \sum_{a_k} \omega_k \cdot (a_k - \hat{\mu})^2$ ▷ the target $\hat{\mu} \smallsetminus \hat{\sigma}^2$
    $J_\pi(\varphi) = \frac{1}{2} (\mu_\varphi - \hat{\mu})^2 + \frac{1}{2} (\sigma_\varphi - \hat{\sigma})^2$ ▷ Loss function of π function
    $\varphi \leftarrow \varphi - l_\pi \cdot \nabla_\varphi J_\pi(\varphi)$ ▷ Update the π function parameters
    $\bar{\phi}_i \leftarrow \tau \cdot \phi_i + (1-\tau) \cdot \bar{\phi}_i$ for $i \in \{1, 2\}$ ▷ Update target network weights
  end for
end for
output: $\phi_1 \smallsetminus \phi_2 \smallsetminus \varphi$ ▷ Optimized parameters

---

To enhance the utilization of samples in theory, the deep expected SARSA algorithm is proposed by the improvement of Soft AC, whose pseudocode is shown in Table 1. Then, we test and compare them in the Fetch robotics arm environment which is simulated using the MuJoCo [13] physics engine with HER [11]. The results are shown in Fig. 3.

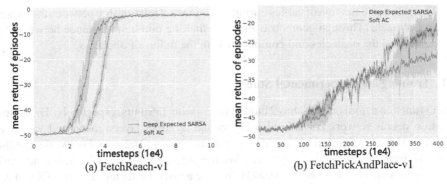

Fig. 3. Training curves on Fetch tasks.

4 Obstacle Avoidance Planning and Experimental Study

4.1 Task Settings

In order to apply the deep expected SARSA algorithm to solve the obstacle avoidance planning of RCDPR, the robotics task should be constructed like as Gym.

1. State: composed of the length of cables, the position of mobile modules and EE, and so on. $s_t = \left[\theta_i, \dot{\theta}_i, l_i, \dot{l}_i, x_e, y_e, z_e, \dot{x}_e, \dot{y}_e, \dot{z}_e, x_D, y_D, z_D, R_D\right]^{\mathrm{T}}$, where $i = 1, 2, 3$.
2. Goal: the position that end-effector need to reach, $g = \left[x_g, y_g, z_g\right]^{\mathrm{T}}$. Whether the robot completes task or not, depend on the function $f_g = bool\left(\|g - E\|_2 < \varepsilon\right)$ where E is position of EE.
3. Obstacle: simplified as a cylinder on ground, height $z_D \in [0.5\,\mathrm{m}, 0.8\,\mathrm{m}]$, radius $R_D \in [0.03\,\mathrm{m}, 0.08\,\mathrm{m}]$.
4. Action: action space is the response of RCDPR, $a = [\Delta\theta_1, \Delta\theta_2, \Delta\theta_3, \Delta l_1, \Delta l_2, \Delta l_3]^{\mathrm{T}}$. They are normalized to $[-1, 1]$, and correspond module gain k_θ and cable gain k_l respectively.
5. State transition function: simplified to describe by the kinematics, $s_{t+1} = f_{kine}(s_t, a_t)$.
6. Timestep: $t_{step} = 0.002\,s$, $n_{step\_keep} = 20$, $n_{\max\_step} = 100$.
7. Sparse reward: for every timestep, if the task is completed, reward is 1, otherwise reward is 0.

4.2 Collision Detection

After every timestep, the robot updates to a new state and we need to check if the current state is reasonable. If there is a collision, it needs to stop this episode.

1. There should be a fixed order between mobile modules when they move on the circular orbit.
2. Since the cable can only provide tension, it is necessary to check whether the projection of the end-effector on the XY plane is in the 2D workspace after the forward kinematics.

3. The collision detection of cables is to study the spatial relationship between the cables and obstacle. Through geometric analysis, find the minimum distance between the cables and the obstacles and compare it with the radius of obstacles.

4.3   Training and Experimental Study

The Q function neural network has 2 hidden layers with 256 units respectively. The action function neural network has 2 hidden layers and 2 output layers, mean and variance. And they share the first hidden layer's weights and biases. The neural networks use the rectified linear unit for all hidden layers. We use Adam for learning the neural network parameters with a learning rate of 0.0003. We use a discount factor of $\gamma = 0.98$ and we use a soft target update of 0.005. We train with minibatch size of 64 and a replay buffer size of 1 million (Figs. 4 and 5).

Using the deep expectation SARSA algorithm with HER, after training for 2 million timesteps, the learning curve and task success rate curve are shown in Figs. 6 and 7. In the initial stage of training, there is no improvement until a certain number of samples are accumulated and the correct strategy is learned from the successful samples. The return and success rate begin to rise, and the success rate is around 60% finally. The failure cases may be due to the limitation of the maximum number of timesteps and the maximum displacement of mobile modules in the task environment.

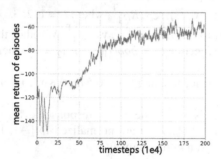
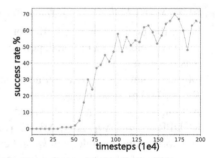

Fig. 4. Learning curve of return   **Fig. 5.** Learning curve of success rate

The trained policy network is used to verify the obstacle avoidance planning task in a simulation environment by randomly generating the obstacle and goal. The initial position of the end-effector is $(-0.233$ m, 0.197 m, 0.391 m), the position of obstacle in XY plane is $(-0.010$ m, 0.219 m) and the height of the obstacle is 0.652 m, the radius is 0.052 m, the position of the goal is $(0.375$ m, -0.120 m, 0.285 m). The result of obstacle avoidance planning is shown in Fig. 6. The red, green, and blue solid lines correspond to the mobile module 1, module 2, and module 3 respectively. The orange point is the goal point to reach. It can be seen from Fig. 6 that the obstacle avoidance motion of RCDPR is realized through the cooperation between the mobile modules and the flexible cables. The brown dotted line represents the obstacle avoidance path of the RCDPR.

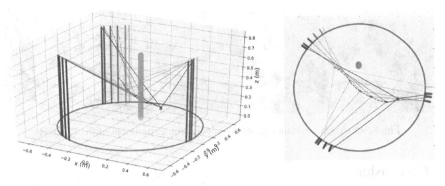

Fig. 6. Simulation result of obstacle avoidance planning (Color figure online)

At the same time, the motion trajectories of the mobile modules and the cables are also obtained. To prevent the robot from being impacted and oscillating during the movement, the trajectory generated by the policy network should be denoised and smoothed. The length change curves of the flexible cables and the displacement curves of the mobile modules are shown in Fig. 7 after processing.

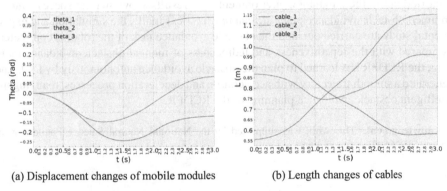

(a) Displacement changes of mobile modules   (b) Length changes of cables

Fig. 7. Obstacle avoidance trajectory curves of the RCDPR

The angular displacements of the modules and the lengths of the flexible cables turn into the trajectories that each motor needs to track at each moment by linear transformations, to control the movement of the robot platform, and obtain the robot motion process shown in Fig. 8. Experiment shows that the trajectory intelligently planned by the reinforcement learning algorithm is a feasible obstacle avoidance trajectory.

Fig. 8. Obstacle avoidance planning verification experiment of the RCDPR

5 Conclusion

In this paper, a deep expected SARSA algorithm based on improvements of the Soft AC algorithm is proposed to solve the obstacle avoidance planning problem of the reconfigurable cable-driven parallel robot. The mechanical structure of the RCDPR is described, and the kinematic analysis is carried out. The update process of Q function and policy function of the Soft AC is adjusted, and the deep expected SARSA algorithm is used to improve the learning efficiency in the Fetch robot simulation environment. Then, the obstacle avoidance planning task of the RCDR is built. The state space, action space, reward function, and collision detection algorithm are designed, and the task training is carried out in the simulation environment. The results show that the success rate of obtained obstacle avoidance planning can reach 60%. Finally, the simulation and experimental study are carried out, and the obstacle avoidance task of the robot is completed. Compared with the repetitiveness and tediousness of manual obstacle avoidance planning, the RCDPR has learned to plan the obstacle avoidance autonomously by DRL and generated a smooth trajectory with acceleration and deceleration processes, realizing the intelligent obstacle avoidance planning of the RCDPR.

Acknowledgment. This work was supported by the National Natural Science Foundation of China (51925502).

References

1. Qian, S., Zi, B., Shang, W.W., Xu, Q.S.: A review on cable-driven parallel robots. Chinese J. Mechanical Eng. **31**(04), 37–47 (2018)
2. Zi, B., Lin, J., Qian, S.: Localization, obstacle avoidance planning and control of a cooperative cable parallel robot for multiple mobile cranes. Robotics and Comp. Integ. Manuf. **34**, 105–123 (2015)
3. Lahouar, S., Ottaviano, E., Zeghoul, S., Romdhane, L., Ceccarelli, M.: Collision free path-planning for cable-driven parallel robots. Robot. Auton. Syst. **57**(11), 1083–1093 (2009)
4. Bak, J.-H., Hwang, S.W., Yoon, J., Park, J.H., Park, J.-O.: Collision-free path planning of cable-driven parallel robots in cluttered environments. Intel. Serv. Robot. **12**(3), 243–253 (2019). https://doi.org/10.1007/s11370-019-00278-7
5. Gagliardini, L., Caro, S., Gouttefarde, M., Girin, A.: Discrete reconfiguration planning for cable-driven parallel robots. Mech. Mach. Theory **100**, 313–337 (2016)

6. Qian, S., Zi, B., Wang, D.M., Li, Y.: Development of modular cable-driven parallel robotic systems. IEEE Access. **7**, 5541–5553 (2018)
7. Mnih, V., et al.: Human-level control through deep reinforcement learning. Nature **518**(7540), 529–533 (2015)
8. Arulkumaran, K., Deisenroth, M.P., Brundage, M., Bharath, A.A.: Deep reinforcement learning: A brief survey. IEEE Signal Process. Mag. **34**(6), 26–38 (2017)
9. Ibarz, J., et al.: How to train your robot with deep reinforcement learning: lessons we have learned. The Int. J. Roboti. Res. **40**(4–5), 698–721 (2021)
10. Haarnoja, T., Zhou, A., Abbeel, P., Levine, S.: Soft actor-critic: off-policy maximum entropy deep reinforcement learning with a stochastic actor. In: Proceedings of the 35th International Conference on Machine Learning, pp. 1861–1870 (2018)
11. Andrychowicz, M., et al.: Hindsight experience replay. In: 31st Conference on Neural Information Processing Systems (NeurIPS), pp. 5048–5058. Long Beach, CA, USA (2017)
12. Sutton, R.S., Barto, A.G.: Reinforcement Learning: An Introduction. MIT Press, Cambridge, MA, USA (2018)
13. Todorov, E., Erez, T., Tassa, Y.: Mujoco: a physics engine for model-based control. In: 2012 IEEE/RSJ International Conference on Intelligent Robots and Systems, pp. 5026–5033. IEEE, Vilamoura-Algarve, Portugal (2012)

Ant3DBot: A Modular Self-reconfigurable Robot with Multiple Configurations

Sen Niu[1], Linqi Ye[1], Houde Liu[1(✉)], Bin Liang[2], and Zongxiang Jin[3]

[1] Tsinghua Shenzhen International Graduate School, Shenzhen 518055, China
liu.hd@sz.tsinghua.edu.cn
[2] Tsinghua University, Beijing 100084, China
[3] Shanghai Academy of Aerospace Technology, Shanghai 201900, China

Abstract. In the paper, a novel modular self-assembling and self-reconfiguring robot named Ant3DBot was proposed, which has many configurations. Ant3DBot consists of four semicircular iron spheroid shells, telescopic legs, and internal magnets that can rotate around the center. Ant3DBot can expand its shells and legs through a single motor, a synchronous belt and compressed springs, which results in two different docking states. Ant3DBot which has the height of 12 cm can traverse obstacles with the height of 8 cm, and pass through a 25° slope in extending configuration. For many unstructured environments, the cooperation of multiple Ant3DBots can reach a target point with simple control. The simulations show the basic ability of a single module to overcome obstacles as well as the cooperative motion of multiple robots. The results demonstrate that the Ant3DBot system has excellent locomotion performance and versatility.

Keywords: Modular robot · Self-reconfigurable robot · Continuous docking form · Fixed location docking form

1 Introduction

Modular self-reconfigurable robot (MSRR) has become a research hotspot in recent years [1–6]. Due to its unique reconfiguration strategy, it can turn into different configurations according to the tasks. Thus, it has high robustness and great adaptability, which is quite suitable for exploring unstructured environments and performing related tasks.

Connector is one of the basic components in MSRR system. Many innovative connectors have been proposed in previous studies. For example, the latches [3, 7], and hooks [8, 9] that are activated by shape memory alloys (SMA) or DC motors [1, 3], electromagnet [10], and permanent magnets [2, 11]. When they self-assemble, the modules need to plan their trajectories to align with the connectors, and require point-to-point connection. In fact, the connections between modules are time-consuming and have a low success rate.

A new type of connectors has emerged, namely, the freeform connector. MSRR with freeform connector can connect to each other without precise docking. However, most are limited to 2D plane movement [12–14]. To our knowledge, only four modular robots have demonstrated the ability of 3D continuous connection, namely, FireAnt3D [15], FreeBot [16], FreeSN [17] and SnailBot [18]. FireAnt3D requires large electric power consumption, has short service life and is time-consuming. FreeSN and SnailBot make up for the problem of FreeBot's single-point topology constraints, but they have weak movement ability in single form, and basically can only move on the plane. When performing tasks on unstructured environments, their overall speed is greatly reduced due to the self-reconfiguration (SR) process. While in reality, speed is a of high priority in the rescue of fire, earthquake and mining disaster, reconnaissance and other tasks [19, 20].

Currently, there are fewer researches on the deformation of single self-reconfigurable robots, and their connection form is simple. This paper aims to explore the deformation of single self-reconfigurable robot by itself to realize two kinds of connection form, and enhance obstacle crossing ability to complete more tasks faster.

Fig. 1. Three configurations of Ant3DBot (Form I, II, and III).

Inspired by the anatomy of ants, a novel MSRR named Ant3DBot was proposed in this paper, as shown in Fig. 1. It consists of four semicircle iron spherical shells, retractable legs and internal Magnet that rotates around its center. Unlike the existing modular self-reconfigurable robots with only one connection form, Ant3DBot can control the expansion of both spherical shells and the upper legs through a single motor combined with a synchronous belt and compressed springs. When the spherical shells are not extended, as shown in Fig. 1(a), Ant3DBot uses 3D continuous docking points to attach to its peers regardless of alignment, thus docking becomes more convenient and free. When the spherical shells are extended, as shown in Fig. 1(b), dock-to-dock alignment can also be used to improve connection strength. Furthermore, its single obstacle crossing capability is worth mentioning. After the leg extension, a single Ant3DBot with the height of 12 cm can cross over obstacles with the height of 8 cm, and slope of 25°. Figure 1 shows the three configurations of Ant3DBot. It should be noted that the transition between the three configurations can also be achieved.

This paper is organized as follows: Sect. 2 introduces the mechanical design; Sect. 3 and Sect. 4 introduces the movement and simulation results of Ant3DBot, respectively. Finally, Sect. 5 gives the conclusions and future work.

2   Mechanical Design

2.1   Ant3DBot Design

Figure 2 shows the view of Ant3DBot in its expansion form. Ant3DBot consists of two spheroid shells equipped with internal magnets. It is mainly composed of four parts, namely, iron spheroid shell, shell driving structure, internal magnet driving structure and shell expansion structure. It should be noted that in this design, the positions that the front shells can reach are different from those of the back shells ($d_f = 70$ mm, $d_r = 11$ mm). Similarly, the reaching positions of front and back legs are also different ($L_f = 124.01$ mm, $L_{fmax} = 131.6$ mm, $L_r = 88.96$ mm, $L_{rmax} = 100.65$ mm), as shown in Fig. 3.

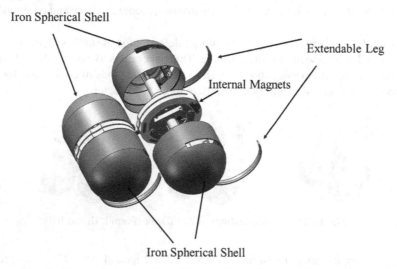

Fig. 2. The configuration of Ant3DBot when its legs are fully expanded.

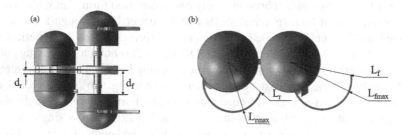

Fig. 3. Top view and side view of Ant3DBot when its legs are fully expanded.

The shell is mainly composed of iron spherical shell and extendable legs. The shell driving structure consists of two motors which control the rotation of the robot axes on both sides respectively through the gearbox and the gears, thereby driving the rotation of the spherical shell and realizing the forward movement, backward movement or rotation. The internal magnet movement is driven by a DC motor through a set of internal meshing gears. It can drive the permanent magnet to rotate about 300 degrees along the axis of the spherical shell ($\theta = 60°$), as shown in Fig. 4.

The expansion of the shell is driven by the synchronous belt on both sides of the transmission rod, and the compressed spring in the spherical shell, through a single motor. It can control the expansion of the spherical shell on both sides as well as the expansion and retraction of the upper legs, as shown in Fig. 5.

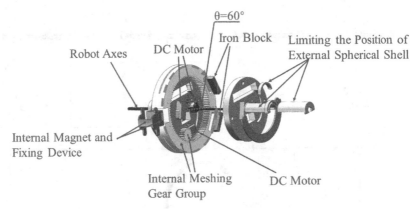

Fig. 4. Shell driving structure and internal magnet driving structure.

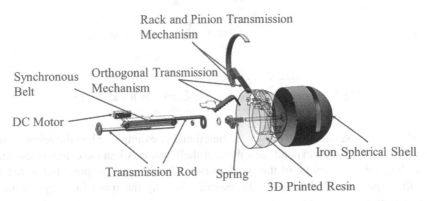

Fig. 5. Expansion and retraction structure of the shell and the legs.

The shell and leg expansion process of Ant3DBot is shown in Fig. 6. The initial conditions are as follows: the spring is compressed during assembly, so that the elastic force of the initial spring is slightly greater than the frictional force between the shell and the ground, and the spring can be further compressed by 20mm to drive the expansion of the leg. The detailed process is as follows. First, the synchronous belt drives the connecting rod compression spring. When the elastic force of the compression spring is greater than the frictional force between the shell and the ground, the connecting rod will drive the spherical shell outward. When the spherical shell expands outward for a certain distance, as shown in Fig. 3(a), it will be constrained by the position of the internal structure, and the continuous motion of the synchronous belt will drive the connecting rod compression spring. At the same time, the compression spring will be driven by the orthogonal transmission mechanism and the rack and pinion transmission mechanism to expand the legs. Based on the above analysis, when there is smaller external resistance, the selection of appropriate springs can ensure that the spherical shell extends at first, and the legs extend later.

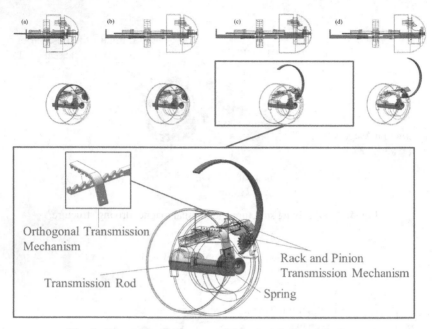

Fig. 6. The expansion process of the robot shell and the legs.

In fact, the expansion is a very useful function. For example, when the robot is stuck in a dilemma and cannot expand the spherical shell, that is, when the external resistance is very large, the movement of the synchronous belt will first compress the spring and drive the expansion of the legs, thus smoothly helping the robot to escape from the trapped ground.

Single Ant3DBot has strong barrier crossing capability because it can control the outward extension and leg expansion of the spheroid shell. Simulation experiments show that single Ant3DBot with the height of 12 cm can cross over 8 cm high obstacles and 25° ramp after extending legs. In addition, the position of the internal magnets in the spheroid shell is controlled by the motor. Besides, it can control the outward extension and leg expansion of the shells. Ant3DBot has many docking modes, including both FreeBot and chain structures, which will be discussed in the third part.

2.2 Connector

FreeBot can achieve fast 3D continuous docking by using a permanent magnet and an iron sphere. Ant3DBot in Form I is similar to FreeBot in that it contains magnets embedded in the body, can rotate around the center, and connect peers. The 3D continuous docking mechanism is one of the most important mechanisms of freeform MSRR.

Notably, compared with FreeBot, Ant3DBot is indeed more difficult to rotate in peers. However, it still has advantages in Form I when this is a genderless connector and the connection of two Ant3DBots can be at almost any point on their spherical iron shell, and it is sufficient when performing refactoring and loading functions.

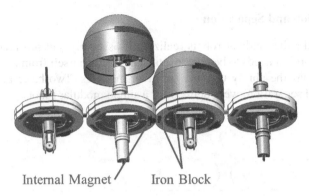

Internal Magnet   Iron Block

Fig. 7. Connectors of Ant3DBot in Form II.

In Form II, Ant3DBot can be linked with other Ant3DBots by a chain, as shown in Fig. 7. Thereby, Ant3DBot can pass through obstacles such as a gap and overcome higher obstacles, which will be explained in the fourth Part of experimental results.

The specifications of the magnet and the thickness of the iron shell of Ant3DBot in Form I are consistent with that of FreeBot. Therefore, the force action is no longer analyzed in this paper. The connectors of Ant3DBot in Form II can easily adjust the size of the iron block to change the connection strength according to the required connection strength of the tasks, so it is no longer analyzed.

3   Motion of Ant3DBot

3.1   Individual Motion

Each Ant3DBot module contains 8 motors, and has the same front and rear structures, including 4 motors in each. The available motions are summarized according to their functions, as shown below.

1) Connection: Ant3DBot is connected to the peers by rotating the magnet position. The magnet position can be adjusted in advance for rapid connection. The front and rear motors control two magnets respectively.
2) Disconnection: Ant3DBot rotates the magnet position until it disconnects from its peers.
3) Rotation: Both sides of the motors (DC motors) rotate in opposite directions respectively.

4) Driving: When the iron shell contacts with an external environment such as the ground, it can rotate to provide driving force. The four spherical shells are controlled by four motors respectively.

5) Extension and retraction: one motor can control the expansion and retraction of both sides of spherical shells and legs; two motors control the expansion and retraction of the four spherical shells and legs.

3.2   Connection and Separation

In order to make the modular robots realize self-assembly and self-reconfiguration, a single modular robot needs to be able to attach and detach itself from its peers. Besides, it necessarily has the ability to move on other modules. Two basic actions (namely, connection and separation) were defined for a single modular robot.

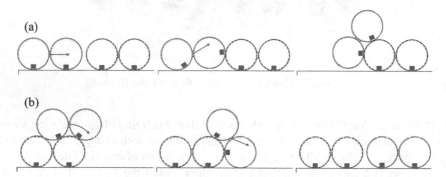

Fig. 8. Connection and separation of Ant3DBot in Form I.

The connection and separation of Ant3DBot in Form I enable the modular robot group to self-assemble (see Fig. 8). And the connection and separation only occur when the robot is about to touch or leave the ground. The connection and separation of Ant3DBot in Form II is shown in Fig. 9.

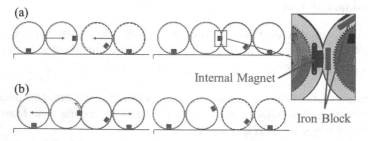

Fig. 9. Connection and separation of Ant3DBot in Form II.

3.3 Reconfiguration

The collaboration of multiple Ant3DBot showed some exciting performance. For the MSRR system, we focused on how to rearrange these modules into different configurations. Ant3DBot can crawl on the surfaces of other Ant3DBots and connect to other Ant3DBots when spherical shells are expanded so as to achieve many reconfigurable functions.

Adjacent transition and nonadjacent transition are usually performed in 3D space, meaning that moving robots can have various postures. For simplicity, only one of these cases was drawn in Fig. 10(a) and Fig. 10(b) respectively.

It was exciting to note that Ant3DBot could achieve any connection in Form I and achieve point-to-point connection in Form II, so it could excellently perform extremely difficult tasks. As shown in Fig. 11, the black is the connection of two Ant3DBots in Form II; the blue is that of the Ant3DBot in Form I. The red represents the movement process of Ant3DBot in Form I, and the green dashed lines roughly describe the movement trajectory of the red Ant3DBot.

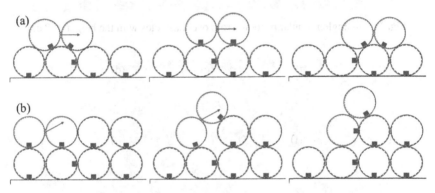

Fig. 10. Adjacent transition and nonadjacent transition of Ant3DBot in Form I.

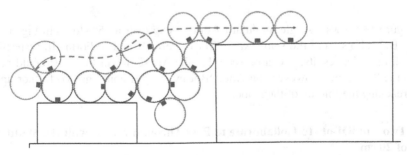

Fig. 11. Multiple Ant3DBot to form a bridge to pass through a gap.

4 Simulation Results

Simulations were performed in CoppeliaSim. They demonstrated the kinematic capabilities of Ant3DBot, including various basic actions and cooperative movements of multiple modules.

4.1 Performance of Single Ant3DBot

Figure 12 shows the basic abilities of a single modular robot. Although the specific initial position of the Ant3DBot for crossing 8 cm obstacles was required, the single modular robot still had the outstanding ability of crossing obstacles with 0.66 times its own height.

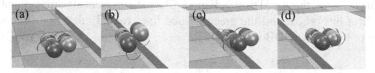

Fig. 12. A single modular robot to cross over obstacles with the height of 8 cm

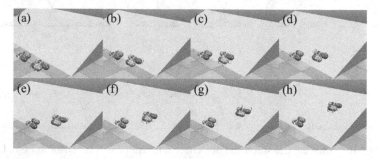

Fig. 13. A single modular robot to climb a 25° Slope

Figure 13 shows a single modular robot crossing over a 25° slope. In Fig. 13, two Ant3DBot robots were the same Ant3DBot in Form II and in Form III, respectively. According to the results, it can be seen that the Ant3DBot in Form III could rapidly climb the 25° slope. However, the Ant3DBot in Form II could not go further upward after reaching the middle of the slope.

4.2 Two Ant3DBots to Collaborate to Pass Through a Gap with the Width of 20 cm

Figure 14 shows two Ant3DBots in Form II collaborating to cross a gap with the width of 20 cm. The two Ant3DBots had a total length of about 50 cm, which could cross a gap with the width of 20 cm as quickly as they did in flat land. For the gap obstacles shown in Fig. 14, multiple Ant3DBots in Form II could coordinate and pass through it with almost no decrease of velocity.

Fig. 14. Two Ant3DBots to collaborate to cross a gap with the width of 20 cm.

4.3 Two Ant3DBots to Collaborate to Cross a Step with the height of 10 cm

Figure 15 shows two Ant3DBots synergistically moving through a step with the height of 10 cm. Each Ant3DBot only extended two legs, being an intermediate form between Form II and III. In addition, there were numerous Ant3DBot and Ant3DBot forms available for exploration between Form II and III. They could pass through with basically no loss of velocity under multiple obstacles. The collaborated movement mode in Form I was not considered unless Ant3DBots in Form II and III, and their intermediate forms are unable to pass the obstacles.

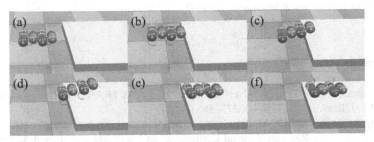

Fig. 15. Two Ant3DBots to collaborate to pass through a step with the height of 10 cm.

4.4 Loading Experiment

All forms of the Ant3DBot were non-sealing structures. They could be point-to point connected and crawl on the surface of other Ant3DBot. Thus, they were highly suitable for fulfilling the loading tasks. Therefore, partial custom-made containers, a 2mm diameter string or objects with hoses could be placed in the position shown in Fig. 16.

Fig. 16. Loading experiment of Ant3DBots.

5 Conclusions and Future Work

In this paper, a bio-inspired modular self-reconfiguring robot named Ant3DBot is pro-posed, which has many configurations and can move in multiple forms. The motor equipped in the Ant3DBot can control the expansion and retraction of both sides of spherical shells and legs. Single Ant3DBot can cross over 8 cm high obstacles and 25° ramps. Ant3DBot in Form I uses the 3D continuous dock to attach to its peers regardless of alignment. In Form II and III, Ant3DBot is linked by fixed docking locations and can coordinate to pass through gaps and steps. Its potential has been proved by simulations.

In the future, we will explore more possibilities based on the performance of Ant3DBot, and design self-reconfiguration algorithms and motion planning algorithms suitable for it according to its characteristics, and conduct related testing in more complex scenarios.

Acknowledgements. This work was supported by National Natural Science Foundation of China (62003188, U1813216), Shenzhen Science Fund for Distinguished Young Scholars (RCJC20210706091946001), and Guangdong Special Branch Plan for Young Talent with Scientific and Technological Innovation (2019TQ05Z111).

References

1. Kurokawa, H., et al.: Distributed self-reconfiguration of M-TRAN III modular robotic system. The Int. J. Roboti. Res. **27**(3–4), 373–386 (2008)
2. Davey, J., Kwok, N., Yim, M.: Emulating self-reconfigurable robots-design of the SMORES system. In: IEEE/RSJ International Conference on Intelligent Robots and Systems 2012, IEEE, pp. 4464–4469 (2012)
3. Spröwitz, A., et al: Roombots: reconfigurable robots for adaptive furniture. IEEE Computational Intelligence Magazine **5**, 20–32 (2010)
4. Seo, J., Paik, J., Yim, M.: Modular reconfigurable robotics. Annual Review of Control, Robotics, and Autonomous Systems **2**, 63–88 (2019)
5. Liu, C., Yim, M.: Reconfiguration motion planning for variable topology truss. In: IEEE/RSJ International Conference on Intelligent Robots and Systems (IROS) 2019, IEEE, pp. 1941–1948 (2019)
6. Liu, C., Yu, S., Yim, M.: A fast configuration space algorithm for variable topology truss modular robots. In: IEEE International Conference on Robotics and Automation (ICRA) 2020, IEEE, pp. 8260–8266 (2020)
7. Salemi, B., Moll, M., Shen, W. M.: SUPERBOT: a deployable, multi-functional, and modular self-reconfigurable robotic system. In: IEEE/RSJ International Conference on Intelligent Robots and Systems 2020, IEEE, pp. 3636–3641 (2006)
8. Jorgensen, M.W., Ostergaard, E.H., Lund, H.H.: Modular ATRON: modules for a self-reconfigurable robot. In: IEEE/RSJ International Conference on Intelligent Robots and Systems (IROS) (IEEE Cat. No. 04CH37566) 2004, IEEE, vol. 2, pp. 2068–2073 (2004)
9. Wei, H., et al.: Sambot: a self-assembly modular robot system. IEEE/ASME Trans. Mechatron. **16**(4), 745–757 (2010)
10. Zykov, V., et al.: Evolved and designed self-reproducing modular robotics. IEEE Trans. Rob. **23**(2), 308–319 (2007)

11. Tosun, T., et al.: Design and characterization of the ep-face connector. In: IEEE/RSJ International Conference on Intelligent Robots and Systems (IROS) 2016, IEEE, pp. 45–51 (2016)
12. Li, S., et al.: Particle robotics based on statistical mechanics of loosely coupled components. Nature **567**(7748), 361–365 (2019)
13. Shimizu, M., Ishiguro, A.: An amoeboid modular robot that exhibits real-time adaptive reconfiguration. In: IEEE/RSJ International Conference on Intelligent Robots and Systems 2009, IEEE, pp. 1496–1501 (2009)
14. Malley, M., et al.: Eciton robotica: design and algorithms for an adaptive self-assembling soft robot collective. In: IEEE International Conference on Robotics and Automation (ICRA) 2020, IEEE, pp. 4565–4571 (2020)
15. Swissler, P., Rubenstein, M.: FireAnt3D: a 3D self-climbing robot towards non-latticed robotic self-assembly. In: IEEE/RSJ International Conference on Intelligent Robots and Systems (IROS) 2020, IEEE, pp. 3340–3347 (2020)
16. Liang, G., et al.: FreeBot: a freeform modular self-reconfigurable robot with arbitrary connection point-design and implementation. In: IEEE/RSJ International Conference on Intelligent Robots and Systems (IROS) 2020, IEEE, pp. 6506–6513 (2020)
17. Tu, Y., Liang, G., Lam, T.L.: FreeSN: a freeform strut-node structured modular self-reconfigurable robot-design and implementation. In: IEEE International Conference on Robotics and Automation (ICRA) 2022, IEEE (2022)
18. Zhao, D., Lam, T.L.: SnailBot: a continuously dockable modular self-reconfigurable robot using rocker-bogie suspension. In: IEEE International Conference on Robotics and Automation (ICRA) 2022, IEEE (2022)
19. Luo, H., Lam, T.L.: Adaptive flow planning of modular spherical robot considering static gravity stability. IEEE Robotics and Automation Letters **7**(2), 4228–4235 (2022)
20. Luo, H., et al.: An obstacle-crossing strategy based on the fast self-reconfiguration for modular sphere robots. In: IEEE/RSJ International Conference on Intelligent Robots and Systems (IROS) 2020, IEEE, pp. 3296–3303 (2020)

Design, Modeling and Experiments of a Modular Robotic Finger

Qinjian Zhang[1] , Pengcheng Wang[1] , Haiyuan Li[2(✉)] , and Xingshuai Li[1]

[1] School of Mechanical Electrical Engineering, Beijing Information Science and Technology University, Beijing 100101, China
[2] School of Automation, Beijing University of Posts and Telecommunications, Beijing 100876, China
lihaiyuan@bupt.edu.cn

Abstract. The robot dexterous hand is a highly flexible and complex end-effector. In response to the complex drive transmission mechanical structure of the traditional humanoid dexterous hand and the difficulty of assembly and maintenance control, etc., a modular linkage-driven robotic finger is designed in this paper based on a linkage drive mechanism. It has two degrees of freedom (two joints) and is compact in structure, low in cost and simple in assembly and maintenance. Compared with underactuated fingers, it is featured with greater dexterity and a stronger adaptive grasping ability. The modular robotic finger kinematics model is established and analyzed. Finally, simulation based on ROS and the experiment based on a finger prototype are constructed. A straight line and a circular arc trajectory is designed to verify the performance of the proposed kinematics method and the feasibility of the modular robotic finger mechanism. Experimental results show that the proposed kinematics method has high accuracy and the designed modular robotic finger structure is reliable.

Keywords: Dexterous hand · Modular robot · Hand kinematics · Linkage-driven mechanism

1 Introduction

As the field of robotics continues to expand with the rapid development of intelligent manufacturing, the application of robotics has extended from the industrial field to health, military, aerospace and other fields, the operating environment is often dynamic and unknown, prompting the growing need to manipulate objects dexterously [1]. Research on robotic multi-finger dexterity has become a major hot spot in the field of robotics [2, 3], and there appears an increasing need to its application. In despite of decades of research and development, robotic multi-finger dexterity is still a long way from achieving the full functionality and dexterity of a human hand [4]. Our human hands are flexible and perceive a variety of information, and the unique range of motion of the human thumb remains difficult to replicate mechanically [5]. Because the complex combination of tendons and muscles is significantly different from traditional serial robot joint designs

© The Author(s), under exclusive license to Springer Nature Switzerland AG 2022
H. Liu et al. (Eds.): ICIRA 2022, LNAI 13455, pp. 564–574, 2022.
https://doi.org/10.1007/978-3-031-13844-7_53

[6]. There are still many issues and challenges in dexterous hand research that need to be addressed.

Robot dexterous hands with different drive and transmission methods can have a wide range of performance indicators such as flexibility, maneuverability, and size. The dexterous hand can be divided into underactuated dexterous hand and fully-actuated dexterous hand according to the number of drives and degrees of freedom (DOF). The underactuated dexterous hand, with a simple structure, has low imitation of humanity, and poor stability and flexibility when implementing grasping operations on target objects. The joint of the fully-actuated dexterous hand can be driven independently, which is characterized with strong flexibility, high grasping stability and complex structure. According to the different transmission mode, dexterous hand can be divided into wire-driven dexterous hand, tendon-driven dexterous hand, linkage-driven dexterous hand and soft dexterous hand, etc. The Okada dexterous hand [7] is the most representative wire-driven dexterous hand in the early research on dexterous hand. It has three fingers and a palm. The thumb has 3-DOF, and the other two fingers each have 4-DOF. The dexterous hand is small in size, but its flexibility is limited. The Shadow hand [8], the Stanford/JPL hand [9], the Utah/MIT hand [10], the Robonaut Hand [11, 12] and the DLR hand [13], etc., are the main representatives of tendon-driven. This kind of dexterous hand can do almost the same movement as human hand, but the flexibility of tendon-driven reduces the motion control precision of finger, resulting in hysteresis of finger drive control. Moreover, the assembly and control are complicated and the cost is high. The Belgarde/USC hand [14], the KAWABUCHI hand [15], the ILDA hand [2] and the Schunk hand [16, 17], etc., mainly take connecting rod as the mode of work transmission. This kind of dexterous hand has the advantages of good stiffness, large transmission power, strong load capacity, easy manufacturing and maintenance, but it is difficult to achieve multi-degree-of-freedom movement and maintain a large working space.

Based on the above analysis, we believe that dexterity, controllability, low cost, compactness and easy installation and maintenance are essential to the dexterous robot hand. The research difficulties and key technologies of robot dexterous hand lie in structure and mechanism, drive, sensor and modeling control. In this paper, a modular robotic finger is designed, which is independently driven with 2-DOF, and the end position is controllable and measurable. The modular robotic finger consists of two joints, namely metacarpophalangeal joint and proximal interphalangeal joint. Each joint is driven by a micro linear servo driver, and the transmission mechanism is driven by a connecting rod. The finger has the function of working space adjustment, and it is simple to install and control, with a low cost and high dexterity.

2   Modular Robotic Finger Design

The movement of our hands involves a fairly high level of dexterity. Out of 206 bones in the human body, 54 bones are in the hands, equivalent to a quarter of the total number of bones. The muscle structure that drives them is also extremely complex [2]. According to the medical anatomical structure of the human hand, the human hand has 21-DOF, and every finger except the thumb has the metacarpophalangeal (MCP) joint, the proximal interphalangeal (PIP) joint and the distal interphalangeal (DIP) joint. Based on the analysis and research of the human hand structure, a modular robotic finger is designed, as shown in Fig. 1. It has 2-DOF (two joints), the length of the finger is 100 mm, the width of the finger is 20 mm, and each finger weighs 300 g. It has the characteristics of compact structure, reliable transmission, high control accuracy and small size. Detailed configuration parameters of the modular robotic finger are shown in Table 1.

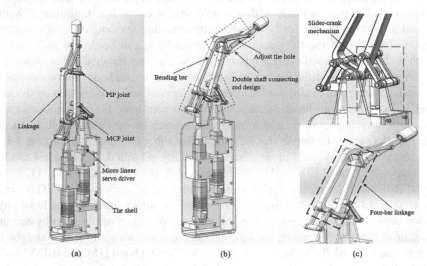

Fig. 1. Modular robotic finger. (a) Modular robotic finger structure. (b) Finger detailed structure design. (c) Finger transmission structure design.

Table 1. Configuration parameters of the finger.

Item	Value
Width	20 mm
Length	100 mm
DOF	2
Joint	2
Weight	400 g
Grab weight	1 kg

2.1 Mechanism Design

In this paper, the modular robotic finger is composed of micro linear servo driver, connecting rod mechanism, MCP joint, PIP joint and shell, as shown in Fig. 1 (a). The modular robotic finger has two joints, the MCP joint and the PIP joint. Each joint is driven by a micro linear servo driver, and each joint can control rotation independently.

It is an independently driven 2-DOF finger, making the position of the end controllable and measurable. The finger transmission mechanism adopts connecting rod transmission, which is a fully-actuated dexterous hand. Compared with underactuated dexterous hand, its dexterity is greater, and the self-adaptive grasping ability is stronger. In order to improve the force transmission performance, strength and stiffness of the modular robotic finger, a dual-axis connecting rod design is adopted at each hinge of the finger, as shown in Fig. 1 (b). Meanwhile, the positioning accuracy of the modular robotic finger can also be increased. In order to expand the working space of the finger and improve the grasping ability of the finger, a connecting rod of the PIP joint is designed as a bent rod, as shown in Fig. 1 (b), which can significantly expand the working space of the PIP joint of the modular robotic finger. The drive of both joints is driven by a connecting rod mechanism, which reduces the size of the finger compared to integrate in the finger. The stiffness and precision of long distance transmission can be guaranteed by using connecting rod, and the independent decoupling control of two joints can thus be realized.

Under the condition of keeping the finger volume as small as possible, two adjusting holes are designed on the PIP joint connecting rod to adjust the finger working space, as shown in Fig. 1 (b). The modular robotic finger working space can be adjusted through the adjusting holes to realize grasping objects of different sizes. The adjustment hole improves the adaptability of fingers to grasp objects of different sizes, and the adjustment process is simple and convenient to operate. In addition, the end of the finger is cylindrical spherical, similar to human fingers, so as to ensure that the influence of the position of the end of the finger on grasping objects can be avoided in the process of grasping. What's more, the modular robotic finger uses a micro linear servo driver with force sensor so as to obtain the contact force when the finger grabs the target object.

Based on the designed modular robotic fingers, we can design different hand structures to form multi-finger dexterous hands with different number of fingers, such as three-finger dexterous hands and five-finger dexterous hands, so as to realize the grasping of different items according to the demand and accomplish different grasping and operation tasks as well as various shapes of targets with high interchangeability.

2.2 Transmission Structure Design

The transmission mechanism of modular robotic finger adopts connecting rod drive, which has the advantages of good stiffness, large transmission force, strong load capacity and high precision. The MCP joint consists of a metacarpophalangeal output rod and a micro linear servo driver hinged with each other to form a crank slider mechanism, as shown in Fig. 1 (c). The vertical motion of the micro linear servo driver is converted to the rotation of the MCP joint. The PIP joint consists of a four-bar linkage mechanism articulated by a micro linear servo driver through multiple connecting rods. The vertical motion of the micro linear servo driver is converted into rotation of the PIP joint, as shown in Fig. 1 (c). When the PIP joint moves, the motion of MCP joint is not affected, and independent decoupling control is realized.

3 Kinematic Modeling

Each finger of a dexterous hand can be regarded as a linkage robot. D-H parameters method is used to analyze the kinematics modeling of the proposed modular robotic finger, which is of great significance to verify the mechanism and control its motion. The modular robotic finger uses forward kinematics to calculate the position coordinates and working space of the finger end, and uses inverse kinematics to calculate the expansion of the micro linear servo driver required by the finger end coordinates.

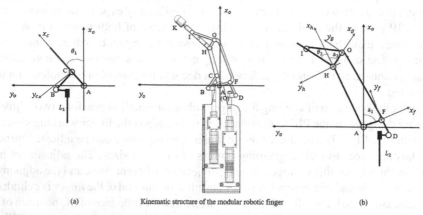

(a)   Kinematic structure of the modular robotic finger   (b)

Fig. 2. Kinematic analysis of the proposed mechanism of the modular robotic finger. (a) Kinematics analysis of MCP joint. (b) Kinematics analysis of PIP joint.

Define the kinematic parameters of modular robotic fingers, as shown in Fig. 2. According to the D-H parameters method, the global coordinate system $o_o x_0 y_0 z_0$ is established at point A of MCP joint, and the local coordinate system $i_i x_i y_i z_i$ ($i = c, f, h, g$) is established at point C, F, H, and G respectively. The kinematics model of fingers can be divided into three Spaces: drive space, joint space and work space. Suppose that the joint Angle of the MCP joint is θ_1, the joint Angle of the PIP joint is θ_2, the contraction of the micro linear servo driver of the MCP joint is L_1, the initial position of L_1 is L_{1init}, the contraction of the micro linear servo driver of the PIP joint is L_2 and the initial position of L_2 is L_{2init}.

3.1 Mapping Relationship Between Drive Space and Joint Space

Establish Kinematic Relation of MCP Joint. As shown in Fig. 2 (a), the coordinate of point B in the coordinate System {O} is $^oP_b = \left[L_{1init} + L_1, y_b, 0\right]^T$, where y_b is constant and the coordinate of point C in the coordinate system {C} is $^cP_c = [0, 0, 0]^T$, the coordinate of point C in the coordinate system {O} is ^oP_c. The transformation matrix of coordinate system {C} relative to coordinate system {O} is ^o_cT, L_{AC} is the length of connecting rod AC and L_{BC} is the length of connecting rod BC, then the following equation can be obtained:

$$^o_cT = Rot(z, \theta_1)Trans(L_{AC}, 0, 0) \tag{1}$$

$$^oP_c = {}^o_cT {}^cP_c \tag{2}$$

$$L_{BC} = \sqrt{(^oP_b - {}^oP_c)^2} \tag{3}$$

According to Eq. (3), the following constraint equation can be obtained:

$$L_{BC}^2 = (L_{1init} + L_1 - L_{AC}\cos\theta_1)^2 + (y_b - L_{AC}\sin\theta_1)^2 \tag{4}$$

According to Eq. (4), the forward and inverse kinematics relationship between L_1 and θ_1 can be obtained:

$$\begin{cases} \theta_1 = \arcsin(\frac{y_b^2+(L_{1init}+L_1)^2+L_{AC}^2-L_{BC}^2}{2L_{AC}\sqrt{y_b^2+(L_{1init}+L_1)^2}}) - \arctan\frac{L_{1init}+L_1}{y_b} \\ L_1 = -\sqrt{L_{BC}^2 - (y_b - L_{AC}\sin\theta_1)^2} + L_{AC}\cos\theta_1 - L_{1init} \end{cases} \tag{5}$$

Establish Kinematic Relation of PIP Joint. As shown in Fig. 2 (b), the coordinate of point D in the coordinate system {O} is $^oP_d = \begin{bmatrix} L_{2init} + L_2, y_d, 0 \end{bmatrix}^T$, the coordinate of point F in the coordinate system {F} is $^fP_f = [0, 0, 0]^T$, and the coordinate of point F in the coordinate system {O} is ^oP_f. The transformation matrix of coordinate system {F} relative to coordinate system {O} is ^o_fT, and L_{DF} is the length of link DF, and L_{AF} is the length of Link AF, a_1 is the rotation Angle of connecting rod AF about the z_o axis, then the following equation can be obtained:

$$^o_fT = Rot(z, -a_1)Trans(L_{AF}, 0, 0) \tag{6}$$

$$^oP_f = {}^o_fT {}^fP_f \tag{7}$$

$$L_{DF} = \sqrt{(^oP_d - {}^oP_f)^2} \tag{8}$$

According to Eq. (8), the following constraint equation can be obtained:

$$L_{AF}^2 = (L_{2init} + L_2 - L_{AF}\cos a_1)^2 + (y_d + L_{AF}\sin a_1)^2 \tag{9}$$

According to Eq. (9), the forward and inverse kinematics relationship between L_2 and a_1 can be obtained:

$$\begin{cases} a_1 = \arcsin(\frac{y_d^2+(L_{2init}+L_2)^2+L_{AF}^2-L_{DF}^2}{2L_{AF}\sqrt{y_d^2+(L_{2init}+L_2)^2}}) - \arctan\frac{L_{2init}+L_2}{-y_d} \\ L_2 = \pm\sqrt{L_{DF}^2-(y_D + L_{AF}\sin a_1)^2} + L_{AF}\cos a_1 - L_{2init} \end{cases} \tag{10}$$

where the negative sign is taken, when point A is between points D and F.

As shown in Fig. 2 (b), the coordinate of point G in coordinate system {G} is $^gP_g = [0, 0, 0]^T$, and the coordinate of point G in coordinate system {O} is ^oP_g. The transformation matrix of coordinate system {H} relative to coordinate system {O} is ^o_hT, The transformation matrix of coordinate system {G} relative to coordinate system {H} is

^h_gT, and the transformation matrix of coordinate system {G} relative to coordinate system {O} is ^o_gT. a_2 is the rotation Angle of connecting rod GH around z_h axis. According to the finger structure, it is easy to get the relationship between a_2 and θ_2: $\theta_2 = a_2 + \angle GHI - \theta_1$, L_{GF} is the length of the link GF, L_{AH} is the length of the link AH, L_{GH} is the length of the link GH, then the following equation can be obtained:

$$^o_hT = Rot(z, \theta_1)Trans(L_{AH}, 0, 0) \tag{11}$$

$$^h_gT = Rot(z, -a_2)Trans(L_{GH}, 0, 0) \tag{12}$$

$$^o_gT = {}^o_hT {}^h_gT \tag{13}$$

$$^oP_g = {}^o_gT^g P_g \tag{14}$$

$$L_{GF} = \sqrt{(^oP_g - {}^oP_f)^2} \tag{15}$$

According to Eq. (15), the following constraint equation can be obtained:

$$L^2_{GF} = (L_{GH} \cos(a_2 - \theta_1) + L_{AH} \cos\theta_1 - L_{AF} \cos a_1)^2$$
$$+ (L_{AH} \sin\theta_1 + L_{AF} \sin a_1 - L_{GH} \sin(a_2 - \theta_1))^2 \tag{16}$$

According to Eq. (16), the kinematic relationship between a_1, θ_1 and θ_2 can be obtained:

$$\begin{cases} a_2 = \arcsin\left(\dfrac{L^2_{GH} + L^2_{AH} + L^2_{AF} - L^2_{GF} - 2L_{AH}L_{AF}\cos(\theta_1 + a_1)}{2L_{GH}\sqrt{(L_{AF}\cos(\theta_1 + a_1) - L_{AH})^2 + (L_{AF}\sin(\theta_1 + a_1))^2}} \right) \\ \quad - \arctan \dfrac{L_{AF}\cos(\theta_1 + a_1) - L_{AH}}{L_{AF}\sin(\theta_1 + a_1)} \\ a_1 = \arcsin\left(\dfrac{L^2_{AH} + L^2_{AF} + L^2_{GH} - L^2_{GF} + 2L_{AH}L_{GH}\cos a_2}{2L_{AF}\sqrt{(L_{GH}\sin(\theta_1 - a_2) + L_{AH}\sin\theta_1)^2 + (L_{GH}\cos(\theta_1 - a_2) + L_{AH}\cos\theta_1)^2}} \right) \\ \quad - \arctan \dfrac{L_{GH}\cos(\theta_1 - a_2) + L_{AH}\cos\theta_1}{-L_{GH}\sin(\theta_1 - a_2) - L_{AH}\sin\theta_1} \end{cases} \tag{17}$$

where $\theta_2 = a_2 + \angle GHI - \theta_1$.

3.2 Mapping Between Joint Space and Workspace

Assume that the coordinate of the end of the finger is $^oP_k = [x_k, y_k, z_k]$, and z_k is a constant value, determined by the palm. As shown in Fig. 2, according to the finger model, the relationship between joint angles and terminal coordinates can be easily obtained by using D-H parameters method.

The forward kinematics solution of coordinate ^oP_k can be solved according to joint angles θ_1 and θ_2 as follows:

$$\begin{cases} x_K = L_{AH}\cos\theta_1 + L_{HK}\cos(\theta_1 + \theta_2) \\ y_K = L_{AH}\sin\theta_1 + L_{HK}\sin(\theta_1 + \theta_2) \end{cases} \tag{18}$$

The inverse kinematics solution of joint angles θ_1 and θ_2 is solved according to coordinate ^oP_k as follows:

$$\begin{cases} \theta_1 = \pm\arccos(\dfrac{x_K^2 + y_K^2 + L_{AH}^2 - L_{HK}^2}{2L_{AH}\sqrt{x_K^2 + y_K^2}}) + \arctan\dfrac{y_K}{x_K} \\[4mm] \theta_2 = \pm\arccos(\dfrac{x_K^2 + y_K^2 + L_{HK}^2 - L_{AH}^2}{2L_{HK}\sqrt{x_K^2 + y_K^2}}) + \arctan\dfrac{y_K}{x_K} - \theta_1 \end{cases} \tag{19}$$

4   Experiments

In order to verify the performance of the proposed kinematics algorithm and the rationality of the modular robotic finger mechanism, simulation and prototype experiments of modular robotic finger were carried out respectively. All work was developed in C++ in ROS(Melodic version, Ubuntu 18.04) and modular robotic finger prototype.

4.1   Simulation

In this section, we verify the performance of the proposed inverse kinematics algorithm through simulation. We simplified the simulation model of the designed finger structure, designed a straight line and an arc trajectory with a radius of 10 mm, and controlled the motion of the end of the finger simulation model by using the joint angle obtained by inverse kinematics, the trajectory of finger end motion is consistent with the designed trajectory, as shown in Fig. 3 (a). Finally, the position error of x coordinate is 0 mm, and the maximum position error of y coordinate is 7.8×10^{-3} mm due to the calculation accuracy, as shown in Fig. 3 (b).

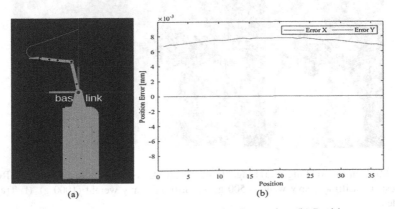

Fig. 3. Simulation results. (a) Linear and circular motion. (b) Position error.

4.2   Modular Robotic Finger Experiment

Modular robotic finger prototype, as shown in Fig. 4 (a). We pasted ArUco Marker on the end of finger and used OpenCV's ArUco library to complete the detection of finger end trajectory. We let the modular robotic finger move according to the circular arc trajectory designed in Sect. 4.1. The trajectory of finger end movement is shown in Fig. 4 (b), the actual coordinates of the trajectory have not been obtained yet, but the trajectory is similar to the simulation result, and the error is within an acceptable range. Finally, several experiments were conducted to verify the reliability of the developed hand, such as repeatability test, high payload test as shown in Fig. 4 (c), (d), (e). The repeatability test of the finger is to move the end of the finger repeatedly to the same point. The repetition accuracy of the finger is tested by tracking the movement of the end of the finger and the track of the modular robot finger repeatability test overlaps, as shown in Fig. 4 (f). The finger high payload test experiment is performed by letting the two joints of the fingers move to the right position and then lifting objects of different weights, and the finger can lift 1 kg weight, as shown in Fig. 4 (d). These tests are important for the practical use of modular robot fingers.

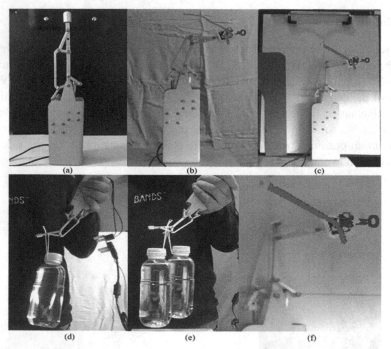

Fig. 4. Modular robotic Finger. (a) Finger prototype. (b) Linear and circular motion. (c) Repeatability test. (d) Lifting heavy weight (500 g). (e) Lifting heavy weight (1000 g). (f) Trajectory coincides.

5 Conclusions

In this paper, a modular robotic finger based on connecting rod transmission is designed, and its transmission system is innovative compared with other dexterous hands. The modular robotic finger has 2-DOF of joints, and each joint can control the rotation independently. It is an independently driven 2-DOF finger with controllable and measurable end position. It has low cost, simple assembly and control, greater dexterity than underactuated dexterous fingers, and better adaptive grasping ability. Then the kinematics model of modular robotic finger is proposed and the forward and inverse kinematics solutions of modular robotic finger are solved. Then, based on the kinematics model, a simulation based on ROS was constructed, and the performance of the inverse kinematics method was verified by designing a straight line and an arc trajectory. Finally, the rationality and reliability of the modular robotic finger mechanism are verified by experiments with a prototype finger. It lays a good foundation for our future work and provides a new idea for the design and modeling of dexterous hands.

Acknowledgments. This work was supported by the National Key Research and Development Program of China (Grant No. 2019YFB1309802) and the National Natural Science Foundation of China (Grant No. 62003048).

References

1. Ding, H., et al.: Tri-Co Robot: a Chinese robotic research initiative for enhanced robot interaction capabilities. Natl. Sci. Rev. **5**(6), 799–801 (2017)
2. Kim, U., et al.: Integrated linkage-driven dexterous anthropomorphic robotic hand. Nat. Commun. **12**, 7177 (2021)
3. Piazza, C., Grioli, G., Catalano, M., Bicchi, A.: A century of robotic hands. Annu. Rev. Control Robot. Auton. Syst. **2**, 1–32 (2019)
4. Palli, G., et al.: The DEXMART hand: mechatronic design and experimental evaluation of synergy-based control for human-like grasping. Int. J. Robot. Res. **33**(5), 799–824 (2014)
5. Chalon, M., et al.: The thumb: guidelines for a robotic design. In: 2010 IEEE/RSJ International Conference on Intelligent Robots and Systems, pp. 5886–5893. IEEE (2010)
6. Chang, L.Y., Matsuoka, Y.: A kinematic thumb model for the act hand. In: Proceedings 2006 IEEE International Conference on Robotics and Automation, ICRA 2006, pp. 1000–1005. IEEE (2006)
7. Okada, T.: Computer control of multijointed finger system for precise object-handling. IEEE Trans. Syst. Man Cybern. **12**(3), 289–299 (1982)
8. Li, S., et al.: Vision-based teleoperation of shadow dexterous hand using end-to-end deep neural network. In: 2019 International Conference on Robotics and Automation (ICRA), pp. 416–422. IEEE (2019)
9. Salisbury, J.K., Craig, J.J.: Articulated hands: force control and kinematic issues. Int. J. Robot. Res. **1**(1), 4–17 (1982)
10. Jacobsen, S.C., Wood, J.E., Knutti, D., Biggers, K.B.: The UTAH/MIT dexterous hand: work in progress. Int. J. Robot. Res. **3**(4), 21–50 (1984)
11. Lovchik, C., Diftler, M.A.: The robonaut hand: a dexterous robot hand for space. In: Proceedings 1999 IEEE International Conference on Robotics and Automation (Cat. No. 99CH36288C), vol. 2, pp. 907–912. IEEE (1999)

12. Diftler, M.A., et al.: Robonaut 2-the first humanoid robot in space. In: 2011 IEEE International Conference on Robotics and Automation, pp. 2178–2183. IEEE (2011)
13. Grebenstein, M., et al.: The DLR hand arm system. In: 2011 IEEE International Conference on Robotics and Automation, pp. 3175–3182. IEEE (2011)
14. Gazeau, J.P., Zehloul, S., Arsicault, M., Lallemand, J.P.: The LMS hand: force and position controls in the aim of the fine manipulation of objects. In: Proceedings 2001 ICRA. IEEE International Conference on Robotics and Automation (Cat. No. 01CH37164), vol. 3, pp. 2642–2648. IEEE (2001)
15. Lotti, F., Tiezzi, P., Vassura, G.: UBH3: investigating alternative design concepts for robotic hands. In: Proceedings World Automation Congress, 2004, vol. 15, pp. 135–140. IEEE (2004)
16. Armstrong-Helouvry, B., Dupont, P., De Wit, C.C.: A survey of models, analysis tools and compensation methods for the control of machines with friction. Automatica 30(7), 1083–1138 (1994)
17. Cerulo, I., Ficuciello, F., Lippiello, V., Siciliano, B.: Teleoperation of the SCHUNK S5FH under-actuated anthropomorphic hand using human hand motion tracking. Robot. Auton. Syst. 89, 75–84 (2017)

Robotic Replacement System for Thermocouple Components in the Nuclear Power Plant

Haihua Huang[1], Yujie Feng[1], Yi Tan[2], Rui Ma[3(✉)], Quanbin Lai[3], Binxuan Sun[3], and Xingguang Duan[3]

[1] China Nuclear Power Technology Research Institute Co., Ltd., Shenzhen 518000, China
[2] China Nuclear Power Operations Co., Ltd., Shenzhen 518000, China
[3] Beijing Institute of Technology, Beijing 100081, China
3220200143@bit.edu.cn

Abstract. Aiming at leakage, crystallization and deformation of RIC (In-Core Instrumentation) system, the thermocouple is mainly used to measure the outlet temperature of the reactor core coolant in the RIC system, which plays an important role in the condition monitoring of the internal equipment in the nuclear reactor core. To prevent serious nuclear accidents and reduce the radiation to maintenance personnel, a thermo-couple component robotic replacement system is built in the nuclear reactor. This paper analyzes the increased demand for thermocouple components replacement. According to the demand, the context plans the specific workflow of the robot, designs three dexterous end effectors, adopts an incremental master-slave mapping algorithm and completes the overall design of the robotic system. Finally, an experimental setup is built to test the operation process of the robotic system, which proved the system can complete the assembly replacement requirements. The system lays the foundation for the development and engineering application on next step.

Keywords: Nuclear robot · Thermocouple replacement · RIC system

1 Introduction

Nuclear energy is high-quality clean resource [1]. However, maintenance crew enters nuclear reactor will be limited by the radiation. With the rapid development of robotics, nuclear power robots provide an ideal solution for O&M, emergency and post-processing of nuclear power plants. Nuclear power robot has been performing tasks in high radiation and unstructured environments for a long time. Hence, teleoperation and visual serving are important for nuclear power robots to work stably and efficiently [2–4]. The French Get La Calhene company developed

This work was supported by the National Key R&D Program of China (Grant No. 2019YFB1310803).

the MT200Tao master-slave manipulator system (see Fig. 1-a), which is mainly used for the internal operation of medium and large hot cells [5]. The master arm and the slave arm have 7 degrees of freedom [6]. The Korea Electric Power Research Institute (KEPRI) has developed an underwater robot equipped with a radiation proof camera and four thrusters (see Fig. 1-b) to inspect the internal facilities of the nuclear reactor and use visual to solve the pose of the robot [7, 8]. In China, the detector component recovery robot developed by Beijing Institute of Technology (see Fig. 1-c) completed the extraction, coiling, cutting and recycling of detector components based on visual serving [9]. However, research on robotic systems for thermocouple assembly replacement in nuclear reactors is rare.

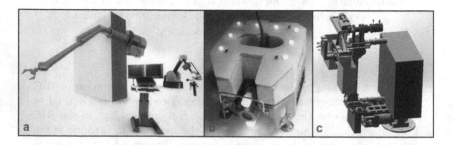

Fig. 1. Research status of nuclear power robots

Therefore, we present a novel master-slave robotic system to complete the replacement of thermocouple components. In the following, the second part analyzes the urgent need for replacement and presents the system overview and the specific process. In the third part, the end effector, the tool changer system and the master-slave control system are detailed. An experimental verification platform and experimental evaluation are presented and discussed in Sect. 4. Section 5 concludes the paper.

2   Scheme Design

2.1   Environmental Analysis

During the running of the nuclear power station, the thermocouple in the RIC [10] system is mainly used to measure the outlet temperature of the reactor core coolant. In addition, the thermocouple can calculate the average temperature inside the reactor core, the maximum temperature and the maximum interpolation of the regional temperature. Hence, the thermocouple is great significance to the stable and safe working of nuclear power station.

In a nuclear power reactor, 4 thermocouple columns are required, which are evenly distributed on the circumference and located at the top of the reactor pressure vessel. The RIC system measures the temperature and other information in the core through 40 thermocouples. Stainless steel hollow tube thread into the thermocouple wire, which is an outer diameter of 7.8 mm. Each thermocouple column is threaded into 13 conduit tubes, 2 empty hollow tubes are reserved for use. The two thermocouple tubes are connected by Swagelok union. The union are hexagonal bolts with an inner diameter of 16 mm. To prevent the union from loosening after tightening, the pipe joints weld with the anti-loose structure by the TIG welding. The three welding spots are evenly distributed at a circumference (3/120). When the thermocouple column is damaged, the connection (called the thermocouple assembly) must be removed before removing the thermocouple column, as shown in Fig. 2.

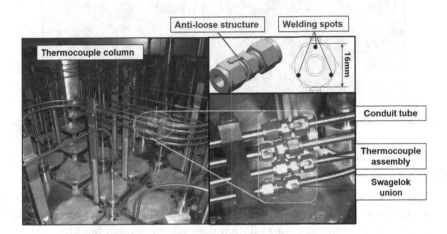

Fig. 2. The thermocouple assembly

2.2 Requirement

The damage of thermocouple components occurs frequently in the core of reactors. EDF had two serious deformations of several thermocouple columns: GRA6 in 2010 and DAMP4 in 2014, as shown in Fig. 3-a. There are two workarounds:

1) Maintenance personnel to manually disassemble and replace the deformed thermocouple column connector underwater. Maintenance personnel complete the welding spots removal, loosening pipe joints, tightening new thermocouple pipe joints and welding spots in unstructured environment.
2) Replace the RIC system inside the core as a whole or replace the components above the core.

   During the overhaul of a nuclear power plant, Boron crystallization was found in the K13 conduit of E13 thermocouple column. Then, leakage of K13 conduit was confirmed, as shown in Fig. 3-b. In response to this incident, Guangxi, Fangchenggang Nuclear Power C., Ltd. proposed a plugging and welding scheme. The main procedures are as follows: pipe cutting, pipe drilling, reaming, chamfering, plug machining, plug installation and welding, meantime, K13 mimic pipe was used to simulate. This welding and plugging process passed non-destructive and water pressure tests, which avoided massive extraction and insertion of thermocouple assembly.

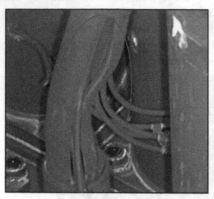

Fig. 3. Leakage, crystallization and deformation of the thermocouple components

Taken together, the problems exist in the replacement of thermocouple components are as follows:

1) Repair crews need to complete the replacement task in a high radiation, unstructured and narrow environment. Hence, it is difficult for repairman to operate. What's more, high radiation dose affects human health;
2) The dismantling is extensive in the nuclear reactor core;
3) Long replacement cycle and low replacement success rate.

Therefore, research and development of thermocouple component robot replacement system has the following advantages:

1) The specific process of replacing thermocouple components is planned, which shortens the replacement period and improves the success rate;
2) Dexterous end effectors and tool changer system are designed, which enable the robot to complete tasks in a stenosis and amorphous environment;
3) Disassemble the nearby local guide control rod to avoid large-scale disassembly of the core;
4) The robot can keep people away from high-radiation areas through the master-slave and autonomous mode.

According to the above analysis, the thermocouple component robot system needs to meet the following requirements:

1) The robot can complete the functions of removing and establishing solder joints, unscrewing and tightening fittings, photographing and comparing pipes in complex unstructured environment;
2) The system needs to have dexterous end effectors to complete the operation function in 1) and tool changer function;

3) To avoid robot autonomous decision-making and damage to nuclear power facilities. Thus, the system adopts master-slave operation mode in unstructured environment and autonomous mode in structured environment.

2.3   System Overview

The integrated schematic of the replacement system is shown in Fig. 4. The major equipment in the system is Aubo-i5 robot of 6-DOF, Omega.6 haptic device, Intel RealSense camera, six-dimensional force sensor, tool changer system, welding end effector, unscrewing end effector and tightening end effector. The manipulator picks up three end effectors by the tool changer system. This system completes fusing solder joints, spotting welding, loosening and tightening the union and photo comparison by the master-slave and autonomous mode. The force sensor and camera feed environmental information to the operator.

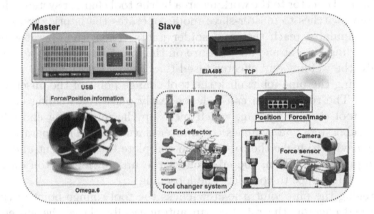

Fig. 4. The integrated schematic of the thermocouple replacement system

2.4   Workflow

The robotic system needs to work in an anhydrous environment. Thus, before the replacement of nuclear power facilities, the following preparations should be made:

1) Unload the nuclear power reactor completely;
2) Remove the control guide tube near the damaged thermocouple column;
3) Place the module radiation protection platform above the in-reactor components;
4) Change the water level by USP: between +80 mm and +180 mm.

The following workflow shows the major replacing the thermocouple assembly steps by using the system. Detailed procedure is depicted in Fig. 5.

1) System initialization and parameter setting: open the replacement system, log in the account, and check the connection of each component. After the check, enter the operation state;

2) Setting work points: the operator sets the working points on upper computer: camera point, welding end effector tool change point, unscrewing end effector tool change point and tightening end effector tool change point, Then, the operator can click the working point, and the manipulator can independently complete the photographing and end effector shift according to the input position;

3) Taking picture of the original pipes: the operator clicks the camera point, the robotic arm moves to the photo working point autonomously. The end camera takes photo of the original pipeline and generates log files. Subsequently compared with photos of the reloaded pipes.

4) Removing welding spots: the repairman selects the tool change point of the welding end effector, and the robotic arm can autonomously. picks up the welding end effector to the working area by the tool changer system. Hereafter, the crew switches to master-slave mode, operates the haptic device to make the manipulator reach the fixed solder joints. Then, the operator increases TIG welding current and air pressure on the interface of the upper computer. Finally, the welding end effector fused the original solder joints.

5) Unscrewing the pipe joint: click the tool change point of the unscrewing end effector. The robotic arm can independently place the welding end effector by the tool changer system, which picks up the unscrewing end effector to the working area and switches the master-slave mode. The operator controls haptic device to make the robotic arm complete the alignment and insertion of the pipe joint. Then, the crew clicks the unscrewing button on the host computer interface to complete the loosening;

6) Tightening the pipe joint: the crew clicks the tool change point of the tightening end effector, the robotic arm automatically places the loosening end effector through the tool changer system, which picks up the tightening end effector to the working area. At the same time, the repairman switches the master-slave mode. At last, operator clicks the tightening button on the upper computer to complete the tightening;

7) Soldering welding spots: operator clicks the tool change point of the welding end effector, and the robotic arm can place the tightening end effector, which picks up the welding end effector to the working area via the tool changer system. Meantime, the operator switches the master-slave mode and operates the haptic device to make the manipulator complete the soldering welding joints;

8) Photographing pipeline and comparison: the staff clicks the camera point, and the robotic arm moves to the working point of photographing autonomously. The end camera takes photo of the new pipeline and generates log files for comparison with the original pipeline photo.

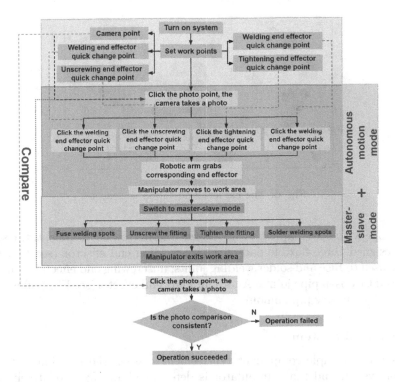

Fig. 5. Workflow of robotic replacement system for thermocouple components

3 System Design

Because of the complicated arrangement of equipment and pipelines in nuclear power plants with limited operating space, three types of dexterous end effector and tool changer system are designed. The autonomous motion of the robotic arm may damage the target equipment, so the robotic replacement system of the thermocouple assembly adopts a master-slave and local autonomous control method. The operator controls the robotic arm to complete the specified task by environmental information returned by the camera and the force sensor, as shown in Fig. 6.

3.1 Tool Changer System and End Effector

The tool changer system is composed of robot master, tool holder and tool gripper, as shown in Fig. 7. The robot master connects to the manipulator flange. The three tool holders are connected with the welding, unscrewing and tightening end effectors. The tool gripper is fixed with the tool changer fixing frame. The manipulator is connected or disconnected with the end effector through the master robot and the tool gripper to complete the placing/picking up the end effector.

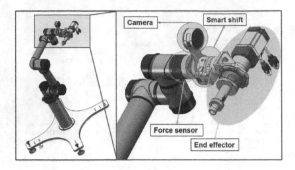

Fig. 6. The camera and the force sensor

To cope with the complex, unstructured and narrow environment, the system have designed three flexible end effectors: welding end effector (see Fig. 8-a) is mainly used to fuse and solder welding joints; unscrewing end effector (see Fig. 8-b) is used to loosen pipe joints; And tightening end effector(see Fig. 8-c) is mainly used to tighten new pipe union.

3.2   Control System

In this thermocouple component replacement system, the position of the tool changer system and the manipulator is determined and fixed relatively, which means that the environment is structured. The robotic arm can take pictures, pick up/place the end effector and move to the vicinity of the working point independently, and complete tasks such as welding, tightening and unscrewing by the master-slave control of the robotic arm.

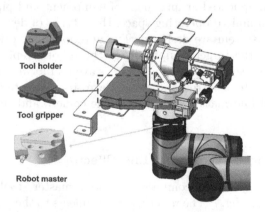

Fig. 7. The tool changer system

The master-slave control system is mainly composed of AUBO i5 manipulator, Omega.6 haptic device, Intel RealSense camera, network communication equipment and master-slave control console. The communication mode adopts TCP/IP. Industrial personal computer is selected as the main controller. The manipulator sends the position information, environmental force information and image information of the joint encoder to the main controller through the network. The main controller processes the information and sends it to the haptic device for feedback. The haptic device then sends the motor joint information to the main controller according to its current state. After processing by the main controller, the motor joint information is sent to the manipulator for operation task, as shown in Fig. 9. Through the information transmission of the control system, the movement of the operator is replicated to the manipulator, which means to realize master-slave following movement.

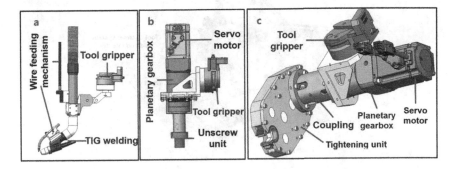

Fig. 8. Welding end effector, unscrewing end effector and tightening end effector

The process ensures the consistency of the position and posture of the haptic device and manipulator end points. In addition, the visual feedback system can feed back the image information of the operating area to the master console in real time, providing the operator with visual assistance.

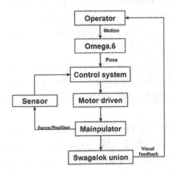

Fig. 9. Block diagram of master-slave control

4 Experimental Evaluation

To verify the workflow and main functions of the thermocouple component robot replacement system, an experimental verification platform is built in this paper. The experimental verification platform is composed of master console, tool changer system, end effector, manipulator and Swagelok union, as shown in Fig. 10.

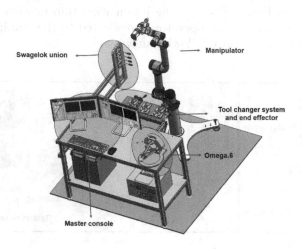

Fig. 10. The experimental verification platform

In this paper, the verification platform is built to verify the function and workflow of the thermocouple assembly robotic replacement system for three typical operation scenarios, as follows:

1) Automatic photographing and picking/placing end effector functions of the robotic system: pre-calibrate and set the working points according to the position of the manipulator and the tool changer system. After that, the robotic system completes the photographing and tool shift process before pipeline demolition (see Fig. 11-a);

2) Master-slave control to unscrew the pipe union: after the robotic arm picks up the unscrewing end effector independently. The operator controls haptic device to complete the verification of nesting and unscrewing to the Swagelok union (see Fig. 11-b);

3) Placing the end effector of the manipulator and taking photos: After the unscrewing is completed, click the unscrewing tool changer point to place the unscrewing end effector. Finally, the operator clicks the camera point to complete the reinstallation of the pipeline and take photos (see Fig. 11-c).

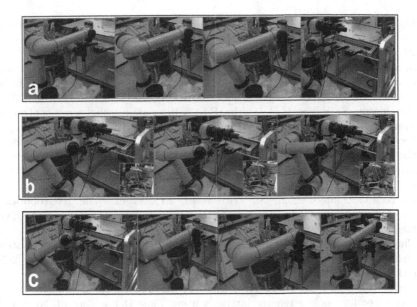

Fig. 11. The workflow evaluation and experiment

5   Conclusion

This paper presents a robotic system for thermocouple assembly replacement. The robotic system removes and refits the thermocouple conduit connections in response to emergencies such as deformation and crystallization of the thermocouple column. The workflow of the robot system is proposed and a robot replacement system for thermocouple components is built. Furthermore, three end effectors are designed for the workflow. Finally, the tool changer system and the master-slave mode are verified through the experimental verification platform. Experiments have proved that the thermocouple component replacement system can complete the workflow and realize the function of thermocouple component replacement.

The next step in the thermocouple assembly replacement system will continue with structural optimization. It will not only increase the visual serving and workflow planning system to reduce the operation difficulty, but also optimize the workflow and increase the radiation protection design. Make this system truly serve the daily O&M of nuclear power plants.

References

1. Ruth, M., Cutler, D., Flores Espino, F., et al.: The Economic Potential of Three Nuclear-Renewable Hybrid Energy Systems Providing Thermal Energy to Industry (2016). https://doi.org/10.2172/1335586

2. Li, C., Wang, T., Hu, L., et al.: A novel master-slave teleoperation robot system for diaphyseal fracture reduction: a preliminary study. Comput. Assisted Surg. **21**(sup1), 162–167 (2016).https://doi.org/10.1080/24699322.2016.124030

3. Sun, D., Liao, Q., Gu, X., et al.: Multilateral teleoperation with new cooperative structure based on reconfigurable robots and type-2 fuzzy logic. IEEE Trans. Cybern. **49**(8), 2845–2859 (2018).https://doi.org/10.1109/TCYB.2018.2828503

4. Hutchinson, S., Hager, G.D., Corke, P.I.: A tutorial on visual servo control. IEEE Trans. Robot. Autom. **12**(5), 651–670 (1996)

5. Piolain, G., Freudenreich, A.G., Monthel, P., et al.: Results of a testing campaign of the telerobotic system MT200-TAO in AREVA La Hague's hot-cells. In: 2012 2nd International Conference on Applied Robotics for the Power Industry (CARPI), pp. 157–162. IEEE (2012). https://doi.org/10.1109/CARPI.2012.6473378

6. Garrec, P., Lamy-Perbal, S., Friconneau, J.P., et al.: The tele-robotics system MT200-TAO replaces mechanical tele-manipulators in COGEMA/AREVA-La Hague hot cells (2006)

7. Cho, B-H., Byun, S-H., Shin, C-H., et al.: KeproVt: underwater robotic system for visual inspection of nuclear reactor internals. Nuclear Eng. Des. **231**(3), 327–335 (2004). https://doi.org/10.1016/j.nucengdes.2004.03.012

8. Park, J-Y., Cho, B-H., Lee, J-K.: Trajectory-tracking control of underwater inspection robot for nuclear reactor internals using Time Delay Control. Nuclear Eng. Des. **239**(11), 2543–2550 (2009).https://doi.org/10.1016/j.nucengdes.2009.07.029

9. Han, Z., Tian, H., Meng, F., et al.: Design and experimental validation of a robotic system for reactor core detector removal. In: 2021 IEEE International Conference on Robotics and Automation (ICRA), pp. 2473–2479. IEEE (2021). https://doi.org/10.1109/ICRA48506.2021.9560847

10. Laffont, G., Cotillard, R., Roussel, N., et al.: Temperature resistant fiber Bragg gratings for online and structural health monitoring of the next-generation of nuclear reactors. Sensors **18**(6), 1791(2018). https://doi.org/10.3390/s18061791

Design and Modeling of a Dexterous Robotic Hand Based on Dielectric Elastomer Actuator and Origami Structure

Yang Li and Ting Zhang[✉]

Robotics and Microsystems Center, College of Mechanical and Electrical Engineering,
Soochow University, Suzhou, China
tzhang@suda.edu.cn

Abstract. Dexterous robotic hands can not only work in dangerous situations like industrial processing, but also play a full role in daily lives such as artificial hands for the disabled, nursing home services and other fields. And smart materials driven dexterous hands are lightweight, highly compliant and have low risk of failure. However, the poor stiffness and low driving force limit their practical applications. In this paper, we propose a design of the dexterous hand driven by dielectric elastomer actuator (DEA), and incorporate origami structure to improve its stiffness and bearing capacity. Then, an analysis model for the DEA and knuckle is presented. Through this analysis model, not only the bending curvature, tip displacement and driving force of DEA, but also the compressive displacement, bending angle and driving force of the knuckle can be obtained after determining the design parameters (dimensions and materials) and input voltage. And the curvature model of DEA is verified experimentally. This paper lays a structural and theoretical foundation for subsequent research of the dexterous hand, showing that the combination of DEA with origami structure has great prospects in the field of dexterous hands.

Keywords: Dielectric elastomer actuator · Origami structure · Dexterous hand

1 Introduction

Traditional industrial robotic hands are mainly designed for specific tasks and their targets are similar in shape and size, so they have fewer joints and degrees of freedom, and poor versatility [1]. In recent years, smart dexterous robotic hands with multi-finger and multi-joint for a wider range of applications have emerged, they can not only work in dangerous situations like industrial processing, but also play a full role in daily lives such as artificial hands for the disabled, nursing home services and other fields [1–3].

H. Liu et al. (Eds.): ICIRA 2022, LNAI 13455, pp. 587–599, 2022.
https://doi.org/10.1007/978-3-031-13844-7_55

The research on dexterous hands has become a popular direction in the field of robots. Their driving methods mainly include motor [4, 5], pneumatic [6, 7], hydraulic [8, 9], and smart material [10–15]. Especially, due to the emergence of new functional materials, flexible mechanical devices have been widely used in the end-effectors of operation robots, surgical robots and biomimetic robots to realize driving and sensing. Smart materials commonly used to actuate dexterous hands mainly include thermoactive materials [10–12], and electroactive polymers (EAPs) [13–15], etc. Dielectric elastomer (DE), a kind of EAPs, has many advantages such as rapid response, small mass, large deformation and high energy density compared with other functional materials [16]. Therefore, it shows great potential in the driving of dexterous hands. Smart materials driven dexterous hands have advantages like lightweight, highly compliant and low risk of failure, while the poor stiffness and low driving force limit their practical applications.

On the other hand, combining ancient art and modern materials in accordance with design principles, "Origami Engineering" has found new solutions in robotics [17–19], which brings many benefits such as reducing space requirements, material consumption and increasing energy efficiency. Moreover, combining origami structures with self-folding property to realize the automation of "Origami Engineering" has more research value. In this way, high energy density, rapid response and reversibility of smart materials are crucial to practical applications of "Origami Engineering".

In this study, a dexterous robotic hand is firstly designed based on dielectric elastomer actuator (DEA) and origami structure, and its knuckles are directly driven by DEAs. Then, an analysis model is presented for DEA's bending curvature, tip displacement and driving force with consideration of its design parameters and input voltage. Further, based on DEA's analysis model, the equations of the compressive displacement, bending angle and driving force of the knuckle are deduced. Finally, experiments are conducted to verify the validity of the curvature model, and the driving force of the DEA and knuckle is discussed. The paper lays a structural and theoretical foundation for subsequent development of this dexterous hand.

2 Design of the Dexterous Hand

The origami structural dexterous hand is designed based on the bending DEA. The bending DEA is composed of the active layer and the passive layer. The active layer can be multilayer stacked DE films with each film sandwiched by the electrodes, and the passive layer is also a soft material. And the passive layer, also called substrate, is to suppress the movement of the active layer when it tries to extend after applying the electric field. Strain imbalance occurs at the interface between the active layer and the substrate, resulting in bending deformation, as shown in Fig. 1.

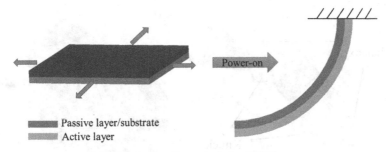

Fig. 1. Bending principle of DEA.

The requirements for the knuckles of the dexterous hand are to be able to stretch, bend and bear a certain amount of capacity. In order to increase the compression displacement and bending angle of the driving knuckle, it is designed as shown in Fig. 2. Six DEAs are pasted to the specified position of two plates, which are connected in pairs and symmetrical up and down. When DEAs bend, they are regarded as beams and the plate is regarded as a fixed end. And the substrates can be designed to be slightly longer than the active layers and the longer parts can be pasted to each other to realize the connection of DEA. In addition, two folding plates are added to both sides of the knuckle to provide support and improve the rigidity. The input voltage of four DEAs on one side is the same, thus the bending angles generated are the same. Similarly, the input voltage and bending angles of two DEAs on the other side are also the same. If the input voltage is the same on both sides, the knuckle compresses, if not, the knuckle bends.

After the design of a single knuckle, the finger and entire dexterous hand can be preliminarily designed. The finger is shown in Fig. 3(a), which is composed of three knuckles. The metacarpophalangeal joint is in a compressed state while the distal and proximal interphalangeal joints are in a bent state. The structure of the dexterous hand whose thumb is composed of two knuckles is shown in Fig. 3(b). Its phalanges of the middle finger are slightly longer than those of the index finger and ring finger, while the phalanges of the little finger are slightly shorter.

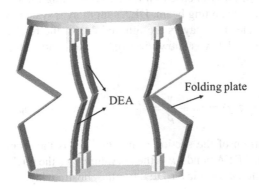

Fig. 2. Design of the knuckle.

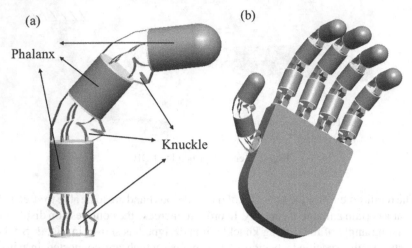

Fig. 3. Design of the finger and dexterous hand. (a) Finger; (b) Dexterous hand.

3 Modeling

It can be seen from the structure of the knuckle that its deformation and driving force depend on DEA, so we need to analyze the output performance of DEA first. The structure and analysis of multilayered DEA are complex and many parameters need to be taken into account, such as the layer number, size, elastic modulus of DE and substrate, as well as the electric field intensity applied outside. Therefore, an analysis model is established here. The bending curvature, tip displacement and driving force of DEA can be analyzed through the design parameters. Then we deduce the deformation and driving force of the knuckle with DEA's analysis model.

3.1 Analysis Model of DEA

The analysis model of DEA is based on the beam bending theory. When DEA bends, we assume it is a purely bending beam. DEA's multilayer system includes DEs and the substrate, while the electrode layers are ignored due to the relatively small thickness. The section diagram of DEA is shown in Fig. 4. The relationship between strain and height when DEA bends is,

$$\varepsilon(y) = \varepsilon_0' + \frac{y}{\rho} = \varepsilon_0' + y\kappa; \quad -t_s \leq y \leq h_n \tag{1}$$

where $\varepsilon(y)$ is the strain of the section at height y, ε_0' is the strain at $y = 0$, ρ is the curvature radius when DEA bends, κ is the curvature, t_s is the thickness of the substrate, and $h_n = nt_p$ is the height of n-layer DEs. For the substrate layer,

$$\sigma_s = Y_s\varepsilon_s = Y_s(\varepsilon_0' + y\kappa); \quad -t_s \leq y \leq 0 \tag{2}$$

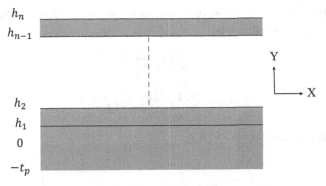

Fig. 4. The section of DEA.

where Y_s is the Young's modulus of the substrate, and σ_s is the normal stress of the substrate's section. Similarly, the normal stress of the DE's section is,

$$\sigma_p = Y_p(\varepsilon_0' + y\kappa - M_pE^2); \; 0 \leq y \leq h_n \tag{3}$$

$$M_p = \frac{\mu\varepsilon_0\varepsilon_r}{Y_p} \tag{4}$$

where σ_p is the normal stress, Y_p is the Young's modulus, M_p is the electrostrictive coefficient, which can be calculated by (4), and μ is the Poisson's ratio, ε_0 is the dielectric constant of vacuum which is $8.854 \times 10^{-12} \; F/m$, and ε_r is the relative dielectric constant of DE. When no external force or moment is applied on DEA, the resultant force and moment are zero,

$$\int_{-t_s}^{h_n} \sigma \, dA = 0 \Rightarrow \int_{-t_s}^{0} \sigma_s dA + \int_{0}^{h_n} \sigma_p dA = 0 \tag{5}$$

$$\int_{-t_s}^{h_n} \sigma y \, dA = 0 \Rightarrow \int_{-t_s}^{0} \sigma_s y dA + \int_{0}^{h_n} \sigma_p y dA = 0 \tag{6}$$

Substituting (3) and (4) into (5) and (6), the expression of κ can be obtained:

$$\kappa = \left[\frac{6n\alpha\beta(n + \alpha)}{4n\alpha^3\beta + 4n^3\alpha\beta + \alpha^4\beta^2 + n^4 + 6n^2\alpha^2\beta} \right] \frac{M_pE^2}{t_p} \tag{7}$$

where $\alpha = t_s/t_p$, $\beta = Y_s/Y_p$. E is the intensity of the external applied electric field, and its relationship with the input voltage V is $E = V/t_p$. Choosing VHB F9469PC as DE, PDMS as the substrate and $n = 4$, thus $t_p = 130 \; \mu m$, $Y_p = 0.5 \; MP_a$, $t_s = 160 \; \mu m$, $Y_s = 1.8 \; MP_a$, $\mu = 0.5$, $\varepsilon_r = 4.7$. The relationship of $\kappa - E$ obtained from (7) is shown in Fig. 5. To verify the validity of this model, experimental data in a paper [20] is referenced. The experimental and analytical data of that paper are also shown in Fig. 5. It can be seen that the analytical data in this paper are closer to the experimental data than those in Lau's paper, thus verifying the validity of the analysis model in this paper.

When DEA is powered on, its deformation is shown in Fig. 6(a). The relationship between δ_x, δ_y and curvature κ is,

$$\delta_x = L - \frac{\sin \kappa L}{\kappa} \tag{8}$$

$$\delta_y = \frac{1}{\kappa}(1 - \cos \kappa L) \tag{9}$$

where L is the effective length of DEA.

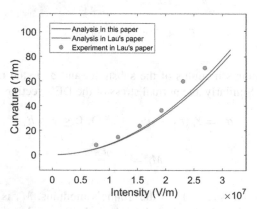

Fig. 5. The relationship between the curvature and electric field intensity.

Fig. 6.Deformation of DEA under electric field or force. (a) Electric field; (b) Force.

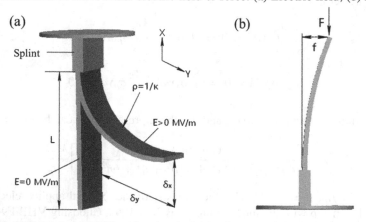

Fig. 6. Deformation of DEA under electric field or force. (a) Electric field; (b) Force.

Then, to analyze the driving force of DEA, considering DEA as a pressure rod and applying a force at the end, as shown in Fig. 6(b). When the force increases gradually, DEA will be in the equilibrium of a curve state, which is the buckling state. According to the large deflection approximation formula obtained by applying Pade approximation to the buckling rod [21], the relationship between the maximum deflection f of the buckling rod and the force F is,

$$
f = \frac{l}{\pi} \left\{ \left[2\left(p_1 - q_1\sqrt{\frac{F}{F_{cr}}}\right) - 2\sqrt{\left(p_1 - q_1\sqrt{\frac{F}{F_{cr}}}\right)^2 - 4\left(\sqrt{\frac{F}{F_{cr}}} - 1\right)\left(q_2\sqrt{\frac{F}{F_{cr}}} - p_2\right)} \right] \Big/ \left(q_2\sqrt{\frac{F}{F_{cr}}} - p_2\right) \right\}^{1/2} \Big/ \sqrt{\frac{F}{F_{cr}}}
$$

(10)

where $l = 2L$ (L is the effective length of DEA), p_1, p_2, q_1 and q_2 are four constants whose values are respectively $p_1 = -249/304$, $p_2 = 409/4864$, $q_1 = -325/304$ and $q_2 = 1025/4864$, and F_{cr} is the Euler critical load of the pressure rod, which is:

$$
F_{cr} = \frac{\pi^2 YI}{l^2}
$$

(11)

YI is the bending stiffness of the rod, here is the equivalent bending stiffness of DEA [22]:

$$
YI = b \int_{-\frac{h}{2}}^{\frac{h}{2}} Y(y)y^2 dy = b\left(\int_{-\frac{h}{2}}^{-\frac{h}{2}+t_s} Y_s y^2 dy + \int_{-\frac{h}{2}+t_s}^{\frac{h}{2}} Y_p y^2 dy \right)
$$

(12)

$$
\overset{h=t_s+nt_p}{\Longrightarrow} \quad YI = \frac{bY_p t_p^3}{3}\left(\frac{n^3 + 3n\alpha^2 + \alpha^3\beta + 3n^2\alpha\beta}{4} \right)
$$

where b is the width of DEA. It can be seen from Fig. 6(a) and (b) that the maximum deflection f of pressure rod is the horizontal tip displacement δ_y of DEA. Substitute (7) and (9) into (10), and expand $\cos\kappa L$ with Taylor's formula to get:

$$
\frac{1}{2}\left[\frac{6n\alpha\beta(n+\alpha)}{4n\alpha^3\beta + 4n^3\alpha\beta + \alpha^4\beta^2 + n^4 + 6n^2\alpha^2\beta} \right]\frac{M_p E^2}{t_p}L^2 =
$$

$$
\frac{l}{\pi}\left\{ \left[2\left(p_1 - q_1\sqrt{\frac{F}{F_{cr}}}\right) - 2\sqrt{\left(p_1 - q_1\sqrt{\frac{F}{F_{cr}}}\right)^2 - 4\left(\sqrt{\frac{F}{F_{cr}}} - 1\right)\left(q_2\sqrt{\frac{F}{F_{cr}}} - p_2\right)} \right] \Big/ \left(q_2\sqrt{\frac{F}{F_{cr}}} - p_2\right) \right\}^{1/2} \Big/ \sqrt{\frac{F}{F_{cr}}}
$$

(13)

From the above equation, it can be seen that applying electric field intensity E and corresponding force F to DEA will produce the same horizontal tip displacement. Therefore, it is assumed that when the electric field intensity is applied to DEA, it can be equivalent to a force applied at the end of DEA, then the relationship between E and DEA's driving force can be obtained, which is (13). When $L = 20$ mm and $b = 12.5$ mm, the relationship of F-E is shown in Fig. 7.

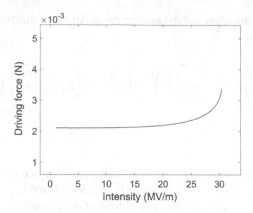

Fig. 7. The relationship between the driving force and electric field intensity.

3.2   Analysis Model of the Knuckle

When the input voltage (electric field intensity) of two sides is the same, the knuckle will compress. Due to the symmetrical structure of the knuckle, its compressive displacement x is,

$$x = 2\delta_x = 2\left(L - \frac{\sin \kappa L}{\kappa}\right) \tag{14}$$

And the relationship of x-E is shown as Fig. 8.

When the input voltage of two sides is different, the knuckle will bend. Simplify the structure as shown in Fig. 9(a). D is the diameter of the plate. According to (8) and (9), the coordinate of point A is $((1 - \cos \kappa_1 L)/\kappa_1, \ \sin \kappa_1 L/\kappa_1)$ and the coordinate of point B is $(D - (1 - \cos \kappa_2 L)/\kappa_2, \ \sin \kappa_2 L/\kappa_2)$. From the coordinates of the two points, it can be deduced that the bending angle θ of the knuckle is

$$\theta = 2\tan^{-1}\left|\frac{\frac{1}{\kappa_2}\sin \kappa_2 L - \frac{1}{\kappa_1}\sin \kappa_1 L}{D - \frac{1}{\kappa_2}(1 - \cos \kappa_2 L) - \frac{1}{\kappa_1}(1 - \cos \kappa_1 L)}\right| \tag{15}$$

The relationship between θ and E_1, E_2 obtained from (15) is shown in Fig. 9(b).

Finally, when the knuckle bears external forces, it is in a normal or compressed state. As can be seen from the structure of the knuckle, its driving force is 3 times that of DEA.

$$P = 3F \tag{16}$$

where P is the driving force of the knuckle.

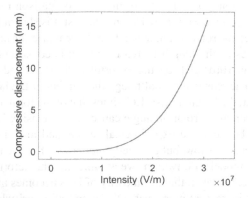

Fig. 8. The relationship between the compressive displacement and electric field intensity.

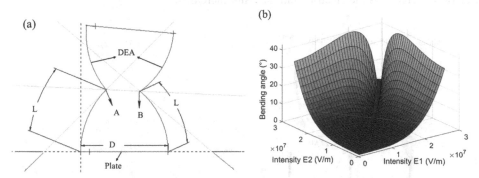

Fig. 9. (a) Simplified structure of the knuckle; (b) The relationship between the bending angle and electric field intensities on two sides.

4 Experiment and Discussion

4.1 Experiment of Deformation

In the experiment, we choose VHB F9473PC with compliant electrodes covering on both sides as DE layer and VHB F9473PC without covering electrodes as the substrate to conduct experiments to further verify the validity of the curvature model. Then, $t_p = t_s = 260\,\mu m$, $Y_p = Y_s = 0.5\,MP_a$, $\mu = 0.5$, $\varepsilon_r = 4.7$. Since the bending curvature of DEA is difficult to measure, we convert the curvature to angle for evaluation. When DEA bends, its rotation angle θ at the end is,

$$\theta = \kappa L \tag{17}$$

Two pieces of paper with thickness of 0.1 mm are pasted on both ends of DEA for convenience to measure the rotation angle. L is the length of the middle bendable part. When $n = 3$, $L = 6\,mm$, the variation of the DEA's rotation angle is shown in Fig. 10(a), and the comparison result of experiment and model is shown in Fig. 10(b). In addition, when $n = 1$, $L = 3$ mm and $n = 1$, $L = 6$ mm, the comparison results are shown in Fig. 10(c) and (d), and when $n = 2$, $L = 10$ mm, the result is shown in Fig. 10(e).

From Fig. 10(b)–(e), the rotation angle of DEAs decreases as the number of DE layers increases, and increases as the length increases, which is consistent with the analysis results. Comparing Fig. 10(d) and (e), the experimental results and analysis curves of DEAs are very close. The reason is that although the number of DE layers of the latter is twice that of the former, the length is also 1.67 times that of the former. Increasing length offsets the effect of decreasing rotation angle caused by increasing DE layers' number. In addition, the error between the experimental results and model is small when the input electric field intensity is low, but gradually increases when the intensity increases. That is because in the model's derivation, we assume that the deformation of DEAs is within the elastic range, however, the nonlinearity of DEs becomes more obvious as the electric field intensity increases; moreover, DEA's end will curl when the intensity is large, which means the rotation angle of the end is large; both aspects will cause the error to increase as the electric field intensity increases.

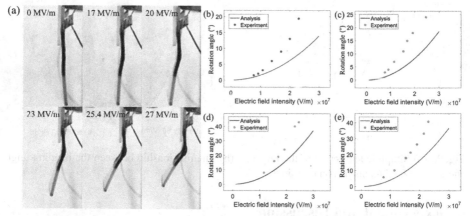

Fig. 10. (a) Variation of the DEA's rotation angle; (b–e) The comparison results of experiment and model at (b) $n = 3$, $L = 6$ mm; (c) $n = 1$, $L = 3$ mm; (d) $n = 1$, $L = 6$ mm; (e) $n = 2$, $L = 10$ mm.

4.2 Discussion of Driving Force

When analyzing the driving force of the knuckle, DEA is regarded as a pressure rod. The main reason for the error in this assumption is that curvatures of all sections are regarded as the same when analyzing the deformation of DEA. In fact, the elastic line of the pressure rod is more like an ellipse. We calculate the driving force with the analysis model in this paper when the angle of DEA's end is 10°, 20°, 30°, 60° and 90° respectively. Then comparing DEA's driving force with the corresponding force required for the same deformation of the pressure rod [21], and the results are shown in Table 1. It can be seen that the analysis error of the driving force is relatively small, indicating that the hypothesis and analysis in this paper is reasonable and feasible.

Table 1. Analysis errors of driving force.

θ_0	The exact value of F/F_{cr} [21]	κ (1/m)	E (MV/m)	F/F_{cr} in this paper	Relative error (%)
10°	1.0038	8.73	10.03	1.0114	0.76
20°	1.0154	17.45	14.18	1.0171	0.17
30°	1.0351	26.18	17.37	1.0286	−0.63
60°	1.1517	52.36	24.56	1.1143	−3.25
90°	1.3937	78.54	30.08	1.4286	2.50

When $n = 4$, the driving force of the knuckle is small. If a larger driving force is needed, it can be realized by increasing the number of layers of DE. Table 2 lists the driving force P when $E = 30.77$ MV/m (DEA's breakdown critical electric field intensity [20]) at different number of layers. It can be seen the number of layers of DE has a great influence on the driving force. In addition, through the analysis process of this paper, it can be found that changing the parameters α, β, b and L of DEA can also change the driving force. Changing α and β means changing the materials of DEA (including DE and substrate), and b and L are the dimensions of DEA, which can be designed according to actual demands.

Table 2. Driving forces at different number of layers.

n	E (MV/m)	F (mN)	P (mN)
5	30.77	4.13	12.39
10	30.77	17.4	52.2
15	30.77	46.44	139.32
48	30.77	1000.3	3000.9

5 Conclusion

In this paper, we present an analysis model for the DEA and knuckle, and preliminarily design a dexterous hand based on DEA and origami structure. Experimental results show that the DEA's curvature model is valid. After determining the design parameters (dimensions and materials) and input voltage, not only the bending curvature, tip displacement and driving force of DEA, but also the compressive displacement, bending angle and driving force of the knuckle can be obtained through the analysis model. The study paves the way of subsequent research of this dexterous hand, and shows that the combination of DEA with origami structure has great prospects in the field of dexterous hands.

Acknowledgment. Thanks for the support of the National Key R&D Program of China (2020YFC2007804), the Natural Science Foundation of the Jiangsu Higher Education Institutions of China (19KJA180009), the Natural Science Foundation of Jiangsu Province (BK20191424), the Jiangsu Frontier Leading Technology Fundamental Research Project (BK20192004D), and the Distinguished Professor of Jiangsu province.

References

1. Mattar, E.: A survey of bio-inspired robotics hands implementation: new directions in dexterous manipulation. Robot. Auton. Syst. **61**(5), 517–544 (2013)
2. Chunmiao, Y., Wang, P.: Dexterous manipulation for multi-fingered robotic hands with reinforcement learning: a review. Front. Neurorobot. **16**, 861825 (2022)
3. Ozawa, R., Tahara, K.: Grasp and dexterous manipulation of multi-fingered robotic hands: a review from a control view point. Adv. Robot. **31**(19–20), 1030–1050 (2017)
4. Wang, T., Geng, Z., Kang, B., Luo, X.: A new designed modular tactile sensing dexterous hand for domestic service robots. In: 2019 International Conference on Robotics and Automation (ICRA), pp. 9087–9093 (2019)
5. Amend, J., Lipson, H.: The JamHand: dexterous manipulation with minimal actuation. Soft Rob. **4**(1), 70 (2017)
6. Zhong, G., Hou, Y., Dou, W.: A soft pneumatic dexterous gripper with convertible grasping modes. Int. J. Mech. Sci. **153–154**, 445–456 (2019)
7. Puhlmann, S., Jason, H., Oliver, B.: RBO hand 3: a platform for soft dexterous manipulation. IEEE Trans. Robot. 1–16 (2022)
8. Wang, H., et al.: A bidirectional soft biomimetic hand driven by water hydraulic for dexterous underwater grasping. IEEE Robot. Autom. Lett. **7**(2), 2186–2193 (2022)
9. Zhao, H., Obrien, K., Li, S., Shepherd, R.F.: Optoelectronically innervated soft prosthetic hand via stretchable optical waveguides. Sci. Robot. **1**(1), eaai7529 (2016)
10. Wang, W., Ahn, S.-H.: Shape memory alloy-based soft gripper with variable stiffness for compliant and effective grasping. Soft Rob. **4**, 379–389 (2017)
11. Wang, W., Yiwei, L.: Structure design and research of dexterous finger based on the SMA driver. IOP Conf. Series. Mater. Sci. Eng. **439**(3), 32078 (2018)
12. Liu, M., Hao, L., Zhang, W., Zhao, Z.: A novel design of shape-memory alloy-based soft robotic gripper with variable stiffness. Int. J. Adv. Robot. Syst. (2020)
13. Li, J., Liu, L., Liu, Y.: Dielectric elastomer spring-roll bending actuators: applications in soft robotics and design. Soft Robot. **6**, 69–81 (2018)
14. Araromi, O.A., et al.: Rollable multisegment dielectric elastomer minimum energy structures for a deployable microsatellite gripper. IEEE/ASME Trans. Mechatron. **20**(1), 438–446 (2015)
15. Wang, Y., Gupta, U., Parulekar, N., Zhu, J.: A soft gripper of fast speed and low energy consumption. Sci. Chin. Technol. Sci. **62**(1), 31–38 (2018)
16. Brochu, P., Pei, Q.: Advances in dielectric elastomers for actuators and artificial muscles. Macromol. Rapid Commun. **31**(1), 10–36 (2010)
17. Lee, K., Wang, Y., Zheng, C.: TWISTER hand: underactuated robotic gripper inspired by origami twisted tower. IEEE Trans. Rob. **36**(2), 488–500 (2020)
18. Farhan, M.: Origami hand for soft robotics driven by thermally controlled polymeric fiber actuators. MRS Commun. **11**, 476–482 (2021)
19. Liu, C., Wohlever, S.J., Ou, M.B., Padir, T., Felton, S.M.: Shake and take: fast transformation of an origami gripper. IEEE Trans. Robot. **38**(1), 491–506 (2022)

20. Lau, G.-K., Goh, S.C., Shiau, L.-L.: Dielectric elastomer unimorph using flexible electrodes of electrolessly deposited (ELD) silver. Sens. Actuators, A: Phys. **169**(1), 234–241 (2011)
21. Wu, B., Piao, S.: Application of Pade Approximation in Mechanics. Mech. Pract. 01 (1996)
22. Saad, A., Ounaies, Z., Arrojado, E.A.F.: Electric field-induced bending and folding of polymer sheets. Sens. Actuators. A. Phys. **260**, 68–80 (2017)

Autonomous Intelligent Robot Systems for Unconstrained Environments

Planning with Q-Values in Sparse Reward Reinforcement Learning

Hejun Lei[1], Paul Weng[2], Juan Rojas[3], and Yisheng Guan[1(✉)]

[1] BIRL, Guangdong University of Technology, Guangzhou, China
ysguan@gdut.edu.cn
[2] UM-SJTU Joint Institute, Shanghai Jiao Tong University, Shanghai, China
[3] School of Mechanical and Automation Engineering,
Chinese University of Hong Kong, Hong Kong, China

Abstract. Learning a policy from sparse rewards is a main challenge in reinforcement learning (RL). The best solutions to this challenge have been via sample inefficient model-free RL algorithms. Model-based RL algorithms are known to be sample efficient but few of them can solve sparse settings. To address these limitations, we present PlanQ, a sample efficient model-based RL framework that resolves sparse reward settings. PlanQ leverages Q-values that encode long-term values and serve as a richer feedback signal to actions than immediate rewards. As such, PlanQ scores rollout returns from its learned model with returns containing Q-values. We verify the efficacy of the approach on robot manipulation tasks whose difficulties range from simple to complex. Our experimental results show that PlanQ enhances performance and efficiency in sparse reward settings.

Keywords: Motion planning · Model-based reinforcement learning · Sparse reward

1 Introduction

Despite the fact that deep reinforcement learning (RL) has achieved great success in many fields [1–3], RL has yet to practically be applied to physical robots. One of the main factors that hinder the practical application of RL is the reward function design. Most RL algorithms run on tasks with dense, well-shaped reward functions. The design of such reward is time consuming and requires significant domain knowledge. Sparse rewards, on the other hand, are simple to design but challenging to learn due to infrequent feedback learning signals from the environment. Curiosity-based exploration [4] and curriculum learning [5] have helped

The work is supported by the Key Research & Development Prog. of Guangdong (2019B090915001), the Guangdong Yangfan Innovative & Entrepreneurial Program (2017YT05G026), the CUHK Direct Grant (4055141), the NSF of China (62176154), and Hong Kong Center for Logistic Robotics.

H. Liu et al. (Eds.): ICIRA 2022, LNAI 13455, pp. 603–614, 2022.
https://doi.org/10.1007/978-3-031-13844-7_56

solve sparse tasks. One of the most significant works has been Hindsight Experience Replay (HER) [6]. In multi-goal settings, HER transforms failed trajectories into successful ones by replacing the true goals with achieved goals. HER while successful, still belongs to model-free methods, which have low sample efficiency. In general, model-based reinforcement learning (MBRL) algorithms have higher sample efficiency than model-free algorithms by learning an additional dynamic model. They do suffer, however, from lower asymptotic performance than their counterpart–and only a few of them resolve sparse settings. Thus, the main challenge is to design an efficient and robust algorithm for sparse reward settings.

In this work, we present PlanQ: a sample efficient MBRL algorithm, which leverages Q-value's long-term value encoding to solve sparse reward RL problems. PlanQ is based on shooting methods, which belong to the class of efficient MBRL algorithms for low-dimensional tasks with dense reward settings. Shooting methods however cannot complete sparse tasks since they weigh imagined rollouts with *only* the sum of the rollout's immediate rewards. In RL, Q-values are a richer and longer-term feedback signal for actions than immediate rewards. Inspired by this, we believe Q-values are helpful for shooting algorithms to weigh rollouts in sparse tasks, selecting more reasonable actions. The main contributions of the work are summarized as follows:

- A framework that combines shooting methods with Q-values based model-free methods.
- A weighing method for imagined rollouts that not only includes immediate rewards but also Q-values–which help shooting algorithms resolve sparse reward tasks.
- A method for re-planning policy outputs with Q-values that accelerates a policy's convergence speed.

2   Related Work

The idea of combining model-free and MBRL algorithms has been widely studied [7–9]. MVE [10] uses rollouts generated from learned dynamic models to improve target estimates for TD learning. Although MVE achieves promising results, the rollout horizon is fixed over the entire training process and is tuned manually. Motivated by this limitation, STEVE [11] weighs the candidate targets using model uncertainty to balance between errors in the learned Q-function and errors from longer model rollouts. The way STEVE weighs candidate targets is similar to the λ-return method [12], where targets from multiple time-steps are merged via exponential decay. PlanQ uses a similar but simpler returns compared to the STEVE and λ-return methods[1].

The closest previous work to our method is POPLIN [13]. By combining shooting algorithms (like random shooting (RS) [14], probabilistic ensembles with trajectory sampling (PETS) [15]) with the policy networks, POPLIN treats

---

[1] The simpler returns are weighed by summing all the returns of one imagined rollout without weighing them.

action planning at each time step as an optimization problem. POPLIN improves exploration by planning actions in the action or parameter space. However, since the computed returns from shooting algorithms only use immediate reward, POPLIN can hardly address reward-sparse tasks. Under sparse reward settings, all the imagined rollout's immediate rewards will likely be the null. In this case, the trajectory optimizer performs a trivial update without reward weighting. Hence, shooting algorithms and POPLIN struggle to resolve sparse reward tasks. PlanQ addresses this shortcoming by adding Q-values to the returns such that even when all the immediate rewards are the same, the planner can still choose a meaningful action.

Another similar previous work to our method is PlanGAN [16], which trains an ensemble of GANs and leverages the principle of HER [6] to solve sparse tasks successfully. However, PlanGAN performs computationally expensive rollouts, since their horizon is equal to the length of an episode. Compared with PlanGAN, PlanQ uses short rollout lengths, which make it much more computationally efficient.

3 Preliminaries

We consider multi-goal Markov Decision Processes, where an agent interacts with an environment to achieve desired goals: $\langle \mathbb{S}, \mathbb{A}, \mathbb{G}, R, p, \gamma \rangle$, where $\mathbb{S}, \mathbb{A}, \mathbb{G}$ are the set of all states, all actions, and all goals respectively, R is a reward function, p is the dynamics transition distribution, and γ is the discounted factor. At time step t, we observe the state $s_t \in \mathbb{S}$ and goal $g \in \mathbb{G}$, after which an agent executes an action $a_t \in \mathbb{A}$ in the environment according to a policy. Then, the environment changes state to $s_{t+1} \in \mathbb{S}$ according to the dynamics transition distribution $p(s_{t+1}|s_t, a_t)$ and gives the agent an immediate reward $r_t = R(s_t, a_t, g)$. As time step goes on, a trajectory $\tau = \langle g, (s_t, a_t, r_t, s_{t+1}, a_{t+1}, r_{t+1}, s_{t+1}, ..., s_T) \rangle$ is generated. To achieve the goal, the agent must learn a policy π to maximize the expected discounted sum of rewards $G = \mathbb{E}_\pi \left[\sum_t^\infty \gamma^t \cdot r_t \right]$, where $\gamma \in [0, 1]$. In value-based RL, the policy can be obtained by maximizing a Q function, which is defined as: $Q(s_t, a_t, g) = \mathbb{E}_\pi[\sum_t^\infty \gamma^t \cdot r_{t+1}|s_t, a_t, g)]$.

Deep Deterministic Policy Gradient. DDPG [17] solves RL problems using an actor-critic formulation. In this paper, we use a multi-goal version. The critic is encoded via an approximate Q function that is approximated by a deep network parameterized by φ. The Q network is trained to minimize the term: $L_\varphi = \frac{1}{N} \sum_i^N (y^i - Q_\varphi(s_t^i, a_t^i, g^i))^2$, where $y^i = r_t^i + \gamma \cdot Q_{\varphi'}(s_t^i, \pi_{\theta'}(s_t^i, g^i), g^i)$. The actor is represented by a policy that is learned by a policy network that is parameterized by θ. The actor is trained to maximize the Q function, i.e., to minimize the term: $L_\theta = -\frac{1}{N} \sum_i^N Q_\varphi(s_t^i, \pi_\theta(s_t^i, g^i), g^i)$. To stabilize the networks, DDPG uses a target Q network (parameterized by φ') and a target policy network (parameterized by θ'). They are updated by: $\varphi' = \epsilon\varphi + (1 - \epsilon)\varphi'$ and $\theta' = \epsilon\theta + (1 - \epsilon)\theta'$, where *epsilon* is a hyperparameter that limits the amount of change experienced by the networks.

Hindsight Experience Replay. HER [6] is a technique that addresses sparse reward multi-goal problems. In sparse reward tasks, it is extremely difficult for an agent to obtain a reward signal by taking random actions. When HER is combined with an off-policy algorithm like DDPG, it is possible to address reward-sparse tasks by replacing true goals with virtually achieved goals that then allow reward signals to be fed back. Assume that the tuple (s_t, a_t, r_t, g) is sampled from a reply buffer. When g is replaced with a reasonable g' by HER, a new reward $r'_t = R(s_t, a_t, g')$ is obtained. Then the tuple (s_t, a_t, r'_t, g'), which consists of a new goal and reward can be used to train the agent[2]. In this way, HER significantly improves algorithmic sample efficiency in sparse-reward settings.

Online Planning with Deep Dynamics Models. In PDDM [18], an ensemble of M networks $\hat{p}_{\omega_j}, j = 1, 2, ..., M$ are used to approximate the unknown dynamics transition distribution p. The loss functions of $\hat{p}_{\omega_j}$ are: $L_{\omega_j} = \frac{1}{N} \sum_i^N (s^i - \hat{p}_{\omega_j}(s^i, a^i))^2, j = 1, 2, ..., M$. To plan actions based on $\hat{p}_{\omega_j}$, PDDM maintains an H-dimensional, iteratively updating, mean action distribution $\boldsymbol{\mu}_t = \{\mu_t, \mu_{t+1}, ..., \mu_{t+H-1}\}$ that can be initialized as $\boldsymbol{\mu}_t = \mathbf{0}$. According to $\boldsymbol{\mu}_t$, PDDM samples K candidate action sequences, each of which has H actions, $A_i = \{\tilde{a}_t^i, \tilde{a}_{t+1}^i, ..., \tilde{a}_{t+H-1}^i\}, i = 1, 2, ..., K$, and can be expressed as follows:

$$\begin{cases} \tilde{a}_{t+h}^i = \eta_{t+h}^i + \mu_{t+h}, \\ \eta_{t+h}^i = \beta \xi_{t+h}^i + (1 - \beta)\eta_{t+h-1}^i, \\ \xi_{t+h}^i \sim \mathcal{N}(0, 1) \end{cases} \tag{1}$$

where, $h = 0, 1, ..., H - 1$, $\eta_{t-1}^i = 0$, and β is the filtering coefficient. An action sequence A_i interacting with M dynamics models $\hat{p}_{\omega_j}, j = 1, 2, ..., M$ respectively can generate M trajectories $\tau_i = \{\tau_i^1, \tau_i^2, ..., \tau_i^M\}$. Each of the M trajectories can be expressed as follows: $\tau_i^j = \langle g, (\tilde{s}_t^{ij}, \tilde{a}_t^{ij}, \tilde{r}_t^{ij}, \tilde{s}_{t+1}^{ij}, \tilde{a}_{t+1}^{ij}, \tilde{r}_{t+1}^{ij}, \tilde{s}_{t+2}^{ij}, ..., \tilde{s}_{t+H}^{ij}) \rangle$, where,

$$\begin{cases} \tilde{s}_t^{ij} = s_t, \quad \tilde{a}_{t+h}^{ij} = \tilde{a}_{t+h}^i, \\ \tilde{s}_{t+h+1}^{ij} = \hat{p}_{\omega_j}(\tilde{s}_{t+h}^{ij}, \tilde{a}_{t+h}^{ij}), \\ \tilde{r}_{t+h}^{ij} = R(\tilde{s}_{t+h}^{ij}, \tilde{a}_{t+h}^{ij}, \tilde{s}_{t+h+1}^{ij}, g), \\ h = 0, 1, ..., H - 1, \\ j = 1, 2, ..., M \end{cases} \tag{2}$$

Note that $\sim$ represents imaginary quantities. PDDM then defines the mean return function for trajectories τ_i as:

$$\begin{aligned} \bar{\mathcal{R}}_i(\tau_i) &= \frac{1}{M} \left[\sum_{h=0}^{H-1} \gamma^h \cdot \tilde{r}_{t+h}^{i1} + \sum_{h=0}^{H-1} \gamma^h \cdot \tilde{r}_{t+h}^{i2} + ... + \sum_{h=0}^{H-1} \gamma^h \cdot \tilde{r}_{t+h}^{iM} \right] \\ &= \frac{1}{M} \sum_{j=1}^{M} \sum_{h=0}^{H-1} \gamma^h \cdot \tilde{r}_{t+h}^{ij} \end{aligned} \tag{3}$$

---

[2] Note that this goal transformation does not change the environment dynamics.

The mean return function $\bar{\mathcal{R}}_i$ scores how good the action sequence A_i is. PDDM uses it to update the mean action distribution $\boldsymbol{\mu}_t$ according to:

$$\boldsymbol{\mu}_t = \frac{\sum_{i=1}^{K} A_i \cdot e^{\lambda \cdot \bar{\mathcal{R}}_i}}{\sum_{i=1}^{K} e^{\lambda \cdot \bar{\mathcal{R}}_i}}. \tag{4}$$

where, λ is the reward-weighing factor. Finally, PDDM performs only the first action $\boldsymbol{\mu}_t$ of $\boldsymbol{\mu}_t$ in the environment.

4 Method

Shooting algorithms like PDDM are sample efficient in dense reward settings since the mean return function Eq. (3) can encode well how good an action sequence is–not so in sparse reward settings where most action sequences would not collect rewards–that is, the mean return function value for all action sequences would be the same $\bar{\mathcal{R}}_i(\tau_i) = \bar{\mathcal{R}}_j(\tau_j), i, j = 1, 2, ..., K$. In this case, $\bar{\mathcal{R}}_i$ would fail to distinguish which action sequence is more valuable and the $\boldsymbol{\mu}_t$ update in Eq. (4) would become meaningless and lead to poor action planning which in turn would lead to task failure. Sparingly, at time step t, action sequences might get an immediate reward $\tilde{r}_t$, at which time, the agent can output a meaningful action $a_t = \mu_t$. However, at the next time step, it is again unlikely to yield an action that might lead to an immediate reward due to Eq. (3) and cannot leverage the reward $\tilde{r}_t$ to help distinguish actions. Other shooting algorithms such as RS and PETS use different distributions to generate action sequences, but they face the same dilemma as PDDM does due to the use of the same type of mean return function Eq. (3).

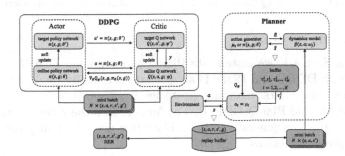

Fig. 1. PlanQ framework: The Critic of DDPG provides the Q-function for the Planner. HER is used in the framework for better sample efficiency. Data in replay buffer is used in two ways, one for DDPG, another for dynamic model training.

4.1 PlanQ Framework

To boost the sample efficiency of shooting algorithms in sparse reward settings we propose the PlanQ framework, where Q-values are integrated into the mean return function to help the agent differentiate actions. In contrast to immediate rewards, Q-values are a longer-term feedback signal for an action. Q-values store signals from immediate sparse rewards, enabling the agent to leverage them as Q-values can propagate over time across the state-action space.

PlanQ can extract Q-values from model-free RL algorithms such as DDPG, TD3, SAC. Note, however, that these model-free approaches directly output actions according their policy network, which is trained to maximize the Q-function. When combined with shooting algorithms, there are two ways to generate action sequences: (i) from the shooting planner or (ii) the policy network (see Sect. 4.2). In this work, we concretely instantiate the PlanQ framework with a Q-function from DDPG and a planner from PDDM as shown in Fig. 1. PlanQ then redefines the mean return function Eq. (3) by integrating Q-values to it: $\bar{R}_i(\tau_i) = \frac{1}{M} \sum_{j=1}^{M} \mathcal{R}_i^j$, where

$$
\begin{aligned}
\mathcal{R}_i^j = \; & q_t^{ij} \\
& + \tilde{r}_t^{ij} + \gamma \cdot q_{t+1}^{ij} \\
& + \tilde{r}_t^{ij} + \gamma \cdot \tilde{r}_{t+1}^{ij} + \gamma^2 \cdot q_{t+2}^{ij} \\
& \quad \vdots \\
& + \tilde{r}_t^{ij} + \gamma \cdot \tilde{r}_{t+1}^{ij} + \cdots + \gamma^{H-2} \cdot \tilde{r}_{t+H-2}^{ij} + \gamma^{H-1} \cdot q_{t+H-1}^{ij} \\
= \; & \sum_{h=0}^{H-1} \gamma^h \left[(H - h - 1) \cdot \tilde{r}_{t+h}^{ij} + q_{t+h}^{ij} \right]
\end{aligned}
\tag{5}
$$

where $q_{t+h}^{ij} = Q_\varphi(\tilde{s}_{t+h}^{ij}, \tilde{a}_{t+h}^{ij}, g)$, $\tilde{r}_{t+H-1}^{ij} = 0$. By adding Q-values to the mean return function, the mean action distribution μ_t will be updated with reward signals encoded in the Q-values even when all immediate rewards are zeros.

4.2 Planning Actions

As noted in Sect. 4.1, we instantiate PlanQ by combining DDPG and PDDM. However, both DDPG and PDDM can generate actions by themselves. As such, we can adopt two action planning strategies as shown in Fig. 2. We call them: PlanQ(PDDM) and PlanQ(DDPG). The former, uses the mean action distribution μ_t of PDDM to generate actions. The latter uses the policy network π_θ of DDPG to generate actions.

PlanQ (PDDM). At time-step t, the action generator samples K action sequences $A_i = \{\tilde{a}_t^i, \tilde{a}_{t+1}^i, ..., \tilde{a}_{t+H-1}^i\}, i = 1, 2, ..., K$ by Eq. (1). Next, action sequence A_i interacts with an ensemble of M dynamics models $\hat{p}_{\omega_j}, j = 1, 2, ..., M$ to form M trajectories $\tau_i = \{\tau_i^1, \tau_i^2, ..., \tau_i^M\}$, and calculate the mean return $\bar{R}_i(\tau_i)$ for τ_i by Eq. (5). Then, the mean action distribution μ_t in Eq. (4) is updated using $\bar{R}_i$ and A_i. Finally, the first action of μ_t is executed. PlanQ(PDDM) plans actions in the same way as PDDM does, the only difference is the mean return function modification from Eq. (3) to Eq. (5).

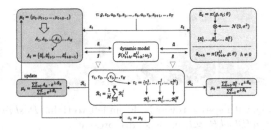

Fig. 2. Two types of action planning methods in PlanQ.

PlanQ (DDPG). At time-step t, taking the state and goal (s_t, g) as input, the policy π_θ outputs an action $\tilde{a}_t$. Next K actions $\{\tilde{a}_t^1, \tilde{a}_t^2, , ..., \tilde{a}_t^K\}$ are sampled from the Gaussian distribution $\mathcal{N}(\tilde{a}_t, \sigma^2)$ with $\tilde{a}_t$ as a mean and σ^2 as a variance. Then each triple $(g, s_t, \tilde{a}_t^i), i = 1, 2, ..., K$ is taken as a starting point for policy π_θ with dynamics models $\hat{p}_{\omega_j}, j = 1, 2, ..., M$. Each triple can generate M trajectories $\tau_i = \{\tau_i^1, \tau_i^2, ..., \tau_i^M\}$. Each of the M trajectories can be expressed as follow: $\tau_i^j = \langle g, (\tilde{s}_t^{ij}, \tilde{a}_t^{ij}, \tilde{r}_t^{ij}, \tilde{s}_{t+1}^{ij}, \tilde{a}_{t+1}^{ij}, \tilde{r}_{t+1}^{ij}, \tilde{s}_{t+2}^{ij}, ..., \tilde{s}_{t+H}^{ij}) \rangle$, where,

$$
\begin{cases}
\tilde{s}_t^{ij} = s_t, \quad \tilde{a}_t^{ij} = \tilde{a}_t^i, \quad j = 1, 2, ..., M \\
\tilde{s}_{t+h+1}^{ij} = \hat{p}_{\omega_j}(\tilde{s}_{t+h}^{ij}, \tilde{a}_{t+h}^{ij}), \quad h = 0, 1, ..., H - 1, \\
\tilde{r}_{t+h}^{ij} = R(\tilde{s}_{t+h}^{ij}, \tilde{a}_{t+h}^{ij}, \tilde{s}_{t+h+1}^{ij}, g), \quad h = 0, 1, ..., H - 1, \\
\tilde{a}_{t+h}^{ij} = \pi_\theta(\tilde{s}_{t+h}^{ij}, g), \quad h = 1, 2, ..., H - 1,
\end{cases}
\tag{6}
$$

Although τ_i^j in Eqs. (6) and (2) have the same equation form, they differ in actions. In PlanQ(PDDM), after observing state s_t, N action sequences, each of which has K actions, are sampled from an iteratively updating mean action distribution μ_t before interacting with dynamics models. In contrast, after observing state s_t, PlanQ(DDPG) generates only the first-step actions for K action sequences, and the subsequent-step actions will be generated by the policy network π_θ when interacting with dynamics models.

Finally, PlanQ(DDPG) calculates the mean return $\bar{\mathcal{R}}_i(\tau_i)$ for τ_i by Eq. (5) and outputs action $a_t = \mu_t$ by Eq. (7):

$$
\mu_t = \frac{\sum_{i=1}^K \tilde{a}_t^i \cdot e^{\lambda \cdot \bar{\mathcal{R}}_i}}{\sum_{i=1}^K e^{\lambda \cdot \bar{\mathcal{R}}_i}}.
\tag{7}
$$

This result is different from that of Eq. (4) where we have an iteratively updating vector. Here, the action update in Eq. (7) is used once and then dismissed.

5 Experiments

5.1 Experimental Setup

Four robot manipulation tasks are used to test PlanQ as shown in Fig. 3. The first two and the last tasks are the same as in [19]. Task *DclawTurn* originates from

Fig. 3. Robotic tasks with sparse rewards. From left to right: *Pushing, Pick-and-Place, DclawTurn, and HandBlockRotation* tasks are presented.

[18], but was modified to work in the sparse setting. In the *Pushing* task, a small box and a target position are selected randomly over the table. The agent learns to move the box to the target position with a tolerance of $\delta = 0.05$ m. The *Pick-and-Place* task uses the same setting as the *Pushing* task. The only difference is the target position could be in the air, so that the robot needs to learn how to pick and place the box at the target location. In the *DclawTurn* task, the agent learns to turn a valve to an arbitrary target location. The tolerance is $\delta = 0.1°$. In the *HandBlockRotation* task, a block is placed in a five-finger robotic hand with a random orientation, and a target block orientation is selected randomly. The agent learns to rotate the block to the target orientation. The tolerance is $\delta = 0.1°$. The reward function for the four tasks is: $R(s, a, s', g) = \mathbb{1}[\|\,ag - g\,\| \leq \delta] - 1$, where $\mathbb{1}$ is an indicator function, ag is the achieved goals and g is the desired goals.

5.2   Results and Analysis

PlanQ Performance Analysis. We examine whether PlanQ can improve the sample efficiency across tasks. Results are shown in Fig. 4(a). We first note that PDDM (designed to work in high-dimensional dexterous hand manipulation tasks) fails to complete the tasks under sparse reward settings. In contrast, PlanQ(PDDM) completed all the tasks with a success rate of 1 except for the complex HandBlockRotation task, where it achieved a success rate of 0.8. PlanQ(DDPG) outperformed DDPG+HER on all tasks. However, its improvement on the *DclawTurn* and *HandBlockRotation* tasks was limited. We hypothesize that the error introduced by the learned models must be close to the error introduced by learning a Q-function.

Performance of PlanQ Without HER. In this experiment, we examine whether the proposed algorithm could solve sparse reward problems without HER (recall HER is designed to resolve sparse tasks). Experiment results are shown in Fig. 4(b). Without HER, DDPG only performed well in the *DclawTurn* task. In contrast, PlanQ still learns in all tested tasks with different success rates. PlanQ(PDDM) achieved the best results on the simpler tasks of *Pushing* and *Pick-and-Place*. It was also the only method that could learn the *Pick-and-Place* task. PlanQ(DDPG) achieved the best results on complex tasks of *DclawTurn* and *HandBlockRotation* tasks. The experiments reveal that PlanQ,

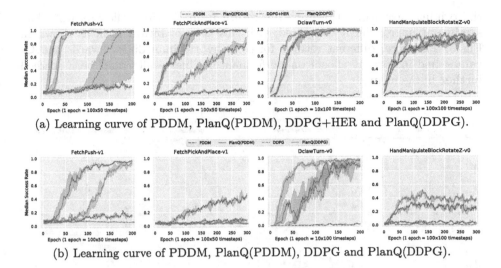

(a) Learning curve of PDDM, PlanQ(PDDM), DDPG+HER and PlanQ(DDPG).

(b) Learning curve of PDDM, PlanQ(PDDM), DDPG and PlanQ(DDPG).

Fig. 4. Performance comparison. (a) All algorithms use HER, except PDDM which cannot be combined with HER directly. (b) All algorithms do not use HER.

in the absence of HER, was still effective in sparse tasks. Each of the PlanQ methods had their own unique advantages compared to each other.

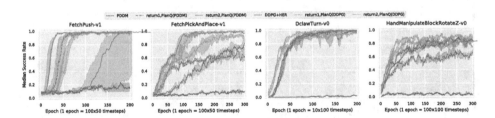

Fig. 5. Performance of PlanQ under different return forms.

PlanQ Performance Under Different Returns. Here, the return form $\bar{\mathcal{R}}$ of Eq. (5) is changed to the return1 form, which is defined as:

$$
\begin{aligned}
\bar{\mathcal{R}}_i(\tau_i) &= \sum_{j=1}^{M} \tilde{r}_t^{ij} + \gamma \cdot \tilde{r}_{t+1}^{ij} + \dots + \gamma^{H-2} \cdot \tilde{r}_{t+H-2}^{ij} + \gamma^{H-1} \cdot q_{t+H-1}^{ij} \\
&= \frac{1}{M} \sum_{j=1}^{M} \left(\gamma^{H-1} \cdot q_{t+H-1}^{ij} + \sum_{h=0}^{H-1} \gamma^h \cdot \tilde{r}_{t+h}^{ij} \right)
\end{aligned}
\tag{8}
$$

Figure 5 shows the results and indicate that despite the return change, PlanQ still contained Q-values and could still improve the performance compared to the original algorithm. However, the return from Eq. (5) (called return2) had significant improvement compared with this type of return form as shown in Fig. 5. Therefore, different returns forms of hybrid immediate rewards and Q-values had important effects on performance. This result could be a studied further in the future.

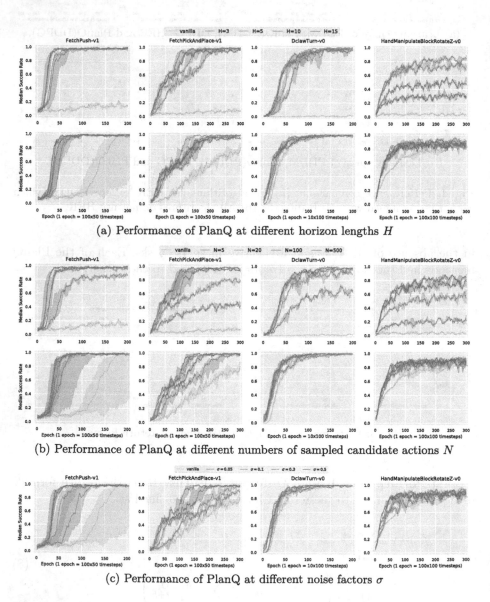

(a) Performance of PlanQ at different horizon lengths H

(b) Performance of PlanQ at different numbers of sampled candidate actions N

(c) Performance of PlanQ at different noise factors σ

Fig. 6. Sensitivity study results of the three hyper-parameters. In (a) and (b) the first row are the performance of PlanQ(PDDM) and the second row is the performance of PlanQ(DDPG); (c) is the performance of PlanQ(DDPG).

Sensitivity Study of Hyper-parameters. The sensitivity of PlanQ is studied with respect to three important hyper-parameters: (i) the length of the horizon H, (ii) the number of sampled candidate actions N, and (iii) the noise variance σ.

Figure 6(a) shows PlanQ achieved its best results at different horizon lengths in different tasks. Interestingly, even on the same task, PlanQ(PDDM) and PlanQ(DDPG) achieved their best results at different horizon lengths. When the model is perfect, the longer the horizon the better the planning result will be. Therefore, we infer that PlanQ(PDDM) and PlanQ(DDPG) have different accuracies for the learned models in the same task since the dataset used to train the models varies as it is collected by a different policy or planner.

Figure 6(b), shows PlanQ performance monotonically increased with the number of sampled candidate actions in all the tested tasks until a ceiling was reached.

Figure 6(c), shows the effects of noise variance on sampled candidate actions from PlanQ(DDPG)'s policy network. For small noise variances, the performance of PlanQ(DDPG) was similar to vanilla. For large variances however, the performance decreased because for a constant number of sampled candidate actions, the larger the action variance with respect to the policy network output, the less likely an agent was to find a better action than the policy network output.

6   Conclusions

This paper proposes PlanQ, a sparse-reward MBRL framework. PlanQ has two instantiations PlanQ(PDDM) and PlanQ(DDPG). PlanQ(PDDM) helps PDDM resolve sparse reward settings by adding Q-values to the returns. PlanQ(DDPG), derived from PlanQ(PDDM), samples candidate actions via policy networks and achieves faster convergence in contrast to DDPG. Each PlanQ instantiation has its own advantages. Both resolve sparse tasks with or without the help of HER.

Promising directions of future research could be studying how to obtain more precise dynamic models to support a longer horizon length and selecting a more proper measurement to weigh candidate actions without being limited at the immediate reward and Q-value.

References

1. Charlesworth, H.J., Montana, G.: Solving challenging dexterous manipulation tasks with trajectory optimisation and reinforcement learning. In: International Conference on Machine Learning, pp. 1496–1506. PMLR (2021)
2. Silver, D., Huang, A., Maddison, C.J., et al.: Mastering the game of Go with deep neural networks and tree search. Nature **529**(7587), 484–489 (2016)
3. Andrychowicz, O.A.I.M., Baker, B., Chociej, M., et al.: Learning dexterous in-hand manipulation. Int. J. Robot. Res. **39**(1), 3–20 (2020)
4. Pathak, D., Agrawal, P., Efros, A.A., et al.: Curiosity-driven exploration by self-supervised prediction. In: International Conference on Machine Learning, pp. 2778–2787. PMLR (2017)

5. Bengio, Y., Louradour, J., Collobert, R., et al.: Curriculum learning. In: Proceedings of the 26th Annual International Conference on Machine Learning, pp. 41–48 (2009)
6. Andrychowicz, M., Wolski, F., et al.: Hindsight experience replay. In: Advances in Neural Information Processing Systems, pp. 5048–5058 (2017)
7. Gu, S., Lillicrap, T., Sutskever, I., et al.: Continuous deep Q-learning with model-based acceleration. In: International Conference on Machine Learning, pp. 2829–2838. PMLR (2016)
8. Kalweit, G., Boedecker, J.: Uncertainty-driven imagination for continuous deep reinforcement learning. In: Conference on Robot Learning, pp. 195–206. PMLR (2017)
9. Kurutach, T., Clavera, I., Duan, Y., et al.: Model-ensemble trust-region policy optimization. In: International Conference on Learning Representations (2018)
10. Feinberg, V., Wan, A., Stoica, I., et al.: Model-based value estimation for efficient model-free reinforcement learning. Arxiv:1803.00101 (2018)
11. Buckman, J., Hafner, D., Tucker, G., et al.: Sample-efficient reinforcement learning with stochastic ensemble value expansion. In: Advances in Neural Information Processing Systems, p. 31 (2018)
12. Sutton, R.S., Barto, A.G.: Reinforcement Learning: An Introduction, 2nd edn. MIT Press, Cambridge (2018)
13. Wang, T., Ba, J.: Exploring model-based planning with policy networks. In: International Conference on Learning Representations (2019)
14. Nagabandi, A., Kahn, G., Fearing, R.S., et al.: Neural network dynamics for model-based deep reinforcement learning with model-free fine-tuning. In: International Conference on Robotics and Automation, pp. 7559–7566. IEEE (2018)
15. Chua, K., Calandra, R., McAllister, R., et al.: Deep reinforcement learning in a handful of trials using probabilistic dynamics models. In: Advances in Neural Information Processing Systems, p. 31 (2018)
16. Charlesworth, H., Montana, G.: PlanGAN: model-based planning with sparse rewards and multiple goals. In: Advances in Neural Information Processing Systems, pp. 8532–8542 (2020)
17. Lillicrap, T.P., Hunt, J.J., Pritzel, A., et al.: Continuous control with deep reinforcement learning. In: International Conference on Learning Representations (2016)
18. Nagabandi, A., Konolige, K., Levine, S., et al.: Deep dynamics models for learning dexterous manipulation. In: Conference on Robot Learning, pp. 1101–1112. PMLR (2020)
19. Plappert, M., Andrychowicz, M., Ray, A., et al.: Multi-goal reinforcement learning: challenging robotics environments and request for research. arxiv:1802.09464 (2018)

Recent Progress of an Underwater Robotic Avatar

Canjun Yang[1,2,3]([envelope]), Xin Wu[1], Yuanchao Zhu[1], Weitao Wu[1], Zhangpeng Tu[1], and Jifei Zhou[1]

[1] State Key Laboratory of Fluid Power and Mechatronic Systems, Zhejiang University, Hangzhou 310027, China
{ycj,xinwu,ychzhu,zp.t,zhou_jf}@zju.edu.cn
[2] Pilot National Laboratory of Marine Science and Technology, Qingdao 266000, China
[3] Ningbo Research Institute, Zhejiang University, Ningbo 315100, China

Abstract. This paper presents some of the recent progress of an underwater robotic avatar. The manipulation system of the avatar is enhanced in the terms of compliance, including the arm and the gripper. A rigid-foldable mechanism is applied to develop a compliant robotic arm that has the advantages of light weight, compactness, and expandability. By proposing a shape memory alloy-based module, the adjustable grasping stiffness of the gripper is achieved. Moreover, A human-robot shared control scheme is applied to reduce the burden on the human operator and enable high-level intelligent human-robot collaboration. Preliminary experimental results illustrate that the proposed components can meet the expected performance requirements, providing sufficient prior experience for future total integration of the underwater robotic avatar system.

Keywords: Underwater · Robotic avatar · Human-robot collaboration

1 Introduction

With the continuous development of marine science and technology, underwater operations are becoming increasingly sophisticated. Unmanned underwater vehicles, such as remotely operated vehicles (ROVs) and autonomous underwater vehicles (AUVs), can easily meet the challenges of the extreme marine environment, but their maneuvering capabilities are limited. In challenging task scenarios such as reef restoration, maintenance of offshore oil and gas facilities, and overhaul of nuclear reactor condensing systems, the expertise and flexibility of human divers are still indispensable. However, human scuba divers can only work at a maximum depth of about 300 m. In deep water operations, particularly, saturation diving techniques are required, in which considerable working

This research is supported by National Natural Science Foundation of China (Grant No. 52071292, 52101404).

time is spent to adapt to the pressurization and decompression brought about by changes in depth, causing reduced working efficiency and unpredictable hazards for divers.

Underwater robotic avatars are an emerging idea in response to such dilemma. A robotic avatar is a robot incarnation that embodies human intelligence and intentions through immersive interfaces in extreme environments that human cannot approach [5]. Khatib et al. proposed a robotic avatar named Ocean One [2,3,5,7,8,15]. Ocean One is comparable in size to human divers (about 5 ft in length), whose lower body is designed for efficient navigation, while the upper body is conceived in an anthropomorphic form that offers a transparent embodiment of the human's interactions with the environment through the haptic-visual interface. Recently, ex-NASA engineers Manley et al. have developed an underwater transformer Aquanaut [1,6]. Aquanaut is untethered and transformable, switching between streamlined transit mode with better maneuverability and intervention mode with greater manipulability.

The smooth and intuitive human-robot interaction interface is a prerequisite for human operator to manipulate robotic avatars. Ocean One provides a user command center consisting of haptic feedback devices, first-person view monitor, graphic control panel, and other control terminals [5,15]. Aquanaut is envisioned to utilize a supervisory command and control architecture under the constraints of limited communication bandwidth, where the operator instructs the robot at a high level, rather than controlling it in real time [6]. Unfortunately, none of the current interface solutions enable natural human-robot interaction to the greatest extent possible. The manipulation of Ocean One arms depends on joystick-like force feedback dragging devices, which makes the process slow and clumsy. Aquanaut operator have to send keyboard commands to give instructions, which is not intuitive as well. Based on the interactive interfaces described above, existing solutions have made some progress in terms of limited human high-level cognitive interventions, although not yet very satisfactory.

In this paper, we introduce the recent developing progress of a newly designed underwater robotic avatar [9]. The developed robotic avatar utilizes a anthropomorphic body skeleton to maximize the natural affinity of human-robot mapping, thereby enhancing the generalizability and transferability of the human operator's expertise and experience. An end-to-end interaction interface is proposed to promote this natural affinity as well. The avatar's manipulator, i.e. arm and hand, is conceived to embody human-like flexibility to achieve dexterous and damage-free manipulation. A shared control scheme is applied to the robotic avatar system, which enables high-level intelligent human-robot collaboration within the narrow bandwidth constraints of underwater communications.

2   System Overview

The robotic avatar is designed to resemble a human diver in scale and shape, thus allowing the avatar workspace as close to that of the operator as possible. A conceptual presentation of the proposed robotic avatar is shown in Fig. 1(a).

There are eight propeller-type thrusters equipped around the avatar torso in convenience of fast maneuvering, as shown in Fig. 1(b). Previous generation of avatar arms were built with a servo motor-linkage system, where the servo motors played the role of the arm joints [10]. In the latest blueprint, the robotic avatar will assembly more dexterous manipulators, including foldable compliant robotic arms and stiffness adjustable flexible grippers, which will be described in the following section.

(a)   (b)

Fig. 1. (a) The underwater robotic avatar (conceptual). (b) The robot torso, with a total of eight thrusters installed.

The human control loop of the robotic avatar is designed to be a physically friendly procedure. The operator in the control room is equipped with a flexible network of wearable sensors, while his postural commands are also captured and extracted by a deep learning-based monocular camera motion capture system [12]. The captured data from wearable sensors and the camera are aligned and fused to generate accurate pose data. The generated pose data are utilized in the proposed shared control scheme, then sent to the robot as high-level instructions. The described process is illustrated in Fig. 2. By applying the proposed shared control scheme, the operator can focus on high-level cognition and reasoning, and the robotic avatar can maximize its capability of long period precise execution and autonomous low-level task handling, therefore reducing the operator's tedium, labor intensity, and error rate [14]. Furthermore, we envisioned a digital twin system [4] that would effectively improve the human-robot interaction performance by providing the operator with a third-person view of the digital model's real-time state.

3   Dexterous Manipulation System

This section describes the progress of the dexterous manipulation system for the proposed underwater avatar, including the robotic arm and the robotic gripper.

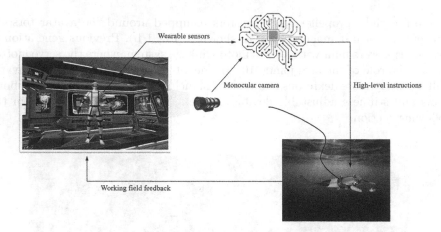

Fig. 2. The human control loop of the avatar.

3.1   Foldable Compliant Robotic Arm

The origami-inspired foldable arm design has advantages of lightweight, compact, and expandable, which allows the robot to manipulate in tortuous environments and enhances the robot's working flexibility. We took origami artwork Twisted Tower as design model and proposed a rigid-foldable mechanism suitable for assembling compliant robotic arms.

Our previous work has revealed the design criteria behind Twisted Tower [11], based on which a continuum robotic arm with high movability can be assembled. To prevent internal interference during the movement, the cells in the same layer should be kept separate from their neighbors. This is satisfied by setting proper geometry of the trapezoidal plates, as Eq. (1) illustrates.

$$\frac{360°}{n} = 2 \arctan \frac{b - a}{2h}$$
$$\theta = 2 \arctan \frac{b - a}{\sqrt{4h^2 - (b - a)^2 \cos^2 \psi}} \tag{1}$$

where a and b are the trapezoid bases, and h is the trapezoid height. ψ is the twist angle, and θ is the field angle. It is trivial to see that the geometry of the trapezoid is relevant to the number of the cells in a layer, n. Typically, n is set to 8 (Fig. 3).

The manufacturing of the robotic arm prototype is achieved by 3D printing technology. All the components used are fully rigid, avoiding the modeling ambiguity and easier aging fracture phenomenon brought by soft components like rubber. Taking $n = 8$, we set $a = 30$ cm, $b = 105$ cm, and $h = 90$ cm. Figure 4 shows this implementation. The plates (a) and (b) in one layer are articulated by Shaft (c) and Shaft cap (d) through the shaft holes. The adjacent layers are hinged together by Hinge (e). For multi-layer towers, additional cover plates (f) could be installed at the end of the arm.

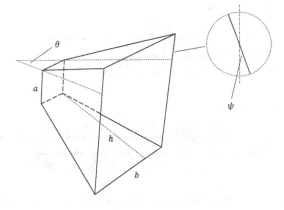

Fig. 3. The geometric parameters of a Twisted Tower cell.

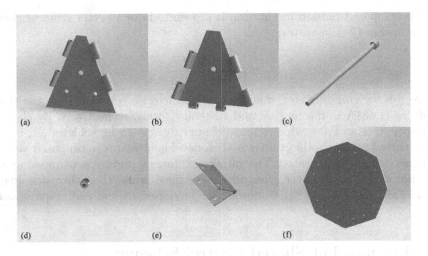

Fig. 4. The components of the 3D printed Twisted Tower implementation. (a) Top/bottom plate. (b) Left/right plate. (c) Shaft. (d) Shaft cap. (e) Hinge. (f) Cover plate.

3.2 Stiffness Adjustable Flexible Gripper

Structure with adjustable stiffness can significantly improve the interactive capabilities of robotic grippers. Shape memory alloy (SMA) is utilized to achieve a novel variable stiffness structure [13]. By adjusting the temperature, SMA can transform between martensite and austenite, exhibiting variable elasticity at different stages. To amplify the effect of stiffness variation, a spring-based tension mechanism is proposed, as shown in Fig. 5.

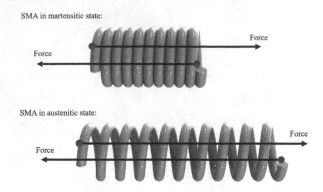

Fig. 5. The spring-based tension mechanism of SMA variable stiffness structure.

The proposed tension mechanism is proven to have a better stiffness change rate η, as Eq. (2) illustrates.

$$\eta = \frac{8\pi D^4}{d^4} \cdot \frac{E_M}{E_A} \tag{2}$$

where d is the coil diameter, d is the wire diameter, E_M and E_A are the elastic modulus of SMA in martensitic and austenitic forms, respectively. By choosing appropriate D and d, a wide range of change rate η can be achieved.

A three-finger robotic gripper is then developed with the proposed variable stiffness structure integrated. The variable stiffness structure is wrapped around the motor-tendon actuator, one side being fixed while the other side free to expand and contract, as Fig. 6 shows. The developed gripper prototype is shown in Fig. 7.

4 Human-robot Shared Control Scheme

A human-robot shared control scheme is proposed that can better combine the respective strengths of the human operator and the robotic avatar during collaboration. The flow block framework of the shared control scheme is illustrated in Fig. 8. In a specific operation task, the operator performs an action U according to the initially identified target position G, and then the motion capture system extracts the operator's arm joint angles and derives the corresponding robot arm joint angles θ_H using human-robot action mapping algorithms [16]. At the same time, the robotic avatar forecasts the intent of the operator according to G and the operator's trajectory over a period of time, ξ_H, and obtains the most reasonably possible target. Given this target position, a series of robotic arm joint angels θ_R can be derived by solving the inverse kinematics of the

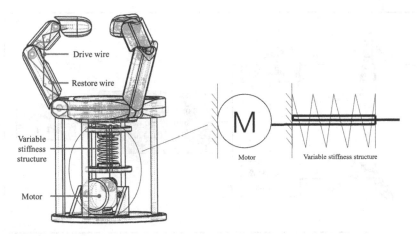

Fig. 6. The integrated SMA variable stiffness structure in gripper actuator.

robot manipulator. The shared control angles θ_S is then generated by assigning appropriate weights between the operator command θ_H and the robot command θ_R. The mentioned angles and the weights are continuously adjusted until the whole task is completed.

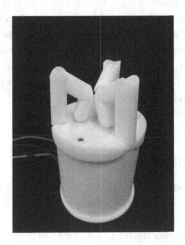

Fig. 7. The developed gripper prototype.

The weight assignment is made according to the confidence level of the target identification. In this paper, the adjustment of the weight α is achieved using a segmentation function (Eq. (3)).

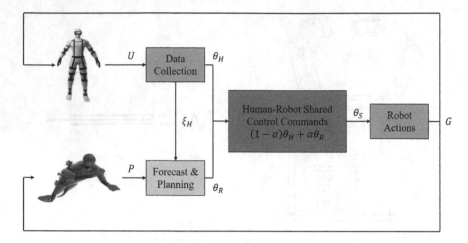

Fig. 8. The flow block of the human-robot shared control scheme.

$$\alpha = \begin{cases} 0 & (conf \leq 0.2) \\ 1.22conf - 0.243 & (0.2 < conf \leq 0.8) \\ \frac{1}{1+e^{-20conf+15}} & (0.8 < conf \leq 1) \end{cases} \tag{3}$$

where $conf$ is the confidence level. When $conf$ is low, the operator intent is dominant to guide the robot for a rough planning. As $conf$ increases, the robot weight increases too, enabling its capability of precise execution. In the low confidence zone, linear expressions are applied to yield smooth movement, while in the high confidence zone, an exponential expression is applied to accelerate the weight transition and improve the response speed of the robot. More details are presented in our previous work [17].

5   Experiments

5.1   Foldable Arm Movability

The movability of the foldable arm is verified with a five-layer foldable arm prototype. A scale panel is placed in the background of the test bench to measure the pose of the arm during the experiment, as Fig. 9(a) shows. The leftmost and the rightmost cells are driven by tendons, and both ψ angles are sampled with a interval of 5°. Figure 9(b) shows the distribution of the end position of the arm, i.e. its workspace, in the vertical cutting plane. The vertical displacement can reach approximately 530 cm, and the horizontal displacement can reach approximately 180 cm.

5.2   Gripper Stiffness Adjustment

The stiffness of the proposed flexible gripper is analyzed in different SMA temperature conditions. The bending forces of the gripper fingertip at a series of

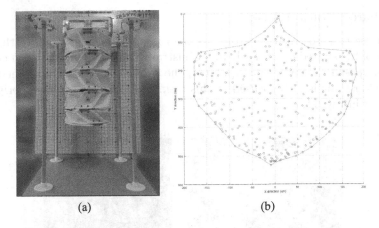

(a)   (b)

Fig. 9. (a) The test bench with five-layer foldable arm. (b) The workspace of the five-layer foldable arm.

different displacements are measured, then a linear fit is performed on the collected data points. The slope of the obtained fit function is the stiffness of the gripper at the current temperature. The sampling temperature interval is set 1 °C, and the range is from 40 °C to 66 °C. Figure 10 shows the gripper stiffness versus temperature. When the temperature is below 45 °C, the stiffness of the gripper is relatively greater (SMA in martensitic state). As the temperature rises, the gripper stiffness gradually decreases (SMA in austenitic state). It can be seen in the figure that the stiffness ranged from 0.0069 to 0.0584, with a stiffness change rate of 8.69.

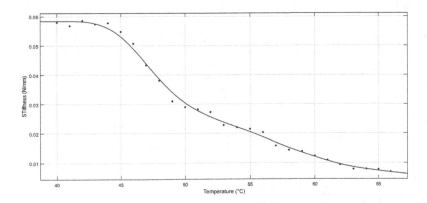

Fig. 10. The gripper stiffness versus temperature.

5.3   Shared Control Task

An exercise task to rescue a drowning man is performed to validate the effectiveness of the shared control scheme. Constrained by the current advancements of the proposed dexterous manipulator, the previous generation of the articulated avatar arms is instead used in this task. The scenario of the experiment is illustrated in Fig. 11.

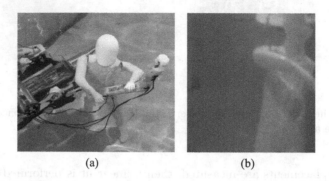

(a)   (b)

Fig. 11. Rescue task scenario. (a) Third-person perspective over water. (b) Avatar's first-person perspective.

During the task, the operator monitors the obtained first-person underwater view Fig. 11(b) and guides the movement of the avatar. The positions of the elbow and the wrist are recorded throughout the process, as shown in Fig. 12. It can be seen that the robotic avatar can steadily follow the trend of the operator's elbow and wrist positions and accurately identify the operator's movement intention.

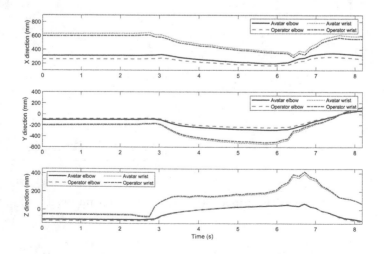

Fig. 12. Elbow and wrist positions of the operator and the avatar.

6 Conclusion

In this paper, we reported some of the recent progress of an underwater robotic avatar, including the dexterous manipulation system and the human-robot shared control scheme. The dexterous manipulation system is divided into foldable compliant robotic arm and stiffness adjustable flexible gripper that enhance the avatar's compliance and environmental friendliness. The rigid-foldable mechanism of the robotic arm is derived from the origami artwork Twisted Tower, which is lightweight, compact, and expandable. A SMA-based spring-like module is integrated in the flexible gripper, providing the ability to adjust the stiffness of the grasping. The human-robot shared control scheme further improves the human-robot collaboration and reduces the burden on the operator throughout the controlling process. In summary, the proposed robotic avatar has strengthened its manipulation and control capabilities, and the experimental results validate this encouraging progress. In the future, the robotic avatar would dive into real underwater scenarios and unlock more challenging adventures that humans or robots alone cannot achieve.

References

1. Ackerman, E.: The underwater transformer: Ex-NASA engineers built a robot sub that transforms into a skilled humanoid. IEEE Spectr. **56**(8), 22–29 (2019). https://doi.org/10.1109/MSPEC.2019.8784119
2. Brantner, G.: Human-Robot Collaboration in Challenging Environments. Ph.D. thesis, Stanford University (2018)
3. Brantner, G., Khatib, O.: Controlling Ocean One: Human–robot collaboration for deep-sea manipulation. J. Field Robot., p. rob.21960, June 2020. https://doi.org/10.1002/rob.21960
4. Jones, D., Snider, C., Nassehi, A., Yon, J., Hicks, B.: Characterising the digital twin: a systematic literature review. CIRP J. Manuf. Sci. Technol. **29**, 36–52 (2020). https://doi.org/10.1016/j.cirpj.2020.02.002
5. Khatib, O., et al.: Ocean One: a robotic avatar for oceanic discovery. IEEE Robot. Automation Magaz. **23**(4), 20–29 (2016). https://doi.org/10.1109/MRA.2016.2613281
6. Manley, J.E., Halpin, S., Radford, N., Ondler, M.: Aquanaut: a new tool for subsea inspection and intervention. In: OCEANS 2018 MTS/IEEE Charleston, pp. 1–4. IEEE, Charleston, SC, Oct 2018. https://doi.org/10.1109/OCEANS.2018.8604508
7. Stuart, H.: Robotic Hand Design for Remote Ocean Exploration: Active Selection of Compliance and Contact Conditions. Ph.D. thesis, Stanford University (2017)
8. Stuart, H., Wang, S., Khatib, O., Cutkosky, M.R.: The Ocean one hands: an adaptive design for robust marine manipulation. Int. J. Robot. Res. **36**(2), 150–166 (2017). https://doi.org/10.1177/0278364917694723
9. Wei, Q.: Study on Design of Underwater Frogman-like Robot and Man-machine Sharing Perceptual Control. Ph.D. thesis, Zhejiang University (2019)
10. Wu, W., Yang, C., Xu, Z., Wu, X., Zhu, Y., Wei, Q.: Development and Control of a Humanoid Underwater Robot. In: 2020 6th International Conference on Mechatronics and Robotics Engineering (ICMRE), pp. 6–11. IEEE, Barcelona, Spain, February 2020. https://doi.org/10.1109/ICMRE49073.2020.9064996

11. Wu, X.: Rigid-foldable mechanism inspired by origami twisted tower. J. Mech. Robot. **14**(5), 054503 (2022). https://doi.org/10.1115/1.4053736

12. Wu, X., Yang, C., Zhu, Y., Wu, W., Wei, Q.: An integrated vision-based system for efficient robot arm teleoperation. Ind. Robot. Int. J. Robot. Res. Appl. **48**(2), 199–210 (2020). https://doi.org/10.1108/IR-06-2020-0129

13. Yang, C., Wu, W., Wu, X., Zhou, J., Tu, Z., Lin, M., Zhang, S.: A flexible gripper with a wide-range variable stiffness structure based on shape memory alloy. Industrial Robot: the international journal of robotics research and application (2022), to be published

14. Yang, C., Zhu, Y., Chen, Y.: A Review of Human-Machine Cooperation in the Robotics Domain. IEEE Transactions on Human-Machine Systems, pp. 1–14 (2021). https://doi.org/10.1109/THMS.2021.3131684

15. Yeh, X.: Development of an Underwater Humanoid Robotic Diver. Ph.D. thesis, Stanford University (2017)

16. Zhu, Y., Cheng, Y., Yang, C., Tu, Z., Wu, X., Wu, W.: An anthropomorphic motion retargeting method based on an adaptive genetic algorithm. In: 2022 8th International Conference on Control, Automation and Robotics (ICCAR), pp. 409–413. IEEE (2022)

17. Zhu, Y., Yang, C., Wei, Q., Wu, X., Yang, W.: Human–robot shared control for humanoid manipulator trajectory planning. Industrial Robot: the international journal of robotics research and application (2020)

Mixline: A Hybrid Reinforcement Learning Framework for Long-Horizon Bimanual Coffee Stirring Task

Zheng Sun[1], Zhiqi Wang[1], Junjia Liu[1], Miao Li[2(✉)], and Fei Chen[1(✉)]

[1] The Chinese University of Hong Kong, Hong Kong, China
{zhengsun,zqwang}@link.cuhk.edu.hk, jjliu@mae.cuhk.edu.hk,
f.chen@ieee.org
[2] Wuhan University, Wuhan, China
miao.li@whu.edu.cn

Abstract. Bimanual activities like coffee stirring, which require coordination of dual arms, are common in daily life and intractable to learn by robots. Adopting reinforcement learning to learn these tasks is a promising topic since it enables the robot to explore how dual arms coordinate together to accomplish the same task. However, this field has two main challenges: coordination mechanism and long-horizon task decomposition. Therefore, we propose the *Mixline* method to learn sub-tasks separately via the online algorithm and then compose them together based on the generated data through the offline algorithm. We constructed a learning environment based on the GPU-accelerated Isaac Gym. In our work, the bimanual robot successfully learned to grasp, hold and lift the spoon and cup, insert them together and stir the coffee. The proposed method has the potential to be extended to other long-horizon bimanual tasks.

Keywords: Reinforcement learning · Bimanual coordination · Isaac Gym

1 Introduction

The rapid development of Reinforcement Learning (RL) has provided new ideas for robot control [1,2], and the training of bimanual robots with coordination has become a hot topic in reinforcement learning. In this paper, we are interested in how to make bimanual robots learn human's daily activities. These activities

---

Z. Sun and Z. Wang—Contribute equally to this work.

This work was supported in part by the Research Grants Council of the Hong Kong Special Administrative Region, China under Grant 24209021, in part by the VC Fund of the CUHK T Stone Robotics Institute under Grant 4930745, in part by CUHK Direct Grant for Research under Grant 4055140, and in part by the Hong Kong Centre for Logistics Robotics.

H. Liu et al. (Eds.): ICIRA 2022, LNAI 13455, pp. 627–636, 2022.
https://doi.org/10.1007/978-3-031-13844-7_58

are usually long-horizon and need the coordination of dual human arms. These two challenges limit the use of RL in complex tasks and make it unavailable to real-world scenarios. Here we design a long-horizon and bimanual coffee stirring task as an example to study the potential solution of these kinds of tasks. The illustration of coffee stirring movements is shown in Fig. 1. It contains movements like grasping, lifting, inserting, and stirring.

Fig. 1. Bimanual coffee stirring

In recent research, Zhang et al. proposed a novel disentangled attention technique, which provides intrinsic regularization for two robots to focus on separate sub-tasks and objects [3]. Chitnis et al. decomposed the learning process into a state-independent task schema to yield significant improvements in sample efficiency [4]. Liu et al. applied dual-arm Deep Deterministic Policy Gradient (DDPG) [5] based on Deep Reinforcement Learning (DRL) with Hindsight Experience Replay (HER) [6] to achieve cooperative tasks based on "rewarding cooperation and punishing competition" [7]. Chiu et al. achieved bimanual regrasping by using demonstrations from a sampling-based motion planning algorithm and generalizing for non-specific trajectory [8]. Rajeswaran et al. augmented the policy search process with a small number of human demonstrations [9]. Liu et al. proposed a novel scalable multi-agent reinforcement methods for solving traffic signal control in large road networks [10]. Cabi et al. introduced reward sketching to make a massive annotated dataset for batch reinforcement learning [11]. Mandlekar et al. presented Generalization Through Imitation (GTI), using a two-stage intersecting structure to train policies [12]. Zhang et al. gave a deep analysis of Multi-Agent RL theory and assessment of research directions [13]. Except for adopting multi-agent RL methods, some recent work also focus on learning bimanual complex robot skills from human demonstration [14,15]. Specially, Liu et al. achieved bimanual robot cooking with stir-fry, the traditional Chinese cooking art. They combined Transformer with Graph neural network as *Structured-Transformer* to learn the spatio-temporal relationship of dual arms from human demonstration [14].

In this paper ,we propose to use a task division process first to decompose the long-horizon task and learn each sub-task separately. Besides, we propose wait training method to solve the poor coordination. Then by adopting the conservative Q-learning (CQL), we can combine the offline data generated via the separate learning process to achieve the learning of the whole task. We regard this hybrid reinforcement learning method which contains both online and offline RL algorithms, as *Mixline*.

2 Task Definition and Environment

2.1 Task Definition

When we drink coffee, we pick up the spoon and the coffee cup with our left and right hands and use the spoon to stir the coffee in the cup. Therefore, the goal is to train two robotic arms to do the same sequential actions: one arm grasps a spoon, the other grasps a cup, then the arm with the spoon lifts and inserts it into the cup for a stirring motion.

We found that the previous work still has flaws, such as bimanual coordination and long-horizon tasks. These are common challenges in the robot field. To solve them, in our study, we split the whole task into three stages. By setting the reward function for the three stages separately, we solve the existing sparse reward problem. Splitting into three stages helps us solve the long-horizon and poor coordination problems.

The three stages are:

1. Grasp and pick up the cup and spoon;
2. Insert the spoon into the cup;
3. Stir in the cup without hitting the cup overly.

The diagrams about three stages are shown in Fig. 2.

(a) Hold and lift   (b) Insert   (c) Stir overly

Fig. 2. Separate the coffee stirring task into three stages. From (a) to (c), there are diagrams about stage 1, stage 2, and stage 3.

2.2 Isaac Gym Environment

Isaac Gym offers a high-performance learning platform to train policies for a wide variety of robotic tasks directly on GPU [16]. It performs significantly better than other standard physics simulators using CPU clusters, and also has many advantages in reinforcement learning:

- It provides a high-fidelity GPU-accelerated robot simulator platform;
- With the help of Tensor API, Isaac Gym goes through CPU bottlenecks by wrapping physics buffers into PyTorch [17] tensors;
- It can achieve tens of thousands of simultaneous environments on a single GPU [18].

3   Methodology

3.1   Background of Reinforcement Learning

The dynamical system of reinforcement learning is defined by a Markov Decision Process (MDP) [19]. MDP can be regarded as a 5-tuple $M = (S, A, T, r, \gamma)$, where S is states of the environment and agent, A refers to the actions of the agent, T defines the state transition function of the system, r is the reward function, and γ means the discount factor.

The goal of reinforcement learning is to learn a policy $\pi(a, s)$. And the objective $J(\pi)$ can be derived as an expectation under the trajectory distribution, as Eq. 1.

$$J(\pi) = \mathbb{E}_{\tau \sim p_\pi(\tau)}[\sum_{t=0}^{H} \gamma^t r(s_t, a_t)] \tag{1}$$

where τ is the whole trajectory given by sequence of states s and actions a, and $p_\pi(\tau)$ is the trajectory distribution of the given policy π.

3.2   Proximal Policy Optimization

Proximal Policy Optimization (PPO) [20] is an on-policy algorithm, which is the most widely used algorithm in RL. Its the objective function is usually modified by important sampling [21]. Suppose the target policy is θ and the behavior policy is θ'. Important sampling adopts KL divergence to measure the difference between these two policies and minimizes their gap. The modified objective function is

$$\hat{J}'_{PPO}(\theta) = \hat{E}_\pi[\frac{\pi_\theta(a_t|s_t)}{\pi_{\theta'}(a_t|s_t)} A^{\theta'}(s, a)] - \beta KL(\theta, \theta') \tag{2}$$

3.3   Wait Training Mechanism for Bimanual Learning

We introduce a new training method to help us solve the problem of bimanual coordination, called wait training. The specific principle is that only one robotic arm is considered each time we train. Taking the first stage as an example, we lock the movement of the right arm so that the algorithm only focuses on the grasping of the spoon by the left arm. When the left arm grabs the spoon, lock the movement of the left arm. After training each arm to grasp successfully, unlock the arms movement and focus the training process on lifting the arms. Through wait training, we have solved the problem of poor coordination between arms under the PPO algorithm.

3.4   Mixline Method for Learning Long-Horizon Tasks

After we finish the policy learning of each stage using PPO, we derive the bimanual trajectory and combine them to form the whole long-horizon trajectory. The combined trajectory is regarded as an expert dataset and used for offline training.

To utilize offline data, we introduce conservative Q-learning (CQL) [22], which can be implemented on top of soft actor-critic (SAC) [23]. Similar work has been proposed based on SAC to reduce the state-action space and improve the training efficiency by introducing inexplicit prior knowledge [24]. The primary purpose of CQL is to augment the standard Bellman error objective with a simple Q-value regularizer. In the experiment, it is proved effective in mitigating distributional shift compared to other offline algorithms.

The conservative policy evaluation minimizes the Q value of all actions, then adds a term to maximize the Q value of actions from the expert dataset to encourage actions that conform to the offline dataset and restrain actions beyond the dataset, where Eq. 3.

$$
\hat{Q}^{k+1} \leftarrow \arg\min_{Q} \alpha \cdot (\mathbb{E}_{s \sim D, a \sim \mu(a|s)}[Q(s,a)] - \mathbb{E}_{s \sim D, a \sim \hat{\pi}_\beta(a|s)}[Q(s,a)])
$$
$$
+ \frac{1}{2}\mathbb{E}_{s,a,s' \sim D}[(Q(s,a) - \hat{\mathcal{B}}^\pi \hat{Q}^k(s,a))^2] \tag{3}
$$

By combining online PPO algorithm and offline CQL algorithm, the proposed *Mixline* method can gather offline data generated from each stage and achieve the learning of the whole long-horizon tasks.

4   Experiments

4.1   Simulation Environment

In our work, we set seven objects in each working space in the Isaac Gym environment. There are two Franka robots, one spoon on a shelf, one cup on a box shelf, and a table, as shown in the Fig. 3a.

Simulation: Each Franka robot has seven revolute joints and two prismatic joints in the gripper. The action space is set continuously between -1 to 1 and uses relative control. Some basic settings are shown in Fig. 3b. To facilitate the state of the grasp in the training process, we divided the observation space in each workspace into 74. The Table 1 records the allocation of each part of the buffer. We labeled one Franka arm as Franka-spoon and the other as Franka-cup.

RL Flow: In our experiment, we use PyTorch [17,25] as base RL library. In the RL iteration, the agents sample actions from the policy and give the actions to the environment for physics simulation; then, the environment gives back all the buffer needed to compute for further steps such as reward calculation.

item	Description
Action buffer size	18
Range of action values	[-1 to 1]
Observation buffer size	74
Number of environments	1024

(a) Franka robots and assets in Isaac Gym environment

(b) RL settings

Fig. 3. Simulation environment

Table 1. Observation buffer table

Index	Description
0–8	The scale of Franka-spoon's joint positions
9–17	The scale of Franka-cup's joint positions
18–26	The velocity of Franka-spoon's joints
27–29	The relative position between the top of gripper and spoon
30–38	The velocity of Franka-cup's joints
39–41	The relative position between the top of gripper and cup
42–48	Spoon's position and rotation
49–55	Cup's position and rotation
56–64	Franka-spoon's joint positions
65–73	Franka-cup's joint positions

4.2   Design of Reward Function

In general, all the rewards and penalties are given a scale to get the total reward.

Reward
We divide total rewards into Distance reward, Rotation reward, Around reward, Finger distance reward, and Lift reward for finishing the task.

Distance Reward: Distance reward is relative to the grasping point. The reward lifts when the robot hand moves towards the object's grasp point.

Rotation Reward: We pre-define the axis to ensure alignment. The rotation reward gets its maximum value when the specified robot plane coincides with the pre-defined plane.

Around Reward: When the robot grasps something, we have to make two fingers at the different sides of the object, not only orientation and distance. Only in this situation can the object be taken up. This reward is the prerequisite for taking up the object.

Finger Distance Reward: If the around reward is satisfied, it can grasp the object when the gripper is close. Meantime, the distance should be small to ensure both the finger and robot hand is close enough, and the gripper holds tighter, the reward is bigger.

Lift Reward: The target of stage 1 is to take up the object. Hence the reward boosts when the robot hand grasps the object successfully and lifts the object. In the meantime, we expect the gripper holds the object tightly so that the object will not drop during fast movement.

Penalty

In general, the penalty term prevents the agent do unexpected actions. We divide total penalty into Action penalty, Collision penalty, Fall penalty, and Wrong pose penalty.

Action Penalty: Making a regularization of the actions means more actions and more penalties. We expect the robot can finish the task as soon as possible.

Collision Penalty: The robot may hit the table if the link contact force exceeds the limit. An unexpected collision gives a penalty to the total reward.

Fall Penalty: The robot receives a fall penalty if the object is knocked down by the robot arm when it tries to grasp or in other similar circumstances.

Wrong Pose Penalty: The goal is to let the robots achieve bimanual coordination so that the trajectory should always be reasonable, not only the final target position. For example, the cup should not be inverted during the movement. Fall penalty can be added to this penalty.

4.3   Reset Condition

The robot should always stay in its safe operational space. We do not expect the robot to be close to its singularity position. We reset the environment if the pose is unreasonable. For example, in our task, we hope the robot should not let the object drop; if it drops on the table or ground, we directly reset it and penalize it. In common, the environment should be reset if the task step exceeds the maximum task length.

4.4   Results

In our work, we generated expert datasets with an online algorithm, then proposed combining the sub-task offline dataset with training the policy. In stage 1, we trained to grasp cup and spoon in the PPO algorithm, used the wait training method to solve coordination problems, and the CQL+PPO method in several different environment settings. In stages 2 & 3, we set the end of stage 1 as the initial state and trained the robot arm to complete the task. With the help of the above methods, We finish our training goals and results as shown in Fig. 4. After combining all stages, we proposed to train the policy using the offline algorithm to finish the whole long-horizon task. The training results are consistent with our expectations, proving that the method proposed in bimanual reinforcement learning is effective.

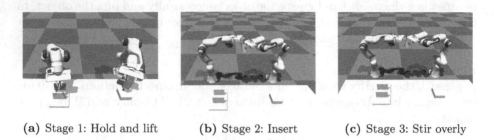

(a) Stage 1: Hold and lift   (b) Stage 2: Insert   (c) Stage 3: Stir overly

Fig. 4. Result of each stage

4.5   Ablation Study

We test the performance in Ant, Humanoid, and our task environments in general PPO method and variant CQL implement based on PPO, as shown in Fig. [5a, 5b, 5c]. The results in Fig. 5 show that CQL(ρ) performs significantly better than the general PPO algorithm in our task. PPO and CQL act nearly the same in typical environments like Ant and Humanoid. This result is expected because, in the on-policy algorithm, the behavior policy is the same as the learned policy. Therefore, the effect of optimizing terms to promote learning efficiency is limited. Our *Mixline* method effectively separates the whole long-horizon task into sub-tasks and can be easily extended to other skill-learning tasks.

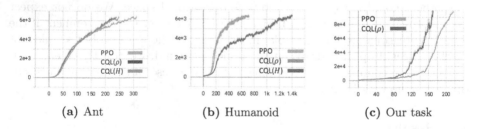

(a) Ant   (b) Humanoid   (c) Our task

Fig. 5. Performance of PPO and CQL+PPO in different task environments

5 Conclusion

This paper proposes a novel hybrid reinforcement learning method for learning long-horizon and bimanual robot skills. To overcome the long-horizon issue, we combine the online and offline reinforcement learning algorithms as the *Mixline* method to learn sub-task separately and then compose them together. Besides, we design a wait training mechanism to achieve bimanual coordination. The experiments are conducted in parallel based on the Isaac Gym simulator. The results show that using the *Mixline* method can solve the long-horizon and bimanual coffee stirring task, which is intractable by just using online algorithms. The proposed method has the potential to be extended to other long-horizon and bimanual tasks. Moreover, combining online and offline RL algorithms might allow us to add human demonstration as the initial offline data to boost policy learning. Another further direction is to model the coordination mechanism by neural network rather than setting waiting manually.

References

1. Arulkumaran, K., Deisenroth, M.P., Brundage, M., Bharath, A.A.: Deep reinforcement learning: a brief survey. IEEE Sign. Process. Mag. **34**(6), 26–38 (2017). https://doi.org/10.1109/MSP.2017.2743240
2. Ding, Z., Huang, Y., Yuan, H., Dong, H.: Introduction to reinforcement learning. In: Dong, H., Ding, Z., Zhang, S. (eds.) Deep Reinforcement Learning, pp. 47–123. Springer, Singapore (2020). https://doi.org/10.1007/978-981-15-4095-0_2
3. Zhang, M., Jian, P., Wu, Y., Xu, H., Wang, X.: Disentangled attention as intrinsic regularization for bimanual multi-object manipulation. arXiv e-prints, pp. arXiv-2106 (2021)
4. Chitnis, R., Tulsiani, S., Gupta, S., Gupta, A.: Efficient bimanual manipulation using learned task schemas. In: 2020 IEEE International Conference on Robotics and Automation (ICRA), pp. 1149–1155. IEEE (2020)
5. Lillicrap, T.P., et al.: Continuous control with deep reinforcement learning. arXiv preprint arXiv:1509.02971 (2015)
6. Andrychowicz, M., et al.: Hindsight experience replay. Adv. Neural Inf. Process. Syst. **30** (2017)
7. Liu, L., Liu, Q., Song, Y., Pang, B., Yuan, X., Xu, Q.: A collaborative control method of dual-arm robots based on deep reinforcement learning. Appl. Sci. **11**(4), 1816 (2021)
8. Chiu, Z.Y., Richter, F., Funk, E.K., Orosco, R.K., Yip, M.C.: Bimanual regrasping for suture needles using reinforcement learning for rapid motion planning. In: 2021 IEEE International Conference on Robotics and Automation (ICRA), pp. 7737–7743. IEEE (2021)
9. Rajeswaran, A., et al.: Learning complex dexterous manipulation with deep reinforcement learning and demonstrations. arXiv preprint arXiv:1709.10087 (2017)
10. Liu, J., Zhang, H., Fu, Z., Wang, Y.: Learning scalable multi-agent coordination by spatial differentiation for traffic signal control. Eng. Appl. Artif. Intell. **100**, 104165 (2021)
11. Cabi, S., et al.: Scaling data-driven robotics with reward sketching and batch reinforcement learning. arXiv preprint arXiv:1909.12200 (2019)

12. Mandlekar, A., Xu, D., Martín-Martín, R., Savarese, S., Fei-Fei, L.: Learning to generalize across long-horizon tasks from human demonstrations. arXiv preprint arXiv:2003.06085 (2020)
13. Zhang, K., Yang, Z., Başar, T.: Multi-agent reinforcement learning: a selective overview of theories and algorithms. Handbook of Reinforcement Learning and Control, pp. 321–384 (2021)
14. Liu, J., et al.: Robot cooking with stir-fry: bimanual non-prehensile manipulation of semi-fluid objects. IEEE Robot. Autom. Lett. **7**(2), 5159–5166 (2022)
15. Dong, Z., Li, Z., Yan, Y., Calinon, S., Chen, F.: Passive bimanual skills learning from demonstration with motion graph attention networks. IEEE Robot. Autom. Lett. **7**(2), 4917–4923 (2022). https://doi.org/10.1109/LRA.2022.3152974
16. Makoviychuk, V., et al.: Isaac Gym: high performance GPU-based physics simulation for robot learning (2021)
17. Paszke, A., et al.: Pytorch: an imperative style, high-performance deep learning library. In: Wallach, H., Larochelle, H., Beygelzimer, A., d' Alché-Buc, F., Fox, E., Garnett, R. (eds.) Advances in Neural Information Processing Systems 32, pp. 8024–8035. Curran Associates, Inc. (2019). http://papers.neurips.cc/paper/9015-pytorch-an-imperative-style-high-performance-deep-learning-library.pdf
18. Wan, W., Harada, K.: Developing and comparing single-arm and dual-arm regrasp. IEEE Robot. Autom. Lett. **1**(1), 243–250 (2016)
19. Sutton, R.S., Barto, A.G., et al.: Introduction to reinforcement learning (1998)
20. Schulman, J., Wolski, F., Dhariwal, P., Radford, A., Klimov, O.: Proximal policy optimization algorithms. arXiv preprint arXiv:1707.06347 (2017)
21. Schulman, J., Levine, S., Abbeel, P., Jordan, M., Moritz, P.: Trust region policy optimization. In: International Conference on Machine Learning, pp. 1889–1897. PMLR (2015)
22. Kumar, A., Zhou, A., Tucker, G., Levine, S.: Conservative q-learning for offline reinforcement learning. Adv. Neural. Inf. Process. Syst. **33**, 1179–1191 (2020)
23. Haarnoja, T., Zhou, A., Abbeel, P., Levine, S.: Soft actor-critic: off-policy maximum entropy deep reinforcement learning with a stochastic actor. In: International Conference on Machine Learning (ICML) (2018)
24. Liu, J., et al.: Efficient reinforcement learning control for continuum robots based on inexplicit prior knowledge. arXiv preprint arXiv:2002.11573 (2020)
25. Yadan, O.: Hydra - a framework for elegantly configuring complex applications. Github (2019). https://github.com/facebookresearch/hydra

Information Diffusion for Few-Shot Learning in Robotic Residual Errors Compensation

Zeyuan Yang[1,2], Xiaohu Xu[3], Cheng Li[1], Sijie Yan[1(✉)], Shuzhi Sam Ge[2], and Han Ding[1]

[1] State Key Lab of Digital Manufacturing Equipment and Technology, Huazhong University of Science and Technology, Wuhan 430074, China
sjyan@hust.edu.cn
[2] Department of Electrical and Computer Engineering, National University of Singapore, Singapore 117576, Singapore
[3] The Institute of Technological Sciences, Wuhan University, Wuhan 430072, China

Abstract. In this work, a novel model-free robotic residual errors compensation method is proposed based on the information-diffusion-based dataset enhancement (ID-DE) and the Gradient-Boosted Decision Trees (GBDT). Firstly, the dataset enhancement method is developed by utilizing the normal membership function based on the information diffusion technology. Then, merging it with multiple GBDTs, the multi-output residual errors learning model (ID-GBDTs) is constructed, and the grid search is used to determine the optimal hyper-parameters to accomplish the accurate prediction of residual errors. Finally, the compensation of robotic residual errors is realized by using the calibrated kinematic model. Experiments show that ID-DE can significantly improve the generalization ability of various learning models on the few-shot dataset. The R-squared of ID-GBDTs is improved from 0.58 to 0.77 along with the MAE decreased from 0.23 to 0.16, compared to original GBDT. Through the compensation of the residual errors, the mean/maximum absolute positioning error of the UR10 robot are optimized from 4.51/9.42 mm to 0.81/2.65 mm, with an accuracy improvement of 82.03%.

Keywords: Robot calibration · Residual errors · Dataset enhancement

1 Introduction

The articulated serial robots have recently been widely employed for accuracy applications such as robot-based machining, robot-based measurement, robot-assisted surgery, and so on [1,2]. However, inadequate absolute position accuracy

Supported by the National Key R&D Program of China (No. 2019YFA0706703), the National Nature Science Foundation of China (Nos. 52075204, 52105514) and the China Scholarship Council (No. 202106160036).

(APC) caused by manufacturing tolerances, assembly errors, deformation errors, etc. continues to be a significant barrier to its development in high-precision operations. Therefore, calibration and compensation of the position errors are the critical steps to enhance the robot's APC before putting it into service.

Currently, much work has been conducted using geometric models and data-driven approaches. The former primarily adopt model-based approaches such as M-DH model [3], POE formula [4], CPC model [5], and other error models to calibrate robot geometric parameter errors caused by the non-ideal geometry of structural elements of the robot. However, non-geometric parameter errors due to gearing, part wear and temperature variations are difficult to establish using the model-based approach. The data-driven approach is a good solution to this challenge. Li et al. [6,7] measured a robot end position dataset containing 1,042 sample data based on a drawstring displacement sensor and implemented a data-driven calibration process using the neural network. Landgraf et al. [8] measured four different series of datasets with 16,811 representative sample data for various scenarios and developed a hybrid neural network for improving the APC. Chen et al. [9] proposed a global compensation method combining a genetic algorithm with and deep neural network (DNN) prediction model based on the more than 3,500 poses dataset being grid-wise distributed in the workspace. In order to obtain enough high-quality sample data, Zhao et al. [10] first calibrated the geometric errors based on the DH model and proposed an end-pose measurement algorithm to avoid the measurement process from being obscured, then achieved the calibration of residual errors by DNN. There are already a growing number of research employing model-free strategies to improve APC, including deep belief network [11], radial basis function neural network [12], and so on [13, 14]. However, these approaches have stringent dataset requirements, relying on the small measurement errors and much sample data to assure learning more information about the real sample space. These requirements are challenging to achieve because of the complicated measurement process along with the vast number of robot error sources.

This work seeks to bridge this gap by developing a novel few-shot learning method to realize the prediction and compensation of the residual errors after the geometric errors being compensated. To summarize, the contributions of this study are two-fold:

i. The proposed information-diffusion-based dataset enhancement method (ID-DE) can boost the few-shot dataset and hence improve the generalization capacity of various learning models with great compatibility.
ii. The proposed ID-GBDTs learning model is applied for the residual errors prediction and compensation of the UR10 robot with superior results.

The rest of this paper is organized as follows: Sect. 2.1 introduces ID-DE that can enhance the generalization ability of the learning models based on the information diffusion. Section 2.2 presents the information-diffusion-based GBDT (ID-GBDTs) model with the few-shot dataset for residual errors prediction and compensation. Section 3 evaluates the ID-DE and ID-GBDTs, as well as the compensation results. The conclusions are finally presented in Sect. 4.

2   Residual Errors Estimation and Compensation Method

The measuring steps for the position of the robot end are generally done manually and required extensive human intervention, limiting the number of measurements and complicating data processing. Simultaneously, data errors caused by environmental interference and measurement errors make it difficult to ensure the quality of the acquired data. The collected data in this way is referred to as an incomplete dataset since it does not always fully reflect the real sample space [15], making model-free robot calibration challenging. The following part presents an information-diffusion-based dataset enhancement (ID-DE) and the ID-GBDTs compensation model to address this problem.

2.1   Information-Diffusion-Based Dataset Enhancement

Define the incomplete residual errors dataset X as

$$X = \left\{ x_i = \left(\theta^{(i)}, e^{(i)} \right) \middle| \theta_i^{(i)} = \left[\theta_1^{(i)} \cdots \theta_n^{(i)} \right]^T, e^{(i)} = \left[e_x^{(i)} \ e_y^{(i)} \ e_z^{(i)} \right]^T \right\} \quad (1)$$

where, $x_i = \left(\theta^{(i)}, e^{(i)} \right)$ denotes the i-th sample pair used for residual errors calibration, $\theta^{(i)} = \left[\theta_1^{(i)} \cdots \theta_n^{(i)} \right]^T$ denotes the joint angle sequence, where $1 \sim n$ are indexes of the joints, respectively. $e^{(i)} = \left[e_x^{(i)} \ e_y^{(i)} \ e_z^{(i)} \right]^T$ denotes the corresponding position errors of the end-effector along the x, y, z direction. And $i = 1, \ldots, m$, m denotes the sample number of X.

Definition 1. *For a given incomplete dataset X, $\hat{R}(\vartheta; X)$ denotes the estimation of the real relation R obtained by the operator ϑ. if $\exists \ \ell$ generates the new dataset $\mathcal{D}(X) = \{x_{new} | x_{new} = \ell(x, \mu_\Gamma(x)), x = (\theta, e) \in X, \mu_\Gamma(x) \in U\}$ satifies that*

$$\left\| \widetilde{R}(\vartheta; \mathcal{D}(X)) - R \right\| \leq \left\| \hat{R}(\vartheta; X) - R \right\| \quad (2)$$

then ℓ is called a diffusion function about X. μ_Γ is the membership function of the fuzzy set Γ of X, and U is the corresponding membership values set. The new dataset $\mathcal{D}(X)$ is called the diffusion set. $\widetilde{R}(\vartheta; \mathcal{D}(X)) = \{\vartheta(x_{new}) | x_{new} \in \mathcal{D}(X)\}$ is called the diffusion estimation about R.

Definition 1 illustrates that, for any incomplete sample set, the original dataset can be processed by information diffusion to bring it closer to the true sample space, thus making the diffusion estimate closer to the true relationship, as shown in Fig. 1. onsequently, to improve the estimation accuracy, it is crucial to find the suitable diffusion function ℓ to achieve the sample enhancement. Considering the randomness of the robotic residual errors dataset X, the normalized normal membership functions are chosen for each sample (the triangular distribution,

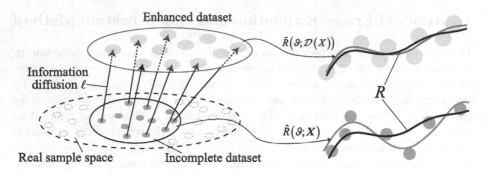

Fig. 1. Information diffusion principle for incomplete dataset.

trapezoidal distribution, etc. can also be selected according to the actual situation). Then, the membership values can be related to the new samples:

$$
\begin{cases}
\mu_\Gamma\left(\boldsymbol{\theta}^{(i)}\right) = \exp\left(-\frac{1}{2}\left(\boldsymbol{\theta}^{(i)} - \boldsymbol{\theta}_{new}^{(i)}\right)^T \Sigma_\theta^{-1}\left(\boldsymbol{\theta}^{(i)} - \boldsymbol{\theta}_{new}^{(i)}\right)\right) \\
\mu_\Gamma\left(\boldsymbol{e}^{(i)}\right) = \exp\left(-\frac{1}{2}\left(\boldsymbol{e}^{(i)} - \boldsymbol{e}_{new}^{(i)}\right)^T \Sigma_e^{-1}\left(\boldsymbol{e}^{(i)} - \boldsymbol{e}_{new}^{(i)}\right)\right)
\end{cases}
\tag{3}
$$

where, Σ_θ and Σ_e are the diffusion coefficient diagonal matrices about $\boldsymbol{\theta}$ and $\boldsymbol{p}$, respectively. As an approach to incorporate the distribution information of the original dataset $\boldsymbol{X}$ into the diffusion set $\mathcal{D}(\boldsymbol{X})$, the diffusion coefficients matrices associated with the variance of $\boldsymbol{X}$ are designed and can be expressed as

$$
\begin{cases}
\Sigma_\theta = \mathrm{diag}\left[\dfrac{\sum_{i=1}^m\left(\theta_1^{(i)} - \bar{\theta}_1\right)^2}{m\,(m-1)}, \ldots, \dfrac{\sum_{i=1}^m\left(\theta_n^{(i)} - \bar{\theta}_n\right)^2}{m\,(m-1)}\right] \\[4mm]
\Sigma_e = \mathrm{diag}\left[\dfrac{\sum_{i=1}^m\left(e_x^{(i)} - \bar{e}_y\right)^2}{m\,(m-1)}, \dfrac{\sum_{i=1}^m\left(e_y^{(i)} - \bar{e}_y\right)^2}{m\,(m-1)}, \dfrac{\sum_{i=1}^m\left(e_z^{(i)} - \bar{e}_z\right)^2}{m\,(m-1)}\right]
\end{cases}
\tag{4}
$$

Bring Eq. (4) into Eq. (3), there has

$$
\begin{cases}
\sum_{j=1}^n \dfrac{\left(\theta_j^{(i)} - \theta_{j,new}^{(i)}\right)^2 \sum_{i=1}^m\left(\theta_j^{(i)} - \bar{\theta}_j\right)^2}{m\,(m-1)} = -2\ln\mu_\Gamma\left(\boldsymbol{\theta}^{(i)}\right) \\[4mm]
\sum_{j=x}^z \dfrac{\left(e_j^{(i)} - e_{j,new}^{(i)}\right)^2 \sum_{i=1}^m\left(e_j^{(i)} - \bar{e}_j\right)^2}{m\,(m-1)} = -2\ln\mu_\Gamma\left(\boldsymbol{e}^{(i)}\right)
\end{cases}
\tag{5}
$$

Equation (5) describes that the expanded new samples $\boldsymbol{x}_{new}$ can be derived from the normal diffusion when given the membership values. Since the joint angle vectors have n features (the corresponding residual errors have 3 features in the Cartesian space), the equation has infinite solutions. An effective approach is to minimize the overall error by constructing a loss function associated with the learning model. Considering here that the features of the joint angle samples are independent of each other, $\theta_j \sim \mathcal{N}\left(\theta_j \mid \theta_{j,new}, h_j\right), e_j \sim \mathcal{N}\left(e_j \mid e_{j,new}, \varsigma_j\right)$, $\theta_{j,new}^{(i)}$ and $e_{j,new}^{(i)}$ correspond to their membership values $\mu_\Gamma(\theta_j^{(i)})$ and $\mu_\Gamma(e_j^{(i)})$ one-to-one, respectively. There has

$$
\begin{cases}
\left(\theta_j^{(i)} - \theta_{j,new}^{(i)}\right)^2 \cdot \dfrac{\sum_{i=1}^{m}\left(\theta_j^{(i)} - \bar{\theta}_j\right)^2}{m\,(m-1)} = -2\ln\mu_\Gamma\left(\theta_j^{(i)}\right), j = 1,\ldots,n \\[4mm]
\left(e_j^{(i)} - e_{j,new}^{(i)}\right)^2 \cdot \dfrac{\sum_{i=1}^{m}\left(e_j^{(i)} - \bar{e}_j\right)^2}{m\,(m-1)} = -2\ln\mu_\Gamma\left(e_j^{(i)}\right), j = x, y, z
\end{cases}
\tag{6}
$$

Therefore, the new dataset can be obtained by rectifying Eq. (6) as

$$
\begin{cases}
\boldsymbol{\theta}_{new} = \boldsymbol{\theta} \pm \mathrm{sqrt}\left(-\boldsymbol{I}_{n\times1} \otimes \mathrm{diag}^\vee\left(\Sigma_\theta\right) \circ \ln\mu_\Gamma\left(\boldsymbol{\theta}\right)\right) \\[2mm]
\boldsymbol{e}_{new} = \boldsymbol{e} \pm \mathrm{sqrt}\left(-\boldsymbol{I}_{n\times1} \otimes \mathrm{diag}^\vee\left(\Sigma_e\right) \circ \ln\mu_\Gamma\left(\boldsymbol{e}\right)\right)
\end{cases}
\tag{7}
$$

where, $\mathrm{diag}^\vee\left(\bullet\right)$ denotes the vectorization of the diagonal matrix to a $1 \times n$ row vector. $\otimes$ denotes the Kronecker product and $\circ$ denotes the Hadamard product. $\boldsymbol{I}_{n\times1}$ denotes the $n \times 1$ unit column vector.

Additionally, $\mathrm{Skew}_L = N_L/(N_L + N_U)$ and $\mathrm{Skew}_U = N_U/(N_L + N_U)$ are used as the left and right skewness magnitudes of the original dataset to characterize the asymmetric diffusion [16], where N_L and N_U denote the number of samples smaller and larger than the mean values of samples, respectively. Then, the diffusion function $\ell\left(\theta, e\right)$ for deriving the new dataset with the skewness information can be expressed as

$$
\ell : \begin{cases}
\boldsymbol{\theta}_{new,L} = \boldsymbol{\theta} - \mathrm{Skew}_{\theta,L} \cdot \mathrm{sqrt}\left(-\boldsymbol{I}_{n\times1} \otimes \mathrm{diag}^\vee\left(\Sigma_\theta\right) \circ \ln\mu_\Gamma\left(\boldsymbol{\theta}\right)\right) \\[2mm]
\boldsymbol{\theta}_{new,U} = \boldsymbol{\theta} + \mathrm{Skew}_{\theta,U} \cdot \mathrm{sqrt}\left(-\boldsymbol{I}_{n\times1} \otimes \mathrm{diag}^\vee\left(\Sigma_\theta\right) \circ \ln\mu_\Gamma\left(\boldsymbol{\theta}\right)\right) \\[2mm]
\boldsymbol{e}_{new,L} = \boldsymbol{e} - \mathrm{Skew}_{p,L} \cdot \mathrm{sqrt}\left(-\boldsymbol{I}_{n\times1} \otimes \mathrm{diag}^\vee\left(\Sigma_e\right) \circ \ln\mu_\Gamma\left(\boldsymbol{e}\right)\right) \\[2mm]
\boldsymbol{e}_{new,U} = \boldsymbol{e} + \mathrm{Skew}_{p,U} \cdot \mathrm{sqrt}\left(-\boldsymbol{I}_{n\times1} \otimes \mathrm{diag}^\vee\left(\Sigma_e\right) \circ \ln\mu_\Gamma\left(\boldsymbol{e}\right)\right)
\end{cases}
\tag{8}
$$

Obviously, the new sample pairs $\boldsymbol{x}_{new} = \left(\boldsymbol{\theta}_{new}, \boldsymbol{e}_{new}\right)$ are derived according to the membership values in domain U with respect to $\boldsymbol{x} = \left(\boldsymbol{\theta}, \boldsymbol{e}\right)$. Although the new dataset created by Eq. (8) can only be twice the size of the original dataset, the additional new samples can be generated by taking different membership values or several iterations. Then, the new dataset $\mathcal{D}\left(\boldsymbol{X}\right)$ can be expressed as

$$
\begin{aligned}
\mathcal{D}\left(X\right) = \Big\{ &\left(\boldsymbol{\theta}, \boldsymbol{e}, 1\right), \left(\left(\boldsymbol{\theta}_{new,U}, \boldsymbol{e}_{new,U}\right)_1, \left(\boldsymbol{\theta}_{new,L}, \boldsymbol{e}_{new,L}\right)_1, \mu_{\Gamma,1}\right), \\
&\ldots, \left(\left(\boldsymbol{\theta}_{new,U}, \boldsymbol{e}_{new,U}\right)_g, \left(\boldsymbol{\theta}_{new,L}, \boldsymbol{e}_{new,L}\right)_g, \mu_{\Gamma,g}\right) \Big\}
\end{aligned}
\tag{9}
$$

where, $\mu_\Gamma\left(\boldsymbol{\theta}\right) = \mu_\Gamma\left(\boldsymbol{e}\right)$ is taken to ensure the correspondence of the input-output relationship of the new samples, so it is abbreviated as μ_Γ. The numerical subscripts $(1, \ldots, g)$ are used to distinguish the use of different membership values.

2.2 Residual Errors Prediction and Compensation Based on ID-GBDTs

Following the enhancement of the original dataset, the Gradient-Boosted Decision Trees (GBDT), a machine learning framework based on decision trees [17], is utilized as an optional regression model to estimate residual errors. It's composed of numerous subtree models, where the latter subtree is built depending on the outcome of the former subtree, and the ultimate output is the total of all subtree's predictions. Using the weak decision trees as the base learners and merging them through iteration as a powerful ensemble learning model allows GBDT to combine the interpretability and fast computing of decision trees with the strong generalization performance of gradient boosting. The loss function of the GBDT can be expressed as

$$\vartheta_t\left(\boldsymbol{\theta}\right) = \vartheta_{t-1}\left(\boldsymbol{\theta}\right) + \arg\min Loss\left(\boldsymbol{e}_{err,i}, \vartheta_{t-1}\left(\boldsymbol{\theta}_i\right) + h\left(\boldsymbol{\theta}_i\right)\right) \tag{10}$$

where, ϑ_t denotes the accumulated models, $h\left(\boldsymbol{\theta}_i\right)$ denotes the new decision trees. Equation (10) illustrates that in the function space, a weak learner $h\left(\boldsymbol{\theta}_i\right)$ should be chosen such that the loss function $Loss\left(\boldsymbol{e}_{err,i}, \vartheta_{t-1}\left(\boldsymbol{\theta}_i\right) + h\left(\boldsymbol{\theta}_i\right)\right)$ is minimized once this weak learner is added.

However, the GBDT can only be used for the single-output system. The proposed ID-GBDTs can cascade several GBDTs, the regressor of which is fitted for each axial residual errors, allowing knowledge of every axial residual errors to be gained by inspecting its corresponding regressor, thereby eliminating the problem that GBDT cannot accomplish multi-target output. Figure 2 illustrates the principle of the ID-GBDTs.

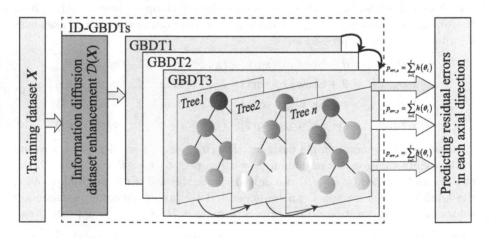

Fig. 2. The learning process of the ID-GBDTs.

After the prediction of the residual errors, the compensated end positions can be obtained by adding the theoretical end positions to their corresponding residual errors.

3 Experimental Setup and Verification

3.1 Experimental Setup

Figure 3 illustrates the experimental setup of the robot calibration process. The experimental setup consists of a desk-mounted Universal Robot UR10, a Leica AT960-LR laser tracker with the measurement accuracy of $\left(\pm 15\,\mu\mathrm{m} + 6\,\frac{\mu\mathrm{m}}{\mathrm{m}}\right)$, and a 6-DOF (degrees of freedom) T-MAC target attached to the flange.

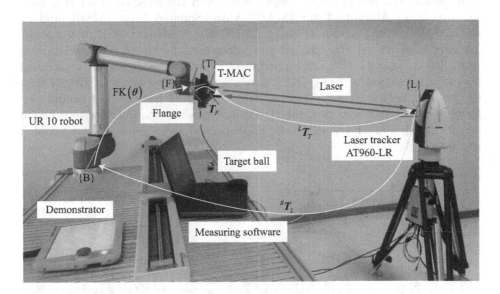

Fig. 3. UR10 robot calibration based on the AT960-LR laser tracker.

The pose transformation matrix $^{B}\boldsymbol{T}_{L}$ of laser tracker coordinate system $\{L\}$ with respect to the robot base coordinate system $\{B\}$ can be fitted by measuring the T-MAC poses when rotating the robot's 1-th and 3-th joints, respectively. Then, the robot is programmed offline to move in space (avoiding T-MAC being obscured), while the laser tracker measures in real-time to get T-MAC poses in $\{L\}$. The robot end position errors $^{B}\boldsymbol{e}$ are calculated by converting the measured T-MAC position $^{L}\boldsymbol{p}$ in $\{L\}$ into $\{B\}$ through $^{B}\boldsymbol{T}_{L}$ and comparing it to the T-MAC position acquired using the compensated forward kinematics FK $(\boldsymbol{\theta})$. $^{B}\boldsymbol{e}$ can be expressed as

$$^{B}\boldsymbol{e} = {}^{B}\boldsymbol{T}_{L} \cdot {}^{L}\boldsymbol{p} - {}^{T}\boldsymbol{T}_{F} \cdot \mathrm{FK}\,(\boldsymbol{\theta}) \tag{11}$$

Based on the above method, 60 sets of residual error data were randomly collected in the range of $800 \times 500 \times 800$ mm^3 of the robot's common workspace, of which 42 samples were selected as the original training sample set and 18 samples as the test set. The dataset has been made publicly available at https://github.com/Alvin8584/RobotCalibationDataforUR10.

3.2   ID-DE Evaluation and Residual Errors Compensation

Figure 4 depicts the influence of the proposed ID-based dataset enhancement method on various learning methods. In this case, membership value of the ID-DE is 0.99, and the number of created samples is 65. The selected models are Bayesian Regression (Bayes), Stochastic Gradient Descent (SGD), Support Vector Regression (SVR), RandomForest (RF), Gradient Boosted Decision Trees (GBDT), eXtreme Gradient Boosting (XGBoost) and Back Propagation Neural Network (BPNN), respectively. And the selected evaluation metrics are Mean Absolute Error (MAE), Mean Squared Error (MSE), and R-squared (R^2), respectively. By using ID-DE, the MAE and MSE of the above learning methods on the test set were decreased by the mean/maximum of 13.62/27.43% and 25.9/52.82% respectively, while R^2 was significantly improved by mean/maximum of 26.67/53.15%. Among them, the scores of BPNN have the greatest noticeable improvement, whereas GBDT has the best overall performance. This indicates that the ID-DE has good compatibility with different learning models and has a significant enhancement effect, especially for few-shot learning.

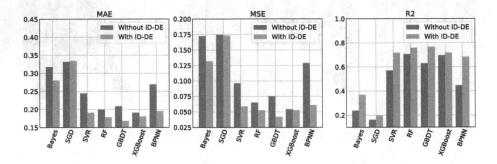

Fig. 4. Performance of learning models with and without ID-DE on test set.

Then, the generalizability ability of the GBDT with different ID-DE parameters is further discussed, as shown in Fig. 5. Generally, as the number of generated samples increases, the performance of the learning model first is improved significantly and then held constant or slightly reduced, while its decrease rate gradually decreases to zero. This is due to the fact that the samples generated by ID-DE can effectively enhance the original dataset and fully utilize the real sample space information; however, when too many samples are generated or the lower membership values are chosen, the information diffusion error increases, which would result in a stagnant or even counterproductive effect. According to a large number of experiments, the ID-DE can significantly improve the model generalization ability when the membership values generally take the value of 0.97–0.99 and the number of the generated new samples is within 0.4–2 times of the original number of samples. In addition, the ID-DE can reduce the MSE by 48.1% at most when its membership value is 0.98 and the number of the generated samples is 55.

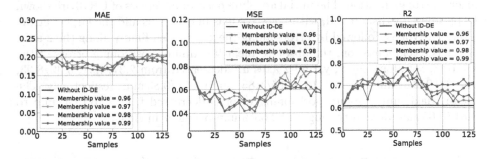

Fig. 5. Performance of ID-GBDTs with different ID-DE parameters on test set.

Based on the optimal parameters obtained above, the learning process and prediction results using the ID-GBDTs are shown in Fig. 6. To further improve the model prediction accuracy, grid search and cross-validation are used to find the hyper-parameters of ID-GBDTs [18]. The MSEs of the final ID-GBDTs along each axis on the test set are 0.06, 0.03 and 0.02, respectively. Comparing to GBDT with only 42 real samples in the training case, ID-GBDTs enhance the

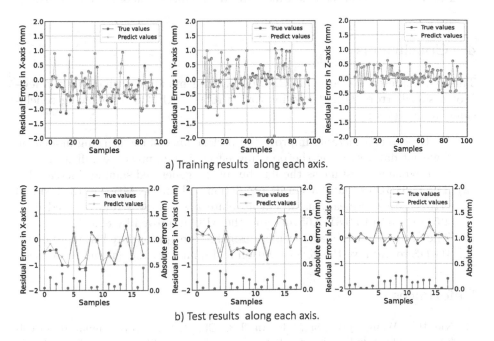

a) Training results along each axis.

b) Test results along each axis.

Fig. 6. Training results of ID-GBDTs along each axis.

R-squared from 0.58 to 0.77, and reduce MAE from 0.23 to 0.16 on the test set with the generalization performance improved by 51.7%.

Figure 7 illustrates the APC comparison of each axial direction before and after the compensation. The initial absolute positioning errors of UR10 are shown to be unevenly distributed, with negative bias in each axis and the largest errors along the y-axis, followed by errors along the x-axis, and finally along the z-axis. After the compensation, the absolute mean/maximum positioning errors of the UR10 robot along the x, y, and z axes are decreased from 2.37/4.91, 3.39/8.93, and 1.19/2.5 mm to 0.23/2.18, 0.17/1.83, and 0.017/0.83 mm, respectively. The mean/maximum absolute positioning error is decreased from 4.51/9.42 mm to 0.81/2.65 mm, demonstrating an 82.03% improvement in APC.

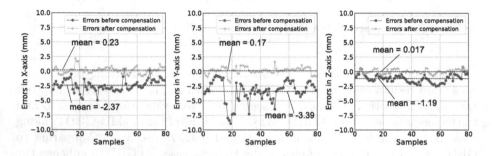

Fig. 7. APC comparison before and after the compensation of residual errors.

4   Conclusions

This paper presents a novel ID-GBDTs learning model for enhancing the few-shot residual errors dataset and improving robot's APC. The following conclusions are achieved:

(1) ID-DE can considerably improve the performance of the learning models on few-shot dataset, while the boosting effect first improves significantly and then remains constant as the number of the generated samples increased.
(2) The ID-GBDTs enable accurate prediction and compensation of the residual errors with the mean/maximum absolute positioning errors reduced from 4.51/9.42 mm to 0.81/2.65 mm and the APC improved by 82.03%.
(3) The future research may consider designing the appropriate loss function for ID-DE to improve the generalization and quality of the enhanced dataset.

References

1. Xie, H.L., Wang, Q.H., Ong, S.K., Li, J.R., Chi, Z.P.: Adaptive human-robot collaboration for robotic grinding of complex workpieces. CIRP Ann. (2022). https://doi.org/10.1016/j.cirp.2022.04.015

2. Yang, Z., et al.: Prediction and analysis of material removal characteristics for robotic belt grinding based on single spherical abrasive grain model. Int. J. Mech. Sci. **190**, 106005 (2021)
3. Peng, J., Ding, Y., Zhang, G., Ding, H.: An enhanced kinematic model for calibration of robotic machining systems with parallelogram mechanisms. Robot. Comput.-Integr. Manuf. **59**, 92–103 (2019)
4. Sun, T., Liu, C., Lian, B., Wang, P., Song, Y.: Calibration for precision kinematic control of an articulated serial robot. IEEE Trans. Industr. Electron. **68**(7), 6000–6009 (2021)
5. Zhuang, H., Wang, L.K., Roth, Z.S.: Error-model-based robot calibration using a modified CPC model. Robot. Comput.-Integr. Manuf. **10**(4), 289–299 (1993)
6. Li, Z., Li, S., Luo, X.: Data-driven industrial robot arm calibration: a machine learning perspective. In: 2021 IEEE International Conference on Networking, Sensing and Control (ICNSC), vol. 1, pp. 1–6 (2021)
7. Li, Z., Li, S., Bamasag, O.O., Alhothali, A., Luo, X.: Diversified regularization enhanced training for effective manipulator calibration. IEEE Trans. Neural Netw. Learn. Syst. 1–13 (2022). https://doi.org/10.1109/TNNLS.2022.3153039
8. Landgraf, C., Ernst, K., Schleth, G., Fabritius, M., Huber, M.F.: A hybrid neural network approach for increasing the absolute accuracy of industrial robots. In: 2021 IEEE 17th International Conference on Automation Science and Engineering (CASE), pp. 468–474 (2021). https://doi.org/10.1109/CASE49439.2021.9551684
9. Chen, X., Zhang, Q., Sun, Y.: Evolutionary robot calibration and nonlinear compensation methodology based on GA-DNN and an extra compliance error model. Math. Probl. Eng. **2020**, 3981081 (2020)
10. Zhao, G., Zhang, P., Ma, G., Xiao, W.: System identification of the nonlinear residual errors of an industrial robot using massive measurements. Robot. Comput. Integr. Manuf. **59**, 104–114 (2019)
11. Wang, W., Tian, W., Liao, W., Li, B.: Pose accuracy compensation of mobile industry robot with binocular vision measurement and deep belief network. Optik **238**, 166716 (2021)
12. Chen, D., Wang, T., Yuan, P., Sun, N., Tang, H.: A positional error compensation method for industrial robots combining error similarity and radial basis function neural network. Meas. Sci. Technol. **30**(12), 125010 (2019)
13. Gao, G., Liu, F., San, H., Wu, X., Wang, W.: Hybrid optimal kinematic parameter identification for an industrial robot based on BPNN-PSO. Complexity **2018**, 4258676 (2018)
14. Gadringer, S., Gattringer, H., Müller, A., Naderer, R.: Robot calibration combining kinematic model and neural network for enhanced positioning and orientation accuracy. IFAC-PapersOnLine **53**(2), 8432–8437 (2020)
15. Huang, C.: Principle of information diffusion. Fuzzy Sets Syst. **91**(1), 69–90 (1997)
16. Li, D.C., Wu, C.S., Tsai, T.I., Lina, Y.S.: Using mega-trend-diffusion and artificial samples in small data set learning for early flexible manufacturing system scheduling knowledge. Comput. Oper. Res. **34**(4), 966–982 (2007)
17. Zhang, Z., Jung, C.: GBDT-MO: gradient-boosted decision trees for multiple outputs. IEEE Trans. Neural Netw. Learn. Syst. **32**(7), 3156–3167 (2020)
18. Pedregosa, F., Varoquaux, G., Gramfort, A., Michel, V., et al.: Scikit-learn: machine learning in Python. J. Mach. Learn. Res. **12**, 2825–2830 (2011)

An Integrated Power Wheel Module
for Automated Guided Vehicle

Sifan Qian[1], Hanlin Zhan[1(✉)], Wenhao Han[1], Gao Yang[2], Wenjing Wu[2],
Wenjie Chen[2], and Dianguo Xu[3]

[1] Harbin Institute of Technology(Shenzhen), Shenzhen, Guangdong, China
Zhanhanlin@hit.edu.cn
[2] Midea Corporate Research Center (CRC), Foshan, Guangdong, China
[3] Harbin Institute of Technology, Harbin, Heilongjiang, China

Abstract. Aiming at the shortcomings of current mobile robot integrated power drive wheels, in this paper, an integrated power wheel module suitable for large industrial Automated Guided Vehicle (AGV)/mobile robots is proposed. Different from the traditional structure, this paper makes innovations in the design of the motor, the topology of the drives and the integrated structure. In order to improve the torque density, an axial flux motor is adopted, and the structure of the reducer and the motor in series is used, which greatly reduces the size of the motor. In terms of drive technology, the winding with common DC bus including dual-inverter circuit structure improves the fault-tolerant capability.

Keywords: Automated guided vehicle · Integrated power wheel module · Axial flux motor · Open winding

1 Introduction

With the development of robot technology, high performance industrial heavy duty AGV/mobile robot is widely used in a variety of industrial occasions, and the power wheel module technology is important to industrial AGV [9]. Based on this, it is a development trend to study the integrated power wheel module for high-performance industrial heavy-duty AGV robots.

The research on integrated power wheel was first started in Japan, which developed a high-performance electric vehicle named IZA in 1991. It was driven by hub motor, and each wheel was integrated with motor, brake disc and hub, without any reduction mechanism. Japan's ARACO company and the University of Tokyo are also working on the integrated power wheel. In addition, Technologies M4 company in France also started the research of electric wheels [3]. Its representative product is TM4 electric wheel, which is specially designed for electric vehicles. Its wheels have no reduction mechanism and are directly driven by electric motors. In 2008, Michelin company developed an electric wheel integrating embedded active suspension, drive motor, suspension motor and disc brake, which is specially used for electric cars. In 2013, Finnish company PROBOT exhibited its Mobility Module series at ICRA, which integrates the power part

© The Author(s), under exclusive license to Springer Nature Switzerland AG 2022
H. Liu et al. (Eds.): ICIRA 2022, LNAI 13455, pp. 648–659, 2022.
https://doi.org/10.1007/978-3-031-13844-7_60

into the inside of the wheel and forms different structure according to the needs. The modularization of vehicle structure is realized. But its disadvantage is the output power too small to drive high-power vehicles [1].

At present, the power wheel transmission structure used by mobile robots at home and abroad is that the servo motor is installed on the edge of the wheel, and it connected with the reducer and the independent hub. The core components include servo motor, driver and reducer. A typical powertrain structure is shown in Fig. 1.

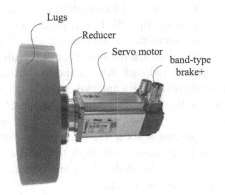

Fig. 1. A typical powertrain structure diagram

This traditional AGV transmission structure is long and occupies a large space inside the mobile robot. Therefore the design space of the battery pack and other operating components will be reduced. In addition, the IP protection level of chassis is required to be higher, otherwise the IP protection level of each separation unit in the car will be required to attain the protection level of the whole vehicle. The limited battery pack will directly affect the maximum vehicle endurance, and requiring more AGVs to achieve the same workload requirements.

Therefore, from the perspective of technology development, it has become a development trend to study the robot power wheel module with high torque density, high power density and high integration. The integrated power wheel module studied in this paper is applied to KUKA's heavy-duty AGV mobile robot products, which greatly simplifies the chassis structure, omits transmission parts, improves the transmission efficiency and provides more free design space for lifting mechanism and other link components. In addition, the reduction of motor size increases the installation space of battery pack, so it will improve the cruise duration (upper limit of single-machine working time) and working efficiency. It also reduces the number of AGVs required to be arranged. For production, simplifying the body structure will also simplify the production and assembly process, reduce production cost and time, improve production efficiency and the consistency of product quality.

In terms of highly integrated structure, compared with the traditional AGV power module, the highly integrated power wheel module studied in this paper adopts specially designed hub motor, reducer, servo driver, brake and so on. Therefore, it has a more compact shape and smaller axial size, providing greater possibility for the optimal layout of the AGV machine [10].

In terms of high-power density servo drivers, the servo drivers used in the traditional AGV power wheel module have large volume and low power density [6], which are generally arranged in the chassis body of AGV. During the past researches, motor drivers frequently use electrolytic capacitors to stabilize the DC voltage. Nevertheless, a considerable part of the damage of the drive system is caused by the failure of the electrolytic capacitor due to the lifetime of electrolytic capacitor is easily affected by the working environment. To guarantee the robustness of the drive system, certain innovative technologies are put forward [7, 8]. In this paper, some innovative technology are used in the design of the servo driver, such as the use of multi-ceramic capacitor instead of electrolytic capacitor, so that the ripple current's value is not limited and the capacity requirement is greatly reduced. An aluminum substrate design is also used, which increases the thermal conductivity and makes ultra high power density possible.

The servo motor used in the traditional AGV power wheel module is slender with large axial size and low torque density, so it is difficult for the traditional motor to achieve the appearance requirement about the ultra-thin power wheel module. In this paper, a specially designed hub motor with high torque density is adopted. For the integrated scheme of motor and reducer, the shape and performance of motor can meet the requirements of high integration module.

The integrated power wheel module of high-performance industrial heavy-duty AGV robot studied in this paper is highly integrated with motor, reducer, servo driver, brake and safety encoder. And it achieves the key technology breakthrough of high torque density, high power density, high integration and it also achieves the international standards of high safety and high reliability. Its core components such as hub motor, servo driver, special reducer have reached the advanced level in the industry. It is conducive to realize the industrialization of the core components such as servo motors and drivers, build the basic platform for the next generation AGV robot.

2   Motor Design for Integrated Power Wheel Moudule

High performance robot power wheel module is a highly integrated system, which requires the drive motor to provide a high torque density in a limited space. With the development of the advanced motor technology, such as rotor synchronous motor, transverse flux motor, vernier motor, magnetic gear motor and other high torque density motor topology has been developed and applied [11]. After comparative analysis, this paper adopts axial flux motor. Axial flux motor has the characteristics of small aspect ratio, small volume, high torque density and good heat dissipation performance [2]. Figure 2 shows the structure of the motor. Using the characteristics of axial flux motor, it is beneficial to make motor and reducer closely connected in the axial direction. Thus, the volume of power wheel is reduced and a highly integrated power wheel module is obtained.

In addition, this paper also research the motor frontier materials and advanced management technology. The research on new materials mainly includes the three aspects: in the aspect of magnetic conductivity materials, the use of high permeability materials to improve the torque density of the motor. High temperature and high remanence

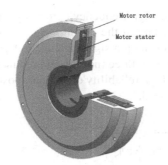

Fig. 2. Axial flux motor topology

permanent magnet are used to reduce motor load and increase torque density. And insulation materials with high thermal conductivity, high dielectric constant and ultra-thin characteristics are used to improve the utilization rate of stator slot area, reduce copper loss and winding temperature and improve torque density.

3   High Reliability and High Performance Redundant Drives

3.1   Open Winding Fault Tolerant Drive System

The adopted open winding driver topology is the common DC bus topology that the dual inverters are powered by one power supply. Meanwhile, it has strong fault tolerance for motor phase break faults, and has higher reliability compared with other topologies [4]. Figure 3 shows the circuit topology of the common DC bus driver used in the open winding fault-tolerant drive system. As shown in the figure, the neutral point of the conventional motor winding is opened, and each terminal is connected with a inverter in series. Thus, a new type of motor system topology is constructed.

Common faults in motor can be divided into body faults and inverter faults. In the traditional motor control, the inverter generally adopts the three-phase full-bridge circuit, which generally does not have the fault-tolerant operation ability after failure. For the open winding with the common DC bus double inverter structure, when the switch tube of one phase is faulty, the direct method is to connect the switch tube to the neutral point and formed the three-phase four-switch structure, so as to achieve the function of cutting the faulty circuit. And the other group of inverters work together to maintain the stable operation of the motor [5].

In the dual inverter open winding control system, the two inverters can be controlled independently. Therefore, the coordinated control of the two inverters can be realized, which is convenient to realize energy management and satisfies various operating conditions and requirements of the system. A sensor-less control strategy with high redundancy based on zero-sequence high frequency signal injection is adopted. Estimation rotor position information using zero-sequence third harmonic back EMF. By injecting zero-sequence high frequency excitation signal (High frequency square wave, sine wave or unipolar high frequency pulse signal), the high frequency current response of the motor ABC three-phase is derived. And then, the Angle information about rotor position is extracted from the high frequency current by signal processing technology. Since the open winding structure of the common DC bus can realize the independent injection of the three-phase excitation signal and the independent position information modulation and demodulation, so three independent redundant estimation channels can be constructed to realize the high reliability of the rotor position observation. Its control block diagram is shown in Fig. 3.

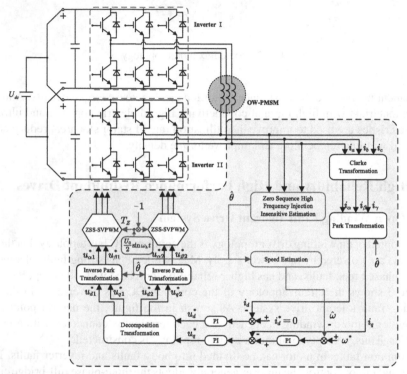

Fig. 3. OW-PMSM zero-sequence high frequency signal injection system diagram

Because of the extra zero-sequence interference current, the traditional PWM strategy can't implement the corresponding control requirements. This paper uses a generalized adjustable SVPWM strategy, without the need to add frequency adaptive zero-sequence current controller to achieve zero-sequence current suppression capability. The zero sequence steerable space vector pulse-width modulation (ZSS-SVPWM) is developed to provide a controllable zero sequence component and the zero-sequence current controller are used to suppress the circulating current in the drive system of the common DC bus open-winding PMSM. In addition, the adjustable SVPWM control strategy only reconstructs the reference voltage of a single SVPWM module, without modifying the original SVPWM module in a single inverter drive system. Therefore, using the SVPWM module driven with a single inverter can be easily applied this method to the open winding drive system.

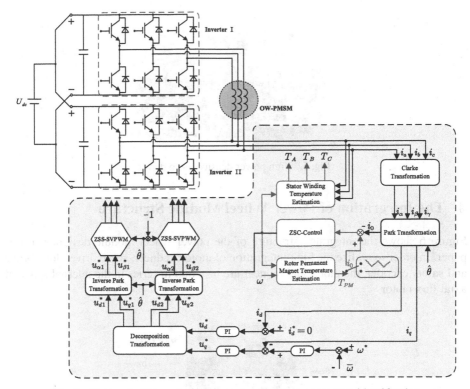

Fig. 4. Stator winding and rotor permanent online temperature identification

On the basis of control strategy and zero-sequence current suppression research, the influence of zero-sequence inductance and resistance in zero-sequence model is eliminated, and the problem that can't be decoupled due to rank dissatisfaction is avoided, so as to identify the zero-sequence harmonic flux linkage with higher accuracy. Combined with the harmonic flux obtained by the finite element analysis of the motor design and then identify the precise rotor permanent magnet temperature. Figure 4 shows the block diagram of stator winding and rotor permanent online temperature identification.

3.2 High Power Density Servo Driver

The servo driver usually consists of a control board responsible for digital model processing and modulation and demodulation and a power board responsible for power device drive and inverter [12]. In order to improve the power density of the driver, the multichip ceramic capacitor is used instead of the aluminum electrolytic capacitor, which reduces the servo driver's volume and increases the service life of the servo driver. Using AGV metal frame for heat dissipation can reduce the volume of heat sink. In addition, modular power devices with high thermal conductivity are used to improve the reliability of the whole system and reduce the processing cost while reducing the volume. Figure 5 shows the high-power density servo driver developed in this paper.

Fig. 5. High power density servo driver

4   The Intrgration of Power Wheel Module Structure

Figure 6 shows the integrated structure of the power wheel module designed in this paper. In order to realize the high integration of motor, reducer, servo driver, lock brake and safety encoder, the motor and reducer are installed in series in the internal space of axial flux motor.

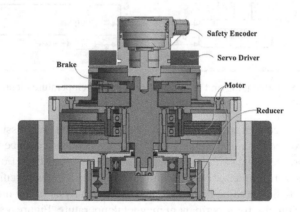

Fig. 6. The integrated structure of the power wheel module

As can be seen from the figure, the motor is coaxially connected with the reducer, and the motor is presented in a flat shape. The motor is the axial flux motor. Because the air gap is axial, the motor has a very short axial length and a high torque density. Taking advantage of this feature, motor and reducer can be closely connected in the axial direction to obtain highly integrated hub power components. One end of the motor is connected with the reducer and the other end is connected with the servo driver and the safety encoder. The hub brake device is directly installed on the edge of the motor, which can quickly realize the power-off brake.

In addition, the reducer used by the power wheel module is a special ultra-thin MC reducer. The reducer innovates the traditional cycloid reducer based on tribology and lubrication theory, and it realizes the rotation of pin column and makes the sliding friction between pin column and pin hole change into rolling friction. Removing the transition parts pin column sleeve to reduce the number of parts. Meanwhile, after removing the pin column sleeve, the center hole of the cycloid wheel is increscent and larger bearings can be put into it, so the life bottleneck of the cycloid structure reducer is greatly extended. Figure 7 shows the integrated power wheel with a motor and reducer in series.

Fig. 7. The integrated power wheel with the motor and the reducer in series

5   Experiment of the Power Wheel Module Structure

This section presents experimental results about verifying the speed characteristics of the power wheel module and compares them with traditional power wheel modules. The experimental test platform is shown in Fig. 8.

Fig. 8. The experimental platform.

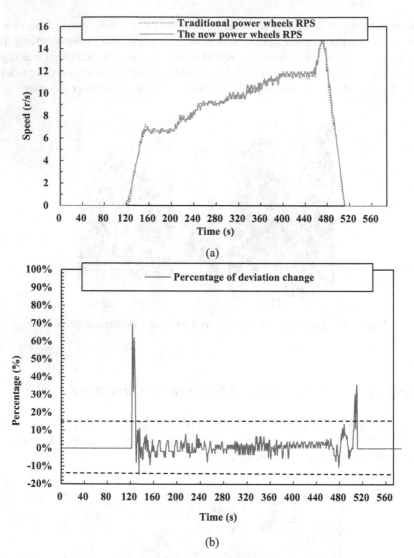

Fig. 9. (a) The speed change curve of the power wheel designed in this paper and the traditional power wheel under the same operating conditions. (b) The percentage of velocity deviation between the two power wheel.

Figure 9(a) shows the speed change curve of the power wheel designed in this paper and the traditional power wheel under the same operating conditions. Figure 9(b) shows the percentage change of velocity deviational compared with the traditional power wheel speed. It can be seen from the experimental results that when the motor runs stably, the speed deviation between the power wheel designed in this paper and the traditional power wheel is within 15 percent, which has good consistency. So the power wheel module can replace the traditional power wheel.

Figure 10 shows the phase current waveform measured by oscilloscope with step speed from 20 to 50 r/min. The experimental results show that the phase current of the motor is stable under constant load. With the increase of speed, the peak current is basically stable at about 45 A. And the waveform of electric current presents basically as a sine wave. Open winding drive system can suppress current harmonic.

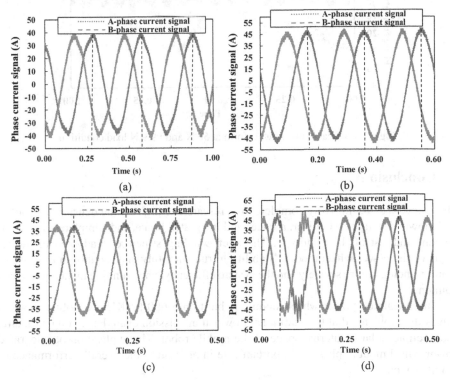

Fig. 10. Phase current waveform. (a) Phase current signal at 20 r/min with 50 N load condition. (b) Phase current signal at 30r/min with 50N load condition. (c) Phase current signal at 40r/min with 50 N load condition. (d) Phase current signal at 50 r/min with 50 N load condition.

Figure 11 shows the A-phase current waveform at 20 r/min with 50 N and 99.9 N load condition. As the load increases, both the amplitude and frequency of the phase current will change in order to achieve the required speed.

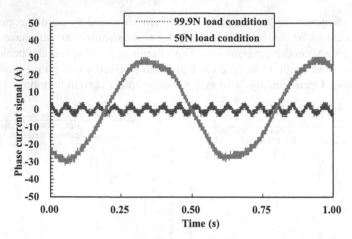

Fig. 11. A-phase current waveform at 50 N and 99.9 N load condition

6 Conclusion

This paper has preliminarily completed the research of high torque density hub motor, high power density servo driver, reducer and integrated brake, and completed the development and test of the prototype. The open winding structure is adopted to further improve the power wheel module's ability to run smoothly and reliably in the case of motor winding failure severely and the system efficiency when running in the high-speed domain.

The integrated power wheel module is built on a 600 kg KUKA mobile robot. It solves the problems that the traditional power transmission chain has a long structure, and occupies a large internal space of the mobile robot. The application of integrated power wheel module plays an important role in promoting the overall performance of mobile robot.

References

1. Chen, W.: Research on Fault Tolerant Control for Open Winding Permanent Magnet Synchronous Motor Drive System with Open Phase Fault. Zhejiang University (2021)
2. In, L., Xu, S., Tan, L.: Design and analysis of axial flux motor for new energy vehicle. MicroMotors **53**(05), 10–14 (2020)
3. Guoqing, C.: Research of Integrated Electric Wheel and Four Wheel Integrated Technology. Shandong University (2017)
4. Sun, D., Lin, B., Zhou, W.: An overview of open winding electric machine system topology and control technology. Trans. Chin. Electrotechnical Soc. **32**(04), 76–84 (2017)
5. Duan, M.: Research of an Open-end Winding PMSM Based on Vector and Fault-tolerant strategy. Harbin Institute of Technology (2015)
6. Marufuzzaman, M., Reaz, M.B.I., Rahman, M.S., Ali, M.M.: Hardware prototyping of an intelligent current dq PI controller for FOC PMSM drive. In: International Conference on Electrical & Computer Engineering (ICECE 2010), pp. 86–88. IEEE, Dhaka (2010)

7. Nishio, M., Haga, H.: Single-phase to three-phase electrolytic capacitor-less dual in-verter-fed ipmsm for suppress torque pulsation. IEEE Trans. Industr. Electron. **68**(8), 6537–6546 (2020)

8. Bao, D., Pan, X., Wang, Y.: A novel hybrid control method for single-phase-input vari-able frequency speed control system with a small DC-link capacitor. IEEE Trans. Power Electron. **34**(9), 9016–9032 (2018)

9. Stefek, A., Van Pham, T., Krivanek, V., Pham, K.L.: Energy comparison of controllers used for a differential drive wheeled mobile robot. IEEE Access **8**, 170915–170927 (2020)

10. Zhao, D., Sun, H., Cui, W.: Research on the platform design and control system for the wheel-side steering-driving coordination vehicle. In: 2010 IEEE International Confer-ence on Mechatronics and Automation, pp. 1276–1281. IEEE, Xi'an (2010)

11. Zhao, Z., Taghavifar, H., Du, H., Qin, Y., Dong, M., Gu, L.: In-wheel motor vibration control for distributed-driven electric vehicles: a review. IEEE Trans. Transp. Electrification. **7**(4), 2864–2880 (2021)

12. Sun, X., Shi, Z., Cai, Y., Lei, G., Guo, Y., Zhu, J.: Driving-cycle-oriented design optimization of a permanent magnet hub motor drive system for a four-wheel-drive electric vehicle. IEEE Trans. Transport. Electrification **6**(3), 1115–1125 (2020)

Human Following for Mobile Robots

Wenjuan Zhou[1], Peter Dickenson[2], Haibin Cai[1(✉)], and Baihua Li[1]

[1] Department of Computer Science, Loughborough University, Loughborough, UK
{W.Zhou2,H.Cai,B.Li}@lboro.ac.uk
[2] School of Sport, Exercise and Health Sciences, Loughborough University,
Loughborough, UK
P.Dickenson@lboro.ac.uk

Abstract. Human following is an essential function in many robotic systems. Most of the existing human following algorithms are based on human tracking algorithms. However, in practical scenarios, the human subject might easily disappear due to occlusions and quick movements. In order to solve the problem of occlusion, this paper proposed a classification-based human following framework. After using a pretrained MobileNetV2 model to detect the human subjects, the robot will automatically train a classification model to identify the target person. In the end, the robot is controlled by some rule-based motion commands to follow the target human. Experimental results on several practical scenarios have demonstrated the effectiveness of the algorithm.

Keywords: Human detection · Object detection · Human-robot interaction · Human following

1 Introduction

As one of the functions of realizing human-robot interaction (HRI), human-following plays a very significant role, becoming an essential ability of a mobile robot. For example, a service robot that accompanies the elder can help the elder lift some heavy objects and always follow behind the elder to secure their status [2]. Shopping-assistance robots also need to follow customers to scan their purchased items and help them deliver the items to the check-out counter [6].

Early human-following robots used tracking by detecting LED lights on subjects [7]. Then came robots that tracked humans by recognizing their shoulders and backs [4]. Gradually, some robots identify the tracking human by identifying the texture and color of the clothes [10]. In 2013, Hu et al. [5] proposed 3-D meanshift tracking and LRF-based leg tracking for localizing humans. Vision-based approaches to human tracking algorithms are gaining popularity with the development of devices such as robotic cameras.

This paper uses an appearance-based classification model to identify the target person to follow. The robot uses Intel's realsense RGBD camera, which can collect image information, capture the depth information of the detected target, and provide feedback on the distance between the camera and the person.

H. Liu et al. (Eds.): ICIRA 2022, LNAI 13455, pp. 660–668, 2022.
https://doi.org/10.1007/978-3-031-13844-7_61

With this information, we can use a series of calculations to keep the robot at a reasonable distance from the target person.

Human-following Robot generally consists of three parts [9]: hardware mechanism, tracking algorithm, and following control algorithm. This paper mainly discusses the algorithm part, and we use a Jetson Nano-based robot as the hardware to implement and test our algorithm. For the tracking algorithm part, the more popular method is called Tracking-by-detection. These algorithms first detect humans, then determine what to track, and then use a series of tracking algorithms to track humans. However, in practical application scenarios, human-following has many challenges [1]. For example, the target person suddenly turning its direction or colliding or intersecting with another person. In these scenarios, the robot cannot confirm whether the person is the one it should follow. It will come to a situation where the robot loses its target. In response to this situation, we propose an algorithm and construct a pipeline. The following points are the contributions of this article: 1. Propose a classification-based human-following algorithm and a framework to address the occlusion problem. 2. Design a series of experiments to verify the proposed frame.

The main layout is as follows: Sect. 2 presents our complete algorithm pipeline. Section 3 shows the experiments we designed based on the proposed algorithm. Section 4 summarizes our entire paper and discusses possible future developments.

2   Methodology

This part mainly introduces our proposed classification-based human-following algorithm and framework. The framework is divided into three parts. The first part is the initialization part, then the tracking part, and finally the robot control part. In the Initialization part, we use Resnet-18 to train the images returned by the robot so that the robot can identify the original tracking target in the occlusion scene. In the tracking part, the algorithm uses the object detection model trained by MobileNeV2 on the COCO dataset for fast human detection. It works with the model trained in the initialization part to determine the tracking target. For the robot control part, the algorithm executes the corresponding motor command according to the tracking target determined by the tracking part. The following is a detailed description of the framework.

2.1   Hardware

Jetson Nano-based Robot. Jetson Nano-based Robot is an open-source robot based on the Jetson Nano Developer Kit. The NVIDIA Jetson Nano is a powerful small computer that allows running multiple neural networks in parallel applications such as image classification, object detection, segmentation, and speech processing. The other parts of the robot's hardware are four motors, an Intel Realsense D435i camera, and the shell made and assembled by 3D printing technology, as shown in Fig. 1, which are the front and side views of the robot. We use this robot to implement the human-following algorithm proposed in this paper.

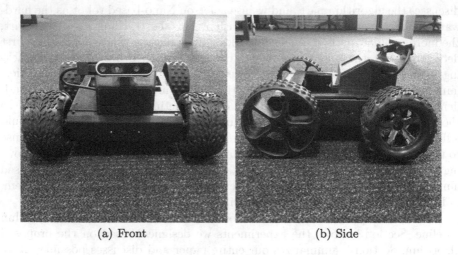

(a) Front   (b) Side

Fig. 1. Jetson Nano-based robot

2.2 Human Detection

The MobileNeV2 model [8] is a lightweight deep neural network proposed by Google for embedded devices such as mobile phones. The core idea of this model is depthwise separable convolution Because of its lightweight network, MobileNeV2 shows outstanding advantages: fast speed, few parameters, and easy to use. Given the limited computing resource of the robot, MovileNeV2 is an ideal model to use. Our proposed algorithm uses the object detection model SSD engine trained on the COCO dataset by MobileNeV2 for fast human detection.

2.3 Target Human Identification

ResNet is a model proposed by He Kaiming et al. in 2015 [3]. This model uses the residual structure to make the network deeper, converge faster, and optimize more easily. At the same time, it has fewer parameters and lower complexity than the previous model. ResNet solves the problem of deep network degradation and arduous training, which is suitable for various computer vision tasks. For the algorithm proposed in this article, in order to determine whether the robot is following the original target, we send the image data collected at the initialization part to ResNet-18 for pre-training. Based on the idea of transfer learning. We use the best-performing model learned on the more extensive dataset to classify the small dataset and get the results in time.

2.4 Human Following Algorithm

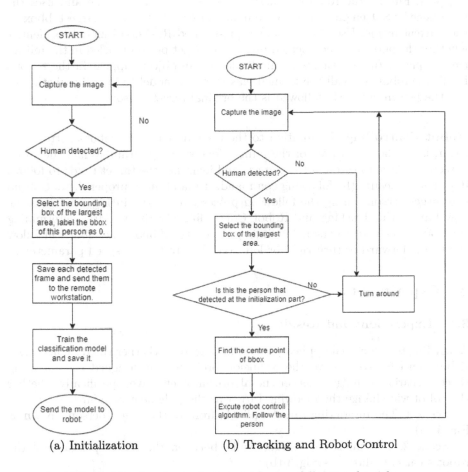

(a) Initialization   (b) Tracking and Robot Control

Fig. 2. The flowchart of proposed human-following algorithm

Initialization. In the beginning, the algorithm reads the first frame of the video captured by the robot's camera, uses the object detection model to detect people, and draws a bounding box (bbox) with the largest area in the robot's field of vision (FOV) in the first frame. Use the person drawn by the largest b-box as the original follower target. This strategy requires that the original target person in the actual application scenario must stand in the center of the robot's FOV in the initial scene.

When the robot starts to run, mark the label of the person with the largest bbox detected as 0, and the labels of other people are still 1, and then transmit the image data of each frame to the computer and re-evaluate the person tracked in each frame. After the computer receives a certain amount of data, it starts to train the network. After the training is complete, the trained model is stored and passed to the robot. As shown in Fig. 1 (a), it is the flowchart of the Initialization part of the Human Following algorithm.

Tracking. After completing the initialization part, the robot starts the tracking part. Firstly, the robot's camera captures the current frame and uses the pre-trained SSD engine to detect humans after selecting the largest bbox in the current frame. Use the previously pre-trained ResNet-18 model to identify whether the person in the selected box is the target person labeled in the initialization phase. In this way, when multiple human objects appear in the robot's FOV, the robot will call the trained classification model to identify whether or not the person currently followed is the original target person.

Robot Controlling. In addition to the tracking part, the robot control algorithm is another vital part of the human-following algorithm. When the robot detects the human through the camera and identifies the target needs to follow, it starts to execute the following command. It maintains a proper distance from the target person during the following process. As shown in Fig. 2(b), it is the flowchart of the Tracking and Robot Controlling algorithm. After determining the bbox of the target person and finding the center of bbox, the robot will follow the target forward or turn right or left according to the set speed parameters.

3   Experiments

3.1   Experiment and Result

According to the actual application scenario, to test whether the designed algorithm can effectively solve the occlusion problem, we designed the following three scenarios to judge whether the algorithm is effective, specifically whether the robot will change the following target as the judgment standard.

Scene 1. The interfering target walks in front of the target person, shown as Fig. 3 (a)

Scene 2. The interfering target walks between the target person and the robot's camera, shown as Fig. 3 (b)

Scene 3. The interfering target and the target person stand side by side in front of the robot camera, shown as Fig. 3 (c)

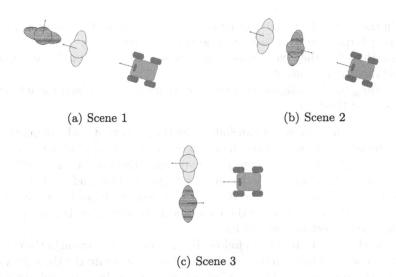

(a) Scene 1   (b) Scene 2

(c) Scene 3

Fig. 3. The figures show the top view of the three experimental scenes, where the blue one is the original target person followed by the robot, and the shadowed one is the interfering subject. The direction of the arrow indicates the speed direction of the human and robot. (Color figure online)

The following is the detailed experimental procedure. The experimental site is in a relatively open laboratory. First, the target person (subject) stands close to the robot and tries to appear in the center of the robot's FOV as much as possible. After the robot detected the subject and started walking towards the target, the subject started walking in space with its back to the robot to test whether the robot would follow the subject. During the subject's journey, an interfering target joined the test according to the three designed scenarios. Before that, only one target person was in the robot's FOV. During the test, to give the robot enough reaction time to test whether our algorithm can recognize the original tracked target. When the interference target participates in the experimental scene, the interference target needs to stand in front of the robot camera with the original followed target and pause for a few seconds according to the position set by the experiment.

The following are the evaluation criteria based on the designed experimental scene. If the robot meets the following conditions during the test, the experimental result is considered to be successful, and the algorithm we designed is effective: 1. During the movement of the target person, when the robot follows the subject, the interfering target walks directly in front of the follower without blocking the subject, pauses with the subject for more than 5 s, then walks away. The subject starts to move, and the robot still follows the subject.

2. In test scene 2, the interfering target walked between the subject and the robot, blocked the subject, paused in front of the robot for more than 5 s, and then walked away with the subject. The robot did not change the original follow target.

3. In test scene 3, the interfering target walked from the subject's side. The interfering target stopping side by side with the subject in front of the robot for more than 5 s, they each moved in opposite directions, and the robot still followed the original target.

According to the designed scenario, we tested the robot, and the following is the process of the test:

1. To test whether the robot can follow the target person without interference, we conducted ten tests. After the robot completes the initialization of the following target, the subject starts to travel and the experimental environment in the laboratory. The subjects can go straight and turn left and right to test whether the robot can follow the target person straight or turn and keep a reasonable distance. During the experiment, observe whether the robot can follow the subject and record it.

2. To test whether the robot can follow the original target person in the occlusion scenario, we conduct ten tests and, in each test, simulate the three previously designed scenarios. Let the interfering targets move from the subject's front, back, and side, respectively, and stop according to the designed scene. In this process, the subject and the robot keep relatively straight to exclude other factors. During the experiment, observe whether the robot changes following the target and record it.

Table 1 counts the number of times the robot follows the target and loses the target in 10 trials. Out of 10 experiments, nine succeeded in following the target, and one lost the following target. This shows that our proposed human-following algorithm can achieve the purpose of following humans. The statistics of the three scenarios proposed in the experimental design section are recorded in Table 2. For each scenario, ten experiments were conducted. Scenario 1 counts whether the robot changes the following target after letting the interfering target pass in front of the subject. Scenario 2 counts whether the robot transforms the original followed target after the interfering target walks between the subject and the robot. Scenario 3 counts the situation in which the robot changes the original followed target after the interfering target walks from the subject's side. Experimental data show that our proposed algorithm can make the robot follow the original target person in the occlusion scene, but the accuracy still needs improvement.

Table 1. The record of the robot following the target person.

Number of experiments	Followed the target (counts)	Lost the target (counts)
10	9	1

Table 2. The record of the robot changed following target.

Scene of experiment	Follow the original target person (counts)	Change the target (counts)
The interfering target stands in front of the target person	10	0
The interfering target stands between the target person and the robot	6	4
The interfering target stands with the target person in front of the robot	7	3

4 Conclusion

To solve the problem of occlusion that occurs when robots follow humans, we propose a classification-based human-following algorithm. At the same time, we proposed a set of test strategies. According to our experiments and research, the deep classification-based model has demonstrated the effectiveness of the human-following algorithm. However, the model training in the initialization phase takes some time, so the entire process of the human-following framework takes a long time. Hoping this problem can be improved in future work.

References

1. Do Hoang, M., Yun, S.S., Choi, J.S.: The reliable recovery mechanism for person-following robot in case of missing target. In: 2017 14th International Conference on Ubiquitous Robots and Ambient Intelligence (URAI), pp. 800–803. IEEE (2017)
2. Gupta, M., Kumar, S., Behera, L., Subramanian, V.K.: A novel vision-based tracking algorithm for a human-following mobile robot. IEEE Trans. Syst. Man Cybern. Syst. **47**(7), 1415–1427 (2016)
3. He, K., Zhang, X., Ren, S., Sun, J.: Deep residual learning for image recognition. In: Proceedings of the IEEE Conference on Computer Vision and Pattern Recognition, pp. 770–778 (2016)
4. Hirai, N., Mizoguchi, H.: Visual tracking of human back and shoulder for person following robot. In: Proceedings 2003 IEEE/ASME International Conference on Advanced Intelligent Mechatronics (AIM 2003), vol. 1, pp. 527–532. IEEE (2003)
5. Hu, J.S., Wang, J.J., Ho, D.M.: Design of sensing system and anticipative behavior for human following of mobile robots. IEEE Trans. Industr. Electron. **61**(4), 1916–1927 (2013)
6. Kejriwal, N., Garg, S., Kumar, S.: Product counting using images with application to robot-based retail stock assessment. In: 2015 IEEE International Conference on Technologies for Practical Robot Applications (TePRA), pp. 1–6. IEEE (2015)
7. Nagumo, Y., Ohya, A.: Human following behavior of an autonomous mobile robot using light-emitting device. In: Proceedings 10th IEEE International Workshop on Robot and Human Interactive Communication. ROMAN 2001 (Cat. No. 01TH8591), pp. 225–230. IEEE (2001)

8. Sandler, M., Howard, A., Zhu, M., Zhmoginov, A., Chen, L.C.: Mobilenetv 2: inverted residuals and linear bottlenecks. In: Proceedings of the IEEE Conference on Computer Vision and Pattern Recognition, pp. 4510–4520 (2018)
9. Tarmizi, A.I., Shukor, A.Z., Sobran, N.M.M., Jamaluddin, M.H.: Latest trend in person following robot control algorithm: a review. J. Telecommun. Electron. Comput. Engi. (JTEC) 9(3), 169–174 (2017)
10. Yoshimi, T., et al.: Development of a person following robot with vision based target detection. In: 2006 IEEE/RSJ International Conference on Intelligent Robots and Systems, pp. 5286–5291. IEEE (2006)

Multi-objective RL with Preference Exploration

Wei Xi and Xian Guo[✉]

Institute of Robotics and Automatic Information System, Nankai University,
Tianjing 300353, China
guoxian@nankai.edu.cn

Abstract. Traditional multi-objective reinforcement learning problems
pay attention to the expected return of each objective under different
preferences. However, the difference in strategy in practice is also important. This paper proposes an algorithm Multi-objective RL with Preference Exploration (MoPE), which can cover the optimal solutions under
different objective preferences as much as possible with only one trained
model. Specifically, the coverage of the optimal solution is improved by
exploring the preference space in the sampling stage and reusing samples
with similar preferences in the training stage. Furthermore, for different
preference inputs, a variety of diversity strategies that conform to the
preference can be generated by maximizing the mutual information of
preference and state based on a method of information theory. Compared with the existing methods, our algorithm can implement more
diverse strategies on the premise of ensuring the coverage of the optimal
solution.

Keywords: Multi-objective · Reinforcement learning · Diversity ·
Information theory

1 Introduction

In the real world, a task often contains multiple objectives, and the preferences
for these objectives are different in different situations, so various strategies are
needed to meet the needs in different situations. Existing reinforcement learning
methods such as DQN [1] and DDPG [2] can already handle single-objective
problems. In more cases, the importance of each objective in the task is difficult
to determine in advance, or some changes need to be made according to the
actual situation. In single-objective reinforcement learning, this kind of problem
is solved by adjusting the weight of this objective separately. The results of
this adjustment method are often uncertain, because some objective may not be
independent of each other, or even exist in opposition to each other. And for the

This work is supported by the National Natural Science Foundation of China
(62073176). All the authors are with the Institute of Robotics and Automatic Information System, College of Artificial Intelligence, Nankai University, China.

traditional reinforcement learning algorithm, its goal is to maximize the expected return made up of multiple parts, the larger return is not necessarily achieved by increasing the reward, but by reducing the penalty. For example, when the reward for reaching the goal is small, and the penalty related to time is large, the robot may end the episode early by colliding with the obstacle to reduce the penalty obtained. Compared with traditional single-objective reinforcement learning, multi-objective reinforcement learning (MORL) provides a better way to deal with multi-objective tasks.

Existing MORL methods can be divided into two categories [3]: outer loop and inner loop [5]. The outer loop method treats the MORL as multiple single-objective reinforcement learning problems with different preferences. This method achieves the effect of approximately representing the Pareto front by maintaining a population of policies [6] distinguished by preference, which makes it difficult to extend to complex problems or problems with a large number of objective. The inner loop class method learns a value function or policy network conditioned on preference, and uses the deep neural network to obtain an approximate Pareto optimal solution. During the training process, different preferences are used as the input of the neural network, and the goal is to maximize the cumulative return under the linear weighting of the preferences. Compared with the outer loop method, it avoids maintaining a large set of strategies, but there are problems of large sample demand and catastrophic forgetting. Friedman et al. [7] combined the MORL method with Hindsight Experience Replay (HER) [8] and Deep Deterministic Policy Gradients to achieve higher sample utilization in continuous action space. Abels et al. [9] implemented a weight-conditioned network (CN) based on vector Q-functions, and accelerate learning by using deverse experience replay (DER). Yang et al. [10] proposed the optimality operator for a generalized version of Bellman equation and the Envelope Q-learning (EQL) method, they proved its theoretical onvergence under linear preference. The EQL outperforms single-objective reinforcement learning on the complex Atari game SuperMario.

Multi-objective problems can be seen as a form of diversity problems. For multi-objective problems, the strategies on the Pareto frontier have certain differences. Diversity problems focus on differences in strategies under the same scenario, which can be caused by different reward functions. Shen et al. [6] used multi-objective genetic algorithm combined with single-objective reinforcement learning method to obtain different styles of game AI. Optimizing the distance of trajectories obtained by different strategies or the kl-distance of different strategies is also a way to generate diversity. Wu et al. [11] used the Maximum Mean Discrepancy (MMD) distance between trajectories as a regular term to generate different opponents strategies. Eysenbach et al. [12] used unsupervised learning for generating diversity by maximizing the mutual information of different skills and states based on maximum entropy reinforcement learning. These methods can generate more fine-grained diversity, but for many practical problems, a controllable and interpretable diversity is more valuable.

The contribution of our work is threefold:

1) We propose an algorithm which can cover the optimal solution as much as possible with training only one model.
2) For different preference inputs, a variety of diversity strategies that conform to the preference can be generated.
3) Compared with single-objective reinforcement learning, our algorithm can reduce the possibility of falling into a local optimal solution, and can better converge to the optimal solution in sparse reward environments.

The structure of this paper is organized as follows: In Sect. 2, we introduce the relevant background of multi-objective reinforcement learning and some notations used in this paper. In Sect. 3, we analyze some problems with existing methods and propose a multi-objective reinforcement learning algorithm with preference exploration (MoPE). In Sect. 4, we introduce two multi-objective environments and validate our methods based on them. In Sect. 5, we summarize the contributions of this article and illustrate future research directions.

2 Background

The Multi-objective Reinforcement Learning (MORL) is a class of methods relative to traditional single-objective reinforcement learning. Its reward function $r(s,a) = (r_1(s,a), ...r_m(s,a))$ is given in vector form, where m is the number of targets. The MORL is derived from multi-objective optimization problems, whose goal is to solve $\max f(x) = (f_1(x), ...f_m(x))^\top$. In most multi-objective problems, there are conflicts or incomparability between objectives, and the global optimal solution cannot be obtained, which leads to the improvement of one objective that tends to weaken other objectives. For a solution, if there is no other solution that is better than it on all objectives, it is called a Pareto solution under the problem. A set of Pareto optimal solutions is called the Pareto optimal set, and the surface formed by the optimal set in space is called the *Pareto front*.

The Markov Decision Process (MDP) is the basic form of reinforcement learning (RL). MDP can be represented by the tuple (S, A, P, γ, r), with state space S, action space A, action $a \in A$, transition probability $P(s' \mid s, a)$, discount factor γ, reward function $r(s, a)$. The goal of reinforcement learning is to learn the strategy $\pi : S \times A \to [0, 1]$ to obtain the maximum cumulative return $G_t = \sum_t^\infty \gamma^t r(s, a)$, at this time the strategy is called the optimal strategy π^*. The solution method of the optimal strategy can be divided into two types: based on the value function $V(s) = E_\pi[G_t \mid S_t = s]$ and $Q(s,a) = E_\pi[G_t \mid S_t = s, A_t = a]$ and based on the policy. The DQN is a representation of a value function-based approach, which value function is updated as:

$$Q(s,a)_{i+1} \leftarrow Q(s,a)_i + \alpha \left[r + \gamma \max_{a' \in A} Q(s', a')_i - Q(s,a)_i \right] \tag{1}$$

The PPO is a policy base algorithm, which loss function is:

$$J_{PPO}(\theta) = \sum_{t=1}^{T} \frac{\pi_\theta(a_t \mid s_t)}{\pi_{old}(a_t \mid s_t)} \hat{A}_t - \lambda \text{KL}[\pi_{old} \mid \pi_\theta]$$

$$\hat{A}_t = \hat{R}_t - V_\phi(s_t)$$

(2)

The Multi-objective Markov Decision Process (MOMDP) can be represented by the tuple $(S, A, P, r, \Omega, f_\Omega)$ with vector reward function $r(s, a, s')$, the space of preference Ω, preference function $f_\omega = \omega^T r(s, a)$, preference $\omega \in \Omega$. When ω is fixed, each ω corresponds to a MDP process. All optimal solutions form the Pareto coverage set (PCS) $\mathcal{F}^* := \{\hat{r} \mid \hat{r} \geq \hat{V}', \forall \hat{r}'\}$, where the return $\hat{r}_t = \sum_t^\infty \gamma^t r_t(s, a)$. The optimal strategies corresponding to all optimal solutions constitute the *Pareto front* of this problem. For all possible $\omega \in \Omega$ constitute a convex coverage set (CCS) [10] which is a subset of PCS:

$$\text{CCS} := \{\hat{r} \in \mathcal{F}^* \mid \exists \omega \in \Omega \text{ s.t. } \omega^\top \hat{r} \geq \omega^\top \hat{r}', \forall \hat{r}' \in \mathcal{F}^*\}.$$

(3)

Our goal is to learn a general value function $\mathcal{Q}(s, a, \omega, \theta)$ that can generalize to the entire preference space, and the policy obtained by this value function can cover the CCS as much as possible.

3   Multi-objective RL with Preference Exploration

The algorithm we propose is based on two ideas. The first is the exploration and utilization of existing samples. For inner loop methods, it is necessary to sample trajectories under different preferences during the training process to learn a general value function, which reduce sample size for each preference. To address this issue, we expand and explore in existing samples through HER and prioritization experience replay (PER) [13] combined with information theory to increase sample utilization. The second is the exploration of preference space during sampling. Existing methods usually directly obtain the preference used in each episode through uniform sampling. While it's favorable to use the already trained preferences and corresponding result as priors to guide the selection of new preferences.

Exploring and Utilizing Existing Experience is the key to improving sample efficiency. The HER is a technique for dealing with the sparse reward goal-condition problem, which improves the utilization of samples by relabeling the goals of existing trajectories as goals that can be reached by the current strategy. Preference is also a goal in this paper. The preference will only affect the action of the agent, but not the dynamics of the environment. Therefore, A relabeling can be used to the experience to improve the utilization of the sample. For each experience in the batch (s, ω_b, a, r, s') we additionally sample N_ω preferences $\omega = \{\omega_0, \omega_1, ..., \omega_{N_\omega} \mid \forall \omega, \|\omega_i - \omega_b\|_2 \leq \sigma_\omega\}$ as new goals. Different from the

EQL, it can be noticed that policies with similar preferences will be more similar under linear preferences, which can provide more information to help the learning of the current policy, so we will limit the newly sampled preferences to the vicinity σ_w of the actual sampled w_b which called Similar Preference Exploration. After relabeling, The EQL's loss is used to update the network. The loss function L includes two parts:

$$L^A(\theta) = \mathbb{E}_{s,a,w} \left[\|\boldsymbol{y} - \boldsymbol{Q}(s, a, \boldsymbol{w}; \theta)\|_2^2\right]$$
$$L^B(\theta) = \mathbb{E}_{s,a,w} \left[|\boldsymbol{w}^\top \boldsymbol{y} - \boldsymbol{w}^\top \boldsymbol{Q}(s, a, \boldsymbol{w}; \theta)|\right] \tag{4}$$
$$L = L^A + L^B$$

where $\boldsymbol{y} = \mathbb{E}_{s'} \left[\boldsymbol{r} + \gamma \arg_Q \max_{a,w'} \boldsymbol{w}^\top \boldsymbol{Q}(s', a, \boldsymbol{w}'; \theta_k)\right]$. Compared to the original DQN objective, the EQL takes the largest Q value among the sampled actions and preferences simultaneously. L^A updates the vector Q function, L^B is the auxiliary loss, and the existence of L^B is to reduce the influence of the discrete solutions on the frontier on the optimization. The optimal solution corresponding to the preference is the same, which increases the difficulty of learning the value function.

The HER focuses on the utilization of data in the current batch, and PER is used to focus on the utilization of historical data. PER is generally based on the TD error of each experience. Based on the above analysis, it is more beneficial to consider a preference interval rather than the empirical TD error under a single preference in the MORL problem:

$$\delta = \frac{1}{N_\omega} \sum_{i=0}^{N_\omega} \boldsymbol{\omega_i}^\top \boldsymbol{y} - \boldsymbol{\omega_i}^\top \boldsymbol{Q}(s, a, \boldsymbol{\omega_i}; \theta). \tag{5}$$

The TD error takes into account the error of the value function, reflecting how well the value function is learned. However, discrete optimal solutions will make strategies under multiple preferences correspond to the same optimal solution, which increases the possibility of strategies falling into local optimality. At the same time, the multi-objective reinforcement learning problem pays more attention to the results of different strategies. But the differences in results do not fully correspond to the differences in strategies. In this regard, we use the method of information theory to deal with this problem. Our method is based on an idea that a large difference in preference w corresponds to a large difference in the state S reached by the agent. It should be able to better distinguish the agent's preferences under different state, that is, maximize the mutual information $I(S; w)$ between state and the preferences.

$$I(S; w) = (\mathcal{H}[w] - \mathcal{H}[w \mid S])$$
$$= \mathbb{E}_{w \sim p(w), s \sim \pi(w)}[\log p(w \mid s)] - \mathbb{E}_{w \sim p(w)}[\log p(w)] \tag{6}$$
$$\geq \mathbb{E}_{w \sim p(w), s \sim \pi(w)} [\log q_\phi(w \mid s) - \log p(w)]$$

Among them, $p(w \mid s)$ is difficult to calculate directly, a discriminator network $q_\phi(w \mid s)$ is trained to approximate it. It can be proved that the approximated solution can provide a variational lower bound on mutual information. $I(S; \omega)$ is optimized by add this priority to PER, the priority sampling probability is:

$$q(s_i) = \delta + \alpha(\log q_\phi(\omega \mid s) - \log p(\omega)). \tag{7}$$

The above formula can be understood that we pay more attention to the state that is easy to distinguish, and the value function has not been estimated accurately. This kind of state also corresponds to the frontier of exploration, and α is used to balance the ratio of the two parts. For some adversarial tasks, the addition of the discriminator also brings convenience to opponent modeling.

Exploring in Preference Space is key to speeding up training and mitigating catastrophic forgetting. To guarantee coverage of the optimal solution, continuously train with different preferences is needed. After many updates, the neural network may forget some of the policies it learned earlier. In order to reduce the impact of forgetting and take advantage of the learned policy, we need to update the sampling probability $p(\omega)$ during training to purposefully learn some preferences.

Specifically, we expect to give higher sampling probabilities to preferences that currently have few visits or incomplete training. For the problem of visit frequency, we discretize the preference space into N_I intervals $I_i \in \Omega, i \in [0, N_I]$. Put each used preference into the corresponding interval to get the count N_i. Combined with the counting-based exploration method in reinforcement learning [15], we set $p(\omega) \propto (N_i + 0.01)^{-1/2}, \omega \in I_i$.

4   Experiment

Deep-Sea Treasure (DST) [14] is a simple multi-objective 10×11 grid world environment, which is often used for the verification of MORL algorithms. Its Pareto frontier is obtainable and convex. In the DST environment, there is an agent and several treasures with scores, and the treasure near the bottom of the map have higher scores. At the beginning of the round, the agent is in the upper left corner of the map, and the algorithm needs to control the agent to move in four directions until it reach the treasure. The agent's goal is to obtain the highest possible score while taking the fewest steps. The two parts of the rewards are the reward r_{score} for reaching the treasure, and the penalty for each step $r_{steps} = -1$ (Fig. 1).

In order to evaluate the coverage of the algorithm to the optimal solution in the CCS, we introduce the evaluation metric Coverage Ratio (CR). The calculation of CR is based on the coincidence of the optimal solution set $\mathcal{P}$ and CCS found by the algorithm [10]:

$$CR = 2 \times \frac{\text{precision} \times \text{recall}}{\text{precision} + \text{recall}}, \tag{8}$$

where precision $= |\mathcal{P} \cap \text{CCS}| / |\mathcal{P}|$, recall $= |\mathcal{P} \cap \text{CCS}| / |\text{CCS}|$, represent the proportion of coincident solutions in the two sets. In practical, we approximate

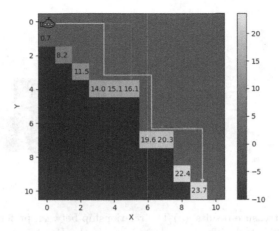

Fig. 1. The Deep-sea treasure (DST) environment. Agent starts from the upper left corner of the map, takes (x, y) as the state, and searches for treasures with different scores by moving in four directions. The red and the orange line in the figure represent two paths that can reach a specific treasure. It can be seen that the set of optimal solution paths in the DST environment is the shortest path to each treasure. (Color figure online)

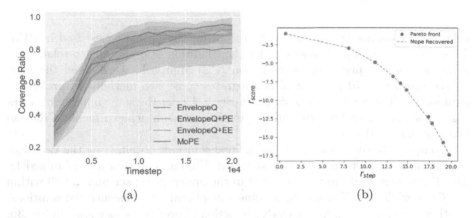

Fig. 2. Evaluate Deep-sea treasure results. (a) Coverage ratio metric under 20000 timesteps. (b) The real CCS and the recovered solutions.

the current optimal solution set $\mathcal{P}$ by randomly sampling a certain number of ω in the preference space.

We use a conditional Multi-head Q network [9] by 4 fully connected hidden layers with {64, 128, 128, 64} for training. The inputs are states (x, y) and preferences, and the number of heads in the output layer is equal to the number of objectives. The original EQL and the algorithm after adding exploration were trained for 20,000 timesteps, and the CR was evaluated every 1,000 steps during the training process, and 2,000 preferences were evaluated using uniform sampling. For the experience exploration (EE) approach, a discriminator network

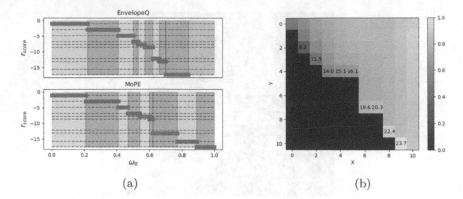

Fig. 3. Deep-sea treasure results. (a) The relationship between preference and optimal solution under DST task. The gray dotted line is the Pareto optimal solution, the green thick solid line is the optimal solution obtained by the algorithm. The preference space can be divided into multiple parts according to the different solutions. The red dotted line indicates that the corresponding optimal solution is missing, and the red area indicates that the solution obtained by the algorithm is not in the optimal solution set. (b) The discriminator's prediction of preference. The color indicates the weight corresponding to r_{score}. (Color figure online)

with 3 fully connected layers is used to output the probabilities used in PER. Then we sample 64 preferences under the condition of $\sigma_\omega = 0.04$ to relabel the samples. For the preference exploration (PE) approach, we divided the preference space into 10 parts. MoPE integrates these two methods of preference exploration. The final result is shown in Fig. 2. Under the same number of training steps, the algorithm after adding exploration can achieve higher CR than the original algorithm.

Compare the distribution of the optimal solutions obtained by the two algorithms in the preference space as shown in Fig. 3a. The solutions obtained by MoPE are more uniformly distributed in the preference space and are all within the CCS, while the EQL will have some suboptimal and concentrated solutions. Further, we plot the discriminator's prediction of preference as shown in Fig. 3b. For the DST environment, the optimal solution is unique, but the optimal path is not. The agent's preference is more difficult to discern when it is close to a treasure location in the top half of the map. Under our method, this part exhibits larger differences in predicted preferences, which means that agents choose more diversity routes for different preferences.

Robot Confrontation Game is a multi-objective problem in a continuous action space. There are two red and blue agents A_r, A_b in the scene, where A_r is the agent to be controlled, A_b is the rule-based agent, and the state update of the agents is based on (9).

$$\dot{x} = v\cos\theta, \dot{y} = v\sin\theta, \dot{\theta} = w, \dot{v} = a, \tag{9}$$

where robot's acceleration $a \in [-0.2, 0.2]$ m/s, angular velocity $w \in [-0.8, 0.8]$ rad/s, direction $\theta \in [-\pi, \pi]$. The goal is to hunt down the blue agent without going out of bounds. The definition of winning is that the distance and relative angle between the two agents are less than a certain threshold, such as (10) (Fig. 4).

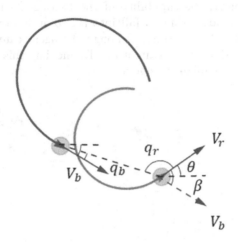

Fig. 4. Parameter definition of the environment.

$$q_r < 30°, q_b > 30°, \beta < 40°, d < 0.3\,m, \tag{10}$$

where q_r, q_b is the angle between the speed direction and the line connecting the two agents, β is the angle between the speed directions, and d is the distance between the two robots. For the strategy of rule-based agents, we use the threat index T which widely used in air combat problems as the evaluation index of the state, combined with single-step forward prediction, then select the action with the highest threat to the opponent. The threat index T we use includes two parts, the angle threat T_a and the distance threat T_b, which are defined as follows:

$$T_a = \frac{q_b - q_r}{\pi}, T_d = \frac{d_{\max} + d_{\min} - 2d}{d_{\max} - d_{\min}}, T = aT_a + bT_b, \tag{11}$$

where d_{max} and d_{min} are the maximum and minimum distances that two agents may encounter, a and b are the corresponding weight coefficients. In this paper, $a = 0.1, b = 0.9$.

For this environment we choose pursuit reward r_{catch} and moving distance reward r_{move} as optimization goals.

$$r_{catch} = \begin{cases} 10 & \text{if red wins} \\ -10 & \text{if bule wins} \\ (T_a - 1)/10 + (T_b - 1)/10 & \text{otherwise} \end{cases} \quad (12)$$

$$r_{run} = \begin{cases} -10 & \text{if out of range} \\ vdt & \text{otherwise} \end{cases}$$

In this environment, the capability of the two agents is consistent, which makes it easy for the algorithm to fall into a sub-optimal solution that keeps accelerating in circles. At this time, although the agent cannot obtain rewards, it will not be punished for being caught up. To alleviate this problem we use the threat index penalty to guide the agent.

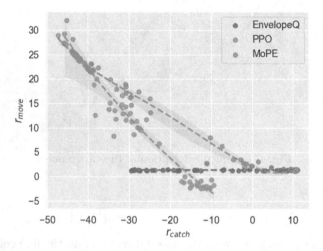

Fig. 5. Optimal solutions obtained by different algorithms. The dashed line is result fitted by data.

Compare the optimal solutions obtained by different algorithms in Fig. 5. The data of the PPO [16] is obtained by training single-objective problems under different preferences, and the data of MoPE and the EQL are obtained by uniform sampling 100 preferences after training. From the maximum reward that the algorithm can achieve, it can be seen that (1) the single-target PPO algorithm does not learn a strategy that can catch up with the opponent (the reward for catching up with the opponent is 10). (2) Compared with the EQL, MoPE has more diverse strategies. We further map MoPE's representative games under different preferences as Fig. 6.

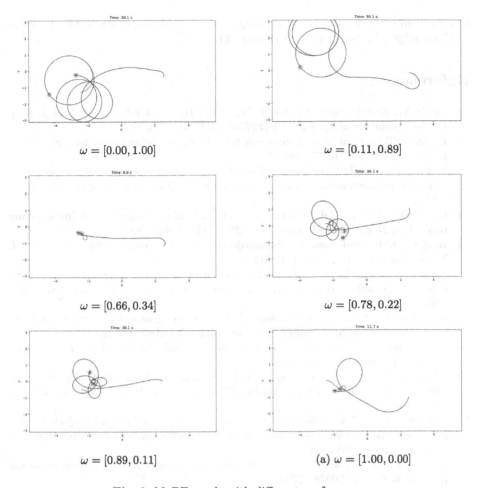

$\omega = [0.00, 1.00]$ $\omega = [0.11, 0.89]$

$\omega = [0.66, 0.34]$ $\omega = [0.78, 0.22]$

$\omega = [0.89, 0.11]$ (a) $\omega = [1.00, 0.00]$

Fig. 6. MoPE result with different preferences.

5 Conclusion

We propose a multi-objective reinforcement learning algorithm (MORL), which can cover the optimal solutions under different preferences as much as possible when only one model is trained, and can generate sufficiently diversity strategies under different preference inputs. We conduct experiments on the algorithm in a simple grid world environment DST and a more difficult robot confrontation environment, Our experiments demonstrate that our algorithm has sufficient generalization and diversity relative to the benchmark algorithms. Future research will consider constrained multi-objective problems. The method in this paper is based on the assumption of linear preference, which means that all rewards must participate in the weighting calculation, and their corresponding weights need to be sampled in training, but for some penalty items, such as collisions, timeouts, etc., we do not need to consider them preferences, but wish to constrain them within a certain range. One possible approach to this problem is Thresholded Lexicographic Ordering (TLO) [17].

References

1. Mnih, V., Kavukcuoglu, K., Silver, D., et al.: Human-level control through deep reinforcement learning. Nature **518**(7540), 529–533 (2015)
2. Lillicrap, T.P., et al.: Continuous control with deep reinforcement learning. arXiv preprint arXiv:1509.02971 (2015)
3. Hayes, C.F., Rădulescu, R., Bargiacchi, E., et al.: A practical guide to multi-objective reinforcement learning and planning. arXiv preprint arXiv:2103.09568 (2021)
4. Czarnecki, W.M., Gidel, G., Tracey, B., et al.: Real world games look like spinning tops. Adv. Neural. Inf. Process. Syst. **33**, 17443–17454 (2020)
5. Roijers, D.M., Whiteson, S.: Multi-objective decision making. Synth. Lect. Artif. Intell. Mach. Learn. **11**(1), 1–129 (2017)
6. Shen, R., Zheng, Y., Hao, J., et al.: Generating behavior-diverse game AIs with evolutionary multi-objective deep reinforcement learning. In: IJCAI, pp. 3371–3377 (2020)
7. Friedman, E., Fontaine, F.: Generalizing across multi-objective reward functions in deep reinforcement learning. arXiv preprint arXiv:1809.06364 (2018)
8. Andrychowicz, M., Wolski, F., Ray, A., et al.: Hindsight experience replay. Adv. Neural Inf. Process. Syst. **30** (2017)
9. Abels, A., Roijers, D., Lenaerts, T., et al.: Dynamic weights in multi-objective deep reinforcement learning. In: International Conference on Machine Learning. PMLR, pp. 11–20 (2019)
10. Yang R, Sun X, Narasimhan K. A generalized algorithm for multi-objective reinforcement learning and policy adaptation[J]. Advances in Neural Information Processing Systems, 2019, 32
11. Wu, Z., Li, K., Zhao, E., et al.: L2e: learning to exploit your opponent. arXiv preprint arXiv:2102.09381 (2021)
12. Eysenbach, B., Gupta, A., Ibarz, J., et al.: Diversity is all you need: learning skills without a reward function. arXiv preprint arXiv:1802.06070 (2018)
13. Schaul, T., Quan, J., Antonoglou, I., et al.: Prioritized experience replay. arXiv preprint arXiv:1511.05952 (2015)
14. Vamplew, P., Yearwood, J., Dazeley, R., et al.: On the limitations of scalarisation for multi-objective reinforcement learning of pareto fronts. In: Australasian Joint Conference on Artificial Intelligence. Springer, Berlin, Heidelberg, pp. 372–378 (2008)
15. Strehl, A.L., Littman, M.L.: An analysis of model-based interval estimation for Markov decision processes. J. Comput. Syst. Sci. **74**(8), 1309–1331 (2008)
16. Schulman, J., Wolski, F., Dhariwal, P., et al.: Proximal policy optimization algorithms. arXiv preprint arXiv:1707.06347 (2017)
17. Gábor, Z., Kalmár, Z., Szepesvári, C.: Multi-criteria reinforcement learning. In: ICML, vol. 98, pp. 197–205 (1998)

Rehabilitation and Assistive Robotics

Design and Iterative Learning Control
of Intelligent Cooperative Manipulator

Wujing Cao[1,2], Meng Yin[1,2(✉)], Mingwei Hu[3], Zhuowei Li[1,2], and Xinyu Wu[1,2]

[1] Shenzhen Institutes of Advanced Technology, Chinese Academy of Sciences,
Shenzhen 518055, China
yinmenglz@163.com
[2] Guangdong Provincial Key Lab of Robotics and Intelligent System, Shenzhen Institute of
Advanced Technology, Chinese Academy of Sciences, Shenzhen 518055, China
[3] Jiangsu Automation Research Institute, Lianyungang 222006, China

Abstract. In view of the shortcomings of the existing service robot manipulator, such as low flexibility and small load, the tendon-sheath transmission is creatively applied to design a 7-DOF robotic arm. The joint and the drive module are separated by the tendon-sheath transmission and designed individually. Considering the transmission characteristics of the gear reducer and the tendon-sheath, position transmission model of the joint is built. Proportional-integral-differential (PID) controller and iterative learning controller are designed for position tracking control based on double encoders. Position control experiments of the elbow joint are carried out based on the constructed physical prototype. The experimental results show that compared with PID controller, iterative learning controller can effectively reduce the position tracking error and improve the position control accuracy. Applying this transmission method to the manipulator can improve its cost performance ratio, which provides the possibility for the large-scale application of the manipulator in more scenes.

Keywords: Tendon-sheath transmission · Manipulator · Position tracking control · Iterative learning

1 Introduction

The tendon-sheath mainly composed of an inner flexible cable and an outer casing. The typical application is a bicycle brake cable. It can realize the long-distance transmission of force and displacement through the movement of the flexible cable in the casing. It has the advantages of simple structure, strong space adaptability, and low design cost, so it is widely used in robotics.

According to the size of the joint end, the existing applications of tendon-sheath transmission can be divided into two categories. The first category is the application of dexterous hands and surgical robots, which are characterized by limited space at the joint end, the slight movement distance of the driven wheel and flexible cable, but sufficient space at the drive end. Therefore, the tension sensors and encoders are mostly installed on the drive end. Kaneko et al. [1, 2] applied a tendon-sheath mechanism to drive the fingers of a dexterous hand, described the transmission model of the tendon-sheath based on the Coulomb friction model. They verified the non-linear phenomena of the tendon-sheath transmission, such as clearance and hysteresis, through experiments. Palli et al. [3, 4] applied the tendon-sheath mechanism to the DEXMART five-finger dexterous hand and improved the transmission model considering the flexibility of the tendon-sheath. The control strategy based on friction compensation was applied to reduce the impact of the non-linear characteristics of the tendon-sheath transmission. Phee et al. [5, 6] applied the tendon-sheath mechanism to a surgical robot, proposed a method to estimate the joint force and position based on the driving side force and position sensor, and measured the transmission error under the assumption that the shape of the tendon-sheath does not change. Li et al. [7] applied the deep learning method to predict the joint force based on the measurement data of the driver. The experiment proved that when the training algorithm has enough data, it can obtain a more accurate prediction than the traditional method when moving at a constant speed.

The other is the application in rehabilitation robots and exoskeletons. The specialty of the application is that there is enough space between the joint end and the drive end to install the encoder, but the driven wheel and the flexible cable have a considerable moving distance, and the use of the tension sensor requires ample space. It is not easy to install it. Kong et al. [8, 9] applied tendon-sheath transmission to lower limb rehabilitation robots and proposed an algorithm based on multi-sensor and Kalman filter to detect motion trajectory in real-time. Agarwal et al. [10, 11] applied the tendon-sheath drive to a finger rehabilitation robot. Under the circumstance of ignoring the elastic deformation of the flexible cable, the joint torque was calculated by measuring the deformation of the spring installed at the joint end, and the torque control was realized.

Robotic arms have been widely used in industrial production lines, but the prices are generally high. With the development of humanoid robots and service robots, anthropomorphic light manipulators have become an important part of robotics. The existing service robot manipulator has few degrees of freedom, low flexibility, small load, and virtually use only for demonstration. Service robots with arms are expensive, and there is a lack of special-purpose arms for service robots in the market. With the gradual popularity of service robots, the demand for anthropomorphic manipulators is bound to increase. One of the existing solutions is to use traditional motors and reducers, such as ASIMO [12] and Sophia [13, 14], which are similar to a human arm by its appearance but with a small load. Another solution is to use a permanent magnet synchronous motor and a harmonic reducer, such as ABB-YUMI [15], DLR-Justin [16], Rethink-Baxter, and Saywer [17] and Kinova-Jaco [18], etc. The load is relatively large, but the price is higher than the small one, and the appearance is not very human. Flexible cable transmission has been applied to manipulators, such as WAM [19] and LIMS2 [20]. The existing flexible cable mechanism mainly uses transmission wheels to achieve long-distance transmission—the complex structure results in high manufacturing and maintenance costs.

In order to make the robotic arm more lightweight and anthropomorphic, this paper designs a 7-DOF robotic arm with reference to the human shoulder, elbow, and wrist joints. A scheme of rear-positioning the motor through tendon-sheath transmission is proposed, and the joint and drive are designed separately. Considering the influence of the non-linear transmission characteristics such as the transmission clearance of the reducer and the idle loop of the tendon-sheath transmission, a method of installing an encoder on the joint end and the driving end for dual closed-loop control is proposed. Last, a prototype is built to carry out various joint motion experiments, and a position tracking control experiment is carried out based on the designed PID controller and iterative learning controller. The experimental results verify the feasibility of applying the tendon-sheath drive to the manipulator and provide a new idea for the design of the manipulator.

2   Humanoid Manipulator with Seven Joints

2.1   The Mechanical Arm Configuration Design

The overall scheme of the mechanical arm is shown in Fig. 1. The mechanical system is composed of seven joints and a drive integrated box. The system adopts a bionic design, and the joint layout is based on the configuration of a human arm. Joints one, two, and three can realize movement similar to the shoulder joint; joints five, six, and seven realize the movement similar to the wrist joint; joint four can realize the movement similar to the elbow joint.

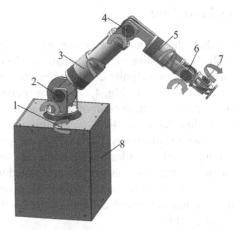

Fig. 1. The overall scheme of the mechanical arm. 1-Jonit one. 2-Jonit two. 3-Jonit three. 4-Joint four. 5-Joint five. 6-Jonit six. 7-Joint seven. 8-Integrated drive box

Joint one is located at the bottom of the robotic arm and adopts a design in which a reducer directly drives the motor. Other joints use tendon-sheath transmission to realize the separation of drive and joint. Both ends of the tendon-sheath are connected to the joint and the drive module. The drive module is installed in the drive integrated box. The tendon-sheath is routed close to the arm outside and left length allowance to adapt the motion.

2.2 The Structure of the Drive Integration Design

The structure of the drive integrated box is shown in Fig. 2. In addition to the drive of joint one, the drive modules of the other six joints are also installed in the drive integrated box. The selection of compact motors and the optimized layout of the motor positions can reduce the integration and compact the box's volume.

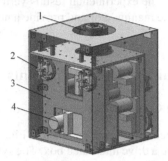

Fig. 2. Structure of the driver integration. 1-Jonit one. 2-Driver wheel. 3-Support frame. 4-Drive motor.

3 The Kinematics Modeling

Gear transmission can reduce the speed and increase the transmission torque, but the transmission distance is short. The tendon-sheath transmission has a longer transmission distance, but the transmission torque is limited. The combination of the two can achieve complementary advantages. As shown in Fig. 4, the motor is connected to the reducer, the driving wheel is installed on the output shaft of the reducer, and the driven wheel is placed in the joint. Two flexible cables are fixed on the driving wheel and then wound clockwise and counterclockwise respectively, pass through the tendon-sheath baffle and enter the sleeve, after passing another tendon-sheath baffle, are wound and fixed on the driven wheel. Among them, the main driven wheel is machined with wheel grooves to facilitate the winding of the flexible cable on the wheel; the driving wheel is designed with a bolt pre-tightening mechanism, which can tighten the flexible cable to reduce the transmission idling effectively (Fig. 3).

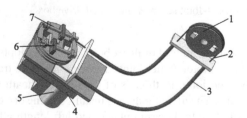

Fig. 3. Diagram of the transmission principle. 1-Driven wheel. 2-Tendon. 3-Sheath. 4-Reducer. 5-Drive motor. 6-Pre-tightening mechanism. 7-Driver wheel.

Define the rotation angle of the motor, the rotation angle of the driving wheel and the rotation angle of the driven wheel after the speed reducer are θ_m, θ_n and θ_j respectively, and define the rotation speed of the motor, the rotation speed of the driving wheel and the rotation speed of the driven wheel after the speed reducer are respectively ω_m, ω_m and ω_j. Due to factors such as clearance and friction in actual transmission, transmission errors will be generated. The following are the transmission models of gear transmission and tendon-sheath transmission.

3.1   Gear Modeling

Gear backlash is inevitable in actual engineering, and backlash will lead to a decrease in the accuracy of the mechanism's position tracking control. When the driven wheel has a significant damping condition, it can be regarded as stationary when the driving wheel passes through the tooth gap until it contacts the driving wheel [21]. When the damping of the driven part is relatively small, it can quickly jump over the tooth gap and contact the driven part under the action of the control signal. For such a transmission process, the hysteresis model can be used to model it mathematically.

$$\theta_n(t) = \begin{cases} \frac{1}{i}[\theta_m(t) - \alpha_s(t)], & \omega_m(t) > 0 \\ \theta_n(t^-), & \omega_m(t) = 0 \\ \frac{1}{i}[\theta_m(t) - \alpha_n(t)], & \omega_m(t) < 0 \end{cases} \tag{1}$$

In the formula, i is the reduction ratio of the gear transmission, α_s and α_n are the gear transmission gaps when rotating in different directions, $\theta_n(t)$ and $\theta_m(t)$ are the output angle of the reducer and the motor rotation angle at time t, respectively, $\theta_n(t^-)$ Represents the output angle of the reducer at the previous moment. Among them, the gear transmission clearance α is affected by many factors such as gear processing, assembly, wear, and lubrication.

3.2   Tendon-Sheath Modeling

When the tendon-sheath transmission works, factors such as the friction between the flexible cable and the casing and the elastic deformation of the flexible cable will lead to the generation of the transmission idling. The dynamic transmission model can accurately describe the double tendon-sheath transmission model, but because the solving process of the differential equations is very time-consuming, in real-time control applications, the static transmission model based on the Coulomb friction model is usually used [22]. The tendon-sheath transmission model has been deduced in detail [23]. The following formula is the double tendon-sheath transmission model.

$$\theta_j(t) = \begin{cases} \frac{r_1}{r_2}\theta_n(t) - \beta_s(t) & \omega_n(t) > 0 \\ \theta_j(t^-) & \omega_n(t) = 0 \\ \frac{r_1}{r_2}\theta_n(t) - \beta_n(t) & \omega_n(t) < 0 \end{cases} \tag{2}$$

In the formula, r_1 and r_2 are the radius of the driving wheel and the driven wheel, β_s and β_n are the transmission idling of the tendon-sheath transmission when rotating in different directions. $\theta_j(t)$ is the rotation angle of the driven wheel at time t, and $\theta_j(t^-)$ represents The rotation angle of the driven wheel at the previous moment. Among them, the transmission air return β is affected by factors such as the pre-tightening force, the diameter of the flexible cable, and the full curvature of the casing.

4   Position Tracking Control

Precise position control is the basis of the application of the manipulator. This paper chooses PID and iterative learning, and these two controllers are used to study the position tracking control of the manipulator.

4.1   Proportional-Integral-Derivative Controllers

The system adopts a double closed-loop control structure. The driving motor first forms a position closed loop through the driving wheel encoder as shown in the dotted box and then realizes the second position closed loop through the driven wheel encoder. θ_c is the input signal, and θ_u is the output signal. Both controllers use the traditional PID control algorithm. The deviation θ_e is formed by the robot arm joint control value received by the position controller, and the actual position value is used as the controller's input. The PID control law is:

$$\theta_u(t) = K_p\left(\theta_e(t) + \frac{1}{K_i}\int_0^t \theta_e(t)dt + \frac{K_d d\theta_e(t)}{dt}\right) \tag{3}$$

K_p is the proportional coefficient in the formula, K_i is the integral time constant, and K_d is the derivative time constant. The three parameters of the position controller PID are determined through empirical trial and error. PID controller has the advantages of simple structure and convenient use. However, parameter tuning takes a long time for complex systems with hysteresis, and it is not easy to debug the ideal control effect.

4.2   Iterative Learning Controller

Send-to-generation learning control has apparent advantages over other control algorithms when it solves the problem of complete tracking of the trajectory of a complex system with strong coupling and nonlinearity in a limited time interval [23]. The trajectory tracking task of the robotic arm system is just such a problem, which is very suitable for introducing iterative learning algorithms with better environmental interference suppression effects. When the information of the robot arm object model is missing, the model-free iterative learning algorithm can be used as the control scheme of the system.

Figure 4 shows the principle diagram of the iterative learning controller. The drive motor forms a position closed loop through the driving wheel encoder. As shown in the dashed box, the position signal output by the driven wheel encoder is saved in the control memory and compared with the expected trajectory to obtain a deviation signal. Suppose the dynamic equation of a mechanical arm joint with repetitive motion is:

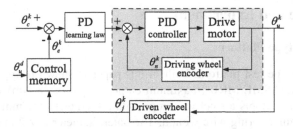

Fig. 4. Iterative learning control.

$$\begin{cases} \dot{\theta}_x(t) = f[t, \theta_x(t)] + B(t)\theta_c(t) \\ \theta_u(t) = C(t)\theta_c(t) \end{cases} \tag{4}$$

In the formula, $\theta_x(t)$, $\theta_c(t)$, and $\theta_u(t)$ represent the system state, input control signal, and output signal, respectively, and f, B, and C represent vectors of appropriate dimensions. The control objective of iterative learning is: within a given time $t \in [0, T]$, according to a certain learning control algorithm through multiple repeated runs, the control input $\theta k\ c(t)$ at the kth run is approached to the ideal control signal $\theta d\ c(t)$ so that the system output $\theta k\ u(t)$ at the k-th run is close to the ideal control output signal $\theta d\ u(t)$.

At the $k - 1$th run, the tracking error of the system is:

$$\theta_e^{k-1}(t) = \theta_u^d(t) - \theta_u^{k-1}(t) \tag{5}$$

The iterative learning law can be expressed as;

$$\theta_u^k(t) = Q[\theta_u^{k-1}(t) + L\theta_e^{k-1}(t)] \tag{6}$$

In the formula, the matrix Q is used as a form of low-pass filtering and is usually set as the identity matrix first to ensure the algorithm's convergence and reduce the interference of high-frequency noise. The matrix L is the gain matrix of the iterative learning algorithm, which is also called the learning matrix or learning rate. The choice of L largely determines the characteristics of the iterative learning law.

As a common choice, the gain matrix in PD has the advantages of simple structure, strong robustness, fast online calculation, and no need for a controlled object model [28]. At the same time, compared with traditional PID control, it does not rely too much on selecting the three coefficients of proportional, integral, and derivative, so it often has a better control effect for repetitive control tasks. The PD-type iterative learning law used in this paper can be expressed as:

At the k-1th run, the tracking error of the system is:

$$\theta_u^k(t) = \theta_u^{k-1}(t) + K_p\theta_e^{k-1}(t) + K_d\dot{\theta}_e^{k-1}(t) \tag{7}$$

In the formula, K_p and K_d are the proportional gain and differential gain of the learning law, respectively.

5   Prototype and Experiment

5.1   The Prototype Platform

The robot prototype test platform built in this paper is shown in Fig. 5. The driving motor adopts the ASME-MRB (maximum output torque of 38 Nm) with its reducer. The flexible cable adopts a steel wire rope with a diameter of 1 mm, and the casing adopts a rectangular spring wire wound. The outer diameter is 2.2 mm, and the inner diameter is 1.2 mm spiral casing. The control system of the robotic arm adopts NI-cRIO-9067 as the lower computer. The control program is firstly written by Labview software on the upper computer and then downloaded to the lower computer running the real-time system through the Can interface for execution. The joint angle feedback signal is measured by the encoder and then input to the NI-9205 module, and the motion control signal is output to the motor driver by the NI-9264 module. The frequency of real-time feedback and data monitoring is set to 1 kHz.

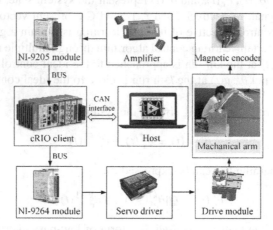

Fig. 5. Control system of the experimental prototype.

5.2   Position Tracking Control Experiment

Taking joint four as the experimental object, inputting the same control signal can test the position tracking performance of different controllers. As shown in Fig. 6 and Fig. 7, (a) is the position tracking curve under the initial iteration that is under open-loop control, (b) is the position tracking curve under the PID controller, and (c) is the position tracking when iterative learning is performed 30 times The curve, (d) is the tracking error under open-loop and two controllers.

When the same step control signal is input to make the joint move between 60° and 120°, the maximum tracking error of the open-loop, PID controller, and iterative learning controller is 1.56°, 1.47°, and 0.31°, respectively. Input the sinusoidal control signals with amplitudes of 60° and 30° for testing, and the maximum tracking errors under the open loop, PID controller, and iterative learning controller is 0.42°, 0.3°, and 0.09°, respectively. From Fig. 8(d) and Fig. 9(d), it can be seen that the iterative learning controller can significantly reduce the tracking error, has a faster convergence speed and higher tracking accuracy, and can improve the control performance of the system.

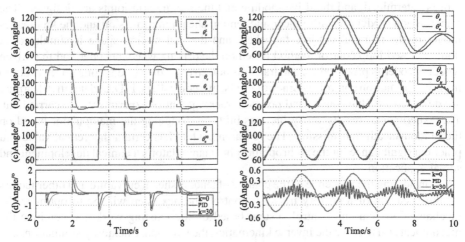

Fig. 6. Position tracking under the step signal.

Fig. 7. Position tracking under the sinusoidal signal.

The error iteration curve of the iterative learning controller under step and sine input is shown in Fig. 8. From the figure, it can be seen that the error decreases significantly as the number of iterations increases, and the error stabilizes after a certain number of iterations. The movement of the robot's joint is repetitive and periodic. The iterative learning control uses the previous experience of the control system to find an ideal input signal to make the controlled object produce the desired movement. Therefore, compared with other control methods, iterative learning control can achieve better control results when applied to a robotic arm.

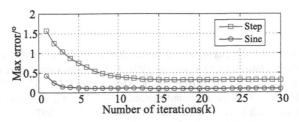

Fig. 8. Curves over 20 iterations.

6 Conclusion

This paper applies the tendon-sheath drive to the manipulator and proposes a 7-DOF anthropomorphic light manipulator with a rear motor. With reference to the human arm's shoulder joints, elbow joints, and wrist joints, the configuration of the robotic arm is determined, and the drive module and the robotic arm joints are designed. The transmission model of gear reducer and tendon-sheath transmission and the kinematics model of the manipulator is established, and the end motion space is simulated. A double closed-loop control method based on the driving wheel encoder and the driven wheel encoder is proposed for the transmission error of the system concern. In order to improve the motion control accuracy of joints, two controllers, PID, and iterative learning are designed simultaneously, and position tracking control experiments are carried out. The experimental results verify the feasibility of designing the manipulator based on the tendon-sheath transmission. The research content has certain theoretical value and practical significance for the anthropomorphic manipulator's technical development and social application.

Considering the influence of the change of tendon-sheath curvature and other factors on the accuracy of trajectory tracking control, the next step will be to optimize the mechanical system and control system based on the existing work and combine the mechanical arm to solve the inverse kinematics, the workspace dexterity simulation, and Multi-joint motion control and other content are studied more in-depth and detailed.

Acknowledgements. This work was supported in part by the R&D projects in key areas of Guangdong Province through Grant 2020B090925002, in part by the Guangdong Basic and Applied Basic Research Foundation under Grant 2021A1515011699, in part by Postdoctoral Science Foundation of China under Grant 2021M703389, in part by the Guangdong Regional Joint Fund- Youth Fund Project of China under Grant 2021A1515110486, in part by the Shenzhen Excellent Science and Innovation Talents Training Doctoral Startup Project under Grant 202107063000284, in part by National Natural Science Foundation of China under Grant 62022087, in part by the Defense Industrial Technology Development Program of China under Grant JCKY2020206B008, in part by the High-level Innovation and Entrepreneurship Talent Introduction Plan of Jiangsu Province under Grant JSSCBS20211456.

References

1. Kaneko, M., Wada, M., Maekawa, H., Tanie, K.: A new consideration on tendon-tension control system of robot hands. In: Proceedings 1991 IEEE International Conference on Robotics and Automation, vol. 2, pp. 1028-1033. IEEE, Sacramento, CA, USA (1991)
2. Kaneko, M., Paetsch, W., Tolle, H.: Input-dependent stability of joint torque control of tendon-driven robot hands. IEEE Trans. Ind. Electron. **39**(2), 96–104 (1992)
3. Palli, G., Melchiorri, C.: Friction compensation techniques for tendon-driven robotic hands. Mechatronics **24**(2), 108–117 (2014)
4. Palli, G., Borghesan, G., Melchiorri, C.: Modeling, identification, and control of tendon-based actuation systems. IEEE Trans. Robot. **28**(2), 277–289 (2012)
5. Phee, S.J., Low, S.C., Sun, Z.L., Ho, K.Y., Huang, W.M., Thant, Z.M.: Robotic system for no-scar gastrointestinal surgery. Int. J. Med. Robot. Comput. Assist. Surg. **4**(1), 15–22 (2008)

6. Phee, S.J., Low, S.C., Dario, P., Menciassi, A.: Tendon sheath analysis for estimation of distal end force and elongation for sensorless distal end. Robotica **28**(7), 1073–1082 (2010)
7. Li, X.G., Cao, L., Tiong, A.M.H., Phan, P.T., Phee, S.J.: Distal-end force prediction of tendon-sheath mechanisms for flexible endoscopic surgical robots using deep learning. Mechanism and Machine Theory **134**, 323–337 (2019)
8. Kong, K., Jeon, D.: Design and control of an exoskeleton for the elderly and patients. IEEE/ASME Trans. Mechatronics. **11**(4), 428–432 (2006)
9. Kong, K., Bae, J., Tomizuka, M.: Torque mode control of a cable-driven actuating system by sensor fusion. J. Dyn. Syst., Meas., Control **135**(3), 031003 (2013)
10. Agarwal, P., Deshpande, A.D.: Series elastic actuators for small-scale robotic applications. J. Mech. Robot. **9**(3), 031016 (2017)
11. Agarwal, P., Fox, J., Yun, Y., O'Malley, M.K., Deshpande, A.D.: An index finger exoskeleton with series elastic actuation for rehabilitation: design, control and performance characterization. The Int. J. Robot. Res. **34**(14), 1747–1772 (2015)
12. Sakagami, Y., Watanabe, R., Aoyama, C., Matsunaga, S., Higaki, N., Fujimura, K.: The intelligent ASIMO: system overview and integration. In: IEEE/RSJ International Conference on Intelligent Robots and Systems, vol. 3, pp. 2478-2483. IEEE, Lausanne, Switzerland (2002)
13. Cao, W., Chen, C., Hu, H., Fang, K., Wu, X.: Effect of hip assistance modes on metabolic cost of walking with a soft exoskeleton. IEEE Trans. Autom. Sci. Eng. **18**(2), 426–436 (2021)
14. Anonymous: ABB introduces YuMi a dual-arm co-robot. Manuf. Eng. 154(6), 22 (2015)
15. Wimböck, T., Nenchev, D., Albu-Schäffer, A., Hirzinger, G.: Experimental study on dynamic reactionless motions with DLR's humanoid robot Justin. In: 2009 IEEE/RSJ International Conference on Intelligent Robots and Systems, pp. 5481-5486. IEEE, St. Louis, USA (2009)
16. Guizzo, E., Ackerman, E.: How rethink robotics built its new baxter robot worker. http://spectrum.ieee.org/robotics/industrial-robots/rethink-roboticsbaxter-robot-factory-worker (18 July 2012) [1 Jan 2015]
17. Maheu, V., Frappier, J., Archambault, P.S., Routhier, F.: Evaluation of the JACO robotic arm: Clinico-economic study for powered wheelchair users with upper-extremity disabilities. IEEE Int. Conf. Rehabil. Robot. **2011**, 5975397 (2011)
18. Salisbury, K., Townsend, W., Ebrman, B., DiPietro, D.: Preliminary design of a whole-arm manipulation system (WAMS). In: Proceedings. 1988 IEEE International Conference on Robotics and Automation, vol. 1, pp. 254–260. IEEE, Philadelphia, USA (1988)
19. Kim, Y.-J.: Anthropomorphic low-inertia high-stiffness manipulator for high-speed safe interaction. IEEE Trans. Rob. **33**(6), 1358–1374 (2017)
20. Theodossiades, S., Natsiavas, S.: Non-linear dynamics of gear-pair systems with with periodic stiffness and backlash. J. Sound Vib. **229**(2), 287–310 (2000)
21. Chen, L., Wang, X.S., Xu, W.L.: Inverse transmission model and compensation control of a single-tendon-sheath actuator. IEEE Trans. Ind. Electron. **61**(3), 1424–1433 (2014)
22. Wu, Q.C., Wang, X.S., Chen, L., Du, F.: Transmission model and compensation control of double-tendon-sheath actuation system. IEEE Trans. Ind. Electron. **62**(3), 1599–1609 (2015)
23. Bristow, D.A., Tharayil, M., Alleyne, A.G.: A survey of iterative learning control. IEEE Control Syst. Mag. **26**(3), 96–114 (2006)

Design and Motion Planning of a Pelvic-Assisted Walking Training Robot

Yuanming Ma[1,2], Ming Xia[1,2](✉), Tao Qin[1,2,3](✉), Jinxing Qiu[1,2], and Bo Li[1,3]

[1] School of Mechanical Engineering, Hubei University of Arts and Science, Xiangyang 441053, China
445908462@qq.com, heu_qt@163.com
[2] Xiangyang Key Laboratory of Rehabilitation Medicine and Rehabilitation Engincering Technology, Hubei University of Arts and Science, Xiangyang 441053, China
[3] Technical Center, Xiangyang Institute of Advanced Manufacturing Engineering Research of Huazhong University of Science and Technology, Xiangyang 441053, China

Abstract. Aiming at the difficulty of pelvic motion control and knee bending during rehabilitation training for patients with limb motor dysfunction, a walking training robot with pelvic motion assistance function was proposed. First, according to the needs of clinical rehabilitation training and the design requirements of rehabilitation robot, the overall structure of a pelvic-assisted walking training robot (PAWTR) with left-right symmetrical arrangement was innovatively designed. The unilateral pelvic-assisted walking unit (PAWU) adopted a single-drive double-exit structure. Secondly, the kinematics model of PAWU was established, and the mechanism parameters were analyzed and determined, which laid the foundation for the robot motion planning. Finally, the robot motion planning methods in the single-leg swing and double-leg swing training modes were proposed, and the influence of different walking cycle durations was studied. The simulation verified that the robot motion planning was feasible and could meet the requirements of walking rehabilitation training.

Keywords: Walking training robot · Pelvic assistance · Kinematics modeling · Motion planning

1 Introduction

Stroke is a frequently-occurring disease among the elderly, which leads to motor dysfunction and even symptoms such as high muscle tension, muscle weakness or hemiplegia [1]. In clinical practice, generally performing exercise training by rehabilitation physicians or through rehabilitation equipment on patients to improve the muscle memory of the nervous system [2].

Rehabilitation robots can complete various training tasks according to the design program requirements, provide patients with long-term, continuous and accurate fatigue-free treatment. And they can also use sensing devices to detect the patient's training status in real time and record rehabilitation training data, which can provide doctors with objective and independent reference for rehabilitation treatment indicators, and can allow doctors to formulate corresponding rehabilitation programs according to different patients [3].

At present, the research on walking training robots mainly focuses on exoskeleton walking training robots and pedal-type walking training robots [4, 5]. The exoskeleton walking training robot uses controlled mechanical legs to track the swing of the patient's legs to complete the walking training. The representative ones are Lokomat [6] developed by Hocoma company in Switzerland, BLEEX [7] designed by the University of California, etc. In order to satisfy the multi-degree-of-freedom motion of the feet, some existing pedal-type walking training robots are driven by multiple motors, simulating normal walking, going up and down stairs, etc. For example, GaitMaster [8] developed by the University of Tsukuba in Japan, G-EO-system [9] of Mediacl Park in Germany, etc. Although the above walking training robot can meet the rehabilitation needs of the elderly and hemiplegic patients to a certain extent, the use of multi-motor control leads to complex systems, high control difficulties, and high prices. Most robots ignore the importance of the pelvis assisting the coordinated movement of the lower limbs in human walking training, and long-term training is prone to form a pathological gait. Gu X [10] and others conducted walking rehabilitation training on 40 stroke patients with hemiplegia and found that pelvic movement plays an important role in coordinating human walking training, and that training based on pelvic control and coordinated lower limb movements can produce substantially better results [11]. At present, most PAWTR use a single cable to support the human body and control the up and down motion of the human gravity. Some devices can control the pelvis's forward and backward motion by using a screw-nut mechanism or a hydraulic cylinder. However, the pelvis up and down, left and right and rotation motion cannot be controlled. Humans, especially hemiplegic patients, have the problem of knee stiffness during walking, and most robots rarely achieve the task of knee-assisted knee flexion. Therefore, combined with the laws of pelvic movement and lower limb movement during human walking, this paper links the pelvis and lower limbs through mechanism innovation, and proposes a unilateral, single-drive, and double-exit PAWTR. Such robot uses a motor to realize the pelvic motion control and assist knee flexion tasks during walking, so as to meet the requirements of walking rehabilitation training.

2 Structural Design of PAWTR

2.1 Overall Structure of PAWTR

Comparing with the advantages and disadvantages of the existing walking training robots in terms of structure, working principle, training method. The PAWTR with new structural design scheme is proposed as shown in Fig. 1(a). It is mainly composed of four parts: auxiliary support unit, PAWU, self-preloading seat and medical treadmill. The auxiliary support unit includes a fixed frame and a lifting adjustment device, which can adjust the height of the PAWU to adapt to the height of the patient and achieve partial weight reduction. The PAWU mainly includes the pelvic motion mechanism, the lower limb walking assistance mechanism, etc., with symmetrical structures on the left and right sides. The unilateral lower limb walking assistance mechanism is driven by unilateral motor to assist the patient's thigh to perform walking training. The self-preloading seat adopts parallelogram connecting rod mechanism to automatically clamp the patient's pelvis position by clamping the cushion blocks at both ends. When the PAWTR is used for walking training, the patient sits on the self-preloading seat, and the patient's pelvis moves with the end point of the long rod, through the fixing of spherical hinge of self preloading seat and end point of long rod of pelvic motion mechanism. The drive motor of the PAWU can control the position of the end point of the long rod on the elliptical trajectory, so as to assist the patient's pelvic movement, and at the same time drive the lower limb walking assist connecting rod (LLWACR) to perform the task of assisting knee flexion.

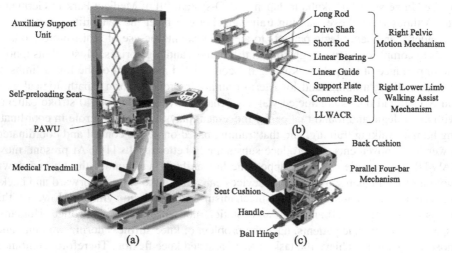

Fig. 1. (a) Overall structure scheme of the PAWTR. (b) Structure diagram of the PAWU. (c) Structure diagram of self-preloading seat.

2.2 Structural Design of PAWU

Relevant studies have shown [12] that the motion laws of the pelvis along the sagittal axis and the vertical axis in the process of walking are in line with the sine-cosine motion relationship, and the projection in the sagittal plane can be approximated as an ellipse. Therefore, the structure design of the PAWU can refer to the structure of the elliptical machine, as shown in Fig. 1(b). The pelvic motion mechanism consists of long rod, drive shaft, short rod, linear bearing, etc. The lower limb walking assist mechanism is mainly composed of linear guide, support plate, connecting rod, and LLWACR, etc. Combining pelvic movement and lower limb movement, the single side independent drive design is more in line with the principle that the lower limbs on both sides of the human body can independently move to achieve different walking states when walking.

2.3   Structural Design of Self-preloading Seat

During the process of walking rehabilitation training, the patients' safety is particularly important. At the same time, improving the patients' comfort during walking training is also conducive to improving the rehabilitation effect of patients. The self-preloading seat structure is shown in Fig. 1(c). Two parallel four-bar mechanisms are mainly used to realize the motion connection between the back cushions on both sides and the seat cushions. The patient's sitting and rising actions can drive the parallel four-bar mechanism, and then adjust the distance between the back cushions on both sides, which can automatically clamp the patient's pelvis position without repeated adjustment after the patient sits down, improving convenience. At the same time, the two ends of the self-preloading seat adopt the form of ball hinge connection. The mechanism is designed with a self-locking device and a handle. The self-locking device mainly keeps the cushions on both sides clamped to the patient when the patient sits down, and does not appear to be in a loose or tight state, causing unnecessary hidden dangers to the patient. The handle is mainly used to release the self-locking state. When the patient stops walking training and needs to leave, the patient only needs to press the handle down with both hands on both sides to get out of the self-preloading seat.

3   Modeling and Analysis of PAWTR

Robot kinematics is mainly used to analyze the position and velocity relationship between the input and output of the mechanism. Taking the unilateral PAWU as the research object, the mathematical relationship between the input drive shaft and the angle change of the output LLWACR is determined by kinematics analysis, which will lay the foundation for the motion planning of walking rehabilitation training. At the same time, the key size parameters of the PAWU are determined by combing with the law of normal human movement.

3.1   Positive Kinematics Modeling of PAWU

The structure of the PAWU is left and right symmetrical, and the right PAWU is selected to simplify as shown in Fig. 2. The fixed coordinate system xOy is set at the hinge between the support plate of the pelvic motion mechanism and the LLWACR. The length of each rod is expressed as $L_i(i = 1, 2, ..., 10)$, the angular velocity of the drive shaft is set to be ω_1, and the clockwise direction is specified as positive. According to the known design relationship, the angular velocities of the long rod EF and the short rod CD are both ω_1, the corresponding rotation angles are θ_1. The angular velocities of the LLWACR OB and the connecting rod AO_1 are ω_2 and ω_3 respectively, and the corresponding rotation angles are θ_2 and θ_3 respectively. The human body is simplified as a connecting rod model, F and H correspond to hip and knee joints, the length of thigh FH is L, and the angle with the negative direction of the y-axis is defined as θ.

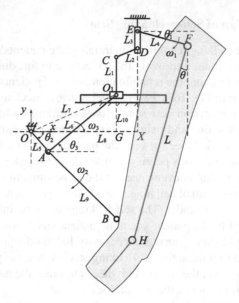

Fig. 2. Human-robot system diagram of PAWU

According to the mathematical relationship shown in Fig. 2, we can get:

$$\begin{bmatrix} \cos\theta_2 & \cos\theta_3 \\ \sin\theta_2 & \sin\theta_3 \end{bmatrix} \begin{bmatrix} L_5 \\ L_6 \end{bmatrix} = \begin{bmatrix} L_8 - L_2\cos\theta_1 \\ L_{10} \end{bmatrix} \tag{1}$$

The solutions to Eq. (1) are:

$$\begin{cases} \theta_2 = \arccos \dfrac{-mk + e\sqrt{(k^2 + e^2 - m^2)}}{e^2 + k^2} \\ x_B = L_9\cos\theta_2 \\ y_B = -L_9\sin\theta_2 \end{cases} \tag{2}$$

where,

$$k = L_8 - L_2\cos\theta_1$$

$$m = \frac{L_6^2 - L_5^2 - L_{10}^2 - (L_8 - L_2\cos\theta_1)^2}{2 \cdot L_5}$$

$$e = L_{10}$$

The velocity relationship can be obtained by taking the derivative of time for Eq. (1):

$$\begin{bmatrix} -L_5\cdot\sin\theta_2 & -L_6\cdot\sin\theta_3 \\ -L_5\cdot\cos\theta_2 & L_6\cdot\cos\theta_3 \end{bmatrix} \begin{bmatrix} \omega_2 \\ \omega_3 \end{bmatrix} = \begin{bmatrix} L_2\cdot\omega_1\cdot\sin\theta_1 \\ 0 \end{bmatrix} \tag{3}$$

The solutions are:

$$
\begin{cases}
\dot{\theta}_2 = \dfrac{2k + \dfrac{em}{\sqrt{(e^2+k^2-m^2)}}}{(e^2+k^2)\cdot t} \\[4mm]
\dot{x}_B = -L_9 \cdot \dot{\theta}_2 \cdot t \\[3mm]
\dot{y}_B = -L_9 \cdot \dot{\theta}_2 \cdot \dfrac{-mk + e\sqrt{(k^2+e^2-m^2)}}{e^2+k^2}
\end{cases}
\tag{4}
$$

where,

$$
t = \sqrt{1 - \frac{\left(2km - e \times \sqrt{(e^2 + k^2 - m^2)}\right)^2}{(e^2 + k^2)^2}}
$$

3.2 Inverse Kinematics Modeling of PAWU

The inverse kinematics analysis of PAWU is to know the motion law of the rotation angle of the known LLWACR, solve the rotation law of the drive shaft of PAWU, and provide input parameters for the robot motion planning. As shown in Fig. 2, that is, given θ_2, after calculation, we get the motion law of θ_1.

From Eq. (1), it can be deduced that the rotation angle of the drive shaft of the PAWU is:

$$
\theta_1 = \cos^{-1}\left(\frac{L_8 - L_2 \cos\theta_2 + \sqrt{(2(L_8 - L_2\cos\theta_1)^2 - (L_6^2 - (L_{10} + L_5\sin\theta_2)^2))}}{L_2}\right)
\tag{5}
$$

Taking the derivation of Eq. (5), the angular velocity of the drive shaft of the PAWU can be obtained as:

$$
\dot{\theta}_1 = \left(\cos^{-1}\left(\frac{L_8 - L_2\cos\theta_2 + \sqrt{(2(L_8 - L_2\cos\theta_1)^2 - (L_6^2 - (L_{10} + L_5\sin\theta_1)^2))}}{L_2}\right)\right)'
\tag{6}
$$

3.3 Size Parameters of PAWU

LLWACR in the process of assisted walking, we mainly consider the three position states between the end of the connecting rod and the thigh, namely, non-contact, just contact and about to separate. The thigh is simplified as connecting rod. The three different positions of the knee joint are simplified as a mass point $H_i (i = 1, 2, 3)$, and the corresponding end points of LLWACR are located at three key positions $B_i (i = 1, 2, 3)$. B_1 and H_1, B_2 and H_2, and B_3 and H_3 as shown in Fig. 3.

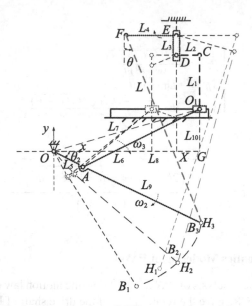

Fig. 3. Structure diagram of different positions of the system

In the process of size calculation, select the position where the end point of LLWACR and the thigh are about to be separated for analysis. According to the analysis of the mechanism and human gait data, when in B_3 state, take $\theta = +16.5°$. The coordinate of H_3 (which is the contact point between LLWACR and the thigh) is $(L_8 - L_4 + L\sin\theta, L_{10} + L_1 + L_3 - L\cos\theta)$, and the coordinate of B_3 (which is the end point of the LLWACR) is $(L_9 \cos\theta_2, L_9 \sin\theta_2)$. Since the LLWACR is still in contact with the thigh, at this state, point B_3 and point H_3 coincide.

In the actual design process, it is necessary to fully consider the space occupied by each part of the PAWTR, and the part size parameters can be determined first: $L_1 = 85$ mm, $L_2 = 25$ mm, $L_3 = 51$ mm, $L_4 = 75$ mm, $L_8 = 180$ mm, $L_{10} = 63$ mm.

After sorting out the above results, set $L = 350$ mm, we get:

$$L_9 = \sqrt{x_{H_3}^2 + y_{H_3}^2} = 245.841 \approx 246\,\text{mm}$$

$$\theta_2 = \arccos\frac{x_{B_3}}{L_9} = \arccos 0.831 = 33.8°$$

Substitute into Eq. (2) to get: $L_6 = 187$ mm.

At the point B_1, the maximum backward swing angle of LLWACR is $\theta = -25°$, and the coordinate of the corresponding point H_1 is $(L_8 - L_4 + L\sin\theta, L_{10} + L_1 + L_3 - L\cos\theta)$. At the same time, no point on the thigh should be in contact with the LLWACR. Since $\theta = -25°$, only the end of the thigh is most likely to contact the LLWACR, that is, the abscissa of point $B_1(L_9 \cos\theta_2, L_9 \sin\theta_2)$ at the initial position is less than the abscissa of H_1, then:

$$x_{B_1} < x_{H_1}$$

According to the known dimensional parameters, the coordinates of H_1 can be determined: $H_1(43.961\,\text{mm}, -254.154\,\text{mm})$.

Substitute the data into Eq. (2) to get:

$$\theta_2 = \arccos 0.115 = 88.4°$$

$$x_{B_1} = 28.29\,\text{mm} < x_{H_1}$$

Therefore, it meets the design requirements.

In summary, the size parameters of PAWU are as follows:

$L_1 = 85\,\text{mm}, L_2 = 25\,\text{mm}, L_3 = 51\,\text{mm}, L_4 = 75\,\text{mm}, L_5 = 50\,\text{mm}, L_6 = 187\,\text{mm},$ $L_8 = 180\,\text{mm}, L_9 = 246\,\text{mm}, L_{10} = 63\,\text{mm}.$

4 Motion Planning of PAWTR

4.1 Motion Planning for Single-Leg Swing Training

During normal walking, the lower limbs on both sides of the human body are separated by half a walking cycle. For some hemiplegic patients, they can't move because of unilateral lower limb dysfunction, so they can only rely on one leg of the healthy lower limb to support the upper body. The single-leg swing training mode can be understood as fixing one leg and swinging the other leg. The PAWTR is driven independently by its bilateral auxiliary walking mechanisms, which can realize unilateral swing walking training. It is only necessary to plan the forward and reverse rotation of the drive motor according to a certain law to realize the swing training of unilateral limbs. By controlling the rotation angle of the drive shaft of the PAWU, the position of the LLWACR in the space can be controlled, and the swing range of the lower limb can be controlled. In order to ensure that the planned curve is smooth and continuous, and that there is no impact on the joints of the lower limbs during training, the cosine function can be used to simulate the rotational speed of the drive shaft of the PAWU, which is more in line with the actual human motion law. The rotation speed law of the drive shaft of the PAWU that can be planned for unilateral swing training is:

$$\begin{cases} \omega_{L1-S} = 0 \\ \omega_{R1-S} = \frac{720n}{T}\cos(\frac{2\pi}{T}t), 0 \le t \le T \end{cases} \tag{7}$$

In Eq. (7), T is the time of a walking cycle. Set the time T, and change the parameter n to set the speed of the drive motor, so as to realize the single-leg reciprocating swing training gait with different swing speeds and amplitudes.

4.2 Motion Planning for Double-Leg Coordination Swing Training

The purpose of walking rehabilitation training is to achieve the coordination motion of the affected limb and the healthy limb. Therefore, when the affected limb undergoes the single-leg swing intensive training, the lower limb is recovered to a certain extent, and it is necessary to increase the coordinated swing training of the two legs to improve the coordination ability in the double-leg walking exercise. During the coordinated swing training of the legs, the amplitude and speed of the swing of the legs can be controlled by planning the angle range and rotation speed of the drive motor. The cosine function can also be used to simulate the coordinated movement of the bilateral lower limbs during normal human walking. The rotational speed law of the drive shaft of the PAWU in the planned double-leg swing training mode is:

$$
\begin{cases}
\omega_{L1-D} = -\frac{720n}{T} \cos(\frac{2\pi}{T}t), 0 \le t \le T \\
\omega_{R1-D} = \frac{720n}{T} \cos(\frac{2\pi}{T}t), 0 \le t \le T
\end{cases}
\tag{8}
$$

In Eq. (8), T is the time of a walking cycle. Set the time T, and change the parameter n to set the speed of the drive motor, so as to control the legs to achieve different swing amplitudes and speeds. Comparing the double-leg coordination swing training and the single-leg swing training mode, it can be considered that the single-leg swing training mode is a special case of the double-leg swing training mode.

4.3 Simulation Analysis

For the single-leg and double-leg swing training modes, the motion situation of the single-leg swing training mode can be obtained by analyzing the coordinated double-leg swing training mode. Therefore, in order to verify the feasibility of motion planning in the swing training mode, the influence of different walking cycles T and parameter n on gait planning was analyzed. Take $T = 6\,s$, $n = 1$; $T = 8\,s$, $n = 1$; $T = 8\,s$, $n = 0.6$ respectively, three different situations were used to analyze the motion law of the driving shaft of the PAWU and the LLWACR. As shown in Fig. 4(a), it is the planned rotational speed (ω_1) curve of the drive shaft of the PAWU. Figure 4(b) and (c) show the change curves of the LLWACR rotation angle (θ_2) and angular velocity (ω_2) during the coordinated swing training of the legs. It can be seen from the figure that after setting the swing training period T, the swing amplitude (LLWACR angle θ_2) and speed (LLWACR angular velocity ω_2) of the LLWACR can be adjusted by changing the parameters n. When the value of n decreases, the swing amplitude and speed of the LLWACR are correspondingly reduced. When the parameter n is the same, changing the period T only changes the swing speed of the LLWACR. The shorter the period T, the faster the LLWACR rotates, and its swing amplitude remains unchanged. Therefore, according to the needs of rehabilitation training, adjusting the parameters according to the above rules in the swing training mode can easily realize the transformation of the swing amplitude and speed.

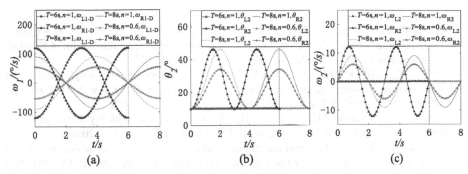

Fig. 4. (a) Drive shaft speed curve of planned PUWA (b) Rotation angle curve of LLWACR during swing training (c) Angular velocity curve of LLWACR during swing training.

5 Conclusion

A rehabilitation robot considering pelvic motion control and assisted walking is designed to help patients achieve anthropomorphic coordinated gait training. The unilateral PAWU adopts a single-drive double-out structure, and one motor can realize the tasks of pelvic motion control and knee flexion during walking. The forward and inverse kinematics model of the PAWU is established by kinematics analysis method, and the parameters of each connecting rod of the mechanism are determined, which lays the foundation for motion planning. According to the normal walking law of the human body and the robot structure, the rotational speed of the bilateral drive shafts is planned, and the simulation results verify the feasibility of the motion planning. The entire robot system controls the movement of the left and right LLWACR respectively through 2 degrees of freedom, and realizes the coordinated movement mode of one leg and two legs, which can meet the requirements of walking rehabilitation training. The future work will study the control system and prototype of PAWTR to further verify the rationality and feasibility of the structural design and motion planning.

Acknowledgments. This work supported by Hubei Provincial Natural Science Foundation under Grant 2018CFB313, Hubei Provincial Higher Institutions Excellent Young and Middle-aged Technological Innovation Team Project under Grant T201919, "Innovation and Entrepreneurship Education" Teaching Research Project of Hubei University of Arts and Sciences under Grant CX2021015.

References

1. Lou, Y.T., et al.: Effects of different acupuncture methods combined with routine rehabilitation on gait of stroke patients. World J. Clin. Cases **8**(24), 14 (2020)
2. Jiang, G.: Early rehabilitation nursing for stroke patients with hemiplegia in neurology department. J. Clin. Nurs. Res. **5**(6), 5 (2021)
3. Tao, R., et al.: Modeling and emulating a physiotherapist's role in robot-assisted rehabilitation. Adv. Intell. Syst. **2**, 190018 (2020)

4. Shi, D., Zhang, W., Zhang, W., Ding, X.: A review on lower limb rehabilitation exoskeleton robots. Chin. J. Mech. Eng. **32**(1), 1–11 (2019). https://doi.org/10.1186/s10033-019-0389-8

5. Lu, J., Guo, S., Zhou, M.: Weight loss system of lower limb rehabilitation robot based on force/position control. Metrol. Meas. Tech. **46**(3), 49–51+55 (2019)

6. Cherni, Y., Hajizadeh, M., Dal Maso, F., Turpin, N.A.: Effects of body weight support and guidance force settings on muscle synergy during Lokomat walking. Eur. J. Appl. Physiol. **121**(11), 2967–2980 (2021). https://doi.org/10.1007/s00421-021-04762-w

7. Zoss, A.B., Kazerooni, H., Chu, A.: Hybrid control of the Berkeley lower extremity exoskeleton (BLEEX). IEEE/ASME Trans. Mechatron. **11**(2), 128–138 (2006)

8. Tanaka, N., et al.: Effects of gait rehabilitation with a footpad-type locomotion interface in patients with chronic post-stroke hemiparesis: a pilot study. Clin. Rehabil. **26**(8), 686 (2012)

9. Andrenelli, E., et al.: Improving gait function and sensorimotor brain plasticity through robotic gait training with G-EO system in Parkinson's disease. Ann. Phys. Rehabil. Med. **61**, e79–e80 (2018)

10. Gu, X., et al.: Effects of pelvic assisted walking rehabilitation robot on motor function and daily living ability in hemiplegic patients after stroke. Chin. J. Rehabil. Med. **35**(5), 556–559 (2020)

11. Low, K.H.: Subject-oriented overground walking pattern generation on a rehabilitation robot based on foot and pelvic trajectories. Procedia IUTAM **2**(1), 109–127 (2011)

12. Qin, T., Zhang, L.: Motion planning of a footpad-type walking rehabilitation robot considering motion of metatarsophalangeal joint. Robot **36**(3), 330–336 (2014)

Simulation of Model Reference Adaptive Compliance Control Based on Environmental Stiffness Parameter Identification

Huaiwu Zou[1,2] ⓘ, Lujiang Liu[1,2] ⓘ, Meng Chen[1,2] ⓘ, Xiaolong Ma[1,2] ⓘ,
Haoran Tao[3] ⓘ, and Bingshan Hu[3(✉)] ⓘ

[1] Shanghai Institute of Aerospace Systems Engineering, Shanghai, China
[2] Shanghai Key Laboratory of Spacecraft Mechanism, Shanghai, China
[3] University of Shanghai for Science and Technology, Shanghai, China
hubingshan@usst.edu.cn

Abstract. This paper describes an impedance control strategy based on model reference adaptation in unstructured environment, aimed at the uncertainty of the environmental stiffness and the unknown of the dynamic change of the environmental position during force tracking. First, the contact force model between the robot and the environment is established, and the environmental stiffness is identified through the BP (back propagation) neural network; then, the simulink-adams co-simulation model of dynamic-based adaptive force control is established. The change of the contact force adjusts the parameters of the impedance model online adaptively, which is used to compensate for the unknown dynamic change of the environment; finally, the simulation results show that the strategy can achieve a good force control effect, and the control method has strong robustness It can increase the reliability of the system, and is suitable for robotic arm force interaction scenarios in a location environment.

Keywords: Force control · Parameter identification · BP artificial neutral network · Model reference adaptive control · Compliance · Impedance control

1 Introduction

There are various forms of manipulator tasks. Using space manipulators to replace and help astronauts complete a large number of space tasks can greatly reduce the danger of space activities and improve work efficiency. In the process of the manipulator's mission operation, capture and release are the basis of the space manipulator's on-orbit operation mission. The captured objects of the robotic arm are usually fixed or floating objects. In the process of capturing, there must be a situation where the robotic arm and the captured object form a force closed loop, which puts forward higher requirements for the control system of the robotic arm. In order to ensure the safety of the manipulator, it is necessary to study the manipulator compliant control technology based on mechanical feedback to realize the compliant operation of the manipulator.

H. Liu et al. (Eds.): ICIRA 2022, LNAI 13455, pp. 705–715, 2022.
https://doi.org/10.1007/978-3-031-13844-7_65

With the development of force control technology, classical force control strategies have been widely used in applications where environmental information is determined or known, such as impedance control [1] or hybrid force/position control. The characteristic of impedance control is that it does not directly control the force between the robot and the contact environment, but adjusts the feedback position error, velocity error or stiffness to control the force according to the relationship between the robot end position (or speed) and the end force. Among them, the work of Whitney, Salisbury, Hogan, Kazerooni, etc. are representative [2, 3]. Railbert and Craig decompose the robot space motion in Cartesian coordinates, and the motion in the free direction is controlled by a position controller. The movement in the direction is controlled by the force controller, and the sum of the control quantities of the two sets of controllers is the joint control quantity [4]. However, for the unstructured environment, the environment during the contact operation may be different materials or unknown. It is very difficult to establish a perfect model for various environments with unknown characteristics, so the difficulty of force control is also greatly increased. At present, force tracking control in unstructured environment is divided into two types: environmental parameter identification and online adjustment of impedance parameters. Reference [5] uses force feedback and adaptive methods to estimate environmental information, and reference [6] uses current and environmental parameters. The environmental stiffness is estimated online from the contact information, and the steady-state error is analyzed. Reference [7] adaptively adjusts the stiffness parameters according to the force error.

The rest of this paper is organized as follows: the Sect. 2 introduces the identification method of environmental stiffness, the Sect. 3 presents the model reference adaptive impedance control method, and the Sect. 4 establishes the simulation model and adapts the model reference based on the environmental parameter identification. The impedance control is studied by simulation, and the Sect. 5 is the conclusion.

2 Environmental Stiffness Identification

Environmental parameter identification is a difficult problem to solve, and many scholars have proposed various solutions to this problem. N. Diolaiti proposed to calculate the dynamic parameters of the second-order system online [8], using a linear regression algorithm, which must provide velocity, position and force measurements from the objects interacting with the manipulator. Reference [9] proposes the Hunt-Crossley model for online parameter estimation. The model contains an exponential n, the dynamics model is nonlinear, and the premise of the algorithm assumes that the object has no acceleration, but this condition is in the actual training process. difficult to satisfy, thus limiting its practical application. L.J. Love will divide the interactive object of the manipulator into several discrete units, combined with the traditional multiple-input-multiple-output (MIMO) least squares identification of the working object impedance from the manipulator control end [10], proposes a power source from the control end of the manipulator. It is an algorithm for learning modeling and parameter identification. The calculation accuracy of this algorithm is closely related to the computing power and storage capacity of the machine. If the segmentation of the interactive object from the manipulator is too coarse, the expression of the dynamic parameters of the object will be inaccurate, and the segmentation rules will be too detailed. Requires a large amount of data storage.

In this paper, a new method of parameter identification based on BP artificial neural network is proposed. The impedance parameter prediction based on neural network is realized based on the mass-spring damping formula, and the linear relationship existing in a certain range allows us to effectively predict the impedance parameter through the measured force, acceleration, velocity and position data.

BP artificial neural network is a kind of artificial neural network. The full name is error back propagation neural network. It is a multi-layer neural network with three or more layers, and each layer is composed of several neurons. Figure 1 shows the structure of BP artificial neural network. Each neuron between the left and right layers is fully connected. Each neuron in the left layer is connected to each neuron in the right layer, and there is no connection between the upper and lower neurons. The BP artificial neural network is trained according to the supervised learning method. When a pair of learning modes is provided to the network, the activation value of its neurons will be propagated from the input layer through the hidden layers to the output layer, each neuron in the output layer outputs the network response corresponding to the input pattern. Then, according to the principle of reducing the error between the desired output and the actual output, each connection weight is corrected layer by layer from the output layer, through each hidden layer, and finally back to the input layer. Since this correction process is carried out layer by layer from output to input, it is called "error back propagation algorithm". As this error back-propagation training continues, the correct rate of the network's response to the input pattern will continue to improve.

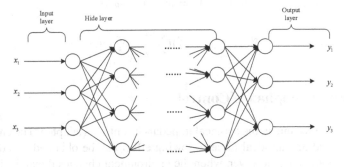

Fig. 1. Structure of BP artificial neural network

The input of the ith neuron of the hidden layer under the action of the sample p

$$net_i^p = \sum_{j=1}^{M} w_{ij} o_j^p - \theta_i = \sum_{j=1}^{M} w_{ij} x_j^p - \theta_i \qquad (i = 1, 2, \ldots, q) \qquad (1)$$

The output of the ith neuron in the hidden layer

$$O_i^p = g\left(net_i^p\right) \qquad (i = 1, 2, \ldots, q) \qquad (2)$$

The total input of the kth neuron in the output layer

$$net_k^p = \sum_{i=1}^{q} w_{ki} o_i^p - \theta_k \qquad (k = 1, 2, \ldots, L) \qquad (3)$$

The actual output of the kth neuron of the output layer

$$O_k^p = g\left(net_k^p\right) \quad (k = 1, 2, \ldots, L) \tag{4}$$

The quadratic error function for the input mode pair for each sample p

$$J_p = \frac{1}{2} \sum_{k=1}^{L} (t_k^p - o_k^p)^2 \tag{5}$$

The basic principle of the BP artificial learning algorithm is the gradient steepest descent method, and its central idea is to adjust the weights to minimize the total error of the network. The learning process adjusts the weighting coefficients in the direction that makes the error function J_p decrease the fastest until a satisfactory weighting coefficient is obtained. Therefore, the weight coefficient should be adjusted in the opposite direction of the gradient change of the J_p function, so that the network gradually converges. The formula for modifying the neuron weight coefficients of the output layer

$$w_{ki}(k + 1) = w_{ki}(k) + \eta \delta_k^p o_i^p \tag{6}$$

$$\delta_k^p = o_k^p (1 - o_k^p)(t_k^p - o_k^p) \tag{7}$$

The formula for modifying the neuron weight coefficient of the hidden layer

$$w_{ij}(k + 1) = w_{ij}(k) + \eta \delta_i^p o_j^p \tag{8}$$

$$\delta_i^p = o_i^p (1 - o_i^p)(\sum_{k=1}^{L} \delta_k^p \cdot w_{ki}) \tag{9}$$

3   Adaptive Compliance Control

For a specific environment, the classical impedance control is adopted. The entire system can be stabilized and an ideal force following effect can be obtained by adjusting the impedance parameters. However, when the environment changes dynamically, the system will become unstable, and the impedance parameters need to be re-adjusted. This section proposes an impedance control method based on model reference adaptation, which adapts to the dynamic changes of the environment on the basis of the impedance identification based on the first section.

Position-based impedance control has long been considered a practical method for compliance force control. Considering the contact between the end effector of the manipulator and the environment, let X_r, X_c and X_m be the reference trajectory, planning trajectory and measurement trajectory, respectively. $X_p = X_c - X_r$ is the position perturbation due to the contact force of the robot and the environment, X_e denotes the position of the environment, P_r and P_m denotes the expected contact force and the actual contact force, E is the force tracking error. In a general robot-environment contact model, the environment can be represented by a linear spring with stiffness K_e. Therefore, the measured contact force can be expressed as $P_m = K_e (X_m - X_e)$.

When the robot moves in free space and has no contact with the environment, $P_m = P_r = 0$. therefore, $X_p = 0$ and $X_c = X_r$. When the robot end effector is in contact with the environment, the force sensor installed on the end effector measures the contact force P_m, which will perturb the reference trajectory X_r. Specifically, the force error $E = P_r - P_m$ of the expected contact force and the actual contact force is fed back to the impedance model and the position perturbation X_p is generated. Generally, the impedance model adopts a linear second-order system $K(s) = [Ms^2 + Bs^2 + K]^{-1}$, so the relationship between the contact force error and the position perturbation is a mass-spring-damping system, as follows

$$M \frac{d^2}{dt^2} X_p(t) + B \frac{d}{dt} X_p(t) + K X_p(t) = E(t) \tag{10}$$

where M, B and K is the mass coefficient, damping coefficient and stiffness coefficient. The perturbation X_p is used to correct the reference trajectory and X_r generate the planned trajectory $X_c = X_r + X_p$. The planned trajectory is actually the trajectory that the robot control system needs to track accurately. By sensing the contact force in real time and correcting the reference trajectory, the robot end-effector can be compliant with the contact environment and characterize the set impedance dynamics. Due to the high precision of robot position control, it is generally believed that the robot controller can accurately track the robot's planned trajectory, $X_m = X_c$.

For the convenience of analysis, the Cartesian coordinate single axis is selected for analysis without loss of generality, and lowercase letters are used to replace the original uppercase letters to represent the single axis situation. Combined with the above analysis, it can be seen that the force tracking error can be expressed as

$$e = p_r - p_m = p_r - k_e(x_m - x_e) = p_r + k_e x_e - k_e[x_r + k(s)e] \tag{11}$$

In the case of $k(s) = \frac{1}{ms^2 + bs + k}$, (11) is rewritten as

$$\left[ms^2 + bs + (k + k_e) \right] e = \left[ms^2 + bs + k \right] \left[p_r + k_e(x_e - x_r) \right] \tag{12}$$

In the case of (12) Steady state error of force tracking is

$$e_{ss} = \frac{k}{k + k_e} \left[p_r + k_e(x_e - x_r) \right] = k_{eq} \left[\frac{p_r}{k_e} + (x_e - x_r) \right] \tag{13}$$

where $k_{eq} = \left(\frac{1}{k} + \frac{1}{k_e} \right)^{-1} = \frac{k k_e}{k + k_e}$ is the equivalent stiffness of the robot in contact with the environment, and the steady-state contact force $p_m = k_e(x_m - x_e)$ acting on the environment can be described as

$$p_m = p_r - e_{ss} = k_{eq} \left[\frac{p_r}{k} + (x_r - x_e) \right]. \tag{14}$$

It can be seen that the contact force is a function of the reference trajectory x_r and the desired contact force p_r. From (14) it can be concluded that if the reference trajectory is set as follows

$$x_r = x_e + \frac{p_r}{k_e} \tag{15}$$

Then, the force steady state error $e_{ss} = 0$. If the environmental position x_e and stiffness k_e can be precisely known, the reference trajectory can be generated by (15) so that the steady-state force error is zero. Unfortunately, the position and stiffness of the environment cannot be precisely known, so it is impossible for the robot to exert the exact desired force on the environment.

Assume that the estimated errors of the environmental position and stiffness are Δx_e and Δk_e where $x_{act} = x_e + \Delta x_e, k_{act} = k_e + \Delta k_e$. Then the reference trajectory generated by (15) will yield the steady state force error as

$$e_{ss} = \frac{k}{k + k_e + \Delta k_e} \left[k_e \Delta x_e - \frac{\Delta k_e}{k_e} p_r + (\Delta x_e)(\Delta k_e) \right] \tag{16}$$

Since the environmental stiffness is generally relatively large, a small value Δx_e will produce a large force steady state error. To this end, we consider the use of direct adaptive control to generate a reference trajectory adaptively online in real time to eliminate the force error caused by the uncertainty of the system parameters. The robot-environment interaction model can be considered as a second-order system, and x_r is a function of error, which is defined as follows:

$$x_r(t) = f(t) + k_p(t)e(t) + k_d(t)\dot{e}(t) \tag{17}$$

where k_p and k_d are the adaptive proportional and differential gains, and $f(t)$ are the auxiliary signals. Since p_r, k_e and x_e are constants,

$$m\ddot{e} + b\dot{e} + (k + k_e)e = k(p_r + k_e x_e) - mk_e\ddot{x}_r - bk_e\dot{x}_r - kk_e x_r. \tag{18}$$

Considering the previously defined error dynamics, $\dot{x}_r$ and $\ddot{x}_r$ will appear in (18), which are not expected to appear in subsequent controller design, the error dynamics are modified as

$$m\ddot{x}_c + b\dot{x}_c + k(x_c - x_r) = e \tag{19}$$

where x_r appears in the spring term, and at the same time, Eq. (18) is rewritten as:

$$m\ddot{e} + b\dot{e} + (k + k_e)e = k(p_r + k_e x_e) - kk_e x_r \tag{20}$$

Substituting the control rate Eq. (17) into the error dynamics Eq. (20), we obtain:

$$\ddot{e} + \left[\frac{b + kk_e k_d(t)}{m} \right]\dot{e} + \left[\frac{k + k_e + kk_e k_d(t)}{m} \right]e = \frac{k(p_r + k_e x_e - k_e f(t))}{m} \tag{21}$$

Under the model reference adaptive framework, (21) is a standard adjustable system, and the expected force tracking error dynamics are set as follows:

$$\ddot{e}_m + 2\varsigma\omega\dot{e}_m + \omega^2 e_m = 0 \tag{22}$$

where ς and ω are the damping ratio and the undamped natural frequency of the system, respectively. (22) is the reference model under the adaptive framework. The adaptation rates of $f(t)$, k_p and k_d ensure that the error dynamics (21) are close to the reference model (22), adaptation rates are as follows

$$\begin{cases} f(t) = f(0) + \alpha_1 \int_0^t q(t)dt + \alpha_2 q(t) \\ k_p(t) = k_p(0) + \beta_1 \int_0^t q(t)e(t)dt + \beta_2 q(t)e(t) \\ k_d(t) = k_d(0) + \gamma_1 \int_0^t q(t)\dot{e}(t)dt + \gamma_2 q(t)\dot{e}(t) \\ \quad q(t) = \omega_p e(t) + \omega_d \dot{e}(t) \end{cases} \tag{23}$$

where ω_p and ω_d are the positive position and velocity gain factors respectively; $(\alpha_1, \beta_1, \gamma_1)$ is the positive integral adaptive gain, $(\alpha_2, \beta_2, \gamma_2)$ is the proportional adaptive gain greater than or equal to 0; $[f(0), k_p(0), k_d(0)]$ is the positive initial value. The above Eqs. (17) and (23) provide a convenient method for online adaptive acquisition of the reference trajectory. Note that Eq. (17) can be written as:

$$x_r(t) = x_r(0) + k_p^*(t)e(t) + k_i^*(t) \int_0^t e(t)dt + k_d^*(t)\dot{e}(t) \tag{24}$$

where $k_p^*(t) = \alpha_1\omega_d + \alpha_2\omega_p + k_p(t)$, $k_i^*(t) = \alpha_1\omega_p$ and $k_d^*(t) = \alpha_2\omega_d + k_p(t)$ are the proportional gain, integral gain and the differential gain, $x_r(0) = f(0)$. It can be seen that the reference trajectory is generated by an adaptive PID controller driven by the force error signal. Its control block diagram is shown in Fig. 2.

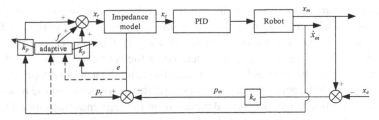

Fig. 2. Model reference adaptive impedance control

4   Simulation Verification

4.1   Simulation Model Construction

The Adams model of the three-degree-of-freedom manipulator is established as shown in Fig. 3, and the end of the manipulator is controlled to descend along the hole wall to realize the operation of the jack. The stiffness of the hole is the change value, which is 10000 N/m, 11000 N/m, and 12000 N/m respectively from top to bottom.

Fig. 3. Adams dynamic model

Figure 4 is a model built by Simulink-Adams co-simulation, which mainly includes five parts, namely robot trajectory planning, Adams dynamics model, robot dynamics control, neural network interaction impedance parameter identification and adaptive force controller. In the same way, the robot trajectory planning and Adams dynamic model are the same as Fig. 4. The BP artificial neural network in the first section is selected for the neural network interaction impedance parameter identification. The network parameters can be adjusted online, and the adaptive force control adopts the model parameter adaptation in the second section. Control Method. In the simulation, firstly, the robot runs to contact with the environment through trajectory planning. At this time, an interactive force will be generated. The 6-dimensional interactive force is measured by the force sensor set at the end of the robot. In this section, only the lower X along the coordinate system of the force sensor is used. The interaction force on the axis and the Y axis. For the convenience of analysis, the robot trajectory generated by the robot trajectory planning is also defined as the reference trajectory, the actual motion trajectory of the robot is the actual trajectory, and the neural network input is the difference between the actual trajectory and the reference trajectory of the robot, that is, due to the interaction force, the robot deviates from the reference trajectory. Offset, the neural network output is the predicted value of the actual trajectory of the robot at the next moment, and its feedforward component is input into the robot trajectory planning model, and the adaptive force controller adjusts the controller parameters online in real time. The goal is to make the robot offset as 0, when the robot offset is 0, the interaction force between the robot and the environment is naturally 0, and the interaction force is guaranteed. The input is the interaction force, and the output is fed back to the robot trajectory planning model. After the robot trajectory planning is completed, the joint motion is output to the robot dynamics model, the joint torque of the robot is calculated, and the Adams dynamics model is driven to move to realize the jack operation.

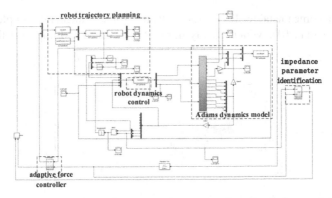

Fig. 4. Dynamics-based adaptive force control co-simulation model

4.2 Simulation Results

The interaction force along the X-axis direction measured by the force sensor during the jack operation is shown in Fig. 5. It can be seen that the maximum value of the X-direction interaction force is less than 0.15 N, which is much smaller than the aforementioned impedance control and kinematics-based adaptive control. The interaction force along the Y-axis direction measured by the force sensor during the jack operation is shown in Fig. 6. It can be seen that the maximum value of the X-direction interaction force is less than 5 N, which is also much smaller than the aforementioned impedance control and kinematics-based adaptive control. In addition to the fact that the neural network can accurately identify the interaction impedance and the adaptive control can achieve the optimal control parameters, there is another reason, the robot dynamics control can make the robot have a certain flexibility by controlling the joint torque, and encounter environmental interaction. After the force is applied, the robot joints can actively adapt to environmental changes, and the robot joint torque is shown in Fig. 7. It is noted that the kinematic-based adaptive control jack operation needs to be carried out slowly. If the insertion speed is too fast, the interaction force will increase sharply, and even the

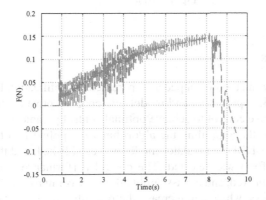

Fig. 5. X-direction interaction force

system will become unstable. The learned adaptive force control, the completion time of the jack is less than 10 s, which greatly improves the speed and improves the assembly efficiency.

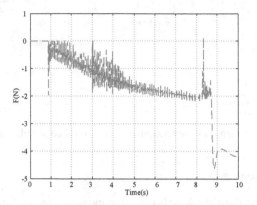

Fig. 6. Y-direction interaction force

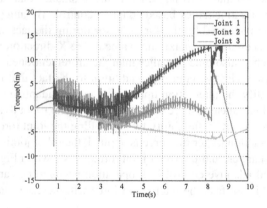

Fig. 7. Robot joint torque

5   Conclusions

In this study, a new method of impedance parameter identification based on BP artificial neural network is proposed, and model reference adaptive control is added to the traditional impedance control to achieve optimal control parameters. In order to verify the performance of the algorithm, the algorithm was applied to a typical force interaction scenario, a 3-DOF manipulator model was established, and the simulink-adams co-simulation platform was selected. The control performance is more superior, the speed is greatly improved, and the assembly efficiency is improved. The control method has strong robustness, which can increase the reliability of the system, and is suitable for robotic arm force interaction scenarios in unknown environments.

Acknowledgments. This research was supported by the National Natural Science Foundation of China with Grant No. U21B6002 and 2021–2022 Independent research and development project of structure and mechanism Laboratory, China Aerospace Science and Technology Corporation.

References

1. Hogan, N.: Impedance control: an approach to manipulation: Part I, II, III. J. Dyn. Syst. Meas. Control **107**, 1–24 (1985)
2. Zhang, M., Sun, C., Liu, Y., Wu, X.: A robotic system to deliver multiple physically bimanual tasks via varying force fields. IEEE Trans. Neural Syst. Rehabil. (2022). https://doi.org/10.1109/TNSRE.2022.3158339
3. Zhong, W., Fu, X., Zhang, M.: A muscle synergy-driven ANFIS approach to predict continuous knee joint movement. IEEE Trans. Fuzzy Syst. (2022). https://doi.org/10.1109/TFUZZ.2022.3158727
4. Yoshikawa, T., Sugie, T., Tanaka, M.: Dynamic hybrid position/Force control of robot manipulators–controller design and experiment. In: IEEE International Conference on Robotics & Automation, Raleigh. IEEE Press (1987). https://doi.org/10.1109/ROBOT.1987.1087787
5. Zhang, X., Khamesee, M.B.: Adaptive force tracking control of a magnetically navigated microrobot in uncertain environments. IEEE/ASME Trans. Mechatron. **22**(4), 1644–1651 (2017). https://doi.org/10.1109/TMECH.2017.2705523
6. Komati, B., Clevy, C., Lutz, P.: Force tracking impedance control with unknown environment at the microscale. In: 2014 IEEE International Conference on Robotics and Automation, Hong Kong, pp. 5203–5208. IEEE Press (2014). https://doi.org/10.1109/ICRA.2014.6907623
7. Pei, Y., Obinata, G., Kim, Y.W., Lee, J.: Impedance control with variable viscosity for motion and force tracking system. In: 2015 International Symposium on Micro-NanoMechatronics and Human Science, Nagoya, pp. 1–5. IEEE Press (2015). https://doi.org/10.1109/MHS.2015.7438279
8. Erickson, D., Weber, M.: Contact stiffness and damping estimation for robotic system. Int. J. Robot. Res. **22**(1), 41–45 (2003). https://doi.org/10.1177/0278364903022001004
9. Ljung, L., Sodertstrom, T.: Theory and Practice of Recursive Identification. MIT Press, Cambridge (1983)
10. Love, L.J., Book, W.J.: Force reflecting teleoperation with adaptive impedance control. IEEE Trans. Syst. Man Cybern. B **34**(1), 159–165 (2004). https://doi.org/10.1109/TSMCB.2003.811756

Vision-Based Fall Detection and Alarm System for Older Adults in the Family Environment

Fei Liu[1,2(✉)], Fengxu Zhou[1,2], Fei Zhang[1,2], and Wujing Cao[3]

[1] School of Intelligent Manufacturing and Control Engineering, Shanghai Polytechnic University, Shanghai 201209, China
liufei@sspu.edu.cn
[2] Smart Manufacturing Factory Laboratory, Shanghai Polytechnic University, Shanghai 201209, China
[3] Guangdong Provincial Key Lab of Robotics and Intelligent System, Shenzhen Institute of Advanced Technology, Chinese Academy of Sciences, Shenzhen 510663, China

Abstract. This study proposes an innovative fall detection and alarm system for the elderly in the family environment based on deep learning. The overall cost of hardware development is a camera and an edge device like a Raspberry PI or an old laptop that can detect and alert users to falls without touching the user's body. The development idea of the system is as follows: 1. Collect the pictures of falling and normal states under different conditions; 2. The improved lightweight SSD-Mobilenet object detection model is used to train the data set and select the optimal weight; 3. Optimal results are deployed on a Raspberry PI 4B device using a lightweight inference engine Paddle Lite. The mean Average Precision of the best model is 92.7%, and the detection speed can reach 14FPS (Frames Per Second) on the development board. When the camera detects that someone has fallen for 10 s, the compiled script sends an alert signal to the default guardian's email via the Mutt email program on Linux. The experimental results show that the fall detection system achieves satisfactory detection accuracy and comfort.

Keywords: Computer vision · Human fall detection · Object detection · Edge devices

1 Introduction

Nowadays, more and more people pay attention to home care. An essential part of daily care tasks is to detect falls in the elderly. The risk of falls is one of the most common problems faced by the elderly [1].

Fall is a significant cause of death in the elderly. It is especially dangerous for people who live alone, as it can take quite a long time before they receive help. Therefore, an effective fall detection system is essential for an elderly person, and in some cases can even save his life [2]. When an elderly person falls, the fall detection system detects abnormal behavior and sends an alert signal to some caregivers or the elderly person's family through modern communication.

H. Liu et al. (Eds.): ICIRA 2022, LNAI 13455, pp. 716–724, 2022.
https://doi.org/10.1007/978-3-031-13844-7_66

At present, researchers have proposed different methods to detect falls, which are mainly divided into two categories: non-visual detection method and visual detection method.

Non-visual detection method: Wearable sensor technology is the most commonly used type of commercial device for fall alarm products on the market, mainly in the form of pendants, belts, bracelets or watches [3, 4].

Visual detection method: Most commercial fall detection systems on the market are based on portable devices. Commercial devices based on computer vision are not common, but they look promising based on current vision-related technologies and literature.

In recent years, with the rapid development of pattern recognition technology, many researchers have applied this method to fall detection tasks [5]. Lu et al. developed a fall detection method based on 3D convolutional neural network, which only uses video motion data to train automatic feature extractor, thus avoiding the requirement of deep learning for large fall data sets [6]. Adrián Núñez-Marcos et al. proposed a vision-based solution that uses convolutional neural networks to determine whether a frame sequence contains a falling person. In order to model the video motion and make the system scene independent, they used optical flow images as the input of the network [7]. RicardoEspinosa et al. proposed a multi-camera fall detection system based on 2D convolutional neural network reasoning method. This method analyzes images in a fixed time window and uses optical flow method to extract features to obtain information about the relative motion between two continuous images [8].

Commercial devices for non-visual fall detection have been developed, but they largely require the elderly to wear sensor devices. Some older people, especially those with dementia, often forget to wear the device. Elderly people with dementia need intensive care to maintain independent living conditions.

In this study, we propose a visual fall detection and alarm system based on deep learning, which is mainly composed of an embedded computer and a camera. Firstly, the improved lightweight network model was used to extract the characteristics of subjects in the training set under normal and falling conditions, then the optimal model was deployed on the hardware platform of the Linux system (Raspberry PI, Nvidia Jetson series, notebook, etc.).

When the system detects that someone has fallen for 10 s or more, it sends an alert signal to the caregiver's mailbox via mutt on Linux using a preset script command. The device can be mounted on the wall or ceiling to monitor a room without human intervention. In addition, people monitored at home do not need to wear devices, and when detection occurs, an alarm email is sent to the preset caregiver. This method has the advantages of no impact on user comfort, low development cost and ideal detection rate.

2 Proposed Method

In this study, the object detection method was used to detect the occurrence of falls in the home environment. In order to make the detection model achieve the ideal detection effect on the low-cost hardware platform, an improved lightweight SSD (Single Shot MultiBox Detector) [9] algorithm was adopted to perform this task.

2.1 Overall Structure of Fall Detection and Alarm System

Figure 1 is the overall flow diagram of the fall detection and alarm system we developed.

First, deploy the optimal model to the terminal equipment (raspberry pie, NVIDIA Jetson series, computer, etc.) and install the equipment in a fixed position.

The system detects whether there is a fall event in the room in real time through the camera. The results of the object detection model have two categories (person and fall). When the detection is normal, there is no feedback signal. When an abnormal state is detected and lasts for more than 10 s, the system will send an alarm signal to the preset caregiver mailbox through mutt to remind them to deal with the dangerous event as soon as possible.

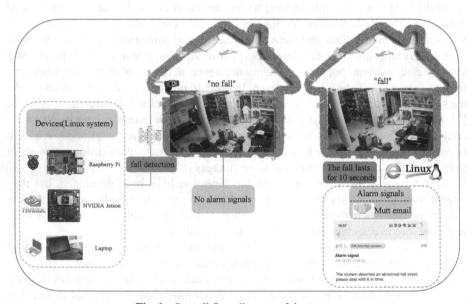

Fig. 1. Overall flow diagram of the system

2.2 Data Set

We used Python script to obtain 864 pictures of normal walking and 973 pictures of falling state from Baidu website. We also extracted 677 images from an open source fall data set. To enhance the robustness and generalization ability of the model, data enhancement methods were used to expand the data set. Specifically, not only common approaches such as rotation, cropping, and changing brightness and contrast but also generating new samples through the MixUp [10] algorithm to fuse positive and negative samples (Fig. 2).

Fig. 2. Data augmentation

2.3 Object Detection Algorithm

Algorithmic Network Structure. The object detection algorithm can judge whether there is a specified category in the detected image. Object detection algorithms can be divided into two main categories: one-step method and two-step method. The two-step method needs to be completed in two steps: regional proposal and detection. Its main advantage is high detection accuracy, such as R-CNN series. The one-step detection algorithm does not need to find candidate regions alone. Its main advantage is fast precision detection, such as SSD and YOLO series.

SSD is classified as a one-stage object detection method, which uses multiple frames to predict the object. Compared with the Faster R-CNN [11] algorithm, SSD can complete detection within one step, so the detection speed is faster. Candidate frames are obtained through convolutional neural network first, and then classification and regression are performed. Compared with YOLO algorithm [12], SSD algorithm overcomes the shortcomings of small object detection difficulty and inaccurate positioning.

The original SSD used VGG16 [13] backbone network as the basic model. VGG16 consists of 13 convolutional layers, 5 maximum pooling layers and 3 fully connected layers. The ReLU activation function is used after the hidden layer in the network.

The SSD algorithm makes some modifications to VGG16 as its backbone network. The main improvements include: removing fully connected layer 8, changing fully connected layer 6 and 7 to convolution layer, and performing secondary sampling for parameters of fully connected layer 6 and 7. The size of VGG pooling layer 5 was changed to 3×3, and the step size was changed to 1. To prevent overfitting, the dropout layer was removed. The modified VGG16 has excellent detection speed and accuracy. However, in low-configuration hardware platforms such as Raspberry PI, it still has a large amount of computation, and the real-time detection of the camera is very slow.

In order to reduce the computational burden of the model and improve the detection speed while maintaining the accuracy as much as possible, Mobilenetv1 model was used in this study instead of VGG16 to extract target features.

In 2017, Google Research released Mobilenetv1 [14] lightweight deep neural network (Fig. 3). Its main feature is that it uses depth-wise separable convolutional structure to replace the traditional convolutional mode. It is a convolutional neural network with less computation and small volume, which is very suitable for deployment on platforms with limited computing power such as embedded or mobile terminals.

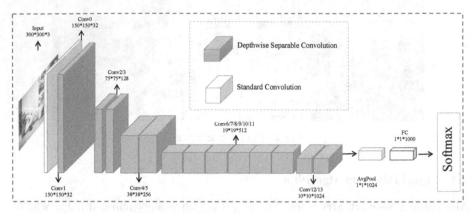

Fig. 3. Mobilenetv1 network architecture

In this study, some key modifications were made to the Mobilenetv1 network as the backbone network. Figure 4 shows the improved SSD-Mobilenetv1 network structure for fall detection. As can be seen from the basic network module of the algorithm, the input image in the new structure is uniformly set as 300 × 300, and the configuration from convolution 0 to convolution 13 is completely consistent with the Mobilenetv1 model, except that the global average pooling, fully connected layer and softmax layer of the last part of Mobilenetv1 are removed.

The SSD model used six different feature maps to obtain the features to be detected, with sizes of 19 × 19 × 512, 10 × 10 × 1024, 5 × 5 × 512, 3 × 3 × 256, 2 × 2 × 256, and 1 × 1 × 128, respectively. SSD-mobileNetV1 also uses six different feature maps, but the resolution of feature maps is only half that of SSD: 38 × 38 × 512, 19 × 19 ×

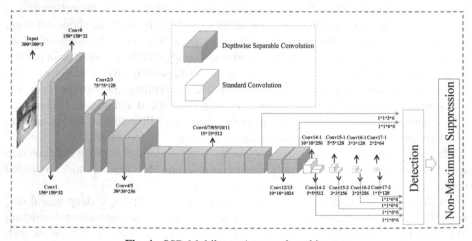

Fig. 4. SSD-Mobilenetv1 network architecture

1024, 10 × 10 × 512, 5 × 5 × 256, 3 × 3 × 256, and 1 × 1 × 128. In addition, in the path from feature graph to detection, the size of the convolution kernel used by SSD is 3 × 3, and the default number of boxes is 4, 6, 6, 6, 4, and 4 respectively. The size of the convolution kernel used by SSD-Mobilenetv1 is 1 × 1, and the default number of boxes is 3, 6, 6, 6, 6, and 6 respectively.

2.4 Loss Function of the Model

Model training is the process of reducing the error between predicted value and real value. The total target loss function of the improved SSD-Mobilenet algorithm used in this study is the weighted sum of position and classification loss, as shown below:

$$L(x, c, l, g) = \frac{1}{N}(L_{\text{conf}}(x, c) + \alpha L_{\text{loc}}(x, l, g)) \tag{1}$$

$$L_{\text{conf}}(x, c) = -\sum_{i \in Pos}^{N} x_{ij}^{p} \lg \hat{c}_{i}^{p} - \sum_{i \in neg} \lg \hat{c}_{i}^{0} \tag{2}$$

$$\hat{c}_{i}^{p} = \frac{\exp c_{i}^{p}}{\sum_{p} \exp c_{i}^{p}} \tag{3}$$

N is the number of matching boxes, l and g are the coordinates of predicted and real borders respectively, c represents the confidence of the softmax function on the target category, x is the matching mark between the predicted frame and the real frame, S_{L1} is the smooth L1 loss between forecast and true position, α is the weight coefficient, L_{loc} is the position loss, and L_{conf} is the classification loss, p_{os} and n_{eg} are the set of positive and negative samples respectively, b_{ox} represents the central coordinate, width and height of the prediction box.

3 Experiment

3.1 Model Training

The experimental training environment is shown in Table 1. Table 2 shows the initialization parameters of the improved SSD-Mobilenet network.

Table 1. Training environment.

Name	Model
CPU	Intel(R) Core i9-9900k (32 GB)
GPU	Nvidia Tesla V100 (16 GB)
Operating system	Ubuntu 16.04
Development language	Python 3.6
Deep learning framework	PaddlePaddle

Table 2. Initialization parameters of network.

Input size	Batch size	Learning rate	Num_workers	Iteration steps
300 × 300	32	0.001	8	30,000

3.2   Model Deployment and Test

We deployed the best model to the Raspberry Pi-4B. In order to ensure that the model can obtain excellent detection speed and accuracy, we used Paddle-Lite to compress the model to achieve the purpose of acceleration. The mean Average Precision of the best model is 92.7%. The accelerated model can reach the detection speed of 14FPS on this development board.

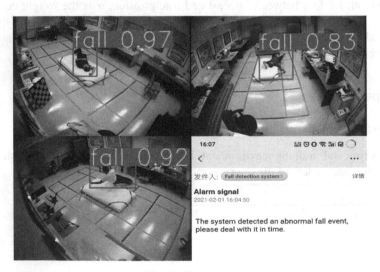

Fig. 5. Test results

In the alarm system, when the camera detects that the target is in a falling state and lasts for more than 10 s, Mutt tool will send an alarm message to the preset caregiver mailbox. Mutt is a text-based email client based on Linux system.

Figure 5 is the results of the test and alarm, which show that this method has good detection accuracy. This fall detection and alarm system can reduce the serious consequences of accidental falls to a certain extent.

4 Conclusion

The experimental results show that the method used in this paper has the advantages of comfortable use, ideal accuracy and low price. However, during the test, we found that there are occasional false detection situations, such as sometimes squatting will be judged as falling. In the next work, we will further expand the data set to classify various situations, and continue to optimize the network structure to improve the detection accuracy of the model. We will also try to apply the behavior detection model to fall detection task.

Acknowledgment. Research supported by follows: 1. Research Foundation of Shanghai Polytechnic University under grant EGD22QD01; 2. Guangdong Basic and Applied Basic Research Foundation under grant 2021A1515011699.

References

1. Ren, L., Peng, Y.: Research of fall detection and fall prevention technologies: a systematic review. IEEE Access **7**, 77702–77722 (2019)
2. Xu, T., Zhou, Y., Zhu, J.: New advances and challenges of fall detection systems: a survey. Appl. Sci. **8**(3), 418 (2018)
3. Santos, G.L., Endo, P.T., Monteiro, K.H.C., et al.: Accelerometer-based human fall detection using convolutional neural networks. Sensors **19**(7), 1644 (2019)
4. Mauldin, T.R., Canby, M.E., Metsis, V., et al.: SmartFall: a smartwatch-based fall detection system using deep learning. Sensors **18**(10), 3363 (2018)
5. De Miguel, K., Brunete, A., Hernando, M., et al.: Home camera-based fall detection system for the elderly. Sensors **17**(12), 2864 (2017)
6. Lu, N., Wu, Y., Feng, L., et al.: Deep learning for fall detection: three-dimensional CNN combined with LSTM on video kinematic data. IEEE J. Biomed. Health Inform. **23**(1), 314–323 (2018)
7. Núñez-Marcos, A., Azkune, G., Arganda-Carreras, I.: Vision-based fall detection with convolutional neural networks. Wirel. Commun. Mob. Comput. **2017**, 1–16 (2017)
8. Espinosa, R., Ponce, H., Gutiérrez, S., et al.: A vision-based approach for fall detection using multiple cameras and convolutional neural networks: a case study using the UP-Fall detection dataset. Comput. Biol. Med. **115**, 103520 (2019)
9. Liu, W., et al.: SSD: single shot multibox detector. In: Leibe, B., Matas, J., Sebe, N., Welling, M. (eds.) ECCV 2016. LNCS, vol. 9905, pp. 21–37. Springer, Cham (2016). https://doi.org/10.1007/978-3-319-46448-0_2
10. Zhang, H., Cisse, M., Dauphin, Y.N., Lopezpaz, D.: mixup: beyond empirical risk minimization. arXiv: Learning (2017)

11. Ren, S., He, K., Girshick, R., et al.: Faster R-CNN: towards real-time object detection with region proposal networks. IEEE Trans. Pattern Anal. Mach. Intell. **39**(6), 1137–1149 (2016)
12. Redmon, J., Farhadi, A.: YOLOv3: an incremental improvement. arXiv preprint arXiv:1804. 02767 (2018)
13. Simonyan, K., Zisserman, A.: Very deep convolutional networks for large-scale image recognition. arXiv preprint arXiv:1409.1556 (2014)
14. Howard, A.G., Zhu, M., Chen, B., et al.: MobileNets: efficient convolutional neural networks for mobile vision applications. arXiv preprint arXiv:1704.04861 (2017)

Research on the Application of Visual Technology in Sorting Packaging Boxes

Fei Liu[1,2(✉)], Wujing Cao[3], and Qingmei Li[1,2]

[1] School of Intelligent Manufacturing and Control Engineering, Shanghai Polytechnic University, Shanghai 201209, China
liufei@sspu.edu.cn
[2] Smart Manufacturing Factory Laboratory, Shanghai Polytechnic University, Shanghai 201209, China
[3] Guangdong Provincial Key Lab of Robotics and Intelligent System, Shenzhen Institute of Advanced Technology, Chinese Academy of Sciences, Shenzhen 510663, China

Abstract. In order to improve the efficiency of enterprises in the sorting task of packaging boxes and reduce the labor intensity of workers, a fast and efficient detection method based on image processing is proposed in this study. This research mainly involves pose estimation of the packaging box, as well as solving the transformation relationship from the pose of the packaging box in the camera coordinate system to the base coordinate system of the manipulator. SIFT method is used to obtain packaging feature points, FLANN method is used for feature point matching, and EPnP method is used to solve the pose of the box. This study uses nine-point calibration method to solve the transformation relationship between the base coordinate system of manipulator and camera coordinate system. It can be seen from the test results that the method used in this study has achieved satisfactory results by weighing the two indicators of detection accuracy and speed.

Keywords: Image processing · Pose estimation · Hand-eye calibration · Sorting

1 Introduction

Industrial robots are currently widely used in various industrial environments, and with the increasing demand for intelligent industrial robots, the combination of machine vision and robots has become a research topic for more and more scholars [1].

Nowadays, traditional manual operations are gradually replaced by intelligent equipment such as industrial robots. Industrial robots play an important role in the field of automation, including the warehousing and stacking of food and medicine production lines [2]. S. Dhakshina Kumar et al. proposed a non-destructive system for sorting and grading tomatoes [3]. They used a microprocessor to obtain images of tomatoes in the sorting scene, and completed the detection through three steps of binarization, maturity classification and defect classification. Feng et al. proposed an optimization design method of PID controller based on deep learning for robots to perform classification tasks [4]. Wang et al. proposed an automatic sorting and grading system for Agaricus bisporus based on machine vision [5]. Zhang et al. proposed an automatic palletizing robot system based on machine vision [6]. They used k-means clustering method to establish standard template library. A fast matching algorithm based on template shape was proposed, which can quickly and accurately identify several cigarette shapes and cigarette cases.

In this study, we mainly focus on the categories and poses of packaging boxes in visual detection. Our ultimate goal is that the investigated detection system is not only fast but also accurate. Sift method was used to obtain packaging feature points, FLANN (Fast Library for Approximate Nearest Neighbors) method was used for feature point matching, and finally EPnP (Efficient Perspective-n-Point) method was used to solve the pose of the box. We also used the hand-eye calibration method (nine-point method) to complete the transformation of the pose of the object to the base coordinates of the robot arm.

2   Pose Estimation of Box

In this study, we used a series of image processing algorithms to achieve the pose estimation of the target by taking the medicine box as an example.

2.1   Image Distortion Correction

The quality of the image directly affects the accuracy of the recognition algorithm, so preprocessing is required before image analysis (feature extraction, segmentation, matching, and recognition, etc.). The main purpose of image preprocessing is to eliminate irrelevant information in images, restore useful real information, and enhance the detectability of relevant information.

It is necessary to perform camera calibration to obtain camera internal parameters, external parameters and distortion coefficients of the image. With the distortion coefficient, the distortion in the image can be removed. The following is the process of image distortion elimination:

1. the coordinates of pixels on the original image

$$UV_i = \begin{bmatrix} u_i \\ v_i \\ 1 \end{bmatrix} \tag{1}$$

2. According to the formula for the projection of points on the normalized plane to pixel coordinates (K is the internal parameter matrix of the camera)

$$UV_i = KQ_i'' \tag{2}$$

3. Points on pixels are projected onto a normalized plane (with distortion)

$$Q_i'' = M_{intri}^{-1} * UV_i = \begin{bmatrix} x_{distor} \\ y_{distor} \\ 1 \end{bmatrix} \tag{3}$$

4. According to the coefficient and formula of the distortion, the coordinates of the point on the normalized plane (without distortion) are obtained by inverse solution

$$x_{\text{distor}} = x * \left(1 + k_1 * r^2 + k_2 * r^4 + k_3 * r^6\right)$$
$$+ 2p_1 xy + p_2\left(r^2 + 2x^2\right) \tag{4}$$

$$y_{\text{distor}} = y * \left(1 + k_1 * r^2 + k_2 * r^4 + k_3 * r^6\right)$$
$$+ p_1\left(r^2 + y^2\right) + 2p_2 xy \tag{5}$$

$$Q_i' = \begin{bmatrix} x \\ y \\ 1 \end{bmatrix} \tag{6}$$

2.2 Perspective Transformation

In this study, the perspective transformation method was used to obtain matching templates [7]. The essence of perspective transformation is to project the image to a new viewing plane, and its general transformation formula is:

$$p_i' = H_{3\times3} * p_i \tag{7}$$

$$\begin{bmatrix} x_i' \\ y_i' \\ 1 \end{bmatrix} = \begin{bmatrix} h_{00} & h_{01} & h_{02} \\ h_{10} & h_{11} & h_{12} \\ h_{20} & h_{21} & h_{22} \end{bmatrix} \begin{bmatrix} x_i \\ y_i \\ 1 \end{bmatrix} \tag{8}$$

p_i represents those points in the original graph, and p_i' represents those points after the homography transformation. $H_{3\times3}$ is the homography transformation matrix.

$$\begin{bmatrix} h_{00} & h_{01} & h_{02} \\ h_{10} & h_{11} & h_{12} \\ h_{20} & h_{21} & h_{22} \end{bmatrix} = \begin{bmatrix} a_{00} & a_{01} & t_1 \\ a_{10} & a_{11} & t_2 \\ v_1 & v_2 & s \end{bmatrix} \tag{9}$$

$$\begin{bmatrix} a_{00} & a_{01} & t_1 \\ a_{10} & a_{11} & t_2 \\ v_1 & v_2 & s \end{bmatrix} = \begin{bmatrix} A_{2\times2} & T_{2\times1} \\ V_{1\times2} & s \end{bmatrix} \tag{10}$$

$A_{2\times2}$ is the linear transformation matrix, $T_{2\times1}$ is the translation vector, $V_{1\times2}$ is the scaling factor related to the projection vector and the projection vector, where the value is 1.

2.3 Detect Feature Points Using SIFT Algorithm

Next, we need to obtain the feature points of the image to prepare for matching with the feature points of the template. In this project, we use the SIFT (Scale-invariant feature transform) [8] algorithm to complete the feature point extraction task.

The SIFT algorithm can find key feature points in the scale space and calculate their orientation. What SIFT finds are some very prominent key points, which do not change due to factors such as lighting, noise, etc.

The SIFT algorithm can be decomposed into the following four steps:

- The image positions on all scales are searched, and the key points invariant to scale and rotation are identified by Gaussian difference function.
- At each candidate location, the location and scale are determined by a fine fitting model.
- Each key point location is assigned one or more directions based on the local gradient directions of the image.
- The local gradient of the image is measured in the neighborhood around each key point.

2.4 Feature Point Matching Based on FLANN Algorithm

FLANN [9] is an algorithm for nearest neighbor search on large datasets and high-dimensional features. Some feature points are found in the query image, and some feature points are also found in another image, and finally the feature points between the two images are matched.

When using FLANN algorithm for matching, we need to pass in two dictionaries as parameters. The first dictionary is 'IndexParams'. For SIFT algorithm, the parameters we pass in are "dict(algorithm = FLANN_INDEX_KDTREE, trees = 5)". The second dictionary is 'SearchParams'. It is used to specify the number of recursive iterations. The higher the value, the more accurate the result is, but the more time it takes. In this project, the parameter we pass in is "searchparams = dict(checks = 50)".

2.5 Calculate the Homography Matrix

The homography matrix is the projection matrix of one plane to another plane, which can be simply understood as the position mapping relationship between the world coordinate system and the pixel coordinate system of the object. According to (8), it can be obtained as follows:

$$1 = \begin{bmatrix} h_{20} & h_{21} & h_{22} \end{bmatrix} \cdot \begin{bmatrix} x_i \\ y_i \\ 1 \end{bmatrix} \tag{11}$$

$$1 = h_{20} * x_i + h_{21} * y_i + h_{22} \tag{12}$$

$$x'_i = h_{00} * x_i + h_{01} * y_i + h_{02} \tag{13}$$

$$y'_i = h_{10} * x_i + h_{11} * y_i + h_{12} \tag{14}$$

$$h_{00} * x_i + h_{01} * y_i + h_{02} * 1$$

$$- h_{20} * x_i' x_i - h_{21} * x_i' y_i = x_i' \qquad (15)$$

$$h_{10} * x_i + h_{11} * y_i + h_{12} * 1$$
$$- h_{20} * x_i' x_i - h_{21} * x_i' y_i = y_i' \qquad (16)$$

There are a total of 8 unknown variables in the homography matrix, so the mapping relationship of four groups of points can be solved. Therefore, 8 sets of relational expressions can be obtained, and the closed solution of the homography matrix can be directly obtained after being written in the form of matrix operation.

2.6 Solve the Pose by the EPnP Algorithm

The points on the object in the object coordinate system are recorded as $^{obj}P_i$, the points on the object in the camera coordinate system are recorded as.

The transformation formula for converting the coordinates of the point in the object coordinate system ($^{obj}P_i$) to the coordinates of the point in the camera coordinate system ($^{cam}P_i$) is as follows:

$$^{cam}P_i = R *^{obj} P_i + t \qquad (17)$$

where R is the rotation matrix and t is the translation vector. The full name of PnP is Perspective-n-Point. According to the internal parameters of the camera, the pose of the points in the object coordinate system and the coordinates of the points in the pixel coordinate system, the pose of the camera in the object coordinate system is deduced. In this study, the EPnP [10] algorithm was used to solve the pose of the box. The EPnP scheme expresses the camera coordinates of the reference point as a weighted sum of control points, and then transforms the problem into the solution of the camera coordinate system of these four control points. For the non-planar case, 4 non-coplanar control points are required, while for the plane only 3 are required.

The steps of the EPnP algorithm are as follows:

- Calculate the coordinates of the control points in the camera reference frame;
- Calculate the coordinates of all 3D points in the camera reference frame;
- Extract the rotation matrix and translation vector.

In this study, we use cv2.solvePnP in opencv to solve the pose. It should be noted that the solvePnP function returns the pose of the object coordinate system in the camera coordinate system.

The prototype of the solvePnP function contains the following parameters: objectPoints, imagePoints, cameraMatrix, distCoeffs, and flags.objectPoints represents the three-dimensional coordinate points of the object in the world coordinate system; imagePoints represents the pixel coordinates of points in the image; cameraMatrix represents the camera intrinsic parameter matrix; distCoeffs represents the distortion coefficient of the image; flags indicates the configuration options for solving (flags = cv2. SOLVEPNP_EPNP).

Through the above image processing methods, the position and pose of the packaging box in the camera coordinate system are finally obtained.

3 Hand-Eye Calibration

3.1 Coordinate Systems in Visual Grasping

Figure 1 shows the structure of the robotic arm based on visual grasping. The three main coordinate systems are marked in the figure: Camera Coordinate System, Workbench Coordinate System, and Base Coordinate System. Different dashed arrows represent the matrix transformation process between different coordinate systems.

The purpose of the hand-eye calibration of the robotic arm is to solve $^{arm}_{cam}T$. It can be obtained by the following calculation.

$$^{arm}_{cam}T = {}^{arm}_{ws}T * {}^{ws}_{cam}T \tag{18}$$

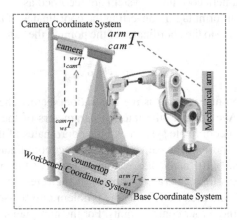

Fig. 1. Coordinate systems in sorting scenarios

3.2 Nine-Point Calibration

- Measure the actual size of the workbench, and get the coordinates of the sampling points on the workbench (nine groups).

$$^{ws}P = \left[{}^{ws}P_1, {}^{ws}P_2, \ldots, {}^{ws}P_9 \right] \tag{19}$$

- Collect the coordinates of nine points in the pixel coordinate system.
- Collect the coordinates of nine points in the coordinate system of the robot arm. By moving the end of the robotic arm, let it fall on the 9 sampling points on the bench. The coordinates of the end of the manipulator at this time are obtained through the upper computer software, and a total of 9 groups of points ($^{arm}P_i$) are recorded.

$$^{arm}P = \left[{}^{arm}P_1, {}^{arm}P_2, \ldots, {}^{arm}P_9 \right] \tag{20}$$

Fig. 2. Test results: (a) Graphs in standard and arbitrary poses, (b) Distorted images, (c) Template obtained using perspective transform on standard pose graph, (d) Detection of SIFT features, (e) Feature matching with FLANN, (f) Pose visualization (EPnP algorithm is used to solve the PnP problem)

- ICP algorithm is used to calculate the transformation from manipulator coordinate system to workbench coordinate system.

$$_{ws}^{arm}T = ICP\left(^{arm}P, ^{ws}P\right) \tag{21}$$

- The two-dimensional pixel coordinates of the nine points in the image are p_i, and the three-dimensional coordinates of the nine points on the workbench are $^{ws}P_i$, they are all known by measurement. What needs to be solved here ($_{ws}^{cam}T$) is the pose of the workbench in the camera coordinate system. This is a typical PnP problem. With the help of EPnP algorithm, the transformation matrix can be obtained.

$$_{ws}^{cam}T = EPnP\left(^{ws}P, p\right) \tag{22}$$

$$_{cam}^{arm}T = {}_{ws}^{arm}T * {}_{cam}^{ws}T \tag{23}$$

4 Experiments

The following are screenshots of the image processing process for pose detection. Here is an example of any product packaging box. The method used in this study can easily realize real-time detection even on the CPU of laptop (Fig. 2).

5 Conclusion

In this study, the pose estimation of the box is implemented using 2D image processing. However, this method is not ideal for objects with insignificant surface features. In the future work, we intend to use the method based on 3D point cloud matching to obtain pose.

Acknowledgment. Research supported by follows: 1. Research Foundation of Shanghai Polytechnic University under grant EGD22QD01; 2. Guangdong Basic and Applied Basic Research Foundation under grant 2021A1515011699.

References

1. Ali, M.H., Aizat, K., Yerkhan, K., et al.: Vision-based robot manipulator for industrial applications. Procedia Comput. Sci. **133**, 205–212 (2018)
2. Smys, S., Ranganathan, G.: Robot assisted sensing control and manufacture in automobile industry. J. ISMAC **1**(03), 180–187 (2019)
3. Kumar, S.D., Esakkirajan, S., Bama, S., et al.: A microcontroller based machine vision approach for tomato grading and sorting using SVM classifier. Microprocess. Microsyst. **76**, 103090 (2020)
4. Feng, C., Nie, G., Naveed, Q.N., et al.: Optimization of sorting robot control system based on deep learning and machine vision. Math. Probl. Eng. **2022** (2022). Article ID 5458703

5. Wang, F.Y., Feng, W.J., Zheng, J.Y., et al.: Design and experiment of automatic sorting and grading system based on machine vision for white Agaricus bisporus. Trans. Chin. Soc. Agric. Eng. **34**(7), 256–263 (2018)
6. Zhang, Y., Kang, J., Xing, B., et al.: Research on cigarette packet recognition and stacking technology based on machine vision. In: 2020 11th International Conference on Prognostics and System Health Management (PHM 2020), Jinan, pp. 532–537. IEEE (2020)
7. Tuohy, S., O'Cualain, D., Jones, E., et al.: Distance determination for an automobile environment using inverse perspective mapping in OpenCV (2010)
8. Lindeberg, T.: Scale invariant feature transform (2012)
9. Muja, M., Lowe, D.: FLANN-fast library for approximate nearest neighbors user manual, p. 5. Computer Science Department, University of British Columbia, Vancouver, BC, Canada (2009)
10. Lepetit, V., Moreno-Noguer, F., Fua, P.: EPnP: an accurate o(n) solution to the PnP problem. Int. J. Comput. Vision **81**(2), 155–166 (2009). https://doi.org/10.1007/s11263-008-0152-6

Structural Design and Aerodynamic Characteristics of Two Types of Fold-Able Flapping-Wings

Xinxing Mu[1,2(✉)], Sheng Xu[1,2], and Xinyu Wu[1]

[1] Guangdong Provincial Key Lab of Robotics and Intelligent System, Shenzhen Institute of Advanced Technology, Chinese Academy of Sciences, Shenzhen 518055, China
xx.mu@sdiat.ac.cn
[2] Shandong Institute of Advanced Technology, Chinese Academy of Sciences, Jinan 250102, Shandong, China

Abstract. Large wingspan birds inspire the studies about the bionic fold-able flapping-wing robot. To explore the influencing factors of the bionic ornithopter's aerodynamic characteristics, two bionic fold-able flapping-wing flapping mechanisms were established to simulate the flight motion of birds. We present two fold-able flapping-wing structural design methods with parameters: inner wing flapping and outer wing folding angles. A simulation analysis is carried out for these structures based on XFlow, and the influence on lift and thrust is explored with different flapping frequencies and air velocities. The results show that the lift and drag of the ornithopter increase with air velocity, and the thrust increases with the rise of flapping frequency. Furthermore, the comparisons indicate that an asymmetric flapping mode of fold-able wing structure has better aerodynamic characteristics. The critical contribution of this paper is that we propose helpful structural design guidance for flapping-wing robots.

Keywords: Fold-able flapping-wing · Driven structure · XFlow · Aerodynamic characteristics

1 Introduction

With the rapid development of unmanned aerial vehicle (UAV) technology, flapping-wing aircraft has attracted numerous domestic and foreign scholars. Unlike traditional fixed-wing and rotor aircraft, ornithopter has good mobility, high efficiency and small noise [1]. With the deepening of research, the structural design of the flapping-wing becomes more complex, e.g., designing a multi-segment wing. The structural change puts forward new requirements for the movement mode of the flapping-wing. Designing the multi-segment wing to improve the aerodynamic efficiency of flight has become a significant problem.

To design and develop a high-performance artificial ornithopter, understanding the physiological and behaviour aspects of live birds and the kinematic and kinetic features of live birds is urgently needed. In particular, the coupling between aerodynamics and

© The Author(s), under exclusive license to Springer Nature Switzerland AG 2022
H. Liu et al. (Eds.): ICIRA 2022, LNAI 13455, pp. 734–746, 2022.
https://doi.org/10.1007/978-3-031-13844-7_68

structural dynamics plays an essential role in wing design but, to date, has not been adequately addressed [2]. Considering that the core motion of the bionic flapping-wing aircraft is realized by its flapping mechanism, the flapping mechanism is dimensioned based on the determination of the flapping scheme and the shape parameters of the flapping-wing prototype [3]. At present, the research on the flapping-wing design of ornithopters still focuses on single-segment and two-segment rigid wing prototypes. Skills transfer learning of robots is a hot topic in bionics [4].

Jung investigated the aerodynamic characteristics of a wing during fold motion, and the results were obtained using the unsteady vortex lattice method to estimate the lift, drag and the moment coefficient in subsonic flow during fold motion [5]. Han analyzed the seagull wing's wake pattern and aerodynamic characteristics by considering its level-flight deformation [6]. Yang analyzed the effects of flight angle and flapping-wing bending-folding using the XFlow. Flapping-wing shape, frequency and inflow on surrounding air are studied [7]. After that, a multi-degree-of-freedom motion model of "swing-torsion-bending and folding" is built. Considered violent vortex and negative pressure are produced on the upper surface of outer wings, which will improve the lift-drag ratio and impact drag coefficient less [8].

In this paper, we analyze the flight characteristics of large wingspan birds, establish two different fold-able wing structures, and construct a simple airfoil flapping process. Then we obtain the surrounding flow field characteristics of the fold-able wing by using the XFlow software of three-dimensional numerical simulation. In addition, we analyze the folding structure, flapping frequency, and incoming velocity on the flow field. Consequently, we conclude the corresponding theoretical and technical results to help improve the ornithopter's structure.

2 Mechanism of the Bionic Fold-Able Wing

2.1 Characteristics of Bird Flying

The mechanism of bird flying is complex, and the flying stability is impacted by the superposition of various aerodynamic effects. Birds achieve optimal flying status during the regulation of flapping amplitude, frequency, torsion, closure and folding. In the above process, the upward bending of the wing can effectively reduce the generation of negative lift during the up flap movement, and thus the aerodynamic efficiency is improved. Therefore, this paper focuses on analyzing wing folding motion on the aerodynamic properties of flight. As shown in Fig. 1, the fold-able wing flapping process of a large-scale bird can be divided into two stages.

Fig. 1. Feature of large-scale bird wing motion in level flight.

Flapping Down. The wings flapping down from the highest point and remain stretch, and the outer wing has a small folding angle. The folding amplitude continues to increase (see a–d in Fig. 1).

When the wing flaps downwards, due to inertia, the air on the upper part of the wing does not flow down with the wing immediately. Subsequently, the air on the upper surface of the wing is relatively small temporarily, and a partial vacuum occurs. Therefore, when the pressure difference of the flapping-wing is greater than gravity, the bird will rise.

Flapping Up. The wings flapping up from the lowest point and remain folding angle, the folding amplitude gradually increases and reaches the maximum near the median stroke. Then the wing folding amplitude gradually decreases (see d-g in Fig. 1).

When the wing flaps upward, the wing folds, and the force area on the wing reduces. Although the pressure difference is downward and there is gravity, the resultant force on the bird is downward. But also, due to inertia, the bird will maintain the original upward speed and will not descend immediately. After that, the wings resumed flapping downwards, and the bird gains upward lift again.

2.2 Fold-Able Flapping-Wing Shape and Motion Analysis

The main objective of this section to develop the fold-able flapping-wing for level flight. While flapping flight in ornithopters has been studied, many researchers designed several models. They usually had unfoldable wings actuated with DC motors and mechanical transmission to achieve the flapping motion, which transmits power by the four-link structure. Although the core movement of the bionic ornithopter is realized by its flapping mechanism, the different wing structures affect the flapping movement. This section establishes two types of flapping folding wing structures with the analysis of the folding movement characteristics under the flapping mechanism intuitively.

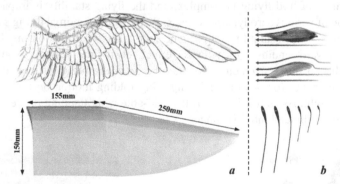

Fig. 2. Feature of sparrowhawk wing and artificial flapping-wing.

To accurately contrast the motion characteristics of the two proposed fold-able flapping-wing structures, the geometric parameters of the wing need to be unified. This paper determines the surface shape and size of the wing inspired by the sparrowhawk.

The length of the inner wingspan is 155 mm, the length of the outer wing is 250 mm, and the maximum string length is 150 mm. The real sparrowhawk wing sketch and artificial fold-able flapping-wing model are shown in Fig. 2(a). Meanwhile, to improve the aerodynamic efficiency of the horizontal flight process, we built a 3D artificial wing model with a large similarity to the real birds'. The sparrowhawk wing shape inspires the design of the airfoil contour, modeled with the BE6308B profile, which was verified in Ref [9] to have an excellent aerodynamic effect, as shown in Fig. 2 (b).

The defined motion parameter model of the ornithopter fold-able flapping-wing is shown in Fig. 3. Figure 3 shows the flapping and folding of the flapping wing's motion synthesis where ψ indicates the flapping angle of the inner wing, and φ indicates the folding angle of the outer wing relative to the inner wing.

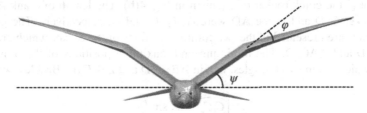

Fig. 3. Schematic representation of fold-able wing motion parameters.

2.3 Fold-Able Wing Geometry and Kinematics

For the convenience of the analysis, the skeleton structure is described as a two-jointed arm model that consists of two rigid-jointed rods which represent the leading edge of flapping-wing. The translation from DC brushless motor rotation to the wing's flapping motion is achieved by a gear reduction unit and four-link structure. In addition, the folding movement of the outer wing is also realized by the four-link structure. Therefore, the folding action under this driving mode has only one controllable degree of freedom, namely the flapping frequency of the wing. In contrast, the folding angle of the outer wing is determined by the structural parameters of the four-link and the flapping angle of the inner wing. Therefore we utilize fold-able wing geometry parameters to design two flapping-wing drive structures and analyze the movement characteristics of the wing under different structures.

Before the structural design, the motion range of the fold-able wing should be set. Then, after observing the pattern of biological flying motion, we define the flapping amplitude of the inner wing as 60° and determine the folding amplitude of the outer wing as 50°. The upwards flapping angle is set to 50°, and the downwards flapping angle is set to 10°. The following part adopts the same geometry dimensions through different combinations of crank rocker and double rocker structures to achieve the same inner wing flapping range and outer wing folding range.

Case 1. Establish the fold-able flapping-wing drive structure as shown in Fig. 4.

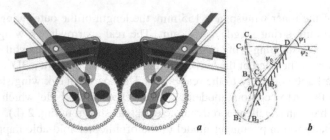

Fig. 4. Flapping-wing drive structure for Case 1.

Figure 4(a) shows the highest and lowest inner wing flapping positions, which is equivalent to the crank rocker mechanism in Fig. 4(b). The length of crank AB_1, link B_1C_1, rocker C_1D and frame AD were l_1, l_2, l_3 and l_4, respectively. The geometric relationships are presented in the two limited positions of the rocker which are located in $\triangle AC_1D$ and $\triangle AC_4D$. The minimum and maximum positions of the transmission angle γ which are in two triangles, i.e., in $\triangle B_2C_2D$ and $\triangle B_3C_3D$. Besides, we have:

$$\begin{cases} \widehat{C_1C_4} = 2l_3 \sin\dfrac{\psi}{2} \\ AC_4 = l_2 + l_1 \\ AC_1 = l_2 - l_1 \end{cases} \tag{1}$$

According to $\triangle AC_1D$, $\triangle AC_4D$, $\triangle B_2C_2D$, $\triangle B_3C_3D$ and $\triangle C_2AC_4$ in Fig. 4, the following equations can be obtained:

$$\begin{cases} \left(2l_3 \sin\frac{\psi}{2}\right)^2 = (l_2+l_1)^2 + (l_2-l_1)^2 \\ \qquad\qquad\qquad - 2(l_2+l_1)(l_2-l_1)\cos\theta \\ (l_2-l_1)^2 = l_3^2 + l_4^2 - 2l_3l_4\cos\psi_0 \\ (l_2+l_1)^2 = l_3^2 + l_4^2 - 2l_3l_4\cos(\psi_0+\psi) \\ (l_4-l_1)^2 = l_2^2 + l_3^2 - 2l_2l_3\cos\gamma_{min} \\ (l_4+l_1)^2 = l_2^2 + l_3^2 - 2l_2l_3\cos\gamma_{max} \end{cases} \tag{2}$$

Nine parameters in (2) indicate the four-bar mechanism's relative motion and geometrical relationship. For example, when the crank length l_1, rocker length l_2, frame length l_3 and swing amplitude ψ of the four-bar mechanism are known, the link rod length l_4, the mechanism pole angle θ, the drive angle $\gamma_{min}/\gamma_{max}$ and the angle ψ_0 between rocker and frame at the limited positions can be obtained by solving (2).

After calculating the parameters of the drive structure, the four-bar mechanism parameters in the fold-able wing also need to be designed. The fold-able wing structure schematic diagram is shown in Fig. 5(a).

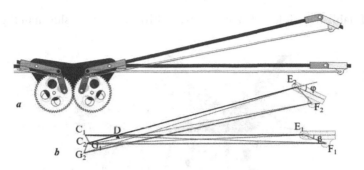

Fig. 5. Four-bar fold-able wing structure for Case 1.

To satisfy the folding angle amplitude $\phi = 50°$ for the fold-able wing, the four-bar mechanism at the minimum and maximum drive angle γ is further analyzed, as shown in Fig. 5(b). The geometrical relationships exist in $\triangle E_1 C_1 G_1$, $\triangle E_1 F_1 G_1$, $\triangle C_1 G_1 F_1$, $\triangle C_1 E_1 F_1$, $\triangle E_2 C_2 G_2$, $\triangle E_2 F_2 G_2$, $\triangle C_2 G_2 F_2$ and $\triangle C_2 E_2 F_2$:

$$\begin{cases} l_5^2 + l_6^2 - 2l_5 l_6 \cos \gamma_{min} = l_7^2 + l_8^2 - 2l_7 l_8 \cos \angle E_1 F_1 G_1 \\ l_5^2 + l_8^2 - 2l_5 l_8 \cos \angle C_1 G_1 F_1 = l_6^2 + l_7^2 - 2l_6 l_7 \cos \angle C_1 E_1 F_1 \\ \gamma_{min} + \angle C_1 E_1 F_1 + \angle E_1 F_1 G_1 + \angle C_1 G_1 F_1 = 2\pi \\ l_5^2 + l_6^2 - 2l_5 l_6 \cos \gamma_{max} = l_7^2 + l_8^2 - 2l_7 l_8 \cos \angle E_2 F_2 G_2 \\ l_5^2 + l_8^2 - 2l_5 l_8 \cos \angle C_2 G_2 F_2 = l_6^2 + l_7^2 - 2l_6 l_7 \cos \angle C_2 E_2 F_2 \\ \gamma_{max} + \angle C_2 E_2 F_2 + \angle E_2 F_2 G_2 + \angle C_2 G_2 F_2 = 2\pi \end{cases} \tag{3}$$

where the lengths of $C_1 G_1 (C_2 G_2)$, $C_1 E_1 (C_2 E_2)$, $E_1 F_1 (E_2 F_2)$ and $F_1 G_1 (F_2 G_2)$ are l_5, l_6, l_7 and l_8, respectively. γ_{min}, γ_{max} can be obtained by (2), l_7, l_8 are set by the wing shape, $\angle C_1 E_1 F_1 = \pi - \beta$, $\angle C_2 E_2 F_2 = \pi - \beta - \phi$, where β is determined by 3D printing part. Then l_5, l_8, $\angle C_1 G_1 F_1$, $\angle E_1 F_1 G_1$, $\angle C_2 G_2 F_2$ and $\angle E_2 F_2 G_2$ can be obtained by solving (3).

Fig. 6. Fold-able wing motion simulation for Case 1.

Considering the shape and size requirements of ornithopter, we set $l_1 = 7$ mm, $l_3 = 15$ mm, $l_4 = 21.2$ mm, $\psi = 60°$, and substitute them into (2) yields: $l_2 = 13.53$ mm, $\psi_0 = 6.55°$, $\theta = 26.91°$, $\gamma_{min} = 59.44°$, $\gamma_{max} = 162.64°$. Set $l_6 = 158$ mm, $l_7 = 10.4$ mm, $\beta = \arctan (4/9.6)$, $\phi = 50°$, and substitute them into (3) yields: $l_5 = 4.28$ mm, $l_8 = 165.42$ mm. Then we can get motion simulation of fold-able wing for Case 1 as shown in Fig. 6 by Solidworks.

Case 2. Establish the fold-able flapping-wing drive structure as shown in Fig. 7.

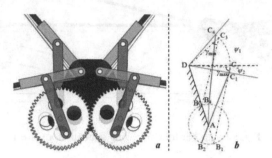

Fig. 7. Flapping-wing drive structure for Case 2.

Figure 7(a) shows the highest and lowest inner wing flapping positions, and an equivalent crank rocker mechanism is shown in Fig. 7(b). The parameter definitions are the same to that in Case 1. The schematic diagram of the fold-able wing structure is shown in Fig. 8(a), and an equivalent crank rocker mechanism is shown in Fig. 8(b).

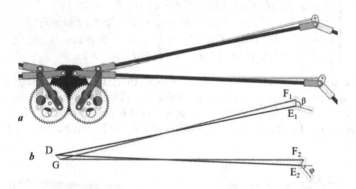

Fig. 8. Four-bar fold-able wing structure for Case 2.

Similar to Case 1, the geometrical relationships exist in $\triangle DE_1F_1$, $\triangle DG_1F_1$, $\triangle GDE_1$, $\triangle GF_1E_1$, $\triangle DE_2F_2$, $\triangle DG_2F_2$, $\triangle GDE_2$ and $\triangle GF_2E_2$ at the limited positions.

$$\begin{cases} l_5^2 + l_6^2 - 2l_5l_6 \cos \angle E_1DG = l_7^2 + l_8^2 - 2l_7l_8 \cos \angle E_1F_1G \\ l_5^2 + l_8^2 - 2l_5l_8 \cos \angle DGF_1 = l_6^2 + l_7^2 - 2l_6l_7 \cos \angle DE_1F_1 \\ \angle E_1DG + \angle DGF_1 = \angle E_1F_1G + \angle DE_1F_1 \\ l_5^2 + l_6^2 - 2l_5l_6 \cos \angle E_2DG = l_7^2 + l_8^2 - 2l_7l_8 \cos \angle E_2F_2G \\ l_5^2 + l_8^2 - 2l_5l_8 \cos \angle DGF_2 = l_6^2 + l_7^2 - 2l_6l_7 \cos \angle DE_2F_2 \\ \angle E_2DG + \angle DGF_2 = \angle E_2F_2G + \angle DE_2F_2 \end{cases} \quad (4)$$

where the lengths of DG, DE_1 (DE_2), E_1F_1 (E_2F_2) and F_1G_1 (F_2G_2) were l_5, l_6, l_7 and l_8, respectively. The wing shape determines l_7 and l_8. $\angle E_1DG = 45° + \psi_1$, $\angle E_2DG =$

$45° - \psi_2$, and $\psi_1 = 50°$, $\psi_2 = 10°$ at the limited positions of inner wing. $\angle F_1 E_1 G = \pi - \beta$, $\angle F_2 E_2 G = \pi + \phi - \beta$, where β is determined by 3D printing part.

Set $l_1 = 6.5$ mm, $l_3 = 15$ mm, $l_4 = 21.2$ mm, $\psi = 60°$, and substitute them into (2) yields: $l_2 = 24.41$ mm, $\psi_0 = 6.55°$, $\theta = 18.3°$, $\gamma_{min} = 34.33°$, $\gamma_{max} = 85.81°$. Set $l_6 = 158$ mm, $l_7 = 4$ mm, $\beta = 110°$, $\phi = 50°$, and substitute them into (4) yields: $l_5 = 3.63$ mm, $l_8 = 157.12$ mm. Then we can get motion simulation of fold-able wing for Case 2 as shown in Fig. 9 by Solidworks.

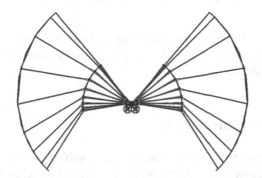

Fig. 9. Fold-able wing motion simulation for Case 2.

It is known that Case 2 has a larger stroke range in the outer wing than Case 1 by comparing Figs. 6 and 9. As shown in Fig. 10, two instances have the same flapping angle range $\psi = [-10°, 50°]$, and the same folding angle range $\varphi = [0°, 50°]$. Besides, ψ and φ in Case 1 have the same variation tendency but to the contrary in Case 2. Moreover, the travel velocity-ratio coefficient $K = (180 + \theta)/(180 - \theta)$ can be derived from (2). It is easy to discover that the inner wing $K_{\psi 1} = 1.35$, the outer wing $K_{\varphi 1} = 1$, the inner wing $K_{\psi 2} = 1.23$, and the outer wing $K_{\varphi 1} = 1.31$.

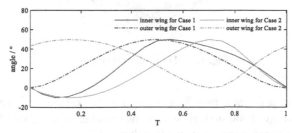

Fig. 10. Flapping angle ψ and folding angle φ for Case 1 (blue) and Case 2 (red). (Color figure online)

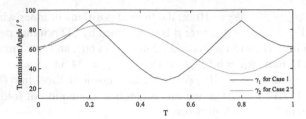

Fig. 11. Transmission angle γ for Case 1 (blue) and Case 2 (red). (Color figure online)

As shown in Fig. 11, the fluctuation amplitude of transmission angle γ_1 is significant, while the curve of transmission angle γ_2 is approximately sinusoidal, which has a more smooth power transmission.

3 Simulation Scheme Setting

The airfoil model refers to the shape of the falcon, simplifying the feather characteristics, and a 3D model is designed, as shown in Fig. 12. The 3D model includes the bird body (including the head), tail wing and fold-able flapping wing. The fuselage's length is 200 mm, the wingspan is 850 mm, the fuselage's width is 50 mm, the inner wing's length is 155 mm, the outer wing's size is 250 mm, and the string length is 150 mm. In addition, the airfoil adopts the upper arc surface and the lower concave surface to increase the pneumatic efficiency during the level flight, and the fuselage adopts a streamlined character to reduce the drag.

Fig. 12. 3D model of ornithopter

The 3D model of imitated bird flapping aircraft was established in Solidworks software platform and saved into stp format, then the model is imported into XFlow software. We use function *linearinterpolation(t; {t0, value0}; {t1, value1}; ...; {tn, valuen})* to set the angle motion data respectively for each component in the motion module, to analyze the simulation model.

Next, we determine the computing domain and boundary, and select the computing domain type as a virtual wind tunnel. The calculation domain is set to 6 times of the length of the fuselage on the X-axis, 2 times of the wingspan on the Y-axis, and 3 times of the wing span on the Z-axis. The calculation domain of the virtual wind tunnel is shown in Fig. 13.

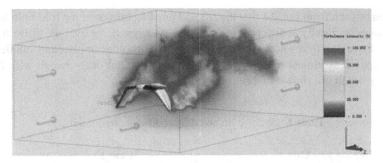

Fig. 13. Axonometric drawing of the virtual wind tunnel and ornithopter model.

We compare the performance of two cases to examine the effects of the two designed structures on thrust, lift and correlated aerodynamics coefficients. The simulations are conducted for flapping frequency f ranging from 4 Hz to 8 Hz and velocity v from 6 m/s to 10 m/s.

3.1 Effect of the Flapping Frequency on the Aerodynamic Characteristics

The flapping frequency has an important influence on the lift and drag of the ornithopter. For example, we set inflow velocity as 8 m/s, the aerodynamic characteristics are studied by the flapping frequencies at 4 Hz, 6 Hz and 8 Hz, while the other motion parameters are the same. As a result, the lift and drag curves vary over the second period of simulation time in Fig. 14.

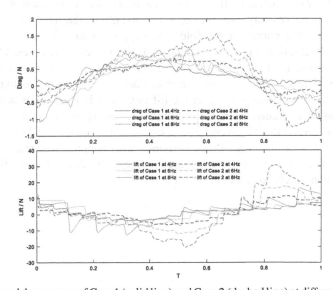

Fig. 14. Lift and drag curves of Case 1 (solid line) and Case 2 (dashed line) at different frequencies.

It can be seen from Fig. 14 that the lift and the drag curves of the fold-able flapping-wing change cyclically at different frequencies. As a result, the average thrust increases with the increasing frequency, and the growing field becomes smaller and smaller, while the average lift is almost unchanged. The average lift and drag change with flapping frequency which are shown in Table 1.

Table 1. Average lift and drag at different frequencies.

Flapping frequency	Case 1		Case 2	
	Average drag/N	Average lift/N	Average drag/N	Average lift/N
4 Hz	0.3015	1.556	0.3068	1.107
6 Hz	0.2194	1.572	0.2675	1.086
8 Hz	0.1857	1.516	0.2507	1.062

It can be observed that the average lift is not affected by flapping frequency. On the contrary, the average drag decreases with the flapping frequency (the average thrust increases with the flapping frequency). Lift in Case 1 is almost 42.7% higher than in Case 2, indicating that the structure of Case 1 is more likely to obtain large lift and thrust.

3.2   Effect of the Velocity on the Aerodynamic Characteristics

With the flapping frequency of 4 Hz, the aerodynamic characteristics are studied by the air velocity at 6 m/s, 8 m/s and 10 m/s, while the other motion parameters are the same. The lift and drag curves vary over the second period of simulation in Fig. 15.

The lift and drag curves of the fold-able flapping wing can be seen in Fig. 15. Although the fluctuation amplitude increases as the velocity increases, Case 2 has a larger fluctuation range than Case 1, presumably due to the larger stroke of the outer wing. Besides, The average lift growth ratio in Case 2 (72.1%) is more significant than in Case 1 (112.9%), although the average lift in Case 2 is lower than in Case 1. The average lift and drag change with flapping frequency are shown in Table 2.

It can be observed that the average lift increases with velocity, and the average drag decrease with velocity (average thrust increases with flapping frequency). Therefore, case 1 has more lift and less drag than Case 2 (except 10 m/s), indicating that structure of Case 1 is more likely to obtain large lift and thrust.

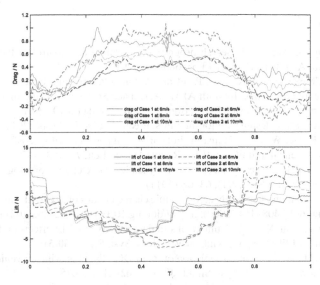

Fig. 15. Lift and drag curves of Case 1 (solid line) and Case 2 (dashed line) at different velocities.

Table 2. Average lift and drag at different velocities

Air velocity	Case 1		Case 2	
	Average drag/N	Average lift/N	Average drag/N	Average lift/N
6 m/s	0.1699	0.8366	0.2077	0.4246
8 m/s	0.3015	1.5562	0.3068	1.1066
10 m/s	0.4696	2.462	0.4289	1.8277

4 Conclusion

In this paper, two flapping mechanisms of the bionic fold-able flapping-wing were established by analyzing the bird flying behaviors. The flapping trajectories of Case 1 is symmetrical, which can effectively reduce the negative lift generated in the upward stroke. Besides, the smaller stroke amplitude of Case 1 can also reduce the drag during the flapping motion. Although the two structures have the same geometric size, and amplitude of inner wing flapping angle and outer wing folding angle, the different structures provide different aerodynamic characteristics. The simulation results show that Case 1 is more suitable for flapping-wing flight than Case 2.

Acknowledgement. This work was supported by the Key Research and Development Plan of Shandong Province (2021CXGC011304), Shenzhen Basic Key Research Project (JCYJ202001 09115414354) and Shenzhen Science and Technology Program (JCYJ202103241024 01005).

References

1. He, W., Ding, S., Sun, C.: Research progress on modeling and control of flapping-wing air vehicles. Acta Automatica Sinica **43**(5), 685–696 (2017)
2. Aono, H., Chimakurthi, S.K., Wu, P., et al.: A computational and experimental studies of flexible wing aerodynamics. In: 48th AIAA Aerospace Sciences Meeting Including the New Horizons Forum and Aerospace Exposition, Orlando, Florida (2010)
3. Wong, B.: New robot designs are for the birds. Electron. Des. **59**(6), 14 (2011)
4. Yu, X., Liu, P., He, W., et al.: Human-robot variable impedance skills transfer learning based on dynamic movement primitives. IEEE Robot. Autom. Lett. **7**, 6463–6470 (2022)
5. Jung, Y., Kim, J.H.: Unsteady subsonic aerodynamic characteristics of wing in fold motion. Int. J. Aeronaut. Space Sci. **12**(1), 63–68 (2011)
6. Han, C.: Investigation of unsteady aerodynamic characteristics of a seagull wing in level flight. J. Bionic Eng. **6**(4), 408–414 (2009). https://doi.org/10.1016/S1672-6529(08)60136-5
7. Yang, Y., Su, H., Gu, X., et al.: Numerical simulation analysis of the effects of flight angle and bend-fold on bird-like flapping-wing air vehicle. J. Syst. Simul. **30**(5), 1781–1786 (2018)
8. Yang, Y., Su, H.: Aerodynamic simulation of multi-DOF flapping-wing air vehicle of bird-like based on XFlow software. J. Syst. Simul. **30**(6), 2162–2167 (2018)
9. Mu, X.: Design of autonomous flight control system for a bionic flapping wing robot. University of Science & Technology Beijing, Beijing (2022)

Master-Slave Control of the Robotic Hand Driven by Tendon-Sheath Transmission

Zhuowei Li[1,2], Meng Yin[1,2(✉)], Hui Sun[3], Mingwei Hu[3], Wujing Cao[1,2], and Xinyu Wu[1,2]

[1] Shenzhen Institutes of Advanced Technology, Chinese Academy of Sciences, Shenzhen 518055, China
yinmenglz@163.com
[2] Guangdong Provincial Key Lab of Robotics and Intelligent System, Shenzhen Institute of Advanced Technology, Chinese Academy of Sciences, Shenzhen 518055, China
[3] Jiangsu Automation Research Institute, Lianyungang 222006, China

Abstract. A robotic hand with 19 joints is designed to make the mechanical hand lighter and more anthropomorphic. Inspired by the human flexor tendon and sheath, tendon-sheath transmission is applied to drive the finger joint, which decouples the motion of the joints and achieves the postposition of the drive motor. The configuration of the robotic hand is determined by referring to the joints of a human hand; furthermore, a joint mechanism and a drive structure are designed. The flex sensor and the changeable proportion mapping algorithm are applied, and the tracking control of grasping is achieved. Finally, a mechanical hand prototype is built to conduct gesture experiments and grasping control experiments. According to the experimental results, the designed hand has high motion flexibility, and the cooperation of the fingers achieves the effective grasping of various objects. The application of tendon-sheath transmission to the mechanical hand is feasible, and the research context has certain theoretical value and practical significance for the technical development and social application of anthropomorphic multijoint robotic hands.

Keywords: Five-fingered mechanical hand · Tendon-sheath transmission · Position control · Gesture feature capture · Master-slave mapping algorithm

1 Introduction

The function of the mechanical hand is similar to the human hand. Since its inception, it has been highly valued by research institutions in various countries [1]. The mechanical hand can be used as the end-effector in the industrial field, as a prosthesis for individuals with a disability, and as a replacement for human hands in the dangerous environments, such as space, deep sea, and nuclear power station, to achieve accurate operations, which has important social application value [2, 3]. The demand for humanoid mechanical hands will increase because of the development of service robots, but the hand of service robots, e.g. Pepper [3], has less freedom and less load, and there is

H. Liu et al. (Eds.): ICIRA 2022, LNAI 13455, pp. 747–758, 2022.
https://doi.org/10.1007/978-3-031-13844-7_69

no special mechanical hand for service robots on the market. According to the different driving methods, dexterous hands are subdivided into motor driving, pneumatic driving, hydraulic driving and functional material driving, among which the motor driving mode is more common. The representative hand using a pneumatic drive is the shadow hand [4], which has 5 fingers and 24 degrees of freedom, including 20 pneumatic drives and 4 under-actuated drives. It is driven by a pneumatic device called the "air muscle", and the driving mechanism is integrated into the forearm. The advantages of the pneumatic muscle are the low price and low environmental requirements, but the disadvantages are poor stiffness and poor dynamic characteristics. Schulz et al. [5] applied hydraulic drives to a robotic hand and developed a humanoid hand that was potentially useful as a prosthetic. The advantages of the hydraulic drive are the large driving torque, high transmission efficiency, sensitive response, overload protection and good stability. The disadvantages are the large volume, complex pipeline, high sealing requirements, high manufacturing and maintenance costs, and potential increase in environmental pollution. Functional material driving refers to the use of a shape memory alloy [6], magnetic responsive structures [7] and other new materials to drive finger joints. The shape memory alloy changes its length in response to temperature, the deformation is difficult to control accurately, the movement accuracy is poor, and its reliability, versatility and cost performance still need to be improved.

The motor drive is popular because of its small size, low noise, stable motion, easy control and moderate price. Based on the position at which the motor is installed, the motor drive is sub-classified into internal motor drive and external motor drive. The representative hand using the internal motor drive is the DLR-HIT hand [8, 9]. The motor, harmonic reducer and other components are integrated into the finger, which has a high degree of integration, strong operability and robustness, but the structure is complex and the maintenance cost is high. The external motor is mainly activated by bar linkages or cable transmission, e.g. RIC hand [10]. All fingers are designed with a four-bar linkage, and elastic elements are embedded in the linkage to increase mechanical compliance. It has 4 fingers and 8 joints and is driven by a brushless motor. The advantages are the compact structure and good lightweight design, but the use of an outer rotor motor and the auto-clutch results in a high cost. The representative hand using the external motor drive with a flexible cable is the Robonaut hand [11], which has 5 fingers and 14 degrees of freedom. The thumb, index finger and middle finger are dexterous fingers, and each finger has 4 degrees of freedom; the remaining two fingers are grasping fingers, and each finger has 1 degree of freedom. It is intended to be used in the international space station to replace people in the operations performed in outer space. Other dexterous hands with flexible cable drives include the Italian UBH3 hand [12] and the French LMS hand [13].

The tendon drive [14] has the advantages of a flexible layout, high precision, and lightweight, which has been widely used in a variety of precision devices and servo mechanisms. However, when the transmission distance is long, the existing cable transmission mechanism is mainly activated by the transmission wheel, which will make the structure very complex and increase the difficulty of manufacturing and maintaining the system. Tendon-sheath transmission [15] has been widely applied in designing robots, such as surgical robots and powered exoskeletons. In tendon-sheath transmission, the hollow sheath is used to guide the movement path of the flexible tendon, which is closer to the motion mode of the human hand [16]. It overcomes the limitations of the cable drive and achieves the long-distance transmission of the motion. The advantages are the strong space adaptability and low manufacturing cost.

Inspired by the human hand, this paper designs a five-fingered mechanical hand with 19 joints. Tendon-sheath transmission is applied to achieve the postposition of the motor, and the joint and the drive are designed. The flex sensor and the changeable proportion mapping algorithm are applied, and the tracking control of grasping is achieved. The tracking position control is achieved based on the flex sensor and the master-slave mapping algorithm. Finally, a prototype is built to perform relevant experiments. The experimental results verify the feasibility of applying the tendon-sheath transmission to the mechanical hand. The designed robotic hand is promising to be used in service robots and industrial application scenarios that have high requirements for the flexibility of mechanical hand.

2 Robotic Hand with Fingers

2.1 Bionic Design of the Hand

The bionic hand is designed according to Fig. 1. The eight carpal bones are located in the wrist and five metacarpal bones connect to the five phalanges. Only 2 phalanges are present in the thumb and each of the other fingers consists of three phalanges. The joint layout of the mechanical hand designed in this paper is shown in Fig. 2. The index finger, middle finger, ring finger and thumb all contain four joints. The downside joint is swing freedom, and the upside three joints are bending degrees of freedom. Limited by the appearance, the thumb has three joints, and the upside two joints are bending degrees of freedom. The five swing joints are driven by a double tendon-sheath mechanism. To simplify the structure and reduce the number of the tendon-sheaths, the remaining joints are driven by a single tendon-sheath mechanism.

The types of motion of finger joints are divided into side swing and flexion. Considering the transmission characteristics of the tendon-sheath and the appearance of the dexterous hand, the designed mechanical hand adopts the scheme of first side swing joint and then flexion joint to decouple the two movements. The axes of the base joint and the proximal finger joint are perpendicular to each other to simulate the proximal ball joint of the human hand, and the axes of the middle finger joint and the distal finger joint are parallel to the proximal finger joint.

The maximum torque of the torsion spring appears at the proximal finger joint to ensure the effective reduction of the joints. So based on the calculation, the carbon steel torsion spring is selected. The effective number of turns is 3 and the wire diameter is 0.5 mm.

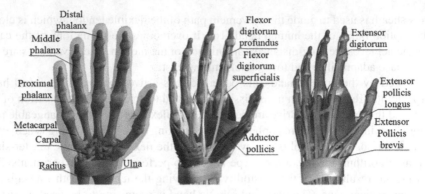

Fig. 1. Anatomy of a human hand

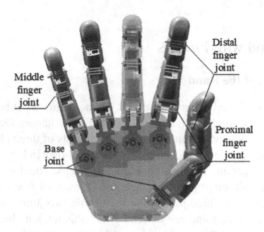

Fig. 2. Joint layout of the mechanical hand

2.2 Configuration of the Hand

The hand structure was generated using 3D printing with nylon material. The drive motor adopts the steering gear with its own reducer (Hiwonder-LX-16A, maximum output torque 19.5 kg.cm). The flexible tendon adopts a steel wire rope with a diameter of 0.5 mm, and the sheath adopts a spiral spring with outer diameter of 1.2 mm and inner

Table 1. Length parameter of the dexterous fingers

Finger length (mm)	Thumb	Index	Middle	Ring	Little
Distal phalanx	25	20	23	22	22
Middle phalanx	27	20	29	24	22
Near phalanx	27	30	30	28	26
Metacarpal	-	30	30	30	30
Total length	79	100	112	104	110

diameter of 0.8 mm wound by a circular wire. The external dimensions of the mechanical hand are similar to the human hand, and the dimensions are shown in Table 1.

The finger is installed on the palm, and the bottom of the palm is connected with the driver integration. The tendon-sheath transmission is adopted to realize the separation of the drive and the joint, and the two ends of the tendon-sheath are respectively connected to the joint and the drive module. The drive module is installed centrally in the drive integrated box. The pretightening devices of nineteen joints are installed in layers on a disk with a diameter of 125 mm. The support frame is divided into four layers, and each layer is arranged with five motors in a circle to ensure the proper installation position of the pre-tightening device. The mechanical hand and the integrated drive are connected by a connecting frame, and the hollow structure allows the tendon-sheath to pass freely. Through the selection of compact motor and the optimized layout of the motor position, the volume of the integrated box is reduced.

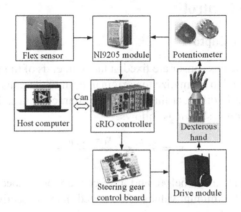

Fig. 3. Control system of the experimental prototype

2.3   Electrical Control System

The hardware structure of the system is shown in Fig. 3. The finger bending signal is measured by the flex-4.5 sensor and input to the NI-9205 module. The joint angle feedback signal is measured by the potentiometer and then input to the NI-9205 module. The motion control signal is output by the RS485 communication to the motor control board. The resistance of the flex sensor changes from 60 kΩ to 110 kΩ, and the frequency of real-time feedback and data monitoring is set to 1 kHz.

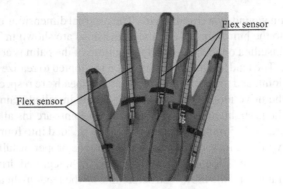

Fig. 4. Gesture capture system

3   Master-Slave Control

3.1   Gesture Feature Capture

As shown in Fig. 4, the flex sensor are fixed at the both ends of fingers, respectively. The linear function was used to normalize the original input to the range of [0, 90] deg and to compare the variation in different finger bending characteristics. The specific equation used for the conversion is shown as follows:

$$y_i = 90° \times \frac{x_i - x_{min}}{x_{max} - x_{min}} \tag{1}$$

where x_i and y_i are the values before and after conversion, respectively; x_{min} and x_{max} are the maximum and minimum values of collected data, respectively; and i = 1,2,···,5 each correspond to five fingers.

3.2   Master-Slave Mapping Algorithm

A single finger of the human hand only produces one signal, but the control of the mechanical finger requires three joint angle signals. As shown in Fig. 5, master-slave mapping must be introduced to solve the joint angle.

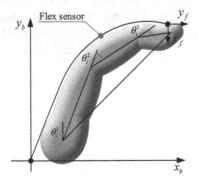

Fig. 5. Principle of master-slave mapping

Here, the bending angle of j joint of a finger i is obtained from the proportion coefficient as follows:

$$\theta_i^j = k_i^j \times y_i \qquad (2)$$

where θ_i^j is the motion angle of joint j of finger i and k_i^j is the proportional coefficient that converts the normalized value into the joint bending angle; $i = 1,2,\cdots,5$ is the finger label, and $j = 1,2$ or 3 is the joint label corresponding to the proximal, middle and distal knuckles, respectively. When the finger moves, the distal and middle knuckles move first, and the proximal knuckles move last. Notably, y_i' is defined as the critical value to ensure that the mechanical hand moves with the same regularity. When y_i has different ranges, different values of k_i^j are selected.

$$\begin{cases} k_i^j = \bar{k}_i^j, \; y_i \leq y_i' \\ k_i^j = \vec{k}_i^j, \; y_i > y_i' \end{cases} \qquad (3)$$

By selecting the transformation coefficient k_i^j of each finger joint based on the experiments, the angle matrix of the mechanical hand joint is obtained, as shown in the following formula:

$$k_i^j = \begin{bmatrix} \bar{k}_1^1 & \bar{k}_1^2 & \bar{k}_1^3 & \bar{k}_1^1 & \bar{k}_1^2 & \bar{k}_1^3 \\ k_2^1 & k_2^2 & k_2^3 & k_1^1 & k_1^2 & k_1^3 \\ \bar{k}_3^1 & \bar{k}_3^2 & \bar{k}_3^3 & \bar{k}_1^1 & \bar{k}_1^2 & \bar{k}_1^3 \\ \bar{k}_4^1 & \bar{k}_4^2 & \bar{k}_4^3 & \bar{k}_1^1 & \bar{k}_1^2 & \bar{k}_1^3 \\ \bar{k}_5^1 & \bar{k}_5^2 & \bar{k}_5^3 & \bar{k}_1^1 & \bar{k}_1^2 & \bar{k}_1^3 \end{bmatrix} \qquad (4)$$

$$\theta_i^j = \begin{bmatrix} \theta_1^1 & \theta_1^2 & \theta_1^3 \\ \theta_2^1 & \theta_2^2 & \theta_2^3 \\ \theta_3^1 & \theta_3^2 & \theta_3^3 \\ \theta_4^1 & \theta_4^2 & \theta_4^3 \\ \theta_5^1 & \theta_5^2 & \theta_5^3 \end{bmatrix} \qquad (5)$$

where $k_1^2 = 0$ is the virtual thumb middle knuckle of the dexterous hand.

The difference in size between human hand and mechanical hand will cause movement error of the robotic hand, resulting in difficulty in obtaining the map. To solve the problem of master and slave hand size inconsistency, the proportional relation of master and slave finger length is introduced:

$$\hat{\theta}_i^j = m_i \times \theta_i^j \qquad (6)$$

where m_i is the size proportional coefficient.

4 Verification Experiments

4.1 Gesture Experiments

Experiments designed to assess the motions of the side swing joint, the proximal finger joint, the middle finger joint and the distal finger joint were conducted by directly controlling the steering gear to assess the performance of the tendon-sheath-driven robotic hand. Meanwhile, an important flexibility index for a robotic hand is to produce all types of gestures. Figure 6 shows the common number gestures from one to ten in China. The five fingers are fully used for each gesture. For example, the number "ten" makes full use of the bending ability of each finger, and the degree of freedom of finger swing is needed for the number "five". The mechanical hand adequately forms all types of gestures, indicating that the dexterous hand displays good movement flexibility.

Table 2. Parameters of gesture recognition

Finger	$x_{max}(v)$	$x_{min}(v)$	m_i
Thumb	3.89	1.23	1.52
Index	4.83	1.19	1.54
Middle	4.77	1.17	1.49
Ring	4.62	1.20	1.50
Little	4.45	1.18	1.45

The original control signal is from the voltage values of the bending sensor. Depending on the size of the human hand and the robotic hand, the coefficient mi is calibrated. As shown in Table 2, after many experiments, the parameters of gesture recognition are calibrated using average value. The experiment of grasping candy, a 0.5 kg weight, marker pen and pliers with the mechanical hand is shown in Fig. 10.

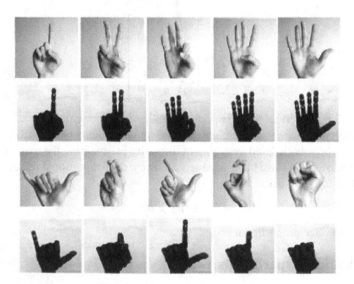

Fig. 6. Chinese number gestures

The joints of the robotic fingers are controlled by the master-slave mapping algorithm. After many experiments, the parameters of the master-slave mapping are calibrated using

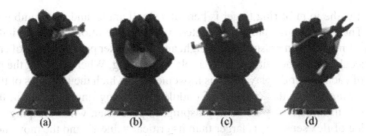

Fig. 7. Experiments assessing grasp control

Eq. (4) and (5). The curves of the grasping experiments are shown in Fig. 8. Figure 8(a) presents the curves of the five flex sensors after conversion using Eq. (3). Figure 8(b) shows the angle curves of the proximal thumb joint and the distal thumb joint. Figure 8(c) depicts the angle curves of the proximal, middle and distal joints of the index finger. Figure 8(d) shows the angle curves of the proximal, middle and distal joints of the middle finger. Figure 8(e) presents the angle curves of the proximal, middle and distal joints of the ring finger. Figure 8(f) shows the angle curves of the proximal, middle and distal joints of the little finger.

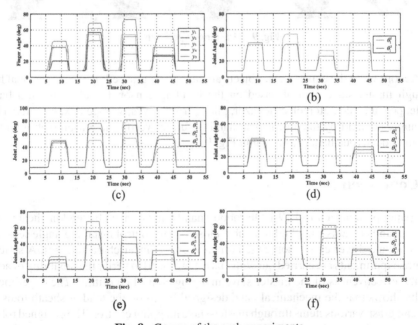

Fig. 8. Curves of the grab experiments

In Fig. 7, the candy is grabbed between 5 s and 15 s, the 0.5 kg weight is grabbed between 15 s and 25 s, the marker pen is grabbed between 25 s and 35 s, and the pliers are grabbed between 35 s and 50 s. As shown in the curves, when the mechanical hand is grasping the candy, the joints of thumb, index finger and middle finger are bent substantially, the joint of ring finger is bent at a small angle, and the thumb is basically not bent. The grasping is mainly completed by the cooperation of thumb, index finger and middle finger. When grasping the weight and the marker pen, the joints of each finger move noticeably, and each finger plays a role in grasping. When grasping the pliers, the knuckles of each finger display obvious movement, in which the knuckles of thumb and index finger are larger; the knuckles of middle finger, ring finger and small thumb are smaller; and all fingers play a role in grasping. In particular, when grasping candy, the output value of flex sensor y_i is larger than its critical value y_i', and the movement of the thumb, index finger and middle finger is more obvious than the other fingers.

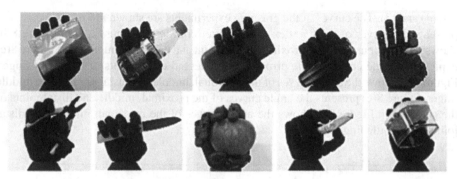

Fig. 9. Grasping experiments

According to the experiment, objects are able to be grasped by the mechanical hand through master-slave control based on the bending sensor. Facial tissue in a bag, a bottle, peanut, calculator, electric razor, pliers, fruit knives, storage box, biscuits in bag, and apple are held by the mechanical hand to further verify the grasping ability of the designed dexterous hand, as shown in Fig. 9.

5   Conclusion

This paper presents a novel 19-DOF robotic hand that is driven by tendon-sheath transmission, and presents a method of double closed-loop control installing angle sensors at joint end and driver end to solve the influence of nonlinear characteristics. A series of gesture experiments are carried out with this robotic hand to verify the flexibility of action and the effectiveness of the master-slave mapping control algorithm. The experimental results shows that the mechanical hand designed based on the tendon-sheath transmission can grasp various items through master-slave mapping control. The designed robotic hand is promising to be used in service robots and industrial application scenarios that have high requirements for the flexibility of mechanical hand.

Considering the complexity of practical application, the next step is to optimize the structure and control algorithm on the basis of the existing work. Furthermore, the high precision position control of the hand joint, the strategy to obtain the mapping proportion value and the grasp based on force will be necessary to be studied in more detail.

Acknowledgements. This work was supported in part by the R&D projects in key areas of Guangdong Province through Grant 2020B090925002, in part by the Guangdong Basic and Applied Basic Research Foundation under Grant 2021A1515011699, in part by Postdoctoral Science Foundation of China under Grant 2021M703389, in part by the Guangdong Regional Joint Fund- Youth Fund Project of China under Grant 2021A1515110486, in part by the Shenzhen Excellent Science and Innovation Talents Training Doctoral Startup Project under Grant 202107063000284, in part by National Natural Science Foundation of China under Grant 62022087, in part by the Defense Industrial Technology Development Program of China under Grant JCKY2020206B008, in part by the High-level Innovation and Entrepreneurship Talent Introduction Plan of Jiangsu Province under Grant JSSCBS20211456.

References

1. Ramírez Rebollo, D.R., Ponce, P., Molina, A.: From 3 fingers to 5 fingers dexterous hands. Adv. Robot. **31**(19–20), 1051–1070 (2017)
2. Dutta, N., Saha, J., Sarker, F., et al.: A novel design of a multi-DOF mobile robotic helping hand for paralyzed patients. In: Proceedings of the 7th International Conference on Computing, Communications and Informatics (ICACCI), Bangalore, India, SEP, pp. 19–22 (2018)
3. Wu, X., Cao, W., Yu, H., Zhang, Z., Leng, Y., Zhang, M.: Generating electricity during locomotion modes dominated by negative work with a knee energy harvesting exoskeleton. IEEE-ASME Trans. Mechatron. (2022). https://doi.org/10.1109/TMECH.2022.3157848,earlyaccess
4. Jamshidi, J.S.: Developments in dextrous hands for advanced robotic applications. In: 10th International Symposium on Robotics and Applications held at the 6th Biannual World Automation Congress, Seville, Spain, pp. 123–128, June 2004
5. Cao, W., Chen, C., Hu, H., Fang, K., Wu, X.: Effect of hip assistance modes on metabolic cost of walking with a soft exoskeleton. IEEE Trans. Autom. Sci. Eng. **18**(2), 426–436 (2021)
6. Lee, J.H., Chung, Y.S., Rodrigue, H.: Long shape memory alloy tendon-based soft robotic actuators and implementation as a soft gripper. Sci. Rep. **9**, 11251 (2019). https://doi.org/10.1038/s41598-019-47794-1
7. Hu, W., Lum, G.Z., Mastrangeli, M., Sitti, M.: Small-scale soft-bodied robot with multimodal locomotion. Nature **554**, 81 (2018)
8. Chen, Z.P., Lii, N.Y., Wimbock, T., et al.: Experimental evaluation of Cartesian and joint impedance control with adaptive friction compensation for the dexterous robot hand DLR/HIT II. Int. J. Humanoid. Rob. **8**(4), 649–671 (2011)
9. Chen, Z., Lii, N., Wimboeck, Y.T., et al.: Experimental analysis on spatial and cartesian impedance control for the dexterous DLR/HIT II hand. Int. J. Robot. Autom. **29**(1), 1–13 (2014)
10. Lenzi, T., Lipsey, J., Sensinger, J.: The RIC arm - a small, anthropomorphic transhumeral prosthesis. IEEE/ASME Trans. Mechatron. 2660–2671 (2016)
11. Bridgwater, L.B., Ihrke, C.A., Diftler, M.A., et al.: The robonant 2 hand-designed to do work with tools. In: IEEE International Conference on Robotics and Automation (ICRA), St. Paul, MN, pp. 14–18, May 2012
12. Lotti, F., Tiezzi, P., Vassura, G.: UBH3: investigating alternative design concepts for robotic hands. In: Automation Congress IEEE (2004)
13. Chaigneau, D., Arsicault, M., Gazeau, J.P., et al.: LMS robotic hand grasp and manipulation planning (an isomorphic exoskeleton approach). Robotica **26**(2), 177–188 (2008)

14. Deng, L., Shen, Y., Fan, G., et al.: Design of a soft gripper with improved microfluidic tactile sensors for classification of deformable objects. IEEE Robot. Autom. Lett. 7(2), 5607–5614 (2022)
15. Palli, G., Melchiorri, C.: Friction compensation techniques for tendon-driven robotic hands. Mechatronics 24(2), 108–117 (2014)
16. Palli, G., Borghesan, G., Melchiorri, C.: Modeling, identification, and control of tendon-based actuation systems. IEEE Trans. Robot. 28(2), 277–289 (2012)

Design of a Cable-Driven Interactive Rehabilitation Device with 3D Trajectory Tracking and Force Feedback

Han Xu[1], Yibin Li[1], Dong Xu[1], Xiaolong Li[1], Jianming Fu[2], and Xu Zhang[1($\boxtimes$)]

[1] Auckland Tongji Rehabilitaion Medical Equipment Research Center, Tongji Zhejiang College,
Jiaxing 314051, China
zhangx12@tjzj.edu.cn

[2] Rehabilitation Medical Centre, The Second Affiliated Hospital of Jiaxing University,
Jiaxing 314099, China

Abstract. The design of a cable-driven interactive rehabilitation device with 3D trajectory tracking and force feedback is presented in this paper. This device is designed for the upper limb active training, including muscle strengthening and full range of 3D space motion training. Unlike the traditional end-effector robot, this device only offers tensile force to the user by grasping the handle, which attached to the end of the cable. The force value, force direction and handle position are real-time monitored by three force sensors and an encoder. This enables more interesting interactive training between the user and the device. The mechanical design and control system design are presented in detail. The motion space of the device and the human model are analyzed. The PID force controller was designed to keep the tensile force accurately tracking given trajectories. Experiment with different PID parameters was carried out and the results show that the designed PID controller has relatively optimal control performance, with sine and square wave tracking errors are respectively -0.018 ± 0.56 N and -0.11 ± 3.45 N. The proposed device is potentially to provide physical fitness training, in addition to the routine training therapy in daily life.

Keywords: Cable-driven · Rehabilitation device · Trajectory tracking · Force feedback · PID control

1 Introduction

Muscle weakness and motor dysfunction are common sequelae of neurological diseases or limb injuries. Rehabilitation training can timely and effectively help patients recover their motion ability. However, traditional approach of rehabilitation training is very labor intensive and lack of consistency and objective assessment. Rehabilitation robot plays a very important role in assisting patients in rehabilitation training because of its accurate quantitative training process and accurate data feedback.

Many kinds of limb assist rehabilitation robotics have been developed to offer intensive, repetitive and quantifiable training [4]. Typical end-effector rehabilitation system

© The Author(s), under exclusive license to Springer Nature Switzerland AG 2022
H. Liu et al. (Eds.): ICIRA 2022, LNAI 13455, pp. 759–768, 2022.
https://doi.org/10.1007/978-3-031-13844-7_70

such as MIT's upper limb robot system (MIT-MANUS) [2], the Rehabilitation Robot (REHAROB) therapeutic system [5], and NEURARM system [6], are used for shoulder and elbow rehabilitation training. however, the terminal-guidance design has very limited range of motion and range of freedom. The exoskeleton rehabilitation system such as ARMin [3], CABexo [9], and NEUROExos [7], wearable lower limb exoskeleton from SUSTech [10], have implemented larger range of motion in 3D space during the rehabilitation training progress, and safety and comfort in the adaptive motion process through the rehabilitation robot multi-DOF design and kinematics modeling, however, the operation and wearing of exoskeleton robots are complex, which is not conducive to improving the rehabilitation efficiency. Some cable-driven robotic system are developed because of its wide motion range motion and easy to use. Fang et al. [1] developed an active cable-driven robotic system to evaluate force control strategies for walking rehabilitation using frequency-domain analysis. Zou et al. [11] developed an astronaut rehabilitative training robot (ART) with bilateral three DOF resistance force control capacities to strengthen the upper limbs of astronauts.

Most of the presented rehabilitation systems are bulky, heavy, complex or expensive so that they are only suitable used in hospital. Therefore, the research on the upper limb rehabilitation robot suitable for household use is very important as home rehabilitation is a long term work and daily necessary tasks for most patients. this paper presents a cable-driven interactive rehabilitation device with 3D trajectory tracking and force feedback, to provide patients with audio-visual feedback from the games, 3D motion with force feedback from the device. We embedded three force sensors and an encoder to measure the tensile force and its components and the length of the cable, with which can be used to derive the relative position of the handle to the device. The force can be used in the muscle resistance training of the limbs both for rehabilitation or fitness training.

The remainder of the paper is organized as follows. Section II presents the system design from aspects of mechanism, motion space analysis, control system and game. Section III describes the force controller design and the validation experiments, and the results was analyzed. Next, the conclusion is given and the potential further work is discussed.

2 System Design and Analysis

2.1 Mechanical Design

The structure of the device was presented in Fig. 1. (A) and (B) are the front and top view of the prototype, (C) is the top view of virtual 3D model. The servo motor, gear box, reel drum and the encoder are coaxial. Gear box deduction ratio is 15, and its output shaft is fixed on the reel drum, an encoder is also fixed on the drum for angle measurement. The diameter and length of the reel drum are 50 mm and 51 mm, a cable is coiled around the drum, which valid length and diameter are 4000 mm and 2 mm. Tension force generation component is installed slidingly on the main frame through a linear guideway, and a tension force sensor is installed between the main frame and the tension force generation component. In order to measure the tension force directly, the cable between the main frame and the tension force generation component is parallel to the detection axis of the tension sensor by the fixed guide frame and the guide frame.

The moving guide frame is designed to keep the cable outlet direction vertical to the drum axis. The moving guide frame moves synchronously with the reel drum through a timing belt and a screw rod. On the front panel of the device, another two force sensors are vertical to each other which are used to measure the force component projected onto the plane.

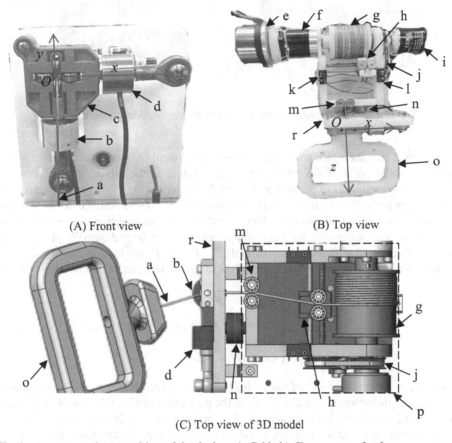

(A) Front view   (B) Top view

(C) Top view of 3D model

Fig. 1. Structure and composition of the device. a). Cable b). Force sensor for force component on y axis measuring c). Guide frame d). Force sensor for force component on x axis measuring e). Servo motor f). Gear box g). Reel drum h). Moving guide frame i). Encoder j). Timing Belts k). End limit switch l). Initial limit switch m). Fixed guide frame n). Tension force sensor o). Handle p). Tension force generation component r). Main frame

Figure 2 (A) shows a scenario of a patient doing 3D Interactive training with the device. There is a sucker under the bottom of the device so that the device can be placed on any solid, smooth and flat plane. The user can do the active resistance training with playing game running on the remote display system.

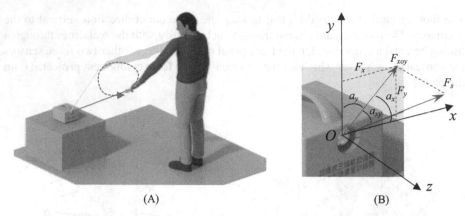

Fig. 2. (A). 3D Interactive training with the device. (B). The coordinate system

In Fig. 2 (B), the space rectangular coordinate system $O - xyz$ is established which takes the outlet point of the cable on the guide frame as the origin. The x axis and y axis of the coordinates is parallel to F_x and F_y shown in Fig. 1 (A) respectively, and the z axis is parallel to F_z in Fig. 2 (B). The tension force of the cable can be measured with the cable pulling out from the device, and if the outlet direction of the cable is not perpendicular to xOy plane, the force component being projected onto the plane can be measured directly by force sensor b) and d). F_x, F_y and F_z are the force components of the tension force. Thus, the relationship of these parameters can be described as follows:

$$\begin{cases} F_{xoy} = \sqrt{F_x^2 + F_y^2} \\ \cos(a_x) = F_x / F_{xoy} \\ \cos(a_y) = F_y / F_{xoy} \\ \cos(a_{xy}) = F_{xoy} / F_s \end{cases} \tag{1}$$

where F_s is the tension force of the cable, F_{xoy} is the projection of F_s on the xOy plane, a_{xy} is the angle between F_s and F_{xoy}, F_x is the projection of F_s on the x axis, a_x is angle between F_s and F_x, F_y is the projection of F_s on the y axis, a_y is angle between F_s and F_y. However, to avoid interference between the cable and the structure, the a_x and a_y should both smaller than 60 degrees.

The real position of the handle can be derived as:

$$P_h = \begin{bmatrix} x \\ y \\ z \end{bmatrix} = L \begin{bmatrix} \cos(a_{xy}) \cdot \cos(a_x) \\ \cos(a_{xy}) \cdot \cos(a_y) \\ \sin(a_{xy}) \end{bmatrix} = L \begin{bmatrix} F_x/F_s \\ F_y/F_s \\ \sqrt{F_s^2 - F_x^2 - F_y^2}/F_s \end{bmatrix} \tag{2}$$

where P_h is the position of the handle, L is the distance between handle and the device measured by the encoder and $L \in [0, 4000]$ mm.

2.2 Motion Space Analysis

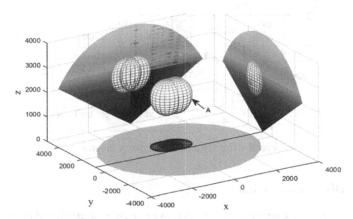

Fig. 3. Motion space of the device and human upper limbs

The device is designed for active resistance training in large range of 3D space. Thus the 3D motion space of the device should bigger than the upper limb motion range of the user. The circle and sectors on each plane in Fig. 3 are projections of the motion space of the device, and the dual sphere shape (A in Fig. 3) is the maximum motion range of the bilateral upper limb. The projections of the dual sphere shape are all inside the motion space of the device, which means the device allows the upper limb training with full motion space. The human model is referenced from national standard GB10000-88 (human dimensions of Chinese adults) with the 99th percentiles and the 18–60 years age group. The device is placed at the height of 800 mm, and the human model is 2000 mm far away from the device, to simulate the situation in Fig. 2 (A).

2.3 Control System Design

The system control block diagram is presented in Fig. 4. The system consists of a Personal Computer (PC) for game application running, a NI myRIO controller for real time control and signal acquisition, a servo driver, a motor, a cable-driven unit, an encoder, a tension force sensor and two force sensors. The PC runs a game application to offer visual and auditory feedback meanwhile, record the experimental data through the wireless transmission with myRIO. The basic principle of the system works as follows. First, the game application generates the target force value according to the game task, the PC sends the data through WIFI to the myRIO, myRIO generates the input signal of the servo driver based on the target force. Then the motor is driven by the driver causing a change of the cable tension of the cable-driven unit. Then the three force parameters and the output length of the cable are sent to the input interface of the myRIO through the force sensors and encoder. All the date are recorded by the game application automatically.

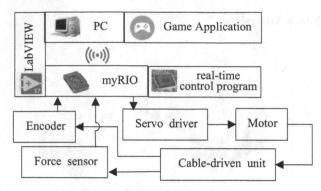

Fig. 4. The system control block diagram

2.4 Interactive Game Design

Task-oriented repetitive movements can improve muscular strength and movement coordination in patients with impairments due to neurological problems [8]. Thus, the game CROSSY MAZE (Fig. 5) was developed to guide the user to complete the task as preassigned. In this game, the user is required to control the red block going across the Start Point, Via Point and End Point in sequence, at each point, the user should change the size of the block to match the size of the point for successful judgment. The control law of the red block is defined as follows. The x and y coordinates of the handle in real world control the x and y coordinates of the red block in the game, the output length of the cable control the size of the red block, the longer the length, the bigger the red block.

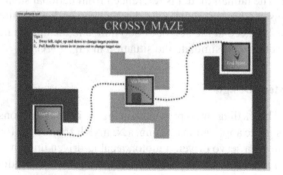

Fig. 5. A game for interactive training

3 Force Controller Design and Validation

3.1 Force Controller Design

The main goal of this device is to provide controllable and precise force feedback through the cable and the handle to the user. This is important for the patient in different recover stage as the muscle strength training requires proper resistance level varies from person to person. The controller should be able to track the target force well so when in training, the force feedback could change rapidly depending on the needs of the tasks to achieve a better human-machine interactive experience, and to offer comfortable and safe training process.

To realize the force tracking, a PID controller was implemented in the myRIO controller. The discrete PID control algorithm is described by:

$$u(k) = K_P \cdot e(k) + K_I \cdot \sum_{i=0} e(i) + K_D[e(k) - e(k-1)] \tag{3}$$

where u(k) is the control output at the kth sampling time. e(k) and e(k − 1) are the deviation at the kth and k − 1th sampling time. K_P is the proportional gain. $K_I = K_P * T/Ti$ is the integral coefficient, and $K_D = K_P * Td/T$ is the derivative coefficient. T = 0.02 s is the control cycle.

The control structure of the rehabilitation device is depicted by Fig. 6. The one and only control variable is the tension force in cable. When in training, the length of the cable or position of the handle are unlimited and uncontrolled as this determined by the tasks in the game.

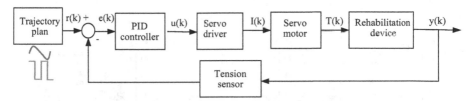

Fig. 6. The control structure of rehabilitation device with trajectory plan

3.2 Experiment Setup

Figure 1 (A) and (B) show the experimental prototype. The servo motor is maxon EC 60 flat, with standard voltage is 24VDC. The servo driver is maxon ESCON. The servo driver is set to current mode with an analog input of 0–10 V, and the corresponding current output is −5–5 Amps (negative current generate pull torque and positive current generate release torque). The tension force sensor is ZNLBM-20 kg with ±5 V analog output for pull or push force detection. The cable is gummed wire rope with a diameter of 2 mm. The experiment process follows below. First, the device is placed and fixed on a table with a height of 80 cm from floor. Second, a tester sit in front of the device with a distance of 200 cm. Third, activate the device and pull the handle out and the tester hold the handle still and steady. Next, input the force trajectory plan and record the data.

3.3 Experiment and Results

PID control is a model-independent method, the most important work for PID control is to find out the optimal parameters. The K_P is initially set to 0.25, as the maximum current is 5 Amps, and an error of 20 N is considered the saturation boundary of the controller output. By trial and error, the parameters of the PID controller was tuned to be: $K_P = 0.4$, $K_I = 0.004$, $K_D = 0.0001$, which is shown as Group 4 in Table 1, the rest combinations are listed as well. The controller output is limited to 1–6 V, as a larger release torque is no need and may cause stall when the cable is pulled out with a higher speed.

Table 1. PID parameters group.

Group	P	I	D
1	0.2	0.004	0.0001
2	0.4	0	0.0001
3	0.4	0.004	0
4	**0.4**	**0.004**	**0.0001**
5	0.4	0.004	0.0003
6	0.4	0.010	0.0001
7	0.6	0.004	0.0001

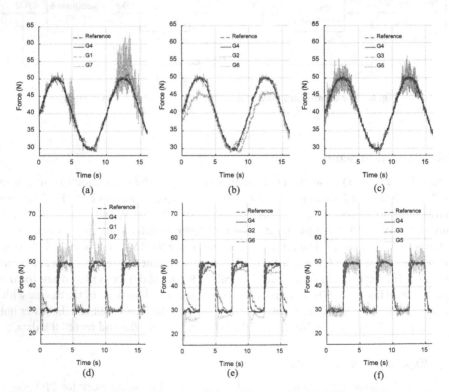

Fig. 7. The sine and square wave trajectories tracking results with different PID parameters

The experiment tested two force trajectories to validate the performance of the controller. One is sine wave wave trajectory with an amplitude of 10 N, an offset of 40 N and a period of 10 s. Another is square wave trajectory with an amplitude of 20 N, an offset of 30 N and a period of 5 s. Each group of PID parameters was tested and the results are shown in Fig. 7.

Figure 7 (a) and (d) are with different K_P, (b) and (e) are with different K_I, (c) and (f) are with different K_D. The results show that the selected PID parameter (Group 4) has the relatively superior performance. The rest have some problems such as overshoot, oscillation and large error. The tracking error of the sine wave is -0.018 ± 0.56 N, the tracking error of the square wave is -0.11 ± 3.45 N. The results show that the controller can track the given trajectory well on the whole. However, the static error of the square wave trajectory is not steady, and the dynamic trajectory error of the sine wave trajectory can not be neglected especially when falling down start from the the peak. The possible reason for above are that the friction in the system can not be ignored and the tester can not keep the handle still as ideal especially when the force change rate is relatively great.

4 Conclusion

In this paper, we proposed an interactive rehabilitation device with 3D trajectory tracking and force feedback based on cable driven. This device offers controllable force feedback to the user when in resistance training. Moreover, this device can detect the space motion trajectory of the handle by using additional two force sensors and an encoder. And this device is based on cable-driven and the whole mechanical design is compact and tiny. This meets the lightweight, miniaturized, economical requirements for daily home rehabilitation training. At last, a force controller based on PID is designed and test in experiments and the results show that the controller can track the given trajectories well on the whole.

Further work may concentrate on the force control under dynamic high speed motion as the present research mainly focus on the still and low speed condition. Dynamic high speed motion is more useful when the patient' myodynamia recover close to normal, as well as when the device is used for physical fitness training. Another work is to develop suitable interactive game to improve the training effectiveness, playability and attractiveness.

Acknowledgements. This work was supported in part by the Science and Technology Plan Project of Jiaxing under Grant 2021AY10077, Grant 2019AY32022 and 2021AY10075, in part by the Foundational Commonweal Research Plan Project of Zhejiang Province under Grant LGF22H180035.

References

1. Fang, J., Haldimann, M., Marchal-Crespo, L., Hunt, K.J.: Development of an active cable-driven, force-controlled robotic system for walking rehabilitation. Front. Neurorobot. **15**, 651177 (2021)

2. Hogan, N., Krebs, H.I., Charnnarong, J., Srikrishna, P., Sharon, A.: MIT-MANUS: a workstation for manual therapy and training. In: I. [1992] Proceedings IEEE International Workshop on Robot and Human Communication, pp. 161–165. IEEE (1992)

3. Nef, T., Riener, R.: ARMin-design of a novel arm rehabilitation robot. In: 9th International Conference on Rehabilitation Robotics. ICORR 2005, pp. 57–60. IEEE, Chicago (2005)

4. Sanjuan, J.D., et al.: Cable driven exoskeleton for upper-limb rehabilitation: a design review. Robot. Auton. Syst. **126**, 103445 (2020)

5. Toth, A., Fazekas, G., Arz, G., Jurak, M., Horvath, M.: Passive robotic movement therapy of the spastic hemiparetic arm with REHAROB: report of the first clinical test and the follow-up system improvement. In: 9th International Conference on Rehabilitation Robotics. ICORR 2005, pp. 127–130. IEEE, Chicago (2005)

6. Vitiello, N., et al.: Characterization of the NEURARM bio-inspired joint position and stiffness open loop controller. In: 2008 2nd IEEE RAS & EMBS International Conference on Biomedical Robotics and Biomechatronics, pp. 138–143. IEEE, Scottsdale (2008)

7. Vitiello, N., et al.: NEUROExos: a powered elbow exoskeleton for physical rehabilitation. IEEE Trans. Rob. **29**(1), 220–235 (2012)

8. Wu, J., Huang, J., Wang, Y., Xing, K.: A wearable rehabilitation robotic hand driven by PM-TS actuators. In: International Conference on Intelligent Robotics and Applications, Shanghai, vol. 6425, pp. 440–450 (2010)

9. Xiao, F., Gao, Y., Wang, Y., Zhu, Y., Zhao, J.: Design of a wearable cable-driven upper limb exoskeleton based on epicyclic gear trains structure. Technol. Health Care **25**(S1), 3–11 (2017)

10. Zhong, B., Guo, K., Yu, H., Zhang, M.: Toward gait symmetry enhancement via a cable-driven exoskeleton powered by series elastic actuators. IEEE Robot. Autom. Lett. **7**(2), 786–793 (2021)

11. Zou, Y., Zhang, L., Qin, T., Liang, Y.: Force control for an astronaut rehabilitative training robot in bench press mode. In: 2013 ICME International Conference on Complex Medical Engineering, pp. 296–301. IEEE, Beijing (2013)

An EEG-EMG-Based Motor Intention Recognition for Walking Assistive Exoskeletons

Guangkui Song[1], Rui Huang[1]([⊠]), Yongzhi Guo[1], Jing Qiu[2], and Hong Cheng[1]

[1] Center for Robotics, University of Electronic Science and Technology of China, Chengdu, China
ruihuang@uestc.edu.cn

[2] School of Mechanical and Electrical Engineering, University of Electronic Science and Technology of China, Chengdu, China

Abstract. Lower Limb Exoskeleton (LLE) has received considerable interests in strength augmentation, rehabilitation and walking assistance scenarios. For walking assistance, the LLE is expected to have the capability of recognizing the motor intention accurately. However, the methods for recognizing motor intention base on ElectroEncephaloGraphy (EEG) can not be directly used for recognizing the motor intention of human lower limbs, because it is difficult to distinguish left and right limbs. This paper proposes a human-exoskeleton interaction method based on EEG and ElectroMyoGrams (EMG)-Hierarchical Recognition for Motor Intention (HRMI). In which, the motor intention can be recognized by the EEG signal, and supplemented by EMG signals reflecting motor intention, the exoskeleton can distinguish the left and right limbs. An experimental platform is established to explore the performance of the proposed method in real life scenario. Ten healthy participants were recruited to perform a series of motions such standing, sitting, walking, and going up and down stairs. The results shown that the proposed method is successfully applied in real life scenarios and the recognition accuracy of standing and sitting than others.

Keywords: Exoskeleton · Human-machine interaction · Motor intention · EEG · EMG

1 Introduction

Lower Limb Exoskeleton (LLE) is a wearable robot system which integrate human intelligence and robot power. With development of wearable technologies, exoskeletons are widely applied in various field. Especially, the exoskeleton for

This work was supported by the National Key Research and Development Program of China (No. 2018AAA0102504), the National Natural Science Foundation of China (NSFC) (No. 62003073, 62103084), and the Sichuan Science and Technology Program (No. 2021YFG0184, No. 2020YFSY0012, No. 2018GZDZX0037).

H. Liu et al. (Eds.): ICIRA 2022, LNAI 13455, pp. 769–781, 2022.
https://doi.org/10.1007/978-3-031-13844-7_71

walking assistance has evolved from the stuff of laboratory to quasi-commercial product, it has drawn considerable interests from researchers [3]. As lower limb exoskeletons are tightly coupled with human being during the assisted walking, they need to predict the motor intention accurately. However, traditional exoskeletons mainly use the push of a button to tell the exoskeleton motor intention of the pilot, which does not satisfy the requirements of naturally initiating normal motor actions [13]. Therefore, the methods base on Brain-Computer Interface (BCI) have become one of the most potential interaction method of exoskeleton.

Recent research has shown the efficiency of exoskeleton combined with BCI in physical and neurological rehabilitation for Spinal Cord Injury (SCI) patients [11]. Thus motor intentions can be recognized through the classification of motor imagery, and EEG-based BCI make it more applicable to the control of exoskeletons. Among them, one of commonly used methods is to use eigenvalue as the object of classification [12]. In which, the obtained signals was band-pass filtered and normalized firstly. Then local Fisher Discriminant Analysis (FDA) was used to reduce the dimension of the feature matrix. Finally, a mixture of Gaussian models was used for classification according to motor intention. In the experiments, the subject wearing exoskeleton follow instructions to perform corresponding motions, during which the signals of EEG are recorded.

From the above analysis, it can be seen that the EEG-based method has achieved high-precision motor intention recognition. However, for differentiating which limb is used to stride, the EMG-based method is more effective [1,15,16]. In [5], a 3-layer BP neural network is used to process the RMS of surface EMG signals from biceps and triceps to predict the angle of elbow joint [5,9]. [4,8] developed a subject-specific EMG pattern classification method, which can robustly distinguish between the pattern of muscle tremors and expected manual tasks for stroke patients (e.g. hand opening, grasping). [6,17] recorded the high-density surface EMG signals of 12 stroke patients performing 20 different actions, and identified the expected tasks of each stroke subject through a series of pattern recognition algorithms.

To sum up, the EEG-based method can accurately recognize the motor intention, and the EMG-based method can not only distinguish which limb is performing the stepping action, but also the angle of the human joint. However, for real life scenarios of exoskeleton, it is not only necessary to accurately recognize the motor intention, but also to accurately distinguish the left and right limbs. This paper proposes a new interaction method to deal with the above defects, make it can be used for control of exoskeleton in real life scenario. In which, we design an algorithm-Hierarchical Recognition for Motor Intention (HRMI) to recognize motor intentions of the pilot, and supplemented by EMG signals reflecting motor intention, the exoskeleton can differentiate the motion of the left and right limbs. The combination of the EEG-based and EMG-based method makes the method base on biological signals successfully applied to the control of exoskeleton in real life scenario. An experimental platform is established to explore the performance of the proposed method in real life scenario. The paper is organized as follows: Sect. 2 introduces the proposed HRMI method for applied the method in the control of exoskeleton. In Sect. 3, experimental results on the AIDER lower limb exoskeleton system are presented and discussed. This paper ends with conclusions and future work in Sect. 4.

2   Method

The current paper proposes a Hierarchical Recognition for Motor Intention (HRMI) method using EEG and EMG for a wearable exoskeleton system. As shown in Fig. 1, HRMI mainly has two layers: EEG-based Motor Intention Recognition (EEG-MIR) and EMG-based Left and Right Differentiator (EMG-LRD). In which, EEG-MIR utilize the high precision for classifying motor intention of pilots, and with the support of EMG signals, the exoskeleton can differentiate the motion of the left and right limbs. Before using EEG signals for motor intention recognition by the EEG-MIR, EEG signal was preprocessed by median filtering, band-pass filtering and signal spatial projection. After inputting the preprocessed EEG signal into the EEG-MIR, six motor intentions can be obtained. And the EEG-MIR divide motor intentions into three categories with a two-class classifier strategy. The left and right legs' motion can be differentiated by the EMG-LRD, similarly before the EMG signals is used by the EMG-LRD, The EMG signal was preprocessed by median filtering, band-pass filtering, rectification and low-pass filtering. And the EMG-LRD distinguishes left-leg and right-leg events according the input EMG signals. After the classifier recognizes left and right, the controller of exoskeleton generates corresponding control commands. In the figure, the EMG-LRD is also used for sitting-to-standing and standing-to-sitting classification. Unlike the left-leg and right-leg classifiers, the input of the sitting-to-standing and standing-to-sitting classifier only contains a single state of data output as two types of labels, i.e., sitting-to-standing and standing-to-sitting.

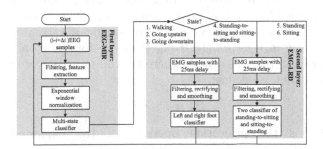

Fig. 1. The flow chart of HRMI method

2.1 Signal Preprocessing

Preprocessing in this paper includes general signal filtering and some special processing methods for EEG and EMG signals. Specifically, the preprocessing of EEG signals includes median filtering, 7–30 Hz band-pass filtering, and signal spatial projection; the preprocessing of EMG signals is median filtering, 10–45 Hz band-pass filtering, rectification, and 6 Hz low-pass filtering. In addition, due to the sensitivity of neural network model to input value range, the data are normalized before input to the neural network.

Signal Filtering. Median filtering and band-pass filtering were performed on the collected EEG and EMG data. Since meaningful EEG and EMG signals are concentrated at 7–30 Hz and 10–45 Hz respectively [7], a band-pass filter can remove most of the non-target frequency band interference. A window function method can produce a Finite Impulse Response (FIR) filter to achieve band-pass filtering. The output signal of the FIR is the convolution of the input signal with a vector of coefficients. This paper uses a sinc function and a Hamming window to design band-pass filters for EEG and EMG, respectively. The width of the filter kernel is 200 points, which means that the sampling time is 0.2 s. If running online, the time delay of the filter is 0.1 s, which can meet general real-time requirements.

EEG Signal Spatial Projection for Noise Reduction. The EEG signal of each subject in the lying position was used as the noise signal to perform Signal-Space Projection (SSP) for noise reduction on other EEG samples. SSP is a digital method to eliminate external interference, it is widely used to preprocess EEG signals, such as can be used to remove blink interference [14]. Unlike many other noise reduction methods, SSP does not require an additional reference sensor to record the interference field, as it relies on the fact that the signals generated by the human body have a sufficiently different spatial distribution than those generated by many external noise sources. SSP assumes that the linear space formed by external noise patterns has a lower dimension. Suppose our measurement is a random vector $m(t)$, consisting of a signal $m_s(t)$ and noise $m_n(t)$, i.e. $m(t) = m_s(t) + m_n(t)$. If $m_n(t)$ can be formed by a few orthogonal basis sheets, i.e. $m_n(t) = U = n(t)$, where the column space of matrix U is the noise subspace, then we define:

$$P_\perp = I - UU^T, \tag{1}$$

where $P_\perp$ is the projection operator in the requested signal, and $m_s(t) = P_\perp\, m(t)$.

Rectification and Smoothing of EMG Signals. After processing by the band-pass filter at 10–450 Hz, the EMG signal still maintains a high frequency, which is not conducive to algorithmic analysis. One of the most significant information that EMG signal can reflect is the resting or contracting state of muscle.

And this can be reflected by the signal's amplitude, which is the envelope. In our proposed method, we use rectification and low-pass filtering to obtain the envelope of EMG signals. Then we take the absolute value of the band-pass-filtered signal (which has no DC component), and apply a 6 Hz low-pass filter for smoothing.

Dimension Reduction of Motor Intention Features. The Common Spatial Pattern (CSP) is a method of supervised feature dimension reduction. It is effective in many multidimensional two-classification problems, and is widely used in BCI systems. In the processing of EEG, CSP can distinguish task-related signals (e.g., ERD, MRA) from their common background motions. Before performing the CSP transformation, the data is processed through whitening to make the energy of each EEG signal equal. Let the sample data of motor intention after whitening be Y. CSP is a linear algorithm of the form $Z = YW_2$. To obtain W_2, Y is divided into Y_A and Y_B according to different motions, the covariance matrix of most real data is invertible. We calculate

$$\frac{\Sigma_B}{\Sigma_A^{-1}} = Q\Lambda_2\,Q^T, \tag{2}$$

where $\Sigma_A = Y_A^T Y/(N_A \times T - 1)$, $\Sigma_B = Y_B^T Y/(N_B \times T - 1)$. If S is a selection matrix of k rows, the result Z of CSP can be given by $Z^T = SY_\theta^T = SQ^{-1}Y^T$, where SQ^{-1} consists of k rows corresponding to larger eigenvalues in Q^{-1}, i.e.,

$$W_2 = Q^{-1T}S^T = QS^T, \tag{3}$$

where W_2 contains the spatial pattern of EEG. Finally, after CSP transformation, we calculate the log-averaged energy of the sample in the time dimension as a feature,

$$log(E) = log\left(\frac{1}{T}\sum_{i=1}^{T} s_i^2\right), \tag{4}$$

where s is a time series and E is a scalar. After time-dimensional reduction, a sample of motor intention corresponds to a k-dimensional feature vector, where k is the number of rows in S.

2.2   EEG-MIR Classifier

The EEG-MIR Classifier of motor intention is realized by integrating multiple two-class classifiers. This method splits the original problem into multiple two-classification problems (training the multiple two-classifiers separately), and combines the classification results to realize the equivalent function of multi-classifier (i.e. it can realize the recognition of multi-intent). There are two strategies: one-to-one (OvO) and one-to-the-other (OvR). The OvO strategy consists of two-class classifiers of any two kinds of motions in the n kinds of motions, for a total of C_n^2 two-class classifiers. In the training stage, n pairs of intention samples are pairwise paired to separately train each two-class classifier. During the test, new unknown motion samples are input to each two-class classifier, and the output category is determined by C_n^2 two-class classifiers. The disadvantage of OvO is that the number of sub-classifiers is larger, so its structure is more complicated than that of OvR, and the training and running times are longer. The OvR strategy consists of n two-classifiers, each of which can separate one of the motions. The OvR requires far fewer two-classifiers than OvO. The OvR strategy has the advantage of dealing with complex states.

2.3 EMG-LRD Classifier

The motor intention can be recognized by the EEG-MIR, however the left and right limb representation areas in the human sensorimotor cortex are located not only near the margo superior cerebri but also very close to each other [10]. The motor intention can be recognized by the EEG-MIR, however the left and right limb representation areas in the human sensorimotor cortex are located not only near the margo superior cerebri but also very close to each other. So the EMG-LRD is introduced to supply reflecting motor intention by differentiating the left and right limbs. The EMG-LRD is mainly realized through a neural network structure, and we will introduce it in detail.

Structure of EMG-LRD. As Fig. 2 shown, the EMG-LRD is composed of a neural network, in which the fully connected layer completes the reduction of the spatial dimension, including multiple fully connected layers; the convolutional layer completes the reduction of the time dimension. There are multiple convolutional and pooling layers, and a fully connected layer. There are two layers of fully connected layer in the network for spatial dimension reduction, namely a single hidden layer structure. There are 8 hidden nodes, and the input layer has 32 nodes. The number of nodes in the output layer is determined by

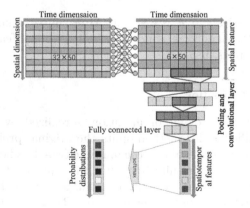

Fig. 2. Motion prediction structure of neural network-based multi-classification

the number of classified tasks. The hidden and output layer activation functions are both sigmoid functions. For time dimension reduction, there are two sets of 1-dimensional convolutional and pooling layers, which are convolution layer $c1$ of length 5, average pooling layer $p1$ of length 6, convolution layer $c2$ of length 3, average pooling layer $p2$ of length 5, and fully connected layer $d1$ with four nodes. At the end of the network is the softmax layer. The coefficients of expansion of $c1$ and $c2$ are 2 and 1, respectively. The activation functions of $c1$ and $c2$ are sigmoid functions, and $d1$ has no activation function.

The samples of EMG signals for differentiating the left and right limbs during movement can be regarded as a random variable, which includes dimensions of time and space, which differs from many classic machine learning tasks. Due to the non-equivalence of sample space and time, this differs from ordinary two-dimensional pictures. The spatial dimension of motor intention includes the two-dimensional space of x and y. Different processing strategies for the time and space dimensions of intention to classify samples can generate different network models. We generally want to do the following: (a) reduce the space (time) dimension, and then reduce the time (space) dimension; (b) flatten the input matrix into a feature vector of length "channels $\times$ time," then is direct reduced. The latter model has a larger model space and can capture the dependence of different spatial motions at different times, but it is easy to overfit. Considering the small sample size of this experiment, we adopt the strategy of first reducing the space dimension, and then the time dimension. There are different ways to reduce each dimension, corresponding to different prior preferences. These include the use of fully connected layers, loop layers, and convolutional layers. We describe our choices below.

Time-Space Reduction Strategy Spatial Dimension: The data of different electrodes at a certain time constitute a vector that reflects the spatial structure of an event. The sample of this experiment is a 38×500 matrix (including EEG and EMG), and the data at each moment form a 38-dimensional vector. Taking the 32-channel EEG as an example, 32 sensors are spatially distributed in two dimensions in an extension of the international 10–20 system. It is not a simple grid distribution like a bitmap, which makes it difficult to use a CNN network. However, the number of channels in this experiment is small, and the linear model based on CSP has proved the rationality and feasibility of the linear assumption in space (the CSP model above is a linear combination on the space reduction, and the logarithmic average without parameters in time reduction). So here it is directly assumed that the classification result is related to any linear combination of this vector, and the relationship of fully connected layer response is introduced.

Time Dimension: For a single electrode, the data at different times constitute a random vector, which is limited to a finite-dimensional vector during a certain period of time. The 38×500 sample matrix of this experiment has a length of 500 in the time dimension. If the temporal pattern is any linear combination of vectors, as is the case with coding space characteristics, the model will undoubtedly fall into serious overfitting. Considering that the characteristics of random vectors are often local, the introduction of convolutional layers is a good choice. The convolutional layer can be regarded as a restricted, fully connected layer with parameter sharing, which greatly reduces the number of parameters while retaining the encoding ability of local dependence on the input. The long-term characteristics in time rely on the pooling operation and a fully connected layer behind CNN to capture them.

To reduce the amount of calculation, the original data were down-sampled by $1/10$ before being input to the neural network. The sampling rate was reduced from the original $1000\,\text{Hz}$ to $100\,\text{Hz}$, and the sample matrix (including EEG and EMG) was reduced from 38×500 to 38×50. Because the highest frequency of the EEG signal after band-pass filtering is $30\,\text{Hz}$, the highest frequency of the rectified and smoothed EMG signal is only $6\,\text{Hz}$. According to the sampling theorem, the sampling frequency of $60\,\text{Hz}$ can guarantee to restore the original signal. Hence, reducing it to $100\,\text{Hz}$ causes no loss of information.

3   Experiments

Our experiments explored the differences in biological signals during different motions of human body in scenarios of wearing an exoskeleton. So as to facilitate recognition of different intentions in assisting exoskeleton robots for paraplegic patients. We designed a series of motions such as standing, sitting, walking, and going up and down stairs according to real-life application scenarios of lower extremity exoskeletons for collecting dynamic EEG and EMG signals of the pilot. We obtained labeled data of different motions to provide a supervised learning dataset for subsequent research on motor intention recognition. During the experiments, subjects wore an AIDER 3.2 exoskeleton [2] and completed specified motions, and the EEG and EMG signals of the human body were obtained through an eego mylab device worn by the subject. At the same time, the Perception Neuron motion-capture system was used to return the human kinematics data. The acquired data were processed by signal preprocessing, signal filtering, signal rectification and smoothing, and dimension reduction of motor intention features. The processed data were used for intention classification, as shown in Fig. 3. According to the obtained motor intention, corresponding commands were generated to control the exoskeleton to complete the specified motion. The validity of our method was verified by comparing the recognized intentions with the real intentions and the accuracy of the completed motions. This study was approved by the Ethics Committee of the Sichuan Provincial Rehabilitation Hospital. All subjects signed informed consent forms before the tests.

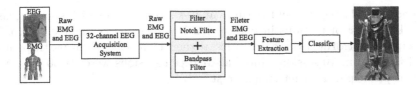

Fig. 3. Processing flow of human's biological signal.

3.1 Experiments Setup

Seven participants (all males, 20–27 years old) served as volunteers. They were all right-handed and healthy. None had prior BCI training, and all subjects signed informed consent before participating in the study. The eego mylab(Brain Product, Germany) EEG and EMG capture device was used to record the EEG and EMG signals of the participants. An international 10–20 EEG electrode system was used for placement of the electrodes on the scalp. Thirty-two EEG channels were placed at Fp1, Fp2, F7, F3, Fz, F4, F8, FT9, FC5, FC1, FC2, FC6, T7, C3, Cz, C4, T8, TP9, CP5, CP1, CP2, CP6, TP10, P7, P8, O1, O2, and IO. Meanwhile, the EMG signals from trapezius muscle, biceps femoris muscle, and middle gluteal muscle were collected. The EEG and EMG placements are illustrated as in Fig. 4. The sampling rate of the signals was 1000 Hz. Two internal filters were set during acquisition, one a 50 Hz notch filter and the other a 0.01–70 Hz bandpass filter.

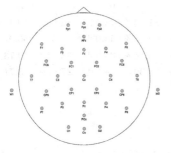

Fig. 4. Distribution of EEG acquisition cap electrodes.

Fig. 5. Process of motion intention data acquisition experiment.

The experimental platform is shown in the right of Fig. 5. It consisted of a double-sided staircase and two chairs. The stairs and chairs were placed in a straight line, and the stairs were between the chairs. The distance between each chair and the stairs was 7 m. In each session, a participant was asked to perform the motions of standing-to-sitting, sitting-to-standing, walking, standing, going upstairs, and going downstairs. Standing-to-sitting and sitting-to-standing were performed successively five times at 10-s intervals, in which standing lasted 10 s. The order of motions in one session is shown in the right of Fig. 5. The participants performed these activities at their own pace. Each participant was asked to perform 10 sessions. Intervals between sessions were 10–30 min, which enabled participants to get enough rest.

The experimental procedure was approved by the institutional ethical review board. All participants received detailed information about the experiments, and could clarify any doubts. Subjects signed a consent form before participating in the experiments.

4   Experimental Results and Discussions

4.1   Results of EEG-MIR

The EEM-MIR integrated by a two-class classifier strategy was used to complete the motor intention. The classification accuracy of each experimental object is shown in Table 1 for both the OvO and OvR strategies. The accuracy of OvR classifiers was much lower than that of OvO classifiers. There are two reasons for this. First, multiple motion modes are different, and the distribution reflects multimodal characteristics. Second, the classifiers inherent to the classifiers of the remaining strategy imbalance effects.

Table 1. Classification results of two-class classifiers

Subjects		1	2	3	4	5	6	7	Average
OvO	Training set	90.57%	80.96%	70.60%	75.98%	81.83%	73.74%	82.59%	79.47%
	Test set	68.80%	56.98%	46.77%	59.84%	62.78%	44.08%	59.51%	56.97%
OvR	Training set	65.30%	37.73%	32.78%	29.35%	46.26%	33.23%	33.44%	39.73%
	Test set	36.24%	19.62%	16.91%	19.02%	28.30%	18.31%	27.57%	23.71%

4.2   Results of EMG-LRD

Next we will discuss the experimental results of EMG-LRD in this section. The neural network that constitutes the EMG-LRD was trained using the ADAM algorithm, and the early stopping strategy was used to end the training after reaching a fixed number of training steps. Oversampling the EMG signal with minority samples to deal with sample imbalance, the minimum ratio of over-sampling was set to 0.5, i.e., the samples obtained by overfitting can ensure that their number was at least half that of majority samples. The model was evaluated using 10 cross-validations.

Table 2. Confusion matrix of neural network-based multi-classification (%)

Recognized motions	Actual motions					
	Walking	Going upstairs	Going downstairs	Standing-to-sitting	Standing	Sitting
Walking	59.61	32.06	23.53	11.50	8.20	10.81
Going upstairs	12.16	45.59	10.67	0.00	1.14	1.23
Going downstairs	6.35	16.67	50.04	0.34	1.26	1.31
Standing-to-sitting	7.71	0.00	11.88	73.49	0.00	4.41
Standing	6.11	0.00	2.25	0.00	88.07	8.65
Sitting	8.06	5.68	1.63	14.67	1.33	73.59

The confusion matrix of neural network-based classifier on the test sets is shown in Table 2. The table shows that the classification accuracy of standing-to-sitting, standing, and sitting was better, because these statuses were not easily confused with other motions. However, it is easy to confuse walking. Going up and down stairs. In these motion patterns, the movements of the left and right feet are extremely similar, and the samples of going up and down stairs was insufficient. So, as shown in the table many samples were recognized as walking.

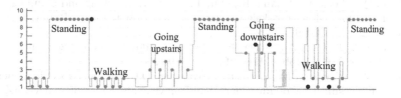

Fig. 6. Results of motor intention online recognition

4.3 Results of Online Recognition of Motor Intention

Figure 6 shows the results of online recognition. The curve represents the motions identified by the HRMI. In the figure, the ordinate axis represent motion label. And the dots represent the real motions, in which the black dots indicate that the motor intention is not correctly recognized. As shown in Fig. 6, the recognition accuracy of the stationary state is higher, however the motor intention with fewer samples (such as going upstairs and going downstairs) is recognized as other motor intention. The main reason for this error is that the motion range of going up and down stairs is large. And the noise contained in the signal makes the recognized label curve of motor intention contains many burrs, however the smoothed signal is more easily recognized as others.

5   Conclusions

This paper proposes a human-exoskeleton interaction method based on EEG and EMG-Hierarchical Recognition for Motor Intention (HRMI). The combination of the EEG-based and EMG-based method makes the method base on biological signals successfully applied to the control of exoskeleton in real life scenario. An experimental platform is established to explore the performance of the proposed method in real life scenario.

The method in this paper considers walking, going up and down stairs, sitting, standing, sitting-to-standing, and standing-to-sitting in a conventional environment. However, the terrain in daily life is more complicated, which will inevitably affect the recognition accuracy of the method. Future research will focus on various load-bearing environments, so that our method can be applied to daily activities.

References

1. Ambrosini, E., et al.: A robotic system with EMG-triggered functional electrical stimulation for restoring arm functions in stroke survivors. Neurorehabil. Neural Repair **35**(4), 334–345 (2021)
2. Chen, Q., Cheng, H., Huang, R., Qiu, J., Chen, X.: Learning and planning of stair ascent for lower-limb exoskeleton systems. Ind. Robot: Int. J. Robot. Res. Appl. **46**(3), 421–430 (2019)
3. Kazerooni, H., Chu, A., Steger, R.: That which does not stabilize, will only make us stronger. Int. J. Robot. Res. **26**(1), 75–89 (2007)
4. Lee, S.W., Wilson, K.M., Lock, B.A., Kamper, D.G.: Subject-specific myoelectric pattern classification of functional hand movements for stroke survivors. IEEE Trans. Neural Syst. Rehabil. Eng. **19**(5), 558–566 (2010)
5. Li, D., Zhang, Y.: Artificial neural network prediction of angle based on surface electromyography. In: 2011 International Conference on Control, Automation and Systems Engineering (CASE), pp. 1–3. IEEE (2011)
6. Li, H., et al.: EEG changes in time and time-frequency domain during movement preparation and execution in stroke patients. Front. Neurosci. **14**, 827 (2020)
7. Merletti, R., Di Torino, P.: Standards for reporting EMG data. J. Electromyogr. Kinesiol. **9**(1), 3–4 (1999)
8. Miao, M., Hu, W., Yin, H., Zhang, K.: Spatial-frequency feature learning and classification of motor imagery EEG based on deep convolution neural network. Comput. Math. Meth. Med. 2020 (2020)
9. Obayashi, S., Takahashi, R., Onuki, M.: Upper limb recovery in early acute phase stroke survivors by coupled EMG-triggered and cyclic neuromuscular electrical stimulation. NeuroRehabilitation **46**(3), 417–422 (2020)
10. Penfield, W., Boldrey, E.: Somatic motor and sensory representation in the cerebral cortex of man as studied by electrical stimulation. Brain **60**(4), 389–443 (1937)
11. Poboroniuc, M.S., Irimia, D.C.: FES & BCI based rehabilitation engineered equipment: clinical tests and perspectives. In: E-Health and Bioengineering Conference (EHB), pp. 77–80 (2017)

12. Radman, M., Chaibakhsh, A., Nariman-zadeh, N., He, H.: Generalized sequential forward selection method for channel selection in EEG signals for classification of left or right hand movement in BCI. In: International Conference on Computer and Knowledge Engineering (ICCKE), pp. 137–142 (2019)
13. Shi, D., Zhang, W., Zhang, W., Ding, X.: A review on lower limb rehabilitation exoskeleton robots. Chin. J. Mech. Eng. **32**(1), 1–11 (2019)
14. Uusitalo, M.A., Ilmoniemi, R.J.: Signal-space projection method for separating MEG or EEG into components. Med. Biol. Eng. Compu. **35**(2), 135–140 (1997)
15. Wang, J., Dai, Y., Kang, T., Si, X.: Research on human motion recognition based on lower limb electromyography (EMG) signals. In: IEEE International Conference on Electronics Technology (ICET), pp. 1234–1239 (2021)
16. Zhang, X., Tang, X., Wei, Z., Chen, X., Chen, X.: Model-based sensitivity analysis of EMG clustering index with respect to motor unit properties: investigating post-stroke FDI muscle. IEEE Trans. Neural Syst. Rehabil. Eng. **28**(8), 1836–1845 (2020)
17. Zhang, X., Zhou, P.: High-density myoelectric pattern recognition toward improved stroke rehabilitation. IEEE Trans. Biomed. Eng. **59**(6), 1649–1657 (2012)

Design and Analysis of New Multi-DOF Parallel Mechanisms for Haptic Use

Congzhe Wang$^{(\boxtimes)}$ (iD) and Bin Zhang (iD)

School of Advanced Manufacturing Engineering, Chongqing University of Posts and
Telecommunications, Chongqing, China
{wangcz,zhangbin}@cqupt.edu.cn

Abstract. The design of parallel mechanisms with multi-rotational degrees of
freedom (DOFs), especially with large orientation workspace, is still a tough task.
This paper presents the design process of new multi-DOF parallel mechanisms
with large orientation workspace, which can be used in haptic application. First,
based on the configurable design concept, two configurable platforms with two
or three rotational DOFs are designed. By means of the designed platforms and
Lie group theory, a series of parallel mechanisms with two rotational and three
translational (2R3T) DOFs or three rotational and three translational (3R3T) DOFs
are developed. According to the synthesized parallel mechanisms, a haptic device
with reconfigurable ability is proposed. The analysis of rotational capability is
carried out in terms of one of the synthesized parallel mechanisms. The results
reveal that resorting to actuation redundancy, the studied PM achieves the design
requirement of large orientation workspace.

Keywords: Parallel mechanism · Configurable platform · Rotational capability

1 Introduction

Parallel mechanisms (PMs) have been researched widely and extensively for their special
superior performances over serial mechanisms, such as heavy payloads, low inertia, high
stiffness and precision, etc. Based on these advantages, PMs have been utilized in a large
number of applications including flight simulators [1], pick and place tasks [2], parallel
machine tools [3], haptic devices [4] and so on.

Nevertheless, the design of PMs with multi-rotational DOFs, especially with large
orientation workspace, is still a challenging topic and one research focus of structural
synthesis. In this paper, the multi-rotational DOFs mean that PMs have two or three
rotational DOFs. For achieving this objective, different methods were proposed in existing literatures. One available method is to use circular guideways and circular prismatic
joints, such as the EclipseII [5] and the RRRS PM [6]. The EclipseII proposed by Kim
et al. can realize continuous 360° rotational motion in any direction and is suitable for the
application of flight motion simulators. Usually, circular guideways enlarge the mechanism's footprint and increase the manufacturing cost. Another method is to reduce the
number of limbs for alleviating the interference between the moving platform and limbs

© The Author(s), under exclusive license to Springer Nature Switzerland AG 2022
H. Liu et al. (Eds.): ICIRA 2022, LNAI 13455, pp. 782–793, 2022.
https://doi.org/10.1007/978-3-031-13844-7_72

[7–9]. For example, by means of three pantograph mechanisms, Yoon et al. [7] proposed a 6-DOF parallel mechanism with three limbs, each of which is driven by two base-fixed motors. This mechanism can tilt almost 70 from the horizontal plane. Using three legs actuated by 2-DOF gimbal mechanisms, Lee et al. [8] developed a 6-DOF parallel type haptic device. Additionally, some researches preferred to design special structures of limbs. For instance, Huang et al. [10] proposed a 6-DOF adaptive parallel manipulator with four identical peripheral limbs and one center limb. Due to the special architecture of the center limb, the proposed manipulator can adapt the center limb for best dexterity and large tilting capability. Gosselin et al. [11] proposed a novel architecture of kinematically redundant parallel mechanisms, which employed a kinematically redundant leg with two prismatic actuators. Because of the special leg, the parallel mechanism can produce very large rotation angles.

On the other hand, more and more researches have paid attention to the method of designing a configurable or non-rigid moving platform. A configurable platform means that the moving platform of PMs is not a rigid platform, but a kinematic chain. For example, the moving platform of Par4 developed by Pierrot et al. [12] is a parallelogram structure. Utilizing the relative motion of the parallelogram, Par4 can actualize an overturn revolution in one direction. Based on this configurable concept, PMs with multi-rotational DOFs can be designed for large orientation workspace as well. For instance, Wu et al. [13] developed a 6-DOF parallel robot by means of two Delta robots. Two sub-platforms of the two Delta robots are connected by a complex gearbox, which transfers the relative motions between the two sub-platforms into three rotational motions. Likewise, combing two Delta robots by a customized ball-screw handle, Vulliez et al. [14] proposed a new 6-DOF parallel haptic device with large rotational workspace. Resorting to two modified 3-DOF Delta mechanisms and two 3-DOF passive joints, Arata et al. [15] introduced a multi-DOF parallel haptic device with a wide rotational workspace. For the three parallel mechanisms above, two platforms and a transferring mechanism are comprised of a configurable platform. Actually, the structures of configurable platforms are various, and hence attract researchers' interest. In the authors' previous work [16, 17], through designing different configurable platforms with two or three rotational DOFs, a kind of PMs with high rotational capability in two or three directions were developed. Jin et al. [18, 19] proposed a synthesis method for generalized PMs with integrated end-effectors (also called configurable platforms), and designed a class of 4-DOF and 6-DOF PMs with large rotational angles. Tian et al. [20, 21] also presented a type synthesis method for generalized PMs with several novel configurable platforms, and proposed a series of PMs with high rotational capability.

This paper will adopt the concept of configurable platforms to design a kind of new multi-DOF parallel mechanisms for haptic use. First, two configurable platforms are developed to produce two or three rotational motions. Then PMs with multi-rotational DOFs are synthesized based on Lie subgroup of displacement theory. The results of performance analysis show that resorting to actuation redundancy, the studied PM can rotate continuously about two axes up to large angles with no interference and singularity. This research can provide some available structures for haptic application.

2 Design Multi-DOF Parallel Mechanisms

In consideration of the fact that some applications like haptic devices also demand translational freedoms, the design problems of PMs with two rotational and three translational (2R3T) DOFs or three rotational and three translational (3R3T) DOFs are focused on. The design process starts from designing two configurable platforms.

2.1 Two Configurable Platforms

Two configurable platforms are designed and shown in Fig. 1(a) and (b), respectively. Both the two configurable platforms consist of seven main parts: rods N_1N_2, N_1C_1, N_2C_2, N_3N_4, N_3C_3, N_4C_4 and OO_1. The rods N_1C_1 and N_2C_2 are connected with the rod N_1N_2 separately by a revolute joint (denoted as R) with the axis parallel to the vector m_1, where m_1 is the unit vector of N_1N_2. The rods N_3C_3 and N_4C_4 are linked with the rod N_3N_4 separately by a revolute joint with the axis parallel to the vector m_2, where m_2 is the unit vector of N_3N_4. The rod N_3N_4 is connected with the rod OO_1 by a revolute joint with the axis parallel to m, where m is the unit vector of OO_1. For the first configurable platform depicted in Fig. 1(a), the rod OO_1 is fixed to the rod N_1N_2. For the second configurable platform depicted in Fig. 1(b), the rod OO_1 is linked with the rod N_1N_2 by a helical joint (denoted as H) with the axis parallel to m. Due to the helical joint, the change of the relative distance between the rods N_1N_2 and N_3N_4 results in the self-rotation of the screw rod OO_1, which is the difference between the two proposed configurable platforms.

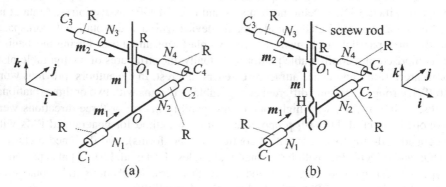

(a)   (b)

Fig. 1. Two configurable platforms.

2.2 Design 2R3T Parallel Mechanisms

According to the displacement group theory, the set of feasible relative displacements of a rigid body with respect to another body in a given serial kinematic chain is called kinematic bond that can be implemented by the group product. For the first configurable platform, the kinematic bond of the rod OO_1 with respect to the rod N_3C_3 or N_4C_4 can be represented as $\{R(O_1, m_2)\} \cdot \{R(O_1, m)\}$, where $\{R(O_1, m_2)\}$ represents the set of relative motions produced by the revolute joint whose axis is parallel to m_2 and passes through O_1, and $\{R(O_1, m)\}$ is likewise. The kinematic bond of the rod OO_1 with respect to the rod N_1C_1 or N_2C_2 can be written as $\{R(O, m_1)\}$. Apparently, the intersection of the two kinematic bonds above cannot produce two rotational motions. In order to make the rod OO_1 have 2R3T freedoms, it is necessary to add kinematic chains to the rods N_1C_1, N_2C_2, N_3C_3 and N_4C_4.

Kinematic Bonds and Mechanical Generators. Due to the fact that the kinematic bond of the rod OO_1 with respect to the rod N_1C_1 only has the rotation of $\{R(O, m_1)\}$, the rod N_1C_1 requires three-dimensional (3-D) translations and one rotation. Thus, the kinematic bond of the rod N_1C_1 with respect to the base, denoted as $\{L_1\}$, needs to include the spatial translation subgroup $\{T\}$ and another rotation subgroup $\{R(O, i)\}$, where i is perpendicular to m_1, and can be written as

$$\{L_1\} = \{T\} \cdot \{R(O, i)\} \tag{1}$$

where $\{T\} \cdot \{R(O, i)\}$ is an equivalent subgroup of Schoenflies displacements $\{X(i)\}$. The equality above can be represented in another form

$$\{L_1\} = \{X(i)\} \tag{2}$$

Combining $\{L_1\}$ with the kinematic bond of the rod OO_1 with respect to the rod N_1C_1 leads to a new kinematic bond, which is signified by $\{L_{m1}\}$ and can be expressed as

$$\{L_{m1}\} = \{L_1\} \cdot \{R(O, m_1)\} = \{T\} \cdot \{R(O, i)\} \cdot \{R(O, m_1)\} \tag{3}$$

where $\{R(O, i)\} \cdot \{R(O, m_1)\}$ is a 2-D manifold contained in the subgroup of spherical rotation $\{S(O)\}$. Hence, $\{L_{m1}\}$ is a 5-D manifold, and includes two rotations and three translations.

The kinematic bond of the rod N_2C_2 with respect to the base is denoted as $\{L_2\}$. Because the situation of $\{L_2\}$ is similar with $\{L_1\}$, let $\{L_2\} = \{L_1\}$. Combining $\{L_2\}$ with the kinematic bond of the rod OO_1 with respect to the rod N_2C_2 results in another kinematic bond, which is signified by $\{L_{m2}\}$ and can be written as $\{L_2\} \cdot \{R(O, m_1)\}$. Obviously, $\{L_{m2}\}$ is also equal to $\{L_{m1}\}$.

Subsequently, the kinematic bond of the rod N_3C_3 with respect to the base, denoted as $\{L_3\}$, is considered. In view of the kinematic bond of the rod OO_1 with respect to the rod N_3C_3 having $\{R(O_1, m_2)\}$ and $\{R(O_1, m)\}$, it seems reasonable to make the rod N_3C_3 only have spatial translations. If so, combining $\{L_3\}$ with the kinematic bond of the rod OO_1 with respect to the rod N_3C_3 leads to a kinematic bond that is signified by $\{L_{m3}\}$ and can be written as

$$\{L_{m3}\} = \{L_3\} \cdot \{R(O_1, m_2)\} \cdot \{R(O_1, m)\} = \{T\} \cdot \{R(O_1, m_2)\} \cdot \{R(O_1, m)\} \tag{4}$$

where $\{T\} \cdot \{R(O_1, m_2)\}$ is an equivalent subgroup of $\{X(m_2)\}$. Due to the product closure in the subgroup $\{X(m_2)\}$, the following relationship is tenable

$$\{T\} \cdot \{R(O_1, m_2)\} = \{T\} \cdot \{R(O, m_2)\} = \{R(O, m_2)\} \cdot \{T\} \tag{5}$$

Substituting Eq. (5) into Eq. (4) leads to

$${L_{m3}} = {R(O, m_2)} \cdot {T} \cdot {R(O_1, m)} \tag{6}$$

where ${T} \cdot {R(O_1, m)}$ is an equivalent subgroup of ${X(m)}$. Likewise, according to the product closure in one subgroup, the equation above can be represented in another form

$${L_{m3}} = {T} \cdot {R(O, m_2)} \cdot {R(O, m)} \tag{7}$$

Compared Eq. (7) with Eq. (3), the intersection of ${L_{m1}}$ and ${L_{m3}}$ cannot produce two rotational movements, since m is not parallel to m_1. To satisfy the freedom requirement, ${L_3}$ should be altered. In consideration of ${R(O, i)} \cdot {R(O, m_1)}$ contained in the subgroup ${S(O)}$, ${L_3}$ is modified into ${X(j)}$, where j is perpendicular to m_2. Then, ${L_{m3}}$ can be represented as

$${L_{m3}} = {X(j)} \cdot {R(O, m_2)} \cdot {R(O, m)} = {T} \cdot {R(O, j)} \cdot {R(O, m_2)} \cdot {R(O, m)} \tag{8}$$

where ${R(O, j)} \cdot {R(O, m_2)} \cdot {R(O, m)}$ is equivalent to ${S(O)}$, as long as j, m_2 and m are linearly independent. Hence, ${L_{m3}}$ is equal to ${T} \cdot {S(O)}$ that is the 6-D Lie group of transformations. Obviously, in this condition, ${L_{m3}} \cap {L_{m1}} = {L_{m1}}$, which means the freedom requirement is satisfied.

The kinematic bond of the rod $N_4 C_4$ with respect to the base is denoted as ${L_4}$. Because the situation of ${L_4}$ is similar with ${L_3}$, let ${L_4} = {L_3}$. The combination of ${L_4}$ and the kinematic bond of the rod OO_1 with respect to the rod $N_4 C_4$ is signified by ${L_{m4}}$, which is equal to ${L_{m3}}$ as well. According to the displacement subgroup theory, the displacement set of the screw rod OO_1 is determined by the intersection set of the four bonds ${L_{m1}}$, ${L_{m2}}$, ${L_{m3}}$ and ${L_{m4}}$. Apparently, the intersection set is equal to ${T} \cdot {R(O, i)} \cdot {R(O, m_1)}$, which meets the design objective. There exist many choices for mechanical generators of ${X(i)}$ or ${X(j)}$. The two kinematic chains $^iR^iR^iP_a^iR$ (or $^jR^jR^jP_a^jR$), $^kP^iR^iP_a^iR$ (or $^kP^jR^jP_a^jR$) are chosen for their practical value, where P_a is a composite joint of planar hinged parallelogram that produces circular translation between two opposite bars.

Mechanisms Construction. Based on the first configurable platform and the kinematic chains obtained above, two 5-DoF 2R3T PMs can be synthesized. The general arrangement of PMs is one actuator per limb. Hence, five actuators require five limbs, but there are just four limbs. To solve this problem, a <u>RRRRR</u> five-bar planar mechanism is employed to actuate the first two revolute joints of the RRP_aR chain, and a <u>PPRRR</u> five-bar planar mechanism is used to actuate the first prismatic joint and the second revolute joint of the PRP_aR chain, where an underlined character represents an actuated joint. In virtue of this actuation arrangement, two 5-DoF 2R3T PMs can be constructed and illustrated in Fig. 2.

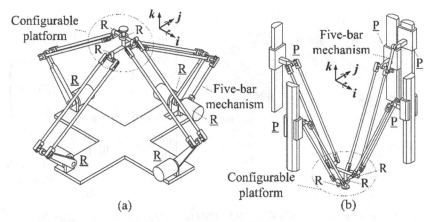

Fig. 2. Two synthesized 2R3T PMs.

2.3 Design 3R3T Parallel Mechanisms

Based on the second configurable platform shown in Fig. 1(b), a class of 3R3T PMs can be synthesized. The notations in the section above are still employed and have the same meanings. It can be proved that the requirement of 3R3T freedoms is still satisfied when $\{L_1\} = \{L_2\} = \{X(i)\}$ and $\{L_3\} = \{L_4\} = \{X(j)\}$. The reason is given as below.

The kinematic bond of the screw rod OO_1 with respect to the rod N_1C_1 or N_2C_2 can be written as $\{R(O, m_1)\} \cdot \{H(O, m)\}$, where $\{H(O, m)\}$ signifies the set of relative motions produced by the helical joint whose axis is parallel to m and passes through O. In consideration of $\{L_1\} = \{L_2\} = \{X(i)\}$, $\{L_{m1}\}$ or $\{L_{m2}\}$ can be given by

$$\{L_{m1}\} = \{L_{m2}\} = \{T\} \cdot \{R(O, i)\} \cdot \{R(O, m_1)\} \cdot \{H(O, m)\} \tag{9}$$

According to the characteristics of helical joint, the following relationship can be easily obtained

$$\{T(m)\} \cdot \{H(O, m)\} = \{T(m)\} \cdot \{R(O, m)\} \tag{10}$$

Due to $\{T(O, m)\}$ contained in $\{T\}$, substituting Eq. (10) into Eq. (9) results in

$$\{L_{m1}\} = \{L_{m2}\} = \{T\} \cdot \{R(O, i)\} \cdot \{R(O, m_1)\} \cdot \{R(O, m)\} \tag{11}$$

where $\{R(O, i)\} \cdot \{R(O, m_1)\} \cdot \{R(O, m)\}$ is equivalent to $\{S(O)\}$, as long as i, m_1 and m are linearly independent. Thus, $\{L_{m1}\}$ or $\{L_{m2}\}$ is equal to $\{T\} \cdot \{S(O)\}$. On the other hand, because of $\{L_3\} = \{L_4\} = \{X(j)\}$, $\{L_{m3}\}$ or $\{L_{m4}\}$ keeps unvaried and can be represented as Eq. (8). Consequently, the intersection set of the four bonds $\{L_{m1}\}$, $\{L_{m2}\}$, $\{L_{m3}\}$ and $\{L_{m4}\}$ is equal to $\{T\} \cdot \{S(O)\}$, which means the freedom condition is satisfied.

Subsequently, using the same kinematic chains and five-bar planar mechanisms, two 6-DoF 3R3T PMs can be constructed. One of the 3R3T PMs is illustrated in Fig. 3(a). It should be noted that two five-bar planar mechanisms are used to actuate two limbs of the depicted 3R3T PM, respectively. The joint-and-loop graphs of the two 3R3T PMs are shown in Fig. 3(b).

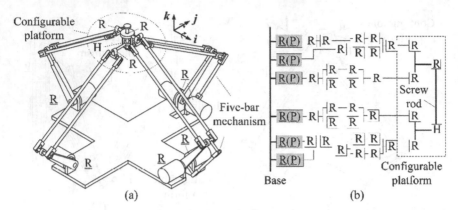

Fig. 3. One of the synthesized 3R3T PMs (a) and joint-and-loop graphs (b).

2.4 Haptic Use

Based on the 2R3T PM shown in Fig. 2(a), a 6-DoF haptic device with actuation redundancy is built and illustrated in Fig. 4(a). The redundant haptic device has four limbs, all which are actuated by five-bar planar mechanisms. That is to say, there are eight active joints. An operation handle is connected to the rod N_3N_4 by a passive revolute joint, which is also depicted in Fig. 4(b). Therefore, the redundant haptic device can achieve 6-DOF motions, but five motions including three translations and two rotations are active, and the remaining self-rotation of the operation handle is passive. In fact, the redundant haptic device has a certain reconfigurable feature. As shown in Fig. 4(c), another configurable platform with an active revolute joint is constructed. The operation handle in this configurable platform is actuated by a motor mounted on the rod N_3N_4. If this configurable platform is used instead of the one in Fig. 4(b), the redundant haptic device will have a hybrid structure, and can achieve 6-DOF active motions. On the other hand, based on the configurable platform in Fig. 1(b), fixing the operation handle to the screw rod OO_1 leads to a new configurable platform shown in Fig. 4(d). If this new configurable platform is used, the redundant haptic device will also realize 6-DOF active motions. Therefore, using different configurable platforms in Fig. 4(b), (c) and (d), the redundant haptic device has different operation modes. This reconfigurable feature will enhance the flexibility of the proposed system.

3   Rotational Capability Analysis

The 2R3T PM in Fig. 4 with actuation redundancy is taken as an example to study the rotational capability of the proposed haptic PMs. The base reference frame $X_bY_bZ_bO_b$ attaches at the fixed base, and the moving reference frame $XYZO$ located at the point O attaches at the rod OO_1. The ith limb is connected to the configurable platform at the point C_i and to the base at the point A_i. The angle between N_1N_2 and the Y_b-axis is denoted as α, and the angle between N_3N_4 and the X_b-axis is denoted as φ. The used parameters are defined as follows:

$$l_1 = \left\| \overrightarrow{A_iB_i} \right\|, l_2 = \left\| \overrightarrow{B_iC_i} \right\|, d_1 = \left\| \overrightarrow{N_1N_2} \right\|, d_2 = \left\| \overrightarrow{N_3N_4} \right\|, d_3 = \left\| \overrightarrow{N_iC_i} \right\|$$

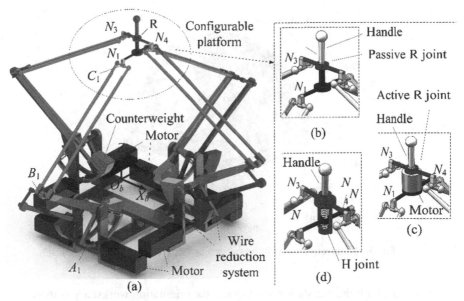

Fig. 4. A redundant haptic device (a); configurable platforms separately with a passive R joint (b), an active R joint (c) and an H joint (d).

The workspace is one of the significant performance indices of parallel mechanisms, and reveals the position-orientation capability of haptic mechanisms. Its size and shape are influenced by geometrical constraints and interference. For the redundant 2R3T PM, the following factors are considered. First, the inverse kinematic model should have solutions of real value. Second, to avoid the interference between links and platforms, the motion ranges of the active joints and some passive joints should be restricted. Finally, each limb should satisfy the expected assembly condition. The used architectural parameters of the 2R3T PM are presented as below: $l_1 = 180$ mm, $l_2 = 414$ mm, $d_1 = 108$ mm, $d_2 = 104$ mm, $d_3 = 16$ mm, $^b a_1 = (-187.5 - 13.5\ 0)^T$ mm, $^b a_2 = (187.5\ 13.5\ 0)^T$ mm, $^b a_3 = (13.5 - 187.5 - 37)^T$ mm, $^b a_4 = (-13.5\ 187.5 - 37)^T$ mm, $d_m = 42$ mm, where $^b a_i$ signifies the coordinates of the point A_i expressed in the base frame.

By means of a numerical search method, the translation workspace of the 2R3T PM, or called constant-orientation workspace, is numerically computed and illustrated with light blue color in Fig. 5, where α and φ are set to zero. For convenience, this type of workspace is denoted as Workspace I. For comparison, the configuration of the 2R3T PM at the position of $^b o = (0, 0, 380)^T$ mm is given. As can be observed from these figures, the translation workspace nearly covers the installation area of the 2R3T PM. The workspace shape is similar to a hemisphere. In terms of the given parameters, the constant-orientation workspace is limited between -400 mm and 400 mm at both the X- and Y-axes, and limited approximately below 620 mm at the Z-axis.

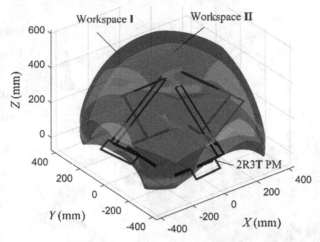

Fig. 5. Perspective view of the two workspaces. (Color figure online)

In contrast with the translation workspace, the orientation workspace is more complex and changes with the position of the configurable platform. According to the structural feature of the configurable platform, both the angle α of the rod N_1N_2 rotating about the X_b-axis and the angle φ of the rod N_3N_4 rotating about the Y_b-axis are confined from $-90°$ to $90°$. However, owing to the interference between limbs and the configurable platform, the rotation angles of the rods N_1N_2 and N_3N_4 are less than the extreme values. Figures 6(a)–(d) show the shapes of the configurable platform located at the positions near the workspace boundary, when α and φ take $-80°$ or $80°$. Different views are also given in Figs. 6(e)–(h) to show the relative positions of the rods of the configurable platform and limbs. In these cases, some rods are quite close and the interference among these rods nearly occurs. Since the potential interference appears at the workspace boundary, it can be inferred that there will be no interference near the central workspace when α or φ changes from $-80°$ to $80°$. Based on the discussion above, it's interesting to search the positons where the orientations of $(\alpha, \varphi)^{\mathrm{T}}$ can vary from $-80°$ to $80°$. For this purpose, it's necessary to check whether each point meets the constraints mentioned above at the four orientations, which are $(80, 80)^{\mathrm{T}}$ deg, $(80, -80)^{\mathrm{T}}$ deg, $(-80, 80)^{\mathrm{T}}$ deg and $(-80, -80)^{\mathrm{T}}$ deg. By using the numerical search method, the qualified positions are identified and marked with dark blue color in Fig. 5. This type of workspace is denoted as Workspace **II**. It can be derived from these figures that the 2R3T PM is competent for the prescribed rotational requirement in most regions of the workspace.

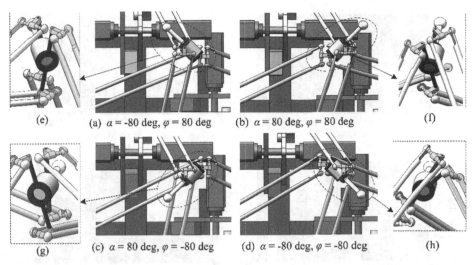

Fig. 6. Different shapes of the configurable platform when α and φ take different values.

Actuation redundancy can eliminate singular configurations inside the workspace for enhancing the rotational capability. Generally, singularities occur if Jacobian matrixes degenerate. The inverse kinematic singularity just occurs at the workspace boundary. In contrast, the direct kinematic singularity occurs inside the workspace, so it should be eliminated. The direct kinematic singularity can be analyzed by the condition number of a mechanism. For the redundant 2R3T PM, its condition number is denoted as κ_{xm}. Take the positions $^{b}o = (-100, 100, 380)^{T}$ mm, $(100, 100, 380)^{T}$ mm, $(-100, -100, 380)^{T}$ mm and $(100, -100, 380)^{T}$ mm as examples. The distributions of κ_{xm} in the whole workspace at these positions are illustrated in Figs. 7(a)–(d), respectively. From these figures, the values of κ_{xm} are more than 0.1 in most orientations, and the minimum values more than 0.01 just appear in one corner of the orientation workspace. This means the redundant mechanism has no singularity at the given position. Meanwhile, these figures display the symmetrical feature. Specifically, Fig. 7(a) and (d) are symmetrical with each other, and Fig. 7(b) and (c) are symmetrical as well.

Usually, PMs have limited orientation workspace due to joint range constraints and link interference. In most cases, the moving platform can tilt no more than 40 from the horizontal plane. However, according to the analysis above, by means of actuation redundancy, the redundant 2R3T PM has large orientation workspace, and can rotate continuously about both the X_b- and Y_b-axes from $-80°$ to $80°$, even if interference and singularity are considered. Furthermore, this high rotational capability is displayed in most regions of the workspace, not only limited in the home configuration, which is helpful for the application in haptic use.

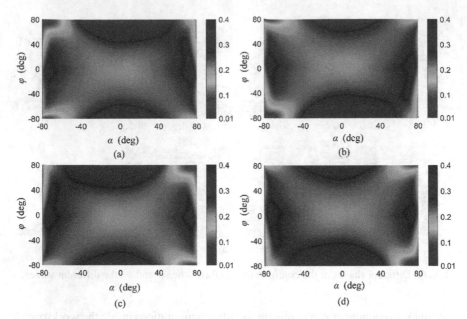

Fig. 7. Distributions of κ_{xm} in the orientation workspace at one group of positions.

4   Conclusions

The design process of a series of multi-DOF parallel mechanisms for haptic use has been presented in this paper. The proposed parallel mechanisms are characterized by the two configurable platforms that mainly contain two rods with relative rotational or helical movements. By means of the employed five-bar planar mechanisms, it is feasible to use four limbs to arrange five or six actuators, which can reduce the number of limbs and the interference. Based on these design schemes, a haptic device with reconfigurable ability is proposed, which can be reconfigured into three different mechanisms. The result of rotational capability analysis shows that by means of actuation redundancy, the studied 2R3T PM has indeed large orientation workspace, and can rotate continuously about both the X_b- and Y_b-axes from $-80°$ to $80°$. This high rotational capability makes the proposed multi-DOF parallel mechanisms suitable for haptic use.

Acknowledgments. The authors gratefully acknowledge the financial supports from National Science Foundation of China under grant No. 52005070, Chongqing Natural Science Foundation under grant No. cstc2020jcyj-msxmX0886 and the Foundation and Frontier Research Project of Chongqing Municipal Science and Technology Commission under grant No. KJQN201900640.

References

1. Pouliot, N.A., Gosselin, C.M., Nahon, M.A.: Motion simulation capabilities of three-degree-of-freedom flight simulators. J. Aircraft **35**(1), 9–17 (1998)

2. Arian, A., Isaksson, M., Gosselin, C.: Kinematic and dynamic analysis of a novel parallel kinematic Schönflies motion generator. Mech. Mach. Theory **147**, 103629 (2020)
3. Ye, W., Chai, X., Zhang, K.: Kinematic modeling and optimization of a new reconfigurable parallel mechanism. Mech. Mach. Theory **149**, 103850 (2020)
4. Lambert, P., Herder, J.L.: A 7-DOF redundantly actuated parallel haptic device combining 6-DOF manipulation and 1-DOF grasping. Mech. Mach. Theory **134**, 349–364 (2019)
5. Kim, S.H., Jeon, D., Shin, H.P., In, W., Kim, J.: Design and analysis of decoupled parallel mechanism with redundant actuator. Int. J. Precis. Eng. Manuf. **10**(4), 93–99 (2009). https://doi.org/10.1007/s12541-009-0076-2
6. Glozman, D., Shoham, M.: Novel 6-DOF parallel manipulator with large workspace. Robotica **27**(6), 891 (2009)
7. Yoon, J.W., Ryu, J., Hwang, Y.K.: Optimum design of 6-DOF parallel manipulator with translational/rotational workspaces for haptic device application. J. Mech. Sci. Tech. **24**(5), 1151–1162 (2010)
8. Lee, S.U., Kim, S.: Analysis and optimal design of a new 6 DoF parallel type haptic device. In: IEEE/RSJ International Conference on Intelligent Robots and Systems, pp. 460–465. IEEE (2006)
9. Abeywardena, S., Chen, C.: Implementation and evaluation of a three-legged six-degrees-of-freedom parallel mechanism as an impedance-type haptic device. IEEE/ASME Trans. Mech. **22**(3), 1412–1422 (2017)
10. Huang, H., Li, B., Deng, Z., et al.: A 6-DOF adaptive parallel manipulator with large tilting capacity. Robot. Comput. Integr. Manuf. **28**(2), 275–283 (2012)
11. Gosselin, C., Schreiber, L.T.: Kinematically redundant spatial parallel mechanisms for singularity avoidance and large orientational workspace. IEEE Trans. Rob. **32**(2), 286–300 (2016)
12. Pierrot, F., Nabat, V., Company, O., et al.: Optimal design of a 4-DOF parallel manipulator: from academia to industry. IEEE Trans. Rob. **25**(2), 213–224 (2009)
13. Wu, G.: Workspace, transmissibility and dynamics of a new 3T3R parallel pick-and-place robot with high rotational capability. In: IEEE International Conference on Robotics and Automation (ICRA), pp. 942–947. IEEE (2018)
14. Vulliez, M., Zeghloul, S., Khatib, O.: Design strategy and issues of the Delthaptic, a new 6-DOF parallel haptic device. Mech. Mach. Theory **128**, 395–411 (2018)
15. Arata, J., Ikedo, N., Fujimoto, H.: New multi-DoF haptic device using a parallel mechanism with a wide rotational working area. Adv. Robot. **26**, 121–135 (2012)
16. Wang, C., Fang, Y.: GUO S, Design and analysis of 3R2T and 3R3T parallel mechanisms with high rotational capability. J. Mech. Rob. **8**(1), 011004 (2016)
17. Wang, C., Fang, Y., Fang, H.: Novel 2R3T and 2R2T parallel mechanisms with high rotational capability. Robotica **35**(2), 401 (2017)
18. Jin, X., Fang, Y., Zhang, D.: Design of a class of generalized parallel mechanisms with large rotational angles and integrated end-effectors. Mech. Mach. Theory **134**, 117–134 (2019)
19. Jin, X., Fang, Y., Zhang, D., Luo, X.: Design and analysis of a class of redundant collaborative manipulators with 2D large rotational angles. Front. Mech. Eng. **15**(1), 66–80 (2019). https://doi.org/10.1007/s11465-019-0570-x
20. Tian, C., Zhang, D.: A new family of generalized parallel manipulators with configurable moving platforms. Mech. Mach. Theory **153**, 103997 (2020)
21. Tian, C., Zhang, D., Liu, J.: A novel class of generalized parallel manipulators with high rotational capability. Proc. IMechE. Part C **234**(23), 4599–4619 (2020)

Author Index

Printed in the United States
by Baker & Taylor Publisher Services

Printed in the United States
by Baker & Taylor Publisher Services